SHALLOW GRAVES

SHALLOW GRAVES

TWO WOMEN AND VIETNAM

Wendy Wilder Larsen
Tran Thi Nga

RANDOM HOUSE
NEW YORK

 Published in the United States by Random House, Inc., New York and simultaneously in Canada by Random House of Canada Limited, Toronto.

Portions of this work first appeared in *Hawaii Review* and *13th Moon*.

Grateful acknowledgment is made to the following for permission to reprint previously published material:

The Asia Society: "Poor Matchmaking" and excerpts from "Lament of the Warrior's Wife," published in *A Thousand Years of Vietnamese Poetry*, ed. by Nguyen Ngoc Bich, tr. by Burton Raffel and W. S. Merwin. Alfred A. Knopf, Inc., 1975.

Columbia Pictures Publications: Excerpts from the lyrics to "Fire and Rain" by James Taylor, Copyright © 1969, 1970 by Blackchord Music, Inc. and Country Road Music, Inc. Administered by Blackchord Music, Inc.

Farrar, Straus & Giroux, Inc., and Faber and Faber, Ltd.: Excerpt from "Losses," by Randall Jarrell. From *The Complete Poems of Randall Jarrell*. Copyright 1948, renewed copyright © 1975 by Mrs. Randall Jarrell. Reprinted by permission of the publishers.

The New York Public Library: One-page excerpt from "The Vietnamese Language," by Nguyen Dinh Hoa, Vietnam Culture Series, No. 2, 1961. Reprinted by permission of the General Research Division, The New York Public Library, Astor, Lenox and Tilden Foundations.

Warner Bros. Music: Lyrics excerpted from "Ballad of a Thin Man," by Bob Dylan. © 1965 Warner Bros. Inc. All Rights Reserved. Used By Permission.

Library of Congress Cataloging-in-Publication Data

Larsen, Wendy Wilder, 1940–
Shallow graves.

1. Vietnamese Conflict, 1961–1975—Poetry.
I. Tran, Thi Nga, 1927– . II. Title.
PS 3562.A745S5 1986 811'.54 85-14534
ISBN 0-394-54985-6

Manufactured in the United States of America

2468753

FIRST EDITION

Book design by Carole Lowenstein

TO

Nguyen Thi Toan
Nguyen Hung Vuong
Katherine Burton
Katharine Herrick Metcalf

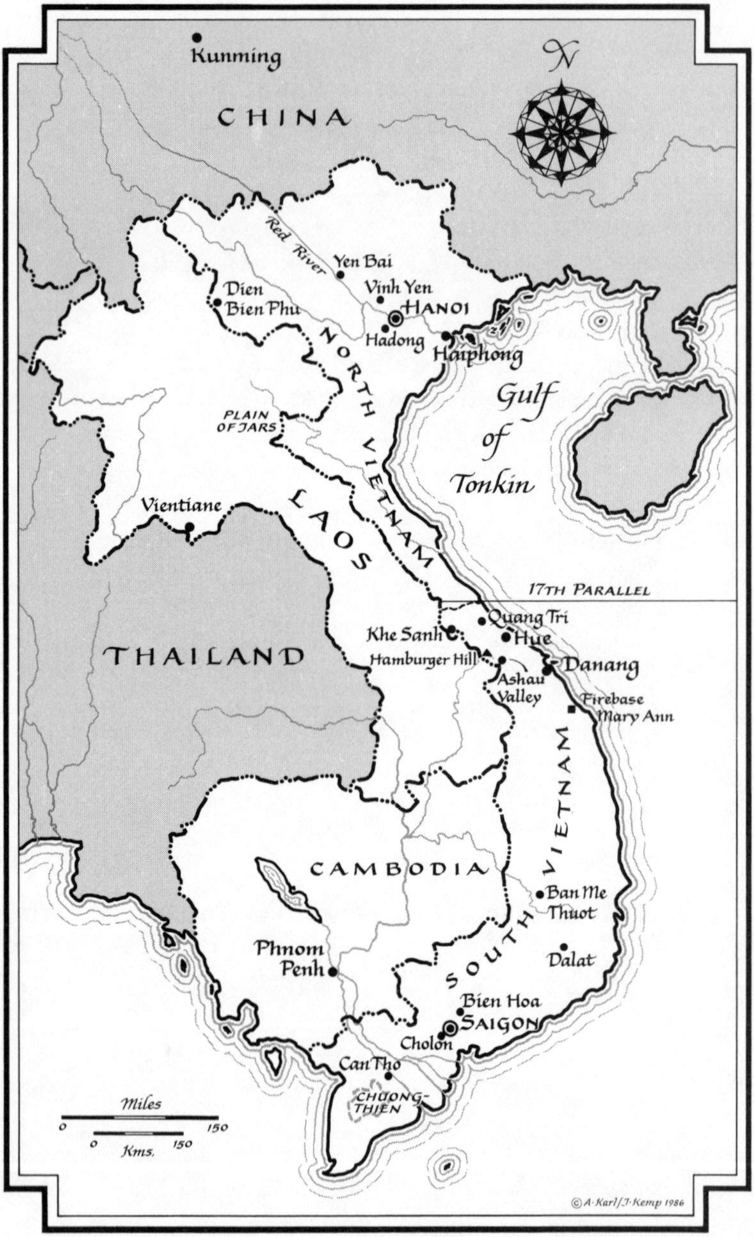
Kunming
CHINA
N
Red River
Yen Bai
Vinh Yen
Dien Bien Phu
HANOI
Hadong
Haiphong
NORTH VIETNAM
Gulf of Tonkin
PLAIN OF JARS
LAOS
Vientiane
17TH PARALLEL
Quang Tri
Khe Sanh
Hue
THAILAND
Hamburger Hill
Danang
Ashau Valley
Firebase Mary Ann
CAMBODIA
SOUTH VIETNAM
Ban Me Thuot
Phnom Penh
Dalat
Bien Hoa
SAIGON
Cholon
Can Tho
CHUONG-THIEN
Miles
0
150
0
Kms.
150
© A·Karl/J·Kemp 1986

PREFACE

As early as the fifteenth century, it was a common practice in Vietnam for a band of singers, sometimes even a single performer—often a blind person—to travel from village to village reciting from a repertoire of verse novels. The verse novel, or *truyen*, is a Vietnamese form, but the stories were adapted from Chinese prose tales.

I feel like the performer of Mrs. Nga's story as well as my own. I first met this remarkable woman when my husband was a journalist covering Vietnam, and I was teaching English literature at the School of Pedagogy in Saigon. Mrs. Nga was the bookkeeper in my husband's office.

Our paths crossed then, and again later when she fled from her country to mine and together we began work on *Shallow Graves*.

—W.W.L.

CONTENTS

Preface

BA LARSEN'S STORY

SAIGON • 1970–1971 *3*
PHNOM PENH AND VIENTIANE *61*
BACK TO SAIGON *75*
NEW YORK CITY • 1971–1975 *97*

NGA'S STORY

KUNMING • HANOI • YEN BAI • HADONG • 1927–1940 *105*
HADONG • KUNMING • HANOI • 1940–1954 *147*
SAIGON • SWANSEA • RANGOON • SAIGON • 1954–1975 *179*
LEAVING SAIGON • 1975 *223*
THE UNITED STATES: GUAM • FORT CHAFFEE •
NEW YORK CITY • GREENWICH • COS COB • 1975–1980 *239*

NEW YORK CITY 1980 *275*

NOTES

Glossary *281*
Vietnam: A Chronology *283*
Vietnamese Names *289*
Sources *291*

BA LARSEN'S STORY

SAIGON
1970-1971

ASSIGNMENT

I remember the night you came back from dinner
(we were living in Hollywood then)
and said, "It's going to be Vietnam."
Somehow I had pictured London.

As a sophomore, I had gone to hear the Dragon Lady,
Madame Nhu, speak at Harvard.
All I can remember now
is that her dress was brilliant yellow silk
and her red nails so long
they curved backward.

POP! a black-and-white photograph
in my brain
Diem and Nhu, brothers
dead in the back of a truck somewhere
blood streaming from their mouths.

My other images came from television.
I pictured me in a flak jacket
diving down a manhole
dodging shrapnel;
buildings falling
and burning all around me.

I pictured tank patrols in the jungle
booby traps and poison pungi sticks.
Medics lifting wounded soldiers
into waiting helicopters
the wind from the blades
flattening tall grasses
into circles.

Or was that in a movie?

CAPTURE

Vacationing in New England
two weeks before we left,
we got the news:
our predecessor had been captured
a prisoner of the Khmer Rouge
held somewhere in Cambodia.

I dream I'm running.
I'm running in a jungle at night.
Palm trees clatter overhead.
My feet are bleeding.
I cannot understand the order.

We took our guests on a picnic
to a meadow near our house.
Their voices crisscrossed
overhead like bees.

"British soldiers,"
my friend said, pointing to lichen
with bright red hats
and straight gray bodies,
"Perfect for your terrarium."

We sat on granite
drinking too much white wine
under an apple tree.

Two mornings before,
I'd watched a fat blue jay
rip the blossoms from that tree
shredding them with such gusto
the pink spilled from his beak.

Alone then,
I heard his satisfied scoldings
patrol the tall grasses of the meadow,
the borders of the woods.

ADVICE

I waited in the hall
on the 24th floor
for my turn to see
the Chief of Correspondents,
my arms shot full
of plague, cholera, yellow fever.
His face floated up
from behind his desk
like one of those answers
in a fortune globe.

"Any questions?" he asked.
"What about the water?"
"People do live there," he said.

A map of the world
big as the wall
the countries tinted blue
the oceans green
spun over his left shoulder.

I focused on pushpins
stuck on the map.
Across the Atlantic
beyond Europe, Turkey, Afghanistan's Hindu Kush
beyond India
down past Thailand
east to the bulge
in a peninsula floating in green
stood two red ones.

One of them would be us.

ADVICE 2

"Call your friend, the expert," my husband said.
"She'll know. She's been out there
and back four times."

I reported her words:
"There are no gynecologists in Vietnam."

"B.Y.O.G.Y.N." My husband laughed.

ADVICE 3

"You'll like it there.
Saigon's not scary at all.
All that humidity's marvelous for the skin
and those wonderful little seamstresses
come to your house, work all day
and eat like gerbils."

SAIGON HOUSEKEEPING

I arrived at Christmas time.
The cook left the first day.
She was part Chinese
would not work with Chi Phuc,
Vietnamese.

I sat in a chair
watching her carry past me
our pots and pans
stainless-steel knives and forks
pottery plates
our colander.

She took the same turns,
one load at a time,
out of the kitchen
across the living room
down the stairs—
an ant to her mound.

I drew the line
at a large earthenware crock
used to hold the water
we boiled each day.
She had somehow strapped it to her back.

When she wasn't looking
I'd get up, throw Hong Kong tinsel
on the Christmas tree
to hang there
with the colored lights
the twisted dragons.

OPERATION FIRST STEPS

"O.K. this is it.
Only a block to the office.
No more standing at the window, kid."

I watched my legs
in a slow replay
move down the dark steps

past the women
washing laundry in plastic tubs,
their voices shrill as shrapnel
caught in the stairwell.

I moved
first right leg, then left
past the one-eyed guard

out onto the street
and the Pacific sun
that hurts on impact,

over the broken concrete,
head down, muttering

"Step on a crack!
Break your mother's back"

as if that childhood chant
could make me brave

past vendors
selling packs of stolen Marlboros

our WWII veterans sent from home
complete with messages

"We in Sioux City, Iowa
love you boys"

past lepers.
One had a hole in his cheek.

I rounded the corner
touched the white column
of the Continental Palace Hotel
like the home tree in "capture the flag."

From the open veranda
voices breathed behind the potted palms,
behind the gin-and-tonics
that sweated like the soldiers.

I heard my husband,
whom I could talk to,
debriefing the office Vietnamese reporter
on Kill Ratios, Task Forces, ARVN movements in I Corps.

THE GAME

Our first social event
we played a war game
in a journalist's flat
above the market street.

A free-lancer made the rules.
There were cards for troop deployment.
Points for Pacification.
Cards to call in air strikes.

I think my chair
was Quang Tri or Ban Me Thuot.
I can't remember now.

But I took my cards.
I rolled the dice.
I played the game.

LEARNING THE WAR

I never made friends faster.
We foreigners were learning the war,
cramming it in
breakfast, lunch and dinner.

We learned the abbreviations:
USAID, JUSPAO, MACV, DMZ,
ARVN, NLF, GVN.

We learned the names of battles:
Dien Bien Phu
Ashau Valley
Khe Sanh
Hamburger Hill
Firebase Mary Ann.

We peppered our speech
with militarese

with roger this
and roger that
with dust off
blown away and neutralize

to give us courage—
warriors painting our faces
before battle.

We learned to rate hamlets
praise Ruff-Puffs
recognize Kit Carson scouts
laugh at White Mice.

We learned it all
and we couldn't speak to anyone
when we got home.

THE LANGUAGE

Vietnamese is a tonal language, that is to say, a given syllable may be pronounced in any of the six tones, thus multiplying the number of vocables by six. To take a classic example, **ma**, pronounced in the high level tone, means «ghost». The same word pronounced with the high rising tone refers to the « cheek ». It means « but », « grave », «horse» or «rice seedling», depending on whether it is given the low falling, low rising, broken rising, or low constricted tone, respectively. Following are the six forms of the syllable **/ma/** pronounced in the six tones :

ma **má** **mà** **mả** **mã** **mạ**

«ghost» «cheek» «but» «grave» «horse» «rice seedling»

WATCH

Most of the journalists
wore army-issue watches
with large waterproof faces
and khaki-colored straps.

When I got mine on the black market,
I turned it over and read
"This watch is non-maintainable."

SAVING FACE

I had a problem with my staff in Saigon.
The maid, Chi Phuc, my favorite, cried most of the day.
The new cook, higher up the pecking order,
was forcing her to do his chopping, his dishes.
I called the office and spoke to Mrs. Nga,
the only woman there.

"It's 'Nga' like 'ma,' " she corrected me.
I had pronounced it 'naga' like Naugahyde.

"Give me a week," she said
and came up with this solution.

"Scold Chi Phuc in front of the cook.
Say the Big Boss, your husband, is upset.
His laundry isn't getting done perfectly."
I got mad at the person I wasn't mad at,
saved everyone's face
and brought peace to my Asian household.

RIDING TO SCHOOL

I taught literature in Saigon then
at the School of Pedagogy.

My students rode to school on Hondas.

The women wore silk ao dai
black satin pants.

The pastel panels floated out
behind them as they drove

pink, blue, green
like so many dragonfly wings.

They wore black gloves
pale conical hats

tied with maroon ribbons
under their chins.

Their backs were straight.

From my window I wanted to call
like a riding instructor,

"Nice hands. Good seat."

I watched them each morning
drive through the puddles

and park in a circle
under the flamboyant tree.

STAR-CROSSED

They stood when I entered the classroom,
called me Ba Larsen,

which means "Mrs." or "Lady"
a sign of respect.

I concentrated on appearance
and reality, textual analysis of *Romeo and Juliet*.

Late one afternoon Miss Hoa
came to the apartment on Le Thanh Ton.

I remember her white dress
black hair to her waist.

She had never been in an elevator before.

She said she was in love with her cousin
had been since she was thirteen

explained that many Vietnamese love their cousins,
the extended family.

Such love was forbidden by the church.
Should she kill herself like Juliet?

She drank the Coke I offered.

From the balcony we watched
magnesium flares fall beyond the harbor.

TEACHING

My students brought ca dao to class,
folk poems, centuries old,
told over and over
passed on from one generation to another.

Ca Dao to Hoa Sen To the Lotus

In the pond there is nothing more beautiful than the lotus.
Green leaves, white petals, yellow anthers.
Yellow anthers, white petals, green leaves.
Growing out of mud, yet not giving off the mud smell.

Trong đầm gì đẹp bằng sen
Lá xanh bông trắng lại chen nhị vàng.
Nhị vàng bông trắng lá xanh
Gần bùn mà chẳng hôi tanh mùi bùn.

I announced:
"Clearly this poem speaks of appearance and reality."

Mr. Thung raised his hand in protest,
"Excuse me, Ba Larsen.
It is you who do not understand.
We live here.
We know the lotus flower
grows in stinky mud.
For us, the poem's about reality.
For you, who do not know our land,
it is about appearances."

STUDENT PAPER

I have to say that ca dao cannot be translated. It's the meaning and the feeling it gives to the reader that forbids the translation. Only people in the Vietnamese culture can fully understand and enjoy ca dao, but I will give you my favorite.

> *"Oh my darling, over there by the side of the path,*
> *why do you scoop up and throw away yellow moonlight*
> *shining on the water's surface?"*

This is a question on a summer moonlit night asked by a passer-by to a hard-working young girl using her draining can to take water from a flooded field to a dry field.

TO MARKET, TO MARKET

Scared to enter the big market, that noisy covered maze, alone,
I asked Mrs. Nga if she would be my guide.

She showed me the fruit ladies, seated on their platforms
among pyramids of mangosteens, papayas and smelly durian.

Heads wrapped in turbans, teeth red with betel,
they balanced their brass scales

bartering in high-pitched voices like so many exotic birds,
like puppets banging their heads together.

She led me through hot tunnels. No air.
Things jostled from all sides. Chairs hung from the ceiling.

Everywhere the smell of scallions and ginger
the stench of meat rotting in the sun.

We threaded our way. Black catfish flopped on the tile floor.
Crabs wriggled their blue claws through slats in straw baskets.

Tiny striped snails clung to the sides of aluminum buckets.
Her favorite fish vendor smiled the red-toothed smile of easy money.

We pressed past bins of turmeric and cloves, bolts of lavender and
  tangerine silk,
opium trays, black-market Kiwi shoe polish, Chinese blue-and-white
  porcelain

past one woman who sold individual garlic buds
displayed on a plaid handkerchief.

Exhausted, we collapsed into a pedi-cab and let an old man
pedal us home through noonday heat.

Over the market, a huge suspended sign floated:
a smiling black man with enormous white teeth

advertising Hynos, a Vietnamese toothpaste. She told me
"All Vietnamese know that blacks have the whitest teeth."

MULTIPLES

Along the Bien Hoa Highway
I saw shacks
made from aluminum sheets.

In the USA, we cut the metal
into soda-pop cans
that we toss on the side of our roads.

Here, for miles and miles
their red and green houses
spelled out *Coca-Cola* *7 Up*.

CALLING HOME

I called my family from the USO
decorated like a high school gym.
Chains of red white and blue crepe paper
sagged in the heat.
The room was thick with the smell of fries
Osterizers blending chocolate shakes
the snap of shuffled cards.

I'd wait in line
with GI's sweating half-circles
down to their khaki waists.
Together we'd count the time difference
to the States.

"We're all sitting in the blue room
on my big bed upstairs,"
I heard my mother's voice
break over the line
like surf over rocks.
"The ducks and geese are flying.
You know how I dread September."

September—Rhode Island.
I pictured my family on cool evenings
rocking on the porch
in black wicker chairs
under Japanese lanterns.
The lawn curved down to the rocks
where the fishermen waited in the fog
for the blues to come in.

That morning in my dream
our white frame house stood
at the edge of a jungle.
Its windows lit up
like a child's eyes.

CONSCIOUSNESS-RAISING

Saigon was a natural place
to start a consciousness-raising group.
We were eight women
all wives of journalists.

I remember sitting in a hot small room
a punkah fan creaking overhead,
our knees forming a circle
as we discussed why baby girls
are dressed in pink,
boys in blue.

Outside, a peasant woman
driven into the city by the bombing
slept in the street
on a newspaper
a child pulling at her breast.

BOYS

This is the land
where they dye eggs red
when a son is born.

This is the land
where the birth of a boy
brings a week's celebration.

In this land
when a girl is born
the mother is quiet.

ASSIGNMENT FROM BA LARSEN

Compare William Blake's "London" to Saigon in 1970

LONDON

I wander thro' each charter'd street,
Near where the charter'd Thames does flow,
And mark in every face I meet
Marks of weakness, marks of woe.

In every cry of every Man,
In every Infant's cry of fear,
In every voice, in every ban,
The mind-forg'd manacles I hear.

Now the Chimney-sweeper's cry
Every black'ning Church appalls,
And the hapless Soldier's sigh
Runs in blood down Palace walls.

But most thro' midnight streets I hear
How the youthful Harlot's curse
Blasts the new born Infant's tear,
And blights with plagues the Marriage hearse.

—William Blake

STUDENT'S RESPONSE

Where is the traditional and peaceful Saigon?
Where is the Pearl of the Orient—that sweet name?

In every street I see bar-girls in mini-skirts
shocking every passer-by.

At midnight I hear feverish jazz music
rocking with the pounding of the far-away cannons.

I smell in every corner the stink of scattered garbage.

Corruption touches every level of society
while the poor starve.

Where is the Pearl of the Orient?

Refugees bombed from their villages fill her sidewalks.
Pollution and horns disturb her treeless avenues.

Large foreigners live in her houses.
Men in green uniforms patrol her streets, sleep with her women.

Juveniles, uprooted from their families, steal from her people.
The rush of disorder shows on every face.

I wish I had not been born to live in this time.

I am worn out.
My city is worn out.
My country is worn out.

PROTOCOL

Downstairs, at the embassy party,
there were place cards with embossed gold crests
antimacassars on the backs of stuffed chairs
talk of commitment.

Upstairs, in the bedroom after dinner,
there was a refrigerator filled with champagne
and bar-girls dancing
to Mick Jagger's rock 'n' roll.

"Welcome to the turd world,"
the diplomat winked.

BAR-GIRL'S SONG TO A GI

I love you beaucoup.
  You love me titi.
You give me baby.
  I give you V.D.

MONEY TALKS

The office had a fixer.
Nothing he couldn't do.

His bag of tricks was exquisite.
If your smallpox vaccination expired,
he got you the stamp
without the office visit.

When our colleague was caught
with marijuana for example
he said, "You're doing a story on drugs
say you were collecting samples."

He could save you from jail
from any disaster,
get you through customs
in under two hours.

All you needed
was an extra briefcase of piasters.

FOR CHI PHUC

You ironed my shirts
in my living room.
Two women
in one apartment.
You ironed.
I read about your country.
We could not speak one word to each other.
When you almost died
of your eighth pregnancy at 27,
I found you at home sitting on a rush mat.
Your deserter husband
hid behind a wardrobe
plastered with *Playboy* centerfolds.
I took you to the Tan Son Nhut Hospital.
When they laid you on the gurney cart
and I saw you in my missing silk underpants
you shrugged.

A NAME

In Vietnamese,
Mrs. Nga explained,
chi means “maid” or “sister”
depending on the relationship.

I thought it was a name.

CHI AI

Ai, the seamstress, was creepy.
She weighed as much as a mynah bird
and looked like one.
She could copy anything.
She stopped sewing
only to eat plain rice,
nothing on it.
She'd swish the last kernel
from her bowl
with cold brown tea.

My mother's words
floated up to me
like lyrics from some song.

> "Eat everything on your plate.
> Remember the starving children of China."

I was told this over bowls of oatmeal
brown sugar and heavy cream.
At the bottom of the dish,
Beatrix Potter's Peter Rabbit,
the prize for finishing.

JEANNETTE

Jeannette stopped by "the Nam"
on her way home
from temples in Burma.
Each morning the seamstress
came to her villa
fitting the tea-colored pajamas
until they lay on her body—a silk skin.

"Darling, why bother teaching them English?
We taught them French.
Next they will have to learn Russian."
She knew her antiques.
"Not that one," she'd roar,
pointing to a blue-and-white teapot,
"that's early Chiang Kai-shek."

She wore a Nikkormat
around her neck
like an ornament.
Her portraits of us
came out silhouettes.
She took her readings on the sun.

ORPHANAGE

When I visited the orphanage
I went with balloons, hard candies
old *National Geographics*.

The children grabbed for everything.
I gave one a candy, others screamed
until seven or eight were clawing at my legs.

They popped the balloons
choked on the candies
shredded the magazines.

I looked over to the nun for help.

She stopped ladling gruel into the communal trough
put down the long tin spoon
and came across the room to tell me,

"Next time, if you come,
bring enough for everyone, or bring nothing."

THE WHEEL OF BRIE

For my first office party
I hunted down a wheel of Brie.
When none of the Vietnamese touched it,
I called Mrs. Nga, who told me:

"Some Vietnamese hate dairy products.
We like fruit and vegetables.
We think you Americans
smell of rich butter and milk."

POTTERY FACTORIES

One Thursday each month
my friends and I hired a CBS car
to visit pottery factories in "friendly" villages.

A family enterprise—children carried parts
of clay elephants on boards
placed on their heads

the trunk, the ears, the legs
all separate—carried in procession
an offering to be assembled and fired in the kilns.

In the last stages, tiny boys kneeled
beside the glazed green elephants
painting their toenails gold.

A river flowed by the factory.
We watched narrow boats being loaded
with hundreds of plates and saucers for the city.

Across the river on a porch above the bank
a grandmother rocked a baby in a hammock
by a string attached to her big toe.

"Their babies never cry," my friend said.

On the way back, I coveted her bowls,
the ones with the dancing roosters painted on the sides.
She admitted later she wanted mine with the dragons.

PIDGIN

Bob worked with Brown and Root,
carved out the roads we left there
with earthmovers flown from home.

He had an affair
with a bar-girl called Twiggy
he said spoke only pidgin.

They giggled a lot.
Took Polaroids of each other.
Studied them and giggled some more.

When they came to my apartment,
she said, "You remind me of a housewife.
I remind myself of that flower"—

and pointed to a single red rose
in a tall green vase.

DAVE'S OCELOT

Dave, our journalist friend,
bought a baby ocelot
from the animal market.

Before he got home,
the rain had washed away
its spots.

WINNING THEIR HEARTS AND MINDS

We rehearsed our *Macbeth*
four scenes from four acts.
I'd cast Lady Macbeth, Banquo, the witches.

They made costumes
bought knives as daggers
memorized their lines.

The day of the performance
the first act was perfect.
I sat proudly in the back.

For Act II
a second Lady Macbeth appeared,
another Banquo, different witches.

Stunned, I spoke to them
when it was all over.
They said their way was more democratic.

I told my friend the expert.

"Calm down," she said.
"You'll get it. But here's a hint.
There are 50 daily newspapers in Saigon."

SHRINE

I played tennis at the Cercle Sportif
with one of the justices of the Supreme Court—
the only Vietnamese to ask me
to his house for dinner.

In the living room
his refrigerator
covered in a blue brocade cloth
was locked.

THE HONDA REVOLUTION

Looking down from my window
I watched lovers
seated on their motorbikes
kissing under the sacred banyan tree.

At siesta, the woman who guarded the bikes
took her nap, lying across the seats
a cone-shaped hat over face.

I played a game with my friend—
who could count
the most people on one Honda.

At Tet, I counted seven
including a grandmother and presents.
I won.

THE HOUSE ON TU DO STREET

"Something is happening here,
but you don't know what it is.
Do you, Mr. Jones?"
—Ballad of a Thin Man
BOB DYLAN

We called their place
on Tu Do Street "the crash pad."
It had been Graham Greene's.

Something was always going on there
not the John-Wayne-rerun
frozen-chicken-à-la-king-French-poodle
white-wall-to-wall carpeting
of the American compound.

They were young Americans
who came to Vietnam and stayed.
Sam came in the army
worked for an alternative news service.
Skye read me my first ca dao.
She knew the language
had her baby in a Vietnamese hospital.

More Vietnamese than the Vietnamese
they hunkered down
on the backs of their calves to chat
slept on the floor
ate with wooden chopsticks
made cha gio and pho.

There was a difference.
Rolling papers lay among their dictionaries.
Our go-betweens
they knew the way to opium
as well as Buddha's path.

DAO DUA THE COCONUT MONK

The Dao Dua picked Sam
to be his American successor.
One weekend he led us on his dark-red motorcycle
out into the countryside.

From the brown river, Paradise Island,
the Dao Dua's kingdom, rose like a mirage—
a river platform with painted dragons,
spiral staircases and strings of colored lights.

Monks in maroon and brown pajamas,
their hair pulled forward like elves' caps,
made bells from bullet casings,
grew their trees in jerry cans.

The Dao Dua prayed for peace for ten years.
He lived in two symbolic towers;
slept in Hanoi, prayed in Saigon.
Beneath him lay a papier-mâché map of Vietnam.

Hearing the astronauts had gone to the moon,
he had himself lifted in a basket.
All day people came to him for advice
though he had not spoken in five years.

I climbed the tower to bring him *Life* magazine.
He found a colored picture of Disneyland at night,
pointed out over his world and smiled.

We wore maroon pajamas all day
slept on the floor
with a plastic brick for a pillow.
Monks left bowls of vegetables outside the door.

In the candlelight Sam made a shadow figure
of a praying mantis on the wall.
The insect danced higher and higher
until I heard him say,

"Our countries are both whores.
We deserve each other."
The sound of bells drifted over the river
answered by gunshots from the shore.

WORDY

I had been teaching "wordiness." My students' essays dripped with "It can be said of the mannerisms of Romeo that he had a violent personality."

At the end of the hour, I asked Mr. Phuc to comment on Romeo's speech:

Two of the fairest stars in all the heaven,
Having some business, do entreat her eyes
To twinkle in their spheres till they return.
What if her eyes were there, they in her head?
The brightness of her cheek would shame those stars,
As daylight doth a lamp.

"Shakespeare is wordy," he said, making the whole class laugh.

MILITARY INTERPRETER'S HANDBOOK

The Vietnamese words
for "birthday suit"
were translated
"Nude as a worm in a cocoon."

"Send to Siberia" as
"Send to the place
where the monkeys cough
and the flamingos sing."

Two-bit	*Rẻ tiền*
Two bits	*25 xu*
Two-time	*Đánh lừa*
Typewriter	*Tiểu liên*

U

U-drive-it car	*Xe hơi cho thuê không tài-xế*
Unbleached American	*Người Mỹ da đen*
Uncle benny	*Tiệm cầm đồ*
Uncle sam's pokey	*Nhà ngục liên-bang*
Undercover	*Bí-mật*
Unky	*Chú, bác*
Unscramble	*Mã-dịch một điện-văn*
Up-and-upper	*Người liêm-khiết*
Upchuck	*Nôn-oẹ*

V

Varnish remover	*Cà-phê pha thật đậm*
V.D. (Venereal Disease)	*Bệnh lậu*
Vetmobile	*Xe hơi đặc-biệt dành cho các thương-binh què quặt*
Vice cops	*Cảnh-sát kiểm-tục*
V.I.P. (Very Important People)	*Những nhân-vật rất quan-trọng*
V.U.P. (Very Unimportant People)	*Những người rất tầm thường*

W

Wade in	*Bắt đầu*
Wage hike	*Tăng lương*

Walking dandruff	*Chấy, rận*
Wampum	*Tiền*
War-hawks	*Người theo phe điều-hâu, chủ chiến*
War horse	*Chính-trị-gia lão thành*
Waterloo	*Thất-bại, sự thất trận*
When my ship comes in	*Khi nào tôi giầu*
When the cows give beer	*Không bao giờ*
Whodidit	*Tiểu-thuyết hay là phim trinh-thám*
Whodunist	*Tác-giả tiểu-thuyết hay là phim trinh-thám*
Why, sure!	*Là cái chắc!*
Wobbly hole	*Số không (xe hơi)*
Wooden overcoat	*Áo quần*

X

X-eyes	*Mắt lé*

Y

Yes-man	*Người ba phải*
Y-gun	*Đại-bác chống tầu ngầm*
You are all wet	*Anh nhầm to rồi*
You are so right!	*Anh nói đúng quá!*
You bet!	*Dĩ nhiên rồi!*

Z

Zipper your kisser	*Im họng đi!*
Zipper	*Nhanh nhẹn*

DINNER PARTY

I asked my brother, who came out to stay,
what he would like for dinner.
The cook, I told him, could produce
French, Chinese or American.

"Why not Japanese?" he joked.
"Too short an occupation?
No time to teach the culinary arts?"

"Duck *à l'orange*," I ordered
in French that made the cook wince.

That afternoon, my brother watched three ducks,
one white, two black-and-white,
follow the cook up the balcony steps
into the kitchen.

He left the house to avoid
what he knew was coming.

The next morning, inside the refrigerator,
he found a glass of fresh dark blood
drained from their necks.

LETTER FROM MY BROTHER

Dear Wendy,

Back in my own time-zone, the journey has come full circle, and all that is left is great memories, a little better understanding, 18 cases of photographs and incoming American Express bills.

I feel like a returning veteran filled with stories of war and horror. But perhaps the real horror of the thing was to be in a city where war is taken so for granted. I guess really it's no different here, where we watch killing every night before dinner and let it bounce off into inaction.

I find myself viewing more closely not so much for answers, but places that are familiar. I guess I've forsaken all answers, but at least I know now where Vietnam ends and Cambodia begins and that there are real people living there and that they don't all look alike.

Our latest "confrontation" is that our neighbors who think *Hair* is "disgusting" think that we are disgusting too for letting our kids go to see it. It takes all kinds.

I'm watching the news now and you wouldn't believe the height of Tricia Nixon's wedding cake.

You were a great guide. Keep the blood out of the icebox.

Your cowardly brother,

Michael

CHECK-POINTS

Hot nights we'd lie awake
in a room that smelled of mildew and insecticide
watching the blade of the punkah turn overhead,
listening to the rumble of outgoing in the distance,
waiting for Linh, the telex operator, to call from the office.

In the reign of a previous bureau chief
Linh had called in the night
to check on the name of a town.

Awakened, the former Big Boss hollered into the phone:

"You can tell those bastards in New York
in case they've forgotten, there's 13 hours difference between
there and Saigon. That makes it 4 A.M. here.
If they expect me to get up and get dressed
in the middle of the night and walk alone after curfew
through these rat-infested streets to check-point some fact
in a story they'll never run. You can tell them."

In the morning when he came into the office
he saw Linh had telexed his message verbatim.

THE LION

Before breakfast when it was still cool
I joined my neighbor on her roof
for Yoga exercises.

In turquoise leotards and black tights
we crouched,
hands dug into our knees like claws,

then crossed our wide-open eyes
stuck our tongues out and down
as far as we could, leaned forward

and roared into the Saigon air—
two blue Danskin lions
panting to lift our sagging chins.

HOARDING

My friend the expert downstairs
lived in Asia 13 years.
She knew the ropes.

When the PX got in artichokes
she'd call. We'd hire a car
and race to secure one case each.

Sometimes she didn't call till she got back.

VIETNAMESE CA DAO

Buffalo, listen to me.
Go to the fields and work with me.
Plowing is the farmer's destiny.
Here I am. There you are.
Neither of us complains of hard work.
If the rice still has flower,
you still have grass in the field to eat.

PHNOM PENH
AND
VIENTIANE

THE ROYAL HOTEL

The sign at the Phnom Penh airport warned,
"It is unsafe to visit Angkor Wat."

We were driven in a white Mercedes
to the Royal Hotel
where waiters in white uniforms
carried tall drinks
to us journalists sprawled in lounge chairs
by the swimming pool.

In huge rooms upstairs
we spread out maps of Cambodia on the floor
dotted with names of towns and rivers
we couldn't pronounce
without interpreters.

INCOMING

The night they shelled the airport I was there.
I hadn't meant to be. I was on my way to the hotel.

No time, the journalist driving said. He'd been cleaning
grass with his headphones on, almost missed the shelling.

The guards that stopped us were fourteen-year-olds.
They held their weapons like heavy toys.

I was dressed in a light-blue Lilly Pulitzer dress
and open-toed sandals.

From the pitch-black night, someone yelled
"Get down. That's incoming."

I remember thinking the Asians are all in front of the wall,
everyone else crouched behind it. Which was better?

I guess I asked too many times.
A man yelled, "Get down and shut up."

Something heavy whistled overhead.
It came too fast to be scared.

I thought, who's out there in the dark?
who are those guys?
who wants to kill me?

and then came rage
and the shakes
and Oh God please get me out of this.

In the distance the fuel tanks exploded
shooting huge orange balls into the air.

One of the network men got up and screamed
to his Korean camera crew, "Get closer. I want you closer."

and then, "I don't know what possesses me at times like this.
Maybe it's the Devil."

With that he jumped the wall and ran toward the fire
his right arm circling a cavalry charge.

DAWN SOW

After hours, I heard a grunt.
Lifting my face from the dirt,
I watched a pink sow in the half light
slog toward me through a mud puddle,
her enormous swollen tits
touching the ground,
her six piglets squealing behind her.

I remember laughing,
I'm alive.
There's a pig coming toward me.
I'm alive.
There's a pig and her babies coming toward me.

As the sun came up,
I saw the silhouettes of families,
hundreds of them on the one road
leaving their homes,
the men pulling crude wagons
filled with their children,
chickens, a prized sewing machine.

There was an awful stillness
except for the typing of the Reuters man
kneeling by the side of the road
his blue portable on a turned-over crate.

PHNOM PENH DANCING CLASS

The day after the rocket attack
I went alone to the palace

to watch a dancing class
forty children, aged three to fourteen

their purple harem pants
tucked into orange cummerbunds.

Bare curve of shoulder
backs as straight as bamboo

they practiced hour after hour
forcing their delicate fingers back.

An old woman clipped them lovingly
on the ankles with her stick.

All morning, birds flew in and out
resting on the wooden carvings

of the coffered ceiling.
A breeze blew across the river

over the palms
onto the open gallery.

The only sounds were the gamelan—
clear notes trickling over each other

like stream water over rocks—
and the tap tap tapping of the teacher's stick.

THE ROYAL THRONE ROOM

It was not dying—no, not ever dying;
But the night I died I dreamed that I was dead,
And the cities said to me: "Why are you dying?
We are satisfied, if you are; but why did I die?"

—RANDALL JARRELL, "Losses"

A gnome-shaped white-haired man
touched me on the shoulder.

I started from my trance.

He beckoned with his finger
as in a fairy tale.

I followed him down palace halls
until he unlocked a simple door.

The Royal Throne Room,
inlaid with mother-of-pearl, shimmered.

His dark eyes shone as he showed
the silver floors

woven peacock feathers on the walls,
golden Buddhas their legs smooth from touching.

He said across the dark,
"My family has guarded these treasures
for generations. What will happen?

Many of my people will die.
My country will die."

He looked to me for help.
Then locked the door.

RECALLED

Sitting in a lounge chair by the pool,
the wife of a TV correspondent said,
"We've just been recalled.
I've got to beat it down
and pick up some of those silver animals,
those gorgeous little elephants,
before the plane takes off."

HANDMADE IN LAOS

Outside the hotel in Vientiane
I bought an embroidered bag
from an old mountain woman.

Her brown curled hands
had sewed a thousand perfect stitches
on strips of pink and black appliqué.

From the bottom hung plastic beads,
French coins
République Française 1937
Indochine, they read.

Liberty sits draped on Her throne
a torch in Her hand
a crown on Her silver head.

I felt the mountain lady's presence
as, teeth clenched, I smiled
through diplomatic receptions
my new bag jangling at my side.

What would her people find
to sew on when my country left?
What would they weave
into the tree-of-life design—

film canisters
pop-top rings
rusted casings of M-16's?

OPIUM DENS AND GOLDEN EGGS

One night we tried an opium den.
There were more than 200 in Vientiane.
The place looked like a hut.
To get there we walked a plank across a ditch.

Dark inside, the addicts lay on mats.
The bare-chested opium man's skin glowed.
The tiny coal of his fire-maker lit one side
of his green face with the raked light of a Caravaggio.

My turn.

I lay beside this stranger
as he heated the sticky brown wax.
Next to me, the brass spittoon
where I'd watched others throwing up.

Inhale cough. Inhale cough.
The pipe went out.
I talked too much
where silence was the rule.

The others wanted theirs.
A French correspondent yelled *shut up*.
Two woman rolled together.
I could hardly walk the plank to leave.

Afraid, I lay awake all night
in a strange hotel room
listening to the rain
feeling my veins tighten around my blood.

Next morning
temples greased in Tiger Balm
we were the only round-eyes
on the plane to Saigon.

  The Plain of Jars.
  It could be Mars.

  The Plain of Jars.
  It could be Mars

stuck in my head
like a record going round and round
like my own blood through my body
the night before.

Then through the crack in the seats ahead of us
I thought I saw a woman as thin as bamboo
slipping Elizabeth Arden lipsticks
and solid-gold eggs to other Asians.

Golden eggs.

In the opium afterhaze
I saw the yellow spun-sugar eggs
left by the Easter bunny
at the foot of my bed.

I remember holding them up to my eye
and through the magic window seeing
tiny bunnies on their hind legs
pushing wheelbarrows filled with colored eggs
across a bright green lawn.

The Plain of Jars.
It could be ours.

The woman's cohorts went to the bathroom
returning with nothing.
I poked my husband and whispered
"We're in the middle of a smuggling ring."

"Where do you suppose they're putting them?"
"Three guesses," he said.

The Queen of Hearts.
She stole some tarts.

The Plain of Mars.
The Plain of Jars.

We reported the racket to customs
but no one was ever caught.
"The goose that laid the golden egg,"
my husband said.

BACK TO SAIGON

LETTER TO MY SISTER IN WASHINGTON, D.C.

Saigon

Dear Sis,

Janie, the weather person on the Armed Services Station, is showing 95° in Danang, snow falling in Washington, and I'm sitting here thinking of you and wondering how a Thomas's English muffin tastes in the morning.

I'd give anything to be cold. Sometimes when I wake up in the middle of the night, I go to the kitchen, open the refrigerator door and just stand there in my nightgown letting the cool air hit my skin.

I wish I were there. We could take a walk. Old Dusty could pull us around Cleveland Park on her red leash. The huge oaks up by the Washington Cathedral would be weighted down with snow.

Afterwards, we'd sit around your kitchen table, drinking coffee, watching "General Hospital" and gossiping about everything as fast as we could. I'm so t i r e d of speaking s l o w l y.

Yesterday on my way to the market, I was walking along like a true colonialist in my straw hat, when a cyclo man jumped on my back. I don't know why I didn't buckle to the pavement—but those cyclo men smoke so much opium they weigh nothing. His egret legs wrapped around my waist as he pounded on me yelling, "Get out. Get out. Get out of my country."

I can't blame him. "Troi oi." We say this all the time. Literally, it means "Oh Heaven," but I think it means "It's all too much." No doubt it loses something in translation. Sometimes I think I'm losing something in translation.

Write to me—anything—from home. How's Ali MacGraw's mustache?

Troi-oi
Wendell

TAPES

When the bigwigs flew out from New York
to interview President Thieu,
my husband was allowed to sit in.

The cassette he brought to the palace
had Bob Dylan singing on it.

When the tape was transcribed
we heard Dylan wailing in the background,
"Hey, Mr. Tambourine Man, play a song for me"

as Thieu droned on
about progress in Vietnamization,
assurances of his landslide victory.

VICTORY

After President Thieu won the election
by 99.4% of the vote,
we crowned him "Ivory Snow"
$99^{44}/_{100}\%$ pure.

JOHNNIE WALKER TO THE RESCUE

President Thieu had an aide
who spoke perfect English
wore a baseball cap.

When he had the press to dinner
he had the menu printed on the table
so we knew what we were eating:

hedgehog
duck's feet
crisp baby sparrows from the nest.

I gagged down the first duck's foot
with Scotch.
He saw and ordered me another.

GI JOE

One afternoon three GI's came to my balcony.
The blond, from Iowa City, looked like Gary Cooper.
I told him I had a boyfriend once
who went to college in Des Moines.

It was exciting just to say the names.

I told him I raised a black Angus heifer for 4-H.
Never could train her either.
She pulled me through the sawdust
at the fairgrounds in Santa Ynez, California.

I won a red ribbon.
We laughed about ribbons hanging in barns
all across America.
He talked about his high school basketball team

and in the same breath
asked if I minded his smoking heroin.
As he tapped white powder onto a Kool cigarette,
I expected to see the Man with the Golden Arm.

Instead he kept on talking about home
said he started smoking the Big H
the first day in the Nam,
the smell of marijuana was too easy to detect.

SOLDIER'S GRAFFITO

"I think I'm falling in love
with my right hand."

DUNCAN'S HORSES

I taught the Elizabethan concept of order in *Macbeth*,
The Great Chain of Being,
every speck of creation a link in nature's chain.
When disorder erupts, the links break
moving along the chain in a ripple movement.

When Macbeth murders Duncan
night strangles day
mousing owls kill falcons
Duncan's horses break from their stalls
and eat each other.

I taught this theory to Vietnamese teachers
while we defoliated their land
napalmed their children
burned their villages to save them.

Black powder	*Thuốc súng đen*
Blank ammunition	*Đạn thuốc không*
Blasting effect	*Hiệu-lực hơi thổi*
Booster	*Kíp nổ*
Bursting charge	*Thuốc nổ phá*
Bursting effect	*Hiệu-lực phá vỡ*
Coarse grained powder	*Thuốc súng hột to*
Chlorated powder	*Thuốc súng cờ-lo-rát*
Colloidal powder	*Thuốc súng keo*
Complete round	*Phát đạn đầy đủ*
Concrete-piercing shell	*Trái đạn xuyên phá bê-tông*
Delayed action fuze	*Đầu nổ chậm*
Detonator	*Kíp nổ*
Dummy ammunition	*Đạn giả*
Fine grained powder	*Thuốc súng hột nhỏ*
Fulminating powder	*Thuốc súng fu-mi-nát*
Gas shell	*Trái đạn hơi độc*
Graze burst shell	*Trái đạn chạm nổ*
Gun cotton	*Bông thuốc súng*
High explosive powder	*Thuốc nổ phá*
High explosive shell	*Trái đạn nổ phá*
Illuminating shell	*Trái đạn chiếu sáng*
Incendiary shell	*Trái đạn lửa*
Increment	*Thuốc bồi*
Instantaneous fuze	*Đầu nổ tức khắc*
Live ammunition	*Đạn thật*
Lacrymatory shell	*Trái đạn cay mắt*
Mechanical fuze	*Đầu nổ cơ-vận*
Mercury fulminate	*Ful-mi-nát, thủy-ngân*
Nitrocotton	*Bông thuốc súng*
Nitrogen powder	*Thuốc đạm-tố*

Piercing effect	*Hiệu-lực xuyên phá*
Powder bag	*Túi thuốc nạp*
Primer mixture	*Thành phần thuốc nổ*
Propelling charge	*Thuốc tống*
Proximity fuze	*Đầu nổ sóng điện*
Quick burning powder	*Thuốc súng nhạy*
Rocket	*Hỏa-tiễn*
Safety pin	*Chốt an-toàn*
Saltpeter	*Hỏa-tiêu*
Shape charge	*Thuốc nổ lõm*
Shell	*Trái đạn*
Shrapnel shell	*Trái đạn ghém*
Smoke shell	*Trái đạn khói*
Smokeless powder	*Thuốc súng không khói*
Sympathetic detonation	*Nổ vì giao-cảm*
The base	*Đuôi đạn*
The body	*Thân đạn*
The case	*Vỏ đạn*
The fuze	*Đầu nổ*
The primer	*Hạt nổ*
The rotating band	*Đai đạn*
Time fuze	*Đầu nổ cao*
T and P (Time and Percussion) fuze	*Đầu nổ lưỡng tính*
To set a fuze	*Điều-chỉnh đầu nổ*
Trinitrotoluene T. N. T.	*Thuốc nổ TNT*
Training ammunition	*Đạn huấn-luyện*

INVASION

The morning of the Laotian invasion
I got up with my husband at dawn
took his picture on the balcony.
He looked small and pale
wrapped in an army-issue camouflage poncho
we kept on the bed.
The press was forbidden to file stories home.
There was even an embargo on the embargo.

When his friend came to tell me
that the first helicopter had gone down
that everyone on it was dead
that the pilots were Vietnamese
that they flew north into enemy fire
that my husband was on the second and O.K.
I wanted to sleep with this messenger.

Instead, we stayed up
smoking strong grass
listening to Sweet Baby James

I've seen fire and I've seen rain
I've seen sunny days that I thought would never end
I've seen lonely times when I could not find a friend
but I always thought that I'd see you again . . .

The music burned in
                    dodged
scored along my nerves
new, three-dimensional
guitar   notes   words
cascading over each other
rising like the heat
held there.

VIETNAMIZATION

The name of the operation
was changed
from Dewey Canyon II
to Lam Son 719.

EDITOR

In his air-conditioned room
24 floors above the Avenue of the Americas
the editor waits for the story.

He tells his researcher,
"I've heard from my Pentagon division.
Now I'm waiting for my flower children in Saigon."

LETTER FROM A SOLDIER

Five flights below me
the landlady's daughter
received a letter
from her fiancé fighting in Laos.

"We are running scared. We cannot hold the line. Everyone is running. No one even stops to dig in. We call in American support. Nothing happens. I doubt that I will make it home."

I heard about the letter
told her my husband
was doing a story
on the invasion of Laos.

When I asked if he could quote from her letter,
she took the paper from her pocket
and burned it on the table
with a look beyond disgust.

GECKOS

Evenings, waiting for you
I watched pale geckos
belly their way
across my ceiling.

Slowly three, sometimes five
(their large eyes never blinked)
manoeuvered to surround
a fluttering moth.

After hours of upside-down stalking,
by some signal I never saw,
one would uncurl his thin tongue
and strike! Swallow the insect whole.

This happened every night in silence.

It was strange how at the end
I looked forward to the geckos' coming out.

THE AMERICAN ADVISER

We met an American adviser
in a French café
on the southern coast of Vietnam.
Over a bowl of soupe Chinoise
he told us about his dog.

It seems he raised a large retriever
in his village in the jungle
on vitamins and cases of Alpo
his mother sent from home.

The dog was the wonder of the village.
Children stood in line
to touch his golden hair.

When I asked him what would happen
to the dog when he left,
he said not even the village elders
could afford to feed it.
He would have to shoot it.

EXAMS

During examination week
there was a demonstration
in the more radical
School of Science.

I decided to hold my orals anyway.

I was asking Mr. Phuc
to explain the role of the witches in *Macbeth*
when we heard an explosion
and both dived under my desk.

He pointed to the book in his hand.
Through tear-gassed eyes,
I read the title dimly:
Shakespeare without Tears.

We held on to each other
under my desk
our cheeks wet
with laughing and crying.

REST AND RECREATION

After all the dragon jars
the rows of Buddha smiles

gold leaf plastered
on guard dogs outside temples

after all the burning sandalwood
cobras, firebirds
teacups of the moon palace

I climbed the steps
of a Portuguese church in Macao.

Cut in gray stone
above the door
ox, eagle, lion, and winged man

Matthew, Mark, Luke, and John
I recognized them!

BACK IN THE WORLD

In a French restaurant in Saigon,
I overheard a GI
say to his Vietnamese date,

"You see what I mean?
Why I have to get out?
Back in the world,
they have cabbages *this* big."

He stared through the empty
circle of his arms
at the Brussels sprouts
piled on his plate.

THE NOODLE CART

My friends sent back rain drums from Laos,
lacquered trays with goldfish, ceramic elephants.
Once I knew we were leaving
I wanted a noodle cart

the old kind,
like the one I passed each morning on Le Thanh Ton,
with the stained-glass panels
of dragons and oceans and mythic sword fights.

I loved the giant ladles
the blue-and-white bowls in racks
the pots of boiling soup
over the charcoal braziers
the tiny stools on the street.

I loved the way the vendor
knew his clients
knew their favorite noodles
what they liked on top
like a waitress knowing you like your eggs
"sunny-side up" in an American coffee shop.

I asked Mrs. Nga to help me find a noodle cart.
After a month she said she had.
To buy one, she had to talk a family out of theirs.
The son was all in favor, but not the father
who was dead against selling the family business.

Now the noodle cart stands
on my brother's porch in California
stocked with little green bottles of Perrier water
Mr. and Mrs. T's Bloody Mary Mix.

NEW YORK CITY
1971-1975

PACKERS

When our shipping crate arrived at home,
our cameras, lenses,
tape recorders, cassettes, typewriters
and drip-dry shirts were gone.

In our living room I stared at a black X
inked on the outside of the half-empty box.
Above it, a hole, axed in the plywood
stared back like a skull.

The men who'd worked three days
in our Saigon apartment
wrapping our possessions
carefully in newspaper

put all the black market stuff
in one place and marked it
so that their cohorts at the docks
would know just where to go in
and scoop it out.

LETTER FROM A FRIEND STILL IN SAIGON

Dear Wendy,

In answer to your question, I've had it here. If I come around the corner one more time to see a cyclo driver pissing on the sidewalk or if the god-awful smell of frying nuoc mam wafts through the window one more breakfast, I'll throw up on the whole village of people parked outside my walls.

Everyone we knew and loved in the press corps has moved on. We are stuck here one more year.

We are in a new villa since you left. The cook took everything that was not nailed down except a mutt we did not want and the lawn.

Papayas are coming into season. The strawberries from Dalat are here. Otherwise, you can have this Pearl of the Orient.

This will have to be short. We're going to Hong Kong in two days for R&R. I can't wait to call Mandarin room service from the bathtub then jump into those pressed linen sheets.

Otherwise, you're lucky to be back in the world of round-eyes and Rexall Drugs.

Miss you,

Susan

REUNION

Late January. Tet.
It's been four years.
Mrs. Nga is coming toward me
on the Avenue of the Americas.
The Christmas decorations are down
in New York City
where buildings slice the sky
streets smoke from underneath
doors open automatically.

She's wearing a red nylon ski parka.
She looks small and alone
beside all the reflecting glass.
I remember my first walk in Saigon
asking everyone I met for directions
to Na Goo Yen Huey Street.
I was on it. Nguyen Hue
pronounced *When Way*.

It's snowing.
Vietnamese fear the cold.
When I was living there,
I dreamt of snow
dreamt of diving into a river of crystals
like an otter on a slide
covering myself from head to toe
in soft white powder.

Inside a restaurant, snowflakes melt
on the smooth red surface of her coat.
"From the rummage sale," she says
hanging it on a hook.

For some reason, I tell her
that as Saigon fell, the coded message
played on the U.S. radio
for Americans to go to their evacuation stations
was "the temperature report for Saigon
is 105° and rising"
followed by the first thirty seconds
of "I'm Dreaming of a White Christmas."

She tells me how she managed to escape
four days before the Americans,
how she misses her country, her mother,
how the church helped her find a house in Greenwich.
She says now it is she who has a problem.
Her son has fallen in love
with the daughter of their American tutor.

They stay upstairs in his room all day
playing loud music, will not be part of the family
not even to come down to dinner.
"Troi oi," I sigh and she laughs.
Remembering her advice to me in Vietnam,
I say "give me a week"
hoping I'll come up with something
to bring peace to her American household.

NGA'S STORY

KUNMING
HANOI
YEN BAI
HADONG
1927-1940

THE SCROLL

My father owned a Chinese scroll
big as a wall
nine different birds
painted on silk
some flying, some standing
some building nests.
He named all of us,
six boys and three girls,
after the birds in the scroll.

Phuong for phoenix
Nhan for skylark
Hac for heron
Bang for eagle
Cau for dove
Nga for swan
Hai for seagull
and later
Yen for swallow
Tuoc for robin.

Whenever we moved
he rolled it up himself
carried it on his shoulders
from one place to another
even when the silk had faded yellow.

LEAVING CHINA

I was born in China in 1927.
My father was sent there to teach.
He graduated with honors from the University of Hanoi,
should have been allowed to choose his post,
but his French superior wanted a bribe.

My father was honest
influenced too much by Confucius.
When he refused to give money, he was sent to Kunming
a province on the border of Vietnam.
He always said it was a punishment.

I remember the day we left China for Hanoi.
I was the youngest in the family then.
The whole town came to say goodbye to my father.
His students lit firecrackers
hung flowers from the train.

My mother's friends cried.
She lay down in the dark
all the way to Hanoi.
The train burned charcoal.
When I stuck my head out the window
dust blew in my eyes.

RIDING WITH MY FATHER

I remember the days
in the waterfall highlands
riding through the jungle
in front of my father's saddle
feeling his arms around me.
Together we'd cross mountain passes:
wild orchids in the morning mist
chattering monkeys
pythons sunning on the rocks.
Below us, transparent streams
where the soldiers, our escorts,
would stop to catch tiny striped fish
in their hands.

I'd carry them in the cold pool
of a wrapped banana leaf
watching the water move from side to side.
When I was scared, I'd cover my eyes.
At the steepest places, he'd dismount
and lift me on his shoulders
leading his brown horse
over the narrow mountain passes
going to inspect the schools
in Yen Bai.

Few of the fish
ever reached home alive.

MY FATHER'S TREASURES

Each time my father gambled with his boss,
the Province Chief,
I was to bring the silver betel box.
In it were betel, lime, the bitter bark of a tree,
tobacco and two sweet-smelling flowers from our garden.
My parents encouraged us to try it
said the lime would make our teeth strong.
They chewed, then spat red juice
into a brass pot polished bright each day.

My father stored his medicines in wooden boxes—
white cinnamon, dark cinnamon, ginseng root.
One day he brought home a python.
He kept its bile sac in a jar of alcohol.
After several weeks, he took it out
and dried it in the sun.
When we were sick,
he smashed the dried bile into little pieces
making us swallow the bitter medicine.
Sometimes he sucked strength
from young deer antlers
throwing his head back like a giant.
Deer antlers, he said, would give you many children.

Each morning before school
my job was to polish the antiques
kept in a drawer in the lacquer chest.
My father was afraid of being poisoned.
He always carried his special chopsticks
on his trips to the countryside.
They were black with silver tips.
A mountain chief gave them to him

promising that the tips would change color
if there was poison.

I was never sure whom he thought would kill him,
the French or the Vietnamese.

VISITING MY AUNTIE LAN

My father and I visited my auntie in Vinh Yen.
The cyclo man ran rhythmically
through the immense flat fields
of rice and corn—all yellowing.
Wind blew through the rice like waves.

Young girls cut the rice with their long scythes
piling it up
singing ritual folksongs
of the landscape to their sweethearts.

First the girls sang:

> *Can you guess how many rice plants we have?*
> *Do you know how many tributaries the river has?*
> *Who can sweep all the leaves in the forest?*

Then the boys would call back:

> *Before I answer you,*
> *you answer me.*
>
> *In how many years will the moon be old?*
> *How many years before we can say*
> *the mountain is old enough to stay forever?*

They would tease:

> *Oh young miss with the bucket on your shoulder*
> *could you please give me a bucket*
> *to water my evergreen plants?*
> *If the evergreen gets more leaves,*
> *a phoenix can stand on each branch.*

At night my cousins walked me through the rice fields.
The sound of the gongs from the harvest festival got closer and closer.
We watched the boys and girls dance in the moonlight
to the beat of the drums that hung from their necks.

Too excited to sleep
I'd lie awake in the strange bed
listening to the dogs barking in the village.

POLITICS

My father told me that when he was twenty
he taught himself French
so he could make more money
become a big man, a mandarin,
a Minister of Education.
Education, examination, administration:
that was the Confucian way.

We learned French too
like birds who cannot speak a human tongue.
We learned like parrots
and did not understand—
the alphabet, the verbs.

We hated the French
though Father worked with them.
We especially hated their long noses
called them *mui lo*,
which means, the nose looks at the mouth.

We never had them in our houses.
We saw them in the streets
heard they would rape and torture us
put electric strings on our fingers.
The most savage were the Algerians.
We named them *red gullets*.
When they killed you,
they ripped your belly out.

I never understood politics.
In the highlands Father warned us
not to take any leaflets.
They were guerrilla propaganda

would ruin our family's name.
His look scared us into silence.

Actually, many people entered our house at night.
They never went out in the day.
They talked quietly,
left in the black of night.
When I asked Father, he said
they were my aunties and uncles.
I wondered why I had so many.

THE EXECUTION

My elder brother remembers the day of the execution
in Yen Bai when I was very young.
Everyone in the house got up so early
it was still dark outside.

Father was serious.
He had received an invitation
from the French to watch an execution.
The French cut the throats of thirteen people
with a big machine—a guillotine.

The roads were blocked for miles.
There was no school.
I was not allowed to go.
The sky was dark and gloomy
the mountain covered with clouds.

My brother escaped from the house to watch.
When he came home,
he dared not sleep alone.
Father was very pale.

Years later, I understood
they had killed Nguyen Thai Hoc
and his sweetheart, Co Giang
and her sister, Co Bac—
national heroes and heroines
who fought against the French.

When he spoke of the highlands,
my father said,
"Difficult geography makes heroes."

SON NU—MOUNTAIN GIRLS

My elder sister
will remember
happier mornings
in the highlands.
Awake
before school
we'd look
through the window
up at the blue mountain
see the girls
in their long
navy blue skirts
their embroidered vests
big straw baskets
on their heads,
weaving their way
single file
slowly
down the path
covered with dew
in the coming sunlight.

We'd race from the house
to buy the sweet sim fruit
which turned our tongues purple.

OUR HOUSE IN HADONG

Our best house, the house where we were happy,
was our brick house on Ha Van Street
with its two hectares of land
lichee and mangosteen and starfruit in the back,
the two Hoa Moc trees white as snow in the front.
We'd put the petals in our tea to sweeten our breath.

From far down the road
I could smell the heavy jackfruit.
Father never allowed us to eat them
said they were too rich for the climate.
He'd give them to the soldiers outside the walls.
When he was away, we ate until we got fevers.
My younger sister climbed the apple trees
and shook the apples down.

We had everything.
There was a flower garden
with dark red roses, orchids and yellow mimosa.
We had our own cauliflower, tomatoes,
the artichokes my father loved,
chickens, pigs, ducks and pigeons.
We needed the market only for beef
and rice kept in giant brown jars in the storeroom.

We even had two ponds.
Each New Year
we'd let the water out of the big pond
to catch the butterfish
we'd fed all year.

On a tiny island in the middle of the smaller pond,
the cook built an imitation mountain

with caves, bamboo, porcelain angels,
and two old matchmakers playing chess.
When the moon came up,
we'd watch the goldfish move in the warm water
and listen to night noises
remembering the sounds of the jungle.

MY MOTHER

My mother always dressed with care.
She'd wrap her long black hair
into a black velvet turban
secured with a long gold pin.
She wore gold earrings
and a necklace of 1,000 fine gold beads.
(We'd count them round her neck.)
Embroidered in red beads
on her tiny velvet shoes
were her name and my father's.

As a child, her mother
encouraged her to dye her teeth black—
a sign of wealth and beauty.
My father dyed his, too.
When he became more westernized,
he wanted his white teeth back.
He went to bed
with a special leaf in his mouth,
but he never could get rid of the black.
His teeth remained a strange in-between color.

Each afternoon Mother would go gambling
with the Province Chief's wife
as was the duty of a mandarin's wife.
She'd be introduced as Ba Doc Hoc,
wife of the Minister of Education,
or as Ba Lon, Big Lady.

I watched from the window
as she settled in the rickshaw
first straightening the long skirt of her brown ao dai
over the pale pink one underneath.

Then the rickshaw man
would hand her the umbrella
with the gold handle
and out the gate they'd go.

THE FOUR DEMEANORS

When she was home, my mother instructed
my sister and myself in the four demeanors
as her mother had instructed her,
believing a woman should sacrifice for her husband.

Cong—manage the household within the budget
including cooking, sewing, knitting, care
of the husband, education of the children
all to save the husband's face

Dung—maintain an attractive and cheerful appearance
most particularly for the husband
(She showed us how to fix our hair, keep
our bodies clean.)

Ngon—speak properly, never raise one's voice
in front of the servants or other family
members

Hanh—know one's place
show respect and gratitude for parents and elders
faithfulness and sacrifice for the husband

She knew parts of the "Warrior's Wife" by heart
and made us learn it
to show how a brave wife behaves
when her husband goes to war to serve his country.

from "THE LAMENT OF THE WARRIOR'S WIFE"

Dang Tran Con (18th century)

The farewell cup is not empty, but you shake your sword;
Spear lowered, you point at the den of wild beasts.
Like Chieh-tzu, who fought the Lou-lan,
Like the Conqueror of Waves who held down the Man-chu,
Like them, you say, so you.
Red: your coat is as red as cinnabar,
White: Your horse is as white as new snow,
His bells begin to shake in time to the drums.
We stood facing each other. Now you are gone.
When I see the bridge I will see our parting.
I stand alone on the road, sadly watching your banners flutter away.
The first chariots draw near Chi-liao
But the cavalry to the rear is still wandering through
the Ch'ang-yang valley

. . .

This confinement is my destiny—
But who has decreed that you remain so far away?
I expected to live with you like a fish in water:
How could I know we were to be as separate as water and clouds?
I had no dream of being a warrior's wife,
Nor did you expect to be forever away.
Why must we be apart
And lonely in the morning, in the night?
We were young, we lived elegantly and well
in our happy marriage.
Who could bear to separate such lovers?
Now days warm you, nights chill you,
But there are mountains between us.
When you left there were no orioles in the willow trees.
You told me you would return with the cuckoos.
The cuckoos have come, the orioles have gone,

And there are swallows warbling in front of the house.
When you left the plum trees had felt no cold winds.
You told me you would return when the peach tree blooms.
Winter had blown on the peach trees,
Along the river the rose mallows are all withered.
You told me to wait on Lung-hsi hill,
And I waited from early dawn, and saw no one:
Only dry leaves fluttered down on my hairpin.

. . .

MY GRANDMOTHER

My mother missed her mother so much
she convinced my father to let her live with us.
We loved her and held her in respect.

Before we had electric heat,
my mother ordered one of us to lie
in Grandmother's bed to warm it up for her.

Grandmother would instruct us daily, especially the girls.

> "Be khong vin ca gay canh"
> A young branch must be put into shape
> lest it break when it's old.
>
> Girls, do not hang your underwear
> on a man's door.
> If your father or your brother pass under it,
> he will have bad luck.
>
> On your wedding day, your guests will chew the betel.
> If the color runs red, you will have great happiness.
> If not, your guests will be silent and worry for you.
>
> Remember.
> Once you go to your husband's house,
> you must wait on everyone,
> even the dog.

We had few toys, no radio.
We would sit on her lap
listening to her stories.

GRANDMOTHER'S FABLE

Once upon a time there lived a farming family.
The mother died, leaving three sons
to live with their father.
When the father became ill
and thought he was going to die,
he called his children to his bedside
and handed each of them
a large bunch of chopsticks tied together.

He said, "Whoever can break this,
I will reward."
Not one was able to.

The father then handed each of them
only one set.
This they broke easily.
The father said, "If you remain united,
no one can harm you,
but if you separate, then you will be hurt.
This is the advice I leave with you.
The heritage I have for you
is in the rice fields."

After the father's death,
the three brothers stayed together
even after they married.
They did not find any golden treasures
buried in the rice fields.
They plowed and planted
and the ground gave successful harvests.
They realized working together
and working hard were life's riches.

OUR RICKSHAW MAN

Anh Nhi was our rickshaw man.
"Anh" means brother.
He wore a cone-shaped straw hat
tied under his chin.
His smooth legs were wrapped
in red ribbons.
I never told my mother,
but I liked his fluffy rice
better than the finer rice
up at the big house.

He was loyal to our family,
but gambling was his weakness.
Sometimes he'd disappear for a week.
He'd come back so tired,
he would sleep under the high bed
with the legs carved to look like dragons,
afraid my mother would find him.

MY NURSE

My vu em
who nursed me from her breasts
stayed with our family most of her life
after her own baby died.
Even when I grew up,
she'd come and meet me at the gate
just as she did in the old days.
Nothing had changed—
not the smell
not the dress
not the sweets she hid under her waistband.

One night I heard my mother scream
and all the lights came on.
I asked my vu em what was happening
and she said mother was having a baby.
I saw my father running in and out
asking for hot water, more towels.
I ran to ask my sister where babies came from.
She told me from Mother's armpit.
I ran around the house telling everyone,
"Mother's having a baby from her armpit."

My vu em terrified me
with stories of the phantom
who lived in the Hoa Dai tree
and would stand at the head of my bed,
where I slept with my sister,
sticking its tongue,
as red as blood, out at us,
threatening to curl around my legs

and squeeze me to death
unless I slept.

I was old before I dared to sleep alone
and would run by any Hoa Dai tree.

ELEVEN YEARS OLD

My mother said I was growing up.
I looked at myself in the mirror
and I knew I was.
My eyes were big and brown
my cheeks very pink.
I smiled all the time.
My brothers would pinch me
saying "come on, daughter-in-law."
I did not understand
and would run into my room.

I began to like music,
reading poems and novels.
My third brother had a huge collection.
I loved *les livres roses*,
a series for children,
especially one about the vengeance of snakes,
one where the students go to fairyland
and *Tam Cam*, our *Cinderella*,
about the real sister and the stepsister and the prince.
I was a dreamer.

MY ELDEST BROTHER, PHUONG

I remember the day my eldest brother left,
the first separation in the family.
My parents rented a car
and took him to boarding school.
There was no high school where we lived.
Each night I passed his room, I cried.

He was the one who taught me to sing.
The one who lost his lover to his best friend
and put his sadness in his songs.
The one who knew when I was sad
watching the sun set behind the blue mountains,
happy when the morning sunshine
lit the tops of trees.

I knew my father would beat me for singing.
    "Singing is doing nothing.
    Nice girls from good families do not sing."
We met in secret.
    "Brothers and sisters must not sit together.
    Brothers and sisters must sit far from each other
    unless accompanied."

After school, I'd take a bath
change my clothes,
pretend to be visiting a friend
next door across the wall.
Instead, I'd run to my brother
waiting for me with his guitar
at the far end of the yard
in the summer thatch house
under the cool palm-leaf roof.

MY BROTHER'S STORY OF *Quynh Hoa*, THE PRINCESS FLOWER

This princess was so lovely
her own brother fell in love with her.
Because of his lust,
she felt she was no longer a virgin
and that he had sinned
against their ancestors.
She asked their forgiveness
then killed herself.

A mysterious flower
grew from the spot where she died.
The flower bloomed at night,
but never when her brother was there
though he sent special guards to tend it.
She wished to punish her brother
show the kingdom
she was still a virgin.

The first time our princess flower bloomed
we invited our friends to the courtyard
by the imitation mountain.
We circled the flower
with its fragile cream and pink blossoms,
played our guitars and sang,
watching its petals come out
little by little in the moonlight.

THE SCHOOL PLAY

One of our best-kept secrets
was that I was the head angel in the school play
and Father did not know it,
though he was head of the education board.

Everyone in the area came,
even the Province Chief.
When the curtain was raised
on the beautiful landscape
there stood twenty angels,
all dressed in white
with white flowers in their long black hair.

We sang the story of a romantic king
who journeyed out with these maidens
to go sightseeing.
Since he was a human king,
he drank too much wine.
Enchanted by the moonlight,
he journeyed to the heavens.
I was the angel who showed him the way back.

My eldest brother was the head of the orchestra.
My second played the flute,
my third the Spanish guitar.

At the end we sang farewell
to the king, played by our teacher.
Everyone clapped warmly.
As he walked off,
his crown slipped from his head
he tripped on his robe
and fell from the stage.

I stood there laughing
until I saw my father
give the signal to pull down the curtain.

That afternoon a soldier came to summon Father
to the Province Chief's house.
I watched him leave the yard.
He wore the long black topcoat
Mother had given him
with the blue brocade one underneath.
From the collar hung an ivory nameplate
engraved with his position in red characters.
I knew the summons was my fault.
I had caused my family ridicule
and ran to my brother for protection.

That evening we were all called to the table.
We invited our parents to eat first,
as is our custom.
My father took his chopsticks in his long fingers.
He looked at me with a little smile
and said to my mother,
"From now on, you will have the driver
take Nga in the afternoons
to the Province Chief's house
to teach his children music."
My eyes shone as I looked at my brother.

MATCHMAKERS

We had a formal relationship with our mother.
We never sat next to her,
but stood behind her chair.
Her days were filled with social obligations,
gambling with the Big Boss's wife.
Hour after hour they played *To Tom*,
a Vietnamese game for five players
120 pieces of red and black characters.

As they played, the women discussed
their children's fate.
"My son is so good at school,
he will become a mandarin."
"My daughter is so capable,
she runs the house without me."
Sometimes a real matchmaker would join in
praising her latest bride-to-be.

Even in my day, we did not pick our own husbands.
That was our parent's choice.
Once married, your fate was sealed.
You could not return to your home.
Everyone would think you had been rejected for a reason.
This would bring shame to your family.

TO THE EMPEROR

Once every three years in the spring,
my father would go to Hue, the ancient capital,
to pay homage to the Emperor Bao Dai.

My mother explained
this was the Nam Giao ceremony.
The Emperor was the Son of Heaven.

He communicated with the Universe
asking for blessings for his people.
The mandarins assisting him at court

were not allowed to look at him.
This was a sign of disrespect
in the old days punishable by death.

My mother brought down a special box
from its high place
unpacked father's deep blue brocade robe.

The soldiers warmed the heavy iron
in a clay oven filled with charcoal,
handed it to my mother.

As she smoothed the folds of the robe,
I stared at its embroidered double herons.
My job was to dust my father's black cloth boots.

KHAM THIEN,
THE STREET OF THE TEA HOUSES

There was a street called Kham Thien
between Hanoi and Hadong.
We were forbidden to go there
forbidden to even mention the name.
This was the street of the tea houses.
A senior geisha trained the younger geishas
to entertain the guests, only men.
They would play games
sing poems to the beat of a drum
My father loved the music.
He would go to these places often with Mr. van Phuc.

One day my mother said,
"Didn't you know your daddy had a friend
who was not a good friend?
Mr. van Phuc knew that your father was generous
that he had money.
Mr. van Phuc did not.
He spent days and days on the Kham Thien road
looking for the geisha who was the best singer
and reported back to your father."

Mother knew that if that man came to our house
Father would dress and leave in five minutes.
She tried to stop him, but it was no use.
He said he would only go for a little while
but he would always go for the whole night
and come home in the morning.
I hated that man.
One day when I saw him at the door
instead of asking him into the sitting room

and telling my father
I turned my head and went into my own room.

One night when Father came home late
I heard my mother's voice talking loudly.
Each one yelled at the other
and then my mother started to cry.
Father left the bedroom and slept on the couch.
The next morning when Father went out,
Mother ordered Anh Nhi, the rickshaw man,
to follow without letting Father know.

She told me and my sister to come with her
saying, "Hurry. Hurry, we have important work to do."
The three of us sat in the rickshaw
following close behind my father.
My mother said nothing.
Her face looked sad.

After one half hour we reached the country.
On either side were fields of rice
turning yellow and smelling so sweet.
Each time the breeze blew
the rice bent its head
like a wave on the river.
Birds flew here and there over the fields.
I spent my time daydreaming
wondering if I had time to run
deep into the fields picking up the ripe rice
to bring home to burn in our ovens.

Suddenly the rickshaw man stopped
at a row of houses.

There was one very tiny house.
Outside the white door was a fence and bushes of roses.
My mother hurried up to the house
followed by my sister and myself.
She knocked urgently on the door,
but no one answered.
Finally she pushed the door with all her strength
opening it onto a bed
a small sitting room and a closet.

When she saw my father's clothes in the closet,
she began to tremble.
She took the clothes from the hanger
then turned and ran from the house
seizing my hand
as we ran down the street after the lady
who had escaped from her house.
My mother cried over and over
"Oh, how selfish man is. How savage."
When we came close to the lady,
my mother stood in front of her and cried.
My sister said something and shook her head.
I was a machine following my mother and sister.

When we got home, Father was waiting for us
in his favorite chair.
His face was very very angry.
He said my mother was a big lady.
Why should she go running after another lady?
He said he was ashamed to have such a wife.
She said she had not meant to behave in such a way
but since my father was showing his unfaithfulness

she had to protect her happiness.
They were both talking and the noise got louder and louder.

When my brother came from his room,
all was silent.
We did not go to school.
There was sadness in the atmosphere of our family.

MY ELDER SISTER

Nhan was six years older than me.
I cried when she first went to school
leaving me alone at home.
She left school at fourteen.
Father did not believe in education for women.
It is our tradition that the eldest girl
learns to care for the house and the children
to prepare to become a good wife herself.

My mother turned over all powers to her.
She took care of the house money, made our clothes,
planned and cooked our meals.
She practiced French embroidery
and even took French cooking lessons,
a sign of status in the provinces.
My father thought no one was good enough for her.
She wore a white silk suit
with flowers embroidered on the cuffs.

She was strict
would beat us, even my brothers,
with a rattan rope.
I was beaten for being late,
and once for spilling violet ink on my clothes.
We did not have ballpoint pens.
We carried our own ink to school
in little glass bottles.

LOVE LETTERS

Sister and I slept in the same bed.
In the summer when it was hot,
we slept on polished boards with no sheets.
I was still afraid of the phantom.
Knowing this, my sister threatened
not to sleep with me
unless I delivered letters to her boyfriends.

Sometimes, I would deliver them.
Other times, embarrassed near boys,
I'd drop them down a hole
in between the bricks that covered the ditch
at the back of the house.
I'd watch the dark water carry them away.

When I was 12 and she was 18,
my father caught me with a letter.
He took it from me,
then beat us till we both bled.
Gradually, I came to understand
he wanted to stop us from loving the wrong person,
a person who would not be approved by the family.

In our country a girl should be pure
when she marries.
The purer she is
the more she is worth.
A big wedding means much face.
Parents raise their daughters
many years for that day.

AUNTIE LAN'S SON

Auntie Lan sent her tiny quiet son
from the countryside to live with us
to be educated by my father up to university.

When he was five years old,
she came to take him home
to marry a woman twenty-two years old.

She said her husband needed another strong woman
to work in his rice fields.
My father could not change her mind.

At the wedding the bride held her husband
in her arms. After the ceremony,
she gave him a bath.

The peasants joke about such marriages:

A husband and wife are walking in a field.
They come to a ditch.
The wife jumps over easily,
but the tiny husband falls in.
The water is high and rushing.
She calls out,
"Friend, come help me.
Lend me a bucket
to scoop up my husband."

FOLK POEM
OF THE MISMATCHED BRIDE

You love money so much
you would marry a little boy.
In the upper village
in the lower village
count the men.
Why bring your body to a little boy?
Can he massage your breasts?
In the wintertime
the boy tries to warm himself
by lying near you
and you must cover him.
Nine out of ten nights
you sleep alone.

I cannot tell anyone of my situation.
My youth is wasted,
my cheeks no longer rosy
all because of a tiny boy.
In the middle of the night
I rub him
waste my time.
Sad, I try to wake him.
He is too small. It is no use.
He snores gently into the next morning.

Dear Sister,
how many times will the flower blossom?

AUNTIE MAI

My father's younger sister was my favorite.
I wanted to go live with her in Hanoi.
She was westernized
had many French friends
who came to her house.
When she came to our house
she and father whispered in his room.
Once we did not see her for three months.
Father said she was busy.

Later he told me
she traveled in disguise all over Vietnam
as a nun, a nurse, a village teacher.
Much later I found out
her house was the headquarters
of the Quoc Dan Dang.
She passed on information
learned from the French.
She was arrested and tortured.
They put wires in her breasts
ants in her lower parts
but she never told them anything.
Eventually, they killed her.

HADONG
KUNMING
HANOI
1940-1954

MEETING BAO IN HADONG

The electric train that took us to school
passed by every fifteen minutes.
We heard the clang and ran to catch it.
Sometimes I stood the whole way,
one brother in front, one in back to protect me.
On the crowded train we met students
from other school levels.
We could tell by the labels on their books.

A man always offered me a seat.
I looked closely at him
though even that was not allowed.
He was handsome, with a high nose and bright eyes.
One morning he asked to borrow my novel.
From then on we began talking about books.
That was our relationship—
his explaining Lamartine to me.

One day he returned my book.
I saw a blue envelope
as sweet-smelling as a flower.
When I read it, my ears grew hot,
my cheeks red and my eyes thrilled.
It was my first love letter.
Then I remembered Father
beating my sister and myself for the letters
I'd carried for her as a go-between.
I hid my letter in the bottom drawer of my desk.

NIGHT-LISTENING

I remember the airplanes coming everyday.
I thought they had come to attack the Japanese
who were everywhere—
in the streets
in the barracks near our house.
We feared them
thought them savage
called them *Chu lun,* midgets.
I trusted the French more than them.
My father stayed home now.

The planes were Allied planes.
My father had shelters dug in the yard
up against the wall under the fruit trees.
They were five meters long
covered over with palm leaves.
When the rains flooded them,
he had concrete ones built.

We learned night-listening
how to tell the heavy bombers
from the inspection planes.

On moonlit nights they'd come.
We'd wake to the alert,
run into the garden
covering our heads.
At first it was so exciting.
We had never seen planes.
Everything seemed so far away
the noise
the shells
the fire.

We'd peek from our shelters
through the trees in the moonlight
to watch the planes shoot shells through the air
in the night sky.
When they'd passed over,
we'd hear the two short whispers of the all-clear sign
and we'd come out
walking past the fish ponds
back to our beds.

VIET MINH

The war between the French and the Viet Minh
came nearer and nearer.
One day, going to school,
I heard an explosion and ran to a ditch
already filled with people.
I lay outside the ditch
watching people run by me
shouting and crying through the smoke.

I did not move until the all-clear signal.
Then I saw people lying on the ground
blood everywhere
hands and legs hanging in a tree.

I yelled and fainted.
When I woke up,
I was in a strange house.
Bao was looking down at me
trying to wipe my face with a handkerchief.

We began to whisper more and more
about arrests.
Many anti-French leaflets
were passed out at school.
Teachers left. My best friend, Dung,
did not come to school.
At first I thought she was sick.
Then I found out she had been arrested.

When friends were arrested,
we were never to speak of that person again.

MUC

One night, caught in the fighting
between the French and the Viet Minh,
we were forced to run.
I was carrying my little brother.
Our dog followed us from house to house, barking.
The neighbors yelled, "Kill him. Kill him.
Otherwise he will get us all killed
with his barking."

My second brother had to shut his eyes
and stab Muc with a knife.
Muc, our trusting dog,
his hair bright and black as velvet.
The look in his eyes
as he opened them wide
just before my brother stabbed him,
so helpless, so pitiful—
it followed me for years.

HIDING AT HOME

The Viet Minh came to power.
Bao Dai was dethroned.
People began to parade by my house.
They sang a special song.
Other people left their houses,
joined in the march.
My sister and I peeked through the gate.

The Province Chief lost his job.
My father lost his.
They'd worked for the French.
Everything stopped for us.
There was no office, no school.
We had no radio.
My younger brother would bring us news
from the street each day.
We stayed home. We had each other.

We stored corn for our animals.
The cook was almost killed on his way to market
for the money he carried.
Nothing was safe.
We heard the Viet Minh buried the French alive.
We were nothing now.
My mother read her Buddhist prayers
over and over.
She would not go to the door.

THE CHINESE

Then the Chinese came to occupy our country,
disarm the Japanese.
We are a small country, but every other country
feels it can treat us like its own home.
Just walk in. Do what you please.

The Chinese frightened me.
Many of them had walked from their country.
Their legs were swollen and festering.
They marched through the streets
in their gray cotton jackets and dirty pants.

Hundreds of them moved to the barracks
near our house where the Japanese had been.
My sister and I climbed the apple tree
to stare down over the wall at them.
When we thought they looked up,
we ducked behind the bricks.

FAMINE

Worse for us than the bombs
was the famine.
We had money,
but there was no rice to buy.
People ate grass.
We read that out in the countryside
peasants were stealing from landlords.
Father told us the French and Japanese
had overstocked rice in the warehouses.
Tons and tons of rotted grain
had to be dumped into the Red River.

When Father tried to fire our servants,
they begged to stay.
They had been loyal.
Where would they go?
How could they eat?
In the end he let them stay
gave them what he could.

When Father had his high position
teachers bought him gifts—
baskets of fruit
lichee and longan.
We stored them in giant vases in the hall,
cut the mooncakes into pieces to be eaten later.
Now he ordered us to eat less rice.
We made rice balls from what we saved
to give to the people outside the walls.

One day when I opened the gate
for Father to go out,
there were corpses collapsed against the wall.

I fainted.
Father offered soldiers money to remove the corpses.
Sometimes they took bodies that were still alive.
People would call from the carts,
"Don't take me. Don't take me.
I'm not dead yet."

INSIDE OUR COURTYARD

I played music in the courtyard
near the imitation mountain
with its caves and its angels
and two matchmakers playing chess.

I played my guitar
at night by the fountain
where carp swam in the pool
and leaves rustled on the bamboo fence.

I sang in the moonlight
smelling the sweet perfume
of the princess flower
carried on the night breeze.

I sang my eldest brother's songs
to express my inside feelings:
"There is a boat floating
with nowhere to land."

Though no one saw me,
I knew they heard my music.
The servants told me the neighbors asked,
"What happened to your second lady last night?"

THE CHINESE GENERAL

We heard a knock one morning.
Father opened the door
and there stood three Chinese officers.
One had so many stars,
I did not know his rank.
"General," my brother whispered.
He was huge, broad-shouldered
with bright eyes that looked straight at you.
My brother and father spoke Chinese.
The general said he heard such sweet music
he followed the sound around the walls
to our front door.
He was surprised to learn
it was a young girl playing the music.
He asked permission to come and listen.
I did not like to play in front of strangers.
Father said I could play in my room
and the general would listen outside the door.

When he wanted to hear me,
I had to dress up and say hello
then return to my room.
He came for several weeks.
I did not understand.
I asked my brother, "Why does he come
and sit outside my room?
Why isn't it boring?"
I felt angry, but could say nothing more
as he was a big man.
He came to our house for four weeks.
On the fifth he went away.

SACRIFICE

One day a colonel came to tell my father
the general wanted to marry me.
Father said I was engaged.
My little sister ran around the table calling,
"Sister General. Sister General."
The colonel said father was needed to translate
a certain military document.
Nobody else could do it.
His Chinese was so excellent.

We were frightened when he did not return
after three days, four days, five days.
We had nowhere to turn.
There were no French, no Province Chief, no government.
They said they would release him
if I would marry the general.

Our house was like a funeral house.
My brother wanted to hide me.
Should we run away?
Where would we go?
My eyes were swollen with crying.

Finally, like our national heroine, Kim Van Kieu,
I realized I had no choice.
I had to pay my debt to my parents
for what they had done for me.
I would sacrifice my happiness
to save my father. I said yes.
My family demanded a large dowry
hoping the general would change his mind.

My father begged for time, saying,
"I am a big man.
I cannot marry my daughter in such haste.
I will lose face."
The general answered,
"You have three days to prepare the wedding.
I must return with my troops to China
to fight the communists."

THE WEDDING

It is the custom in an important family
for the bride to have as many clothes as possible.
Father asked for 30 ao dais,
all velvets and satins,
hoping they could not be made.
Chinese soldiers went with pistols
into the homes of the seamstresses
forcing them to sew the dresses.
They were ready by evening.

My mother's friend chose a necklace
and a diamond ring of many carats.
The whole town was forced to come to the wedding
whether they wanted to or not.
The city museum was the only place large enough.
The general ordered his troops to move everything out—
king's clothes, hats, antiques
great Cham heads and statues.

They took chairs and tables from everyone's house.
I did what I was told blindly.
The dresses were ready
jewels were brought
place was decorated
our friends were invited.
I was sent to the hairdresser.

I could not say one word to the general.
I cried silently.
My brothers refused to go to the wedding
said I was too young and innocent.
The Chinese cooks from the barracks prepared the feast.
In a dream I dressed in my red velvet dress

the white Western veil over my eyes.
There was an orchestra and the governor's piano
but no one dared to dance
with the Chinese troops all around the room.

WEDDING NIGHT

After the wedding I did not want to be alone.
I begged my father, my sisters, my mother to stay.
I pleaded with my little sister to sleep with me
all night at the barracks.
She said she would, but my mother pulled her away.
I was alone with the general.
I cried silently.

In front of me lay my guitar,
my music books, my jewels,
my new clothes—all piled up.
I told the two interpreters I would not sleep.
The general said, "Do not worry.
No one will disturb you."
After midnight he dismissed them.
I cried out loud then.
I refused to go to his bed.
All night we stayed awake at either end of a table.

It is our custom to return to our parents
the day after the wedding
to say thanks to them.
Mother looked at me.
"Are you happy?" she asked.
"Happy?" I thought.
My little sister, knowing nothing,
asked me what I did at night.
I told her I slept at the table.
She cried out, "Why did you sleep at the table
when you could have come home and slept with me?"

HONEYMOON

Each night I brought my guitar to bed
to divide me from the general.
If I felt something at night,
I would scream.
He said, "Please, please. I will do nothing.
Do not scream. The soldiers outside will laugh."

I thought of Bao.
I had seen his face at the wedding,
but said nothing
surrounded by troops and guests.

On our honeymoon at the beach in Haiphong,
the general asked my parents if I loved somebody else.
They did not know about Bao.
I told only my sister about him,
asked her to please tell him my situation
that I did not love the general.

My parents said I was the general's wife now
that the guitar between us
would not stop him
if he wanted to love me
that he must love me
not everything could be said through the interpreter.

He was tall. I was short.
He was 32. I was 18.
The moment we stepped outside the door,
we were saluted.

POOR MATCHMAKING—
A FOLK POEM

I'm climbing a ladder with a stick to catch you,
old Man in the Moon, and give you ten whacks.
After the beating I'll lash you to a tree
and give you the third degree:
Is this what you call a red thread?
Here's for your threads linking East and North!
Here's more for the ones binding husbands and wives!
Do I deserve an old hag, you matchmaking moron?
I'm climbing a ladder with a torch to burn down your house,
old bungler, old Man in the Moon.

TO CHINA

The commander general ordered my husband back to China
to Hoang Thu Phu, Kunming, not far from where I was born.
When we dropped down safely,
I did not even know the name of the airport.
The general told me not to say a word to anyone.
He did not want them to know I was Vietnamese.
He left me at a hotel.
I could not express hunger
or the need for a bath.
I learned to use signs.

Everyone was Chinese with long hair in pigtails.
It was January—cold and gloomy.
I could hear something in my ears,
but I could say nothing.
People kept toasting us as is the custom.
I could not drink
and always the same little glass was there,
the people standing and smiling.

After four weeks at the hotel
three horse-drawn buggies came to the door.
Was I going home?
The horses didn't answer.
They hung their heads as we loaded the carriages.
We drove out to the countryside.
Where we stopped, thirty people
came out to greet us.

I saw an ancestor's altar.
Nearby was a lady staring at me,
not too old and not too young.
She was as small as I

with a round face, small eyes
and a big mouth covered in red lipstick.
She wore a blue Chinese dress.
Was it his sister?

Then I knew. It was the other wife.
The general made a motion I did not understand—
to pay respects to the other wife,
the little wife to the bigger one.
He looked at me, motioning to nod my head.
Then his whole family came out,
his three children,
and the old men with beards.
They all knelt on the floor to me.

OUR MARRIED LIFE

The house was surrounded by rice fields.
A mountain stood in the distance.
In the front courtyard was a well
and a flower garden with orange trees.
A mirror hung on the front door
to ward away spirits.
An inner door protected the house from evil
as evil follows a straight line.
Yet, only a fortuneteller knew
from which direction evil would come.

I lived on the first floor,
the first wife on the second floor.
Whenever the general came to my room,
she would throw things, make a scene.
Once she tried to poison me.
The general, suspecting her,
gave my rice to the dog
who vomited and died.

He moved me to a different house
where Mai and Vinh were born.
He was fighting then in the West
against Mao's troops.
I stayed at home with the children
and two soldiers he left with me.

I knew the Chinese characters
and at last could speak and write.
I kept my pencil and ink in the study room.
Thin paper was specially divided for each character.
When he was home on leave,

the general taught me handwriting
said I had an inborn sense of it.

His sister, my friend, helped me,
saying, "It is not a sin to have two wives.
My brother has no sons."
When Vinh was born, we celebrated for three months
dyed the eggs red.
I began to like the general better.
He was my closest friend now
who taught me everything I knew.

SEA MOUNTAIN

In China I traveled with two soldiers
who carried me up my favorite Sea Mountain.
At the base we ate raw snails
covered with nut seasoning, chopped mint.
We climbed the path of Five Mountains
until the clouds ran between our knees
until the sound of the brass bells
echoing across the mountains
rang closer and closer.

We climbed little steps
higher and higher
until the stream shone silver
and the people below us were tiny.
At the top stood a beautiful pagoda
with five hundred gold-leaf Buddhas.
People came to the pagoda
to burn incense, to ask their fortune
gain answers from the Buddhas
from papers at the base of each statue.

I would stay there for days
in a house built in the rocks.
I fished in the small streams.
In the summer we played mah-jongg in the rock house.
We played five so one person could sleep.
All night we shuffled the ivory pieces
under the light of the kerosene lamps.

Once coming home from there,
pirates robbed my jewelry.
They took everything—

gold chains, diamond rings, jade.
When I dared to tell my mother years later,
she cried, "You have lost yours
and your children's property."

OUTSIDE MY HOUSE

Revisiting the clear pond of my childhood,
I looked down from above
on the two stone dragons.
From the mouth of one came green water,
from the other black.

As a child
I wanted to hold the cold water in my hand.
My mother stopped me,
whispering, "The dragons are sacred.
You must not touch them."

I remember in mountain lakes
the protected fish
black, pink, silver—
their mouths breaking the surface
of the still water
to eat the popped corn we threw.

The pond and lakes seemed small when I grew up,
but I still loved the spring peach blossoms
green willows in my courtyard
the warm summer rain
giant chrysanthemums in autumn.

I was happy outside my house.

BURNING OUR HOUSE IN HADONG

I received a letter from my mother saying
my second brother had burnt down our beloved house.
The Viet Minh, in their fight against the French,
ordered my family to destroy our dwelling.
My brother poured gasoline over the walls of the house
then set a torch to it.

As the flames leaped up,
he remembered the piano
so he tried to pull it through the door.
When he realized he could not save the piano,
he began beating it with a hammer—
all the time laughing and crying.

My family was forced to run from the house
by Allied bombing against the Viet Minh.
They heard the alert and ran, sometimes for miles
through the rice fields and jungle around Hadong.
When they saw the planes overhead,
they would lie down in the ditches
at the borders of the rice fields,
pretending to be dead.

The planes would dive out of the sky
and fire along the ground.
My father threw away the rice
when it got too heavy.
My mother threw away her sandals
when they broke on the rocky paths.
They cooked very little
for fear the planes would see the smoke
from their small fires.

They stayed where they could
in a rice field, in a village hut.
The people knew of my father and welcomed him.
When the place was unsafe, they ran again—
from the bombing, from the French, from the Viet Minh,
it did not matter, they had to run.
Sometimes their new hosts ran with them.
For one year they lived this way.

My family and others like them
were caught in the middle:
afraid the French would think them Viet Minh
and kill them,
afraid the Viet Minh would think them French agents
and kill them.

Far away in China, I held onto my new baby daughter
and prayed for my family.

RETURN TO HANOI

When the general was surrounded
at Tien Sy in the mountains,
he sent his captain galloping back
with word for me to leave China.
I took my two children and my guitar
and flew home to Hanoi.

My mother and my elder sister were at the airport.
My sister said, "This is my baby and this is my husband."
I saw Bao standing beside her
and then could see nothing else
only people calling my name in the distance.
I said I was airsick from the long trip.

I tried to avoid him
not wishing any complications,
but he wrote me every day
saying he never expected to see me again.
He said he had told my sister he still loved me
and that we should marry.
I said, "I have a husband.
Let bygones be bygones."

I was back in Hanoi only one month
when I received word my husband had been killed.
The whole family cried,
but tears did not come to my eyes.
They could not.
Bao kept writing for months and months.
I kept refusing
afraid my sister might kill herself.
She had slashed her wrist once before.

MARRIAGE TO BAO

Bao still wanted to marry me
after three years of formal mourning for the general.
He said many people in his family had two wives
including his father.
He was the son of the second wife.
My father said he had not known
of my love for Bao,
but now that he did, we should marry.
He said it was normal in our country
for two sisters to have one husband.
Bao's mother agreed.
I said yes reluctantly,
not wanting anyone outside the family to know.
We were married and had two children.
After the second, we became like brother and sister.
I could not stand my sister's long face,
her jealousies, her unhappiness.
Blood runs thick in my country.

Bao decided that since I was more educated,
I would be the outside wife,
my sister the inside wife.
I would entertain his friends and business associates.
She would take care of his house.
We lived this way in different houses for six years.
I was eager to work, but was forbidden by Father and Bao.
My father tore up my acceptance
from the Ministry of Education.
I had to teach music at home.

SAIGON
SWANSEA
RANGOON
SAIGON
1954-1975

GENEVA AGREEMENTS

We were told in 1954
that anyone not wishing
to live with the communists
could go south by plane or by boat.

My father wanted to leave,
said he knew the communists.
My mother had spent much of her life
in the four walls of our houses.
She did not want to go
to a strange new place.

My younger sister's husband
had been in Saigon.
He warned us against
the unfriendly people there
said he would never go back.

We were given 300 days to decide.

SEEING MY THIRD BROTHER, BANG

We received word that my third brother
whom we had not heard from in many years
wanted to see us.
He said he could not come to our house
so Father and I rented a rickshaw.
We left early in the morning
reaching his village in the afternoon.

A bamboo hedge surrounded the village.
We have an ancient saying,
"The power of the Emperor stops at the bamboo hedge."
We walked through a bamboo gate
down a dirt path until we reached a thatched house.

Two men came toward us.
One held back a barking dog.
The other led us to my brother.
He looked so thin and different
as he bowed to my father.
I stood behind my father.
We all cried.

When Father was asleep,
my brother asked me to come into the yard.
We remembered our childhood together.
We called him *mot sach,* the bookworm.
He said the Viet Minh were good people
who believed in giving to the poor
saving the country for the Vietnamese.

I said I had no contact with them,
but that Father said they were against families.

My brother said the nationalists were sentimentalists,
just like we were, with a strong sense of family.
He promised if I stayed he'd help me build a new life,
take care of the children.

We talked through the night
and I decided to stay in the North,
I remember sitting in the moonlight
watching the chickens go back and forth in the yard.
He drew me a map of our rendezvous spot
told me not to bring much luggage.
I would not need many things.

I WAS CAUGHT

The night of the 18th July
all the family was packed
to go to Gia Lam airport.
I could not sleep.
I had packed my bags
and put them a little to one side.
My mother sensed my plan.
She came over to my bed and asked,
"You are not coming with us?"

She cried out, waking everyone
and brought my father to my bed, saying,
"Here is your daughter
who will not come with us."
He asked if I planned to stay behind
with my third brother.
I tried to say no, but the tears came.

Father said we must stick together
at least share our troubles.
The communists would divide the family.
This way we would die together.
The whole family slept near me that night.
In the morning, they put me in the car first
with the little children.
I could not get a message to my brother.

WHAT WE LEFT, WHAT WE TOOK

We were leaving Hanoi by American military planes.
We were each allowed forty pounds.
We took no furniture, only gold.
Father took his scroll with the nine birds.
His second wife went separately.
Unknown to us, he had married
the woman we had chased down Kham Thien Street.

Bao's sister had no children.
She loved babies.
She was my friend, loved me more than my sister.
I told her I was going South
and planned to work, against everyone's wishes.
I feared I could not do it all
with a small child.
At the last minute, I left Bao's little girl with her.

SAIGON MARKET

I was scared to go out at first,
even to the market.
We spent the day looking from the window
at people going back and forth.
There were huge Cambodian women
who talked very loud
staring at you from head to toe
as if they would swallow you up.
They spoke Vietnamese,
but we could not understand them.
Their minds had been poisoned against us.
"Why do you come here?" they asked.
"It is too crowded already.
You just want to follow the westerners
for their bread and butter."
They recognized us by our voices,
our clothes, our skin.
When they saw us, they raised their prices
and we did not dare bargain.

One day at the market,
my long ao dai knocked over a woman's lichee basket.
She scolded me until a mob came
and started ripping my dress
calling out, "Hurt that northerner.
They have come to make us suffer."
A policeman came.
When they saw he too was from the North,
they yelled, "Kill him. Kill them both."
Finally a third came, from the South.
He tried to calm the mob, saying,
"This lady is your countrywoman.

She has left everything behind.
She suffers too. Please."

It was a long time before I went back
to the market. When I did,
I always took a southerner with me.
I carried my plastic bag in silence.

OUR HOUSE IN CHOLON

It was hard to find a house in Saigon.
One million people had moved south.
At first we stayed in part of a friend's house
across from the old cinema.
Father said we could not stay there forever.
Every day we went searching for a house.
We finally found one in Cholon,
the Chinese city within Saigon.
We could speak to few of the Chinese there.
They spoke Cantonese, not Mandarin.

We all contributed our gold, our jewelry.
Nine of us squeezed into the tiny place—
only two rooms and a kitchen.
The dining room became wall-to-wall cots.
At night the baby would wake everyone.
To get up we would crawl from one cot to another.
Outside, was a public outhouse,
really a big dirty can.
You had to wait in line.
I was so shy I would get up at five.

Soon we looked for a new house.
I found one on Nancy Street.
The French had used it for a school.
There were 36 houses in a row—all in ruins,
36 families worked to clean them up.
The market was in the front,
gambling in the back.
This was the house my father liked.
He was 63 when we moved to Saigon.
He died there at 84.

SOUTHERNERS AND NORTHERNERS

The South has only two seasons
dry and rainy.
In the North we had four.
In the South they eat sweeter food
with more coconut sauce.
In the North farmers rise at 3
to go to the rice paddies
no matter how cold it is.

Northerners work harder.
They plan for the future.
If I make 1000 piasters, I save 300
one day to buy a tael of gold.
In the South they spend it all.
They do not take life as seriously,
do not have death on their minds.
Even the farmers move easily
through their sunny fields.

A POEM ABOUT THE NORTH

(memorized from a schoolbook when I was 8)

December is the month we grow potatoes.
January we grow beans.
February we grow eggplant.
March we harrow the fields.
April we prepare the rice seedlings.
Everyone works.
The husband harrows.
The wife plants.
We are happy.
In May we finish harvesting.
Thanks to heaven each hectare yields
5 full buckets of rice.
I must grind and beat the full bucket.
The husk we use for cooking.
We beat it again, removing the second layer
producing the very white rice.
The hull we feed to the pigs
mixed with water lilies from the ponds.
I must pay the tax from the harvest
for my husband.
If we be hungry or full
we must be together always.
Better to be poor and together than alone.

GOING TO WORK

I went to work in the Ministry of Social Welfare.
My mother was furious.
Being old-fashioned, she thought other people
would think she and my father
did not have enough to feed me.
They would lose face.

I trained as a midwife and social assistant
helping poor families in hospitals
and in their homes where they suffered family breakdowns.
I helped some of the million people from the North
find their lost relatives.

Mother scolded me for leaving my house and children.
I explained I needed something for myself,
needed to have a job and responsibility,
money to provide for my children.
She refused to talk to me.
Ridiculed at home, I advanced at work
from door-to-door fieldwork
to planning in the hospitals.

FIGHTING

I cannot forget one night in March of 1955.
It was midnight.
The whole family was asleep.
We heard guns,
the sound of people running toward the Y Bridge.
We all woke up and looked out the window.
We saw soldiers running.
At first we thought it was the military.
We saw different uniforms.
Then we thought it was the communists.
We all hid under our thick dining-room table.
We covered the top of the table
with our pillows and blankets.
The fighting went on around us until morning.
Then the shots got less and less
and we dared to open the door.
The neighbors said one side was the military police,
the other the Binh Xuyen, Vietnamese against the government.
At 2 o'clock I decided I must go to work
or the government would question me.
Tanks were lined up near the bus.
Suddenly the fighting started again.
There were people all around me
and I was caught in the middle
unable to get back to my house.
A soldier behind me
dropped to the ground covered with blood.
I started running,
not knowing in which direction.

RUNNING TO ESCAPE

I came to a flooded place,
the houses all on stilts.
We call them *pierres sur pilotes*.
I climbed up into the houses.
Then I saw the fire at my back.
Trying to jump over the water,
I landed in it, waves slapping all around me.
I ripped my green-and-white ao dai,
lost my new sandals
but managed to run, wet and barefoot over small stones.
I heard people shouting, but I did not see them.
I crawled into a bunker
covered with wide planks.
It was dark in there, but I heard a noise.
I turned and there was a yellow dog
as scared as I was.
He put his paw in my hand
to show that he needed me.
We both knelt in the dark hole, listening.
I heard a wind whirling over us.
I poked my head out
to see all the roofs on fire.
I knew I would have to run from my safe place.
The dog ran out with me.
The two of us, running, running.
He barking, me too scared to cry.
After hours I saw the Saigon market
and knew I had run in a circle.
The fire was chasing me
smoke billowing all around
until I fell down unconscious.
The shots seemed further away.
It was cooler.

WAR IN THE STREETS

When I woke up,
I saw a man on a bicycle.
I stopped him, begged him to help me.
"Please. I cannot run or walk."
He asked if I knew how to ride a bike.
I said no but I could sit behind him.
He said he could not ride toward the fire.
It would be suicide.
On the way to his sister's, I recognized a road
and got off, thanking the man.

My mother's friend cried when she saw me
walking alone toward her house.
"Where is your family?
Where are your children?
You live where the fire comes from."
I stayed the night, returning home the next day.
I said I would rather die with my family.
I walked home slowly in sandals borrowed from their daughter.

The police tried to stop me from going near my house,
but I begged them to let me see my family.
Then I saw all of them alive—standing outside the door.
They were so happy to see me. Mother thought I was dead.
They had been trapped by the fire,
but our house was saved by the wind turning suddenly.
The ones at the back were burnt to the ground.
The wall of our house was full of bullet holes.

We believe in destiny.
Mother said she had prayed to Buddha.
For many generations our family had done nothing wrong
so this time Buddha protected us.

LOOKING FOR VOTES

We always thought we would go home to Hanoi.
Two years in the South, then with America's help
we would defeat the communists.
With America on our side, how could we lose?

In 1955 Diem proclaimed us a republic.
We were sent in groups from the ministries
to the villages to influence people
to vote for Diem as president.

We would bring food, explain his aims,
said we would vote for him.
At first I was afraid to speak.
They would know I was from the North.
They'd accuse me of taking a good government job.

The women in the South smoke and drink
and are generally easygoing.
We could hardly keep from laughing
when they offered us their cheap cigars.

They called their children
by where they came in the family
number two, three, four, five:
cau hai, cau ba, cau tu, cau nam

but never number one.
Number one son was called number two.
The name *number one* was reserved
for the head of the village, *ong ca*, Mr. One.

I would walk through the rice fields,
ask to enter their wooden houses,
sit with them as their children crawled
across the floor with the pigs and the chickens.

HOMESICK

In the South, I lost my interest in playing music.
The family was split up.
The heat burnt.
The streets were filled with noise and fighting.

At night I would stare from my bed
through the window
at the moonlight shining on the leaves.

I felt lonely.
Parts of Hoang Duong's song of the North
drifted over me with the breezes.

"Hanoi, oh my darling,
from an immeasurable distance I think of you
a city decorated with brilliant lights
and the colored, floating flaps of the ao dai.

"Hanoi, oh my darling,
in the endless raining evenings,
remember there is someone alone
in silence watching the floating clouds
my heart broken from missing you."

I thought of the house of my childhood.
Clear nights singing with my brothers and sisters
in the courtyard by the imitation mountain.

LEARNING ENGLISH

I decided to learn English.
Bao taught me one hour a day.
He learned from the radio.
My parents did not understand.
"What are you learning that for?"
they would ask in scorn.
"The sound is so strange to us.
Your place is in the home.
You should not be seen with foreigners."

When Bao was given a scholarship
to study administration in the States,
I encouraged him to go.
He wrote me saying,
"The longer I am in the States,
the more I realize how poor our country is.
There is no civil war here.
If you have a will, you can succeed.
Women have more freedom
and divorce is easier."

THE AMERICAN CAPTAIN

In Washington Bao met an American colonel
on his way to do duty in Saigon.
He wanted to know Vietnamese people
and became a friend to me.
His wife taught me English.
I would help them buy Vietnamese things,
ceramics, elephants, tortoise-shell, lacquer work.
I also attended English classes
at the Vietnamese-American Association.
Our teachers were officers
who came from the camps to teach us.
My teacher was a black captain.
He was a doctor.
He looked at me all the time in class.
My friends said he was in love with me.
He began to walk with me,
to follow me to the bus station.
I did not know what to do—
a foreigner and black.
I was scared of him,
only bar-girls walked with foreigners.
I convinced my friend Mr. Tuan
from the Finance Ministry to walk home with me.

LOSING FACE

One day after the captain had been absent,
he asked in front of the whole class,
"Nga, you have not even asked me what happened.
Every night when I close my eyes, I see your image."
I wanted to disappear.
My face was red; my fingers numb.
I stood up, took my books and left.
Angry and sick for the whole week,
I could not go to class.
One day I saw him pass by my house.
I wanted to hide.
He had something under his arm,
candy for the children, perfume, soap,
everything from the PX.
The family and neighbors were shocked.
No foreigners had been to our neighborhood.
They all came out to watch.
We were surrounded by people.
I said, "This is my English teacher.
He has come to visit me, to see my children."
He asked me where I had been
said I must return to class
that he had done nothing wrong
except love me.

I had nowhere to turn.
I asked the American colonel for help.
He asked for the captain's name and serial number
and had him transferred.
I did not go back to the training classes.

MY CAREER

I wanted to leave my country
to train in another, hopefully in the States.
I passed six different tests
but my Big Boss refused to recommend me.
I think he kept my tests in his desk drawer.
I became so enraged that I finally asked him
why he did not send me.
This was considered very blunt in my country.
(I did not know then that he was anti-American
the leader of a Buddhist league.)

He said I must stay in my country
go to the provinces and help our poor.
Once I had proven myself, I could go abroad.
I was so furious, I volunteered for Chuong Thien,
one of the most dangerous provinces.
It was a poor area, attacked daily by the communists.
The roads were mined.
I arranged through USAID
to fly back and forth by plane.

The Chief of the Province had a bomb shelter under his house.
He too preferred to spend his nights in Saigon.
He was a good military officer, but spoke no English.
I became his interpreter to the Americans.
To build his own reputation,
he asked for material goods,
food, blankets and building materials.

Trained in the social services,
I knew we needed a headquarters
to receive people, to meet them.
Within three months, I set up a day-care center

and a sewing class
much to the surprise of the Big Boss
who had to sign the papers
for my scholarship to England.

ENGLAND

I studied in Swansea in South Wales.
England was freezing even in July.
They took us to a shopping center to buy new coats.
The streets were dark and gloomy—
all stone and centuries old.
I felt lonely, quiet and strange.

My Vietnamese friend and I stayed in the attic
of a professor's house.
The flower pot on the table froze.
We used all our money in electric heaters.
We put pennies in the machines,
burned our money all winter.

Studying juveniles, neglected children,
I spent many hours with my face in a dictionary.
The library was a huge place
with 36,000 books.

At night I would cover my feet
with a hot-water bottle.
Listening to the English wind
howl under my door,
I'd think of the soft air in my country,
the songs of our village.

MY HOME VILLAGE—A SONG

Golden sunshine glitters through the trees
in the late afternoon.

Birds sing their jovial songs.

Leaning on doors, villagers stand and sit
sharing memories of their lives.

Across the sky wind hums through bamboo flutes
attached to paper kites.

The golden rice dances as if joining in the gaiety.

O afternoon in my country, how tranquil and peaceful you are.

I wait in the silence, watching the blue smoke rise,
waiting to fall in love.

BURMA

Before I reached home, I visited Rangoon as a tourist.
When I arrived at the Vietnamese consulate, Bao was there.
Without my knowing, he had transferred
to the Ministry of Foreign Affairs,
Vice-Consul to Burma.

In Saigon he had seen my application for another scholarship
to allow me to stay out of the country longer.
He had put it away in a drawer.
I was surprised and furious.
I was happier alone.

My son had been expelled from school.
He was intelligent and trusted no one,
not the government, not the school, not me.
He did not want to serve in the army.
When I said, "How can we beat the communists
if you do not fight?"

He answered
"Whom will I fight—my uncle?
Big shots do not have to fight.
Why should I?
You will not have to go to the battlefield.
You know nothing."
My father blamed me for his attitudes,
said I neglected him when I went to work.

All my plans for my own career were ruined.
Bao organized a big party
introduced me as his wife
told me diplomatic wives cannot work
and sent for his mother and the older children.
My sister stayed with the younger children in Saigon.

CORRUPTION

In Rangoon we stayed in the same house
as the Consul General.
We had a cook, a gardener and a driver.
The house had two stories
and a garden where I spent most of my time.
There were snakes and scorpions
that lay on the rocks in the sun.
The Burmese, Buddhists, do not believe in killing snakes.

My job was to entertain guests.
The consul would say we had 150 guests, instead of 50.
He rented the house with dollars from the Saigon government.
He changed the money on the black market
and kept the difference.
He claimed false renovations on the villa.
By these corrupt means, he made thousands.

He offered my husband money
asked him to falsify a document.
When Bao refused, the Consul made a report back to Saigon
that I was a mistress.
We have a saying:

"Once you fight with a snake,
you must smash his head.
Otherwise, he will kill you."

Without the Consul's permission
Bao returned to Saigon to plead his case.
When he arrived, his name was already smeared.
They said he was a playboy
flitting from one woman to another.

The Consul had stolen so much money,
he could "please" the commission.

We have another saying,
"A dog always finds his way home."

TET
JANUARY 31, 1968

We had to come back to Saigon for Tet.
Everyone was meeting at my mother's and father's.
I could see my children.
My daughter was in boarding school in Dalat.
My son would be home from the Air Force.

Tet, New Year's, is our celebration day.
The whole family gathers
dressed in their best clothes
to give thanks to Heaven
and to our ancestors.
We have a saying:
Birds have nests.
People have ancestors.

Everything must be ready
before the end of the lunar year.
Our tradition says
we must be quiet on that night
at peace to receive the new spring.

We prepare special food.
In the North, we have sweet oranges,
in the South, mangosteens, watermelon, tangerines.
We invite our ancestors to eat
offering them the feast at an altar
the best place in the house.

We light incense on the altar.
When the sticks burn to the end,
we light others.

When they have burned,
our ancestors have finished.
We remove the food and serve ourselves.

On the fifth day
we prepare another big feast.
We burn red tissue paper
covered with gold and silver paint—
false money for our ancestors
to spend on transportation to their world.

To prepare for Tet,
we made sticky rice together.
This takes 24 hours
and must cook at the same temperature.
We put logs around a huge pot
which holds 50 rice cakes.
Someone must watch the pot all night
to keep the rice from drying out.

Early in the morning
during my turn to watch the rice cakes,
I heard shots far away.
The next day there was fighting
on the Y Bridge again
people crying and running,
uniforms everywhere.

We learned through a radio
this was a surprise attack by the Viet Cong.
They attacked the American embassy,
American bases, every town and city in South Vietnam.
Many of them came into Saigon in trucks

hidden under Tet watermelons.
Like my son, many South Vietnamese soldiers
were home for the New Year.

We stayed together in our concrete house,
not daring to look out the window.

CORRUPTION

After the Tet Offensive,
the corruption grew worse and worse.
What we had seen in Burma
was a mirror of life in Saigon.
Always the Americans worked hand-in-glove
with the Vietnamese.

All the buses leaving Long Binh Base
had false hollows under the seats
filled with steaks, chickens, bacon.
As soon as the buses were out the gate,
everything was sold.
There was no bargaining then.

I had a woman friend
who bought a truck for 2 million piasters.
People inside the American warehouse
would load the truck with goods.
No guard would inspect it.
Everyone was in on the deal.

They drove to the jungle, distributed the goods.
Once they loaded hundreds of boxes
thinking they were radios.
When they opened the boxes and found computers
that no one could understand,
they threw them in the river.

THE SYSTEM

The Americans were too rich.
They thought they could buy everything.
They were poor psychologists.
They gave lots of money to the man on top
and did not watch down the line.
On paper, the projects looked good,
but the money went out the door.

The Project Chief drew up a plan
for a Community Center.
He said he needed so many sewing machines,
so many blankets.
In the meeting with the American advisor,
the translator would say
we need fifty sewing machines.

The place was built.
There was a big celebration.
Everyone came and lots of pictures were taken.
Ten sewing machines were in the showroom,
the other forty had been sold.
Who was there to check?

It was simple.
If you were corrupt, you stayed on top,
had money for your family.
If you worked under these corrupt officials
and were not,
you were sent to the battlefields.

If you had money, you were not sent.
If you failed a course at the university,
you could buy a pass and avoid the army.

I knew someone who flunked
and ended up teaching French to a general's children.

If you deserted and the MPs found you hiding,
you bribed the MPs.
If you went to the doctor, you paid him
to falsify your check-up.
You drank something that showed up
on the X-ray of your lung.

We have a saying:
*"Money can go through paper
no matter how thick."*

TWO DEATHS

When my father's second wife died,
he begged us to come to the funeral,
said she had never done us any harm.
My mother was stone-faced, but we went.

Soon after the funeral, father had a stroke.
Suddenly when he was gambling,
his hands went down.
He could not answer my mother.

I rushed home to give him massage,
but he could not speak.
He came to stay with me for three years.
We cared for him, washed him every day.

He showed great courage, regained his speech
and even helped my daughter with her French,
but he remained paralyzed and could not travel.
He died six months before we left the country.

Otherwise, we might still be there.

MY FATHER'S FUNERAL

We believe the devil may come
to lead the soul of the dead to Hell
before the burial.

We wrapped my father's body
in Buddha's orange robe
so Buddha would lead his soul to Heaven.

A monk circled the coffin.
The family, dressed in white gauze mourning clothes
and white turbans, chanted prayers.

The eldest son walked in front of the coffin
carrying an incense burner.

The grandchildren wore white headbands.
The great-grandchildren wore yellow.
The great-great-grandchildren red.

Old friends brought flowers and banners—
more than 100 of them—
with words for the dead.

The coffin was closed and nailed shut.
The family walked behind it to the grave.

We believe the dead must be buried deep and tight
so the soul will be secure and go to Heaven
and bless the family.

If not, the soul will become a monster
and haunt the family.

We believe members of the family
with the same sign
must stay away at the closing of the coffin.

My father was the sign of the buffalo.
One of my brothers was also.
We fear the dead wants one of his own for company.

100 DAYS

For 100 days after my father died,
we prepared his favorite dishes
worshiped at his house altar
with the huge incense burner
the white candles
his picture wrapped in black satin.

We believe after the body is buried properly,
the soul floats with nowhere to go for 49 days.
It must be fed so as not to do mischief.

For the next 51 days, the soul goes to the intermediate state
where the good deeds are weighed against the bad.
If bad, it will be reincarnated as an animal,

if good, as a human again.
If best, it will go to Paradise
never to be reborn again.

MY SIXTH BROTHER, TUOC, RETURNS TO HANOI

During the Paris Accords,
my seventh brother was assigned by the government
to go to Hanoi on an observation trip
to check on the North's claims about prisoner exchange.

He was chaperoned by communists
but managed to pass by our last house
hoping to see our brothers and sister.

The house was the same pale color.
All the windows were closed.
Tall weeds grew on the path.
He felt no life there
only silence and gloom.

He wished there had been a bird.
He would tie a note to its leg
to carry up to the window.

The note would say:

"Here I am. I have come back
to visit my sister and my brother
and my country. Where are they?"

THE MAGAZINE

When the American magazine came to me,
I was ready to leave my job.
I'd hoped to do family planning,
new foster homes for children.
I'd seen them work in other countries.

I knew the fraud in mine.
The women in Saigon who moved the same 200 children
from orphanage to orphanage
receiving money from the state each time.

My boss laughed at my ideas
said I lived in a dream world.
Our country was at war.
I should put my ideas away for a decade.
He used me as an interpreter
to talk to the Americans.

In my country, one cannot resign
from civil service during war.
It would mean jail.
I had to show I was incapable
with a report of five doctors
who said I had a mental disturbance.

Then I resigned.
The magazine hired me to watch over the books,
make sure nobody was stealing from the company.
They called me Madame Nga.

THE AMERICANS

The Americans came to Vietnam
and turned our country upside down
with their money and their army.

Their soldiers slept with our women.
Their generals patted our generals on the heads
as if they were children.

Bao and I had a successful business at first
selling Vietnamese handicrafts at the PX,
silver, ceramics, lacquerware.

Inflation rose higher and higher.
I thought we should get out.
Bao said no.

"America is so strong,
the richest, most powerful country in the world.

Number one in the world. She will never desert us.
She cannot. She is in too deep.

She will send more ammunition.
NBC and CBS say so.

She will bring more phantoms and battleships
and B-52s to bomb Hanoi."

THE NOODLE CART

My boss's wife was educated.
She taught English literature at the university.
She called the office and asked questions,
"Why is Chi Phuc crying?
Why don't Vietnamese eat cheese?"
One day she asked me to find a noodle cart
to take home to the United States.
She was my boss's wife. Of course I would do it.

It took me three weeks of searching.
I would go from cart to cart
asking where to buy one.
No one would tell me.
I got Bao to drive me through Cholon
way out to the countryside to PhuLam
where I had never been.

Every week I went to the same noodle man
pretending I went for noodles.
Soon he knew what I liked
and we started talking.
He asked if I wanted to start a business.
I explained my boss's wife
wanted the cart as a souvenir.
He said the Chinese would never sell
except to another Chinese.
After 14 bowls, he told me where to go look.

Bao said I was spending too much time on the project.
I said I had made a promise and I would keep it.
I would go by cyclo if he would not take me.
One Saturday we drove round and round for two hours
to a place where there were few houses.

Far away, all lined up in a field, we saw the noodle carts.
There were only Chinese there.
They said no carts would be ready for six months.

Finally I found a man in Saigon
who wanted to sell his cart.
He had a second wife in Can Tho
and wanted to move down with her.
The father and son fought.
The father refused to sell.
The son said he had to. The father cried.
The son told me to sneak back in the evening
and take the cart.
I had to find people to push it to the warehouse.

My boss's wife was pleased with the noodle cart.
"It's perfect," she said.
She had it shipped home to the United States.

LEAVING SAIGON 1975

THE GAME OF CHESS

The Bureau Chiefs came and the Bureau Chiefs went.
We had to get used to them.

One played chess with my colleague.
My colleague always won.

The Big Boss's face would turn red.
Then he'd come over and kick my desk.

The Americans expressed themselves
more than the Vietnamese.

One day my colleague said, "This isn't worth it,"
and let the Big Boss win.

DECIDING

We went to the office every day.
Though the situation was critical,
people at work said nothing.
Province Chiefs were running.
We told the Big Boss our country would be lost.
We told him we would blow ourselves up
if we could not leave.

I sat at my desk doing the financial report.
My thoughts went round and round.

Should I leave?
Should I go alone?
Should I take my mother?
She did not want to go.
She feared they wouldn't let her chew the betel.
Should I leave my children?
How would I make a living?
What would happen when the communists came?

When I made up my mind,
pictures of my childhood floated to the surface
as clear and strong as dreams.

Our old house in Hadong.
The bamboo in the backyard.
We ate the shoots.
The soldiers made a fence from the stalks.
My sister and I painted the fence
first white, then blue, then her favorite yellow.
The small antigonon vine we planted
with its pink blossoms in spring.

Our ponds.
The many steps down
to the small bridge
where we'd sit hour after hour
letting our hands dip into the water
trying to catch the silver-brown fish.

Airplanes bombing
running from our house
people dying, people calling from outside the walls
don't take me. I'm not dead yet.
The family hiding together in our house in Cholon
sunlight coming through the bullet holes.

THE SECRET LIST

The Big Boss said a plane would come
and fly us to Hong Kong.

We were to make a list of our family.

Only the staffers and the immediate family
could be on the list.

We were to talk to no one
or the plan would fail.

THE TELEX OPERATOR

Linh, the telex operator, could not be on the list.
He was not a full-time staffer.
He worked in the evenings,
sometimes all night, sleeping on the couch
because of the time difference to the States.
He asked me what are they doing in New York
buying bread and shipping merchandise to Hong Kong?
I could not tell him
we were the bread and the merchandise.
That was the code.
Someone must have told him.
His wife came to the office crying,
"Sister, sister are you trying to run away?
Would you leave us behind?"
I knew she had ten children.
She said she would bring them all
to lie down in front of my door.

We knew that if there were too many of us,
we would all be caught.
Linh had been there eight years,
one year longer than I.
He was from the North.
I knew if he were left behind,
he would throw a grenade
and blow his whole family up.
I brought his case to the Big Boss.
When the confidential came over the wire
from New York saying he could go,
we all cried. He was overhappy,
said I had saved his whole family.
After that, all plans were kept secret from me.

FIRST, WE MUST TAKE OURSELVES

At the end I was so scared,
I did not feel like myself.
I did not know what to take,
what to leave behind.
I told the children,
"First, we must take ourselves."

We were silent for two-and-a-half months.
No one talked.
My sister had swollen eyes.
We had no appetite.
I made my son a waistband
to carry our gold.

The manager of the Continental Hotel
stopped me and asked,
"You look sad. Are you all right?
Are you planning to go away?"
"No," I said. "Are you?"
He said no. "I am old.
It will not be too bad."

PHOTOGRAPHS

We could bring only
what fit into one small bag.
They warned us not to take too much.
"They have things in the States,"
the Big Boss said.

For days I burnt documents on my terrace,
papers from when I worked for my government
papers from when I worked for the Americans.
I couldn't think
except to destroy whatever would bring trouble.

I burnt photographs
of the whole family at Tet,
year after year
all of us together
my father's nine birds.

I stared at the black-and-white pictures:
me—tiny, smiling
a pigtail on both sides
holding my eldest brother's hand,

me—the angel in the school play
a tiara on my head,
me in China at the bottom of Sea Mountain
my children standing beside me.

As the pile of ashes floated away
I felt I was burning my life.

PACKING

I packed strange things
sandalwood soap from Hong Kong,
12 of my best ao dai,
my collection of tiny perfume bottles.

We all wanted to bring our mothers.
None of us could.
We had so many false starts
I never said goodbye to her.

One morning I made an incense offering
on my father's altar.

"You going today?" Mother asked.
"No," I said. "I just missed him
dreamt about him
wanted him to wish us luck."

I left my mother in our house on the street
that had been named General de Gaulle,
then Cong Ly, or Justice Street,
and then Cach Mang, Revolution Street.

I left my money on the outside porch
and never saw her again.

PAPER MONEY

One of Bao's daughters saved a million piasters.
She kept it too long.

On the last day
she carried the money in a bag
running through the streets of Saigon
trying to exchange it for anything.

The boy at the Continental Hotel
gave her $2.00 for it.

If he hadn't,
she would have thrown the bag away
money and all.
It was too heavy to carry.

OUTSIDE THE GATES

In the end, we had falsified documents.
I had to pretend I was the wife
of one of the American correspondents,
who came to plan our escape.
On the appointed day, we were the lead car,
four others followed.
When the correspondent asked if I minded saying
I was his wife, I just laughed.
We went through the security gate without stopping.
The guards whistled,
put their guns at the ready.
I said, "Please stop."
They ordered us from the cars.
I said I had come to see my husband off.
They said I could go, not my children.
They had new orders,
no Vietnamese allowed at the airport.
Had they seen our sons' real papers,
they would have been jailed.
They were supposed to be in the army.
We tried all the gates.
The Big Boss put 500,000 piasters
in with our papers.
The money was returned.
The guard said, "A few days ago
these papers would have been legal. Not now."
We tried dollars.
Nothing worked.
Five hours and we were still outside the gates.

INTO THE AIRPORT

There were 23 in our group,
all from foreign news agencies.
Bao and my sister went separately.
By late afternoon our chartered plane had departed
with us still outside the gates.

We regrouped and returned
this time in an embassy car
its windows covered on all sides by curtains.
No one could see in.
We were stopped by a Vietnamese MP
before reaching the hangar,
but he was told by an American
to let us pass.
We were in!

All the planes had gone.
The Big Boss told us to stay,
made me responsible for the group,
said he would look for us in Guam,
gave us 20,000 piasters for dinner,
wished us luck and left.

THE AIRPORT

In the yard outside the hangar
were hundreds of Vietnamese
lying on their mats with their luggage
and their children all around them.
We were worried about the crowds,
about being searched,
about the gold and dollars on our persons,
about what we would say if we were caught.
We walked to the snack bar for dinner
and paid 19,000 piasters for noodles.
When we got back, it was dark.
Our spot was crowded with people,
embassy people, MACV people.
My son thought he recognized a secret agent
and hid his face.
Men with walkie-talkies were everywhere.

When an official Vietnamese asked us
to leave our place,
I pleaded with an American Lt.-Colonel
who allowed us to stay.
We had a tiny baby with us, my granddaughter.
I told him we had missed our charter
and wanted to go as soon as possible.
He said the sooner the better.
I said the office could not blame us
if we did not take the plane they had chartered.
He said to stay together
and go to the Philippines, not to Guam.
I said, anywhere but Vietnam.

ESCAPE

We made lists.
That was the manifest,
name, sex, age.
When the captain came for us,
we went quickly to the bus,
squeezed into the front
with all our luggage on one seat
as he had told us to.
A man asked who could speak English.
I was quiet.
It was dark.
He told us to be silent
or we would be shot.
We held our breath.
There wasn't a sound on that crowded bus.

As we approached, the plane made a huge noise,
like a C-130.
It opened at the back, a mouth.
We were thrown in like packets.
The pilot ordered *stop*
just as the last of our group was in.
Hundreds of us sat on the floor,
a huge string tied around us,
our babies on our laps.
Many were sick.

We arrived at Clark Field, Philippines, at 1:30 A.M.
Everyone was quiet.
We were handed medicine, blankets, mattresses.
People were everywhere.
There was much red tape,
name, sex, age.

I heard over the radio
soon after we left, the Vietnamese MPs,
not wanting any more people to leave the country,
arrested everyone at the airport.

THE UNITED STATES: GUAM FORT CHAFFEE NEW YORK CITY GREENWICH COS COB 1975-1980

GUAM

We flew the next day to Guam
packed in side by side
our possessions on our laps.
There, we slept on our luggage,
not knowing the other people,
afraid they would steal from us.
We were greeted by American officers,
who took us to a church,
and in bad Vietnamese
we could not understand
read us the regulations.
Most of the children were asleep.
We had been flying for hours and hours.
Still we had to line up for papers.
My granddaughter was sick with diarrhea.
She could not cry, not even suck.

In the acres and acres of tents,
blue-green nylon as far as the eye could see,
we had to find ours.
I was given a paper with our tent number.
We started walking in the bright sunlight,
carrying all the baggage and the sick baby.
Tiny stones on the path hurt my feet.
At the end of the long line of tents,
we could not find our number.
Since I was not afraid to speak English,
I was chosen to walk all the way back
over the stones
past the other tents
where people were settling in
under the burning sun.

CAMP

This time an American returned with me.
He could not find the number either.
Back I went to wait in the long lines.
I found our new number,
but the tent was not put up.
I laid the baby on a newspaper,
and we raised the tent ourselves.
As soon as it was up,
they called over the *haut-parleur*, the loudspeaker,
"Come fill out your papers."
We did not go. We did not care.
Too tired to move again, we fell asleep.

Much later, they called us for dinner
in English and in Vietnamese.
There was no time to wash.
Men and women shared the few bathrooms.
The women were so shy
they would go only at night.
In the day, we used a can
with water in it
just as at the market.

We waited in lines for food.
When it came,
we could not swallow some of it.
The rice was cooked in a way
that scared us,
very soft, filled with water and minced fish.
It had a horrible smell.
Even the children shook their heads.

The Americans spent a lot of money,
but they did not know our diet—
mostly fresh vegetables
and fruit with fluffy rice.
If you had money
there was "meals on wheels"
a cart from which they sold sandwiches,
hot dogs and ice cream.

LOST

We are a hot people from a hot country.
Even we could not take the Guam sun
burning through the nylon tent.
Our family collected empty food boxes
left by the Americans.
We put them on the roof to shield the sun.
Others near us copied the idea.

The magazine did not know where we were.
Half of my family did not know.
I had everyone make signs with colored pencils.
We all worked, putting them on tents,
nailing them to trees.

The sign said,
"Nga is in Tent 1005
at location such and such.
Please get in touch."
We heard nothing.

Once in a queue for food,
I saw my nephew, who called,
"Auntie, Auntie, I am out.
My wife and children are stuck behind.
I must fill the papers."
Then he was swallowed by the door.

Many families were separated.
Children wandered from tent to tent
crying for their parents.

SAIGON FALLS

On the night of the 30th
we heard on the little radio I always carried
that Big Minh, the last president of South Vietnam,
had given up.

Sitting on the floor of the blue tent in Guam,
all of us cried, even the boys.
We had thought we would be gone only a short time.
Now we knew we would never return,
never see our friends and family.
Our country was lost.

We worried about Bao, my sister, the other children.
All night long, whenever we'd see the lights of a bus
driving by with other refugees,
we'd go out to ask about our relatives.
I never saw a familiar face.

Americans forget
there are all kinds of Vietnamese,
fishermen, farmers
doctors and lawyers
educated and uneducated.
We lived in constant fear of being robbed
by our own countrymen.

FORT CHAFFEE

After days and days
I saw Harold from the office
driving down the long rows of tents
calling out my name.
We told him what we needed
and he returned with powdered milk,
20 pairs of rubber sandals,
(ours were ruined by the tiny stones)
oranges and apples.
When the children saw the fruit,
they jumped up and down saying,
"Now we will survive.
We have fruit!"

Harold promised to help us with the paperwork.
Before we left Saigon, our family made a plan
to meet in California.
I did not know California
but I thought it was a warm place.
We wrote *San Francisco* on our papers.

On the way to the airport,
I read on my papers *Fort Chaffee*.
I asked the officer, "What does this mean?"
He answered, "Fort Chaffee means Fort Chaffee.
You are going to Arkansas."
I said, "But I want to go to San Francisco."
"You have no choice," he said.
We resigned ourselves to going
though we did not know what it meant
or how it would be.
"Don't be worried," Linh said,
"We have our mouths. We can talk."

Many people were sick on the flight.
We arrived at 3 A.M.
went right to work on the papers.
There were eight people at the desk.
For hours they asked about our private lives.
We were treated like beasts
standing to sleep
standing in categories—
Files, Pictures, Health.

Finally we were settled,
eight of us—all in one room.
We were almost asleep
when the loudspeaker called out,
"Everybody up to do the paperwork."
They threatened to send us back to Vietnam.
I said, "Send us back. I do not care.
I will not move. I cannot move."

BAO

My daughter volunteered to translate
so she could see the lists of newcomers
hoping to find word of the family.

With 20,000 people, Fort Chaffee was overflowing.
For days and nights we did paperwork.
I helped others who did not speak English.

I worried about Bao and my sister
but could only say with the fates,
"If they're lucky, they'll make it."

One day the New York office called
and spelled Bao's name over the phone.
He had called the Red Cross.

They were in Indian Town Gap, Pennsylvania.
My sister had been separated from the group
and ended up on Wake Island.

I had mixed feelings,
happy she was out,
unhappy I could not live with Bao.

VIETNAMESE GENERAL

I recognized a general.
He was said to have been one of the richest
men in Vietnam.
If you did not want to be enlisted,
you would pay him money.
If you did not want to be transferred
to the battlefield,
you would pay him money.
If you wanted your husband, or brother, or son
to go abroad for further training,
you would pay him money.
He was said to have over 100 million dollars.

One morning in the camp
a mob of women came up to him.
They took off their high-heeled wooden shoes
and began beating him about the head
screaming, "Because of you, my son,
my brother, my husband was left behind."
They beat him
until the MPs came and stopped them.

LIFE AT FORT CHAFFEE

Our food was dished out
with an ice-cream scoop.
There were no vegetables
but we learned fast what was good.

Word would go around,
"Beef today, get the beef."
"Canned fish, no good."
The children took extra apples
on apple days.

We could buy ham sandwiches
candy bars and ice-cream on a stick
at a small snack bar
called "The Hitching Post."

By the second month we enjoyed ourselves.
The couple next to us had a stove
and access to outside food.

We cooked chicken, ready-made soup,
toasted soft white American bread
until it was hard like French bread.

My granddaughter recovered
drinking special milk from a can
with a smiling blond mother and baby
photographed on pink paper.

We saw Elizabeth Taylor
and Sophia Loren on a huge outdoor screen—
all of us sitting on the grass
watching movies in the sky.

My son fell in love
with Linh's daughter.
We saw them sneak off
into the night holding hands.

Linh spent his days fishing
in a small brook behind the barracks.
He used a branch, string
and a paper clip made into a hook.
Once he caught a snake.

FAREWELL TO FORT CHAFFEE

We did not know why our papers took so long.
Maybe the authorities had to go to Washington
to see if we had ever been in jail in Vietnam.
They asked about our business, our schooling,
our private lives. I told everything.

When my bossman from the magazine arrived,
the red tape disappeared.
He arrived on a Saturday.
After months of waiting,
the papers came out of hiding.
We could leave the next day.

By now we loved our barracks
had made friends with other people.
A woman near us,
a bar-girl from the countryside,
wanted my address.
She said she was alone
and would need friends once out of the camp.
Her husband was an American GI
who said he would pick her up
in Naples, Florida.

We all sat on the porch
talked about our country
and wondered about our future.
Some of us would go East
and some West,
wherever there was work.

THE RAMADA INN

We drove in three cars
past the armed guards
out of the gates of Fort Chaffee
down the highway to the Ramada Inn.

With only two of us in a room,
a colored T.V., a private bathroom
and a swimming pool,
it seemed like a palace.

We sat at a long table
eating like we would never eat again.
Only the lovers were sad.
Linh and his family were going to California,
my family and I to New York.

NEW YORK CITY

We stayed at the Alden Hotel
on the West Side of New York City.
My son was fascinated.
"How big it is,"
he kept saying
looking out the windows
at the tall houses,
"like huge boxes of matches."

I would not let them down on the street.
I knew New York was full of crime
especially in the dark.
The children asked what floor we were on.
"Sixteen," I answered.
They said in awe,
"This is so much bigger than our Caravelle Hotel."

We heard a knock.
I hurriedly opened the door.
Our friends warned,
"Never open a door like that.
One day you will get into trouble.
In this country, first look
through the small hole
and then open the door."
They brought us chopsticks,
nuoc mam, and bags of oranges.

THE OFFICE

After a Chinese dinner, our American friends
showed me the office building
all made of glass
with fountains on the outside.
In the night my eyes looked
up and up into the sky
at the hundreds of lit windows.
The children said,
"Mummy, will you work here
in this huge building?"
I said yes,
but I was scared.
I was not good at figures.
I had to feed my children.
By the third day
I was at work
on the 27th floor
in Accounts Payable.

MY BROTHER'S ESCAPE

When we were reunited with my younger brother
he told us he and his family
could not leave by the airport.
The rocketing was too heavy.
They went by sampan from Nha Be.

After floating eight days and nights
with no food and little water,
they were picked up by an American battleship.
To board they had to climb a rope one by one
while the huge ship pitched from side to side
on the rough seas.

Everyone wanted to be first up the rope.
People crawled over other people.
Many fell into the ocean.
His wife was pregnant
does not know how she found strength
to climb the rope.

No one could carry anything.
Fathers threw their babies up to the mothers.
With luck they made it.

Two months after I left the base
my brother ended up in Fort Chaffee
in my same room!
The woman next door asked,
"Do you know Mrs. Nga? You look like her."
"She is my sister," he replied.

THE CHURCH

The church helped us find a place to live.
We were afraid the community would not understand us,
so many people living together—Asians.
In New York City, the places we wanted to live in
were too expensive, the cheap places too dangerous.
A kind family let us live in their house
in Connecticut, which is a good place
full of green grass and birds singing.
If we could be together, we were happy.

When the church ladies came to talk,
I was afraid to tell them about the two wives.
Bao and my sister and their children
had gone from the camps to Massachusetts
where they had contacts.
I talked to the church women about ordinary things,
not my whole life.

They warned me not to let my little grandchildren
watch "The Incredible Hulk" on the television.
They said they admired me, making "do" on my own.
They said we were a brave family,
honest and hardworking.

We needed the church.
Without it, the houses we read of in the papers
would shut their doors to us.
We were grateful to the church.
They paid some of the rent,
but we are proud and do not like
finding our clothes at the rummage sale.
People will give one shoe to a rummage sale.

ALLISON

Our sponsors helped us find our first house
on Old Church Road in Greenwich, Connecticut.
I kept my little bottles of perfume
on the bureau in my bedroom.
My children teased me, saying,
"You thought there was no perfume
in the United States."

Through the church,
a family offered to tutor us in English.
At first they all came,
the husband, and the wife and the daughter, Allison.
My son studied with Allison.
She soon moved into his room.
We offered her our food and hospitality.
She criticized me, turned my son against me.

I rode the commuter train to New York every morning
leaving at 6:30, returning in the evening.
One night Allison said,
"I accept you as an educated woman.
How could you let yourself
become a second wife?"
I was shocked.
She was not my mother, not my sister
only a guest in my house.

They began to stay in his room all day,
never sharing meals with us
never talking to us
drinking and smoking
listening to loud music at night.
She played a guitar, slept late.

I could hear her step out of bed
over my head, above me.

I had to send for Bao in Massachusetts.
He said, "This is not a bar,
not a hotel. This is our home."
He threatened to throw the tape recorder
they played all night out the window.
She pushed my son to fight back.
"How can you let him talk to you that way?"
"He is my father," my son answered.

Finally the rest of us had to move
to get away from her.

MRS. LARSEN'S APARTMENT

After we talked about my life,
Mrs. Larsen said, "Nga, your father
should have named you
Phuong for phoenix, not Nga for swan."

She went to the red bookcase
took down two glass boxes.
In them lay perfect musical instruments,
miniatures, glued on purple brocade.

My father's masterpieces!

I'd watched him by the window in Cholon
as he sat hour after hour
carving the tiny violin bows
dying the silks himself.

He made one set for each child.
Even in old age, his eyes were perfect,
his hands steady.

The office staff had presented the Larsens
with a set when they left Saigon,
one of eastern instruments, one of western.
My brother had given the office his,
thinking Father could make him another.

"I wish I could help you more with your son.
I really don't know what you should do,
but I want you to have this," Mrs. Larsen said
and handed me the case with the ti ba and the sao.

She kept the western case.

DEATH DAY

Each year we celebrated my father's death day.
We burnt imitation money
so he would have it to spend,
paper clothes
so he would have them to wear,
left his favorite meals on the altar.

We did this
to show we had not forgotten him.
We did this
to teach his grandchildren
and his great-grandchildren
to respect their elders.

JOBS

We took the jobs available.
My son-in-law, who had a law degree,
sold the Electrolux vacuum cleaner
demonstrated door to door.
American people are afraid of Asians.
They would not let him in.

My sons worked as mechanics,
sold gasoline at night for extra money
until they were robbed.
My daughter worked in a training program
for a cosmetics company.
Bao and my sister started a small grocery store
near the university, selling notebooks, cigarettes,
cookies, ice cream, newspapers for the students.

My brother is an electrician.
My daughter-in-law stayed home
to cook and watch the babies.
We all studied English at night.
One of our friends in Saigon
was Chief Justice of the Supreme Court.
He was trained in France
spoke four languages.
He wrote me:
"I am a watchman in Houston.
When they hired me,
they felt uneasy with my title,
called me a telephone operator.
When anyone knocks on the door
of the company, I open it.
They call me a telephone operator,

but to tell you the truth,
I am a watchman."

From what I have seen in the States,
education means less than in my country.
There, if you are well educated,
you are sure of a high position and respect.
We say with the Chinese,
*"Learn to handle a writing brush
and you will not handle a begging bowl."*
Here a skilled worker makes a lot of money.
America is an industrial society.

TET IN AMERICA

The whole week of Tet
I prepared our favorite dishes
three times a day every day.
After the incense burned,
I removed the food from the altar,
put it on the table.

How silly I felt each noontime
alone in my house
surrounded by little saucers of food,
no one to share them with
no neighbors around me celebrating.

I'd asked my children to take time off
the way I had.
They said, "What for?
So we can sit around the table
and stare at each other?"

I said I did this not for them
but for our ancestors.
Inside I was sad
feeling myself on a desert
knowing my customs will die with me.

LETTER TO MY MOTHER

Dear Mother,

I do not know if you are receiving my letters, but I will keep writing to you as you are always in my mind.

We have been here three years now. I have moved from Greenwich and have a wooden shingled house in Cos Cob. We have a garden in the back where we plant vegetables, flowers in the front the way we used to when we were together. I have a pink dogwood tree that blooms in spring. It looks like the Hoa dai tree, but has no leaves, only flowers.

We worked for months to clear away the poison ivy, a plant that turns your skin red and makes you itch.

We are near a beach, a school and a shopping center. Green lawns go down to the streets and there are many cars and garages. I am even learning to drive.

When we got our new house, people from the church came and took us to "Friendly's" for ice cream. Americans celebrate with ice cream. They have so many kinds—red like watermelon, green for pistachio, orange sherbet like Buddha's robes, mint chocolate chip. You buy it fast and take it away to eat.

Our house is small, but a place to be together and discuss our daily life. At every meal we stare at the dishes you used to fix for us and think about you. We are sorry for you and for ourselves.

If we work hard here, we have everything, but we fear you are hungry and cold and lonesome. Last week we made up a package of clothes. We all tried to figure out how thin you must be now. I do not know if you will ever receive that package wrapped with all our thoughts.

I remember the last days when you encouraged us to leave the country and refused to go yourself. You said you were too old, did not want to leave your home and would be a burden to us. We realize now that you sacrificed yourself for our well-being.

You have a new grandson born in the United States. Thanh looked beautiful at her wedding in a red velvet dress and white veil, a yellow turban in her dark hair. She carried the chrysanthemums you love.

You always loved the fall in Hanoi. You liked the cold. We don't. We have just had the worst winter in a century, snow piled everywhere. I must wear a heavy coat, boots, fur gloves, and a hat. I look like a ball running to the train station. I feel that if I fell down, I could never get up.

Your grandson is three, in nursery school. He speaks English so well that we are sad. We made a rule. We must speak Vietnamese at home so that the children will not forget their mother tongue.

We have made an altar to Father. We try to keep up our traditions so that we can look forward to the day we can return to our country, although we do not know when that will be.

Here we are materially well off, but spiritually deprived. We miss our country. Most of all we miss you. Should Buddha exist, we should keep praying to be reunited.

Dear Mother, keep up your mind. Pray to Buddha silently. We will
have a future and I hope it will be soon.

We want to swim in our own pond.
Clear or stinky, still it is ours.

Your daughter,

Nga

LETTER FROM VIETNAM, HAND-CARRIED TO FRANCE, MAILED TO THE U.S.

Dear Daughters and Sons,

I received your letter and am glad you are happy. Here things are getting worse. We live from day to day. We have spent our savings, sold our antiques and jewelry. Last week your brother sold the last silver cup of the family.

We have to work very hard here now. There are so many new rules. Each family is allowed to change only 5000 piasters. Thousands of people became bankrupt, including us. Many killed themselves. Some put their money in sacks with stones and let it sink under the river rather than give it back to the government.

The government controls everything, food, clothes and housing. They put many people to live in your sister's house. Each family (not a comrade family) is allowed each month to buy at the official rate

1 dozen eggs
1 kilo of meat
10 kilos of rice
1 kilo of sugar

and 5 meters of material. The food lasts our family only a few days and then we must buy at the blackmarket rate which is 5 or 6 times higher.

Your brothers are not allowed to work for the government. They say jobs are scarce and are kept for the comrades. My retirement pension from your father is not paid. We are considered deserters, belonging to the old regime. We could not live without the money you send through our "friend."

We pray not to be sick. The hospital and all good medicine is not for us. It is for the comrades.

I must tell you, recently an order from the government said that all tombs in Saigon and its vicinity should be removed or they will be dug up. We will sacrifice anything, but not your father's tomb. Although it is on private land, I am worried.

I received the package three months after you sent it from the United States. The blouse is too big, but I wear it. The soup was all spoiled even in those little packages.

My favorite carnations are in full bloom. I think of when we were all together. I love my country, but I miss my family. Please let me come with you.

Your Mother

BLUE CABLE

Washington D.C. accepted my application.
My mother had a chance to come to America.
My heart sang.
Back from work, I shared the news with my family.

Everyone wanted her.
We agreed she would stay three months with each group.
We carried our happiness everywhere
even in our dreams.

Late April. I was in the backyard in the garden
admiring my new red tulips.
The postman had me sign a blue cable.

"Mother died. March 26. Funeral Saturday."

> My mother dead for one month.
> My mother so far away
> did our relatives perform the ceremony?
> Did they dig her tomb deep?
>
> O my country!
>
> O my countrymen
> so many of you left in shallow graves
> in time of war
> your souls wandering ceaselessly.

THE DEAD MUST NOT GO HUNGRY

In Cos Cob, we worshiped Mother every day.
We made an altar in the living room
put up her picture, burnt incense
left a bowl of rice and one hard-boiled egg.

The dead must not go hungry.
From the egg will come a chicken
from the chicken an egg.
The dead will have plenty.

I looked at her picture,
the last one ever taken,
and thought of her children
in Hanoi, in Saigon, in the U.S.

Did my elder brother in Hanoi know of her death?
How many letters I had sent.
From him, only one short note saying,
"I thought you would want to keep this."

Attached was my father's note in 1954
explaining how he was moving to the South
because he believed the communists
would break up the family.

"If Buddha is good," he wrote,
"Pray for him to unify us.
One day we will be together again
in one country."

I stared at my mother's picture

saw the translucent blue jade bracelet
she always wore on her left wrist.

We have a saying,
"You do not know how beautiful your jade is
when you are wearing it."

"Mother," I prayed, "Your one hundred days are past.
We invite your spirit
to go to the pagoda in Washington
where Buddha will take care of your soul."

WASHINGTON PAGODA

There were no dragons, no phoenix on the roof
no good and evil spirit-gods
guarding the front door.

Just a red two-storied house with pine trees in the front
a parking lot in the back.
A young woman in brown monk's robes greeted us.

In the central room a golden Buddha sat on a platform
his head reaching to the ceiling.
Burning sandalwood drifted through the room.

We changed into our white funeral clothes,
washed off our lipstick and makeup.
The monk entered and read Mother's names out loud,

her maiden name, her married name, her death date.
He recited all her good deeds
then summoned her soul to be with Buddha for a blessing.

At the sound of a bell,
we stood and chanted, kneeled and prayed.
I thought of Saigon.

Was my father's tomb still intact
with the white elephants at the four corners?
Did they bury my mother next to him
under the jackfruit trees
near the pagoda she loved?

The ceremony was over.
We packed our mourning clothes

into a little suitcase
and climbed into the second-hand stationwagon.

Looking out the window
at the lights on the New Jersey Turnpike
I prayed that we children

though across the world from one another
had followed the ancient traditions
so her spirit would rest with Father's in Paradise.

NEW YORK CITY 1980

IN THE AMERICAN MUSEUM OF NATURAL HISTORY

An equestrian statue of Theodore Roosevelt
guards the entrance.
On one side stands an Indian,
on the other a Negro.
Roosevelt rises head and shoulders above them,
his bronzed gunbearers.
The Negro exposes a naked leg,
the Indian a bare shoulder;
he wears moccasins, the Black, sandals.
Roosevelt wears boots and spurs and packs a pistol.
Behind the groomed tail of the horse,
swings a red dragon on an orange banner
announcing the opening of the Hall of Asian Peoples.

To reach the rooms
Mrs. Nga and I pass through
the darkened Hall of Asiatic Mammals.
Each diorama lights a world.
We stop before a leopard killing a peacock.
The bird's neck is broken
snapped against a rock.
The leopard stares straight ahead.
His mate watches from below.
Copper feathers lie upon the ground,
their turquoise eyes stare out.
A pair of peacocks flies into the painted jungle.

We find the Hall of Asian Peoples
just past the elephants.
Finding Vietnam is more difficult;
one small window

buried between India and China.
Black-and-white drawings show
a traditional wedding procession,
a typical farmer plowing with a water buffalo,
rice growing in a Vietnamese landscape,
four Vietnamese faces.
The only statue is a grinning Money God.
Its caption says
small change is dropped in his back for good luck.

Leaving the Hall of Asian Peoples,
Mrs. Nga smiles as she says,
"I think your country wants to forget about mine."

I picture us, Ba Larsen and Madame Nga,
arm in arm walking through the skeleton
of the dinosaur upstairs.
She has a flute and I a drum.
We carry no flags
and we make a sad song
as we pluck on the bones
dancing over the sides of the universe
past the bison and the bear
and the five-clawed dragon
and its burning pearls of wisdom.

NOTES

GLOSSARY

ANGKOR WAT: Magnificent temple complex in Cambodia, built in the twelfth century

AO DAI: Vietnamese silk dress, worn over long black or white pants

ARVN: (Pronounced R-VEN) Army of the Republic of Vietnam

BA: Mrs. or Lady

BETEL: A climbing pepper plant whose leaves wrapped around the nut from a betel palm and combined with the bark of a tree and lime is chewed as a stimulant

CA DAO: Vietnamese folk poem

CERCLE SPORTIF: Private Saigon club with swimming pool and tennis courts frequented by Vietnamese and foreigners

CHA GIO: Vietnamese egg roll

CYCLO: Tricycle cab

DMZ: Demilitarized zone dividing North and South Vietnam

DURIAN: A large oval fruit having a delicious flavor and an offensive odor

DUST OFF: Medical evacuation helicopter

GAMELAN: An East Asian percussion instrument, akin to the xylophone

GVN: Government of South Vietnam

HAMBURGER HILL: Peak of Apbia mountain in the Ashau Valley near the Laotian border, so named because the grinding battle there killed and wounded so many GI's

HOA SEN: Lotus

I CORPS: (Pronounced eye corps) the northernmost of the four military regions in South Vietnam

JACKFRUIT: A large East Indian tree bearing immense fruit. It is related to the breadfruit tree.

JUSPAO: Joint U.S. Public Affairs Office

KHE SANH: Once an outpost to recruit local tribesmen. Resupplied by General Westmoreland with Marine battalion. Scene of controversial and costly siege of the Marines by the North Vietnamese in 1968.

KHMER ROUGE: Communist guerrillas in Cambodian countryside, so named by Prince Sihanouk

KIM VAN KIEU: Nguyen Du's classic verse novel of filial devotion, written in 1813. Thuy Kieu, the heroine and eldest daughter, sacrifices herself, leaving behind her true love, Kim Trong, to marry her younger sister, Thuy Van, while she suffers slavery and prostitution to save her father. The title comes from the three different characters.

Kit Carson scouts: Vietnamese military defectors who worked with U.S.
Lam Son: Ancient Vietnamese triumph over China
longan: A pulpy fruit related to the lichee
macv: (Pronounced MAC-V) Military Assistance Command Vietnam. U.S. military headquarters in Vietnam, formed in 1962.
Man in the Moon: In Vietnamese legend, the Man in the Moon ties couples together with the red thread of the marriage bonds.
mangosteen: Dark, reddish fruit. It has a thick rind and is very juicy.
Madame Nhu: Wife of Ngo Dinh Nhu, brother of Ngo Dinh Diem, President of South Vietnam
nlf: National Liberation Front
nuoc mam: Favorite Vietnamese sauce made from fermented fish
nva: North Vietnamese Army
Pacification: A complex U.S. program of security and economic measures started in 1958 for government control of the villages. Elaborate systems such as the "Hamlet Evaluation System" were created to measure success at winning Vietnamese "hearts and minds."
piasters: Vietnamese money. In 1970, 118 to the U.S. dollar; blackmarket 175.
pho: Vietnamese soup
Plain of Jars: High plain in the center of Laos where hundreds of urns 2,000 years old, thought to be funeral urns, were found. Scene of frequent battles and U.S. air raids.
Pungi stick: A bamboo stick about 20 inches long, used as a kind of booby trap by the Viet Cong. Both ends were sharpened. One end was buried about 6 inches deep; the other, having previously been dipped in human excrement, was exposed.
r&r: Rest and Recreation. Since Vietnam was considered a hardship post, every six weeks or so, depending on company policy, journalists got a week's vacation somewhere else in Asia.
Ruff-Puffs: Vietnamese regional and popular forces. (RF's and PF's.) Regional forces were company size and protected district areas; popular forces were platoon size and protected home villages.
sao: Flute
Tet: Vietnamese New Year, at the end of January or the beginning of February, based on the lunar calendar.
Ti Ba: Oval-shaped mandolin
titi: Pidgin for *petit*
usaid: United States Agency for International Development
white mice: Saigon police, so called because of their white gloves and shirts and apparent lack of martial spirit
world: What the GIs called the U.S.

VIETNAM: A CHRONOLOGY

LEGEND OF ORIGINS

Once upon a time
Lac Long Quan, the King of the Dragons,
married Au Co, the Queen of the Fairies.
She gave birth to one hundred eggs
from which came one hundred children.

Then Lac Long said,
"I am a dragon. I like the sea.
You are a fairy. You like the mountains.
We cannot live together.
Let us divide the children and part."

He took fifty children to the Southern Sea
the other fifty went north with their mother
to the mountains near Hanoi.
There, the eldest male was elected king
beginning the Hong Bang dynasty
which lasted 2,000 years.

2897–258 BC	Hong Bang dynasty. Country was known as Van Lang.
257–208 BC	Thuc Dynasty. Country known as Au Lac.
208 BC	Trieu Da, a Chinese general, conquers Au Lac in Northern Vietnam. Proclaims himself emperor of "Nam Viet," Land of the Southern Viets, a people of Mongolian origin who had migrated south.
111 BC–39 AD	1st Chinese Occupation. Nam Viet incorporated into Chinese empire as Giao Chi.
40–43	Trung sisters lead major insurrection against Chinese. Set up independent state, lasting only two years.
43–544	2nd Chinese Occupation. In 248, 23-year-old Trieu Au, the Vietnamese Joan of Arc, wearing gold armor and riding an elephant, leads another revolt against China.

603–939	3rd Chinese Occupation.
939–967	Ngo Quyen drives Chinese out. Becomes emperor, establishing Ngo Dynasty, beginning 900 years of Vietnamese independence.
968	After defeating the other 11 warlords, Dinh Bo Linh proclaims himself emperor. Calls his state Dai Co Viet, Kingdom of the Watchful Hawk, but pays tribute to China.
1010–1225	Ly Dynasty. Ly Thai To proclaims himself emperor. Moves to the new capital, Thang Long (now Hanoi). Thang Long means "a dragon rising up," from a dream the emperor had about the place.
1225–1400	Tran Dynasty. Tran Hung Dao defeats the Mongols twice.
1306	The king of the Champa, the Indianized kingdom of central Vietnam, gives up Thua Thien province to the Tran, beginning the southward march of the Vietnamese.
1414–1427	Chinese Occupation (Ming dynasty).
1428	Emperor Le Loi, Vietnam's great hero, defeats China.
1460–1497	Le Thanh Tong rules. Initiates many legal reforms.
1553–1788	Two and a half centuries of civil strife between regional factions. 1627 first of many clashes between the Trinh rulers in the North and the Nguyen in the South.
1787	Pigneau de Behaine, Bishop of Adran, leads an expedition to back his protégé, the Nguyen leader Nguyen Anh. Louis XVI at first finances the expedition and then withdraws his support.
1788	Nguyen Hue defeats the Chinese in Hanoi. Overthrows the last of the Le.
1802	Nguyen Anh becomes emperor under the name Gia Long. Calls country Vietnam. Bao Dai is a descendent of Gia Long.
1862	Treaty of Saigon. French acquire Cochin China (Mekong Delta area).
1883	Treaty of Hue. French protectorate extended to include Tonkin (North Vietnam) and Annam (Central Vietnam).
1887	Cochin China, Cambodia, Annam and Tonkin administratively united as Indochinese Union.
1900	French control all levels of administration.
1927	Viet Nam Quoc Dan Dang, Vietnamese Nationalist Party, organized in North. Founded by Nguyen Thai Hoc.
1930	Yen Bai uprising by the VNQDD. French reprisal fierce. VNQDD leaders guillotined. The Indochinese Communist Party under Nguyen Ai Quoc, better known as Ho Chi Minh, established in Hong Kong.
1932	Bao Dai, theoretically emperor since 1925, returns to Vietnam from France to ascend the throne under French.
1940	Japanese enter Vietnam after France falls to Germany. New Vichy government gives Japanese right to move through Indochina in return for Japanese recognition of French sovereignty there.
1941	Ho Chi Minh forms Viet Nam Doc Lap Dong Minh Hoi, called Viet Minh Front. Fights Japanese and French.
1945	FEB.–MARCH Two million people die of famine in the north. MARCH Japanese unseat French in Indochina and declare Cambodia, Laos and Vietnam independent under Bao Dai.

	JULY	Potsdam Agreement. Chinese Kuomintang occupy North Vietnam for six months to supervise the surrender of Japanese troops in North Vietnam. British to disarm them in the south.
	AUG.	Viet Minh occupies Hanoi.
	SEPT.	Ho Chi Minh proclaims Democratic Republic of Vietnam.
	OCT.	French return, reconquer much of South Vietnam. Viet Minh resist.
1946	Indochina War begins between French and Viet Minh.	
1949	JULY	With French approval, Bao Dai forms the first government of the state of Vietnam.
	OCT.	Mao Tse Tung achieves victory in China.
1950	President Truman signs legislation granting $15 million in military aid to the French war in Indochina. 35 American advisors are sent to Vietnam.	
1954	MAY 7	French defeated by Ho's forces at Dien Bien Phu.
	JUNE	Diem named Prime Minister by Bao Dai.
	JULY	Geneva Agreement. French and Democratic Republic of Vietnam meet at international conference of Great Britain, United States, Soviet Union, and China plus State of Vietnam, Kingdom of Cambodia, Kingdom of Laos (called Three Associated States of Indochina). Agree to divide Vietnam at 17th parallel. Both sides to evacuate troops. Truce declared. People given 300 days to decide whether to live in the North or the South. Elections to be held in 1956 to reunify the country.
	SEPT.	The Southeast Asia Treaty Organization (SEATO) formed by the United States, Great Britain, France, Australia, New Zealand, Pakistan, Thailand, Philippines for defense of Southeast Asia.
1955	JAN.	U.S. sends direct aid to Saigon government and agrees to train South Vietnamese army.
	MARCH–SEPT.	Ngo Dinh Diem consolidates his power by putting down various sects, the Cao Dai, the Hoa Hao, and the Binh Xuyen. The Cao Dai was a fusion of Confucianism, Taoism and Buddhism modeled on the Catholic Church with a "pope" as head. They claimed 2 million followers, an army of 20,000 and controlled much of the Delta. The Hoa Hao, another political-religious sect of reformed Buddhists, had 1 million followers and an army of 15,000. The Binh Xuyen were gangsters, with an army of 25,000, who controlled the Saigon police and underworld.
	JULY	Diem rejects Geneva Accords and refuses to participate in nationwide elections.
	OCT.	National referendum held in the South. Bao Dai deposed. Diem promotes himself Chief of State.
1956	New constitution adopted by referendum in 1956. Diem elected 1st President of the Republic of Vietnam in accordance with the new constitution.	

1957	OCT.	Communist insurgent activity in South Vietnam begins.
1960	APRIL	North Vietnam imposes universal military conscription.
	DEC.	National Liberation Front for South Vietnam officially born.
1961	NOV.	Kennedy increases military advisors to 16,000 over a two-year period.
1962	FEB.	American Military Assistance Command formed in South Vietnam.
1963	MAY	Buddhists demonstrate against Diem's discrimination.
	NOV. 1ST	Coup against Diem and Nhu.
	NOV. 2	Diem and Nhu assassinated.
	U.S. aid increased to $500 million by that year.	
1964	AUG. 2	Johnson Administration reports the USS *Maddox* attacked by North Vietnamese PT boats in Tonkin Bay.
	AUG. 7	Tonkin Gulf Resolution passed in Congress, giving Johnson extraordinary power to act in Southeast Asia.
1965	FEB.	President Johnson orders air attacks on North Vietnam. "Operation Rolling Thunder."
	MARCH	Marines land in Danang; first American combat troops.
	DEC.	American troops number approximately 184,000 in Vietnam.
1967	SEPT.	Nguyen Van Thieu elected President.
		U.S. spending more than $2 billion per month on the war.
1968	JAN.	Tet Offensive. Viet Cong and North Vietnamese attack U.S. Embassy in Saigon and 36 of the provincial capitals.
	MAY	U.S. and North Vietnam hold first formal negotiating session in Paris.
	At the end of the year, American troop strength in Vietnam stands at 540,000.	
1969	JAN.	NLF, North Vietnam, South Vietnam and U.S. agree to meet in Paris.
	JUNE	Nixon and Thieu meet on Midway. Nixon announces 25,000 troops will be withdrawn from South Vietnam by the end of August and emphasizes increased "Vietnamization," South Vietnam taking on additional responsibilities for the war.
	JULY	In Guam, Nixon proclaims "Nixon Doctrine" saying that in the future, unless a major power intervened in a Third World conflict, the U.S., to avoid situations such as Vietnam, will limit its assistance to economic and military aid rather than direct combat involvement.
1970	MARCH	Prince Norodom Sihanouk deposed as ruler of Cambodia. General Lon Nol heads new government.
	APRIL–JUNE	U.S. and South Vietnamese soldiers invade sanctuaries in Cambodia.
1971	FEB.	South Vietnamese invade Laos with U.S. support.
	JUNE–JULY	Secret peace negotiations with North Vietnamese begun by Kissinger.
	OCT.	Thieu reelected President.
1972	AUG.	Last U.S. ground combat troops leave Vietnam.
	DEC.	U.S. bombing of area around Hanoi and Haiphong.

1973	JAN.	Paris Accords signed between Kissinger and Le Duc Tho. The cease-fire begins on Jan. 28.
	MARCH	Last U.S. military personnel leave Vietnam.
	APRIL	American prisoners of war released in Hanoi.
1974	JAN.	Thieu declares war has begun again.
1975	APRIL 17	Phnom Penh falls to the Khmer Rouge.
	APRIL 21	Thieu resigns. Flees Saigon to Taiwan. Now lives in Great Britain.
	APRIL 30	Fall of Saigon.
1976	Vietnam is officially unified as Socialist Republic of Vietnam.	

VIETNAMESE NAMES

Because there are less than a hundred family names in Vietnam, the Vietnamese use their given name as we do our family name. Take, for instance, Tran Thi Nga: *Tran* is the family name, *Thi* means female, and *Nga* is the given name. Married women use their husband's given name. Working married women use their own given names, but in society are called by their husband's name.

SOURCES

The two poems, "Lament of the Warrior's Wife" by Dang Tran Con on page 123 and the ca dao "Poor Matchmaking" on page 166 are from *A Thousand Years of Vietnamese Poetry*, edited by Nguyen Ngoc Bich, translated by Nguyen Ngoc Bich with Burton Raffel and W. S. Merwin, Alfred A. Knopf, New York, 1975.

The military expressions are from the *Cam Nang Thong-Dich Vien Quan-Doi, English-Vietnamese Military Handbook*, Vu-Anh-Tuan.

The description of Vietnamese as a tonal language is from The Vietnamese Culture Series, No. 2, Nguyen Dinh Hoa, Vietnamese Language Series, Department of Education, Republic of Vietnam, 1961.

The chronology is based on the following works:

Committee of Concerned Asian Scholars. *The Indochina Story*. Bantam, 1970.
Cooper, Chester L. *The Lost Crusade*. Dodd, Mead & Co., 1970.
Doan Them. *The Past Twenty Years*. Nam Chi Tung Thu, 1966.
FitzGerald, Frances. *Fire in the Lake*. Little, Brown, 1972.
Herring, George C. *America's Longest War: The United States and Vietnam, 1950–1975*. Alfred A. Knopf, 1979.
Karnow, Stanley. *Vietnam. A History*. Penguin Books, 1984.
Tran Trong Kim. *Summary History of Vietnam*. Tan-Viet-Saigon, 1958.

ABOUT THE AUTHORS

Wendy Wilder Larsen was born in Boston in 1940, moved to California when she was five, and has been traveling ever since. She received a BA in English Literature from Wheaton College and an MAT from Harvard University. She lived in Saigon from 1970 to 1971.

Her poems have appeared in *Dark House, Hawaii Review, The Seattle Review, Tendril, 13th Moon,* and *Manhattan Poetry Review.* She is presently living in New York City.

Tran Thi Nga was born in China in 1927. She was educated at Dong Khanh College, Hanoi, and at Swansea University, South Wales, where she received a diploma in Social Administration. She was a social worker at the Ministry of Social Welfare in Saigon, and later worked for an American magazine, both in Vietnam and in the United States.

She has four children and five grandchildren and lives in Connecticut.

FOUR IN HAND

A QUARTET OF NOVELS

SYLVIA TOWNSEND WARNER

FOUR IN HAND

A Quartet of Novels
Sylvia Townsend Warner

LOLLY WILLOWES

MR. FORTUNE'S MAGGOT

SUMMER WILL SHOW

THE CORNER THAT HELD THEM

Introduction by William Maxwell

W. W. NORTON & COMPANY
NEW YORK

FOUR IN HAND: A QUARTET OF NOVELS
First published by W. W. Norton & Company, Inc.
500 Fifth Avenue New York, NY 10110
Published simultaneously in Canada
by Penguin Books Canada Ltd., 2801 John Street
Markham, Ontario L3R 184

This edition published by arrangement
with Chatto & Windus, Ltd.

Warner, Sylvia Townsend, 1893–1978
Four in Hand: A Quartet of Novels
Library of Congress Catalog Number: 86–5414

ISBN 0-393-02356-7

1 2 3 4 5 6 7 8 9 0

CONTENTS

Introduction by William Maxwell vii

Lolly Willowes 1

Mr. Fortune's Maggot 135

Summer Will Show 265

The Corner That Held Them 565

INTRODUCTION
William Maxwell

In 1926, when *Lolly Willowes* was chosen as the first Book-of-the-Month Club selection, its author, Sylvia Townsend Warner, was thirty years old. The subscribers were told that it was her first book of fiction but that she had published—"as might be guessed"—poetry. In the fullness of time (Miss Townsend Warner died in 1978, at the age of eighty-five) she published six more novels, eight collections of short stories, four volumes of poetry, a biography and several long essays on one subject and another. There have been two posthumous collections of short stories, a fifth volume of poetry and a volume of selected letters.

Early on in *Lolly Willowes* the author observes: "There is nothing more endangering to a young woman's normal inclination toward young men than an intimacy with a man twice her age." She was speaking of the heroine but could conceivably have been speaking of herself as well. Her father, George Townsend Warner, was a handsome, gifted and charming man, and their two minds were wholly congenial. He was a House Master and taught history at Harrow. The school bells and the cricket bat striking the ball were woven into the fabric of household sounds. After a brief experience at kindergarten—she mimicked the teachers and was unresponsive to discipline—her father decided that she should be educated at home. Her mother gave her lessons for two hours every morning, and eventually there was a French governess, whom she didn't like. On holidays her father taught her history. When her mother was out for the afternoon, he would send for Sylvia at tea-time. In his study there was a rocking horse ten hands high. Holding her in his lap, he would read poetry to her while they rocked.

She had the run of his library. In a treatise on popular delusions, which she read when she was not yet ten, she found a chapter on witchcraft and sat on the stairs repeating to her cat the spells for raising the devil, hoping that they would work.

She grew up steeped in the English poets. In music as well.

She meant to go to Vienna to study composing with Arnold Schönberg, but the outbreak of the First World War prevented this, and she went to work in a munitions factory instead. In 1916 her father died, of grief she felt, as one after another of his most talented pupils was killed in the trenches. After the war she lived in London on a very small allowance and was involved in the collecting and editing of Tudor church music.

The novelist David Garnett, who at this time had a literary bookshop in London, has described her as she was then: "Sylvia is dark, lean, and eager, with rather frizzy hair. She wears spectacles and her face is constantly lighting up with amusement and intelligence." Her conversation was full of verbal fireworks. At times ideas, epigrams and paradoxes "poured from her mouth as though she were delirious." He showed her poems to an editor at Chatto and Windus, who accepted them for publication and asked if she had ever thought about writing a novel. She had done more than think about it, and submitted the manuscript of *Lolly Willowes* to him with this note: "Here is my story about a witch, that you were kind enough to say you would like to read. If you like it well enough to think of publishing it, I shall be extremely pleased. If you don't, I shan't be much surprised." The manuscript, so diffidently presented, must have made him rub his eyes with astonishment, for *Lolly Willowes* is clearly the work of a born novelist. It demonstrated that Miss Townsend Warner could tell a story, she could create characters that had the breath of life in them, she had a sense of subject, imagination, irony and wit. She saw the world with a clear eye and she had a flawless prose style.

Some novelists cover their tracks, some don't bother, but very few of them leave an explicit account of the way in which a book came into being. In the mid-1960s Miss Townsend Warner dictated to the poet Valentine Ackland, who lived with her, this recollection of the genesis of *Mr. Fortune's Maggot:*

"When I first went to live in London, in 1917, in a flat over a furrier's at 127 Queen's Road, Bayswater, I was poor and could not afford a lending library subscription. I had the British Museum by day but I wanted something to read in the evenings.

Then I found the Westbourne Grove branch of the Paddington Public Library. It was a very snuffy establishment with a great many biographies of unimportant people and all the books had the same smell (I suppose it was some public disinfectant). One of the books I took out was a volume of letters by a woman missionary in Polynesia. . . . It had only the minimum of religion, only elementary scenery and a mass of details of every-day life. The woman wrote out of her own heart—for instance, describing an earthquake she said that the ground trembled like the lid of a boiling kettle. . . .

"One early morning I woke up remembering an extremely vivid dream. A man stood alone on an ocean beach, wringing his hands in an intensity of despair; as I saw him in my dream, I knew something about him. He was a missionary, he was middle-aged and a deprived character . . . he was on an island where he had made only one convert, and at the moment I saw him he had realized that the convert was no convert at all. I jumped out of bed and began to write this down, and even as I wrote, a great deal that I knew from the dream began to scatter; but the main facts and the man's loneliness, simplicity and despair and the look of the island all remained as actual as something I had really experienced.

"I made a few notes of the development . . . and began to write. The opening, with hardly a word's alteration, is as I wrote it then. This must have been in winter, because I remember Duncan Grant coming to dinner, and we had the gas fire on and ate some kind of stewed game. The moment he had gone I went on writing; and the description of the island, especially its colouring, shows the influence of Duncan's painting, which at that time was particularly brilliant and free.

"My remembrance of the book from the public library was so vivid and substantial that I never felt a need to consult other books. . . . The definition of an umbrella arose from a conversation with Victor Butler, in which he said everything was definable in mathematical terms. How would you define an umbrella? I said. Next day I got a postcard beginning, 'An umbrella, Sylvia,' etc. Victor also supplied the practical bones of the tree-measuring episode. The parrot lived next-door to the cottage in Wayford in Somerset I rented that summer. It sat in a tree and I grew very familiar with its voice and noticed how much quieter unconfined parrots sound.

"There must have been some breaks between Duncan coming to dine and listening to the parrot, but when I went back to London that autumn I wrote steadily and with increasing anxiety: not because I had any doubt about the story but because I was so intensely conscious that the shape and balance of the narrative must be exactly right—or the whole thing would fall and break to smithereens and I could never pick it up again. . . . This was made the more alarming by the way in which things kept on working out right—like the business of Mr. Fortune's watch, for instance. I was in a state of semi-hallucination during the last part of the book—writing in manuscript and taking wads of it to be typed at the Westbourne Secretarial College in Queen's Road. I remember writing the last paragraph and reading the conclusion and then impulsively writing the envoi, with a feeling of compunction, almost guilt, toward this guiltless man I had created and left in such a fix."

There is also a note on *Summer Will Show,* dictated to the same person at roughly the same time: "It must have been in 1920 or '21 that I said to a young man called Robert Firebrace that I had invented a person: an early Victorian young lady of means with a secret passion for pugilism; she attended prize-fights dressed as a man and kept a punching-ball under lock and key in her dressing-room. He asked what she looked like and I replied without hesitation: Smooth fair hair, tall, reserved, very ladylike. She's called Sophia Willoughby.

"And there she was and there she stayed. I had no thought of doing anything with her. A year or so later and equally out of the blue I saw Minna telling about the pogrom in a Paris drawing-room and Lamartine leaning against the doorway. And there she stayed. I had written my first three novels and *Opus 7* and *The Salutation* and was living in Frankfort Manor in Norfolk with Valentine when we went to Paris (1932, I think) and in the Rue Mouffetard, outside a grocer's shop, I found that I wanted to write a novel about 1848. And Sophie and Minna started up and rushed into it.

"When we got back I sent to the London Library for histories and memoirs, as close to the date as I could find. This was a lesson in history. Legitimists, Orleanists, Republicans all told incompatible versions of the same events and several times didn't even agree on dates. But their prejudices made them what I needed. It was from one of these that I read how Marie-Amélie urged poor Louis-Philippe to go out and confront the mobs, adding, 'I will call down blessings on you from the balcony.' I reflected that this nonsense coincided with the Communist Manifesto, and this shaped the argument of the book. I read several guidebooks of that date, too, and discovered Columbin who sold English buns, and the Dames Réunies; and I reread Berlioz's *Mémoires,* and with an effort put the French novelists out of my mind.

"Caspar came out of the Scotch branch of my own family tree. My grandmother remembered his black hand beside her white one when he arrived in Edinburgh as the little boy Uncle Alexander was interested in. She remembered, too, being held over a lime kiln for whooping cough. The character I most enjoyed creating was Léocadie: she was so detestable and so estimable. . . .

"I drafted the book in Norfolk, continued it in Dorset, ended it at Lavenham in Suffolk, where I had gone to be alone with it. Once it began, I wrote it with great impetus—too much impetus, for there are some howlers. The Sabbath candle should have been lit by Minna's mother, for instance. But mainly I was lucky. If one goes fast enough, one is less likely to trip."

The material of a novel—the *action*—is an experience which the novelist lives through and is permanently affected by. Nothing in Miss Townsend Warner's first three novels suggests the emotional power of *Summer Will Show.* Confronted by the horror and violence that erupted during the period she had chosen to write about, her imagination rose to the occasion, producing a strength and toughness that could deal with bloodshed, grinding poverty, death, the ultimate isolation of the soul, and the failure of worthy causes to live up to the hopes that people invest in them.

If the claims on Miss Townsend Warner's attention had continued to be of the ordinary kind, *The Corner That Held Them* would probably have been written at the same white heat as the others. But she was overtaken by history as it exists before the historians have caught up with it and produced their conflicting interpretations. At night the sky over Dorset was lit up with gunfire ("Gunfire light is quite different to lightning, it doesn't twitch, it just glares and goes and glares and goes"). If they were sufficiently far off, the bump bump bump of bombs falling in the still air sounded like apples falling from a tree. If they were close by, the house shook like an old buggy.

In September, 1942, she wrote to the American composer Paul Nordoff: "Please don't mind if I write back to you on the verso of your letter, it is not heartlessness or inattention, just paper-saving. I still have quite a fair amount of paper, but I want to husband it, as I seem to be really writing a book this time. After endless false starts and false scents. It is about fourteenth-century England, almost all the characters are professionally religious, nuns, or parsons, or bishops. I am interested to find how much I know about these people, there is practically no love in the book, and no religion, but a great deal of financial worry and ambition and loneliness and sensitivity to weather, with practically no sensitivity to nature. If you have no sensibility to nature the rain seems much wetter, the cold much colder, etc. It is not in any way a historical novel, it hasn't any thesis, and so far I am contentedly vague about the plot. But it is being very obliging in the way it presents itself to me as I write it, lots of good fortunes about counter-subjects that turn out to be invertible or perfectly good canons, and so on."

At various times she had families of Londoners billeted in her not very large house at the edge of the village of Maiden Newton. She served as a fire warden and coped with the matter of three meals a day in a place where the local population was always soaring above the allotment of food. There being very little petrol, she sold her car and at the age of forty-six learned to ride a motorized bicycle. Two days a week she sat filling out forms in the Dorchester office of the Public Assistance Committee. The house was, for a brief time, full of feathers because an incendiary bomb landed on a bed, tearing open the pillows and eiderdown quilt. So much of London was gone that it made her feel like a ghost.

("There has never been more beautiful summer weather. The air is full of the scent of cut hay, and now the smell of the elder blossom has been added to it. And our garden is crammed with clove pinks, and presently we shall be crammed with raspberries. Perhaps it is a trifle like the hearty breakfast you get on the morning you are going to be hanged; but that is no reason for not enjoying it.") She gave talks on history and English literature to working women and soldiers. And she was sometimes blue with fear. Like the nuns in her novel—for, what with the Hundred Years' War, the epidemic of bubonic plague known as the Black Death that carried off a third of the population of England, and the Peasants' Revolt (all of which figure in *The Corner That Held Them*), the fourteenth century was quite as full of mayhem and wanton destruction as our own.

In May 1946, by which time people had returned to their former habit of looking at the sky for signs of a change in the weather and not for planes with a swastika on them, she again wrote to Nordoff: "I thought my novel was almost finished; then I went back to the beginning, and now I find I want to rewrite a great deal of it, perhaps the whole of it. Because having spent so long on it and written it at such divers times and under such distracting circumstances, though all the characters in it are solid and consistent, the lighting, so to speak, has an inconsistency, the shadows are sometimes to the east sometimes to the west of an incident, and it needs a long study as a whole to put these discrepancies right. One might almost think that the material of a work of art has the awkward individual vitality of timber; and warps and changes its contours after it has been sawn and fitted and put together."

There is reason to think that, oftener than not, writers do not choose a subject but are chosen by it. In any case, the subject of *The Corner That Held Them*—the daily life of a group of medieval nuns over a period of thirty years—was a particularly difficult one, demanding virtuosity at every turn. The book bears a certain resemblance to a class photograph. It focuses for a few pages on one character, and then the focus shifts to another, and another. Nothing much happens or can happen to any of them to change the repetitious shape given to their days by the religious discipline they have embraced (or that was chosen for them) and the small irritations produced by over-familiarity with their company and surroundings. Only once—in the episode of the stolen altar-hanging—does the fish take the hook, in a manner of speaking, and run with it, and the narrative move along more usual lines, with suspense, surprises and somebody in trouble whom the reader identifies with. Perhaps to avoid this very thing, the author has seen the events from an elevation where the people do not dominate the landscape but both are merely part of the picture. Ostensibly about a small group of women living in a religious establishment of no importance or wealth, the novel is in fact a panorama of the time. One cannot help feeling that the child whose special happiness was to be taught history by her father on holidays in France and Switzerland and Cornwall is passing the gift on, with compound interest.

Miss Townsend Warner published one more novel, about a Victorian family, and at the age of seventy was induced to write a biography of T. H. White, the author of *The Once and Future King,* who at the end of his life was living on an island off the coast of France. One would have said offhand that she and White didn't have a single trait in common, except that they were both writers. "From the moment I went to Alderney," she wrote to a friend, "I knew I was to do it because it was a human obligation. He had been dead less than four months. His suitcases were at the foot of the stairs, as though he had just come back . . . everything was there, defenceless as a corpse. And so was he; morose, suspicious, intensely watchful and determined to despair. I have never felt such an *imminent* haunt." To his anguished soul she brought a compassionate understanding and to his acts a moral sense that is never superior in its tone but only just. Her life of White belongs among the handful of first-rate literary biographies of the twentieth century.

In her eighties Miss Townsend Warner had a flare-up of creative energy and produced a spate of chilling, phosphorescent fairy tales which seem to be based on first-hand information. Common sense says, of course, that it cannot be. And yet there it is.

Miss Townsend Warner's writing life spans more than fifty years. She made no effort to be original; she simply was—in her conversation, in the way she thought and lived. She was asked once why she had left off composing music and answered that she had come to the conclusion that she didn't do it authentically enough, whereas when she turned to writing she never had a doubt as to what she meant to say. A definition, *one* definition, of style.

"But if I were reincarnated," she added, "I think I would like to be a landscape painter." The habit of looking at things carefully was perhaps acquired, perhaps ingrained. Her descriptions have the exactness of a Chinese ink drawing. Her extraordinary fancy existed side by side with and never distorted her profound understanding of human and animal behavior. She stands quite alone among the writers of our period.

L O L L Y   W I L L O W E S

Or The Loving Huntsman

PART 1

When her father died, Laura Willowes went to live in London with her elder brother and his family.

"Of course," said Caroline, "you will come to us."

"But it will upset all your plans. It will give you so much trouble. Are you sure you really want me?"

"Oh *dear,* yes."

Caroline spoke affectionately, but her thoughts were elsewhere. They had already journeyed back to London to buy an eiderdown for the bed in the small spare-room. If the washstand were moved towards the door, would it be possible to fit in a writing-table between it and the fireplace? Perhaps a bureau would be better, because of the extra drawers? Yes, that was it. Lolly could bring the little walnut bureau with the false handles on one side and the top that jumped up when you touched the spring by the ink-well. It had belonged to Lolly's mother, and Lolly had always used it, so Sibyl could not raise any objections. Sibyl had no claim to it whatever, really. She had only been married to James for two years, and if the bureau had marked the morning-room wall-paper, she could easily put something else in its place. A stand with ferns and potted plants would look very nice.

Lolly was a gentle creature, and the little girls loved her; she would soon fit into her new home. The small spare-room would be rather a loss. They could not give up the large spare-room to Lolly, and the small spare-room was the handiest of the two for ordinary visitors. It seemed extravagant to wash a pair of the large linen sheets for a single guest who came but for a couple of nights. Still, there it was, and Henry was right—Lolly ought to come to them. London would be a pleasant change for her. She would meet nice people, and in London she would have a better chance of marrying. Lolly was twenty-eight. She would have to make haste if she were going to find a husband before she was thirty. Poor Lolly! black was not becoming to her. She looked sallow, and her pale grey eyes were paler and more surprising than ever underneath that very unbecoming black mushroom hat. Mourning was never satisfactory if one bought it in a country town.

While these thoughts passed through Caroline's mind, Laura was not thinking at all. She had picked a red geranium flower, and was staining her left wrist with the juice of its crushed petals. So, when she was younger, she had stained her pale cheeks, and had bent over the greenhouse tank to see what she looked like. But the greenhouse tank showed only a dark shadowy Laura, very dark and smooth like the lady in the old holy painting that hung in the dining-room and was called the Leonardo.

"The girls will be delighted," said Caroline. Laura roused herself. It was all settled, then, and she was going to live in London with Henry, and Caroline his wife, and Fancy and Marion his daughters. She would become an inmate of the tall house in Apsley Terrace where hitherto she had only been a country sister-in-law on a visit. She would recognise a special something in the physiognomy of that house-front which would enable her to stop certainly before it without glancing at the number or the door-knocker. Within it, she would know unhesitatingly which of the polished brown doors was which, and become quite indifferent to the position of the cistern, which had baffled her so one night when she lay awake trying to assemble the house inside the box of its outer walls. She would take the air in Hyde Park and watch the children on their ponies and the fashionable trim ladies in Rotten Row, and go to the theatre in a cab.

London life was very full and exciting. There were the shops, processions of the Royal Family and of the unemployed, the gold tunnel at Whiteley's, and the brilliance of the streets by night. She thought of the street lamps, so impartial, so imperturbable in their stately *diminuendos,* and felt herself abashed before their scrutiny. Each in turn would hand her on, her and her shadow, as she walked the unfathomed streets and squares—but they would be familiar then—complying with the sealed orders of the future; and presently she would be taking them for granted, as the Londoners do. But in London there would be no greenhouse with a glossy tank, and no apple-room, and no potting-shed, earthy and warm, with bunches of poppy heads hanging from the ceiling, and sunflower seeds in a wooden box, and bulbs in thick paper bags, and hanks of tarred string, and lavender drying on a tea-tray. She must leave all this behind, or only enjoy it as a visitor, unless James and Sibyl happened to feel, as Henry and Caroline did, that of course she must live with them.

Sibyl said: "Dearest Lolly! So Henry and Caroline are to have you. . . . We shall miss you more than I can say, but of course you will prefer London. Dear old London with its picturesque fogs and its interesting people, and all. I quite envy you. But you mustn't quite forsake Lady Place. You must come and pay us long visits, so that Tito doesn't forget his aunt."

"Will you miss me, Tito?" said Laura, and stooped down to lay her face against his prickly bib and his smooth, warm head. Tito fastened his hands round her finger.

"I'm sure he'll miss your ring, Lolly," said Sibyl. "You'll have to cut the rest of your teeth on the poor old coral when Auntie Lolly goes, won't you, my angel?"

"I'll give him the ring if you think he'll really miss it, Sibyl."

Sibyl's eyes glowed; but she said:

"Oh no, Lolly, I couldn't think of taking it. Why, it's a family ring."

When Fancy Willowes had grown up, and married, and lost her husband in the war, and driven a lorry for the Government, and married again from patriotic motives, she said to Owen Wolf-Saunders, her second husband:

"How unenterprising women were in the old days! Look at Aunt Lolly. Grandfather left her five hundred a year, and she was nearly thirty when he died, and yet she could find nothing better to do than to settle down with Mum and Dad, and stay there ever since."

"The position of single women was very different twenty years ago," answered Mr. Wolf-Saunders. "*Femme sole,* you know, and *femme couverte,* and all that sort of rot."

Even in 1902 there were some forward spirits who wondered why that Miss Willowes, who was quite well off, and not likely to marry, did not make a home for herself and take up something artistic or emancipated. Such possibilities did not occur to any of Laura's relations. Her father being dead, they took it for granted that she should be absorbed into the household of one brother or the other. And Laura, feeling rather as if she were a piece of property forgotten in the will, was ready to be disposed of as they should think best.

The point of view was old-fashioned, but the Willoweses were a conservative family and kept to old-fashioned ways. Preference, not prejudice, made them faithful to their past. They slept in beds and sat upon chairs whose comfort insensibly persuaded them into respect for the good sense of their forbears. Finding that well-chosen wood and well-chosen wine improved with keeping, they believed that the same law applied to well-chosen ways. Moderation, civil speaking, leisure of the mind and a handsome simplicity were canons of behaviour imposed upon them by the example of their ancestors.

Observing those canons, no member of the Willowes family had risen to much eminence. Perhaps great-great-aunt Salome had made the nearest approach to fame. It was a decent family boast that great-great-aunt Salome's puff-paste had been commended by King George III. And great-great-aunt Salome's prayer-book, with the services for King Charles the Martyr and the Restoration of the Royal Family and the welfare of the House of Hanover—a nice example of impartial piety—was always used by the wife of the head of the family. Salome, though married to a Canon of Salisbury, had taken off her embroidered kid gloves, turned up her sleeves, and gone into the kitchen to mix the paste for His Majesty's eating, her Venice-point lappets dangling above the floury bowl. She was a loyal subject, a devout churchwoman, and a good housewife, and the Willoweses were properly proud of her. Titus, her father, had made a voyage to the Indies, and had brought back with him a green parrokeet, the first of its kind to be seen in Dorset. The parrokeet was named Ratafee, and lived for fifteen years. When he died he was stuffed; and perched as in life upon his ring, he swung from the cornice of the china-cupboard surveying four generations of the Willowes family with his glass eyes. Early in the nineteenth century one eye fell out and was lost. The eye which replaced it was larger, but inferior both in lustre and expressiveness. This gave Ratafee a rather leering look, but it did not compromise the esteem in which he was held. In a humble way the bird had made county history, and the family acknowledged it, and gave him a niche in their own.

Beside the china-cupboard and beneath Ratafee stood Emma's harp, a green harp ornamented with gilt scrolls and acanthus leaves in the David manner. When Laura was little she would sometimes steal into the empty drawing-room and pluck the strings which remained unbroken. They answered with a melancholy and distracted voice, and Laura would pleasantly frighten herself with the thought of Emma's ghost coming back to make music with cold fingers, stealing into the empty drawing-room as noiselessly as she had done. But Emma's was a gentle ghost. Emma had died of a decline, and when she lay dead with a bunch of snowdrops under her folded palms a lock of her hair was cut off to be embroidered into a picture of a willow tree exhaling its branches above a padded white satin tomb. "That," said Laura's mother, "is an heirloom of your great-aunt Emma who died." And Laura was sorry for the poor young lady who alone, it seemed to her, of all her relations had had the misfortune to die.

Henry, born in 1818, grandfather to Laura and nephew to Emma, became head of the house of Willowes when he was but twenty-four, his father and unmarried elder brother dying of smallpox within a fortnight of each other. As a young man Henry had shown a roving and untraditional temperament, so it was fortunate that he had the licence of a cadet to go his own way. He had taken advantage of this freedom to marry a Welsh lady, and to settle near Yeovil, where his father bought him a partnership in a brewery. It was natural to expect that upon becoming the head of the family Henry would abandon, if not the Welsh wife and the brewery, at least Somerset, and return to his native people. But this he would not do. He had become attached to the neighbourhood where he had spent the first years of his married life; the ill-considered jest of his uncle the Admiral, that Henry was courting a Welsh-woman with a tall hat like Mother Shipton's who would carry her shoes to church, had secretly estranged him from his relations; and—most weighty reason of all—Lady Place, a small solid mansion, which he had long coveted—saying to himself that if ever he were rich enough he would make his wife the mistress of it—just then came into the market. The Willowes obstinacy, which had for so long kept unchanged the home of Dorset, was now to transfer that home across the county border. The old house was sold, and the furniture and family belongings were installed at Lady Place. Several strings of Emma's harp were broken, some feathers were jolted out of Ratafee's tail, and Mrs. Willowes, whose upbringing had been Evangelical, was distressed for several Sundays by the goings-on that she found in Salome's prayer-book. But in the main the Willowes tradition stood the move very well. The tables and chairs and cabinets stood in the same relation to each other as before; the pictures hung in the same order though on new walls; and the Dorset hills were still to be seen from the windows, though now from windows facing south instead of from windows facing north. Even the brewery, untraditional as it was, soon weathered and became indistinguishably part of the Willowes way of life.

Henry Willowes had three sons and four daughters. Everard, the eldest son, married his second cousin, Miss Frances D'Urfey. She brought some more Willowes property to the Somerset house: a set of garnets; a buff and gold tea-service bequeathed her by the Admiral, an amateur of china, who had dowered all his nieces and great-nieces with Worcester, Minton, and Oriental; and two oil-paintings by Italian masters which the younger Titus, Emma's brother, had bought in Rome whilst travelling for his health. She bore Everard three children: Henry, born in 1867; James, born in 1869; and Laura, born in 1874.

On Henry's birth Everard laid down twelve dozen of port against his coming of age. Everard was proud of the brewery, and declared that beer was the befitting drink for all classes of Englishmen, to be preferred over foreign wines. But he did not extend this ban to port and sherry; it was clarets he particularly despised.

Another twelve dozen of port was laid down for James, and there it seemed likely the matter would end.

Everard was a lover of womankind; he greatly desired a daughter, and when he got one she was all the dearer for coming when he had almost given up hope of her. His delight upon this occasion, however, could not be so compactly expressed. He could not lay down port for Laura. At last he hit upon the solution of his difficulty. Going up to London upon the mysterious and inadequate pretext of growing bald, he returned with a little string of pearls, small and evenly matched, which exactly fitted the baby's neck. Year by year, he explained, the necklace could be extended until it encircled the neck of a grown-up young woman at her first ball. The ball, he went on to say, must take place in winter, for he wished to see Laura trimmed with ermine. "My dear," said Mrs. Willowes, "the poor girl will look like a Beefeater." But Everard was not to be put off. A stuffed ermine which he had known as a boy was still his ideal of the enchanted princess, so pure and sleek was it, and so artfully poised the small neat head on the long throat. "Weasel!" exclaimed his wife. "Everard, how dare you love a minx?"

Laura escaped the usual lot of the new-born, for she was not at all red. To Everard she seemed his very ermine come to true life. He was in love with her femininity from the moment he set eyes on her. "Oh, the fine little lady!" he cried out when she was first shown to him, wrapped in shawls, and whimpering at the keen sunlight of a frosty December morning. Three days after that it thawed, and Mr. Willowes rode to hounds. But he came back after the first kill. " 'Twas a vixen," he said. "Such a pretty young vixen. It put me in mind of my own, and I thought I'd ride back to see how she was behaving. Here's the brush."

Laura grew up almost as an only child. By the time she was past her babyhood her brothers had gone to school. When they came back for their holidays, Mrs. Willowes would say: "Now, play nicely with Laura. She has fed your rabbits every day while you have been at school. But don't let her fall into the pond."

Henry and James did their best to observe their mother's bidding. When Laura went too near the edge of the pond one or the other would generally remember to call her back again; and before they returned to the house, Henry, as a measure of precaution, would pull a wisp of grass and wipe off any tell-tale green slime that happened to be on her slippers. But nice play with a sister so much younger than themselves was scarcely possible. They performed the brotherly office of teaching her to throw and to catch; and when they played at Knights or Red Indians, Laura was dutifully cast for some passive female part. This satisfied the claims of honour; if at some later stage it was discovered that the captive princess or the faithful squaw had slipped away unnoticed to the company of Brewer in the coach-house or Oliver Cromwell the toad, who lived under the low russet roof of violet leaves near the disused melon pit, it did not much affect the course of the drama. Once, indeed, when Laura as a captive princess had been tied to a tree, her brothers were so much carried away by a series of single combats for her favour that they forgot to come and rescue her before they swore friendship and went off to the Holy Land. Mr. Willowes, coming home from the brewery through a sunset haze of midges, chanced to stroll into the orchard to see if the rabbits had barked any more of his saplings. There he found Laura, sitting contentedly in hayband fetters, and singing herself a story about a snake that had no mackintosh. Mr. Willowes was extremely vexed when he understood from Laura's nonchalant account what had happened. He took off her slippers and chafed her feet. Then he carried her indoors to his study, giving orders that a tumbler of hot sweet lemonade should be prepared for her immediately. She drank it sitting on his knee while he told her about the new ferret. When Henry and James were heard approaching with war-whoops, Mr. Willowes put her into his leather arm-chair and went out to meet them. Their war-whoops quavered and ceased as they caught sight of their father's stern face. Dusk seemed to fall on them with condemnation as he reminded them that it was past their supper-time, and pointed out that, had he not happened upon her, Laura would still have been sitting bound to the *Bon Chrétien* pear-tree.

This befell upon one of the days when Mrs. Willowes was lying down with a headache. "Something always goes wrong when I have one of my days," the poor lady would complain. It was also upon one of Mrs. Willowes's days that Everard fed Laura with the preserved cherries out of the drawing-room cake.

Laura soon became very sick, and the stable-boy was sent off post-haste upon Everard's mare to summon the doctor.

Mrs. Willowes made a poor recovery after Laura's birth; as time went on, she became more and more invalidish, though always pleasantly so. She was seldom well enough to entertain, so Laura grew up in a quiet household. Ladies in mantles of silk or of sealskin, according to the season of the year, would come to call, and sitting by the sofa would say: "Laura is growing a big girl now. I suppose before long you will be sending her to a school." Mrs. Willowes heard them with half-shut eyes. Holding her head deprecatingly upon one side, she returned evasive answers. When by quite shutting her eyes she had persuaded them to go, she would call Laura and say: "Darling, aren't your skirts getting a little short?"

Then Nannie would let out another tuck in Laura's ginghams and merinos, and some months would pass before the ladies returned to the attack. They all liked Mrs. Willowes, but they were agreed amongst themselves that she needed bracing up to a sense of her responsibilities, especially her responsibilities about Laura. It really was not right that Laura should be left so much to herself. Poor dear Miss Taylor was an excellent creature. Had she not inquired about peninsulas in all the neighbouring school-rooms of consequence? But Miss Taylor for three hours daily and Mme. Brevet's dancing classes in winter did not, could not, supply all Laura's needs. She should have the companionship of girls of her own age, or she might grow up eccentric. Another little hint to Mrs. Willowes would surely open the poor lady's eyes. But though Mrs. Willowes received their good counsel with a flattering air of being just about to become impressed by it, and filled up their tea-cups with a great deal of delicious cream, the silk and sealskin ladies hinted in vain, for Laura was still at home when her mother died.

During the last few years of her life Mrs. Willowes grew continually more skilled in evading responsibilities, and her death seemed but the final perfected expression of this skill. It was as if she had said, yawning a delicate cat's yawn, "I think I will go to my grave now," and had left the room, her white shawl trailing behind her.

Laura mourned for her mother in skirts that almost reached the ground, for Miss Boddle, the family dressmaker, had nice sensibilities and did not think that legs could look sorrowful. Indeed, Laura's legs were very slim and frisky, they liked climbing trees and jumping over haycocks, they had no wish to retire from the world and belong to a young lady. But when she had put on the new clothes that smelt so queerly, and looking in the mirror saw herself sad and grown-up, Laura accepted the inevitable. Sooner or later she must be subdued into young-ladyhood; and it seemed befitting that the change should come gravely, rather than with the conventional polite uproar and fuss of "coming-out"—which odd term meant, as far as she could see, and when once the champagne bottles were emptied and the flimsy ball-dress lifted off the thin shoulders, going-in.

As things were, she had a recompense for the loss of her liberty. For Everard needed comfort, he needed a woman to comfort him, and abetted by Miss Boddle's insinuations Laura was soon able to persuade him that her comfortings were of the legitimate womanly kind. It was easy, much easier than she had supposed, to be grown-up; to be clear-headed and watchful, to move sedately and think before she spoke. Already her hands looked much whiter on the black lap. She could not take her mother's place—that was as impossible as to have her mother's touch on the piano, for Mrs. Willowes had learnt from a former pupil of Field, she had the *jeu perlé;* but she could take a place of her own. So Laura behaved very well—said the Willowes connection, agreeing and approving amongst themselves—and went about her business, and only cried when alone in the potting-shed, where a pair of old gardening gloves repeated to her the shape of her mother's hands.

Her behaviour was the more important in that neither of her brothers was at home when Mrs. Willowes died. Henry, now a member of the Inner Temple, had just proposed marriage to a Miss Caroline Fawcett. When he returned to London after the funeral it was impossible not to feel that he was travelling out of the shadow that rested upon Lady Place to bask in his private glory of a suitable engagement.

He left his father and sister to find consolation in consoling each other. For though James was with them, and though *his* sorrow was without qualification, they were not likely to get much help from James. He had been in Germany studying chemistry, and when they sent off the telegram Everard and Laura reckoned up how long he would take to reach Lady Place, and planned how they could most comfortingly receive him, for they had already begun to weave a thicker clothing of family kindness against the chill of bereavement. On hearing the crunch of the wagonette in the drive, and the swishing of the wet rhododendrons, they glanced at each other reassuringly, taking heart at the thought of the bright fire in his bedroom, the carefully chosen supper that awaited him. But when he stood before them and they looked at his red twitching face, they were abashed before the austerity of a grief so differently sustained from their own. Nothing they had to offer could remedy that heart-ache. They left him to himself, and sought refuge in each other's society, as much from his sorrow as theirs, and in his company they sat quietly, like two good children in the presence of a more grown-up grief than they could understand.

James might have accepted their self-effacement with silent gratitude; or he might not have noticed it at all—it was impossible to tell. Soon after his return he did a thing so unprecedented in the annals of the family that it could only be explained by the extreme exaltation of mind which possessed him: for without consulting any one, he altered the furniture, transferring a mirror and an almond-green brocade settee from his mother's room to his own. This accomplished, he came slowly downstairs and went out into the stable-yard where Laura and his father were looking at a litter of puppies. He told them what he had done, speaking drily, as of some everyday occurrence, and when they, a little timidly, tried to answer as if they too thought it a very natural and convenient arrangement, he added that he did not intend to go back to Germany, but would stay henceforth at Lady Place and help his father with the brewery.

Everard was much pleased at this. His faith in the merits of brewing had been rudely jolted by the refusal of his eldest son to have anything to do with it. Even before Henry left school his ambition was set on the law. Hearing him speak in the

School Debating Society, one of the masters told him that he had a legal mind. This compliment left him with no doubts as to what career he wished to follow, and before long the legal mind was brought to bear upon his parents. Everard was hurt, and Mrs. Willowes was slightly contemptuous, for she had the old-fashioned prejudice against the learned professions, and thought her son did ill in not choosing to live by his industry rather than by his wits. But Henry had as much of the Willowes determination as either his father or his mother, and his stock of it was twenty-five years younger and livelier than theirs. "Times are changed," said Everard. "A country business doesn't look the same to a young man as it did in my day."

So though a partnership in the brewery seemed the natural destiny for James, Everard was much flattered by his decision, and hastened to put into practice the scientific improvements which his son suggested. Though by nature mistrustful of innovations he hoped that James might be innocently distracted from his grief by these interests, and gave him a new hopper in the same paternal spirit as formerly he had given him a rook-rifle. James was quite satisfied with the working of the hopper. But it was not possible to discover if it had assuaged his grief, because he concealed his feelings too closely, becoming, by a hyperbole of reticence, reserved even about his reserve, so that to all appearances he was no more than a red-faced young man with a moderate flow of conversation.

Everard and Laura never reached that stage of familiarity with James which allows members of the same family to accept each other on surface values. Their love for him was tinged with awe, the awe that love learns in the moment of finding itself unavailing. But they were glad to have him with them, especially Everard, who was growing old enough to like the prospect of easing his responsibilities, even the inherent responsibility of being a Willowes, on to younger shoulders. No one was better fitted to take up this burden than James. Everything about him, from his seat on a horse to his taste in leather bindings, betokened an integrity of good taste and good sense, unostentatious, haughty, and discriminating.

The leather bindings were soon in Laura's hands. New books

were just what she wanted, for she had almost come to the end of the books in the Lady Place library. Had they known this the silk and sealskin ladies would have shaken their heads over her upbringing even more deploringly. But, naturally, it had not occurred to them that a young lady of their acquaintance should be under no restrictions as to what she read, and Mrs. Willowes had not seen any reason for making them better informed.

So Laura read undisturbed, and without disturbing anybody, for the conversation at local tea-parties and balls never happened to give her an opportunity of mentioning anything that she had learnt from Locke on the Understanding or Glanvil on Witches. In fact, as she was generally ignorant of the books which *their* daughters were allowed to read, the neighbouring mammas considered her rather ignorant. However they did not like her any the worse for this, for her ignorance, if not so sexually displeasing as learning, was of so unsweetened a quality as to be wholly without attraction. Nor had they any more reason to be dissatisfied with her appearance. What beauties of person she had were as unsweetened as her beauties of mind, and her air of fine breeding made her look older than her age.

Laura was of a middle height, thin, and rather pointed. Her skin was brown, inclining to sallowness; it seemed browner still by contrast with her eyes, which were large, set wide apart, and of that shade of grey which inclines neither to blue nor green, but seems only a much diluted black. Such eyes are rare in any face, and rarer still in conjunction with a brown colouring. In Laura's case the effect was too startling to be agreeable. Strangers thought her remarkable-looking, but got no further, and those more accustomed thought her plain. Only Everard and James might have called her pretty, had they been asked for an opinion. This would not have been only the partiality of one Willowes for another. They had seen her at home, where animation brought colour into her cheeks and spirit into her bearing. Abroad, and in company, she was not animated. She disliked going out, she seldom attended any but those formal parties at which the attendance of Miss Willowes of Lady Place was an obligatory civility; and she found there little reason for animation. Being without coquetry she did not feel herself bound to feign a degree of entertainment which she had not experienced, and the same deficiency made her insensible to the duty of every marriageable young woman to be charming, whether her charm be directed towards one special object or, in default of that, universally distributed through a disinterested love of humanity. This may have been due to her upbringing—such was the local explanation. But her upbringing had only furthered a temperamental indifference to the need of getting married—or, indeed, of doing anything positive—and this indifference was reinforced by the circumstances which had made her so closely her father's companion.

There is nothing more endangering to a young woman's normal inclination towards young men than an intimacy with a man twice her own age. Laura compared with her father all the young men whom otherwise she might have accepted without any comparisons whatever as suitable objects for her intentions, and she did not find them support the comparison at all well. They were energetic, good-looking, and shot pheasants with great skill; or they were witty, elegantly dressed, and had a London club; but still she had no mind to quit her father's company for theirs, even if they should show clear signs of desiring her to do so, and till then she paid them little attention in thought or deed.

When Aunt Emmy came back from India and filled the spare-room with cedar-wood boxes, she exclaimed briskly to Everard: "My dear, it's high time Laura married! Why isn't she married already?" Then, seeing a slight spasm of distress at this barrack-square trenchancy pass over her brother's face, she added: "A girl like Laura has only to make her choice. Those Welsh eyes. . . . Whenever they look at me I am reminded of Mamma. Everard! You must let me give her a season in India."

"You must ask Laura," said Everard. And they went out into the orchard together, where Emmy picked up the windfall apples and ate them with the greed of the exile. Nothing more was said just then. Emmy was aware of her false step. Ashamed at having exceeded a Willowes decorum of intervention she welcomed this chance to reinstate herself in her brother's good graces by an evocation of their childhood under these same trees.

But Everard kept silence for distress. He believed in good faith that his relief at seeing Laura's budding suitors nipped in their bud was due to the conviction that not one of them was good enough for her. As innocently as the unconcerned Laura might have done, but did not, he waited for the ideal wooer. Now Emmy's tactless concern had thrown a cold shadow over the remoter future after his death. And for the near future had she not spoken of taking Laura to India? He would be good. He would not say a word to dissuade the girl from what might prove to be to her advantage. But at the idea of her leaving him for a country so distant, for a manner of life so unfamiliar, the warmth went out of his days.

Emmy unfolded her plan to Laura; that is to say, unfolded the outer wrappings of it. Laura listened with delight to her aunt's tales of Indian life. Compounds and mangoes, the early morning rides along the Kilpawk Road, the grunting song of the porters who carried Mem Sahibs in litters up to the hill-stations, parrots flying through the jungle, ayahs with rubies in their nostrils, kid-gloves preserved in pickle jars with screw-tops—all the solemn and simple pomp of old-fashioned Madras beckoned to her, beckoned like the dark arms tinkling with bangles of soft gold and coloured glass. But when the beckonings took the form of Aunt Emmy's circumstantial invitation Laura held back, demurred this way and that, and pronounced at last the refusal which had been implicit in her mind from the moment the invitation was given.

She did not want to leave her father, nor did she want to leave Lady Place. Her life perfectly contented her. She had no wish for ways other than those she had grown up in. With an easy diligence she played her part as mistress of the house, abetted at every turn by country servants of long tenure, as enamoured of the comfortable amble of day by day as she was. At certain seasons a fresh resinous smell would haunt the house like some rustic spirit. It was Mrs. Bonnet making the traditional beeswax polish that alone could be trusted to give the proper lustre to the elegantly bulging fronts of tallboys and cabinets. The grey days of early February were tinged with tropical odours by great-great-aunt Salome's recipe for marmalade; and on the afternoon of Good Friday, if it were fine, the stuffed foxes and otters were taken out of their glass cases, brushed, and set to sweeten on the lawn.

These were old institutions, they dated from long before Laura's day. But the gradual deposit of family customs was always going on, and within her own memory the sum of Willowes ways had been augmented. There was the Midsummer Night's Eve picnic in Potts's Dingle—cold pigeon-pie and cider-cup, and moth-beset candles flickering on the grass. There was the ceremony of the hop-garland, which James had brought back from Germany, and the pantomime party from the workhouse, and a very special kind of sealing-wax that could only be procured from Padua. Long ago the children had been allowed to choose their birthday dinners, and still upon the seventeenth of July James ate duck and green peas and a gooseberry fool, while a cock-pheasant in all the glory of tail-feathers was set before Laura upon the ninth of December. And at the bottom of the orchard flourished unchecked a bed of nettles, for Nannie Quantrell placed much trust in the property of young nettles eaten as spring greens to clear the blood, quoting emphatically and rhythmically a rhyme her grandmother had taught her:

"If they would eat nettles in March
  And drink mugwort in May,
So many fine young maidens
  Would not go to the clay."

Laura would very willingly have drunk mugwort in May also, for this rhyme of Nannie's, so often and so impressively rehearsed, had taken fast hold of her imagination. She had always had a taste for botany, she had also inherited a fancy for brewing. One of her earliest pleasures had been to go with Everard to the brewery and look into the great vats while he, holding her firmly with his left hand, with his right plunged a long stick through the clotted froth which, working and murmuring, gradually gave way until far below through the tumbling, dissolving rent the beer was disclosed.

Botany and brewery she now combined into one pursuit, for at the spur of Nannie's rhyme she turned her attention into the forsaken green byways of the rural pharmacopœia. From Everard she got a little still, from the family recipe-books much information and good advice; and where these failed her, Nicholas Culpepper or old Goody Andrews, who might have been Nicholas's crony by the respect she had for the moon, were ready to help her out. She roved the countryside for herbs and simples, and many were the washes and decoctions that she made from sweet-gale, water purslane, cowslips, and the roots of succory, while her salads gathered in fields and hedges were eaten by Everard, at first in hope and trust, and afterwards with flattering appetite. Encouraged by him, she even wrote a little book called "Health by the Wayside" commending the use of old-fashioned simples and healing herbs. It was published anonymously at the local press, and fell quite flat. Everard felt much more slighted by this than she did, and bought up the remainders without telling her so. But mugwort was not included in the book, for she was never allowed to test its virtues, and she would not include recipes which she had not tried herself. Nannie believed it to be no less effective than nettles, but she did not know how to prepare it. Once long ago she had made a broth by seething the leaves in boiling water, which she then strained off and gave to Henry and James. But it made them both sick, and Mrs. Willowes had forbidden its further use. Laura felt positive that mugwort tea would not have made her sick. She begged for leave to make trial of it, but to no avail; Nannie's prohibition was as absolute as that of her mistress. But Nannie had not lost her faith. She explained that the right mugwort for the purpose was a very special kind that did not grow in Somerset, but at the gates of the cobbler in her native village the mugwort grew fair enough. Long after this discussion had taken place, Laura found in Aubrey's *Miscellany* a passage quoted from Pliny which told how Artemis had revealed the virtues of mugwort to the dreaming Pericles. She hastened to tell Nannie of this. Nannie was gratified, but she would not admit that her faith needed any buttressing. "Those Greeks didn't know everything!" she said, and drove a needle into her red cloth emery case, which was shaped like a strawberry and spotted over with small yellow beads.

For nearly ten years Laura kept house for Everard and James. Nothing happened to disturb the easy serenity of their days except the birth of first one daughter and then another to Henry and Caroline, and this did not disturb it much. Everard, so happy in a daughter, was prepared to be happy in granddaughters also. When Henry apologised to him with dignity for the accident of their sex Everard quoted to him the nursery rhyme about what little boys and girls were made of. Henry was relieved to find his father taking so lightly a possible failure in the Willowes male line, but he wished the old man wouldn't trifle so. He could not stoop to give his father the lie over his unscientific theory of sex. He observed gloomily that daughters could be very expensive now that so much fuss was being made about the education of women.

Henry in his fears for the Willowes male line had taken it for granted that his brother would never marry. And certainly if to lie very low about a thing is a sign that one is not thinking about it, James had no thought of marriage. He was nearly thirty-three when he announced with his usual quiet abruptness that he was going to marry. The lady of his choice was a Miss Sibyl Mauleverer. She was the daughter of a clergyman, but of a fashionable London clergyman which no doubt accounted for her not being in the least like any clergyman's daughter seen by Everard and Laura hitherto. Miss Mauleverer's skirts were so long and so lavish that they lay in folds upon the ground all round her when she stood still, and required to be lifted in both hands before she could walk. Her hats were further off her head than any hats that had yet been seen in Somerset, and she had one of the up-to-date smooth Aberdeen terriers. It was indeed hard to believe that this distinguished creature had been born and bred in a parish. But nothing could have been more parochial than her determination to love her new relations and to be loved in return. She called Everard *Vaterlein,* she taught Laura to dance the cake-walk, she taught Mrs. Bonnet to make *petits canapés à l'Impératrice;* having failed to teach Brewer how to make a rock garden, she talked of making one herself; and though she would have liked old oak better, she professed herself enchanted by the Willowes walnut and mahogany. So assiduously did this pretty young person seek to please that Laura and Everard would have been churlish had they not responded to her blandishments. Each, indeed, secretly wondered what James could see in any one so showy and dashing as Sibyl. But they were too discreet to admit this, even one to the other, and contented themselves with politely wondering what Sibyl could see in such a country sobersides as James.

Lady Place was a large house, and it seemed proper that James should bring his wife to live there. It also seemed proper that she should take Laura's place as mistress of the household. The sisters-in-law disputed this point with much civility, each insisting upon the other's claim like two queens curtseying in a doorway. However Sibyl was the visiting queen and had to yield to Laura in civility, and assume the responsibilities of housekeeping. She jingled them very lightly, and as soon as she found herself to be with child she gave them over again to Laura, who made a point of ordering the *petits canapés* whenever any one came to dinner.

Whatever small doubts and regrets Everard and Laura had nursed about James's wife were put away when Sibyl bore a man child. It would not have been loyal to the heir of the Willowes to suppose that his mother was not quite as well-bred as he. Everard did not even need to remind himself of the Duchess of Suffolk. Titus, sprawling his fat hands over his mother's bosom, Titus, a disembodied cooing of contentment in the nursery overhead, would have justified a far more questionable match than James had made.

A year later Everard, amid solemnity, lit the solitary candle of his grandson's first birthday upon the cake that Mrs. Bonnet had made, that Laura had iced, that Sibyl had wreathed with flowers. The flame wavered a little in the draught, and Everard, careful against omens, ordered the French windows to be shut. On so glowing a September afternoon it was strange to see the conifers nodding their heads in the wind and to hear the harsh breath of autumn go forebodingly round the house. Laura gazed at the candle. She understood her father's alarm and, superstitious also, held her breath until she saw the flame straighten itself and the first little trickle of coloured wax flow down upon the glittering tin star that held the candle. That evening, after dinner, there was a show of fireworks for the school children in the garden. So many rockets were let off by Everard and James that for a while the northern sky was laced with a thicket of bright sedge scattering a fiery pollen. So hot and excited did Everard become in manœuvring this splendour that he forgot the cold wind and took off his coat.

Two days after he complained of a pain in his side. The doctor looked grave as he came out of the bed-chamber, though within it Laura had heard him laughing with his old friend, and rallying him upon his nightcap. Everard had inflammation of the lungs, he told her; he would send for two nurses. They came, and their starched white aprons looked to her like unlettered tombstones. From the beginning her soul had crouched in apprehension, and indeed there was at no time much hope for the old man. When he was conscious he lay very peacefully, his face turned towards the window, watching the swallows fly restlessly from tree to tree. "It will be a hard winter," he said to Laura. "They're gathering early to go." And then: "Do you suppose they know where they're going?"

"I'm sure they do," she answered, thinking to comfort him. He regarded her shrewdly, smiled, and shook his head. "Then they're wiser than we."

When grandfather Henry, that masterful man, removed across the border, he was followed by a patriarchal train of manservants and maidservants, mares, geldings, and spaniels, vans full of household stuff, and slow country wagons loaded with nodding greenery. "I want to make sure of a good eating apple," said he, "since I am going to Lady Place for life." Death was another matter. The Willowes burial-ground was in Dorset, nor would Henry lie elsewhere. Now it was Everard's turn. The dead appeared to welcome him without astonishment—the former Everards and Tituses, Lauras and Emmelines; they were sure that he would come, they approved his decision to join them.

Laura stood by the open grave, but the heap of raw earth and the planks sprawling upon it displeased her. Her eyes strayed to the graves that were completed. Her mind told the tale of them, for she knew them well. Four times a year Mrs. Willowes had visited the family burying place, and as a child Laura had counted it a solemn and delicious honour to accompany her upon these expeditions. In summer especially, it was pleasant to sit on the churchyard wall under the thick roof of lime trees, or to finger the headstones, now hot, now cold, while her mother went from grave to grave with her gauntlet gloves and her gardening basket. Afterwards they would eat their sandwiches in a hay-field, and pay a visit to old Mrs. Dymond, whose sons and grandsons in hereditary office clipped the grass and trimmed the bushes of the family enclosure. As Laura grew older the active part of these excursions fell upon her; and often of late years when she went alone she half yielded her mind to the fancy that the dead mother whose grave she tended was sitting a little apart in the shade, presently to rise and come to meet her, having just recalled and delicately elaborated some odd trait of a neighbouring great-uncle.

The bees droned in the motionless lime trees. A hot ginny churchyard smell detached itself in a leisurely way from the evergreens when the mourners brushed by them. The sun, but an hour or so declined, shone with an ardent and steadfast interest upon the little group. "In the midst of life we are in death," said Mr. Warbury, his voice sounding rather shameless taken out of church and displayed upon the basking echoless air. "In the midst of death we are in life," Laura thought, would be a more accurate expression of the moment. Her small body encased in tremendous sunlight seemed to throb with an intense vitality, impersonally responding to heat, scent, and colour. With blind clear-sighted eyes she saw the coffin lowered into the grave, and the earth shovelled in on top of it. She was aware of movement around her, of a loosening texture of onlookers, of foot-steps and departures. But it did not occur to her that the time was come when she too must depart. She stood and watched the sexton, who had set to work now in a more business-like fashion. An arm was put through hers. A voice said: "Dear Laura! we must go now," and Caroline led her away. Tears ran down Caroline's face; she seemed to be weeping because it was time to go.

Laura would have turned for one more backward look, but Caroline prevented her. Her tears ran faster and she shook her head and sighed. They reached the gate. It closed behind them with a contented click, for they were the last to leave.

Opposite the churchyard were the gates of the old home. The drive was long, straight, and formal; it had been a cart-track across a meadow when the old home was a farm. At the end of the drive stood the grey stone house. A purple clematis muffled the porch, and a white cat lay asleep in a bed of nasturtiums. The blinds were drawn down in respect to the dead. Laura looked at it. Since her earliest childhood it had been a familiar sight, a familiar thought. But now she saw it with different eyes: a prescience of exile came over her and, forgetting Lady Place, she looked with the yearning of an outcast at the dwelling so long ago discarded. The house was like an old blind nurse sitting in the sun and ruminating past events. It seemed an act of the most horrible ingratitude to leave it all and go away without one word of love. But the gates were shut, the time of welcome was gone by.

For a while they stood in the road, none making a move, each waiting for the other's lead. A tall poplar grew on the left hand of the churchyard gate. Its scant shadow scarcely indented the white surface of the road. A quantity of wasps were buzzing about its trunk, and presently one of the wasps stung Henry. This seemed to be the spur that they were all waiting for; they turned and walked to the corner of the road where the carriages stood that were to drive them back to the station.

Every one was sorry for Laura, for they knew how much she had loved her father. They agreed that it was a good thing that Henry and Caroline were taking her to London. They hoped that this change would distract her from her grief. Meanwhile, there was a good deal to do, and that also was a distraction. Clothes and belongings had to be sorted out, friends and family pensioners visited, and letters of condolence answered. Beside this she had her own personal accumulation of vagrant odds and ends to dispose of. She had lived for twenty-eight years in a house where there was no lack of cupboard room, and a tradition of hoarding, so the accumulation was considerable. There were old toys, letters, stones of strange shapes or bright colours, lesson-books, water-colour sketches of the dogs and the garden; a bunch of dance programmes kept for the sake of their little pencils, and all the little pencils tangled into an inextricable knot; pieces of unfinished needlework, jeweller's boxes, scraps cut out of the newspaper, and unexplainable objects that could only be remembrancers of things she had forgotten. To go over these hoards amused the surface of her mind. But with everything thrown away she seemed to be denying the significance of her youth.

Thus busied, she was withheld all day from her proper care. But at dusk she would go out of the house and pace up and down the nut alley at the foot of the garden. The cold airs that rose up from the ground spoke sadly to her of burial, the mossy paths were hushed and humble under her tread, and the smells of autumn condoled with her. Brewer the gardener, stamping out the ashes of his bonfire, saw her pass to and fro, a slender figure moving sedately between the unmoving boughs. He alone of all the household had taken his master's death without exclamation. Death coming to the old was a harmless thought to him, but looking at Laura he sighed deeply, as though he had planted her and now saw her dashed and broken by bad weather.

Ten days after Everard's death Henry and Caroline left Lady Place, taking Laura with them. She found the leave-taking less painful than she had expected, and Caroline put her to bed as soon as they arrived in Apsley Terrace, which simplified her unhappiness by making her feel like an unhappy child.

Laura had heard the others agreeing that the move to London would make her feel very differently. She had thought them stupid to suppose that any outward change could alter her mood. She now found that they had judged better than she. In Somerset she had grieved over her father's death. In London her grief was retracted into sudden realisations of her loss. She had thought that sorrow would be her companion for many years, and had planned for its entertainment. Now it visited her like sudden snow-storms, a hastening darkness across the sky, a transient whiteness and rigour cast upon her. She tried to recover the sentiment of renunciation which she had worn like a veil. It was gone, and gone with it was her sense of the dignity of bereavement.

Henry and Caroline did all they could to prevent her feeling unhappy. If they had been overlooking some shame of hers they could not have been more tactful, more modulatory.

The first winter passed by like a half-frozen stream. At the turn of the year it grew extremely cold. Red cotton sandbags were laid along the window-sashes, and Fancy and Marion skated on the Round Pond with small astrakhan muffs. Laura did not skate, but she walked briskly along the path with Caroline, listening to the rock and jar of the skates grinding upon the ice and to the cries of the gulls overhead. She found London much colder than the country, though Henry assured her that this was impossible. She developed chilblains, and this annoyed her, for she had not had chilblains since she was a child. Then Nannie Quantrell would send her out in the early morning to run barefoot over the rimy lawn. There was a small garden at Apsley Terrace, but it had been gravelled over because Henry disliked the quality of London grass; and in any case it was not the sort of garden in which she could run barefoot.

She was also annoyed by the hardness of the London water. Her hands were so thin that they were always a little red; now they were rough also. If they could have remained idle, she would not have minded this so much. But Caroline never sat with idle hands; she would knit, or darn, or do useful needlework. Laura could not sit opposite her and do nothing. There was no useful needlework for her to do, Caroline did it all, so Laura was driven to embroidery. Each time that a strand of silk rasped against her fingers she shuddered inwardly.

Time went faster than the embroidery did. She had actually a sensation that she was stitching herself into a piece of embroidery with a good deal of background. But, as Caroline said, it was not possible to feel dull when there was so much to do. Indeed, it was surprising how much there was to do, and for everybody in the house. Even Laura, introduced as a sort of extra wheel, soon found herself part of the mechanism, and, interworking with the other wheels, went round as busily as they.

When she awoke, the day was already begun. She could hear iron noises from the kitchen, the sound of yesterday's ashes being probed out. Then came a smell of wood smoke—the kitchen fire had been laid anew and kindled in the cleansed grate. This was followed by the automatic noise of the carpet-sweeper and, breaking in upon it, the irregular knocking of the staircase brush against the banisters. The maid who brought her morning tea and laid the folded towel across the hot-water can had an experienced look; when she drew back the curtains she looked out upon the day with no curiosity. She had seen it already.

By the time the Willowes family met at breakfast all this activity had disappeared like the tide from the smooth, garnished beach. For the rest of the day it functioned unnoticed. Bells were answered, meals were served, all that appeared was completion. Yet unseen and underground the preparation and demolition of every day went on, like the inward persistent workings of heart and entrails. Sometimes a crash, a banging door, a voice upraised, would rend the veil of impersonality. And sometimes a sound of running water at unusual hours and a faint steaminess in the upper parts of the house betokened that one of the servants was having a bath.

After breakfast, and after Henry had been seen off, Caroline descended to the kitchen and Laura read the relinquished *Times.* Then came shopping, letter-writing, arranging the flowers, cleaning the canary-cage, and the girls' walk. Such things as arranging flowers or cleaning the canary-cage were done with a kind of precautious routine which made them seem alike solemn and illicit. The flowers were always arranged in the ground-floor lavatory, where there was a small sink; vases and wire frames were kept in a cupboard, and a pair of scissors was strung to a nail. Then the completed affair was carried carefully past the coats that hung in the lobby outside and set down upon some established site.

Every Tuesday the books were changed at the library.

After lunch there was a spell of embroidery and more *Times.* If it was fine, Caroline paid calls; if wet, she sat at home on the chance of receiving them. On Saturday afternoons there was the girls' dancing-class. Laura accompanied her nieces thither, carrying their slippers in a bag. She sat among the other parents and guardians upon a dais which shook to the primary accents of the pianist, watching lancers and polkas and waltzes being performed, and hearing Miss Parley say: "Now we will recommence." After the dancing was over there was a March of Grace, and when Fancy and Marion had miscarried of their curtseys she would envelop their muslin dresses and their red elbows in the grey ulsters, and walk them briskly home again.

They were dull children, though their dullness did not prevent them having a penetrating flow of conversation. Their ways and thoughts were governed by a sort of zodiacal procession of other little girls, and when they came down to the drawing-room after tea it seemed to Laura that they brought the Wardours, or the Wilkinsons, or the de la Bottes with them.

Dinner was at half-past seven. It was a sensible rule of Caroline's that at dinner only general topics should be discussed. The difficulties of the day (if the day had presented difficulties) were laid aside. To this rule Caroline attributed the excellence of Henry's digestion. Henry's digestion was further safeguarded by being left to itself in the smoking-room for an hour after dinner. If he was busy, this hour of meditation would be followed by some law-work. If not, he would join them in the drawing-room, or go to his club. When they were thus left by themselves Laura and Caroline went off to bed early, for they were pleasantly fatigued by their regular days and regular meals. Later on Laura, half asleep, would hear Henry's return from his club. The thud of the front door pulled to after him drove through the silent house, and this was followed by the noise of bolts and chains. Then the house, emptied of another day, creaked once or twice, and fell into repose, its silence and security barred up within it like a kind of moral family plate. The remainder of the night was left at the disposal of the grandfather's clock in the hall, equitably dealing out minutes and quarters and hours.

On Sunday mornings Henry would wind the clock. First one and then the other the quivering chains were wound up, till only the snouts of the leaden weights were visible, drooping sullenly over the abyss of time wherein they were to make their descent during the seven days following. After that the family went to church, and there were wound up for the week in much the same manner. They went to evening service too, but evening service was less austere. The vindictive sentiments sounded less vindictive; if an umbrella fell down with a crash the ensuing silence was less affronted; the sermon was shorter, or seemed so, and swung more robustly into "And now to God the Father."

After evening service came cold supper. Fancy and Marion sat up for this, and it was rather a cheerful meal, with extra trivialities such as sardines and celery. The leaden weights had already started upon their downward course.

Caroline was a religious woman. Resolute, orderly and unromantic, she would have made an admirable Mother Superior. In her housekeeping and her scrupulous account-books she expressed an almost mystical sense of the validity of small things. But like most true mystics, she was unsympathetic and difficult of approach. Once only did she speak her spiritual mind to Laura. Laura was nursing her when she had influenza; Caroline wished to put on a clean nightdress, and Laura, opening the third drawer of the large mahogany wardrobe, had commented upon the beautiful orderliness with which Caroline's body linen was arranged therein. "We have our example," said Caroline. "The graveclothes were folded in the tomb."

Looking into the large shadowy drawer, where nightgowns and chemises lay folded exactly upon each other in a purity that disdained even lavender, Laura shuddered a little at this revelation of her sister-in-law's private thoughts. She made no answer, and never again did Caroline open her mind to her upon such matters.

Laura never forgot this. Caroline seemed affectionately disposed towards her; she was full of practical good sense, her advice was excellent, and pleasantly bestowed. Laura saw her a good wife, a fond and discreet mother, a kind mistress, a most conscientious sister-in-law. She was also rather gluttonous. But for none of these qualities could Laura feel at ease with her. Compared to Caroline she knew herself to be unpractical, unmethodical, lacking in initiative. The tasks that Caroline delegated to her she performed eagerly and carefully, but she performed them with the hampering consciousness that Caroline could do them better than she, and in less time. Even in so simple a matter as holding a skein of wool for Caroline to wind off into a ball, Caroline's large white fingers worked so swiftly that it was she who twitched the next length off Laura's thumb before Laura, watching the diminishing thread, remembered to dip her hand. But all this—for Laura was humble and Caroline kind—could have been overcome. It was in the things that never appeared that Laura felt her inadequacy.

Laura was not in any way religious. She was not even religious enough to speculate towards irreligion. She went with Caroline to early service whenever Caroline's inquiries suggested it, and to morning service and evening service every Sunday; she knelt beside her and heard her pray in a small, stilled version of the voice which she knew so well in its clear everyday ordinances. Religion was great-great-aunt Salome's prayer-book which Caroline held in her gloved hands. Religion was a strand in the Willowes life, and the prayer-book was the outward sign of it. But it was also the outward sign of the puff-paste which had been praised by King George III. Religion was something to be preserved: it was part of the Willowes life and so was the prayer-book, preserved from generation to generation.

Laura was bored by the church which they attended. She would have liked, now that she was come to London, to see the world, to adventure in churches. She was darkly, adventurously drawn to see what services were like amongst Roman Catholics, amongst Huguenots, amongst Unitarians and Swedenborgians, feeling about this rather as she felt about the East End. She expressed her wish to Caroline, and Caroline, rather unexpectedly, had been inclined to further it. But Henry banned the project. It would not do for Laura to go elsewhere than to the family place of worship, he said. For Henry, the family place of worship was the pew upon whose ledge rested great-great-aunt Salome's prayer-book. He felt this less explicitly than the straying Laura did, for he was a man and had less time to think of such things. But he felt it strongly.

Laura believed that she would like Caroline if she could only understand her. She had no difficulty in understanding Henry, but for no amount of understanding could she much like him. After some years in his house she came to the conclusion that Caroline had been very bad for his character. Caroline was a good woman and a good wife. She was slightly self-righteous, and fairly rightly so, but she yielded to Henry's judgment in every dispute, she bowed her good sense to his will and blinkered her wider views in obedience to his prejudices. Henry had a high opinion of her merits, but thinking her to be so admirable and finding her to be so acquiescent had encouraged him to have an even higher opinion of his own. However good a wife Caroline might choose to be she could not quite make Henry a bad husband or a bad man—he was too much of a Willowes for that: but she fed his vanity, and ministered to his imperiousness.

Laura also thought that the law had done a great deal to spoil Henry. It had changed his natural sturdy stupidity into a browbeating indifference to other people's point of view. He seemed to consider himself briefed by his Creator to turn into ridicule the opinions of those who disagreed with him, and to attribute dishonesty, idiocy, or a base motive to every one who supported a better case than he. This did not often appear in his private life, Henry was kindly disposed to those who did not thwart him by word or deed. His household had been well schooled by Caroline in yielding gracefully, and she was careful not to invite guests who were not of her husband's way of thinking.

Most of their acquaintance were people connected with the law. Laura grew familiar with the legal manner, but she did not grow fond of it. She felt that these clean-shaven men with bristling eyebrows were suavely concealing their doubts of her intelligence and her probity. Their jaws were like so many mousetraps, baited with commonplaces. They made her feel shy and behave stiffly.

This was unfortunate, as Henry and Caroline had hoped that some one of them would fall sufficiently in love with Laura to marry her. Mr. Fortescue, Mr. Parker, Mr. Jermyn, Mr. Danby, Mr. Thrush, were in turn selected as suitable and likely undertakers. Every decent effort was made by Henry and Caroline, and a certain number of efforts were made by the chosen. But Laura would make no efforts at all. Henry and Caroline had lost heart when they invited Mr. Arbuthnot to tea on Sunday. They invited him for pity's sake, and but to tea at that, for he was very shy and stammered. To their surprise they saw Laura taking special pains to be nice to him. Equally to their surprise they saw Mr. Arbuthnot laying aside his special pains to observe a legal manner and stammering away quite enthusiastically about climbing Welsh mountains and gathering parsley fern. They scarcely dared to hope, for they felt the time for hope was gone by. However, they invited him to dinner, and did their best to be on friendly terms with him.

Mr. Arbuthnot received their advances without surprise, for he had a very good opinion of himself. He felt that being thirty-five he owed himself a wife, and he also felt that Laura would do very nicely. His aunt, Lady Ross-Price, always tried to get servants from the Willowes establishment, for Mrs. Willowes trained them so well. Mr. Arbuthnot supposed that Mrs. Willowes would be equally good at training wives. He began to think of Laura quite tenderly, and Caroline began to read the Stores' catalogue quite seriously. This was the moment when Laura, who had been behaving nicely for years, chose to indulge her fantasy, and to wreck in five minutes the good intentions of as many months.

She had come more and more to look on Mr. Arbuthnot as an indulgence. His stammer had endeared him to her; it seemed, after so much legal manner, quite sympathetic. Though nothing would have induced her to marry him, she was very ready to talk to him, and even to talk naturally of what came uppermost in her thoughts. Laura's thoughts ranged over a wide field, even now. Sometimes she said rather amusing things, and displayed unexpected stores (General Stores) of knowledge. But her remarks were as a rule so disconnected from the conversation that no one paid much attention to them. Mr. Arbuthnot certainly was not prepared for her response to his statement that February was a dangerous month. "It is," answered Laura with almost violent agreement. "If you are a were-wolf, and very likely you may be, for lots of people are without knowing, February, of all months, is the month when you are most likely to go out on a dark windy night and worry sheep."

Henry and Caroline glanced at each other in horror. Mr. Arbuthnot said: "How very interesting! But I really don't think I am likely to do such a thing." Laura made no answer. She did not think so either. But she was amusing herself with a surprisingly vivid and terrible picture of Mr. Arbuthnot cloaked in a shaggy hide and going with heavy devouring swiftness upon all-fours with a lamb dangling from his mouth.

This settled it. Henry and Caroline made no more attempts to marry off Laura. Trying to do so had been a nuisance and an expense, and Laura had never shown the smallest appreciation of their trouble. Before long they would have the girls to think of. Fancy was sixteen, and Marion nearly as tall as Fancy. In two years they would have to begin again. They were glad of a respite, and made the most of it. Laura also was glad of a respite. She bought second-hand copies of Herodotus and Johnson's Dictionary to read in the evenings. Caroline, still sewing on buttons, would look at her sister-in-law's composed profile. Laura's hair was black as ever, but it was not so thick. She had grown paler from living in London. Her forehead had not a wrinkle, but two downward lines prolonged the drooping corners of her mouth. Her face was beginning to stiffen. It had lost its power of expressiveness, and was more and more dominated by the hook nose and the sharp chin. When Laura was ten years older she would be nut-crackerish.

Caroline resigned herself to spending the rest of her evenings with Laura beside her. The perpetual company of a sister-in-law was rather more than she had bargained for. Still, there she was, and Henry was right—they had been the proper people to make a home for Laura when her father died, and she was too old now to begin living by herself. It was not as if she had had any experience of life; she had passed from one guardianship to another: it was impossible to imagine Laura fending for herself. A kind of pity for the unused virgin beside her spread through Caroline's thoughts. She did not attach an inordinate value to her wifehood and maternity; they were her duties, rather than her glories. But for all that she felt emotionally plumper than Laura. It was well to be loved, to be necessary to other people. But Laura too was loved, and Laura was necessary. Caroline did not know what the children would do without their Aunt Lolly.

Every one spoke of her as Aunt Lolly, till in the course of time she had almost forgotten her baptismal name.

"Say How-do to Auntie Laura," said Caroline to Fancy. This was long ago in the refurbished nursery at Lady Place when Laura knelt timidly before her first niece, while the London nurse bustled round them unpacking soft hair-brushes and pots of cold cream, and hanging linen to air upon the tall nursery fender.

"How-do, Auntie Lolly," said Fancy, graciously thrusting forward a fur monkey.

"She's taken to you at once, Laura," said Caroline. "I was afraid this journey would upset her, but she's borne it better than any of us."

"Journeys are nothing to them at that age, ma'am," said the nurse. "Now suppose you tell your new auntie what you call Monkey."

"Auntie Lolly, Auntie Lolly," repeated Fancy, rhythmically banging the monkey against the table-leg.

The name hit upon by Fancy was accepted by Marion and Titus; before long their parents made use of it also. Everard never spoke of his daughter but as Laura, even when he spoke of her to his grandchildren. He was too old to change his ways, and he had, in any case, a prejudice against nicknames and abbreviations. But when Laura went to London she left Laura behind, and entered into a state of Aunt Lolly. She had quitted so much of herself in quitting Somerset that it seemed natural to relinquish her name also. Divested of her easily-worn honours as mistress of the household, shorn of her long meandering country days, sleeping in a smart brass bedstead instead of her old and rather pompous four-poster, wearing unaccustomed clothes and performing unaccustomed duties, she seemed to herself to have become a different person. Or rather, she had become two persons, each different. One was Aunt Lolly, a middle-aging lady, light-footed upon stairs, and indispensable for Christmas Eve and birthday preparations. The other was Miss Willowes, "my sister-in-law Miss Willowes," whom Caroline would introduce, and abandon to a feeling of being neither light-footed nor indispensable. But Laura was put away. When Henry asked her to witness some document for him her *Laura Erminia Willowes* seemed as much a thing out of common speech as the *Spinster* that followed it. She would look, and be surprised that such a dignified name should belong to her.

Twice a year, in spring and in summer, the Willowes family went into the country for a holiday. For the first three years of Laura's London life they went as a matter of course to Lady Place. There once more arose the problem of how two children of one sex can play nicely with a much younger child of the other. Fancy and Marion played at tea-parties under the weeping ash, and Titus was the butler with a tin tray. Titus would presently run off and play by himself at soldiers, beating martial tattoos upon the tray. But now there was no danger of the youngest member of the party falling into the pond, for Aunt Lolly was always on guard.

Laura enjoyed the visits to Lady Place, but her enjoyment did not go very deep. The knowledge that she now was a visitor where she had formerly been at home seemed to place a clear sheet of glass between her and her surroundings. She felt none of the grudge of the dispossessed; she scarcely gave a thought to the old days. It was as if in the agony of leaving Lady Place after her father's death she had said good-bye so irremediably that she could never really come there again.

But the visits to Lady Place came to a sad end, for in 1905 James died suddenly of heart-failure. Sibyl decided that she could not go on living alone in the country. A manager was found for the brewery, Lady Place was let unfurnished upon a long lease, and Sibyl and the four-year-old heir of the Willowes name and traditions moved to a small place in Hampstead. Sibyl had proposed to sell some of the furniture, for there was a great deal more of it than she needed, and most of it was too large to fit into her new dwelling. This project was opposed by Henry, and with considerable heat. The family establishment must, he admitted, be broken up, but he would allow no part of it to be alienated. All the furniture that could not be found room for at Hampstead or at Apsley Terrace must be stored till Titus should be of an age to resume the tenure of Lady Place.

To Laura it seemed as though some familiar murmuring brook had suddenly gone underground. There it flowed, silenced and obscured, until the moment when it should reappear and murmur again between green banks. She thought of Titus as a grown man and herself as an old woman meeting among the familiar belongings. She believed that when she was old the ghost-like feeling that distressed her would matter less. She hoped that she might not die before that day, if it were only that she would remember so well, as Titus could not, how the furniture stood in the rooms and the pictures hung on the walls.

But by then, she said to herself, Titus would have a wife with tastes of her own. Sibyl would have liked to alter several things, but tradition had been too strong for her. It would be a very different matter in twenty years' time. The chairs and tables and cabinets would come out blinking and forgetful from their long storage in darkness. They would have lost the individuality by which they had made certain corners so surely their own. The Lady Place she had known was over. She could remember it if she pleased; but she must not think of it.

Meanwhile Emma's harp trailed its strings in her bedroom. Ratafee was removed to Hampstead. Titus had insisted upon this.

She wondered if Henry felt as she did. He had shown a great deal of Willowes spirit over the furniture, but otherwise he had not expressed himself. In person Henry, so it was said, resembled his grandfather who had made the move from Dorset to Somerset—the sacrilegious move which the home-loving of the Willowes had so soon sanctified that in the third generation she was feeling like this about Lady Place. Henry seemed to resemble his grandfather in spirit also. He could house all the family traditions in his practical mind, and for the rest talk about bricks and mortar. He concerned himself with the terms of Sibyl's lease, the agreement with the manager of the brewery, and the question of finding a satisfactory place to carry his family to for the holidays.

After some experiments they settled down to a routine that with a few modifications for the sake of variety or convenience served them for the next fifteen years. In spring they went to some moderately popular health resort and stayed in a hotel, for it was found that the uncertainty of an English spring, let alone the uncertainty of a Christian Easter, made lodgings unsatisfactory at that time of year. In summer they went into lodgings, or took a furnished house in some seaside village without any attractions. They did this, not to be economical—there was no need for economy—but because they found rather plain dull holidays the most refreshing. Henry was content with a little unsophisticated golf and float-fishing. The children bathed and played on the beach and went on bicycling expeditions; and Caroline and Laura watched the children bathe and play, and replenished their stock of underclothes, and rested from the strain of London housekeeping. Sometimes Caroline did a little reading. Sometimes Sibyl and Titus stayed with them, or Titus stayed with them alone while his mother paid visits.

Laura looked forward with pleasure to the summer holidays (the Easter holidays she never cared about, as she had a particular dislike for palms); but after the first shock of arrival and smelling the sea, the days seemed to dribble out very much like the days in London. When the end came, and she looked back from the wagonette over the past weeks, she found that after all she had done few of the things she intended to do. She would have liked to go by herself for long walks inland and find strange herbs, but she was too useful to be allowed to stray. She had once formed an indistinct project of observing limpets. But for all her observations she discovered little save that if you sit very still for a long time the limpet will begin to move sideways, and that it is almost impossible to sit very still for a long time and keep your attention fixed upon such a small object as a limpet without feeling slightly hypnotised and slightly sick. On the lowest count she seldom contrived to read all the books or to finish all the needlework which she had taken with her. And the freckles on her nose mocked her with the receptivity of her skin compared to the dullness of her senses.

They were submerged in the usual quiet summer holidays when the war broke out. The parish magazine said: "The vicar had scarcely left East Bingham when war was declared." The vicar was made of stouter stuff than they. He continued his holiday, but the Willoweses went back to London. Laura had never seen London in August before. It had an arrested look, as though the war were a kind of premature autumn. She was extraordinarily moved; as they drove across the river from Waterloo she wanted to cry. That same evening Fancy went upstairs and scrubbed the boxroom floor for the sake of practice. She upset the bucket, and large damp patches appeared on the ceiling of Laura's room.

For a month Fancy behaved like a cat whose kittens have been drowned. If her family had not been so taken up with the war they would have been alarmed at this change in her demeanour. As it was, they scarcely noticed it. When she came in very late for lunch and said: "I am going to marry Kit Bendigo on Saturday," Henry said, "Very well, my dear. It's your day, not mine," and ordered champagne to be brought up. For a moment Laura thought she heard her father speaking. She knew that Henry disapproved of Kit Bendigo as a husband for Fancy: Willoweses did not mate with Bendigos. But now he was more than resigned—he was ready. And he swallowed the gnat as unswervingly as the camel, which, if Laura had wanted to be ill-natured just then, would have surprised her as being the greater feat. Willoweses do not marry at five days' notice. But Fancy was married on Saturday, and her parents discovered that a hasty wedding can cost quite as much as a formal one. In the mood that they were in this afforded them some slight satisfaction.

Kit Bendigo was killed in December 1916. Fancy received the news calmly; two years' war-work and a daughter thrown in had steadied her nerves. Kit was a dear, of course, poor old Kit. But there was a war on, and people get killed in wars. If it came to that, she was working in a high-explosive shed herself. Caroline could not understand her eldest daughter. She was baffled and annoyed by the turn her own good sense inherited had taken. The married nun looked at the widowed amazon and refused battle. At least Fancy might stay in her very expensive flat and be a mother to her baby. But Fancy drew on a pair of heavy gauntlet gloves and went to France to drive motor lorries. Caroline dared not say a word.

The war had no such excitements for Laura. Four times a week she went to a depot and did up parcels. She did them up so well that no one thought of offering her a change of work. The parcel-room was cold and encumbered, early in the war some one had decorated the walls with recruiting posters. By degrees these faded. The ruddy young man and his Spartan mother grew pale, as if with fear, and Britannia's scarlet cloak trailing on the waters bleached to a cocoa-ish pink. Laura watched them discolour with a muffled heart. She would not allow herself the cheap symbolism they provoked. Time will bleach the scarlet from young men's cheeks, and from Britannia's mantle. But blood was scarlet as ever, and she believed that, however despairing her disapproval, that blood was being shed for her.

She continued to do up parcels until the eleventh day of November 1918. Then, when she heard the noise of cheering and the sounding of hooters, she left her work and went home. The house was empty. Every one had gone out to rejoice. She went up to her room and sat down on the bed. She felt cold and sick, she trembled from head to foot as once she had done after witnessing a dog-fight. All the hooters were sounding, they seemed to domineer over the noises of rejoicing with sarcastic emphasis. She got up and walked about the room. On the mantelpiece was a photograph of Titus. "Well," she said to it, "you've escaped killing, anyhow." Her voice sounded harsh and unreal, she thought the walls of her room were shaking at the concussion, like stage walls. She lay down upon her bed, and presently fainted.

When she came to herself again she had been discovered by Caroline and put to bed with influenza. She was grateful for this, and for the darkened room and the cool clinking tumblers. She was even grateful for the bad dreams which visited her every night and sent up her temperature. By their aid she was enabled to stay in bed for a fortnight, a thing she had not done since she came to London.

When she went downstairs again she found Henry and Caroline talking of better days to come. The house was unaltered, yet it had a general air of refurbishment. She also, after her fortnight in bed, felt somehow refurbished, and was soon drawn into the talk of better days. There was nothing immoderate in the family display of satisfaction. Henry still found frowning matter in the *Times,* and Caroline did not relinquish a single economy. But the satisfaction was there, a demure Willowes-like satisfaction in the family tree that had endured the gale with an unflinching green heart. Laura saw nothing in this to quarrel with. She was rather proud of the Willowes war record; she admired the stolid decorum which had mastered four years of disintegration, and was stolid and decorous still. A lady had inquired of Henry: "What do you do in air-raids? Do you go down to the cellar or up to the roof?" "We do neither," Henry had replied. "We stay where we are." A thrill had passed through Laura when she heard this statement of the Willowes mind. But afterwards she questioned the validity of the thrill. Was it nothing more than the response of her emotions to other old and honourable symbols such as the trooping of the colours and the fifteenth chapter of Corinthians, symbols too old and too honourable to have called out her thoughts? She saw how admirable it was for Henry and Caroline to have stayed where they were. But she was conscious, more conscious than they were, that the younger members of the family had somehow moved into new positions. And she herself, had she not slightly strained against her moorings, fast and far sunk as they were? But now the buffeting waves withdrew, and she began to settle back into her place, and to see all around her once more the familiar undisturbed shadows of familiar things. Outwardly there was no difference between her and Henry and Caroline in their resumption of peace. But they, she thought, had done with the war, whereas she had only shelved it, and that by an accident of consciousness.

When the better days to come came, they proved to be modelled as closely as possible upon the days that were past. It was astonishing what little difference differences had made. When they went back to East Bingham—for owing to its military importance, East Bingham had been unsuited for holidays—there were at first a good many traces of war lying about, such as sandbags and barbed-wire entanglements. But on the following summer the sandbags had rotted and burst and the barbed-wire had been absorbed into the farmer's fences. So, Laura thought, such warlike phenomena as Mr. Wolf-Saunders, Fancy's second husband, and Jemima and Rosalind, Fancy's two daughters, might well disappear off the family landscape. Mr. Wolf-Saunders recumbent on the beach was indeed much like a sandbag, and no more arresting to the eye. Jemima and Rosalind were more obtrusive. Here was a new generation to call her Aunt Lolly and find her as indispensable as did the last.

"It is quite like old times," said Caroline, who sat working beside her. "Isn't it, Lolly?"

"Except for these anachronisms," said Laura.

Caroline removed the seaweed which Jemima had stuffed into her work-bag. "Bless them!" she said absently. "We shall soon be back in town again."

PART 2

The Willoweses came back to London about the second week in September. For many years the children's schooling had governed the date of their return; and when the children had grown too old for school, the habit had grown too old to be broken. There was also a further reason. The fallen leaves, so Henry and Caroline thought, made the country unhealthy after the second week in September. When Laura was younger she had sometimes tried to argue that, even allowing the unhealthiness of fallen leaves, leaves at that time of year were still green upon the trees. This was considered mere casuistry. When they walked in Kensington Gardens upon the first Sunday morning after their return, Caroline would point along the tarnishing vistas and say: "You see, Lolly, the leaves are beginning to fall. It was quite time to come home."

It was useless to protest that autumn begins earlier in London than it does in the country. That it did so, Laura knew well. That was why she disliked having to come back; autumn boded her no good, and it was hard that by a day's train-journey she should lose almost a month's reprieve. Obediently looking along the tarnishing vistas, she knew that once again she was in for it.

What It was exactly, she would have found hard to say. She sometimes told herself that it must be the yearly reverberation of those miserable first months in London when her sorrow for her father's death was still fresh. No other winter had been so cold or so long, not even the long cold winters of the war. Yet now her thoughts of Everard were mellowed and painless, and she had long ago forgiven her sorrow. Had the coming of autumn quickened in her only an experienced grief she would not have dreaded it thus, nor felt so restless and tormented.

Her disquiet had no relevance to her life. It arose out of the ground with the smell of the dead leaves: it followed her through the darkening streets; it confronted her in the look of the risen moon. "Now! Now!" it said to her: and no more. The moon seemed to have torn the leaves from the trees that it might stare at her more imperiously. Sometimes she tried to account for her uneasiness by saying that she was growing old, and that the year's death reminded her of her own. She compared herself to the ripening acorn that feels through windless autumnal days and nights the increasing pull of the earth below. That explanation was very poetical and suitable. But it did not explain what she felt. She was not wildly anxious either to die or to live; why, then, should she be rent by this anxiety?

At these times she was subject to a peculiar kind of day-dreaming, so vivid as to be almost a hallucination: that she was in the country, at dusk, and alone, and strangely at peace. She did not recall the places which she had visited in holiday-time, these reproached her like opportunities neglected. But while her body sat before the first fires and was cosy with Henry and Caroline, her mind walked by lonely seaboards, in marshes and fens, or came at nightfall to the edge of a wood. She never imagined herself in these places by daylight. She never thought of them as being in any way beautiful. It was not beauty at all that she wanted, or, depressed though she was, she would have bought a ticket to somewhere or other upon the Metropolitan railway and gone out to see the recumbent autumnal graces of the countryside. Her mind was groping after something that eluded her experience, a something that was shadowy and menacing, and yet in some way congenial; a something that lurked in waste places, that was hinted at by the sound of water gurgling through deep channels and by the voices of birds of ill-omen. Loneliness, dreariness, aptness for arousing a sense of fear, a kind of ungodly hallowedness—these were the things that called her thoughts away from the comfortable fireside.

In this mood she would sometimes go off to explore among the City churches, or to lose herself in the riverside quarters east of the Pool. She liked to think of the London of Defoe's *Journal,* and to fancy herself back in the seventeenth century, when, so it seemed to her, there were still darknesses in men's minds. Once, hemmed in by the jostling tombstones at Bunhill Fields, she almost pounced on the clue to her disquiet; and once again in the goods-yard of the G.W.R., where she had gone to find, not her own secret, but a case of apples for Caroline.

As time went on Laura grew accustomed to this recurrent autumnal fever. It was as much a sign of the season as the falling leaves or the first frost. Before the end of November it was all over and done with. The next moon had no message for her. Her rambles in the strange places of the mind were at an end. And if she still went on expeditions to Rotherhithe or the Jews' Burying-Ground, she went in search for no more than a little diversion. Nothing was left but cold and sleet and the knowledge that all this fuss had been about nothing. She fortified herself against the dismalness of this reaction by various small self-indulgences. Out of these she had contrived for herself a sort of mental fur coat. Roasted chestnuts could be bought and taken home for bedroom eating. Second-hand book-shops were never so enticing; and the combination of east winds and London water made it allowable to experiment in the most expensive soaps. Coming back from her expeditions, westward from the city with the sunset in her eyes, or eastward from a waning Kew, she would pause for a sumptuous and furtive tea, eating *marrons glacés* with a silver fork in the reflecting warm glitter of a smart pastry-cook's. These things were exciting enough to be pleasurable, for she kept them secret. Henry and Caroline would scarcely have minded if they had known. They were quite indifferent as to where and how she spent her afternoons; they felt no need to question her, since they could be sure that she would do nothing unsuitable or extravagant. Laura's expeditions were secret because no one asked her where she had been. Had they asked, she must have answered. But she did not examine too closely into this; she liked to think of them as secret.

One manifestation of the fur-coat policy, however, could not be kept from their knowledge, and that manifestation slightly qualified their trust that Laura would do nothing unsuitable or extravagant.

Except for a gradual increment of Christmas and birthday presents, Laura's room had altered little since the day it ceased to be the small spare-room and became hers. But every winter it blossomed with an unseasonable luxury of flowers, profusely, shameless as a greenhouse.

"Why, Lolly! Lilies at this time of year!" Caroline would say, not reproachfully, but still with a consciousness that in the drawing-room there were dahlias, and in the dining-room a fern, and in her own sitting-room, where she did the accounts, neither ferns nor flowers. Then Laura would thrust the lilies into her hands; and she would take them to show that she had not spoken with ill-will. Besides, Lolly would really see more of them if they were in the drawing-room. And the next day she would meet Laura on the stairs carrying azaleas. On one occasion even Henry had noticed the splendour of the lilies: red lilies, angular, authoritative in form and colour like cardinals' hats.

"Where do these come from?" Caroline had asked, knowing well that nothing so costly in appearance could come from her florist.

"From Africa," Laura had answered, pressing the firm, wet stalks into her hand.

"Oh well, I daresay they are quite common flowers there," said Caroline to herself, trying to gloss over the slight awkwardness of accepting a trifle so needlessly splendid.

Henry had also asked where they came from.

"From Anthos, I believe," said Caroline.

"Ah!" said Henry, and roused the coins in his trousers pocket.

"It's rather naughty of Lolly. Would you like me just to hint to her that she mustn't be quite so reckless?"

"No. Better not. No need for her to worry about such things."

Husband and wife exchanged a glance of compassionate understanding. It was better not. Much better that Lolly should not be worried about money matters. She was safe in their hands. They could look after Lolly. Henry was like a wall, and Caroline's breasts were like towers.

They condoned this extravagance, yet they mistrusted it. Time justified them in their mistrust. Like many stupid people, they possessed acute instincts. "He that is unfaithful in little things . . ." Caroline would say when the children forgot to wind up their watches. Their instinct told them that the same truth applies to extravagance in little things. They were wiser than they knew. When Laura's extravagance in great things came it staggered them so completely that they forgot how judiciously they had suspected it beforehand.

It befell in the winter of 1921. The war was safely over, so was their silver wedding, so was Marion's first confinement. Titus was in his third year at Oxford, Sibyl was at last going grey, Henry might be made a judge at any moment. The Trade Returns and the Stock Exchange were not all that they should be, and there was always the influenza. But Henry was doing well enough to be lenient to his investments, and Aunt Lucilla and her fortune had been mercifully released. In the coming spring Caroline proposed to have the house thoroughly done up. The lesser renovations she was getting over beforehand, and that was why Laura had gone out before the shops shut to show Mr. Bunting a pair of massy candlesticks and to inquire how much he would charge for re-plating them. His estimate was high, too high to be accepted upon her own responsibility. She decided to carry the candlesticks back and consult Caroline.

Mr. Bunting lived in the Earls Court Road, rather a long way off for such a family friend. But she had plenty of time for walking back, and for diversion she thought she would take a circuitous route, including the two foxes who guard the forsaken approach in Holland Park and the lane beside the Bayswater Synagogue. It was in Moscow Road that she began to be extravagant. But when she walked into the little shop she had no particular intention of extravagance, for Caroline's parcel hung remindingly upon her arm, and the shop itself, half florist and half greengrocer, had a simple appearance.

There were several other customers, and while she stood waiting to be served she looked about her. The aspect of the shop pleased her greatly. It was small and homely. Fruit and flowers and vegetables were crowded together in countrified disorder. On the sloping shelf in the window, among apples and rough-skinned cooking pears and trays of walnuts, chestnuts, and filberts, was a basket of eggs, smooth and brown, like some larger kind of nut. At one side of the room was a wooden staging. On this stood jars of home-made jam and bottled fruits. It was as though the remnants of summer had come into the little shop for shelter. On the floor lay a heap of earthy turnips.

Laura looked at the bottled fruits, the sliced pears in syrup, the glistening red plums, the greengages. She thought of the woman who had filled those jars and fastened on the bladders. Perhaps the greengrocer's mother lived in the country. A solitary old woman picking fruit in a darkening orchard, rubbing her rough fingertips over the smooth-skinned plums, a lean wiry old woman, standing with upstretched arms among her fruit trees as though she were a tree herself, growing out of the long grass, with arms stretched up like branches. It grew darker and darker; still she worked on, methodically stripping the quivering taut boughs one after the other.

As Laura stood waiting she felt a great longing. It weighed upon her like the load of ripened fruit upon a tree. She forgot the shop, the other customers, her own errand. She forgot the winter air outside, the people going by on the wet pavements. She forgot that she was in London, she forgot the whole of her London life. She seemed to be standing alone in a darkening orchard, her feet in the grass, her arms stretched up to the pattern of leaves and fruit, her fingers seeking the rounded ovals of the fruit among the pointed ovals of the leaves. The air about her was cool and moist. There was no sound, for the birds had left off singing and the owls had not yet begun to hoot. No sound, except sometimes the soft thud of a ripe plum falling into the grass, to lie there a compact shadow among shadows. The back of her neck ached a little with the strain of holding up her arms. Her fingers searched among the leaves.

She started as the man of the shop came up to her and asked her what she wished for. Her eyes blinked, she looked with surprise at the gloves upon her hands.

"I want one of those large chrysanthemums," she said, and turned towards the window where they stood in a brown jar. There were the apples and pears, the eggs, the disordered nuts overflowing from their compartments. There on the floor were the earthy turnips, and close at hand were the jams and bottled fruits. If she was behaving foolishly, if she looked like a woman roused out of a fond dream, these were kindly things to waken to. The man of the shop also had a kind face. He wore a gardener's apron, and his hands were brown and dry as if he had been handling earth.

"Which one would you like, ma'am?" he asked, turning the bunch of chrysanthemums about that she might choose for herself. She looked at the large mop-headed blossoms. Their curled petals were deep garnet colour within and tawny yellow without. As the light fell on their sleek flesh the garnet colour glowed, the tawny yellow paled as if it were thinly washed with silver. She longed for the moment when she might stroke her hand over those mop heads.

"I think I will take them all," she said.

"They're lovely blooms," said the man.

He was pleased. He did not expect such a good customer at this late hour.

When he brought her the change from her pound-note and the chrysanthemums pinned up in sheets of white paper, he brought also several sprays of beech leaves. These, he explained, were thrown in with her purchase. Laura took them into her arms. The great fans of orange tracery seemed to her even more beautiful than the chrysanthemums, for they had been given to her, they were a surprise. She sniffed. They smelt of woods, of dark rustling woods like the wood to whose edge she came so often in the country of her autumn imagination. She stood very still to make quite sure of her sensations. Then: "Where do they come from?" she asked.

"From near Chenies, ma'am, in Buckinghamshire. I have a sister living there, and every Sunday I go out to see her, and bring back a load of foliage with me."

There was no need to ask now who made the jams and tied on the bladders. Laura knew all that she wanted to know. Her course lay clear before her. Holding the sprays of beech as though she were marching on Dunsinane, she went to a bookseller's. There she bought a small guide-book to the Chilterns and inquired for a map of that district. It must, she explained, be very detailed, and give as many names and footpaths as possible. Her eyes were so bright and her demands so earnest that the bookseller, though he had not that kind of map, was sympathetic, and directed her to another shop where she could find what she wanted. It was only a little way off, but closing-time was at hand, so she took a taxi. Having bought the map she took another taxi home. But at the top of Apsley Terrace she had one of her impulses of secrecy and told the driver that she would walk the rest of the way.

There was rather a narrow squeak in the hall, for Caroline's parcel became entangled in the gong stand, and she heard Henry coming up from the wine cellar. If she alarmed the gong Henry would quicken his steps. She had no time to waste on Henry just then for she had a great deal to think of before dinner. She ran up to her room, arranged the chrysanthemums and the beech leaves, and began to read the guide-book. It was just what she wanted, for it was extremely plain and unperturbed. Beginning as early as possible with Geology, it passed to Flora and Fauna, Watersheds, Ecclesiastical Foundations and Local Government. After that came a list of all the towns and villages, shortly described in alphabetical order. Lamb's End had three hundred inhabitants and a perpendicular font. At Walpole St. Dennis was the country seat of the Bartlet family, faced with stucco and situated upon an eminence. The almshouses at Semple, built in 1703 by Bethia Hood, had a fine pair of wrought-iron gates. It was dark as she pressed her nose against the scrolls and rivets.

Bats flickered in the little courtyard, and shadows moved across the yellow blinds. Had she been born a deserving widow, life would have been simplified.

She wasted no time over this regret, for now at last she was simplifying life for herself. She unfolded the map. The woods were coloured green and the main roads red. There was a great deal of green. She looked at the beech leaves. As she looked a leaf detached itself and fell slowly. She remembered squirrels.

The stairs creaked under the tread of Dunlop with the hot-water can. Dunlop entered, glancing neither at Laura curled askew on the bed nor at the chrysanthemums ennobling the dressing table. She was a perfectly trained servant. Before she left the room she took a deep breath, stooped down, and picked up the beech leaf.

Quarter of an hour afterwards Laura exclaimed: "Oh! a windmill!" She took up the guide-book again, and began to read intently.

She was roused by an unaccustomed clash of affable voices in the hall. She remembered, leapt off the bed, and dressed rapidly for the family dinner-party. They were all there when she reached the drawing-room. Sibyl and Titus, Fancy and her Mr. Wolf-Saunders, Marion with the latest news from Sprat, who, being in the Soudan, could not dine out with his wife. Sprat had had another boil on his neck, but it had yielded to treatment. "Ah, poor fellow," said Henry. He seemed to be saying: "The price of Empire."

During dinner Laura looked at her relations. She felt as though she had awoken, unchanged, from a twenty-year slumber, to find them almost unrecognisable. She surveyed them, one after the other. Even Henry and Caroline, whom she saw every day, were half hidden under their accumulations—accumulations of prosperity, authority, daily experience. They were carpeted with experience. No new event could set jarring feet on them but they would absorb and muffle the impact. If the boiler burst, if a policeman climbed in at the window waving a sword, Henry and Caroline would bring the situation to heel by their massive experience of normal boilers and normal policemen.

She turned her eyes to Sibyl. How strange it was that Sibyl

should have exchanged her former look of a pretty ferret for this refined and waxen mask. Only when she was silent, though, as now she was, listening to Henry with her eyes cast down to her empty plate: when she spoke the ferret look came back. But Sibyl in her house at Hampstead must have spent many long afternoons in silence, learning this unexpected beauty, preparing her face for the last look of death. What had been her thoughts? Why was she so different when she spoke? Which, what, was the real Sibyl: the greedy, agile little ferret or this memorial urn?

Fancy's Mr. Wolf-Saunders had eaten all his bread and was at a loss. Laura turned to him and asked after her great-nephew, who was just then determined to be a bus-conductor. "He probably will be," said his father gloomily, "if things go on as they are at present."

Great-nephews and great-nieces suggested nephews and nieces. Resuming her scrutiny of the table she looked at Fancy, Marion, and Titus. They had grown up as surprisingly as trees since she first knew them, and yet it did not seem to her that they were so much changed as their elders. Titus, in particular, was easily recognisable. She caught his eye, and he smiled back at her, just as he had smiled back when he was a baby. Now he was long and slim, and his hay-coloured hair was brushed smoothly back instead of standing up in a crest. But one lock had fallen forward when he laughed, and hung over his left eye, and this gave him a pleasing, rustic look. She was glad still to be friends with Titus. He might very usefully abet her, and though she felt in no need of allies, a little sympathy would do no harm. Certainly the rustic forelock made Titus look particularly congenial. And how greedily he was eating that apple, and with what disparagement of imported fruit he had waved away the Californian plums! It was nice to feel sure of his understanding and approval, since at this moment he was looking the greatest Willowes of them all.

Most of the family attention was focused on Titus that evening. No sooner had coffee been served than Sibyl began about his career. Had Caroline ever heard of anything more ridiculous? Titus still declared that he meant to manage the family brewery.

After all his success at Oxford and his popularity, could anything be more absurd than to bury himself in Somerset?

His own name was the first thing that Titus heard as he entered the drawing-room. He greeted it with an approving smile, and sat down by Laura, carefully crossing his long legs.

"She spurns at the brewery, and wants me to take a studio in Hampstead and model bustos," he explained.

Titus had a soft voice. His speech was gentle and sedate. He chose his words with extreme care, but escaped the charge of affectation by pronouncing them in a hesitating manner.

"I'm sure sculpture is his *métier,*" said Sibyl. "Or perhaps poetry. Anyhow, not brewing. I wish you could have seen that little model he made for the grocer at Arcachon."

Marion said: "I thought bustos always had wigs."

"My dear, you've hit it. In fact, that is my objection to this plan for making me a sculptor. Revive the wig, and I object no more. The head is the noblest part of man's anatomy. Therefore enlarge it with a wig."

Henry thought the conversation was taking a foolish turn. But as host it was his duty to take part in it.

"What about the Elgin Marbles?" he inquired. "No wigs there."

The Peruke and its Functions in Attic Drama, thought Titus, would be a pretty fancy. But it would not do for his uncle. Agreeably he admitted that there were no wigs in the Elgin Marbles.

They fell into silence. At an ordinary dinner party Caroline would have felt this silence to be a token that the dinner party was a failure. But this was a family affair, there was no disgrace in having nothing to say. They were all Willoweses and the silence was a seemly Willowes silence. She could even emphasise it by counting her stitches aloud.

All the chairs and sofas were comfortable. The fire burnt brightly, the curtains hung in solemn folds; they looked almost as solemn as organ pipes. Lolly had gone off into one of her day dreams, just her way, she would never trouble to give a party the least prod. Only Sibyl fidgeted, twisting her heel about in her satin slipper.

"What pretty buckles, Sibyl! Have I seen them before?"

Sibyl had bought them second-hand for next to nothing. They came from Arles, and the old lady who had sold them to her had been such a character. She repeated the characteristic remarks of the old lady in a very competent French accent. Her feet were as slim as ever, and she could stretch them out very prettily. Even in doing so she remembered to ask Caroline where they were going for the Easter holidays.

"Oh, to Blythe, I expect," said Caroline. "We know it."

"When I have evicted my tenants and brewed a large butt of family ale, I shall invite you all down to Lady Place," said Titus.

"But before then," said Laura, speaking rather fast, "I hope you will all come to visit me at Great Mop."

Every one turned to stare at her in bewilderment.

"Of course, it won't be as comfortable as Lady Place. And I don't suppose there will be room for more than one of you at a time. But I'm sure you'll think it delightful."

"I don't understand," said Caroline. "What is this place, Lolly?"

"Great Mop. It's not really Great. It's in the Chilterns."

"But why should we go there?"

"To visit me. I'm going to live there."

"Live there? My dear Lolly!"

"Live there, Aunt Lolly?"

"This is very sudden. Is there really a place called . . . ?"

"Lolly, you are mystifying us."

They all spoke at once, but Henry spoke loudest, so Laura replied to him.

"No, Henry, I'm not mystifying you. Great Mop is a village in the Chilterns, and I am going to live there, and perhaps keep a donkey. And you must all come on visits."

"I've never even heard of the place!" said Henry conclusively.

"But you'll love it. 'A secluded hamlet in the heart of the Chilterns, Great Mop is situated twelve miles from Wickendon in a hilly district with many beech-woods. The parish church has a fine Norman tower and a squint. The population is 227.' And quite close by on a hill there is a ruined windmill, and the nearest railway station is twelve miles off, and there is a farm called Scramble Through the Hedge . . ."

Henry thought it time to interrupt. "I suppose you don't expect us to believe all this."

"I know. It does seem almost too good to be true. But it is. I've read it in a guidebook, and seen it on a map."

"Well, all I can say is . . ."

"Henry! Henry!" said Caroline warningly. Henry did not say it. He threw the cushion out of his chair, glared at Laura, and turned away his head.

For some time Titus's attempts at speech had hovered above the tumult, like one holy appeasing dove loosed after the other. The last dove was luckier. It settled on Laura.

"How nice of you to have a donkey. Will it be a grey donkey, like Madam?"

"Do you remember dear Madam, then?"

"Of course I remember dear Madam. I can remember everything that happened to me when I was four. I rode in one pannier, and you, Marion, rode in the other. And we went to have tea in Potts's Dingle."

"With sponge cakes and raspberry jam, do you remember?"

"Yes. And milk surging in a whisky bottle. Will you have thatch or slate, Aunt Lolly? Slate is very practical."

"Thatch is more motherly. Anyhow, I shall have a pump."

"Will it be an indoor or an outdoor pump? I ask, for I hope to pump on it quite often."

"*You* will come to stay with me, won't you, Titus?"

Laura was a little cast-down. It did not look, just then, as if any one else wanted to come and stay with her at Great Mop. But Titus was as sympathetic as she had hoped. They spent the rest of the evening telling each other how she would live. By half-past ten their conjectures had become so fantastic that the rest of the family thought the whole scheme was nothing more than one of Lolly's odd jokes that nobody was ever amused by. Henry took heart. He rallied Laura, supposing that when she lived at Great Mop she would start hunting for catnip again, and become the village witch.

"How lovely!" said Laura.

Henry was satisfied. Obviously Laura could not be in earnest.

When the guests had gone, and Henry had bolted and chained the door, and put out the hall light, Laura hung about a little, thinking that he or Caroline might wish to ask her more. But they asked nothing and went upstairs to bed. Soon after, Laura followed them. As she passed their bedroom door she heard their voices within, the comfortable fragmentary talk of a husband and wife with complete confidence in each other and nothing particular to say.

Laura decided to tackle Henry on the morrow. She observed him during breakfast and saw with satisfaction that he seemed to be in a particularly benign mood. He had drunk three cups of coffee, and said "Ah! poor fellow!" when a wandering cornet-player began to play on the pavement opposite. Laura took heart from these good omens, and, breakfast being over, and her brother and the *Times* retired to the study, she followed them thither.

"Henry," she said. "I have come for a talk with you."

Henry looked up. "Talk away, Lolly," he said, and smiled at her.

"A business talk," she continued.

Henry folded the *Times* and laid it aside. He also (if the expression may be allowed) folded and laid aside his smile.

"Now, Lolly, what is it?"

His voice was kind, but business-like. Laura took a deep breath, twisted the garnet ring round her little finger, and began.

"It has just occurred to me, Henry, that I am forty-seven."

She paused.

"Go on!" said Henry.

"And that both the girls are married. I don't mean that that has just occurred to me too, but it's part of it. You know, really I'm not much use to you now."

"My dear Lolly!" remonstrated her brother. "You are extremely useful. Besides, I have never considered our relationship in that light."

"So I have been thinking. And I have decided that I should like to go and live at Great Mop. You know, that place I was talking about last night."

Henry was silent. His face was completely blank. Should she recall Great Mop to him by once more repeating the description out of the guide-book?

"In the Chilterns," she murmured. "Pop. 227."

Henry's silence was unnerving her.

"Really, I think it would be a good plan. I should like to live alone in the country. And in my heart I think I have always meant to, one day. But one day is so like another, it's almost impossible to throw salt on its tail. If I don't go soon, I never shall. So if you don't mind, I should like to start as soon as possible."

There was another long pause. She could not make out Henry at all. It was not like him to say nothing when he was annoyed. She had expected thunders and tramplings, and those she could have weathered. But thus becalmed under a lowering sky she was beginning to lose her head.

At last he spoke.

"I hardly know what to say."

"I'm sorry if the idea annoys you, Henry."

"I am not annoyed. I am grieved. Grieved and astonished. For twenty years you have lived under my roof. I have always thought—I may be wrong, but I have always thought—that you were happy here."

"Quite happy," said Laura.

"Caroline and I have done all we could to make you so. The children—*all* the children—look on you as a second mother. We are all devoted to you. And now, without a word of warning, you propose to leave us and go and live at a place called Great Mop. Lolly! I must ask you to put this ridiculous idea out of your head."

"I never expected you to be so upset, Henry. Perhaps I should have told you more gradually. I should be sorry to hurt you."

"You have hurt me, I admit," said he, firmly seizing on this advantage. "Still, let that pass. Say you won't leave us, Lolly."

"I'm afraid I can't quite do that."

"But Lolly, what you want is absurd."

"It's only my own way, Henry."

"If you would like a change, take one by all means. Go away

for a fortnight. Go away for a month! Take a little trip abroad if you like. But come back to us at the end of it."

"No, Henry. I love you all, but I feel I have lived here long enough."

"But why? But why? What has come over you?"

Laura shook her head.

"Surely you must have some reasons."

"I have told you my reasons."

"Lolly! I cannot allow this. You are my sister. I consider you my charge. I must ask you, once for all to drop this idea. It is not sensible. Or suitable."

"I have reminded you that I am forty-seven. If I am not old enough now to know what is sensible and suitable, I never shall be."

"Apparently not."

This was more like Henry's old form. But though he had scored her off, it did not seem to have encouraged him as much as scoring off generally did. He began again, almost as a suppliant.

"Be guided by me, Lolly. At least, take a few days to think it over."

"No, Henry. I don't feel inclined to; I'd much rather get it over now. Besides, if you are going to disapprove as violently as this, the sooner I pack up and start the better."

"You are mad. You talk of packing up and starting when you have never even set eyes on the place."

"I was thinking of going there to-day, to make arrangements."

"Well, then, you will do nothing of the kind. I'm sorry to seem harsh, Lolly. But you must put all this out of your mind."

"Why?"

"It is impracticable."

"Nothing is impracticable for a single, middle-aged woman with an income of her own."

Henry paled slightly and said: "Your income is no longer what it was."

"Oh, taxes!" said Laura contemptuously. "Never mind; even if it's a little less, I can get along on it."

"You know nothing of business, Lolly. I need not enter into explanations with you. It should be enough for me to say that for the last year your income has been practically nonexistent."

"But I can still cash cheques."

"I have placed a sum at the bank to your credit."

Laura had grown rather pale too. Her eyes shone.

"I'm afraid you must enter into explanations with me, Henry. After all, it is my income, and I have a right to know what has happened to it."

"Your capital has always been in my hands, Lolly, and I have administered it as I thought fit."

"Go on," said Laura.

"In 1920 I transferred the greater part of it to the Ethiopian Development Syndicate, a perfectly sound investment which will in time be as good as ever, if not better. Unfortunately, owing to this Government and all this socialistic talk the soundest investments have been badly hit. The Ethiopian Development Syndicate is one of them."

"Go on, Henry. I have understood quite well so far. You have administered all my money into something that doesn't pay. Now explain why you did this."

"I had every reason for thinking that I should be able to sell out at a profit almost immediately. During November the shares had gone up from 5¾ to 8½. I bought in December at 8½. They went to 8¾ and since then have steadily sunk. They now stand at 4. Of course, my dear, you needn't be alarmed. They will rise again the moment we have a Conservative Government, and that, thank Heaven, must come soon. But you see at present it is out of the question for you to think of leaving us."

"But don't these Ethiopians have dividends?"

"These," said Henry with dignity, "are not the kind of shares that pay dividends. They are—that is to say, they were, and of course will be again—a sound speculative investment. But at present they pay no dividends worth mentioning. Now, Lolly, don't become agitated. I assure you that it is all perfectly all right. But you must give up this idea of the country. Anyhow, I'm sure you wouldn't find it suit you. You are rheumatic—"

Laura tried to interpose.

"—or will be. All the Willoweses are rheumatic. Buckinghamshire is damp. Those poetical beech-woods make it so. You see, trees draw rain. It is one of the principles of afforestation. The trees—that is to say, the rain—"

Laura stamped her foot with impatience. "Have done with your trumpery red herrings!" she cried.

She had never lost her temper like this before. It was a glorious sensation.

"Henry!" She could feel her voice crackle round his ears. "You say you bought those shares at eight and something, and that they are now four. So if you sell out now you will get rather less than half what you gave for them."

"Yes," said Henry. Surely if Lolly were business woman enough to grasp that so clearly, she would in time see reason on other matters.

"Very well. You will sell them immediately—"

"Lolly!"

"—and reinvest the money in something quite unspeculative and unsound, like War Loan, that will pay a proper dividend. I shall still have enough to manage on. I shan't be as comfortable as I thought I should be. I shan't be able to afford the little house that I hoped for, nor the donkey. But I shan't mind much. It will matter very little to me when I'm there."

She stopped. She had forgotten Henry, and the unpleasant things she meant to say to him. She had come to the edge of the wood, and felt its cool breath in her face. It did not matter about the donkey, nor the house, nor the darkening orchard even. If she were not to pick fruit from her own trees, there were common herbs and berries in plenty for her, growing wherever she chose to wander. It is best as one grows older to strip oneself of possessions, to shed oneself downward like a tree, to be almost wholly earth before one dies.

As she left the room she turned and looked at Henry. Such was her mood, she could have blessed him solemnly, as before an eternal departure. But he was sitting with his back to her, and did not look round. When she had gone he took out his handkerchief and wiped his forehead.

Ten days later Laura arrived at Great Mop. After the interview with Henry she encountered no more opposition. Caroline knew better than to persist against an obstinacy which had worsted her husband, and the other members of the family, their surprise being evaporated, were indifferent. Titus was a little taken aback when he found that his aunt's romantic proposals were seriously intended. He for his part was going to Corsica. "A banal mountainous spot," he said politely, "compared with Buckinghamshire."

The day of Laura's arrival was wet and blusterous. She drove in a car from Wickendon. The car lurched and rattled, and the wind slapped the rain against the windows; Laura could scarcely see the rising undulations of the landscape. When the car drew up before her new home, she stood for a moment looking up the village street, but the prospect was intercepted by the umbrella under which Mrs. Leak hastened to conduct her to the porch. So had it rained, and so had the wind blown, on the day when she had come on her visit of inspection and had taken rooms in Mrs. Leak's cottage. So, Henry and Caroline and their friends had assured her, did it rain and blow all through the winter in the Chilterns. No words of theirs, they said, could describe how dismal and bleak it would be among those unsheltered hills. To Laura, sitting by the fire in her parlour, the sound of wind and rain was pleasant. "Weather like this," she thought, "would never be allowed in London."

The unchastened gusts that banged against the side of the house and drove the smoke down the chimney, and the riotous gurgling of the rain in the gutters were congenial to her spirit. "Hoo! You daredevil," said the wind. "Have you come out to join us?" Yet sitting there with no companionship except those exciting voices she was quiet and happy.

Mrs. Leak's tea was strong Indian tea. The bread-and-butter was cut in thick slices, and underneath it was a crocheted mat; there was plum jam in a heart-shaped glass dish, and a plate of rather heavy jam-puffs. It was not quite so good as the farmhouse teas she remembered in Somerset, but a great deal better than teas at Apsley Terrace.

Tea being done with, Laura took stock of her new domain. The parlour was furnished with a large mahogany table, four horsehair chairs and a horsehair sofa, an armchair, and a sideboard, rather gimcrack compared to the rest of the furniture. On the walls, which were painted green, hung a print of the Empress Josephine and two rather scowling classical landscapes with ruined temples, and volcanoes. On either side of the hearth were cupboards, and the fireplace was of a cottage pattern with hobs, and a small oven on one side. This fireplace had caught Laura's fancy when she first looked at the rooms. She had stipulated with Mrs. Leak that, should she so wish, she might cook on it. There are some things—mushrooms, for instance, or toasted cheese—which can only be satisfactorily cooked by the eater. Mrs. Leak had made no difficulties. She was an oldish woman, sparing of her words and moderate in her demands. Her husband worked at the sawmill. They were childless. She had never let lodgings before, but till last year an aunt with means of her own had occupied the parlour and bedroom which were now Laura's.

It did not take Laura very long to arrange her belongings, for she had brought little. Soon after supper, which consisted of rabbit, bread and cheese, and table beer, she went upstairs to bed. Moving about her small cold bedroom she suddenly noticed that the wind had fallen, and that it was no longer raining. She pushed aside a corner of the blind and opened the window. The night air was cold and sweet, and the full moon shone high overhead. The sky was cloudless, lovely, and serene; a few stars glistened there like drops of water about to fall. For the first time she was looking at the intricate landscape of rounded hills and scooped valleys which she had chosen for learning by heart.

Dark and compact, the beech-woods lay upon the hills. Alighting as noiselessly as an owl, a white cat sprang up on to the garden fence. It glanced from side to side, ran for a yard or two along the top of the fence and jumped off again, going secretly on its way. Laura sighed for happiness. She had no thoughts; her mind was swept as clean and empty as the heavens. For a long time she continued to lean out of the window, forgetting where she was and how she had come there, so unearthly was her contentment.

Nevertheless her first days at Great Mop gave her little real pleasure. She wrecked them by her excitement. Every morning immediately after breakfast she set out to explore the country. She believed that by eating a large breakfast she could do without lunch. The days were short, and she wanted to make the most of them, and making the most of the days and going back for lunch did not seem to her to be compatible. Unfortunately, she was not used to making large breakfasts, so her enthusiasm was qualified by indigestion until about four P.M., when both enthusiasm and indigestion yielded to a faintish feeling. Then she turned back, generally by road, since it was growing too dark to find out footpaths, and arrived home with a limp between six and seven. She knew in her heart that she was not really enjoying this sort of thing, but the habit of useless activity was too strong to be snapped by change of scene. And in the evening, as she looked at the map and marked where she had been with little bleeding footsteps of red ink, she was enchanted afresh by the names and the bridle-paths, and, forgetting the blistered heel and the dissatisfaction of that day's walk, planned a new walk for the morrow.

Nearly a week had gone by before she righted herself. She had made an appointment with the sunset that she should see it from the top of a certain hill. The hill was steep, and the road turned and twisted about its sides. It was clear that the sunset would be at their meeting-place before she was, nor would it be likely to kick its heels and wait about for her. She looked at the sky and walked faster. The road took a new and unsuspected turn, concealed behind the clump of trees by which she had been measuring her progress up the hill. She was growing more and more flustered, and at this prick she lost her temper entirely. She was tired, she was miles from Great Mop, and she had made a fool of herself. An abrupt beam of light shot up from behind the hedge as though the sun in vanishing below the horizon had winked at her. "This sort of thing," she said aloud, "has got to be put a stop to." She sat down in the extremely comfortable ditch to think.

The shades that had dogged her steps up the hill closed in upon her as she sat in the ditch, but when she took out her map there was enough light to enable her to see where the nearest inn lay. It was close at hand; when she got there she could just read its name on the sign. Its name was The Reason Why. Entering The Reason Why, she ordered tea and a conveyance to drive her back to Great Mop. When she left the inn it was a brilliant night of stars. Outside stood a wagonette drawn by a large white horse. Piled on the seat of the wagonette were a number of waterproof rugs with finger-rings on them, and these she wrapped round her with elaborate care.

The drive back to Great Mop was more filled with glory than anything she had ever experienced. The wagonette creaked over bare hilltops and plunged downwards into the chequered darknesses of unknown winter woods. All the stars shook their glittering spears overhead. Turning this way and that to look at them, the frost pinched her cheeks.

That evening she asked Mrs. Leak if she would lend her some books. From Mrs. Leak's library she chose *Mehalah,* by the Rev. Sabine Baring-Gould, and an anonymous work of information called *Enquire Within Upon Everything.* The next morning was fine and sunny. She spent it by the parlour fire, reading. When she read bits of *Mehalah* she thought how romantic it would be to live in the Essex Marshes. From *Enquire Within Upon Everything* she learned how gentlemen's hats if plunged in a bath of logwood will come out with a dash of respectability, and that ruins are best constructed of cork. During the afternoon she learned other valuable facts like these, and fell asleep. On the following morning she fell asleep again, in a beech-wood, curled up in a heap of dead leaves. After that she had no more trouble. Life becomes simple if one does nothing about it. Laura did nothing about anything for days and days till Mrs. Leak said: "We shall soon be having Christmas, miss."

Christmas! So it had caught them all again. By now the provident Caroline herself was suffering the eleventh hour in Oxford Street. But here even Christmas was made easy.

Laura spent a happy afternoon choosing presents at the village shop. For Henry she bought a bottle of ginger wine, a pair of leather gaiters, and some highly recommended tincture of sassafras for his winter cough. For Caroline she bought an extensive parcel—all the shop had, in fact—of variously coloured rug-wools, and a pound's worth of assorted stamps. For Sibyl she bought some tinned fruits, some sugar-biscuits, and a pink knitted bed-jacket. For Fancy and Marion respectively she bought a Swanee flute and a box with Ely Cathedral on the lid, containing string, which Mrs. Trumpet was very glad to see the last of, as it had been forced upon her by a traveller, and had not hit the taste of the village. To her great-nephew and great-nieces she sent postal orders for one guinea, and pink gauze stockings filled with tin toys. These she knew would please, for she had always wanted one herself. For Dunlop she bought a useful button-hook. Acquaintances and minor relations were greeted with picture postcards, either photographs of the local War Memorial Hall and Institute, or a coloured view of some sweet-peas with the motto: "Kind Thoughts from Great Mop." A postcard of the latter kind was also enclosed with each of the presents.

Titus was rather more difficult to suit. But by good luck she noticed two heavy glass jars such as old-fashioned druggists use. These were not amongst Mrs. Trumpet's wares—she kept linen buttons in the one and horn buttons in the other; but she was anxious to oblige such a magnificent customer and quite ready to sell her anything that she wanted. She was about to empty out the buttons when Laura stopped her. "You must keep some for your customers, Mrs. Trumpet. They may want to put them in their Christmas puddings." Laura was losing her head a little with excitement. "But I should like to send about three dozen of each sort, if you can spare them. Buttons are always useful."

"Yes, miss. Shall I put in some linen thread too?"

Mrs. Trumpet was a stout, obliging woman. She promised to do up all the parcels in thick brown paper and send them off three days before Christmas. As Laura stepped out of the shop in triumph, she exclaimed: "Well, that's done it!"

For the life of her she could not have said in what sense the words were intended. She was divided between admiration for her useful and well-chosen gifts and delight in affronting a kind of good taste which she believed to be merely self-esteem.

Although she had chosen presents with such care for her relations, Laura was surprised when counter presents arrived from them. She had not thought of them as remembering her. Their presents were all of a warm nature; they insisted upon that bleakness and draughtiness which their senders had foretold. When Caroline wrote to thank Laura, she said:

"I have started to make you a nice warm coverlet out of those pretty wools you sent. I think it will look very cheerful and variegated. I often feel quite worried to think of you upon those wind-swept hills. And from all I hear you have a great many woods round you, and I'm afraid all the decaying leaves must make the place damp."

Heaping coals of fire was a religious occupation. Laura rather admired Caroline for the neat turn of the wrist with which she heaped these.

In spite of the general determination of her family that she should feel the cold Laura lived at Great Mop very comfortably. Mrs. Leak was an excellent cook; she attended to her lodger civilly and kindly enough, made no comments, and showed no curiosity. At times Laura felt as though she had exchanged one Caroline for another. Mrs. Leak was not, apparently, a religious woman. There were no texts on her walls, and when Laura asked for the loan of a Bible Mrs. Leak took a little time to produce it, and blew on the cover before she handed it over. But like Caroline, she gave the impression that her kingdom was not of this world. Laura liked her, and would have been glad to be upon less distant terms with her, but she did not find it easy to break through Mrs. Leak's reserve. She tried this subject and that, but Mrs. Leak did not begin to thaw until Laura said something about black-currant tea. It seemed that Mrs. Leak shared Laura's liking for distillations. That evening she remarked that the table-beer was of her own brewing, and lingered a while with the folded cloth in her hand to explain the recipe. After that Laura was given every evening a glass of home-made wine: dandelion, cowslip, elderberry, ashkey, or mangold. By her appreciation and her inquiries she entrapped Mrs. Leak into pausing longer and longer before she carried away the supper-tray. Before January was out it had become an established thing that after placing the bedroom candlestick on the cleared table Mrs. Leak would sit down and talk for half an hour or so.

There was an indoor pleasantness about these times. Through the wall came the sound of Mr. Leak snoring in the kitchen. The two women sat by the fire, tilting their glasses and drinking in small peaceful sips. The lamplight shone upon the tidy room and the polished table, lighting topaz in the dandelion wine, spilling pools of crimson through the flanks of the bottle of plum gin. It shone on the contented drinkers, and threw their large, close-at-hand shadows upon the wall. When Mrs. Leak smoothed her apron the shadow solemnified the gesture as though she were moulding an universe. Laura's nose and chin were defined as sharply as the peaks of a holly leaf.

Mrs. Leak did most of the talking. She talked well. She knew a great deal about everybody, and she was not content to quit a character until she had brought it to life for her listener.

Mrs. Leak's favorite subject was the Misses Larpent, Miss Minnie and Miss Jane. Miss Minnie was seventy-three, Miss Jane four years younger. Neither of them had known a day's illness, nor any bodily infirmity, nor any relenting of their faculties. They would live for many years yet, if only to thwart their debauched middle-aged nephew, the heir to the estate. Perhaps Miss Willowes had seen Lazzard Court on one of her walks? Yes, Laura had seen it, looking down from a hill-top—the park where sheep were penned among the grouped chestnut trees, the long white house with its expressionless façade—and had heard the stable-clock striking a deserted noon.

The drive of Lazzard Court was five miles long from end to end. The house had fourteen principal bedrooms and a suite for Royalty. Mrs. Leak had been in service at Lazzard Court before her marriage; she knew the house inside and out, and described it to Laura till Laura felt that there was not one of the fourteen principal bedrooms which she did not know. The blue room, the buff room, the balcony room, the needle-work room—she had slept in them all. Nay, she had awakened in the Royal bed, and pulling aside the red damask curtains had looked to the window to see the sun shining upon the tulip tree.

No visitors slept in the stately bedrooms now, Lazzard Court was very quite. People in the villages, said Mrs. Leak coldly, called Miss Minnie and Miss Jane two old screws. Mrs. Leak knew better. The old ladies spent lordily upon their pleasures, and economised elsewhere that they might be able to do so. When they invited the Bishop to lunch and gave him stewed rabbit, blackberry pudding, and the best peaches and Madeira that his Lordship was likely to taste in his life, he fared no worse and no better than they fared themselves. Lazzard Court was famous for its racing-stable. To the upkeep of this all meaner luxuries were sacrificed—suitable bonnets, suitable subscriptions, bedroom fires, salmon and cucumber. But the stable-yard was like the forecourt of a temple. Every morning after breakfast Miss Jane would go round the stables and feel the horses' legs, her gnarled old hand with its diamond ring slipping over the satin coat.

Nothing escaped the sisters. The dairy, the laundry, the glass-houses, the poultry-yard, all were scrutinised. If any servant were found lacking he or she was called before Miss Minnie in the Justice Room. Mrs. Leak had never suffered such an interview, but she had seen others come away, white-faced, or weeping with apron thrown over head. Even the coffins were made on the estate. Each sister had chosen her elm and had watched it felled, with sharp words for the woodman when he aimed amiss.

When Mrs. Leak had given the last touches to Miss Minnie and Miss Jane, she made Laura's flesh creep with the story of the doctor who took the new house up on the hill. He had been a famous doctor in London, but when he came to Great Mop no one would have anything to do with him. It was said he came as an interloper, watching for old Dr. Halley to die that he might step into his shoes. He grew more and more morose in his lonely house, soon the villagers said he drank; at last came the morning when he and his wife were found dead. He had shot her and then himself, so it appeared, and the verdict at the inquest was of Insanity. The chief witnesses were another London doctor, a great man for the brain, who had advised his friend to lead a peaceful country life; and the maidservant, who had heard ranting talk and cries late one evening, and ran out of the house in terror, banging the door behind her, to spend the night with her mother in the village.

After the doctor, Mrs. Leak called up Mr. Jones the clergyman. Laura had seen his white beard browsing among the tombs. He looked like a blessed goat tethered on hallowed grass. He lived alone with his books of Latin and Hebrew and his tame owl which he tried to persuade to sleep in his bedroom. He had dismissed red-haired Emily, the sexton's niece, for pouring hot water on a mouse. Emily had heated the water with the kindest intentions, but she was dismissed nevertheless. Mrs. Leak made much of this incident, for it was Mr. Jones's only act of authority. In all other administrations he was guided by Mr. Gurdon, the clerk.

Mr. Gurdon's beard was red and curly (Laura knew him by sight also). Fiery down covered his cheeks, his eyes were small and truculent, and he lived in a small surprised cottage near the church. Every morning he walked forth to the Rectory to issue his orders for the day—this old woman was to be visited with soup, that young one with wrath; and more manure should be ordered for the Rectory cabbages. For Mr. Gurdon was Mr. Jones's gardener, as well as his clerk.

Mr. Gurdon had even usurped the clergyman's perquisite of quarrelling with the organist. Henry Perry was the organist. He had lost one leg and three fingers in a bus accident, so there was scarcely any other profession he could have taken up. And he had always been fond of playing tunes, for his mother, who was a superior widow, had a piano at Rose Cottage.

Mr. Gurdon said that Henry Perry encouraged the choir boys to laugh at him. After church he used to hide behind a yew tree to pounce out upon any choir boys who desecrated the graves by leaping over them. When he caught them he pinched them. Pinches are silent: they can be made use of in sacred places where smacking would be irreverent. One summer Mr. Gurdon told Mr. Jones to forbid the choir treat. Three days later some of the boys were playing with a tricycle. They allowed it to get out of control, and it began to run downhill. At the bottom of the hill was a sharp turn in the road, and Mr. Gurdon's cottage. The tricycle came faster and faster and crashed through the fence into Mr. Gurdon, who was attending to his lettuces and had his back turned. The boys giggled and ran away. Their mothers did not take the affair so lightly. That evening Mr. Gurdon received a large seed-cake, two dozen fresh eggs, a packet of cigarettes, and other appeasing gifts. Next Sunday Mr. Jones in his kind tenor voice announced that a member of the congregation wished to return thanks for mercies lately received. Mr. Gurdon turned round in his place and glared at the choir boys.

Much as he disliked Henry Perry, Mr. Gurdon had disliked the doctor from London even more. The doctor had come upon him frightening an old woman in a field, and had called him a damned bully and a hypocrite. Mr. Gurdon had cursed him back, and swore to be even with him. The old woman bore her defender no better will. She talked in a surly way about her aunt, who was a gipsy and able to afflict people with lice by just looking at them.

Laura did not hear this story from Mrs. Leak. It was told her some time after by Mrs. Trumpet. Mrs. Trumpet hated Mr. Gurdon, though she was very civil to him when he came into the shop. Few people in the village liked Mr. Gurdon, but he commanded a great deal of politeness. Red and burly and to be feared, the clerk reminded Laura of a red bull belonging to the farmer. In one respect he was unlike the bull: Mr. Gurdon was a very respectable man.

Mrs. Leak also told Laura about Mr. and Mrs. Ward, who kept the Lamb and Flag; about Miss Carloe the dressmaker, who fed a pet hedgehog on bread-and-milk; and about fat Mrs. Garland, who let lodgings in the summer and was always so down at heel and jolly.

Although she knew so much about her neighbours, Mrs. Leak was not a sociable woman. The Misses Larpent, the dead doctor, Mr. Jones, Mr. Gurdon, and Miss Carloe—she called them up and caused them to pass before Laura, but in a dispassionate way, rather like the Witch of Endor calling up old Samuel. Nor was Great Mop a sociable village, at any rate, compared with the villages which Laura had known as a girl. Never had she seen so little dropping in, leaning over fences, dawdling at the shop or in the churchyard. Little laughter came from the taproom of the Lamb and Flag. Once or twice she glanced in at the window as she passed by and saw the men within sitting silent and abstracted with their mugs before them. Even the bell-ringers when they had finished their practice broke up with scant adieus, and went silently on their way. She had never met country people like these before. Nor had she ever known a village that kept such late hours. Lights were burning in the cottages till one and two in the morning, and she had been awakened at later hours than those by the sound of passing voices. She could hear quite distinctly, for her window was open and faced upon the village street. She heard Miss Carloe say complainingly: "It's all very well for you young ones. But my old bones ache so, it's a wonder how I get home!" Then she heard the voice of red-haired Emily say: "No bones so nimble as old bones, Miss Carloe, when it comes to—" and then a voice unknown to Laura said "Hush"; and she heard no more, for a cock crew. Another night, some time after this, she heard some one playing a mouth-organ. The music came from far off, it sounded almost as if it were being played out of doors. She lit a candle and looked at her watch—it was half-past three. She got out of bed and listened at the window; it was a dark night, and the hills rose up like a screen. The noise of the mouth-organ came wavering and veering on the wind. A drunk man, perhaps? Yet what drunk man would play on so steadily? She lay awake for an hour or more, half puzzled, half lulled by the strange music, that never stopped, that never varied, that seemed to have become part of the air.

Next day she asked Mrs. Leak what this strange music could be. Mrs. Leak said that young Billy Thomas was distracted with toothache. He could not sleep, and played for hours nightly upon his mouth-organ to divert himself from the pain. On Wednesday the tooth-drawer would come to Barleighs, and young Billy Thomas would be put out of his agony. Laura was sorry for the sufferer, but she admired the circumstances. The highest flights of her imagination had not risen to more than a benighted drunk. Young Billy Thomas had a finer invention than she.

After a few months she left off speculating about the villagers. She admitted that there was something about them which she could not fathom, but she was content to remain outside the secret, whatever it was. She had not come to Great Mop to concern herself with the hearts of men. Let her stray up the valleys, and rest in the leafless woods that looked so warm with their core of fallen red leaves, and find out her own secret, if she had one; with autumn it might come back to question her. She wondered. She thought not. She felt that nothing could ever again disturb her peace. Wherever she strayed the hills folded themselves round her like the fingers of a hand.

About this time she did an odd thing. In her wanderings she had found a disused well. It was sunk at the side of a green lane, and grass and bushes had grown up around its low rim, almost to conceal it; the wooden frame was broken and mouldered, ropes and pulleys had long ago been taken away, and the water was sunk far down, only distinguishable as an uncertain reflection of the sky. Here, one evening, she brought her guide-book and her map. Pushing aside the bushes she sat down upon the low rim of the well. It was a still, mild evening towards the end of February, the birds were singing, there was a smell of growth in the air, the light lingered in the fields as though it were glad to linger. Looking into the well she watched the reflected sky grow dimmer; and when she raised her eyes the gathering darkness of the landscape surprised her. The time had come. She took the guide-book and the map and threw them in.

She heard the disturbed water sidling against the walls of the well. She scarcely knew what she had done, but she knew that she had done rightly, whether it was that she had sacrificed to the place, or had cast herself upon its mercies—content henceforth to know no more of it than did its own children.

As she reached the village she saw a group of women standing by the milestone. They were silent and abstracted as usual. When she greeted them they returned her greeting, but they said nothing among themselves. After she had gone by they turned as of one accord and began to walk up the field path towards the wood. They were going to gather fuel, she supposed. To-night their demeanour did not strike her as odd. She felt at one with them, an inhabitant like themselves, and she would gladly have gone with them up towards the wood. If they were different from other people, why shouldn't they be? They saw little of the world. Great Mop stood by itself at the head of the valley, five miles from the main road, and cut off by the hills from the other villages. It had a name for being different from other places. The man who had driven Laura home from The Reason Why had said: "It's not often that a wagonette is seen at Great Mop. It's an out-of-the-way place, if ever there was one. There's not such another village in Buckinghamshire for out-of-the-way-ness. Well may it be called Great Mop, for there's never a Little Mop that I've heard of."

People so secluded as the inhabitants of Great Mop would naturally be rather silent, and keep themselves close. So Laura thought, and Mr. Saunter was of the same opinion.

Mr. Saunter's words had weight, for he spoke seldom. He was a serious, brown young man, who after the war had refused to go back to his bank in Birmingham. He lived in a wooden hut which he had put up with his own hands, and kept a poultry-farm.

Laura first met Mr. Saunter when she was out walking, early one darkish, wet, January morning. The lane was muddy; she picked her way, her eyes to the ground. She did not notice Mr. Saunter until she was quite close to him. He was standing bareheaded in the rain. His look was sad and gentle, it reflected the mood of the weather, and several dead white hens dangled from his hands. Laura exclaimed, softly, apologetically. This young man was so perfectly of a piece with his surroundings that she felt herself to be an intruder. She was about to turn back when his glance moved slowly towards her. "Badger," he said; and smiled in an explanatory fashion. Laura knew at once that he had been careless and had left the henhouse door unfastened. She took pains that no shade of blame should mix itself with her condolences. She did not even blame the badger. She knew that this was a moment for nothing but kind words, and not too many of them.

Mr. Saunter was grateful. He invited her to come and see his birds. Side by side they turned in silence through a field gate and walked into Mr. Saunter's field. Bright birds were on the sodden grass. As he went by they hurried into their pens, expecting to be fed. "If you would care to come in," said Mr. Saunter, "I should like to make you a cup of tea."

Mr. Saunter's living-room was very untidy and homelike. A basket of stockings lay on the table. Laura wondered if she might offer to help Mr. Saunter with his mending. But after he had made the tea, he took up a stocking and began to darn it. He darned much better than she did.

As she went home again she fell to wondering what animal Mr. Saunter resembled. But in the end she decided that he resembled no animal except man. Till now, Laura had rejected the saying that man is the noblest work of nature. Half an hour with Mr. Saunter showed her that the saying was true. So had Adam been the noblest work of nature, when he walked out among the beasts, sole overseer of the garden, intact, with all his ribs about him, his equilibrium as yet untroubled by Eve. She had misunderstood the saying merely because she had not happened to meet a man before. Perhaps, like other noble works, man is rare. Perhaps there is only one of him at a time: first Adam; now Mr. Saunter. If that were the case, she was lucky to have met him. This also was the result of coming to Great Mop.

So much did Mr. Saunter remind Laura of Adam that he made her feel like Eve—for she was petitioned by an unladylike curiosity. She asked Mrs. Leak about him. Mrs. Leak could tell her nothing that was not already known to her, except that young Billy Thomas went up there every day on his bicycle to lend Mr. Saunter a hand. Laura would not stoop to question young Billy Thomas. She fought against her curiosity, and the spring came to her aid.

This new year was changing her whole conception of spring. She had thought of it as a denial of winter, a green spur that thrust through a tyrant's rusty armour. Now she saw it as something filial, gently unlacing the helm of the old warrior and comforting his rough cheek. In February came a spell of fine weather. She spent whole days sitting in the woods, where the wood-pigeons moaned for pleasure on the boughs. Sometimes two cockbirds would tumble together in mid air, shrieking, and buffeting with their wings, and then would fly back to the quivering boughs and nurse the air into peace again. All round her the sap was rising up. She laid her cheek against a tree and shut her eyes to listen. She expected to hear the tree drumming like a telegraph pole.

It was so warm in the woods that she forgot that she sat there for shelter. But though the wind blew lightly, it blew from the east. In March the wind went round to the south-west. It brought rain. The bright, cold fields were dimmed and warm to walk in now. Like embers the wet beech-leaves smouldered in the woods.

All one day the wind had risen, and late in the evening it called her out. She went up to the top of Cubbey Ridge, past the ruined windmill that clattered with its torn sails. When she had come to the top of the Ridge she stopped, with difficulty holding herself upright. She felt the wind swoop down close to the earth. The moon was out hunting overhead, her pack of black and white hounds ranged over the sky. Moon and wind and clouds hunted an invisible quarry. The wind routed through the woods. Laura from the hill-top heard the different voices. The spent gusts left the beech-hangers throbbing like sea caverns through which the wave had passed; the fir plantation seemed to chant some never-ending rune.

Listening to these voices, another voice came to her ear—the far-off pulsation of a goods train labouring up a steep cutting. It was scarcely audible, more perceptible as feeling than as sound, but by its regularity it dominated all the other voices. It seemed to come nearer and nearer, to inform her like the drumming of blood in her ears. She began to feel defenceless, exposed to the possibility of an overwhelming terror. She listened intently, trying not to think. Though the noise came from an ordinary goods train, no amount of reasoning could stave off this terror. She must yield herself, yield up all her attention, if she would escape. It was a wicked sound. It expressed something eternally outcast and reprobated by man, stealthily trafficking by night, unseen in the dark clefts of the hills. Loud, separate, and abrupt, each pant of the engine trampled down her wits. The wind and the moon and the ranging cloud pack were not the only hunters abroad that night: something else was hunting among the hills, hunting slowly, deliberately, sure of its quarry.

Suddenly she remembered the goods yard at Paddington, and all her thoughts slid together again like a pack of hounds that have picked up the scent. They streamed faster and faster; she clenched her hands and prayed as when a child she had prayed in the hunting-field.

In the goods yard at Paddington she had almost pounced on the clue, the clue to the secret country of her mind. The country was desolate and half-lit, and she walked there alone, mistress of it, and mistress, too, of the terror that roamed over the blank fields and haunted round her. Here was country just so desolate and half-lit. She was alone, just as in her dreams, and the terror had come to keep her company, and crouched by her side, half in fawning, half in readiness to pounce. All this because of a goods train that laboured up a cutting. What was this cabal of darkness, suborning her own imagination to plot against her? What were these iron hunters doing near mournful, ever-weeping Paddington?

"Now! Now!" said the moon, and plunged towards her through the clouds.

Baffled, she stared back at the moon and shook her head. For a moment it had seemed as though the clue were found, but it had slid through her hands again. The train had reached the top of the cutting, with a shriek of delight it began to pour itself downhill. She smiled. It amused her to suppose it loaded with cabbages. Arrived at Paddington, the cabbages would be diverted to Covent Garden. But inevitably, and with all the augustness of due course, they would reach their bourne at Apsley Terrace. They would shed all their midnight devilry in the pot, and be served up to Henry and Caroline very pure and vegetable.

"Lovely! lovely!" she said, and began to descend the hill, for the night was cold. Though her secret had eluded her again, she did not mind. She knew that this time she had come nearer to catching it than ever before. If it were attainable she would run it to earth here, sooner or later. Great Mop was the likeliest place to find it.

The village was in darkness; it had gone to bed early, as good villages should. Only Miss Carloe's window was alight. Kind Miss Carloe, she would sit up till all hours tempting her hedgehog with bread-and-milk. Hedgehogs are nocturnal animals; they go out for walks at night, grunting, and shoving out their black snouts. "Thrice the brindled cat hath mewed; Thrice, and once the hedgepig whined. Harper cries, ' 'Tis time, 'tis time,' " She found the key under the half-brick, and let herself in very quietly. Only sleep sat up for her, waiting in the hushed house. Sleep took her by the hand, and convoyed her up the narrow stairs. She fell asleep almost as her head touched the pillow.

By the next day all this seemed very ordinary. She had gone out on a windy night and heard a goods train. There was nothing remarkable in that. It would have been a considerable adventure in London, but it was nothing in the Chilterns. Yet she retained an odd feeling of respect for what had happened, as though it had laid some command upon her that waited to be interpreted and obeyed. She thought it over, and tried to make sense of it. If it pointed to anything it pointed to Paddington. She did what she could; she wrote and invited Caroline to spend a day at Great Mop. She did not suppose that this was the right interpretation, but she could think of no other.

All the birds were singing as Laura went down the lane to meet Caroline's car. It was almost like summer, nothing could be more fortunate. Caroline was dressed in sensible tweeds. "It was raining when I left London," she said, and glanced severely at Laura's cotton gown.

"Was it?" said Laura. "It hasn't rained here." She stopped. She looked carefully at the blue sky. There was not a cloud to be seen. "Perhaps it will rain later on," she added. Caroline also looked at the sky, and said: "Probably."

Conversation was a little difficult, for Laura did not know how much she was still in disgrace. She asked after everybody in a rather guilty voice, and heard how emphatically they all throve, and what a pleasant, cheerful winter they had all spent. After that came the distance from Wickendon and the hour of departure. In planning the conduct of the day, Laura had decided to keep the church for after lunch. Before lunch she would show Caroline the view. She had vaguely allotted an hour and a half to the view, but it took scarcely twenty minutes. At least, that was the time it took walking up to the windmill and down again.

The view had taken no time at all. It was a clear day, and everything that could be seen was perceptible at the first glance.

Caroline was so stoutly equipped for country walking that Laura had not the heart to drag her up another hill. They visited the church instead. The church was more successful. Caroline sank on her knees and prayed. This gave Laura an opportunity to look round, for she had not been inside the church before. It was extremely narrow, and had windows upon the south side only, so that it looked like a holy corridor. Caroline prayed for some time, and Laura made the most of it. Presently she was able to lead Caroline down the corridor, murmuring: "That window was presented in 1901. There is rather a nice brass in this corner. That bit of carving is old, it is the Wise and the Foolish Virgins. Take care of the step."

One foolish Virgin pleased Laura as being particularly life-like. She stood a little apart from the group, holding a flask close to her ear, and shaking it. During lunch Laura felt that her stock of oil, too, was running very low. But it was providentially renewed, for soon after lunch a perfect stranger fell off a bicycle just outside Mrs. Leak's door and sprained her ankle. Laura and Caroline leapt up to succour her, and then there was a great deal of cold compress and hot tea and animation. The perfect stranger was a Secretary to a Guild. She asked Caroline if she did not think Great Mop a delightful nook, and Caroline cordially agreed. They went on discovering Committees in common till tea-time, and soon after went off together in Caroline's car. Just as Caroline stepped into the car she asked Laura if she had met any nice people in the neighbourhood.

"No. There aren't any nice people," said Laura. Wondering if the bicycle would stay like that, twined so casually round the driver's neck, she had released her attention one minute too soon.

As far as she knew this was her only slip throughout the day. It was a pity. But Caroline would soon forget it; she might not even have heard it, for the Secretary was talking loudly about Homes of Rest at the same moment. Still, it was a pity. She might have remembered Mr. Saunter, though perhaps she could not have explained him satisfactorily in the time.

She turned and walked slowly through the fields towards the poultry-farm. She could not settle down to complete solitude so soon after Caroline's departure. She would decline gradually, using Mr. Saunter as an intermediate step. He was feeding his poultry, going from pen to pen with a zinc wheelbarrow and a large wooden spoon. The birds flew round him; he had continually to stop and fend them off like a swarm of large midges. Sometimes he would grasp a specially bothering bird and throw it back into the pen as though it were a ball. She leant on the gate and watched him. This young man who had been a bank-clerk and a soldier walked with the easy, slow strides of a born countryman; he seemed to possess the earth with each step. No doubt but he was like Adam. And she, watching him from above —for the field sloped down from the gate to the pens—was like God. Did God, after casting out the rebel angels and before settling down to the peace of a heaven unpeopled of contradiction, use Adam as an intermediate step?

On his way back to the hut, Mr. Saunter noticed Laura. He came up and leant on his side of the gate. Though the sun had gone down, the air was still warm, and a disembodied daylight seemed to weigh upon the landscape like a weight of sleep. The birds which had sung all day now sang louder than ever.

"Hasn't it been a glorious day?" said Mr. Saunter.

"I have had my sister-in-law down," Laura answered. "She lives in London."

"My people," said Mr. Saunter, "all live in the Midlands."

"Or in Australia," he added after a pause.

Mr. Saunter, seen from above, walking among his flocks and heards—for even hens seemed ennobled into something Biblical by their relation to him—was an impressive figure. Mr. Saunter leaning on the gate was a pleasant, unaffected young man enough, but no more. Quitting him, Laura soon forgot him as completely as she had forgotten Caroline. Caroline was a tedious bluebottle; Mr. Saunter a gentle, furry brown moth; but she could brush off one as easily as the other.

Laura even forgot that she had invited the moth to settle again; to come to tea. It was only by chance that she had stayed indoors that afternoon, making currant scones. To amuse herself she had cut the dough into likenesses of the village people. Curious developments took place in the baking. Miss Carloe's hedgehog had swelled until it was almost as large as its mistress. The dough had run into it, leaving a great hole in Miss Carloe's side. Mr. Jones had a lump on his back, as though he were carrying the Black Dog in a bag; and a fancy portrait of Miss Larpent in her elegant youth and a tight-fitting sweeping amazon had warped and twisted until it was more like a gnarled thorn tree than a woman.

Laura felt slightly ashamed of her freak. It was unkind to play these tricks with her neighbours' bodies. But Mr. Saunter ate the strange shapes without comment, quietly splitting open the villagers and buttering them. He told her that he would soon lose the services of young Billy Thomas, who was going to Lazzard Court as a footman.

"I shouldn't think young Billy Thomas would make much of a footman," said Laura.

"I don't know," he answered consideringly. "He's very good at standing still."

Laura had brought her sensitive conscience into the country with her, just as she had brought her umbrella, though so far she had not remembered to use either. Now the conscience gave signs of life. Mr. Saunter was so nice, and had eaten up those derisive scones, innocently under the impression that they had been prepared for him; he had come with his gift of eggs, all kindness and forethought while she had forgotten his existence; and now he was getting up to go, thanking her and afraid that he had stayed too long. She had acted unworthily by this young man, so dignified and unassuming; she must do something to repair the slight she had put upon him in her own mind. She offered herself as a substitute for young Billy Thomas until Mr. Saunter could find some one else.

"I don't know anything about hens," she admitted. "But I am fond of animals, and I am very obedient."

It was agreed that she might go on the following day to help him with the trap-nesting, and see how she liked it.

At first Mr. Saunter would not allow her to do more than walk round with him upon planks specially put down to save her from the muddy places, pencil the eggs, and drink tea afterwards. But she came so punctually and showed such eagerness that as time went on she persuaded him into allowing her a considerable share in the work.

There was much to do, for it was a busy time of year. The incubators had fulfilled their time; Laura learnt how to lift out the newly-hatched chicks, damp, almost lifeless from their birth-throes, and pack them into baskets. A few hours after the chicks were plump and fluffy. They looked like bunches of primroses in the moss-lined baskets.

Besides mothering his chicks Mr. Saunter was busy with a great re-housing of the older birds. This was carried out after sundown, for the birds were sleepy then, and easier to deal with. If moved by day they soon revolted, and went back to their old pens. Even as it was there were always a few sticklers, roosting uncomfortably among the newcomers, or standing disconsolately before their old homes, closed against them.

Laura liked this evening round best of all. The April twilights were marvellously young and still. A slender moon soared in the green sky; the thick spring grass was heavy with dew, and the earth darkened about her feet while overhead it still seemed quite light. Mr. Saunter would disappear into the henhouse, a protesting squawking and scuffling would be heard; then he would emerge with hens under either arm. He showed Laura how to carry them, two at a time, their breasts in her hands, their wings held fast between her arm and her side. She would tickle the warm breasts, warm and surprisingly bony with quills under the soft plumage, and make soothing noises.

At first she felt nervous with the strange burden, so meek and inanimate one moment, so shrewish the next, struggling and beating with strong freed wings. However many birds Mr. Saunders might be carrying, he was always able to relieve her of hers. Immediately the termagant would subside, tamed by the large sure grasp, meek as a dove, with rigid dangling legs, and head turning sadly from side to side.

Laura never became as clever with the birds as Mr. Saunter. But when she had overcome her nervousness she managed them well enough to give her a great deal of pleasure. They nestled against her, held fast in the crook of her arm, while her fingers probed among the soft feathers and rigid quills of their breasts. She liked to feel their acquiescence, their dependence upon her. She felt wise and potent. She remembered the henwife in the fairy-tales, she understood now why kings and queens resorted to the henwife in their difficulties. The henwife held their destinies in the crook of her arm, and hatched the future in her apron. She was sister to the spaewife, and close cousin to the witch, but she practised her art under cover of henwifery; she was not, like her sister and her cousin, a professional. She lived unassumingly at the bottom of the king's garden, wearing a large white apron and very possibly her husband's cloth cap; and when she saw the king and queen coming down the gravel path she curtseyed reverentially, and pretended it was the eggs they had come about. She was easier of approach than the spaewife, who sat on a creepie and stared at the smouldering peats till her eyes were red and unseeing; or the witch, who lived alone in the wood, her cottage window all grown over with brambles. But though she kept up this pretence of homeliness she was not inferior in skill to the professionals. Even the pretence of homeliness was not quite so homely as it might seem. Laura knew that the Russian witches live in small huts mounted upon three giant hens' legs, all yellow and scaly. The legs can go; when the witch desires to move her dwelling the legs stalk through the forest, clattering against the trees, and printing long scars upon the snow.

Following Mr. Saunter up and down between the pens, Laura almost forgot where and who she was, so completely had she merged her personality into the henwife's. She walked back along the rutted track and down the steep lane as obliviously as though she were flitting home on a broomstick. All through April she helped Mr. Saunter. They were both sorry when a new boy applied for the job and her duties came to an end. She knew no more of Mr. Saunter at the close of this association than she had known at its beginning. It could scarcely be said even that she liked him any better, for from their first meeting she had liked him extremely. Time had assured the liking, and that was all. So well assured was it, that she felt perfectly free to wander away and forget him once more, certain of finding him as likeable and well liked as before whenever she might choose to return.

During her first months at Great Mop the moods of the winter landscape and the renewing of spring had taken such hold of her imagination that she thought no season could be more various and lovely. She had even written a slightly precious letter to Titus—for somehow correspondence with Titus was always rather attentive—declaring her belief that the cult of the summer months was a piece of cockney obtuseness, a taste for sweet things, and a preference for dry grass to strew their egg-shells upon. But with the first summer days and the first cowslips she learnt better. She had known that there would be cowslips in May; from the day she first thought of Great Mop she had promised them to herself. She had meant to find them early and watch the yellow blossoms unfolding upon the milky green stems. But they were beforehand with her, or she had watched the wrong fields. When she walked into the meadow it was bloomed over with cowslips, powdering the grass in variable plenty, here scattered, there clustered, innumerable as the stars in the Milky Way.

She knelt down among them and laid her face close to their fragrance. The weight of all her unhappy years seemed for a moment to weigh her bosom down to the earth; she trembled, understanding for the first time how miserable she had been; and in another moment she was released. It was all gone, it could never be again, and never had been. Tears of thankfulness ran down her face. With every breath she drew, the scent of the cowslips flowed in and absolved her.

She was changed, and knew it. She was humbler, and more simple. She ceased to triumph mentally over her tyrants, and rallied herself no longer with the consciousness that she had outraged them by coming to live at Great Mop. The amusement she had drawn from their disapproval was a slavish remnant, a derisive dance on the north bank of the Ohio. There was no question of forgiving them. She had not, in any case, a forgiving nature; and the injury they had done her was not done by them. If she were to start forgiving she must needs forgive Society, the

Law, the Church, the History of Europe, the Old Testament, great-great-aunt Salome and her prayer-book, the Bank of England, Prostitution, the Architect of Apsley Terrace, and half a dozen other useful props of civilisation. All she could do was to go on forgetting them. But now she was able to forget them without flouting them by her forgetfulness.

Throughout May and June and the first fortnight of July she lived in perfect idleness and contentment, growing every day more freckled and more rooted in peace. On July 17th she was disturbed by a breath from the world. Titus came down to see her. It was odd to be called Aunt Lolly again. Titus did not use the term often; he addressed his friends of both sexes and his relations of all ages as My Dear; but Aunt Lolly slipped out now and again.

There was no need to show Titus the inside of the church. There was no need even to take him up to the windmill and show him the view. He did all that for himself, and got it over before breakfast—for Titus breakfasted for three mornings at Great Mop. He had come for the day only, but he was too pleased to go back. He was his own master now, he had rooms in Bloomsbury and did not need even to send off a telegram. Mrs. Garland who let lodgings in the summer was able to oblige him with a bedroom, full of pincushions and earwigs and marine photographs; and Mrs. Trumpet gave him all the benefit of all the experience he invoked in the choice of a toothbrush. For three days he sat about with Laura, and talked of his intention to begin brewing immediately. He had refused to visit Italy with his mother—he had rejected several flattering invitations from editors—because brewing appealed to him more than anything else in the world. This, he said, was the last night out before the wedding. On his return to Bloomsbury he intended to let his rooms to an amiable Mahometan, and to apprentice himself to his family brewery until he had learnt the family trade.

Laura gave him many messages to Lady Place. It was clear before her in an early morning light. She could exactly recall the smell of the shrubbery, her mother flowing across the croquet lawn, her father's voice as he called up the dogs. She could see herself, too: her old self, for her present self had no part in the place. She did not suppose she would ever return there, although she was glad that Titus was faithful.

Titus departed. He wrote her a letter from Bloomsbury, saying that he had struck a good bargain with the Mahometan, and was off to Somerset. Ten days later she heard from Sibyl that he was coming to live at Great Mop. She had scarcely time to assemble her feelings about this before he was arrived.

PART 3

It was the third week in August. The weather was sultry; day after day Laura heard the village people telling each other that there was thunder in the air. Every evening they stood in the village street, looking upwards, and the cattle stood waiting in the fields. But the storm delayed. It hid behind the hills, biding its time.

Laura had spent the afternoon in a field, a field of unusual form, for it was triangular. On two sides it was enclosed by woodland, and because of this it was already darkening into a premature twilight, as though it were a room. She had been there for hours. Though it was sultry, she could not sit still. She walked up and down, turning savagely when she came to the edge of the field. Her limbs were tired, and she stumbled over the flints and matted couch-grass. Throughout the long afternoon a stock-dove had cooed in the wood. "Cool, cool, cool," it said, delighting in its green bower. Now it had ceased, and there was no life in the woods. The sky was covered with a thick uniform haze. No ray of the declining sun broke through it, but the whole heavens were beginning to take on a dull, brassy pallor. The long afternoon was ebbing away, stealthily, impassively, as though it were dying under an anaesthetic.

Laura had not listened to the stock-dove; she had not seen the haze thickening overhead. She walked up and down in despair and rebellion. She walked slowly, for she felt the weight of her chains. Once more they had been fastened upon her. She had worn them for many years, acquiescently, scarcely feeling their weight. Now she felt it. And, with their weight, she felt their familiarity, and the familiarity was worst of all. Titus had seen her starting out. He had cried: "Where are you off to, Aunt Lolly? Wait a minute, and I'll come too." She had feigned not to hear him and had walked on. She had not turned her head until she was out of the village, she expected at every moment to hear him come bounding up behind her. Had he done so, she thought she would have turned round and snarled at him. For she wanted, oh! how much she wanted, to be left alone for once. Even when she felt pretty sure that she had escaped she could not profit by her solitude, for Titus's voice still jangled on her nerves. "Where are you off to, Aunt Lolly? Wait a minute, and I'll come too." She heard his very tones, and heard intensely her own silence that had answered him. Too flustered to notice where she was going, she had followed a chance track until she found herself in this field where she had never been before. Here the track ended, and here she stayed.

The woods rose up before her like barriers. On the third side of the field was a straggling hedge; along it sprawled a thick bank of burdocks, growing with malignant profusion. It was an unpleasant spot. Bitterly she said to herself: "Well, perhaps he'll leave me alone here," and was glad of its unpleasantness. Titus could have all the rest: the green meadows, the hill-tops, the beech-woods dark and resonant as the inside of a sea-shell. He could walk in the greenest meadow and have dominion over it like a bull. He could loll his great body over the hill-tops, or rout silence out of the woods. They were hers, they were all hers, but she would give them all up to him and keep only this dismal field, and these coarse weeds growing out of an uncleansed soil. Any terms to be rid of him. But even on these terms she could not be rid of him, for all the afternoon he had been present in her thoughts, and his voice rang in her ears as distinctly as ever: "Wait a minute, and I'll come with you." She had not waited; but, nevertheless, he had come.

Actually, she knew—and the knowledge smote her—Titus, seeing her walk by unheeding, had picked up his book again and read on, reading slowly, and slowly drawing at his pipe, careless, intent, and satisfied. Perhaps he still sat by the open window. Perhaps he had wandered about, taking his book with him, and now was lying in the shade, still reading, or sleeping with his nose pressed into the grass, or with idle patience inveigling an ant to climb up a dry stalk. For this was Titus, Titus who had always been her friend. She had believed that she loved him; even when she heard that he was coming to live at Great Mop she had half thought that it might be rather nice to have him there. "Dearest Lolly," Sibyl had written from Italy, "I feel quite reconciled to this wild scheme of Tito's, since you will be there to keep an eye on him. Men are so helpless. Tito is so impracticable. A regular artist," etc.

The helpless artist had arrived, and immediately upon his arrival walked out to buy beer and raspberries. Sibyl might feel perfectly reconciled. No cat could jump into the most comfortable armchair more unerringly than Titus. "Such a nice young gentleman," said Mrs. Garland, smoothing his pyjamas with a voluptuous hand. "Such a nice young gentleman," said Miss Carloe, rubbing her finger over the milling of the new florin she received for the raspberries. "Such a nice young gentleman," said Mrs. Trumpet at the shop, and Mrs. Ward at the Lamb and Flag. All the white-aproned laps opened to dandle him. The infant Bacchus walked down the village street with his beer and his raspberries, bowing graciously to all Laura's acquaintances. That evening he supped with her and talked about Fuseli. Fuseli —pronounced Foozley—was a neglected figure of the utmost importance. The pictures, of course, didn't matter: Titus supposed there were some at the Tate. It was Fuseli the man, Fuseli the sign of his times, etc., that Titus was going to write about. It had been the ambition of his life to write a book about Fuseli, and his first visit to Great Mop convinced him that this was the perfect place to write it in. The secret, Titus said, of writing a good book was to be cut off from access to the reading-room of the British Museum. Laura said a little pettishly that if that were all Titus might have stayed in Bloomsbury, and written his book on Good Fridays. Titus demurred. Suppose he ran out of ink? No! Great Mop was the place. "Tomorrow," he added, "you must take me around and show me all your footpaths."

He left his pipe and tobacco pouch on the mantelpiece. They

lay there like the orb and sceptre of an usurping monarch. Laura dreamed that night that Fuseli had arrived at Mr. Saunter's poultry-farm, killed the hens, and laid out the field as a golf-course.

She heard a great deal about Fuseli during the next few days, while she was obediently showing Titus all her footpaths. It was hot, so they walked in the woods. The paths were narrow, there was seldom room for two to walk abreast, so Titus generally went in front, projecting his voice into the silence. She disliked these walks; she felt ashamed of his company; she thought the woods saw her with him and drew back scornfully to let them pass by together.

Titus was more tolerable in the village street. Indeed, at first she was rather proud of her nephew's success. After a week he knew everybody, and knew them far better than she did. He passed from the bar-parlour of the Lamb and Flag to the rustic woodwork of the rector's lawn. He subscribed to the bowling-green fund, he joined the cricket club, he engaged himself to give readings at the Institute during the winter evenings. He was invited to become a bell-ringer, and to read the lessons. He burgeoned with projects for Co-operative Blue Beverens, morris-dancing, performing *Coriolanus* with the Ancient Foresters, getting Henry Wappenshaw to come down and paint a village sign, inviting Pandora Williams and her rebeck for the Barleighs Flower Show. He congratulated Laura upon having discovered so unspoilt an example of the village community.

After the first fortnight he was less exuberant in the growth of his vast fronds. He was growing downwards instead, rooting into the soil. He began his book, and promised to stand godfather to the roadman's next child. When they went for walks together he would sometimes fall silent, turning his head from side to side to browse the warm scent of a clover field. Once, as they stood on the ridge that guarded the valley from the south-east, he said: "I should like to stroke it"—and he waved his hand towards the pattern of rounded hills embossed with rounded beech-woods. She felt a cold shiver at his words, and turned away her eyes from the landscape that she loved so jealously. Titus could never have spoken so if he had not loved it too. Love it as he might, with all the deep Willowes love for country sights and smells, love he never so intimately and soberly, his love must be a horror to her. It was different in kind from hers. It was comfortable, it was portable, it was a reasonable appreciative appetite, a possessive and masculine love. It almost estranged her from Great Mop that he should be able to love it so well, and express his love so easily. He loved the countryside as though it were a body.

She had not loved it so. For days at a time she had been unconscious of its outward aspect, for long before she saw it she had loved it and blessed it. With no earnest but a name, a few lines and letters on a map, and a spray of beech-leaves, she had trusted the place and staked everything on her trust. She had struggled to come, but there had been no such struggle for Titus. It was as easy for him to quit Bloomsbury for the Chilterns as for a cat to jump from a hard chair to a soft. Now after a little scrabbling and exploration he was curled up in the green lap and purring over the landscape. The green lap was comfortable. He meant to stay in it, for he knew where he was well off. It was so comfortable that he could afford to wax loving, praise its kindly slopes, stretch out a discriminating paw and pat it. But Great Mop was no more to him than any other likeable country lap. He liked it because he was in possession. His comfort apart, it was a place like any other place.

Laura hated him for daring to love it so. She hated him for daring to love it at all. Most of all she hated him for imposing his kind of love on her. Since he had come to Great Mop she had not been allowed to love in her own way. Commenting, pointing out, appreciating, Titus tweaked her senses one after another as if they were so many bell-ropes. He was a good judge of country things; little escaped him, he understood the points of a landscape as James his father had understood the points of a horse. This was not her way. She was ashamed at paying the countryside these horse-coping compliments. Day by day the spirit of the place withdrew itself further from her. The woods judged her by her company, and hushed their talk as she passed by with Titus. Silence heard them coming, and fled out of the fields, the hills locked up their thoughts, and became so many grassy mounds to be walked up and walked down. She was being boycotted, and she knew it. Presently she would not know it any more. For her too Great Mop would be a place like any other place, a pastoral landscape where an aunt walked out with her nephew.

Nothing was left her but this sour field. Even this was not truly hers, for here also Titus walked beside her and called her Aunt Lolly. She was powerless against him. He had no idea how he had havocked her peace of mind, he was making her miserable in the best of faith. If he could guess, or if she could tell him, what ruin he carried with him, he would have gone away. She admitted that, even in her frenzy of annoyance. Titus had a kind heart, he meant her nothing but good. Besides, he could easily find another village, other laps were as smooth and as green. But that would never happen. He would never guess. It would never occur to him to look for resentment in her face, or to speculate upon the mood of any one he knew so well. And she would never be able to tell him. When she was with him she came to heel and resumed her old employment of being Aunt Lolly. There was no way out.

In vain she had tried to escape, transient and delusive had been her ecstasies of relief. She had thrown away twenty years of her life like a handful of old rags, but the wind had blown them back again, and dressed her in the old uniform. The wind blew steadily from the old quarter; it was the same east wind that chivied bits of waste paper down Apsley Terrace. And she was the same old Aunt Lolly, so useful and obliging and negligible.

The field was full of complacent witnesses. Titus had let them in. Henry and Caroline and Sibyl, Fancy and Marion and Mr. Wolf-Saunders stood round about her; they recognised her and cried out: "Why, Aunt Lolly, what are you doing here?" And Dunlop came stealthily up behind her and said: "Excuse me, Miss Lolly, I thought you might like to know that the warning gong has gone!" She stood at bay, trembling before them, shaken and sick with the grinding anger of the slave. They were come out to recapture her, they had tracked her down and closed her in. They had let her run a little way—that was all—for they knew they could get her back when they chose. They had stood grinning behind the bushes when she wept in the cowslip field.

It had been quite entertaining to watch her, for she had taken herself and her freedom so seriously, happy and intent as a child keeping house under the table. They had watched awhile in their condescending grown-up way, and now they approached her to end the game. Henry was ready to overlook her rebellion, his lips glistened with magnanimity; Caroline and Sibyl came smiling up to twine their arms round her waist; the innocent children of Fancy and Marion stretched out their hands to her and called her Aunt Lolly. And Titus, who had let them in, stood a little apart like a showman, and said, "You see, it's all right. She's just the same."

They were all leagued against her. They were come out to seize on her soul. They were invulnerably sure of their prey.

"No!" she cried out, wildly clapping her hands together. "No! You shan't get me. I won't go back. I won't. . . . Oh! Is there *no* help?"

The sound of her voice frightened her. She heard its desperate echo rouse the impassive wood. She raised her eyes and looked round her. The field was empty. She trembled, and felt cold. The sultry afternoon was over. Dusk and a clammy chill seemed to creep out from among the darkening trees that waited there so stilly. It was as though autumn had come in the place of twilight, and the colourless dark hue of the field dazzled before her eyes. She stood in the middle of the field, waiting for an answer to her cry. There was no answer. And yet the silence that had followed it had been so intent, so deliberate, that it was like a pledge. If any listening power inhabited this place; if any grimly favourable power had been evoked by her cry; then surely a compact had been made, and the pledge irrevocably given.

She walked slowly towards the wood. She was incredibly fatigued; she could scarcely drag one foot after the other. Her mind was almost a blank. She had forgotten Titus; she had forgotten the long afternoon of frenzy and bewilderment. Everything was unreal except the silence that followed after her outcry. As she came to the edge of the wood she heard the mutter of heavy foliage. "No!" the woods seemed to say. "No! We will not let you go."

She walked home unheedingly, almost as though she were walking in her sleep. The chance contact with a briar or a tall weed sent drowsy tinglings through her flesh. It was with surprise that she looked down from a hillside and saw the crouched roofs of the village before her.

The cottage was dark; Laura remembered that Mrs. Leak had said that she was going out to a lecture at the Congregational Hall that evening. As she unlocked the door she smiled at the thought of having the house all to herself. The passage was cool and smelt of linoleum. She heard the kitchen clock ticking pompously as if it, too, were pleased to have the house to itself. When Mrs. Leak went out and left the house empty, she was careful to lock the door of Laura's parlour and to put the key under the case with the stuffed owl. Laura slid her fingers into the dark slit between the bottom of the case and the bracket. The key was cold and sleek; she liked the feel of it, and the obliging way it turned in the lock.

As she entered the room, she sniffed. It smelt a little fusty from being shut up on a warm evening. Her nose distinguished Titus's tobacco and the hemp agrimony that she had picked the day before. But there was something else—a faintly animal smell which she could not account for. She threw up the rattling window and turned to light the lamp. Under the green shade the glow whitened and steadied itself. It illuminated the supper-table prepared for her, the shining plates, the cucumber and the radishes, and neat slices of cold veal and the glistening surface of the junket. Nameless and patient, these things had been waiting in the dark, waiting for her to come back and enjoy them. They met her eye with self-possession. They had been sure that she would be pleased to see them. Her spirits shot up, as the flame of the lamp had cleared and steadied itself a moment before. She forgot all possibility of distress. She thought only of the moment, and of the certainty with which she possessed it. In this mood of sleepy exaltation she stood and looked at the supper-table. Long before she had come to Great Mop, the shining plates had come. Four of them, she knew from Mrs. Leak, had been broken; one was too much scorched in the oven to be presentable before her. But these had survived that she might come and eat off them. The quiet cow that had yielded so quietly the milk for her junket had wandered in the fields of Great Mop long before she saw them, or saw them in fancy. The radishes and cucumbers sprang from old and well-established Great Mop families. Her coming had been foreseen, her way had been prepared. Great Mop was infallibly part of her life, and she part of the life of Great Mop. She took up a plate and looked at the maker's mark. It had come from Stoke-on-Trent, where she had never been. Now it was here, waiting for her to eat off it. "The Kings of Tarshish shall bring gifts," she murmured.

As she spoke, she felt something move by her foot. She glanced down and saw a small kitten. It crouched by her foot, biting her shoelace, and lashing its tail from side to side. Laura did not like cats; but this creature, so small, so intent, and so ferocious, amused her into kindly feelings. "How did you come here? Did you come in through the keyhole?" she asked, and bent down to stroke it. Scarcely had she touched its hard little head when it writhed itself round her hand, noiselessly clawing and biting, and kicking with its hind legs. She felt frightened by an attack so fierce and irrational, and her fears increased as she tried to shake off the tiny weight. At last she freed her hand, and looked at it. It was covered with fast-reddening scratches, and as she looked she saw a bright round drop of blood ooze out from one of them. Her heart gave a violent leap, and seemed to drop dead in her bosom. She gripped the back of a chair to steady herself and stared at the kitten. Abruptly pacified, it had curled itself into a ball and fallen asleep. Its lean ribs heaved with a rhythmic tide of sleep. As she stared she saw its pink tongue flicker for one moment over its lips. It slept like a suckling.

Not for a moment did she doubt. But so deadly, so complete was the certainty that it seemed to paralyse her powers of understanding, like a snake-bite in the brain. She continued to stare at the kitten, scarcely knowing what it was that she knew. Her heart had begun to beat once more, slowly, slowly; her ears were dizzied with a shrill wall of sound, and her flesh hung on her clammy and unreal. The animal smell that she had noticed when first she entered the room now seemed overwhelmingly rank. It smelt as if walls and floor and ceiling had been smeared with the juice of bruised fennel.

She, Laura Willowes, in England, in the year 1922, had entered into a compact with the Devil. The compact was made, and affirmed, and sealed with the round red seal of her blood. She remembered the woods, she remembered her wild cry for help, and the silence that had followed it, as though in ratification. She heard again the mutter of heavy foliage, foliage dark and heavy as the wings of night birds. "No! No!"—she heard the brooding voice—"We will not let you go." At ease, released from her cares, she had walked homeward. Hedge and coppice and solitary tree, and the broad dust-coloured faces of meadowsweet and hemlock had watched her go by, knowing. The dusk had closed her in, brooding over her. Every shadow, every deepened grove had observed her from under their brows of obscurity. All knew, all could bear witness. Couched within the wood, sleeping through the long sultry afternoon, had lain the Prince of Darkness; sleeping, or meditating some brooding thunderstorm of his own. Her voice of desperate need had aroused him, his silence had answered her with a pledge. And now, as a sign of the bond between them, he had sent his emissary. It had arrived before her, a rank breath, a harsh black body in her locked room. The kitten was her familiar spirit, that already had greeted its mistress, and sucked her blood.

She shut her eyes and stood very still, hollowing her mind to admit this inconceivable thought. Suddenly she started. There was a voice in the room.

It was the kitten's voice. It stood beside her, mewing plaintively. She turned, and considered it—her familiar. It was the smallest and thinnest kitten that she had ever seen. It was so young that it could barely stand steadily upon its legs. She caught herself thinking that it was too young to be taken from its mother. But the thought was ridiculous. Probably it had no mother, for it was the Devil's kitten, and sucked, not milk, but blood. But for all that, it looked very like any other young starveling of its breed. Its face was peaked and its ribs stood out under the dishevelled fluff of its sides. Its mew was disproportionately piercing and expressive. Strange that anything so small and weak should be the Devil's Officer, plenipotentiary of such a power. Strange that she should stand trembling and amazed before a little rag-and-bone kitten with absurdly large ears.

Its anxious voice besought her, its pale eyes were fixed upon her face. She could not but feel sorry for anything that seemed so defenceless and castaway. Poor little creature, no doubt it missed the Devil, its warm nest in his shaggy flanks, its play with imp companions. Now it had been sent out on its master's business, sent out too young into the world, like a slavey from an Institution. It had no one to look to now but her, and it implored her help, as she but a little while ago had implored its Master's. Her pity overcame her terror. It was no longer her familiar, but a foundling. And it was hungry. Must it have more blood, or would milk do? Milk was more suitable for its tender age. She walked to the table, poured out a saucer full of milk and set it down on the floor. The kitten drank as though it were starving. Crouched by the saucer with dabbled nose, it shut its pale eyes and laid back its ears to lap, while shoots of ecstasy ran down its protuberant spine and stirred the tip of its tail. As Laura watched it the last of her repugnance was overcome. Though she did not like cats she thought that she would like this one. After all, it was pleasant to have some small thing to look after. Many lonely women found great companionship with even quite ordinary cats. This creature could never grow up a beauty, but no doubt it would be intelligent. When it had cleaned the saucer with large final sweeps of its tongue, the kitten looked up at her. "Poor lamb!" she said, and poured out the rest of the milk. It drank less famishingly now. Its tail lay still, its body relaxed, settling down on to the floor, overcome by the peaceful weight within. At last, having finished its meal, it got up and walked round the room, stretching either hind leg in turn as it walked. Then, without a glance at Laura, it lay down, coiled and uncoiled, scratched itself nonchalantly and fell asleep. She watched it awhile and then picked it up, all limp and unresisting, and settled it in her lap. It scarcely opened its eyes, but burrowing once or twice with its head against her knees resumed its slumber.

Nursing the kitten in her lap Laura sat thinking. Her thoughts were of a different colour now. This trustful contentment, this warmth between her knees, lulled her by example. She had never wavered for an instant from her conviction that she had made a compact with the Devil; now she was growing accustomed to the thought. She perceived that throughout the greater part of her life she had been growing accustomed to it; but insensibly, as people throughout the greater part of their lives grow accustomed to the thought of their death. When it comes, it is a surprise to them. But the surprise does not last long, perhaps but for a minute or two. Her surprise also was wearing off. Quite soon, and she would be able to fold her hands upon it, as the hands of the dead are folded upon their surprised hearts. But *her* heart still beat, beat at its everyday rate, a small regular pulse impelling her momently forward into the new witch life that lay before her. Since her flesh had already accepted the new order of things, and was proceeding so methodically towards the future, it behoved her, so she thought, to try to readjust her spirit.

She raised her eyes, and looked at her room, the green-painted walls with the chairs sitting silently round. She felt herself inhabiting the empty house. Through the unrevealing square of the window her mind looked at the view. About the empty house was the village, and about the village the hills, neighbourly under their covering of night. Room, house, village, hills encircled her like the rings of a fortification. This was her domain, and it was to keep this inviolate that she had made her compact with the Devil. She did not know what the price might be, but she was sure of the purchase. She need not fear Titus now, nor any of the Willoweses. They could not drive her out, or enslave her spirit any more, nor shake her possession of the place she had chosen. While she lived her solitudes were hers inalienably; she and the kitten, the witch and the familiar, would live on at Great Mop, growing old together, and hearing the owls hoot from the winter trees. And after? Murk! But what else had there ever been? Those green grassy hills in the churchyard were too high to be seen over. What man can stand on their summit and look beyond?

She felt neither fear nor disgust. A witch of but a few hours' standing, she rejected with the scorn of the initiate all the bugaboo surmises of the public. She looked with serene curiosity at the future, and saw it but little altered from what she had hoped and planned. If she had been called upon to decide in cold blood between being an aunt and being a witch, she might have been overawed by habit and the cowardice of compunction. But in the moment of election, under the stress and turmoil of the hunted Lolly as under a covering of darkness, the true Laura had settled it all unerringly. She had known where to turn. She had been like the girl in the fairy tale whose godmother gave her a little nutshell box and told her to open it in the hour of utter distress. Unsurmised by others, and half forgotten by the girl, the little nutshell box abided its time; and in the hour of utter distress it opened of itself. So, unrealised, had Laura been carrying her talisman in her pocket. She was a witch by vocation. Even in the old days of Lady Place the impulse had stirred in her. What else had set her upon her long solitary walks, her quests for powerful and forgotten herbs, her brews and distillations? In London she had never had the heart to take out her still. More urgent for being denied this innocent service, the ruling power of her life had assaulted her with dreams and intimations, calling her imagination out from the warm safe room to wander in darkened fields and by desolate sea-boards, through marshes and fens, and along the outskirts of brooding woods. It had haled her to Wapping and to the Jews' Burying Ground, and then, ironically releasing her, had left her to mourn and find her way back to Apsley Terrace. How she had come to Great Mop she could not say; whether it was of her own will, or whether, exchanging threatenings and mockeries for sweet persuasions, Satan had at last taken pity upon her bewilderment, leading her by the hand into the flower-shop in the Moscow Road; but from the moment of her arrival there he had never been far off. Sure of her—she supposed—he had done little for nine months but watch her. Near at hand but out of sight the loving huntsman couched in the woods, following her with his eyes. But all the time, whether couched in the woods or hunting among the hills, he drew closer. He was hidden in the well when she threw in the map and the guide-book. He sat in the oven, teaching her what power she might have over the shapes of men. He followed her and Mr. Saunter up and down between the henhouses. He was nearest of all upon the night when she climbed Cubbey Ridge, so near then that she acknowledged his presence and was afraid. That night, indeed, he must have been within a hand's-breadth of her. But her fear had kept him at bay, or else he had not chosen to take her just then, preferring to watch until he could overcome her mistrust and lure her into his hand. For Satan is not only a huntsman. His interest in mankind is that of a skilful and experienced naturalist. Even human sportsmen at the end of their span sometimes declare that to potter about in the woods is more amusing than to sit behind a butt and shoot driven grouse. And Satan, who has hunted from eternity, a little jaded moreover by the success of his latest organised Flanders battue, might well feel that his interest in a Solitary Snipe like Laura was but sooner or later to measure the length of her nose. Yet hunt he must; it is his destiny, and whether he hunts with a gun or a butterfly net, sooner or later the chase must end. All finalities, whether good or evil, bestow a feeling of relief; and now, understanding how long the chase had lasted, Laura felt a kind of satisfaction at having been popped into the bag.

She was distracted from these interesting thoughts by the sounds of footsteps. The kitten heard them too, and sat up, yawning. The Leaks coming back from their lecture, thought Laura. But it was Titus. Inserting his head and shoulders through the window he asked if he could come in and borrow some milk.

"I haven't any milk," said Laura, "but come in all the same."

She began to tickle the kitten behind the ears in order to reassure it. By lamplight Titus's head seemed even nearer to the ceiling, it was a relief to her sense of proportion when he sat down. His milk, he explained, the jugful which Mrs. Garland left on the sitting-room table for his nightly Ovaltine, had curled into a sort of unholy junket. This he attributed to popular education, and the spread of science among dairy-farmers; in other words, Mr. Dodbury had overdone the preservative.

"I don't think it's science," said Laura. "More likely to be the weather. It was very sultry this afternoon."

"I saw you starting out. I had half a mind to come with you, but it was too hot to be a loving nephew. Where did you go?"

"Up to the windmill."

"Did you find the wind?"

"No."

"You weren't going in the direction of the windmill when I saw you."

"No. I changed my mind. About the milk," she continued (Titus had come for milk. Perhaps, being reminded that he had come in vain, he would go. She was growing sleepy): "I'm sorry, but I have none left. I gave it all to the kitten."

"I've been remarking the kitten. He's new, isn't he? You ugly little devil!"

The kitten lay on her knees quite quietly. It regarded Titus with its pale eyes, and blinked indifferently. It was only waiting for him to go, Laura thought, to fall asleep again.

"Where has it come from? A present from the water-butt?"

"I don't know. I found it here when I came back for supper."

"It's a plain-headed young Grimalkin. Still, I should keep it if I were you. It will bring you luck."

"I don't think one has much option about keeping a cat," said Laura. "If it wants to stay with me it shall."

"It looks settled enough. Do keep it, Aunt Lolly. A woman looks her best with a cat on her knees."

Laura bowed.

"What will you call it?"

Into Laura's memory came a picture she had seen long ago in one of the books at Lady Place. The book was about the persecution of the witches, and the picture was a woodcut of Matthew Hopkins the witch-finder. Wearing a large hat he stood among a coven of witches, bound cross-legged upon their stools. Their confessions came out of their mouths upon scrolls. "My imp's name is Ilemauzar," said one; and another imp at the bottom of the page, an alert, ill-favoured cat, so lean and muscular that it looked like a skinned hare, was called Vinegar Tom.

"I shall call it Vinegar," she answered.

"Vinegar!" said Titus. "How do you like your name?"

The kitten pricked up its ears. It sprang from Laura's knee

and began to fence with Titus's shadow, feinting and leaping back. Laura watched it a little apprehensively, but it did him no harm. It had awakened in a playful frame of mind after its long sleep, that was all. When Titus had departed it followed Laura to her bedroom, and as she undressed it danced round her, patting at her clothes as they fell.

In the morning the kitten roused her by mewing to be let out. She awoke from a profound and dreamless sleep. It took her a little time to realise that she had a kitten in her bedroom, a kitten of no ordinary kind. However it was behaving quite like an ordinary kitten now, so she got out of bed and let it out by the back door. It was early; no one was stirring. The kitten disappeared with dignity among the cabbages, and Laura turned her thoughts backward to the emotions of overnight. She tried to recall them, but could not; she could only recall the fact that overnight she had felt them. The panic that then had shaken her flesh was no more actual than a last winter's gale. It had been violent enough while it lasted, an invisible buffeting, a rending of life from its context. But now her memory presented it to her as a cold slab of experience, like a slab of pudding that had lain all night solidifying in the larder. This was no matter. Her terror had been an incident; it had no bearing upon her future, could she now recall it to life it would have no message for her. But she regretted her inability to recapture the mood that had followed upon it, when she sat still and thought so wisely about Satan. Those meditations had seemed to her of profound import. She had sat at her Master's feet, as it were, admitted to intimacy, and gaining the most valuable insight into his character. But that was gone too. Her thoughts, recalled, seemed to be of the most commonplace nature, and she felt that she knew very little about the Devil.

Meanwhile there was the kitten, an earnest that she should know more.

"Vinegar!" she called, and heard its answer, a drumming scramble among the cabbage leaves. She wished that Vinegar would impart some of his mind to her instead of being so persistently and genially kittenish. But he was a familiar, no doubt of it. And she was a witch, the inheritrix of aged magic, spells rubbed smooth with long handling, and the mistress of strange powers that got into Titus's milk-jug. For no doubt that was the beginning, and a very good beginning, too. Well begun is half-done; she could see Titus bending over his suit-case. The Willowes tradition was very intolerant of pease under its mattress.

Though she tried to think clearly about the situation—grapple, she remembered, had been Caroline's unpleasantly strenuous word—her attention kept sidling off to other things: the sudden oblique movements of the water-drops that glistened on the cabbage leaves, or the affinity between the dishevelled brown hearts of the sunflowers and Mrs. Leak's scrubbing-brush, propped up on the kitchen window-sill. It must have rained heavily during the night. The earth was moist and swelled, and the air so fresh that it made her yawn. Her limbs were heavy, and the contentment of the newly-awakened was upon her. All night she had bathed in nothingness, and now she was too recently emerged from that absolving tide to take much interest in what lay upon its banks. Her eyelids began to droop, and calling the kitten she went back to bed again and soon fell asleep.

She was asleep when Mrs. Leak brought her morning tea.

Mrs. Leak said: "Did the thunder keep you awake, miss?"

Laura shook her head. "I never even heard it."

Mrs. Leak looked much astonished. "It's well to have a good conscience," she remarked.

Laura stretched herself, sat up in bed, and began to tell Mrs. Leak about the kitten. This seemed to be her real awakening. The other was a dream.

Mrs. Leak was quite prepared to welcome the kitten; that was, provided her old Jim made no unpleasantness. Jim was not Mr. Leak, but a mottled marmalade cat, very old and rather shabby. Laura could not imagine him making any unpleasantness, but Mrs. Leak estimated his character rather differently. Jim thought himself quite a Great I Am, she said.

After breakfast Laura and Vinegar were called into the kitchen for the ceremony of introduction. Jim was doing a little washing. His hind leg was stuck straight up, out of the way, while he attended to the pit of his stomach. Nothing could have been more suitable than Vinegar's modest and deferential approach. Jim gave him one look and went on licking. Mrs. Leak said that all would be well between them; Jim always kept himself to himself, but she could see that the old cat had taken quite a fancy to Miss Willowes's kitten. She promised Vinegar some of Jim's rabbit for dinner. Mrs. Leak did not hold the ordinary view of country people that cats must fend for themselves. "They're as thoughtful as we," she said. "Why should they eat mouse unless they want to?" She was continually knocking at the parlour door with tit-bits for Vinegar, but she was scrupulous that Laura should bestow them with her own hand.

Since Titus had come to Great Mop Laura had seen little of Mrs. Leak. Mrs. Leak knew what good manners were; she had not been a housemaid at Lazzard Court for nothing. Taken separately, either Titus or his aunt might be human beings, but in conjunction they became gentry. Mrs. Leak remembered her position and withdrew to it, firmly. Laura saw this and was sorry. She made several attempts to persuade Mrs. Leak out from behind her white apron, but nothing came of them, and she knew that while Titus was in the village nothing would. Not that Mrs. Leak did not like Titus; she approved of him highly; and it was exactly her approval that made her barricade of respect so insuperable. But where Laura had failed, the kitten succeeded. From the moment that Jim sanctioned her kindly opinion of him, Mrs. Leak began to thaw. Laura knew better than to make a fuss over this turn in the situation; she took a leaf out of the Devil's book and lay low, waiting for a decisive advance; and presently it came. Mrs. Leak asked if Miss Willowes would care to come out for a stroll one evening; it was pleasant to get a breath of air before bedtime. Miss Willowes would like nothing better; that very evening would suit her if Mrs. Leak had nothing else to do. Mrs. Leak said that she would get the washing-up done as soon as possible, and after that she would be at Miss Willowes's disposal. However, it was nearly half-past ten before Mrs. Leak knocked on the parlour door. Laura had ceased to expect her, supposing that Mr. Leak or some household accident had claimed her, but she was quite as ready to go out for a walk as to go to bed, and Mrs. Leak made no reference to the lateness of the hour. Indeed, according to the Great Mop standard, the hour was not particularly late. Although the night was dark, Laura noticed that quite a number of the inhabitants were standing about in the street.

They walked down the road in silence as far as the milestone, and turned into the track that went up the hillside and past the wood. Others had turned that way also. The gate stood open, and voices sounded ahead. It was then that Laura guessed the truth, and turned to her companion.

"Where are you taking me?" she said. Mrs. Leak made no answer, but in the darkness she took hold of Laura's hand. There was no need for further explanation. They were going to the Witches' Sabbath. Mrs. Leak was a witch too; a matronly witch like Agnes Sampson, she would be Laura's chaperone. The night was full of voices. Padding rustic footsteps went by them in the dark. When they had reached the brow of the hill a faint continuous sound, resembling music, was borne towards them by the light wind. Laura remembered how young Billy Thomas, suffering from toothache, had played all night upon his mouth-organ. She laughed. Mrs. Leak squeezed her hand.

The meeting-place was some way off; by the time they reached it Laura's eyes had grown accustomed to the darkness. She could see a crowd of people walking about in a large field; lights of some sort were burning under a hedge, and one or two paper garlands were looped over the trees. When she first caught sight of them, the assembled witches and warlocks seemed to be dancing, but now the music had stopped and they were just walking about. There was something about their air of disconnected jollity which reminded Laura of a Primrose League gala and fête. A couple of bullocks watched the Sabbath from an adjoining field.

Laura was denied the social gift, she had never been good at enjoying parties. But this, she hoped, would be a different and more exhilarating affair. She entered the field in a most propitious frame of mind, which not even Mr. Gurdon, wearing a large rosette like a steward's and staring rudely and searchingly at each comer before he allowed them to pass through the gate, was able to check.

"Old Goat!" exclaimed Mrs. Leak in a voice of contemptuous amusement after they had passed out of Mr. Gurdon's hearing. "He thinks he can boss us here, just as he does in the village."

"Is Mr. Jones here?" inquired Laura.

Mrs. Leak shook her head and laughed.

"Mr. Gurdon doesn't allow him to come."

"I suppose he doesn't think it suitable for a clergyman."

Perhaps it was as well that Mr. Gurdon had such strict views. In spite of the example of Mr. Lowis, that old reading parson, it might be a little awkward if Mr. Jones were allowed to attend the Sabbath.

But that apparently was not the reason. Mrs. Leak was beginning to explain when she broke off abruptly, coughed in a respectful way, and dropped a deep curtsey. Before them stood an old lady, carrying herself like a queen, and wearing a mackintosh that would have disgraced a tinker's drab. She acknowledged Mrs. Leak's curtsey with an inclination of the head, and turned to Laura.

"I am Miss Larpent. And you, I think, must be Miss Willowes."

The voice that spoke was clear as a small bell and colourless as if time had bleached it of every human feeling save pride. The hand that rested in Laura's was light as a bird's claw; a fine glove encased it like a membrane, and through the glove Laura felt the slender bones and the sharp-faceted rings.

"Long ago," continued Miss Larpent, "I had the pleasure of meeting your great-uncle, Commodore Willowes."

Good heavens, thought Laura in a momentary confusion, was great-uncle Demetrius a warlock? For Miss Larpent was so perfectly witchlike that it seemed scarcely possible that she should condescend to ordinary gentlemen.

Apparently Miss Larpent could read Laura's thoughts.

"At Cowes," she added, reassuringly.

Laura raised her eyes to answer, but Miss Larpent had disappeared. Where she had stood, stood Miss Carloe, mincing and bridling, as though she would usurp the other's gentility. Over her face she wore a spotted veil. Recognising Laura she put on an air of delighted surprise and squeaked like a bat, and immediately she too edged away and was lost in the darkness.

Then a young man whom she did not know came up to Laura and put his arm respectfully round her waist. She found herself expected to dance. She could not hear any music, but she danced as best she could, keeping time to the rhythm of his breath upon her cheek. Their dance was short, she supposed she had not acquitted herself to her partner's satisfaction, for after a few turns he released her, and left her standing by the hedge. Not a word had passed between them. Laura felt that she ought to say something, but she could not think of a suitable opening. It was scarcely possible to praise the floor.

A familiar discouragement began to settle upon her spirits. In spite of her hopes she was not going to enjoy herself. Even as a witch, it seemed, she was doomed to social failure, and her first Sabbath was not going to open livelier vistas than were opened by her first ball. She remembered her dancing days in Somerset, Hunt Balls, and County Balls in the draughty Assembly Rooms. With the best intentions she had never managed to enjoy them. The first hour was well enough, but after that came increasing listlessness and boredom; the effort, when one danced again with the same partner, not to say the same things, combined with the obligation to say something rather like them, the control of eyelids, the conversion of yawns into smiles, the humbling consciousness that there was nothing to look forward to except the drive home. That was pleasant, and so was the fillip of supper at the drive's end, and the relief of yielding at last to an unfeigned hunger and sleepiness. But these were by-blow joys; of the delights for which balls are ordained she knew nothing.

She watched the dancers go by and wondered what the enchantment was which they felt and she could not. What made them come out in the middle of the night, loop paper garlands over the trees, light a row of candles in the ditch, and then, friends and enemies and indifferents, go bumping round on the rough grass? That fatal comparison with the Primrose League recurred to her. She was not entertained, so she blamed the entertainment. But the fault lay with her, she had never been good at parties, she had not got the proper Sabbath-keeping spirit. Miss Larpent was enjoying herself; Laura saw the bonnet whisk past. But doubtless Miss Larpent had enjoyed herself at Cowes.

These depressing thoughts were interrupted by red-haired Emily, who came spinning from her partner's arms, seized hold of Laura and carried her back into the dance. Laura liked dancing with Emily; the pasty-faced and anaemic young slattern whom she had seen dawdling about the village danced with a fervour that annihilated every misgiving. They whirled faster and faster, fused together like two suns that whirl and blaze in a single destruction. A strand of the red hair came undone and brushed across Laura's face. The contact made her tingle from head to foot. She shut her eyes and dived into obliviousness—with Emily for a partner she could dance until the gunpowder ran out of the heels of her boots. Alas! this happy ending was not to be, for at the height of their performance Emily was snatched away by Mr. Jowl, the horse-doctor. Laura opened her eyes and saw the pale face disappearing in the throng as the moon sinks into the clouds.

Emily was in great request, and no wonder. Like a torch she was handed on from one to another, and every mutation shook down some more hair. The Sabbath was warming up nicely now, every one was jigging it, even Laura. For a while Mrs. Leak kept up a semblance of chaperonage. Suddenly appearing at Laura's elbow she would ask her if she were enjoying herself, and glancing at her would slip away before she could answer. Or with vague gestures she indicated some evasively bowing partner, male or female; and silently Laura would give her hand and be drawn into the dance, presently to be relinquished or carried off by some one else.

The etiquette of a Sabbath appeared to consist of one rule only: to do nothing for long. Partners came and went, figures and conformations were in a continual flux. Sometimes the dancers were coupled, sometimes they jigged in a circle round some specially agile performer, sometimes they all took hands and galloped about the field. Half-way through a very formal quadrille presided over by the Misses Larpent they fell abruptly to playing Fox and Geese. In spite of Mr. Gurdon's rosette there was no Master of Ceremonies. A single mysterious impulse seemed to govern the company. They wheeled and manœuvred like a flock of starlings.

After an hour or two of this Laura felt dizzy and bewildered. Taking advantage of the general lack of formality she tore herself from Mr. Gurdon's arms, not to dance with another, but to slip away and sit quietly in the hedge.

She wondered where the music came from. She had heard it quite clearly as she came over the hill, but upon entering the field she had lost it. Now as she watched the others she heard it once more. When they neared it grew louder, when they retreated into the darkness it faded with them, as though the sound issued from the dancers themselves, and hung, a droning exhalation, above their heads. It was an odd kind of music, a continuous high shapeless blurr of sound. It was something like mosquitoes in a hot bedroom, and something like a distant threshing machine. But besides this, it had a faintly human quality, a metallic breathing as of trombones marking the measure; and when the dancers took hands and revolved in a leaping circle the music leaped and pounded with them, so much like the steam-organ music of a merry-go-round that for a moment Laura thought that they were riding on horses and dragons, bobbing up and down on crested dragons with heads like cocks, and horses with blood-red nostrils.

The candles burnt on in the dry ditch. Though the boughs of the thorn-trees moved above them and grated in the night-wind, the candle flames flowed steadily upwards. Thus lit from below, the dancers seemed of more than human stature, their bodies extending into the darkness as if in emulation of their gigantic upcast shadows. The air was full of the smell of bruised grass.

Mrs. Leak had forgotten Laura now. She was dancing the Highland Schottische with a lean young man whose sleeves were rolled up over his tattooed forearms. The nails in his boots shone in the candle-light, and a lock of hair hung over his eye. Mrs. Leak danced very well. Her feet flickered to and fro as nimbly as a tongue. At the turn of the figure she tripped forward to be caught up and swung round on the young man's arm. Though her feet were off the ground they twitched with the movements of the dance, and set down again they took up the uninterrupted measure. Laura watched her with admiration. Even at a Witches' Sabbath Mrs. Leak lost none of her respectability. Her white apron was scarcely crumpled, she was as self-contained as a cat watching a mouse, and her eyes dwelt upon the young man's face as though she were listening to a sermon.

She preserved her dignity better than some of the others did. Mr. Gurdon stood by himself, stamping his foot and tossing his head, more like the farmer's bull than ever. Miss Carloe was begging people to look at the hole in her leg where the hedgehog sucked her; and red-haired Emily, half-naked and holding a candle in either hand, danced round a tree, curtseying to it, her mouth fixed in a breathless corpse-like grin.

Miss Minnie and Miss Jane had also changed their demeanour for the worse. They sat a little retired from the dancers, tearing up a cold grouse and gossiping with Mrs. Dewey the midwife. A horrible curiosity stretched their skinny old necks. Miss Minnie had forgotten to gnaw her grouse, she leant forward, her hand covered the lower half of her face to conceal the workings of her mouth. Miss Jane listened as eagerly, and questioned the midwife. But at the answers she turned away with coquettish shudders, pretending to stop her ears, or threatening to slap her sister with a bone.

Laura averted her eyes. She wriggled herself a little further into the hedge. Once again the dancers veered away to the futher side of the field, their music retreating with them. She hoped they would stay away, for their proximity was disturbing. They aroused in her neither fear nor disgust, but when they came close, and she felt their shadows darkening above her head, a nameless excitement caught hold of her. As they departed, heaviness took its place. She was not in the least sleepy and yet several times she found herself astray from her thoughts, as though she were falling asleep in a train. She wondered what time it was and looked up to consult the stars. But a featureless cloud covered the sky.

Laura resigned herself. There was nothing to do but to wait, though what she waited for she did not know: whether at length Mrs. Leak would come, like a chaperone from the supper-room, and say: "Well, my dear, I really must take you home,"—or if, suddenly, at the first cock-crow, all the company would rise up in the air, a darkening bevy, and disperse, and she with them.

She was roused by a shrill whistle. The others heard it too. Miss Minnie and Miss Jane scrambled up and hurried across the field, outdistancing Mrs. Dewey, who followed them panting for breath and twitching her skirts over the rough ground. The music had stopped. Laura saw all the witches and warlocks jostling each other, and pressing into a circle. She wondered what was happening now. Whatever it was, it seemed to please and excite them a great deal, for she could hear them all laughing and talking at once. Some newcomer, she supposed—for their behaviour was that of welcome. Now the newcomer must be making a speech, for they all became silent: a successful speech, for the silence was broken by acclamations, and bursts of laughter.

"Of course!" said Laura. "It must be Satan!"

As she spoke she saw the distant group turn and with one accord begin running towards where she sat. She got up; she felt frightened, for their advance was like a stampede of animals, and she feared that they would knock her down and trample her underfoot. The first runner had already swooped upon her, she felt herself encompassed, caught hold of, and carried forward. Voices addressed her, but she did not understand what was said. She gathered that she was being encouraged and congratulated, as though the neglectful assembly had suddenly decided to make much of the unsuccessful guest. Presently she found herself between Mrs. Leak and red-haired Emily. Each held an arm. Mrs. Leak patted her encouragingly, and Emily whispered rapidly, incoherently, in her ear. They were quite close to the newcomer, Satan, if it were he, who was talking to Miss Minnie and Miss Jane. Laura looked at him. She could see him quite clearly, for those who stood round had taken up the candles to light him. He was standing with his back to her, speaking with great animation to the old ladies, bowing, and fidgeting his feet. As he spoke he threw out his hands, and his whole lean, lithe body seemed to be scarcely withheld from breaking into a dance. Laura saw Miss Jane point at her, and the stranger turned sharply round.

She saw his face. For a moment she thought that he was a Chinaman; then she saw that he was wearing a mask. The candle-light shone full upon it, but so fine and slight was the modelling that scarcely a shadow marked the indentations of cheek and jaw. The narrow eyes, the slanting brows, the small smiling mouth had a vivid innocent inexpressiveness. It was like the face of a very young girl. Alert and immobile the mask regarded her. And she, entranced, stared back at this imitation face that outwitted all perfections of flesh and blood. It was lifeless, lifeless! But below it, in the hollow of the girlish throat, she saw a flicker of life, a small regular pulse, small and regular as though a pearl necklace slid by under the skin. Mincing like a girl, the masked young man approached her, and as he approached the others drew back and left her alone. With secretive and undulating movements he came to her side. The lifeless face was near her own and through the slits in the mask the unseen eyes surveyed her. Suddenly she felt upon her cheeks a cold darting touch. With a fine tongue like a serpent's he had licked her right cheek, close to the ear. She started back, but found his hands detaining her.

"How are you enjoying your first Sabbath, Miss Willowes?" he said.

"Not at all," answered Laura, and turned her back on him.

Without glancing to left or right she walked out of the field, and the dancers made way for her in silence. She was furious at the affront, raging at Satan, at Mrs. Leak, at Miss Larpent, with the unreasoning anger of a woman who has allowed herself to be put in a false position. This was what came of attending Sabbaths, or rather, this was what came of submitting her good sense to politeness. Hours ago her instinct had told her that she was not going to enjoy herself. If she had asserted herself and gone home then, this odious and petty insult would never have happened. But she had stayed on, deferring to a public opinion that was not concerned whether she stayed or went, stayed on just as she used to stay on at balls, stayed on to be treated like a silly girl who at the end of a mechanical flirtation is kissed behind a palm.

Anyway, she was out of it now. Her feet had followed the windings of a little path, which crossed a ditch by a plank bridge: it passed through a belt of woodland, and led her out on to a space of common that sloped away into the darkness. Here she sat down and spread out her palms upon the cool turf.

She had been insulted and made a mock of. But for all that she did not feel truly humiliated. Rather, she was filled with a delighted and scornful surprise at the ease with which she had avenged her dignity. The mask floated before her eyes, inscrutable as ever, and she thought no more of it than of an egg-shell that she could crush between her finger and thumb. The Powers of Darkness, then, were no more fearful than a herd of bullocks in a field? Once round upon them and the sniffing encumbering horde made off, a scramble of ungainly rumps and foolish tails.

It had been a surprising night. And long, endlessly long, and not ended yet. She yawned, and felt hungry. She fancied herself at home, cutting large crumbling slices from the loaf in the cupboard, and spreading them with a great deal of butter and the remains of the shrimp paste. But she did not know where she was, and it was too dark to venture homewards with no sense of direction. She grew impatient with the night and strained her ears for the sound of cock-crow. As if her imperious will had wrenched aside the covering of cloud, a faint glimmer delineated part of the horizon. Moonset or sunrise, westerly or easterly she did not know; but as she watched it doubtfully, thinking that it must be moonset, for it seemed to dwindle rather than increase, a breeze winnowed the air, and looking round her she saw on every side the first beginnings of light.

Sitting up, her hunger and sleepiness forgotten, and all the disappointments and enigmas of the Sabbath dismissed from her mind, she watched the spectacle of the dawn. Soon she was able to recognise her surroundings, she knew the place well, it was here that she had met the badger. The slope before her was dotted with close-fitting juniper bushes, and presently she saw a rabbit steal out from one of these, twitch its ears, and scamper off. The cloud which covered the sky was no longer a solid thing.

It was rising, and breaking up into swirls of vapour that yielded to the wind. The growing day washed them with silver. Every moment the web of cloud seemed to rise higher and higher, as though borne upward by a rising tide of light. The rooks flew up cawing from the wood. Presently she heard the snap of a dead twig. Somebody was astir. Whistling to himself, a man came out of the wood. He walked with a peculiarly slow and easy gait, and he had a stick in his hand, an untrimmed rod pulled from the wood. He switched at the head of a tall thistle, and Laura saw the dew fly off the astonished blossom. Seeing her, he stopped short, as though he did not wish to intrude on her. He showed no surprise that she should be sitting on the hillside, waiting for the sun to rise. She smiled at him, grateful for his good manners, and also quite pleased to see a reasonable being again; and emboldened by this, he smiled also, and approached.

"You are up very early, Miss Willowes."

She did not recognise him, but that was no reason why he should not recognise her. She thought he must be a gamekeeper, for he wore gaiters and a corduroy coat. His face was brown and wrinkled, and his teeth were as white and even as a dog's. Laura liked his appearance. He had a pleasant, rather detached air, which suited well with the early morning. She said:

"I have been up all night."

There was no inquisitiveness in his look; and when he expressed the hope that she felt none the worse for it, he spoke without servility or covert amusement.

"I liked it very much," said Laura. Her regard for truth made her add: "Particularly when it began to be light. I was growing rather bored before then."

"Some ladies would feel afraid," said he.

"I'm not afraid when I'm alone," she answered. "I lived in the country when I was a girl."

He bowed his head assentingly. Something in his manner implied that he knew this already. Perhaps he had heard about her in the village.

"It's pleasant to be in the country again," she continued. "I like Great Mop very much."

"I hope you will stay here, Miss Willowes."

"I hope so too."

She spoke a little sadly. In this unaccustomed hour her soul was full of doubts. She wondered if, having flouted the Sabbath, she were still a witch, or whether, her power being taken from her, she would become the prey of a healthy and untroubled Titus. And being faint for want of food and want of sleep, she foreboded the worst.

"Yes, you must stay here. It would be a pity to go now."

Laura nearly said, "I have nowhere to go," but a dread of exile came over her like a salt wave, and she could not trust herself to speak to this kind man. He came nearer and said:

"Remember, Miss Willowes, that I shall always be very glad to help you. You have only to ask me."

"But where shall I find you?" she asked, too much impressed by the kindness of his words to think them strange.

"You will always find me in the wood," he answered, and touching his cap he walked away. She heard the noise of swishing branches and the scuff of feet among dead leaves growing fainter as he went further into the wood.

She decided not to go back just yet. A comfortable drowsiness settled down upon her with the first warmth of the risen sun. Her mind dwelt upon the words just spoken. The promise had been given in such sober earnestness that she had accepted it without question, seeing nothing improbable in the idea that she should require the help of a strange gamekeeper, or that she should undertake to give it. She thought that people might be different in the early morning; less shy, like the rabbits that were playing round her, more open-hearted, and simpler of speech. In any case, she was grateful to the stranger for his goodwill. He had known that she wanted to stay on at Great Mop, he had told her that she must do so. It was the established country courtesy, the invitation to take root. But he must have meant what he said, for seeing her troubled he had offered to help. Perhaps he was married; and if Mrs. Leak, offended, would keep her no longer, she might lodge with him and his wife in their cottage, a cottage in a dell among the beech-woods. He had said that he lived in the woods. She began to picture her life in such a cottage, thinking that it would be even better than lodging in the village.

She imagined her white-washed bedroom full of moving green shades; the wood-smoke curling up among the trees; the majestic arms, swaying above her while she slept, and plumed with snow in winter.

The trees behind her murmured consolingly; she reclined upon the sound. "Remember, Miss Willowes" . . . "Remember," murmured the trees, swaying their boughs muffled with heavy foliage. She remembered, and understood. When he came out of the wood, dressed like a gamekeeper, and speaking so quietly and simply, Satan had come to renew his promise and to reassure her. He had put on this shape that she might not fear him. Or would he have her to know that to those who serve him he appears no longer as a hunter, but as a guardian? This was the real Satan. And as for the other, whom her spirit had so impetuously disowned, she had done well to disown him, for he was nothing but an impostor, a charlatan, a dummy.

Her doubts were laid to rest, and she walked back through the fields, picking mushrooms as she went. As she approached the village she heard Mr. Saunter's cocks crowing, and saw the other cock, for ever watchful, for ever silent, spangle in the sun above the church tower. The churchyard yews cast long shadows like open graves. Behind those white curtains slumbered Mr. Jones, and dreamed, perhaps, of the Sabbath which he was not allowed to attend.

As Laura passed through Mrs. Leak's garden she remembered her first morning as a witch when she had gone out to give the kitten a run. The sunflowers had been cut off and given to the hens, but the scrubbing-brush was still propped on the kitchen window-sill. That was three weeks ago. And Titus, like the scrubbing-brush, was still there.

During those three weeks Titus had demanded a great deal of support; in fact, being a witch-aunt was about twice as taxing as being an ordinary aunt, and if she had not known that the days were numbered she could scarcely have endured them.

At her nephew's request she made veils of butter-muslin weighed with blue beads to protect his food and drink. Titus insisted that the beads should be blue: blue was the colour of the Immaculate Conception; and as pious Continental mothers dedicated their children, so he would dedicate his milk and hope for the best. But no blue beads were to be found in the village, so Laura had to walk into Barleighs for them. Titus was filled with gratitude, he came round on purpose to thank her and stayed to tea.

He was no sooner gone than Mrs. Garland arrived. Mrs. Garland had seen the veils. She hoped that Mr. Willowes didn't think she was to blame for the milk going sour. She could assure Miss Willowes that the jugs were mopped out with boiling water morning *and* evening. For *her* part, she couldn't understand it at all. She was always anxious to give satisfaction, she said; but her manner suggested less anxiety to give than to receive. Laura soothed Mrs. Garland, and sat down to wait for Mr. Dodbury. However, Mr. Dodbury contented himself with frowning at that interfering young Willowes's aunt, and turning the bull into the footpath field. Laura thought that the bull frowned too.

Though veiled in butter-muslin, the milk continued to curdle. Titus came in to say that he'd had an idea; in future, he would rely upon condensed milk out of a tin. Which sort did Aunt Lolly recommend? And would she make him a kettle-holder? Apparently tinned milk could resist the Devil, for all was peace until Titus gashed his thumb on the raw edge of a tin. In spite of Laura's first aid the wound festered, and for several days Titus wore a sling. Triumphant over pain he continued the Life of Fuseli. But the wounded thumb being a right-hand thumb, the triumph involved an amanuensis. Laura hated ink, she marvelled that any one should have the constancy to write a whole book. She thought of *Paradise Lost* with a shudder, for it required even more constancy to write some one else's book. Highly as she rated the sufferings of Milton's daughters, she rated her own even higher, for she did not suppose that they had to be for ever jumping up and down to light the poet's cigarette; and blank verse flowed, flowed majestically, she understood, from his lips, whereas Titus dictated in prose, which was far harder to punctuate.

Nor did it flow. Titus was not feeling at his best. He hated small bothers, and of late he had been seethed alive in them. Every day something went wrong, some fiddle-faddle little thing.

All his ingenuity was wasted in circumvention; he had none left for Fuseli.

Anyhow, dictation was only fit for oil-kings! He jumped up and dashed about the room with a fly-flap. Fly-flapping was a manly indoor sport, especially if one observed all the rules. The ceiling was marked out in squares like a chess-board, and while they stayed in their squares the flies could not be attacked. The triangle described by the blue vase, the pink vase, and the hanging lamp was a Yellowstone Park, and so was the King's Face, a difficult ruling, but Titus had decided that of two evils it was more tolerable that the royal countenance should be crawled over by flies than assaulted by the subject. All this from a left-handed adversary—the flies had nothing to complain of, in his opinion. Laura owned his generosity, and sat, when she could, in the Yellowstone Park.

By the time Titus had recovered the use of his right hand the flies had lost their sanctuaries one by one, and could not even call the King's Face their own. They swarmed in his sitting-room, attracted, Mrs. Garland supposed, by the memory of that nasty foreign cheese Mr. Willowes's Mr. Humphries had brought with him when he came to stay. They swarmed in his bedroom also, and that—Mrs. Garland said—was what brought in the bats. Laura told Titus the belief that if a bat once entangles itself in a woman's flowing hair there is no remedy but to cut away hair and bat together. Titus turned pale. That afternoon he went up to London to visit his hairdresser, and returned with hair cropped like a convict's.

All this had unsettled her victim a good deal; but it had not unseated him, and meanwhile it was sufficiently unsettling for her. So far, she thought, the scheme and its execution had been the kitten's—she could recognise Vinegar's playful methods. She gave him credit for doing his best. But he was young and inexperienced, this was probably his first attempt at serious persecution; it was not to be wondered at if his methods were a little sketchy. Now that the Devil had taken matters into his own hands—and of this she felt assured—all would soon be well. Well for her, well for Titus. Really, it was time that poor boy was released from his troubles. She felt complete confidence in the Devil, a confidence that the kitten had never inspired. There was a tinge of gratuitous malice in Vinegar's character; he was, as one says, rather a cat. She suspected him of meditating a scratch which would give Titus blood-poisoning. She remembered with uneasiness what cats are said to do to sleeping infants, and every night she was careful to imprison Vinegar in her bedroom, a useless precaution since he had come in by the keyhole and might as easily go out by it. The Devil would get rid of Titus more speedily, more kindly (he had no reason to be anything but kind: she could not imagine Titus being of the smallest interest to Satan), more economically. There would be no catastrophe, no pantechnicon displays of flood or fire. He would proceed discreetly and surely, like a gamekeeper going his rounds by night; he would remove Titus as imperturbably as Dunlop had removed the beech-leaf. She could sit back quite comfortably now, and wait for it to happen.

When Titus next appeared and complained that he had been kept awake for two nights running by a mouse gnawing the leg of his bedstead, Laura was most helpful. They went to Mrs. Trumpet's to buy a mouse-trap, but as Mrs. Trumpet only kept cheese they walked very pleasantly by field-paths into Barleighs, where Denby's stores had a larger range of groceries. During their walk Titus recalled anecdotes illustrative of mice from Soup from a Sausage Peg, and propounded a scheme for defending his bed by a catskin valance. The day was fine, and at intervals Titus would stop and illustrate the landscape with possessive gestures.

He was particularly happy. He had not enjoyed himself so much for some time. The milk and the mice and the flies had checked his spirits; he was not doing justice to Fuseli, and when he went out for long encouraging walks an oppressed feeling went with him. Twice or thrice he had felt horribly frightened, though at what he could not tell. The noise of two iron hurdles grating against each other in the wind, a dead tree with branches that looked like antlers, the stealthy movement of the sun towards the horizon: quite ordinary things like these were able to disquiet him.

He fell into the habit of talking aloud to himself. He would reason with appearances. "I see you, old Horny," he said to the dead tree. And once, as dusk pursued him homeward, he began repeating:

As one that on a lonesome road
Doth walk in fear and dread,
And having once turned round, walks on,
And turns no more his head;
Because he knows a frightful fiend
Doth close behind him tread:

when the sound of a crackling twig made every nerve in his body stiffen with terror. Some impulse not his own snatched him round in the path, only to see old Luxmoor going out with his snares. Old Luxmoor touched his cap and grinned in an embarrassed way. Every one knew that Luxmoor poached, but it was not polite to catch him at it. He did not appear to have overheard Titus or noticed his start of terror. But there had been one instant before recognition when Titus had almost known what he dreaded to see.

So it was pleasant to find that the company of his aunt could exorcise these ghostly enmities. Clearly, there was nothing in it. To-morrow he would go for a long walk by himself.

Laura also went for a walk that afternoon. It was a hot day, so hot and still that it felt like a Sunday. She could not do better than follow the example of the savages in *Robinson Crusoe:* go up on to a hill-top and say O! No pious savage could have ejaculated O! more devoutly than she did; for the hill-top was scattered over with patches of that small honey-scented flower called Tailors' Needles, and in conjunction with the austere outlines of the landscape this perfume was exquisitely sweet and surprising. She found a little green pit and sat down in it, leaning her back against the short firm turf. Ensconced in her private warmth and stillness she had almost fallen asleep when a moving figure on the opposite hillside caught her attention. Laura's grey eyes were very keen-sighted, she soon recognised that long stride and swinging gait. The solitary walker was Titus.

There is an amusing sense of superiority in seeing and remaining unseen. Laura sat up in her form and watched Titus attentively. He looked very small, human, and scrabbly, traversing that imperturbable surface. With such a large slope to wander upon, it was faintly comic to see Titus keeping so neatly to the path; the effect was rather as if he were being taken for a walk upon a string.

Further on the path was lost in a tangle of brambles and rusty foxglove stems which marked the site of Folly Wood, a larch plantation cut down during the war. In her map the wood had still been green. She had looked for it on one of her early explorations, and not finding it had felt defrauded. Her eyes now dwelt on the bramble tangle with annoyance. It was untidy, and fretted the hillside like a handful of rough-cast thrown on to a smooth wall. She turned back her gaze to see how Titus was getting on. It struck her that he was behaving rather oddly. Though he kept to the path he was walking almost like a drunken man or an idiot, now hurrying his pace, now reforming it into a staid deliberation that was certainly not his natural gait. Quite abruptly he began to run. He ran faster and faster, his feet striving on the slippery turf. He reached the outskirts of Folly Wood, and Laura could gauge the roughness of the going from his leaps and stumbles. Midway through the wood he staggered and fell full-length.

"A rabbit-hole," she said. "Now I suppose he's sprained his ankle."

But before any thought of compunction could mitigate the rather scornful bewilderment with which she had been a spectator of these antics, Titus was up again, and behaving more oddly than ever. No amount of sprained ankle could warrant those raving gestures with which he beat himself, and beat the air. He seemed to be fending off an invisible volley of fisticuffs, for now he ducked his head, now he leaped to one side, now he threatened, now he quailed before a fresh attack. At last he made off with shambling speed, reeling and gesticulating as though his whole body bellowed with pain and fear. He reached the summit of the hill; for a moment he was silhouetted against the sky-line in a final convulsion of distress; then he was gone.

Laura felt as if she were releasing her gaze from a telescope.

Her glance strayed about the landscape. She frowned and looked inquiringly from side to side, not able to credit her eyes. Blandly unconscious, the opposite hillside confronted her with its familiar face. A religious silence filled the valley. As the untroubled air had received Titus's roarings and damnings (for it was obvious that he had both roared and damned) without concerning itself to transmit them to her hearing, so her vision had absorbed his violent pantomime without concerning itself to alarm her brain. She could not reason about what she had seen; she could scarcely stir herself to feel any curiosity, and still less any sympathy. Like a masque of bears and fantastic shapes, it had seemed framed only to surprise and delight.

But that, she knew, was not Satan's way. He was not in the habit of bestowing these gratuitous peep-shows upon his servants, he was above the human weakness of doing things for fun; and if he exhibited Titus dancing upon the hillside like a cat on hot bricks, she might be sure that it was all according to plan. It behoved her to be serious and attend, instead of accepting it all in this spirit of blank entertainment. Even as a matter of bare civility she ought to find out what had happened. Besides, Titus might require her ministrations. She got up, and began to walk back to the village.

Titus, she reflected, would almost certainly have gone home. Even if he did not run all the way he would by now have had time to settle down and get over the worst of his disturbance. A kind of decency forbade her to view too immediately the dismay of her victim. Titus unmenaced, Titus invading her quiet and straddling over her peace of mind, was a very different thing from Titus melting and squirming before the fire of her resentment. Now that she was walking to his assistance she felt quite sorry for him. My nephew who is plagued by the Devil was as much an object for affectionate aunt-like interest as my nephew who has an attack of measles. She did not take the present affliction more seriously than she had taken those of the past. With time, and a change of air, she was confident that he would make a complete recovery.

As for her own share in the matter, she felt no shame at all. It had pleased Satan to come to her aid. Considering carefully, she did not see who else would have done so. Custom, public opinion, law, church, and state—all would have shaken their massive heads against her plea, and sent her back to bondage.

She reached Great Mop about five o'clock. As she turned up Mrs. Leak's garden-path, Titus bounded from the porch.

"There you are!" he exclaimed. "We have just come to have tea with you."

She perceived that Titus was not alone. In the porch playing with the kitten was Pandora Williams, Pandora Williams whom Titus had invited to play the rebeck at the Flower Show. Before Laura could welcome her Titus was exclaiming again.

"Such an afternoon as I've had. Such adventures! First I fell into a wasps'-nest, and then I got engaged to Pandora."

So that was it. It was wasps. Wasps were the invisible enemies that had beset and routed him on the hill-side. O Beelzebub, God of flies! But why was he now going to marry Pandora Williams?

"The wasp-nest was in Folly Wood. I tripped up, and fell smack on top of it. My God, I thought I should die! They got into my ears, and down my neck, and up my trousers, they were everywhere, as thick as spikes in soda-water. I ran for my life, I ran nearly all the way home, and most of them came with me, either inside or out. And when I rushed up the street calling in an exhausted voice for onions, there was Pandora!"

"I had been invited to tea," said Pandora rather primly.

"Yes, and I'd forgotten it, and gone out for a walk. Pandora, if I'd had my deserts, you would have scorned me, and left me to perish. Pandora, I shall never forget your magnanimous way of behaving. That was what did it really. One has to offer marriage to a young woman who has picked dead wasps out of one's armpit."

Laura had never seen Titus so excited. His face was flushed, his voice was loud, the pupils of his eyes were extraordinarily dilated. But how much of this was due to love and how much to wasps and witchcraft it was impossible to say. And was Pandora part of the witchcraft too, a sort of queen wasp whose sting was mortal balm? Why should Titus offer her marriage? Why should Pandora accept it? They had always been such friends.

Laura turned to the girl to see how she was taking it. Pandora's smooth cheeks and smooth lappets of black hair seemed to shed calm like an unwavering beam of moonlight. But at Laura's good wishes she started, and began nervously to counter them with explanations and apologies for coming to Laura's rooms for tea. She had dropped Titus's teapot, and broken it. Laura was not surprised that she had dropped the teapot. It was clear to her that Pandora's emotions that afternoon had been much more vehement than anything that Titus had experienced in his mental uproar. How well—thought Laura—she has hidden her feelings all this time! How well she is hiding them now!

These fine natures, she knew, always found comfort in cutting bread-and-butter. Pandora welcomed the suggestion. She covered three large plates, and would have covered a fourth if the butter had not given out. There were some ginger-bread nuts as well, and a few bull's-eyes. Mrs. Leak must have surmised a romance. She marked her sense of the occasion by the tea, which was almost purple—as strong as wedding-cake, Titus said.

It was a savagely plain tea. But had it consisted of cocoa and ship's-biscuit, Laura might have offered it without a qualm to guests so much absorbed by their proper emotions. Titus talked incessantly, and Pandora ate with the stealthy persistence of a bitch that gives suck. Meanwhile Laura looked at the new Mr. and Mrs. Willowes. They would do very well, she decided. Young as she was, Pandora had already the air of a family portrait; such looks, such characters change little, for they are independent of time. And undoubtedly she was very much in love with Titus. While he talked she watched his face with the utmost attention, though she did not seem to hear what he was saying. Titus, too, must be considerably in love. Despite the unreality of his behaviour, and a swelled nose, his happiness gave him an almost romantic appearance. Perhaps it was that too recently she had seen him dancing on the Devil's strings to be able to take him quite seriously; perhaps she was old-maidishly scornful of the authenticity of anything that a man may say or do; but at the back of her mind Laura felt that Titus was but a proxy wooer, the ambassador of an imperious dynastic will; and that the real match was made between Pandora and Lady Place.

Anyhow, it was all very suitable, and she must be content to leave it at that. The car from the Lamb and Flag was waiting to take them to the station. Titus was going back to London with Pandora to see her people, as Pandora had refused to face their approval alone. The Williamses lived pleasantly on Campden Hill, and were typical of the best class of Londoners, being almost indistinguishable from people living pleasantly in the country. What, indeed, could be more countrified than to be in town during September? For a moment Laura feared that she would be obliged to travel to London. The lovers had insisted upon her company as far as the station.

"You must come," said Titus. "There will be all sorts of things I shall remember to ask you to do for me. I can't remember them now, but I shall the moment the car starts. I always do."

Laura knew this to be very truth. Nevertheless she stood out against going until Pandora manœuvred her into a corner and said in a desperate whisper: "O Miss Willowes, for God's sake, please come. You've no idea how awful it is being left alone with some one you love."

Laura replied: "Very well. I'll come as a thank-offering."

Pandora's sense of humour could just contrive a rather castaway smile.

They got into the car. There was no time to spare, and the driver took them along the winding lanes at top speed, sounding his horn incessantly. It was a closed car, and they sat in it in perfect silence all the way to the station. Before the car had drawn up in the station yard Titus leaped out and began to pay the driver. Then he looked wildly about for the train. There was no train in sight. It had not come in yet.

When Laura had seen them off and gone back to the station yard she found that in his excitement Titus had dismissed the driver without considering how his aunt was to get back to Great Mop. However, it didn't matter—the bus started for Barleighs at half-past eight, and from Barleighs she could walk on for the rest of the way. This gave her an hour and a half to spend in Wickendon. A sensible way of passing the time would be to eat something before her return journey; but she was not hungry, and the fly-blown cafés in the High Street were not tempting. She bought some fruit, and turned up an alley between garden walls in search of a field where she could sit and eat it in peace. The alley soon changed to an untidy lane and then to a cinder-track running steeply uphill between high hedges. A municipal kindliness had supplied at intervals iron benches, clamped and riveted into the cinders. But no one reposed on them, and the place was unpeopled save by swarms of midges. Laura was hot and breathless by the time she reached the top of the hill and came out upon a bare grassy common. Here was an obvious place to sit down and gasp, and as there were no iron benches to deter her, she did so. But she immediately forgot her exhaustion, so arresting was the sight that lay before her.

The cinder-track led to a small enclosure, full of cypresses, yews, clipped junipers and weeping-willows. Rising from this funereal plumage was an assortment of minarets, gilded cupolas and obelisks. She stared at this phenomenon, so byronic in conception, so spick and span in execution, and sprouting so surprisingly from the mild Chiltern landscape, completely at a loss to account for it. Then she remembered: it was the Maulgrave Folly. She had read of it in the guide-book, and of its author, Sir Ralph Maulgrave, the Satanic Baronet, the libertine, the atheist, who drank out of a skull, who played away his mistress and pistolled the winner, who rode about Buckinghamshire on a zebra, whose conversation had been too much for Thomas Moore. "This bad and eccentric character," the guide-book said, disinfecting his memory with rational amusement. Grown old, he had amused himself by elaborating a burial-place which was to be an epitome of his eclectic and pessimistic opinions. He must, thought Laura, have spent many hours on this hillside, watching the masons and directing the gardeners where to plant his cypresses. And afterwards he would be wheeled away in his bath-chair, for, *pace* the guide-book, at a comparatively early age he lost the use of his legs.

Poor gentleman, how completely he had misunderstood the Devil! The plethoric gilt cupolas winked in the setting sun. For all their bad taste, they were perfectly respectable—cupolas and minarets and cypresses, all had a sleek and well-cared-for look.

They had an assured income, nothing could disturb their calm. The silly, vain, passionate heart that lay buried there had bequeathed a sum of money for their perpetual upkeep. The Satanic Baronet who mocked at eternal life and designated this place as a lasting testimony of his disbelief had contrived to immortalise himself as a laughing-stock.

It was ungenerous. The dead man had been pilloried long enough; it was high time that Maulgrave's Folly should be left to fall into decent ruin and decay. And instead of that, even at this moment it was being trimmed up afresh. She felt a thrill of anger as she saw a gardener come out of the enclosure, carrying a flag basket and a pair of shears. He came towards her, and something about the rather slouching and prowling gait struck her as being familiar. She looked more closely, and recognised Satan.

"How can you?" she said, when he was within speaking distance. He, of all people, should be more compassionate to the shade of Sir Ralph.

He feigned not to hear her.

"Would you care to go over the Folly, ma'am?" he inquired. "It's quite a curiosity. Visitors come out from London to see it."

Laura was not going to be fubbed off like this. He might pretend not to recognise her, but she would jog his memory.

"So you are a grave-keeper as well as a game-keeper?"

"The Council employ me to cut the bushes," he answered.

"O Satan!" she exclaimed, hurt by his equivocations. "Do you always hide?"

With the gesture of a man who can never hold out against women, he yielded and sat down beside her on the grass.

Laura felt a momentary embarrassment. She had long wished for a reasonable conversation with her Master, but now that her wish seemed about to be granted, she felt rather at a loss for an opening. At last she observed:

"Titus has gone."

"Indeed? Isn't that rather sudden? It was only this afternoon that I met him."

"Yes, I saw you meeting him. At least, I saw him meeting you."

"Just so. It is remarkable," he added, as though he were politely parrying her thought, "how invisible one is on these bare green hill-sides."

"Or in these thick brown woods," said Laura rather sternly.

This sort of satanic playfulness was no novelty; Vinegar often behaved in the same fashion, leaping about just out of reach when she wanted to catch him and shut him up indoors.

"Or in these thick brown woods," he concurred. "Folly Wood is especially dense."

"Is?"

"Is. Once a wood, always a wood."

Once a wood, always a wood. The words rang true, and she sat silent, considering them. Pious Asa might hew down the groves, but as far as the Devil was concerned he hewed in vain. Once a wood, always a wood: trees where he sat would crowd into a shade. And people going by in broad sunlight would be aware of slow voices overhead, and a sudden chill would fall upon their flesh. Then, if like her they had a natural leaning towards the Devil, they would linger, listening about them with half-closed eyes and averted senses; but if they were respectable people like Henry and Caroline they would talk rather louder and hurry on. There remaineth a rest for the people of God (somehow the thought of the Devil always propelled her mind to the Holy Scriptures), and for the other people, the people of Satan, there remained a rest also. Held fast in that strong memory no wild thing could be shaken, no secret covert destroyed, no haunt of shadow and silence laid open. The goods yard at Paddington, for instance —a savage place! as holy and enchanted as ever it had been. Not one of the monuments and tinkerings of man could impose on the satanic mind. The Vatican and the Crystal Palace, and all the neat human nest-boxes in rows, Balham and Fulham and the Cromwell Road—he saw through them, they went flop like card-houses, the bricks were earth again, and the steel girders burrowed shrieking into the veins of earth, and the dead timber was restored to the ghostly groves. Wolves howled through the streets of Paris, the foxes played in the throne-room of Schönbrunn, and in the basement at Apsley Terrace, the mammoth slowly revolved, trampling out its lair.

"Then I needn't really have come here to meet you!" she exclaimed.

"Did you?"

"I didn't know I did. I thought I came here to be in the country, and to escape being an aunt."

"Titus came here to write a book on Fuseli, and to enjoy himself."

"Titus! I can't believe you wanted *him.*"

"But you believe I wanted you."

Rather taken aback she yet answered the Devil honestly.

"Yes! I do believe you wanted me. Though really I don't know why you should."

A slightly malevolent smile crossed the Devil's face. For some reason or other her modesty seemed to have nettled him.

"Some people would say that you had flung yourself at my head."

"Other people," she retorted, "would say that you had been going about seeking to devour me."

"Exactly. I even roared that night. But you were asleep while I roared. Only the hills heard me triumphing over my spoil."

Laura said: "I wish I could really believe that."

"I wish you could, too," he answered affably; "you would feel so comfortable and important. But you won't, although it is much more probable than you might suppose."

Laura stretched herself out on the turf and pillowed her head on her arm.

"Nothing could feel more comfortable than I do, now that Titus is gone," she said. "And as for importance, I never wish to feel important again. I had enough of that when I was an aunt."

"Well, you're a witch now."

"Yes. . . . I really am, aren't I?"

"Irrevocably."

His voice was so perfectly grave that she began to suspect him of concealing some amusement. When but a moment before he had jested she had thought a deeper meaning lay beneath his words, she almost believed that his voice had roared over her in the thunder. If he had spoken without feigning then, she had not heard him; for he had stopped her ears with a sleep.

"Why do you sigh?" he asked.

"Did I sigh? I'm puzzled, that's all. You see, although I'm a witch, and although you sitting here beside me tell me so, I can't really appreciate it, take it in. It all seems perfectly natural."

"That is because you are in my power. No servant of mine can feel remorse, or doubt, or surprise. You may be quite easy, Laura: you will never escape me, for you can never wish to."

"Yes, I can quite well believe that; I'm sure I shall never wish to escape you. But you are a mysterious Master."

"You seem to me rather an exacting servant. I have shaped myself like a jobbing gardener, I am sitting on the grass beside you (I'll have one of your apples if I may. They are a fruit I am particularly fond of), I am doing everything in my power to be agreeable and reassuring . . . What more do you want?"

"That is exactly what I complain of. You are too lifelike to be natural; why, it might be Goethe's Conversations with Eckermann. No! if I am really a witch, treat me as such. Satisfy my curiosity. Tell me about yourself."

"Tell me first what *you* think," he answered.

"I think"—she began cautiously (while he hid his cards it would not do to show all hers)—"I think you are a kind of black knight, wandering about and succouring decayed gentlewomen."

"There are warlocks too, remember."

"I can't take warlocks so seriously, not as a class. It is we witches who count. We have more need of you. Women have such vivid imaginations, and lead such dull lives. Their pleasure in life is so soon over; they are so dependent upon others, and their dependence so soon becomes a nuisance. Do you understand?"

He was silent. She continued, slowly, knitting her brows in the effort to make clear to herself and him the thought that was in her mind:

"It's like this. When I think of witches, I seem to see all over England, all over Europe, women living and growing old, as common as blackberries, and as unregarded. I see them, wives and sisters of respectable men, chapel members, and blacksmiths, and small farmers, and Puritans. In places like Bedfordshire, the sort of country one sees from the train. You know. Well, there they were, there they are, child-rearing, housekeeping, hanging washed dishcloths on currant bushes; and for diversion each other's silly conversation, and listening to men talking together in the way that men talk and women listen. Quite different to the way women talk, and men listen, if they listen at all. And all the time being thrust further down into dullness when the one thing all women hate is to be thought dull. And on Sunday they put on plain stuff gowns and starched white coverings on their heads and necks—the Puritan ones did—and walked across the fields to chapel, and listened to the sermon. Sin and Grace, and God and the—" (she stopped herself just in time), "and St. Paul. All men's things, like politics, or mathematics. Nothing for them except subjection and plaiting their hair. And on the way back they listened to more talk. Talk about the sermon, or war, or cock-fighting; and when they got back, there were the potatoes to be cooked for dinner. It sounds very petty to complain about, but I tell you, that sort of thing settles down on one like a fine dust, and by and by the dust is age, settling down. Settling down! You never die, do you? No doubt that's far worse, but there is a dreadful kind of dreary immortality about being settled down on by one day after another. And they think how they were young once, and they see new young women, just like what they were, and yet as surprising as if it had never happened before, like trees in spring. But they are like trees towards the end of summer, heavy and dusty, and nobody finds their leaves surprising, or notices them till they fall off. If they could be passive and unnoticed, it wouldn't matter. But they must be active, and still not noticed. Doing, doing, doing, till mere habit scolds at them like a housewife, and rouses them up—when they might sit in their doorways and think—to be doing still!"

She paused, out of breath. She had never made such a long speech in the whole of her life, nor spoken with such passion. She scarcely knew what she had said, and felt giddy and unaccustomed, as though she had been thrown into the air and had suddenly begun to fly.

The Devil was silent, and looked thoughtfully at the ground.

He seemed to be rather touched by all this. She continued, for she feared that if she did not go on talking she would grow ashamed at having said so much.

"Is it true that you can poke the fire with a stick of dynamite in perfect safety? I used to take my nieces to scientific lectures, and I believe I heard it then. Anyhow, even if it isn't true of dynamite, it's true of women. But they know they are dynamite, and long for the concussion that may justify them. Some may get religion, then they're all right, I expect. But for the others, for so many, what can there be but witchcraft? That strikes them real. Even if other people still find them quite safe and usual, and go on poking with them, they know in their hearts how dangerous, how incalculable, how extraordinary they are. Even if they never do anything with their witchcraft, they know it's there—ready! Respectable countrywomen keep their grave-clothes in a corner of the chest of drawers, hidden away, and when they want a little comfort they go and look at them, and think that once more, at any rate, they will be worth dressing with care. But the witch keeps her cloak of darkness, her dress embroidered with signs and planets; that's better worth looking at. And think, Satan, what a compliment you pay her, pursuing her soul, lying in wait for it, following it through all its windings, crafty and patient and secret like a gentleman out killing tigers. Her soul—when no one else would give a look at her body even! And they are all so accustomed, so sure of her! They say: 'Dear Lolly! What shall we give her for her birthday this year? Perhaps a hot-water bottle. Or what about a nice black lace scarf? Or a new workbox? Her old one is nearly worn out.' But you say: 'Come here, my bird! I will give you the dangerous black night to stretch your wings in, and poisonous berries to feed on, and a nest of bones and thorns, perched high up in danger where no one can climb to it.' That's why we become witches: to show our scorn of pretending life's a safe business, to satisfy our passion for adventure. It's not malice, or wickedness—well, perhaps it *is* wickedness, for most women love that—but certainly not malice, not wanting to plague cattle and make horrid children spout up pins and—what is it?—'blight the genial bed.' Of course, given the power, one may go in for that sort of thing, either in self-defence, or just out of playfulness. But it's a poor twopenny house-wifely kind of witchcraft, black magic is, and white magic is no better. One doesn't become a witch to run round being harmful, or to run round being helpful either, a district visitor on a broomstick. It's to escape all that—to have a life of one's own, not an existence doled out to you by others, charitable refuse of their thoughts, so many ounces of stale bread of life a day, the workhouse dietary is scientifically calculated to support life. As for the witches who can only express themselves by pins and bed-blighting, they have been warped into that shape by the dismal lives they've led. Think of Miss Carloe! She's a typical witch, people would say. Really she's the typical genteel spinster who's spent herself being useful to people who didn't want her. If you'd got her younger she'd never be like that."

"You seem to know a good deal about witches," remarked Satan. "But you were going to say what you thought about me."

She shook her head.

"Go on," he said encouragingly. "You compared me to a knight-errant. That's very pretty. I believe you have also compared me to a hunter, a poaching sort of hunter, prowling through the woods after dark. Not so flattering to my vanity as the knight-errant, but more accurate, I daresay."

"O Satan! Why do you encourage me to talk when you know all my thoughts?"

"I encourage you to talk, not that I may know all your thoughts, but that you may. Go on, Laura. Don't be foolish. What do you think about me?"

"I don't know," she said honestly. "I don't think I do think. I only rhapsodise and make comparisons. You're beyond me, my thought flies off you like the centrifugal hypothesis. And after this I shall be more at a loss than ever, for I like you so much, I find you so kind and sympathetic. But it is obvious that you can't be merely a benevolent institution. No, I must be your witch in blindness."

"You don't take warlocks so seriously, I know. But you might find their point of view illuminating. As it's a spiritual difficulty, why not consult Mr. Jones?"

"Poor Mr. Jones!" Laura began to laugh. "He can't call his soul his own."

"Hush! Have you forgotten that he has sold it to me?"

"Then why did you mortgage it to Mr. Gurdon? Mr. Jones isn't even allowed to attend the Sabbath."

"You are a little dense at times. Hasn't it occurred to you that other people might share your sophisticated dislike for the Sabbath?"

"You don't attend the Sabbath either, if it comes to that."

"How do you know? Don't try to put me in your pocket, Laura. You are not my only conquest, and I am not a human master to have favourites among my servants. All are souls that come to my net. I apologise for the pun, but it is apt."

She had been rebuked, but she did not feel particularly abashed. It was true, then, what she had read of the happy relationship between the Devil and his servants. If Euphan Macalzean had rated him—why, so, at a pinch, might she. Other things that she had read might also be true, she thought, things that she had till now been inclined to reject. So easy-going a Master who had no favourites among his servants might in reality attend the Sabbath, might unbend enough to eat black-puddings at a picnic without losing his dignity.

"That offensive young man at the Sabbath," she remarked, "I know he wasn't you. Who was he?"

"He's one of these brilliant young authors," replied the Devil. "I believe Titus knows him. He sold me his soul on the condition that once a week he should be without doubt the most important person at a party."

"Why didn't he sell his soul in order to become a great writer? Then he could have had the party into the bargain."

"He preferred to take a short-cut, you see."

She didn't see. But she was too proud to inquire further, especially as Satan was now smiling at her as if she were a pet lamb.

"What did Mr. Jones—"

"That's enough! You can ask him that yourself, when you take your lessons in demonology."

"Do you suppose for one moment that Mr. Gurdon would let

me sit closeted with Mr. Jones taking lessons in plain needle-work even? He would put his face in at the window and say: 'How much longer are them Mothers to be kept waiting?' or: 'I should like to know what your reverence is doing about that there dung?' or: 'I suppose you know that the cowman's girl may go off at any minute.' And then he'd take him down to the shrubbery and scold him. My heart bleeds for the poor old gentleman!"

"Mr. Jones"—Satan spoke demurely—"will have his reward in another life."

Laura was silent. She gazed at the Maulgrave Folly with what she could feel to be a pensive expression. But her mind was a blank.

"A delicate point, you say? Perhaps it is bad taste on my part to jest about it."

A midge settled on Laura's wrist. She smacked at it.

"Dead!" said Satan.

The word dropped into her mind like a pebble thrown into a pond. She had heard it so often, and now she heard it once more. The same waves of thought circled outwards, waves of startled thought spreading out on all sides, rocking the shadows of familiar things, blurring the steadfast pictures of trees and clouds, circling outward one after the other, each wave more listless, more imperceptible than the last, until the pool was still again.

There might be some questions that even the Devil could not answer. She turned her eyes to him with their question.

Satan had risen to his feet. He picked up the flag basket and the shears, and made ready to go.

"Is it time?" asked Laura.

He nodded, and smiled.

She got up in her turn, and began to shake the dust off her skirt. Then she prodded a hole for the bag which had held the apples, and buried it tidily, smoothing the earth over the hole. This took a little time to do, and when she looked round for Satan, to say good-bye, he was out of sight.

Seeing that he was gone she sat down again, for she wanted to think him over. A pleasant conversation, though she had done most of the talking. The tract of flattened grass at her side showed where he had rested, and there was the rampion flower he had held in his hand. Grass that has been lain upon has always a rather popular bank-holidayish look, and even the Devil's lair was not exempt from this. It was as though the grass were in league with him, faithfully playing-up to his pose of being a quite everyday phenomenon. Not a blade of grass was singed, not a clover-leaf blasted, and the rampion flower was withering quite naturally; yet he who had sat there was Satan, the author of all evil, whose thoughts were a darkness, whose roots went down into the pit. There was no action too mean for him, no instrument too petty; he would go into a milk-jug to work mischief. And presently he would emerge, imperturbable, inscrutable, enormous with the dignity of natural behaviour and untrammelled self-fulfilment.

To be this—a character truly integral, a perpetual flowering of power and cunning from an undivided will—was enough to constitute the charm and majesty of the Devil. No cloak of terrors was necessary to enlarge that stature, and to suppose him capable of speculation or metaphysic would be like offering to crown him with a few casual straws. Very probably he was quite stupid. When she had asked him about death he had got up and gone away, which looked as if he did not know much more about it than she did herself: indeed, being immortal, it was unlikely that he would know as much. Instead, his mind brooded immovably over the landscape and over the natures of men, an unforgetting and unchoosing mind. That, of course—and she jumped up in her excitement and began to wave her arms—was why he was the Devil, the enemy of souls. His memory was too long, too retentive; there was no appeasing its witness, no hoodwinking it with the present; and that was why at one stage of civilization people said he was the embodiment of all evil, and then a little later on that he didn't exist.

For a moment Laura thought that she had him: and on the next, as though he had tricked himself out of her grasp, her thoughts were scattered by the sudden consciousness of a sort of jerk in the atmosphere. The sun had gone down, sliding abruptly behind the hills. In that case the bus would have gone too, she might as well hope to catch the one as the other. First Satan, then the sun and the bus—*adieu, mes gens!* With affectionate unconcern she seemed to be waving them farewell, pleased to be left to herself, left to enter into this new independence acknowledged by their departure.

The night was at her disposal. She might walk back to Great Mop and arrive very late: or she might sleep out and not trouble to arrive until to-morrow. Whichever she did Mrs. Leak would not mind. That was one of the advantages of dealing with witches; they do not mind if you are a little odd in your ways, frown if you are late for meals, fret if you are out all night, pry and commiserate when at length you return. Lovely to be with people who prefer their thoughts to yours, lovely to live at your own sweet will, lovely to sleep out all night! She had quite decided, now, to do so. It was an adventure, she had never done such a thing before, and yet it seemed most natural. She would not sleep here: Wickendon was too close. But presently, later on, when she felt inclined to, she would wander off in search of a suitable dry ditch or an accommodating loosened haystack; or wading through last year's leaves and this year's fern she would penetrate into a wood and burrow herself a bed. Satan going his rounds might come upon her and smile to see her lying so peaceful and secure in his dangerous keeping. But he would not disturb her. Why should he? The pursuit was over, as far as she was concerned. She could sleep where she pleased, a hind couched in the Devil's coverts, a witch made free of her Master's immunity; while he, wakeful and stealthy, was already out after new game. So he would not disturb her. A closer darkness upon her slumber, a deeper voice in the murmuring leaves overhead—that would be all she would know of his undesiring and unjudging gaze, his satisfied but profoundly indifferent ownership.

MR. FORTUNE'S MAGGOT

To Theo

maggot 2: A whimsical or perverse fancy; a crotchet

The scenes and characters of this story are entirely imaginary. In the island names the vowels should be pronounced separately with the Italianate vowel-sounds. Words of three syllables are accented on the second: Fanua, Lueli.

I am greatly obliged to Mr. Victor Butler for his assistance in the geometrical passages, and for the definition of an umbrella.

Though the Reverend Timothy Fortune had spent three years in the island of Fanua he had made but one convert. Some missionaries might have been galled by this state of things, or if too good to be galled, at least flustered; but Mr. Fortune was a humble man of heart and he had the blessing which rests upon humility: an easy-going nature. In appearance he was tall, raw-boned, and rather rummaged-looking; even as a young man he had learnt that to jump in first doesn't make the 'bus start any sooner; and his favourite psalm was the one which begins: 'My soul truly waiteth still upon God.'

Mr. Fortune was not a scholar, he did not know that the psalms express bygone thoughts and a bygone way of life. In his literal way he believed that the sixty-second psalm applied to him. For many years he had been a clerk in the Hornsey branch of Lloyds Bank, but he had not liked it. Whenever he weighed out the golden sovereigns in the brass scales, which tacked and sidled like a yacht in a light breeze, he remembered uneasily that the children of men are deceitful upon the weights, that they are altogether lighter than vanity itself.

In the bank, too, he had seen riches increase. But he had not set his heart upon them: and when his godmother, whose passbook he kept, died and left him one thousand pounds, he went to a training-college, was ordained deacon, and quitted England for St. Fabien, a port on an island of the Raratongan Archipelago in the Pacific.

St. Fabien was a centre of Christianity. It had four missions: one Catholic, one Protestant, one Wesleyan, and one American. Mr. Fortune belonged to the Protestant mission. He gave great satisfaction to his superiors by doing as he was bid, teaching in the school, visiting the sick, and carrying the subscription list to the English visitors, and even greater satisfaction when they had discovered that he could keep all the accounts. At the end of ten years Archdeacon Mason was sorry to hear that Mr. Fortune (who was now a priest) had felt a call to go to the island of Fanua.

Fanua was a small remote island which could only be seen in imagination from that beach edged with tin huts where Mr. Fortune walked slowly up and down on evenings when he had time to. No steamers called there, the Archdeacon had visited it many years ago in a canoe. Now his assistant felt a call thither, not merely to visit it in the new mission launch, but to settle there, and perhaps for life.

The two clergymen strolled along the beach in the cool of the evening. The air smelt of the sea, of flowers, and of the islanders' suppers.

'I must warn you, Fortune, you are not likely to make many converts in Fanua.'

'What, are they cannibals?'

'No, no! But they are like children, always singing and dancing, and of course immoral. But all the natives are like that. I believe I have told you that the Raratongan language has no words for chastity or for gratitude?'

'Yes, I believe you did.'

'Well, well! You are not a young man, Fortune, you will not expect too much of the Fanuans. Singing and dancing! No actual harm in that, of course, and no doubt the climate is partly responsible. But light, my dear Fortune, light! And not only in their heels either.'

'I am afraid that none of the children of men weigh altogether true,' said Mr. Fortune. 'For that matter, I have heard that many cannibals are fond of dancing.'

'Humanly speaking I fear that you would be wasted in Fanua. Still, if you have felt a call I must not dissuade you, I won't put any obstacles in your way. But you will be a great loss.'

The Archdeacon spoke so sadly that Mr. Fortune, knowing how much he disliked accounts, wondered for a moment if God would prefer him to wait still in St. Fabien. God tries the souls of men in crafty ways, and perhaps the call had been a temptation, a temptation sent to try his humility. He turned his eyes towards where he knew the island of Fanua to lie. What his superior had said about it had not displeased him, on the contrary he liked to think of the islanders dancing and singing. It would be a beautiful estate to live among them and gather their souls as a child gathers daisies in a field.

But now the horizon was hidden in the evening haze, and Fanua seemed more remote than ever. A little cloud was coming up the heavens, slowly, towards the sunset; as it passed above the place of Fanua it brightened, it shone like a pearl, it caught the rays of the sun and glowed with a rosy rim. Mr. Fortune took the cloud to be a sign.

Heartened by a novel certainty that he was doing the right thing, he disappointed the Archdeacon quite unflinchingly and set about his preparations for the new life. Since the island was so unfrequented it was necessary to take with him provisions for at least a year. In the ordinary course of things the Mission would have supplied his outfit, but he had a scruple against availing himself of this custom because, having kept the accounts, he knew their poverty and their good works, and also because he was aware that the expedition to Fanua was looked on as, at best, a sort of pious escapade. Fortunately there were the remains of his godmother's legacy. With feelings that were a nice mixture of thrift and extravagance he bought tinned meat, soup-squares, a chest of tea, soap, a tool-box, a medicine chest, a gentleman's housewife, a second-hand harmonium (rather cumbrous and wheezy but certainly a bargain), and an oil-lamp. He also bought a quantity of those coloured glass baubles which hang so ravishingly on Christmas trees, some picture-books, rolls of white cotton, and a sewing-machine to make clothes for his converts. The Archdeacon gave him a service of altar furniture and the other mission-workers presented him with a silver teapot. With the addition of some plate-powder Mr. Fortune was now ready to embark.

In fancy he had seen himself setting foot upon the island alone, though he knew that in fact some one must go with him if only to manage the launch. But that some one would be a sailor, a being so aloofly maritime as scarcely to partake in the act of landing. He was slightly dashed when he discovered that the Archdeacon, accompanied by his secretary, was coming too in order to instal him with a proper appearance of ceremony.

'We cannot impress upon them too early,' said the Archdeacon, 'the solemn nature of your undertaking.' And Mr. Fortune hung his head, a grey one, old and wise enough to heed an admonition or a rebuke.

The voyage was uneventful. The Archdeacon sat in the bows dictating to the secretary, and Mr. Fortune looked at the Pacific Ocean until he fell asleep, for he was tired out with packing.

About sunset he was aroused by the noise of surf and by peals of excited laughter; and opening his eyes he found that they were close in under the shadow of the island of Fanua. The launch was manœuvring round seeking for an inlet in the reef, and the islanders were gathered together to view this strange apparition. Some were standing on the rocks, some were in the sea, others were diving from cliff to water, in movement and uproar like a flock of seagulls disturbed by a fishing-boat.

It seemed to Mr. Fortune that there must be thousands of them, and for a moment his heart sank. But there was no time for second thoughts; for behold! a canoe shot forward to the side of the launch, a rope was thrown and caught, the Archdeacon, the secretary, and himself were miraculously jumped in, the sea was alive with brown heads, every one talked at once, the canoe turned, darted up the smooth back of a wave, descended into a cloud of spray, and the three clergymen, splashed and stiff, were standing on the beach.

Now Mr. Fortune was properly grateful for the presence of the Archdeacon, for like a child arriving late at a party he felt perfectly bewildered and would have remained in the same spot, smiling and staring. But like the child at a party he found himself taken charge of and shepherded in the right direction until, in the house of the chief islander, he was seated on a low stool with his hat taken off, a garland round his neck, and food in his hands, smiling and staring still.

Before dark the luggage was also landed. The evening was spent in conversation and feasting. Every one who could squeeze himself into Ori's house did so, and the rest of them (the thousands did not seem above a few hundreds now) squatted round outside. Even the babies seemed prepared to sit there all night, but at length the Archdeacon, pleading fatigue, asked leave of his host to go to bed.

Ori dismissed the visitors, his household prepared the strangers' sleeping place, unrolling the best mats and shooing away a couple of flying foxes, the missionaries prayed together and the last good-nights were said.

From where he lay Mr. Fortune could look out of the door. He saw a tendril of some creeper waving gently to and fro across the star Canopus, and once more he realised, as though he were looking at it for the first time, how strangely and powerfully he had been led from his native land to lie down in peace under the constellations of the southern sky.

'So this is my first night in Fanua,' he thought, as he settled himself on his mat. 'My first night . . .'

And he would have looked at the star, a sun whose planets must depend wholly upon God for their salvation, for no missionary could reach them; but his eyes were heavy with seafaring, and in another minute he had fallen asleep.

As though while his body lay sleeping his ghost had gone wandering and ascertaining through the island Mr. Fortune woke on the morrow feeling perfectly at home in Fanua. So much so that when he stood on the beach waving farewell to the launch he had the sensations of a host, who from seeing off his guests turns back with a renewed sense of ownership to the house which the fact of their departure makes more deeply and dearly his. Few hosts indeed could claim an ownership equally secure. For when the Archdeacon, visited with a sudden qualm at the thought of Mr. Fortune's isolation, had suggested that he should come again in three months' time, just to see how he was getting on, Mr. Fortune was able to say quite serenely and legitimately that he would prefer to be left alone for at least a year.

Having waved to the proper degree of perspective he turned briskly inland. The time was come to explore Fanua.

The island of Fanua is of volcanic origin, though at the time of Mr. Fortune's arrival the volcano had been for many years extinct. It rises steeply out of the ocean, and seen from thence it appears disproportionately tall for its base, for the main peak reaches to a height of near three thousand feet, and the extremely indented coast-line does not measure more than seventy miles. On three sides of the island there are steep cliffs worked into caverns and flying buttresses by the action of the waves, but to the east a fertile valley slopes gently down to a low-lying promontory of salt-meadow and beach where once a torrent of lava burst from the side of the mountain and crushed its path to the sea; and in this valley lies the village.

The lower slopes of the mountain are wooded, and broken into many deep gorges where the noise of the cataract echoes from cliff to cliff, where the air is cool with shade and moist with spray, and where bright green ferns grow on the black face of the rock. Above this swirl and foam of tree-tops the mountain rises up in crags or steep tracts of scrub and clinker to the old crater, whose ramparts are broken into curious cactus-shaped pinnacles of rock, in colour the reddish-lavender of rhododendron blossoms.

A socket of molten stone, rent and deserted by its ancient fires and garlanded round with a vegetation as wild as fire and more inexhaustible, the whole island breathes the peculiar romance of a being with a stormy past. The ripened fruit falls from the tree, the tree falls too and the ferns leap up from it as though it were being consumed with green flames. The air is sleepy with salt and honey, and the sharp wild cries of the birds seem to float like fragments of coloured paper upon the monotonous background of breaking waves and falling cataract.

Mr. Fortune spent the whole day exploring, and when he felt hungry he made a meal of guavas and rose-apples. There seemed to be no end to the marvels and delights of his island, and he was as thrilled as though he had been let loose into the world for the first time. But he returned with all the day's wonders almost forgotten in the excitement and satisfaction of having discovered the place where he wanted to live.

It was a forsaken hut, about a mile from the village and less than that distance from the sea. It stood in a little dell amongst the woods, before it there was a natural lawn of fine grass, behind it was a rocky spur of the mountain. There was a spring for water and a clump of coco-palms for shade.

The hut consisted of one large room opening on to a deep verandah. The framework was of wood, the floor of beaten earth, and it was thatched and walled with reeds.

Ori told him that it could be his for the taking. An old woman had lived there with her daughter, but she had died and the daughter, who didn't like being out of the world, had removed to the village. Mr. Fortune immediately set about putting it in order, and while he worked almost every one in the island dropped in at some time or other to admire, encourage, or lend a hand. There was not much to do: a little strengthening of the thatch, the floor to be weeded and trodden smooth, the creepers to be cut back—and on the third day he moved in.

This took place with ceremony. The islanders accompanied him on his many journeys to and from the village, they carried the crate containing the harmonium with flattering eulogies of its weight and size, and when everything was transported they sat on the lawn and watched him unpacking. When he unpacked the teapot they burst into delighted laughter.

Except for the lamp, the sewing-machine, and the harmonium, Mr. Fortune's house had not an European appearance, for while on the island he wished to live as its natives did. His bowls and platters and drinking-vessels were made of polished wood, his bed (Ori's gift) was a small wooden platform spread with many white mats. When everything was completed he gave each of the islanders a ginger-bread nut and made a little formal speech, first thanking them for their gifts and their assistance, and going on to explain his reasons for coming to Fanua. He had heard, he said, with pleasure how happy a people they were, and he had come to dwell with them and teach them how they might be as happy in another life as they were in this.

The islanders received his speech in silence broken only by crunching. Their expressions were those of people struck into awe by some surprising novelty: Mr. Fortune wondered if he were that novelty, or Huntley and Palmers.

He was anxious to do things befittingly, for the Archdeacon's admonition on the need for being solemn still hung about the back of his mind. This occasion, it seemed to him, was something between a ceremony and a social function. It was a gathering, and as such it had its proper routine: first there comes an address, after the address a hymn is sung, then comes a collect and sometimes a collection, and after that the congregation disperses.

Mr. Fortune sat down to his harmonium and sang and played through a hymn.

His back was to the islanders, he could not see how they were taking it. But when, having finished the hymn and added two chords for the Amen, he turned round to announce the collect, he discovered that they had already dispersed, the last of them even then vanishing noiselessly and enigmatically through the bushes.

The sun was setting behind the mountain, great shafts of glory moved among the top-most crags. Mr. Fortune thought of God's winnowing-fan, he imagined Him holding the rays of the sun in His hand. God winnows the souls of men with the beauty of this world: the chaff is blown away, the true grain lies still and adoring.

In the dell it was already night. He sat for a long time in his verandah listening to the boom of the waves. He did not think much, he was tired with a long day's work and his back ached. At last he went indoors, lighted his lamp and began to write in his diary. Just as he was dropping off to sleep a pleasant thought came to him, and he smiled, murmuring in a drowsy voice: 'To-morrow is Sunday.'

In the morning he was up and shaved and dressed before sunrise. With a happy face he stepped on to his lawn and stood listening to the birds. They did not sing anywhere near so sweetly as English black-birds and thrushes, but Mr. Fortune was pleased with their notes, a music which seemed proper to this gay landscape which might have been coloured out of a child's paint-box.

He stood there till the sun had risen and shone into the dell, then he went back into his hut; when he came out again he was dressed in his priest's clothes and carried a black tin box.

He walked across the dell to where there was a stone with a flat top. Opening the box he took out, first a linen cloth which he spread on the stone, then a wooden cross and two brass vases. He knelt down and very carefully placed the cross so that it stood firm on the middle of the stone. The vases he carried to the spring, where he filled them with water, and gathering some red blossoms which grew on a bush near by he arranged them in the vases, which he then carried back and set on either side of the cross. Standing beside the stone and looking into the sun, he said in a loud voice: 'Let your light so shine before men, that they may see your good works, and glorify your Father which is in heaven.'

The sun shone upon the white cloth and the scarlet flowers, upon the cross of wood and upon the priest standing serious, grey-headed and alone in the green dell all sparkling with dew as though it had never known the darkness of night.

Once more he turned and went back to the hut. When he came out again he carried in either hand a cup and a dish which shone like gold. These he put down upon the stone, and bowed himself before them and began to pray.

Mr. Fortune knelt very upright. His eyes were shut, he did not see the beauty of the landscape glittering in the sunrise, the coco-palms waving their green feather head-dresses gently to and fro in the light breeze, the wreaths of rosy mist floating high up across the purple crags of the mountain—and yet from the expression on his face one would have said that he was all the more aware of the beauty around him for having his eyes shut, for he seemed like one in an ecstasy and his clasped hands trembled as though they had hold of a joy too great for him. He knelt on, absorbed in prayer. He did not see that a naked brown boy had come to the edge of the dell and was gazing at him and at the stone which he had decked to the glory of God—gazing with wonder and admiration, and step by step coming softly across the grass. Only when he had finished his prayer and stretched out his hands towards the altar did Mr. Fortune discover that a boy was kneeling at his side.

He gave no sign of surprise, he did not even appear to have noticed the newcomer. With steadfast demeanour he took from the dish a piece of bread and ate it, and drank from the cup. Then, rising and turning to the boy who still knelt before him, he laid his hand upon his head and looked down on him with a long look of greeting. Slowly and unhesitatingly, like one who hears and accepts and obeys the voice of the spirit, he took up the cup once more and with the forefinger of his right hand he wrote the sign of the cross upon the boy's forehead with the last drops of the wine.

The boy did not flinch, he trembled a little, that was all. Mr. Fortune bent down and welcomed him with a kiss.

He had waited, but after all not for long. The years in the bank, the years at St. Fabien, they did not seem long now, the time of waiting was gone by, drowsy and half-forgotten like a night watch. A cloud in the heavens had been given him as a sign to come to Fanua, but here was a sign much nearer and more wonderful: his first convert, miraculously led to come and kneel beside him a little after the rising of the sun. His, and not his. For while he had thought to bring souls to God, God had been beforehand with His gift, had come before him into the meadow, and gathering the first daisy had given it to him.

For a long while he stood lost in thankfulness. At last he bade the kneeling boy get up.

'What is your name?' he said.

'Lueli,' answered the boy.

'I have given you a new name, Lueli. I have called you Theodore, which means "the gift of God." '

Lueli smiled politely.

'Theodore,' repeated Mr. Fortune impressively.

The boy smiled again, a little dubiously this time. Then, struck with a happy thought, he told Mr. Fortune the name of the scarlet blossoms that stood on either side of the cross. His voice was soft and pleasant, and he held his head on one side in his desire to please.

'Come, Theodore, will you help me to put these things away?'

Together they rinsed the cup and the dish in the spring, folded the linen cloth and put them with the cross and the vases back into the black tin box. The flowers Mr. Fortune gave to the boy, who with a rapid grace pulled others and wove two garlands, one of which he put round Mr. Fortune's neck and one round his own. Then discovering that the tin box served as a dusky sort of mirror he bent over it, and would have stayed coquetting like a girl with a new coral necklace had not Mr. Fortune called him into the hut.

In all Lueli's movements there was a swiftness and a pliancy as though not only his mind but his body also were intent on complaisance and docility. A monkey will show the same adaptability, deft and pleased with his deftness, but in a monkey's face there is always a sad self-seeking look, and his eyes are like pebbles unhappily come alive. Birds, or squirrels, or lizards whisking over the rock have a vivid infallible grace; but that is inherent, and proper to their kind; however much one may admire or envy them, they do not touch one into feeling grateful to them for being what they are. As Mr. Fortune watched Lueli folding up the priestly clothes, patting them smooth and laying them in their box, he felt as though he were watching some entirely new kind of being, too spontaneous to be human, too artless to be monkey, too sensitive to be bird or squirrel or lizard; and he wished that he had been more observant of creation, so that he could find out what it was that Lueli resembled. Only some women, happy in themselves and in their love, will show to a lover or husband this kind of special grace; but this Mr. Fortune, whose love affairs had been hasty and conventional, did not know.

While they were breakfasting together in the verandah the missionary had a good look at his convert.

Lueli was of the true Polynesian type, slender-boned and long-limbed, with small idle hands and feet: broad-minded persons with no colour prejudices might have described him as aristocratic-looking. This definition did not occur to Mr. Fortune, who had had no dealings with aristocrats and was consequently unaware of any marked difference between them and other people; but he reflected with satisfaction that the boy looked very refined for one who had been so recently a heathen. His eyes were rather small and his nose was rather snub, but these details did not mar the general good effect of regular features and a neatly shaped head. Though when he talked he pulled very charming faces, in repose his expression was slightly satirical. In colour he was an agreeable brown, almost exactly the colour of a nutmeg; his hair was thick but not bushy, and he wore it gathered up into a tuft over either ear, in much the same manner as was fashionable at the French Court in the year 1671.

In spite of his convert's advantageous appearance and easy manners Mr. Fortune judged that he was not the child of any one particularly rich or distinguished; for in these islands where the poorest are scrupulously clean and the richest may wear for sole adornment the sophisticated elegance of freshly gathered flowers, social standing may yet be deduced from the degree of tattooing. Lueli had greaves and gaiters of a pattern of interlacing bamboo-shoots, and in addition a bracelet round his left wrist and on his right shoulder-blade an amusing sprig. But this was all. And from the elegance of the designs and their wilful disposition it seemed as though he had been decorated for no better reason than the artist's pleasure.

When Mr. Fortune came to make inquiries he found that he had judged rightly. Lueli was one of a large family, which is rare in these islands. His mother was a fat, giggling creature, without a care in the world; even among the light-hearted people of Fanua she and her brood were a byword for their harum-scarum ways. Their dwelling was a big tumble-down hut in which there was scarcely ever any one at home except a baby; and though they had no apparent father or other means of sustenance, that was no obstacle to well-being in this fertile spot where no one need go hungry who could shake fruit off a tree or pull fish out of the water.

All of the family were popular. Lueli in particular for his beauty and amiability was a regular village pet. But, whether it be that an uncommon share of good looks, like a strain of fairy blood, sets their owners apart, or whether beautiful people are in some way aware of the firebrand they carry with them and so are inclined to solitariness, Lueli, like other beauties, had for all his affability a tincture of aloofness in his character. Although he was a pet, it was not a pet dog he resembled, solicitous and dependent, but a pet cat, which will leap on to a knee to be fondled and then in a moment detach itself, impossible to constrain as a beam of moonlight playing bo-peep through a cloud. So when he deserted the village and attached himself to the newcomer no one was hurt or surprised, they took it for granted that he would go where he pleased.

This complaisance had slightly shocked Mr. Fortune, particularly as it fell in so conveniently for his wishes. It was most desirable, indeed almost necessary, that his convert should live with him, at any rate for the present, in order to assure and perfect the work of conversion. Afterwards the finished product could be let loose again, a holy decoy, to lure others into salvation's net. But good men do not expect silver spoons to be slipped into their mouths. Easy fortune finds them unprepared and a trifle suspicious.

Mr. Fortune sought to inoculate his good luck by a scrupulous observance of formalities. He put on his black felt hat and went to pay a call on Lueli's mother. On the fourth visit he happened to find her at home. Taking off the hat and bowing, he addressed her with a long speech in which he drew a careful distinction between obedience to God and obedience to lawful authority. Lueli, said he, having become a Christian, any attempts on her part to discourage him would be tempting Lueli to disobey God, therefore as God's priest it would be his duty to oppose them. On the other hand, as Lueli's only visible parent and lawful guardian she had an absolute right to decide whether Lueli should remain at home, and if she wished him (Lueli) to do so, far from opposing her he (Mr. Fortune) would enforce her authority with his own and insist upon the boy's return.

Lueli's mother looked rather baffled, and crumpled her face exactly as Lueli crumpled his in the effort to follow Mr. Fortune's explanation. But when he had finished she brightened, said that it was all a very good scheme, and asked if Mr. Fortune would like a netful of shrimps?

He spoke a little longer of his affection for the boy, and his plans for teaching him, explaining that though perhaps an European education might not be much use in Fanua, wherefore he was not proposing to trouble him with much arithmetic, yet a Christian education is useful anywhere, and so Lueli must soon learn the Catechism; and then carrying the shrimps he set off to visit Ori.

Ori was the chief man of the island and it would be only civil and politic to consult him. Besides, there was always the chance that Ori might put a spoke in his wheel, a chance not to be missed by any conscientious Englishman. But when Ori had listened to the speech about obedience to God and obedience to lawful authority which Mr. Fortune delivered all over again (with, of course, suitable omissions and alterations) he also said that it was all a very good scheme. Wouldn't Mr. Fortune like a girl too?

Mr. Fortune refused, as politely as his horror would allow, for he had had more than enough of the girls of Fanua. He wished them no harm, it was his hope to live in charity with all men, girls included, and he had no doubt that when they were converted they would become as much better as they should be. But in their present state they were almost beyond bearing. Once upon a time when he was still a bank clerk and had leisure for literature the phrase 'a bevy of young girls' had sounded in his ears quite pleasantly, suggesting something soft as 'a covey of partridges' but lighter in colour. Now it sounded like a cross between a 'pack of wolves,' 'a swarm of mosquitoes,' and 'a horde of Tartars.'

The girls of Fanua always went about in bevies, and ever since his arrival they had pestered him with their attentions. He had but to put his nose into the village for a score of brown minxes to gather round him, entangling him in garlands and snatching at his hat. If he walked on the beach at sunset repeating to himself that sonnet of Wordsworth's:

It is a beauteous evening, calm and free,
The holy time is quiet as a Nun
Breathless with adoration; the broad sun
Is sinking down in its tranquillity;
The gentleness of heaven is on the sea:

long before he had got to:

Dear Child! dear Girl! that walkest with me here,

he was sure to be interrupted by sounds of laughter and splashing, and to find himself encompassed by yet another bevy, naked from the sea, and begging and cajoling him to go bathing with them.

If he fled to the woods they followed him, creeping softly in his tracks. When he thought himself safe and sat down to rest a head and shoulders would be thrust through the greenery; soon there would be half a dozen of them watching him, commenting and surmising on his person, and egging each other on to approach nearer. If he got up to walk away they burst out after him and taking hands entrapped him in the centre of a dance wanton enough to inflame a maypole.

Once these nymphs surprised him bathing. Fortunately the pool he was in was only large enough to hold one at a time, so while it continued to hold him he was tolerably safe. But it was tiresome to have them sitting all round gazing at him as though he might shortly turn into a satyr. He told them to go away, he even begged them to do so, for the water was cold and as modesty compelled him to sit with as much of his person in the water as possible he was growing cramped. But all was in vain; they sat there as expectant as a congregation, and for once sat in silence. His zeal told him that, tiresome as it all was, this opportunity for proselytising should not be missed. Accordingly he began to preach to them with chattering teeth, only his shoulders appearing above the surface of the water, draped in a sort of ruff or boa of water-weed. He preached for an hour and twenty minutes, and then, seeing that they would neither be converted nor go, he reared up out of the pool, strode over the shoulder of the nearest girl and proceeded (the word is more dignified than walked), blue and indignant, toward his clothes. Thank Heaven the young whores had not noticed them!

The best thing that could be said for the girls of Fanua (unless judged as trials of temper, mortifications, and potential stumbling-blocks, in which case they would have received very high marks) was that they afforded an admirable foil to Lueli's maidenly demeanour. Day by day he unrolled such a display of the Christian virtues, was so gentle, so biddable, so deft to oblige, so willing to learn, and just sufficiently stupid to be no trouble, that Mr. Fortune felt that he could have endured even twice as many girls as the price of being soothed by one such boy. He had never beheld, he had never dreamed of such a conversion. Indeed, if it had been his own work he would have been uneasy, wondering if it were not too good to be true. But he acknowledged it to be the Lord's doing and so he was prepared for anything.

But he was not prepared for his paragon to disappear without a word of warning and stay away for three days and four nights.

For the first twenty-four hours he thought little or nothing of it: Lueli was gone birding or gone fishing: he was playing with his friends in the village, or he might be on a visit to his mother. Mr. Fortune had no objection. On the contrary, he was rather pleased that the convert should thus hie him back to the company of his old acquaintance. There had been something disquieting, almost repulsive, in the calm way Lueli had given his former life the go-by. He would not like to think him lacking in natural affection. So he slept through the first night and dabbled through the first day without feeling any uneasiness; but on the second night he dreamed that Lueli had come back, and waking from his dream he ran out into the dell to see if it were a true one.

There was no one there. He called—at first loudly, then he thought that Lueli might be hiding in the bushes afraid to come out lest he should be angry, so he called softly. Then he sat down in the verandah, for he knew there would be no more sleep for him that night, and began to worry, imagining all the dreadful things that might have befallen the boy, and reproaching himself bitterly for having allowed so much time to slip by before he awoke to the possibility of danger. Perhaps Lueli had been drowned. Mr. Fortune knew that he could swim like a fish, but he thought of drowning none the less. Perhaps running through the woods he had been caught like Absalom, or perhaps he had broken his leg and now, tired of calling for help, was lying snuffling with his face to the wet ground. Perhaps he had been carried off in a canoe by natives from some other island to serve as a slave or even as a meal.

'This is nonsense,' said Mr. Fortune. 'The boy is probably somewhere in the village. I will go down as soon as it is day and inquire for him. Only when I know for certain that he is not there will I allow myself to worry.'

For all that he continued to sit on the verandah, shredding his mind into surmises and waiting for the colour of day to come back to the whispering bushes and the black mountain. 'In a little while,' he thought, 'the moon will be in her first quarter and Lueli will not be able to see his way back if he comes by night.'

As soon as he decently could (for he had his dignity as a

missionary to keep up) he walked to the village and made inquiries. No one had seen Lueli; and what was worse, no one could be persuaded into making any suggestions as to his whereabouts or being in the least helpful. There was some sort of feast toward; people were hurrying from house to house with baskets and packages, and the air was thick with taboos. Mr. Fortune hung about for a while, but no one encouraged him to hang on them. Presently he returned to the hut, feeling that the Fanuans were all very heathen and hateful.

Anxious and exasperated he spent the greater part of the day roaming about the woods, harking back every hour or so to the dell and the bathing-pool on the chance that Lueli might have reappeared. In the dell the shadows moved round from west to east and the tide brimmed and retrenched the pool; everything seemed to be in a conspiracy to go on as usual. By sunset he had tormented himself out of all self-control. His distress alternated with gusts of furious anger against his convert. Blow hot, blow cold, each contrary blast fanned his burning. At one moment he pictured Lueli struggling in the hands of marauding cannibals: in the next he was ready to cast him off (that is if he came back) as a runagate, and he began to prepare the scathing and renouncing remarks which should dismiss him. 'Not that I am angry,' he assured himself. 'I am not in the least angry. I am perfectly cool. But I see clearly that this is the end. I have been deceived in him, that is all. Of course I am sorry. And I shall miss him. He had pretty ways. He seemed so full of promise.'

And instantly he was ravaged with pity for the best and most ill-prized convert the world had ever seen, and now, perhaps, the world saw him no longer. Even if he had run away and was still frolicking about at his own sweet will, there was every excuse to be made for him. He was young, he was ignorant, he had not a notion how much suffering this little escapade had entailed on his pastor, he belonged to a people to whom liberty is the most natural thing in the world. And anyhow, had he not a perfect right to run away if he chose to? 'Good heavens, do I want him tethered to me by a string?' So his passion whisked him round again, and he was angrier than ever with Lueli because he was also angry with himself for being ridden by what was little better than an infatuation, unworthy of a man and far more unworthy of a missionary, whose calling it is to love all God's children equally, be they legitimated or no. And he remembered uneasily how in visiting the village that morning he had not breathed a word of conversion.

The idea of having to worry about his own conduct as well as Lueli's agitated him so extremely that he fell on his knees and took refuge in prayer, imploring that his deficiencies might be overlooked and that his sins might not be visited upon Lueli; for it was no fault of the child's, he began to point out to the All-Knowing, that his pastor had chosen to erect him into a stumbling-block. But he was in too much of an upset to pray with any satisfaction, and finding that he was only case-making like a hired barrister he opened his Prayer Book and set himself to read the Forms of Prayer to be Used by Those at Sea, for these seemed appropriate to his case. Thence he read on through the Form and Manner of Making, Ordaining, and Consecrating of Bishops, Priests, and Deacons, and had persevered into the Accession Service when there was a noise behind him. He leapt up to welcome the truant. But it was only a stray pig, looking curiously in on him from the doorway.

'O pig!' Mr. Fortune exclaimed, ready just then to disburden himself to anybody. But the emotion betrayed in his hurt voice was so overwhelming that the pig turned tail and bolted.

He addressed himself once more to the Accession Service. The Prayer Book lay face downward, something had fallen out of it and lay face downward too. It was a little old-fashioned picture with a lace-paper frame, one of those holy valentines that lurk in pious Prayer Books, and in course of time grow very foxed. He looked at it. It was a print of the Good Shepherd, who with His crook was helping a lost sheep out of a pit. Careless of His own equilibrium, the Good Shepherd leant over the verge of the rocks, trying to get a firm grip on the sheep's neck and so haul him up into safety.

Smitten to the heart and feeling extremely small, Mr. Fortune closed up the print in the Prayer Book. He had a shrewd suspicion that this incident was intended as a slightly sarcastic comment on his inadequacies as a shepherd. But he took comfort too, for he felt that God had looked on his distress, even though it were with a frown. And all night (for he lay awake till dawn) he held on to this thought and endeavoured to wait still.

Having been so tossed up and down, by the morrow he was incapable of feeling anything much. He spent the day in a kind of stoical industry, visiting the islanders and preaching to them, though they heard him with even less acceptance than usual, for they were all engaged in sleeping off the feast. During the afternoon he washed his clothes and cleaned the hut, and in the evening he practised the harmonium till his back smouldered with fatigue; and all night he lay in a heavy uncomfortable sleep, imprisoned in it, as though he were cased up in an ill-fitting leaden armour.

He awoke stupefied to bright daylight. He could scarcely remember where he was, or who he was, and his perplexity was increased by finding a number of presences, cold, sleek, and curved, disposed about his limbs. Serpents! In a panic that was half nightmare he sat up. His bed was full of bananas, neatly arranged to encircle him as sausages are arranged to encircle a Christmas turkey. Who had put bananas in his bed? Could it be—? He went swiftly and silently to the door and peered into the dell. There by the spring sat Lueli, arranging shells round the water's edge as though he were laying out a garden. His back was turned, he was so absorbed in his game that he did not discover that he was being watched. Presently he rolled over and lay on his stomach, gently kicking his heels in the air.

Mr. Fortune had a good stare at him. Then he tiptoed back again and began to dress.

As a rule Mr. Fortune was rather careless about his appearance, and compared to the islanders he was decidedly dirty, for whereas they would bathe themselves three times a day or more, he considered that once was enough. But now he made his toilet with extraordinary circumspection and deliberation. He shaved himself as minutely as though he were about to attend an archidiaconal meeting, he parted his hair, he fastened every button with a twitch, he pulled his coat forward so that it should sit well on his shoulders, he wound up his watch and knotted his boot-laces so that they should not come undone. He even put on a hat.

All the while he had a curious sensation that he was dressing a man of stone that must needs be dressed like a dummy, for of itself it was senseless and immovable. Yet *he* was the man of stone, his fingers that slowly and firmly pushed the buttons through the button-holes and knotted the bootlaces were so remorselessly and stonily strong that if he had not been managing them with such care they would have ground the buttons to powder; and if he had allowed them for one moment to tremble the bootlaces would have snapped off in his grasp like black cotton threads.

Walking terribly and softly, and still in this curious stony dream, he stepped into the dell and advanced on Lueli. Lueli turned round. It seemed to Mr. Fortune that he was looking frightened, but he could not be sure of this for his eyes also were partaking of the nature of stone, they did not see very clearly. He came up to Lueli and took hold of him by the shoulder and jerked him on to his feet.

Then, still holding fast to Lueli's shoulder, he said:

'Where have you been?'

Lueli said: 'I have been fishing with my two cousins. For three days we went in our boats and at night we sang.'

But Mr. Fortune did not seem to have heard him, and said again:

'Where have you been?'

Lueli said: 'We paddled round this island and away to the north-west to an islet of shells. I have brought you back these —look!—as a present.'

For the third time Mr. Fortune asked:

'Where have you been?'

But this time he did not wait for an answer. Putting his face close to Lueli's and speaking with his eyes shut and in a low, secret voice, he began to scold him.

'Don't tell me where you've been. I don't care. Why should I care where you go? You made off without asking my leave, so what is it to me where you go to or how long you stay away? Nothing! For I cannot allow myself to love a boy who flouts me. While you were good I loved you, but that goodness didn't last long and I don't suppose it meant much. Why did you run away?

If you had told me, if you had asked my leave, I would have given it gladly. But of course you didn't, you went off without a word, and left me to worry myself half out of my mind. Not that I worried for long. I soon saw that you didn't care a snap of your fingers for me. If you were sorry I would forgive you, but you are not sorry, you are only frightened. I am very angry with you, Lueli—for I cannot call you Theodore now.'

Mr. Fortune's eyes were shut, but he knew that Lueli was frightened for he could feel him trembling. After a minute he began again:

'I can feel how you tremble, but that is silly of you, it only shows how little you understand me. You have no reason to be frightened, don't think I would punish you with blows for I would never do such a thing, I don't approve of it. But something I must do. I must tell you when you do wrong, for it seems that you yourself don't know the difference between good and bad. Why did you run away without telling me where you were going? Was that like a Christian? Was that like a child of God? Do you suppose Samuel would have behaved so, whom you pretend to take such an interest in?'

Mr. Fortune had almost talked himself out. He was feeling dazed by the sound of his own voice, sounding so different too, and he wished Lueli would take a turn. But Lueli continued to tremble in silence, he did not even wriggle, so Mr. Fortune exerted himself to say a few last words.

'Come now, Lueli, what is it to be? Don't be frightened of me. I mean you nothing but good. Perhaps I spoke too angrily, if so, you must forgive me. I was wrong to scold; but you really are maddening, and I have been very anxious about you and not slept much since you ran away. Anxiety always makes people seem stern.'

Now he spoke almost pleadingly, but he still had his hand fast on Lueli's shoulder. At length he noticed this, for his hand was no longer stone but flesh and blood which ached from the intensity of its grip. He withdrew it, and in an instant Lueli had ducked sideways, and with a spring like a frightened deer he fled into the bushes.

Mr. Fortune was in a state to do anything that was desperate, though what, he had not the slightest idea. But suddenly, and completely to his surprise, he found himself convulsed with laughter. He did not know what he was laughing at, till in a flash he remembered Lueli's bolt for safety, and the ludicrous expression, half abject, half triumphantly cunning, with which he had made off. To run away again when he was in such disgrace for running away—this stroke, so utterly unexpected, so perfectly natural, rapt him into an ecstasy of appreciation. He forgave everything that had gone before for leading up to this. And the brat had done it so perfectly too. If he had practised nothing else for years he could not have surpassed that adroit, terror-stricken bound, nor the glance he cast over his shoulder—deprecating, defiant, derisive, alive.

He had never been so real before.

Mr. Fortune propped himself against a tree and laughed himself weak. He had laughed his hat off, his ribs ached, and he squealed as he fetched his breath. At last he could laugh no more. He slid to the ground and lay staring up into the branches with a happy and unseeing interest. He was looking at his thoughts: thoughts that at a less fortunate juncture might have pained him but that now seemed as remote and impersonal a subject for consideration as the sway and lapse of the fronds moving overhead.

How near he had gone to making an irremediable fool of himself, and perhaps worse than a fool! This came of letting oneself get into a fuss, of conscientiously supposing oneself to be the centre of the universe. A man turned into stone by a fury of self-justification, he had laid hold of Lueli and threatened him with pious wrath whilst all the time his longing had been to thrash the boy or to smite his body down on the grass and ravish it. Murder or lust, it had seemed that only by one or the other could he avenge his wounded pride, the priestly rage against the relapsed heretic. And then by the grace of God Lueli had leapt aside with that ludicrous expression, that fantastic agility: and by a moment's vivid realisation of his convert's personality, of Lueli no longer a convert but a person, individual, unexpected, separate, he was released, and laughed the man of stone away.

He looked back on it without embarrassment or any feelings

of remorse. Remorse was beside the point for what was so absolutely over and done with. Lueli had nothing to fear from him now—unless it were indigestion; for he proposed to make him some coco-nut buns as a peace-offering. They were quite easy to make. One just grated the coco-nut into a bowl, added a little water, and drove the contents round with a spoon till they mixed. Then one formed the mixture into rocks, made each rock into a package with leaves, and baked them under the ashes. The results were quite palatable while they remained hot. And Lueli would take it as a compliment.

He would set about it presently. Meanwhile he would lie here, looking up at the tree and taking an interest in his sensations. 'I suppose it is partly reaction,' he thought, 'but I do feel most extraordinarily happy. And as mild as milk—as mothers' milk.' He was not only happy, he was profoundly satisfied, and rather pleased with himself, with his new self, that is.

'And why shouldn't I be? It is a great improvement on the old. It would be absurd to pretend now that I am not entirely different to what I was then. I might as well refuse to feel pleased at waking from a nightmare. A nightmare, a storm of error. The heavens after a thunderstorm, and the air, are so radiant, so fresh, that they seem to be newly created. But they are not: the heavens and the eternal air were created once for all, it is only in man, that creature of a day, so ignorant and fugitive, that these changes can be wrought. The great thing, though, is not to make too much fuss about it. One should take things as they come, and keep reasonably busy. Those buns . . . How I must have frightened that pig!'

This time there were no bananas round him when he woke, and no sign of Lueli. He did not fret himself; knowing how very unfrightening he was he could not seriously apprehend that his convert was much frightened of him.

Nor was he. For hearing his name called he came out from where he had been reconnoitring in the bushes with scufflings so soft and yet so persistent that they might have been self-commendatory: serene, perfectly at his ease, with a pleasant smile and his head only slightly to one side. He showed no tactless anxiety to sound himself in Mr. Fortune's good graces.

Only when Mr. Fortune ventured on a few words of apology did he seem at a loss, frowning a little, and wriggling his toes. He made no answer, and presently introduced a new topic. But he made it quite sufficiently clear that he would prefer an act of oblivion.

From that day the two friends lived together in the greatest amity. True, the very next week Lueli disappeared again. But this time Mr. Fortune remembered his psalm and waited with the utmost peacefulness and contentment. Indeed he found himself quite pleased to be left to the enjoyment of his own society. It had never seemed very enjoyable in old days but it was now. For on this enchanting island where everything was so gay, novel, and forthcoming, his transplanted soul had struck root enough to be responding to the favouring soil and sending up blossoms well worth inspection.

Beyond a few romantic fancies about bathing by moonlight and a great many good resolutions to keep regular hours, Mr. Fortune had scarcely propounded to himself how he would be suited by the life of the only white man on the island of Fanua. In the stress of preparation there had been no incitement to picture himself at leisure. It seemed that between converting the islanders and dissolving soup-squares he would scarcely have an unoccupied minute. Now he found himself in possession of a great many—hours, whole days sometimes, without any particular obligation, stretching out around him waste and tranquil as the outstretched blue sky and sparkling waves.

Leisure can be a lonely thing; and the sense of loneliness is terrifically enhanced by unfamiliar surroundings. Some men in Mr. Fortune's position might have been driven mad; and their madness would have been all the more deep and irrevocable because the conditions that nursed it were so paradisal. A delightful climate; a fruitful soil; scenery of extreme and fairy-tale beauty; agreeable meals to be had at the minimum of trouble; no venomous reptiles and even the mosquitoes not really troublesome; friendly natives and the most romantic lotus—these, and the prospect of always these, would have mocked them into a melancholy frenzy.

But Mr. Fortune happened to be peculiarly well fitted to live on the island of Fanua. Till now there had been no leisure in his life, there had only been holidays; and without being aware of it, in body and soul he was all clenched up with fatigue, so that it was an intuitive ecstasy to relax. He could not have put a name to the strange new pleasure which was come into his existence. He supposed it was something in the air.

As it was with leisure, so it was with luxuriance. Most Englishmen who visit the South Sea Islands are in the depths of their hearts a little shocked at the vegetation. Such fecundity, such a largesse and explosion of life—trees waving with ferns, dripping with creepers, and as it were flaunting their vicious and exquisite parasites; fruits like an emperor's baubles, flowers triumphantly gaudy or tricked out with the most sophisticated improbabilities of form and patterning: all this profusion unbridled and untoiled for and running to waste disturbs them. They look on it as on some conflagration, and feel that they ought to turn the hose on it. Mr. Fortune was untroubled by any such thoughts, because he was humble. The reckless expenditure of God's glory did not strike him as reckless, and his admiration of the bonfire was never overcast by a feeling that he ought to do something about it. Indeed, the man who ten years ago had been putting down in Mr. Beaumont's pass-book: Orchid Growers, Ltd., £72, 15s. od., had presently ceased to pay any special attention to the vegetables of Fanua, and was walking about among them as though they were the most natural thing in the world; which, if one comes to reflect on it, in that part of the world they were.

But though he came to disregard the island vegetation he never ceased to be attentive to the heavens. To have time to watch a cloud was perhaps the thing he was most grateful for among all his leisurely joys. About a mile or so from the hut was a small grassy promontory, and here he would lie for hours on end, observing the skies. Sometimes he chose out one particular cloud and followed it through all its changes, watching how almost imperceptibly it amassed and reared up its great rounded cauliflower curves, and how when it seemed most proud and sculptural it began to dissolve and pour itself into new moulds, changing and changing, so that he scarcely had time to grasp one transformation before another followed it. On some days the clouds scarcely moved at all, but remained poised like vast swans floating asleep with their heads tucked under their wings. They rested on the air, and when they brightened, or changed their white plumage to the shadowy pallor of swans at dusk, it was because of the sun's slow movement, not their own. But those days came seldom, for as a rule the sea wind blew, buoying them onward.

Lying on his stomach Mr. Fortune would watch a cloud come up from the horizon, and as it approached he would feel almost afraid at the silent oncoming of this enormous and towering being, an advance silent as the advance of its vast shadow on the sea. The shadow touched him, it had set foot on the island. And turning on his back he looked up into the cloud, and glancing inland saw how the shadow was already climbing the mountain side.

Though they were silent he imagined then a voice, an enormous soft murmur, sinking and swelling as they tumbled and dissolved and amassed. And when he went home he noted in his diary the direction of the wind and any peculiarities of weather that he had noticed. At these times he often wished, and deeply, that he had a barometer: but he had never been able to afford himself one, and naturally the people of the Mission had thought of a teapot.

On the first really wet day however, he rushed out with joy and contrived a rain-gauge. And having settled this in and buttered its paws, he went for a long rejoicing walk, a walk full of the most complicated animal ecstasy, or perhaps vegetable would be the truer word; for all round him he heard the noise of the woods guzzling rain, and he felt a violent sympathy with all the greenery that seemed to be wearing the deepened colour of intense gratification, and with the rich earth trodden by the rain and sending up a steam of mist as though in acknowledgment. And all the time as he trudged along he was pretending to himself how hardy he was to be out in such disagreeable weather, and looking forward to how nice it would be to get back to the hut and change into dry clothes and boil a kettle for tea.

He was behaving as though he had never been out in the rain

before. It had rained quite often in St. Fabien, indeed there were times when it seemed never to do anything else. But rain there had been a very different matter, veiling the melancholy quay-side, clanking on the roofs of the rabble of tin church premises, and churning the soft grit of the roads into mud. It had rained in St. Fabien and he had constantly been out in it, but with no more ecstasy than he had known when it rained in Hornsey. No doubt the ownership of a rain-gauge accounted for much; but there was more to it than that—a secret core of delight, a sense of truancy, of freedom, because now for the first time in his life he was walking in the rain entirely of his own accord, and not because it was his duty, or what public opinion conceived to be so.

Public opinion was waiting for him in the hut when he got back. While he was still shaking himself like a dog in the verandah, Lueli appeared in the doorway, looking very dry and demure, and began to pet and expostulate in the same breath.

'How very wet! How very silly! Come in at once! Why do you go out when it rains?'

'It is healthy to go for a walk in the rain,' replied Mr. Fortune, trampling firmly on public opinion.

'It would be better to stay under a roof and sleep.'

'Not at all. In England it rains for days at a time, but every one goes out just the same. We should think it very effeminate to stop indoors and sleep.'

'I haven't been asleep the whole time,' Lueli remarked in a defensive voice. 'That new pot of yours—I've been out to fetch it in case it got spoilt.'

While he was drinking his tea (Lueli drank tea also, because his affection and pride made him in everything a copy-cat, but he sipped it with a dubious and wary expression), Mr. Fortune found himself thinking of England. He thought about his father, a sanguine man who suddenly upped and shot himself through the head; and thence his thoughts jumped to a Whitsuntide bank holiday which he had spent in a field near Ruislip. The sky was a pale milky blue, the field was edged with some dowdy elms and beyond them was a view of distant gasworks. At two o'clock he had eaten his lunch—a cold pork chop; and clear as ever he could recall the exquisite unmeaning felicity of that moment.

How little pleasure his youth had known, that this outing should remain with him like an engraved gem! And now he scarcely knew himself for happiness. The former things were passed away: the bank with its façade trimmed with slabs of rusticated stone—a sort of mural tripe; his bed-sitting-room at 'Marmion,' 239 Lyttleton Road, N.E., so encumbered and subfusc; and the horrible disappointment of St. Fabien. There had passed the worst days of his life; for he had expected something of them, he had gone there with an intention of happiness and doing good. But though he had tried his best he had not been able to love the converts, they were degenerate, sickly, and servile; and in his discouragement he had thought to himself: 'It's a good thing I know about book-keeping, for I shall never be fit to do anything better.' And now he was at Fanua, and at his side squatted Lueli, carving a pattern on the rain-gauge.

The next day it rained again, and he went for another walk, a walk not so ecstatic as the former, but quite as wet and no doubt quite as healthy. Hollow peals of thunder rumbled through the cold glades, the chilling South wind blew and the coco-nuts fell thumping from the trees. He walked to his promontory and stood for some time watching the clouds—which were to-day rounded, dark, and voluminous, a presentation to the eye of what the thunder was to the ear—and the waves. He felt no love for the sea, but he respected it. That evening the rain-gauge recorded 1.24.

The project of bathing by moonlight never came to much, for somehow when the time came he was always too sleepy to be bothered; but he was extremely successful in keeping regular hours, for all that so many of them were hours of idleness. Morning prayers, of course, began the day, and after prayers came breakfast. A good breakfast is the foundation of a good day. Mr. Fortune supposed that a great deal of the islanders' lack of steadfastness might be attributed to their ignorance of this maxim. Lueli, for instance, was perfectly content to have no breakfast at all, or satisfied himself with a flibberty-gibberty meal of fruit eaten off the bushes. Mr. Fortune made tea, softened and sweetened at once by coco-milk, and on Sundays coffee. With this he had three boiled eggs. The eggs were those of the wild pigeon, eggs so small that three were really a quite moderate allowance. Unfortunately there was no certainty of them being new-laid, and very often they were not. So it was a notable day when it occurred to him that a native dish of bread-fruit sopped into a paste was sufficiently stodgy and sticky to be perfectly well eaten in lieu of porridge.

After breakfast and a pipe shared with Lueli—he did not really approve of boys of Lueli's years smoking, but he knew that pipe-sharing was such an established Polynesian civility that Lueli's feelings would be seriously wounded if he didn't fall in with the custom—the hut was tidied, the mats shaken in the sun, and the breakfast things put away. Then came instruction in befitting branches of Christian lore; then, because the pupil was at hand and it was well to make sure of him while he had him. For all that there were a good many holidays given and taken. With such an admirable pupil he could afford himself the pleasures of approbation.

Since the teaching had to be entirely conversational, Lueli learnt much that was various and seemingly irrelevant. Strange alleys branched off from the subject in hand, references and similes that strayed into the teacher's discourse as the most natural things in the world had to be explained and enlarged upon. In the middle of an account of Christ's entry into Jerusalem Mr. Fortune would find himself obliged to break off and describe a donkey. This would lead naturally to the sands of Weston-super-Mare, and a short account of bathing-machines; and that afternoon he would take his pupil down to the beach and show him how English children turned sand out of buckets, and built castles with a moat round them. Moats might lead to the Feudal System and the Wars of the Barons. Fighting Lueli understood very well, but other aspects of civilisation needed a great deal of explaining; and Mr. Fortune nearly gave himself heat apoplexy by demonstrating in the course of one morning the technique of urging a golf ball out of a bunker and how English housewives crawl about on their hands and knees scrubbing the linoleum.

After dismissing Lueli from his lessons Mr. Fortune generally strolled down to the village to enlarge the work of conversion. By now he had given up general preaching and exhortation—not that he thought it a bad way to go to work, on the contrary, he knew that it had been sanctioned by the best Apostolic usage; but preaching demands the concurrence of an audience, even though it be one of fishes or pigs; and since he was no longer a novelty the islanders had become as slippery as the one, as artful and determined in dodging away as the other. He practised instead the Socratic method of pouncing upon any solitary and defenceless person who happened to pass by. And like Socrates he would lead them aside into the shade and ask them questions.

Many charming conversations took place. But nothing ever came of them, and the fields so white for the harvest continued to ripple and rustle in the sun, eluding all his efforts to reap and bind them into sheaves and carry them into God's barn in time for the harvest-home.

He had now been on the island for nearly six months, and every day he knew himself to have less attractive power. How he wished that he had thought of bringing some fireworks with him! Two or three rockets touched off, a green Bengal light or a Catherine wheel, he would have been sure of a congregation then. And there is no religious reason why fireworks should not be used as a means to conversion. Did not God allure the fainting Israelites by letting Himself off as a pillar of fire by night? He thought, though, that had he fireworks at his command he would draw the line at that variety which is known as British Cannon. They are very effective, but they are dangerous; and he did not wish to frighten his flock.

From midday till about two or three in the afternoon there was no possibility of converting anybody, for the islanders one and all went firmly to sleep. This was the time when Mr. Fortune went for his daily walk. After so much endeavour he would have been quite pleased to take a nap himself; but he knew the value of regular exercise, and by taking it at this time of day he was safe from molestation by the bevies. He usually ate a good deal of fruit on these walks, because he had not yet accustomed himself to such a long stretch between breakfast and dinner. Indeed for some time after his arrival on the island he felt rather underfed. Dinner consisted of more bread-fruit, messes prepared by Lueli, fish sometimes, roots flavoured with seawater.

Lueli preferred his fish raw. Sometimes Mr. Fortune made soup or opened a tin of sardines.

Dinner was immediately followed by afternoon tea. Mr. Fortune would not forego that comfortable meal, so they had it as a sort of dessert. Then followed a long sub-afternoon, spent in various ways of doing nothing in particular. Lueli always went bathing then. He had no theories about it being dangerous to bathe on the heels of a large meal, and after an interval for digestion Mr. Fortune bathed too. Sometimes they paid visits, or received them. On these occasions Mr. Fortune never spoke of religion. He produced his pocket magnifying-glass and showed them his pores. At other times they went sailing or took a stroll.

These were all pleasant doings, but perhaps the moment he enjoyed best was when, dusk having fallen, he lit the lamp. He had a peculiar affection for his lamp. It hung from the ridge-pole of the hut, and he felt about it much as Sappho felt about the evening star. It shone as though with a kindness upon everything that was dear to him: upon his books and the harmonium; upon the bowls and dishes and woven mats that were both dear in themselves as tokens of the islanders' good-will, and endeared by use; upon the wakeful shine of the teapot and the black tin box, and upon Lueli's sleepy head. He would often walk out into the darkness for the pleasure of seeing his hut lighted up within, the rays of warm light shining through the chinks in the latticed walls as though they were shining through a very large birds' nest. Overhead were the stars trembling with the intensity of their remote fires. The air was very sweet and the dark grass gentle underfoot as he walked round about his home.

He whistled to himself, softly, an air that Delilah sings in the oratorio of *Samson*— a rather foolish, chirruping tune, in which Handel expressed his private opinion of soprano Delilahs: but he liked the words—

How charming is domestic ease,
A thousand ways I'll strive to please:

(after that they ceased to be appropriate).

A thousand, thousand ways he would strive to please until he had converted all the islanders. And planning new holy wiles for the morrow, he re-entered the hut to eat a slight supper, and perhaps to darn a rent or replace a button, and then to write up his diary, to read prayers, and so to end another day.

Saturdays and Saints' days were holidays, for himself and Lueli both. Lueli disported himself as he pleased, and Mr. Fortune watched clouds. On Sundays they performed the services appointed by the Church of England.

There was a week or two when he believed that he was in the way to make another convert. She was a very old woman, extremely ugly, not very agreeable, and rather doting. But she seemed perfectly able to understand about eternal life, and showed great anxiety to lay hold on it. Mr. Fortune visited her daily and tried hard to teach her the love of God, and the Christian belief. But she seemed deaf to all topics save one—and her anxiety to lay hold became as the days went by positively grasping.

One day the wife of Teioa, a sensible woman whom Mr. Fortune had a great respect for, came in with some food for the invalid and overheard part of their colloquy.

'Live for ever,' she remarked rather scornfully to the missionary as they left the house. 'Why, isn't she old enough already? How much more does she want?' And though Mr. Fortune deplored her blindness, yet in this particular instance he admitted to himself that she had perceived clearly enough, and that his old woman was no sort of genuine convert, only very old and frightened and rapacious. None the less he continued to visit her, and to do what he could to comfort her. And often as he sat by her bedside he thought what a mystery this business of eternal life is, and how strangely, though almost all desire it, they differ in their conception of what it is they desire; some, like Shakespeare (and how many others unknown?) coolly confident of an immortality

Where breath most breathes, even in the mouths of men;

some, like Buddha, hoping for an eternal life in which their own shall be absolved and lost; some, like this old woman, desiring an eternity like an interminable piece of string which she could clutch one end of and reel for ever about herself. 'And how do I desire it?' he thought. 'I want to feel it on every side, more abundantly. But I want to die first.'

In the end he grew quite attached to the old creature, and when she died he was sorry. He would have liked, as a mark of respect, to attend her funeral: (he certainly did not feel that he had any claim to conduct it himself). But no one suggested that he should, and he hesitated to suggest it lest he should be offending against some taboo. So he went off by himself for a day in the woods and thought about her, and said a prayer or two. And in the evening he returned to Lueli. One convert at any rate had been granted to him, and perhaps it would be greedy to want more, especially as that one was in every way so exemplary and delightful.

The two friends—for such they were despite more than sixty degrees of latitude and over thirty years between them (and the latter is a more insuperable barrier than an equator)—lived together in the greatest amity. Lueli had now quite give up running away. He settled down to Mr. Fortune's ways, and curled himself up amidst the new customs and regulations as peacefully as though he had never known any other manner of existence. Indeed Mr. Fortune was sometimes obliged to pack him off to the village to play with the other boys, thinking that it would harm him never to be with company of his own age.

Lueli was no anchorite, he enjoyed larking about the island with his friends as much as any boy should do; but what he loved beyond anything was novelty, and for this he worshipped Mr. Fortune, whose every action might reveal some new and august entertainment. The faces he made in shaving, the patch of hair on his chest, his ceremonious method of spitting out pips into his hand, the way in which his boot-laces went round the little hooks, his watch, his pockets and the things he kept in them—Lueli might grow accustomed to these daily delights, but he did not tire of them any more than Wordsworth tired of the Lesser Celandine. And there was more than this, and much more: prayer, the harmonium, the sewing-machine, religious instruction and occasional examples of European cookery. Prayer Lueli had taken to from the beginning, but he needed to acclimatise himself to the harmonium. When Mr. Fortune played to him he would sit as close as possible to the instrument, quivering like a dog and tilting up his chin with such an ecstatic and woebegone look that Mr. Fortune almost expected him to howl; and thinking that he didn't really enjoy it he would leave off playing. But Lueli would then edge a little closer and beg for more, and Mr. Fortune was only too glad to comply.

Like the harpsichord, the harmonium has a repertory of its own, pieces that can only be properly rendered on this instrument. Naturally I do not speak of the harmonium compositions of such recent composers as Schoenberg or Max Reger: these would have been too difficult for Mr. Fortune to play even if they had been stocked by the music-shop he had frequented. But without being in any way a virtuoso—and some think that the harmonium, being essentially a domesticated instrument, sober and of a religious cast, is inherently unsuited for displays of skill—Mr. Fortune played quite nicely and had a repertory of many classical larghettos and loud marches, besides, of course, the usual hymns and chants. Haydn was his favourite composer; and arrangements from the string quartets go rather well on the harmonium.

Lueli too was a musician after a simpler fashion. He had a wooden pipe, rather like a flageolet, of a small compass and a sad, squeaky tone; and the two friends passed many happy evenings entertaining each other with their performances. First Mr. Fortune obliged, leaning forward at an acute angle on the music-stool, his knees rising and falling like parts of a machine, his face very close to the music, his large hands manœuvring among the narrow keys, or sometimes hovering like a bee in a flower border over the ranks of stops, pulling out one, hitting another back with a tap, as though his fingers could read, though rather short-sightedly, in black Gothic lettering on the ivory knobs such names as Gamba, Corno di Bassetto, Bourdon, or Dulciana. And then, when rising he released the last throbbing chord and stretched himself (for he was a tall man, and in order to adjust his body and legs to the instrument he had to assume a rather cramped position), it was pleasant to see Lueli discoursing music in his turn, and a curious study in contrasts. For the boy sat cross-legged on the floor, or leant against the wall in the attitude of the boy in the statue, an attitude so physically nonchalant, so spiritually intent, that whoever looks at the statue, or even a cast of it or a photograph, understands, sometimes with a kind of jealous horror, how musicians are free of a world of their own, inhabiting their bodies as it were nominally or by proxy—just as we say of a house: That is Mr. So-and-So's; but the house is empty save for a sleepy caretaker, the owner is away travelling in Africa.

Lueli's tunes were very long tunes, though the phrases composing them were short; the music seemed to waver to and fro, alighting unexpectedly and then taking another small flight, and listening to it was like watching a bird flitting about in a bush; the music ends, the bird flies away; and one is equally at a loss to explain why the bird stayed so long and seemed so busy or why it suddenly made up its mind that the time had come for a longer flight, for a flight that dismisses it from our vision.

To tell the truth, Mr. Fortune was not as much impressed by Lueli's music as Lueli was by his. His chin even sank further into his chest as he sat, his listening flesh was unmoved, and he never felt the least impulse to howl. Mr. Fortune, in spite of his superior accomplishments, his cultivated taste, and enough grasp of musical theory to be able to transpose any hymn into its nearly related keys, was not so truly musical as Lueli. For instance, he never had the least idea whether Lueli's tunes were lively or sad. They all seemed alike to him. But Lueli learnt almost immediately to distinguish between a march and a sentimental piece, and as the harmonies grew more and more passionate his chin would lift higher, his mouth would contract, and the shadow of his long eyelashes would shorten up over his cheek.

It would have been pleasant if the two musicians could have joined forces. Mr. Fortune by listening very often and pretty intently to Lueli's rambling tunes was able to memorise two of them—as he believed, perfectly. Sending Lueli down to the village he spent an afternoon practising these two melodies on the harmonium and putting in a part for the left hand. It would make an agreeable surprise for his boy, he thought, to hear his tunes played by some one else; and then with Lueli playing his pipe whilst he supported the melody with chords and figurations they could achieve a duet. But the surprise fell quite flat; perhaps Mr. Fortune's European harmonies queered the pitch, perhaps he had misunderstood the time-values; in any case Lueli showed no signs of recognising the tunes, and even when their identity was pointed out to him he seemed doubtful. As for the duet plan it was not feasible, for the harmonium was tuned to the mean tone temperament and Lueli's pipe obeyed some unscientific native scale; either alone sounded all right, but in conjunction they were painfully discordant.

Finding it impossible to convert Lueli's pipe, Mr. Fortune next essayed to train his voice to Christian behaviour. In this he was more successful; Lueli's voice was of a nondescript newly broken timbre. He couldn't always control it, and Mr. Fortune had to smoke his pipe very hard in order not to laugh at the conjunction of Lueli's expression, so determined in well-doing, and the vagaries of his voice wandering from the straight path and ricochetting from note to note.

He also taught him to whistle, or tried to, for he was rather shocked at the idea of a boy not knowing how to whistle, explaining to him beforehand the secular nature of the act, and forbidding him to whistle tunes that had any especially sacred associations. But though Lueli screwed up his lips and almost burst himself taking in breath his whistling remained of a very girlish incompetent kind. On the other hand he showed an immediate aptitude for the vulgar kind of whistling which is done with a blade of grass. The first hearing of this was one of the pleasantest surprises that his pastor gave him. He mastered the technique in a few minutes and raced off to show the new accomplishment to his friends in the village. The fashion caught on like wildfire, and soon every boy on the island was looking for the proper blades of grass, which are called squeakers. The woods rang with their performances, and the parrots looked down with awe and astonishment at hearing men producing sounds so much more ear-splitting than anything they could achieve themselves.

The fashion raged like wildfire, and like wildfire burnt itself out. The groves were peaceful again, that is to say peaceful as any groves can be with parrots in them (not that the reader should suppose that the parrots at Fanua were like the parrots in the Zoological Gardens: oppression makes them much noisier); and every one was out in the salt-meadows, passionately flying kites.

The islanders were like that; enthusiastic and fickle, they would wear a whim to shreds and cast it away in the course of a week. Lueli was as bad; if it had not been for Mr. Fortune he would never have persevered in anything. It was provoking for a master to find his pupil so changeable and inconstant, all the more so because of Lueli's extraordinary docility and aptitude in learning. Nothing could have exceeded the readiness with which he accepted a new idea; and finding him so swift to become a Christian Mr. Fortune used to wonder why the other islanders would not respond as pleasantly to his teaching, for at this time he was still in hopes of converting the whole island. He preached to them, he prayed among them, every night and morning he prayed for them, he gave them biscuits and showed them pictures. They behaved themselves to him most charmingly, tactfully overlooking his blunders in etiquette, accepting him as their friend, though an unaccountable one. But his message they would not accept, it slid off them as though their very innocence and guilelessness had spread a fine impermeable film over their souls.

'After all,' thought Mr. Fortune, 'I have not made a single convert in this island though it is now almost a year since I came. For I did not convert Lueli, God gave him to me (by the way I must remember to call him Theodore). And God still withholds the others.'

This was a comfortable point of view. It satisfied Mr. Fortune, all the more so since it agreed so aptly with his psalm, of which the last verse runs: 'And that Thou, Lord, art merciful: for Thou rewardest every man according to his work.' And he quoted this verse of it in the report which he handed to Archdeacon Mason on returning to St. Fabien to buy more stores and give an account of his ministry.

The Archdeacon frowned slightly when he laid down the report, which was a pretty piece of work, for Mr. Fortune had written it in his neatest hand and Lueli (under his direction) had tinted blue, fawn-colour, and green the little sketch-map of the island which embellished it as a frontispiece.

The next day Mr. Fortune called upon his superior. 'My dear Fortune,' said he after a few polite questions about the soil of Fanua and its marriage ceremonies, 'this is excellent' (here he tapped the report which lay on the table). 'Indeed I may say it is idyllic. But you must allow me to make one comment, you must let me tell you that there is such a thing as being too modest. Believe me, conversions at the rate of one *per annum* are not an adequate reward of your works. God's grace is infinite, and I am sure that your labours have been most truly conscientious; and yet you say you have made only one convert. This is not enough—mind, I would not speak a word of blame. I only say—if I may so express myself—that there must have been a leakage somewhere, a leakage!'

He paused. Mr. Fortune looked at his hands and realised how sunburnt they had become.

'Compel them to come in, you know.'

Mr. Fortune wondered if he should confess to his superior the one so nearly disastrous occasion when he had tried to use compulsion. But the Archdeacon's metaphor about the leakage had pained him and he decided not to. Instead he asked the Archdeacon how he would advise him to act in order to convert the whole island.

It was rather a shock to him to be recommended to take a leaf out of the Jesuits' book. However on the first evening of his return to the island he began to make some discreet inquiries of Lueli about what gods the islanders worshipped, though being very careful to convey by his tone and choice of words that he thought it a terrible pity that they should not worship his.

'Oh, they,' said Lueli, offering him some more fruit, which Mr. Fortune refused, since he had been stuffed with gifts in kind ever since the moment he got out of the launch. 'Oh, they—they only worship one god.'

This answer did not sound quite as it should; and in deference to his recent memories of the Archdeacon, Mr. Fortune ran his convert through the Apostles' Creed before proceeding with his inquiries. It was quite all right. Lueli remembered the creed without a single lapse, and on further questioning Mr. Fortune discovered that the islanders worshipped one god each, a much more suitable state of affairs for heathens; although on thinking it over before he fell asleep the missionary reflected that in the island of Fanua conversion must necessarily be a slow business since he would have to break the faggot stick by stick. Just before he lost consciousness he began to wonder what sort of god Lueli had worshipped.

In the morning he remembered his curiosity. He said to Lueli: 'What god had you before I came and taught you to know the true God?'

'I'll show him to you,' said Lueli; and running into the bushes he presently returned with an idol about two foot long.

Mr. Fortune looked at the idol very seriously, almost respectfully, as though he were measuring swords with an adversary. It was a rather well-looking idol, made of wood and nicely polished, and he was pleased to note that it was not obscene; but for all that a slight shudder ran through his flesh, such as one feels on looking at a dead snake even though one knows that it is a dead one.

'Drop it,' he commanded, and the boy laid it down on the grass between them. Mr. Fortune remembered the words of a female missionary from China who had visited St. Fabien on a tour. 'The first thing I make my converts do,' she had said, and as she spoke she clenched her hands till the knuckles showed up as bones, 'is to destroy their idols. Then I can feel sure of them. And not till then.'

Talking over her lecture afterwards Mr. Fortune had been of the opinion of the majority: that the lady missionary had been right. 'I don't agree at all,' said his friend, Henry Merton. 'We teach that idols are the works of men's hands, things of wood and stone. To insist on their destruction is to show our converts that we believe in them ourselves, that we look on them with anxiety and attribute power to them. No, no, it is silly to take any idol so seriously!' And Mr. Fortune, who was humble before others, thought that after all he had judged too hastily and that his friend was in the right of it.

Soon after that Henry Merton had died, and the words of the dead have a special value. Mr. Fortune remembered his friend's opinion, but he also remembered the female missionary. She had spoken with an air of authority; and for all he knew she might be dead too, she might even be a martyr. He stood and looked at Lueli's idol which lay on the grass between them and he wondered if he should tell Lueli to burn it. At last, without saying anything, he walked into the hut. When he came out again Lueli was scouring a wooden bowl with sand and the idol was gone.

One of the Archdeacon's first questions about the convert of Fanua was: Had Mr. Fortune dressed him properly? And Mr. Fortune had replied with perfect candour that he had been too busy caring for his soul to think of his clothing. This too the Archdeacon had objected to, saying that dress made a great difference, and that when the other islanders saw Lueli dressed befittingly they would become aware of their nakedness and wish to be converted and wear white raiment.

'But they have seen me, *I* have never omitted to dress myself since I have lived on Fanua.'

'No, no, of course not,' answered the Archdeacon, a little testily, for really the missionary's simplicity was making him very argumentative and tiresome. 'But that is not to the point, for you surely don't suppose that they look on you as one of themselves. You must clothe that boy, Fortune, you must make him wear trousers and a tunic. And at night he must wear a night-shirt.'

So now, seeing that the idol was gone, Mr. Fortune called Lueli into the hut and began to measure him. He had never learnt tailoring; however he supposed that by taking great care and doing his best he could turn out a suit of clothes which might insinuate the fact of their nakedness to the islanders of Fanua, even if it had no other merit. He measured Lueli, he wrote down the measurements, he made his calculations and drew a sort of ground plan. Then he fetched a roll of white cotton and having laid it upon the floor and tethered it with some books he crawled about on all fours cutting out the trousers and the tunic with a pair of nail-scissors; for he thought that the night-shirt might rest in abeyance for the present.

The nail-scissors could only manage very small bites, and by the time the cutting-out was completed he was rather dizzy and very hot from taking so much exercise on his knees. 'That will do for the present,' he thought, rolling up the pieces. 'This afternoon I will visit my parishioners. Perhaps as they have not seen me for a week they will be more inclined to listen to my teaching. And I must keep my eyes open for idols.'

But early on the morrow Mr. Fortune got out the sewing-machine and continued his career as a tailor. The sewing-machine was suffering from the sea-air, it needed a great deal of oil and adjustment before it could be got to run smoothly, but he mastered it in the end and began to sew up the seams. As time went on he grew more and more excited. He worked the treadles faster and faster, he had never, even for the most spirited march, trodden the pedals of his harmonium so frantically; the machine rocked under his zeal and all the time the needle kept darting up and down, piercing the cotton with small accurate stabs in a way that seemed to express a kind of mechanical malevolence. The seams were all finished, the hems were turned up; now it was evening, there was nothing left but the buttons. Those he must put on by hand.

All day Lueli had sat beside him watching his performance with rapture. It was the machine which ravished him, he was not so much interested in the clothes. But when Mr. Fortune called him in a rather solemn voice and began to dress him, holding up the tunic above his head as though it were a form of baptism, he too began to put on looks of solemnity and importance.

The tunic fitted tolerably enough though there was no elegance about it; but alas! the trousers were a sad blow to Mr. Fortune. For he had designed them on a two-dimensional basis, cutting out the back and the front in one operation on a doubled fold of the cloth, and forgetting that even the slimmest boy is bulkier behind than in front; so that when attired in these unfortunate garments it was difficult for Lueli to move and almost impossible for him to sit down. He, in his innocence, thought the trousers all that they should be, and late as it was he wished to run down to the village in order to wake up his friends and show them his fine clothes. But Mr. Fortune bade him take them off. It made his heart bleed to see his boy made such a figure of fun, and when the living Lueli emerged from his white cotton sepulchre he privately called the Archdeacon a fool and forswore the idea of the night-shirt for good and all. But on the next day and on the next again he struggled to make a practicable pair of trousers, and in the end he produced a pair that were rather on the baggy side perhaps, but still they were tolerable.

Unfortunately by this time his convert's ardour was somewhat quenched. He had been measured so often, he had stood still to be fitted when he wanted to go fishing, he had had pins run into him, and all this had made this particular novelty seem rather a tedious example of his pastor's odd ways. So though he put on his white raiment at command and walked decorously through the village beside Mr. Fortune to be an object lesson, his demeanour, while admirably meek and civil, wasn't much of an advertisement for the happiness of those who are clothed in the whole armour of God.

The Archdeacon's theory was not borne out by events. The islanders were too much struck and roused to speculation by the sight of Lueli's apparel to spare a thought for their own nakedness. At first they were of the opinion that this was some new and powerful taboo invented by the stranger. They shrank back, and averted their eyes as if from some improper spectacle. Lueli's mother was actually moved to a display of maternal feeling. She rushed weeping from the crowd, hurled herself at Mr. Fortune's knees and began to implore him not to ruin the boy's prospects. Disentangling himself a little pettishly from her pleadings, Mr. Fortune explained that clothing such as this would do Lueli nothing but good: indeed, she herself would be none the worse for something of the sort. She took him at his word; before he could stay her she had torn the clothes off her son and was squirming into them. She was several sizes too fat, and Mr. Fortune saw his seams being rent open in all directions. He had to bribe her with a promise of the blue glass mulberries from his Christmas tree selection before she would consent to undress. Finally he had to ease her out himself. It was a good thing that the Archdeacon was not present, but for all that Mr. Fortune half wished that he had been.

On their return he sewed up the seams once more and called Lueli. The boy began to protest and argue. Then he changed his methods and started coaxing. Mr. Fortune had his own ideas as to how Lueli should be managed. Rising discreetly he opened the harmonium and said that it was time to study another hymn.

That night he lay awake, wondering what he would do if his convert rebelled. He had already decided to drop the Archdeacon's tactics at the first seemly opportunity; but he wished to choose the opportunity and do the dropping himself. He might have spared himself this anxiety. On the morrow Lueli donned the trousers and the tunic with a very matter of course air, and half an hour later went off to bathe. And it was a sure thing that if formerly he had bathed twice or thrice a day he now bathed as often again, undressing with a bland smile and folding up his white raiment with the utmost neatness. Of course it was a pretext; and the missionary wondered if his charge was learning to be deceitful. But Lueli's deceitfulness was so very open and unconcerned that it could scarcely be reckoned as the genuine article.

The clothes were always deposited very carefully in some place where they would have every opportunity of happening to fall into the sea. At the end of a week they were so saturated with brine as to be quite unwearable. Exercising his authority, Mr. Fortune forbade Lueli to wear them any more.

Lueli would bathe anywhere, he seemed equally happy lolling on the Pacific Ocean or folded up in a pool the size of a bedroom basin with a little waterfall splashing on his head. Mr. Fortune was more ceremonious. It was he who instituted the bathing-pool as a regular adjunct to their life.

About half a mile from the hut and near the cloud observatory was a small rocky cove with a half-moon of white shell-beach and a slope of fine sward running back into the woods. A small rivulet debouched here, very convenient for washing off the sea-salt in; and as the mouth of the cove was guarded by a barrier of coral-reef the water within was almost as still as a lake, and so clear that one could look down and see the weeds twenty feet below slowly twirling their vast brown or madder-coloured ribbons, and the fish darting among them.

Mr. Fortune often thought of Robinson Crusoe and his man Friday as he sat on the rocks watching Lueli at his interminable diversions in the pool. Living on an island alone with his convert, spiritually alone at any rate, for though he had not given up hope of the other Fanuans and still visited them pretty frequently, he could never feel the kinship with them which he felt so securely with Lueli, the comparison could scarcely fail to occur to him. And he thought gratefully how much happier he was than the other man. *He* was ideally contented with his island and with his companion, he had come there by his own wish, and he liked the life so well that he proposed to continue in it until his death. So little did it distress him to be away from civilisation that he was of his own will paring away the slender bonds that tied him to the rest of the world. For after the first visit to St. Fabien he had paid no more, and for the last twelvemonth he had not even bestirred himself to write a report to be sent by canoe to the island of Maikalua, where a local steamer touched once a month. But poor Crusoe had no such contented mind. His is a tragic story, albeit considered so entertaining for schoolboys: and though his stay on the island taught him to find religion it did not teach him to find happiness, but whether at work or at leisure he was always looking with a restless and haggard stare at the rigid horizon, watching for a sail, enemy or friend, he knew not.

'I see numbers of goats. Melancholy reflections.' What a world of sombre and attentive ennui, thought Mr. Fortune, is summed up in those words! The goats might supply him with suppers and raiment, but not with a cheerful thought. Their antics were wasted on him, he observed them without a smile, without sympathy, as unresponsive to natural history as the traduced Alexander Selkirk of Cowper's poem; for the real Alexander was a much more genial character who sometimes danced and sang with his troop of pet animals. True, Robinson was fond of his dog, and kind to him, setting him on his right hand at meal-times even after he was grown 'very old and crazy.' He also gave decent burial to the two cats. But these were English animals, fellow-countrymen, assuring relics of the time when he had been knolled to church with other Christians: and it was for this he cherished them, clinging to them with a trivial and desperate affection.

No! In spite of his adventurous disposition and his knowledge of the world, he was not really suited to life on an island, this man who is for all time the representative of island-dwellers. Of course, his island was very different from Fanua: larger, not so beautiful probably; certainly not so convenient. And no doubt the presence of natives would have made a great difference to him. He was the sort of man who would soon marry. 'But to be honest with myself,' thought Mr. Fortune, 'though I came here to convert the islanders, except for my Friday I don't think I should miss their company if it were withdrawn. My happiness is of a rather selfish and dream-like kind and I take my life very much for granted. Why, I have not even walked round the island. That would seem strange to some, they would not believe in me. I should seem as absurd and idyllic as those other Robinsons, that Swiss family, who whenever they needed anything found it cast up on the shore or growing on a tree. I should be even more unlikely than Leila."

And he began to ponder on how many years had gone by since he last thought of Leila. She came in a book belonging to his step-sister, and he had read it secretly and rather bashfully, because it was a book for girls. But he had been obliged to read on, for the subject of islands had always enthralled him. Leila was shipwrecked on a desert island with her papa, her nurse, a spaniel, and a needle. One day the needle was dropped by Leila and lost in the sand. Here was a sad to-do! But the nurse, a very superior politic woman, bade the spaniel 'Go seek'; and presently he uttered a yelp and came running towards them with the needle sticking in his nose.

A very thin story! Yet it might have happened for all that it was so fortunate. Things do sometimes fall out as we would have them, though perhaps not often, for it is always the happy coincidences which are hardest to credit. Man, however gullible and full of high ideals for his own concerns, is suspicious of good-fortune in general. If Robinson had enjoyed himself on the island he would not have been received as somebody in real life.

'But I am in real life,' thought Mr. Fortune, adroitly jerking a limpet to assure himself of being so, 'although I am so happy in my lot. I am real too, as real as Robinson. Some people might even say I was more real than he, because my birth is mentioned in the church register, and I used to pay income-tax, whereas he was only entered at Stationers' Hall. But I don't agree with them. I may seem to have the advantage of him now, but it is only temporary. In twenty years' time, maybe less, who will even remember my name?'

From such reflections he would be diverted by Lueli politely handing him a long streamer of seaweed, dripping and glistening, and freshly exhaling its deep-sea smell—a smell that excites in one strongly and mysteriously the sense of life—or beckoning to him with a brown hand that held a silver fish. These advances meant that Lueli thought it time for Mr. Fortune to bathe too, and to take his swimming-lesson—a turning of the tables which the convert considered extremely amusing and satisfactory.

He was a very poor pupil. As a child he had never done more than paddle about, and now he was too old to learn easily. He did not lack goodwill or perseverance, but he lacked faith. Faith which can remove mountains can also float. Mr. Fortune had not enough of it to do either. In the depths of his heart he mistrusted the sea, an ambiguous element. The real sea beyond the reef he never dreamed of venturing in, he could imagine how the long nonchalant rollers would pick him up and hurl him with their casual strength upon the rocks. Even in this sheltered pool he could gauge their force; for though scarcely a ripple traversed the surface, to every leisurely surge that crashed on the reef the pool responded throughout its depth with a thrill, a tremor, an impulsion, and the streamers of seaweed turned inland one after another as though they were obeying a solemn dance music.

But for all his mistrust he enjoyed bathing, indeed the mistrust put a tang into his enjoyment. And with looks of derring-do he struck out into the middle of the pool, his teeth set, his eyes rolling, splashing horribly and snorting a good deal, labouring himself along with uncouth convulsions, while Lueli swam beside him or round him or under him as easily as a fish and with no more commotion, seeming like a fish to propel himself and change his direction with an occasional casual flip.

The further half of the pool, under the wall of rock whence Lueli used to dive, was extremely deep. Whenever he had got so far Mr. Fortune was afraid and not afraid. He had a natural fear, but he had a reasonable trust; for he knew that while Lueli was by he would never drown. It was sweet to him to be thus relying upon his convert—that was part of the pleasure of bathing. On shore it was fit and proper that Lueli should look up to him and learn from him; but every affectionate character, even though it be naturally a dominant one, spending itself by rights in instruction and solicitude, likes sometimes to feel dependent. People, the most strong-minded people, perfectly accustomed to life, being ill may discover this; and as they lie there, passive, tended, and a little bewildered, may be stirred to the depths of their being by finding themselves wrapped once more in the security of being a good child. Mr. Fortune bathing in the pool did not go quite so far as this. His dependence was not quite so emotional and he was too busy keeping himself afloat to analyse his feelings very carefully; but he liked to depend on Lueli, just as he liked Lueli to depend on him.

Though so ready to learn swimming from Lueli he was less favourably inclined to another of his convert's desires: which was to oil him. He would not for the world have had Lueli guess it; but at the first proposal of these kind offices he was decidedly shocked. Lueli oiled himself as a matter of course, and so did everybody on the island. They also oiled each other. Mr. Fortune had no objection. It was their way. But below all concessions to broad-mindedness his views on oiling were positive and unshakable. They were inherent in the very marrow of his backbone, which was a British one. Oiling, and all that sort of thing, was effeminate, unbecoming, and probably vicious. It was also messy. And had Hector and Achilles, Brutus and Alexander defiled before him, all of them sleek and undeniably glistening as cricket-bats, he would have been of the same opinion still.

'No, thank you,' he said, firmly putting aside the flask of scented coco-nut oil (scented, too!). Or: 'Not just now, Lueli, I am going for a walk. Exercise is the best thing after bathing.' Or again: 'Unfortunately oil has a very painful effect on my skin.'

But he knew all the time that sooner or later he would have to muffle up his prejudices and give in, for every day Lueli began to look, first more hopeful and then more hurt, and was perpetually (if figuratively) standing on his head in the attempt to produce some unguent which could not injure his friend's sensitive skin. So when he sprained his knee jumping off a rock he welcomed the pretext with feelings intricately compounded of relief and apostasy. For some weeks he confined the area of effeminacy to his left knee, and on one occasion he was base enough to lacerate the flesh in secret with a fish-hook in an attempt to justify the statement about his skin. But Lueli was so piteously full of compunction and so certain that if he climbed a yet higher tree or went in a canoe to another island he would be able to procure a balm entirely blameless, that Mr. Fortune was ashamed of the prank and counterfeited no more. Indeed he was beginning to enjoy what he assured himself was not oiling, nothing of the sort, but a purely medicinal process. And by the time he had finished with the sprain it struck him that something of the same kind might be good for his rheumatism. After all there was nothing but what was manly and might quiet him in Elliman's Embrocation—used extensively by many athletes and as far as he could remember by horse-doctors.

Mr. Fortune kept his rheumatism up and down his back, but inevitably a little of the embrocation slopped over his shoulders. By the end of six months he was stretching himself out for Lueli's ministrations as methodically as when in the old days at the corner of the Hornsey Parade he offered one foot and then the other to the boot-black. It did him a great deal of good, and improved his appearance tenfold, though that did not matter to him. Nothing could make him fat, but he began to look quite well-liking. The back of his hands grew smooth and suent, he ceased to have goose-flesh on his thighs, and one day, regarding himself more attentively than usual in the little shaving mirror, he discovered that somehow his expression had changed. How and why he would not stoop to examine into; but Lueli could have told him. For when he came to the island his face was so parched and wrinkled that it was like a mask of rough earthenware, and his eyes, being the only surface in it that looked alive, also looked curiously vulnerable. But now his face had come alive too, and instead of wrinkles had rather agreeable creases that yielded and deepened when he laughed. And his eyes were no longer vulnerable, but just kind.

But if Mr. Fortune had altered during his three years on the island, Lueli had altered a great deal more. Not in character though—he was still the same rather casual compendium of virtues and graces; nor in behaviour; for he still hung affectionately and admiringly round Mr. Fortune with a dependence which, for all its compliance and intimacy, yet remained somehow gaily and coolly aloof, so that the priest felt more and more that what he was rearing up was in truth a young plant, a vine or a morning glory, which, while following all the contours of the tree it clings to, draws from its own root alone a secret and mysterious life in which the very element of dependence is as secret and mysterious as the rest.

In the beginnings of an intimacy one seems to be finding out day by day more about another person's inner life and character. But after a certain stage has been reached not only does further exploration become impossible but things which one thought were discoveries become suddenly quite meaningless and irrelevant, and one finds that one really knows nothing about them, nothing at all. They sit beside one, they turn their heads and make some remark, and the turn of the head and the tone of the voice and even what they say seem all familiar and already recognised in one's heart: but there can be no knowing why they turned and spoke at that moment and not at another, nor why they said what they did and not something totally different. Though one might expect this realisation to be agonising, it is so much part of the natural course of things that many people do not notice it at all, and others, whilst acknowledging that something has happened, account for it perfectly to their own satisfaction by hypotheses which are entirely inapplicable.

Mr. Fortune, for instance, finding that he knew no more of Lueli than at the moment when he first beheld him kneeling on the grass, said to himself that he now knew him so well that he had grown used to him. In the same breath he was able to rejoice in a confidence that no phase of Lueli's development could catch him napping; and he plumed himself on his acuteness in observing that Lueli was growing older every day and was now of an age to assert himself as a young man.

For all that, Mr. Fortune could never quite compass thinking of him as such. Time in this pleasant island where the seasons passed so lightly and where no one ever showed the smallest sense of responsibility was like a long happy afternoon spent under the acacia with the children. However, Lueli was grown up (or would be, the moment he noticed the fact himself), and something would have to be done about it. Something, particularly—for in matters of this sort it is best to go straight to the point—must be done about providing him with a wife.

A Christian wife. And of late he had made several inspections of the village with this end in view, keeping an open eye for all the young women, scanning them as searchingly as Cœlebs, artfully devising the like cheese-paring tests for them and pondering which would be the most eligible for conversion and holy matrimony. There were plenty of charming possibles—by now he had quite got over his empirical aversion to them as bevies —though at first sight they seemed more eligible for holy matrimony than for conversion, being, one and all, smiling, wholesome, and inclined to giggle. But of course convertibility was the prime consideration. Perhaps by catching his hare and making a special effort? Mr. Fortune admitted that during this last year his labours as a missionary had been growing rather perfunctory.

Not that he loved his flock less. Rather he loved them more, and to his love was added (and here was the rub) a considerable amount of esteem. For seeing the extraordinarily good hand they made at the business of living to their own contentment—a business that the wise consider so extremely laborious and risky—and reflecting that for all their felicity they yet contrived to do nobody any harm, he felt some diffidence in his mission to teach them to do better.

And then he would pull himself up with a jerk and remember fiercely that they were loose livers and worshipped idols. Moreover they had rejected the word of God, and had made their rejection if anything worse by making it with such flippancy and unconcern. The seed he scattered had fallen into a soil too rich and easy, so that the weeds sprang up and choked it. Alas, all their charming good qualities were but a crop of fragrant and exotic groundsel, and their innocence was like the pure whiteness and ravishing classical contours of the blossom of the common bindweed, which strangles the corn and looks up from the crime with its exquisite babyface.

Yet after all (he consoled himself by thinking), the apparent reluctance of the Fanuans to become Christians might all be part of God's dealings. God proceeds diversely in divers places, and where His servants have prepared the ground for wheat He may overrule them and set barley. In some islands He may summon the souls with a loud immediate thunderclap; in others He would go about it differently, knowing the secrets of all hearts. God's time is the best. And perhaps it was His intention in Fanua to raise up a people from the marriage of Lueli as He had prepared Himself a people in the seed of Abraham and Sarah. At this thought Mr. Fortune went off into one of his dreams, and he grew cold with emotion as he gazed into the future, seeing in a vision Lueli's children and grandchildren and great-grandchildren, mild and blessed, stretching away into the distance like a field of ripened wheat which the wind flows over and the sun shines on. They would remember him, for their fathers would have told them. But No (he thought), there was no need for them to remember him. For it is only the unsatisfied who want to be remembered: old Simeon in the fullness of his joy, beholding the light and the glory, had no plea but to depart in peace.

Meanwhile, which girl? Ori's tall daughter, gentle Vaili, or the little plump one who laughed so much that he could never remember her name? It occurred to him that since it was Lueli's wife he was choosing Lueli might well be consulted.

Lueli was out fishing. Mr. Fortune sat till dusk by the spring, thinking out what he would say and choosing his metaphors and turns of speech with unusual pleasure and care as though he were preparing a sermon.

The long shadows had merged into shadow and the western sky was a meditative green when Lueli returned. In one hand he held a glistening net of fish and in the other a bough of fruit, so that he looked like some god of plenty, a brown slip of Demeter's who had not got into the mythology.

Mr. Fortune admired the fish and admired the fruit; but inwardly he admired Lueli more, this beautiful young man smelling of the sea. He gave a little cough and began his speech.

Marriage, he said, was a most excellent thing. It was God's first institution, and in the world's loveliest garden the flowers had asked no better than to be twined into a wreath for the bride. Men's stories commonly end with a marriage, but in God's story the marriage comes at the beginning. The ancient poets when they would celebrate the sun compared him to a bridegroom, the saints could find no tenderer name for Christ than the spouse of the soul, and in the vision of the last things John the Evangelist saw the church descending out of Heaven like a bride, so that God's story which begins with a mortal marriage ends with a marriage too, but an immortal one.

What did Lueli think? Did he not agree that marriage was a good thing?

Lueli nodded. His face wore an admiring and far-away expression, as though he were listening to the harmonium.

Marriage, Mr. Fortune continued, is a gracious act, a bestowal, and a token of man's gratitude to his Maker. When we are happy we needs must give; Lueli himself was always giving, be it fruit or fish, a strand of seaweed or a flower. These gifts are transient and incomplete: the weed begins to lose its gloss from the moment it is taken out of the ocean; the fish and the fruit (unless, of course, eaten) go bad; the flower is broken from the stem, its petals will discolour and fold up in death; but whoever begets children gives life itself, gives that from which all gifts are drawn.

The procreation of children is the first end for which marriage is ordained. But that was not all. There was also the love of man and woman and the pleasure they had in one another's company. When he was a young man, Mr. Fortune said, he had often wished for a wife to be merry with. Now he was too old to think much of such things, but none the less marriage did not seem to him less desirable, for now he understood as he did not and could not in his youth how sweet it would be to have the faithful company of one with whom he had shared his best days, if it were only, as a celebrated English Divine once expressed it in a sermon, that he might have some one to whom he could say: 'How our shadows lengthen as our sun goes down!'

Mr. Fortune stopped. Lueli's silent consenting and his own thoughts had led him too far. He had not meant to introduce such serious considerations into a discourse on marriage, and the mournful sound of his own voice alone in the shadow of night suddenly revealed to him that he was sorrowful, although he had not thought he was.

'Tell me, Lueli, have you thought at all about whom you would prefer?'

'Vaili is a nice girl and her father would give her a good dowry—'

Lueli pressed up the tip of his nose with the tip of his finger and spoke in a soft considering voice.

'Or there is Fuma, or Lepe who loves singing. But I think Vaili would suit you best, so you had better marry her.'

'I marry! No, no, Lueli, you are mistaken, I was not talking of myself but of you. It is your marriage I was thinking about.'

'Oh! Were you?'

'Wouldn't you like a wife, Lueli? As you were saying, Vaili is a nice girl. She is gentle and fond of children, we could soon teach her to become a Christian if we gave our minds to it. I'm sure you could be very happy with Vaili.'

A decided shake of the head.

'Fuma, then.'

Another shake.

'Well, what about Lepe or Tialua?'

Mr. Fortune proceeded to recite the names of all the girls on the island, feeling not very respectable as he did so, but going steadfastly on because he was in for it now, he could not go back on his own sermon. But he might as well have recited the Kings of Israel and Judah or the Queens consort of England from Matilda of Flanders down to Adelaide of Saxe-Meiningen for all the effect it had on Lueli, who sat beside him listening decorously as though to a lesson and silently waving away each one of Mr. Fortune's nominees.

'But, Lueli, if you don't approve of any of these, whom do you want?'

A terrible possibility had flashed upon him. Suppose, like the traditional young man, Lueli had placed his affections on some mature married woman? What steps should he take, indeed what steps could he take? He would not even have public opinion on his side.

'I don't want any one. I am quite happy as I am.'

'But, Lueli, you are young and vigorous. This is not natural and I don't think it is at all advisable. Why, St. Paul himself —' And Mr. Fortune gave a short summary of St. Paul's views on the marrying or burning question, toning them down a little, for privately he considered the saint's conclusions a trifle acrid. But there was no shaking Lueli, who continued to asseverate that he found chastity an easier matter than St. Paul supposed, and in any case preferable to the nuisance of taking a wife.

It seemed rather odd and improbable to Mr. Fortune, but he let the matter drop and did not speak of it again. Lueli would change his tune all in good time no doubt. Meanwhile things could go on as before, and certainly nothing could be pleasanter. Of course he was properly desirous to see the beginnings of that Christian family, and he was much looking forward to becoming a godfather. He had already settled that since the proper consecrated kind of mugs were unprocurable, the first child should have the teapot and the second the sovereign he still kept for luck. After that he supposed he would have to sacrifice the magnifying-glass and the tuning-fork, and after that again—well, he still had time to think about it. Indeed, at present even the teapot seemed to be indefinitely postponed.

He was puzzled by Lueli, but he was not uneasy about him; when he went off by himself he did not speculate as to what he was up to, nor ask strategic questions on his return. He trusted the boy and he also trusted himself. He did not think he could be deceived in Lueli.

And so things went kindly and easily on till the day when he was to find out his mistake.

It was very hot weather. Mr. Fortune had been suffering from a severe headache, and had spent the whole day lying down in the shade with wet cloths on his head. About sundown he decided to go for a short stroll, hoping that the dusk and the cool airs from the sea would refresh him. He called for Lueli to come too, but Lueli was nowhere about, so he set forth alone, crossing the dell and going down toward the sea. As he went he admired the brilliance of the after-glow, a marvellous rose-coloured bloom that seemed to hang on the air like a cloud of the finest metallic dust. Perhaps his eyes were weakened by headache and so more sensitive to light than usual; but as he roamed up and down the shadowy strand, at each turn that brought him to face the west he marvelled, thinking that in all his evenings at Fanua he had never beheld the sky so vibrating with colour nor so slow to fade—for sunsets in the tropics are fleeting things, but to-night there was a strange steadfastness in the west. He admired it so much that it was not possible for him to admire it for very long, and there was still light in the sky as he turned homeward.

Ordinarily he kept to the same routes as faithfully as though they had been ruled for him with red ink. But to-night, lost in thoughts of he knew not what, he strayed from his direction and found himself approaching a little grove of coco-palms. They grew prettily together, laced with creepers and thickened with an undergrowth of ferns; there was something about the innocence of their arrangement which reminded him of an English copse, and the resemblance was increased by a little path that turned and twisted its way in among them. But in an English copse even the slenderest path is wide enough for two lovers to walk it with their arms about each other, while this path was so narrow that it was clearly the path of one who visited the thicket alone.

A parrot flew off from a bough above his head, uttering a loud cry. Mr. Fortune roused himself from his dream. He was not in an English copse, looking for bluebells and being careful not to tread on a nightingale's nest, he was in a grove of coco-palms on the island of Fanua, an island in the midst of the Pacific Ocean like an island in a story-book. And he was looking for—? He was not looking for anything; for in all his time at Fanua though he admired the flowers he had rarely picked any. It did not occur to him to do so. One picks only the flowers that one learned to pick as a child—cowslips and primroses and cuckoopint, and pale star-wort that grows in the dusty summer hedge and fades before one can carry it home.

Lueli was always picking flowers. Perhaps he came here for them, perhaps he had been along this path but an hour ago? At any rate some flower-gatherer had; for lying at his feet Mr. Fortune observed a dark-coloured blossom like a stain. He stooped and picked it up. Yes, it was freshly gathered, it had not begun to wither yet, but it was moist with dew and felt cold and forsaken.

Presently Mr. Fortune came on a trail of lilac-flowered creeper caught up on a fern. He disentangled this and carried it along with him.

'Extravagant creature!' he said; for now he felt sure that he was on Lueli's track. 'I could make myself a bouquet out of what he spills and scatters.'

He still followed the path, wondering what next he would pick up. A little further on he perceived a whole garland lying on a patch of greensward. He was in the heart of the little wood, and here the path seemed to end.

'I declared that he's still child enough to be playing at houses. And this is the young man I've been trying to find a wife for!'

It looked exactly as though Lueli had been playing at house. The ferns and bushes around were hung with trailing sprays of blossom which looped them into a pretence of being walls, and in the midst beside the garland was a platter arranged with fruits and leaves.

'What a child!' exclaimed the priest. 'Yet after all it may not be Lueli. Why should I be so sure that this is his fancy-work?'

In an instant he was to be made quite sure. Something slim and dusky and motionless was reared up behind the platter of fruit. He looked closer. It was dreadfully familiar. He snatched it up and stared close into its face, a face he had seen before. And trampling on the garland he stood glaring at Lueli's idol, which looked back at him with flowers behind its ears.

It was quite obvious, quite certain. There was no chance of being mistaken, no hope of doubt. For all these years Lueli had been playing a double game, betraying him, feigning to be a Christian, and in secret, in the reality of secretness, worshipping an idol.

'It is my fault,' said the priest, speaking aloud because of his desperate loneliness. 'Not his at all, nor yours either,' and he gave the idol a sort of compassionate shake.

'I have deluded myself wilfully, I have built my house on the sand. . . .'

'I have forgotten the fear of God,' he went on. 'All this time I have gone on pretending that religion is a pleasant, is a gentle thing, a game for good children.'

'But it is an agony!' he suddenly shouted out.

There was no echo. The sultry twilight was closing in on him like a dark fleece. He could scarcely see the idol now, but in his mind's eye he could see it, a face coldly and politely attentive, and the narrow polished shoulders over which a doll's necklace slipped and sidled as it shook with his trembling hands.

'It is torments, wounds, mutilation, and death. It is exile and weariness. It is strife—an endless strife—it is bewilderment and fear and trembling. It is despair.'

Turning abruptly he left the thicket by the path which had led him in, and stumbling in the dark and feeling his body heavy and cold in the hot night he made his way back to the hut.

It was all dark; but that was no reason why Lueli should not be within, for he had been so often warned to handle the lamp carefully that he was a coward about it and never touched it if he could avoid doing so.

Mr. Fortune threw down the idol and lit the lamp from his tinder-box. Then he looked round. Lueli was curled up on his mat. He had been asleep, and now he opened his eyes and looked drowsily at his friend. Mr. Fortune said nothing. He stood in the centre of the hut under the hanging lamp and waited for Lueli to notice the idol.

Lueli parted his lips. He was just about to speak when he saw what lay on the ground. He raised his eyes to Mr. Fortune's countenance, for a moment he put on a confused smile, then with an ill-feigned yawn he turned over and pretended to have fallen asleep again.

'Deceit,' said Mr. Fortune, as though he were reading from a note-book.

A faint grunt answered him.

'Lueli, my poor Lueli, this is useless. You can't get out of it like this. Get up and tell me what it is that I have found.'

Lueli sat up. The pupils of his eyes were still distended by sleep and this gave him a frightened look; but his demeanour was perfectly calm.

'That?'

He shook his head as if to say that he really couldn't tell what it was.

'Look again.'

Mr. Fortune spoke curtly, but it was from pure sorrow.

'It is an idol.'

'Yes, and it is your idol.'

Lueli gave a sigh of distress. Mr. Fortune knew exactly how much that was worth. Lueli hated any unpleasantness.

'You don't ask me how I came by it. I found it in a thicket near the beach, the lonely one. And there were flowers round it, and offerings of fruit, and look, there are flowers stuck behind its ears.'

'So there are.'

'Is this your doing? Why do I ask you, for I know it is. Lueli, you mustn't lie to me. I implore you not to lie. Is this your doing, have you been worshipping this object?'

'I picked the flowers.'

Mr. Fortune groaned. Then he sat down like one who foresees a long and weariful business before him. Lueli edged himself a little nearer. He had rumpled up his brow into a grimace of condolence, he looked like a beautiful and sympathetic marmoset.

He said in a voice at once tender and sly:

'But why are you unhappy? I have done nothing, it is only my idol, and I just happened to pick it a few flowers. That is all.'

'Listen. I will tell you why I am unhappy. When I came to Fanua I came to teach you not to worship idols but to worship God. I came to teach you all, but the others would have none of me. You were my only convert, you received my teaching, I thought you loved it, and I trusted you. Now I have found out my mistake. If you worship your idol still I am to blame. It is my fault. If I had done my duty by you you would have known better. But I have not shown you the true God, so you have kept to the old one, the false one, a wooden thing, a worship so false that you can treat him like a toy. As I came back to-night I was tempted with the thought that perhaps after all your fault was only childishness. And for a moment (to spare myself and you) I had half a mind to pretend to God that your idol was only a doll. But we will have none of that.'

Now he spoke sternly, and at the last words he beat one fist against the other. Lueli started.

'I blame myself, I say, not you. I should have been on my guard. When I saw that thing two years ago I should have acted then. But I shut my eyes (I am most horribly to blame), and now, see what has come of it. You are in fault too, for you have been deceiving me. But I know you are rather cowardly and very affectionate; your deceitfulness after all is not so surprising.'

He could have gone on talking like this for some time and finding it soothing, but he knew by experience that Lueli would find it soothing too. He raised his eyes from his heavily folded hands and looked at the boy. Sure enough, there was the familiar expression, the lulled face of one who listens to a powerful spell.

He stopped short, nerved himself to deliver the blow, and said in a slow, dull voice:

'You must destroy your idol. You had better burn it.'

With a vehement gesture of refusal Lueli sprang to his feet.

'Burn it,' repeated the priest.

Such a wild and affronted antagonism defied him from the tautened brown body and the unswerving, unbeholding gaze that for a moment the priest was appalled. But his looks gave back defiance for defiance. They bore the other's down, and averting his eyes Lueli gave a sudden shrug and made as though to walk out of the hut.

Mr. Fortune was between him and the door. He jumped up and barred the line of retreat. Lueli wavered. Then he went back to his corner and sat down without a word. Mr. Fortune half-expected him to weep, but he did nothing so obliging.

For a good hour Mr. Fortune talked on, commanding, reasoning, expostulating, explaining, persuading, threatening. Lueli never answered him, never even looked at him. He sat with downcast eyes in utter stubbornness and immobility.

The night was sultry and absolutely still. Mr. Fortune dripped with sweat, he felt as though he were heaving enormous boulders into a bottomless pit. He continued to heave his words into silence, a silence only broken by the hissing of the lamp, or the creak of his chair as he changed from one uneasy position to another, but the pauses grew longer between each sentence. He was weary, and at his wits' end. But he could see nothing for it but to go on talking. And now he became so oppressed by the silence into which he spoke that he could foresee a moment when he would have to go on talking because he would be afraid to hold his tongue.

A frightful imagination took possession of him: that Lueli was become like his idol, a handsome impassive thing of brown wood, that had ears and heard not, that had no life in its heart. Would nothing move him? He would have been thankful for a look of hate, for a curse or an insult. But with the same show of inanimate obstinacy Lueli continued to bend his look upon the ground, a figure too austere to be sullen, too much withdrawn into itself to be defiant.

Mr. Fortune heard himself say at the top of his voice: 'Lueli! Don't you hear me?'

It seemed that his outcry had broken the spell. Lueli suddenly looked up and began to listen, to listen with such strained, absorbed, animal attention that Mr. Fortune found himself listening too. There was a sound: a sound like a violent gust of wind strangely sweeping through the motionless night. It came rapidly, it came near, brushing its way through the tree-tops. Like an actual angry presence the wind came vehemently into the hut and, as though an invisible hand had touched it, Mr. Fortune saw the hanging lamp begin to sway. It swayed faster and faster, widening its sweep at every oscillation; and while he stared at it in a stupor of amazement he felt the earth give a violent twitch under his feet as though it were hitting up at him, and he was thrown to the ground. There was a noise of rending and bellowing, the lamp gave a last frantic leap, again he felt the ground buffet him like the horns of a bull, and then with a crash and a spurt of fire the roof of the hut caved in.

At the same moment he felt something large and heavy topple across his body.

He could not move and he could not think. He saw flames rising up around him and heard the crackle of the dried thatch. Again the ground began to quiver and writhe beneath him, and suddenly he knew what was happening—an earthquake!

The bulk that lay on top of him was the harmonium. He was pinned beneath it—presently the flames would reach him and he would be burnt to death.

He felt no kind of fear or emotion, only a calm certainty as to what was happening and with it a curious detached satisfaction at being able to understand it all so well. The flames would enclose him and he would be burnt to death, unless the ground opened first and swallowed him up. Then he remembered Lueli. What of him? He struggled again, but he could not get out from under the harmonium. The struggle reminded him that he was a human being, not only an intelligence but a creature defencelessly sentient that must perish by fire. Fear came on him, and self-pity, and with it a sort of pique; for he said to himself: 'I know now he never cared for me. He has made off and left me to burn, just what I should expect.' And at the same moment he heard himself cry out: 'Save yourself, Lueli! Be quick, child! Never mind me, I am all right.' And then, seeing Lueli bending over him, he said in a voice of command: 'Lueli, I tell you to save yourself. Get out of this while there's time.'

He saw Lueli in the light of the flames, he saw him put his shoulder against the harmonium and begin to heave it up; he saw the muscles leap out along the thrusting body—all with a sort of anger and impatience because his friend would not attend to what he was saying. Even when the harmonium was jolted backward and he was freed he lay where he had fallen, half-stunned, with no definite thought except to compel Lueli to obey him and get away before the next tremor sent the whole hut crashing down on them.

He felt Lueli put his arms round his shoulders, shaking him and hauling him on to his feet, and he noticed with surprise how stern the boy looked, not frightened, but extraordinarily stern, like a stranger, like an angel. The earth began to quake again, another sheaf of thatch slid from the roof and the flames leaped up to seize upon it. Mr. Fortune suddenly came out of his stupor. Stumbling and losing his footing on the wavering floor he caught hold of Lueli's arm and together they ran out of the hut.

Three times in crossing the dell they were thrown to the earth. There was something horribly comic in this inability to stand upright. It was as though they were being tossed in a blanket. They did not speak to each other; all thought of speech was forbidden by the appalling novelty of the uproar that was going on, rumblings and bellowings underground, trees beating against each other or crashing to the earth, the cries of terror-struck creatures. Lueli dragged him on, hastening toward the mountain. There was a little path that led up by the ravine, difficult to mount at any time and more difficult still in an earthquake.

'Why do you go this way?' Mr. Fortune asked, when the tremor had subsided enough for him to be able to remember how to speak. Lueli turned on him a face of terror.

'The sea,' he said. 'The sea.'

Mr. Fortune had forgotten the sea. Now he remembered what he had read in books of adventures as a boy: how after an earthquake comes a tidal wave, a wall of water frantically hurling itself upon the land. And not daring to look behind him he followed Lueli up the steep path as though the sea were at his heels.

At last they came out upon a little grassy platform overlooking the ravine. They were only just in time, for the earthquake began again. They sat side by side, holding on to one another. Mr. Fortune discovered that it was a brilliant and impassive moonlight night. He looked toward the ocean. It seemed strangely calm, incredibly vast, more solid than the tormented earth. A glittering path of silver across it reflected the moon.

They were close to the cataract. Tonight, instead of the usual steady roar of falling water, the noise was coming in curious gouts of sound, now loud, now almost nothing. He turned his eyes and saw the slender column of falling water all distorted, and flapping like a piece of muslin in a draught. For some reason this sight was overwhelmingly piteous and a sort of throe hollowed him as if he were going to cry.

At every shock thousands of birds flew up from the tossing tree-tops. In wild excitement they circled overhead, flying in droves, sweeping past with a whirr of innumerable wings, soaring higher and higher, then suddenly diving aslant, shot from the wake of their own vortex. Their continual angry clamour, passionate and derisive, swayed above the uproar of trampling earth and clashing forest. One bird came volleying so close to Mr. Fortune that he saw its beak flash in the moonlight and put up his hand to shield his face. As it passed it screamed in his ear like a railway whistle. He thought: 'I should like to scream like that.'

Although he and Lueli sat holding on to each other, Mr. Fortune had no sense of companionship. In this appalling hour there did not seem to be any one alive save himself. He was the Last Man, alone in an universe which had betrayed him, abandoned on the face of an earth which had failed under his feet. He was isolated even from himself. There was no Mr. Fortune now, a missionary who had been a bank-clerk, an Englishman and a member of the Church of England. Such a one would have been behaving quite differently. At the best he might have been behaving much better, he might have been in the village keeping troth with his fellow-men; at the least he would have been trembling for his own skin and calling on God. But this man sat on the reeling mountain side with but one sensation: a cold-hearted excitement, a ruthless attentive craving that at the height of horror would welcome another turn of the screw, another jab of the spur, another record broken.

The shocks were now coming so continuously that it was scarcely possible to say when one followed another; but he went on keeping count and comparing them, and if they seemed to be slackening off he was disappointed. He sat with his eyes shut, for so he could both feel and hear more unmitigatedly. At intervals he looked out seaward for the coming of the tidal wave. But the sea was always calm, as coldly calm as himself and a great deal more solid. 'Yet it must come,' he told himself. 'It is certain to come.' And after a terrific shock, accompanied by sounds of rending and shattering as though the whole island were splitting asunder, he thought with certainty: 'It will come now,' and opened his eyes once more.

Something had happened. There was a difference in the air, in the colour of the night. Had dawn come already? His faculties were so cramped with attention that he could scarcely receive a new sensation, still less analyse it. Yet he felt that there was something he must account for, some discrepancy between this light and the light of dawn. The sun rose—yes, the sun rose in the east, over the sea: but this light seemed to come from behind him. He turned and saw the sky lit up with the light of fire.

'The mountain is on fire!' he cried out. And at the sound of his own words he suddenly understood what had happened. The mountain was on fire. Its ancient fires had come back to it, Fanua was once more an active volcano.

Below the bed of the cold and heavy sea, below the foundations of the great deep, into an unimaginable hell of energy and black burning those fires had withdrawn. They had rejoined the imprisoned original frenzy that lies in the heart of the earth, working and wallowing in unknown tides. And once more the fiery spring had mounted, revolting against the encompassing pressure, fumbling in darkness, melting its way, flooding along its former channels until now it flared on the crest of the island, brightening and brightening upon the sky, a glow of such intense and vivid rose-colour that by contrast the moonlight turned to an icily-piercing blue. Cloud upon cloud of smoke rolled upwards, and at every fresh surge of fire the vault of heaven appeared to grow more vast and haughty, and the stars seemed recoiling into space. The mountain shouted and bellowed as though it were triumphing because its fires had come back to it.

Mr. Fortune leapt to his feet. He waved his arms, he stood on tiptoe in order to see better. Though the next moment might engulf him he was going to make the most of this. But there was no need to be so provident, so economical. This bonfire had been preparing for decades, it would not burn out in a minute or two. Realising this, he sat down again and relinquished himself to an entire and passive contemplation, almost lulled by the inexhaustible procession of fire and smoke, warming his mind at the lonely terrific beauty of a mountain burning by night amid an ocean.

Clouds began to gather at daybreak. Only a pallor showed where the sun groped upwards among them, and the sea, which but a few hours ago had looked so lustrous, and solid like a floor of onyx, was now pale and weltering.

The earthquake seemed to be over; sometimes the ground gave a sort of a twitch and a tremble like an animal that dreams a bad dream, but this happened at longer and longer intervals and each disturbance was fainter than the last. Except for the plume of foul smoke that issued from the crater and sagged over the mountain side as it was checked by the morning airs there was nothing to distinguish this daybreak from any other, unless, thought Mr. Fortune, that it was a peculiarly dreary one.

He was chilled with watching, and oppressed with the indigestion common to those who have sat up all night. He was also bruised with so much falling about, and his ribs ached from being crushed under the harmonium. But his excitement, which in spite of all the adventures of the last twelve hours was still a deferred excitement, unsatisfied and defrauded of its prey, wouldn't let him settle down into a reasonable fatigue, but still kept his muscles strung up and his vision strained.

It seemed an age since he had last thought of Lueli. He looked at him now as though from a long way off, and rather crossly, and it seemed as though his vague irritation were in a way to be justified. For Lueli lay as though asleep.

That Lueli should sleep while he waked was enough. It showed that he was inconsiderate, incapable of true sympathy, an inferior being who hadn't got indigestion. Mr. Fortune heaved a loud short sigh. Lueli didn't stir. No doubt of it. He was asleep. He lay so that Mr. Fortune could only see the curve of his cheek and half his mouth, which bore the sad resigned expression of those who slumber. But bending a little over him to make sure, Mr. Fortune discovered that the boy's eyes were open and fixed mournfully upon the empty and unquiet sea. There was something so devastated about that blank and unmoving gaze that the priest was awed. Why did Lueli look so old, so set and austere? The face so well known seemed that of a stranger; and suddenly he recalled Lueli bending over him in the burning hut as he lay helpless under the harmonium, and remembered that then his face had worn the same look, grave and stern.

Lueli had saved his life at the risk of his own, he had shown that greatest love which makes a man ready to lay down his life for his friend. And now the rescued one sat coldly beside the rescuer, eyeing his unknown sorrow, and but a moment ago seeking some pretext for scorning and disliking him.

'What a hateful creature I am!' thought Mr. Fortune, 'and how this earthquake has shown me up! But Lueli has behaved well throughout, he saved my life, he kept his head, he didn't want to cheer and behave like a tripper when the mountain exploded.' And in his thoughts he begged Lueli's pardon.

Still Lueli lay beside him, staring out to sea with the same mournful look. His silence was like a reproach to Mr. Fortune. It seemed to say: 'You have slighted me unjustly and now I must forget you.' Mr. Fortune waited patiently, he had a confused idea that his patience now must repair his former impatience. But at length his love could endure no longer, and he laid his hand gently on Lueli's arm. There was no response. Lueli didn't even turn his eyes.

'He is tired out,' thought the priest. 'That is why he looks so miserable.' He said aloud: 'Wake up, Lueli, you will make yourself ill if you lie there any longer so still on the cold ground. Wake up. Rouse yourself. It is all over now.' And he gave him an encouraging slap on the shoulder.

At last Lueli sighed and stretched himself and turned and met Mr. Fortune's anxious gaze.

'I think the earthquake is over,' he remarked in an everyday voice.

'Just what I said a minute ago,' thought Mr. Fortune. 'But he doesn't know I said it. What can he have been thinking of that he didn't hear me?'

He still felt slightly worried about the boy.

'We had better walk about a little,' he said. 'Ow! I've got a cramp.'

Taking Lueli's arm he staggered down the little rocky path. The morning was cold and now it began to rain. The rain was dirty rain, full of smuts and fine grit from the volcano. It might have been raining in London or Manchester.

Exercise soon restored Mr. Fortune to an ordinary frame of mind. He looked with interested horror at the wood they passed through. Many trees were uprooted or hung tottering with their roots half out of the ground, the shrubs and grass were crushed and trampled, boughs and torn creepers were scattered everywhere. It was as though some savage beast had run amuck through the glades, tearing and havocking and rooting up the ground with its horns. Lueli picked up a dead parrot, and once they skirted by a swarm of angry bees. Their hive had been broken in the fall of its tree, the honeycomb was scattered on the grass, and the affronted insects were buzzing hither and thither, angrier than ever because now the rain was making its way through the dishevelled green roof.

'But it will soon quench them,' thought Mr. Fortune. 'And if some bees and some parrots are the only deaths by this earthquake we shall be well out of it.'

He was uneasy about the villagers, all the more so because he felt that he had run away from them in their hour of peril. Also he wanted to talk to some one about the stream of lava which he knew would soon flow down from the crater. 'Provided it only flows to the south!' he thought. He questioned Lueli but could learn nothing; Lueli had never been in an earthquake before, he had heard the old men of the island talking about them but the last earthquake had happened long before his day.

On nearing the village Mr. Fortune heard a great hubbub, but it was impossible to discover from the noise of every one talking at once whether they were lamenting or merely excited; all he could conclude was that at any rate they were not all dead.

When he appeared, with Lueli following sedately behind, a crowd of gesticulating islanders rushed forward, all waving their arms and shouting. The thought leapt up in his mind: 'Suppose they think that *I* am responsible for this earthquake? Perhaps they will kill me to appease the mountain!'

He had never felt less in the mood for martyrdom. The last

twelve hours had given him more than enough to cope with. Yet even if the fervour of his faith were lacking, he could make a shift to die decently: and he stiffened himself and went forward. But Lueli? Suppose they wanted to martyr him too? No! That he would not allow. While there was a kick left in him he would see to that. He glanced back as though to reassure him, but as he caught sight of him he remembered that Lueli was not a Christian, nor ever had been one. What a sell if they should sacrifice him before there was time to explain! Well, this made it even more urgent a matter to defend him: martyrdom was one thing, miscarriage of justice quite another.

But Mr. Fortune need not have been agitated. The islanders had no intention but to welcome him and Lueli, and to rejoice round them over their safety, which they did with the pleasanter excitement and conviction, since naturally in the emotions of the night they had not given them a thought till now.

Half-smothered and quite deafened, Mr. Fortune pushed through the throng, saying: 'Where is Ori?' For having lived so long on the island he had fallen into the proper respect for a chief, and depended on Ori rather more than he would have liked to admit. 'He is almost like another European'—so the priest explained to himself. At this juncture Ori was behaving very much like an European, for he was partaking of one of those emergency breakfasts, sketchy in form but extremely solid and comprehensive in content, with which the white races consummate and, as it were, justify any fly-by-night catastrophe. Seeing Mr. Fortune he politely invited him to sit down and take a share. 'But the flow of lava?' inquired Mr. Fortune, wiping his mouth. 'Do you think it will come this way?' Ori took another handful of stirabout. 'There are no signs of it so far, and if it comes this way it will not come here yet.'

'But do you think it will come this way?'

'My god says, No.'

When breakfast was finished Ori got up and went off with the other men of consequence to make an inquisition into the damage done by the pigs. They had come bolting down from the woods and wrought even more serious havoc than the earthquake, which had only shaken down a house or two, whereas the pigs had trespassed into every enclosure and eaten all the provisions. Mr. Fortune felt a little slighted that he was not invited to go too. Apparently Ori did not quite regard him as another Fanuan. 'Oh well,' he said, 'perhaps they meant it politely, seeing that I had not finished my breakfast.' But thought he felt as if he were hungry he had no real appetite, and rising he prepared to walk back to his hut.

It was as though the earthquake had literally shaken his wits. All his recollections were dislodged and tumbled together; he knew they were there somewhere, but he could not find them —just as he had mislaid the discovery of overnight until, turning to view Lueli as a possible martyr, he beheld and recognised him as the idolater he was and always had been. Now he was walking to the hut in the same kind of oblivion. He must have remembered the lamp tossing its flame up to the roof, the burning sheaves of thatch falling down around him, for he had a very clear vision of Lueli's face bending over him, so violently modelled by the flames that it had looked like the face, sad and powerful, of a stranger, of an angel. But his thoughts went no further; and even when the smell of charred wood came sadly to his nostrils through the falling rain he did not put two and two together.

'I wonder if those pigs have messed up my place too,' he said. A sigh out of the air answered him. He had not noticed till then that Lueli was following.

'Poor Lueli, you must be so tired!' There was no answer and still the boy lagged behind. He must be tired indeed. Mr. Fortune stopped. He was about to speak once more, bidding Lueli to lean on him and take heart, when suddenly the boy shot past him, running desperately, and whispering to himself as he ran as though he were imploring his own mind.

Mr. Fortune hastened after him. Would all this strangeness, this bewilderment, this nightmare of familiar living confounded and turned backward never come to an end? He hastened on into the smell of burning, and pulling aside the drooping fronds of a banana tree which, uprooted, had fallen and lay across the pathway like a screen, he beheld the ruins of the hut.

One wall was still standing, a few pale flames licking wistfully over it. The rest was charred logs and hummocks of grey ash sizzling under the rain—for now it was raining more and more heavily. Looking round on the devastation he began to recognise the remains of his belongings. Those shreds of tinder were his clothes. That scrap of shrivelled leather, that wasting impalpable bulk of feathery print, was his Bible; there lay the medicine chest and there the sewing-machine; and this, this intricate ruin of molten metal tubes, charred rubber, and dislocated machinery, was the harmonium, its scorched ivory keys strewed round about it like teeth fallen from a monstrous head.

Lueli was there, but he seemed to have no thought for the unfortunate priest amid the ruins of his home. Wading among the hot ashes, crouching close to the wreckage, turning over this and that with rapid and trembling hands, Lueli was searching with desperate anxiety for—Mr. Fortune knew not what. At length he gave a bitter cry and cast himself down upon the ground.

Instantly Mr. Fortune was kneeling beside him, patting his shoulder, trying to lift the averted head.

'What is it, Lueli? What is it, my dear, dear friend?'

Lueli sat up and turned on him a face discoloured and petrified into an expression of such misery that he could hardly endure to look at it.

'What is it? Are you hurt? Are you ill?'

The expression never changed.

'Are you frightened, Lueli? Has it upset you to find our home burnt to the ground? But never mind! We will soon have another, it is nothing to grieve for.'

He would have said that Lueli did not hear him, so unmoving he sat, so utterly aloof, but that at these last words a very slight smile of scorn quivered on the dry lips.

Then Mr. Fortune remembered. He hung his head; and when he spoke again it was with the grave voice in which we address the bereaved.

'Is it your god you were looking for? Is he gone?'

Lueli did not answer. But it was clear that he had both heard and understood, for he fixed his eyes on the priest's face with the look of an animal which knows itself at man's mercy but does not know what man intends to do to it.

'My poor Lueli! Is that it? . . . Is it so dreadful? Yes, I know it must be, I know, I know. I would do anything to comfort you, but I cannot think how, I can only tell you how I pity you with my whole heart. I do, indeed I do. Believe me, though I told you to burn your god, yet at this moment, if it were possible for me, I think I would even give it to you again.'

He spoke very slowly, scarcely daring to lift his gaze to the sorrow which sat beside him, not answering, not crying out, meek with the meekness of despair. And still Lueli listened, and still looked, with his expression wavering between timidity and antagonism.

'Lueli, I spoke very harshly to you last night, not like a Christian, not as one sad human being should speak to another. In blaspheming against your god I blasphemed against my own. And now I can't comfort you. I don't deserve to. I can only sit beside you and be sorry.'

Lueli never answered, and Mr. Fortune acted his last words, sitting mournfully beside him in the rain. After an hour or so Lueli began to topple forward, then suddenly he lay down and fell asleep.

Now Mr. Fortune had time to think, and though he was dog-tired think he must. For after a while Lueli would wake again, and then the missionary must have some settled reasonable comfort for him, some plan of consolation. On the face of it nothing could be clearer. He should say something of this sort: 'Your god, Lueli, was only made of wood, perishable and subject to accidents, like man who is made of flesh. He is now burnt, and his ashes are lost among the other ashes. Now will you not see that my God is a better God than yours, and turn to Him? For my God is from everlasting, even though the earth shakes He cannot be moved.'

Yes, that was the sort of thing to say, but he felt a deep reluctance to saying it. It seemed ungentlemanly to have such a superior invulnerable God, part of that European conspiracy which opposes gunboats to canoes and rifles to bows and arrows, which showers death from the mountains upon Indian villages, which rounds up the negro into an empire and tricks him of his patrimony.

Mr. Fortune remembered the Man of Sorrows. Would Lueli accept in the place of his wooden god a God that had once been made flesh? In the old days Lueli had enjoyed hearing about Jesus, though Mr. Fortune had always suspected him of preferring Joshua. Many, very many, must have taken Jesus to their hearts out of pity, following the example of the woman who washed His feet, although to her they were most likely but the feet of a wayfaring man. But it was rare to find a Polynesian accepting Him for these mortal motives, they themselves were not sorrowful enough. Probably, despite the loss of his god, Lueli would still prefer the more robust and stirring character of Joshua.

The trumpet that shall awaken the dead with the sanction of the resurrection is louder than all the rams' horns that blew down Jericho. As an honest priest it was Mr. Fortune's duty to preach not only Christ crucified but also Christ arisen to comfort His followers awhile with neighbourly humanity ere He ascended to His Father. If this were all, it might suit Lueli very well: but in a twinkling it would lead him on to the Trinity, a mysterious sign revolving in the heavens from everlasting, a triangle that somehow is also a sphere. And so he was back again where he started from, embarrassed with a God so superior to poor Lueli's that to insist upon Him now would be heartless boasting, would be exploiting an unfair advantage, wouldn't be cricket.

'If I were a proper missionary,' he burst out in a cross voice. And then with a wry grin he added: 'It doesn't look as though I were any sort of missionary. Lord, what a mess I've made of it!'

He had indeed. The mess amid which he sat was nothing to it. Disconsolately he looked at his watch. It had stopped. In the stress of overnight he had forgotten to wind it up, and now it recorded the epoch at which his last link with European civilisation had been snapped—eight hours thirty-five minutes. It could not be much later than that now. But a miss is as good as a mile, and for the rest of his sojourn on the island, for the rest of his life maybe, he would not know what o'clock it was. This circumstance, not serious in itself and not to be compared with the loss of the medicine chest or his books, upset him horribly. He felt frightened, he felt as small and as desperate as a child lost. 'I must set it as best I can,' he thought. 'After all, time is a convention, just like anything else. My watch will measure out my days and remind me to be up and doing just as well though it be a little askew. And no doubt I shall die at my appointed hour, however erroneously I reckon to it.'

But what time was it? The sky was overcast, he could not guess by the sun and he could not guess by his own time-feeling either, for his body had lost touch with ordinary life. He sat debating between nine-seventeen, five past ten, ten-forty-three, eleven-twenty—indecisive times which all seemed reasonably probable—and noon exactly, which was bracing and decisive, a good moment to begin a new era—but too good to be true. At last he settled on ten-twenty-five; but even so he still delayed, for he felt a superstitious reluctance to move the hands and so to destroy the last authentic witness his watch could bear him. Five minutes, he judged, had been spent in this weak-minded dallying: so resolutely he set the hands to ten-thirty and wound the poor machine up. It began to tick, innocently, obediently. It had set out on its fraudulent career.

It was a good watch, painstaking and punctual, its voice was confident, it had an honest face; but henceforth its master had lost his trust in it, and though he wore it (like a wife) at bed and at board and wound it up regularly and hung it on a tree when he went bathing, yet he never could feel it was his true wife (watch, I mean) again.

Still Lueli slept.

'I make all this fuss,' thought Mr. Fortune, 'I even feel helpless and abandoned, because I have lost my reckoning of time. How much worse to lose one's god!'

Thus, the watch diversion over and done with, and the new time being ten-thirty-one, he was back on the old problem. What could he do for poor Lueli who had lost his god? 'And it was for me that he lost it,' he thought, with a poignancy of feeling that was almost irritation. 'He might have picked up his god and run out of the hut with it, but he would not leave me under the harmonium.' It was heroic, desperately heroic. . . . Yet there might have been time to save both? A god that could be picked up in one hand. Had Lueli in the flurry of the moment forgotten that the idol lay on the floor of the hut? 'But No, one would not forget one's god,' thought he, 'even in an earthquake.'

Now he could understand why Lueli had seemed so cold in the early morning, so aloof and unlike his usual self. When he had lain staring out to sea with that strange expression he had been tasting what it feels like to be without a god. And when they approached the hut that was why he had lagged behind until the last explosion of hope had sent him running to seek his god among the wood-ashes. Now he was asleep. But he would not sleep much longer. Already he had stirred once or twice, and sighed, as those do who must soon awaken. And still Mr. Fortune had not settled how to deal with him when he awoke. Would the Man of Sorrows fit his sorrowful case, He who had once cried out, *Eloi, Eloi, lama sabachthani?* Or would it be better to try Jehovah, a tribal character whose voice was in the clouds, whose arrows stuck very fast? The worst of it was that Lueli knew all about them already. For three years he had been living on the terms of the greatest intimacy with them, he was even at home with the Trinity. And so all that Mr. Fortune could tell him now would be but a twice-told tale; and that was not likely to be of much effect, for Polynesians are fickle, they tire as easily as children and must be bribed with novelties.

Mr. Fortune grew increasingly despondent. He was even growing bored, and more and more quickly he turned over in his mind the various expedients of Godhead which might appeal to Lueli, like a woman tossing over a piece-bag in search of something she cannot find. The blue print, the grey merino, the long and ever more tangled trail of metal lace, a scrap of corduroy: none of these is what she looks for, and what she looks for is not there.

'I can do nothing,' he cried out; and then an inner voice finishing the quotation for him added, 'without Thee.'

Of course he could do nothing without God. Why had he not thought of that before? Why, instead of vain thinking, hadn't he prayed?

He looked about him. He was alone in a mesh of rain. For

leagues around the rain was falling, falling upon the quenched ashes of his homestead where were mingled and quenched too the ashes of Lueli's god, falling upon the motionless forest, falling upon the moving ocean, on that vast watery and indivisible web of tides and currents, falling everywhere with an equal and unstaying pressure. Only upon the newly open mouth of the pit was the rain not falling, for there the flames rushed up and caught and consumed it.

There had been an earthquake and now it was raining. Both events were equally natural, equally accountable for, equally inevitable. There was nowhere any room for chance; no happening from the greatest to the least could be altered or provoked or turned aside. And why should he specify into greatest or least? In causation there is no great or small. He himself was as great as the mountain, as little as the least of the ashes of Lueli's god.

Still he looked about him. But he was not looking for anything now, nor did he need to raise his eyes to heaven or close them before any presence unseen. The God who had walked with him upon the island was gone. He had ascended in the flames that had burst roaring and devouring from the mountain-top, and hiding His departure in clouds of smoke. He had gone up and was lost in space.

Mr. Fortune no longer believed in a God.

It had all happened quite quietly, just like that. Once he put out his hand as though to arrest something that was floating away out of reach, but in a moment it dropped again. And there it was before him, resting upon his knees, the hand of a man who didn't any longer believe in a God, with fingers idly patting out a slow and flagging rhythm, tick-tock, like a time-piece that is running down. The real time-piece went on nimbly enough, it was now (he noticed) five minutes to eleven of the new era. If his diary had not been burnt he could have mentioned in it with impressive accuracy: 'At 10:54 A.M. (N.T.) I ceased to believe in God.' This quaint fancy gave him pleasure.

How differently to Lueli was he taking his loss! The reason must be that Lueli though losing his god had kept his faith. Lueli had lost something real, like losing an umbrella; he had lost it with frenzy and conviction. But *his* loss was utter and retrospective, a lightning-flash loss which had wiped out a whole life-time of having. In fact the best way of expressing it, though it sounded silly and paradoxical, was to say that what he had lost for ever was nothing. 'Forever is a word that stretches backward too,' he explained to himself. If any proof were needed his own behaviour was supplying it. He had ceased to believe in God, but this was making no difference to him. Consequently what he had ceased to believe in had never been.

He sighed—the loud horse's sigh of one who has come to the end of a long stint. Then he stood up amid the rain and the ashes and stretched himself. He had got pins and needles in his leg from sitting still for so long, but it was a pleasure to his body to stretch and he stretched once more. The air struck cold on the muscles and skin which had, as it were, started to live again. He felt at once both tired and vigorous. In an odd way he was feeling rather pleased with himself, a pleasure that was perhaps the independent pleasure of his flesh which had waited patiently around his motionless thinking as a dog waits at the feet of its master absorbed in writing. The pen is thrown down rather wantonly, so that the ink may give a little spurt on to the page that a moment ago was all the world, that now is finished and prostrate and floutable. The master gets up and stretches, the dog gambols round him with congratulation. 'Now you have come home to your senses again, now we can be reasonable and go for a walk!'

He leant down and gave Lueli a little shake, affectionate but brisk.

'Wake up, wake up. We are going down to the village now to find a lodging. You cannot sleep here in the rain all day or you will get rheumatism."

A policeman could not have been kinder, a mother more competent. He had got Lueli up and walking through the wet woods and eating stirabout by Ori's fire before he had time to bethink him of his unhappiness.

Lueli sat swallowing and blinking and looking very debauched and youthful while Mr. Fortune and Ori made arrangements. For the present they could live under the chief's ample roof. Meanwhile the burnt hut could be rebuilt, or some dwelling could be fitted up to receive them as lodgers, whichever Mr. Fortune thought best. As for the volcano, that would not interfere with anybody's plans. The pigs had been corralled once more, the earthquake was already half-forgotten. Ori had sent an old woman up to the mountain to make a reconnaissance, and she had reported that the lava was flowing down the south side of the mountain where nobody lived. Everything was all right again, and the rain would freshen things up nicely. To-morrow he would invite a few friends in, and there would be roast meat and a party in honour of his guest.

Personally Mr. Fortune would have preferred to have the former hut rebuilt and to go on living there, much as of old except for religion, the harmonium, and other European amenities. But he feared that Lueli would mope and be miserable. It would be better for him to have a change of scene, company and gaiety. Accordingly, he arranged that for the future they should lodge with Teioa, a lesser chief, whose family included several lively sons and daughters and an extremely vivacious great-grandmother.

Unfortunately this plan worked badly. Mr. Fortune was much happier than he expected to be. He was now engaged in growing a beard, and freed from any obligation to convert his housemates he found their society very agreeable. The great-grandmother was especially good company. She was a celebrated story-teller, and when she had exhausted her stock of scandals about everyone in the village she fell back upon legends and fairy-tales. Mr. Fortune was interested to find that many of these were almost word for word the stories of the Old Testament. One hot afternoon as they sat bathing their legs in a pool and waving away the flies from each other she recounted the story of Joseph and his Brethren. Joseph was called Kila and was carried to the land of Egypt in a canoe, but all the familiar characters were there, all the familiar incidents, even to where Kila turned away from his brothers he was threatening to hide the tears which he could no longer keep back. The only variation was in the character of Isaac, who had changed his sex and split into Joseph's mother and aunt. But in truth the change made little difference, nor did it detract from the dignity of the story, for in spite of our English prejudice there is nothing inherently ridiculous about a mother's sister. Mr. Fortune was not perturbed to hear the history of the Jews from the lips of a wrinkled and engraved old Polynesian harridan. He reflected that everywhere mankind is subject to the same anxious burden of love and loneliness, and must in self-defiance enchant their cares into a story and a dream. In return for Joseph and his Brethren he told the old dame of the adventures of Mr. Pickwick, many of which were new to her.

But while Mr. Fortune was getting on so nicely Lueli was very unhappy. His playmates had soon found out his misfortune. They teased him, saying that he had lost his god and would soon go to Hell. Every day the boy grew more dispirited. He shunned his fellows and went slinking off to hide himself in the woods, where he could mope in peace and quiet. Late in the evening he would creep back, smelling of damp forest earth and wild spices; and without a word he would lie down on his mat and fall into a dreary slumber.

One day Teioa remarked to Mr. Fortune: 'That boy has lost his god. I expect he will die soon.'

'What nonsense!' shouted Mr. Fortune in a loud rude voice. He felt too suddenly sick to choose his words. He remembered what he had once read in a book about the Polynesians: that they can renounce life at their own will, not with the splash of suicide, but slowly, sullenly, deliberately, driving death into themselves like a wedge. Was Lueli doing this—gay, inconsequent, casual Lueli? But since the loss of his god Lueli was gay no longer, and his casualness had taken on a new and terrible aspect, as though it were the casualness of one who could not be bothered to live, who was discarding life as naturally and callously as he had picked flowers and thrown them down to die.

Just then a troop of boys and girls danced by. They were dancing after Lueli and pelting him with small glittering fishes. 'Catch!' they cried; 'here's a god for you, Lueli. Catch him!'

Lueli walked on as if he hadn't noticed them. He looked down and saw one of the fish lying at his feet. Like an animal he picked it up and began eating it, but he ate inattentively, without appetite. He was like a sick dog that snatches listlessly at a tuft of grass. Mr. Fortune stepped out from the verandah. His intention had been to drive the dancers away, but instead of that he put his arm through Lueli's and began walking him down to the beach.

'Let us bathe together,' he said. 'It is a long time since you gave me a swimming-lesson.'

Lueli swam so beautifully that it was hard to believe he was not happy. Mr. Fortune surpassed himself in flounderings. He tried to catch a fish in his mouth.

When they were sitting on the beach again he said: 'Where shall we live when we leave Teioa's house? Shall we make a new hut or shall we build up our old one again?'

'Go back to the old,' Lueli replied instantly in a soft fearful whisper.

'Yes, I think so too. Our own bathing-pool is much the best.'

'Yes. It's deeper than the one here.'

'I think the fish are tamer too.'

'Yes.'

'I was wondering if we couldn't make a small wicker-work bower on a pole and teach the parrots to sleep in it. In England people do so, only the birds are doves, not parrots. Perhaps you remember me telling you about our doves and pigeons?'

'They take messages.'

'Yes, those are the carrier pigeons. There are also pouters and fantails and tumbling pigeons that turn head over heels in the air. But parrots would be very nice too. You could feed them.'

'Won't they be able to feed themselves?'

'Oh yes, certainly. But they would be more apt to stay with us if we fed them.'

'Must they stay?'

'Now, am I diverting him from his grief,' thought Mr. Fortune, 'or am I only boring him?'

The new hut that rose on the place of the old had a faint whiff of burning. Mr. Fortune had superintended the building of it, and because the islanders were fond of him they allowed him to introduce several novelties, such as window-boxes and a kitchen dresser. He also threw out a bay. The parrot-cote stood in a corner of the lawn, and leading up to it was a narrow serpentining path with crazy paving made out of flat shells. On the other side of the house to balance the parrot-cote was a pergola, constructed in bamboo. In front of the house, in fact exactly where it always had been, but uprooted by the earthquake, was the flat stone on which he had celebrated Holy Communion on that first Sunday morning. He looked at it a little sadly. He bore it no malice, although it reminded him of a special kind of happiness which he could taste no more. He decided that he would make it the headstone of a rock-garden.

Mr. Fortune attached a special importance to these European refinements because he felt that to the eyes of the world he must now present such an un-European appearance. The earthquake had left him nothing save the clothes he stood up in, the contents of his pockets, and a good-sized rubbish-heap. As for the rubbish-heap, he had with his own hands grubbed a large hole among the bushes and buried therein the bones of the harmonium, lamp, sewing-machine, etc., also the molten images of the communion plate and the teapot. He had done this by night, working by moonlight in the approved fashion of those who have a past to put away, and when he had covered in the hole and stamped down the earth he went back and forth from the ruins to the bushes, scooping up the ashes in a gourd and scattering them in the undergrowth.

His clothes he had folded and put away, thinking that as they were all he had, he had better save them up for future emergencies, such as a shipwreck, a visit of American tourists, the arrival of a new missionary or somebody dropping in from a flying machine. In their stead he wore a kilt and a mantle of native cloth, soberly contrived without any fringes or fandangos, and sandals of plaited bark. Since this new garb was pocketless, the contents of his pockets were ranged on the shelf of honour of the kitchen dresser—a pocket magnifying-glass, a whistle, a nailfile, a graduated medicine spoon, a flint-and-steel lighter, a copper medal commemorating Parnell which Henry Martin had brought from Ireland as a curiosity, nineteen mother-of-pearl counters in a wash-leather bag, a pencil-sharpener blunted by sand getting into it, a tape-measure that sprang back into a boxwood nut, several buttons, a silver pencil-case with no pencil, and a small magnet painted scarlet. There was also a knife with two blades, but this he carried on a string round his neck.

He looked on this array without sentiment. The parrot-cote and the pergola were also without charms for him. His intentions were severely practical. These things were all part of his designs on Lueli, they were so many fish-hooks to draw him from despair. Not by their proper qualities, of course; Mr. Fortune was not so simple as to expect that, even of the magnet. But indirectly they would build up around their owner and designer a compelling spiritual splendour, a glamour of mysterious attributes, fastidious living, and foreign parts. After three years of such familiarity it would not be easy to reconstruct his first fascination as something rich and strange. But it must be done if he were to compete successfully with his rival in Lueli's affections. It must be done, because that rival was death.

He thought as little as he could help about his progress in this contest. He dared not allow himself to be elated when he seemed to be gaining a little, he dared not admit the possibility of failure. He fought with his eyes turned away from the face of the adversary, like Perseus attacking the Gorgon. He fought by inches, by half-hours; he dared not attempt a decisive victory for he could not risk a decisive defeat. And when he crept out of the hut at night to refresh himself with solitude and darkness, the sullen red light kindling and wavering above the blackness of the crags betokened to him that his enemy was also awake and weaving his powerful spells of annihilation.

He had no time to think of his own loss. He was entirely taken up with solicitude for Lueli, a soul no longer—as he supposed—immortal, and for that reason a charge upon him all the more urgent, as one is more concerned for a humming-bird than for a tortoise. Only at such times as when he had received a serious set-back or was feeling especially desperate did he find himself on the point of taking refuge in prayer; and then remembering the real state of things he would feel exactly like a person who makes to cast himself down on a chair but recalls just in time (or maybe just too late) how all the furniture has been moved, and that the chair is no longer in its old place.

It was sometimes hard for him with his English prejudices not to grow irritated at Lueli's abject listlessness and misery. He could not have believed that his friend could be so chicken-hearted. And since when one is down everything falls on one, circumstances seemed to conspire in twitting and outraging the luckless youth.

Mr. Fortune thought he would try games. Lueli was agile and dexterous, surely it would comfort him to exhibit those qualities. Mr. Fortune introduced him to ping-pong. They played with basket-work bats and small nuts. On the second day a nut hit Lueli and made his nose bleed. He turned green, cast down his bat and began to whimper.

Since ping-pong was too rough, what about spillikins? He carved a set of pieces out of splinters, dyed them with fruit juice to make them look more appetising, and made a great show of excitement to tempt the other on. Whenever it was Lueli's turn to hook a piece from the tangle he sighed and groaned as though he had been requested to move mountains. Dicing and skittles were no better received.

Deciding that neither games nor gaming (they diced for the mother-of-pearl counters) were likely to rouse Lueli from his dejection, Mr. Fortune cast about for some new expedient. Perhaps a pet animal might have charms? He caught a baby flying fox and reared it with great tenderness on guavas and coco-milk. The flying fox soon grew extremely attached to him and learnt to put its head out of the cage when he called 'Tibby!' But whenever Lueli could be induced to take an interest in it and to prod it up with a cautious finger, it scratched and bit him. Still persevering with natural history Mr. Fortune spat on the magnifying-glass, polished it, and began to show off the wonderful details of flowers, mosses, and water-fleas. Lueli would look, and look away again, obediently and haplessly bored.

Though the idea of such cold and rapacious blood-thirstiness was highly repugnant to him, he resolved to sacrifice his own feelings (and theirs) and make a moth collection. He prepared a mess of honey and water and took Lueli out that evening on an expedition to lime the trees. Two hours later they went out again with a string of candle-nuts for a lantern and collected a quantity of moths and nocturnal insects, poignantly beautiful and battered with their struggles to escape. But he stifled his sense of shame, all the more in that Lueli seemed inclined to rise to this lure, of his own accord suggesting a second expedition. He had not quite grasped the theory, however. Two days later Mr. Fortune, returning from an errand in the village, was surprised to hear a loud and furious buzzing proceeding from the dell. It was full of wild bees, and Lueli, very swollen and terrified, came crawling out of the bushes. He had smeared the parrot-cote and the posts of the verandah with honey, and it seemed as though every bee and wasp on the island were assembled together to quarrel and gorge themselves. It was not possible to approach the hut until after nightfall, and drunk and disorderly bees hovered about it for days, not to speak of a sediment of ants.

Worse was to come. Since his arrival on the island Mr. Fortune had never ailed. But now, whether by exposure to night dews and getting his feet damp out mothing or by some special malignity of Fate, he found himself feeling sore at the back of the throat and sneezing; and presently he had developed a streaming cold. Lueli caught it from him, and if his cold were bad, Lueli's was ten times worse. He made no effort to struggle against it; indeed, he was so overwhelmed that struggling was practically out of the question. He crouched on his mats, snorting and groaning, with a face all chapped and bloated, blear eyes, a hanging jaw, and a sullen and unhealthy appetite; and every five minutes or so he sneezed as though he would bring the roof down.

Mr. Fortune was terrified, not only for Lueli, but for the whole population of the island. He knew how direly European diseases can rampage through a new field. He set up a rigid quarantine. Since the loss of his god Lueli had been at pains to avoid his friends, but naturally he was now seized with a passionate craving for their society; and there was some excuse for him, as Mr. Fortune was not just now very exhilarating company. But he did his best to be, in spite of an earache which followed the cold, and between Lueli's paroxysms of sneezing he strove to cheer him with accounts of the Great Plague and the Brave Men of Eyam.

At last they were both recovered. But though restored in body Lueli was as mopish as ever. Mr. Fortune went on bracing, and beat his brains for some new distraction. But he had lost ground in this last encounter, and the utmost he could congratulate himself upon was that Lueli was still, however indifferently or unwillingly, consenting to exist. The worst of it was that he couldn't allow himself to show any sympathy. There were times when he could scarcely hold himself back from pity and condolence. But he believed that if he were once to acknowledge the other's grief he would lose his greatest hold over him—his title of being some one superior, august and exemplary.

And then one morning, when they had been living in the new hut for about six weeks, he woke up inspired. Why had he wasted so much time displaying his most trivial and uncompelling charms, opposing to the magnetism of death such fripperies and tit-bits of this world, such gewgaws of civilisation as a path serpentining to a parrot-cote (a parrot-cote which hadn't even allured the parrots), or a pocket magnifying-glass, while all the time he carried within him the inestimable treasures of intellectual enjoyment? Now he would pipe Lueli a tune worth dancing to, now he would open for him a new world. He would teach him mathematics.

He sprang up from bed, full of enthusiasm. At the thought of all those stretches of white beach he was like a bridegroom. There they were, hard and smooth from the tread of the sea, waiting for that noble consummation of blank surfaces, to show forth a truth; waiting, in this particular instance, to show forth the elements of plane geometry.

At breakfast Mr. Fortune was so glorified and gay that Lueli caught a reflection of his high spirits and began to look more lifelike than he had done for weeks. On their way down to the beach they met a party of islanders who were off on a picnic. Mr. Fortune with delight heard Lueli answering their greetings with something like his former sociability, and even plucking up heart enough for a repartee. His delight gave a momentary stagger when Lueli decided to go a-picnicking too. But, after all, it didn't matter a pin. The beach would be as smooth again to-morrow, the air as sweet and nimble; Lueli would be in better trim for learning after a spree, and, now he came to think of it, he himself wouldn't teach any the worse for a little private rubbing-up beforehand.

It must be going on for forty years since he had done any mathematics; for he had gone into the bank the same year that his father died, leaving Rugby at seventeen because, in the state that things were then in, the bank was too good an opening to be missed. He had once got a prize—the Poetical Works of Longfellow—for algebra, and he had scrambled along well enough in other branches of mathematics; but he had not learnt with any particular thrill, or realised that thrill there might be, until he was in the bank, and learning a thing of the past.

Then, perhaps because of that never-ending entering and adding up and striking balances, and turning on to the next page to enter, add up, and strike balances again, a mental occupation minute, immediate, and yet, so to speak, wool-gathering, as he imagined knitting to be, the absolute quality of mathematics began to take on for him an inexpressibly romantic air. 'Pure Mathematics.' He used to speak of them to his fellow-clerks as though he were hinting at some kind of transcendental debauchery of which he had been made free—and indeed there does seem to be a kind of unnatural vice in being so completely pure. After a spell of this holy boasting he would grow a little uneasy; and going to the Free Library he took out mathematical treatises, just to make sure that he could follow step by step as well as soar. For twenty pages, perhaps, he read slowly, carefully, dutifully, with pauses for self-examination and working out the examples. Then, just as it was working up and the pauses should have been more scrupulous than ever, a kind of swoon and ecstasy would fall on him, and he read ravening on, sitting up till dawn to finish the book, as though it were a novel. After that his passion was stayed; the book went back to the Library and he was done with mathematics till the next bout. Not much remained with him after these orgies, but something remained: a sensation in the mind, a worshipping acknowledgment of something isolated and unassailable, or a remembered mental joy at the rightness of thoughts coming together to a conclusion, accurate thoughts, thoughts in just intonation, coming together like unaccompanied voices coming to a close.

But often his pleasure flowered from quite simple things that any fool could grasp. For instance, he would look out of the bank windows, which had green shades in their lower halves; and rising above the green shades he would see a row of triangles, equilateral, isosceles, acute-angled, right-angled, obtuse-angled. These triangles were a range of dazzling mountain peaks, eternally snowy, eternally untrodden; and he could feel the keen wind which blew from their summits. Yet they were also a row of triangles, equilateral, isosceles, acute-angled, right-angled, obtuse-angled.

This was the sort of thing he designed for Lueli's comfort. Geometry would be much better than algebra, though he had not the same certificate from Longfellow for teaching it. Algebra is always dancing over the pit of the unknown, and he had no wish to direct Lueli's thoughts to that quarter. Geometry would be best to begin with, plain plane geometry, immutably plane. Surely if anything could minister to the mind diseased it would be the steadfast contemplation of a right angle, an existence that no mist of human tears could blur, no blow of fate deflect.

Walking up and down the beach, admiring the surface which to-morrow with so much epiphany and glory was going to reveal the first axioms of Euclid, Mr. Fortune began to think of himself as possessing an universal elixir and charm. A wave of missionary ardour swept him along, and he seemed to view, not Lueli only, but all the islanders rejoicing in this new dispensation. There was beach-board enough for all and to spare. The picture grew in his mind's eye, somewhat indebted to Raphael's Cartoon of the School of Athens. Here a group bent over an equation, there they pointed out to each other with admiration that the square on the hypotenuse equalled the sum of the squares on the sides containing the right angle; here was one delighting in a rhomboid and another in conic sections; that enraptured figure had secured the twelfth root of two, while the children might be filling up the foreground with a little long division.

By the morrow he had slept off most of his fervour. Calm, methodical, with a mind prepared for the onset, he guided Lueli down to the beach and with a stick prodded a small hole in it.

'What is this?'

'A hole.'

'No, Lueli, it may seem like a hole, but it is a point.'

Perhaps he had prodded a little too emphatically. Lueli's mistake was quite natural. Anyhow, there were bound to be a few misunderstandings at the start.

He took out his pocket-knife and whittled the end of the stick. Then he tried again.

'What is this?'

'A smaller hole.'

'Point,' said Mr. Fortune suggestively.

'Yes, I mean a smaller point.'

'No, not quite. It is a point, but it is not smaller. Holes may be of different sizes, but no point is larger or smaller than another point.'

Lueli looked from the first point to the second. He seemed to be about to speak, but to think better of it. He removed his gaze to the sea.

Meanwhile Mr. Fortune had moved about, prodding more points. It was rather awkward that he should have to walk on the beach-board, for his footmarks distracted the eye from the demonstration.

'Look, Lueli!'

Lueli turned his gaze inland.

'Where?' said he.

'At all these. Here; and here; and here. But don't tread on them.'

Lueli stepped back hastily. When he was well out of the danger zone he stood looking at Mr. Fortune with great attention and some uneasiness.

'These are all points.'

Lueli recoiled a step further. Standing on one leg he furtively inspected the sole of his foot.

'As you see, Lueli, these points are in different places. This one is to the west of that, and consequently that one is to the east of this. Here is one to the south. Here are two close together, and there is one quite apart from all the others. Now look at them, remember what I have said, think carefully, and tell me what you think.'

Inclining his head and screwing up his eyes Lueli inspected

the demonstration with an air of painstaking connoisseurship. At length he ventured the opinion that the hole lying apart from the others was perhaps the neatest. But if Mr. Fortune would give him the knife he would whittle the stick even finer.

'Now what did I tell you? Have you forgotten that points cannot be larger or smaller? If they were holes it would be a different matter. But these are points. Will you remember that?'

Lueli nodded. He parted his lips, he was about to ask a question. Mr. Fortune went on hastily.

'Now suppose I were to cover the whole beach with these; what then?'

A look of dismay came over Lueli's countenance. Mr. Fortune withdrew the hypothesis.

'I don't intend to. I only ask you to imagine what it would be like if I did.'

The look of dismay deepened.

'They would all be points,' said Mr. Fortune impressively. 'All in different places. And none larger or smaller than another.

'What I have explained to you is summed up in the axiom: a point has position but not magnitude. In other words, if a given point were not in a given place it would not be there at all.'

Whilst allowing time for this to sink in he began to muse about those other words. Were they quite what he meant? Did they indeed mean anything? Perhaps it would have been better not to try to supplement Euclid. He turned to his pupil. The last words had sunk in at any rate, had been received without scruple and acted upon. Lueli was out of sight.

Compared with his intentions, actuality had been a little quelling. It became more quelling as time went on. Lueli did not again remove himself without leave; he soon discovered that Mr. Fortune was extremely in earnest, and was resigned to regular instruction every morning and a good deal of rubbing-in and evocation during the rest of the day. No one ever had a finer capacity for listening than he, or a more docile and obliging temperament. But whereas in the old days these good gifts had flowed from him spontaneously and pleasurably, he now seemed to be exhibiting them by rote and in a manner almost desperate, as though he were listening and obliging as a circus animal does its tricks. Humane visitors to circuses often point out with what alacrity the beasts run into the ring to perform their turn. They do not understand that in the choice of two evils most animals would rather flourish round a spacious ring than be shut up in a cage. The activity and the task is a distraction from their unnatural lot, and they tear through paper hoops all the better because so much of their time is spent behind iron bars.

It had been a very different affair when Lueli was learning Bible history and the Church Catechism, *The King of Love my Shepherd is* and *The Old Hundredth.* Then there had been no call for this blatant submission; lessons had been an easy-going conversation, with Lueli keeping his end up as an intelligent pupil should and Mr. Fortune feeling like a cross between wise old Chiron and good Mr. Barlow. Now they were a succession of harangues, and rather strained harangues to boot. Theology, Mr. Fortune found, is a more accommodating subject than mathematics; its technique of exposition allows greater latitude. For instance, when you are gravelled for matter there is always the moral to fall back upon. Comparisons too may be drawn, leading cases cited, types and antetypes analysed, and anecdotes introduced. Except for Archimedes, mathematics is singularly naked of anecdotes.

Not that he thought any the worse of it for this. On the contrary he compared its austere and integral beauty to theology decked out in her flaunting charms and wielding all her bribes and spiritual bonuses; and like Dante at the rebuke of Beatrice he blushed that he should ever have followed aught but the noblest. No, there was nothing lacking in mathematics. The deficiency was in him. He added line to line, precept to precept; he exhausted himself and his pupil by hours of demonstration and exposition; leagues of sand were scarred, and smoothed again by the tide, and scarred afresh: never an answering spark rewarded him. He might as well have made the sands into a rope-walk.

Sometimes he thought that he was taxing Lueli too heavily, and desisted. But if he desisted for pity's sake, pity soon drove him to work again, for if it were bad to see Lueli sighing over the properties of parallel lines, it was worse to see him moping and pining for his god. Teioa's words, uttered so matter-of-factly, haunted his mind. 'I expect he will die soon.' Mr. Fortune was thinking so too. Lueli grew steadily more lack-lustre, his eyes were dull, his voice was flat; he appeared to be retreating behind a film that thickened and toughened and would soon obliterate him.

'If only, if only I could teach him to enjoy an abstract notion! If he could once grasp how it all hangs together, and is everlasting and harmonious, he would be saved. Nothing else can save him, nothing that I or his fellows can offer him. For it must be new to excite him and it must be true to hold him, and what else is there that is both new and true?'

There were women, of course, a race of beings neither new nor true, yet much vaunted by some as a cure for melancholy and a tether for the soul. Mr. Fortune would have cheerfully procured a damsel (not that they were likely to need much of that), dressed her hair, hung the whistle and the Parnell medal round her neck, dowered her with the nineteen counters and the tape-measure, and settled her in Lueli's bed if he had supposed that this would avail. But he feared that Lueli was past the comfort of women, and in any case that sort of thing is best arranged by the parties concerned.

So he resorted to geometry again, and once more Lueli was hurling himself with frantic docility through the paper hoops. It was really rather astonishing how dense he could be! Once out of twenty, perhaps, he would make the right answer. Mr. Fortune, too anxious to be lightly elated, would probe a little into his reasons for making it. Either they were the wrong reasons or he had no reasons at all. Mr. Fortune was often horribly tempted to let a mistake pass. He was not impatient—he was far more patient than in the palmiest days of theology—but he found it almost unendurable to be for ever saying with various inflections of kindness: 'No, Lueli. Try again'; or: 'Well, no, not exactly'; or: 'I fear you have not quite understood'; or: 'Let me try to make that clearer.' He withstood the temptation. His easy acceptance (though in good faith) of a sham had brought them to this pass, and tenderness over a false currency was not likely to help them out of it. No, he would not be caught that way twice.

Similarly he pruned and repressed Lueli's talent for leaking away down side-issues, though this was hard too, for it involved snubbing him almost every time he spoke on his own initiative.

Just as he had been so mistaken about the nature of points, confounding them with holes and agitating himself at the prospect of a beach pitted all over, Lueli contrived to apply the same sort of well-meaning misconceptions to every stage of his progress—if progress be the word to apply to one who is hauled along in a state of semi-consciousness by the scruff of his neck. When the points seemed to be tolerably well established in his mind Mr. Fortune led him on to lines, and by joining up points he illustrated such simple figures as the square, the triangle, and the parallelogram. Lueli perked up, seemed interested, borrowed the stick and began joining up points too. At first he copied Mr. Fortune, glancing up after each stroke to see if he had been properly directed. Then growing rather more confident, and pleased—as who is not?—with the act of drawing on sand, he launched out into a more complicated design.

'This is a man,' he said.

Mr. Fortune was compelled to reply coldly:

'A man is not a geometrical figure.'

At length Mr. Fortune decided that he had better take in sail. Pure mathematics were obviously beyond Lueli; perhaps applied mathematics would work better. Mr. Fortune, as it happened, had never applied any, but he knew that other people did so, and though he considered it a rather lower line of business he was prepared to try it.

'If I were to ask you to find out the height of that tree, how would you set about it?'

Lueli replied with disconcerting readiness:

'I should climb up to the top and let down a string.'

'But suppose you couldn't climb up it?'

'Then I should cut it down.'

'That would be very wasteful; and the other way might be dangerous. I can show you a better plan than either of those.'

The first thing was to select a tree, an upright tree, because in all elementary demonstrations it is best to keep things as clear as possible. He would never have credited the rarity of upright trees had he not been pressed to find one. Coco-palms, of course, were hopeless: they all had a curve or a list. At length he remembered a tree near the bathing-pool, a perfect specimen of everything a tree should be, tall, straight as a die, growing by itself; set apart, as it were, for purposes of demonstration.

He marched Lueli thither, and when he saw him rambling towards the pool he recalled him with a cough.

'Now I will show you how to discover the height of that tree. Attend. You will find it very interesting. The first thing to do is to lie down.'

Mr. Fortune lay down on his back and Lueli followed his example.

Many people find that they can think more clearly in a recumbent position. Mr. Fortune found it so too. No sooner was he on his back than he remembered that he had no measuring-stick. But the sun was delicious and the grass soft; he might well spare a few minutes in exposing the theory.

'It is all a question of measurements. Now my height is six foot two inches, but for the sake of argument we will assume it to be six foot exactly. The distance from my eye to the base of the tree is so far an unknown quantity. My six feet, however, are already known to you.'

Now Lueli had sat up, and was looking him up and down with an intense and curious scrutiny, as though he were something utterly unfamiliar. This was confusing, it made him lose the thread of his explanation. He felt a little uncertain as to how it should proceed.

Long ago, on dark January mornings, when a septic thumb (bestowed on him by a cat which he had rescued from a fierce poodle) obliged him to stay away from the bank, he had observed young men with woolen comforters and raw-looking wind-bitten hands practising surveying under the snarling elms and whimpering poplars of Finsbury Park. They had tapes and tripods, and the girls in charge of perambulators dawdled on the asphalt paths to watch their proceedings. It was odd how vividly fragments of his old life had been coming back to him during these last few months.

He resumed:

'In order to ascertain the height of the tree I must be in such a position that the top of the tree is exactly in a line with the top of a measuring-stick—or any straight object would do, such as an umbrella—which I shall secure in an upright position between my feet. Knowing then that the ratio that the height of the tree bears to the length of the measuring-stick must equal the ratio that the distance from my eye to the base of the tree bears to my height, and knowing (or being able to find out) my height, the length of the measuring-stick, and the distance from my eye to the base of the tree, I can, therefore, calculate the height of the tree.'

'What is an umbrella?'

Again the past flowed back, insurgent and actual. He was at the Oval, and out of an overcharged sky it had begun to rain again. In a moment the insignificant tapestry of lightish faces was exchanged for a noble pattern of domes, blackish, blueish, and greenish domes, sprouting like a crop of miraculous and religious mushrooms. The rain fell harder and harder, presently the little white figures were gone from the field and, as with an abnegation of humanity, the green plain, so much smaller for their departure, lay empty and forsaken, ringed round with tier upon tier of blackly glistening umbrellas.

He longed to describe it all to Lueli, it seemed to him at the moment that he could talk with the tongues of angels about umbrellas. But this was a lesson in mathematics: applied mathematics moreover, a compromise, so that all further compromises must be sternly nipped. Unbending to no red herrings, he replied:

'An umbrella, Lueli, when in use resembles the—the shell that would be formed by rotating an arc of curve about its axis of symmetry, attached to a cylinder of small radius whose axis is the same as the axis of symmetry of the generating curve of the shell. When not in use it is properly an elongated cone, but it is more usually helicoidal in form.'

Lueli made no answer. He lay down again, this time face downward.

Mr. Fortune continued: 'An umbrella, however, is not essential. A stick will do just as well, so find me one, and we will go on to the actual measurement.'

Lueli was very slow in finding a stick. He looked for it rather languidly and stupidly, but Mr. Fortune tried to hope that this was because his mind was engaged on what he had just learnt.

Holding the stick between his feet, Mr. Fortune wriggled about on his back trying to get into the proper position. He knew he was making a fool of himself. The young men in Finsbury Park had never wriggled about on their backs. Obviously there must be some more dignified way of getting the top of the stick in line with the top of the tree and his eye, but just then it was not obvious to him. Lueli made it worse by standing about and looking miserably on. When he had placed himself properly he remembered that he had not measured the stick. It measured (he had had the forethought to bring the tape with him) three foot seven, very tiresome—those odd inches would only serve to make it seem harder to his pupil. So he broke it again, drove it into the ground, and wriggled on his stomach till his eye was in the right place, which was a slight improvement in method at any rate. He then handed the tape to Lueli, and lay strictly motionless, admonishing and directing, while Lueli did the measuring of the ground. In the interests of accuracy he did it thrice, each time with a different result. A few minutes before noon the height of the tree was discovered to be fifty-seven foot nine inches.

Mr. Fortune now had leisure for compassion. He thought Lueli was looking hot and fagged, so he said:

'Why don't you have a bathe? It will freshen you up.'

Lueli raised his head and looked at him with a long dubious look, as though he had heard the words but without understanding what they meant. Then he turned his eyes to the tree and looked at that. A sort of shadowy wrinkle, like the blurring on the surface of milk before it boils, crossed his face.

'Don't worry any more about that tree. If you hate all this so much we won't do any more of it, I will never speak of geometry again. Put it all out of your head and go and bathe.'

Still Lueli looked at him as though he heard but didn't understand. Then in the same sleep-walking fashion he turned and went down towards the bathing-pool.

Presently, looking between the trees, Mr. Fortune saw him reappear on the rock above the deep part of the pool. He was going to dive. Very slowly and methodically he took off everything that was on him, he even took off his earrings. Then he stretched his arms in a curve above his head and leapt in.

A beautiful dive—Mr. Fortune found himself thinking of the arc of a stretched bow, the curve and flash of a scimitar, the jet of a harpoon—all instruments of death, all displaying the same austere and efficient kind of beauty, the swiftness to shed blood. A beautiful dive—and a long one. Had he come up already? Hardly; for from where he sat Mr. Fortune could see almost the whole surface of the bathing-pool. Perhaps, though, he had come up behind the rock, swimming back under water.

Mr. Fortune rose to his feet. Instantly, with the movement, agonising fear took hold of him. He ran down to the pool, and out along the rocks, shouting and calling. No sign, only the quietly heaving water under the impervious blue sky. No sound, except the parrots and sea-birds squawking in answer to his disturbing voice. Lueli was staying down on purpose. He was holding on to the seaweed, drowning himself, with the resolute fatal despair of his light-hearted race.

Mr. Fortune leapt over his own fear of deep water. Where Lueli had dived he could dive too. He hurled himself off the rock, he felt the water break like a stone under him, he felt himself smothered and sinking; and the next moment he was bouncing about on the surface, utterly and hopelessly afloat. He kicked and beat the water, trying to force a passage downward. It would not let him through.

He swam to the rock and scrambled out into the weight of air and dived for a second time. Once more the sea caught him and held him up.

'Damn!' he said, softly and swiftly, as though he were pursuing a pencil which had rolled into a dark corner out of reach.

Since diving was out of the question he must run to the village to fetch helpers. The village was nearly a mile away, there might be no one there but old women and babies, he would be breathless, every one would shout and wave their arms, by the time he got back with a rescue party it would be too late, Lueli would be drowned.

This time it was harder to haul himself out of the water, for he had forgotten to throw off his large draperies and they were now water-logged. After the shadow of the pool the sunlight seemed black and blinding. He started to run, loosening the knots as he went, for he would run quicker naked. As he threw off the cloak he caught sight over his shoulder of a canoe out to sea. It was heading away from the island, but perhaps it was still within earshot. He shouted and waved the cloak and shouted and coo-eed again. Each cry came out of his body like a thing with jagged edges, tearing him inwardly. The canoe kept on its course. The sweat ran down and blinded him, so that he thought for a moment that the canoe had changed its direction and was coming towards him: but it was only the sweat in his eyes which had enlarged it.

He began to run again. It was a pity that he had wasted so much good breath shouting. He was among the trees now, rushing down a vista of light and shadow. Each tall tree seemed to gather speed as he approached it till it shot past him with a whirr of foliage and a swoop of darkness. His going shook the ground, and the fruit fell off the bushes as he ran by.

The path began to wind downhill and grew stonier. He was about half-way to the village, he could hear the noise of the brook. He shot round a corner, tripped over something, and fell headlong into a group of human beings, falling among smooth brown limbs and cries of astonishment. It was one of those bevies, half a dozen young women who had come out to the brook to net crayfish. To his horror they all leapt to their feet and began to run away. Lying along the ground as he fell, with his head in the brook, he caught hold of an ankle.

'Stop! Don't be little fools!' he cried out, sobbing for breath. 'Lueli is drowning in the bathing-pool. You must come back with me and save him.'

The ankle belonged to Fuma, a hoyden whom he had once loathed beyond words; but now he adored her, for she was going to play up. She called back the other girls, rallied them, sent one back to the village, and bade the others run as fast as they could to the pool; and in a twinkling she and Mr. Fortune were following them up through the woods. Fuma caught hold of his arm and patted it encouragingly.

'He is in the deep hole under the black rock,' he said. 'He is lying there holding on to the weed. I have been shouting, and I may not be able to keep up with you. But you must run on without me and dive until you find him.'

'Silly boy! Silly Lueli! He told me three days ago that he meant to die. Such nonsense! Never mind, we will pull him up and breathe him alive again.'

They ran on side by side. Presently Mr. Fortune said: 'You know, Fuma, this is all my fault.'

Fuma laughed under her breath. 'Lueli thinks the world of you,' she said. 'He is always telling us how lovable you are.'

After a few more yards Mr. Fortune said: 'Fuma, you must run on alone now.'

She gave his arm a gentle nip and shot ahead. He saw her join the others as a starling flies into the flock, and then they were out of sight. He could only think of quite small immediate things, Fuma's eyebrows, a beautiful clear arch, and the soft quick sound of her breathing. He was thinking more of her than of Lueli. She seemed more real.

He was still running, but now every time that he put a foot down it was with a stamp that disintegrated his balance, so that he could not guide his direction. Then he heard a splash, and another and another. They had reached the pool and begun diving. Then he heard Fuma's voice crying: 'Further to the left. He's down here.' Then a babble of voices and more splashings. Then silence.

He gathered up his will for the last thirty yards, was down on to the beach and out breast high into the water. He saw a girl's head rise above the surface of the empty pool. She shook the hair from her eyes, saw him standing there, and came swimming towards him.

'We've got him,' she said. 'But Fuma has to cut the weed with a shell for we can't loosen his hands.'

Mr. Fortune took the pocket-knife from his neck and held it out to her. Then he saw a strangely intricate and beautiful group emerge and slowly approach. They had brought up Lueli and were bearing him among them. His head lolled and dipped back into the water from Fuma's shoulder where it lay. His eyes were open in a fixed and piteous stare, his mouth was open too, and a little trickle of blood ran down from his lip where he had bitten it. His inanimate body trailed in the water with gestures inexpressibly weary. But two long streamers of weed still hung from his clenched hands.

Death comes with her black ruler and red ink and scores a firm line under the long tale of more or less, debit and credit, all the small multitudinous entries which have made up the relationship between one's self and another. The line is drawn, the time has come to audit; and from the heart of her shadow a strange clarity, dream-like and precise, is shed upon the page, so that without any doubt or uncertainty we can add up the account which is now at an end, and perceive the sum-total of the expenditure of time. While the others were ministering around the body of Lueli, squeezing the water out of his lungs, rubbing him, breathing into his nostrils, burning herbs and performing incantations, Mr. Fortune sat under a tree, a little apart, and audited the past. In the tree sat a parrot, uttering from time to time its curious airy whistle—a high, sweet, meditative note. It seemed to Mr. Fortune that the bird was watching the process of his thoughts, and that its whistle, detached from any personal emotion, even from that of astonishment, was an involuntary and philosophic acknowledgment of the oddity of men's lives and passions.

'I loved him,' he thought. 'From the moment I set eyes on him I loved him. Not with what is accounted a criminal love, for though I set my desire on him it was a spiritual desire. I did not even love him as a father loves a son, for that is a familiar love, and at the times when Lueli most entranced me it was as a being remote, intact, and incalculable. I waited to see what his next movement would be, if he would speak or no—it was the not knowing what he would do that made him dear. Yes, that was how I loved him best, those were my happiest moments: when I was just aware of him, and sat with my senses awaiting him, not wishing to speak, not wishing to make him notice me until he did so of his own accord because no other way would it be perfect, would it be by him. And how often, I wonder, have I let it be just like that? Perhaps a dozen times, perhaps twenty times all told, perhaps, when all is put together, for an hour out of the three years I have had with him. For man's will is a demon that will not let him be. It leads him to the edge of a clear pool; and while he sits admiring it, with his soul suspended over it like a green branch and dwelling in its own reflection, will stretches out his hand and closes his fingers upon a stone—a stone to throw into it.

'I'd had a poor, meagre, turnpike sort of life until I came here and found Lueli. I loved him, he was a refreshment to me, my only pleasant surprise. He was perfect because he *was* a surprise. I had done nothing to win him, he was entirely gratuitous. I had had no hand in him, I could no more have imagined him beforehand than I could have imagined a new kind of flower. So what did I do? I started interfering. I made him a Christian, or thought I did. I taught him to do this and not to do the other, I checked him, I fidgeted over him. And because I loved him so for what he was I could not spend a day without trying to alter him. How dreadful it is that because of our wills we can never love anything without messing it about! We couldn't even love a tree, not a stone even; for sooner or later we should be pruning the tree or chipping a bit off the stone. Yet if it were not for a will I suppose we should cease to exist. Anyhow it is in us, and while we live we cannot escape from it, so however we love and whatever we love, it can only be for a few minutes, and to buy off our will for those few minutes we have to relinquish to it for the rest of our lives whatever it is we love. Lueli has been the price of Lueli. I enslaved him, I kept him on a string. I robbed him of his god twice over—first in intention, then in fact. I made his misery more miserable by my perpetual interference. Up till an hour ago I was actually tormenting him with that damned geometry. And now he is dead. . . . Yes, parrot! You may well whistle. But be careful. Don't attract my attention too much lest I should make a pet of you, and put you in a cage, and then in the end, when you had learnt to talk like me instead of whistling like a wise bird, wring your neck because you couldn't learn to repeat *Paradise Lost.*'

At these words the parrot flew away, just as though it had understood and wished to keep on the safe side; and looking up

Mr. Fortune saw some of the islanders running towards him. He got up and went to meet them. 'Well, is he dead?' he asked, too deeply sunk in his own wan hope to pay any attention to their looks and greetings.

It was some time before they could make him understand that Lueli was alive. He followed them, dumb, trembling, and stupefied, to where Lueli was sitting propped up under a tree. He looked rather battered, and rather bewildered, and slightly ashamed of himself, like a child that has been at a rich tea-party, grown over-excited and been sick. But the hag-ridden look he had worn since the earthquake was gone, and he was answering the congratulations and chaff of those around him with a semblance of his old gaiety.

Mr. Fortune stood looking down on him in silence, confused at meeting him whom he had not thought to meet again. Lueli was infected by his embarrassment, and the two regarded each other with caution and constraint, as dear friends do who meet unexpectedly after long separation. Lueli was the first to speak.

'How ill you look. Your face is all holes.'

'Lueli, you would have laughed if you could have seen me trying to dive in after you. Twice I threw myself in, but I could do nothing but float.'

'I expect you let yourself crumple up.'

'Yes, I expect I did.'

'But it was very kind of you to try.'

'Not at all.'

The situation was horrible. Mr. Fortune was tongue-tied, very jealous of the others, and haunted with the feeling that behind all this cause for rejoicing there was some fatal obstacle which he ought to know all about but which his mind was shirking the contemplation of. Lueli fidgeted and made faces. The awkwardness of being raised from the dead was too much even for his *savoir faire.*

'Why can't I be natural?' thought Mr. Fortune. 'Why can't I say how glad I feel? And why don't I feel my gladness? What have I done? Why is it like this, what is the matter with me?'

Lueli's thoughts were something like this: 'He has a blemish on his neck, but didn't I ever notice it before? It must have grown larger. I hope they won't begin to laugh at him because he can't dive. I love him, but, oh dear! what a responsibility he is. I don't think I can bear it much longer, not just now. I don't want responsibilities. I only want to go to sleep.'

Round them stood half the population of the island, raging with congratulations, jokes, and inquiries. Even when they had escorted them back to the hut, superintended Lueli's falling asleep, and eaten all the provisions which Mr. Fortune brought out to them, they would not go away but sat among their crumbs and on the rock-garden imploring Fuma to tell them once more how Mr. Fortune had come bounding through the wood and fallen headlong into the girls' laps.

For no reason that he could see he had suddenly become immensely popular. And as he walked to and fro in the twilight waiting for his guests to take themselves off he heard his name being bandied about in tones of the liveliest affection and approval. He had one consolation: by the morrow he would be out of fashion again. As for Lueli, they scarcely mentioned him. If he had been drowned they would have spent the evening wailing and lamenting: not for him but for themselves, at the reminder of their own mortality, after the natural way of mourning. And there would have been just as much gusto, he thought—but tenderly, for he felt no animosity to them now, only a desire to get rid of them and be left to his own soul—and just as many crumbs.

The moon had set before they went away. Mr. Fortune stole into the hut and listened for a while to Lueli's quiet breathing, a slight human rhythm recovered that day from the rhythm of the sea. He knelt down very quietly and creakingly, and taking hold of Lueli's limp warm hand he put it to his lips. 'Good-bye, my dear,' he murmured under his breath. Lueli stirred, and uttered a drowsy inarticulate Good-night.

Both rhythms were in Mr. Fortune's ears as he lay down to rest. He did not sleep, at least not for some hours; but he lay unharried in a solemn and dream-like repose, listening to the gentle fanning of Lueli's slumber and the slow tread of the sea.

Thus, tranquil and full of long thoughts, he had lain on his first night in Fanua, gazing at the star Canopus and watching the trail of creeper stir at the sweet breath of night. All that he had then of hope and faith was lost. But now at the last he seemed strangely to have resumed the temper of that night, and the thought of his renunciation was as full and perfect as the former thought of his vocation had been. 'It is not one's beliefs that matter,' he told himself, 'but to be acting up to them. To have come to Fanua and now to have made up my mind to go away—it is the decision that fills me with this amazing kind of joy.'

To go away. It was the only solution, he had the parrot's word for it. The slow tread of the sea told him the same story. 'I brought you here,' it said, 'and presently I shall bear you away. My ebbing tides will return to Fanua, and ebb and return again and ebb and return again. But for you there will be no return.' And the tread of the sea became the footfall of a warder. It was this necessity, still implicit and unrealised, which had lain like a stone in his heart when he saw Lueli brought back from the dead. If he had not thought of Lueli as being dead he would never have understood. But Death had vouchsafed him a beam of her darkness to see clearly by; and having seen, he could not sin against that light. He must go away, that was the only stratagem by which love could outwit its own inherent treachery. If he stayed on, flattering himself with the belief that he had learnt his lesson, he would remember for a while no doubt; but sooner or later, inevitably he would yield to his will again, he would begin to meddle, he would seek to destroy.

To see everything so clearly and to know that his mind was made up was almost to be released from human bondage. This must be the boasted calm joy of mathematicians which he had once pretended to share. Euclid had failed him, or he had failed Euclid; but the contemplation of his own reasoning and resolved mind gave him a felicity beyond even that which the rightness of right-angles could afford. He would keep awake a little longer and make the most of it. He could be sure it would not last. But when it had shattered and desolation came in its stead there would still be common sense and common manliness and several practical preoccupations with which to keep desolation at bay.

First he must get a message to St. Fabien. In the pocket of the coat he had worn on the night of the earthquake were a couple of sheets torn out of an exercise book. He had carried them on his stroll on the chance that he might feel impelled to write a sonnet (Petrarchan Sonnets were the only poetical form he attempted, because they were so regular, and even so he did them very badly) On The Setting Sun, or To a Hermit Crab. He had not done so, partly because he had forgotten to take a pencil too; but now, when he had smoothed the crumples out these sheets would come in handy for his letter to the Archdeacon.

In the morning he gathered some purple fruit whose juice he knew from experience to be indelible, squeezed them into a bowl, and with a reed pen wrote as follows:

'Fanua.

'My Dear Archdeacon,—I am sorry to trouble you, but I must ask that the launch may be sent to fetch me away from Fanua. My ministry here has been a failure. I have converted no one, moreover I think that they are best as they are.

'I am aware that I shall seem to you an unprofitable servant, and I am prepared for reproof. But I must tell you that in my present state of mind nothing that you can say, either of blame or consolation, is likely to make much difference.

'I should be very much obliged if you could send with the launch a pair of stout black boots (size eleven), some collars (sixteen and a half inch), and a bottle of Aspirin tablets.

—Yours sincerely,
'Timothy Fortune.

'P.S.—Also some bone collar-studs. There was an earthquake and I lost those which I had.'

When the letter was written he put it away. His mind was quite made up as to leaving Fanua, there was no danger that a week's delay or so in sending off the letter would weaken his resolution. Indeed if he had consulted his own feelings he would not have delayed for an hour. But he did not wish to leave Lueli until he was quite certain the boy was able to stand on his own feet.

One thing was beyond doubt: Lueli would not try to kill himself again. He had been frightened by the dark look of

Death under the water. Though he said nothing about his drowning or his rescue it was obvious that he had set himself to get on good terms with the life he had then thought fit to abandon. Never before had he been so beautiful, nor moved so lithely, nor sprawled so luxuriously on the warm grass. Sleek, languid and glittering, he was like a snake that has achieved its new skin. He was grown more sociable too, and with a quite new form of sociability; for instead of seeking the company of others he exerted himself to make others seek his. Although his drowning had done him no harm whatsoever and he had never been in better trim, he chose to preen himself as an interesting invalid. At all hours of the day the youth and beauty of the island would appear with offerings of fruit and invalid delicacies. Since the Fanuans are a people unequalled in kindness and idleness this was not such a great tribute to Lueli's fascinations. But what was really remarkable was the success with which he imposed himself upon them as a young hero. Even Fuma, who had stood out against his pretensions for several days, laughing at him and pulling his hair and making sarcastic remarks about people who couldn't swim, suddenly dropped her sisterly airs and attended on him as devoutly as the rest. As though this were the last plum that he had been proposing should drop into his mouth Lueli began to feel a little better now; was able to go sailing or swimming—not even the waters that drowned him could quench his love for water—or to take a stroll in the woods. Presently he was addressing Fuma as 'Child.'

If he had not so utterly forsworn meddling, if the letter to the Archdeacon were not put away in his coat pocket, Mr. Fortune might have yielded himself to a glow of match-making. Perhaps Fuma was not quite the girl he would have chosen; perhaps for that matter Lueli's choice of her was not quite to the exclusion of other girls; but having been so heart-rent over the defeated estate of that spiritless and godless boy whom even his own younger brothers had been able to tease out of the village, it would have been sweet now to abet the happiness of this triumphant young man.

As things were, Lueli's recovery must be the waving of the

flag which signalled his departure. So one morning he set off to find Ori and explained to him that he wished to send a message by canoe to Maikalua. Would Ori as usual see about it and oblige?

Early in the morning the canoe was launched: and singing and shouting the boatmen set out on their voyage.

As he watched them depart Mr. Fortune had a sudden vision of a pillar-box. It seemed to spring up before him, a substantial scarlet cylinder, out of the glittering untenanted beach. He remembered how long ago, one August afternoon, he had posted a note accepting with pleasure an invitation to play tennis, an invitation which came from some people called Tubbs who lived at Ealing; and how, having done so, he stood with the sun beating down upon him, just outside the station, with people jostling past him and the newspaper man shouting: 'Star, Standard, Westminster! Surrey all out!'—wishing with despair that he could get his note back, for it seemed to him that nothing could be more distasteful than to play tennis at Ealing with those rollicking Tubbses.

But now he had no wish to recall his letter, though he was still sick with the wrench of definitely despatching it. His only thought was to leave Fanua as soon as possible; and until the moment of departure came he could not imagine how he would pass away the time. Gradually the pillar-box faded out before him and he saw the ocean-waste, the narrow diminishing boat, the empty indifferent sky. His head was aching again and he put his hand to his forehead. There was that deluded watch, mincing complacently on. It was much better at passing away time than he. Half-past seven. Another thirteen hours and he would be getting himself supper, and Lueli might come in or he might not. And after supper he would be going to bed. But if he fell asleep too soon he would wake early with another shining unending morning before him. No! It would be better to sit up late, to midnight if possible. For time passes more tolerantly at night when the body is drowsy and the mind tired; but in the morning hours there is no release from one's faculties, and every second is a needle-prick to consciousness.

The sand had dribbled out between his fingers, he found himself staring at the palm of his hand. It would be the better for washing; and he turned back toward the bathing-pool. While he was still the headache was not so bad; but every step jolted it and sent a heavy sick tingle up his spine to jar against his temples.

As the bathing-pool came in sight through the lattice of ferns and bushes he paused, for it came into his mind that Lueli might be there with his friends. And dropping on his hands and knees he crawled through the undergrowth, holding his breath and cautiously poking out his head from the greenery to scout if the coast were clear. He need not have been so discreet. The pool was empty. There was no footprint on the sandy rim.

He undressed and bathed his body wearily in the cool water —it was always exquisitely cool under the shadow of the rock. It did not occur to him that by going a little further he could drown. He hauled himself up on a ledge and began to clean his toes with a wisp of seaweed.

The shade of his wet limbs, the sound of the sea, the breathing murmur of the woods in the soft steady wind was comforting to his headache. He began to feel slightly lachrymose and a good deal better, and with the tenderness of a convalescent he watched the fish darting in and out of the streaming weed. Of course he might have gone himself by the canoe instead of sending his request for the launch. But though he now realised that it would have been perfectly feasible to have done so, something within him assured him that it would not really have been possible. Things must take their course: and thus to wait still in Fanua for the launch to come and fetch him away was the natural course for his departure. He could see himself leaving the island in the launch, but not any other how.

That bull-faced fish had dodged in and out from the weed a dozen times at least. It was as persistent as a swallow. His body was dry now and his headache smoothed away. Only the heartache remained; and he was getting used to that.

All this while, as he was crawling through the bushes, and cleaning his toes, and watching the fish, there had been but one deep preoccupying thought at the back of his mind—the thought of Lueli and a longing for his presence. It was on the chance that Lueli might come down to bathe that he was waiting now. And he imagined the conversation that must take place between them.

'Lueli, I am going away from Fanua.'

'But you will come back again?'

'No. I am going away for ever.'

It would be quite simple—as simple as that. 'I am going away from Fanua.' Above all he was determined that there should be no explanations. It would never do to tell Lueli that he was going away because of him. No smirch of complicity, no blight of responsibility should fall upon Lueli, happy Lueli, who had done him no wrong, and whom so often he had sought to injure from the best, worst, most fatal and affectionate motives. How could he have so teased his misery with that idiotic geometry—a misery, too, in which he was the agent, for it was through him that Lueli had lost his idol. That was bad enough, at any rate it was damnably silly. Though what else could he have done? Something equally senseless, no doubt. But what was it to his behavior in the hut, when the idol lay between them, and Lueli crouched in his last refuge of silence while he sought with menaces and blackmailing to rob him of his faith, and bade him cast his god into the fire? Ah! of the two gods who had perished that night it was the wooden one he would now fetch back again.

But this he could never say. He must not give any reason for his departure lest he should at length fall into giving the true one and seeming to involve Lueli in his own blunders. 'I am going away from Fanua.' That must be all. Little to say: so little that he must postpone saying it till the last hour came, the hour when one says good-bye. And for that reason he must shun Lueli's presence, hide from him if need be and crawl through bushes; for if he once allowed himself to resume their old familiar intercourse he would not be able to keep back the words: 'Lueli, I am going away. I am going away for ever.'

He said it aloud, and as it were heard the words for the first time. He put on his clothes and began mechanically to walk back toward the hut. Then he had a good idea. Since he was leaving the island it would be a pity not to go up the mountain and have a look at the crater. Very likely he would never have another opportunity of inspecting an active volcano.

It would be a taxing expedition, and not without danger. He put up some food, cut himself a stout walking-stick and gathered a bunch of plantain leaves to stick in his boots—for it was decidedly an occasion for boots. Preparations always pleased him, for he had a housewifely mind, and by the time he set out he was feeling, if not less miserable, at any rate a point or two deflected from his misery.

The new crater was on the further side of the mountain. He decided that the best way of approach would be to walk up through the woods by tracks which he knew and thence to skirt round under the foot of the crags, keeping against the wind in order to avoid the smoke and fumes. As he mounted through the woods he could hear, at first the sea and the tree-tops, presently the murmuring tree-tops alone. Soothed by their company and their shade he climbed on peacefully enough for a couple of hours, keeping a sharp look-out for rents and fissures; for however weary one may be of life one would not choose to discard it by starving, or suffocating in a deep crevice as hot as an oven.

At last he came out upon the tract of scrub and clinker which covered the upper slopes of the mountain. After the cool depth of the woodland it was like a pale hell, a prospect bleached and brittle such as even the greenest garden will offer if one sits up and looks at it suddenly after lying with the sun strong on one's eyelids. After a moment of dizziness the garden will revive again, but the longer Mr. Fortune looked at this landscape the more spectral and repellent it seemed. And because the air quivered with heat the face of the mountain side seemed to be twitching with fear.

There were the crags, some two miles away yet, but looking as though he could throw a stone and splinter them. They were not rhododendron-coloured now, but a reddish and scabby mottle. They reminded him of a group of ruined gas-vats with the paint scaling off them, standing in the middle of a brickfield. It smelt of brickfields too; and in the place of the former sounds of the sea and the tree-tops new sounds came to his ear, ugly to match the landscape, and of a kind of baleful insignificance like the landscape—far-off crashes and rumblings, the hiss and spurt of escaping steam: the noise of a flustered kitchen.

Now was the moment to put the plantain leaves in his boots.

Those which he had gathered were faded, he threw them away and gathered fresh. Then, with a heart beating harshly and remotely, he set forth on the second stage of his climb.

It was a hateful going—slippery bents, bristling scrub, sharp-edged clinker which hurt his feet. He tripped and fell constantly, and when he fell the clinker cut his hands. Twice he remained crumpled on the ground just as he had fallen, gasping for breath and cowed by the frantic beating of his heart, which did not seem to belong to him, behaving like some wild animal which, terrified and apprehensive, is dragged struggling to the summit of the mountain to be sacrificed there. And as he went on the brickfield smell grew stronger, and the kitchen noises grew louder, and the sun, striking down on him from the motionless sky, striking up at him from the ground, reverberating upon him from the parched landscape, enclosed him in its burning net.

He remembered the story of the woman Kapiolani, the Christian convert of Hawaii. Followed by a crowd of trembling islanders she had gone up the burning mountain to manifest her faith in the true God. When she was come to the crater of Kilauea she had scrambled down to the very edge of the burning lake, and there, half hidden in clouds of smoke, she called on Pele the Fire-goddess, and flouted her, calling her an impostor and challenging her, if goddess she were, to rise up out of her everlasting fiery den and overwhelm her accuser with its waves. Pele did not answer: she sulked in the heart of her fire, powerless before the name of Christ. And when she had waited long enough Kapiolani climbed up again out of the pit and showed herself once more to the crowd who had been cowering at the crater-side, trembling, and listening to the loud voice of her faith. And when they saw her, they believed.

Her faith, thought Mr. Fortune, had carried her lightly up the mountain side, and over the lava-flow which she had trodden with scorched and bleeding feet. But he, though a man, and born free from the burden of heathen fears, and wearing boots, was already tired out and reluctant, and only a cold tourist's curiosity could carry him onward, and a bargain-hunting spirit which told him that having gone so far it would be a waste not to go on to the end.

Kapiolani had made her act of faith in the year 1825. And

after that, as though for her courage she were like the prophetess Deborah, the land had peace for thirty years. Then Pele shook herself contemptuously, and fell to her tricks again. At her first shake the island trembled, as though it knew what was to come. 'Yet a little,' said the Fire-goddess; and slept for another ten years. This time she woke angrier. The island quivered like the lid of a boiling pot; a river of fire, flowing terribly underground, rent open a green and fertile plain, and five times a tidal wave reared up and fell upon the helpless land. And once more Pele fell asleep, but fell asleep to dream; snarling to herself, and hotly, voluptuously, obscurely triumphing in a dream of what her next awakening would be.

Kapiolani would not know of that awakening at any rate. It was to be hoped that she had been spared the others. Simple faith like hers would be cruelly jolted by such ambiguities in God's law. She might even have lost it thereby, as did Voltaire, another blunt, straightforward thinker, at a rather similar exhibition; for she could hardly be expected to take the subtler view of those long-standing and accustomed believers who can gloss over an eruption as a very justifiable protest against the wickedness of their neighbours. And as for saying that it is all a mystery—well, there is not much satisfaction to be got out of that.

These thoughts carried him over the last mile, and looking up he was surprised to find himself under the crags. He began to skirt round them. Now the noises and the smells were so strong that as he rounded every jut of the crags he expected to come on the new crater. Just as he had climbed on to the top of a large rock a gust of wind, veering among the crags, brought with it a volley of foul smoke, which rose up from beneath him and smothered him round, just as smoke comes suddenly belching out of the vent of a tunnel. He stood for a moment coughing and stifling: and then the wind shifted again, and the smoke lifted away from him, and looking out underneath it he saw that he was come to the end of his search.

The rock on which he stood was the last westernmost redoubt of the crags, and before him extended the other side of the island of Fanua. Far off and strangely high up he saw the sea-line. The ocean seemed to fall steeply and smoothly downhill to where it broke upon the reef in a motionless pattern of foam. Stretching away down the mountain side was a long, serpentining slab of lava—the thickly-burning torrent which had torn apart the flanks of the mountain on the night of the eruption, wallowing downward with an ever more heavy and glutted motion until now it was solidifying into rock; a brutal surface of formless hummocks and soppy and still oozing fissures. Everything around was deep in ashes, and here and there little gushes of steam showed where the heat still worked under the outer crust. It was like the surface of a saucepan of porridge which has been lifted off the fire but still pimples and undulates with its own heat.

Another jet of smoke belched up. Holding his breath Mr. Fortune crept over the rock on his hands and knees and looked down into the crater.

By night the spectacle might have had a sort of Medusa's head beauty, for ever wakeful and writhing and dangerous; but in the light of day it was all sordid and despairing. Thick smoke hung low over the burning lava, and thin gaseous flames flickered on the surface, livid and cringing, like the ghosts of bad men still haunting around the corrupting body. Below this play of dun smoke and shadowy flame the lava moved unceasingly, impelled to the south, on and on and over and over as though its torment were bound upon an axle. Every now and then two currents would flow into each other with a heavy impact, a splash and a leap of fire. And then it was as though it clapped hands in its agony.

Slowly, because he was cramped with having watched it so long, Mr. Fortune raised himself to his feet and turned away. He had no thoughts, no feelings. What he had seen was something older than the earth; but vestigial, and to the horror of the sun what the lizard is to the dragon: degenerate. Shuddering and cold he went down past the shadow of the crags and over the scorched expanse of hell-ground towards the woods, hastening, still having in his ears the growlings and concussions of the pit and with that foul smell still in his nostrils.

When he came into the woods he stopped and looked up. The

green boughs hid away the skies. He was glad. He did not want to look at anything eternal just now. He sat down on a fallen tree. Moss covered it, and creepers and tree-ferns were springing out of it; but he parted the ferns and creeper and scratched away the moss and put down his nose to snuff up the scent of decay. Everywhere in the woods was the odour of mortality; it was sweet to him, like a home-coming. He lay down and buried his face in the leaf-mould, pressing his eyelids to the warm mouldering softness, trying to forget the rock.

When he felt better he went on again; and coming to a stream he bathed himself, and ate some fruit. He was not very sure of his whereabouts, so to follow the stream seemed the best plan. It was a pleasant guide. He heard it singing ahead as he followed its windings. All this part of the woodland was unknown to him. It seemed very venerable and solitary. The solemn girth and glossy great leaves of the bread-fruit trees pleased him all the better because he was thinking of them as beings transient and subject to laws of growth and decay. They were steadfast, he thought, because they knew of their appointed end. They soothed him, bearing faithful witness that his own should be no other—that he too should one day lie along the earth and be gathered into it.

It occurred to him for the first time that now he would not, as he had hoped, be buried in Fanua. And as though the thought had called up a vision he saw what appeared to be a graveyard before him. It was a sort of pound or enclosure, built of rough stones. Whatever the purpose of the place, it was clearly unfrequented, perhaps forsaken; for the mossy walls were breached and tumbled and the grass grew clean and untrodden in the entry. Overhead the bread-fruit trees mingled their large boughs like a roof of wings. He turned and went in. He found himself surrounded by ranks of idols, idols of all sizes and all fashions, idols of wood and stone, all very old, subdued with weather, moss-grown, with the grass tangling round their bases. He knew well what they must be: in this island where every one had his own god these were the gods of the dead. At the death of their worshippers the gods were carried here and left to their repose till they too in their time failed and sank into the earth. He remembered who had died since he came to the island and peered among the idols for some more recent than the others which might be those of his acquaintances. Yes, that was Akau's god perhaps, and that pot-bellied fellow with the humorous squint might be the god of poor old Live for Ever. Only Lueli's god would never come here.

Sad Lueli! Just now in his flourish of youth and affability he might forget his lost god and do quite as well without him; but one day Lueli would be growing old, and then—then he would feel his loss. For the day must come when a man turns from the companionship of flesh and blood, be it flesh and blood failing like his own or the flesh and blood he has begotten, and seeks back into the traditions of his race for a companionship more ghostly and congenial—old habits, old beliefs, old stories—the things his childhood accepted and his forefathers lived by. In that day Lueli would need his god. The lack of it would be a kind of disgrace, a mutilation.

'I cannot go from Fanua,' said Mr. Fortune, standing among the idols, 'until I have given Lueli back his god.'

The knife hung round his neck: it would be easy to take one of the idols, re-trim its features, scrape off the moss and made a new idol of it. But a feeling of decorum stayed his hand. However, he might study them, for he would need an example. He spent half an hour or so in the enclosure, kneeling before the idols, examining the details of their workmanship and trying to acquire the convention. Then, for it was still afternoon, he spent some time wandering round in search of a suitable piece of wood. It must be about two foot long, straight, without knots, not so fresh as to tear, not so old as to crumble, of an easy grain to carve, and for choice, of a pleasant colour. He sought out several pieces and experimented on them with his knife before he found one to his liking. It was of rather dark, sweet-smelling wood, of what tree he knew not, for he found it lying beside the stream. A freshet must have carried it there, perhaps from the hands of some other woodman; for there seemed to be cutting-marks about one end of it.

He sat down and began to rough out the image he had in his mind: a man with a bird perched on his wrist, his head a little inclined towards the bird as though it were telling him something; and seated at his feet a plain smooth dog, also looking at the bird, but quite kindly. After so many failures, great and small: the trousers, the introduction to mathematics, all his very indifferent attempts at cookery, boiled bad eggs and clammy coco-nut buns, the conversion of the islanders and the domestication of the parrots, it might have been expected of Mr. Fortune that he would put forth on sculpture with diffidence. But his heart was in it; he had never attempted anything of the kind before; and anyhow, it is the vainglorious people who expect difficulties. Mr. Fortune in his modesty supposed that cookery, conversion, etc., were really quite easy matters, and that it was only he who made a botch of them. So when after an hour or so of whittling and measuring and whittling again, he found himself possessed of a considerable aptitude for wood-carving, and the man, the dog, and the bird emerging from the billet with every promise of looking very much as he intended them to, he was pleased, but without any amazement.

He worked while there was light; then wrapping the idol carefully in soft grasses and leaves and tying it into a parcel with vines he set out to follow the stream by starlight.

Now into the solemn caverns of the wood came rolling solemnly the noise of the ocean. Wafts of sweet scent wandered to him from flowering shrubs whose flowers he could not discern, and large soft moths brushed across his face. He was footsore and perhaps sorrowful, and he knew that soon he must quit this island which was so beautiful and romantic under its crown of horror, and go, he knew not whither, but certainly never again to any place like this; but nothing disturbed his enjoyment of the hour. His thoughts were slow and peaceful, and looking up through the trees he saw the heavens without disquiet, although they were eternal. The stream laughed and ran joyously forward to the waterfall. He looked about him and knew where he was. The stream which had borne him such pleasant company was the same whose torrent he had seen wavering and distorted on the night of the earthquake.

He hitched the god a little closer up under his arm and turned into a path he knew. As he neared the village he heard voices not far off. He stopped. Yes, that was Fuma's voice: and the laugh—only Lueli could laugh like that. Standing in the darkness he blessed them. The god weighed on his arm, and it occurred to him that this was the first time he had ever returned from a walk bringing with him a present for Lueli. Lueli never came back without some gift or other; he was as prodigal as his native clime. Trails of flowers which festooned the doorway and wound themselves round Mr. Fortune's neck whenever he went in or out; shells, which were casually thrown down on his mat and ran into his sleep when he turned over in the night; perfectly uneatable shellfish because they were so pretty; feathers and fantastic ornaments which he wore with gratified embarrassment round his neck. He too had sometimes brought things back with him, but things practical or edible: never real presents, objects perishable, useless and inconvenient, friendship's tokens, emblems of love, that passion which man, for all his sad conscience and ingenuity, will never be able quite to tame into something useful.

Well, at last he was making some atonement where he had been so remiss. He was a poor hand at presents: an Englishman, with a public school training still lurking in his heel, he would never be able with any sort of grace or naturalness to offer garlands of morning glories or small gay striped crabs. But he was doing his best; he was bringing Lueli a god.

When Lueli came into the hut Mr. Fortune had eaten his supper and was almost asleep.

'Where have you been all day?' inquired Lueli. 'I kept on looking for you, and wondering where you had gone. I was growing very anxious, I assure you.'

'I have been to the mountain.'

'To the mountain?'

'Yes, right to the top of it.'

'Oh! did you see the flames and the smoke they talk about? What's it like? Are there a great many flames? Does it make a great noise? Did you feel frightened? I hope you were careful not to fall in. Tell me all about it.'

'It is a very impressive sight.'

'Well? Go on!'

'I will tell you the rest to-morrow. Now it is time you went to bed. You needn't trouble about Tibby. I've fed her.'

He turned over and fell asleep. All night he lay with the idol close against his side.

For three days he worked on it in secret, chipping and scooping and shaving, rubbing it smooth with fine sand, oiling it, treating it as tenderly as a cricket-bat. As he worked, intent and unflurried, strange thoughts concerning it stole into his mind. Sometimes he thought that the man was himself, listening to the parrot which told him how the doom of love is always to be destroying the thing it looks upon. At other times the man seemed to be Christ, and the bird on his wrist the Holy Ghost. In these suppositions there was no part for the dog, save as an adjunct to the design, steadying the base of the composition and helping it to stand upright. But there was yet a third fancy; and then the man was Lueli, the bird neither parrot nor dove but the emblem of his personality, while the dog was he himself, looking up at Lueli's bird but on trust not to snatch at it or frighten it away.

On the afternoon of the third day the idol was finished. So far it had been his, the creature of his brain, the work of his hands. In an approving look he took his farewell of it, and dismissing it from his care he put it to stand upright on the rock before the hut. Then, moving very quietly, for inside the hut Lueli was taking his afternoon nap and must not be disturbed till everything was ready, he went to the bush by the spring where the red flowers grew. Of these he wove a rather uncouth garland, after the style of the daisy-chains that children make, but a daisy-chain like slow drops of blood. He arranged this round the idol and walked into the hut.

'Lueli.'

Under the smooth brown eyelids the eyes flickered and awakened. Lueli blinked at him, shut his eyes once more and stretched protestingly. It was all most right: he would hear the words as he should hear them, he would hear them as in a dream.

'Lueli, on the rock outside there is something waiting for you. Go out and see what it is.'

He was conscious of Lueli rising and passing him by, and pausing for a moment on the threshold. He sat down with his face to the wall, for he dared not watch an encounter that must be so momentous. Even the eyes of his mind he turned away, and sat in a timeless world, listening. Then, at last, he heard and was released—for what he heard, a murmur, a wandering wreath of sound, was Lueli talking softly to his god.

He made a movement to arise, and then stayed himself. This time he would not intrude, would not interefere. Lueli should be left in peace. He too was at peace, wasn't he? His atonement had been accepted, his part was done. Now there was nothing left for him but to go away. He began to reckon the days. His letter had caught the boat, he knew; for last night the canoe had returned and Moki told him that he had seen the Captain and put the letter into his hands. That was two days ago, and so by now Archdeacon Mason had hitched on his gold-rimmed eyeglasses and was scanning the letter at arm's length in that dignified way he had, a way of reading letters which was as much as to announce: 'Whilst reserving my judgment I remain perfectly infallible.' At any rate by tomorrow morning he would learn that Mr. Fortune wished to be recalled from Fanua: for though the boat touched at two or three ports before reaching St. Fabien, she was never more than half a day out of her time. By this reckoning the launch might be expected, perhaps tomorrow evening, perhaps on the day following. Then the canoe would push out to the opening of the reef and dodge forward between two waves. He would stand up in the canoe, catch hold of a rope, push against that footing, buoyant and unsteady almost as the sea. He would be on the launch, looking at the neat life-belt, and smelling brass-polish again and warm machine-oil. He would be off, he would be gone.

Outside among the birds and the sliding shadows of the palm-fronds Lueli was still talking to his god—a happy noise. Mr. Fortune listened for a minute or two and then went on thinking. He would have no luggage and that was a pity, for he felt the need for doing something business-like, packing would have been a solace. Stay! There would of course be presents: the islanders would not allow him to depart without gifts. They would give him mats, carved bowls and platters, a pig-sticker hung with elaborate tassels, a pipe. A pleasant people, and very beautiful, with their untrammelled carriage and arabesqued nakedness. He glanced down at his forearm where he had allowed old Hina to prick out a vignette of a fish with whiskers. While she was jabbing and chattering he had thought: 'A man who has lost his faith in God may perfectly well allow himself to be tattooed.' After Lueli, Hina was the islander with whom he had gone nearest to a feeling of intimacy. In extreme old age, as in infancy, distinctions of nationality scarcely exist; and Hina had seemed to him very little different to any legendary old lady in an English chimney-corner. She might almost have been his god-mother, grown so aged as to be grown gay, and without her wig.

To-morrow he must go round and bid good-bye to everybody. They would be very surprised, very exclamatory: he did not think that they would be very much upset. If they had seemed rather unreal to him, how much more unreal must he have seemed to them! They had been on easy terms with him—they would be on easy terms with anybody; they had accepted his odd ways without demur. While he still preached they had sometimes listened, and when he ceased preaching they asked no questions. When he was happy they smiled back, and when he was parched with anxiety they had not appeared to notice much difference. And at all times they continued to supply him with food and to perform any services he required of them.

They had grown accustomed to him but they had not assimilated him; and his odd ways they had taken as something quite natural since he himself was an oddity. His departure would affect them much as if a star had fallen out of their sky: that is to say, it wouldn't really affect them at all. There were once three stars where now you see two: there was once a white man with a magic box which groaned when he trampled it who came to Fanua. In the course of time the few remaining people who had seen the lost star would brag a little about its superior size and lustre, saying that there were no such stars in these days; and similarly in times to come a black and white being ten foot high and able to speak in a voice of thunder for seven days and seven nights might haunt the groves of Fanua. The ginger-nuts, they too might be commemorated in the fact that he fed men with red-hot pebbles. All he hoped was that they would not use him to frighten children with. But alas! he was fooling himself. There would soon be plenty of white men to frighten the children of Fanua, to bring them galvanised iron and law-courts and commerce and industry and bicycles and patent medicines and American alarm clocks, besides the blessing of religion. The island could not hope to keep its innocence much longer. Had he not come, a single spy? And soon there would come battalions. Poor islanders! He almost said: 'Poor flock!' Well, to-morrow he must bid them good-bye, and to-morrow too, before he bade farewell to the rest, he must say: 'I am going away, Lueli, I am going away for ever.'

And then—*suppose the launch didn't come?* Suppose that the earthquake at Fanua had been but a ripple of an enormous earthquake which had swallowed up St. Fabien?

It would not do to fancy such things. He got up and walked out of the hut. Lueli was gone and had taken his god with him; maybe he had carried him off to the little copse where he had cherished the old one. Absently Mr. Fortune sat down on the altar. His hand touched something cold and flabby. It was the garland of red flowers which he had woven in order to give the idol a more festive and Christmas-tree appearance—for a present is a present twice over if it be tied up prettily. He smiled, and hung it round his neck.

He was still sitting on the altar when Lueli came strolling back for supper. He came singing to himself, and as he walked he tossed a couple of small fish from hand to hand.

'Why didn't you come and bathe too? Look! I caught these in my fingers.'

'How beautiful they are!'

They were silvery fish with black and vermilion markings and rose-coloured fins. Their strange blue eyes were yet bright, and they retained the suppleness and shine of life. One does not admire things enough: and worst of all, one allows whole days to slip by without once pausing to see an object, any object, exactly as it is.

'We will have them for supper,' he said. 'I am sorry that I forgot to come bathing. But I'll tell you what. There will be a moon to-night, we might bathe after supper by moonlight. Unless you want to go down to the village.'

'No. It would be a lark to bathe.'

The night was so mild that after bathing they lounged on the rocks, dangling their legs in the water, which felt even more surprisingly tepid because its black and silver pattern looked so cold. The ledge where they sat was padded with the soft tough growth of sea-plants. Out on the reef some gulls were complaining.

The shadow hid his own face but Lueli sat in full moonlight. It was a good moment to speak.

'Lueli, I am going away from Fanua.'

There would be no need to add: 'I am going away for ever.' Somehow, from the tone of his voice or by some curious sympathy, Lueli had guessed. He started so violently that he lost his balance and slipped off the rock. He swam a few strokes out into the pool and then turned and came back again and caught hold of Mr. Fortune's knees to moor himself.

'But if you go you will leave me,' he said, lying along the water and looking up into his friend's face. 'Don't go!'

'I must, my dear. It is time.'

'Are you going back to your own country?'

'Yes. I expect so. Anyhow, I must go. A boat will come for me, the same boat which brought me when I came to the island. Perhaps to-morrow, perhaps the day after.'

'Not to-morrow!' Lueli cried out, his face suddenly convulsed with distress.

Mr. Fortune nodded.

'To-morrow or the next day.'

'But why do you only tell me now? Now there will be no time to do anything, I can't even make you a pipe. Stay longer! Stay even a little longer! I thought you would stay for ever.'

'I'm sorry if I have left it too late. I did it for the best. I didn't want to spoil our last days.'

'But when did you know that you would go away?'

'A long time ago. A bird—' He stopped. It would not do to

tell Lueli what the bird had said to him. He would not understand, he was incapable of understanding, because he was incapable of feeling that sad, civilised and proprietary love which is anxious and predatory and spoil-sport. Even now, despite his distress at hearing that his friend was about to leave him, he wasn't attempting to interfere or to do anything about it.

'Lueli, you know how sorry I am to be leaving you. I will not speak of it much, I don't think we need upset each other by telling our feelings. We know them already. But I have one consolation. I am not leaving a weakling, some one that I should have to feel uneasy about. When I think of you, as I shall do constantly, it will be with admiration and confidence.'

He looked down at the face raised toward his. Affection, grief, the most entire attention were depicted thereon; but for all these Lueli's countenance still kept its slightly satirical air. And this, because it was the expression most essentially and characteristically his, the aspect that nature had given him, was dearest of all.

'When I came here you were still almost a child. How the three years have changed you! You are as tall as I am now, and a great deal stronger. You are almost as strong as Kaulu whom you used to tell me about—Kaulu the strong boy, who broke the waves with his hands and forced open the jaws of the King Shark who had swallowed his brother. And you are intelligent too, and as you grow older you will become more so. Perhaps you may become as wise and prudent as Kana, who rescued the sun and moon and stars and put them back into the sky. And when he held up the sun the cock crowed. Do you remember telling me that? And as for charm—why, I think you the most popular young man on the island and the best-loved. It delights me to see it.'

'You flatter me,' answered Lueli in a pleased voice.

Then he sighed. 'I wish you were not going,' he said. 'I shall miss you. I shall miss you terribly. Oh, why must you leave me?' And he hung his head and kicked his heels disconsolately.

The water splashed up, drops of spray fell on Mr. Fortune. He shivered, but it was not the falling spray which chilled him. What could he say, how was he to comfort this child?

'Do you remember how I used to tell you about my God?'

'Yes, of course I remember.'

'I haven't spoken of Him lately, and perhaps you have noticed that.'

'Yes.'

'Well, the reason why I didn't speak of Him was—I have lost Him. I lost Him on the same night that you lost yours, the night of the earthquake. No!'—Lueli had made a sudden movement of inquiry. 'He wasn't anything in the hut, He wasn't any of the things that were burnt. He wasn't the kind of God that could be burnt. But He was the kind of God that could perfectly well be lost; and, as I say, I have lost Him.'

'But perhaps you will find Him, perhaps He will come back. I—my god—'

Lueli's voice sank into a warm cautious silence, the silence of a lover.

Mr. Fortune put out a hand and stroked the wet head.

'No. I am quite sure I shall never find Him. But I have no doubt He is somewhere around, and that is why I am telling you of my loss. Because, you see, when I go I shall leave Him behind; my God will remain here on the island where I lost Him. And while He remains, a part of me will remain too. I do not leave you utterly.'

'Like a keepsake?' ventured Lueli after thinking it over.

'Yes. Like a keepsake. But rather more than a keepsake. Almost like leaving part of myself.'

'Yes. I think I understand.'

'So now do you feel happier?'

'Not now. But I shall later on.'

It had not been anywhere near as bad as he had dreaded that it would be. It had even been a rather comfortable conversation, and one that he would be able to look back upon with kindness.

The next day, the last day, was spent in packing and leave-taking. The news of his approaching departure was received with genuine regret, and from every one he met with such kind concern that it would have been impossible not to feel gratified even if he had wished to be above that sort of feeling. Ori, Teioa, and the other important islanders got up a farewell feast in his honour. Speeches were made, his health was drunk, and afterwards Mr. Fortune sat on the best mats, flushed with praise and wearing as many garlands as a May Queen or a coffin, while presentations were made to him. A necklace of carved sharks'-teeth, bracelets of scented nuts, mother-of-pearl earrings, several pipes, spears, paddles and carved walking-sticks, rolls of tapa and fine mats, coloured baskets, polished bowls, sweetmeats and cosmetics, several remembrance-knots of curiously plaited hair, and charms of all sorts—these were piled up on his lap and all around him. Only Lueli brought no gift. He sat beside him, examining and praising the gifts of the others and pointing out their beauties.

'I do hope he isn't feeling out of it because he has brought no present,' thought Mr. Fortune. 'My blessed child, he is too generous to have anything left to give. But I can't bear to think that he might be put out of countenance. I could almost wish—'

At that moment he became aware that Lueli was no longer by his side. The conversation suddenly died down, there was a conscious, premonitory pause and people were looking toward the door of the house. They wriggled to either side, opening a sort of lane. And then Lueli stepped over the threshold, carrying a resplendent head-dress of straw-coloured and scarlet feathers.

Walking solemnly, with a rapt and formal face, he advanced down the lane, bearing on high the softly-waving and coloured crown, till with a deep bow he laid the head-dress at Mr. Fortune's feet.

'But, Lueli!' exclaimed Mr. Fortune, too much overcome for words of thanks. 'This lovely thing, this marvellous thing! Is it —can it be—?'

'Lueli is your especial friend,' said Ori. 'It is right that he should make you the best gift.'

There was a loud hum of approval. Mr. Fortune raised the head-dress, admired it all round, and put it on. The hum of approval swelled into acclamations and loud cheers.

Then it was Mr. Fortune's turn to produce gifts. He had spent most of the forenoon going over his possessions, such as they were, and in between spells of working on the idol he had contrived to make an assortment of pipe-stoppers, tooth-picks, bodkins, and such-like small items. With these and the mother-of-pearl counters and almost all his buttons he was enabled to produce a tolerable array; and though he apologised a great deal over their inadequacy there was no need to apologise, for the recipients were overjoyed with objects so distinguished and far-fetched.

The knife, at once his most personal and valuable possession, was naturally for Lueli, and so was his pipe. Ori received the magnifying-glass and his two sons the whistle and the flint-and-steel lighter respectively. To Teioa he presented the magnet and to Mrs. Teioa the medicine spoon. Lueli's mother went into fits of rapture over the measuring-tape; Tekea, a handsome, rather taciturn fellow, who had helped a great deal with the new hut, was much gratified by the nail-file; the Parnell medal was hung round Fuma's neck and the pencil-case round Vaili's. The pencil-sharpener he gave to Lei-lei, village sorceress, doctoress and midwife, who declared that it would be an invaluable asset. At the last moment he remembered Hina, the old story-teller. He gave her the wash-leather bag.

After songs and dances the party broke up at a late hour; and still wearing his crown Mr. Fortune walked home with Lueli by moonlight. The other gifts he had left behind, for Ori had undertaken to see that they were packed properly, ready for the morrow. A night bird was calling among the trees—a soft breathy note like an alto flute—and the roof of the hut shone in the moonlight.

'Will you go on living here, Lueli?'

'Of course. Where else should I like to live so well?'

'I am glad. I shall know how to picture you when I am thinking of you.'

'When I think of you I shall not know where you are.'

'Think of me here.'

As a result of the party they overslept themselves, and they were still breakfasting when Tekea came running up to say that the launch had been sighted. Mr. Fortune became a man of action. He knew instantly that no one from St. Fabien could be allowed to set foot on his island. He gave instructions to Tekea accordingly: a canoe might go out to the reef to keep them in play, but no one was to be taken off the launch on any account.

'What shall I tell them,' asked Tekea, 'if they want to land?'

'Tell them—' What could they be told? Small-pox, tigers, taboos, hornets in swarm; he ran over a few pretexts but nothing seemed quite suitable. 'Tell them,' he said, 'tell them I say so. By the way, you might take them out a few bananas.'

Tekea grinned. He was an understanding fellow. He ran back to the village while Mr. Fortune and Lueli followed at a more leisurely pace. There was nothing to delay them: Mr. Fortune was already dressed in his European clothes, and the feather head-dress was carefully packed in a large leafy frail. Just as they were crossing the dell he stopped. 'Wait a minute,' he said, 'we never washed up the breakfast things.'

'I can do that afterwards.'

'No indeed! That would be dismal. We will do it now, and shake out the mats. There is plenty of time, and if there isn't it won't hurt them to wait. They'll have the bananas to amuse them.'

Together they put all straight and tidy, folded up Mr. Fortune's island clothes, threw away the garlands of overnight and the unused twigs and vines that had been plucked for the packing of the head-dress, and removed every trace of departure. Then they set forth for the village once more.

Every one was out to see Mr. Fortune off and wish him good luck. The launch was outside the reef and his luggage was being conveyed on board. There was a vast amount of it, and it seemed even more numerous because of the quantity of helping hands outstretched to deal with it. It was all so exactly like what he had foreseen that he felt as though he were in a dream—the beach, the lagoon, thronged with excited well-wishers, canoes getting their outriggers entangled and nearly upsetting, hands thrust out of the water to right them, every one laughing and exclaiming. Every one, that is, except Lueli: Mr. Fortune had not been able to include him in his foreseeing of the last act. He had been lively and natural at breakfast; but now he was silent, he was pale, he was being brave. 'If I say something cheerful,' thought Mr. Fortune, 'I may upset him. What shall I say?' At the water's edge he turned to him. 'Forgive me if—' He got no further for Lueli's arms were flung about his neck. Mr. Fortune gently patted him on the back.

He got into the canoe and the dream began again. The canoe manœuvred at the opening of the reef, it dodged forward between the waves. He stood up, he felt the sea sidle and thrust under him as the earth had done on the night of the earthquake, the rope was thrown, he touched the side of the launch, he was on board.

In the launch was the secretary, grown bald and corpulent, who immediately began to tell Mr. Fortune about the Great War, saying that the Germans crucified Belgian children, were a disgrace to humanity, and should be treated after the same fashion themselves.

Mr. Fortune sat listening and saying at intervals: 'Indeed!' and 'How terrible!' and: 'Of course I have heard nothing of all this.' His eyes were fixed upon the coral reef where Lueli stood, poised above the surf, and waving a green frond in farewell. As the launch gathered speed Lueli's figure grew smaller and smaller; at last he was lost to sight, and soon the island of Fanua appeared to be sinking back into the sea whence it had arisen.

Now the secretary was abusing the French; and from them he passed to the Turks, the Italians, and King Ferdinand of Bulgaria. Mr. Fortune could not yet gather who was fighting who, still less what they were all fighting about. However, there seemed no doubt but that it was a very comprehensive dog-fight.

'Shall I go back to Europe?' he thought. 'I couldn't fight, but perhaps I might pick up the wounded. No! I am too old to be of any use; and besides, I have no money to pay my passage.'

The launch scurried on with a motion that might have been described as rollicking if it had not also been so purposeful and business-like. The paint which used to be white picked out with dark blue was now buff picked out with chocolate. The mechanic was a new one. He had stared at Mr. Fortune when the latter came aboard, and now he came out of the engine-house with a rag in his hand and began polishing the brass-work, turning round at frequent intervals to have another look at him.

'Perhaps he expected me to carry a goatskin umbrella,' thought Mr. Fortune.

The secretary displayed no such interest. He asked no questions about Fanua, a negligible peaceful spot, not like Europe, not to be compared to St. Fabien, where there was a gunboat and a fermenting depot for the Red Cross Fund. And as for Mr. Fortune, he had known years ago all that there was to know about him, and that wasn't much.

His conversation shifted from the wife of an ex-prime minister who was certainly in the pay of the Germans to the proprietor of the Pension Hibiscus who had attempted to charge for teas served to the ladies of the Swab Committee and was probably a spy. Meanwhile the island of Fanua was sinking deeper into the Pacific Ocean.

At last he stopped talking. Mr. Fortune knew that he ought now to say something, but he felt incapable of comment. He did not seem to have an idea left. Everything that was real, everything that was significant, had gone down with the island of Fanua and was lost for ever.

No. After all there was one thing he might ask, one small interest which had been overlooked in the pillaging of his existence.

'By the by, can you tell me the exact time?'

He was an hour and twenty minutes out. A bad guess on his part. But perhaps it was not quite such bad guessing as it now appeared to be; for he had spent three and a half years in Fanua, and his watch might well have lost half an hour or so in that time. It was a good watch once; but Time will wear out even watches, and it had seen its best days.

ENVOY

My poor Timothy, good-bye! I do not know what will become of you.

SUMMER WILL SHOW

To Valentine Ackland

"Winter will shake, spring will try,
Summer will show if you live or die."

ONE

It was on this very day—the thirteenth of July—and in just such weather that Sophia Willoughby had been taken to see the Duke of Wellington. At ten o'clock precisely the open barouche came to the door, and Sophia, who had been dressed and ready and punctual, it seemed for hours, ran down the steps to admire the turnout. Walking stiffly, her legs well apart in order not to crumple the fluted frills of her long white muslin drawers, she had inspected the vehicle and the horses from all sides. Her scrutiny was searching, a child's exacting curiosity, sharpened and stiffened by the consciousness of being an heiress, the point advancing on the future, as it were, of that magnificent triangle in which Mr. and Mrs. Aspen of Blandamer House, Dorset, England, made up the other two apices.

But even under her eyes there was nothing to be found amiss. The wheels were spotless, Henry's white silk calves were blamelessly symmetrical (and that was her doing, since only two days before she had pointed out that the stuffing of his left leg extended quite an inch farther down than that of his right leg), every button winked in the sun, cockades and nosegays were spruce as they could be. Moreover, John coachman had remembered to shave the back of his neck. This array of manflesh was highly gratifying, but it was the horseflesh that fuelled her greatest satisfaction. The two chestnuts had never looked better. Pools of reflected light gleamed on their shining flanks with a lustre like treacle, it was a deep physical pleasure to see the veins on their close-clipped bellies, they tossed their proud heads in the air, and their snorts of well-being mingled with the fine clatter of bits.

And then Mamma and Papa had come from the house, Mamma wearing a new dress of shot silk, a bonnet with feathers, a lace scarf, and purple kid gloves. The sunlight flashed, sudden as a viper's bite, from the gold half-hunter watch opened in Papa's hand.

"Augusta, it is seven minutes past ten precisely."

The footman arranged the shawl round Mamma's feet, shut

the door, and sprang up behind; and the barouche, with its grand freight of the Aspen triangle, rolled down the drive towards the west gate of the park.

Now, down the same drive, walked she, Sophia Willoughby of Blandamer House, Dorset, England, and the new Damian and Augusta ran before her, bowling a hoop between them. The same sun burned unconsumed overhead, and thanks to the good forestry of Job Saunders scarcely a tree was missing from that avenue of lime and beech whose shade had spattered the barouche party with hot and cold. 1826, 1847—twenty-one years to a day—a majority's measure.

How little the place had changed! The drive a trifle mossier, perhaps, the trees in the park holding out a larger shade under which the sheep might gather from the sun, and this year the lime-blossom not quite so forward. But I . . . I am changed indeed from that proud and happy child, sitting between Mamma smelling of orris root and Papa smelling of Russian eau-de-Cologne, and going to see the Great Duke. And a sense of what was due to her position made her heave a sigh.

As though her thoughts had walked into the sun again a feeling of pride and well-being swept her on from the melancholy which befitted her. Glancing from side to side she acknowledged the added richness and maturity which twenty-one years had bestowed upon her property, and her mind busied itself with the improvements which she could and should bring about before the new Damian came of age.

Further plantations, an improved breed of cows at the home farm, the lake dredged and a walk of mown grass and willow trees carried round it, the library windows enriched with coloured glass, and a more respectable tenantry—to these schemes and others time and income should be adjusted. For now the Aspen triangle was reversed, and she, the hind apex, propelled forward its front of Damian and Augusta, even as now she was propelling them towards the lime-kiln.

During the early spring they had developed whooping-cough, and the remnants of the disease still hung about them. Sophia's own whooping-cough had been dealt with by the traditional method of being dangled over a lime-kiln to inhale the fumes;

she could recollect the exciting experience, and the hands of the man who had lifted her up—hard hairy hands, powdered with lime, the fingers with their broken nails meeting on her bosom under the fur-edged tippet. Her whooping-cough had come in winter, and had been a matter of a week or two. All her due childish ailments had been after that fashion: thoroughly taken, and swiftly dismissed, like the whippings which had fallen to her lot.

For all that doctors and valetudinarian ladies might say, Sophia held by old-fashioned manners with children. Crusts, cold water, cold rooms, scanty clothing, rough romping games to harden them, philosophical conversations to enlarge their minds. She herself had been brought up under the dispensation of *Émile,* and it had answered admirably. Walking swiftly under the gashes of sunlight that striped the avenue, she smiled to think that the stables and sheepfolds and kennels of Blandamer House had not produced a more vigorous or better-trained animal than she.

She slowed her steps, turning to the children's nurse, who was already lagging behind.

"Hannah! I am positive that the lime fumes are what the children need. I only regret that we have not done it before."

"Yes, Madam. They do seem better today, certainly. Under Providence."

Fool! thought Sophia with decision. And as though her father had spoken, a voice said within her, a voice from the Regency penetrating into mid-century, "That, my dear, is what you may expect, if you choose your maid-servants from Sunday-school families."

"I should have done it before," she reasserted.

The system which had strengthened her childhood she had faithfully imposed upon her children, in every case of doubt consulting the practice of her father, and doing as he would have done. It was a pity (for many reasons it was a pity) that she was not a man; for then she could have known with more assurance how Papa would have brought up a boy. Before Damian could walk he had been given a go-cart and a goat—a goat which had also supplied the nursery with milk. As soon as his legs could straddle a pony, a pony was his. But for all her care she had not yet succeeded in striking a spark of horsemanship from the boy, and he was fast turning into that most ignoble type of rider: a rider who knows how to avoid falling off. Damian had been given a miniature tool-chest, and encouraged to visit the carpenter's shop; he had a little gun, and a fishing-rod, and a stretch of the park had been levelled into a cricket pitch, where Damian might play with the village boys; but for all she could do, he remained childish. Nor was there any hope that the criticism or scorn of his playfellows would spur him on to greater daring, since his peculiar charm of confidingness and affability made him an idol among those of whom she designed him to be the leader. Only last week she had met little Larkins coming up the backdrive with a young owl which Master Damian had been scared to take from the nest for himself.

She commandeered the bird and as soon as the boy was out of sight tossed it up into the air. Then she had sought out Damian.

"Damian! Bill Larkins has brought your young owl. But if you cannot get a bird for yourself you cannot be fit to keep it, so I have let it go."

The child sighed.

"Oh dear! I wanted it for Sister."

It had been difficult to turn away, so ravaging had been the sudden impulse to caress him, to bow down the lids of those clear hazel eyes with a kiss. She had to be careful not to make a pet of Damian. Everyone seemed irresistibly moved to indulge and befriend him; pliable and affectionate, he lent himself to cosseting, just as his sleek brown curls twined themselves round the fingers of any hand that rested on his head. But petting would do him no good, it would be no true kindness to the child, for soon he must go to school, and he must not go there a milksop. He should have gone this year, but Doctor Hervey said he was still too delicate. The hardening system, so admirable, so well proved and well accredited, so successful in her own case, did not apply so perfectly to her children. On the nursery door the notches recording her own growth from year to year were still visible; and year by year Damian and Augusta fell short of them.

The clatter of the hoop-stick had failed. Looking out from her thoughts she saw that the children played no longer. Hannah was carrying the hoop, and the boy and the girl walked staidly beside her. Their cropped hair (Augusta's hair had been cropped to make it grow more strongly) showed the hollows in their slender necks. They had sloping shoulders, both of them. Their father had just such shoulders; yet he was vigorous enough, when he liked to bestir himself. The two forward apices of the Aspen triangle looked much too much like Willoughbys, at that moment; and she was glad of the lodge gates and the road beyond. It would be hotter there, but the change of surroundings would free the current of her thoughts, fretting so uselessly round the fact of her husband.

Here, when they had been driving to see the Duke, the barouche had passed a cluster of the villagers of Blandamer Abbotts, those who, being too childish or too infirm to walk to the route along which he would pass, had gathered about the gates of Blandamer House for the minor spectacle of the Squire and his Lady and the little Miss; and as the lodge gates had swung open a shrill fragmentary cheer had been raised. Papa bowed, Mamma bowed, Sophia bowed repeatedly until Papa had bidden her not to ape grand manners. A flush of confusion at the rebuke had been submerged in the more thorough flush of being suddenly tossed out into the full heat of the sun, and Mamma had put up a sunshade. Now the sun fell upon her with the same emphasis.

Augusta said, "I think this road was nicer when the may was in bloom."

"Much nicer," the boy replied. "And look at that chestnut tree. It is quite ugly now that there are no more flowers."

"I disdain July," the girl remarked, with something of her mother's decision.

The chestnut trees grew at the north-west corner of the park, so massive that they completely dwarfed the heavy stone wall that bounded it. Under their bulk of foliage it shrank to the value of a wicker paling. In the July sun their green was dark and formidable. They have lost their flowers, thought Sophia. I like them better so. Her mind, clumsy at anything like a metaphor, dwelt heavy and slow on the trees, and under the shade of her straw bonnet she blinked her eyes as though dazzled. The chestnuts had out-grown their flowers, rather, and now stood up against the full strength of the summer, unbedizened, dark, castellated, brooding, given over to the concern of ripening their burden of fruit. Like me, exactly, she thought. I admire them, and I am glad to resemble them. I am done with blossoming, done with ornament and admiration. I live for my children—a good life, the life my heart would have chosen.

Out here, where the road ran among the large swelling fields, it was as though one were in a different world from that bounded by the park wall. Only an occasional hedgerow elm or elder-bush shadowed the road. The grass banks were whitened with dust, and the flowers that grew there, chalk-white milfoil, and feverfew, looked like spattered handfuls of a thicker dust. The sun flashed on the flints in the fields, the loose straws on a rick glittered like shreds of glass. It was the landscape that Sophia had known all her life long. She liked it for acquaintance' sake, but knew that it was ugly. The land was poor, its bones showed through, its long history of seedtime and harvest had starved it, it had the cowed ungainly outlines of a woman gone lean with over-much childbearing. Except for the park-lands of Blandamer House it was unwooded, and the hills where the sheep-walks lay had none of the dignity of proper hills; they were round-shouldered slouching hummocks. However, it was all familiar to her, and a considerable part of it belonged to her, and did its duty and was productive. Just as she desired a more respectable tenantry, Sophia might have desired a more suave and fertile landscape; but in the depth of her heart she knew that one was as unimprovable as the other, and the consciousness of having no illusions made her content with what she had.

Now, by a thicket of elder and dog-roses, the path that led to the lime-kiln branched off. It ran on a grassy ridge between two fields. On the one side was a crop of barley, ripening well, but poor in straw. The poppies growing among it made the green of the barley seem almost sea-blue by contrast. On the other side was a turnip field. Two men were hoeing there, their hoes ringing against the flints. As the party from the house filed along the ridge the younger of the men turned round and came towards them, pulling his forelock. The sweat stood on his burned skin, his shirt clung damply to his shoulders. Tucked in at the back of his collar was a wad of dockleaves, wilted and discoloured.

"Good day, Madam. Good day, little Master and Miss. Here's a fine day for your walk."

The children hesitated politely, embarrassed to see such a hot man so close.

"How the little Master do grow!"

"Go on, children," said Sophia.

So that's the excuse you make to leave off working, she thought to herself. If the children had come out with Hannah only, the rogue would have talked for half an hour. She turned to look back. The man was still standing idle, catching her eye he pulled his forelock again; but at the persistence of her look he went back to his work.

After two more fields the path ran into the stony track that led uphill to the lime-kiln. The cleft in the hillside was filled with elder-bushes and blackthorns. The children, who had been silent in the fields, began to chatter again now that they were shaded from the sun. At intervals they coughed. Twice the party had to halt for a coughing-fit to be got over. Sophia, chafing at all this dawdling, and obliged to make some answer to Hannah's chit-chat, oh-dears, and grievings, and condolences, felt a rising exasperation. It was one thing to live for one's children; another to go walks with them, and converse with their nursemaid. She pined for something decisive, for the moment when she should exercise her authority. Thankfully she stepped from the climbing track to the small grassy platform where, in a nook of the hills, the lime-kiln stood.

"But where's the man?" cried Hannah. "Oh, Madam, how unfortunate if he's not here!"

"Of course he's here. There he is."

She called to him, and heard with pleasure her voice carry its command over the silent hillside. The man did not raise his head. He was sitting on the grass by the kiln, with his arms crossed on his knees, and his head bowed as though he were asleep. She advanced alone across the grassy platform, and only when her shadow fell across him did he raise his head. She noticed how dilated his pupils were, and that as he rose to his feet he staggered.

"You should not fall asleep in the sun, my man."

He raised his head and stared at her. His face twitched, he swallowed as though his throat were too stiff for him to speak. He has been drinking overnight, she thought. However, she must make the best of him; having got the children to the kiln, she must carry out her purpose, whether this fellow were sober or no.

"I have brought my children here, to breathe the lime fumes," she said, speaking slowly to drive the words into his head. "Is the kiln working?"

"Kiln be working, Mum."

She beckoned to Hannah to bring forward the children, who were hanging back, frightened. Hannah began to comfort them, and their faces grew paler.

"It won't hurt, my lamb, now don't get into a fuss. It's nothing, it will be over in a minute, it won't hurt you. I dare say you'll like the smell, and you'll be able to see inside, and all. Why, you'll quite enjoy it."

"Children, come here."

She seated herself on the grass, composedly, as though in smoothing her silk skirts she would allay their fears. Impressed by her dignity they stood before her, their faces stupid with heat, but docile and calm, now that they were under her spell.

"Damian, do you remember the lesson on lime in your Natural Science?"

"Yes, Mamma."

"Then tell Augusta what you remember of it."

Damian turned to Augusta with a company smile.

"There are two sorts of lime, Augusta. One is slacked lime, and that is dug into the fields. The other is quicklime, and that is more interesting, I think. It is hot, burning hot. Once a man who was drunk fell into a pit of quicklime, and when he was pulled out his face, his hands, everything, was burned right away."

Augusta's mouth opened appreciatively.

"And another time a poor little cat fell in. And all its hair was burned off, and—"

"No! Oh, Damian! Mamma!"

"You foolish baby, do you suppose I would bring you here to be hurt?"

She took the child in her arms, and held her close. With Augusta's wet eyelashes scrabbling softly against her cheek she continued,

"And, Damian, do you remember why lime is spread on the soil?"

"To kill insects, Mamma?"

"Yes, and to purify it. Lime purifies the ground, and purifies the air. That is why I had the Pond Cottages lime-washed after the fever had been there. That is why all our cow-sheds are lime-washed every six months. And that is why I have brought you and Augusta here to snuff up the fumes from this lime-kiln. The smell of the burning lime will go into your lungs, and strengthen and purify them, so that you will be cured of your coughs. Now do you understand?"

"Yes, Mamma."

"And you, Augusta, have you understood?"

Against her neck Augusta's head nodded drowsily. She yawned, stretched herself, and sidled down into her mother's lap; in another moment she would have been asleep if a fit of coughing had not waked her.

Hannah had not listened to the lesson in Natural Science. She was fanning herself with her pocket-handkerchief, and looking with disapproval at the man of the lime-kiln, every now and then drawing in her breath and shaking her head. For he had sunk down onto the grass again, and sat in his former attitude, sprawling there, in a way that was not respectful to gentry. Stepping to his side she prodded him swiftly, and whispered,

"Can't you get up? Don't you know you're wanted?"

He answered her prod with an oath, but rose the moment after.

"You're drunk, you beast!" she whispered. But for all her scorn and reprobation, her class loyalty made her add,

"Pull yourself together, lad. Don't you know that this is Mrs. Willoughby? Better not let *her* see you in this state."

"I bain't drunk. How can I afford to be drunk before midday?

But I've got a headache as would split a stone. What do they want of me?"

"She told you. You're to hold the children over the kiln, so's they can breathe it. Here! Wipe your hands on the grass and do up your shirt a bit. What's that on your wrists?"

"Bug sores."

Now all together they walked towards the kiln, moving slowly under the weight of the sun. To Hannah's religious mind it seemed as though they were advancing towards an altar of Moloch. Not that she had any doubts as to the rightness of the proceedings: she also had grown up in the knowledge that lime fumes were good for whooping-cough. But the conjunction of fire, children, and this solemn advance upon the kiln made her remember Moloch. The look of the kiln, too, was ecclesiastical in a heathen way. Squarely built of stone, solidly emerging from the turf, its walls were blackened and ruddied with stains of burning; and above the vent the fumes trembled upon the air, glassy, flickering, spiritual, as though they were rising up from the power of a mysterious altar.

They seemed to be a long time marching towards it, falling, with every slow step, deeper into its domain of heat and heavy odour. The man went in front. Following him went Sophia with a child on either side, and Hannah walked after.

"If you will stand on the steps," said Sophia, "we will lift the children up to you. Now, Damian, you can go first. Shut your eyes, and breathe deeply."

Returned to earth, Damian whispered to Augusta,

"I looked."

"What is it like? Is it like Hell?" she asked softly.

There was no time to hear, for now in her turn she was taken hold of, and hoisted towards the man's grasp. She gave a sudden cry, wriggled, and made her escape.

"What is it, Augusta? You are not afraid, surely? Damian was not afraid."

The child's face was pale, but her look was less of fear than of some suspicion and bewilderment in which she was deeply absorbed.

"Mamma! I don't quite like the man. He's so queer."

"But he's the kiln-man. His work makes him look like that."

Her face working in an attempt to find words, the child whispered,

"It's not him that I mind. But there's something about him so very auspicious."

At the second hoisting she made no resistance; and whether the man had overheard her or no, he knew his place well enough to show no consciousness of her words. Standing priest-like and impassive upon the steps, his head and shoulders dark against the background of trembling air, he stretched out his arms for the light burden, and Augusta was held above the opening of the kiln.

Her face, lit by the flickering fires below, wore the same bewildered and cogitative expression, and her eyes did not open for a single glance of curiosity at what was beneath.

"Why didn't you look?" inquired Damian. "Were you afraid?"

"I forgot."

"Miss Augusta kept her eyes shut as she was told," improved the overhearing Hannah. "Miss Augusta behaved properly, and God will cure her cough because she was obedient."

Lost in her musing dream, the child stood pale and unhearing.

The man having been given the shilling for his pains, and dismissed from their world, the little party moved away, slowly and religiously, as they had approached. No one spoke. Sophia was the first to rouse herself. The fumes must have made us sleepy, she thought, suddenly conscious that there was something odd, something pompous and bewitched about the way they were all behaving. And she began to walk faster, and to sweep her glance this way and that over the wide view from the terrace of the hill.

At the entrance of the lane she looked back. The man was standing where they had left him, staring after them. Hannah looked back too.

"How he stares, Madam! But no wonder. He might be here year in, year out, and scarcely be visited by a soul, let alone little gentry children. He'll think of this till supper-time, I dare say."

Sophia nodded her assent. Even as she did so, her mind glancing casually at the lot of the lime-kiln man, she received a sudden and violent impression that, however fixedly he had stared after them, and stared still, he did not really see them, and that their coming was already wiped from his mind like a dream. . . . A fancy, and she disliked fancies. . . . But even before she had time to rebuke it Damian coughed, and her thoughts were tilted back again to what was actual.

What childishness to have expected that the children would be cured of their coughs immediately. She was no wiser than a poor papist, that would hope to nail up a waxen leg or a goitre before a shrine, like dead vermin nailed up on a gamekeeper's tree. Walking ahead, listening for coughs, she began to reason herself into common sense, damping down her present fears by a reckoning of what illnesses the children had already been through, what remained for them yet to combat. It should be comforting to know how greatly the former outnumbered the latter. Damian aged nine, Augusta aged seven, might be looked upon as scarred and salted veterans in these wars of youth. It is best to get such things over early in life, everyone was agreed as to that. Later on they might affect the constitution, and certainly interfered with schooling. So she might count herself lucky among mothers.

"Excuse me, Madam, but the children are rather tired. I think it would be best for them to sit in the shade for a while."

The sycamore by the gate between the two fields made a small separate world of shade in the glaring whitish landscape. In its shelter the two children stood islanded, looking out on the brightness all round as though they were looking from a fortress on some beleaguering danger. They had drawn close together, and stood in silence, their bright eyes flickering in their pale faces, their bony knees seeming years older than their thin legs. Augusta loosened her straw bonnet; as it fell back it showed her hair, plastered dark and limp on her forehead.

"Certainly, Hannah. Let us rest by all means. I expect you are tired too."

"Oh no, Madam."

However, she retreated with alacrity to the shade of the

sycamore, sat down, spread out her skirts for the children to sit on, and took out her knitting.

"Hannah, my head thumps," said Damian.

"Never mind, dear. It will soon be better."

From a neighbouring field a bull blared. The noise, so thick and shrill and dully furious, seemed the very voice of the mid-day heat. It was as though the sun thrust its voice from the heavens. The cows in the meadow went on feeding, whisking their tails against the flies that pestered them, and snatching at the herbage. The bull blared again and again, and the cows cropped on, uninterested. Sensible cows, thought Sophia. She was tearing up grasses also, and mechanically stripping off the *Loves-me, Loves-me-not* seed-heads. This waiting irked her, this waiting for the next cough. She disliked sitting down in the middle of a walk, she disliked any kind of dawdling. A slow and rigid thinker, to sit still and contemplate was an anguish to her. Presently she jumped to her feet, saying,

"Children, I shall walk on. You can stay here with Hannah until you have rested enough, then you can walk slowly to the end of the path. Meanwhile, I shall have reached home, and sent the carriage to bring you the rest of the way."

I wonder how Hannah will like listening to that bull, she thought with amusement as she climbed the stile and set out briskly along the grass ridge. But the amusement faded from her mind, and with a few more steps she was teased by cares again. Suppose the lime-kiln treatment did not work, what was she to try next? And presently there would be that boy from the West Indies that Uncle Julius was sending. True, he would not be in the house for more than a week, but in that week a number of things might go wrong: he might tease Augusta, or corrupt Damian. For however necessary it was to be broadminded about Negroes and half-castes, the necessity to be broad-minded about bastards was not so imperative; and now she half wished that she had not undertaken to look after the brat. Well, it was another responsibility, another care—and she straightened her shoulders, and walked more erectly, feeling herself with every step deepening her hold upon the earth that she trod upon and owned, and resolutely absorbing the rays of the down-beating sun. It was an extraordinary thing that she, who had been so strong all her life, should have given birth to two such delicate children. Nor was Frederick delicate either, though he had fussed inordinately about his health. No, the delicacy was not inherited. It was struck out in the conjunction of the parents; it was the worst, the only enduring result of that deplorable mating.

She could still hear the bull blaring—a furious monotonous cry, a wail almost, ringing through the unmoved countryside. It was Dymond's bull, she supposed, not a good beast at any time, and ageing. Dymond must be spoken to. A place in service must be found for Topp's eldest girl, who was doing herself no good, hanging about among the farm-hands. Mamma's tomb must be scrubbed again, and a room (the red dressing-room would do) made ready for that Caspar, Gaspar, whatever the child was called. She was a land-owner, and a mother, and every day there was more to do, more to oversee the doing of. Duties came out of thought, one after another, swift as bees coming out of a hive. She was a mother, and a land-owner; but fortunately she need no longer be counted among the wives.

Now she saw her hand as it had been eighteen months ago, a hand whitened with winter and indoor living, holding the quill that moved swiftly and decisively over the paper. She could see the very look of the four pages, neatly filled with her even Italian script, and her signature, exactly filling the calculated space at the bottom of the fourth page—the four pages on which she had stated to her husband her exact reasons for wishing not to live with him again, her exact decision never to do so. She could remember everything: the look of the winter room, the fire rosy on the white marble hearth, the yellow flames of the candles she had lit, and the uncurtained window reflecting them, presenting its illusion of bright fire and sallow candle-flames alight in the dusky February garden, where the evergreens bent toppling under the rainy wind. She could remember the dress she wore, the bracelet on her wrist with its staring onyx, the new scratch, raw and blatant, on the green leather of the escritoire. With a veer of wind the rain had spattered against the windows, and on that streaming surface the reflection of the fire and the candle-flames had brightened. She could remember the smell of the sealing-wax, and the exact imprint of the seal, and the look of the letter, lying sealed, stamped, and addressed, on the summit of the other letters she had written that afternoon.

Frederick Willoughby, Esquire.
Hôtel de l'Étoile,
rue Ste-Anne,
Paris.

So clear, so authentic, was the recollection that walking along the road between the dusty hedgerows and the parched fields she yet had a feeling of a rainy afternoon and of the safe pleasure of being withindoors by a fire. It was only what she had said that she could not remember. Out of all that letter, so swimmingly written, so clear-headedly willed, that letter which was to decide the remainder of her life, she could not remember a single phrase, a single sentence.

If I had been jealous, thought Sophia, if the last angry embers of love had smouldered in me when I wrote, I should remember my letter still. And if there had been a twinge of hope left, I should have kept a copy of it. But as it was, I wrote it as one writes a business letter, a letter dismissing a servant, or refusing an application.

Now the lodge gates had swung to behind her, and the shade of the avenue dappled her progress. I go to my house, she said to herself, alone. I rule and order it alone. And no one doubts my sufficiency, no one questions my right to live as I do. I am far safer than if I were a widow. For at my age, and in my position, I should be pestered with people wanting to marry me; I should have to live as cautiously as a girl. But now I can stand up, and extend my shade, my suzerainty, unquestioned as a tree. No cloistered fool of a nun could live freer from the onslaught of love than I, and no queen have a more absolute sway.

She turned off to the stables, to order the carriage which was to fetch Hannah and the children. While the horse was being put in she stood by, making desultory conversation with the coachman, and looking round the stable-yard. Here she had run as a child, to strut over the cobbles with her legs apart in an imitation of old Daniel, to plunge her bare arm into the bins of corn and oats, to sniff saddle-soap and the bottles of liniment and horse-medicine, to dabble in the buckets and, when no one was looking, to lick the polished metal on the harness, so cold and sleek to the tongue. Again she felt the sense of escape; for here everything was clean, bare, and sensible; there was no untidiness, and no doubt. Her horses (she did not admit it but the thought was there) were everything that her children should have been: strong, smooth-skinned, well-trained, well-bred. The texture of the muzzle searching her hand for sugar, so delicately smooth, so dry and warm and supple, satisfied something in her flesh which the kisses of her children left unappeased. To them she responded with tenderness, with pity, with conscience, with a complicated anguish of anxiety, devotion, and solicitude. Even in bending to kiss Damian the thought would spring up: *His forehead is very hot. Has he a fever?* But to this contact her own vigorous well-being could respond with an immediate and untrammelled satisfaction.

At the stroke of the stable-clock the pigeons flew off with a whirr. In a moment, even while the vibrations of the metal still hung on the midday stillness, they would fly back to the roof and sit sunning there; but she was bidden away. What next to do? Dymond's bull, Topp's girl, Mamma's tomb . . .

Mamma's tomb came into the province of the gardener. He was in the tomato-house pinching off the lesser fruits. A good servant, she thought, watching how unerringly he nipped away the poor, the imperfect, the superfluous growths. A heavy smell, spiced and pungent, flowed from the vines, and from his hands. The sun beat through the glass upon the whitewashed wall, the shadows of the vines with their dangling fruits were sharply patterned. The grey-green foliage was hung with swags of orange and scarlet fruit.

"A good yield, Brewster. Better than last year, I think."

He nodded, and said in a voice that, for all his years of service in England, retained its Scottish whine,

"There'll be too many, I'm thinking, for the house to eat them."

He seemed to be reproaching her for living alone, for not keeping up the state which his tomatoes, his peaches, his melons and nectarines, deserved. She countered him swiftly.

"In that case, the rest can be sold."

It might not be genteel to sell one's superfluous fruit. Neither was it genteel to live apart from one's husband. But the one and the other was sensible, was rational, was concordant with Sophia's views as to the conduct of life. Brewster had intended no reproach, she could see that now, for it was without any reservation that he began to speak of a fruiterer in Weymouth who would make a good offer. It was foolish of her to have thought that he would reproach her. She lived singularly uncriticized by her household, so calmly enforcing her will upon them that they felt themselves supported by it. Every inch of Sophia's body, tall, well made, well finished, her upright carriage, her direct gaze, her slow, rather loud voice and clear enunciation, warded off criticism.

"Good. Then you will see to that this afternoon, Brewster."

"Yes, Madam."

Mamma's tomb had been troublesome from the first, owing to Mamma's odd wish that a weeping willow should be planted over it. The willow dripped, cast its leaves, and stained the white marble. Moreover, in Sophia's opinion, it looked rather silly and sentimental. It was strange how Mamma, in her two years of widowhood, had remodelled her character, on that first flood of forsaken tears sailing off into a new existence of being fashionably feeling. She had read poetry, she had read novels. She had covered pages of hot-pressed lilac paper with meditations and threnodies of her own composition, and had pressed mournful flowers between the pages. Refusing carriage exercise, she had taken to wandering about the garden in the evenings, and at her bidding an arbour had been put up, where she could sit in the dusk, catching colds and looking at the moon. When fetched indoors by Sophia, instead of knitting or embroidering, she would play the piano—not very well, since she had not touched the keys since her marriage, except to play quadrilles and waltzes, but with prolonged enjoyment and great expressiveness. She became as finicking as a girl over her meals, grew thin, developed a cough, and declared on the slightest provocation her intention of dying as soon as possible of a broken heart; and after two years of this conduct she had done so, withering mysteriously, with the strongest resemblance to a snapped-off flower that could have been achieved by human suggestibility and human obstinacy.

Sophia had watched this behaviour with bewilderment, embarrassment, and disapproval. It was not new to her that people could behave like this. At her boarding-school several of the young ladies had complied with all the dictates of fashion in being romantic and sentimental, and during the short season in London in which she met and married Frederick she had worn the prevailing mode of feeling as duly as she had worn flowers in her hair. One was foolish, and the other was messy; but while they were the mode it would have been eccentric not to make a show of compliance. Mamma had approved her demeanour; Papa, philosophically, had approved her compliance; but there had never been, at any point of the Aspen triangle, the slightest yielding of heart to these whims of behaviour and feeling. Sophia might gaze at the moon as much as she thought fit; but she gazed at it through the drawing-room windows. Sophia might visit a waterfall, or a ruin; but she must change her stockings and have some hot wine when she returned. Sophia might refuse her food, pine, burst into unexpected tears, copy poetry into albums and keep pet doves, while her marriage was being arranged and her trousseau ordered; but once married it was understood that she would put away these extravagancies and settle down into the realities of life once more.

No one had understood this more whole-heartedly than Sophia, and in the second week of her honeymoon, as she and Frederick strolled under the archway of their twelfth Rhine castle, she had come to a sudden decision to cut short their travels and return to Blandamer House, where the settling down could be more effectively put into action. Seated upon a block of crumbling masonry and prodding the earth with the tip of her parasol, she listened to Frederick reading aloud legends of robber barons and mysterious maidens. It had taken another week to move him: legends by day and roulette and the opera-house in the evening made up a life that Frederick was loath to relinquish; but at last, seated in their travelling carriage on the deck of the Channel boat, she beheld the chalk cliffs of Kent, whose whiteness promised her the chalk downs of Dorset. She could not turn to her husband to express her pleasure, since he was walking up and down with his cigar; but indeed she had not needed to; her pleasure was sufficient without expression.

Already she had been quite well able to do without Frederick; and returning to her father's house, she seemed to be bringing her husband with her like one of the objects of art which she had bought on her travels. Inevitably a return to sensible real life meant a return to Blandamer. The Willoughby house, too large and traditionally splendid for the Willoughby means, was let on a long lease to a Person from the North who had made a fortune during the wars. Edward Willoughby and his wife, flourishing on the rental in London, had no mind to encourage a younger brother and his country wife to settle near by. A visit or two had shown Sophia that she was not popular with them; and hearing them speak of the Person from the North she had suspected that to them she had seemed socially little better than he, since to a mind so elegant as Mrs. Edward Willoughby's the production of military small-clothes and the ownership of an estate in the West Indies were almost equally commercial and suspect. Conscious of this, she had determined to make a country gentleman of Frederick; and since he would one day or other share with her the ownership of Blandamer, it seemed to her, and to Papa too, sufficiently conscious of that dowry of debts which Frederick had brought to the marriage, proper that her husband should begin at once to accustom himself to the life which the course of time must entail upon him.

So they had settled down. To her this process meant arranging the west wing as their peculiar domain, teaching the servants to address her as Madam instead of Miss, holding her own with Mamma, choosing her clothes for herself, and awaiting the birth of her first child. Now, looking back upon those years, she could admit that for Frederick things might not have been so easy. Re-rooted in her old life, the more strongly settled there by the additional weight of marriage and maternity, she had watched

Frederick fidget—at first watching with compunction, then with annoyance, at last with indifference. Then, scarcely noticing his absence, she had let him go again. Frederick was in Northamptonshire, staying with friends for the shooting season; Frederick was at Brighton for his health; Frederick was at Aix-les-Bains being a companion to an uncle from whom he had expectations. From these absences he would return, affable, wearing new clothes, and laden with gifts, to admire the growth of his children, to exercise his riding horse, to lounge and twiddle through a spell of bad weather until he went off again. Sometimes, taking pity on his aimlessness, she would put aside her work and play a match of billiards with him; she was a better player than he, though not so well in practice; and their rivalry under these circumstances was almost the only thing that made their relations real and living. Meanwhile, Mamma ate, slept, netted, and fondled her grandchildren, and Papa, suddenly grown old, laid every day more and more of the cares of the estate upon Sophia's shoulders. In the evenings, before the tea-equipage was brought to the drawing-room, the four would play whist together, and Sophia and her father would beat Frederick and Mamma.

She was too haughty to deny herself that luxury of the proud-minded—a sense of justice. Justice made her admit that things were not too easy for Frederick. And on the day when the growing sympathy of the neighbourhood for that poor neglected young Mrs. Willoughby first penetrated the calm of Blandamer it had been natural for her to reply that no sensible person could expect Frederick to stay perpetually tied to her apron-strings. Resenting this first waft of criticism, she had written to her husband encouraging him to prolong his stay at Aix. Frederick immediately returned. Sophia engaged lodgings in Mayfair, provided herself with clothes of the latest fashion, and took him off for a month of gaiety, leaving behind her full and exact directions for everything that should be done in the nursery, the home farm, the Sunday-school, and the hot-houses during her absence. With the same method and resolution she had arranged four weeks of exemplary fashion and enjoyment—dinners, balls, breakfast-drums, the races, the opera, Hyde Park, and the hair-dresser; and during the first week she had as unflinchingly stormed her sister-in-law for introductions and invitations. But this had not been necessary, after all; Frederick knew already every man, woman, and head-waiter they encountered.

Filling her diary with careful accounts of everything seen, done, heard, and visited, Sophia had thought to herself, as day after day was written down and disposed of: Once back at Blandamer I can be happy and sensible again; and it was with a feeling of nearing the winning-post that she left her farewell cards, paid the bills, and dropped kid-gloves and bon-bon boxes into the wastepaper basket.

That visit to London had done much to stay local criticism. The pity due to a neglected wife faltered before the aspect of such a fashionably dressed young woman who had heard Grisi and seen Vestris. But the excursion, so well calculated to circumvent the doubts of others, had done as much, or more, to breed uneasiness in herself. Heretofore an absent Frederick had been a shadowy creature, a something dismissed to wander in exile from the real life and centre of life at Blandamer, to drink watered milk and eat stale vegetables, breathe bad air and keep unhealthy hours. Now the place of this spectre was taken by the Frederick she had seen in London, a Frederick popular, sought after, light-hearted, affable, open-handed, and probably open-hearted—her satellite of Blandamer changed to a separate and self-lit star.

A weaker or an idler woman might have been jealous; a woman in love would certainly have been so. Indifference and responsibility preserved her from any sharper pang than annoyance and the grim admission that the current opinion as to her pitiable state must be, in the eyes of the world, well founded. Papa's death, the growth and illnesses of her children, the cholera, the potato disease, and Mamma's strange florescence of widowhood distracted her attention from the increasing frequency and length of her husband's absences, his uneasy behaviour, half-frivolous and half-servile, when he was with her. Even when she knew for certain that he had been many times unfaithful to her, and was again neck-deep in an adultery, she was not jealous. She was furious.

Her fury had been intensified by his choice of a woman.

For even to Dorset the name of Minna Lemuel had made its way. Had the husband of Mrs. Willoughby chosen with no other end than to be scandalous, he could not have chosen better. A by-word, half actress, half strumpet; a Jewess; a nonsensical creature bedizened with airs of prophecy, who trailed across Europe with a tag-rag of poets, revolutionaries, musicians, and circus-riders snuffing at her heels, like an escaped bitch with a procession of mongrels after her; and ugly; and old, as old as Frederick or older—this was the woman whom Frederick had elected to fall in love with, joining in the tag-rag procession, and not even king in that outrageous court, not even able to dismiss the mongrels, and take the creature into keeping.

Her fury lasted still. Walking swiftly and heedlessly, she had made her way from the tomato-house to the park. And now she stood under the wasp-droning shade of a lime tree with a dozen sheep staring at her. The leader moved a step nearer, the others shuffled after it. She must have been here a long while for their timid curiosity to have brought them so close. If I were to speak as I feel, she thought, eyeing them sardonically, how you would scatter! She kept silence, silent as she had been from the moment she first heard the news, scornfully silent before the sheepishness of mankind. For all that anyone knew, Mrs. Willoughby was still patiently and unresentfully awaiting her husband's return from the Continent.

It was fortunate that Mamma's death had taken place when it did—before Sophia's discovery of Minna Lemuel. Mamma, a rather stupid and trifling woman, the slave of her grandchildren, the gull of any village slut who chose to wear a tattered bodice and lose a husband, amply deceived by her son-in-law, and constantly buying tender green-house rarities which turned out to be chickweed, had yet been able to keep her daughter almost in awe by a power of reading the most carefully concealed thoughts. From the moment when Sophia had first suspected Frederick, Mamma had known of it; and though not a word had been spoken, Sophia was made aware of Mamma's knowledge. For a shawl had been handed, like a shelter; a "Thank you, my dear," at the passing of a cup of tea had murmured: "My poor forsaken child, I know all, and feel for you as only a mother can"; a second glass of port accepted with, "Well, Sophia, since you insist," had said: "But you always were headstrong." And day by day Sophia had felt herself more like some strong rustic animal entangled in a net. The net was never drawn close. She had but to stamp or bellow a little, and it shrank to the silken twist of Mamma's netting, which had again trailed off that black silk lap and needed to be picked up. With the rather pompous disapproval of a strong character, Sophia deplored her mother's feminine intuition. It was too subtle, it was the insight of a slave. Exercised upon her childhood it had fostered her with subtle attentions, gratifying her wishes before she herself was aware of them. But slaves, it is well known, make the most admirable attendants to young children.

So it was a good thing that Mamma had died, her silken net sinking into the grave after her as a dead leaf is drawn under the mould by earthworms, before the first, the only and final rupture with Frederick. Even after the funeral Sophia had walked cautiously, suspecting the net might be trailing still, that, put away among gloves, or her own baby clothes, or in a letter-case or jewel-case, she might find a letter from Mamma, saying what only impregnable death would give her the daring to say, condoling or counselling. Such a letter, and most of all, a letter of counsel, was a thing to dread. For Sophia respected death, that final and heavily material power, as greatly as she despised finesse and feminine intuition; and however little the living mother had been honoured, the dead mother was another matter. But there was nothing either of sympathy or counsel. Mamma had betaken herself bag and baggage to the grave, even the lilac-paged albums were inscribed: To Be Burned Unread after My Death. Nothing had been left over except a packet of letters that slipped through the lining of an old dressing-case, letters written by Mamma to Papa shortly before their marriage. Sophia had read them, a little guiltily, carrying them to the stale window-light of the winter dusk, for to light candles would have illuminated the act into an impropriety. But she had not read long. They were cold and insipid, reading them was like eating jelly.

The sheep were within a hand's breadth now, and her fury

had died down. She was glad. She had no wish to feel anger, when anger was so unavailing. Of the two moods possible to her, such rage, and the icy disdain in which her letter to Frederick had been written, she preferred disdain. It was more dignified, and it allowed her to get on with her work. For now all her passion of life should be poured into what she had to do: bring up her children, order the house and the estate, govern the village. That should be enough, surely, for any woman who had outgrown her follies; and cool enough now to smile at herself, she considered what small half-hearted follies hers had been. For though while Frederick was wooing her she had been quite thoroughly and properly in love with him, from the day of the marriage she had known without illusion what lay before her: respectable married life with its ordered contacts and separations, the attentive acceptance that a married woman should feel for a man who must be made allowances for, a man much like other men—a compromise that one might hope would in time solidify into something positive and convenient. Nor, from these soberly chilling ashes, had the sudden explosion even of Minna Lemuel raised up a flame of that folly of loving too well. It was not that Frederick had ceased to love her, but that he should love such a one as Minna, that had tormented her, and must be at intervals her torment still.

Over her luncheon of cold chicken and claret Sophia found herself pondering the conduct of Uncle Julius Rathbone with unexpected approval. Julius Rathbone was her father's half-brother. At her father's death she had, so to speak, inherited him, and with the inheritance had come something of Papa's masculine tolerance. Julius was part owner and manager of the estate in the West Indies which supplied the Aspen wealth; and twice a year or so he sent large consignments of guava jelly, molasses, preserved pineapple, and rum. These were for general family consumption, and so were the portraits of his elegant sharp-nosed wife and his three plain daughters. Other consignments were of a kind more confidential—accounts of his scrapes, financial and amatory; and now he was entrusting to Sophia his illegitimate son, a half-caste. "*He is now fourteen years old,*" wrote Uncle Julius, "*and I do not want him to get false ideas into his head. I should be very grateful if you could place him in some moderate establishment where he could receive a sound commercial education."* Then, as though with a waving of the hand, the letter had turned to a more detailed account of the guava jellies, etc., which would accompany the boy across the Atlantic and ended with *"your dear Aunt, as usual, sends her fondest love, and so do the Girls."*

It was scarcely a matter in which she could consult with people of her own standing, even had she felt inclined to do so. She told her solicitor to advertise the requirements, and send the answers to her. They came in hundreds; it seemed as though England's chief industry was keeping boarding-schools where religion and tuition had united to put into the heads of bastards all the suitable ideas and no false ones. Most of the prospectuses came from Yorkshire, but finally she settled upon a school in Cornwall; and though Uncle Julius had begged her not to put herself out in any way, Sophia could no nothing without becoming conscientious and determined to do it thoroughly, so workmanly pride as well as humaner considerations made her travel to Cornwall to inspect the Trebennick Academy. It was a tall house standing alone on a sweep of moorland, having on one side of it a lean garden filled with cabbages. The moorland sloped to a valley, and on the opposite slope, against the skyline, was a prick-eared church with a well-filled graveyard. She saw the Trebennick Academy on an April afternoon but, unless a gardener's eye were to find it in the condition of the cabbages, there was no sign of spring in the landscape. Stones of various sizes were tumbled over the moor, rusty bracken was plastered against them by the winter's rain, and a fine mist limpened the folds of her pelisse and bloomed her gloves. The air was such as she had never smelt before, very fresh and smelling of earth. Her first impression was one of distaste, almost of fear; and that evening, coughing over the peat-fire of the Half Moon Inn, she all but decided against the Trebennick Academy. Yet on the morrow, smelling again that fresh, earth-scented air, she found herself queerly in love with the place, and reluctant to leave it so slightly tasted, as when a child she had felt reluctant to leave, half-eaten, some pot of stolen jam.

There was no doubt that, in some unsuspected way, she could have been very happy at Trebennick. That air, so pure and earthy, absolved one back into animal, washed off all recollection of responsibilities; one waft of wind there would blow away the cares from one's mind, the petticoats from one's legs, demolish all the muffle of imposed personality loaded upon one by other people, leaving one free, swift, unburdened as a fox. At intervals during the summer Sophia had found herself betrayed by fancy into Cornwall, and leading there a wild romantic life, in which, unsexed and unpersoned, she rode, sat in inns, slept in a bracken bed among the rocks, bathed naked in swift-running brooks, knocked people down, outwitted shadowy enemies, poached one night with gipsies, in another went a keeper's round with a gun under her arm. Out of these rhapsodies she would fall as suddenly as she had fallen into them, and without a moment's pause go on with what she was doing: a memorandum for the bailiff, a letter to the dressmaker, the paper boat her hands had been folding and fastening for Augusta to sail on the pond. In a space no longer than it takes to open one's eyes she was back in her accustomed life, in a leap was transferred to daylight from darkness. And yet, as by the mere closing of eyelids one can surmise a darkness stranger than any star has pierced, a darkness of no light, which only the blind can truly possess, she knew that by a moment's flick of the mind she could levant into a personal darkness, an unknown aspect of Sophia as truly hers as one may call the mysterious sheltering darkness of one's eyelid one's own.

However well a life in Cornwall might suit her (not, though, that it was a life that the real and waking Sophia could anywhere find), seeing Caspar, she doubted if the Trebennick Academy could possibly do for him. She had arranged her mind before his coming, telling herself that black blood is stronger than that of the white races, that the boy would bear little or no resemblance to Julius, and might well be no more than a woolly Negro. But the boy who stepped from the carriage and walked towards her up the sunlit steps might have come, not from any surmisable country, but from a star, and before his extreme beauty and grace she felt her mouth opening like that of any bumpkin.

Could this beauty be for her sight alone? She heard a servant whisper, "What a little blackamoor!" Fools! she said to herself; and like one with something at stake she awaited the moment when her children should be introduced to the new-comer.

The minds of Damian and Augusta had also been arranged beforehand. They had been told something of the colour question, and of the rational humanitarianism which forbids that any race should toil as slaves when they would toil more readily as servants; they had been told, more practically, not to stare and not to be shy. They had also been told (though the question of bastardy had been left undiscussed) not to be too familiar.

Augusta's conduct was all that could have been asked of her. She had come forward prettily, said her greetings, held out her hand, glanced with her blue eyes as though they beheld nothing out of the ordinary. Damian had both stared and been shy, but his conduct had better pleased his mother. It was obvious that the arrival of this dusky piece of romance had stirred him deeply; and Sophia found herself moved towards her son not as a child but as a companion. His admiration corroborated hers, sanctioned it almost; she was knit to Damian, not by the common bond that tethers a mother to her child, but by the first intimation of the stronger link that time might forge, the close tremulous excited dependence of the woman upon the male she has brought forth. Flying out into the future, launched there the faster by the weighted impetus of her practical character, she decided that Caspar must be present, and honoured, too, at Damian's coming of age.

Meanwhile the two boys were walking across the lawn, Damian a little stiffly holding the new-comer's hand.

Augusta's carefully adjusted sigh intimated that she wished to receive attention.

"How do you like Caspar? Do you think you will be friends with him?"

"I like him very much. Is he a heathen?"

"No, of course not."

"Oh!"

Regret was implied.

"Did you want him to be a heathen, Augusta?"

"No, not exactly. But if he had been I had a plan, that's all."

"To convert him?"

Sophia's voice had gone a little dry. Once again Papa's cool shade had neared her, remarking on what one might expect if one chose the nurse for respectable piety. Religion was all very well, and a certain amount of it was necessary, no doubt, if only to comply with custom. Papa himself would have been the first to agree to that. But Sophia did not wish her children to be too religious. Untimely piety, not only in story-books, allured untimely deaths.

"No."

"Why did you want him to be a heathen, then, my darling?"

Augusta did not answer. She fidgeted, and stared across the lawn. Suddenly she began to cry.

"My love, my little one, what is it? What is the matter? Don't you feel well?"

"Mamma, Mamma! Don't let us ever go to that place again."

"The lime-kiln?"

There was no doubt in Sophia's mind as to what place Augusta meant. The child's long shudders vibrated against her bosom. This life she encompassed with her anxious arms was separate and inarticulate to her as an animal's; it was as though the fiddle should suddenly take a personal life upon it, wailing against the player's shoulder.

"Of course we won't go there again if it frightens you. There will be no need to go. Your cough is almost cured, isn't it?"

Though a child be born, nursed, the creature and study of endless nourishing days, she thought, it is never one's own to understand. Its every movement bruises one, is as terrifying and incomprehensible as the first movement in the womb, as alien as that first announcement of a separate life. And as though it were her own mysterious pain she rocked and comforted, Sophia rocked and comforted her child. Her mind, despairingly detached from her emotions, surveyed the lawn before her, noticed that a bough had withered on the copper beech and must be lopped off, wondered when Damian and Caspar would come in sight again, beheld Caspar's little trunk being lifted from the carriage, recollected the list of clothes that were considered necessary by the Trebennick Academy, revised her own supplementary list, and wondered again if it would be right to send the boy there. But if one cannot understand even one's own children, how hope to judge best for the bastard of one's half-uncle and some unknown quadroon, passionate and servile, her gold ear-rings swinging proudly, and the marks of the lash, maybe, on her back?

And how hope, her thought went on, to trace or elicit the connexion in Augusta's mind between Caspar being a heathen and the visit to the lime-kiln? No, no, distraction was the only hope: to be busy, to do the next thing, and the next thing. And already Damian and the half-caste were in sight, and the child in her arms wept no longer.

During the week that Caspar stayed at Blandamer the household disapprobation hardened, and behind it, rearing up like a range of further mountains, ice-summits of the neighbourhood's disapproval disclosed themselves. That the child should be viewed askance because he was coloured and a stranger was no more than natural; but he had more than that to call down wrath. He was not more black than vivid, not more of a stranger than of a phoenix.

Everyone who came in contact with him—and no one could keep away—must needs call out some achievement, as people prod monkeys at a fair; and then, angered by the brilliant response, sulk, grumble, and belittle it. The boy could ride. The groom took him from Damian's pony, mounted him on the bay mare, and set him at a jump. Over and over the boy went and cantering back slid off the excited beast like a silk shawl dropping to the ground. Roger went off snarling and talking of circus-riders. Mr. Foscot, the curate of the next parish, who came once a week when the weather was fine to give Damian swimming lessons, challenged the visitor to dive. From the first plunge Caspar came up discoloured and quivering, his body aghast at the chilly lake-water; but for all that, being anxious to please, and vain, he dived repeatedly, and in swimming outstripped the curate, looking back from the end of the course, his chattering teeth displayed in a smile of pleasure at having done well. Mr. Foscot praised him duly; but also admonished him against staying in the water too long, since to do so would be bad for Damian and inconsiderate.

Mr. Harwood, the rector, also noticed the boy, inquiring if he knew his catechism. Caspar had never heard of the catechism. "I don't know what Church he belongs to," Sophia had interposed, coldly. Mr. Harwood was well enough in his proper place, in his restored Gothic, cushioned by her supplies of red felt and green velvet, and admirable in the parish; but this interview took place in her dining-room.

"I am a Protestant, please."

"Then you should know your catechism, my boy."

Damian only was privy to what followed. Not till later in Caspar's visit did Sophia hear how, having borrowed Damian's prayer-book and learned the catechism by heart, adding several collects as a gratuity, Caspar, accompanied by Damian, called upon Mr. Harwood and insisted upon a hearing.

"Very glib, remarkable quickness," the rector had added, telling this story. "But such facility—I expect, Mrs. Willoughby, that you share my opinion—is not altogether desirable. Light come, light go, you know."

Seeing her frown he added that he preferred Damian's type of mind. But even this sop did not appease Sophia; and with irony she amused herself by taking the old man to the conservatory and picking him a bouquet of her gaudiest and most delicate tropical plants. "I am afraid these are all I can offer you," she said. "There are no violets left." But delighted and admiring he did not perceive the insinuation.

With the same shortsighted partisanship all the household set themselves to match one boy against the other. And Caspar was always the readier, the more agile, the more daring. Each new feat increased their bile against him. They seemed bent on calling out his best in order to trample on it.

But Damian showed only the purest delight in the successes of the elder boy, and if Caspar had had no other gifts his music would have been enough to birdlime the English child. He had brought a small beribboned guitar on which he accompanied his ditties, singing in a thrilling over-sweet treble, forgetful of himself, as a bird sings, his slender fingers clawing the wires with the pattering agility of a bird's footing. He sang every evening, sitting on the terrace, his head leaning against the balustrade, his eyes half closed, singing hymns and love songs and melancholy Negro rants, his fingers pattering over the dry wires. And Damian, like an entranced dog, would sit as close as possible, his lips moving with the singer's, his whole being rapt and intent. Sophia lacked the instinct of music; Caspar's songs were apt to be particularly irritating to her since she could not understand the words. But she was glad to make one of the music party, soothed by the sight of her child's pleasure, caressed by the outer wave-lengths of a world into which she could not enter; and while the music lasted she would stay, gazing at the picture the children made—the picture of two white cherubs and a black.

Often she told herself that it was impossible to dismiss this being to the Trebennick Academy. Yet she did nothing. With Caspar's coming something came into her life which supplanted all her disciplined and voluntary efficiency, a kind of unbinding spell which worked upon her lullingly as the scent of some opiate flower. His beauty—a bloom of youth and of youth only—his character, so pliable, sweet, and shallow, and the wide-open flattery which he gave to her, all worked her into a holiday frame of mind. It was not possible, while Caspar was in the house, to do anything but enjoy; enjoy the ample summer weather, the smooth-striped lawns over which they strolled, the waving of the full-flourished boughs, the baskets of warm raspberries, the clematis pattern of stars, the smooth-running gait of her household, the sweet cry of one crystal dish jarred against another, the duskier bloom coming upon the outdoor peaches along the south wall, her children's laughter, the cool amethysts she clasped about her neck. Seeing Caspar unharmed by slights and snubs, she troubled herself no more about them; and the sense of being superior to such foolish things heightened her pleasure, seeming to make her move more grandly and freely above their pettiness, as though she were invulnerable as one of those vast white clouds that ambled so nobly overhead. It was all a dream, it could not last, soon her anxious days would repossess her—and surely Augusta had a little snuffle, one sneeze would bring down this enchanted world about her ears; but till the sneeze, till the crash, she would lie basking, trouble herself about that place in Cornwall no more than Caspar troubled himself.

So, doing nothing, too deep in living for action, she swam through the week of the visit until its last day. Then her warm world was rent away from her by a sudden outcry of anger from Damian. The three were playing on the lawn, and she jumped up and ran through the open French window, alert with anger at this threat to her content, furious and ready to pounce. Like a hawk she was on them. Augusta was in tears, Damian was pulling her hair. She heard the half-caste implore, his voice urgent with fear, "Don't be angry, don't quarrel, loveys. Oh, don't!"

"What's all this?"

They were silent, Augusta checking her tears with surprise at the sudden onslaught.

"Caspar! Were you teasing them? Is this your fault?"

He shook his head despairingly.

"What has happened?"

Still he did not answer, wringing his small hands and casting deploring looks from one child to the other. Then Augusta began to weep again.

"Horrid Damian, hateful boy! You are a bad brother, you hurt me."

"Hold your tongue, silly!"

"You did hurt me, you did, you did! You pulled my hair, and it's given me a headache, and you aren't sorry in the least, for you didn't stop, even when Caspar begged you. Caspar is a fool. He ought to have knocked you down. But he can do nothing, he can only play his silly guitar."

She turned to the half-caste, and tried to make a face at him, but more tears ruined the attempt. He had come towards her on his knees, and with a cry of sympathy began to stroke the jangled curls.

"Go away! I don't want you. You're *black!*"

"Augusta!"

But before the word was out of Sophia's mouth Damian hurled himself upon his sister, scratching and buffeting her.

"How dare you, Augusta, how dare you? I'll kill you for that. Caspar is my friend, and he isn't black, and I'll kill you for saying so."

"Black, black! He is black. A blackamoor! And he's not a proper boy either, he's only a bastard. Harlowe said so. I heard her. A black bastard, that's all your Caspar is."

She railed out of the tumult of Damian's assault, her cropped hair tangled over her face, wet with spittle, a furious fighting mane, which she shook over her flushed cheeks. A long scratch leaped out on her arm, and began to bleed. Damian thrust his face against hers, snarling, speechless with rage.

It was all Sophia could do to unclench their combat. Raging herself, locked into a stone of anger, she hauled them towards the house.

"Kneel down," she commanded, trembling with fury, forcing them down with hands that were like stone against their slight shaken flesh. "Stay there and quiet yourselves."

After that struggle under the midday sun the shaded air of her sitting-room was cold as a tomb. She trembled as she sat down behind her desk, entrenching herself as against two savage animals. Presently she took her Commonplace Book and began turning over the pages. The children knelt quietly now, subdued by the austere cool of the shaded room. Under her lashes she saw that they had begun to exchange glances, allied again, now that they had her wrath to look forward to.

"Listen.

> *"On Tuesday last Samuel Turvey, a boy of nine years of age, apprentice to a chimney sweep, was suffocated in the chimney of a house at Worksop. His master declares that the boy, having gone a little way up the chimney, called down that he was wedged, and could go no further. As he had shown sullenness before, and refused other chimneys, a fire of damp straw was kindled on the hearth, in order that he might be obliged to mount. He still expostulated, though he was heard attempting to go further. To the horror of those present, his body then fell to the hearth, he having been rendered unconscious by the smoke, and loosing his hold. Plucked from the fire he was discovered to be badly burned, and died the same day in the workhouse infirmary."*

She read coldly and slowly. After a pause she asked,

"Do you understand that?"

"Yes, Mamma."

"Would you like to be a chimney sweep?"

"No, Mamma."

The boy's answer was mechanical. He knelt and trembled, his face was ashen, every now and then it quivered. Her words had fallen on ears almost deaf, he was still absorbed in the bodily aftermath of the quarrel. Augusta cried out,

"What a horrible wicked man!"

"He had his living to make. And chimneys have to be swept. And some chimneys are so built that a brush cannot be put up them, so a boy must go instead. Only it happens that I am rich, and so such things do not happen to you or your brother."

It was difficult to speak. Her own wrath still kept her throat clenched, her tongue heavy. Her hand trembled, clattering the paper of the book. She laid it aside, and hid the shaking hands in the folds of her shawl. Outside, shrunken in the violent sunlight, she could see Caspar, standing where they had left him, staring at his shadow with hanging head. The gardener's boy was shearing the edges of the lawn, glancing sometimes over his shoulder at the half-caste, eyeing him with a complacent gulping grin as though the child were a penny spectacle at a fair.

"On just such a morning as this, some unfortunate child has been driven up a dark chimney. And you—you can find nothing better to do than quarrel like wild beasts. Worse! For no animal quarrels without reason, for food, or for supremacy. Be ashamed of yourselves. Now, get up. Go to Hannah, and tell her to put you both to bed, and to draw the blinds. There you shall spend the rest of the day."

They glanced at each other, as though consulting, and rose. Lagging, they moved towards the door. Then Damian turned back.

"But Caspar. I must say good-bye to him."

"No."

An hour later Hannah came to say that the boy was still weeping. Sophia shook her head. A profound disgust and weariness held her back from yielding.

"But I am afraid it will make him ill, Madam. He does take on so. Now Miss Augusta, she's asleep."

Sophia shook away the plea. He is always ill, she thought, bitterly impatient; and going to the medicine chest she mixed a sedative. Hannah carried it off, divided in her mind between pity for her nursling and gratification at any sunderance between the white child and the coloured.

The table was laid for two, and during luncheon Sophia kept the conversation upon the Trebennick Academy. Still locked in cold rage, she spoke to Caspar severely and practically, explaining that if he wished to gain favour with his teachers and fellows it would not do to play the guitar, dance, or sing. The carriage appeared before the windows, the small luggage was loaded on, it was time to start. In the hall the boy hesitated, looked round questioningly. "Your cousins are in disgrace," she said, and he followed her submissively, hanging his head.

During the journey she spoke little, thought little, still brooding furiously over the morning's incident. Arriving at Exeter, naked there of the dignity which clothed her on the platform of her own railway station, she was for a moment aware of herself as a spectacle: an English lady travelling with a little black boy. Her mind waved a grim acknowledgement towards Uncle Julius Rathbone, who managed the affairs of his heart so competently. At St. Austell the railway ceased; for the rest of the journey they must drive. They drove in a small closed wagonette, cold as the tomb. It was strange to look out of this mouldy box and see the blazing landscape through which they moved. Armies of ravelled late-summer foxgloves grew beside the stone walls; as the day wore on their purple turned melancholy and discoloured against the hues of a flaming sunset. She leaned her head out of the window, interrogating the air, searching for the romance of her previous visit. It was there still, but the long summer's warmth had changed it, and now it was turned from an excitement to a menace. With something like fear she felt that her body was heavy, her mind slow, that she was strong and helpless as a stone, strong only to be trampled on and to endure. The boy beside her, so quick, so vulnerable, was better equipped for life than she. Now she would have been glad to talk to him, would have clutched at any expedient which might carry her away from this obsession of being cold and heavy and helpless; but he was listless, half asleep, and doleful, gone crumpled and dead as suddenly as a tropical blossom.

"Here is Caspar Rathbone," she said at last, standing before the smouldering peat-fire which seemed to be identical with the fire she had noticed on Mr. Gulliver's hearth six months ago. She had done her errand, now she could say good-bye, drive back to the Half Moon Inn, fall exhausted into the strange uncomfortable bed. It was all something done by rote, done before and quite unreal. As she looked back from the wagonette, and saw that Caspar had already been swallowed up by the Trebennick Academy, the sense of doom and predestination which had, all the journey long, rested so leaden upon her sharpened suddenly into the thought: *The child will die there. I shall never see him again.* But this, a moment after, she drove out as sentiment; and she knew also that, even without this expunging explanation, she could not, for the life of her, have turned back then to rescue him, or to make any attempt to turn destiny aside, so deeply had this hallucination of puppetry and rote enforced itself upon her.

Shivering and stupefied, she sat alone in the dining-parlour of the Half Moon Inn, unable to eat the food set down before her. "I believe I am going to be ill," she said to herself; and, rousing, she ordered a glass of hot brandy and water. It was cold before she remembered to drink it; and having drunk it she sat on, staring at a glass picture of Britannia, and a bunch of dying foxgloves in a white jug, sat until a tap on the door roused her as though with a thunder-clap, and the landlady came in, awkward and timid, to say that it was past midnight, and would the lady be sitting up much longer.

Almost the next thing that she knew was another tap, which roused her to morning and the recollection that of the day's two eastward trains from St. Austell she was catching the earlier. The boxlike wagonette was waiting for her, it had spent the night at Trebennick also, the same ravelled foxgloves awaited her along the hilly winding roads. But yesterday's cloud had evaporated. With renewed delight she smelt the exciting soulless air, and watched the shaggy contours of the hills. She was in Cornwall, unknown, and without responsibilities. Her body rejoiced and grew impatient, chafing at the joggling wagonette; and telling the man he should spare his horse, she alighted and walked up a hill. The rough road underfoot delighted her, the dust flew up like an incense, the light of morning seemed spilled on the lonely country for her alone. At St. Austell she paid off the man, and saw her dressing-case put in the office. Thence she went on to a tobacconist, and bought some cheroots. She had four hours to spend, four hours in which her soul could be at liberty.

Any road would do, and the road she chose took her out of the town, and past a slated farmhouse under a group of sycamores, and over a suddenly humped stone bridge. The stream was small, brilliant, and swift-running; she left the road and followed it through the steep small fields towards a dome of rough moorland. Here, scrambling over the last stone wall, she sat down in the sun, settled herself against an outcrop of granite, and lay basking, stripping bracken fronds between her fingers, and listening to the chatter of the brook. Its waters were exquisitely cold and sweet; she drank, at first from her hand, then, stretching herself along the warm turf, from the stream itself, where the water arched, glassy and smooth, over a rock. It ran so strongly that at the first essay she plunged her mouth too deeply into the flow, and spattered her face and hair. She was hungry now, and glad of the parcel of sandwiches put up by the Half Moon Inn. Then she took out a cheroot, lit it, and began to smoke. It was not such a good cheroot as those she had stolen, long ago, from Papa's cabinet. But it was passable, and had this advantage over the others, that she would not be whipped for it.

The cheroot was half finished when a company of gipsies crossed the shoulder of the moor, not seeing her in her shelter of rock and fern. They loped along in single file, picking their way over the waste as though they followed a scent. They were at home in the landscape like animals. Yet though I should like to stay here for ever, she thought, spreading out her palms to feel the sun, I should never want to be a gipsy. But I would build a house here, no larger than that ruined cottage I passed, live alone, and do everything for myself. Perhaps a woman coming in to do the cooking and make the bed. But everything else I would do, and at night sit by a fire of wood that I had chopped myself. Her mind went back to the hours she had spent with old Saunders, the estate woodman, and to the day when, suddenly yielding to her persuasions, he had allowed her to fell a tree. The noise of the axe chiming through the silent plantation was in her ears, and the cry and harsh rustle of the falling tree. That afternoon her parents had given a dinner-party, and she had been allowed to sit with the ladies in the drawing-room, pulling the silk mittens over her blistered palms, thinking to herself: Today I felled a tree. Saunders, no wonder, had kept his own counsel, and no one else had ever known. Now she went the round of her woods with young Saunders, nodding her agreement as he chalked the trees due for felling; but still her glance could find the mossy hollow whence the root of her tree had been stubbed out. "For it is my own mark I want to leave," she exclaimed, striking her hand against the rock. "Not always to work my will through others."

She had still more than an hour of liberty before she must remember the second train and walk back; yet already a liberty in which she had nothing to do was irksome to her. Should she walk further? paddle her feet in the stream? The one was pointless, the other childish. It was boring to be a woman, nothing that one did had any meat in it. And her peculiar freedom, well incomed, dishusbanded, seemed now only to increase the impotence of her life. Free as she might be to do as she pleased, all her doings were barrened. Should she have her horse saddled in the middle of the night, ride through the dark and the rough weather till morning, she rode to no end. Should she enforce her will over convention, go out into her woods and cut down another tree, the deed would be granted to her only on the terms that it was a woman's whim, a nonsense to be tidied up as soon as possible by the responsible part of the world. If she were to shoot a poacher, the Justices of the Peace would huddle it away as an accident. Yes, they would say that she was frightened, a timid female acting in fear of her life. She could do nothing out of doors, a woman's sphere was the home. Yet, there, what could she do to appease her desire to leave a mark? The cook made the jams, which anyhow were eaten by the following summer; she had no talent for painting in water-colours, and certainly she could not write a novel. Needlework and embroidery? Often her longing had turned to these, and fingering the quilts and bed-hangings worked by the bygone women of her race she had most passionately envied them their power to leave behind them something solid and respectable, envied them the solace which could accompany them through the long idleness of a woman's life. Her bureaux were filled with beginnings: lace-pillows with rusty pins, crumpled canvases with half a parrot's wing embroidered; but her hands, so strong and shapely, could not manage a needle, bungled and grew weak before their natural employment.

In thoughts like these her last hour of liberty trailed by, and at last she was glad to get up, shake out her skirts, tie on her bonnet, and go. The stream kept her company down the valley, an idle influence, turning no millwheels, running happily to waste. She had drunk of it; but she could not drink of its brilliant peace.

During the journey she stared sometimes at the landscape through the mesh of her veil, sometimes at the mesh itself, eyeing this needle-run entanglement as though it were something alien and inexplicable, a puzzle set before her in a dream. At Exeter a young woman got into the carriage who carried a baby and was in tears. As soon as the train started she broke into conversation. Her talk was perfectly insipid, alternately self-pity and brag, and Sophia found herself listening with pleasure, glad of any distraction from her own thoughts. For any forward thinking travelled only to boredom, and she would not let her thoughts turn backward, lest they should recall the events of yesterday, the iron sense of doom which had so oppressed her, that terrifying evening at the Half Moon Inn.

Mrs. Henry Woolby, daughter of the late Canon Pawsey, lasted till Dorchester, where Sophia got out, hearing as she did so that life was so cruelly full of partings, and that Mrs. Woolby's address was 7, Marine Terrace, Dawlish.

Her groom was beside her, holding the dressing-case. She turned to give him her ticket.

"Good evening, Roger. Is all well?"

She heard him catch his breath, and now looked at him. His face was flushed, she thought he had been drinking.

"Master Damian, Madam, and Miss Augusta. They're queer."

"What?"

"Miss Augusta, Madam, she was took queer late last night. And this morning Master Damian was queer, too."

"Has the doctor been sent for?"

"Yes, Madam. Grew fetched him this morning."

"What did he say?"

"I'm sure I don't know, Madam. But I understand he said it might be the smallpox."

She saw again the blank face of the Trebennick Academy, the staring sunset, the empty porch whence Caspar had already been whisked. But it was not he whom she would never see again. It was her own children, the fruit of her forsaken womb.

Once I am at the house, she thought, driving between the ripened cornfields, I can get to work. I am only a little late, four hours' delay cannot count for so much. Already she felt the need to exculpate herself; and since destiny cannot be wheedled, and since in any crisis her nature turned not to God but to destiny, she would brazen it out. Yet in turning rather to destiny she was like one who seeks shelter. God, an enormous darkness, hung looped over half her sky, an ever-present menace, a cloud waiting to break. In the antipodes of God was destiny, was reason —a small classical temple in a clear far-off light, just such a temple as shone opposed to a stormcloud in the landscape by Claude Lorrain that all her life long had hung in the dining-room. Small and ghostly were the serene figures that ministered there, a different breed to the anxious pilgrims who in the foreground rested under the gnarled tree, turning, some, to the far-off temple, some to the cloud where lightnings already flashed. God was a cloud, lightnings were round about his seat; and though the children must pray to Jesus, and Mrs. Willoughby support the Church of England, Sophia, even in her childhood, had disliked God exactly as she disliked adders, earthquakes, revolutions—anything that lurked and was deadly, any adversary that walked in darkness. For God, her being knew, meant her no good. He had something against her, she was not one of those in whom he delighted. Now in his cloud he had come suddenly close, had reared up close behind her—at her back, as usual, for God was not an honest British pugilist. But once at the house, she thought—and already the carriage was turning in at the lodge gate—she could get to work.

Seeing the children, all her sense of competence fell off her. They were not her children who lay there, her children biddable and comprehensible. They were the fever's children, they were possessed; devils had entered into them, and looked with burning sullen glare from their heavy eyes. A devil strengthened Augusta's hand to strike at her when she bent down to smooth the damp curls; a devil with a thick strange voice answered her from Damian's mouth—mocking her with answers at random.

The doctor was there, waiting for her arrival. He had sent for a Mrs. Kerridge, who would do everything, who understood these cases.

"The less you see them," said he, "the better."

"Infection? I don't fear it. I never catch anything," she answered.

He shook his head. "Even so, a stranger is best. In any fever, the essential is discipline."

His voice was grim, but his eyes pitied her.

"Have you no one to be with you?" he said.

She shook her head. She knew what would come next—a hint, an inquiry, about Frederick. She put out her will and stopped it. Later that evening, wearing a flustered mixture of every-day clothes and a best pelisse and gloves, came the doctor's wife—a flimsy little boarding-school creature, much too young and genteel, thought Sophia, to be any good to the broad-backed bottle-nosed doctor, a man as stolidly cunning as his hairy-legged hunter. And she could hear the conversation between them. "You must go, my dear. You're at home in a drawing-room, you'll understand her better than I." And then, "Oh no, Henry, I couldn't dare such a thing. I'm far too shy." However, the faculty had prescribed her—or perhaps she was the pink colouring. Anyhow, there she sat, crumpling a lace pocket-handkerchief, staring at Sophia and hurriedly averting her gaze to the tea-urn. "I do so feel for you. It is so terrible that you should be alone," was as far as she got. Yet, silly, common, timid as she might be, there was a certain reviving quality about her company. Like a glass of *eau sucrée,* thought Sophia. It is deplorable that one should find solace in such wash, yet in that year of being finished in Paris under the guardianship of great-aunt Léocadie she had often found pleasure in *eau sucrée.* And those were beautiful eyes, eyes that could be admired without any social embarrassment, for eyes are enfranchised from any question of breeding, a variety of flesh so specialized as to transcend what else conditions a face into being well-bred or common, worn, a precious jewel, in any head. The lips might simper, the hands twist uneasily; but the beautiful eyes dwelt on her with an attention beyond curiosity or adulation. I never want to see you again, thought Sophia, duly begging her visitor to stay a little longer, but I shall never forget your eyes.

But she was gone, almost running from the room after a sudden awkward embrace. "Mrs. Willoughby, I can't express to you how I feel!" Hot, a little roughened, her lips had been like those of a child. "She might be in love with me," said Sophia, picking up the childish glove, so creased and warm. "Now I suppose she will go home and dash off some verses in her album. For she certainly keeps an album. Poor little creature, she must get out of these sentimental ways if she is to be a doctor's wife." And putting away the glove in a drawer, she wrote in her notebook a memorandum that tomorrow a glove must be returned, flowers sent to Mrs. Hervey. Left to herself again, the terrors of her situation—strange that a chit like this should have been able to keep them at bay—thundered back on her again, and God was again a lowering cloud, and she must do all she could to establish herself as methodical and undismayed.

The clock struck eleven, its calm silver voice suddenly enlarging the expanse of the empty room. She looked up, raising her forehead from her hand, opening her eyes. She stared about her, searching for a bunch of dying foxgloves in a white jar. Her being had sunk back to the previous night, she was again in the sitting-room of the Half Moon Inn, with the lamplight hot on her cold sweating forehead and the moths flying in at the open window; she was locked in the same desperate cold trance. But now she knew what it was that oppressed her so deathlily. Not Caspar's death, nor her own, but the death of her children had breathed so cold on her. For they would die, they would die! And through what untold stretches of time she must stumble, bearing the load of this knowledge, while yet they lived. Every minute was there to be lived through, methodical as the bricks in a prison wall. There could be no escape from this torment until despair came after it. How long did it take for a child to die of smallpox? A week, perhaps, or longer. Everything would go on, the fields be reaped, fruit ripen, meals appear and be taken away. The grass would grow, stealthily the grass would grow, as it grows on lawns, as it grows on graves. Two days ago, while her children had been quarrelling, the lawn had been mown and its edges sheared. It would need to be mown again, once, twice, before they were dead. For a blade of grass cannot be turned aside, any more than the scythe death swings so steadily, so skilfully. With this to come, with this to endure before its coming, how could she pass the time until the death of her children? There was nothing she could do. Mrs. Kerridge was perfectly qualified, could take charge of everything in the sick-room. The laundrymaid could wash bed-linen, the cook could make gruel, the housemaid empty slops, the scullion scour dishes. Everyone else was provided for, had something to do to pass the time, some service to mitigate their care. But for her, the mother, there was nothing. She must wait, idle, and alone.

Treading like a thief she went through her house so strange to her, and up the stairs, and along the passage to the night nursery door. A chink of light shone from under it, there was no sound within. They are dead already, she thought, waiting outside. But no, they were asleep, in a sound sleep, the two of them, a sleep that would do them good. Being so well asleep, she might open the door, steal in, look at them? But then they might waken, and the good of their sleep be undone. She must stay outside. Shivering and burning she waited, and down the hall the clock ticked. Suddenly there was a whimper, a stir, a weak melancholy whining that seemed as though it must go on for ever. She turned the handle, and went in. Mrs. Kerridge, enormous in the candlelight, was bending over Augusta's cot. She turned, and moved heavily and noiselessly towards the door, her finger to her lips.

"How are they?"

"The boy's asleep. The girl has just awakened, she's fretful. But I don't mind that, that's a good sign."

"Let me come to her."

"No, Madam. It's best not. Maybe she wouldn't know you. If she did, she'd fret worse. She's thirsty, you see. Best leave her alone, and she'll go off again."

The door was closed upon her, she stood again in the passage, listening to that endless whine. At last, sighing like some oppressed animal, she turned and went obediently downstairs. Stupid with anguish she unlocked the garden door, and walked up and down the lawn, looking at the dim wavering light from the night nursery windows. Once the shadow of Mrs. Kerridge crossed the blind, slow and towering.

It seemed on the morrow that everyone she encountered had only two things to say: first, the children's illness; next, fine weather for the harvest. Even Dr. Hervey, patting his horse's neck, sunk in a final silence which rebuffed any further question from her, and yet apparently unable to mount and leave her, must needs at last say: "Splendid weather, this. Just what the farmers want. If only it lasts."

It seemed as though it would last for ever, as though the unmoving air were a block of heat set down on the earth. Time could scarcely press its way through it, the minute-hand of the clock flagged, seemed wavering to a standstill. All the windows stood open, but no refreshment came in. Through the countryside, on the burning upland fields, the harvest was being reaped, the men stooping, sickle in hand, working like automatons, only pausing at the hedgerows to gather another handful of docks to plaster under their sweaty shirts. For such God-sent weather as this was not to be wasted. The overseers were among the men, seeing to it that they kept to their labour. To and fro from the cornfields trailed little processions of women, carrying water, or cold tea. Into some fields a farmer might cause a cask of soured cider to be carried. But this was a dubious measure. Though at first the men might seem to work the better for it, by the end of the day half a dozen of the weaker would be lying under the hedge, writhing and powerless with colic.

The trees of the park, heavily mustering, cut off the world of the Aspens from the drought of the working world. Deep in the branches the wood-pigeons cooed. Shoots of iridescent spray filled the green-houses, the little fountain plashed, at dusk the flower-beds were watered. But thirst was in this world also. From the night nursery sounded the endless weak wail of the children, craving for the water that their treatment denied them. Mrs. Kerridge, who knew everything, knew that fever patients must not be allowed to drink beyond a regulated allowance. A little wine they might have, a little warm soup; but not water lest the fever being for a moment checked, the eruption should be driven inward.

For five days the heat never slackened, and only on the sixth day did a thin brownish vapour begin to steal up from the westward, muffling the sun as it lowered. With dusk, a furtive wind got up, stirring the hot air. All day long Sophia had been framing in her mind the letter which must be sent to Frederick. It must be sent, it was a matter of propriety, of self-respect. Yet the day was over, and she had not set pen to paper. It was not wounded pride that prevented her. She had more pride than the pride that had been wounded, she was proud as a woman as well as proud as a wife; and woman's pride knew that it had more to suffer by Frederick's absence than by his recall. Were he not to come, people would talk, would surmise. Already they must be doing so; their silence before her was the index of how they prated behind her back. That Mrs. Willoughby's children should be in danger of death and that Mr. Willoughby should remain on the Continent would drag her through a shame far deeper, far more sullying than the private disgrace of having beckoned him to return.

But the summons pride would have sent, envy kept back. Too well she knew what the quality of Frederick's grief would be;

how naturally, how purely his sorrow would run, how spontaneously he would feel all that she must feel with anguish, with difficulty and torment. He would melt, where she must be ground small. His heart's-blood would run freely, where hers stagnated like old Seneca's. For as she had given birth to her children, she would lose them: with throe after sickening throe, with effort, and humiliation, with clumsy, furious, disgraceful striving, with hideous afterbirth of all her hopes. But for Frederick it would be all an emotion, a something that afterwards music could call up, or the first snowdrops, or a page of poetry. And lanced for his spirit's health by the death of his children, he would go back, quiveringly consolable, to be comforted by Minna Lemuel.

But write I will, she said to herself. There was the escritoire, and the inkstand, and the mother-of-pearl blotter which she had used when last she wrote to Frederick. I will write, and Roger shall take in the letter the first thing tomorrow morning. But the room was heavy with her resentment, she would walk in the park a little, to clear her head.

The light shone from the nursery windows, the wailing cry hung on her hearing. She turned her back, and walked swiftly across the parched turf, her glance on the ground, walking without direction. Presently she knew that the glimmer of water was before her. She had come to the boat-house by the lake. A screen of poplars grew beside it, the hot wind stirred them, slightly, raspingly, as though it were a cat's tongue, licking. Against the piles of the boat-house the water slapped, lightly and rhythmically. Then, in a moment, as though a hand had grasped their trunks and shaken them, the poplars swayed violently, bending almost to earth, struggling to rear again against the grip of air that held them, a wave, and a second wave, smacked against the echoing boat-house, and staring into the water she saw a brilliant sword of light strike up at her.

In a moment the thunder-clap was about her ears. She turned and ran, remembering only her children's terror of thunderstorms. In the distance between the lake and the house the rain had come, drenching her to the skin. Into the house and up the stairs the lightning pursued her, brandishing before her steps. But the house was silent, they must still be asleep.

As she pushed open the heavy door, a voice came into her hearing.

"Don't drop me, don't drop me! I will keep my eyes shut, I promise not to look. Oh! . . . Burning! That's hell, sister! But I didn't look, I kept my eyes shut. Don't drop me! I saw nothing, only those hairy arms. O Devil, don't drop me. *That's Satan, you know.* For in six days the Lord made heaven and earth, thy man-servant and thy maid-servant, thy cattle and all the stranger that is within thy gates. No! For in six days the Lord made heaven and earth. . . . Don't drop me, don't drop me! My mouth's hot. I looked at hell with my mouth, my mouth's burning. Hannah! Come and take hell out of my mouth, take it out, I say! And our mouths shall show forth thy praise. For in six days. . . . Three sixes are eighteen, are eighteen, four sixes are twenty-four, five sixes are hairy. In among the hairs are spots, like little hot mouths. Don't drop me, *don't drop me!*"

His hands were fastened, that he might not tear himself to pieces. His face and neck were covered with sores, sores were on his eyelids, sealing up his eyes. His hair stood out, stiff and bristling, as though the fever had singed it. Out of this horrible body, speckled with sores, swollen as though the poison within might at any moment explode it, the clear childish voice bubbled senseless as the tinkle of a fountain.

"Poor little lamb," said Mrs. Kerridge, tightening the bedclothes with her bleak hands. "It's wonderful how he keeps on about hell. But they often do, children. Not that they know what they're talking about, you know, for they don't. You couldn't expect that."

Sophia turned to the other bed. Out of the circle of the candle-light, its semi-darkness was lanced by the quivering blue flare of the lightning. Augusta lay there unstirring, unafraid. Her mouth was open and she snored, and choked with phlegm. As the lightning flickered out and the thunder pealed, obliterating the noise of her breath, she seemed to go under like someone drowning, wearily rising to the surface again with the ensuing silence.

Mrs. Kerridge had followed Sophia, and stood behind her, shaking her head slowly.

"She doesn't fight like her brother do."

"I was afraid the storm would wake her. She is terrified of thunder-storms."

Mrs. Kerridge did not answer.

Which of them will die first? The question rose to her lips, but she did not utter it. If the woman could say, she would not speak truly. No one ever spoke the truth in a sickroom. And they would both die, and since die they must, the sooner the better. For already her own children, the children she loved, were dead. This tinkling little maniac, corrupting under her eyes, this snoring choking slug that lay couched so slyly under the lightning, these were not her children. Her own life had ceased in them, they were fever's children, not hers. Through the smell of the vinegar she could smell the foulness of their disease. "When did I love them last?" she asked herself. "Not when I left them to go to Cornwall. I was ashamed of them then. When Caspar was here, yes, for then they were well. But mostly they have been a care to me, a thing that must always be tended, made allowances for, buttressed up, remedied. Like a wound in me that would never quite heal, that must perpetually be cleansed and dressed. No, I have scarcely ever had time to love them, my mind divided between pitying them as they were, and glorifying them as they would be; as they would be when all their ailments and deficiencies were fought through and done with. A devoted mother. That is what I have been, that is what people have said, will say of me. But devotion is not love. It grovels, fears, forebodes, lies to itself or to others. Devotion is a spaniel's trick, it is what the animal feeling of a mother turns into when it is cowed. An animal instinct cowed, that is what I have chiefly known. And now that fails me. My children are dying, and all that I can truly say I feel is resentment that I have been made a fool of. Damian's chatter maddens me, I could not touch either of them without a shudder, though at this moment I could easily lay down my life for them. But that is not love, that is devotion, devotion exasperated to its last act, the spaniel driven mad."

Mrs. Kerridge's stare was gradually propelling her from the room. As the door closed she heard Damian's raving veer back to the lime-kiln again. The sullenness of one unjustly condemned took possession of her thoughts. What a doom, that whatever I have done for the best should turn into whips and scorpions. The lime-kiln that was to cure their whooping-cough is now a hell that he must dangle over, past help of any snatching. The lime-kiln. Under the uproar of the storm she recalled with feverish accuracy every step of that journey; how, setting out, her thoughts had been of that long-ago expedition to see the Duke of Wellington, thoughts turned by the sight of the chestnut tree to an upswelling of maternal pride. She had felt herself stand up, a fortress, drawing out of the earth, out of the past, the nourishment which should feed and forward her ripening children. Dull, brooding, disblossomed, the chestnut had been she. And so they had gone on, walking between the songless July hedges, and over the parched fields, where the hoes had chinked against the flints. Edmunds, leaving his work, had come fawning up, ready to snatch an excuse for idling and gossip even from her austere disapproval. Then leaving the fields they had gone up the steep track to where the lime-kiln stood on its grassy plateau with the heated air trembling above it. He had been asleep, his head bowed on his knees, his hands dangling; even at their departure, as he had stood watching them go down the lane, he had seemed like one sleep-walking. In his attitude, in his fixed stare, he had been like one beholding a vision, some fixed and grim hallucination of fever. For all his stare, she had thought, it is as though he does not see us. Hannah had gossiped a little about him afterwards. A rough solitary man, she had said, choosing of his own accord that life of uncouth solitude, a stranger from across the county, without kith or kin, and going only to the alehouse to buy a bottle to take away. Yet it was said that women would go to him, stealing to him by night, guided by the red glare of his kiln upon the dark hillside. A foul-living man, Hannah said. Had she not noticed the sores upon his wrists?

In the space between the lightning blearing the window and shuddering out again, Sophia knew that it was to this man, to those arms, already opening in the sores of smallpox, that she had entrusted her children. Like the flash of lightning the certainty had dived into her heart and vanished, leaving only darkness. Without a falter her body went on its way, moving neatly and composedly through the sound of the thunder-clap; as though wound up like a toy it carried her up and down the long drawing-room, even remembering, so skilful the mechanical body is, to wring its hands. Someone was there, watching her. She did not know who, or care.

"Oh!"

At the trembling whine of terror she stopped, came to herself. There, pressed into a corner, holding out something in her gloved hands, was Mrs. Hervey. Her drenched clothes hung limp on her, her hair dangled in streaks along her cheeks, her eyes were black with fear and her mouth was open. Now, in a sudden swoop like a terrified bird she rushed forward and fell on her knees before Sophia.

"Oh, Mrs. Willoughby, forgive me, if I've done wrong! But I felt I had to come to you."

With her gloved hands, slimy and cold, she had caught hold of Sophia's hand.

"I don't know what you'll think of me, coming like this. No one knows I'm here, I came in through the window. But I had to come."

"You must have some wine. I'll fetch you some. Or would you rather have tea?"

"Oh no, nothing. I implore you, don't trouble to fetch anything."

"Here are some salts."

When she returned with wine and biscuits, Sophia found the young woman sitting on the smallest chair in the room, snuffing at the vinaigrette. Though she was shaking from head to foot she had composed herself into a ladylike posture, and could stammer out her speech of, "Oh, how very kind of you. No, not as much as that, if you please."

"Drink it down," said Sophia, and tilted the glass at her lips.

The wine was swallowed, biscuits were refused. The storm continued, a musketry of rain rattling against the windows. With so much noise around the house it seemed impossible that any conversation should ever take place. My children are dying, thought Sophia, and I must sit here, dosing this little ninny with port and waiting to hear what hysterical fool's errand brought her. Yet she felt no anger towards the downcast figure, so childish in its grown-up fripperies, so nonsensical in its drenched elegance. You should be at home and in bed, warm beside your snoring old husband, she thought—a sudden dash of tenderness and amusement redeeming her dry misery, so that she was almost glad that, instead, Mrs. Hervey was here, blown in at the window like a draggled bird.

She filled the glass again.

But the bird had revived into a boarding-school miss, and with an exasperating gesture of refinement, waved it away. Then, sitting bolt upright, and opening her eyes as though that must precede opening her mouth she began impressively.

"I have done something that I know is very indiscreet. I am quite prepared to be reproached for it.

"The wife of a medical man," continued Mrs. Hervey, "is in a very delicate position. Officially, she should know nothing. But it is impossible to take *no* interest, especially where one's feelings are engaged."

If you were not so much on your best behaviour, thought Sophia, you would be telling me that I know what husbands are like, don't I. The eyes had no charm for her now. Too disdainful for either a true word or a civil one, she set her lips closer, and inclined her head for sole assent.

But her wrath had showed out. The young woman paled and shrank.

"I have thought of you day and night, ever since that first evening when your children were taken ill and my husband sent me to you. You can't understand, and I can't express it. It's more than pity, than sympathy, for I have heard other people pitying you, people who know you better than I, women with children of their own. But they don't feel as I do. But that's not it, that's not what I came here to say. I would not put myself forward to tell you that."

She stopped on her flow of words as abruptly as a wren ceases in mid-song, and turned her face aside as though to hide her tears.

"Though that had been all you came for, I should be very grateful to you for coming."

Stiff and sincere, the words once spoken seemed completely beside the point, and Sophia had the sensation that she had snubbed without meaning to. If snub it were, the young woman ignored it, preoccupied in nerving herself to speak again.

"Mrs. Willoughby, when I came that evening, I came at my husband's bidding, and I came with a purpose. There was something I had to say to you. But I did not, I could not, say it. You did not guess."

"I did," said Sophia gently. "You came because Dr. Hervey had told you to find out if I had sent for my husband."

"And I wouldn't!" the girl cried out with something like exultation.

"And now, I suppose," continued Sophia, "you have been sent on the same errand."

"No! I have refused. I have told him, nothing would make me do it."

"Why?"

The look that answered this made her ashamed. Like a reflection of her shame a deep flush covered Mrs. Hervey's face. Reddened as a schoolgirl in fault, she drew herself up and began to speak with something of her former stiffness.

"You have asked me why I have come, and no doubt my visit must seem ill-timed and peculiar. I told you that I was prepared for censure. This is my reason for coming."

She held out a letter. It was addressed to Frederick in Dr. Hervey's handwriting.

"I stole it," she said. In her voice there was almost reverence for such a deed, and the pupils of her eyes, suddenly enlarging, seemed to rush towards Sophia like two black moons falling through a cloud.

"He gave it to me yesterday, to post. And I have had it ever since."

But we might be two schoolgirls, thought Sophia, two romantic misses, stolen from our white beds to exchange illicit comfits, and trembling lest amid this stage-rattling thunder-storm we should hear the footsteps of Mrs. Goodchild. The letter, lying so calmly on her lap, seemed to have no real part in this to-do. Some other motive, violent and inexperienced as the emotions of youth, trembled undeclared between them.

"For why should all this be done behind your back?" exclaimed the girl passionately. "What right have they to interfere, to discuss and plot, and settle what they think best to be done? As if, whatever happened, you could not stand alone, and judge for yourself! As if you needed a man!"

The letter fell to the floor as Sophia rose and leaned her arm upon the steady cold of the marble mantelshelf and shielded her face with her hand. There was something to be done, if she could but remember what, something practical, proper and immediate. She had been staring at a white china ornament, and now, as she shut her eyes, its small glittering point of light seemed to pierce through her eyelids, and to become the immutable focus upon which her thoughts must settle and determine. Slowly she composed herself, was presently all composure; and round her steadied mind she felt her flesh hanging cold and forlorn, as though in this conflict she had for ever abandoned it.

The girl had risen too. As Sophia turned to her she said,

"I see you want me to go. Forgive me."

"There is nothing to forgive. You have acted very well. It is a long time since anyone has dealt by me with such honesty. I wish I could answer your generous impulse with equal truth. But I am too old, too wary of the world, to match you."

She stooped for the letter, and put it back into the unresisting hands.

"This must go. And Dr. Hervey must never know that you brought it here."

The girl sighed.

"Your guess was right, or your instinct. I do not want my husband to return. But whether he comes or no will make little real difference to me. Mine is a spoilt marriage. Yours is not, and I cannot let you endanger it."

The rain had ceased, the storm was retreating. Though the air resounded with the noise of water, it was with the drips splashing from the roof-gutters, or the moisture fitfully cascading from the branches when the dying wind wagged them.

"I will have the horses put in, and you shall be driven back."

"Let me walk," said the girl.

Common sense and civility yielded as Sophia looked at her guest. Unspeaking she picked up a shawl, and as though in some strange pre-ordered consent they left the house by the French window, and walked side by side down the avenue. Iced with the storm, the air was like the air of a new world, the darkness was like the virgin dusk of a new world emerging from chaos, slowly and blindly wheeling towards its first day. Far off the storm winked and muttered, but louder than its thunder was the sipping whistle, all around them, of the parched ground drinking the rain. Half-way down the avenue Sophia took the girl's hand. It was ungloved now, cold and wet, and lay in her clasp like a leaf. So, grave and unspeaking, linked childishly together they went on under the trees, their footsteps scarcely audible among the sounds of the heavily dripping rain and the drinking earth.

She returned alone to the empty lighted drawing-room, to Mrs. Hervey's chair pulled forward, and the decanter and the glass and the biscuits. They must be put away, she thought, all traces of this extraordinary visit; and as she carried the wine and the biscuits to the pantry she found herself stiffening with a curious implacability. No; however touching, such escapades were intolerable. One could not have such young women frisking round one, babbling as to whether or no one needed a husband, declaring on one's behalf that one didn't. From a woman of the village she could have heard such words without offence. Down there, in that lowest class, sexual decorum could be kilted out of the way like an impeding petticoat; and Mary Bugler, whose husband was in jail, and Carry Westmacott, whose husband should be, might declare without offence that a woman was as good as a man, and better. In her own heart, too, unreproved, could lodge the conviction that a Sophia might well discard a Frederick, and in her life she had been ready, calmly enough, to put this into effect. But into words, never! Such things could be done, but not said. And was it for the doctor's wife, an immature little feather-pate, to pipe up in her treble voice, in her tones of provincial refinement, that Mrs. Willoughby did not need Mr. Willoughby?

Setting back the chair, glancing sharply about the room—last time she had left a glove—Sophia shook her head in condemnation. This visit had left no visible trace of Mrs. Hervey. But in this room, the serene demonstration of how a lady of the upper classes spends her leisure amid flowers and books and arts, words had been spoken such as those walls had never heard before. And to hear her own thought voiced she, the lady of the room, had had to await the coming of this interloper, this social minikin, this Thomasina Thumb who, riding on a cat and waving a bodkin, had come to be her champion.

The next morning, she sent off a letter to Frederick, coldly annoyed with herself for neglecting an essential formality—for with the putting of pen to paper it had become no more than that. Absent or present, he could not affect her now. The servants would make his bed, serve his food; she, trained better than they in her particular service of hostess-ship, would entertain him, a guest for the funeral. And then he would be gone again, back to his Minna, the only trace of his visit some additional entries in the household books. For there can be no middle way, she thought, where extremes have been attempted; and Frederick, failing to be my husband, must now be to me less than an acquaintance.

"As if you needed a man." Mrs. Hervey's words renewed themselves in her hearing, spoken with an indignant conviction blazing against the soberer colouring of Sophia's own view of the case: that she could get on better without one. In some ways men were essential. One must have a coachman, a gardener, a doctor, a lawyer—even a clergyman. These served their purpose and withdrew—some less briskly than others, she reflected, seeing Mr. Harwood walking up the avenue. He had visited her daily, to inquire after the children and offer, she supposed, spiritual consolation. Apparently the presence of a clergyman of the Church of England in her morning-room was consolation enough, as though, like some moral vinaigrette, he had but to be filled by a Bishop, introduced, unstoppered, and gently waved about the room, to diffuse a refreshing atmosphere. To visit widows in their affliction, she thought, moving the decanter towards him, was part of his duties. Possibly she was not sufficiently a widow to call out his most reviving gales. But indeed, beyond a pleasant civility and a rather tedious flow of chit-chat, no more was to be expected of him. He gave away very respectable soup, and preached sensible sermons, and his cucumber frames were undoubtedly the most successful in the village. What more to ask, except that he should soon go away? She had often congratulated herself that the parish was served by such a rational exponent of Christianity.

Today, of course, they discussed the storm.

"This cooler air," said he, "must certainly be of assistance to your little invalids. We may, indeed, consider the storm (since you tell me it did not alarm them) as providential. I understand, too, that nearly all the corn was already cut, so that the harvest will not be endangered."

Tithes, thought Sophia.

God was a cloud, lightnings were round about his seat. But Mr. Harwood was unaware of this, and good manners forbade that she should hint it to him. Instead, she found herself thanking him warmly for his promise of balsam seed, well ripened by the hot summer. If brought on under glass and transferred to a southern aspect, she should have a fine show of plants next summer.

For everything would go on, and she with it, broken on the wheeling year. Next summer would come, and she would walk in the silent garden, her black dress trailing, her empty heart stuffed up like an old rat-hole with insignificant cares, her ambition for seemliness and prosperity driving her on to oversee the pruning of trees, the trimming of hedges, the tillage of her lands, the increase of her stock. Urged and directed by her will, everything would go on, though to no end. The balsams would bloom, and she be proud of them.

If I were a man, she thought, I would plunge into dissipation.

What dissipation is to a man, religion is to a woman. Would it be possible to become a Roman Catholic and go into a convent? No, never for her! Of the two alternatives dissipation seemed the more feasible. For though she could not imagine how it might be contrived, since both to wine and the love of man she opposed an immovably good head, yet, could a suitable dissipation be devised, she might find in herself a will for it; but under no circumstances could she yield herself to devotion. There was gaming, she remembered; that was possible to women. And for a moment she paused to consider herself contracted into an anguished ecstasy that the croupier's rake could thrust or gather. Gaming might do; yet in its very fever it was cold, and if she were to survive, she must be warmed—she so frigid to wine and the love of man. There was ambition. That should fit her, with her long-breathed resolution, her clear head and love of dominance. But how should a woman satisfy ambition unless acting upon and through a man—and how control a man by resolution or reason, when any pretty face or leaning bosom could deflect him?

Far off stood the shade of Papa, speaking of philosophy and the calm joys of an elevated mind. True, Papa spoke also of the inconvenience of blue-stockings, pointing to his own mother as a model of all a daughter should be—Grandmamma, thick, dumpy, and perfumed, her creaking stomacher rising and falling under her gloved and folded hands, saying, "Come, little Sophia. You must not run about in the sun. Fetch your needlework, and sit by me." Yet, avoiding blue-stockings, one might yet find some succour from Papa and intellectual pursuits—take up chemistry or archaeology, study languages, travel. A woman cannot travel alone, but two women may travel together; and Sophia for a moment beheld herself standing upon a bridge, a blue river beneath her, a romantic gabled golden town and purple mountains behind, and at her side, large-eyed and delighted and clutching a box of watercolour paints, Mrs. Hervey.

O foolish vision! Even were not Mrs. Hervey stoutly wedded to her apothecary, how could one long endure such a wavering mixture of impulse and impertinence, sensibility and false refinement?

It is because she was kind to me, she thought, that my mind turns to her. She is young, silly, and can do nothing, yet she came to me in kindness, offering to my aridity a refreshment not germane at all to what she really is, but a dew of being young and impulsive. Caspar is such another, if he were here I should cling to him, listen to his music, solace myself with his unconscious grace of being young, and malleable, and alive. Should I adopt him, bring him here in the stead of my children? A black heir to Blandamer? Impossible! Though I have will enough to enforce it, the resentment of those I force would hound him out, all but his actual black body. And indeed, could I long endure to have this pretty soft wagging black spaniel in the place of my children?

Most of the time it seemed to her inevitable that both children should die. Then, more irrational than the conviction of their doom, would come a conviction of their recovery. Hope would twitch her to her feet, set her running towards the night nursery where she should hear from Mrs. Kerridge indubitable symptoms of a turn for the better. And half-way there fear would stay her, bidding her sit down again, continue what occupation she had, taste, as long as it might linger, the hope so exactly fellowed to the previous hopes which inquiry had demolished.

Damian, Mrs. Kerridge and the doctor said, was making the better fight. Yet it was Damian who died first, collapsing suddenly, and dying with a little gasp like a breaking bubble. Two hours later Frederick entered the house. Sophia expected him, yet when the carriage came to the door she ran out by the long window, spying from behind a tree at the intruder, come so inopportunely upon her misery. Whoever it is, she thought, not recognizing her own horses, I will not see him. I will hide.

A foreigner, her mind said, in the instant before recognition. He ran up the steps and stood talking to Johnson, who had opened the door. She advanced, slowly mounting the steps behind him, knowing herself unseen by him. She seemed to be stalking a prey, and on Johnson's countenance she read with how much surmise and excitement her household awaited this meeting.

Why doesn't he turn round, she thought. I cannot touch him, and I don't want to speak, lest my voice should break, and deliver me over to him.

"Here is Mrs. Willoughby, Sir."

As though I were the coffee, she thought; and her lips were moving into a smile when he turned to her.

"Sophia!"

His voice had altered. There was a new note in it, he had lost his drawl. She said,

"Damian is dead. Do you know? I can't remember if he died before the carriage started for you."

He bowed his head.

"Johnson has told me."

She saw that the horses were sweating. They must go to the stables, life must continue.

"You will be tired with your journey. Come in."

Now which chair will you take, she thought—your old one?

But he remained on his feet, walking up and down the room, as though, again under that roof, the habit of his former listless pacing piped its old tune to him. To the window, and turning, to the portrait of grandpapa Aspen, and back to the window again, his advance and retreat surveyed by that quiet old gentleman, who, as Gainsborough had painted him, seemed with his gun and supple wet-nosed retriever to be watching through the endless bronze dusk of an autumnal evening, paused on the brink of his spinney and listening with contemplative pleasure to the footsteps of the poacher within. *Benjamin Aspen Esq., J. P.,* stated the gold letters below. It had sometimes occurred to Sophia that it was as though Frederick, uneasily treading the Aspen estate, were the tribute of yet another poacher offered up to the implacable effigy. But now the poacher walked with a freer gait, a liberated air; and it was in this new manner, and in his subtly altered tone of voice, that Frederick halted by her chair and said,

"I will not make speeches, Sophia. But you must let me say how grateful I am to you for sending for me, how much I grieve that it is for this reason that you have had to break your resolution."

The moment for a reconciliation, she thought, with the more bitterness and annoyance since her sense acknowledged that never before had Frederick's demeanour expressed so patently, not merely an acceptance of their irreconcilability, but a will to it that might be equal to hers. She stared at his dusty boots, and said sourly,

"There wasn't much hope, Frederick, nor is there for Augusta. They neither have much stamina. The Willoughby constitution, I suppose."

To speak so was abominable, was the last thing she had wished to do. Nothing could retrieve the words, even had she not been too weary for an attempt. And feeling the blood labouring to her cheeks she sat unmoving, scorning to avert her shamed face, and fighting against a flood of self-pity.

"The devil of a disease." He spoke as though thinking aloud, voicing a train of thought which her words had not pierced. "Vaccination or not, it will get you if it has a mind to. And if you creep through it, it may leave a life not worth living." He went on to speak, as a traveller might, of the women in Paris who earned a livelihood as mattress-pickers, women whom smallpox had blinded. "They come from the Quinze-Vingts," he said. "A child leads them to the door, and fetches them again at the end of the day. One morning, one spring morning, I came across two of these women sitting on the floor of an empty bedroom in my hotel. The door was open, and I watched them for a little, thinking how quickly they separated the tufts of wool, and wondering that they should work so silently, for as you know it's queer to find two Parisians at work and not chattering. Their backs were towards me, but when I said 'Good day' they turned. Then I saw their faces, so scarred that it would not have been possible to say if they were old women or girls of nineteen, and instead of eyes, hollow sockets and sores. Death is better than that, Sophia."

How deeply changed he is, she thought. It is as though a stranger were speaking. That woman's influence, I suppose. But disciplined by the recollection of her last, abominable speech, she thrust down the thought of Minna Lemuel, and inquired as a hostess, speaking of food and refreshment.

"May I see Augusta?"

Of the two children Augusta had always been his favourite. More of an Aspen in character than the boy, it had been as though in her he wooed his last hope of her mother. An embarrassment of honour made Sophia turn away and talk to Mrs. Kerridge while Frederick stood by the sick child's bed. He had entered the room, she noticed, with a little parcel in his hand; and now, glancing over her shoulder, she saw that he had unpacked from it a white rose, very delicately contrived from feathers, light as a thistledown and sleek as spun glass. The small hand, so roughened and polluted, opened vaguely at the contact, clutched the toy and crumpled it, and let it fall.

"Speak to her, Frederick. She can't see you, but she may recognize your voice."

"*Ma fleur,*" he said. The small hand stirred on the coverlet, closed as though closing on the words, and presently fell open again.

After he had gone back to Paris and she was left alone with the leisure of the childless, those words, and the tone in which they were spoken, haunted her memory—according to her mood, an enigma, a nettle-sting, a caress. It was as though, at that moment, not Frederick, but someone unknown to her had stood by the bed of her dying child and said, *Ma fleur.* That it was said with feeling, yes. Frederick had always been sincerely sentimental, had in the early days of their marriage melted his voice even to her. That it was said gravely, Yes again. To have lost one child and know the other past keeping would darken any voice into gravity. But beyond this, and beyond anything her mind could unquarry, there remained a quality, part innocence, part a deep sophistication in sorrow, that must still fascinate and still elude her. The voice of one acquainted with grief. Not, as Frederick had been, suddenly swept into its shadow, but one long acknowledging it, a voice tuned for a lifetime, and for centuries of inherited lifetimes, to that particular note, falling since the beginning of the world in that melancholy acquiescent cadence, falling as wave after wave brings its sigh, long-swelled, and silently carried, and at last spoken and quenched on the shore.

Modelled on that Minna's Jewish contralto, she told herself, angrily stopping her ears against those two grave harp-notes. Accomplished mountebank, no doubt she could manage her voice to any appropriate timbre; and Frederick, who was always a copy-cat, a weathercock to any breeze that tickled him, had heard the right intonation, and unwittingly reproduced it.

To judge by Frederick, Minna must be a model of decorum. Throughout the difficult visit, he was amiable, tactful, unobtrusive. If it were not the Jewess's good effect, she said to herself, she had at last the answer to her old wonder: why Frederick, displeasing as a husband, should be so much in demand as a guest, should be summoned to Lincolnshire and London, Suffolk and Aix-les-Bains. For undoubtedly he was at Blandamer as a guest.

She had dreaded the intimacy which bereavement might engender; but he, avoiding the thistly touch-me-not which encumbered her behaviour, had exactly preserved the distance that must be between them. She had sickened, foreseeing the easy flow of his grief; it had flowed, but not to splash her. She had quailed, forecasting the social awkwardness which the funeral, the visits of condolence, the assemblage of Aspens and Willoughbys concurring to stamp down the turves over the death of a next generation, must entail. Weariness of body and mind, the apathy, half relief, half despair, that follows on bereavement, had partly muffled her; but even so, she had been conscious how well Frederick was managing, how deftly he had walked his slack rope between the head of the house and the outcast whose bag was ready packed, the tragedy once played out, for departure.

Correct as a mute, she told herself; faultless as some town tragedian supplying at a moment's notice the place of a disabled actor in a company of barn-stormers; polished and affable as the Prodigal may have been, returning to shame with his shamefully acquired graces the angry rustic integrity of the stay-at-home. A French polish!

His accent had improved, too. *Ma fleur.* The Frederick of their honeymoon, the heavy English dandy, sheltering behind her flounces with his, Damn it, Sophia, you must do the parley-vooing, had supplied his tongue as well as his wits. Were she to meet Minna, she must say, Madam, I congratulate you upon the progress in your pupil. But no doubt, with such a vast, such a cosmopolitan experience, you could scarcely fail with any sow's ear.

Thus, sooner or later, her thoughts brought her face to face with that woman, there to discharge her rage. Everything she saw, heard, did, in her solitary existence, and the solitariness of that existence itself, must remind her of the children she had lost. And remembering that loss, she must remember Frederick, and remembering, her candour must oblige her to remember how well he had behaved, detached, unobtrusive, unfailing. How when Mrs. Kerridge, resorting more and more to her professional secret gin, had oversipped the mark and come raging downstairs, declaiming in a tipsy fury against that slut of a kitchen-maid who had again, and as a personal affront, forgotten the nutmeg, he had intercepted and silenced her, sluiced her into sobriety, and sent her trembling back to her duties again. How, at the post-funeral luncheon, he had kept talk going, by some legerdemain removing the conversation to Central Europe, and even while speaking of the liberation of Poland managing to keep them all in a good temper. How with that account of the blinded mattress-pickers, he had patched over the afterwards of her atrocious speech, and yet had avoided seeming to change the subject. In the midst of such recollections, swelling under them and exploding through them, her bitterness against him would break out, and all his good behaviour, his detachment, his unobtrusiveness, his readiness, would seem a lackey's virtues and no more.

For it was in dancing attendance on his harlot that he had learned these embellishments—dancing attendance on a harlot, a school how much more rigorous than a wife, his very improvement demonstrated. As in that *Ma fleur,* which for all she could do still rang in her head, Minna Lemuel's voice resounded, in everything he had said or done he had borne witness to Minna, trailed her invisible presence through the house. Every alteration in him made up a portrait of her. What had the old Frederick cared for the liberation of Poland? What would those blinded mattress-pickers have been to him but two scarecrows, to be run away from in disgust and fear? But weak-minded and porous, he had yielded himself to his Minna, was saturated with her, and willy-nilly must exhale her, even in the house of his wife, even at the bedside of his child. It was as though she could smell Minna on him, as though he had brought bodily into the house the odour of his mistress.

But now he had rejoined her, and she was left alone in the leisure of the childless, to oversee her emptied house, methodically to destroy every remnant of her children, every toy and piece of childish apparel; for in her raging loss she could tolerate no sentiment of keepsakes, and in the burning of the bedding, the scouring of the sickroom, she saw a symbol of what her heart should do. Frederick was back with Minna, and she was done with them both. Telling herself this, in the next moment she would relapse, every consideration other than this a blind road that turned her back to the death of the children. If she remembered them, she must remember Frederick; and how remember Frederick without snuffing Minna? The children, Frederick, Minna. Through this order her thoughts ran, and at Minna stayed, ignobly fascinated, ignobly curious, until the next explosion of bitterness hurled her into a rage that could not think at all.

Presently she began to dream of her. Minna driving with Frederick in a painted circus chariot would appear on the horizon of the desert where she stood talking with Job Saunders the bailiff about a sowing of scarcity-root. The chariot would sweep nearer, bouncing lightly as a bubble over the ridges of sand, pass, and vanish, and presently reappear, persistent as a gad-fly. Or she would come on Minna alone, seated in her own morning-room, and suddenly know that she had been established there for weeks. Waking, she kept the sense of the dream's validity; the time of day, the position of a glove, every word spoken, remained. But there was always one blank. However she might interrogate her memory, or try by a stratagem of suddenness to surprise it of its secret, Minna's visage still eluded her.

At last, rather than expose herself to such dreams, she abjured sleeping. For many successive nights she went to her bedroom only that her maid should undress her, and to rumple the bedclothes into a look of having been slept in. Then, after the house was silent, she would get up, dress herself, and creep downstairs, where, lighting one of her secret stores of candles, she would read, or sort papers, or labour at one of those many unfinished pieces of needlework, or sometimes play a match of billiards with herself. Time went fast in these vigils, faster than it went by day, when a hundred insignificant duties nailed her down to this hour and that; and surprised that the night was over she would hear, beyond the curtained windows, the harsh bird-notes of autumn dawnings, and moving heavily with stiff cold limbs hid the traces of her vigil, and went back to her bed just before the household began to stir.

She had almost forgotten Mrs. Hervey. That strange interview on the night of the thunder-storm seemed as irrelevant as the incident of a fever dream, leaving nothing behind it that could supply any link between her and the young woman in the over-feathered bonnet whom she saw in church on Sundays. It needed the coming of quarter-day, and the arrival of Dr. Hervey's bill, to revive its memory. Then, finding her thoughts running on the doctor's wife, she gave them free rein, since it was better to be teased by Mrs. Hervey than by Minna. A visiting acquaintance between them was neither possible nor desirable; although they had walked hand in hand down the avenue, or rather because they had done so, a civil basket of dessert pears of a hothouse melon would be the properest acknowledgement of that evening visit and the misguided impulse which had prompted it.

Yet having chosen the melon Sophia went on from the hothouse to the stable, and left word there that the carriage was to be ready at midday to drive her to Mrs. Hervey's.

The Herveys lived at Long Blandamer, a village with genteel pretensions enough to support half a dozen shops, a neat Wesleyan chapel, and sufficient trim-fronted stucco villas to provide a society of weekly card parties. It represented the new world, as Blandamer Abbotts, with its mud-walled cottages, tithe barn, and one great house, represented the old. Sophia had been brought up to feel at home in the one, and not in the other; and even now she felt a certain stiffening as the carriage, splashed with the mud of country lanes, moved over the smooth turnpike, overtaking groups of self-conscious young women or nursemaids towing be-ribboned children and fat pug-dogs. Dr. Hervey's house had a green-painted trellis over its white front, a pocket-handkerchief lawn with a small conifer planted in its centre, an enormous brass door-knocker, and a cast of the Dying Gladiator turning his back on the road in what was obviously the parlour window.

The door was opened, the card and the melon received; and after a considerable pause Roger came back with the message that Mrs. Ingleby would be so delighted if Mrs. Willoughby would step in. The parlour was exactly as she had forecasted, but its occupant considerably more than she had bargained for.

My dear Mrs. Willoughby, dear Madam, my daughter will be so delighted, such a superb melon, inexpressibly grieved, doctor's orders, you know, her favourite fruit, condescension, necessity of a hot-bed, bereavement, this one more comfortable, a little refreshment . . . the stout matron pranced about the room, assailing her with chairs and unfinished sentences, the flutter of her cap-ribbons seeming to fill the little room.

Waiting for the moment when breath must fail her, Sophia was at last able to inquire,

"I hope Mrs. Hervey is not ill."

"Oh, no, not in the least, only what is quite natural, you know, at such times. But she does not come down till the afternoons."

Then, after glancing towards the Dying Gladiator as though to be assured of his inattention, the matron leant creaking forward, and whispered,

"My daughter is expecting, you know. In April."

It might be April now, she thought, beholding the landscape of fields and hedgerows that with easy flow swept her away from the stucco of Long Blandamer. It was one of those autumn days which seem to have the innocence of spring. She was glad to wash her senses in it, they needed such a lustration. She had left the doctor's house feeling as though she had escaped, and only just in time, from a dusty and airless closet. Yet in such a narrow den of gentility, and with such a mother, a young woman would bear a child. Yes, and another, and another; and grow middle-aged, and grow old, and die, and be buried under a neat headstone, describing her as a beloved wife. But what other lot, said her thoughts scratching nearer home, need any woman look for? What difference, save a larger den and a quieter mother, between Mrs. Hervey's lot and the lot designed for her? With angry reasonings she tried to shake herself free from the sense of intolerable flatness and tedium which Mrs. Ingleby's excited confidence had evoked. It was as though, after long days in a courthouse, she had heard amid the buzzing of flies and the shuffling of feet a sentence of death pronounced, or of that worst death, a life-long imprisonment; and, suddenly stabbed awake from the indifference of scorn and sickness, had realized that the doom had been pronounced upon her.

"I will therefore that the younger women marry, bear children, guide the house . . ."

Though her children were dead, she was not freed from that sentence.

The horses were checked, the carriage drew to one side. She looked out, and saw, advancing through the village, hounds with their tails flickering like shadows on running water, the bright colours of hunting coats and horseflesh. Tall on their shining mounts between the low-thatched cottages of the hamlet, the riders looked like beings of another race, of an angelic stature and nourishment. Behind them came a following of stragglers —men out of work and long-legged girls; and from a cottage door a woman darted, swiftly tying on a clean apron and calling to her children to follow her.

"I will hunt again!" exclaimed Sophia. And in that determination it seemed as though all her cares might be shaken off, and Minna forgotten. She had not hunted since the birth of the children, never easy in leaving them for her own pleasure lest some harm should befall; and now within three months of her bereavement to ride to hounds would be an outrage. However, do it she would, and show openly to all that knew covertly how destiny and death had combined to make a free woman of her. The apostle had not included hunting in his programme for the younger women.

But she must wait for a new habit, she had grown too thin for the old. Three journeys to the county town to be fitted took off the edge from her anticipation, and when at last the morning came she was half defeated before she set out. She looked with envy at Roger the groom. It was his first meet, that is to say the first to which he had gone mounted; and as they rode down the village street she glanced back and saw with amusement how he grinned from side to side, collecting the eyes of his former foot companions, draining their admiration like some tossed-off stirrup-cup.

His livery was the work of old Mr. Trimlett, and it fitted far better than her new habit. In every way Roger was to be envied. But Roger's was a short-lived kingdom. In a couple of hours he was riding home behind her, crestfallen, blinking, and trying to pretend that it was the sharp wind only that made his eyes water.

At the first covert they had drawn a blank; and while the hounds were snuffing and scrambling through Duke's Gorse the wind-baffled bawls of a farmer arriving belatedly across country signalled to them too late that their fox had been lying out in the plough, and had sneaked away. Meanwhile the new habit was irking her more and more, too easy on the shoulders, too tight under the arms; and increasingly conscious of the singularity of her behaviour, and galled by the false heartiness of the welcomes proffered her by the other riders, Sophia discovered in herself a growing impression that she was out on false pretences, having in reality an assignation with the fox. If you'd hunt *me,* she thought, looking round scornfully, I'd give you a run for your money. And before she was aware she had signalled to Roger, and was riding home.

Of its fashion, it was a good enough right and left. By hunting at all she had estranged the goodies, and by deserting she must scandalize the nimrods. She was rather pleased with herself for the thoroughness of this blunder, and for the rest of the day a queer elation floated her along. But that night, having gone to bed whistling, she dreamed again of Minna, and woke next morning to a blacker despair than she had ever known.

Steadfast as a bodily pain it endured all day, an anguish and a tedium. At the day's end she duly allowed herself to be undressed, and lay in her bed long enough to rumple it. Rising for her vigil she had no more feeling than on any other night that what she was doing was not perfectly prosaic and practical; and it was without any idea of a resorting to despair's approved poetry that she did what she had never done before—drew back her curtains, and opened the window, and stared out into the hollow darkness of the night.

Though such a thought did not visit her, it was a night well mated to her mind's night—a dead darkness, without wind or star. It was as though even the earth's motion had come to a stop, a spring run down, and the vast toy for ever stayed from its twirling. A card-case lay on the window-sill, and with an idle whim she picked it up and dropped it into the well of darkness outside. It seemed an endless while before the ground beneath sighed back its confirmation of her act. "The force of gravity," she remarked to the night; and suddenly the foolish words seemed to clinch her despair, shutting her up for ever in the residue of a life without joy, purpose, or possible release; and wringing her dangled hands she bowed herself over the sill, her mind circling downward like a plummet through a pit of misery, her body listening, as it were, to the pain of her breast crushed against the stone.

Opening her eyes at last, she found herself staring at a star; but a red and angry and earthly one—the flare of the distant lime-kiln. Wrought by the day's desperation to a fantastic clear-headedness, she put on her outdoor clothes, saying aloud as she moved about the room, "I will go to him, as those other women do. He robbed me of my children, he shall give me others."

It seemed to her that she was in a perfectly rational frame of mind; and with detached self-approval she observed how methodically her wits were working, bidding her put on stout boots, visit, the potting-shed for the old storm-lantern that hung there, and take the path across the park which would let her out by the wicket gate. Just as her lantern light made real to her only the patch of road on which her feet were set, her consciousness showed her only a moment's world: a gate to be opened, a thistle skirted, a bramble's clutch to be disentangled from her skirts.

The journey, so laggingly long on that July morning, was a short one now, and presently her lantern light showed her the glitter of water running shallow over stones, and that she had reached the bottom of the track which led to the lime-kiln. In the pale chalk mud she saw the large imprints of a man's feet, and all the path as it led upward was speckled with fallen leaves from the bushes, trampled in so that they made a pattern as of black marble inlaid on white. All through her journey she had kept her eyes on the ground. There had been no need for sight to rekindle in her mind the red and angry star she had seen from the window. Now she was treading on the level turf, harsh with winter, and the star was before her, a fluctuating and sullen glare, and the smell of the kiln caught her throat and dried it as though with terror.

She raised her lantern, and sent its light forward. A furze bush seemed to leap towards her, massive and threatening. In the darkness beyond she heard a rustle and the sound of something breathing, the noise of some startled animal making off. Still holding up her lantern she went on, and with a few more paces had caught him in her light. He was sitting on the ground, his back to the kiln wall for warmth, his arms folded, his eyes watching her advance. He made no move to get up, his features did not alter from their look of dull resentment.

She was out of breath with the climb, and the warmth and fumes of the place made her feel suddenly dizzy and unreal. She sat down on the ground, a few feet away from him, settling the lantern beside her. It shone on her ringed hand, and on the muddied hem of her crape flounces.

"You've walked hard," said the man, after a pause. His voice was like his look; dull and proud.

Her limbs were trembling. The cold of the spongy ground was like a wound.

"This is a queer time for a lady like you to be out a-walking—for you are a lady, I reckon."

With an effort she controlled her voice and said,

"I have some reason for it."

"Aye?" said the man. He spoke slowly, dragging out the word, so that it hardly condescended to be an inquiry.

"I have come here once before. But that was by day, and I brought my two children with me."

He shifted himself a little, moving his back against the wall, luxuriously.

"Now they are dead. Dead of smallpox."

His expression changed, though not to pity. Its sullenness strengthened to wrath, a change of countenance impersonal and senseless as a sudden reddening of that canopy of livid and shadowy air beneath which he sat.

"Children do die hereabouts," he said. "There's the smallpox, and the typhus, and the cholera. There's the low fever, and the quick consumption. And there's starvation. Plenty of things for children to die of."

"You speak with little pity, my man."

"I'm like the gentry, then. Like the parsons, and the justices, and the lords and ladies. Like that proud besom down to Blandamer."

He spoke with such savage intent that she leaped to her feet. But he had not moved, nor changed his look from its sullen dull pride.

"Plenty more children, they say, where the dead ones came from. If they die like cattle, the poor, they breed like cattle too. Plenty more children. That's what I say to you. Rich and poor can breed alike, I suppose.

"Eh?" he shouted, lumbering to his feet and thrusting his face into hers.

In her plunge to escape him she forgot her lantern. She stumbled in the darkness, thought he was upon her. But there was no footfall, no sound; and at last she had to go back for her lantern, stooping to pick it up under the reach of his hand. He stood looking after her, she knew. His raging glance was like a goad on her back, driving her on into the darkness. As she reached the track she heard, shrill and fleering, the sound of a woman's laughter, a forced hysterical cackle that taunted her out of ear-shot.

All her life long Sophia had heard it said that the labouring classes were insolent, mutinous, and violent. She had agreed to this as to a matter of course, accepting the rightness of any legislation designed to keep them down, and in her own dealings with the poor at her gate going upon the assumption that even such apparently toothless animals as widows and Sunday school children should be given their pounds of tea or their buns through the bars. Yet until this evening she had never heard a speech that was not respectful. Even the Labourers' Rising of 1830 had shown itself to her as a procession of men wearing their best clothes, men with washed smocks and oily church-going heads. In those ranks she had recognized, reining in her pony to watch them go by, Harry Dymond the blacksmith, who but a week before had shod the pony, old Ironsides who every summer presented her with a peeled and patterned elder-wand, Bill Cobb who was engaged to the laundry-maid, Herring the small-holder, whose hedges she ransacked for white violets. Those of the village who knew her had pulled their forelocks, and the rest had followed suit, eyeing, with the Englishman's pleasure in a smart turn-out, the handsome girl-child and the bright-coated beast. That evening they had marched up the drive and arranged themselves in a semicircle before the house. Mamma had talked of Marie Antoinette, but Papa, tapping his snuff-box, had gone out and addressed them from the top of the steps, assuring them that their behaviour was foolish, and their throats, no doubt, after so much ill-advised shouting, dry. Whereupon he had returned to his Marsala, and a barrel of beer had been rolled out into the kitchen courtyard. This, apparently, had ended the matter, except for the laundry-maid, who presently began to go about red-eyed and weeping. Bill, said Mrs. Perry, the housekeeper, had gone too far. Bill had been transported, and that foolish Ellen should have been thankful for her mercies, and that she was not burnt in her bed, instead of crying into the starch.

Now, in the kiln-man, the insolence of the labouring classes had been demonstrated. Oddly enough, the outrage had left her neither shocked nor angry. Indeed, it seemed to have done her good; for after the moment of terror had blown off she found herself tautened and stimulated, as though a well-administered slap in the face had roused her from a fainting-fit. Her blood ran living again, her wits revived, her natural vitality, which seemed to have died with the death of her children, returned to her, and once again thinking was a satisfaction, and the use of her limbs a pleasure. Not even the fact that a woman had been there in hiding, listening to her discomfiture and laughing over it, could dash her strange sense of something triumphant in this ignominious escapade. "His vixen with him!" she exclaimed, and heard her chuckle sound out over the silent field, coarse and free-hearted, a sound as kindred to the country night as an owl's Tu-whoo, or the barking of a fox.

What strange loves those must be, up there on the hill, canopied by the wavering ruddied smoke: loves bitter and violent as the man's furious mind, but in the upleaping of that undaunted lust of strength which could outface violence and bitterness.

Too rough a sire, perhaps, for the heir of Blandamer. But his words, plain and vile, had served her purpose, fathering a determination in her mind. Plenty more children, he had said. Rich and poor can breed alike. Fate should not defeat her, she would have a child yet. And having already a husband it was certainly best and most convenient that the child should be his. So she would go to Paris, fetch Frederick back, beguile him if needs be, at the barest, explain her purpose and strike a bargain. As other women could trudge up to the lime-kiln, Mrs. Willoughby might go to Paris.

Though more prosaically. A wish, half truly, half ironically felt, arose in her that she could know what manner of love it was that would take one out on a November midnight to lie embracing on the soggy turf. But one could not hope for everything; and what she wanted, what she must have, was a child.

So, on the night before her journey, she uncurtained her window once more, looked towards the ruddy star on the hillside, and nodded to it briefly, the acknowledgement one resolute rogue might give another. The determination set in her by the kiln-man had never wavered or bleached into fantasy. It proved so sturdy that she had been able to delay, trusting it to carry the burden of various postponements—a visit to London to observe fashions and buy new clothes, the conclusion of a purchase of some land adjoining hers, the choice of a parson to replace Mr. Harwood whose Michaelmas goose had carried him off, entertaining Caspar for the Christmas holidays. Seeing him, she had remembered her fancy that the half-caste should step into the shoes of her dead children—a moment's scheme, a doting desperate fancy. He showed nothing to recommend him for her pug's place now, his Sambo charm smudged out by a violent cold in his head, his fingers too heavy with chilblains to twitch more than a few jangling notes from his guitar, his only pleasure to sit by the fire sucking lozenges.

Holding by the belief that she might choose her time, she had allowed time to slip through her fingers, pleased to feel that every day's delay increased the impetus of her dammed-up purpose; and when Harlowe slipped and sprained her wrist, Sophia, firmly bandaging that genteel white flesh, forgot to be annoyed at this further impediment, absorbed in the pleasure of doing something which she knew she did well. To travel without a maid was not possible. So she thought, till a few days without Harlowe's ministrations showed her that she could brush hair and lace stays quite as well as she could wind on a bandage, and then every consideration seemed to point out the superior convenience of travelling alone. Only the world was against it. But since her visit to the lime-kiln Sophia was against the world.

Now it was the third week in February, and in her head still sounded the clamour of bird-song which had run down the sun of her last day at Blandamer. In the space, proper to well-managed journeys, between everything done and only the journey to do, she had gone out for a walk, to be suddenly ravished into the first evening of spring. Drenched with long rains, the meadows were green as emerald in the level light. Clouds, like the dividing folds of a stage curtain drawing up and aside, made all the sky dramatic. Everywhere around her was the excited chatter of running water, every ditch and drain babbling and hastening. Large as toys the birds sat on the bare boughs, or darted through the watery, lake-still air. Their clamour was dazzling, the counterpart to the ear of the brilliant gash of the sunset.

It was as though everything had combined to egg her on—the hastening water and the acclaiming birds, the drama of the clouds and the swell of the fields, where the sun's shadow-play drew a sharper furrow. And to remember that all this seeming concurrence was the accident of the day, and that she amid all the fervid excitement and quickening of the hour walked with her separate secret purpose, doubled her proud fever, her confidence, and her delight in thinking that now at last her will should be unscabbarded and flash free.

On the next night, too, she was to remember the kiln-man and his ruddy signalling star, for then she was at sea, looking towards the lights of Calais. It was a pleasure to be in France again—a light-of-love country which, making no claims on her esteem, was the more likeable and refreshing. That coastline in the dawn might look as English as it pleased, wear a church spire and be trimmed with ample woods; but it was France, a country where one went for pleasure, whose inhabitants, as the children's geography primer said, "were very fond of dancing, wine, and the Pope."

To this toy country toy trains had been added since her last visit; and it was with a confirming acquiescence that she learned at the station that owing to a mechanical misfortune the Paris train would not run until after midday. The train stood in the station, and an old woman with her head bound up in a spotted nightcap shook out a feather whisk from a compartment window. The driver leaned from the cab, conversing with a porter. At intervals he patted the engine with a soothing hand as though it might rear. Since there seemed nothing to stay her from wandering where she pleased, she walked along the track, feeling a cat's impulse to move into the fresh sunlight.

"I'll tell you," said the porter, "we must have a change. We've had altogether too much of the old pear lately. He fattens himself too much, that pear."

"Fat or thin," said the driver, "they're all the same."

Pear must be the station master, she thought, sliding her glance along the bright rails. Monsieur Poire. It was exactly what a French official would be called. But the porter had pursued her, and now was observing that although there was no immediate danger since the Paris train would be for some hours more stationary, yet the promenade she had chosen was not what one could call propitious, and was, in fact, forbidden to passengers.

"I will go and have breakfast," she said, smiling, pleased with herself and with him for pleasing her. For he was young, light, and nimble, his eyes were sleek black-currants, the glib grandeur of his speech was like the polish of a new toy, so that altogether the encounter was like nibbling up a crisp young radish.

Beau pays de France. She felt suddenly happy, lightened in spirits as though a wand had been waved over her. She knew, too, that she was looking handsome, and in her stately mourning, spirited; that her gloves fitted her triumphantly, that she had not forgotten how to speak French. And although there was no one to admire her, she was quite content to admire herself—indeed, a great part of her high spirits and good humour sprang from her solitary and unprotected state. What a mercy it was that Harlowe had sprained that wrist! For with Harlowe tagging after me, she thought, clutching my dressing-case and mouthing with sea-sickness, there would have been no escape. I should not be rambling out for my breakfast, and looking forward to a whole forenoon of picking up entertainment where I please. No! I should be hunting for somewhere that could supply a good English cup of tea, or sitting in the waiting-room. And she had a vision of Harlowe covering the bench with a sheet of newspaper before she would risk her seat on it.

The air was still the air of early morning, the sky a very pale blue. Along the quayside was a crowd of fishing craft. Looking down on them she saw how, amidst a seemingly irreparable filth and untidiness, someone was intently busy at polishing one particular knob. The smell of the sea, melancholy like a whine, rose from the filthy clucking water. Catches were being auctioned, and she listened for a while, holding her skirts about her, yawning with hunger and early rising.

But before breakfasting she must buy a newspaper, a great many newspapers. And over her coffee she read with the sharpened interest which the mind gives to what is passing and alien how a boatload of convicts had left Havre for Belle Isle, how a mayor had been decorated, how a bishop had preached a formidable sermon against secret societies, how Lady Normanby had attended a reception at the Hôtel Talleyrand, how Monsieur Guizot had expressed his disapproval of banqueting. His speech was reported at length, but she did not read it very attentively, only smiling at his Liberal language which compelled him to refer to the throne as *le Fauteuil.* A good description of that well-stuffed prudent monarch. Sophia held due English views of the Orléans dynasty. It carried on the business well enough, no doubt, but it was not the Old Firm, and its concessions to democracy must certainly have impaired the quality of its teas and sugars. Local prejudice too had strengthened her feelings for the Old Firm. Had not Charles X come in exile to her own country, a fragment of history walking slowly between the primroses of the park of Lulworth Castle, walking there with Marie Antoinette's daughter, the man and woman out of the past pacing black as shadows under the spring sky, hearing the indifferent plaudits of the rooks, who had heard the roars of an acclaiming and a bloodthirsty people? After this, one naturally felt that Louis Philippe was rather tame.

But I did not come here to muse about Louis Philippe, she thought, brusquely tidying up her meditations, for with the recollection of that exiled king at Lulworth Castle she had been carried back to Dorset, and to Sophia Willoughby of Blandamer, whose children were dead, whose husband ran in the train of another woman—Sophia Willoughby, that desperate female who had so little to lose that she was now breakfasting alone in a foreign town, landed secretly there to carry out her foray. She did not want to think too much about the reason of her journey. The determination in her was so strong that it was like an actual pain, she would avoid while she might the pressure of a thought upon it. When she reached Paris, she would face the situation; but meanwhile, this unexpected pause seemed tumbled into her lap for the very purpose of truancy and refreshment, and so she would make the most of it, as she had made the most of those stolen hours in Cornwall.

Must every thought twist her back upon the loss of her children, her stratagem to have children again? She paid for her breakfast, and walked out with determination to amuse herself. And almost immediately she found herself invited to think once more of Louis Philippe.

In a narrow street near the quayside there was a group of fishers and working-men who stood watching a young man who was drawing in chalk on a blank wall. He drew swiftly, scraping his chalk over the masonry, and sometimes giving a hasty scratch to his hatless curls, as though he would ferret out the idea of the next line. He drew a tree, a fruit-tree, a pear-tree, since it bore on every branch an enormous swelling pear. Then he drew a man, a peasant, holding a pruning-knife.

The crowd closed up, there were chuckles, and exclamations of approval. The young man stood back with the gesture of one who has said his say, and through a gap in the crowd she saw what his completing strokes had been. For now the outlined pears had been filled with features, and the features were unmistakably of the cast of the royal family—a big Louis Philippe pear in the centre of the tree, with all his lesser pears around him.

The man darted back, and with a violent stroke sharpened the outline of the pruning-knife. And the instant after he fell to rubbing out the drawing, demolishing it as swiftly as he had made it.

The crowd went on, vanishing as the drawing had vanished, the artist was gone too, and she alone was left, staring at a blank wall, her eyes and wits blinking still at the rapidity of the performance. But there, neat as the answer to a riddle, was the identity of the Monsieur Poire whom she had taken to be the station master. It was nice to have it so pat; but to her, a foreigner, of no significance. She knew the French. A nation that must have, throne or armchair, its king, if only to quarrel with.

She walked on, pleased with the adventure, thinking that perhaps the only satisfactory way of life was to live for the minute. According to that she should miss the train to Paris as she had missed the other train, remaining while her pleasure in them endured to wander through these streets, whose gay pallor, whose sharp scents, unmodulated crashes of fish into roasting coffee, printer's ink into tar, entertained her like a fair and welcomed her like a nursery. There would be insular company, too, did she need it. For now, the morning being more advanced, the debt-driven English colony had begun to show itself; marketing mammas, crowned with righteous bonnets, large-faced, large-eyed schoolgirls giggling arm in arm, shabby-genteel old gentlemen carrying newspapers, and over one arm, a travelling rug.

No, this train she dared not miss. To live for the minute . . . That was how these had begun, the improvident others of her race. And here was their end: a vacant exile, tedium and pretentiousness, and the years of idle dallying, staring across the Channel, waiting to see the English boat come in.

She began to tremble, to hate the interval of time before the Paris train started. Long before due time she returned to the station, to make inquiries, to oversee, if need be, that train's departure. And throughout the journey she practised herself in the mood she must take and keep: a mood cool, artful, and determined. For now was no time for romance or enthusiasm. The kiln-man's star, which had guided her so far, might prove a Jack o' Lantern now. There must be nothing in her adventure that could be called adventurous, nothing visionary or overwrought, no sense of destiny to betray her. As other people go to Paris to buy gloves, she was going to Paris to bargain for a child. I must concentrate upon Frederick, she told herself; if possible, not even mention Minna, and certainly not see her. For if I did, my rage might overset me. And in any case it would be beneath my dignity.

The Hôtel Meurice was well calculated to reinforce these resolutions. It enfolded her with all its admonitions of her class and of her race. For here, of course, Papa and Mamma had stayed during her year of being finished in Paris under great-aunt Léocadie's supervision; here she had first drunk champagne and put on a pearl necklace. The wine waiter, having taken her order, hesitated at the door of her sitting-room, politely recognizing. Though he had served so many of her nation, his dwelling eye implied, she was too fine a figure to be forgotten, and with the confidence of a family servant he inquired after her parents.

"There must have been many changes in Paris since we were here."

His glance towards the window seemed to indicate that a few changes might have taken place outside.

She lingered over her dinner, thinking that when she had finished she would go to bed, to sleep long on that solid French mattress, and refresh herself for the morrow. But the noise of the city resounding beyond the curtained windows excited her, and the dinner and the wine had given her a sense of festivity, so that now to go tamely to bed was not possible. But where to go, being a woman, and alone? For a while she dallied with the idea of a long drive, and began to map out the route which should show her, enclosed like some Turk's bride in her moving box of darkness, the greatest display of light and animation; but her knowledge of Paris failed her, or she had forgotten what once she knew, for it was not possible to remember which street debouched into which—and to show her ignorance would be amateurish, and perhaps injudicious.

"Well, at any rate," she exclaimed, rising angrily, "I suppose I may drive to visit my husband." And with this in her mind she began to array herself as though for a battle, putting on her diamond rings, sleeking the bands of her hair, pinning her veil to fall becomingly. The mirror, being French, must have learned flattery, but even so there was no doubt that the severity of her mourning clothes became her well, enhancing the faint pure doll's pink of her cheeks, giving value to her small regular features, ennobling her maypole stature. Once already today she had thought herself handsome; but how far off that early morning seemed she was not to know fully until she crossed the pavement to get into the waiting cab. For now a small snow was falling, fine as the woolly powder which falls from a springtime poplar tree. It fell between her and the dirty brown face of a woman who was selling mimosa and who, scenting a foreigner, hurried forward, her earthy face peering behind the soft golden plumes. On Sophia's skin at the same moment fell the powdering snow and the soft tickle of the mimosa blossom. The shaken pollen made her sneeze, the touch of this cold and this soft falling together sent a thrill through her flesh.

I am in Paris, she said to herself, suddenly warm and happy, as though happiness had just fledged out on her. And holding her foolish bunch of flowers, she leaned back in the cab, touching her face with their softness, trying to hold intact the mood of pleasure so unexpectedly alighted. To her loneliness the flowers were almost like a person, a Cinderella godmother alighting on her desolation and ashes, and assuring her that after all it would be possible for her to dance at the king's palace that night. Twice today I have felt handsome, twice today I have been happy—and with that rarest happiness, at least it has been rare to me, a simple hedgerow happiness that anyone, a child or an old woman shelling peas, might feel. Perhaps at last I am in the way of it. For I know what I want, and that is a very simple thing—a child, a thing anyone might have. It need not even be sent from the South of France, like this mimosa. But if I have a child, this time I must not spoil it all with fuss and ambition.

Yet, having a child, how not to fuss, how not to be stiffened into anxiety and watchfulness? And she was beginning to wonder if it would not be best to bring up this child in France, where the climate was easier, where there would be no pressure from outside, as at Blandamer there must be, to freeze her back into the awkward consciousness of being a wronged wife, when the cab stopped.

More expensive than it looks, she decided, scanning the rather dowdy façade, with its well-scrubbed paint and unobtrusive blazon. It was snowing more heavily now, and the concierge opened an umbrella as he came forward. Mr. Willoughby had gone out.

Sophia heard the money in her purse clink, and her voice say, "To Madame Lemuel's?"

Most probably. He would inquire of his wife.

He came back, bowing, to say it was so.

"Good. Then I shall meet him there. Please tell my driver where to go."

The weight of her bribe had made him so abundantly confidential that though she listened for the address she could not hear it. But it must be some way off, for the driver clicked to his horse as though to mettle it for a long journey.

You triple fool, she arraigned herself. For what could it serve her to follow Frederick to the house of his mistress? How few hours ago was it that she had sealed up that final determination not even to mention Minna, if the mention could be avoided? And now, carried away by this ridiculous impulse, she was allowing herself to be driven to the woman's door. Well, there was time to revise the error. She would pay off this cab, and immediately hire another for the return journey. And Heaven knows, she thought, trying to stiffen herself with practical considerations, what I shall not have to pay for this jaunt—for the bribe had been considerable, and already her cab had crossed the river.

Except for visits to great-aunt Léocadie in the Faubourg St.-Germain, Sophia knew the Left Bank only as a territory into which one was taken to see something historical. She was at a loss in the narrow winding streets, and peered out anxiously, looking for something to recognize, alarmed by the sensation of being in an unknown place, and wondering if it would be as easy as she had supposed to find that cab for the journey back. The streets were narrow, ill-paved and ill-lit; flares of light from street market or wineshop or rowdy café lightened the darkness unconsolingly; and then with a twist to right or left, they were passing between high walls with garden-doors in them, walls over which trees stooped their empty branches; or the solid shape of a dome ballooned up. Then a larger dome, parenting all these, appeared, and with an effort of memory she recognized the Panthéon. The horse slackened its pace; even when the crest of the hill had been reached the driver's click and whip-crack were half-hearted, a convention only, and hearing this she knew that the street into which they turned must be the journey's end. Rue de la Carabine, she saw, lettered on the wall. And at the next moment the cab had stopped.

It was a narrow street. The houses, old and tall, rose up cliff-like, their shutters banding the perspective. Along the bottom of this crevasse three or four private carriages were being slowly driven up and down, the sound of the horses' hoofs falling like stones pattered methodically into a well. A carriage which had arrived just before her cab was now moving off to join in the back and forth of the others; its occupant, a consciously romantic figure in a flowing cloak, was hesitating on the threshold of a stone passage, from which a flight of stairs ascended; but seeing her, he seemed to take it for granted that she also would enter, and stepped back to make way for her. There was a lamp burning just inside the door, and its light showed her a face that was faintly familiar. I do not know you as well as the wine waiter, she thought, but I do know you. His following presence propelled her up the creaking circling staircase. I am done for now, she said to herself, propelled upwards, flight after flight, towards the sound of voices. Fool! And as though her mind dared not acknowledge the extent of such foolishness, it busied itself trying to recollect when and where she had seen the operatic gentleman of the cloak.

Yes. At an evening party, a rather grand evening party, given by one of Papa's *émigré* friends, who had returned with the Restoration. He had stood in a moody attitude near the harp, someone had told her that he wrote—or was it composed music? —his name began with . . . No. She could not recall his name. Half-way up the third flight she recalled that he had been described as a poet. Hollow with fear, and driven on by fear, like a child arriving at a party, she saw lights, and heard voices, and smelled, swaying out on that cold and dirty staircase, the perfumes of civilized society. And here was the party, the party to which she had not been invited.

Some of the party had overflowed onto the landing, and stood grouped round the doorway, looking inward. If I can stay out here, she thought with a last flicker of hope, and let him go past, I can sneak down again unnoticed. And carefully laying down her absurd bunch of mimosa she began to fidget with her shoe-fastening.

"Please go on," she said to the cloak, and heard her English accent ring out like a trumpet. The cloak bowed, and passed her. After what seemed hours of deception with the shoe-fastening, she looked up cautiously. The cloak was standing by the doorway, having opened a path into the room for her. The other door-keepers were regarding her with polite curiosity. She straightened herself, and their expressions changed to surprise at her height, as though, rising so fiercely tall and straight, she had presented them with a fixed bayonet. Like one large family, occupying one large family pew, and she arriving in the middle of the service, they manœuvred her in.

"A chair," said someone. But shaking her head she wedged herself into a corner. If they will leave me alone, she thought. At that moment her bunch of mimosa was handed in after her.

She was in an ante-room, whose doors stood open upon the larger room beyond. Both rooms seemed incredibly crowded, though as she realized, furtively looking about her, this effect was due to the informal way in which people had grouped themselves, and to the extraordinary mixture of people present. Entering, her embarrassment had been given a final wrench by the impression that all the women were in full evening dress; but now, among these islands of glittering silk and lace, she noticed other figures, some habited, as she said to herself, "like artists," others patently of the working class. Immediately in front of her stood a bald-headed old gentleman, wearing a plaid rug over his shoulders. To her left she looked down upon the polished shoulders and swaying fan of a ball-room elegant. Beside her was a Jewish boy, a humpback, with a face that hunger had sharpened into a painful beauty. He had moved aside to make way for her, and seeing her flowers had smiled. Otherwise no one seemed inclined to take the least notice of her.

I may get out of it yet, she said to herself.

There was talk; but it was of a quality, hushed and hesitant, that suggested the talk that rises among people who are waiting through the indeterminate interval between one item of a concert and another. Perhaps it was a concert. In the farther room the strings of a harp had been plucked. For some while her unused ears could make little of what was being said; but as her nerves quieted, and the hope of keeping her anonymity crept higher, she began to prick her ears, saying to herself that Frederick's voice, at any rate, would emerge to her on its familiarity. But it was another voice that she first caught in the entirety of a sentence, a loud fulsome voice that said, speaking French with a German accent,

"Most beautiful Minna, we are here to be enchanted. Will you not wave your wand, will you not tell us one of your beautiful *Märchen?*"

Good God, what a menagerie! exclaimed Sophia to herself, disgusted at the speech and the manner. The little Jew had turned his head and was looking at her compassionately. Why, she wondered. She saw the bunch of mimosa trembling in her grasp. For those words addressed to Minna, *most beautiful Minna,* had brought her rival before her, in a flash making real the hearsay hated one, stabbing into her consciousness the knowledge that the woman lived and breathed, and was in the very room.

The fulsome voice was lost among other voices making the same request. That's Frederick! her mind cried out, and forgot him in the next instant, hearing in reply the voice whose ghost had spoken at her child's bedside, saying, *Ma fleur.*

"No, not a fairy-tale. I have told so many. This, this shall be a true story."

See her she must. And in the jostle of rearrangement which had followed the requesting voices, Sophia shifted her place till she could see from the ante-room into the room beyond. When she could hear again, Minna was already speaking, leaning forward with her elbows on her knees, her face propped between her hands—the attitude of one crouched over a sleepy fire, watching the embers waste and brighten and waste again.

TWO

"But the first thing I can remember is the lighting of a candle.

"It is night, the middle of the night it seems to me, waking as a child does into that different world, mysterious, unfathomable, which night is to a child. A separate world, as though one awaked in the depths of the sea. My father is there, moving softly in the dusky room. He speaks to himself in a language which I have never heard before, and coming to the hearth he takes up an ember with the tongs, and breathes on it, as though he were praying to it. At his breath it awakens and glows, and I see his face, and his lips moving amid his beard. Then with the ember he lights tall yellow candles; and as the flame straightens he straightens also, and begins to chant in the strange language, raising his hand to his forehead, bowing and making obeisance. On his forehead is a little box, and over his head is the praying towel.

"For it is the Sabbath candle he had lit, and alone, in the depth of the night, in secret, he is praying to the God of our race, and glorifying him.

"I cannot understand it, and yet I can understand it well enough to know that it is something secret and precious, a jewel that can only be taken out at night. Afterwards, how long afterwards I cannot remember, I spoke to him of what I had seen. Then he told me how we were of the chosen people, exiles from Jerusalem, captive in this world as the gold is captive in the rock and trodden underfoot by those who go to and fro. And he showed me a book, written in our holy language; and in that book, he said, were the stories of good Jewesses, faithful women: Jael, who slew Sisera, and Judith, who slew Holofernes; Deborah, who led an army, and Esther, who saved a people.

"'It seemed to me that their stories were written against the sky. For our house, our hovel, stood at the edge of a fir-forest, and those black stems and branches, leaning and jagged, line after line, were like the Hebrew letters in the book; and as I ran through the forest, picking up sticks and fir-cones for fuel, I used to make stories to myself, stories of Jewish women, reading them from the book of the trees.

"'But that was in summer, an endless lifetime, when the sky was as blue as a cornflower, when I picked wild strawberries, and sucked flowers for nectar, and heard the contented bleating of our goats as they ate the sweet pasture, and the endless drone of the insects in the forest. And as day and night were different worlds, so were winter and summer. But best of all I remember the first spring.

"'In the night, the wind changed. I woke up, and heard a different voice, loud like the coming of an army, and yet thick and gentle, as though it wrapped one in velvet. I pinched my mother, and said, 'What's that?' She woke with a start, and lay still, listening and trembling. 'It is the thaw-wind,' she said, 'blowing from Jerusalem. With the Holy One is mercy.' And she gathered me closer, and fell asleep again, and the wind seemed like her snores, warm and kind.

"'The wind brought rain, a soft brushing rain like tassels of silk. The hard crust of snow was covered with little pits, and the goats bleated in the shed. The snow began to fall off the roof in great clods that smashed as they fell. Suddenly the flat grey sky was blue, was lofty, with shining clouds, and a bird flew past the door. When I ran out the snow wetted my feet. It was beginning to melt, and I kicked and danced until I had scrabbled a hole, and there at the bottom of the hole was the ground again, with the grasses squashed and stiff and earth-coloured. I knelt by the hole, and rubbed my cheek against the ground, and snuffed it. Then I looked up at the sky, and the clouds were going so fast and so lightly that I felt giddy, as though the earth were sliding away under me. I ran about, kicking the melting snow, and shouting little tags of Hebrew that I had learned from my father.

"'Day after day the wind blew warm, and the snow melted, and the ground appeared, and thawed, and clucked like a hen, drinking the snow-water. Blades of new grass came up, and small bright flowers, flocks of birds came flying, and settled on the patches of cleared ground, or pecked at the glistening tree-trunks. My mother came out into the yard, shading her eyes with one hand, holding on her other arm my little brother, who blinked and sneezed. He had been born in the winter, this was the first time he had felt the sun. I tugged at her skirts. 'Let us go for a walk, let us go a long way,' I begged. 'Tomorrow,' she said.

"'But on the morrow we could not go out at all, for the wind had shifted, hail-storms flew by, one after another like a flight of screaming cranes whose wings stretched over the whole world. The ground was whitened with hailstones, and the birds lay under the bushes, frozen to death. But the spring could not be stopped now, it came back again, the sun shone, clouds of midges sprang up from nowhere, the bushes swayed like dancers, shadows rippled over the earth like running water.

"'When we were out of doors my mother seemed a different woman, walking with a freer step, singing as she walked. She carried her baby on her back, slung in a shawl, and I, thinking always of the women of Jewry, fancied that she was like Judith's handmaid, carrying the tyrant's head over the hills to Bethulia. We went over the heath, farther than ever I had been. It was piebald with snow, and the pools of bog-water we passed, fringed with cat-ice, were so violently blue under the blue sky that I was almost afraid of them. There was colour, too, in the birch copses, as though the stems had been smeared with damson juice. By one of these copses my mother sat down to suckle her baby. The sun shone on her breast, and it was as though her ugly clothes had been thawed away from this smooth strong pushing flower. When the baby was quieted I heard, through the small noises of the wood, other far-off sounds—roarings and crashes. 'The wolves are fighting!' I cried out, but she shook her head. And presently we went on towards the sounds. If it is not wolves, I thought, it must be woodmen; for now among the crashes that were as though a tree had fallen I heard yelling cries like the whine of a saw. And we came to the wood's end, and stood on the bank of a river.

"On either side it was still frozen, the arched ice rearing up above the water like opened jaws. But in the centre channel the current flowed furiously, and borne along on it, jostling and crashing, turning over and over, grating together with long harsh screams, were innumerable blocks of ice. As the river flowed its strong swirling tongue licked furiously at the icy margins, and undermined them, and with a shudder and a roar of defeat another fragment would break away and be swept downstream. It was like a battle. It was like a victory. The rigid winter could stand no longer, it was breaking up, its howls and vanquished threats swept past me, its strongholds fell and were broken one against another, it was routed at last.

"I wept with excitement, and my mother comforted me, thinking I was afraid. But I could not explain what I felt, though I knew it was not fear. For then I knew only the wintry words of my race, such words as exile, and captivity, and bondage. I had never heard the word Liberty. But it was Liberty I acclaimed, seeing the river sweeping away its fetters, tossing its free neck under the ruined yoke."

She stopped abruptly, like the player lifting the bow from the strings with a flourish. Murmurs of admiration arose. She seemed to listen to them as the concerto player listens to the strains of the orchestra he has quitted, half relaxing from the stanza completed, half intent upon what lies before. This is all quite right, her expression said; presently I shall go on again. For she had raised her head, and now Sophia could see her face. It was ugly, uglier than one could have believed, hearing that voice. A discordant face, Sophia's mind continued, analysing while it could, before the voice went on again; for the features with their Jewish baroque, the hooked nose, the crescent eyebrows and heavy eyelids, the large full-lipped mouth, are florid, or should be; but the hollow cheeks forbid them, and she is at once a heavy voluptuous cat and a starved one. Meanwhile she had omitted to look for Frederick. But it was too late, for Minna had begun to speak again.

"When the next spring came, I remembered the river. Another child had been born, my mother was busy, I seemed likely to beg in vain. And this spring, too, was not like the other. A weeping mist covered the land, a mist that brought pestilence.

From the village, where I was not allowed to go, came the sound of the Christian churchbell, tolling for the dead. Noemi, our neighbour, came to our house and told my mother that the Gentile women said that the pestilence had been seen on the heath, a troop of riders with lances, moving in the mist. My father looked up from his work. 'Such tales are idolatrous,' said he. 'Do you, a good Jewess, believe them?' '*I* do not believe them, Reb,' she answered. 'They sicken for their sins and their swine's flesh. But let them believe it, if they will. It is better than if they said we poisoned their wells.'

"'This story of the pestilence riding over the heath made me think better of my resolve that if my mother would not take me to the river I would find my way there alone. I began to pester my father, saying that though I was only a girl, I was the firstborn. And at last he consented. But with him it was a different journey, for he walked fast, talking sometimes to himself but never to me. The air was raw and sunless, my feet hurt me and I almost wished that we had never come, until reaching the birch wood I heard again those thunders and crashings. I ran on ahead, towards the sound, and came by myself to the river bank. A mist hung over the water, flowing with the river, the glory of the year before was not there. Then, as I looked, I saw that on the hurried ice-blocks there were shapes, men and horses, half frozen into the ice, half-trailing in the water. And in the ice were stains of blood. Last year, I remembered, it had seemed like a battle, like a victory. Had there been blood, and corpses then, and had I forgotten them? The full river seemed to flow more heavily, when ice-block struck against ice-block they clanged like iron bells. My father, coming up behind me, spoke to himself in Hebrew, and groaned. 'Who are they, Father?' 'The wrathful, child, the proud, and the enemies of God. . . . So let thine enemies perish, O Lord!' He cried this out in a voice that rang above the tumult of the river. Then he was silent for a long time, shuddering and sighing like an animal. At last he told me that there must have been a battle, perhaps a war—where, who could tell?—and that the bodies of the slain, caught in the frost, may have been locked up winter-long, that now with the thaw were being hurried to the sea.

"'All the way home, and for long after, I pondered over this thought, so new to me, that there were other people in the world, people living so far off that they might fight and perish and no word of it come to us, no splash of their blood. I knew from the Book, and from stories, that there had been peoples and nations; but I thought they were all dead. I was forbidden to go to the village, lest the children should throw stones at me. Our household, and Noemi's and old Baruch's, was Jewry, and the village the Gentiles. But now these dead men had come into my world.

"Soon came more living. For that summer, staggering over the heath and staring about them as if afraid, came a troop of strangers, men, women, and children. They carried bundles and bits of household stuff, pots and pans flashing in the sun, wicker baskets with hens in them; some led goats, or a cow, and an old white horse drew a hooded cart that rocked and jolted on the moorland track. I was picking strawberries when I looked up and saw them; and spilling the fruit I leaped up and ran home, to tell this strange news. 'They are gipsies,' my mother said. 'Run, child, and fetch in the washing.' Somehow I had heard of gipsies, for I said, 'No, they are not gipsies. These people could never dance.' My father went a little way to where he could see them, my mother following him. I saw her start, and wring her hands as if in pity, and then they hastened forward towards the strangers. My father embraced the foremost, an old man whose bald head glistened with sweat, my mother hurried to and fro among the women. I could hear her voice, loud with excitement, exclaiming and condoling.

"For they were a settlement of Jews, who had been driven out of their homes, and had come over the heath looking for some place where they might live unmolested. That night, and for many nights to come, they camped on our meadow, and my mother fed them, and beat up herbs to put on their blistered feet. Their goats quarrelled with ours, their children played and quarrelled with us. In fancy, remembering their coming across the heath, I told myself that they had come like Eliezer's embassy, with servants and camels, to ask for me in marriage. In fact, since their poverty was even more abject than ours, I lorded it over the new-come children, and discovered the sweets of tyranny."

She paused again, but this time gently, and with a sly smile. And you must still savour them, thought Sophia, seeing that mournful dark glance flicker slowly over the listeners, as though numbering so many well-tied money-bags. Our ears are your ducats. You are exactly like a Jewish shopkeeper, the Jew who kept the antique shop at Mayence, staring, gloating round his shelves, with a joy in possession so absorbing that it was almost a kind of innocence. In a moment you should rub your hands, the shopkeeper's gesture.

At that moment the slowly flickering glance touched her, and rested. It showed no curiosity, only a kind of pondering attention. Then, as though in compliance, Minna's large supple hands gently caressed themselves together in the very gesture of her thought. Sophia started slightly. The glance, mournfully numbering, moved on. But answering Sophia's infinitesimal start of surprise there had been a smile—small, meek, and satisfied, the smile of a dutiful child. And again there had been no time to look for Frederick.

"My position among these children was the stronger, since my father, by his learning and orthodoxy, was looked up to by all the new-comers. He led them in prayer, he exhorted them to cherish our faith, he comforted and advised them. By the end of the summer many of the immigrants had built themselves huts out of the forest, and settled near us. I was delighted with this, seeing that it gave us company and consequence. I blamed my poor mother for narrow-heartedness, since she did not rejoice as much as I did. Bending over the loom she would sigh and shake her head; and among the clatter of the pedals I overheard such words as these: 'One or two they will suffer. But not a multitude.' And then she would weep, her tears falling on the growing web. But for all these doubts, which I could see but not understand, she did what she could for our neighbours, our neighbours who were even poorer than ourselves.

"Perhaps because they had opened their hands, my parents began to grow more prosperous. My father started a little shop, selling such things as seed and candles and household gear. Because the wares were good and cheap, people from the village came to buy, saying always that they were cheated and overcharged, but coming again. My mother baked cakes for their Christian feast-days, cakes flavoured with caraways or wild anise, and I, instead of gathering wood strawberries, cherries, and cranberries for myself, gathered them to make into jams, and the money from this little commerce was put by for my wedding dowry. One day my father came back from a journey to the town with a coloured band-box containing a wig for my mother. For when they had married they had been too poor to buy such a thing, and my mother, shaving her head as Jewish women must do on marriage, had ever afterwards worn only a kerchief. Now she had a wig, a grand, an honourable wig. It was of horsehair, dyed chestnut colour, very voluminous and towering, and when she had put it on all her friends came in to congratulate and admire. My father, too, looked at her as though she were beautiful and stately as Queen Esther. His face was full of pride and love. But I hung back, awkward and alarmed; for to me this wig seemed ugly and, worse still, baleful and unlucky.

"Under these glaring tresses I saw for the first time how pale and careworn my mother's face had grown since the coming of these other Jews and our riches, so that I had lost all sight, now, of the mother who had walked singing over the heath and suckled her baby in the birch wood.

"But these thoughts I kept to myself, only saying among those of my own age that the wig was ugly, and that when I married I would wear a kerchief or perhaps keep my long hair. When I said such things as these my playmates tittered and pretended to be shocked. I made them long speeches, saying that Jewry must be freed, and that when I was older I would lead them all back to Jerusalem. Some of the boys jeered at me, saying that I did not know where Jerusalem was (indeed, I did not), and that anyhow I was only a woman and could do nothing but obey my husband. But mostly they followed me, and when my speeches were too much for them I wooed them back with a story. All my stories were of freedom and the overthrowing of tyrants, and so led to my speeches again. And when I tired of their listening faces I would give them the slip, and go over the heath to the river (for it was an easy walk now); and sitting on the river bank I used to say, over and over again, David's words: *Turn our captivity, O Lord, as the rivers in the south.* For I had never forgotten my first sight of the river, so proud and turbulent, bearing away its broken fetters. The river would understand me when I spoke of liberty.

"Eleven times since I was born the ice had crept over the running river and thickened there. And now it was winter again, midwinter, and a winter's evening dusk. Not since the winter of the pestilence had there been such ruthless cold, such famine and distress. The wolves came out in broad daylight, at night they fought among themselves, ravening for each other's flesh. Unknown birds flew over us in bands, driven even out of their north by the cold. Whenever they flew over, a storm followed.

"I was just coming across the yard from the outhouse, where I had gone to carry our goats their feed, when I heard footsteps, a man running and staggering along the frozen path. The running man was my father. He had torn off his mittens as though their weight would encumber him, I saw his red hands flapping against the dusky white of the snow. His mouth was open, he fetched his breath with groaning. He fell down on the icy track, and was up again, and came running on with his face bloodied. He did not see me where I stood motionless in the dusk of the yard, but ran past me and burst open the house door and staggered in. Before he had spoken I heard my mother cry out, a wild despairing cry that yet seemed to have a note of exaltation in it, as though it were recognizing and embracing some terror long foreseen. I went in after him, very slowly and quietly, as though in this sweep of terror I must move as noiselessly as possible. He was leaning over the table, his hands clenching it and trembling. He trembled, his back heaved up and down with his struggles for breath, with every gasp he groaned with the anguish of breathing. Mixed in with his groans were words. Always the same words. 'They're coming!' he said. 'They're coming!' "

"Wolves!" exclaimed Frederick.

"*Christians.*

"My mother with averted eyes as though she dared not look at him was hurrying the younger children into their coats and wrappings. The baby began to cry. 'Hush!' she whispered. I could scarcely hear the word, but it was spoken with such vehemence that the child, a child at the breast, understood, and lay still as a corpse. With arms that seemed to have stretched into the wings of a vast bird she gathered us together. 'Come! Come quickly and softly! We must hide in the forest.' 'The Book,' said my father. 'The candlesticks. The holy things of Israel.' There was no expression on her face as she stood waiting, while trembling and fumbling he collected these together, and wrapped them carefully in a cloth. When this was done she laid her hand on his arm, persuading him towards the door. He stopped. 'The others,' he said. 'They must be warned. I will go to them.' For a moment her set face seemed to fall apart in an explosion of rage and despair. But she said no word, standing by the door with her baby in her arms and her children about her. 'I will go,' I said. 'Send me!'

"'Through the heavy dusk I ran from house to house. Many houses were closed and shuttered, I had to bang and shout to be admitted. I stopped only to say, 'The Christians are coming.' It was all I knew. In every house it was the same. A cry, a lamentation! And then the same desperate haste and smooth making ready to fly, as though, waking and sleeping, winter and summer, a life long, a nation long, this had been expected and rehearsed. I had reached the last house when I saw the darkness suddenly changed to a pattern of ruddy white and leaping black shadows; and turning, I saw torches, flaring pine-knots, and a throng of people, black and hurrying, and heard shouts, and laughter, and curses. No need, at this last door, to cry that the Christians were coming.

"'I heard them calling out my father's name, saying that he was a usurer, and my mother a witch. Then there was a scream. It was one of our goats, I thought; but Dinah, the woman of the last house, thrust a shawl over my head, pressing her hands over my ears, and someone took me by the arm and began to run with me. My head was muffled in the shawl, I could not untie the knot, I could only run, dragged on by this hand on my arm. Sometimes a bundle with sharp edges banged against my legs, I was jostled against, I lost my footing and stumbled, and was hauled up again, blinded and half smothered in the shawl. All round were people running. I heard their feet striving in the snow, the thud of large feet and the patter of small. And behind us came the pursuers, shouting and jeering like cattle-drivers. Suddenly at my side there was a scream like a flash of lightning, and the hand that dragged me forward let go, and I ran on alone, tearing at the knotted shawl.

"Something cold and rigid stopped my flight, and at the same moment I felt a stab in my arm, and the blood running. I thought it was the pike of the Christians, and I fell on the ground and lay still, waiting for the death-stroke. But nothing happened. The flying and the pursuing feet went past, but no one touched me; and presently, feeling about, I found that it was a bush that I had run against, wounding myself against a broken bough, sharp with ice. My hands were too numbed to unfasten the knot, but with my teeth I bit a hole in the shawl, and tore it open and thrust out my head.

"I was at the edge of the forest, all alone. I thought it would be dark, but there was still a faint cringing daylight. The voices and the footsteps were gone far off, the screaming and shouting almost done. At longer and longer intervals there would sound a long wavering cry, or a yelp of anguish; and as I listened I remembered how after a summer thunderstorm I had often sat at the edge of the forest, watching the world flash out in its new revived green, and hearing the last drops of rain fall, splash, splash, here and there, till at last they ceased altogether, or I had tired of counting them. Summer or winter, then or now . . . both were equally real or unreal to me, as I sat under the bush, waiting, since slaughter had passed me by, for wolves or cold to make an end of me. There was a smell of woodsmoke in the air, and through my stupor this comforted me. My wits were so scattered that even when I saw the flames rising on the sky, and knew that it was our houses that burned, the scented smoke was still my comfort. I moved, to settle myself deeper under the bush where I should die. With the agony of that movement I was driven alive again, crying out with pain, struggling to my feet, and felled by the weight of my stiffened blood. Like an animal gone mad I darted over the snow, shaking myself and whining, and running hither and thither. Presently, near the edge of the forest, I came on the body of a woman—dead; and farther on the body of an old man—dead, too; and the bloodied tracks led me from there to something that might have been man or woman or child—but was only blood and a heap of trampled flesh. Like a mad dog I ran from corpse to corpse, snuffing at them and starting away. Darkness had fallen, but the blazing houses gave me light—light enough to find at last a round thing like a fallen bird's-nest, cold and stiff with frost, and rocking lightly in the wind. It was my mother's wig. There was a body near by, but not hers; and searching over the trampled snow I found at last the track of my father's feet, his by the print of the broken heel. The tracks led back towards the hamlet. He had turned, and gone back for me, his firstborn.

"Now I knew where to perish. The Christians should see that a Jewess could be no less faithful than a Jew. And while I ran towards the blazing house my old fancies flared up, and it seemed to me that not only should I die defying them, but that my race should be avenged through me, since I would certainly kill many of them before they killed me.

"I jumped over a smouldering paling, and ran between the burning huts towards our own. As I came in sight I heard a long crackling yell of acclamation. The Christian women had come up, to watch the burning, and to rifle; and now as I neared them they all cried out, 'See, the little Jewess! How she runs, the Devil is after her! Throw her into the fire! No! Don't touch her! She's mad! Look at her eyes. She's mad, and will bite us.'

"I threw myself among them, and they gave way, shrinking back, grabbing at me and letting go, as I struck at them with fists and set teeth. But in an instant I was caught by two fat strong hands, my shoulders caught, and my face pressed into a fat black-draped belly that smelt of onions and incense. It was the priest, who had come up with the women. I kicked his shins, but he held me fast, and the women, flocking up, took hold of my hands and feet, and overpowered me.

" 'Hold her, good Christians, hold her,' he said, coughing because I had butted his belly. 'God has sent her into our hands. We will keep her, and baptize her. Holy Church has always room for another soul.' "

She paused, her eyes staring out from her rigid pose. There was a stir at the back of the room, but no one turned a head. Only when the heavy eyelids drooped over the staring eyes was there a faint sigh, a rustle and exhalation as though a field of corn that had stood all day in the breathless August drought had yielded to a breath of wind. Released from Minna's gaze Sophia felt a sudden giddiness. I will not faint, she thought. A chair was slid towards her. She had forgotten that all this while she had stood. But she would not sit down. Glancing about, trying to ease her stiffened eyes, she saw that the ivory fan of the woman seated near her was snapped in two.

Still looking down, Minna seemed to be summoning a final cold to arise from the depths of a well at her feet. Her face became even paler, her body stiffened as though with frost, her lips narrowed. When she spoke her voice was cold and flat like a snowfield.

"I shall not forget what I suffered in the priest's house. . . ."

But the stir at the back of the room, discreetly swelling, had now arched itself into an inquiring silence. Into that silence broke a preliminary cough, and a dull snuffling voice said,

"Excuse me, ladies and gentlemen. But the people in the street are demanding the carriages for their barricade."

"What?"

Without animation the concierge repeated,

"The people in the street are demanding the carriages for their barricade."

"Good God!" exclaimed Frederick, speaking from the heart of England.

A sort of quenched scuffle arose. Skirts rustled, chairs thrust back squawked on the parquet, voices, hushed but prepared to rise in a minute, questioned and exclaimed. A lady with diamonds called "Stanislas!" and the bald man whose shoulders were draped with a plaid shawl uttered a growl of satisfaction. For already the assembly had split into two parties, the one lightly alarmed, lightly enthusiastic, the other excited, class-conscious, and belligerent. The ill-dressed and the well-dressed, who had been sitting so surprisingly cheek by jowl, began to group themselves after their kind. When the lady with diamonds embraced Minna and cried out, "Ah, my dear! It has come at last, our revolution," the camp of the ill-dressed showed no sympathy.

Nor, thought Sophia, sharply observing this turn of the evening's entertainment, did Minna. Her narrative and her spell broken by the concierge's announcement, she had put on for a moment the look of a cat made a fool of—a massive sultry fury. Rallying, she had matched the situation by a majestic rising to her feet, a lightening of her sombre mask, a deepened breathing and an opening of hands, as though welcoming a day-spring on her darkness. This was havocked by the embrace of the diamonded lady. For a second time balked of the centre of the stage she seemed about to turn her back on her audience, till, catching Sophia's faithful glance, she made a swift, a confidential grimace, walked towards her, and deflecting herself at a few steps' distance, began to talk to the humpbacked little Jew.

Round her oblivion her guests assembled with a growing anxiety to make their farewells. The voices became louder, more unrestrained, above them soared the voice of the revolutionary diamond lady.

"Stanislas! We must give them our carriage. Tell the man."

But the concierge had taken himself off.

"Isn't he there? Tiresome lout! Minna, my angel, we are going down to join in the revolution."

"Good night, countess."

She might have been brushing off a fly. Shivering, frowning a little, she continued her conversation with the little Jew, laying her hand on his arm, seeming to compel herself to speak with animation.

"But, David, you must insist on a proper rehearsal. What does he think your music is? Vaudeville? And of course he can afford a second flute-player. The last of his wretched concerts I went to, I am sure he had hired at least a dozen drummers, all of them butchers or sergeant-majors. No! Either proper rehearsals, you must tell him, or you will take back the score."

"There is a barricade in your street, Minna. And revolutions have no second flute-players to spare," said the man with the shawl.

"Why not, Ingelbrecht? A revolution must have music to match it."

"Street songs. But not symphonies."

"Symphonies! Are the people, a free people, to have nothing better than a tune on the hurdy-gurdy? My dear, the truth is, you don't like music."

Her change of voice might have wheedled open a strong-box, and he smiled and grunted, pleased to have his lack of taste recognized. But the humpbacked boy, grown pale and dejected as though a sudden gale had nipped him, slid from her detaining hand and, coughing, began to wind a scarf round his long thin neck.

The room was emptying fast. The well-dressed party having deposited their farewells had gone, to bestow or to rescue their carriages. The others, talking much louder now, were preparing to follow. Worse manners, Sophia said to herself, I have never seen. However, I suppose that I may walk off without good-byeing, as casually as they. Indeed, since she had come unasked, she could scarcely do otherwise.

It was high time to go. In this emptying room it would not long be possible for Frederick to avoid meeting her eye. He must certainly have discovered her by now, but tactful as at his last visit to Blandamer he made no sign of recognition.

Between her and the door stood Minna, feeding the humpback with cakes and hot wine. Are you the child who ran across the bloodied snow to kill the Christians? Are you the prophetess, the brooding priestess of liberty, who spoke with such passion of the enfranchised river? Are you the woman so bitterly hated, my rival and over-thrower? Sophia stared at the sleek braids of black hair and the smooth milk-coffee coloured shoulders, the drooping yellow scarf lined with rather shabby ermine, the attitude of elegant single-hearted domesticity. She would never know, never know more! And with a pang of the mind she realized that after this false move there was nothing left her but to go back to Blandamer immediately. Hours, ages ago, propelled up the stairs by the man in the cloak, she had recognized the false move, had seen with the chess-player's pang her queen abandoned in the centre of the board, irremediably exposed to capture. She, who had meant to play so cunningly, had lost the game like any tyro. And tomorrow, with what ignominy, she must retreat, without hope of a child, without hope of any rehabilitation in her own esteem, without hope of any future but one of futility, rage, and regret; and without (with the honesty of despair she admitted it) any hope of knowing more about Minna. From all those dreams she had never been able to carry into waking a recollection of the dream-Minna's face; and from this real-life encounter she would depart as tantalized, as unfulfilled.

"Good night then, my dear," said Minna to the humpback.

Now was the moment. Straight as a ramrod, looking neither to right nor left, Sophia took a step towards the door.

"You look so tired. Please drink a little of this hot wine before you go."

How much the taller I am, thought Sophia, looking down on that countenance of candour and solicitude. She saw her hand go out, accepting the wine.

The warm spiced scent, slightly resinous, as though the Jewess had mixed all the summer forests of her childhood in the cup, was like a caress. Round the first sip she felt her being close, haggard and hungry.

"Ah! That will do you good. You look better already."

A creative possessiveness, a herb-wife's glorying in the work of healing, glowed in the words, and in the melancholy attentive gaze. I must speak, thought Sophia, or in another moment she will be putting me to bed. In any case, for mere civility's sake, she must say something.

"You must be tired too. Your narration—it could not have moved us so much without fatiguing you."

There was a gesture of acknowledgement, stately and resigned.

"Tell me. . . . The river, and the forest, where were they?"

"In Lithuania. Almost on the track of the retreat from Moscow. I could tell you something of that, too, of the old man, a deserter from the Grand Army, always limping from his frostbite, who pitied me when I was in the priest's house. I will tell you, one day."

"I wish you had not been interrupted."

"I was sorry to lose such listening as yours. Yes, as yours. Did you not know that I was speaking to you?"

"I am leaving Paris tomorrow."

With her words came a rush of cold air. A window, giving upon a balcony, had been opened.

"Let us look."

With the cold air came the sound of voices, of picks striking upon stone. From the balcony they could look down upon the barricade a-building. Already it stretched almost across the street, a random barrier of sawn-off boughs bristling, tables and chairs piled together, a cab or two (Stanislas seemed to have preserved the carriage), a mangle, and a bedstead. Round it was a group of men, some busy uprooting the paving-stones, others artistically rearranging the confusion of boughs and bedsteads, like demented furniture-removers. Except for these, the street was empty.

"But what is the object of putting it here?" exclaimed Sophia.

"Moral effect." Frederick's voice answered her words, adding,

"Hullo, Sophia! How long have you been in Paris?"

She was saved from answering by a head interposed between them, and a young man's voice saying excitedly,

"I will tell you the object, Madame. Behind that barricade patriots will defend the cause of liberty, will defy the tyrant, will bleed and conquer."

"They have been defying the tyrant all day, you know," added Frederick.

"Gloriously!" exclaimed the young man. "Ah, what a day! I was there, this morning, in the Place de la Concorde, when the processions converged, waves of indignant patriots advancing with majesty, workers who had left their toil, their humble homes, to oppose the threat to their liberties, to intimidate that worthless Guizot with the spectacle of their might. The *rappel* was beaten. But it was sounded for them. They marched to the drumbeat. The National Guards which it summoned either retreated before them, or joined their ranks in sympathy. They met, these waves, before the Chamber of

Deputies. They stood there, immovable, crying out with one voice for reform."

"Some bold spirits climbed the railings," said Frederick.

"It was a voice to strike terror into the heart of any tyrant," continued the young man, raising his own. "But they did not only speak. They acted. The dragoons were powerless before them. In the Champs-Élysées the first barricade went up. Trees were cut down, benches uprooted, the café-keepers hastened to offer their chairs and tables. It was reared in a moment, that first brave barricade."

"An omnibus," Frederick added, "an omnibus, coming from the Barrière de l'Étoile, was seized in an instant and added to the barricade. An omnibus, you know, Sophia, is a very considerable object. Think what an improvement an omnibus or two would be, down there."

The young man was certainly a windbag, and might be a rival. But it seemed to Sophia that Frederick's malice was aimed at Minna herself, who with averted head leaned on the balcony, staring down at the work below. She had pretended not to hear the words, but her body had crouched under them, dejectedly defensive. Jew-baiting. The word rushed into Sophia's mind, and turning on Frederick, she said,

"As an omnibus is out of the question, I wish you would get me a cab."

Ill-considered words: not only laying her own claim on his attentions, but by doing so seeming to dispute Minna's.

"Certainly, Sophia. If a cab is to be found tonight, you shall have it. But it may take a little finding. You may even have to walk."

"I will bring a cab," said the young man, pleased to get the better of the Englishman, and ready to take up any challenge. "Madame, with your permission, I will bring you a cab immediately."

Frederick's stalking footsteps were already descending the stairs, the young man clattered after him. Dignity seen from above cannot hold its own; but ignoring this, the two men issued from the door in simultaneous exclusiveness, and went off in opposite directions, Frederick pausing at the barricade to examine it and talk to the workers. He will hand round cigars and be a success, thought Sophia. The rightness of the guess deepened her hatred against him; and hearing his easy laughter, his mellow flourishing farewells, she gritted her teeth with rage.

Never had she hated him so thoroughly. For now, she thought, for the first time in my life, I am in his power. He can do with me as he pleases, pity me as a fool or ridicule me as a jealous wife, come scolding after him as a village woman goes to the ale-house to rout home a drunken husband. *Let him try!*—said her will. But he had tried already, and succeeded. Already he had made of her—what all convenient wives should be—his stalking-horse, the malice of his words rebounding off her to Minna, her wifely petticoats the shield whence he could attack his mistress. That spluttering young man might be Frederick's butt, but scarcely his rival. And the thought shot up that if Frederick were jealous of anyone, it was of her.

And why not? No doubt it would be a painful sight to any man to see even the smallest attention, the smallest civility, a glass of hot wine and a couple of sentences, bestowed by the mistress upon the wife. And so he had addressed to her his belittling of the revolutionaries, making her seem a party, however silent, to what must wound Minna. Yes, that was natural enough, and he had done it deftly—what more obvious shift than to show a wife in as unpleasant colours as possible? Yet, good Lord, he had had two years to do it in! Could any man, even Frederick, be such a fool as to neglect that essential process until wife and mistress met?

Yes, Frederick could be such a fool. Slothful and ease-loving, it might well be possible that he had not stirred himself to mention her till this moment. For the mention of an ignominious marriage, of an uncongenial wife, might come under the heading of a business conversation; and she knew how cunning the stratagems of his inertia to put off such. Yet, being such a fool, she, by a superior foolery, had enabled him to remain a fool and still be victorious. He had not to put himself out in the least, he need not even labour his wits for a lie. By her insensate escapade she had given herself into his hands—a stick to beat a mistress with. Perhaps they had already quarrelled; she knew nothing of their relations, Frederick's passion might have cooled long since. If that were so, how aptly she had arrived, led by his good star and her bad—an angry wife roaring after her prey. What easier than to retire behind those petticoats, stroll off politely and leave the two women to fight it out and dry each other's tears. Considering the beautiful simplicity of the trick, it was difficult not to snort aloud with anger.

But then, did Minna know who she was? She was not labelled Mrs. Willoughby, not outwardly, for all the inward brandings of the law and the church and society.

Trapped in this new dilemma, she raised her head and looked at Minna.

The sleet had turned to a drizzling rain. The lamplight of the room behind them diamonded the raindrops on Minna's black hair, washed with sleek glimmerings her folded wet hands that drooped over the balustrade. Her shoulders twitched with cold, but the wrap of yellow satin and ermine dangled forgotten. With averted face she seemed to be studying the work in the street below. A barricade, presumably, was a sight to gladden any revolutionary heart, and Minna was a revolutionary; but every line of her figure spoke of dejection.

Why do you let yourself be made miserable by his taunts? asked Sophia's heart, angered to see this vital creature cast down. Or is this, too, a trick to gain my sympathy? For it was too soon to forget those glances of triumphant power, those smiles of satisfied strategy, which had filled the pauses of Minna's narrative; and not even this appearance of drowned cat could allay the suspicion of a seventh life lurking. But meanwhile not a paw moved out to encircle her, there seemed no possibility of twitch in that dispirited tail; and though the completeness of this appearance of misery should have warned, *Artist,* only curiosity held back Sophia's impulse to pity this desolation, succour and rally it.

Never in her life had she felt such curiosity or dreamed it possible. As though she had never opened her eyes before, she stared at the averted head, the large eloquent hands, the thick, milk-coffee-coloured throat that housed the siren voice. Her curiosity went beyond speculation, a thing not of the brain but in the blood. It burned in her like a furnace, with a steadfast compulsive heat that must presently catch Minna in its draught, hale her in, and devour her.

She was still staring when her hostess turned.

"You are getting very wet," remarked Sophia.

"So are they," she answered, pointing downwards to where, round the completed barricade, the builders were huddling into its shelter. They had a brazier, and now a frying-pan had been produced, and the sizzle of fat was audible. With astonishment Sophia realized that the furniture-removers were settling down for the night.

"I must send them some food and drink."

Minna spoke listlessly, almost automatically. Surely it was not like this that the devotees of liberty nourished its warriors? As though the look of inquiry had spoken its satire, Minna started.

"You think I am not very enthusiastic? I have not given them my carriage, I have not exclaimed. . . . Perhaps you think I am not very sincere. But if you have ever longed for a thing, longed with your whole heart, with year after year of your life, longed for it with all that is noblest in you and worked for it with all that is most base and most calculating, you would understand with what desolation of spirit one beholds the dream made flesh."

"I have never longed for anything like that."

Nor ever shall, she added to herself.

"No?"

It was only courtesy, as Sophia knew, that tilted the inflexion of the monosyllable towards inquiry; and only courtesy that turned the head, and directed that sleep-walking gaze; and yet, for all that, she felt a profound impulse to unburden herself of the motive that had brought her to Paris, to explain passionately and exactly all that she had felt, endured, intended, telling all from the expedition to the lime-kiln to the conversation with the porter which had been like eating a radish; as though the Jewess's impassive attention had been a dark sleek-surfaced pool into which, as one is compelled to cast a stone into those waters, she was compelled to cast her confidence.

All the while of her thought, Minna's glance, sombre and

attentive, waited upon her. The desperate riveted attention, thought Sophia, of the hostess who at the end of a too long protracted party dissembles with the last guest their mutual agony over a belated carriage, who stretches her eyes because to close them would open her jaws in a yawn, whose thoughts wander slowly in search of a subject for conversation.

"Why do you want this revolution? What good do you think it will do?"

The milk-coffee-coloured shoulders tossed back the yellow satin scarf in a shrug.

"What good? None, possibly. One does not await a revolution as one awaits the grocer's van, expecting to be handed packets of sugar and tapioca. My river in spring flood brought dead bodies, a hand or foot dismembered, a clot of entrails. So will this flood, maybe. But for all that it is the spring flood."

The image that had been so fine in her narrative flagged in conversation to no more than gimcrack and rodomontade; and suppressing a feeling of disappointment—for why should she expect to be converted to revolutionary views by Frederick's Jewess?—Sophia resorted to polite praise of Minna's eloquence, wishing with increased passion that Frederick would bring the cab.

For a moment it seemed that he had done so. Footsteps hastened up the stairs. Minna turned to the opened door with a look of recognition. But the head rising from the well of the stair was the head of a tempest-tossed poodle, and even on a night like this the news of a cab could not justify lips so dramatically parted, eyes so passionately beady.

"Gaston!"

"Minna!"

Had they been play-acting at conspirators, thought Sophia, their dramatic embrace could not have been more perfunctory.

"Has it begun? Has it really begun?"

"Begun! It is in full flow, nothing can stop it now. Paris is ours! No, not now," he added petulantly, flinging away from the hand maternally patting his arm, "but by tomorrow night it will be, I can promise you that, I have seen to it. Listen, Minna! Tomorrow night there will be bloodshed."

"Not till then?"

The question was asked with melancholy irony.

"No! One must have the night," he exclaimed, shaking back the poodle-locks from his bony countenance. "One must have the effect of torchlight, the Rembrandtesque shadows, the solemnity and uncertainty of darkness. Besides, feelings run higher at night and there are more people at leisure to become spectators," he added, suddenly assuming the tone of an organizer. "What we have decided is this. There must be bloodshed, and it must come from them. It must be forced from them, they must be compelled to fire on the people, it must be decisive, a volley. This show of cottonwool benevolence must be torn away, this sham liberalism shown up. Very well, then. There must be a concentration of troops, and earlier in the day we have an attack on some public building—the Foreign Affairs probably—sufficient to ensure that a detachment is told off to guard it. In the evening our procession forms—one can always manage a procession—a procession of the citizens with their children—children are essential for the right feeling, and I have arranged for the children. It is a peaceable procession, as it might be a picnic, it is full of patriotism and good feeling. Good! They listen to a speech from Marrast of the *National,* a speech of sympathy for their sufferings; they turn into the boulevard des Capucines, they come to the Foreign Affairs, they are confronted by the troops. They are shot down!"

"But if the troops do not fire? There have been orders—"

"They will fire. That will be seen to."

"And then?"

To Sophia, standing unnoticed by the window, this conversation seemed repulsive and silly. People who had arranged their revolutions standing on landings and gabbling at the tops of their voices. . . . She listened with exasperation to the rapid dogmatic tones of the man greeted as Gaston, to the few interposed words from Minna, and the fact that they spoke in a foreign language seemed to set the whole affair further off, to set it in some different time and place wherein she had no concern. The only words which could fall on her ears with relevance would be an announcement of that cab; and at this moment Gaston was babbling about a dray heaped with the bleeding forms of patriots.

Very well, then! She would walk back to the hotel. And with the same movement which turned her towards the door she sank down on a sofa, overborne by fatigue. There was a book by her hand and she took it up and opened it, and thought she was reading until with a jolt she realized that she was falling asleep. In the ante-room the conversation continued, and from below came a dreary yowling, the songs of those manning the barricade, and finding it as hard as she did, she supposed, to watch through a night of such intolerable disjointedness and tedium. I must go, she told herself; and resolvedly keeping her eyes open with such sensations of pain that she might have been holding open two wounds, she stared round Minna's apartment, and could see nothing. The conversation and the singing continued, but she did not hear them. Sleep roared in her ears like the river roaring through Lithuania, and as her eyelids closed the landscape of France began to flash by, seen through the window of the railway carriage; but now, morassed in a wretched dream, the train was bearing her northwards, she was going home, empty, hopeless, and undone. She had not even the child. But in her dream it was not for the loss of the child she mourned so desperately. Something else was lost, there was some other hope, some other promise, irretrievably mismanaged and irretrievably lost; and it was for this something, this unpossessed unknown, that she mourned in such desolation, having not even the comfort of knowing what was for ever left behind and forfeited—a speech unuttered or unheard, a book heavy with the black Hebrew characters, a bunch of tufted mimosa.

"Sleep, you must sleep, my beauty, my falcon," a voice said. And scarcely knowing that she had for a moment awakened she lay passive under the hands that untied her bonnet-strings, and took off her shoes, and covered her with something warm and furry, stroking her, slowly, heavily, like the hands of sleep, stroking her hair and her brow.

It was full morning, the room was vividly alive and alight when she woke, hearing the sound of drums, and smelling coffee. A woodfire newly lit was crackling on the hearth, and with the first glance of her opening eyes she had seen an old woman of operatic ugliness vanishing from the room as though withdrawing in the fringe of a dream.

She was lying islanded in the middle of the room on a gilded sofa upholstered in pink brocade—the sofa, plebeianly capacious, plebeianly pink, of any provincial hotel's drawing-room, but so tarnished and tattered as to present a semblance of the aristocracy of a fallen fortune. Round her shoulders was the yellow ermine-lined scarf, and beyond a stretch of scarlet-dyed sheepskin her feet confronted her, wearing a pair of sky-blue woollen slippers, several sizes too large. It was like waking up in the bosom of a macaw.

With the benevolence of the well-slept she stared round the room. Over a basis of respectable furnished apartment was scattered what looked like the beginnings of a curiosity shop or the studio of a painter in genre. A mandolin leaned against a mounted suit of armour, a Gothic beaker, ecclestiastically embossed with false gems, stood on a Louis Seize trifle-table and propped an Indian doll with tinsel robes, beaded nose-ring, and black cotton features of a languishing cast. Dangling over a harp was a Moorish bridle. On the walls hung scimitars and bucklers, pieces of brilliant embroidery, tapestries, and a quantity of pictures framed or unframed. It was a room calculated to outrage Sophia's orderly sensibilities. Yet she looked round on it with tolerance; for however fantastic the effect it was not with a studied fantasy. Profuse, eclectic, inconsequential, the room had a nomadic quality, as though an evening had split this extemporization over the respectable furnished apartment and as though another evening might sweep it away.

She sat up, snuffling the aroma of coffee, her frame of mind light, complacent, exhilarated. To the lively drumbeats was added the sound of churchbells, a noise that recalled to her the drive of yesternight, the domes she had seen bulging against the sky. She remembered that she was in Paris, that Paris was in a state of revolution. She jumped up, shook herself briskly, opened the window and leaned from the balcony. The shabby gaiety of the houses opposite charmed her. The colouring of the rue de la Carabine, the light-hearted pallor of the tall housefronts, was as reviving as a watercolour after the look of England, so solidly painted in oils.

At the clatter of the opening windows the men on the barricade glanced up, and one of them kissed his hand to her, shouting up a greeting in the name of the revolution to her fair tumbled hair. Like cats who had been out and about all the night, they were sprucing themselves in the merry morning air. One was sputtering over a bucket of water, another was combing his hair with his fingers; and as she watched she saw a third gravely disarray himself of one pair of trousers and put on a smarter pair which a young woman had brought out over her arm. Some tin coffee-pots, long wands of golden bread, a sausage in a paper chemise, gave a domesticated appearance to the barricade, as though the objects had arrived of their own good will in order to assure the beds and tables that there was nothing, after all, so particularly odd or discreditable in having spent a night in the street. But despite the coffee-pots the barricade had taken on a more formidable appearance than on the previous night, and paving-stones were being methodically taken up, and earth heaped.

Round its defenders stood a small shifting crowd of admirers and sympathizers—errand boys, shop-girls, working-men, students, women in shawl and slipper. There was a babble of advice and encouragement, and presently from the vine-painted wine-shop advanced a smiling man with a number of bottles. Leaning against the barricade he uncorked them with splendid gestures. "To the Revolution," he said, and handed the first bottle to the young man who had tossed up his greeting to Sophia's flaxen hair. "To the Revolution," repeated he, and in turn handed the bottle to a woman standing near by. As she raised it to her lips the tilt of the unbonneted head revealed to Sophia that it was her hostess who was drinking from a bottle in the street.

Now a group of men appeared, coming slowly down the street. At every door they paused, and parleyed; and at almost every door they received a weapon of some sort—a gun, or a pistol, or a rusty sabre. These were heaped upon the following hand-cart, and the group moved on, the leader scrawling in chalk upon the quitted door. As he came nearer Sophia could read the inscription: *Armes données.*

The concierge who had overnight so fatalistically announced the building of the barricade was offering a large household hammer and some lengths of iron dog-chain, explaining that the label tied to them carried his name and address, and that he would be glad of their return "after the victory." He was still expatiating on the various uses of a hammer, and the gladness with which he offered it to heroes, when Minna brushed past him. Sophia could hear her feet on the echoing stairs, a gait with a sort of lumbering lightness, and while she was still debating in her mind as to whether a bear who really enjoyed waltzing would not sound much the same, Minna entered.

"You slept?" she said; and holding Sophia's hand she gazed at her with a possessive earnest glance, a glance that instantly recalled the taste of the mulled wine offered overnight.

I cannot understand, thought Sophia, what Frederick could see in you. But *I* can see a great deal. Though it had never been her habit to drink mulled wine in the morning, it was impossible not to be gratified by the persuasive, rather melancholy warmth which flowed from the Jewess, and forgetting the improbability of the situation, forgetting, even, that she stood in a pair of blue woollen slippers several sizes too large for her, she spoke her thanks for the pink sofa.

The words were civil and correct, they were even genial; but at their close the Jewess sighed heavily, and turned away, gathering from the wall an assortment of rapiers and scimitars. Then, with the troubled air of a good housewife weighing out an unusual quantity of stores, she opened a drawer and took up a pair of fine duelling pistols.

Sophia had inherited from Papa a taste for firearms. It seemed to her that even a revolutionary might part from those pistols with regret, and she said so.

"They are by Watson," sighed Minna. "Well, they must go. But I have another pair." Darkly swimming, her eyes rolled for a moment towards Sophia. "A better pair." And in a grand manner she called the old woman and bade her take down the offering, to the men below.

"Now—" she extended the word upon a skilful yawn. "*Now* we can have our chocolate."

For the last nine years of her life Sophia had seen in every human activity death as a factor. Water might drown, fire might burn. A wet stocking might lead to the grave, a raw fruit was a plummet that lowered the eater into that pit. In every tuft of warm grass lurked an adder, in every tuft of damp grass a consumption. Death's sting was in the wasp. Dogs bit, and were mad dogs. The cat might scratch a child's eye out, a pony shying might toss a child and break a neck. The sun had a heavy stroke on a child's head, and a morning fog wafted sickness into the nursery. In exchange for a kiss, or a penny dropped into a cottager's hand, fever and pestilence might be deposited. Rusty nails waited in sheds, falling slates hung patiently from roofs, in the hay a sickle lay craftily. A diet that was not heating was probably lowering, even the medicine bottle must be eyed as a deceiving enemy, and the best-warranted pill might bring on a fatal choking-fit, as easily as a random blue bead picked off the firescreen. In every path death lay in wait: the death that after all had not had to wait for so very long since both Damian and Augusta lay dead.

Yet the day passed, and the February dusk had fallen, and Sophia had not once bethought her that death might wait upon a revolution. The superior pair of duelling pistols shown to her by Minna had roused but one thought only: a determination to visit a shooting-gallery and become a crack shot. That also were possible to her; she could do anything, go anywhere, if she could spend a day in such passionate amity with her husband's mistress. Hers was the liberty of a fallen woman now.

The cloaked man, propelling her up the staircase, had changed her life for her, with his polite gloved hand waving her into a new existence. It could not be of long duration, this new existence; another day even, in Minna's company (yet for no consideration possible would she forgo an hour of it), would madden her or kill her with excitement. No reason, no mortal frame, could long endure the ardour of this fantastic freedom from every inherited and practised restraint, nor the spur of that passionately sympathetic company. It was an air (however long and unknowingly she had panted for it) which must wear out breathing. Talking to Minna she supposed that she must talk herself to death as others bleed to death; and as a person with hæmorrhage feels the blood beating and striving to escape she felt the weight of her whole life throbbing to be recounted; and as a drowning man sees his whole life pass before him, and recognizes as authentically his a hundred incidents and scenes which had lain forgotten in the un-death-awakened mind, her childhood, her youth, her womanhood rose up crowded and clear before her, and must be told—even to the day when she lay under the showering hawthorn watching the year's first scything of the lawn and eating, with such passionate appetite, the sweet grass-clippings, even to the old beggar-woman in Coblenz whose dry lips had grated in a kiss on her casual charitable hand.

Sitting on the pink sofa, her hair still falling about her shoulders, her feet still muffled in the blue slippers, her eyes blackened with excitement, her lips dry with fever, she continued her interminable, her dying speech. At intervals, in some strange non-apparent way, there was food before her, and more wine in the glass, the fire built up or a lighted lamp carried into the room. Sometimes a drum rattled somewhere through the echoing streets beating the *rappel,* or a burst of sudden voices rose from the barricade. And with some outlying part of her brain she recognized that a revolution was going on outside. News of it was brought by hurried visitors; and as though a semi-awakening had blurred the superior reality of a dream she listened drowsily to tidings of a fallen ministry, a stormed building, a palace in terror and disarray. They went. And instantly she began once more to talk and Minna, caressing her hand or with abstracted attention examining the fineness of her flaxen hair as though it were something marketable, to listen. Neither woman, absorbed in this extraordinary colloquy, had expressed by word or sign the slightest consciousness that there was anything unusual about it.

"Well, Minna, well, Sophia."

Frederick, arriving during the afternoon, seemed instantly felled into taking it for granted that his wife and his mistress should be seated together on the pink sofa, knit into this fathomless intimacy, and turning from it to entertain him with an identical patient politeness. Stroking his hat as though it were a safe domestic animal he told them of Guizot's resignation, of the National Guards singing the Marseillaise in the Place de la Bastille, of the preparations for a universal illumination, and how the funeral of a young lady of the aristocracy had been interrupted and her coffin requisitioned for a barricade. Everything, he implied, was proceeding nicely though it was no affair of his; and now he would be going.

Pausing at the door, "By the way, Sophia," said he, "if you are putting up at your respectable Meurice, you won't get much sleep tonight. There are troops all around the Tuileries, and there's sure to be a dust-up. I should stay here with Minna, if I were you."

And with a bland glassy sweep of the eye over the blue slippers he closed the door as on a sick-room.

Instantly forgetting his existence save as a character in her narrative, Sophia went on talking. Minna's clasp tightened upon her hand.

A more effectual interruption came later when the concierge appeared, remarkingly sternly,

"Excuse me. But illuminations are obligatory."

"Illuminations?" said Minna.

"To celebrate the fall of the tyrant. It is all one to me," he added, "but one cannot have the windows broken."

"No, no, of course not. I will see to it. Natalia! Bring all the candles you can find. What news have you heard?"

"They have extinguished the gas in the outer boulevards."

As the door closed behind him they laughed. It was the first laugh that had passed between them, and its occurrence momentarily re-made them as strangers to each other. Minna averted her eyes, and began a rambling, unconvinced account of the absurdities of Égisippe Coton. Forgetting to answer Sophia stared at her hostess. Under the scrutiny Minna began to wilt. Talking with nervous suppliant emphasis she had a harassed, a hunted expression.

They have extinguished the gas on the outer boulevards. The words were insultingly applicable to this wearied visage, jostled with speech. Using the cool patronage and consideration with which she would attend to the needs of something useful and inferior, order a bran-mash for a horse or send a servant to bed, she found herself thinking that for Minna, conscripted all day on this strange impulse to expound her heart, something must be done.

"I should like to take you out to dinner," she said. "Where can we get a good meal?"

Hearing this loud British incivility proceeding so plumply from a good heart and a healthy appetite—and indeed, they had eaten nothing all day save hors-d'œuvres and pastries—her sense of shame was followed by an inward hysteria.

"That would be charming, there would be nothing I should like better. I am not sure if it can be managed, I expect everything is shut. Perhaps Natalia would know, she could go out and fetch something. No, that would not do, though, she shops abominably, she would bring us pickled herrings and lemonade. She has had such a sad life, poor Natalia, it seems to have turned her naturally towards brine. Has it ever struck you that unhappy women always crave for sour pickles?"

Sophia said,

"But why should everything be shut?"

"The revolution . . ."

She had overlooked the revolution again—an affair of foreign politics. But to Minna, of course, being a revolutionary, it must mean a great deal; and she must be allowed to see something of it.

"If we went out we might see what's going on. But we must have a good dinner first, for I suppose we should have to talk."

It was only when she had ordered the filet-steak that Sophia realized that she had commandeered Minna's evening as high-handedly as she had taken her day. Never in my life, thought she, studying the wine list, have I acted quite like this. For though no doubt I have always been strong-minded, and lately, seeing no one but my inferiors, may have got into a trick of domineering, nothing in my past, nothing in my upbringing, parallels this. For she is older than I am, and she is a woman of some eminence, and she is my husband's mistress—and here am I, taking her out to dinner and allowing her to see a little of her revolution as though she were a child to be given a treat —as though she were Caspar.

"A bottle of eighteen," she said.

It had been an axiom of Papa's that under doubtful circumstances it was best to order Beaujolais. These circumstances were admittedly doubtful, nor was this a place where one might hope much of the wine. Nothing in her past, nothing in her upbringing, would have prepared her to sit unescorted in a restaurant, or to walk at night through the streets of Paris. However, with the probably poorness of the wine went probably security from molestation. The restaurant was crowded, humble, and uninterested in the two women.

I wish I knew, thought Sophia, if I seem as odd to you as I do to myself.

As though overhearing the thought Minna remarked,

"How much I like being with English people! They manage everything so quietly and so well."

"And am I as good as Frederick?"

"You are much better."

For an answer to an outrageous, to an unprovoked, insult, it was dexterous. It was more; for the words were spoken with a composure and candour that seemed, in that stroke of speech, to dismiss for ever any need to insult or be insulted, and the smile that accompanied them, a smile of unalloyed pleasure at successful performance, was as absolving as any caper of triumph from a menaced and eluding animal.

She lives on her own applause, thought Sophia, watching Minna's revival into charm. This is what it is, I suppose, to be an artist, cheered and checked by the April of one's own mind. For she is an artist, though there is nothing to show for it but a collection of people going home from an evening party through the streets of a city in revolution each one carrying with him a picture of a child standing beside a river in Lithuania. Yes, she is an artist, what they call a Bohemian. And I, in this strange holiday from my natural self, am being a Bohemian too, she thought with pride, staring about her at the walls painted with dashing views of Italy, at the worn red velvet of the benches, at the other diners, who expressed, all of them, a sort of shabby weariness countered by excitement, at the waiters, darting nimble as fish through the wreaths of tobacco smoke; and yielding again to that wine-like sensation of ease and accomplished triumph which had been with her all day she said,

"But Frederick would never bring you to a place like this."

"No, indeed. He would bring a nice bunch of lilies of the valley, and dine with me."

Damn him, was Sophia's instant thought.

"It is difficult," continued Minna, "for people like us not to misjudge people like Frederick. There is much that is admirable, much that is touching, in such gentleness and domesticity."

"I have not had much opportunity to muse over Frederick's domesticity for the last three years," said Sophia.

"No. And for part of that time I had perhaps rather too much. So you see we must both be biased."

"Poor Frederick!"

"Poor Frederick!"

Minna echoed the words but not the tone of irony.

"However," she added, "our faulty appreciation would not trouble him. Frederick completely despises all women. I think that is why he seems so dull and ineffectual."

The artless analysis coming from lips on which rumour had heaped so many kisses distracted Sophia from the rage she naturally felt on hearing that Frederick despised all women. But the rage was there, and prompted the thought that she should not lag behind in comments of a kind and tolerant sort.

"However dull you found him, you did him an immense amount of good. I have never known him so pleasant, so rational, as he was on his last visit to England—his last visit to me, I mean. I do not know if he has visited England since then."

"When was that?"

"When my children were dying."

"Ah, no wonder! He would be at his best then, you see. For he felt an emotion that was perfectly genuine, and which he could express without any constraint, any *mauvaise honte.* Men, who are so suspicious, so much ashamed, of any other emotion, have no shame in the feeling of fatherhood. It was his *Volkslied* he was singing then. It was no wonder he sang it well.

"I too," she added, drooping her glance, holding tightly to the stem of her wine-glass, "was very sorry."

You are embarrassed, or you are making yourself feel so, thought Sophia. And that is a pity, for the moment you are embarrassed I lose my liking for you.

"This is horrible coffee," she said. "Coffee is a thing we manage much better in England, where we drink it strong. At this moment when I think of my children my chiefest regret is that their lives were so limited, so dreary. Nothing but restrictions and carefully prepared pap. When I was listening to you last night I thought with bitter reproach that they had never walked over a heath in their lives or seen the shedding of blood."

But they were unreal to her at this moment, her children; and Augusta's remembered face, consuming in a rather stodgy resolute excitement as she begged to be allowed to watch the pig-killing, less actual than the sunburned shag-haired visage of the child in Lithuania chanting in her wild treble against the roaring voice of the bloodied river.

Later in the evening she had good bodily reason to remember the Lithuanian childhood, the free wanderings over the heath. Minna still walked as though her foot were on a heath, and as though conducting her from one bird's-nest to another she led Sophia by innumerable short-cuts to various places where the revolution might be expected to make a good showing. At least a dozen barricades were visited, and over these they had been handed with great civility; falling in with a procession they followed it to the Place de la Bastille where they waited for some time, listening to the singing, and then in the wake of another procession, they had trudged to the Hôtel de Ville and listened to shouting. The shouting was all, presumably, that revolutionary shouting should be—loud, confident, and affable. Here and there, bursting upwards from the level of the crowd, an orator would emerge, twine like some short-lived flower to railings, and sum up in a more polished and blossom-like fashion the sentiments of the shouters.

But shaking her head in critical dissatisfaction Minna said, "There is more to see than this."

"Shall we try the Champs-Élysées?" For there at any rate, thought Sophia, there will be a chance to sit down. She was intolerably footsore, and in the reality of that sensation could feel nothing but despising for a revolution that was no concern of hers.

"No."

Minna turned northward again. As they went further it began to seem as though they were the only people walking that way. Here there was little uproar, no illuminations, no processions—but like leaves blown on some steady wind a man, or three men, or six men, would come towards them and pass them. They spoke very little, their faces wore no particular expression except the look of wariness which comes on the faces of all those who have to strive for a living. They seemed in no great hurry, tramping on as though they were going to their work. Among them, moving more swiftly as though they were lighter leaves on the same steady wind, came coveys of children, and groups of women, marching abreast with linked arms. And while their following shadows still trailed on the pavement, on into the circle of lamp-light would come one man, three men, six men.

"Do you see," whispered Minna. "It is the same yet, the old nursery of revolutions."

"It frightens me," said Sophia. "And I believe that you, even, are a little afraid."

"A little? I am horribly afraid. How is it possible to have a good bed to sleep in, food in the larder, furs against the cold, books on one's shelves, money in one's purse, a taste of music, and not be afraid? It is ten years and more, thanks to my good fortune, since I could have looked at these without feeling afraid."

"But you believe in revolution?"

"With all my heart."

They turned back, walking on the same wind as those others. Sophia began to make conversation about Socialism, endeavouring to blame it as coolly as possible, pointing out that equality was a delusion, that the poor in office were the cruellest oppressors of the poor, etc. By the time they struck into the boulevard des Capucines the changed character of the crowd had restored to her enough confidence to let the conversation drop. For here they were back once more in the heartiest display of comic opera. Earlier in the day the property rooms of the theatres had been raided by some enterprising collectors of arms, and under the light of the illuminations gilded spears and pasteboard helmets still wreathed with artificial flowers mingled their classical elegance with the morions and pikes which had last appeared in performances of *I Puritani.* Moving slowly through the crowd were family groups of sightseers, who had come out to enjoy the illuminations.

"That's nice, that one," said a woman behind Sophia, pointing to a house-front garlanded with little coloured lamps, hanging on wires like festoons of fruit and centring in a large and miscellaneous trophy of flags.

"They should include the ground floor," her companion answered with a laugh of superior sarcasm; and looking more attentively Sophia saw that the ground-floor windows had been boarded up, and that a detachment of soldiers was on guard before the house.

Cheerfully, politely, as though the information would make amends for the partial embellishment only, the woman exclaimed,

"Look, Anatole! Another procession, and this one with torches!"

"They've been quadrilling outside the *National,*" replied the well-informed Anatole. "Old Marrast has been letting off another of his speeches to them."

"Children, too. The little darlings, how pleased they look! I hope they won't set fire to anything with those torches. I'm glad now that we left Louise and Albertine at home. They would never be content until—"

The surging of the crowd carried them away from the words. Sophia tightened her hold on Minna's elbow, and stiffened herself protectively. Weary, footsore, sleepy, and bored, she still retained a core of carefulness for her companion, the last ember of emotion left waking from the earlier day.

"Did that fool jostle you?" she asked in a cross voice.

There was no answer. Minna, very pale, her mouth held stiffly open, was staring through the crowd at the approaching procession. It had neared the house with the boarded windows now, and while the children in shrill weary voices continued to sing the Marseillaise, its leader seemed to be haranguing the soldiers who stood before the boarded-up windows. "Minions," he exclaimed. And added something about tyranny.

"How bored those poor soldiers look," said Sophia.

Every hair of the orator's head seemed to be standing on end, and the torchlight, wavering in the children's inattentive grasp, passed romantic shadows and revelations across his pale face, and the faces massed behind him. She recognized him as Minna's hairy friend of the previous evening, the man who had ranted so on the stairs, and had been greeted as Gaston. A wave of jealousy swept over her—of prim, disapproving, schoolmistressly jealousy. She bent a sharp glance upon Minna's countenance.

Minna shut her eyes.

At the same moment there was the crack of a pistol-shot. Upon it came the most extraordinary sound, a unanimous, multiplied, gasping intake of breath, a sound like the recoil of a wave. Into this avid awaiting gasp from the crowd, plumped, as though compelled thither, a word of command, and a volley.

"Ah!"

Before the cries or the exclamations of the wounded could be heard the crowd had spoken, uttering its first word, not of rage or horror, but of profound physical satisfaction, a cry of relief. As though the shock of fulfilment had annihilated every lesser desire there was scarcely a movement around. The children with their torches, the knot of soldiers, the patriots and the sightseers stood grouped as though for ever, staring at the only movement left—the jerks and writhings of the wounded and dying. Into this silence and immobility Gaston began to launch another oration. On his words followed a rising hubbub of anger and sympathy and denunciation; but as it increased Sophia saw the soldiers relax, as it were, from their official inhumanity, and into their abashed and embarrassed looks there came a growing tincture of relief. Only their officer continued to stare before him with an expression of unmitigated dismay.

The crowd began to break up, swinging this way and that; some to escape homewards, others to gather round the bodies on the pavement. Sighing profoundly Minna disentangled herself from Sophia's clutch, ran forward, and joined herself to those who were attending to the wounded. Gaston swooped downward from his harangue to say something to her as she knelt on the pavement, but it was not possible to see how she answered him, for the crowd thickened, and swallowed them up.

"Here, take these," said Sophia, thrusting her smelling salts, a handkerchief, and a long ribbon ripped from her dress into the hands of a shop-girl who was holding out bloodied hands and demanding bandages for the wounded. And when, soon after, a hat was passed round, she put money into it, wishing that at the same time she could offer drinks to the soldiers.

For she found herself entirely impartial, even able to relish the smell of gunpowder as though this were a Blandamer shooting party, and her natural instinct to take charge of any catastrophe was frozen in her. More accurately than she had known, it seemed, her mind had listened to that conversation overnight. So far, everything had fallen out according to plan. Here were the children, and the Rembrandtesque shadows, the peaceable procession, as it were a picnic, and the provoked volley from the soldiers. Even the building—she recognized it now—was the Ministry of Foreign Affairs. I will wait, she said to herself, for the day.

The sediment of peaceful-minded had fallen out of the crowd and it seemed that she was the only person there who was not armed, who was not angry, and who had not a great deal to say. An uncomfortable neutrality. Pinned against the wall she could not but be aware that each glance that fell on her was more disapproving, more antagonistic, than the last. As though challenging her silence a dishevelled young man, glaring under an operatic helmet, inquired of her if it had not been vilely done, this attack on peaceful citizens; and getting no answer, he drove his elbow into her breast as he shoved himself onward. But already his gilded crest was out of sight, and her look of rage now lit upon a countenance so pale with hunger, so wasted with intellectual melancholy, so burning with indignant idealism that she had to catch back an apology. If he had seen her, though, he had not noticed her; and in a moment he was gone, carrying his strange flame with him, as much a solitary in that crowd as I, she thought, her imagination diving after the image which had sunk so deeply and instantaneously into her consciousness. But one cannot meditate in a crowd; and pinned under the light, her conspicuousness of stature and complexion and expensive mourning apparel placarded by her immobility and noncurrence, she realized with annoyance that her position was becoming increasingly dangerous.

If I am not torn in pieces, she reflected, I suppose I shall be shot by accident. For now shots were being exchanged as well as shouts; and it was strange to hear in this earnest and with these town-bred echoes, the sound so reminiscent of peaceful autumn mornings, of the motionless tawny bulk of the woodlands, of all the virgilian romance and dignity of the landscape in which the English landed gentry go out to shoot pheasants. A life rooted in that life, nourished in the pure leaf-mould of land-owning and fenced round with the Game Laws, does not easily let go its hold. In her worst frustration and weariness of soul Sophia had never contemplated death as a consolation; and to have travelled to Paris and taken her room at the Meurice in order to be killed in the boulevard des Capucines was a turn of Fate which had nothing to commend it. With all of her reason and with half of her heart she would have given away the other half in order to do what was the obvious and sensible thing—to extract herself from this unpleasant and dangerous turmoil, walk off to the hotel, and go to bed. But the other half of her heart, the half which had landed her in this situation, held firm, and kept her there.

A sudden acclaiming clamour of rage and emotion swelled out and, like the chord in a progression of music which with its strong gesture tilts the melody from one key into another, turned the weight of mob-feeling into a new and deeper channel. What it was that had called out this cry Sophia could not see, nor could those immediately around her; but for all that their exclamations tuned in with that other, so that it seemed natural and ordained that presently the mob should divide, pressing itself into mournful hedgerows, leaving, as for a procession of something royal or holy, a space down which the raw-boned cart-horse, its white blaze showy in the gaslight, could be led. The dray it drew forward was heaped with bodies, dead or subsiding into death, and marching beside it, and after it, in silence, with solemn, showmanly looks, were children carrying torches, were the patriots, grimed and bloodied, and women over whose furious faces the tears ran down.

The blood, the tears, the dead and dying bodies were real, as real as the dramatic talent which had organized this clinching raree-show. Real too, though by a momentary inattention compromising the dramatic effect, was Gaston, walking arm in arm with Minna among the mourners, deep in conversation.

To see the pair of them so ridiculously trivial, gabbling with their noses together like a couple of schoolgirls, was the last straw to Sophia's patience. Empowered by rage she wrenched herself out of the crowd, darted upon Minna, and catching her by the shoulder tweaked her away from her companion and out of the procession, and hauled her into a doorway.

"The whole thing has been engineered! It is nothing but a cold-blooded farce, it is beyond my comprehension how you can lend yourself to such . . . to such goings-on," she concluded, lamely and violently, and in English.

"Can you deny it, dare you deny it?"

Because in Minna's fixed and mournful stare she seemed to detect a look of pity her rage became even more arrogant.

"Fortunately it is no affair of mine how you manage your glorious triumphs of liberty.

"How will you get back to the rue de la Carabine? Will one of your friends see you home?"

It was the last blow that landed. Wincing from it, putting up her hand to her cheek as though a real blow had struck her, Minna said, "I can go home alone, Sophia."

"Good!"

But still the crowd kept them where they stood; and if moral loss of temper and the deeper rage of disillusionment could have allowed Sophia to feel any pity she must have felt it then, if only for that pilloried embarrassment. Her hand, like a policeman's, still gripped Minna's shoulder, having left it so long she must keep it there still, for so unnaturally vital was the tension between them that a movement towards convention would only make things worse. Under that grip Minna stood passive and resigned, as though to be held in custody, bullied, and abused were nothing out of the way to her. She made no attempt to speak, her glance, suppliant and patient, wandered to Sophia's face and wandered off again, watching the crowd that surged past them. These fawning, persecuted Israelites, thought Sophia, whetting her resentment on that sure stone.

On the twenty-fourth of February Louis Philippe abdicated, hastening through the gardens of the Tuileries on foot and under an umbrella, for it was raining pretty smartly. His wife, weeping and indignant, hung on his arm, and at the little gate of the Pont Tournant he was glad to climb into the cab which was in waiting there. The cab took the route towards Neuilly. There was no attempt to follow it.

A little later his daughter-in-law made her way to the Chamber of Deputies, taking her child with her. She was given a chair, and sat on it for some hours, unnoticed. A few polite voices had mentioned a regency, but no one had time or inclination to attend to her, though it was generally admitted that she had shown great courage and female dignity, besides being a mother, which is always venerable. At length, compelled by the calls of nature, she retired as inconspicuously as possible to the Invalides.

Meanwhile a provisional government of the Left was proposed and agreed on; and other provisional governments were agreed upon with equal enthusiasm and unanimity at the offices of two newspapers, the *National* and the *Réforme.* The adherents of each government, everything being settled so satisfactorily, joined their triumphal processions before the Hôtel de Ville, where there was a vast scene of rejoicing and fraternity.

All this Sophia heard from the valet who brought dinner to her room. He was a young man, and he admitted himself to be moved, saying that the slaughter had been frightful, and would have been worse if it had not been for the refusal of the National Guards to take any part in it, sticking nosegays in the muzzles of their guns to show the harmlessness of their intentions. Tomorrow, he said, a new era would begin.

She listened with exasperation. And yet when he had left the room she could have wished him and his babble back again; for to spend a whole day alone in a hotel bedroom, with the noise of a revolution sounding beneath one's window, is an ordeal which will fray the most resolute nerves. She would receive no one, she had said. No one had come. She was still in the vilest of tempers, footsore, and sour with sleeplessness, for the noise which had gone on all night made sleep impossible, and the slumber on the pink sofa seemed to have taken place in another world, so far removed was it. The day of confidences on that same sofa seemed as unreal, as far forgotten. Had there been any life left in the recollection it must have perished under her will's heel.

Tomorrow a new era would begin, and she would leave Paris. No, she would not. She would stay, order new clothes at the dressmakers', and visit great-aunt Léocadie. There she would find reason, dignity, and routine—everything that is dear to a woman of good sense who has dismissed her husband, lost her children, discarded the sentimental enthusiasms of youth which sit so ill on a woman of twenty-eight. It would be interesting and consoling to hear what Léocadie had to say about the revolution. This was her third.

Curious how affinity of character could abolish differences of age, race, and tradition! Though Sophia had been a child, and great-aunt Léocadie installed in old age, taking as her due an arm to lean on, hot rum, and a chair with ears, though she had insisted on being spoken to in French and revised every faltering sentence, in her company Sophia had enjoyed an intimacy of confidence never known before, an intimacy lifting her from the discomforts of childhood, setting her among the ranks of women grown. How much pleasanter to be great-aunt Léocadie's Sophie than Mamma's Sophia, what satisfaction in those interminable games of piquet! Mamma's Sophia was praised with faint condolence upon being such a good little girl with the old lady. The praises were accepted, and spat out privately, as one spat out a mawkish lozenge; it would not do to disclose to the one woman that one liked the other quite as well. Better, indeed. Sophia much preferred Léocadie, enjoying her smell, so richly ambered, her cold dry hands, her rather flat voice, loftily unmodulated, and admiring with relief a head which never ached, a back which never tired, an imperious digestion which, for all that extravagant greed and extravagant palate, had never met its match.

I must certainly improve on my bonnet, thought Sophia, stalking about the room in long-limbed nakedness, the London bonnet held out at arm's length. Great-aunt Léocadie had attained her third revolution, the least tribute one could pay would be a bonnet in the highest and latest fashion. Warming herself before the hearth Sophia recollected how great-aunt Léocadie had praised her for those long legs; how, coming into the nursery, she had insisted upon viewing them naked, to make sure that there was no trace of rickets. In the nursery also there had been a blaze of logs, and the child had strutted to and fro, holding up her shift, pleased to be shocking the nursemaids, proud of her legs, so long and fine, and the narrow knee-joints which would be in time, so great-aunt Léocadie said, one of her beauties. Léocadie had spoken praises in her flat voice, the nursemaids had clucked like hens, and the child had strutted up and down, lording it over that poultry-yard. Now once more it was a pleasure to warm her legs at the fire, to be free and naked, and to hold that expensive bonnet in her hand, deciding that it would not do. Since she had freed herself of Frederick nakedness was again a pleasure. Mrs. Frederick Willoughby, sharing a great bed with Mr. Frederick Willoughby, or hearing him splashing and crashing in his dressing-room, had been as shy as a nymph, as disobliging as a virgin martyr, armouring herself in great starched dressing-gowns voluminous as clouds.

She tossed the bonnet across the room, and looked at the bed. Abruptly and absolutely, as though a strain of music had been broken off, her mood of excited self-satisfaction was snapped through. A bonnet, a she-septuagenarian . . . it was not for these that she had come to Paris. Everything, everything was over, henceforth she would have nothing better to do than to toss over such trivialities. There was no purpose, no savour in her life, and yesterday she had made a fool of herself.

Another procession was approaching, a procession with drums and singing and a brass band. To those thumps and brazen pantings she dispatched herself to bed, settling rigidly between the cold sheets, forcing down her eyelids.

Yet however trivial these trivialities, she must keep to them, or go altogether to pieces; and hunting a new bonnet presented difficulties enough for the overcoming of them to raise her spirits a little. Every shop was shut, it was not until after midday that she had at last contrived to get herself admitted to a milliner's by a side door. There, in semi-darkness behind the shuttered windows, a trembling hand pinned bows and snatched at the English gold. "Gold is always gold, is it not?" With that voice, mingled of hope and doubt, in her ears Sophia remembered an aspect of the revolution which might well concern her, and went to Daly's Bank. The bank was shut.

Gold is always gold. It was extraordinary to see how already a pious respect for property had manifested itself, as though Paris had said, "It is true that yesterday we sacked two palaces, havocked every nest where golden eggs are laid, broke, burned, and plundered. But see how scrupulously we are preserving the ruins." Wherever she turned Sophia saw pickets and sentinels, cockaded or badged with red, armed and accoutred like comic-opera bandits, but behaving with the utmost decorum. Outside the Tuileries stood several furniture vans, and into these the Polytechnic students were packing pictures, ornaments, chandeliers, wine, and kitchen utensils. On the felled and mangled trees along the boulevards an official hand had scrawled in chalk, *Property of the Republic. Citizens, respect it!* And when a small handcart passed her, conveying a harmonium, Sophia was not astonished to see that its bearers were accompanied by an escort of two gentlemen, their substantial overcoats girded by sword-belts, red cockades in their top-hats. Indeed, it needed a certain adroitness to avoid incurring an escort for herself, so universal was the helpfulness and good feeling through which she picked her way as she scrambled over barricades or waded through the mud where pavements had been.

All this behaviour was most sensible, most praise-worthy. Every countenance beamed with goodwill, every official placard breathed peace and respect for property, never in her life had she read such a quantity of elevated adjectives. Nor could there be any doubt but that this smugness was, for the moment at any rate, perfectly sincere. It was a shock to encounter amidst this respectable hubbub the unchanged indifferent countenance of the river, as though amidst the fuss and clatter of a philanthropic meeting one were to meet a large snake threading its way among the boots and petticoats. However much blood might flow into that river, no tincture, no composition, could possibly result. Blood would not mix with that cold vein of nature. And leaning on the balustrade Sophia thought how, through every city, some river flows, bearing its witness against the human delusion, discouraging as the sight of a snake. Only a romantic charlatan, speaking for effect, could pretend, as Minna had done, that the sight of a river could bolster up ideas of liberty. *Turn our captivity, O Lord, as the rivers in the south!* Turn our metaphors, O Lord, refresh our perorations! And in her fancy Sophia took firm hold of Madame Lemuel, holding her down under that cold tide, keeping her there until, soused and breathless, she had revised her notions about rivers. A silly and dangerous woman. Yes, dangerous, as this moment could prove. For even now, leaning against the balustrade, watching the river which she must presently cross, Sophia found herself thinking how, in setting foot on the Left Bank, she would be entering Minna's territory. What patent nonsense! The Left Bank was as much great-aunt Léocadie's territory as Minna's. But the thought of great-aunt Léocadie would not spread this sensation of excitement through one's limbs, call out this faint cold sweat of anticipation, knock so heavily on one's heart.

The dangerous woman must indeed have endangered her wits, laid some spell on her common sense. Only now did it occur to her that to arrive, without a word of warning, in great-aunt Léocadie's drawing-room, on the heels of a revolution, would demand rather more pretext than a new bonnet could supply. *I came to Paris to extort a child from my husband.* That would hardly do; though great-aunt Léocadie would see the force of it, might even approve of the expediency, she could never tolerate the statement. *I came to Paris to buy a bonnet.* That on the other hand was too feeble an excuse. Bonnet-buying, however necessary, would be preceded by a letter, one did not pounce after bonnets like a hawk or cattle-raider. Some good reasonable reason must be invented, for at all costs Léocadie must be preserved from supposing that the real reason was, *I heard that there was a revolution and came to look after you.* That unmerited insult must never be suggested, could never be forgiven.

Sophia was still framing the pretext which might decently wrap her appearance when the thought came that great-aunt Léocadie, so capable of looking after herself in any difficulty, might have treated this revolution as she had done others, turning her back upon it. Perhaps even now she was arriving at Blandamer. That was why she had come in 1830. Mamma had said, "Your poor aunt Clotilde's mother is coming to live with us for a little while. We must all be very kind to her, poor old lady. She has had so many sorrows." And Papa, adding that respect would be quite as much called for as kindness, explained that there had been another deplorable revolution. The king of France had been obliged to fly to England. England was, etc.

Not even the shades of the guillotine could do much to ennoble the coming shadow of Madame de Saint-Gonval. Aunt Clotilde had been a very washy character; she had had a baby, and died, the baby had died too, and Uncle Julius Rathbone had become a disconsolate widower and married again. The mother of a dull dead aunt promised little to the ten-year-old Sophia. She came, and remained for a year. Sophia learned to play piquet, learned to speak French, learned to admire her long legs, learned what it was to love someone of her own sex. Till then she had loved only Papa and animals. To love great-aunt Léocadie demanded the same respectful application as the performance of a difficult piece of piano music. There must be the same agility, the same watchfulness, the same attention to phrasing and expression-marks, and simultaneously one must sit well upright, keeping the shoulders down, the elbows in, the wrists arched, the knuckles depressed. Moreover, even in the most taxing passages, one must breathe through the nose and preserve a pleasing and unaffected smile. Exercised daily in loving great-aunt Léocadie, Sophia, by the year's end, loved almost without a flaw in execution and deportment. Never since then had she loved so well; and though with course of time her love for great-aunt Léocadie had been put aside, as one puts aside a piece of piano music, the well-learned was still with her, she could still play it by heart.

The metaphor held good. In the instant of hearing that flat familiar voice, of smelling that richly ambered scent, the former amity renewed itself, carrying her smoothly over what she had foreboded as the difficulties of arrival. But in this foreboding Sophia had forgotten one trait of great-aunt Léocadie: that in any circumstances, however odd or unforeseen, Léocadie's chief concern was Léocadie. Sophia, the revolution, the bonnet, all fell back into their place before the fact that great-aunt Léocadie had taken to spinning.

"The only tolerable occupation, my dear, for an old woman. Listen!" She gave the wheel a turn. "That garrulous gentle doting voice. All the satisfaction of listening to a gossip and none of the trouble of saying *yes,* or *Well,* or *And what happened then?* It is traditional, too, it is Gothic. And that makes it tolerably fashionable. It was an inspiration, that I should spin. You look very well in black, my child. Most women do, and it is providential since life compels us to mourn so often."

She raised her head and glanced at the portraits of her son Anne-Victor, who was killed in a duel, of her daughter Clotilde, who died in childbirth. The glance travelled from the one portrait to the other, deft and sure as the toe of a ballet-dancer. With those words and that glance she established her precedence of sorrow. There was no more contestation about it than there would have been over any other uncontestable social precedence.

"I heard it said the other day, that women all like vinegar for the same reason."

"Nonsense! Women recruit themselves with vinegar after love. It is astringent to the nerves. And so you are not living with Frederick?"

"No."

"No. But how do you manage that in England? Don't your acquaintances pretend to be shocked?"

"I have not consulted them."

"That will scarcely prevent them cold-shouldering you. I do not pretend to be shocked myself, still, I should be glad to see you reconciled. While the children were alive it was quite reasonable, I dare say. But now I recommend you to patch things up. There should be an heir to the property."

How far-off, now, the lime-kiln's winking signal, the tumult of spirit in which she had conceived the expedient that came so naturally to great-aunt Léocadie's practical mind! However, she thought, I was being practical, though failing to recognize it.

"I think I shall take to spinning," she said.

"At your age it would be thriftless. Thirty years hence you may certainly spin, meanwhile . . . Hand me that bag, if you please. I need more wool. Meanwhile, Sophie, you should make up your mind to one of three things—religion, love, or family life. Religion would never suit you, your temperament is too cold. Love is out of the question, too, I hope? . . ."

"Quite."

"So you see, there is nothing for it but family life. You will find Frederick considerably improved."

"Do you see Frederick?"

Great-aunt Léocadie looked up from the bag in which she was searching.

"Delighted as I am to see the last of the Orléans pack, I could wish the dynasty had endured until I had received a fresh supply of wool. Never mind! *À brebis tondue Dieu mesure le vent.* When my wool falls short you arrive on a visit. You will stay here of course. I can assure you I shall be very glad of a little protection."

And see Frederick, and be patched up. Not if I know it, thought Sophia.

"A more despicable family! . . . I hear that the great ambition of the rabble at the Tuileries is to wear the late Adelaïde's bonnets. I wish them joy of her bonnets, they would have been welcome to the head for all I care. Have you noticed, my child, that Liberal families are always run by their old women? And the queen, did you hear of her great speech? It appears that they were all in tears, packing for their lives, and falling over each other to hand Papa the pen and the ink-pot that he might sign the abdication. All but she. She took up a nobler attitude, and told him that he should go out into the Carrousel, confront the mob, and die fighting. *'Je vous bénirai du haut du balcon,'* she said. What an inducement!"

Delicately licking her lips she listened unsmiling to Sophia's laughter.

"And who do you think told me that? Your husband! I assure you, he is improved beyond recognition."

"I have no doubt that Madame Lemuel has done him a great deal of good."

"Incontestably. You were far too delicate a file for him. I saw that at a glance, when you brought him here in '39. Besides, my dear, you are too proud and too indolent—too British, in fact—to shape an unsatisfactory husband. Now that little Jewess, she was exactly what he needed. She is supple, she has immense application, she flattered away and filed away. She has been the making of him."

"These Jewish tailoresses," said Sophia, "turn out their wares quite marvellously, I understand. Still, I am not convinced that I want to array myself in a slop-suit."

"You underestimate the woman. Really, she is quite worthy of your jealousy. For one thing, she is certainly an artist. I have been to some of her recitals myself, and her diction gave me real pleasure."

"But how is she an artist? What does she do?"

"She tells fairy-stories and fables. It is something quite particular, a narrow talent, but perfectly cultivated."

"Well?"

"My dear Sophia, for a woman of that sort a perfectly cultivated talent is already a great deal."

"You cannot make me believe that Madame Lemuel has held Frederick spellbound by telling him fairy-stories."

"I should not attempt to believe it myself."

She turned her wheel, letting it laugh for her, a smooth delighted murmur.

"I see that I can do nothing, you will not condescend to poor fairy-story-telling Jewesses, so I say no more. But it is very unselfish of me, for she is really a most extraordinary person, and has had the most interesting career, and I should have enjoyed telling you about her. You see, I am infected myself. I also want to tell stories."

And Frederick had purveyed those stories, no doubt, the pogroms and the lovers, and all the other details of that interesting career, of that narrow talent intensively cultivated. For an instant Sophia experienced a passionate curiosity to hear all that Léocadie had to tell about Minna—O God, as passionate a curiosity as Minna, two days ago, had seemed to feel, hearing Sophia tell all about Sophia!

That was the flea she had caught, sleeping on the pink sofa, a flea that was still lodged somewhere about her, and bit on. And even when the fresh arrivals, an old lady, and a middle-aged lady, and an old gentleman, and Père Hyacinthe, great-aunt Léocadie's spiritual director, had come in, each one arriving triumphantly endangered and out of breath, and bearing, like doves returning with particularly ample olive-branches, each some new story, discreditably ludicrous, of the fall of the dynasty, Sophia found that she was expecting them to speak of Madame Lemuel.

In this Legitimist drawing-room a new era, it seemed, had begun also. The blessing from the balcony was recounted, the Duc de Nemours fainted repeatedly, each time that the clattering tongues hoisted Louis Philippe into his cab he was damper, more trembling, more abject than before. Sophia was applied to for assurances that only the most ignominious charity awaited the Orléans family on the farther side of the Channel, should they get so far. It seemed taken for granted that the Younger Branch had only to go out for the Elder Branch to come in, like the man and the woman in the weathercock. Amidst these carolings the fact of the revolution passed almost unmentioned. The mob's heart was in the right place, it was only wearing a red cockade as a preparatory emphasis to the white ribbon which would come after. And if corroboration were needed, someone remembered to point out that Monsieur de Lamartine was infinitely more elegant than Monsieur Guizot; alternatively, that a week of the provisional government would entail starvation and stoppage, and what could be more rallying than that?

In the trees of the Place Bellechasse a thrush was trying its song in the gusty evening, and against the large pale clouds that moved with a slackening pace across the eastern sky the scaffolding of the unfinished church of Ste. Clotilde asserted its cock-sure right-angles. It is a view that I shall get to know by heart, she thought. But any port in a storm, and still more any port in a calm so leaden, so dispiriting as that into which her life had fallen. Père Hyacinthe, levitating slightly above the things of this world, began to speak of the beauties of architecture, the religious sensations aroused by cusps and flying buttresses, questioning her with an inflexion of congratulation upon the purifying influence of Pugin and Barry. And as she answered him, concealing her ignorance, she looked forward through metaphors of furs laid by with camphor, silver wrapped in green baize, fruit-trees released of their fruit and nailed back against the wall, to the moment when all these people would go and she would begin to play piquet with great-aunt Léocadie.

Any port in a calm. She could stagnate here as well as anywhere else, better, indeed, for she would be living in accordance with every canon of reputable behavior, and pleasing an old woman who had been kind to her and must soon die. As for Frederick he could be kept at arm's length; and the stories about Minna need never be told, she would not knock on the door of that Bluebeard's cupboard.

The wool from Berri came, though the triumph of the Legitimists tarried. The spinning-wheel turned, every day there came a stock of new scandals, new doves flying to the vast dovecot of great-aunt Léocadie's memory, and Père Hyacinthe came daily too, applying himself like a cold-cream to the upkeep of great-aunt Léocadie's spiritual complexion. Sophia observed that in great-aunt Léocadie a change had taken place, a susceptibility to the spirit of the age manifesting itself in her, just as it had manifested itself in Mamma. Léocadie now respected the Church. She went regularly to mass, and distinguished among the different physiognomies of the virgin, finding our Lady of Carmel, for instance, more sympathetic than she of Victories. So Père Hyacinthe came daily, to be applied like the *Secret de Bonne Femme.* He never spoke of religion, but doubtless he breathed it; and in the minute formalities attending his arrival and his departure, his ambassadorial airs and accolade of benediction, there seemed to be a rehearsal of the superior ceremonials which would be restored with the restoration of the House of Bourbon.

"I do not wish to meet Frederick yet," she had said, knowing that great-aunt Léocadie's tactical feelings, if nothing else, would ensure the wish attention. There had been no need to say, "I do not wish to hear about Madame Lemuel"; and it was with a strangely cool heart that she found herself reading the placard of a concert to be given to raise funds for the wounded of the revolution. Mademoiselle Louise Bertin would play a nocturne of her own composition, a bass from the opera would sing, Madame Lemuel would recount a legend.

It was a shabby enough list, second-rate celebrities padded out with pupils of the Conservatory; and the narrow talent, the diction which had won great-aunt Léocadie's approval, was not, it seemed, sufficiently admitted to be granted any emphasis of lettering. The street was empty and lifeless, the placard, cheaply printed, crumpled, and stuck up askew, gave the impression that it never had been read, and never would be. Sophia foresaw the dreariness of a charity concert, the empty seats, the mumping airs of the programme sellers, enraged at having to attend a performance with such poor promise of tips. Every possible expense would be spared, the floor would be dirty, the platform encumbered with the relics of a previous recital, a harp in a bag perhaps, or a bower of paper roses; a barrel-organ would play outside, and only half the lights would be turned on.

Under such conditions the tedium of listening to a quartet by Habeneck, the Overture to *La Vestale* played as a duet, a series of variations on *Là ci darem* for the flute would be immeasurable; and yet it seemed to Sophia that she would be there, and already she felt the draught playing upon her shoulders and saw the glove buttons which she would sum and study.

It seemed to her that she would be alone. Yet when the day of the concert came great-aunt Léocadie sat on one side of her, Frederick on the other, and beyond great-aunt Léocadie sat Père Hyacinthe, and beyond Frederick sat two elderly Legitimist ladies. "Six tickets," great-aunt Léocadie had said with decision.

"It is one's duty to help these poor wounded creatures. Whatever their opinions, they bled to free us of a tyrant. And a quantity of them were wounded by accident."

"Suffering," added Père Hyacinthe, "appeals in a universal language."

"We, in particular," continued Madame de Saint-Gonval, "must not hold back, now that once more we have a duty towards the people."

"They will recognize it," said Père Hyacinthe, "presently. In their hearts they recognize it already. France is as essentially feudal as it is essentially Catholic. In the last few days I have noticed some quite remarkable movements of piety."

Holding a lozenge between his finger and thumb he spoke of the religious demeanour of the crowd who watched the funeral celebrations on March 4, of the black cloth hangings which covered the Madeleine, of the pompous moment when, to the strains of the organ, the clergy came forward to receive the dead. Even the orations, he said, had been free from offence, and in all that vast crowd there had not been a single accident.

"Except to the statue of Liberty," said great-aunt Léocadie. "Didn't it fall off the triumphal car?"

"It might perhaps have been a little more securely fastened." And in popped the lozenge like a reward.

All things wrought together for those who loved Henry V. The statue of Liberty toppled, and six Legitimists in a row would be an oriflamme. Sophia said,

"I am afraid it will be a very dull programme."

"Not to me," answered great-aunt Léocadie. "Is there not a nocturne by the celebrated Mademoiselle Bertin? For ten years at least I have been watching her talents unclose. It is a unique spectacle, imperceptible almost, gradual as the coming of the dawn. She advances on fame with the majestic pace of a planet."

"Is she very celebrated?"

"Her brother, my dear, is the director of the *Journal des Débats.* A little more wool, if you please."

She had decided to go. Should she find her disorderly feelings for Madame Lemuel threatening to be too much for her, no doubt it would be better to be one of a party; nor was it possible to put up much opposition to Frederick being among those who would, if need arose, stuff handkerchiefs into her mouth and sit on her head. For she was Léocadie's guest, and Frederick Léocadie's visitor. Civility—even a sense of the ridiculous—made it scarcely possible to refuse to encounter him. "I can promise," the old lady had said, "that he will come only when others visit me. There can be nothing awkward. And really, my child, it will be less scandalous to meet him on such a footing than be overwhelmed with sudden sick-headache whenever he is announced."

With great-aunt Léocadie Sophia had found everything that she as a woman of good sense had sought there—reason, routine, dignity. Even in another one must admire the qualities one admires in oneself. Sophia, listening to the clock bestridden by a dimpled and gilded Time, lying awake on an impeccable mattress, owned freely that the old lady wielded reason, routine, and dignity far better than she did. As wary singers and dancers go back to their masters for an overhaul of technique she might consider herself returned to the Academy of Madame de Saint-Gonval; and with the humble admiration that tyros cannot feel she admired the precision and deftness of her schoolmistress. She can even manage Frederick, she thought, prostrating herself in a fit of technical admiration. For the promise had held good, there was nothing awkward in the meetings to which she was now growing accustomed. Frederick came only at visiting hours, did not fidget, did not stare, talked, and did not talk too much. His approach was neither stiff nor familiar, he posed neither as husband nor suitor; and if, as she sometimes admitted to herself, great-aunt Léocadie, and under her guidance Frederick, were slowly, delicately, manœuvring her from the position of an offended wife into the position of a misguided one, the pressure was so tactful, the strategy so benevolent, that she must feel that only magnanimity had prompted the manœuvre, and that she was being insinuated into the wrong only that she might step with more dignity into the right. How much more dignified a reconciliation based on reason, brought about by routine, than the climbing-down from a fit of bad temper implicit in a mere vulgar forgiveness, or an equally vulgar continued resentment!

All this she knew, with little more emotional independence than the oyster may be supposed to have, feeling the change of tide under which it will open. A moment would come, she admitted that now, when she would open, when a reunited Mr. and Mrs. Willoughby would return to Blandamer, when all the past would be forgiven or forgotten, one process cancelling out the other. Meanwhile Frederick came, stayed a little, conversed, handed a tumbler or picked up a shawl, and went again. And as though he had been met and made up by great-aunt Léocadie in the ante-room, with each appearance he increased a delicate fard of melancholy. "I bear no resentment," that demeanour said. "I am a little pained. It is said. My wife will not admit me, my children are dead, I am living in a hotel and eat at a restaurant. Exiled from the joys of the hearth and having abandoned the flashy consolations of my mistress, I am naturally dejected. But I accuse no one, I do not murmur, and you must see how grief has refined my manners." If he turned anywhere for consolation, it was to Père Hyacinthe, as though delicacy forbade that his sexual plaint should be confided to any bosom save one which could not feel as a woman's and had renounced to feel as a man's. Even then the plaint was intimated with scrupulous reserve, voicing itself as a gently growing interest in ecclesiology. Together they would look out of the window at the unfinished Ste. Clotilde, and an artistic conversation would take place, Père Hyacinthe with roulades of language expatiating on the beauties of Gothic, Frederick supplying cadences of agreement, till the two voices joined, as it were, in a duet, aspiring in thirds and sixths towards the day when the scaffolding would be removed, and the edifice completed.

Then, when the tenor had taken his hat and departed, the basso allowed himself to observe that Mr. Willoughby had a great deal of heart.

The two carriages which conveyed the oriflamme had their armorial bearings obliterated from the panels . . . a tactful concession to the people whose heart was in the right place through their king, as yet, was not. The concert-room was quite as half-baked as Sophia had guessed it would be, and empty beyond her most cynical guess. Another sign of the times, observed Père Hyacinthe. The arts could never flourish in a soil undermined by social disquiet, unwarmed, if he might say so, by the sun of majesty. The elderly lady beyond him added that no one could buy concert tickets when the country was on the verge of bankruptcy. On this followed an animated lamentation on bank failures, the ruin of those who held railway shares, the price of gold, and the demented theories of Louis Blanc, Frederick adding that Louis Blanc was the illegitimate son of Pozzo di Borgo, deriving his surname from the blank space in the baptismal register. The burst of applause following this statement applied, however, to the appearance of the duettists who were to perform the Overture to *La Vestale.*

It was an archipelago of a concert, quantities of short items isled in long pauses. Long as the pauses were, the financial situation filled them, and Sophia, who had at first felt somewhat hypocritical in her agreement to be alarmed, knowing of the solid English gold which she had ordered to be conveyed to her agent, fell later to pondering what would happen if by some stroke of Communism that gold were laid hands on. She had an independent spirit, and had never lacked for money. The idea of finding herself penniless (even artificially and temporarily penniless) was repulsive and bewildering, and with growing exasperation she turned over such expedients as selling her diamond brooch, giving lessons in English, or journeying to Calais on foot. The knowledge that her panic was unreasonable did not make it less, and the act of thinking to music heightened her disquiet, the quartet by Habeneck dragging her thoughts at its steadily grinding chariot wheels. It was all very well for the others, she assured herself. For them this chaos which they canvassed so freely was like every other development of the revolution: another proof of the incompetency of the late government, another argument against Liberalism, another preliminary darkness on which the restoration must certainly lighten. They could have it their own way; but neither buffet to one regime nor wind to the sails of another would be of the least consolation to Sophia stranded in Paris with an empty purse. Hearing Frederick murmur confidentially, "They're laying it on a bit thick," she glanced at him with real gratitude for the English phrase and the English phlegm.

And he—with what sensations was he waiting for Madame Lemuel's part in the programme? Whatever they were, he gave no indication, listening to the flute variations on *Là ci darem* with such gentlemanly melancholy that he did not even appear to be numbering them.

Nevertheless, thought Sophia, it is a situation. Man and wife cannot sit side by side waiting for the man's mistress to come forward bowing and public-figured without it being a situation. I hate situations. I loathe drama, and I wish I had never come. Frantically, intently, conscience-strickenly aware how little time remained for the process, she began to freeze herself, while the remaining variations, each more hurried, squeaking, and breathless than the last, scampered to the final trill and the final arpeggio. Now there would be applause, and then another of those intervals.

She must have frozen better than she knew. When the crimson curtains parted and Minna came forward, bowing and public-figured, it was as though she had never seen the woman before. Gravely, carefully, almost as though she were telling the story on oath, Minna told the story of Puss in Boots. Like everything else in the programme, her performance fell flat, and the vigour of a few applauding hands only emphasized the inattention of the other applauders. All the way back great-aunt Léocadie spoke with delight of Madame Lemuel's narrative. It was perfect, she said; the very spirit of old France. In her satisfaction she even forgot to mention the nocturne by Mademoiselle Bertin.

I feel, thought Sophia, as though I had visited a churchyard, and it had been the wrong churchyard. She had caught a cold, as people who visit churchyards often do. Dull with fever, she consented willingly enough to Léocadie's diagnosis of *grippe,* and to the prescription of bed and tisane. She was pleased to lie in bed, and had not enough enterprise of spirit left to wish to die.

When she got up again it was as she expected. The negotiations in which her part had been so passive had gone on perfectly without her. Frederick had brought flowers, and the reconciliation was completed. However, her money had arrived safely, that was one comfort—now, presumably, she would need to buy another trousseau. Only the formalities remained, and those were well in hand. "I have a whim," said great-aunt Léocadie, "an old woman's whim, that must be indulged. Seeing you here together, hearing your English accents, has given me the idea how delightful it would be to have a high tea together, an English nursery high tea, all by ourselves. Just such a feast, my Sophia, as I learned to enjoy at Blandamer, when you were a little girl in a tippet. We will get the buns from Columbin. Shall we say, Saturday?"

Buns on Saturday, thought Sophia. Te Deum on Sunday.

Only now did the slow-witted creature realize how patently, appearing without warning and without pretext, she must have seemed to great-aunt Léocadie to have thrown herself upon those managing mercies, mutely holding out a rended matrimony as a child holds a broken toy or a torn pinafore. Her first refusal to meet Frederick, how affected and mawkish that must have appeared!—her yielding, how natural! Tying on her bonnet before the glass, contemplating her face, blankly handsome, Sophia assured herself that for the last month she had indeed been exactly like the fairy-tale goose that ran about ready-roasted with a knife and fork in its back. It was too late to do anything about it now. Casting back her mind she could not discern a moment since her coming to the Place Bellechasse when it had not been too late, so completely had she pulled the net about her. Really, if one were such a fool when left to one's own devices, it might be as well to resume a husband as soon as possible.

Soon it would be. This was Saturday and she was going out to choose the buns. Having left matters so, this was all she could do as a show of interest in the reconciliation so kindly arranged for her. And like everyone who asserts himself too late she had asserted herself too violently, saying, "I will go to Columbin's for the buns," as though she were volunteering to go through fire and water for them.

"Pray do, my child. Choose them yourself. Madeleine will go with you to carry them."

Columbin, the English pastrycook, had his shop in the rue de

Luxembourg; before going there Sophia went to the agent and picked up the money which awaited her. Twenty-five good golden English pounds—a reassuring weight, a comfortable gravity.

"I love money," she told herself, walking obliviously past shop windows. "There, perhaps, the true unexplored passion of my life awaits me." And remembering how Byron had written,

So for a good old-gentlemanly vice,
I think I must take up with avarice.

she took pleasure in imagining herself back again at Blandamer, sitting by the library fire, reading *Don Juan,* and letting her thoughts stray with the turning of a page to rent-roll and consolidated bonds. True, Frederick would be lounging near by: Frederick, who was no buttress to the pleasures of avarice. But it was ill-advised to think of that, better to look on the other side of the penny, better to remember that the honourable estate of matrimony allowed one to read *Don Juan* in honour and ease, rather than by snatches in a cold bedroom.

The pleasures of avarice were emphasized by the surroundings. It was difficult to believe that this was Paris, so nipped and dingy did it look, so down-hearted and down-at-heel. A shrewish wind was blowing, and if the sun had tempted out the café tables and chairs, it had tempted out nothing else; for the few drinkers sat within the glass doors, and seemed to have wrapped newspapers round them for further protection. Certainly they had no mind for the stumpy young man who had been playing his guitar to a set of tables and chairs, and had now gone in to make his collection. As she passed, idly surveying, he came out again, pausing at the door for one more bow and one more soliciting glance around. A voice, protesting against the draught, cut short the poor hope. They met face to face and Sophia supposed he was about to hold out his hat to her, when he put it on in order to take it off, bowing with stiff politeness. Only then, seeing herself recognized, did she recognize him. It was the humpbacked little Jew who had offered her a chair at the rue de la Carabine, and to whom Minna had spoken of his symphony.

Poor child!—she thought. How cold he looks, what agony to press wire strings with such chilblained hands! Pity softened her blank good looks into beauty. Encouraged and romantic, he stood beside her, with his hat in one hand, and his instrument in the other, asking if she were alone, if he might have the honour of escorting her. The revolution, he said, had made Paris less agreeable than of old.

"You can go home, Madeleine," she said, beckoning to the lady's-maid, who had withdrawn herself from the spectacle of Mrs. Willoughby conversing with a street-musician—and on the very eve, too, of her reconciliation with Mr. Willoughby. "I will bring the buns.

"I have been staying," she said, "with an elderly relation in the Faubourg St.-Germain. We play piquet and lament for Charles X. This revolution seems hardly real to me. I wish you would tell me about it, I am as ignorant as the carp at Chantilly."

If I can get you to Columbin's, her thoughts added, I will feed you. A good square meal is what you need, hopping beside me like a famished sparrow.

"It is magnificent. It is not like any other revolution. It is purer, more noble, more idealistic."

She managed to convert an English humph into a more sympathetic noise of assent.

"It is a marvellous experience," he continued, "to live under a republic. One breathes a different air. Freedom of thought, freedom of speech, no more suspicion or hypocrisy, no more—"

A violent fit of coughing interrupted him.

"I fear that the air of a republic has not been very good for your chest."

Protests and coughs brought them to Columbin's door. Would he jib, recollecting his guitar, his shabbiness? Not at all. Hunger, that brings the wolf out of the wood, carried him into the pastrycook's. The hunger, though, was not for the hot chocolate and sandwiches she ordered. Loneliness was the famine which had tamed him; and in the release of having someone to talk to he forgot the where and the when, forgot the unintimacy between them, forgot even the lack of credence which she could not conceal as she listened to his rodomontades. But by degrees his sincerity gained on her, and she began to listen and question in earnest.

"But surely no state can afford to be completely altruistic. Even granting that France has become a good example to the rest of Europe, that is not a national industry. Revenues must be collected, wages earned and paid. I must seem to you very grovelling—but I fear that Europe, instead of looking on France as an example, will be quite as likely to look on her as a warning."

"They should change their spectacles, then, if they are so old that they cannot see beyond their noses. The spirit of a people is more than material prosperity. Besides, the republic is prosperous. It is only a few luxuries that have been lopped off. That is nothing."

"It has been my experience," she answered, "that soon after people pawn the clock and the tea-set they pawn their tools and their bedding. A nation does not lop off luxuries unless it feels a threat to essentials."

"Even if we have pawned the clock, even if our house seems bare, I would rather live in it so. Never before has there been so much room for hope."

At this moment a waiter walked past, ostentatiously skirting the guitar and then returning for another look at it. In a cold angry voice Sophia began to give him her order for buns.

"Poor guitar! I should not have brought it. It offends a waiter and I am afraid it has done worse. Tell me, has not that unfortunate instrument prejudiced you a little against the republic?"

"Tell me, when did you exchange composing symphonies for playing the guitar?"

"I compose still. Better than before."

"I beg your pardon," she said abashed.

"But I admit it," he continued. "You are quite right. I am one of the luxuries that have been lopped off. And sometimes I tremble for the threat to the essentials . . . to the greatest of essentials, to art."

Candour gave a quality almost like blitheness to the story, as he told how surely and swiftly the prophecy of the man in the shawl had been fulfilled. His allowance had ceased, for his father, a jeweller, did no more business. The orchestras were disbanded, no one wished for music-lessons, there was no copying to be got. Revolutions had no need for symphonies, and it was hard enough to pick up a living by playing his guitar. And there were a hundred others, he added, the blitheness falling from his tune, in the same case—others better than he.

"But your friends," said Sophia slowly. "Surely there must be some people who can help you. Madame Lemuel . . ."

"Minna!" For the first time his face, so pinched and pale, lost its bird's look of confidence. And yet, she thought, I have always heard that Jews help Jews. However meanly she had come to think of Minna it had not occurred to her that Minna would practise the good old-gentlemanly vice.

"Minna!" he repeated. "You have hit on the only thing that can make me doubt of the revolution. Minna should not be left to starve."

"To starve?" she said unbelieving.

"To starve twice over. To be so poor that she cannot help others—that is a double starvation to a heart like hers. I would give my right hand," he said, striking the table, "if I could save her from that."

"But—things cannot be so bad with her. How long is it since we met at her apartment? Five weeks?"

"She could beggar herself in a day," he said with pride.

"But what has happened?"

"She is an artist, and there is no time now for art. And because she had a position her plight is the worse, since the younger, the poorer, have gone to her for help. I did myself, more blame to me. She was not in, but five people were waiting to see her. Two of them were duns, three of them beggars like myself. The concierge told me this, licking his vile lips with malice."

"Did you see her?"

"Yes. She came back at last. Back from a charity concert, unpaid, of course. She had done abominably, she said so. And no wonder, for how can one hold an audience like that, an audience of well-fed idlers, on a little salad?"

"I met people who were at that very concert. They were enthusiastic about her. Her talent is so much admired, she is so well known. . . . Would it not be possible . . . ?" She paused, thinking it must be delicately phrased, and some mocker in her mind repeating the rhyme about the big fleas and the little fleas.

"Not they!" said he.

While she was staring at the pattern of the table-cloth he broke out again.

"But that is not the worst of it, she is starving for more than food and drink. The worst of it is that as a revolutionary she is out of fashion. Before, she was an inspiration. But inspiration is not wanted now, it seems. One must be practical, one must be administrative, one must understand economics and systems. She pines. She said to me, that very evening, 'Our Moses was luckier than he knew, to die before he went into the promised land.' "

He stopped. It seemed to him she was no longer listening. And after a moment's silence he saw her making ready to go.

Aware that he had outstayed his welcome, more aware of it than she, he picked up the guitar and followed her to the door. Frowning abstractedly she listened to his thanks, availing herself of a tact which smoothed the finish of their meeting. Not till the river was crossed did she think, fleetingly, that she should have offered—since he could not be tipped—to take singing-lessons.

She was even later than she had expected, but for all that she spent some time arranging herself for the peace-treaty tea, smoothing her hair and polishing her nails. It was as though she must not allow herself to be hurried, as though some heavenly Mamma had admonished, "My dear, in your condition it is imperative to avoid the slightest flurry. Above all, do not trip on the stairs."

Obediently tranquil, she entered the salon, and saw without the least emotion of apology great-aunt Léocadie and Frederick sitting poised above their boiled eggs, and the table spread with cakes and bread-and-butter, and the bouquet of camellias beside her plate. She seated herself in silence. To Léocadie's polite fears that the buns had given her a great deal of trouble she replied politely that they had given her no trouble whatever; and like a good child, seen and not heard, she crumbled bread-and-butter, and listened to the other two conversing. At intervals, as kind elders do, they made an opening for her in the conversation, pausing, casting encouraging glances; but they got nothing beyond "Yes" or "No" for their pains.

Meanwhile their talk became increasingly animated, increasingly a performance in which great-aunt Lèocadie was the ballerina and Frederick the suave athletic partner, respectfully leading her round by one leg as she quivered on the tip-toe of the other.

Now Frederick was doing a little *pas de fascination* on his own, recounting how he had become involved in the planting of a Tree of Liberty. With humour he described the dejected sapling, tied up in the tricolour, the band of squalling schoolchildren, the mayor of the arrondissement who blew his nose continually, the two gentlemen with their rival speeches on fraternity. When the speeches were concluded, and the tree set toppling in its little pit it was discovered that the gardener had gone away, taking his spade with him; but undeterred by this, said Frederick, they began to pass round a hat for contributions. Abstractedly he had put his hand into his pocket, drawn out his case, and dropped a cigar into the hat.

"Ridiculous wool-gatherer!" commented Léocadie tenderly. "You are not fit to look after yourself. Is he, Sophie?"

She still kept silence. Frederick remarked that he could not help being absent-minded. It was a quality that accompanied untidiness, he was untidy too.

"Am I not, Sophia?" he added, with malice.

"Yes, you are untidy."

"You see, Frederick. Even our Sophie condemns you."

"All the same," Sophia continued, and it seemed to her that she must be shouting at the top of her voice, "however casual and ineffable you are, I think you might take the trouble to tidy up your liaisons. You might at least pension off your mistresses before you start dog's-earing your new leaf."

"Sophia!"

"Sophie, my child!"

"Instead of leaving them to starve."

"Sophia, one does not make accusations in such a tone of voice."

"I beg your pardon, great-aunt Léocadie. I should not have shouted. But I hold to the accusation. Today I heard that Madame Lemuel is destitute and starving. And I mean to have this remedied."

"Starving! Poor creature, how terribly sad!"

"Destitute! That's unexpected! Sophia, who did you hear this from?"

"From a friend of hers. A young man, a humpback. He composes music."

"Guitermann!" Frederick gave a spurt of laughter. "How these Jews cling together. They're all penniless, aren't they, each worse than the last? My poor innocent, he was touting for her. How much did he get out of you?"

"It is dreadful, it is tragic," interposed great-aunt Léocadie. "Such an admirable artist, such a rare talent! But these are cruel days for artists, I have heard the most heartrending stories of their plight, poor things! Sophie is right, Frederick, this must be remedied. It can easily be done, she has so many—so many people who appreciate her talent. A commission or two, one might get up a recital, or find her pupils. Perhaps, since she is in such straits, a little purse. It could be given delicately. One would not wish to wound her."

"Perhaps young Guitermann would like a little purse too. His father is a jeweller, and rolling, but for all that I dare say young Guitermann wouldn't be above a little purse, provided it was given delicately enough."

"I don't think I have heard anything by this Monsieur Guitermann. What a musical race they are! Meyerbeer, and Bellini, and . . . Paganini, and . . ."

"Whether it be given delicately or indelicately," said Sophia, "Minna Lemuel cannot be left to starve. And since Frederick can do nothing about his obligations but snigger out of them like a schoolboy, I shall see to it myself.

"Now," she added, rising to her feet.

Presumably they spoke, but no words remained in her memory. When she was out of doors her rage thinned away like the smoke from an explosion, and hurrying through the limpid spring evening she felt as though in the relief of speaking and acting out her rage she had become almost disembodied. But the weight of that good English gold she carried was real, and her heart-beats were real—heavy and full, thudding like coins let fall one after another.

Acts of impulse are of two kinds. Those performed by people of a naturally impulsive character come with the suavity of habit, they are put forth like the tendrils of a vine, and there is time to meditate them a little, to dispose their curvings with grace. However spontaneous, the mind which generates them has done the same sort of thing before, and in the instant between thought and deed there is an unflurried leisure, in which habit and cunning can contrive their adjustments. But when people of a slow or cautious disposition act upon impulse, the impulse surprises them even more than it surprises those upon whom it is directed. Such astonishment leaves no room for thoughts of contrivance, the assent of the will has been so overwhelming that diplomacy and manœuvring seem not so much impossible as out of the question.

Leaving the pastrycook's Sophia had no project whatever, feeling only a sullen fury, an emotion so pure and absorbing that it had given her a sensation almost like complacence. With this to nurse in her lap she had sat blandly through the first stages of the peace-treaty tea, impregnable in bad behavior, and when Frederick's brag of untidiness had tossed her the cue for her outburst the sight of the intention leaping out of her rage had staggered her like a flash of lightning dazzling between her and the tea-pot. Blinded to everything but that suddenly scribbled zig-zag of purpose, the time it must take to reach the rue de la Carabine was no time at all. It was a hiatus, a darkness through which her purpose must travel to its expression as the rocket arches its dark journey between the moments of being touched off and of exploding its fires. The red winking eye of the lime-kiln had let her off on just such another journey. But her mind, for all its natural bent towards the sardonic and belittling, did not remind her now of the ignominious splutter with which that other rocket had turned itself into a squib, nor of all those misfiring impulses, inappropriate and unavailing, which had defaced her career.

Incapable of considering the how, she had not considered the where either. She was going to Minna; and as her imagination showed Minna, so doubtless she would find her—in the house in the rue de la Carabine, standing by the pink sofa, the ermine scarf drooping lopsidedly from her shoulders. With this meeting so clear in mind her impetus towards it carried her past Minna encountered in the street. The recognition that halted her stock-still on the pavement was only at second-sight realized as a recognition of the woman she sought. For the instantaneous, the overwhelming impression was, that for the first time in her life she had seen despair.

Standing open-mouthed on the pavement, holding her burden of English gold, twenty-five pounds, seven hundred and fifty francs, purpose and pity alike were obliterated by an astonishment that was almost like triumph. She had seen what is seen by perhaps one person in a thousand: the unmitigated aspect of a human emotion. And she had seen it in the street, as one sees a lamppost, a brown horse, an umbrella, a funeral. The shock was a challenge to her whole previous existence, to her outlook on life. Life would never be the same again, she would be henceforth always the woman who had seen the authentic look of despair.

It was not until she turned and walked in pursuit of Minna that astonishment fell away and pity took its place. Pity seemed a vague thing, wavering from one speculation to another, and all the energy of her purpose was gone, for why should she be following, with her twenty-five pounds, a person whose air proclaimed a zero that could quell any other ciphers, a not-having beyond the dreams of avarice?—and she began to walk more slowly, putting off the moment when she must overtake her quarry. Yet flesh and blood must live, and the money be given. Wherever Minna Lemuel was going she was not going to her death. One does not saunter to suicide, thought Sophia, studying that rather stocky figure, large-headed and broad-shouldered, a build oddly at variance with a singularly graceful gait and carriage. And since wherever Minna Lemuel was taking her despair through the limpid spring evening, it was not to death, flesh and blood must be succoured, and the money given.

But how? As alms, as recompense, as hush-money? Let that alone, thought Sophia, mastering a swoon of panic. Given it must be.

Like following an animal, she said to herself. If a hind were to be walking in the rue de l'Abbé de l'Épée it could not be more alien, more unmixing than such despair as I saw in her looks. And with the idea of Minna being like an animal her wavering ineffectual pity was abruptly changed into a deep concern, as though it had taken on flesh and blood. A hind would not pass unremarked, it would be admired, stones would be thrown at it or it would be taken to the police-station. So far, no stone had been thrown at Minna. Could it be, suggested concern, quick to snatch at any hope, that she had been mistaken, that Minna's look had not been despairing after all, or that the look had been of the moment only? Care, illness, hunger—these on that mobile and dramatic visage might mimic the other look: but presently she saw a man, passing Minna, turn back and stare at her; and in that second glance there was a greedy astonishment which might well be followed by stone-throwing, for it was clear that he had never seen anything like that before and had a natural mind to assault the wonder. The stone was only a laugh; but it was aimed well enough to make Sophia hasten forward to glare him down.

She was within a hand's touch of Minna as Minna entered the Luxembourg garden. The fountain, thought Sophia, and wondered why she should be so sure of it; for unless water were deep enough to drown in, her imagination had not so far admitted the affinity between water and woe.

Though the trees were so scantly leaved, there was dusk under their branches, and the look of the water in the tank, sifting the reflections of shadow and sky, was profound enough to beckon down any grief. Here, then, she would wait until Minna raised her eyes and saw her. Yet it was anguish to stand in patience, hearing the condoling voice of water, feeling the melancholy chill of evening, while feet scratched by on the gravel and children bowled their hoops, while the stress of her concern grew to a burden heavier than the weight of the gold she carried. She looks worse than desperate, said that concern. She looks dead. Only the dead look so bitterly resigned.

Without raising her eyes Minna moved slowly away.

Yet perhaps to accost her under those trees, and within the spell of the fountain's melancholy voice, would have been too elegiac. For this was real life, and the accompaniments of real life are not water and trees, but clerks hurrying with papers under their arms, children bowling hoops, gentlemen enjoying the spring evening with their hats off. In any case—Sophia shook up her decision—before Minna was out of the gardens of the Luxembourg speak she would.

"Minna."

She has recognized me, she thought, seeing the flicker of those heavy eyelids. Just so one might speak to the dying, and know oneself recognized, though no answer came.

"You look ill. What has happened to you?"

She answered now, speaking slowly after a long examining pause.

"You have got a good memory—to recognize me."

"I have been following you for a long time. I was coming to see you when I recognized you in the rue de l'Abbé de l'Épée."

"You were coming to see me? Why did you follow me for so long?"

"I wanted to watch you, to see for myself if what I heard was true, that you were ill and unhappy."

"And am I?"

"Yes."

People went by them, and giving to the tide of movement they began to walk, arm in arm.

"But have you never felt unhappy in spring? I have, many times."

"I cannot believe that you have often been as unhappy as you looked when I met you. You could not, and survive it."

"I expect I shall survive it. We Jews are very tough."

There was a sombre pride in her tone, and a little malice. You are coming to life, thought Sophia; under your guise of deathbed your cunning has awakened and you have begun to watch me. So you shall be the next to speak.

"Why were you coming to see me?"

"Various reasons. Some good, some bad. One disgraceful."

"Oh! Was that all?"

On her arm she felt Minna's fingers touching out a small ruminative rhythm. Clerks and deputations were going to and from the Palace, to be walking through this businesslike brisk throng was a better privacy than trees and the fountain could have given.

"And this meeting?—Has it fulfilled all your various reasons for coming to see me—some good, some bad, and one disgraceful?"

"Not the disgraceful one. Yet."

But it shall, she thought, swinging her muff, heavy with its golden lining. The woman beside her, so venal, so unaccountably dear, should live as long as twenty-five pounds might warrant, and exercise that unjustifiable enchantment, though others only should feel it. For the money once given, the giver must go.

"And then you will disappear again? Climb into your cloud, and disappear?"

"Then I shall disappear."

On her arm the fingered rhythm began again, soft and pondering, imperturbably patient. As though respecting those private calculations she kept silence.

"Ah! Madame Lemuel!"

The pondering fingertips closed upon her arm, an impact so sharp, so unexpectedly actual, that it was like a wasp-sting. The man who had uttered the greeting spoke in tones of false cordiality, was undersized and overdressed, and carried a large portfolio. And instantly he began to explain with importance that he was about to present to the Executive Committee sitting in the Palace a petition on behalf of the bakers. Their cause—he made this clear—was as good as won since he was forwarding it.

After the bakers, he added, and the night-soil men, and the fish-porters, he proposed to busy himself in the matter of distressed artists.

"And then, dear lady, I shall avail myself of your advice, I shall find it invaluable," he added, with confidence; and bounded forward, leaving them where his eloquence had convoyed them, in the hall of the Palace.

"My God, what an intolerable upstart!" exclaimed Sophia, gazing round with fury at surroundings which seemed part and parcel of the upstart's complacent industry. For on every hand were run-up partitions, desks, notices, waste-paper baskets, ink-pots and coloured forms, clerks and officials. There was also a variety of collecting-boxes, no church could display more, labelled *For the Veterans of the Republic, For the Polish Patriots, For the Belgians, For the Wounded, For the Orphans,* and so forth.

Here, in this den of bureaucracy, the speech should be spoken, the gift should be given, the oddest encounter of her life wound up and ended.

"Before I climb into my cloud," she began in a pedestrian voice. . . .

"I beg your pardon?"

"Before I go," said Sophia, steadily glaring down that smile of melancholy amusement, the grimace of an affectionate and misunderstood ape, "I want, for my own peace of mind, to give you this. Minna, you must take it."

At the weight of the chamois-leather bag, coming so warm from Sophia's muff, Minna's eyebrows flicked upward.

"Gold," she said, and counted the pieces. "Twenty-five English pounds. Well?"

Under her play-acting of Shylock she was trembling violently, as people tremble with famine, with excitement, with intolerable strain of anxiety.

"Well, Sophia?"

"This mangy republic," said Sophia, "that prancing little cur with the portfolio—you'll perish among them, I know it."

"I like English gold," said Minna. "It's so wonderfully sturdy. Thirty francs at the present exchange for each of these. Thirty mangy republican francs."

"I told you," retorted Sophia, "that one of my reasons was a disgraceful one. It is always disgraceful to offer money, and grand to refuse it. But out of my disgrace, Minna, I beg of you not to refuse."

"I haven't refused yet. I might, you know, be holding out for more. For though twenty-five pounds is a handsome alms . . .

"Why do we quarrel like this?" she exclaimed. "It is ignoble, it is untrue. I will take the money and be grateful."

"Take the truth with it, then. It is not as you think, as you have every right to think. I am not trying to pay off Frederick's arrears of honour. When I set out to find you, an hour ago, I thought I was. I was in a rage, I had one of my impulses. I set off at once with all I had. It ought to convince you," she said wryly, "that this is not a meditated insult, since I bring so little. But now it seems to me that if anyone has treated you shabbily, it is I. So it is only fit that the amends should be shabby too."

She had spoken staring at the floor, at the hem of Minna's dress. Now, seeing it stirred, she looked up to say farewell. With the carriage of someone moving proudly through a dance Minna walked towards the collecting-box labelled *For the Polish Patriots.* When the last coin had fallen through the slit she turned on Sophia with a look of brilliant happiness.

"It was all that you had," she said, her voice smoothly quivering like water under the sun, "and there it goes. *Vive la liberté!*"

"*Vive la liberté!*" answered Sophia.

For she was released, God knows how, and could praise liberty with a free mind. Somehow, by that action, so inexplicable, unreasonable, and showy, Minna had revealed a new world; and it was as though from the floor of the Luxembourg Palace Sophia had seen a fountain spring up, a moment before unsuspected and now to play for ever, prancing upwards, glittering and incorruptible, with the first splash washing off all her care and careful indifference to joy.

"Yes, Sophia, I have beggared you now. Till Monday morning, at any rate, you are as poor as I. I dare say you have not enough money, even, to pay for a cab to take you back to the Meurice."

"My uncle's first wife's mother in the Place Bellechasse, Minna."

"Your uncle's first wife's mother in the Place Bellechasse

would not like to see you destitute, and in rags. You had better come to the rue de la Carabine. It is nearer than the Place Bellechasse. We will collect our supper on the way."

"How can we pay for it?"

"We need not pay for it. If you come into the shop with me your bonnet alone will be as good as a fortnight's credit."

Their words, light and taunting, rose up like bubbles delicately exploding from a wine they were to drink together. People whom they encountered turned round to stare after them. It was not common, in those lean days, to see two faces so carelessly joyful.

THREE

"Well, Sophia?"

"I was thinking," answered Sophia, turning back from the window, "how odd it is to see houses, and be on land. For I feel exactly as though I had run away and gone to sea, like a bad youth in a Sunday-school story book."

"You *have* run away," said Minna placidly. "You'll never go back now, you know. I've encouraged a quantity of people to run away, but I have never seen anyone so decisively escaped as you."

And with dusters tied on her feet she made another glide across the polished floor, moving with the rounded nonchalant swoop of some heavy water bird. Her sleeves were rolled up, she wore a large check apron, she had all the majestic unconvincingness of a gifted tragedy actress playing the part of a servant—a part which would flare into splendour in the last act.

"But what have I run away from?"

"From sitting bored among the tyrants. From Sunday schools, and cold-hearted respectability, and hypocrisy, and prison.

"And domesticity," she added, stepping out of the dusters. "This floor's quite polished enough. You would never believe,

Sophia, how filthily that Natalia kept everything. My beautiful dish-cloths all rolled up in dirty balls, my china broken, verdigris on the coffee-pot . . . she would have poisoned me if I had kept her a day longer."

"Was that the servant who ate pickles because she had known so many sorrows?"

"Ate pickles? She engulfed them! She drank the brandy, she stole the linen, she was in league with the concierge, she lowered down bottles of wine to him from the balcony, she had the soul of a snake, the greed of a wolf, the shamelessness of a lawyer. 'Go!' I said to her. 'March off this instant! You have deceived me, you must go.' And even as I spoke, Sophia, such was her malice, she dropped a trayful of wine-glasses and broke every one of them."

With eyes blazing in a face pale with austere horror she leant forward and whispered,

"And after she had gone I found a monkey's tail in the rubbish-bin."

"A monkey's tail?"

"A monkey's tail. Judge for yourself if she was depraved or no."

From sitting bored among the tyrants. . . . The she-party of those tyrants from whom she was now delivered had talked, Sophia recalled, at endless length about their servants. The cook had pilfered the sugar, the laundry-maid had scorched a pillow-case, the underhousemaid had exhibited herself with a coloured ribbon. Now she was listening to talk about servants once again. But search her sensations as she would, sharply as any good housewife examining after dust, she could not find a shred of the former boredom or disdain.

"I suppose," she said, thoughtlessly voicing her thought, "it's because you're so patently a liar."

"A liar? I a liar, my lovely one? Alas, I am incapable of lies. I am a poor recounter of stories only, I cannot make them up."

And she flipped the dusters out of the window, watching the dust scatter down on Madame Coton's ferns, exposed for an airing on the pavement below, murmuring to herself, "Really, those unfortunate Cotons! . . . They have no luck with their horticulture."

"Was it from this balcony," inquired Sophia, "that the wine was lowered?"

Minna feigned inattention to this lure.

"I would lay down my life for the truth," she added serenely.

The last fleck of dust drifted downward to the Cotons' ferns, the April morning air pushed, gentle and infantine, against their faces. Sighing with appreciation Minna stepped out onto her balcony, tilting her face to the sunlight, staring upwards with the gaze, blank and transfigured, of a cat who with a bird in her belly sits watching the birds. Her head, with the black hair fitting so purely to the curve of her brow, seemed, outlined against the sky, another of the domes of Paris, and it was part of her outrageous freedom from anything like conscience that a visage so inharmonious, so frayed with former passions and disfigured with recent want should appear in that very trying full light exaltedly beautiful as the face of an angel.

"How blue! how vast!" she breathed, and it was as though she had stretched the heavens like a canvas, and painted them with one sweep of a calm brush. "And look, Sophia. In all that firmament, so large, so clear, so open to our inspection, I do not see one little cherub, even, getting ready to go to mass.

"No!" She shook her head. "Only sparrows."

Her glance, following the flirting couple, descended towards the street. And with noiseless alacrity she stepped back from the balcony.

"Oh, the devil! Here comes Wlodomir Macgusty, poor soul! But I don't think he's seen me. He's certainly coming here, and he'll stay for the day, and I don't want him."

"Is Wlodomir Macgusty a patriot?"

"He's two patriots. His great-grandfather was an exiled Highlander, and all his other relations were injured Poles. He is really a very noble creature," she added, arranging herself under Sophia's scrutiny, "and has suffered intensely—wait a minute, let me make sure that the door is locked—and has the most interesting scheme for the redistribution of Europe, and altogether, dear Sophia, I could not have given your twenty-five pounds to a worthier object. But not just now, I feel."

"Wouldn't it broaden my mind to meet this fellow free spirit?"

"No, not at all. It would narrow it, for you'd certainly think poorly of him. Besides, you have met him. He was at my party. You must have noticed him. He sobbed. Hush!"

The double patriot was apparently footed to correspond, for two sets of footsteps trod the stairs.

"Minna!" exclaimed a high-pitched voice, and the door-handle was rattled. "Minna! We've brought you a little cheese. Won't you let us in?"

"Who's the other one?"

"I don't know. I didn't notice."

"A little cheese, Minna."

"Minna!"

The second voice called more imperiously. It was a rasping voice, a voice of a quality which once heard its scarcely forgotten. Nor had Sophia forgotten it.

"I think it must be your friend Monsieur Gaston," she said, not troubling to lower her voice. But the descent of her reproach was turned aside by the sight of Minna's embarrassment—the spaniel-like rolling of eyes, the mouth twitched this way and that between distress and an urchin's amusement. And continuing to look severely at Minna she experienced an exquisite sense of flattery.

Meanwhile the two voices were mingling invocation with argument.

"Of course she's in. I heard a voice quite clearly."

"No, no, Gaston! She's not there, I'm sure. Minna! You would not bar your door to me, would you? There! She doesn't answer, you see. She's not there."

"She is there. Min-na!"

"Hush! Perhaps she's asleep. She may talk in her sleep, you know."

"Pooh! She's awake, confound her, but she won't let you in."

"What? Not let me in? Do you really think so? Oh! Oh! Oh!"

"In heaven's name, Macgusty, don't start crying."

"Oh! Oh! Minna!"

And the door was shaken as though by a tempest.

"Let go my dress, Minna. I intend to put a stop to this."

Though she was shaking with laughter, Minna held firm.

"Nor do I think you should laugh at that misery outside."

"Dear Sophia, I wouldn't laugh at him for worlds. It's you I'm laughing at. There you stand, looking so like an English Prime Minister, and all the time I've got hold of your skirt."

"It is extraordinary to me," said Sophia, seating herself with rigidity and emphasis, "why more people who can see jokes are not strangled."

With a hitch of the head and a gesture of the eyebrows Minna assented, laying a finger to her lips. But on the farther side of the door Gaston's voice had reached such a hearty pitch of exasperation that Wlodomir Macgusty's laments were wellnigh smothered, and the two women could have talked as they pleased and remained unheard.

"As for me," repeated Gaston, "I'm going."

And his footsteps tramped towards the stairs, Wlodomir's pattering after them.

"But my cheese, my little cheese! If I leave it there, the concierge will eat it."

"Let him eat it."

"Yes. . . . Yes, I suppose that would be best."

There was a sniff and a sigh. The pattering footsteps paused, breaking from their allegiance to the trampling footsteps. Then they returned, and with a rustle of paper made off down the stairs.

Smoothing her hair as though all this had dishevelled it, Sophia rose with dignity.

"His little cheese!" said Minna in a tone of profound tenderness.

Exasperation compelled Sophia to gasp for breath, and with her hands still clawing her brow she remained, consciously gaping, but for the moment past any redressing of countenance. I am fascinated, she thought. I have never known such freedom, such exhilaration, as I taste in her presence. But she is indubitably out of her wits, and I suppose I shall be out of mine, too, shortly. At the end of this thought, which passed through her mind, complete and glib and unconvincing as a lesson repeated, she was able to lower her hands, fold them resignedly, and clear her throat.

"You should not scorn him, Sophia, poor little Wlodomir and his cheese. You should not scorn him, even though he is ludicrous, and cries through the keyhole, and is abominably treated by all his friends. Do you not see," she went on earnestly, "that there is something noble in being so completely, so inflexibly vulnerable? When I think of Wlodomir I feel with shame how traitorously I have dealt with my own heart."

"But a little self-control . . . !"

"Why, if one has the courage to do without it? Never have I known Wlodomir feign or conceal. What he feels he expresses, when he is hurt he cries out, he is incapable of duplicity, of keeping himself locked up like a mean housewife with a larder. When I am with him I feel like a mousetrap beside a flower. I feel myself unworthy, yes, Sophia, unworthy, to be in his company. Why are you smiling?—Because I did not let him in, him and his cheese? That proves exactly what I say. I am unworthy."

And turning her irrevocably mournful gaze to the window, she smiled a false sleek demonstrator's smile.

"Such a beautiful day. It would be a pity to stay indoors fobbing off bores, you know. I feel more inclined for something noble and silent—a lion, perhaps. Shall we go to the Jardin des Plantes?"

Turning from the uproar of the lions and the gabble of the crowd assembled to watch them fed, they left the cages, the bear-pit, the artists with their easels, the family parties and the other parties whose demeanour proclaimed a freedom from any shadow of being a family.

"Do you come here often?"

"Constantly. To study the animals—I am working now on the fairy stories of Grimm, and in order to tell them one may have to become a fox or a bear—but more often to walk and meditate, and to be peaceful and solitary. I am an expert in the unfrequented alleys, the corners where no one penetrates—"

"You cannot go down there. *Messieurs.*"

"No, no, of course not. You are very observant. The English are, I believe, they are great naturalists, authorities on migration and the rainfall. No Jew would care a tittle for migration, he is always a migrant himself, a swallow means nothing to him. And rain does not mean much to us, either, we are a hardy patient people. Now here, Sophia, is a place that I am particularly attached to."

They halted before a hillock, on which grew a few common wild-flowers and some untidy natural grass. Children were swarming up it and rolling down, there was a great din and a smell of bruised herbage.

"It's like being in the country, isn't it?" she said, raising her face, where rested for the moment a look of perfect sincerity.

It was a hardy and patient little hillock, preserving its natural tough grasses, its coltsfoot and dandelion, speaking its dialect in the midst of the city.

"It reminds me of a donkey," said Sophia.

"Exactly! So uncouth and thistly. Shall we sit here? It's nicer. There's nothing to pay.

"Such a heavenly silence," she said; and added, with the appreciation one artist gives to another artist, "how well those parrots place their voice. One can hear them even here."

In the foreground of sound were the children playing, and in sound's distance the noise of the city—a brass band playing, the hooting of tugs on the river, the steady melancholy thrumming of life lived against a sounding-board of stone. It was odd to hear floating among these the roaring of lions, the screaming of tropical birds, noises so romantically desolate and unassimilated, and not to feel it odder. For now, thought Sophia, I seem able to take everything as a matter of course, as one does in a dream; though no doubt my knowledge that they are in cages must count for a good deal. The hillock was far from comfortable, she had never had much knack for sitting on the ground, and the children were smelly and insistent. Yet it seemed to her that she had never felt a more ample peace of spirit, a securer leisure. Sitting here, and thus, she had attained to a state which she could never have desired, nor even conceived. And being so unforeseen, so alien to her character and upbringing, her felicity had an absolute perfection; no comparison between the desired and the actual could tear holes in it, no ambition whisper, But this is not quite what you wanted, is it?—no busybody ideal suggest improvements. Her black moire flounces seemed settled into an endless repose on the dirty grass, her glove-buttons winked tranquilly in the sun, she saw herself simultaneously as a figure ludicrously inappropriate, and as something exactly fitted into its right station on the face of the globe.

In this amplitude of mind it was a pleasure to meditate upon practical considerations; and as some people, being idle, crown their contentment by taking a piece of knotted string to unravel, she turned herself to the solution of a problem which had first presented itself as they left the Luxembourg, which had since roamed vaguely through her mind as a piece of seaweed appears and sinks again in the wave, which Minna's words, "It's nicer. There's nothing to pay," and her subsequent silence had cast to shore and left high and dry.

How was she to intimate to Minna that the twenty-five pounds devoted to the Polish Patriots was not the ending of her resources? On that triumphant outcry of "I have beggared you now!" it would have been tactless to mention the margin between herself and beggary; and even when the sudden squall of rain overtook them on the way to the wine-shop she had not undermined the assumption of a heaven-bestowed destitution by mentioning that she had quite enough petty cash to pay for both the wine and a cab, thinking, as they hurried under the sharp pellets of rain, the sudden wrath of cold and darkness, that the woman beside her, so ugly and so entrancing, so streaked and freaked with moods, so incandescent with candour and so tunnelled with deceitfulness, was like a demonstration by earth that working in clay she could contrive a match for any atmospheric April.

Yet Minna, however capable of staring facts in the face and denying their existence (and Sophia could see that she was capable of great feats in that kind), could scarcely have been Frederick's mistress and yet suppose that twenty-five pounds was all that stood between Mrs. Frederick Willoughby and indigence. Besides, she was a Jewess, one of a race who can divine gold even in the rock; she should be able to divine it in a bank too. Ridiculous, thought Sophia, still turning and twiddling the problem; ridiculous that one should feel obliged to break it gently to her that one is blessed with comfortable means. Of all people, she should digest such information most naturally; for she is a Jewess, with a proper esteem for money, and she is an artist, with no hoity-toity scruples about taking it. Most certainly, money must by some means or other be injected into Minna's way of living; she could not be allowed to go on drinking bad wine and eating messes of sour cabbage spiced with caraway, paddling through the wet streets in broken slippers, and over her own parquet in dusters, ogling jellied eels as though they were quails, and fencing her heavy quaking shoulders against the cold with a wrap that should be at the cleaner's.

Even allowing for dramatic instinct, a terrific virtuosity of rhetorical effect, Minna must be painfully poor. All the curiosity-shop trimmings of her apartment, the old masters and the embroideries, the Gothic beaker and the damascened andirons, were gone—gone too, most probably, most regrettably, those superior duelling pistols. Natalia also was gone—a good riddance, maybe, but, since she had no replacer, a bad sign; and despite the curtain-fire of Sophia's bonnet, and sealskin muff and pelerine, and well-funded demeanour, Madame Coton's glance was superciliously inquisitive, and the man in the wine-shop far too affable.

And only someone, thought Sophia with a flash of intuition, only someone who has felt authentic destitution could throw away twenty-five good pounds as soon as look at it.

You must be fed, properly fed, clothed and warmed, she resolved, glancing under her eyelashes at Minna. Her mind almost added, cleaned; for poverty had laid a tarnish on that skin, turned its warm milk-coffee-colour towards sallowness, dulled those jet-black locks to the black of a cheap coffin. In that glance love re-absorbed her, and the knot, turning suddenly in her exploring fingers, presented its aspect of how at all costs she must not let a Midas-touch strike stiff, strike cold and dead, the happiness which that exulting "Sophia, I have beggared you," had brought to life. Poverty in some way warded their relationship, was the battered Aladdin's lamp which had unlocked the undreamed-of riches.

So on the whole the best plan would be to pawn her diamonds, the ring on her hand, the brooch on the dressing-table in the Place Bellechasse. The money resulting from a visit to the Mont-de-Piété would be, in some mystical way, cleansed from the sin original of wealth; it would not offend Minna, or flaw the illusion of poverty on which, she supposed, everything depended; and it would be quite enough for her present purpose.

Pleased to have arranged everything so well, she stretched herself and turned with a smile to her companion.

"Tell me, Sophia. Have you ever stolen anything?"

"Never. Why?"

"Because at this moment you look exactly as though you had been robbing an orchard. Your expression is sly and self-satisfied. Would you thieve, Sophia?"

"Yes, I expect so."

"So would I. When I was in the priest's house I stole like an angel—cigars, money, his bandannas, the wine for the sacrament, everything I could lay hands on. If I had not discovered my talent for thieving I could never have kept my self-respect. But when I looked at the things I had stolen it re-established me. *Le vol, c'est la propriété.*"

"What did you do with the things you stole?"

"Oh, threw them away—except the wine and the cigars. Or put them back again when they were missed. It was the sensation I wanted, I could not hazard that by being found out."

"And the priest?"

"Exorcized the house against the *Poltergeist.* He was a fat man, full of gas, he rumbled like a goat. He drew in coloured chalks, pictures of hell, and showed me a new one every day, saying that there was a special hell for the Jews. At night I was locked into a cupboard, and sometimes he would come in with a candle and another picture. Then he would pray, and weep, and enjoy himself. He drew like a schoolboy, his devils and his damned had hay-fork fingers and bodies like turnips, his chalks were the brightest colours, yellow, and purple. . . ."

Caught by her voice, one of the children playing on the hillock approached, and stood listening openmouthed. His playmate called to him, and finding that of no avail, came up, and tugged him by the arm. The first child shook his head. The second child stayed.

"The priest's housekeeper was a very old woman called Rosa. She had a long plait of grey hair, and into it she twined leaves of mountain ash and elder, as charms to keep away the wood-spirits. She had charms in her pockets, charms round her neck, charms sewn into her slippers to prevent her falling into the well. In one eye she had a cataract, that eye seemed to me to be made of snow, dirty snow pressed into a pellet and beginning to thaw."

One after another the children left their play and came nearer, the bolder shoving forward the timid. Two women went by, and Sophia heard the one say to the other, "Look, the pretty dears! How children love a fairy-story."

"She was pious and cruel, that old woman. Before she thrashed me she made the sign of the cross over my back. But I got even with her. One day . . ."

The story was animated and indecent. The children pressed closer, giggling, nudging each other in delight. Passers-by stopped. Arrested by curiosity, they stayed for entertainment, and at the end of the anecdote the shrill titters of the children were reinforced by several adult guffaws.

"Yes, I avenged myself. But even victory is a poor thing when one is alone, with one's back to the wall. Good God, how unhappy I was! How endless the winters were, how agonizing the nights when I lay shivering, thinking the night as long as a winter. And I no older than these children here," she said, turning to Sophia, her voice lowering its lights, trailing under a weight of woe. "No, I should have gone under, I should have died of misery if it had not been for Corporal Lecoq. A little old fellow, Sophia, limping with a quick step, holding himself upright, his chin always well-shaved, his moustaches curled like ram's horns, his eyes bulging wrathfully from his scarred face. The ice had scarcely melted when he came to the village, limping through the slush, beating a quick-step on his drum, his two dogs following him, wearing coats of red velvet trimmed with gold braid, tarnished but splendid. Outside the church he came to a stop. He unfolded a piece of carpet and laid it down on the slush, and immediately the two dogs sat up to attention. He beat a flourish on his drum and cried out, with a loud voice, with a strange accent, 'Ladies and Gentlemen, good people all, you shall see something worth seeing.

These are my two celebrated dogs, Bastien and Bastienne. And before your delighted eyes they will dance the minuet, as it is danced in all the politest courts of Europe.'

"He drummed out the rhythm of a minuet, *Tra, la-la-la-la, Tra, la,* and the dogs stood up and danced, their haunches trembling, their front paws dangling with affectation from the cuffs of their red velvet coats. At the end of the dance they dropped on their four legs, became dogs again, running round him and barking with excitement, rousing every watch-dog in the village. At the noise of the drumming everyone ran out, the women and children, the men from the tavern. They chattered and screamed, and said that it was witchcraft; and the village idiot, a woman of fifty with the face of an infant, declared that just so was the minuet danced in the courts of Europe. I only dared not go near. But I hung over the paling of the priest's yard, knocking my hatchet against the wood so that Rosa might think I was still at work. Corporal Lecoq said, 'I see a young lady yonder who has a fine ear for music. Bastien, go and make your bow to the young lady,' and he pointed with his finger, and the dog ran to the priest's palings, rose on its hind-legs and made me a bow. Alas, it did me no good! There was an uproar of voices, saying that I was a Jewess, a scapegrace, a good-for-nothing; and Rosa took hold of my arm and sent me whirling into the house.

"Outside the drumming went on, marches and mazurkas, and the villagers laughed and exclaimed. And then I heard the quickstep, the dogs barking, his voice hallooing to them, friendly and imperious; and they were gone.

"For ever, so I thought. Music, red velvet, a dog that bowed, a human being that spoke me kindly—such things were not likely to come my way again. But a few evenings later I felt something touch my leg, and turning, there was the dog Bastien, standing beside me, striking me gently with his paw. 'Good evening,' said a voice, soft and rough like the touch of moss. Corporal Lecoq was leaning on the palings, his curling moustaches silhouetted against the sky. 'Is the priest in?' said he. 'I want to make my confession.'

"Ah, thought I, you are no friend after all. You are another

Catholic, another of those leagued against me. And when he and the priest came out of the church later, roaring with laughter, arm in arm, I hated them alike—no, I hated the corporal worse of the two, for of the priest I had never expected anything but ill. He came often, boasting himself a good Catholic, he and the priest used to sit together, telling stories and drinking sloe gin, and to Rosa he gave a miraculous plaster statue so that after that she fed his dogs when they came into the kitchen. But he never spoke to me, nor I to him, until one hot summer afternoon when I was ironing the church linen, alone for once. 'Hot work?' said he. For answer I spat on the surplice. 'So you are still a Jewess?' 'Always a Jewess,' said I. 'Foolish child,' said he, *'Paris vaut bien une messe.'* And he told me the story of Henry IV, and how, if I would seem to yield a little, Rosa might allow me to talk with him, since he was such a good Catholic, and that he would tell me about Paris, and teach me to speak French. My tears fell on the linen, but I went on ironing. I gave no answer.

"'Later again he brought Rosa the two red velvet coats, asking her to mend them. 'I mend for your filthy animals?' cried she. 'Never! Give the coats to the Jewess. Dogs defile Jews, let her mend the coats.' 'I have mended the cassock,' I said. 'I will mend the dogs' coats too.'

"'There was this to be done, that to be done, holes darned, the gilt braid re-stitched, new linings; and he seemed to make a great fuss, and however I worked was not satisfied. I must do it over again to his liking, and at last he must oversee it all, since I worked so doltishly. That day he sat by me as I sewed, talking of Napoleon, whose soldier he had been, of the retreat from Moscow, and how he was left behind, frost-bitten, as good as dead. But he had been sheltered, and had picked up a living since, tramping from fair to fair with his dogs and his drum, or singing in taverns, or in choirs. For he had a great bass voice; Greek chants, or Roman, or Lutheran psalms were all alike to him. And he could shave too, and dress hair; for in his youth he had been apprenticed to a hair-dresser in Paris, leaving that profession to become a strolling actor. And then he talked to me of the theatre, of the lamps and the dresses, the tragedies of Voltaire and Grétry's operas.

"'I have finished the coats,' said I.

"'Rip them up,' he said. 'And then I will bring them again, and teach you a speech from a tragedy.'

"All that summer he came to the priest's house. We had a language of signals; for I had a quick ear, he had only to tap out the rhythm of some tune we had agreed upon and I would know what he meant, and answer it, banging my hatchet on the wood, or clattering one dish against another at the sink. I stole comfits for his dogs, and cigars for him. I began to be a little happy, for I had a friend. One day he said to Rosa, 'My dogs have fleas, come with me to the sheep-washing trough and hold them while I wash them.' 'Let the Jewess do that,' said she, 'and be defiled.' I put on a sulky face and went with him.

"'Now we will fall to work,' he said, when we got to the sheep-washing trough. And on the grass he laid out soap, and a towel, and a comb, pomade in a china box, and a pair of curling-tongs. 'What, do you curl the dogs' hair?' said I. 'No,' he answered. 'But I curl young ladies'.' And taking me by the scruff of the neck he pushed my head into the cool running water and lathered my hair, scolding at the lice, and the dirt, and the tangles. For a long while he soaped, and rinsed, and soaped and rinsed again, and I, forgetting my first fear, gave myself up to the pleasure of feeling myself so well handled, shivering with voluptuousness when he rubbed the nape of my neck, arching my head back against his strong hand. Then he rubbed it dry with a towel, combed it, and smeared on the pomade that smelled of violets. Last of all he kindled a little fire of sticks, heated the tongs, and curled my hair into ringlets.

"'There,' said he, standing back to look at me well. 'Those ringlets are called *anglaises.* And now for the finishing touch.' Out of his pocket he pulled an artificial rose, frayed and crumpled, and stuck it behind my ear.

"When I looked in the sheep-trough, I did not know myself. He too seemed changed, singing a song in French, pretending to pluck the strings of a guitar which was not there. Then he picked up the soap, what was left of it, the towel, and the rest of his gear, and marched off, still singing, waving his arms and staggering. I guessed then that he was a little drunk.

"I, poor little fool, went dreaming back to the priest's house with my ringlets and my false rose, and my odour of violets which surrounded me like a cloud. 'Harlot!' cried Rosa, 'bedizened little infidel, stinking trumpery, you are not fit to be clean!' And slobbering with rage she tore the rose out of my hair, and a handful of my hair with it, and began to daub my face with dirty pig's lard from the frying-pan."

"No!" exclaimed a solemn voice from the crowd. "That was too much, that was infamous." "Old hag," said another voice.

"But this time I did not submit. I kicked her shins, I hit her in the breast with my bony knuckles till she howled with anger and astonishment. Her howls fetched the priest into the kitchen, puffing and snorting. Out of my face, daubed with pig's lard, through my dishevelled heroine's ringlets, I glared at him. 'Tremble, tyrant!' I cried. And as though it were a charm, an exorcism, I began to repeat a French tragedy speech which I had learned from Corporal Lecoq. I remembered the gestures he had taught me, the raising of the arm, the tossing back of the hair, the furling of the imaginary mantle, the hand laid on the heart. I swelled my voice to the clang of an organ. I made it cold with scorn, exact and small with menace as a dagger's point. And while I spoke, my glance resting upon them as though they were a long way off, I saw them begin to shrink, and draw back, and cross themselves.

"Coming to the end of my speech, I went through it again. Still reciting, still making the right gestures, rolling out my Alexandrines, dwelling terribly upon the cæsuras, I began to step backwards, haughtily, towards the door. And on the threshold I finished my tirade, and rolled my eyes over them once more. And so I walked off, free and unimpeded, to find Corporal Lecoq at the inn."

She had risen to her feet, shaking out her crumpled skirts, rising as though from the ocean of a curtsy. And holding her bonnet before her she moved among the crowd, graciously accepting their congratulations and their contributions, her face pale and noble, her demeanour stately as a sleepwalker's.

To Sophia she returned more briskly, holding out the bonnet as though she were a retriever and the bonnet a pheasant.

"For the Polish Patriots, Minna?"

"Oh no! For our supper. I have always allowed my talent to support me."

"I had been thinking of pawning my diamond brooch for our supper."

"Don't, I beg of you! Keep it till we really need it, keep it"—she said earnestly—"till I break my leg."

Enraptured with her own performance, floating on the good-will of the self-approved, she insisted upon visiting and feeding the bears, the monkeys, the camels, the vultures, the crocodile, the buffaloes, and the sloth; and infected, as captive animals will be, by the mood of their visitor, the gentry behind the bars greeted her with congratulating interest, even the crocodile, it seemed to Sophia, coming leering up from its muddy tank like an approving impresario.

The funds in the bonnet allowed them to take a cab, a proceeding that seemed ordinary enough until Sophia noticed the driver's face assume an expression of dreamlike bewilderment. Minna, it seemed, had again been studying for Grimm's fairy-tales, and had chosen the moment of directing the driver to transform herself into a bear.

"All I ask, Minna, is that you should not be a wolf when it comes to paying him."

"No, no! Then I will be a princess."

Emerging from his onion-scented den Égisippe Coton handed each lady a large formal bouquet. The gentleman had expressed his regrets at not finding the ladies at home.

Dangling from each bouquet was Frederick's card, each card inscribed in his large easy handwriting, *"With Kind Inquiries."* Another of his lucky cannons, thought Sophia; and a sort of affable appreciation spread itself over her first annoyance. She had always preferred Frederick when some waft of rogue's luck puffed out his sails—any development of impertinence, of brag, of manly floridity was an improvement on his usual tedious good manners. Accepting her own roses and lilies in this spirit, it was disturbing to see Minna flinch as though she had been smacked in the face.

"Ridiculous nosegays," she said soothingly.

"What is so frightful to me, Sophia, what upsets me, is to think of the cost of these flowers. What cynicism to spend all this on flowers at a time when people round us lack fire, lack bread! Only a hard heart, only a character stupefied by a false arrangement of society, could throw away money like this. Twenty francs, I dare say, or more."

"Besides the tip to Coton. That must have been considerable."

"My God, yes! That Coton! At our very doors we have these individuals, these parasites. We must pass them whenever we go in or out, as peasants stump past their dunghills."

As she spoke her hands, moving with Jewish nimbleness, tweaked out the wires from the bouquet, snipped the rose stalks, arranged the blossoms to show at their best.

"I am wondering, Minna, if we could do anything to redress the state of society by making up these flowers into buttonholes, and selling them in the street."

Minna turned, her mouth twitching with laughter, her eyes angry with tears.

"I am sincere, I am far more sincere than you think. It does truly shock me, this waste of money on flowers. But how can you expect me to be truthful while you are so calm. We were so happy, so simple, on our hillock like a donkey. And then to come back and find this sophisticated sneer, this crack of the whip."

"Infuriating," agreed Sophia, herself infuriated by those last words. "But quite insignificant. Frederick has these happy thoughts occasionally, but he can never follow them up. This is just another of his runaway knocks."

For there are some circumstances in which it is useless to attempt tact; and since Frederick's runaway knocks had been bestowed on either of them as impartially as his nosegays, wife and mistress might as well avail themselves of the enfranchisement warranted by this. Nor had the words carried any scathe with them. Minna's sigh was for the wire's strangle-hold on the best rose of Sophia's bouquet—for having arranged her own she was now briskly at work on the other.

Leaning against the mantelpiece, staring at Minna's hands,

Sophia mentored herself against anger. For what could be sillier than to waste a moment of her consciousness in the stale occupation of feeling angry with Frederick when she stood here, centred in this exciting existence of being happy, free, and passionately entertained? From the time when they left the Luxembourg Palace she had breathed this intoxication of being mentally at ease, free to speak without constraint, listen without reservation. She would be a triple fool to stoop out of this air to that old lure of being annoyed by Frederick, even though the old lure had been smeared over to seem a new one—for with all the force of her temper she could imagine what it would be like to hate Frederick on Minna's behalf.

"In a way I am sorry we missed him. He could have carried my note to my great-aunt Léocadie—the note I have not yet written."

"Your great-aunt Léocadie?"

"Madame de Saint-Gonval. I was living with her, you know, when I broke out and came to you. I must write to her. Though Frederick by now will have allayed any alarms she may have felt."

"Madame de Saint-Gonval? Yes, indeed you must write."

"I doubt if she has lost a wink of sleep through not knowing my whereabouts."

"Perhaps not. I dare say she has not much heart. But what polish, what discrimination! I have spoken to her once or twice —she introduced herself to me at one of my recitals—and I thought her charming, charming and intelligent."

"She's shrewd. But do you really consider her intelligent?"

"Indeed I do. Her taste is so pure. Narrow, of course—what would you expect?—but exquisitely cultivated."

"Yes, I think her taste is good."

"Sophia, I assure you that a cultivated taste is already a great deal, especially in that class of society. Sophia, why are you laughing?"

"Because you talk about my great-aunt Léocadie exactly as my great-aunt Léocadie talks about you."

"And you laugh at us both. There!"

The two flower vases were completed and set, formal splendours, on either side of the mantelshelf. In her admiring voice, in her admiring survey, there was no overtone of rancour or ironical forgiveness. The flowers were beautiful and she had arranged them beautifully, and now she stood admiring them, delighted as a child.

"I could bow down before you," said Sophia. "You are genuinely good, good as bread."

"One ought to be, you know," replied the other, seriously. And putting up her large hand she pulled away the last noosing wire.

Into the pause that followed, her words came with a rustic earnestness and urgency.

"For how else can one nourish others?"

The letter to great-aunt Léocadie was not written. Wlodomir Macgusty came in, and on his heels came the bald-headed man still wearing the Scotch shawl, the man who had told Minna that revolutions have no second flute-players to spare. As the room filled up Sophia recognized many faces which she had seen on her first visit; but the general aspect of the company was changed, there were no ball-dresses now, no elegant escorting young gentlemen. A change for the better, she thought. Though she had yet no sympathy for republican opinions, she preferred any opinion grave and ungarnished. She was impressed by the way these strangers accepted her, feeling apparently none of the awkward hostility which she could not but feel towards them. They were cordial, sincere, dispassionate; discovering that she was English they began to question her about the Chartists, the poor-law, the franchise, the Fenians, the amount of bacon eaten by English peasants, the experiments of the Co-operatives. With surprise she discovered that they thought highly of the British Constitution and with embarrassment she realized that she knew rather less about it than they did. She found herself ignorant on other counts, too, forced to admit to one young man, whose broad forehead, slow eyes, and cockade of heavy close-cropped curls gave him a singular resemblance to a young bull, that she knew nothing of the work of an artist called Blake. "You should," he said, gravely and sadly. "He is formidable." As one young bull might speak of another, she thought.

Though without any particular concurrence, she was enjoying herself when Égisippe Coton, his countenance bleak of all personal opinion, breathed in her ear that a footman from the Place Bellechasse had brought her luggage, and a note from Mr. Willoughby. Letting the conversation drift away from her, she opened it.

Dear Sophia,

I was sorry not to see you this afternoon as I had hoped to gather from you some information about your plans for the future, and possibly some message of common politeness to your great-aunt. We suppose that you are not likely to return to the Place Bellechasse, at any rate for the present, so your belongings are being packed and sent to you.

I have told Madeleine, by the way, not to send your jewel-case, or any of your valuables. While Minna continues to keep "open house" the risk of losing them would be too great. So you must depend on your beauty unadorned—more than adequate—to enchant the revolutionary bobtail.

Your affectionate husband, Frederick.

P.S. Homage to Minna, of course.

"Well, I'm blowed," she murmured.

Nothing pained Frederick more than to hear vulgarity on a woman's lips, the phrase came naturally, and was comforting. With a deepened conviction she repeated it.

Wlodomir Macgusty, sitting patiently at her side, remarked on the beautiful sounds of the English language, a tongue at once so expressive and sonorous. Nothing, he said, could equal the pleasure with which he listened to readings from Moore and Shakespeare, a pleasure which was not impaired by ignorance of the sense, for it was possible, was it not, to listen with the soul? What she had said just then, for instance, he had not understood; but it had been perfectly clear to him that the ejaculation expressed wonder and reverence, a deep but tranquil movement of the spirit such as one experiences, for example, in looking at the ocean, or the Alps.

Did he listen much to Shakespeare, she asked?

In his youth, often. In his youth he had been employed as a secretary in the household of a Russian nobleman, and an English governess had also been one of the count's household. They met frequently in the garden, two exiles meeting to mix their sighs, she nostalgic for her England, he for the Poland of his ideals. In her walks she carried a book in her hand, and when conversation failed them she would read aloud; for hours, sometimes, readings only broken by his cries of appreciation and her coughing fits. For she coughed, daily she grew thinner, daily her pink and white complexion grew more alarmingly vivid. After her death he had composed an elegy. *"Elle était jeune,"* it began, *"elle était belle, elle s'appelait Miss Robinson."*

The remainder of the elegy did not live up to this arresting beginning, and while it lasted she could look through the letter again. Wlodomir Macgusty had shown discernment: as a specimen of insolence the letter was indeed an Alp. So long accustomed to despising Frederick, even now she could not pay him the tribute of an unmixed anger. Astonishment, an almost congratulating astonishment, qualified her rage. As a specimen of firm and blackguardly advantage-taking, this was beyond what she would have given him credit for. Yet it must certainly be all his own; Léocadie had no more hamper of scruples than he, but her unscrupulousness would have gone otherwise to work.

Strategic sense granted that the advantage Frederick had taken she had given; nothing could have been more uncivil or more unwise than her behaviour towards the Place Bellechasse, nothing could have given him a better-justified stick to beat her with. But that the stick should have been raised, should indeed have fallen—for the jewel-case had been kept back, the husbandly thump administered—surpassed her theory of Frederick.

The elegy had concluded with vows of testifying celibacy.

"You have never married, Monsieur Macgusty?"

"Twice," said he. "One angel after another. They stayed with me no longer than angels would. One died. The other spread her wings. She died too, after a while; but not in my arms."

"Which do you consider the most essential quality in a husband—firmness, or sensibility?"

"Firmness, Madame. Woman demands it. Without it, she pines."

Without it she—spreads her wings. "For I do not see myself flying back to Frederick," she said to herself. "He has put out his arresting firmness a little too late." Her anger, like a rapid wine, had flown to her head; she felt herself mettled, sleek as the oiled wrestler, affable as only the powerful may be. She looked round on the assembly with bonhomie, she found herself rising, like any triumphant tippler, to make a speech.

"Minna! I have a little proposal to make. Will you not allow me to offer your guests some supper?"

The candid pleasure at this proposal made her feel even more warmly towards the guests.

"Unfortunately, as you know, I have no money. But I have this ring, it must be worth something. Perhaps one of these gentlemen would take it to the pawn-shop for me. It is not too late for that, I hope?"

As with one voice her guests could assure her as to the closing hour of the offices of the Mont-de-Piété, as with one pair of legs they were ready to go on her errand. Pleasant creatures, she thought, kindly and unaffected. It was a pity that they were all so crazy, so improvident, so surely doomed to end in the jail or the gutter.

"I suppose you know, young lady," said the bald shawled one, speaking with fatherly gruffness, "that you will make a very bad bargain over this? Diamonds are not what they were. Socially speaking, this is excellent. But for you it is unfortunate."

Meanwhile it was being canvassed with great earnestness whose pawn-shop technique best equipped him for the errand. Strange that in a company where so many were Jews no Jewish candidate was proposed. The choice lay, it seemed, between a mouse-mannered student of engineering and the bull-fronted young man who had spoken about an artist called Blake.

The choice fell on the latter. Tying the ring into a corner of his handkerchief, and pressing the handkerchief down his boot, he remarked, "You see in me, Madame, the triumph of the Latin over the Semite. And if I may say so"—here he bowed courteously to the mouse—"of the peasant over the Parisian."

The writing on the wall, she supposed, had been there long enough for these affable gentry to be able to revel without as much as a glance at it; practically delighting in an unexpectedly good supper they discussed the progress of a republic which had from poverty made them poorer yet, and the only acrimonious note was struck by the bald man of the shawl (whose name, it seemed, was Ingelbrecht) when the mouse disputed his prophecy that except in Paris the elections would go flat against the republic. For while the peasant, said he, thinks the best thing he can do is to work like a beast, while he would rather skulk in virtuous industry than expose himself to the danger of thinking, any republic will be of the town only and in a state of siege. Even Dury, there, was as bad a peasant as the rest of them. He laboured his canvases as though they were his fields, he asked nothing better than to paint from dawn to sundown.

"I am not ashamed of being a peasant," said Dury pleasantly. "He is an astute animal, the peasant, and art demands a great deal of low cunning."

Marching over the protests which this statement roused from Macgusty, Ingelbrecht turned to Sophia, "And what do you think of the peasant? You have some of your own, I understand."

"I find them almost intolerable," she replied.

"There, you see. She finds them almost intolerable. And so you let them die of starvation, eh, harness them in carts and send them to the poorhouse?"

In his grumpy voice with its snarling Belgian accent, in his staring angry eyes, there was considerable kindliness.

"She does nothing of the sort, I'll swear," interposed Minna. "She has a heart and can feel pity, she is not like you, you old humgruffin."

"It seems to me," said Sophia, "that if you wish to help these peasants it is fatal to pity them. Once shown compassion for their misfortunes and they will persist in them to get whatever almsgiving your compassion throws. When a horse is down you beat it to get it up again, pity will never raise it."

"Excellent, excellent!" shouted Ingelbrecht. "I wish more republicans thought like this aristocrat. But your brains are in the wrong place. They should be under a red cap instead of a fashionable bonnet. Why were you not born one of your own poachers, Mrs. Willoughby?"

"I have wished it myself."

He continued to stare at her, growling under his breath. Though the allusion to the bonnet rankled, she liked him. Frederick had left her with her beauty unadorned to enchant the revolutionary bobtail; she would have been glad to discard that also, the bonnet and the sleek hood of flaxen hair beneath it; she would have pawned her pink fingernails along with the diamond ring. It irked her to find that even in this circle her petticoats beringed her first and foremost.

"Should there be no brains under bonnets?"

"Yes, if you please. But the woman of the future will demand to own not brains but vigour. Yes, yes, I dare say you are vigorous too. But unless you are careful your brains will step in first and tell you that it is more dignified and reasonable to remain passive."

"I see. I will be on my guard, then."

She was sorry when with another twinkling glare he walked off. She found him the most congenial of all her diamond's guests; and afterwards with a certain sleeking of pride she listened to Minna's congratulations, learning that even among revolutionaries Ingelbrecht was considered to go too far.

"He would destroy you without a moment's compunction if you did not accept his ideas. Me too," she added as an afterthought.

"And do you?"

"Do I? Oh, accept his ideas. I do not understand them, they are harsh and abstruse and I—alas!—can grasp only the first quality. But I know"—and her expression was one of piety—"that he has been obliged to fly from twelve European countries, and that is enough for me."

They were standing in the middle of the room, a room made cold and oppressive by the departure of so many people. Minna took her hand and caressed it.

"Beautiful hand, so smooth and reckless. I love it better without the ring. How much did Dury bring you?"

"Enough to take me back to the Meurice. What time is it, Minna?"

Even before she heard her voice so flatly speaking them, she had known the craven falsity of those words, words only spoken because to act on them would spare her the humiliation of admitting herself compromised by Frederick's malice. To Mrs. Frederick Willoughby of Blandamer it was one thing to stay under Madame Lemuel's roof as a benefactress, quite another to remain there as a possible beneficiary.

It was as though, shooting off what she knew to be a popgun, she had seen the spurting authentic answer of blood. In an instant Minna had become the desolate ghost of the Medici fountain, the resigned outcast she had bullied on that night of February; and the hand, still holding hers, became cold as death in the moment before it loosed its hold.

"You wound me," she murmured, and fell insensible.

Even more than in sleep her face in unconsciousness became unmistakably ugly, unmistakably noble. The look of life receding from those features left the hooked nose, the florid melancholy lips, the grandiloquent sweep of the jaw from ear to chin, as time leaves the fragmentary grandeur of a forsaken temple, still rearing its gesture of arch and colonnade from drifting sand, from slowly heaping mould. It was unbelievable that those features could ever have worn cajoling looks.

Equally baffling was Minna's behaviour when she had been brought to. Shaking in every limb, passionately complaining of cold, she sat humped on the pink sofa, talking with deriding eloquence on any and every subject save subjects which Sophia would have discussed. She would not eat nor drink, nor go to bed, nor move nearer the fire. She would do nothing but smoke and talk.

After the second cigar, she rose to her feet, sallow and shaking.

"I see I bore you," she said furiously.

"You do not bore me, you exasperate me. How can I attend to what you are saying when I am thinking all the time what should be done with you?"

"I have never met an English person yet," cried Minna, "man

or woman, who was not heartless. And who did not mask that heartlessness with an appearance of practical philanthropy."

With the aim of a savage or a schoolboy she threw Sophia's vinaigrette at Frederick's flowers, burst into a fit of weeping, and rushed from the room. An instant after Sophia heard her being violently sick.

"Oh, how the devil," said Sophia, speaking loudly to the echoing unhearing walls, "am I to save you now?"

A groan like a mortally stricken animal's answered her; and kneeling on the floor, holding Minna's body across her lap, she remembered the grotesque couples she had watched at sheep-shearing: the man crouched over his victim, working with the brutal fury of skill, the sheep sullen with terror, lying lumpish and inert under that heavy grasp, that travelling bite of steel.

The sheep lay still out of cunning. Let the grasp slacken ever so little, and it would leap away, trailing its flounce of half-severed fleece; and searching Minna's countenance her imagination watched for some kindred sign of animal strategy, while ruthless and methodical she continued to dribble brandy over those clenched teeth, or slap those icy hands.

"If I could only warm you," she exclaimed, measuring Minna's weight against her own, measuring the distance from floor to bed. It was too far; but fetching the blankets and eiderdowns she padded Minna round with them, and then laid herself down alongside her in a desperate calculated caress.

It was shocking to smell on that deathly body the scent of the living Minna—the smoky perfume of her black hair, the concocted exhalation of irises lingering on the cold neck, as though the real flowers were there, trapped in a sudden frost. It was spring, she remembered. In another month the irises would be coming into flower. But now it was April, the cheat month, when the deadliest frosts might fall, when snow might cover the earth, lying hard and authentic on the English acres as it lay over the wastes of Lithuania. There, in one direction, was Blandamer, familiar as a bed; and there, in another, was Lithuania, the unknown, where a Jewish child had watched the cranes fly over, had stood beside the breaking river. And here, in Paris, lay Sophia Willoughby, lying on the floor in the draughty passageway between bedroom and dressing-closet, her body pressed against the body of her husband's mistress.

"But it is I, *I,* who will save her," she murmured. After a while, like a leisurely answer to those words, came the cold chiming of a church-clock. Save her wherefor, save her for what?

It was three o'clock, the hour of Napoleon's courage, the hour when people die. How much longer could she hold out? Cautiously she slid her cheek against her shoulder. There was still warmth there, she still had warmth to give. But opposing it, quite as positive, was this deadly cold she embraced, a body of ice in which, like some device at the fishmonger's, a clock-heart beat, a muted tick-tock of breath stirred.

The quarter chimed, continuing the conversation between them. *Where-for?* it said on an interval of a major third. Why, indeed? Immediately, the answer was simple enough. When one finds oneself with someone at the point of death one naturally does what one can to help them. Not from liking, necessarily; not from Christian compassion, not from training, even. A more secret tie compels one in the presence of death, one falls into rank against the common enemy, exerting oneself maybe for the life of one's worst foe in order to demonstrate a victory over that adversary. . . . One's worst foe. In the eyes of the world Minna might be exactly that; and to preserve her now, if she could preserve her, an act of idiocy, magnanimity, and destiny.

The candle was on the point of going out, shooting up a flapping flame. Cautiously she raised herself on her elbow, as though in this last allowance of sight she might surprise the answer to the church-clock's inquiry. As though she had never noticed them before she found herself absorbed in admiring Minna's eyelashes, the only detail in her face that corroborated the suavity of her voice. From the moment I got wind of your voice, she thought, from the moment that Frederick, standing by Augusta's deathbed, echoed those melancholy harp-notes, I have been under some extraordinary enchantment, I have hastened on, troubled, uncomprehending, and resolute, from one piece of madness to another. I have thought I could have a child by the lime-kiln man, more demented still I have proposed to have a child by Frederick. I have sketched myself sailing among the islands of the South Seas with Caspar and his guitar, voyaging on the Rhine with Mrs. Hervey, disguising myself as a poacher and foraying among my own woods, dwelling meekly at the Academy Saint-Gonval. I have left Blandamer as though I should never return, I have been in a street battle, I have pawned my diamond ring in order to entertain a collection of revolutionary ragamuffins. From sheer inattention I have been on the brink of a reconciliation with my husband, and as inattentively I have got myself into a position in which he seems able to cast me off. And now I am lying on the floor beside you, renewing the contact which, whenever I make it, shoots me off into some fresh fit of impassioned wool-gathering.

The candle had gone out. In the darkness Minna stirred and sighed, a rational deploring sigh of one in pain.

"What is it?"

"My head—aches."

Now we are off again, thought Sophia, the thought exploding within her like triumph; and it was with only rather more pity than impatience for life to recommence that she asked,

"But how do you feel? Do you feel better? Let me light a candle."

"No!"

"But, Minna, you can't lie here on the floor."

"I can."

The tone was at once meek and grim. So might an animal have spoken, lying limp and leaden in its burrow.

"Well then, let me arrange you more comfortably. Let me make you a cup of tea."

"On a spirit-lamp, like an Englishwoman in the desert." Her teeth chattered as she spoke, her attempted laugh was broken off sharp by pain.

"Lie beside me, Sophia."

Obediently, and with an embarrassment bred of finding herself obedient, she laid herself down, the pain in her limbs teaching her how to lie as she had lain before, finding again the scent of the irises, the smoky perfume of the loosened hair. Her mind was at war with her reposing attitude, she listened suspiciously to Minna's breathing, and laid a caressing hand upon her wrist in order to measure the pulse-beats.

Battened down, her triumph and impatience still raged inside her, sharpening her thoughts to a feverish practicality. This must be done, the other must be done, done by her, for the time had come for her to assert herself, she must be no longer jerked hither and thither by the electrical propulsion of contact with Minna. Somehow this wildfire force must be appeased, must be granted a *raison d'être* which would release it from accident into purpose. Scurrying thus briskly, her thought suddenly lighted upon the vision of her trunk and her dressing-case, standing in the entry where Égisippe Coton had set them down. Frederick must be dealt with too.

No. On second thoughts, that obligation was over. She could see no reason why she need ever deal with Frederick again. The necessary treaty for her jewels and valuables could be carried on by some third party. That would be the more dignified method. Most dignified of all would be to relinquish to him all that he thought so compelling: the pearl bracelets, the amethyst parure, the gold net reticule, the brooch. But the original Aspen in her would not give so far. Frederick had leeched quite enough during the years of their marriage, she would not trouble to climb to the apex of dignity in order to gratify him with a pair of pearl bracelets.

No burden more fidgeting than an impecunious husband. Her pride had always snarled at seeing him spend what was in truth her money, and her prudence had snarled to see him spending it so lavishly. He was as wasteful as a servant. She remembered the blank sniffing look on her father's face, his voice saying coldly and hastily, "Certainly, Frederick, by all means"; as though he would deny like an ill odour the spectacle of an insolvent son-in-law; and with the same distaste and embarrassment he had whisked over the question of the marriage settlements, depositing me, she thought, with the same haughty embarrassment as he might drop a shilling into the hand of an importunate widow, come over from Ireland with her brats for the hay-making. Why ever had Papa countenanced the marriage?—what could have softened him towards that dowerless beauty, that lad with a long pedigree? Not her own vehemence, that sudden imperious curiosity to know what the love of man and woman might be, which at the first learning had shrivelled away and left her cold and unamorous. Mamma. Her breath had fanned the match, her steadfast gentle talk, like a woollen web, so meek, so muffling, had trawled them all towards that altar where Papa had given this woman to be married to this man. Clear out of the past leapt the recollection of those overheard words, "My dear, for Sophia an early match is the safest match"; and Papa's face, his look of incredulity traversed with alarm. And so, for Sophia's safety, he had given that woman to be married to that man, overlooking even the whiskers. For to Papa, socketed in a smooth-cheeked era, those whiskers had been perhaps what went down his gullet with the greatest difficulty.

Papa, Mamma. . . . She looked back at them now with the peculiar tenderness which ripens only on the farther side of an irreparable estrangement. There they were in her memory, far off, so far off that they were almost blue, walking beside the lake at Blandamer as the gentleman and the lady walked beside the lake on the blue transfer breakfast service. Henceforth she could think of them only with this particular secreted tenderness, seeing them away on their side of the water, they on their side, she on hers. Their departure into death seemed almost immaterial, so greatly was it transcended by her living departure. They at Blandamer, resuming their rightful ownership from their double-bedded grave, where Mamma's willow murmured and dripped; she here, lying on the floor of an apartment in the rue de la Carabine, her body fostering this enigmatical sleeper, her mind wandering excited and tentative through this newly begun riff-raff existence, as one wanders through a new house, where everything is still uncertain or unknown, where none of the furniture has been unpacked.

It was almost midday before she examined the trunk and the dressing-case. They had been most carefully dealt with, the dressing-case in particular. Even the gold tops had been removed from the flasks and pomade-pots, and corks of assorted sizes rammed down in their stead. Hidden under a silk band—

pious observance of Papa's axiom that one should always keep five pounds against emergency—had been a Bank of England note. This also had been removed. Frederick had been indeed a most thorough and conscientious steward of her goods.

But her anger was insubstantial, muted by the fatigue of the night, bleached by the reality of her relief at Minna's re-emergence to life.

"One of my migraines," she had said. Her voice was tinged with regretful pride, as though, mauled and bloodied, she had said, "One of my tigers." And languid and complaint she had allowed herself to be put to bed, murmuring in her most plaintive stockdove note, "Ah, Sophia! How unfortunate that I broke your vinaigrette!"

No other allusion was made to the night before. It was a morning for practical dealings—Minna in bed, the apartment dishevelled with the party of overnight, her own crumpled estate to be remedied, and as usual, no food in the house.

She was in the porter's lodge, a shopping list in hand, impelling Madame Coton to trudge on her errands when she heard herself saluted, and turned to meet the man called Ingelbrecht.

"*Visite de digestion,*" he said, and bowed with formality.

This old man who had been driven from so many capital cities came welcome to her eyes, his cosmopolitan exile seemed to have given him something of the godlike quality of a head-waiter.

"Minna is ill."

"Ah! I am sorry. I will postpone the visit then, and do your shopping for you instead."

Madame Coton protested that for nothing could she relinquish the privilege of shopping for Madame Lemuel, so endeared and so stricken. But defrauding her of the unconcluded tip he took the list from her hands and walked off.

There on the landing stood the trunk and the dressing-case, unpleasing reminders of obligations unfulfilled. Sooner or later the apology must be made to great-aunt Léocadie, sooner or later the affair of her valuables must be settled. Ingelbrecht, indeed, gave such promise of imperturbable reliability that he might well be the third party empowered to treat for them; but on the whole it would be simpler to ask him to take her place within earshot of Minna's interminable drowsiness while she went to the Place Bellechasse, did the civil to Léocadie, and at the same time removed her goods.

But seeing his unmoved agreement she felt a compunction at so commandeering him.

"No," said he. "I shall be quite happy here. I shall go on with my writing." And from his pocket he drew a large notebook and a pencil.

"You are writing a book?"

"A treatise on the proper management of revolutions."

As she went on her way the image remained with her of Ingelbrecht, his shawl wrapped about his knees, his wrinkled face intent and unmoved, writing smoothly in his child's exercise book.

Thinking of Minna, of Ingelbrecht, and of herself, she had forgotten to expect the former things of the Place Bellechasse; but entering she saw with no surprise save that she should have forgotten that he would be there, Père Hyacinthe, visiting at his customary hour, his feet, prudently paired like begging friars, resting on the customary flourish of the Aubusson carpet. There, too, in its place, was the spinning wheel, gently whirring, and there was Frederick, still handing great-aunt Léocadie another tod of wool. It was as though they had been sitting there like that ever since her departure, sitting up for her as people sit up for the event of a deathbed, having called in the consolation of the Church in case it might be necessary. There they had sat, through daylight and lamplight, whiling away the time with subdued conversation. One of them, however, had absented himself long enough from the vigil to pack her trunk and pillage her dressing-case.

No professional *croque-morts* could have received her more calmly, manipulated her more suavely. No word was said of her absence, such was their tact that only a nominal reference was made to her presence. Taking a little turn towards the weather the conversation picked her up, as it were, and brought her back, through rain in England, to the discussion of the status of Claremont among the English country houses.

"It has always been used for oddities," said Frederick. "The Prince Consort lived there. The old one."

"With his dowdy Louise's predecessor. Poor creature! Of course one cannot always draw the winning number, but still it must be painful to sink from the only daughter of England to one of the corps-de-ballet of Orléans."

"She is truly religious, I believe. One can but pity her."

"Not his first experience among *les rats,*" said Frederick. "Do you remember the stories about that German barnstormer of his—Caroline something or other—and how she blackmailed him?"

"I suppose she needed the money," remarked Frederick's wife.

She had not been in the room for a couple of minutes before she became aware that her skirts were creased, her gloves dirty, her face flushed, and that she had a stain on her cuff. Even her voice, it seemed to her, had lost its gloss.

Frederick came forward with a footstool. Resting her feet on it she noticed that the tips of her shoes were rubbed.

As well be hanged for a sheep as a lamb. She would be as vulgar as a washerwoman, she would take off her gloves. Off they came, and there were her hands, unmistakably the worse for wear, the hands that had that morning washed glass and china, burned themselves on the charcoal stove, swept up cigar ash, and emptied slops. Such hands would signal the retire to any delicate intelligence. Quite shortly—she knew it—Frederick and Père Hyacinthe would again be aspiring towards the completion of Ste. Clotilde.

They were. The duet proceeded to its cadence. But this time it was the basso who bowed himself away, casting a sprig or two from his bouquet of blessings on those remaining. And this time it was the tenor who eulogized the nice feeling of the basso, remarking,

"Well, he has tact, has Père Hyacinthe. Knows when to take himself off."

"More tact than you, perhaps, my good Frederick. Still, Frederick is right. Let us be open, and admit that we are glad to be alone, and able to express ourselves. My dearest Sophia, how consoling it is to see you again! I was becoming a little anxious, a little impatient. But seeing you returned, I forget all my reproaches."

Though after the first sentence she had duly turned to Sophia it was upon Frederick that her glance still rested.

"I quite agree," said Frederick. "Least said, soonest mended."

"I was relieved, too," said Sophia, "when Père Hyacinthe went. I have something to say to Frederick which I should prefer to say in private. But before anything else, Great-Aunt Léocadie, I must beg your pardon for my bad manners. I should not have flounced off as I did."

"My child, say no more of that. At my age, when one has outlived for so long one's own impetuosity, one is touched to see an act of impulse. It reassures one, it convinces one that there is still youth in the world that one is about to quit. Think no more of it distress yourself no longer, my little Sophie."

"I must ask pardon for more than that. Impetuosity cannot be the excuse for letting two days go by without writing to you."

"No, my child. Frankly, that was badly done. But do not let us niggle over details. The essential thing is that you are here again; and if you have black lines under your eyes, no doubt they are little black marks placed there by your poor guardian angel. So the heavenly honour is satisfied, and we mortals will be satisfied too."

How to fell this old indomitable, wiry-legged, wiry-hearted ballerina? I cannot, thought Sophia. There is Frederick to settle with, on the way back I want to buy more smelling-salts and some oysters, I cannot leave Ingelbrecht waiting indefinitely. Smashing down on these considerations came, *Suppose Minna is really ill?* Abstractedly she leaned down her cheek to the old woman's kiss.

When Frederick had ushered her into the dining-room and closed the door behind them her consciousness, bent on what was to come next, became slowly and embarrassingly aware that what was to come next threatened to be something compromising and bawdy. Looking round with an inquiring frown she saw the whiskered cheek a few inches from her eye, and understood that Frederick also was about to impose a kiss of pardon and peace.

She gave an alert cough, and spoke.

"Frederick! I should like my jewellery. I will take it with me now. And I will take the remaining fittings of my dressing-case too. I find the corks which you supplied very inconvenient."

"And where do you propose to take them, Sophia?"

"To Madame Lemuel's."

"Ah!" said Frederick, and seated himself. Thoughtfully he took out his cigar case and pondered it—then, with a glance round, appeared to bethink himself of Madame de Saint-Gonval's dining-room, and put it back again.

If there had been time she would have opposed her silence to his, frozen him, as she had done so often before, out of his impudence. But Ingelbrecht could not be left to finish out his exercise book, Minna might be worse. She must dispatch.

"If you are thinking out a speech, Frederick, you can spare yourself the trouble. I had your letter. You made yourself sufficiently clear in that."

"Did I, though?"

"Perfectly, I should say."

"Then what the devil are you here for?"

He is going to fight over this trumpery, she thought. What a fool I was to come for it.

"Visite de digestion," she said.

He opened his mouth like an angry fish. How often in times past his gapings at Blandamer had revealed to her those large regular tedious teeth, that healthy pink maw!

"Let us consider it paid, shall we? I will get my things from Madeleine on my way out. You need not trouble to come with me."

"Still after your gimcracks, eh? Let the bride forget her ornaments. . . . Well, Madeleine hasn't got them. *I've got them!"*

Those three words were spoken in a voice so gross, so heavy with plebeian malice, that she turned on him in astonishment. She could not recover her senses as promptly as he recovered his usual manner; and he had been speaking for some time before she brought herself to attend to what he was saying.

"And you must not run away with the idea that I am doing this without consideration, out of spite or anything of that sort. I have discussed it thoroughly with your great-aunt Léocadie, and she quite agrees with me. You will admit *her* knowledge of the world at any rate, whatever your low opinion of mine! I only wish that she was doing the talking, it would come much better from her. This is an awkward sort of thing to discuss with one's wife."

"I'm sorry, Frederick. I'm afraid I've not been attending. What exactly is it that you have discussed with Léocadie and find so awkward to discuss with me?"

"Don't quibble, Sophia. You are not a child, you know perfectly well what people will say of this. Minna Lemuel is not a fit person for you to associate with."

"As you know yourself from personal experience?"

"As I know myself from personal experience."

Trapped by her intonation an appeasing boon-companion's grin spread over his face. The crease was still on his flat cheek when she struck with the whole force of her fist.

"God damn you, Sophia!"

"God damn you, Frederick!"

So long-nursed, so well-established the hatred between them that this declaration of it scarcely interrupted their conversation. The mark of her knuckles was still white on his flushed cheek, and an involuntary tear only half-way down it when he resumed his exposition of himself and great-aunt Léocadie.

"I must suppose that, at present at any rate, it is useless to appeal to your better feelings, to your feeling as a wife and mother—though when I see you, Sophia, still wearing black for those two poor little babies of ours, I should have thought . . ."

Taking advantage of the pause he wiped off the involuntary tear.

"However, I see that any such appeal would be useless. And as that is so I intend to assert one right, at least, as your husband. Go with Minna Lemuel if you please. But you go without what you please to call your property."

"Do you mean to say, Frederick, that you have really been

making all these speeches, holding all these confabulations with Léocadie, about my jewel-case and the tops of my scent-bottles?"

"I mean what I say. I mean that until you mend your manners you can whistle for your jewels and your scent-bottles, and everything else you like to think yours. Not a penny do you get from me. It's mine, do you understand? By the law, it's mine. When you married me it became mine, and now after ten years it's high time you understood it. You don't seem to grasp that very easily, do you? You'd better talk it over with Minna. She's a Jew, she understands money, she'll be able to explain to you which side a wife's bread is buttered. Meanwhile, as I don't want to expose you to any humiliation, let me tell you that it will be useless to write your Sophia Willoughby on any draft. I've written to the bank already and given orders that your signature is not to be honoured."

"Thank you, Frederick. That is very obliging."

She walked to the door and stood waiting.

Holding it open for her to pass through, as though the action constrained him to a resumption of civility, he said in his pleasantest, most affable tones,

"Look here, Sophia, can't we patch it up? Lord knows, I don't want to do the heavy husband. But really, what else am I to do? I must be responsible for you, I can't let you compromise yourself without asserting myself in some way. Your great-aunt Léocadie . . ."

In the ante-room was a little table with a salver on it for visiting cards. Taking out her card and a pencil she dog's-eared the card and wrote on it, *p.p.c.*

"*Pour prendre congé,*" she explained. "The usual etiquette."

Stronger than rage, astonishment, contempt, the pleasurable sense that at last she had slapped Frederick's face, the less pleasurable surmise that his slap back would be longer-lasting; stronger even than the desire to see Minna was her feeling that of all things, all people, she most at this moment wished to see Ingelbrecht, and the sturdy assurance that she would find in him everything that she expected. If she had gone up the stairs in the rue de la Carabine on her knees, she could not have ascended with a more zealotical faith that there would be healing at the top; and when he opened the door to her, inquiring politely if her errands had gone well, she replied with enthusiasm, "Perfectly. My husband—it was he I went to see—has just threatened to cut me off with a penny."

"A lock-out," said Ingelbrecht. "Very natural. It is a symptom of capitalistic anxiety. I suppose he has always been afraid of you."

She nodded, and her lips curved in a grin of satisfaction.

"How is Minna?"

"Still asleep. In that matter, Minna is superb. Her physical aplomb is infallible, when anyone else would go to pieces, she develops a migraine and goes to sleep. If only—but it is a gift, and it is idle to envy gifts. The rest of us must do what we can. . . . You had better have some coffee."

There, on the table beside the closed exercise book, was the coffee-tray, neatly arranged.

He is everything, she thought, that I expected, everything that I desired; grim and flat, positive without any flavour, a man like plain cold water.

"And can your husband cut you off with a penny?"

"I suppose so."

"You do not know for certain?"

"No."

"Then you must find out. He may be bluffing you. You had better write to your man of business and inquire exactly how you stand."

She looked at him abashed but contented.

"You take the wind out of my sails."

"No, I don't," he replied. "But I think you may be leaving the harbour with too much canvas."

"I should like some coffee, too."

It was the voice of the convalescent, velveted with sleep. A yawn followed it, a rustle; and Minna strolled into the room, wearing the sleek shriven look of the healthily awakened. Her brown ankles emerged from the blue woollen slippers with an astonishing authenticity of colour, they seemed still tanned and supple from her barefoot childhood. Over her nightgown she wore a purple velvet pelisse, through her hair, hanging in elf-locks, glittered the shallower black of her jet earrings.

"He has watched over me like a guardian angel. But more peaceably."

Sophia glanced at the book and the pencil.

"Perhaps more like a recording angel."

"More like a recording angel than she knows."

"Why, Ingelbrecht, am *I* in your book?"

Flowers for me? asked the prima donna. Only a natural aptitude for domination polished by years of practice could have achieved that note of candid gratification. Only an aptitude quite as pronounced and the imperturbable unaffectedness of a long vocation could have replied with such simplicity,

"Not your name, Minna. Your defects, in so far as they are typical and instructive."

Answering a look of genuine grief, he added,

"You will be of great value to future insurgents, my dear."

What I feel, thought Sophia, is what I have seen painted sometimes on the faces of people listening to Beethoven; the look of those listening to a discourse, to an argument carried on in entire sincerity, an argument in which nothing is impassioned, or persuasive, or reasonable, except by force of sincerity; and there they sit in a heavenly thraldom, as blind people sit in the sun making a purer acknowledgement with their skin than sight, running after this or that flashing tinsel, can ever make. I cannot for the life of me see what Minna and Ingelbrecht are after; to me a revolution means that there is a turmoil and after it people are worse off than they were before; and yet as I see them there, Minna looking like someone in a charade and Ingelbrecht like a respectable Unitarian artisan, it is as though I were listening to music, able to feel and follow the workings of a different world. For it is there, that irrefutable force and logic of a different existence. In Ingelbrecht's every word and gesture it is manifested, and in this instant I have seen it touch Minna and change her from the world's wiliest baggage to someone completely humble and sincere.

"What have you written about Minna?" she asked. "I should like to hear it."

Watching Ingelbrecht turn over the pages of his book, and Minna settling herself to attend, it seemed incredible to her that human beings should ever mince, belittle themselves, or expostulate.

"*There are some revolutionaries, on the other hand, who seem incapable of feeling a durable anger against the conditions which they seek to overthrow. In these characters the imagination is too rich, the emotional force too turbulent. The anger which they undoubtedly feel is neutralized by the pleasure they experience in expressing it. They are speech-makers, they are frequently assassins; but when they have finished their speech, or poignarded their tyrant, they are in such a mood of satisfied excitement that they are almost ready to forgive the state of society which allows them such abuses on which to avenge themselves. And this they themselves commonly admit in such remarks as, 'It is enough,' or, 'I have achieved my destiny.'*

"*In using that antiquated and romantic expression, 'poignarded the tyrant,' I use it with intention. These revolutionaries are penetrated with artistic and historical feeling, they turn naturally to the weapons of the past, and to methods which, by being outmoded, appear to be chivalrous. (I point out that there must be an element of the Gothic in all chivalry. No perfectly contemporary action can be described as chivalrous.) This tendency, which is natural in any such character, and therefore ineradicable by any application of reason or analysis, is abetted by another characteristic proper to persons of this temperament—great technical facility. The argument that it is easier to kill a man with a gun than with a rapier carries little force with them, because they are already so skilful with a rapier; the ancestors of these revolutionaries were such good archers that the invention of gunpowder only bored them, so skilful with the flint bolt that no demonstration of the feathered arrow could have persuaded them to a change of weapon. In consequence of this, these skilful assassins seldom dispatch more than one tyrant; like the bee they sting once, and lose with that injury their power to inflict another.*"

"If I could kill one tyrant," murmured Minna, "I would die happy."

"Exactly." He turned a page. "*The assassination of Galeazzo Maria Sforza in 1476 is a typical piece of work in this kind—*

classical republican sentiments, the choice of a showy moment for the deed itself and, the deed ended, no plan of subsequent action. Even more typical is the enthusiasm which this assassination aroused in Italy, despite the fact that as a political coup *it was an utter failure; it was sufficient for the enthusiasm of society that the assassination had been conceived and carried out on classical lines, and the fact that all three perpetrators died on the scaffold only added sublimity to the spectacle.*

"For the greatest danger to revolutionary work of this class of revolutionaries is not their personal improvidence (the consequences of that as a rule affect only themselves), not their tendency to exhaust themselves in gusts of eloquence and coups de théâtre, *not even their lack of discipline; but in their appeal to bourgeois sympathies. One such revolutionary may attract ten undesirable recruits from the bourgeoisie, sentimentalists, sensation-seekers, idealists, etc. These miserable camp-followers clog action, talk incessantly, make the movement ridiculous, and, parasites themselves, harbour further parasites of spies and* agents provocateurs. *Moreover, they are extremely difficult to dislodge."*

He read without any appearance of authorship, his little grey eyes like shot rolling swiftly back and forth as though they were the only visibly moving part of the machine which was the man. And when the reading was finished and the book closed the eyes rested upon Minna in a steadfastness that betokened trust and goodwill.

"I feel really proud, Ingelbrecht, that any part of your book should have been written under my roof. In a hundred years' time people will be reading your book and thinking, It is universal, as true now as when it was written. . . . No, no! What am I saying? In a hundred years' time, thanks to your book, it will all be different, in 1948 the revolution will be too strong to be endangered any longer by people like me."

"Or by the despicable characters you attract," added Sophia.

"There, you see, Ingelbrecht. You are always right, I have done it again. I have converted Sophia now. She admits it."

Under the easy mischief of her voice was a note of excitement, and the glance she cast on Sophia was at once fostering and predatory.

"I forgot to read you a foot-note," said Ingelbrecht. *"It must be stated, however, that these bourgeois disciples are often both wealthy and generous. Since the character of the party is at all times more important than its finances, this should never be thought a reason for welcoming such recruits. If the party be sufficiently strong it does render their introduction less undesirable, but a weak party should arm itself against them as against a pestilence."*

It seemed unbelievable that such an eye should wink. Wink, however, it did. Untying her bonnet-strings, staring Ingelbrecht resolutely in the face, Sophia said with gravity,

"I will write to my man of business tomorrow."

"Pray do," said he. And having advised Minna to eat more and smoke less, he gathered up the book and the rug, bowed like a benevolent gnome, and went away.

From the balcony she watched him go down the street, and as, watching Minna in the rue de l'Abbé de l'Épée, she had thought of an animal, Ingelbrecht reminded her of an animal too, so swiftly and circumspectly he made his way, seeming to trot on some intent personal errand, true to his own laws and oblivious of all else.

"Does he always wear that shawl?"

"Yes, almost always. He was imprisoned in the Spielberg, you know. And he was so cold there, so wretchedly cold, that it got into his bones, and he has felt chilly ever since."

"Have you ever been in a prison, Minna?"

"Yes, once or twice. But never for anything creditable. Vagrancy and theft and so forth, wretched little poverty offences. When I was a girl, going about with Lecoq and his dogs. But once in Vienna I was nearly had for the real thing. I was being very harmless, I was telling my fairy-stories. I described an ogre, a sleek grey ogre, sleek as ice. Wherever he went, I said, it was like a black frost. Whatever he touched stiffened, birds fell dead, the young fruit dropped off the trees. The name of this ogre, I said, was Mitternacht—you know what they call Metternich. There were some students in the audience, and in an instant they were up, shouting and applauding. A riot!

"It was marvellous," she said, swooping forward like some purple-plumaged bird of prey, her hooked nose impending. "Marvelous! To have such power, to have them up at a word. . . . Just what Ingelbrecht would disapprove of, too."

In the silence that followed both women turned and looked at the empty chair, the table, the inkpot.

"I do, I do appreciate him!" exclaimed Minna. "I appreciate him implicitly. If he were to say to me, Minna, never another word, no more stories of the oppressed, no more of your sorceries with fairy-tales, I would sew up my mouth. But this afternoon how could I help feeling a little dulled? All the time he was here, the pen whispering on, the shadow of the curtain moving over the bald head, I was saying to myself—that Sophia . . . Will she ever come back?"

Into this opening she must dive.

"Minna! Do you feel equal to a piece of tiresome news?"

"One is always equal to that."

"I went to see Frederick. I had to. And Frederick has been asserting himself."

At a nod, wise and parrot-like, the jet earrings began to swing slowly in and out of the black hair.

"He dislikes me being with you—"

"He is jealous of you?"

"Yes. I suppose that is what it is. He is jealous."

"And no wonder." The blue slippers moved into a more dignified position, a deft hand tweaked the purple pelisse into nobler folds. Holding her head aloft she said grandly, "If he were to strive for a lifetime, that poor Frederick, he could not appreciate me as you did in our first five minutes. And no doubt that in his darkened way he knows this."

"No doubt. And so, on the best military models, he has cut off my supplies."

There was a swift gesture, called back. Locking her hands together, staring down on them as though to ward them from further movement, Minna was silent.

"He has cut off my supplies. As he is entitled to do, being my husband. He has told the bank not to honour my signature, he has removed the gold fittings from my dressing-case. So you see, Minna, I am penniless, or soon shall be. I have what is left over from my ring, that will last awhile. I have my clothes, for what they are worth. And my hair. I believe one can always sell one's hair. After that, unless I comply with Frederick's wishes, nothing."

"You will stay? You must, if only to gall him."

"I don't think that much of a reason."

"But you will stay?"

"I will stay if you wish it."

It seemed to her that the words fell cold and glum as ice-pellets. Only beneath the crust of thought did her being assent as by right to that flush of pleasure, that triumphant cry.

"But of course," said Minna a few hours later, thoughtfully licking the last oyster shell, "we must be practical."

This remark she had already made repeatedly, speaking with the excitement of an adventurous mind contemplating a new and hazardous experience. Each time the remark had led to some fresh attempt at practicality, attempts that never got beyond a beginning. On the sofa lay Sophia's dresses, three of them valued with the adeptness of an old-clothes-woman, the rest only admired and exclaimed over. On the table were strewn several manuscript poems and a novel which only needed finishing and a publisher to make their fortune. Mixed in with these and, like these, read aloud in their more striking passages, were various letters, any one of which, she said, would be a goldmine if properly negotiated. And why, she added, this prejudice against blackmail, if the results were to be applied to a good end? Why indeed, had answered Sophia, brooding upon the vileness of those who wrote such letters.

"Yes, we must be practical. No more oysters, no more supper-parties. Ah, how I reproach myself that you sold your ring. I don't suppose Dury got half its value, rushing off like that to a Mont-de-Piété. If we could raise the money to buy it back, then we could sell it again."

"I regretted that ring this afternoon. You see, I lost my temper and hit him in the face. And the moment I had done it I remembered my ring and thought how much more it would have hurt if I had been wearing it."

"Yes. A knuckle-duster. Rings are invaluable, I know, and diamonds most painful of all. Still, I expect you didn't do too badly. You must be very strong. I suppose you wouldn't . . . No. That would be out of the question, I'm afraid."

"What?"

"Appear—under good auspices, you know—as a female pugilist. With your figure and height it would be marvelous. But I see that it wouldn't really do, it is just my natural tendency to turn to circuses. You might not believe it, Sophia, to look at me now, but when I was young and slender as a reed I could go right round the ring in a series of somersaults. And the applause would be like thunder. But now, even if I were to thin, I don't suppose I should be good for much."

"I wonder what Ingelbrecht would suggest?"

"He would tell us to move to a cheaper apartment and work as laundresses."

"In England that is what we prescribe for fallen women. They are all set to laundry work, in institutions. In fact, now that I come to think of it, I am among the patronesses of such an institution myself. But if I am to keep that splendid position, Frederick will have to pay my next subscription for me."

They looked at each other with eyes brilliant with laughter and complicity. Too much excited to finish the meal they began to pace up and down the room arm in arm. Through the long window came the smell of the spring night and the smell of the city. In the windows of the house opposite they could see the life of half a dozen families, a woman in petticoat and camisole washing a pair of stockings in a basin, a young man reading while a girl rubbed her face against the back of his neck, another man yawning and fastening on a night-cap, an elderly couple leaning over the sill with a coffee-pot between them. A newspaper was being cried down the street, from the café where the local club held its sitting came the long vague rumour of declamation and bursts of applause, further away some children marched and sang, and a drum beat fitfully. But drum beats and processions were common noises now. And though they heard, immediately below, a door open, the foot of the cautious Égisippe Coton shuffle on the pavement, nothing followed but his flat voice remarking, "It's nothing. It's only a drum."

During the days that followed Minna continued to rejoice in the prospect of being severely practical, and to the many visitors who came to her apartment and were fed there she explained

Sophia's position and the value which would be set upon any advice they could give. To Sophia it was at first slightly embarrassing to be assured of the nobility of her conduct.

"For it is not true, Minna, that I have left Frederick and renounced my income because my sympathies are with the revolution. I am here as I am because I saw a chance of being happy and took it. As for the revolution, when I smacked my husband's face and sent him to the devil, I never gave it a thought.

"Anyhow," she added, countering a look of triumph on Minna's face, "I had done with Frederick long before. The smack was only a postscript."

"You had done with Frederick, yes. But what is that? So had I. So had dozens of other women. To give up a thing or a person, that is of no significance. It is when you put out your hand for something else, something better, that you declare yourself. And though you may think you have chosen me, Sophia, or chosen happiness, it is the revolution you have chosen."

"As for the money," Sophia persevered, "I regret it most sincerely. Nothing would please me better than to have it back."

"Exactly what Ingelbrecht says. He considers it most unfortunate. I was talking to him about it yesterday evening."

" 'These bourgeois disciples are often both wealthy and generous,' " said Sophia reminiscently.

Minna continued,

"I asked him if he thought it better if you should recover your money by a little compliance to Frederick, if I should try to persuade you to that."

"If he had advised it, would you have tried?"

"Caught! You take it for granted that he did not advise such tactics. A week ago even, you would not have been sure of that."

"Would you have tried?"

"No."

In the matter of being severely practical, it was the young man called Dury who gave it the greatest consideration. Priding himself, he said, upon being a peasant and with a peasant's astuteness, he promised to bend his mind upon the problem, and return in a day or two with a solution.

Returning, he happened to find Sophia alone. His glance

rested upon her with extraordinary satisfaction, as though, for the purpose he had in mind, she were even better suited than he had supposed.

"It is nothing showy, my project," said he. "But it is better to begin in a small way, with no outlay, with a certainty of gains, however small. And this expedient is perfectly reliable, a sitting bird. Doubtless you can sing the hymns of England?"

" 'Rule, Britannia'?"

"No, no. The ecclesiastical hymns. A friend of mine, a sculptor, a young man of real talent, is looking for a fair-haired lady who can sing English hymns."

"I would certainly try, but I doubt if I should be of any use to your friend. I am not much practised in singing hymns, and when I sat for my portrait I found it very difficult to sit still. If I had to sing as well . . ."

"Oh, there is no question of sitting. Actually, at this moment, sculpture presents certain difficulties. Unless one tears up a paving-stone, it is difficult to procure the material for any large work. Buyers, too, are hard to come by. But Raoul can also play the accordion, and talk like a cheapjack, and it is on these talents that he is relying. He wishes to make speeches in the street against the Church—our Church—and especially against this abominable celibacy. It is his idea that you should accompany him, as an escaped nun, thrust into a convent against her will, suffering untold atrocities—you know the sort of thing. And it occurred to us that if you were to be an English Protestant, an heiress, taken and held by force, it would be even more affecting. He would ask nothing more of you than you should sing a hymn or two, and wear your hair in long plaits. Everything else he would be responsible for. There is always a little collection, you know, and this he would share with you. The profits are steady, and as you see, there is no outlay whatsoever. He made quite a success of it during March with a young woman (also escaped from a convent, this time a Spanish one) who danced and played a tambourine. Unfortunately for him one of their sympathizing listeners took such a fancy to her that he took her into keeping. It was a blow to Raoul. Just when they were doing so well. But of course he could not stand in the girl's way. It was a great chance for her."

"But I understood that nuns always have their hair cut short. Surely those long plaits . . ."

"In point of fact, yes. In point of effect, no. It is to the sympathies of the crowd that one appeals rather than to their sense of accuracy. And long tresses are undoubtedly moving. You cannot, for instance, imagine a short-haired Magdalen repenting to any purpose. It is the descent, the long line, the weeping-willow quality. . . ."

With his squat peasant's paws he demonstrated the curves of a willow.

"Then should I not wear my hair unbound?"

"No, Madame. For a Protestant, plaits."

Minna found her standing in the middle of the room, attentively rehearsing hymns in a Sunday-school squall. For a while affection and ear strove together. Ear won.

"My dearest, what a very dismal tumult!"

"Frightful, isn't it? It is an English hymn. That obliging young man who pawned my ring . . ."

She explained the project. Minna's listening looks became slowly overcast. Doubt deepened to a noble desolation, to a grief magnanimously borne.

"I'm afraid you do not approve, Minna. You think, perhaps, I should not sing in the street. Of course it is a most outrageous cheat."

"Cheat! Am I one to discountenance cheating? No, no, Sophia! It is envy that gnaws me. It seems to me that Dury might have cast me also for a little part in this comedy. However . . . Well, at any rate, my past can enrich your future. You don't pitch your voice right for the street."

The more Sophia considered the society in which she found herself, the more puzzled she became. What at first had made them easy to settle among—their inconsequentiality, their rather slipshod affability, the intimacy amongst themselves so easily extended to her, the general impression which they gave of being somehow perched temporarily, like a large family stranded for a night in a waiting-room, made them as time went on very unsettling company.

They were idle, or unoccupied; but that was nothing new; the greater part of her life had been spent among the idle, the society of honest shopkeepers would have been much more alien to her than this.

In their assumption of simplicity they were arrogant: listening to their chatter, their easy turnings upside down of all accepted judgments, she felt herself like a shy governess imported from a foreign land; but this again was nothing new to her, all her life she had been listening to people who could talk more cleverly than she, and despising them.

They were idle and they were arrogant. Often, half closing her senses, she might have fancied herself again in Adelaide Willoughby's drawing-room among Adelaide Willoughby's friends. There, too, people had strayed in and out, too intimate for greetings, hurrying in, it seemed, in order to express an urgent admiration for a new opera singer or a new-moded abhorrence for an established one. And then, having made their little somersault, they would whisk off again, just delaying for a moment of patronage towards the country relation. Pausing at the door they would chatter interminably.

Minna's society was politer, and was more entertaining than Adelaide's. But that was not all. Had it been all, she would not have known, as she did increasingly, this curious anxiety on their behalf. She felt in herself the stirrings of an impulse, half maternal, half missionary, to rally this odd troop, to warn them of danger, call them back from some impending destruction. As for the nature of the destruction, that need not be far to seek. It was obvious to her that if they persevered in this manner of life they would all be dead of starvation in six months' time. As it was, they appeared to be living on air, on credit, on taking in each other's washing, only supplementing these means by occasional more solid mouthfuls of living on Minna. For that matter, how did Minna live? On air, on credit, on what she called "another of my windfalls," on Sophia's sealskin and the remains of her ring. And with these mayflies, she thought, standing blandly in the May sunshine, admiring the new spikes of blossom on the horse-chestnut trees, listening inattentively to Raoul's invectives against celibacy and waiting for her cue to intone another Sunday-school hymn, with these mayflies I too shall go down; for certainly I cannot support myself by singing long-haired hymns on the boulevards, and equally certainly I will never go back to Frederick.

Whoever else might hope to survive a year of the republic, its revolutionaries certainly could not. In this half-baked republic they perched temporarily like a large family stranded for the night in a waiting-room; but the morning would never come, no train would ever take them on to their destination. Here they would remain, arguing passionately about the National Workshops and declaring the inalienable right of man to live by his earnings, without attempt or hope, apparently, of earning a livelihood for themselves. And one cold winter's morning the cold would attract their attention and they would all drop down dead.

"In works of Labour or of Skill
I would be busy too;
For Satan finds some mischief still . . ."

Undoubtedly Satan, that old friend of the family, would be surprised, if he came this way, to discover the present occupation of little Sophia Aspen; though whether my singing, she thought, could be considered either skilful or laborious enough to keep him at bay is questionable. Lord, how that tasking-master of a Satan would be delighted with the Paris of May 1848! And remembering Minna's technical advice she concluded on a heart-rending howl that fetched applause from the crowd—the idle, shabby, sauntering crowd, workmen out of work, housewives away from their houses, students truant from their lectures, Civil Guards straying from their round-houses.

Loftily, pensively, for she was supposed to have a soul above lucre, she gazed at the chestnut blossom while Raoul went round with the hat. Already her ears had learned to distinguish between the noise of a giving and ungiving assembly. A year ago, a little less than a year ago, for chestnuts flower rather later in England, she must have been looking at the chestnuts by the gate of Blandamer, those same trees which, their blossom discarded, had pleased her better so, that morning when she had taken the children to the lime-kiln.

So deeply rooted then, and now so fugitive, it was small wonder that she could say to herself with comparative calm, "In six months' time I, with all these other people, shall be dead of starvation and incompetence."

Arm in arm with the sculptor she walked off to their next station, while he in his intellectual-cum-guttersnipe voice explained why the spirit of France must for choice express itself in the round rather than linearly.

"Boucher's bottoms," she said, acquiescing. Glancing down she saw his eyelashes collide as he blinked away the unwomanly comment.

But it is not desperation, she continued in her thoughts, that makes me so casual. I am undoubtedly enjoying myself. I am happier than I have ever been before. I suppose we are really all going mad, and I have caught the madness and whirl on with the rest as carelessly as they. But I am happier. These people in whose extraordinary company I find such happiness are not happy at all. Their revolution has been no real pleasure to them; their republic, now they have got it, brings them no contentment. Apart from being threatened with starvation, they are not at ease in it. Their idleness is more like some sort of deliberate idling, a killing of time, and their arrogance the jauntiness of children who won't admit a fault, who are waiting to be found out. It is not just peril of starvation that frets them, it is some moral worm, some *malaise* of the spirit. They are like—the thought jumped up, exact and clinching—they are like people sickening for a fever; excited, restless, listless, blown this way and that like windlestraws in the gusts that stir before a thunderstorm.

Idle and arrogant . . . there were only two people in whom the taint, the preliminary sickening, displayed itself in such a way as to suggest that they might escape lightly, that their constitutions would stand it; there was only one person in whom there showed no taint at all. Minna and Dury were the two. Minna, God knows, was idle; but she was completely without arrogance, and her idleness was coupled with such energy that it seemed like the flourish of a vitality too rich to be contained in any doing, a stream too impetuous to turn any mill-wheel. As for Dury, his arrogance was intolerable; but as Ingelbrecht had said, no peasant slaved on his small-holding more savagely than Dury laboured his canvases. Even in conversation his gaze drudged over one's face, harrowed the posture of one's hands, or scythed an expanse of wall, the colour of a curtain, the light falling upon a wine-glass and an apple-paring. There was no advantage too petty for him to take, his pinch-farthing husbandry would wring advantage out of a dirty glove or a cotton reel.

The one wholly untainted was Ingelbrecht. Whatever the sickness, there was no taint of it on him; whatever happened he, resolute, discreet, self-contained, alert, would trot like some secret busy badger along his own path.

The tour was ended, and the gains divided. In Raoul's studio, it was a stable really, she put up her hair and tied on her bonnet, eyeing herself in a speckled mirror that reflected the dirty window, the straggling vine-branch that crossed it, the splendid russet haunches of the drayhorse which was being backed into the shafts outside.

"There's a behind for you," she exclaimed, landing another unwomanly blow. "Better than these incessant human bottoms. Why don't sculptors do more animals?"

"They lack soul," he replied. "There would be no market except in England. May I offer you a little beer? It is thirsty weather."

They drank in the amity of professional fellowship, and when the beer was finished parted as cleanly as a cup and saucer which have been rinsed and set apart till they are next needed in conjunction.

For it would not do, they had decided, for her blond plaits to be exhibited in the rue de la Carabine. Apart from the censorious Cotons, such a display would be bad for business. As a lady she left Minna's dwelling, as a lady she returned to it, as a lady embellished with five francs seventy-five, as a lady footsore but lighthearted. Five francs seventy-five was not too bad, considering the times and the nature of her wares, the limited appeal of Dr. Watts's hymns to a Parisian public; though it was not the winning number which she promised herself to bring back one fine day: the vindictive rapture of having squalled attention, if nothing more, from a strolling Frederick.

The baseness of this aspiration had shocked Minna. There was no doubt that Frederick's late mistress had more elevation of soul than Frederick's late wife.

Sophia had never had much elevation of soul; and that the life she was now leading released her so thoroughly into a low way of living was perhaps one of the main reasons why she was so intensely happy. Like some child who has toppled full-clothed into a stream and, taking to the sensation, only returns to the bank to strip off boots, hat, stockings, petticoats, she who had arrived at the rue de la Carabine with all her prejudices girt about her now only recalled her former life in order to discover that another prejudice was a hamper, and could be discarded.

She had been brought up (and had brought up her own children) to consider the chiefest part of mankind as an inferior race, people to be addressed in a selected tone of voice and with a selected brand of language. Towards the extreme youth and age of the lower classes one adopted a certain geniality, to the rest one spoke with politeness. But to none of them did one display oneself as oneself; be it for approving pat or chastising blow one never, never, removed one's gloves.

Now, in addition to singing in the street she shopped in the street also. The decent veil of shopping in a foreign tongue and under conditions which made such shopping an adventure and a fantasy had soon ravelled away. With her whole soul she walked from stall to stall, countering the wiles of those who sell with the wiles of those who purchase, pinching the flesh of chickens, turning over mackerel, commenting disadvantageously upon the false bloom of revived radishes. Her fine nostrils quivered above cheeses and sniffed into pickle-tubs and the defencelessly open bellies of long pale rabbits. Her glance pried out flaws, the under-ripe or the over-ripe, and her tongue denounced them.

Those who displeased her, learned of it; not in the old tongue, the lofty cold-shouldering of Blandamer days, but roundly. Where she had found good bargains she put forth wiles without conscience, with flattery, exhortations, or shameless appeals to better nature extorting better goods or lower prices. She became —highest boast of those who market—a recognized customer, a person whose tastes and whims were known. Bunches of asparagus were put aside for her, and the one-eyed Madame Lefanu held out to her, above the heads of the crowd, a richly drooping garland of black puddings.

All round her were faces of the kind she liked to see; sharp clear glances, lips taut with cupidity, brows sharply furrowed with exact thought. When people jostled her it was not because she was a fine woman, but because she stood in the way of a fine duckling. All her life she had been more or less accustomed to finding herself the first, now she tasted the rapture of being first among peers. When all was bought, the bag filled, the purse pocketed, and a bunch of flowers for Minna brought intact from the crowd, she would find herself approving with passionate affection the people she had quitted, the buyers and the sellers, whose sea-gull voices still echoed on in the narrow sounding-board alley of the rue Mouffetard.

With a queer glance, now, she looked on people of her own class. Not many such came into their quarter; but on forays into "that other Paris," as she learned to think of it, she saw them, elegant and lifeless as she had been; and sometimes, when she was singing in the streets, such a one would pause for a moment, a fish-like wavering, a stare with glassy eyes, a compassionate glove, maybe, advanced. And her body would tighten with malice, her ribs arch over the singing breath, the corner of her due singer's smile twitch a little further up, as her spirit made long noses at them.

The decorum of class had gone, the probity of class had gone too. At intervals she searched Minna's purse for bad money (none came into hers) and used it for seats in parks, seats in omnibuses, or to bestow on beggars for religious purposes who could not be fobbed off otherwise. Gladly would she have swindled on a larger scale, had she been able to. But she could not invent cheats by herself, and Minna, coming to her aid, swiftly enskied any project into impracticality.

With a step she had ranged herself among the *mauvais sujets,* the outlaws of society who live for their own way and by their own wits. There had been no tedium about her fall, and with a flash every false obligation was gone.

Even the prudence of her class had shrivelled. Day by day they grew poorer, every week they pawned something more, money was a continual preoccupation with her, whether she beat down the price of a sausage, or sat laughing with Minna over their grandiose projects for cozenage. But now the question of how to live seemed no more than some sort of gymnastic, in which daily she suppled herself, sharpening her wits in the same arrogant combat towards perfection as that with which a runner or a wrestler keeps his body in trim. Bread and lodging and the outward adorning might be threatened, but she could feel no menace to her happiness. And anyhow we shall all be dead in six months' time, she repeated to herself; and with the next thought visited an unexplored wine-shop where there was a white cat and a very cheap *vin rosé.*

Her happiness, blossoming in her so late and so defiantly, seemed of an immortal kind. One day, looking over a second-hand bookstall with Minna, she opened a snuffy volume that had English poems in it. Her eye fell on the verse:

My love is of a birth as rare
As 'tis of object strange and high,
It was begotten by despair
Upon impossibility.

"Look," she said, pointing on the withered page.

Minna began to glance about for the vender.

"No. Let me look at the other poems. It is silly to buy a book just for the sake of a verse which one can learn by heart." It seemed to her that the other poems were wilfully annoying, and she would have put down the book, but Minna clung to it, absorbed, her lips fumbling at the English syllables.

"*Un objet bizarre et élevé.* Sophia, I must buy this book. I feel an obligation towards it. Besides, it will improve my English."

To please her Sophia spent some time beating down the bookstall man.

Whatever it did for Minna's English, Sophia did not open the book again; but that one verse, rapidly memorized, stayed in her head, and seemed in some way to sum up the quality of her improbable happiness, just as Minna's absurd *bizarre et élevé* hit off the odd mixture of nobility and extravagance which was the core of the Minna she loved.

Minna was not beautiful, nor young. Her principles were so inconsistent that to all intents and purposes she had no principles at all. Her character was a character of extremes: magnanimous and unscrupulous, fickle, ardent, and interfering. Her speaking voice was exquisite and her talent of words exquisitely cultivated, but she frequently talked great nonsense. Similarly, her wits were sharp and her artfulness consummate, and for all that she was maddeningly gullible. She offered nothing that Sophia had been brought up to consider as loveworthy or estimable, for what good qualities she had must be accepted with their opposites, an inconsequential pell-mell of wheat and tares.

Sophia had been brought up in a world policed by oughts. One ought to venerate age, one ought to admire the beautiful. One ought to love ugly Mary Thompson because she was so clean, God because he was so good, prating Mr. Scarby because he was so honest and paid all his son's debts, scolding cousin Arabella because she was so capable, Mamma because she was so kind, Frederick because he was her husband. One ought to devote oneself to one's children because, if well brought up, they would be a comfort in one's old age. Behind every love or respect stood a monitorial reason, and one's emotions were the expression of a bargaining between demand and supply, a sort of political economy. At a stroke, Minna had freed her from all this. Unbeautiful and middle-aged, unprincipled and not intellectual, vain, unreposeful, and with a complexion that could look greasy, she offered her one flower, liberty. One could love her freely, unadmonished and unblackmailed by any merits of body or mind. She made no more demands upon one's moral approval than a cat, she was not even a good mouser. One could love her for the only sufficient reason that one chose to.

She pleased or entertained or moved one without an extortion upon one's sense of gratitude. Like the work of art, her artfulness was for art's sake, and her flashes of goodness were as painless as an animal's. Calculating with unscrupled cunning upon the effect she might have, her calculations stopped short there, she was unconcerned as to whether the effect of the effect would advantage her or no, receiving with the same brief convention of astonishment the news that she had been charming, had been infuriating. If the effect miscarried, was no effect at all, the astonishment was more genuine. A bruised look would settle upon her face for a minute or two. Then, bearing no more malice than a fountain, she would begin again.

In fact, if one came to examine it, she summed up everything that Sophia had previously disapproved. *My love is of a birth as rare . . .* She hummed the verse softly to herself, fitting it to the tune of the "Old Hundredth" which she had lately been intoning in the rue Monge . . . which was a good place to sing in, for at midday the men from the tanneries came out for a snack and a stroll. In spite of the stink of hides she felt a friendliness to the neighbourhood. The sun was shining, the flavour of the beer she had drunk floated agreeably over her singing thirst. In this shabby merry quarter of Paris the prevalent republican shabbiness could be forgotten. And however shabby, cautious, and downcast, Paris was the Paris of May. Wherever one looked there was a demonstration of green, a tree, a lilac-bush with its heart-shaped petals falling back as though in admiration from the spikes of blossom, a trail of vine leaves dangling from the farther side of some courtyard arch, looped there between the shadow and the sun, playing their trick of green stained-glass and tracery. The houses with their pale dirty faces had the vivacious appearance of town children. This one was trimmed with lemon colour, that with blue, beyond the arabesqued façade of the wine-shop was the sober nut-coloured door of the watchmaker. All his clocks were ticking, but one could scarcely hear them for the song of the canaries caged in the first-floor window under the scroll saying *Midwife.* From the watchmaker's darted a very small kitten, prancing sideways on stiff legs. Sophia stooped to caress it, and noticed that attached to the tartan ribbon round its neck was a tin medal dedicating it to the care of the Virgin and Saint Joseph. But it escaped from her hand and capered on towards the butcher's shop where a woman wearing a claret-coloured shawl stood conversing with the grey-haired proprietress over whose solid bosom and heliotrope gown was tied a muffler of the brightest acid-blue.

In the air was a smell mingled of woodsmoke, wine, coffee, garlic, horsedung, and beeswax. A dray left standing blocked the entrance to the rue de la Carabine, the other vehicles went round it with shouts, insults, and the clatter of hooves, beneath it a white hen moved to and fro, pecking at the chaff which lay among the cobbles. And beyond this, and, so it seemed to her, in some way belonging to it, like a demesne, like a park, curved the stately river, stood the avenues, the statues, the palaces of the other Paris, where the grandees strolled in their silk and their broadcloth. There too, universal as the bland voluminous white clouds overhead, were those volumes of greenery, the clipped and bulging alleys, the volleys of green shot from courtyard and soaring above blank walls. Everywhere this brag of green seemed like an assurance, a consenting signal wagged to her from every quarter of Paris, that it was May, that she was, for the first time in her life, intensely happy, and that she should be so.

In the rue de la Carabine, as though stored there as in a reservoir, her passion of happiness seemed to burst upon her a hundred-fold. In one of Minna's windows stood the potted rose-bush, and it seemed to her that a rose had come out since the morning; from another swelled the houri-like curves of the feather bed. Catching her breath she dived into the dark entry, ran up the twirling stairs.

Minna had company. Someone was strumming a guitar. The company, as Minna's company so often did, had brought its little luggage with it—a small and cheap valise.

The company turned round at her entrance, dropped the guitar, and forestalling Minna's speech of introduction, ran towards her with a cry of joy, and was Caspar.

He had changed almost beyond recognition: to her conscience, accusingly changed. He was lanky and overgrown; his clothes would have been too small for him if they had not given at every seam. His hair had been vilely chopped, and had outgrown the chopping in grotesque tufts and drakes'-tails; his knuckles were discoloured, his nails were broken, one of his teeth had been knocked out, the dusky grape-like bloom which had sat on his skin had been rubbed off, leaving nothing but a sallow complexion with spots. Only his honeyed voice and his rolling eyes declared him to be the Caspar who had played so prettily with Damian and Augusta, ridden the bay mare, confounded the rector, enchanted the house with his presence, and antagonized all the servants.

"It is a romance," said Minna, "how this child has come to us!"

Caspar's rough paws stroked her skirts, he was kissing her hand with his dried lips. Behind him, anxious and moved, stroking her breast, stood Minna. That gesture, hand reassuring heart, those looks of embarrassment and tenderness, it was easy to know on whose account they were. Not for the poor blackamoor, starved and travel-stained; but for her who had dismissed him to such a state, and for her to whom his trust in her had brought him.

"I would not be so vile now," she murmured.

It was as though Minna received the words only with her eyes. But as they were spoken the twining fingers lay still, the look was of tenderness unmixed.

"Such adventures," continued Minna, "such homing-pigeon adventures! He came over in a fishing boat, and for the rest of the way he has walked or had lifts in wagons."

Impossible to tell how much of this statement as to the behavior of homing-pigeons was genuine, was dexterity. And the grimace which followed the speech told nothing either.

"From Cornwall? O Caspar, what a long, long journey."

"From Cornwall. And from Blandamer too. I went there first, after I had run away from the Academy. For I had to leave the Academy," he added swaggering. "It was no place for my father's son."

"Blandamer! Did they look after you properly, did Saunders —"

"There was no one there. The house was shut up."

"No one there?"

"No! Not a soul. I went to the door, I went to all the doors.

I could not look in at the windows, the shutters were up. There was no sound, no smoke from the chimneys—and yet it looked as though the house had people in it, for in the rubbish-pit there were fresh potato peelings, quite new cinders. I stayed a long time—I was tired—looking at the house. Then I went to the stables. They were empty too, but the smell of horses was still there. I walked about the garden, the kitchen garden, pulling up spring onions and young carrots and eating them. And I picked a bunch of flowers, to put on Damian and Augusta's grave. Then I heard a shout, and a dog barking, and there was the gardener and Pilot. Pilot knew me, and jumped on me. And I asked the gardener where you were, and he said you were in France with Mr. Willoughby, and that two days before an order had come from Mr. Willoughby that the house was to be shut up, and the servants dismissed, and everything taken away. He had come up, he said, just to walk round and keep an eye on things. But everything in the hot-houses would die, your flowers and the nectarines. And he said it was unfortunate that I had come just then."

(And Frederick could shut up her house, dismiss her servants.)

"Did Brewster look after you?"

"Yes, he took me to his sister's in the village. And they both said, What was to be done with me, and they must write to you. But when I had got your address I came away. It was melancholy staying there. They did nothing but sigh and wonder. And Pilot did nothing but scratch. He has got a skin disease."

"What address did they give you?"

"16, Place Bellechasse. But they sent me on here. They stared at me, I can tell you."

"They?"

"Célestin and Madeleine."

He pulled out a crumpled cigarette and lit it. That ruined young hand still kept some of its intuitive airs and graces; and leaning back on the pink sofa, pouting his lips in an attempt to blow smoke-rings, he showed still through his ungainliness some of the old suavity of movement. Every way debauched, she thought; his softness gone to a mess, like a bruised lettuce.

Those tatters of childishness, of self-confident grace, had survived only to become somehow morbid and disquieting, just as it was disquieting to see those eyelashes, their silk unimpaired, flourishing in that jaded sickly countenance.

To Minna she said,

"It is my fault that he is like this. I should not have sent him to that place. But you cannot expect me to like him any better because of that."

"He wants food and sleep, then he will be all right. Food, and sleep, and a little luxury—some scented hair-oil—and a quiet wholesome life."

"Will he get that with us, Minna?"

"Certainly. My dear, I assure you, after two or three days of soap and water you will find him as lovable as ever."

"Soap and oil him as you please. You won't get rid of that look, that—that unhealthy look. As if he'd curdled."

"His blood is poor. He wants watercress and spinach and a tisane of young nut-leaves."

"Tisane of dog-grass!

"The truth is"—she burst out—"I am jealous, already."

"But it is *you.* It is you he adores."

"Jealous of him. Jealous because he takes up your time, jealous because he is in our way. It is intolerable to me, when I think how rude I have been about your lame dogs, about your poor Claras and your Macgusties, that I should be the one to encumber you with the lamest dog of all."

Minna spoke truly. All Caspar's love, all his solicitous adulation, was for Sophia. Taking it for granted that Minna should wait on him hand and foot, feed him, groom him, tune the guitar for him, he would leap out of his cushions to pick up Sophia's handkerchief or fold her shawl. In her presence he wheedled, postured, strutted, charmed—and all the while his black eyes watched her with humble desperate anxiety. For all her nonconcurrence, his conversation attached itself to subjects wherein she might be magnified: the splendour of Blandamer, the beauty of Damian and Augusta, the immensity of her bereavement. Even the Trebennick Academy he suppled into a compliment—exclaiming on the audacity of a Mr. Gulliver who could so ill-use the ward of such a patroness, or picturing how Mr. Gulliver would grovel before the wrath of that patroness aroused.

All his wits had been bruised out of him, his one idea was to please and he had no ideas as to how it should be done. If she snubbed him he only redoubled his flatteries, and borrowing money from Minna went out to buy propitiating gifts—stale flowers, bad sweets, execrable gimcrack ornaments with their exorbitant price tickets still proudly dangling from them—for he was always cheated.

To their visitors he was invariably rude, loftily chattering in his snatched-up slangy French about the glories of Blandamer, the beauty of Damian and Augusta, the condescension of their mother in living in the rue de la Carabine. Because they had no room for him he slept with the Cotons. Every night he woke bitterly weeping from dreams of the Trebennick Academy. Madame Coton, hugging him in her scrawny arms, comforting him against her yellow flannel bedgown, deepened her grudge against the English and warned him to beware of the Jewess.

It was not until he had made ten days miserable that Sophia came to her senses and remembered Uncle Julius Rathbone. The shock of emerging from her state of muddle and fury into common sense was so great that she could not contain herself until morning.

"Minna! Minna! I have just realized that I am a fool."

"No, no!" With a soothing murmur, with a warm uncertainly aimed caress, Minna would have sidled back into sleep.

"A flat damned fool. That boy has got a father."

"Yes, you told me. So did he. In the West Indies. But the West Indies"—her voice indicated the utmost limits of space—"are a long way off."

If it were possible, her yawn propelled them even farther.

"And it is his money that pays for Caspar, not mine. Frederick cannot possibly lay claim to that."

In the darkness there was a majestic and cat-like stir: Minna rousing, reassembling her pillows, propping herself to sit up and attend. The body that by day was heavy, ill-framed, and faintly grotesque, at night achieved an extraordinary harmoniousness with its bed, became in suavity and sober resilience the sister of that exemplary mattress.

"Well? No, wait a moment! I think I must have a biscuit. Well?"

"So that all we need do is to find somewhere to put him, and have the bills sent to Frederick. Uncle Julius sends over a remittance twice a year, the money's in the bank at this moment. And Frederick spending it, no doubt. My God, what a fool I've been!"

"Where would you put him?"

"In a school. A boarding school. There must be plenty in the suburbs. Tomorrow I will go out and find one. Uncle Julius only stipulated that the school should give a commercial education. One can get that in any language, I imagine."

"Wouldn't a day school be better?"

"And have him back here every evening? Dangling round our heels and being rude to your friends? Eat another biscuit, you aren't properly awake, you don't understand what this means. Think how happy we were before he arrived, think how glad we shall be to be rid of him."

"But you should consult your uncle."

"I'll write to him, of course, and say what I've done. But there is no need to wait, he gave me *carte blanche.* All he wants is for Caspar to be at school. No! Uncle Julius would be the last person to keep the boy hanging on our petticoat tails."

"Rather than send that child as he is now to another school I would let him sell newspapers, run errands for the wine-shop, apprentice him to any trade—*any* trade."

"A sound commercial education, in fact. Unfortunately, his father wants him schooled. And anyhow, in this flourishing republic no trade can afford apprentices."

"Poor child!"

"Tiresome cub!"

"So unhappy in one school that he runs away. To you. And now you put him in another."

"Minna. Apart from the fact that we don't want him and can't afford him, can you seriously maintain that Caspar is benefiting by his stay with us?"

"Better than a school."

Sophia leaped up in a fury.

"I shall write to Uncle Julius *now.*"

The letter took a little while to compose. She was in the mood, trembling with midnight and angry excitement, to dash off something incisive and eloquent; it was irritating to have to choose words carefully, compose a prudent epistle which would skirt round the facts that Caspar had run away from the Trebennick Academy, that she had run away from Frederick. And darkening over this was her wrath against Minna, her indignation that this solution of the problem of Caspar should be so grudgingly, so doubtfully received.

Signing the letter, laying down the pen, she looked sulkily in front of her. Over the writing table hung a mirror, and there she saw reflected the half-open door into the bedroom, and Minna, candle-lit, in bed. Her hand had just conveyed another biscuit to her mouth. Her eyes were full of tears and she was munching slowly. Seeing that face, melancholy and gluttonous, Sophia forgot the anger of the one who is in the wrong. Her whole being was ravaged with love and tenderness. Still holding the pen she sat and stared into the mirror, beholding as though for a first and a last time the creature who, but a few paces away, hung in the mirror as though in the innocence of a different world.

She felt an intricate repentance. That jibe against the republic was a hit below the belt: not by any fair means would Minna's resources of tongue and temper be so easily put out of action. On this she now heaped the equally illegitimate assault of love. Nevertheless, when the morning came she excused herself from hymn-singing, looked up a number of suburban schools in a directory, arrayed herself in the remains of her best clothes, and set out to find another Trebennick Academy.

In one thing she had reckoned without her host. For though there were any number of obliging establishments, cheap, suitable, ruralized with vines and acacias, and yet not too far beyond the Barriers, not one of these would receive a pupil on the strength of her appearance and word only. There must be money paid down.

"These troubled days," said Professor Jaricot, "these menacing horizons, destroy that confidence which is at once so typical of civilization and so necessary to it. No one regrets this more than I."

His parlour, so tidy, so bare, so polished, so lofty and so shady—for the window was screened with another of those vines—reverberated the noise of three bluebottles circling high above his bald head. Modulating through their conversation came a heavenly smell of onion soup, a solid middle-class proclamation that though May weather, wafts of lilac, tilted summer parasols, cooing of doves, beckoning of blossomed trees, were all very well, yet the stomach demanded more of midday than flowers and flowery exhalations and the squeak of shears snipping suburban lawns to a neat edge.

My God, she thought, how hungry I am! I could lie down and fawn for a bowl of that soup, for a day of this assured middle-class comfort and sober repletion. So much emotion in the middle of the night, so much activity since, had made her indeed appallingly hungry. And while Professor Jaricot continued to expatiate on the political situation, explaining how his fatherly heart grieved for those whose most sensitive years must be exposed to an epoch so tumultuous and subversive, she passed her handkerchief across her lips to conceal the languishing yawns of appetite.

These Englishwomen, thought he, sprinkling a few parting reverences on her retreating flounces, how shameless they are! One would say that she had no maternal feeling, no warmth at all. And yet she had had an illegitimate child by a Negro. Strange! Strange of the Negro, too. Sophia's type of beauty had no appeal for Professor Jaricot, so little impression had it made on him in their first encounter that he did not recognize her as the hymn-singing beggar to whom, in an irresistible impulse of sentiment, he had given a five-centime bit. And as Professor Jaricot's type of beauty had no appeal for Sophia either they parted in ignorance that they had met before.

Money must be paid down. Well, there was nothing else for it. Frederick, who was responsible, must be invoked.

"It would be surer, it would be far less painful, to write to your lawyer."

"It would be much slower. And now that I have made up my mind to get Caspar off my hands and now that you have made up your mind to disagree with me, the sooner it is settled the better. Besides, Minna, Caspar is not so utterly to be pitied. If you had smelled that soup . . ."

"Smelled that soup? I have smelled it a thousand times! There is scarcely a city in Europe where I have not smelled that persuasive, that fatal soup. What is it made of?—ledgers, prayerbooks, dividends, death-sentences, the bones of the poor, the flesh of the young, the tears of prisoners, mouldy bread and black beans; and when it is scummed and cleared and flavoured they serve it up in a plated soup tureen. And you hankered for it. Shameful!"

"A good nourishing soup—not a metaphor in it. And, Minna—can you look at those people there and tell me that they too are not hankering for Professor Jaricot's soup, that a bondage to a regular dinner would not mean a great deal more to them than the liberation of Poland?"

A straggling procession of demonstrators was moving slowly down the street. The cross traffic halted them, and the outmost man heard Sophia's words. He turned towards her a placard which he was carrying. Scrawled on it in large characters were the words, *Bread or Lead.*

"As you say, Madame."

His voice was dry and fatigued, the voice of a schoolmaster nearing the end of a lesson. Hunger had painted him of any age, but he was probably young. He had small adder-coloured eyes, pungently bright.

"A regular dinner, soup without metaphors. That is what the workers want, is it not? The ten-hour day, two francs a day from the National Workshops, the blessing of Marie, and a little organization from Thomas—that is a prospect to keep them peaceable, eh?"

"Two francs?" said Sophia.

"If there *is* work, naturally. We are told that perhaps, in time, with organization, with the good-heartedness of employers, there may even be work every other day."

"I cannot understand," she exclaimed, "why there is no work. For though an old lady and her spiritual director in the Faubourg St.-Germain assured me that the republic was doomed to ruin because no one would have sufficient confidence to buy jewellery or have their window-boxes repainted, I cannot be ninny enough to believe *that.* Work! The paving of this street alone and the repair of these houses should be enough to employ a hundred men. And the town has got to go on, hasn't it?—people be fed, and clothed, whether it is a republic or a kingdom?"

She spoke excitedly, forgetting that she was addressing a perfect stranger; it seemed to her that this wry fellow with the adder-coloured eyes was the sort of person she wanted to question, and that she could get from him tougher answers than Minna's circle could supply. For though it is no affair of mine, she said to herself, yet here I am in the middle of this vaunted republic which is so obviously going wrong; and at least I might know why.

"However, your friends in the Faubourg St.-Germain might have given you an inkling," he said. "They assured you that the republic was doomed to ruin—that is to say, they meant to ruin it. They were even frank enough to inform you how they meant to bring that ruin about. Really, Madame, for an Englishwoman, reared at the very hearth of political economy, you have been a little dense."

While he was speaking the procession had been released, and moved on, he with it. It went the faster for having been stemmed, she had some ado to keep up with him, hauling Minna along with her.

"But their trumpery patronage, their twopenny-halfpenny effect on trade—what difference can that make? And anyhow, they must still buy essentials, they must still buy bread."

"So must others, with shallower purses. . . ." (*Bread or Lead,* he shouted, displaying his placard.) "Have you never heard of a lock-out, Madame? It is a simple enough system. There is a difference of opinion between the workers and their employer, and the employer says, in effect, Since I can afford to go without my profits longer than you can afford to go without your wages I will close the manufactory until such time as hunger shall compel you to agree with me. The employing class, not only of France but of Europe, the investors, the manufacturers, the middlemen, the banks, the officials, mislike the republic. And so they are using the lock-out against it."

"Charmingly clear, is it not?" said the boy beyond him,

gazing on Sophia with fatherly interest. Not even want had dimmed his good-hearted impertinence, he was one of those Gallic radishes like the porter who had so much pleased her at Calais. Suddenly she recollected the man who had drawn on the wall, the tree, hung with dimpled fruits of the Orléans dynasty, the working-man whose axe was laid to its root, and the crowd, giggles rising through their intent excitement like bubbles rising through wine. Joy was it in that dawn to be alive. She also had been pleased with herself that morning, rocking on her toes with the sense of an adventure before her; and her adventure too had miscarried very oddly.

"Yes, I know about lock-outs. It is a device often used in England. But are you going to stand it?" she inquired.

"No!" said the man.

"No," said Minna beside her—a thoughtful echo.

"Decision is a great deal," pondered Sophia. "But not quite sufficient. I should think you would do well to get rid of some of your ridiculous leaders, for a start."

"That idea has occurred to us also, as it happens. The more so, since we do not consider them our leaders. At first, our go-betweens; and now, for some time, our betrayers."

Léocadie to the life, she thought, tingling with an odd sort of pleasure at the rap of his snub.

"And so . . . ?"

Before she could finish the question the boy cried out with a brisk cock-a-doodling voice,

"Bread or lead!"

His voice, so young and impudent, uttering those grim words, fetched from Minna a sudden sigh, a tightening of the hand; and from a Civil Guard who was sourly prowling on the edge of the march, a shouted admonishment to hold his tongue or it would be the worse for him. Other voices took up the cry, the Civil Guard flushed angrily among his whiskers.

Pitching her voice carefully, aiming it to travel under the uproar, Sophia asked,

"Have you got the lead?"

He turned and gave her a full glance of those pungent eyes—long, searching, and ruthless. Then, suddenly casting aside his schoolmaster's voice for the twang of the gutter, he replied,

"That's telling, ain't it?"

The glance, leaving her, discarded her too. They slackened step, dawdled to watch the rest of the demonstration go by, remembered that they must purchase salami. Not till some time had gone by did Minna remark,

"Did you know you were talking to a Communist?"

"Of course."

Grabbing the end of that advantage, she added,

"And, Minna—how did you know?"

"Oh, as you did. By the way he spoke."

"Yes. He reminded me of Ingelbrecht. So—so lucid."

"You are lucid too, Sophia. You always know your own mind. It is one of your qualities that most delights me."

The affable mendacity of this tilted Sophia's thoughts back to the question of Caspar, of how soon he could be deposited with Professor Jaricot and Minna's delight given full scope. The sooner the better, undoubtedly. It was a dubious deed, all her dealings with that luckless mulatto were shoddy enough. But testing, as it were, the resilience of her conscience, she knew that once he was out of the way, and the dubious transaction signed and delivered as her act and deed, she would be able to forget about it, and go forward with enough impetus to carry the gainsaying Minna with her.

Only the method, then, remained to be settled. Discreetest, most dignified, would be to write to Mr. Wilcox, sitting, the soul of dignity and discretion, behind his green-shaded windows, his copperplated brass name-plate, his Georgian house-front, demurely set back a pace or two from the narrow Dorchester street. There he sat, among his documentary band-boxes, his few quiet spiders; and sometimes his eyes, so round and clear and empty of expression that they seemed very much akin to his bald forehead, might rest on the band-box where *Aspen* in white letters had been cancelled with a line and *Willoughby* painted below. Discreetest, most dignified course. Unfortunately it would also be the slowest.

At the other extreme was an appeal to that Willoughby who had cancelled her Aspen. And mid-way, just where she would be, agile and timeless trimmer, was great-aunt Léocadie, who would, no doubt, welcome any opportunity to display her mediating talents, do another little family job. One would show oneself a swine before a pearl not to invoke Léocadie at this juncture.

The decision was speeded up by Caspar's greeting, and his news that during their absence a wretched Jew—a Jew with a humpback, moreover—had come to the door, inquiring for Minna, but had been routed by Caspar's assurance that there were no old clothes for sale today.

His eyes of black velvet travelled from Sophia's rigidly unobserving face to the bunch of lilies of the valley arranged on the table, and piteously back again.

"What lovely lilies! I smelled them the moment I came in. Did you get them, Caspar? Are they for us?"

"I got them for Mrs. Willoughby."

Slowly turning herself from Caspar to Sophia, Minna lifted her shoulders, displayed her emptied hands with the gesture of the advocate whose best plea for his client is the admission that there is nothing to be said for him.

With a sensation that the cat was cajoling on behalf of its kitten and that she did not like cats, Sophia carried the salami into the kitchen. She pulled open the little safe and scrutinized a platter. Yes, exactly! The kitten thieved, into the bargain.

"This brat must go, and soon," she murmured, raging, slicing the salami with the deftness of fury. "If I am to be driven into counting anchovies . . . !

"And of course he's hungry," she added, whisking dry the lettuces, mounting on the wings of her fury into the further a ether of fair-mindedness. "We've not had a respectable meal for a week, no wonder he has to filch anchovies. What he needs is that reliable onion soup. He shall have it."

So great-aunt Léocadie was dismissed with Mr. Wilcox. Those mediating talents of hers might withhold the Caspar claim until some favourable moment, when one was that age time was nothing to one, ripeness, all. Moreover, a demand transmitted through her to Frederick might afford Frederick a good excuse for pretending it had never reached him. Frederick should be directly approached; and since so much depended on it, the treaty letter should be inoffensively, reasonably, tactfully constructed.

It was difficult to write tactful letters from a heart pounding with fury, from a stomach whose void was only taunted by scraps of salami and a flourish of salad, and to the accompaniment of a woman of generous disposition and great dramatic talent teaching an over-excited boy how to dance a bolero and click his own stimulus from castanets. Seven drafts were composed, and pensively corrected, and wholeheartedly torn up.

"Are you going out, Sophia?"

"Yes. To the Catacombs. For a little peace and quiet."

"To the Catacombs? Where all the skeletons are? Oh, Mrs. Willoughby, may I come too? You promised I should see the Catacombs!"

Minna, putting away the castanets, said maternally,

"Unfortunately the Catacombs are always shut on the second Thursday of May. For spring-cleaning. But I will ask Monsieur Macgusty to take you there tomorrow."

It was not till the evening, when Caspar had retired to the flannel bosom of Madame Coton, there to be comforted and warned afresh against the Jewess, that Sophia had time to say,

"I have decided that the best thing to do is to write a tactful letter to Frederick. Here it is."

Minna read it, with the attention, part solicitous, part admiring, which she gave to all Sophia's doings.

"Yes, it is tactful. Perhaps it is a little like a tactful proclamation. But then the grand manner suits you—and it is certainly tactful."

"But yet you disapprove?"

"No. No, I don't disapprove."

"You disapprove sentimentally, you think he will be unhappy?"

"Not more unhappy than he is here. And to be candid, I must consider my own happiness also, and I find the poor little wretch a great burden, and we do nothing but fall out about him. . . . I have no wish to keep him, God knows."

"Minna, what is it?"

She wrinkled her broad forehead, drooped her lower lip, put

on a look sulky and innocent, the look of an animal driven towards the bloody smell of the slaughterhouse.

"A misgiving, Sophia. An intuition, a feeling that this is something we shall have to regret. Do you never have such feelings?"

"Often. Constantly. But I have never found them come to anything."

She knew she was lying. She had never known an intuition in her life, blundering unwarned from one mischance to another.

"And when I have analysed them they have always turned out to be colds coming on or a change in the weather."

"*Enfin!*" Minna rose. "What will be, will be."

As though these time-worn words were a sort of music, her body yielded, melted itself like the snake's heavy coils beginning to shimmer with movement at the sound of the Indian's flute. Leaning her cheek on her clasped hands she began to revolve about the room in a waltz, staring down at the floor, vaguely smiling. The air still pulsated with the heat of the long day, the scent of Caspar's cheap dying lilies filled the room.

"When I remember that you have always been like this, and that I have only known you for the last three months, I could bite off my fingers."

Minna did not answer. But now, as she revolved, her wide-open black eyes floated their glance upon Sophia, and wisely, pensively, she nodded her head.

FOUR

To the letter that might also have been a proclamation Frederick replied with a letter that was all, and no more than, a letter should be. He quite agreed that since Caspar had found his way to Paris, Professor Jaricot's was the place for him. He was sure that in choosing Professor Jaricot's establishment Sophia had chosen the best possible establishment, and only regretted that she should have been put to the inconvenience—an inconvenience which he would gladly have spared her—of hunting it out. He had paid all the necessary fees in advance. And since it seemed probable that Caspar would be the better of a new outfit before departing (the sooner the better, no doubt) he proposed calling at the rue de la Carabine on Monday, a little before noon, to take Caspar out to lunch and then on to the tailor's and the hairdresser. And he was, bridging an awkward passage, hers to a cinder, as the Yankees say, and really it is exceptionally hot for this time of year, Frederick.

"Beautifully curled, isn't it? Especially that little frizz of the tongs just at the end," said Sophia, handing over the letter. On this unfortunate matter of Frederick she would allow no subterfuge, no vulgar discretion.

Minna read the letter without comment. Her caution, the way in which, the letter finished, she refolded it and laid it down without once raising her eyelids or wavering from her air of melancholy self-control, suddenly irritated Sophia. It was the look Minna had worn on the night of the twenty-third of February, pinned against the doorway in the boulevard des Capucines. Then it had been that affair of Gaston and the dray. Now it was Frederick. That look, that plaintive scapegoat air of oppression accepted, of accusations meekly unanswered, Minna sheltered behind it whenever she felt a situation becoming awkward. And according to Sophia's view of the situation, these retreats were melting or infuriating.

"Isn't it?" she repeated sharply.

The eyelids flew up, as though the voice had shaken them.

"I've a letter too, a—a delightful letter. It's from a lawyer in Rouen, saying that I have been left a little property.

"Very small," she added hastily. "A small farm. Think! Fancy me a landed proprietor."

"Who left it to you?"

"An old gentleman."

"How very grateful of him!"

"As a matter of fact," said Minna, colouring furiously, bouncing to her feet with a stamp, "he was one of the few people I haven't lain with. So there!"

She swept into a flood of tears, and simultaneously Caspar

and Wlodomir Macgusty entered the room, exclaiming that the Catacombs had been memorable, had been great fun.

"Min-na!" exclaimed Macgusty, bounding across the room between one syllable and the next, throwing down his hat and falling on one knee beside the pink sofa. "Minna! Unfortunate child, what distresses you? What catastrophe is this? Why do you weep?"

Fumbling in his pocket he drew out a paper bag of sweets and a small flask of smelling-salts. "I use them myself," he said persuasively, holding the smelling-salts to Minna's eye.

Caspar sniggered.

"Heartless boy! Fresh from the Catacombs you laugh at human woe. Can nothing move you?"

"I can," said Sophia, pushing Caspar out of the room and shutting the door on him. It seemed to her that she would have given a fortune to remain on the farther side of the door herself. But on second thoughts nothing, except to explode, would have been adequate, so she stalked back to the sofa again and stood looking down on Minna's heaving shoulders, on Wlodomir's waving paws.

Shifting distractedly from knee to knee, drawing long breaths of smelling-salts and offering the flask again to Minna, he continued to implore her to share her griefs with him, to exclaim that sorrow was sacred, to ask why she wept and to suggest various good reasons why she should do so. Suddenly, out of this tumult and flurry, Sophia became aware that Minna was looking at her with one eye, an eye streaming with tears but at the same time bright with intelligence. Then the handkerchief covered it and there was another interval of tears and entreaties. At last, with a long, increasingly determined snuffle, Minna emerged from the entreaties and said,

"I weep for a benefactor, Wlodomir. For a good old man."

"Well may you weep then. They are few," answered he sympathetically.

"I had almost forgotten him," continued Minna. "For one grows heartless as one grows old."

"No, no!"

"Lately I have not even asked myself if he was dead or alive. Now I learn that he is dead. A lawyer's letter tells me, cold and formal. He is dead. But with a better heart than mine, he remembered me, and has left me a legacy."

Her head was raised, her eyes fixed on the cornice. She was well off on the concerto now.

Oh you baggage, you audacity! cried out Sophia's heart in admiration.

"A small farm," she said, feeling that there was now something for her to say. Do as she would, she could not prevent a tone of congratulation and approval creeping into the words. Two glances were shot at her from the sofa—Wlodomir's a glance of reprobation towards such a mercenary frame of mind, Minna's a flash of intimate gratitude, triumph, and trust. Presently, with the lavishness of the virtuoso, Minna had played another trick and so modulated the situation that it was Wlodomir who needed comfort and soothing; and the balm for his sensitive feelings, still quivering from the shock of another's woe, turned out to be lemonade, biscuits, descriptions of the old gentleman, speculations about the farm, and praise of country life in general. They were all picking butter-cups and daisies and making cream cheeses (and here Sophia with her practical experience of country life could be most usefully invoked) before Caspar occurred to any of their recollections. As usual he had gone to Madame Coton. But it was agreed that he should make one in the excursion to Treilles—a name already so much a place to them that each speaker had a mind's-eye view of it, Minna and Wlodomir already at a misunderstanding over poplars and willow trees, and Sophia privately deciding that the pigsties must be re-roofed.

The farm, a small-holding really, since only one family worked it, was occupied; and for many years had brought in a rent of seven hundred francs. As for old Daniel Boileau, he visited it twice a year, in order to collect the rent, and for the rest lived in a hotel in Rouen, making notes for a book which was to prove that the Jews were the great impediment to civilization. It had been a tract preliminary on this subject which had sent a younger and more impassioned Minna (so she said, pensively folding and refolding a sopping handkerchief) to visit the old Sisera. He had been delighted with her pleading, and perfectly unconvinced by her arguments, a balance of mind, he remarked, impossible to any Jew, lop-sided with monotheism; and at parting he had presented her with the pseudo-Watteau which still hung on the wall.

This account of the benefactor was rather astringent to the veneration which Wlodomir was prepared to feel for the shade of the departed. He hurried back into his willows again, and planted some rustic graves there, an orphan or two, a weeping widow. Death, he said, in a country churchyard, seemed a different, a humaner thing. Minna must keep a green enclosure in her mind wherein to inhume the thought of the late Daniel Boileau, and shed there only tranquil tears. And with renewed entreaties that she should only weep tranquilly he took his leave, promising to supply, against the excursion, some very superior pâté, made by a wonderful old woman who lived, quite unsuspected by epicures, in the rue de la Roquette.

"As if I didn't know his wonderful old women and his wonderful old wine-shops," said Minna. "They stew their own bones, and bottle . . . Sophia!"

Sophia's back was turned, she was examining Daniel Boileau's Watteau. It was a pretty, a harmless fake, plump cat-faced music-makers under autumnal trees. Such gilding poisoned no gingerbread, fell off as easily, as naturally, as the trees' brief gold.

"When I saw that ridiculous Macgusty," she said, still staring into the picture, "I began to be ashamed of myself. He keeps a perpetual cistern of pumped-up feeling, one has only to turn the tap and it flows by force of gravity. I don't propose to let loose any more jealousy. I suspect it of being pumped-up, too. Much better to play away on our fiddles, since we shall all be dead so soon."

She turned from the picture to Minna, who stood behind her, pale and tear-stained, her eyes blackening as though with fear.

"*So soon.* I do not know how you can say it so calmly. Whether I die first or survive you, I lose you."

"I haven't any feeling of immortality whatsoever, have you?"

"Not for years. When I was a child, perhaps. Sometimes I think that those who die young may have immortality, but it perishes in us long before we are thirty."

"My father used to say that the younger the rabbit, the longer it kicked and leaped after it had been shot dead. That is about as much immortality as we can presume on, I suppose. Does it grieve you?"

"Bitterly!"

She spoke in a voice passionately unreconciled.

"But why is death so much in your mind today? Because of Daniel Boileau?"

"No, no! He is well out of it. No. Because of a hundred things which touch us more nearly. Because of this."

Out of her reticule she pulled a small crumpled note, written on a slip of paper with a printed heading.

"It was handed to me in the street yesterday, while you were out singing. I have kept it back all this time, but you must see it, there's no escape."

The heading said, *The Alpine Laundry. 29, rue Javotte. Proprietress Madame Amélie Goulet. All branches of fine laundry-work, moderate terms, bag wash and gentlemen's shirts a speciality.* Under this was written, in pale commercial ink, "If your friend will call at this establishment on Monday morning about 10:30, and inquire for Mademoiselle Martin, she will learn if we have the alternative to bread."

While she was still knitting her brows over this Minna took the paper from her and tore it up.

"The man who said, *Bread or Lead.* Don't you remember him?"

"But . . . but why should he write to *me?* And from a laundry? And why *should* he write to me? He doesn't suppose I am a Communist, does he?"

"I really can't say, my dearest. But it seems unlikely."

"Well, then, why does he send this extraordinary invitation? Is he mad?"

"It doesn't read like the letter of a madman."

"Minna, you know a great deal more about this than you let on about. I can see you do. A mystery is a mouse to you, and you've put on your cat-face. Now tell me how long you've known this fellow."

"I don't know him. I've seen him, and heard him speak. But I have never exchanged a word with him."

"Where did you see him?"

"With Ingelbrecht. It was in March, about a fortnight before I met you at the fountain. That was one reason why I was so terribly unhappy then. I could not forget his words, and I could not deny their truth. But with every word he rent all the beliefs I had, made all my enthusiasm for liberty seem a paper garland, and my idea of a republic a child's Utopia, a house built on a quicksand."

"But Communists are all for liberty and republics."

"Not of my kind, Sophia."

"And so he gave you this note?"

"No, not he. The boy who was with him. He was in the rue de la Carabine with a hand-cart, collecting rags and bones and bottles and old iron—every sort of rubbish—when I went out to do some errands yesterday. And he gave me a handbill, and this with it. Then he went on with his barrow, down the street."

"But why should I be the one to receive this invitation?"

"I don't know. I say to myself, Because I love you, and so, with every movement I make I must be bound to endanger you; stab you if I fasten your brooch, poison you if I cook for you, offer you a death-warrant if I show you this. Already I have lost you your money, your world, your friends—"

"I never had any."

"—hauled you down into this shabby Bohemia, which is all I have to offer you, now, where you go hungry, wear holes in your slippers, sing in the streets—"

"I have never been so happy in my life and you know it."

"—and now, seeing you happy, knowing that in spite of my fatal influence you have never been so happy in your life, now, it seems to me that I am doomed to direct you and your happiness towards what must endanger it, what may endanger you. That is what I say to myself, Sophia. But if you ask me for a reasonable answer as to why you should be invited to the Alpine Laundry, then I am at a loss."

"I like your unreasonable answers much better. I hope you have a *quid pro quo* preference for my reasonable questions. For I must ask you, Minna, what there is so very hazardous about a Communist? What do you know about them?"

"Scarcely anything. Nobody does. But I know they are dangerous, deadly."

"But why? Why more deadly than any of the other species in your menagerie?"

"There are so few of them. Ten here—another ten there—saying so little but all saying the same thing. So few of them. And all knowing their own mind. And all of them dead in earnest. There must be death," she cried out vehemently, "in any such earnestness!

"Look at Ingelbrecht," she continued, lowering her voice to a whisper. "So tranquil, so bald, so resolute. How he goes his own way, keeps his own counsel! When I meet him in the street I feel as though I had met the nose of a steel screw, boring up through the pavement from underground. Think of all the prisons he's bored his way out of. Though I have not dreaded *him* on your account, I knew he didn't want you. But this one . . ."

"Minna. Do you ask me not to go?"

She paused, shook her head.

"No. I make it a rule never to impose my will on other people. Besides, to turn you back now, when we both anticipate so much . . . We should die of a galloping curiosity. And from the moment I read this, I knew it was a destiny."

It was not till some while later that it occurred to them that Sophia might not return from the laundry before Frederick called for Caspar.

"Never mind." Minna spoke soothingly. "At least it will spare him the anguish of seeing us together."

"I suppose he hopes to worm a good deal out of Caspar."

"Of course. Why else should he trouble to take him out to lunch? Has that only just occurred to you? I saw that at once, I meant to point it out, but then my sorrow for poor Daniel drove it from my mind. Yes, he will get a lot out of Caspar. Whom we see, whom we don't see, if we quarrel, how much we have to eat, if we wear each other's petticoats, etc. Frederick likes domestic details. I have never met a man of good breeding who didn't. Whereas your Martin—Caspar could pipe to him all day about the holes in our stockings and never get an encouraging word."

"Oh well, he can pipe and be damned."

"Yes, isn't it a comfort to feel that we are not going to do anything about it?—that one can't do anything about it? Such serenity! One feels like the angels in heaven or poor Monsieur Thomas being kidnapped in his cab."

The abduction of that functionary was still news, and to a certain extent, comic relief. Hardening towards the prospect of a much greater degree of violence the mind of Paris saw in the fate of Monsieur Thomas the rather insignificant horseplay of the clowns who only open the circus—unless one took the view of Égisippe Coton, who said in a tone of gloomy longing, "It might happen to any one of us now." Raoul, who piqued himself on the sensitive ear which he turned to the demands of their public, had indeed suggested to Sophia that the hymns might be dropped in favour of *Partant pour la Syrie,* and anything she knew about exiles; but this change of programme did nothing to improve their takings, which were now steadily diminishing.

"Why can't you come on Monday, Sophia?" he asked. "I always consider Monday one of our favourable days, and for this Monday I was working out . . ."

She shook her head, firmly binding up her plaits, her mouth full of hairpins.

"Why don't you take Minna for a change?"

"No! Minna is a collector's piece now. She's lost any knack she may have had for street work. In another ten years, yes. Then she would be magnificent as a crone, as a destitute grandmother reduced to hawking improper albums. But for the moment Minna is decidedly betweentides."

"How old is Minna?" she said.

"God knows!—the old Medusa!"

How odd, she thought, walking homeward, that I felt no impulse to knock him down and dance on him. It is unlike me to be so reasonable. Nor was there any baseness in my question, however loudly my upbringing must shout to me that such questions are base. It was a practical question. For if Minna is —is old, then I ought to know it. Towards the old, the ageing, one observes a certain line of conduct. One respects them, defers to them, spares them. Translated into action, this entails not contradicting them, concealing from them one's private opinions, and seeing to it that they sit in the easiest chairs. On this last count at any rate, she had nothing to reproach herself with. Suavely as any cat Minna always planted herself in the best chair—unless she reposed on the floor; and though dividing the food with scrupulous equity, if there happened to be any unclaimed *bonne bouche* she would crunch it up with the greatest goodwill, mop up the sauce with bread, with thoughtful greed lick out the dish.

Suavely as any cat. Even cats age, though so imperceptibly that no one agrees on the natural span of a cat's life, some saying ten, some twelve, some a score of years. But age and die they do, dying of heart-failure, dying in their sleep before the kitchen embers as a ripe apple falls on a windless afternoon, or throwing themselves down exhausted, after a rat-hunt through the barton, never to rise up and hunt again. For all their nine lives, their guardian cunning, and their whiskers, the wariest, the sleekest cats grow old and die. Or of a sudden, in their practised prime, a sore on the neck will make them peevish with life, they will turn from their food, exploit their wholesome talent of vomiting, spew up in the end nothing but froth and slime, sit gasping for breath with their blackened gaze fixed on some familiar piece of furniture as though, at long last, they recognized in it the furtive enemy of a lifetime, the unmasked foe.

"I can be sick whenever I please," was Minna's boast. "Like a cat, Sophia."

After all, one need not wait for age—how long was it since she, turning from the imitation Watteau, had spoken so seriously with Minna about death, speaking as though under its shadow? But they had spoken together, with every admission re-establishing their liveliness, their power to speak, hear, communicate. It is one thing to speak of death with those one loves; but to think of it alone, walking through the streets, one does that at a different temperature.

Speaking of death had led them to speak about Martin and the Communists. Now she was thinking again of death, and every step of her thought went with a step leading her towards the Alpine Laundry. She had left Minna at her most exasperating: plunged into a martyrdom of domesticity, counting and darning Caspar's underclothes, washing his handkerchiefs, gloomily bruising her fingers in an attempt to hammer the heel more firmly on his boot. Over her shoulders, despite the heat of the day, she had pinned a little shawl, unbecomingly too skimpy for them. From her ears dangled a pair of disgustingly meagre and lacklustre jet earrings, earrings which, since they had never appeared there before, it was tempting to suppose had been borrowed from Madame Coton—that soul of sour domestic virtues—for dressing this particular part.

And all this, as Sophia knew quite well, was because not Minna but she had been bidden so mysteriously to visit the Alpine Laundry. Thither she could go, flourishing her heels, the child of good fortune, destiny's pet. Whereas Minna the daylong labourer in the vineyard, Minna the nursing mother of revolutions, must stay at home, devoting her slighted talents to Caspar's socks. In this mood Frederick would find her. Then God help Frederick!

She was immoderately early for her appointment, Minna's grand renunciation had begun with the smarting punctuality of any attack at dawn, and despite the muddle which her efficiency bred on every hand it had been impossible not to leave the rue de la Carabine at least half an hour too soon. She leaned her elbows on the parapet of the bridge, staring at the barges below her, watching with approval a man who came out of a cabin with a little mat, and shook out its dust into the river. It was obvious that such a man kept house alone.

A hundred times she had injured Minna intentionally, dealt shamelessly blows below the belt, cuffed her vanity, trapped her into the wrong, trampled over her wishes and her principles—and all without a pang. Now, when really for no fault of hers, Minna was thrusting her breast against the thorns of wounded vanity, and caterwauling beyond the powers of any impassioned nightingale, she must feel her heart wrung with sympathy and a conviction of guilt, cry out, "The poor angel!" But long, long ago, she had thrown her reason into this river flowing beneath her—perhaps even on that winter's afternoon when, crossing from the other bank to visit great-aunt Léocadie, she had wished that she could hold Madame Lemuel beneath the cold flood until she came up gasping, and having revised her metaphors.

Meanwhile, whatever might or might not comfort Minna, to turn back from the Alpine Laundry certainly would not do so.

Thanks to Minna, who knew her way through Paris very much as a mongrel might, she had her directions. But now, staring at the decrepit fortress of the Marais, it seemed to her that she would never disentangle her way thither. But why did the word fortress come to mind? Rat's Castle rather—a quarter even more entangled, tattered, secretive of everything except stinks, than that which lay behind her. They did not even look historical, those tall jostling house-blocks, with their stooping gables and crooked roofs. They were past mark of mouth.

"If I stay here much longer," she said to herself, "I shall begin to feel courageous."

This she had determined not to feel. And with a last glance at the river's clear highway she set forward for the Alpine Laundry.

Before she found it she had grown sufficiently accustomed to the Rat's Castle to be observing the prices of the food on the open shop-counters, and thinking that this would be an even more advantageous place to shop than the rue Mouffetard. The language of the country too was extraordinarily grand, never had she read such lofty sentences in cook-shop windows nor seen such flowery recommendations of wine and butter. It was as though they had picked their phrases from the second-hand shops, she thought, running her eye over a dusty interior where chairs and gilded bedposts in the grandest manner struggled pell-mell with broken mangles, gaping concertinas, old mattresses, and odd coffee-cups. It was from shops like these that Minna liked a fairing. But it would be better to take her something clean; and from a shoemaker's window she selected a pair of magnificent slippers, made of spotted crimson plush and trimmed with sparkling tinfoil cupids. Each slipper cost rather more than the result of a morning of song, and she was, as she agreed with the woman who sold them, highly favoured to buy such slippers so cheap.

This transaction emptied her of time as well as of money.

Reaching the Alpine Laundry a hasty glance told her no more of the exterior than that it was painted blue and white, that the paint was thin but well-scrubbed, that in the window two highly goffered infant's long petticoats flanked a man's shirt whose starched arms extended towards the baby-clothes as though in a gesture of family affection.

Inside also the little office was all that honest poverty should be—well-scrubbed, orderly, a chastened sentimentality manifesting itself in a vase of marguerites on the counter. The air had the bitter-sweet almond tang of starch, and behind a glass-panelled door the top part of some piece of machinery rose slowly, and dropped, and rose and dropped again, and with every rise and fall there was a sighing whistle and a gush of water released.

The woman sitting behind the counter was making up accounts. Her thick red fingers held the pen clumsily, her right hand was ink-stained. As Sophia entered the shop she glanced up with a look at once placid and earnest, and it was obvious that she was holding a thread of addition in her mind.

"*Vous désirez, Madame . . . ?*"

Sophia spoke her wish. The woman made a little tick on the column of her addition, noted a sum on the blotting paper, rose and opened the door, calling for Mademoiselle Martin.

"This lady wishes to inspect the laundry."

Mademoiselle Martin was lame, she threw out her hip as she walked, and with each halting step a cordlike muscle stood out in her neck. Her eyes were dark and beady, her face was pinched, dutiful, and industrious. Her arms below her rolled-up sleeves were extraordinarily full and muscular.

Behind the glass-panelled door there was only whitewash and scabby iron for the blue and white paint of the office. There was a great deal of steam, the squelch of wet clothes, the hissing of irons. Four women were at work, their faces shining with sweat, their skirts bunched round their hips. Moving on pattens over the wet floor they seemed in their bunched white pinafores like the creatures of some queer aviary. They looked at Sophia no more mysteriously than any other washerwomen might, good-dayed her in affable voices.

Limping beside her, glancing up sometimes with her beady mouse's eyes, Mademoiselle Martin showed off to Sophia the washing tubs, the mechanical pump, the mangles, the stove where the irons stood heating, the racks of clean linen. Sophia asked questions, examined, approved; and in the moist heat of the workroom her ears sung, her heart pounded.

"One moment, Victoire."

The woman at the heavy ironing-block stood aside. Thrusting with her strong arms, Mademoiselle Martin swung back the ironing-block; and there was a hole in the floor, a dark square, the tips of two iron uprights just showing.

"If you will go down the ladder . . ." she said. "It is quite easy. Nine rungs. No one will observe you from below."

I am glad it is so decent, thought Sophia, holding on to the uprights, feeling that well-oiled darkness overhead move back into place again. Still, I should like to have some idea of what to expect next.

Rats, said reason promptly.

Standing in the darkness at the foot of the ladder, snuffing up the natural mouldy smell of cellar and with it a queer, a Spanish-Inquisition-like tang of red-hot pokers, waiting for her senses to reassemble themselves, her eyes to gather patches of dusk from patches of darkness, her ears to disentangle the rats below from the clatter of the laundry, the far-off continuing whine and gush of water overhead, it was extraordinary to remember that in this position she was wearing a bonnet, a still quite ladylike bonnet.

"Though really," she said to the rats, "there is nothing extraordinary about it. Considering the matter rationally, it would be more remarkable if I were not wearing a bonnet."

"True," said a voice, the same voice which had cried *Bread or Lead.* And at the same moment she heard a door open and close behind her.

"I am sorry to have kept you waiting. I was delayed for a moment. But there was no wish to be dramatic, we are not Freemasons."

"I don't like drama either."

"If you will step this way? Can you see better now? There is nothing to trip over, no steps."

His voice was brittle and businesslike. In the darkness she remembered those bright adder-coloured eyes.

"You do trust me?"

For answer he pulled open a door, stood back for her to enter.

The cellar was lit by a couple of oil lanterns. It was an old wine-cellar, its walls were arcaded for casks, but in the niches where the casks had been were heaps of scrap-metal, old fire-irons, pots and kettles, a bird-cage, chains and bolts, broken tools, lengths of piping, clockweights and trivets. Against one wall where a gas-pipe ran there was a roughly set-up bench, and on this, tapping the gas-supply, where half a dozen little tubed stands, each with its gas-jet hissing and flaring. Over these they were melting down the metal, like so many intent toffee-makers. The table was strewn with moulds, tools, neat little heaps of bullets and ball. For all that it was crowded and makeshift, it was orderly. And the look of a busy kitchen was enforced by the bottles of cheap wine, the assemblages of food, which stood here and there on the bench.

Other workers were squatting on the floor, sorting the scrap, sawing it up for melting. They were of all ages, as many women as men, and their intent and weary expressions gave her the impression that they were all of the same cast of features, that, however long she stayed and looked at them, she would not be able to distinguish between one and another, carry away with her the recollection of any face that was not a composite face.

The gas-jets flared against this general colouring of drab and dusky with the imperious hue of another element; and over all the room hovered the taint of metal smoke. In this lighting pale faces, red hands, seemed alike livid and unreal. Glancing back at Martin she saw that his face wore the stamp of all the other faces, was intent and weary, and insignificant.

Catching her eye, "Our bakery," he said, with a little bow. "I hope you will give us your custom."

The quip sounded hollow and conscientious. It was clear that he had thought of it some time before, had decided to say it, had forgotten it till this moment when it bolted from his lips. No one laughed. The moulders, the men squatting on the floor, went on with their work, still cutting her dead.

How awful for him, she thought. He has got me here, God knows why, and now he doesn't know how to get rid of me.

And she felt a profound uneasiness, a painful sense of guilt. It seemed terrible to her that this man, so resilient and peremptory, should stand there looking awkward, making jokes that fell flat. For the first time in her life she found no comfort in her sense of the ridiculous. For nearly a week she had been thinking, on and off, of Martin, and always thinking highly of him, more and more highly. Now the bubble was to be pricked; and it was as though she awaited the end of a world.

Well, there was no use in hanging about, waiting to be assured that he was a weakling, just like all the other people in this revolution. She must say something tactful, tactful and feminine, and get away as soon as possible.

"I understand why your young friend goes round with a rag and bone barrow."

"Yes. But it is not a perfect method. The scrap has to be paid for—and we have other things to buy, things that must be bought. Besides, he has to accept a lot of other rubbish, that is inconvenient too."

"I know. Whatever one wants, one always has to accept a great deal of rubbish along with it."

"How strong are you?" he asked. "Could you carry that basket there?"

It was astonishingly weighty. As she lifted it she saw a woman turn from her work and watch her superciliously. Mettled, she gave herself more carefully to balancing the basket, walked across the cellar with it, and had the pleasure of seeing the woman's expression change to surprise.

"In your quarter," he continued, "there must be a great deal of scrap lying about. A bit picked up here, a bit there—between the two of you in a week you could collect a passable deal."

He watched her silence.

"I don't see why you shouldn't change your laundry. The Alpine Laundry does excellent work.

"Don't carry too much to begin with," he recommended. "And don't let Madame Lemuel accompany you. She would probably wish to tie a handkerchief over her head and walk barefoot. That sort of thing would estrange the other clients of the laundry."

Meanwhile she was still holding the basket of scrap, and on her other hand the veins were standing out blue and swollen. The set indifference of her countenance, too, was rapidly turning into a glare. Now he took the basket from her, saying, "Don't attempt to carry as much as that. You don't want chivalrous strangers offering to help you."

"When shall I come?" she said.

"As soon as you please. But come regularly. And wrap up the stuff so that it doesn't clatter. And call for the clean clothes four days later. We will leave you to supply your own basket."

"Thank you," she said, already with the sourness of the conscript.

"Thank *you.* I assure you, you will be doing us a considerable service. We are abominably short of helpers, or it would not have occurred to me to ask you."

"I understand. Now I think I had better go. I don't want to waste your time."

"I will see you up the ladder."

His tone was bland, he was working like a well-oiled machine, smoothly, swiftly, powerfully.

As long as you never make another joke, she said to herself. At the foot of the ladder, "What shall I do at the top?" she inquired childishly.

"They're waiting for you," he said. "Nine rungs."

And he was politely removing himself from her ankles when she demanded,

"Do you all come up and down this ladder?"

"Good Lord, no!"

The trap swung open, the smell of steam, the whistle and gush of the pump, came about her once more. Mademoiselle Martin brushed her skirts down, looked over them attentively for any cobwebs or filings.

"I have decided to bring my linen to your laundry. Will you please tell the proprietress?"

"I am so glad," answered Mademoiselle Martin. "If you will leave the linen with Madame Goulet in the shop she will see to it."

In the office she looked at the clock (her watch had been pawned some while since). It was eleven—there was time to get back to the rue de la Carabine before Frederick should arrive. She went and sat in the church of St. Paul, trying, among the shuffling Masses, the in-and-out of worshippers, to settle her thoughts. Instead, she fell asleep, and did not get to the rue de la Carabine until well after midday.

But though her thoughts were unsettled still, sleep had perfectly tidied up her sensations. And there was no affection, only a genuine tactlessness, in the calm with which she walked in and said,

"Well, I have had a very interesting morning."

"And a nice cup of tea? For pity's sake, Sophia, do ruffle your hair a little. Frederick has only just gone, spare me any more English phlegm."

"How is he?"

"Oh, very sleek. Very manly, too. He didn't bring any flowers this time, not for either of us. But I shouldn't be surprised if he sends us each a magnanimous shawl. The way he let his eyes stray round this room, Sophia . . . the hole in the sofa, the hole in my stocking, the patches on the wall where the trophies were —every glance a figleaf."

"Is that why you brought in the sausage-paper and left it on the table?"

"Yes. But I got into my best clothes before he arrived, except the stockings, he interrupted me there. But I wore gloves all through the interview. I hope you think I look well?—And do you see how beautifully I've polished the mirror and the chairs? Well, in he came, and pretended to be sorry to miss seeing you, but really he was immensely relieved. And, Sophia! He's a Bonapartist now."

"No doubt that will make a great difference to Europe. Has he changed his hatter too?"

"No, you're wrong. It's more significant than that. People like Frederick, people who are perfectly secure and never do anything, never range themselves on one side or another, are good guessers. Just as when you are very rich you always win in the lottery. I don't like it at all, Frederick being a Bonapartist."

"Minna. Does it never occur to you that I am one of those people who never do anything, never range themselves on one side or another?"

"No, if you were, you would never have been so angry on the night of the twenty-third of February."

It was the first time either of them had spoken of that night, tact, sometimes, or prudence, at other times the inattention which happiness has for its past, turning away their talk from the subject.

"I was angry with you, disillusioned with you."

"Not only with me. For you have forgiven me, but you have never forgiven the revolution. If you were one of those people who never take sides, it would have been all one to you whether that volley was stage-managed or no."

"Should it have been?"

Minna's hands washed themselves.

"How can I answer? How can one tell? But I can assure you that those Communists you have been among would not hesitate at much more drastic dealings. Tell me, what did Martin say, what happened?"

"He asked me to change my laundry. And to collect bits of old iron we found lying about."

"Oh! For ammunition!"

In her exclamation was excitement, pleasure at the device, pride at so instantly unriddling it; and at the same time an after-sigh of resignation, despairing acceptance.

"So it will come to that."

She rose, walked about the room, went to the window and stared out as though already there were blood on the cobbles. Then she came back, took Sophia's hand, kissed her gravely.

"You have not asked what I said to his suggestion."

"I need not, my dear. It is exactly what would suit you, it is practical, arduous, and rather dangerous. What intuition he has, that Martin!"

She walked about again, sighing, shaking her head. Then she put on her bonnet, took down the shopping bag.

"What do you want, where are you going?"

"To look for scrap iron. I seem to remember an old bell-pull that some children were playing with in the square."

"You can't do it in broad daylight."

Minna winked. "Can't I? When I was young I could have stolen the hem off your petticoat."

Thieving did Minna a great deal of good. She began to resume those sleek and sumptuous airs which she had worn as by right on the evening when Sophia first arrived at the rue de la Carabine, but since then only fitfully and incompletely. My poor darling, thought Sophia, I must have been constraining her to respectability without knowing it—all this time she has been pining in my bleak northern climate. For it seemed to her that Minna was thieving for theft's sake, and with very little attention to the claims of the Alpine Laundry; and sometimes she speculated on the odd concatenation between Minna's beaming delight over some especially neat filch and the end appointed for these unconsidered trifles—their billet in limb or heart or brain.

She thought too, seeing Minna thieve with such industry and *savoir-faire,* that there had been no justification for that taunt about walking barefoot and tying on a handkerchief, for Minna's technique was essentially serious. However, she went alone twice a week to carry their gains to the Alpine Laundry, grinning to herself as she remembered all those little ministering Christians of the goody-goody books, the Misses Lucy and Emily Fairchild visiting a deserving tenantry with a basket of viands and Bibles, trimly covered over with a white towel.

The deserving tenantry were not up to tradition. However well-laden the basket it was received with a flat impervious civility, and without a word said the woman behind the desk made it clear to her that, the load deposited, the next thing for her to do was to get away immediately. It was only on her third visit that Madame Amélie Goulet looked up with anything like a smile of acquaintanceship, and feared that she must find walking in such heat fatiguing.

"What I don't like is being stared at. You seem to live in a very observant street."

"I am so sorry," said Madame Goulet, as though she would have it put right in the next wash. "The truth is, to be so tall, and if I may say it, so elegant, must make one somewhat conspicuous. In this quarter, we do not see many ladies. And to be patronized by a lady so clearly a lady is a most convincing proof of the respectability of my establishment. One can see at a glance that you would not be connected with anything—with anything unusual."

"But is it not unusual for ladies to carry their own washing?"

"One can see, too, that you are English. It is well known that English ladies are energetic."

And not a word of thanks, thought Sophia on the way back, furtively rubbing an aching arm—just to be told that one is conspicuous and eccentric, and that that will do nicely. My God, how patronizing they are!

Still irate, she retailed this interview to Minna. Minna listened in silence, looked properly awed and pained—perhaps a trifle too much so, but then she was always pitching herself to an imaginary gallery.

"And she said that you looked respectable!—that anyone could see you would have nothing to do with low Communists! No, that is going too far. I don't wonder that you are annoyed.

"By the way," she added rapidly. "You remember Égisippe handing out the dog-chains? No doubt he has more—he would not empty himself at one gush, our Égisippe. Tonight I mean to explore downstairs. I shall probably walk in my sleep."

However worthless and neglected other people's property might be there was no doubt that she preferred it to her own. Letters, increasingly long and noble, came from the lawyer in Rouen, but Sophia had to answer them, frowning over the complications of legal terms in another language, sourly quoting to herself, "But mine own vineyard have I not kept." For it seemed to her shameful and ridiculous that she should be taking so much trouble over Minna's affairs, and writing so painstakingly to Minna's lawyer whilst, in all this lapse of time, she had not written to her own Mr. Wilcox to inquire how much income, if any, Frederick's assumption of the husband had left her; but for all that, she still could not bring herself to that letter, still too fastidiously furious to risk Mr. Wilcox's polite confirmation of Frederick's slap in the face.

How Ingelbrecht would scorn me, she thought. Here am I, hanging round pawnshops, sponging on Minna, living from hand to mouth—and all because I have not the moral courage to write to Mr. Wilcox. Her state was the more pressing since she went out singing no longer. Raoul had said there was no money in it, things must wait until he had another good idea. And it seemed to her that if Ingelbrecht were to appear he would read at one glance her slatternly shame, and that no amount of well-doing in the old-iron business would exculpate her.

He had not visited them for some time—not since Caspar had left them. Apart from her private guilt she could have wished with all her heart that he would come soon, for he might be able to make Minna take her legacy seriously. To Sophia it seemed that a property, however small, however worthless, was a thing to attend to. Its few acres should be walked over with thoughts of crop rotation and manure, its fences examined, its barn ascertained to be rat-proof and rain-proof. "If you will do nothing," she exclaimed, "I shall have to go there myself." Minna replied by forecasting the pleasures of a first visit together, the wild flowers, the swallows building their nests, young lambs, wild strawberries, etc. While she was in this frame of mind the visit might as well be postponed. A few injudicious warblings on the beauties of nature to a tenant-farmer might set back the rent for a quarter.

So she held her tongue for another few days, or only used it to supply assents to Minna's fancy sketches of lambs bounding in the hayfield. When next she gave herself to the serious duty of looking after one's property, she got the answer,

"I wonder if I need go yet. You see, I have talked about it so much, that if we were to go there and find everything as dreadful as you say it will be, pigs dying and the roof falling in, it would be more than I could bear. Perhaps it would be better never to go there at all, but just to take the rent and keep it as a beautiful dream."

Ingelbrecht was what she needed. Perhaps he thought that Caspar was still with them, a thought which might well keep him away. Surely he would have heard from someone? But whom? For lately they had been singularly unvisited, even Wlodomir Macgusty had come but once, and then—so now it struck her —with a rather forgiving and magnanimous air.

Now that the thought was in her head, it would not out. They were being dropped. In any other society poverty would have been explanation enough, but here the excuse would not run. Minna's rapscallionly circle would not leave a board because it had grown bare. And what else they can find to object to, she said to herself, God knows. They are all so outrageously broadminded.

It was broadminded of her, too, to be fretting like this. How often, formerly, her wishes had swept the room clear of them, silenced their chatter! They were Minna's friends, not hers, except for Ingelbrecht she would miss little if she never set eyes on them again. They were Minna's friends. And now that the thought was in her head and would not out, she knew she must do something about it. Maybe a little decisiveness here would serve to drape over that continued indecision over Mr. Wilcox. When anyone does turn up, she determined, I will somehow manage to speak about it.

No one turned up. Then, from the window seeing Dury in the street, she was ready to repent her determination, for no one could be more obdurate to a tactful handling than Dury. But he walked past the door and went on into the wine-shop further down.

Snatching up an excuse she descended in chase of him, ran him to earth. It seemed to her that his answer to her greeting was unwilling, and that he looked at her with antagonism.

"It is a long while since we have seen you. I am afraid that tiresome Caspar was enough to keep any of our friends away."

"He wasn't so bad."

"He's gone now, you know."

"Yes, I know."

Staring at her with solemn dislike and disapproval, he said,

"We think it a pity that you sent him into the Gardes Mobiles."

"Into the . . . ?" She stopped, and remained with her mouth open as this neat piece of trickery by Frederick unfolded itself before her. Two francs a day and keep in the Gardes Mobiles was certainly a better bargain than paying fees to Monsieur Jaricot.

She felt rage flooding her face with scarlet. To gloss things over she ordered a bottle of wine which cost more than the money in her purse. Her bonnet's term of credit was long ago ended, and she had to counterorder it for a cheaper bottle. Turning, she found the bovine young man still breathing on the back of her neck. Imperious with loss of temper she planted the bottle in his hands and marched out of the wine-shop.

Would he think it a gift and walk off with it? But he followed her in silence to the entry, to the foot of the stairs.

His face was a great deal redder than hers as she took back the bottle.

"It was a pardonable mistake. Raoul saw him among them, in full fig. It seemed a serious pity, at such a time as this."

"And so you all instantly believed it?"

"The air is full of mistrust, everyone's nerves are on edge. . . ."

"It is a pity you are all so idle," she remarked, thinking of the old-iron trade.

"That's true."

But at that moment his busy eye was at work on her, his attention wandering among the tubes in his palette box. From the landing above she called down, forgivingly,

"I arranged for him to go to a boarding school."

One by one they came back, a little sheepish some of them, at their first entrance, soon rehabilitated by Minna's unsuspicious greetings. For Sophia had kept her own counsel, even about Caspar and the Gardes Mobiles, sucking her paws in silence over this. One and another, they all reappeared, except Ingelbrecht. And since Minna had no suspicion, and all the rest of them were coming as usual, Sophia could remark in safety,

"It's a long while since Ingelbrecht's been here. I wonder where he is."

"Buried himself," was the answer.

No sooner were they back than Sophia began to curse herself for a marplot—for the worst of marplots; for it was her own plot she had marred. During that unvisited interval she had begun to build up a sort of daily routine, as though the constitution of her relationship with Minna needed an iron tincture which routine would supply. With horror she saw them lost, those habits of the two sprigged coffee-cups on the table by the window, the clock set by the compline bell, the paired plates and glasses that her hand could with certainty take down from the shelf and replace there.

Trained all her life long to look upon order and regularity as convenient, in the last few months she had come to regard them with an almost mystical admiration—and in this change of aspect perspective might have played a part, since to live with Minna swept order and regularity far away. But her plot had gone beyond the pleasure of regular coffee-cups and a reliable timepiece, and it was with more than the disapprobation of a character naturally orderly and precise that she saw it marred. Habit, method, the facets of a daily routine, she had been amassing them against the menace of that day when everything would fall to pieces, when the roof of the waiting-room would fall in.

So quite unreasonably, she had taken hold of her regular visits to the Alpine Laundry as a reassurance against the impending ruin of that queer existence in which she knew such happiness; and while carrying material for that next revolution which must explode beneath their feet had found comfort because she carried it twice weekly. Like a hen, she told herself, like a silly hen walking along a chalked line. And yet, though it was destruction she served, it was a purposed destruction, something foreseen and deliberated; and here, if she could only get herself into the well-scrubbed fortress of the Alpine Laundry, become one of these Communists instead of an eccentric Englishwoman carrying a laundry-basket, might be a safety for the mind.

So, blindly and desperately, she had begun to build up that routine of coffee-cups and clock-setting, fastening these cobweb exactitudes round Minna like a first scaffolding of something that time (but there could not be much more time) might stiffen into a defence.

With the return of Minna's friends, the cobweb fortifications broke. They came back more distracting than ever, those friends, more filled with rumours, theories, and counter-theories. Macgusty had grown very militaristic. War, he said in his melancholy piping voice, a war of liberation, must be the next step. The people must put on their might and liberate Ireland. As he declaimed he glanced at Sophia with fury, and added that the English aristocracy should yet tremble before Smith O'Brien. In another corner of the room Raoul was babbling about a congress of arts, pavilions of industry constructed in a Gothic manner of glass and iron to be erected in the Champ de Mars. For demonstrations of civilization, he said, must be the weapons of a civilized republic, and the setting-up and subsequent demolition of the pavilions would supply the unemployed with labour and livelihood.

"And who will visit your pavilions?" inquired Macgusty. "Who will inspect your inglorious machinery, your demonstration of a servile tutelage to commerce?"

"Not the Irish!" shouted Raoul. "They can keep out of it for all I care. France for the French!"

The lovers of France, the lovers of mankind, joined in a furious quarrel, and were hauled out of it by a newcomer announcing that not only were the workless to be drafted to the wastes of the Sologne, but that the Government had framed a scheme for shipping unemployed builders and paviours to Corsica, to erect fortifications. Their wives and children would accompany them, and rear silkworms.

Now into the most outrageous rumours and theories the question of the workless penetrated, and those words, *Bread or Lead,* clanged through every conversation. Sophia found herself believing, arguing, theorizing, with the rest. The spreading madness had infected her, even while scorning the disputes of the nostrum cheapjacks she beat her brains for some panacea of her own. If only Ingelbrecht would come, or if she could see Martin again! Neither of them had said a word, she recalled, of panaceas; they had laid bare causes only; but in the certainty of that analysis there had been a promise of some remedy they could and would apply. Minna, presumably more case-hardened, sat among her noisy visitors saying little, preserving that air of inspiration which she could always radiate in company. And when she poured out coffee and carried round the dish of cherries she seemed to be dispensing something so much more actual than the substance of those she nourished that it was as though, gravely and pityingly, she dispensed an All Souls' Night meal to a tribe of ghosts.

More and more clearly, during those summer evenings, shone out her air of technique, of being a professional amongst amateurs. They, quarrelsome and excited, waited in all the fidgets of stage-fright, for the rising of a curtain. She, uncommunicatively tranquil, sat wearily in an attitude that, for all her weariness, was from long learning both stately and as comfortable as circumstances would permit; nor was it possible to guess from her demeanour if she were going over her lines, or holding a mental roll-call of her greasepaints.

Had it not been for love and love's lack of faith, Sophia might have drawn from Minna the reassurance she longed to get from Martin or Ingelbrecht; and while others were present Minna's spell, her infallible sense of when to speak and how to move, stayed her. But as soon as they were left alone, solicitude undermined the stately idol, and Minna was once again a creature to ward and think for.

Since it was impossible to guess where safety lay, speaking of danger was idle. They continued to collect their scraps of metal, enjoy the green peas and wood-strawberries that the season had brought into the scope of their means, and discuss the management of Minna's property.

For a while that property had seemed to Sophia the way to safety. She set herself to encourage Minna's peculiar views on country life and to repress her own. Yes, there would be young lambs bounding in the hayfields, nightingales singing in a greengage tree, a vine-shaded dairy, sheets coarse but lavendered, a gnatless willow bower by a brook. Yes, there would be beehives, and nothing is easier than taking the honey. Everything would be as in Minna's childhood only cleaner, greener, more fertile.

Nothing came of these conversations save more conversations. She was trying a new line of approach, speaking of the neglect of roofs, the disrepair of fences, the inordinate negligence and inordinate demands of tenant-farmers, and feeling rather more sanguine as to the effect of it, till the humpback, Guitermann, walked in one evening.

It was some time since they had seen him, and in the interval he had changed a great deal. Just as the flesh had wasted from his bones it had wasted from his manner. . . . Aloof, with glittering eyes, he stared at the company, speaking little, haughtily rebuffing all attempts to draw him into the talk. It was his flouted music, she guessed, working in him, frustrated and corroding; and she recognized the authenticity of the talent by the authenticity of the rage. When he did speak, it was with sneers and bitterness, and the coughing-fits that followed were like defiant cock-crowings. With a herd animosity the others put him in Coventry, patently rallying round Minna as though to protect her from such a guest.

So general a manifestation of dislike must needs include Sophia also, for now she was definitely unpopular among Minna's friends. There was nothing for it but to talk to Guitermann, and she did so, wishing with all her heart that she had never given buns to anyone so capable of resentment, or at any rate that he would not recollect the buns.

"How do you think Minna looks?"

"Badly," said he. "Dulled and stupefied."

Blinking under this, she spoke of country air, Minna's legacy, the project of a visit of inspection.

"I suppose you like the country. Minna would not. An assault of clodhoppers, rural conversation about the culture of beetroot and the swine disease, would be the last blow to her talent. Who would she find to talk to, in the country?"

"Minna's talent is in herself, not in her listeners," she answered.

"Talent!" he exclaimed bitterly.

Hunting her wits for a tolerable subject for conversation she could find not one. So she told him how Caspar, sent to a school, had joined the Gardes Mobiles.

But later in the evening he had sought her out, saying, his manner furious as before, but coloured with concern and a kind of despairing trust,

"Don't let Minna go into the country. It's too dangerous."

"Why? How?"

"The peasants may rise at any moment—a counter-revolution. They are enraged against anyone from Paris, anyone suspected of Liberal ideas. None of us dare say it, but it's true. Here, at any rate, she would have some friends. In the country, none."

"When do you think it will happen, the next outbreak?"

"At any moment, now. Perhaps even while I am still alive."

His youth, grandiose and dramatic, flowered in those words. As he went out it seemed as though his deformity were too great a weight for those threadbare limbs to carry, those wounded lungs to lift. She had seen too many of her tenants' children die in a galloping consumption to have any doubts as to his ending.

From that night she said no more of country pleasures or cheating tenants. Whether she blew from the east or the west, her words had made little impression. A property in Normandy was not so real to Minna as a forest and a heath in Lithuania. Of them she spoke inexhaustibly, able to recall every hour of her childhood.

For now, just when Sophia had trampled out her last illusion of anything to be gained through routine, Dury was actually making his picture of them, a canvas long debated and long postponed. It was easier to paint in summer, he said. Living was cheaper then, it was possible to buy all the paints one needed. The picture, which he persisted in referring to as *Mes Odalisques,* was in truth to be called "A Conversation between Two Women." His design seated them upon the pink sofa, their backs to the window. Sophia must listen, hers was a countenance most characteristic in attention. Minna, to give her something to listen to, must talk.

It was curious to sit there in the charmed circle of his watchfulness, hearing the breeze fluttering the curtains, the living noises of the street reared up to them. There was a kind of precarious immortality in this studied repose, and his painter's aloofness quickened the sense of being for an hour's forever in another world. Minna, inexhaustibly recounting, telling with all her art of incidents grotesque or intimidating, piteous or indecent, might have been a bird singing for all the notice he took of her words; and across her narrative would fall his short commands for the redressing of her head's tilt, the loosening of

Sophia's hands that the course of the narrative had tautened one against the other, his murmured blasphemies, or the thoughtful click of his tongue against the roof of his mouth. What his painting left of him was rudimentary. It was as though one overheard the monologue of a small boy, of an exceedingly stupid and exceedingly self-satisfied small boy, who was spending an afternoon fishing with a bent pin or possibly catching frogs and tearing them in pieces. This scum of words, slowly rising from the simmering of his intent, and Minna's idle noble flow of narrative mixed in Sophia's hearing, and touched as though with a bodily impact her sensations of chill and languor and stiffness.

To sit still and listen—this was a child's part. Towards the end of each sitting a profound self-pity would overcome her, a sentiment of weakness and dependence. Like a religious sentiment, she supposed. The religious, who trust in a God, who lie in his hands and never stir themselves to question the future or combat it, must feel so . . . a shameful and a shameless emotion. But still this meek melancholy, this quietism, would well up in her like the rising of a pure tepid water; and through all the irk of her body her spirit clung, lamenting and satisfied, to these hours of precarious immortality, islanded on the pink sofa.

Out of these sojourns in immortality she would come weakened, even more inept for speech or decisive thinking. Tomorrow, bringing nearer a revolution with all its God-knows-what of what would happen then, would bring another sitting.

Every afternoon Dury lugged off his canvas. They were not to see it, he would have no comments muddying his own view of it. And having dreamed of the finished canvas the dream persisted in Sophia's mind, so that her unscrutinized thoughts beheld it as it had been in the dream: a picture of two swans floating on a pink lake.

It had grown very hot. An acrid dust flew in the streets, drains and gutters stank, windows open on the street level showed summer vistas of tumbled beds, fading salad in basins, women sweating in camisoles. Marketing was no pleasure now. The midsummer richness of the wares was sullied by town conditions into stickiness and greasiness, buyers and sellers looked at each other with the unglossed antagonism of the war to live, or exchanged bad money and bad bargains in a lethargic truce.

There were more crowds in the streets but there was less talking; and the decree against outdoor assemblies kept the people in a dreary purposeless trudging. Through their sullen to-and-fro the sharp squawk and rattle of the Gardes Mobiles, parading to music, cut like a vinegared knife. It was said that in the politer quarters the Gardes were cheered and fêted. Among the workers one needed an extra dose of sentimentality to have any feeling other than annoyance, and the vague dread of ageing or wearied flesh before youth in the mass, for these prancing youngsters.

Twice it seemed to Sophia that she recognized Caspar. And this was likely enough, since Frederick would most probably have deposited him in some Left Bank detachment. But an angry unwillingness kept her from looking too closely, for this was another of Frederick's lucky cannons, and she was in no mood now to appreciate such.

With a stale sense of ignominy she had at length written to Mr. Wilcox, inquiring how her finances stood. Whatever was to befall, lack of money would make it worse. She expected the answer any day, and hoped in her heart that it would not come. Whatever the answer, it must establish her as a fool. A fool to hope anything; a fool not to have written before, and saved herself the discomfort of a needless penury. Above all, a fool to know so little of what had been for so long her own affairs that Frederick could put her, or gull her, into this state.

And he had stolen that five-pound note out of her dressing-case too. To think that there had ever been a time (four months ago, no more) when five pounds was merely a fitting in a dressing-case, like a nail-file or an eyebrow tweezer! Now she hesitated over a twopenny nosegay, thinking how soon the flowers would die, thinking shame to herself for such thoughts. That fancy about the "good old-gentlemanly vice" was bidding fast to grow into a fact, and the return of Minna's useless eating guests made the husbanding of their money even more pressing. At midsummer, she supposed, there should be some rent from Treilles, and midsummer was near, now; but till the money was in Minna's hands (and how soon out of them again?) she must walk by flower-baskets and toyshops. Passing the shop where she had bought the slippers trimmed with tin cupids she shook her head and walked on. But the thought was only a tremble of the mind; her arm chafed by the weight of the basket, the cobbles under foot, the stinks of human living, that poured heavily into the narrow street, took up the chief of her attention. And her first sensation was relief when Madame Goulet said to her,

"I regret that we shall not be able to accept your washing next week.

"We are moving to new premises," she added. "There will be a little interruption."

Staring at the vase on the counter where marguerites had given place to sweet-williams, Sophia felt the earth begin to shake under her feet. There would be a little interruption. She thought what this traffic had meant to her, pride, assertion of performance, a steady prosaic rhythm to rivet together her days.

"You are exhausted. It is the heat," said Madame Goulet firmly. "Will you not wait here a little and repose yourself? It is cool in my parlour—at any rate cooler than in the street."

She opened a door behind the counter and showed Sophia into a minute room, with a waxed floor, walls painted to resemble nut-wood, a horsehair couch, a group of plaster fruit under a glass shade.

In this prim apartment Sophia sat primly, her throbbing hands folded on her lap. This, which she felt as a disaster, must not be thought so. Better to reflect on the cool room, the refreshment of sitting still. The door opened, and Mademoiselle Martin limped in, smelling of starch, carrying a glass of water.

"How is your brother?" asked Sophia.

"He is very grateful to you. He asked me to express his thanks if I should see you."

Damned casual, thought Sophia, downing the instant upleap of her heart. And she said,

"I suppose if you want me to do anything more you will let me know?"

"Yes, you may depend upon it."

The beady timid eyes rested upon her with a queer look of confidence. Mademoiselle Martin appeared to be unconscious of any humiliation to Sophia which such words might impose.

"As though," said Sophia, recounting the interview to Minna, "she also were a glass of pure cold water."

"Yes, you can appreciate that sort of thing better than I. I should find it very difficult to exist without some wine in my water, some tincture of passion or duplicity. It is a flaw in my character, I admit—but there it is. Ah, Sophia! Your laundry would be too Alpine for me. But I envy you that you can be at home on such heights, breathe that air without a shawl over your nose."

"Well, I shall not breathe any more of it, I am afraid. Unless one of them cuts my throat, this is likely to be my last encounter with the Communists.

"And this, too, I owe to you, Minna. There is no end to the extraordinary things you bring out of your horn of plenty."

"It has been worth it?"

She spoke hastily, with a passionate unguarded anxiety. They looked at each other, startled, as though truth had been a lightning in the air.

"Yes, Minna. It has been worth it. . . . So you too think that it is nearly over, that we have reached the time when we can reckon up and say, *It has been worth it?*"

"Sophia, I know no more than anyone else. I only know this feeling of something in the air or under foot, a new day or a disaster. All over Europe, maybe, people are feeling like this. But here's Dury. Now we will sit on our island and be princesses."

"Guitermann's dying," said Dury, setting up his canvas.

"Dead," said Minna, settling into her pose, leaning forward to arrange Sophia's hand.

"I went there this morning, while you were out, Sophia. He moved last week, you know, to a cheaper room after that last quarrel with his parents. It is unusual for Jews to quarrel, the family bond is strong with them. But the elder Guitermanns suddenly had a little stroke of prosperity, an order from some army furnisher to make so many badges, a piece of work any tradesman might do, but by some chance it fell into the hands of old Guitermann, a skilled goldsmith. There was work at last, a great deal of work, and to be done swiftly. They called David to share in it and in the money it would bring. And he refused. He would not work for the army, he said. He had had enough of their trumpets, he had his own music to attend to. There was a bitter quarrel, and David, wrapping himself in a bloodspitting as in a royal mantle, walked out of the place."

"If I can do nothing else, I can paint a cheap brocade and make it look like a cheap brocade. It's those blistered highlights. Go on, Minna."

"To be young, and a genius, and dying, makes people exceedingly kingly. 'He spoke to us like a prince,' the woman said. And she looked back over her shoulder as though she still feared to disturb him. They had two rooms, she and her husband and her children, and David had rented the larger of them. It was small enough. And it looked the smaller for being still crowded with their belongings, a child's go-cart, a ladder, pails and brushes. Her husband was a house-painter, she said. They were hoping to keep these things of his trade in case he found work again.

"The bed took up most of the rest of the room, and she had spread a sheet over the body, and lit a candle. But all round the bed were bloodied rags, the floor was moist and smeary where she had been trying to scrub the blood-stains off the boards. She had shut the window, she said, because of the flies. The room was suffocatingly hot, and smelt like a shambles. And for all her precautions, flies darted over the bed, to and fro, as though death were some sort of magnetic attraction to them, twitching them back, willy-nilly, into its orbit.

"I asked her if he had died alone. She told me, yes. They had heard him, his choking and his death-rattle, but they had not dared to move, they were afraid of waking their baby. It cried so loud, she said. There had been already so many complaints of its cries, and threats to turn them out. On the floor were some sheets of music paper, scrabbled over in pencil, written in every kind of haste. But one could not read them, they were soaked in blood, struck together with blood.

" 'Please look at him,' the woman said. 'I did my best for the poor body, after he was gone.' His hair was singed, he had fallen forward against the candle-flame, I suppose, when the last bleeding began. It gave to that side of his face a curious resemblance to a clown . . . the frizzy top-knot and the estuary of bald scalp beside it. He was like a clown who had whitened his face and forgotten the dab of red on nose and eye-sockets. His expression was snarling and malevolent. For on some faces, Sophia, death descends like a thick snowfall, smoothing every contour, so that we look on the face of the dead as on a landscape made unfamiliar by a fall of snow. But here death had fallen like a scanty rime. She had folded his hands on his breast, and put a shred of dusty palm beneath them. His nails were long, long as a wolf's. It seemed as though they were already sprouting under the impulse of death."

"Sophia, your hair is drooping. Stay still, let Minna put it back for you. Keep your lips like that. They are admirable."

"As I was coming away, I looked at the woman. I saw that she was quite young, five-and-twenty maybe, no older. As I looked, her expression of sympathy and decorum seemed to be snatched off her face. Tears of anger began to stream down her cheeks. 'It is just our luck!' she exclaimed. 'Just our luck that he should move in and die! I told my man that he had paid the rent in advance but he had only paid me one-half of it. Now where am I to get the money? And his blood is all over the floor, I must buy soap to scour it off, and I cannot afford to buy food for my children even. It is our luck all over. Though people come here to die, for us there is nothing but living. We are tough, we cannot die so easily as these artists.' "

Dury looked up.

"I wonder if that's true. I suppose it is. My God, I don't want to die before I've finished this."

"And so I gave her what money I had and came away. I am sorry, Sophia. I ought to have kept it for our own rent, I suppose. I gave her nine francs fifty."

"I began to think we must all be damned," said Sophia. "The way we can endure to hear of these things."

"No sisters of charity flocking to that deathbed," said Dury. "No discriminating philanthropists bringing jellies. Presently, no doubt, we shall see some lover of art bringing round the subscription list for a memorial tablet. Was his music good, Minna?"

"I don't know. I have heard so little of it, only the fragments he played me. And I can't read music in score."

"Sophia's going to faint. We had better break off for a minute or two."

"No, go on! It is only in my mind that I feel faint. I think of all the money I used to have, and what I did with it. New cushions for the pulpit, subscriptions to memorial tablets and Bible Societies."

"When I had money," said Minna, "I gave it away to the poor and to the sick, to artists and beggars and frauds, all in the name of charity. But when I was a child in my father's house I learned some Hebrew, and one of the things I learned was, that in our Hebrew language there was no word for charity. The word I must use, my father said, was Justice. This libertine word, charity! . . . I have used it often enough since, to my shame. But I still sometimes remember what my father taught me. While we cannot give justice, Sophia, it is idle to debate whether or no we have given charity."

"I have heard old Ingelbrecht make the same point," observed Dury.

"Yes, I dare say," answered Minna with gentle pride. "He got it from me."

They were silent. Dury went on painting. Things were not going so well for him now, he grunted, and cursed dejectedly. They were relieved when there was a knock at the door.

"Someone for you, Sophia."

On the landing was Mademoiselle Martin, holding a bandbox. Her face shone with sweat, she had white cotton gloves on her large hands. She gave Sophia a note.

"I am to wait for an answer, Madame."

> *Dear Sophia,* wrote Ingelbrecht in his clear stiff handwriting. *You are a good carrier pigeon, I know, punctual and reliable. I have heard you highly praised. May I ask your long legs to do me this favour? Here are five packets, and I want four of them delivered*

into the hands of the addressees before tomorrow night. They contain tracts, explosive only in the intelligence. As for the fifth packet, I leave it to your wits to scatter the contents about with modesty. Do this on your way back only. The addressed packets are the essential. I am much obliged to you.

Josquin Ingelbrecht.

She crumpled up the note, saw Madamoiselle Martin's beady eyes fix and sharpen. Tearing it to pieces, carefully sifting the shreds from hand to hand, she said in her Mrs. Willoughby of Blandamer voice,

"That will do admirably. I will see to it tomorrow. Do you want the box back?"

"If you please, Madame."

Plotting on a stairhead, she said to herself. Nursing Ingelbrecht's neat packets under her arm, listening to Mademoiselle Martin's uneven footsteps on the stairs and the empty bandbox banging against the rails, she remembered Minna's greeting of the man called Gaston. Here am I, she thought—as gullible as she, for all I know.

The addresses for the packets were on a separate sheet of paper, to be learned by heart, she presumed. It took all Minna's mongrel-dog knowledge of Paris to work out the itinerary, as for the address in La Villette, even Minna had to admit herself baffled.

"I should leave it to the last, if I were you. Work up that way by the address in the rue des Vinaigriers, and then across to the canal to the Cité Lepage, and after that northward. And come back by those sturdy *Dames Réunies.*"

"Who are they?"

"An omnibus. And if you get into any sort of fix, or think you are being followed, remember that the arms of the Church are always open, and that a Christian is safest on his knees. I took part in a full-length funeral once; and I assure you, my grief was an adornment to it. Poor gentleman, they had never suspected him of keeping such a devoted mistress."

"I wish it were you, Minna. You would do it with a great deal more style."

"Would it were!"

Looking back at the house she saw Minna leaning from the balcony, her black hair glittering in the morning sunlight, her large hand waving, and every line of her body expressing an invincible sense of drama.

And I might have taken her after all, she thought, as the omnibus rattled over the cobbles. There was nothing to prevent it, no word of going unaccompanied. With half of her mind she turned back to the rue de la Carabine. But the ticket had been paid for; and when she descended into the boulevard Poissonnière, the sun struck on her with such brutality that she was thankful for the thrifty impulse which had stayed her from haling Minna out for such a day's discomfort.

She had decided to start as early as possible, for the sake of what freshness there might be in the morning air. But there was no freshness, only the same nervous tension which marked every morning now. Those who loitered looked restless, and the walkers hurried. Above the rumble and jangle of the omnibus she had heard the *rappel* beaten, a noise in these days of not much more significance than the chiming of a cuckoo-clock.

Even Minna's sense of drama would have flagged under this. The route so lightly undertaken was another thing under the realism of the midsummer sun. Two packets had been delivered over, one to a frowzy woman in a gunshop, another to the lean proprietor of a lean café. Behind his dusty grove of privet she sat down to rest and drink a glass of tepid beer. Over and over she perused the painted advertisement on the house-front opposite. Walk without Fear, it said. Attach the celebrated metal rings of Beaufoin to your heels and save shoe-leather. Walk without Fear. The air shook with a vehement hot panting, the noise of some heavy machine or other. Through the gap in the privet she could see the clustered garments dangling outside the second-hand clothes shop, and among all the other smells of the street she distinguished their sour taint of dried sweat extorted by the sun. The man of the café leaned in his doorway with looks that bade her begone. She was the wrong sort of customer for him, no doubt of it.

She got up, and joined her footsteps to the other footsteps that lagged by. Like everyone else on these pavements she was down at heel and too heavily clothed for the season.

It was a quarter of tall factories and warehouses, cowed and shabby dwellings. The windows had paper shades, the food exposed for sale was meagre and unenterprising. On stall after stall she noticed the same platters of sliced cooked meats, the same ready-bunched assortments of salad: a head of chicory, a lettuce, six radishes, some spears of spring onions, a sprig of fennel. As though for prison meals, she thought. So much and no more and for everyone the same. *The Institution of Labour*. . . . Somewhere she must have heard that phrase, and now her steps trudged it out on the pavement. Somewhere between prisoners in a jail, paupers in an institution, the workers were pent in the Institution of Labour, to do their stint and get their ration. They could no more escape than grow wings, at a dreary best the best-conducted might hope to become sub-warders over their fellows. Sometimes, as now, the running of the Institution failed: there was a shortage of work and a shortage of food. But that would not break down the walls, within the Institution of Labour they must remain—kick their heels, and starve, and breed on.

What idiocy, what futility, to be carrying revolutionary tracts through these streets! The succession of little grasping shops, butcher, baker, candlestick-maker, butcher, baker, candlestick-maker, the factories like ill-kept barracks, the warrenlike *cités* badged with the spiritless ensigns of family washing, what written word, what thought exploding in the mind, could leaven them? A woman in a gunshop, a man in a café, and between them a mile of mean streets, streets wavering between shabby-sordid and crass-sordid. . . . At least, she had assured herself, Ingelbrecht was not an idealist; but she must revise that opinion now. And it was with something like satisfaction that she took from the receiver of the third packet a mistrusting glare, a word of abuse, a door slammed in her face.

It was not consoling to be told in the rue Furet, La Villette, that Monsieur Georges was out, would not be back until three o'clock at the earliest.

Over the counter, heaped with cheap drugs, ointments for

sores and skin diseases, elixirs for the middle-aged, soothing syrup for infants, the chemist's assistant blinked at her wearily through pale eyelashes. He was pale all over, his voice was pale, his eyes had pink rims. Everything of his physique was noxious and debased, and out of his blinking eyes looked a character of helpless anxious integrity. Scratching his head, stirring his limp straight hair, he repeated,

"No, certainly he will not be back before three. I am very sorry. But it would not do for me to mislead you."

It was a little before noon. The sensible course would be to go back. No woman in her senses would wish to dangle herself in La Villette for three mortal midday hours. Equally, no woman in her senses would perform the journey to La Villette twice in one midsummer day.

I am bound to be a fool anyhow, she said to herself. I will eat something, and pull myself together.

The meal was cheap, gross, highly flavoured. It made her sleepy, and heavier-witted than before. From the cheap restaurant she went to a cheap church, and sat there yawning, too vacant even to open the fifth packet and find out with what doctrines Ingelbrecht proposed to kindle men's minds. While she sat there, two christenings took place. Between the christenings she dawdled round the building, examined the stations of the cross and read a number of obituary cards pinned up on a notice-board. They hung in tattering sheaves, one pinned over another. Death had covered death; few people would come to the church of Our Lady of Perpetual Succour with leisure enough to pray their way through to the bottom-most yellowing pasteboard. The holy water smelled, the church smelled too—the smell of raw new plaster warring with the odour, already antique, of a dirty congregation.

At three she returned to the chemist's shop, where the pale young man, looking pleased, informed her that Monsieur Georges had just come in. Monsieur Georges also looked pleased. His was the first face that day to express anything like vigour. He was a fat little man, middle-aged and jaunty, he apologized for delaying her and offered her a glass of wine, which he handed across the counter. While she drank he talked to her about the elixirs and syrups. They were all traditional remedies, he said, perfectly harmless and perfectly useless.

"My professional hours," said he, "are spent in the vilest cheating and charlatanry. My leisure on the other hand, I lay out to good account." And he winked at her as he refilled her glass.

Revived by the wine, she walked uncomplainingly to the omnibus stop, and watched the horses munching from their nosebags, the driver combing his whiskers and counting over his money. She had been carried some way before she recollected that the fifth packet remained to be distributed, and had been left behind in the church of Our Lady of Perpetual Succour.

Cursing herself and Ingelbrecht, and the perpetual sun, she went back. It was there right enough, but the time was now a quarter past four and Minna would be anxious, and her purse was growing empty. Taking out a hairpin she wasted some time fishing for coins in the collecting-boxes. She had only extracted seven sous, inadequate even as a tip for the cab she meant to take from the Barrier, when a sniffing woman and a talking child entered the church. For exchange, she tore open the last packet, slipped one of the tracts into the rack of pious booklets, and dropped another on the bench outside the church. She spent no time in reading them, she was in a hurry.

In the chemist's shop she explained her predicament, and her poor success at church-robbery. He laughed, and lent her five francs with a gesture that went near to being a chuck under the chin. As she was leaving the shop he whistled her back, come to the door, and looked up the street.

"I thought so!" he exclaimed. "You get to know a trot like that in La Villette. It's a blood-horse. Hi, Carrabas! You give this lady a lift down as far as the Barrier."

The young man addressed as Carrabas was driving a light cart hung with tin-ware. An ancient wild-eyed chestnut was in the shafts.

"Take care of her," said Monsieur Georges fervently. "She's just been robbing Holy Church."

Carrabas flushed to his ears. He seemed unable to speak except to his horse, and as the animal jerked into a trot the clatter of tin-ware seemed to Sophia a sufficient reason to be silent also. However, after about half a mile of swallowing and glancing sideways, he said,

"How far have you to go?"

"Across the river, to the Latin Quarter."

"You'll get there all right," he answered. "Keep round to the west a little, then you'll get through."

"Get through?"

"The fighting has started, you know."

Near the Barrier the streets began to fill up. People stood in their doorways and on the pavement, silent mostly, looking towards Paris. Outside a café she noticed a group of men singing. They sat comfortably behind their table spread with books and dominoes, and sang *Mourir pour la Patrie* with gusto, leaning back in their chairs, opening their lungs, waving their shirt-sleeved arms. Beside them stood a young waiter, patient and furious, his bill-tab in his hand, and a fat dog, tied to the table-leg, barked furiously.

"That sort can sing," observed Carrabas. "They'll burst their tripes, singing!"

At the Barrier he helped her down, apologizing that he could take her no further. And again he told her to keep to the west. Here the street was crowded also, but with a moving crowd. She went with it, towards a noise of firing and the smell of gunpowder. The *rappel* was being beaten hither and thither, a dry bony noise on the stifling air.

The crowd closed about her, thickened, came to a standstill. There was a barricade further along, someone said. Where she stood there was nothing to be seen, but word came back from those in the front, carried from mouth to mouth. Meanwhile the people behind amassed, and pressed forward, and a vacant-faced woman, far gone in pregnancy, kept digging her elbow into Sophia's ribs, and inquiring, "What is it, what is it?"

"Twins, mother," a voice replied. There was a guffaw of laughter, and a bickering. In this heat no one is going to keep his temper for long, thought Sophia, uneasily combating her impulse to beat a way out of the crowd; and it was with a feeling of doing something dangerous that she wriggled and pleaded her way to the right, and escaped into a side street.

She had little idea where she was, and no idea which way to go. But she continued to work westward, guiding herself by the sound of firing and the flux of people in the streets.

After nearly two hours, looking down a side street she recognized the profile of Notre Dame de Lorette. Up the street, howling, and holding his hand to his cheek, ran a boy; and as he passed, she saw there was blood dripping onto his shoulder. She flattened herself against the wall to let him go by. He ran past without seeming to notice her and hurried on, howling still. The street became full of voices, women leaving out of windows to stare and exclaim, walkers suddenly materializing and turning to run in the boy's track.

As far as was possible, she would not allow herself to think, bending all her powers to be an animal, an animal that twists and turns and keeps on its way. But she could not prevent herself from comparing the afternoon of this interminable summer day with the evening of the twenty-third of February. People had talked then, questioning and exclaiming. Everyone had talked, knit together by a common excitement. These crowds were almost silent, if they spoke it was under their breath, bitterly or fearfully. And at a screaming bugle-call a man, a clerk perhaps or a shop assistant, walking a little in front of Sophia, threw up his hand and clasped his forehead, as though the noise had been an agony to him.

As she overtook him he came closer to her, bade her an endearing good-evening, and tried to put his arm round her waist. Looking into his face she saw that his teeth were chattering with terror. And she struck back his hands with fury, as though terror were a plague, and his touch might infect her.

Even here she could hear shots behind her, and the smell of gunpowder hung on the air, pungent and autumnal. But she had outflanked the fighting, and could cross the boulevard des Italiens and be among the streets she knew. The sky had clouded over, a few large drops of rain fell, and the trees along the boulevard stirred their leaves uneasily. She crossed the river. She was on her old track, soon she would be passing below great-aunt Léocadie's windows. The housefronts were shuttered, cautiously impassive. She went up the rue de Grenelle and the noise of fighting roused up again, and the smell of powder.

From the turning into the rue de la Carabine she could see Minna's windows. They stood open, the curtains swayed to and fro. She began to run.

The echo of her feet on the stairs sounded like someone pursuing her, turned into the footsteps of Madame Coton, holding out the key. She unlocked the door and went into the empty room.

On the table was a plate of sandwiches and some wine, a letter addressed to her with an English stamp on it, and a small box of polished walnut, plain and solid. She lifted the lid, saw the blue velvet lining, and the scrolled label saying, J. Watson, Gunsmith, Piccadilly. One of the pistols was gone, and in its cradle lay a folded slip of paper.

She carried it to the window, and read.

My Well-Loved,

You will not blame me that I have gone on. I cannot sit here any longer, in this room full of the echoes of all my speeches about liberty.

Ask for me at the Maison au Four des Brindilles—you remember, that shop where we bought the very good pâté. But you are to eat and drink first.

Minna.

Shaking with fatigue, moving with rigid concentration, she pulled a chair to the table, and poured out a glass of wine. All the time a hollow voice seemed to be prompting her, saying, Now the chair. Now the wine. That's right. Presently the collaborating voice was helping her to change her shoes and put on a wrap, and look to the pistol.

Leaving the house she left the voice behind. "Yet another promenade?" remarked Égisippe Coton. The taunt, and the voice wizened with rancour, gave her the fillip she needed, and blandly she condoled with him that he could not also allow himself a little stroll to see how things were going. One is very possibly safer out of doors, she observed.

For a while that seemed true enough, unless it were for the

risk of breaking one's ankle. Paving-stones and blocks of cobbles had been hacked up at random, and in the half-light it was easy enough to stumble into the gaps that remained.

Out of an alley darted the wood-seller's little girl. Her pallor of town-life, her skinniness of under-nourishment, gave her a resemblance to Augusta, whom neither good air nor good food had forwarded; and she had, too, something of Augusta's elfish decisiveness of diction. Poverty, though, had freed her from any nursery airs. And like a grown woman she greeted Sophia, and stretching upwards, linked arms.

"You are late, Madame Vilobie. You have missed a magnificent spectacle! Such barricades I have never seen before."

Looking more closely at this experienced veteran Sophia saw that she had a patch of plaster on her nose.

"Were you wounded, Armandine?"

"Nothing, nothing," said the child. "A scratch, a graze from a piece of stone sent flying. However, I can say that I have been wounded in the people's defence."

"And the others?"

In her voice of a businesslike bird, Armandine detailed the dead and wounded, the butcher's boy, the pastrycook, the sweep, the wine-merchant's two nephews, and Monsieur Allin, saddler and National Guard.

"They also are with us," she said with a sweep of her hand.

It seemed as though his child knew the defenders of the local barricades as well as she knew her father's clients. These were not disembodied revolutionaries, these men behind the barricades, but the workers of the neighbourhood, figures seen every day. The actual barricades were almost as intimately known to Armandine. In this one was Aunt Zélie's great wardrobe, in that the corn-chandler's bins, in a third cords of wood from Armandine's papa and a great mass of books carried out by an old gentleman whom no one had ever set eyes on previously.

"Look," she exclaimed. "There they are!"

Dark and regular, the barricades traversed the vista of the rue St.-Jacques like waves rolling in upon a lee-shore.

"That is Monsieur Allin's barricade," said the child. "He

came to attack it, but the sweep harangued him, and in a twinkling he was among the defenders. And there, do you see it, is the umbrella of the old gentleman who brought the books. He seems to be a little delicate."

Like a guide finishing his course, Armandine walked away.

Augusta, gloved and wrapped in wool and cherished, might have been like this, Augusta walking staidly intrepid into the waves on Weymouth beach. But convention and riches had made of Augusta a rather dull and didactic child. Frederick had understood her best, calling her The Twopenny Piece. These men behind the barricades had children they loved, wives with whom they were in amity. Unglorified, undisciplined, under the windows of their own homes they walked out to die.

"I have no place here," she said to herself, ashamed to the soul. And her hand fell back from the knocker on the door of the cooked-meats shop. The Maison au Four des Brindilles stood in a quiet by-street near the river, a street of ancient and overhanging houses. The burst of cannonading echoed through it as though from another world.

Cannon! The stature of that sound reared up above the height of the barricades, the minikin height of man. She banged on the door.

"Is Madame Lemuel . . . ?"

The old man had a serious face, large and pale and wrinkled. He trod with the cautious dignity of someone suffering from corns, and on his hand was a wide wedding-ring.

"This way, if you please."

Beyond the kitchen, spotless and orderly, abundant with looped black puddings, casks of brined pork, bunches of herbs and jars of spices, was a woodhouse opening into a small courtyard. Across the courtyard was another back-door, another shed, a room where, in semi-darkness, people were sitting round a table eating and a child whimpered. The shop beyond, shuttered and obscure, smelled of blood; putting out her hand Sophia touched something cold and sticky.

"It is only horse-flesh," said her guide. "Never fear."

She heard a door being unbarred, stepped through it, stood in a street. It was almost as though she had entered another courtyard, so tall was the barricade. She looked for Minna, and in an instant recognized her. And her first impulse was an irresistible impulse to laugh, for Minna was holding a gun.

The impulse to laugh was succeeded by a feeling of acute anxiety when she observed more closely how the weapon was handled. She hurried forward.

"Sophia! You are safe!" exclaimed Minna, and levelled the gun at Sophia's bosom.

"How many people have you killed with that?"

"None! But I have wounded several."

"I can well believe it."

There was a crowd of people, a great noise of conversation. An old man, red-nosed and serious, with military medals pinned on his coat, was tying up a boy's wounded hand. The boy was sitting on the ground, his back against the barricade, tears running down his furious rigid face. An old soldier, three National Guards, several students, artisans, small shopkeepers, many ragged and workless, many women . . . for a moment it seemed to Sophia that a young officer was also among the defenders of the barricade.

"Our prisoner," said Minna.

He was seated on a doorstep, his long thin legs sprawling, on his long thin face a look of bewilderment and dejection. Beside him, and seemingly in charge of him, was a very stout old lady with a hairy chin and a magnificent cap. She was haranguing him, emphatically wagging her head, creasing her double chins. Sophia edged a little nearer and heard her say,

"And that is how one gets piles."

The young officer shut his eyes and swallowed.

The attack which he had led so much too spectacularly ("He came clambering over the barricades, waving a sword, so there was nothing for it but to let him in") had been repulsed. The old man with the medals snorted at this. It was a wretched piece of work, he said, he would have been ashamed to be seen dead in it. It was obvious that he spoke with intent, careful to discourage too much elation among the defenders. At every thud of the cannon he cocked his head, made a wry grimace as though he were trying some bitter flavour on his palate. The cannon, Minna said, was firing from the hospital, the Hôtel Dieu. And she made a joke about pills which had obviously not originated with her.

She had completely assimilated the colour of her surroundings, identifying herself with the barricade, knowing all the news, all the rumours, all the nicknames. It was quite genuine, but slightly overdone, and the effect was as though she were a little tipsy. To Sophia, arriving cold and raw in the midst of this scene already warmed with blood and powder, Minna's demeanour was embarrassing and painful, she could not help feeling that Minna knew everyone behind the barricade much better than she knew her.

"How long have you been here?"

"Three hours."

If I were here as many days, thought Sophia, I should still be out of it. If only there were something for me to do!

As time went on this feeling was augmented by a searching wish that there might be something to eat. And she had her first moment of identification with those around her when the door of the horse-flesh shop opened, and the old man who had let her into the Maison au Four des Brindilles came out, treading with his cautious suffering dignity, and carrying wine and bread and slices of pickled pork.

Then, thinking that these refreshments were for those who had fought, whereas she had done nothing but arrive late, hang about, and look on, she stood back, proud and miserable.

"You look so tired."

Minna was at her elbow with a glass and a hunch of bread and meat.

"Do you know, those are the first words you ever spoke to me?"

"When you came that evening to the rue de la Carabine?"

"Yes."

In the shabby remains of daylight they stared at each other, startled into recognition.

"To arms! To the barricades!"

A barricade to the southward was being attacked. A moment later the noise of firing broke out in the next street.

"They are doing it in style," said the old soldier. "Keep

down, damn you!" he shouted to those who had mounted the barricade and were watching the fighting, and shouting encouragement; and he grabbed the leg of a red-haired boy and hauled him down.

"Oh, but I say! We've got to see how it goes, down there."

"We shall know soon enough. Now listen! If they carry it, it'll be our turn. Wait till they come close. Long shots are no good in this cat-light, nothing but waste of powder. Let them come close, and then give them a real peppering. And don't try any fancy shooting. This is fighting, not target practice. Aim fair and square at their middles."

His bellowing harangue over, he climbed heavily up the barricade, and peered down the street. They listened for his report. He clicked his tongue against the roof of his mouth and climbed down again. Stumping grandly to and fro, he trod on Sophia's foot.

"Hey! Can *you* shoot?"

His voice was so contemptuous that the prisoner vented a sound of protest. Turning her back on this champion, Sophia answered,

"I can load."

"Load, then! Here, Clément, Dujau, Laimable! This lady will load for you.

"As for you, Captain—you'll see some fighting presently, maybe."

The prisoner flinched as though the old man's wrath had caught him a buffet. Then, biting his lip and bridling, he tried to reassert his superior dignity, tossed his head, put on a sneering and haughty expression. The old woman on the camp stool continued her inflexible narrative. She was trudging through a death in child-bed now. If she could keep him an hour or two longer, thought Sophia, she would make mincemeat of him.

It seemed as though they would stand for ever in this smoky dusk, under this confused hubbub of firing and shouting. The echoes rang and rattled through the gully of the narrow street, and a cage of canaries in a window overhead trilled frantically. Suddenly, as though answering the canaries, there was an outburst of shrill cheering.

"Those damned brats!" exclaimed the old soldier. And another voice, snarling and agitated, began to speak of the Gardes Mobiles, trained by the government to savagery like a pack of trained hunting dogs, until a third voice, solid and preemptory, silenced the recital.

The man called Laimable, not turning his head, remarked, "The worst of it is, they ought to be fighting with us."

His tone was philosophical, the flat voice of an intellect, the voice of one accustomed to receive no answers to his statements. There was no answer to this one, either.

The cooked-meat-shop man, having carried in his tray and his bottles, now came out again with a long carving-knife.

"The best I can do," he apologized. "My two boys have taken all the firearms, and everything else they can lay hands on. However, they are making good use of them, no doubt."

Without a pause in her monologue the stout old woman fumbled under her petticoats, produced a chopper, and laid it across her knees.

It seemed that the noise around them constrained them to keep silence. With one accord they moved cautiously, spoke in undertones, coughed under their breaths as though in church. A deepening seriousness pressed on them one and all, and there was scarcely a stir in the common mood when the noise from the barricade down the street changed its tune, was traversed by shrieks and crashes, when the clatter of running feet approached.

Panting and bloodied, a man scrambled up the barricade, was helped over.

"Give me a gun! Mine's jammed."

In a moment Minna had given him hers. There was an unmistakable renunciation in the gesture, and an equally unmistakable triumph in the movement with which she pulled the duelling pistol by J. Watson of Piccadilly, London, from her bosom. Sophia could imagine that melancholy voice remarking with suavity,

"One must be prepared for emergencies."

It was likely to be her last clear impression of Minna, for more runners were being helped over the barricade, and already she was busy loading, comparing with rage the smoothness of Frederick's well-oiled pieces which she had handled in the Blandamer preserves, and the cranky unkempt weapons which must serve now. For we shall all be killed, she said to herself—a purely formal movement of the mind. For hours now, under this imminence of death, the idea of death had been unmeaning, unrealizable. And even when the red-headed boy fell back with a cry and lay struggling beside her she went on loading, knowing that the wetness on her hand was blood exactly as she knew that her legs were cramped with kneeling on cobbles, that her ears were humming like stretched wires, that a cold sweat of excitement had broken out all over her.

But this isolation was no longer an isolation setting her apart from those around her, she was not cased up now in that feeling of being out of it, an anomaly, an intruder. This furious detachment, she had it in common with every other fighter on the barricade. It was the mood of battle.

Bread or Lead. Before long, the ammunition would be running short. This was how one felt when one's children were starving, when there was no more bread in the cupboard, no more milk in the breast. The fighters were lessening too. She had noticed that one particular musket was no longer thrust down to her, and now it fell clattering; and slowly, like an ebb, the body of Laimable drooped from its meditative attitude, the head bowed on one arm, and fell also.

This barricade was not holding out so well as the other, or maybe the time of fighting went more swiftly than the time of waiting. Yet, when the assailants rushed it, the hand-to-hand fighting revived a fierceness that the failing ammunition had belied, and for a minute or two it seemed as though they might be driven back. Then, in the street running parallel, the sound of cannonading burst out, and as though this jarred the rhythm of fighting here, there was a wavering, a pause; and like a swarm of bees the Gardes Mobiles came over, yelling and jeering.

Caspar is one of these, she thought. She was able to think now, there was nothing more she could do. With the certainty of a bad dream, there, when she looked up, was Caspar's profile outlined against the smoky dusk, tilted, just as it had been on those summer evenings at Blandamer House, when he played his guitar, leaning against the balustrade. Lightly he leaped down within a hand's breadth of her, crying *Surrender.*

On the farther side of the barricade a house had been broken into. Trampling steps were heard, shouts and cries. Suddenly the shutters of an upper room were thrown open, and a woman leant out, shrieking with terror, crying that she was going to throw herself down. The gaslight shone out into the street, a livid square of light falling like a trap. She saw Caspar recognize her, and for an instant his face wore a look of sheepish devotion.

"Why, it's Caspar!"

It was Minna's voice, warm, inveterately hospitable. He glanced round. With a howl of rage he sprang forward, thrust with his bayonet, drove it into Minna's breast.

"Drab!" he cried out. "Jewess! This is the end of you."

A hand was clapped on Sophia's shoulder, a voice told her she was a prisoner.

"One moment," she replied, inattentively. With her free arm she pulled out the pistol and cocked it, and fired at Caspar's mouth as though she would have struck that mouth with her hand. Having looked to aim, she looked no further. But she saw the bayonet jerk in Minna's breast, and the blood spurt out.

Even when her hands were caught behind her and tied there, she did not realize that she was a prisoner. Thumped with a musket-butt, kicked and hauled and shouted at, she remained motionless and uncomprehending. And dragged away by force, marching with the other prisoners, she thought she was yet standing by the barricade with Minna lying at her feet.

It was the clatter of the pistol falling from her numbed grasp that roused her. She awoke, looked round to see where she was, and who was with her. They were going by the Hôtel de Cluny. Its windows were lit up, a stretcher was being carried in through the doorway.

"We could have some fun in there."

It was one of the escort who spoke; and they began to quarrel amongst themselves, the blither spirits canvassing the project of hunting through the wounded to see if they could lay hands on any notorious revolutionaries, the duller saying that they had better get rid of this lot first.

"That's easy enough. Shoot them now."

"Excuse me," said a voice, precise and anxious. "Such were not our instructions."

And they were halted, while the dispute continued. In some near-by-belfry churchbells were ringing the tocsin, the peal running its scale backwards, the topmost bell smiting back the ascending jangle.

"Orders are orders," persisted the doctrinaire.

"Quite right!" the old soldier interposed. "Orders are orders, prisoners are shot at dawn. I've been in the army, I know."

While the wrangling continued he added softly,

"Maybe things will have changed again by then."

The boy with the wounded hand looked up.

"Do you think so? Yes, why shouldn't they? Listen! The fighting goes on."

With his bright feverish eyes he stared into the old soldier's face, interrogating it for a look of hope. There was no trace of hope on that bleak countenance, only a great deal of obdurate cunning.

Meanwhile the Gardes Mobiles had taken themselves off into the Hôtel de Cluny. The remaining escort were getting under way, the conscientious National Guard scratching his head, and glancing at the old soldier as though for guidance, when another batch of prisoners came past. This was a very different turnout. The escorting men were regulars, an officer was in charge. With a sigh of relief the doctrinaire shepherded his flock into their wake.

There had been nothing in that moment of revived attention to justify coming to life. Sophia made no further attempts to attend and when they were halted in a courtyard, she sat down on the pavement, leaned against someone's legs, and fell asleep.

When she woke it was morning, the sun already high, the noise of fighting still continuing. She woke with a perfect uncommenting recollection of everything that had happened, and a raging thirst. Others had woken thirsty too. All round her she heard complaints, voices begging for water. Cramped, parched, aching all over, sullen and dull-witted, her only feeling was one of dissatisfaction because there were two facts to which her mind woke unadjusted. One was that it had seemed to her overnight that they had been brought to the courtyard of a massive and stately building; whereas this was no building at all, but the tattered skeleton of a building in demolition, all gaps, and jagged edges, and papery broken walls. The other new aspect of the morning was that her acquaintances of overnight were exchanged for perfect strangers.

She had to look at them several times to make sure of this. They were exactly the same sort of people as those behind the barricade, wearing that general badge of being pale, underfed, shabby, and serious. Here were hands exactly like the hands she had touched, receiving and giving back the guns she loaded—hands scarred and discoloured, with the dirty nails and enlarged dusky knuckles of labour. Here were heads that had gone uncovered in all weathers, the hair strong and coarse like a pelt. There, peering into the world through his dirty spectacles, was just such a timid, short-sighted student as he of overnight, and there was another red-headed boy, and there, tormented with a hiccup, resigned and uncompromising, was Laimable, who had fallen back dead from the barricade.

So powerful was this weaving between the dead of overnight, the living of the morning, that when she recognized Martin she supposed that the Martin she knew must be dead also; and this impression was the stronger since, happening to turn his head in her direction, he looked at her without any alteration of his harsh and thoughtful visage. Yet that peremptory turn of the head, and those adder-coloured eyes, stabbed through her illusion, and she admitted that he, at least, was real and living.

"You are looking for your friends, no doubt?"

It was a rather squeaky voice that made this inquiry, one of those voices which, being used seldom, and diffidently, acquire a false note of patronage. It came from the short-sighted student.

"It is possible that they may be among those who have been shot."

Making conversation, he continued,

"What barricade were you on?"

"Do you know, I cannot remember the name of the street."

"I was on the barricade of the Place Cambrai. Ah! I think it may be our turn now."

Suddenly his hand touched hers. It was impossible to guess, so cold was that hand, whether it sought in that contact to reassure or to be reassured.

"It is curious, isn't it, how clumsily one's mind adapts itself to the thought of death?"

"Very curious, Madame."

They were being shouted to their feet, ranged closely together, as though they were inferior exhibits on the back staging of a flower-show. A sergeant of the Republican Guard reckoned them over with a wagging forefinger. There was one above the reckoning, and with a rapid contemptuous movement of his hand he dismissed him from the group, as though flicking off a grain of dust. The firing squad marched up and fell into position. Behind them an officer walked to and fro, soaping his hands, staring with a vaguely critical glance at the sky.

Suddenly he pricked up his ears, became animated, came down from the heavens to the earth.

"What's that? What's that?"

"Wants a priest, Sir. Wants to make his confession."

"Certainly! Certainly! A very edifying desire. I could only wish that more of these miserable wretches had such an impulse. Fetch a priest at once."

And advancing on the religious young man who, already isolated from his fellows by this movement of piety, was now in tears, the officer remarked with a noble blitheness,

"Quite right, my poor young fellow! Such a wish I will always grant with pleasure. We do not combat against souls, quite the contrary.

"Stand at ease," he added, to the firing squad. And crossing himself withdrew, to walk to and fro and consider the heavens once again.

A very awkward pause ensued. The religious young man continued to weep, those on either side of him drew away as much as they could, somebody whistled softly, someone else gave a disapproving cough. Sophia could hear the student beside her grinding his teeth.

Slowly, his acrid voice most skilfully modulated to the tone of one who, out of courtesy only, seems to be persuading others to an opinion which he knows they hold already, Martin began to speak.

"Someone calls for a priest; and immediately, at this cautious provision for another life, this invocation of eternity, we, who have so little of this life left to us, feel any prolongation of it as an intolerable burden. That seems odd, does it not? Unreasonable, to feel so acutely about so small a fret. If we were to revolt against living, we might well have done so earlier. Our lives have been bitter enough, joyless, imperilled, ignominious, the lives of working-people. We have laboured, and never tasted the fruits of our labours. If we have loved, that love has only compelled us to a more anxious hate. The married man, the man who loves his wife and children, in our class that one love cuts him off from the love of his kind. He sees in his fellows only enemies and supplanters, rivals who may do him out of a job, outbid him with a lower wage, steal the bread from the mouths of his children.

"How often we have declared that our lives were intolerable! How much more often, not even troubled to declare it! And yet, having endured such lives, we feel now that it is beyond the resistance of our nerves to endure the delay of five minutes while a priest is sent for. Here we stand, as in our old days we have often enough wished to stand—idle for once, able to stand about in the sun as though it were a holiday. Here we stand as we have wished often enough, too, to stand—on the brink of the grave, our labour and mistrust and weariness almost at an end.

"But after all, what is this five minutes' burden? The weight of a husk, of a dead leaf. For our lives are over. What purpose we had—and we had, many of us, a purpose—is taken out of our hands. What we had to do and to say, is said and done. The world is with others now, and our purpose in other hands. And so this weight of time upon us, it is only the weight of a husk, of the dry wisp that remains and withers after the fruit has been gathered, or the seed fallen into the ground. It is no more substantial than that. And really it seems to me that we ought to bear it with more patience."

He shook his head, a gentle rebuke. Then his bright eyes perused the faces of the firing squad, and he continued,

"But that is how this delay affects *us.* For you, who are here to execute us, it is probably more tedious, certainly more embarrassing. For this break in the common routine lets in a draught of cold air, it gives an inconvenient leisure in which to reflect on this odd business of killing one's fellow-men, one's countrymen, and people of the same class as oneself, at a word of command. For after all, you and we have much more in common than you and your officer, you and the ruling class whose orders your officer orders you to carry out. That ruling class—you would not marry their daughters, sit at their table. You and they, are different nations. And if you reflect on it, you will see that you and they are constantly at war with each other, and have been during all your lives and the lives of your forefathers. But as it is a war in which, so far, they have always won, you have failed to notice that it is a war.

"And here we wait, face to face, people of the same class, fellow-combatants in this profound war in which, so far, we have never gained a victory—waiting for that word of command at which you kill us. Not that I speak against words of command, to be able to carry out an order is admirable and essential—provided that the order does not come from the enemy. But as things are—no! And it seems to me, a prisoner, that you are pretty much prisoners yourselves, and likely, sooner or later, to die very much as we are going to die—blown to bits because someone of the ruling class has ordered it. You are disciplined and courageous prisoners, I grant it. But we have a boast too in our ragged regiment, and it seems to me better than yours. We know what we are dying for, we have fought and will die at our own word of command, not the enemy's."

The priest had been brought, and Martin fell silent, retiring, as the defending counsel might, to listen impassively to the speech of the prosecuting counsel. Professional as the lick of a mother-cat's tongue the absolution was given, and the officer, hovering in the background, crossed himself more and more devoutly, soaped his hands in an increasing ecstasy of sentiment and grand self-approbation.

It was over, this satisfying interlude, the soul was saved, and the order to prepare given. Suddenly his eye lighted upon Sophia.

"I cannot consent to the death of a woman."

"Death of a woman!" she cried out furiously. "Death of a woman! And how many women are dead already, and how many more will be, with your consent and complaisance? Dead in besieged towns, and towns taken by storm. Dead in insurrections and massacres. Dead of starvation, dead of the cholera that follows starvation, dead in childbed, dead in the workhouse and the hospital for venereal diseases. You are not the man to boggle at the death of a woman."

It seemed to her, and she was glad, that she had screamed this out like a virago of the streets.

But with a bow he reasserted,

"I cannot consent to the death *of a lady.*"

Bitterly humiliated, she found herself taken out of the rank of the doomed. As she stumbled forward the student leaned after her.

"I am to tell you that Martin feels great satisfaction to think you will remain alive."

While they were untying her hands she heard the words of command, and the volley. Then the priest was at her side, saying something about mercies and thankfulness, and the dangerous state of the streets. She ran out of the courtyard, not glancing behind her.

She was her own creature again—flapped back into the farewelled world, to fend for herself, sink or swim.

Martin had not much to congratulate himself upon that she was still alive. Never was there a woman with less heart to live. And maybe I shall be killed yet, she said to herself as a bullet went past her. But there was no conviction in the words. No life so charmed as the life that would be laid down. Creaky doors hang longest.

Probably I shall live to a profound old age. And people will say to me, "Do you know, old Mrs. Willoughby went through the Revolution of '48 in Paris?" And someone else will answer, "How extraordinary! One would never think it."

With a sleep-walking obstinacy her body was taking her back to the barricade. Murderers go back. And if it comes to that, I may be said to have murdered Caspar. "Do you know, in the year '48 old Mrs. Willoughby murdered her uncle's illegitimate son—a boy of fifteen, a poor stupid blackamoor who worshipped the ground she trod on?" "No, really? One would never think it." "Such a dull old woman. Rather cold-hearted, don't you think?" This icy pain in her bosom, this pain of a heart becolded, it would go on and on, she supposed, the counterpart to that flowering crimson on Minna's white muslin gown, that flowering of her warm and generous blood.

It was difficult to get back. Where there was not fighting, there was ruin—houses gutted, streets impassable. Crowds of people had settled upon the ruins, like blue-bottles. She could hear their buzzing voices, their crawling exploring footsteps. People thrust their heads through broken windows, recounting what they had found within, holding out a bloodied rag, a musket, a broken chamberpot, as testimony.

She flinched aside from these, wary as a hunted animal. These carrion sightseers, they might settle on her if she gave them the chance.

There was the place she sought, and there, too, another crawling inspecting crowd. She tried to drive herself forward, began to sicken and tremble, could not go on. Then she remembered the quiet by-street, the stone-hooded door which had let her in. She made her way back, and found the narrow turning. Above a high stone wall a tree, an aspen, whispered and sighed. Paris was full of trees—all those May-time trees which had waved their vivid greeting to her happiness. And actually she must have seen the aspen on the day when they walked together down the narrow by-street and found the unexpected shop with its romantic name of an old-fashioned provinciality, and bought that remarkably good potted hare; but happy and companioned, she had ignored the aspen tree, sighing then as it sighed now, for from the moment the leaves put out the tree utters its whispering plaint. She had not noticed the tree till now.

She reached the stone-hooded porch. The door had been broken, and roughly boarded up. Through the gaps in the boarding she could discern the dusky shop, dishevelled and pillaged. She sat down on the step and buried her face in her hands.

It was nothing out of the way to see a woman in despair. She heard a child's trotting step go by, never pausing, and heavier footsteps went by too, and did not pause either. Yet when at last a heavy and slippered treading stopped beside her, she thought it better to be left alone, and resolutely hid her face.

The slippers shuffled as their wearer eased her weight from one leg to another. Sometimes a staybone creaked, petticoats dragged over the cobbles. With these slight movements a smell detached itself, a humble smell, mixed of oil, and yellow soap, and garlic, and calico. At last, sullenly enough, she raised her head, and looked into the face of the stout old woman who had sat on a camp stool haranguing the young officer.

"There!"

Her voice was a sort of soft rumble, her expression compassionate. With her hands folded over her stomach she stood slowly shaking her head, easing her weight from one leg to another.

"I thought it was you. You aren't the sort of person one is mistaken about. Well, we didn't think it would go like this, did we?"

A sort of cloud, a look of more immediate, more compassionate concern, crossed her face.

"I suppose you've come back about that other poor lady. You were friends, I reckon."

Minna dead. *On some faces, Sophia, death falls like a fall of snow.* Minna sitting up in bed, weeping and munching biscuits. Minna dead.

"Where—"

"She's not here now, my dear."

"What!"

This lance-thrust of hope jerked her to her feet, sent the echo of her voice, hoarse and shrieking, down the alley.

"She's dead, my dear. Don't let yourself think otherwise. Her body's gone, but she was dead for certain sure before that. I saw her with my living eyes, and I wouldn't deceive you."

It was as though she were proffering a comfort, the way she insisted that Minna was dead.

Afterwards, sitting on a small chair in a very small room, and looking at Madame Guy's enormous bed, Sophia began to think that for all her kindness the old woman was not to be trusted;

that for all her protestations she knew, and would conceal, that Minna was still alive.

Instantly she began to tremble again, to drown in an icy faintness. For having been so sure of dying, now to return to life and uncertainty was an agony like the bodily agony of the thawing-out of a frostbitten limb. "And I shan't come back till I hear you having a good cry," the old woman had said, "for that's what you need." Not a tear had come. But for all that Madame Guy presently walked in, her survivor's gregariousness too strong for her good resolutions. I will let her talk, thought Sophia. She's the sort that lets out the truth by accident.

Watchful and antagonized, she listened to the old woman's babble, that flowed on innocent as a brook. But just as a brook may flow, innocent and tinkling, and through the limpidity of its waters one may see on the bed of the stream broken tins, a foul old boot, the jawbone of a dead animal, so under Madame Guy's guileless chatter was death, misery, and exploitation. As she said, she had seen a lot of trouble in her time.

"And it's a terrible thing, you know, to see your good neighbours killed and chopped about, or taken off to prison to be transported maybe. Particularly at my time of life. For though new families may move in—you may be sure of that, for as Jesus said, The poor you shall have always with you, and living in a poor neighbourhood like this, I can vouch for the truth of it—I shan't be able to feel the same interest in them, I'm too old now to make new friends.

"And another thing I can't get over, is taking those boys and teaching them to act like so many young demons. When I saw them scrambling over the barricade last night like wicked monkeys it came over me like a thunder-clap that the rich have no mortal right or justice to turn boys into demons just because boys are poor and plentiful. Your poor friend, too, dead and gone! I could see she was a kind-hearted lady. Stuck through by one of them, wasn't she?"

"I tried to kill him. Did I?"

"I can't tell you, my dear. I was running, by then. And don't my legs know it this morning? But I dare say you did. They carried off several of their dead, so I hear. They didn't carry off our dead, though. Left the poor bodies to lie in the street till their own folk came and found them."

"Where is her body, then?"

"They took it, they took it—maybe because she was a lady. Now, my dear, don't you go and get it into your head that she is still alive. She was dead before they took her, I can swear to it, I saw her lying dead with my own eyes."

"But you were running away. . . . Why do you lie to me like this? She is alive and you know it."

Madame Guy turned pale. Tears began to run down her large face.

"Oh, this world of misery! One can do nothing to better it."

That was all she would say, offering her great wet countenance to Sophia's furious questions as to a succession of blows. At last she turned and walked out of the room.

"You shan't get away from me without an answer."

Madame Guy walked on, walked into the courtyard at the back of the house, and through it, and knocked softly on a door.

"Monsieur Guillaume, Monsieur Guillaume! It's me, it's the old Virginie."

The door opened a very little. They went in. There was the cooked-meat-shop man, with his head bandaged. He was covered with cobwebs and dirt, as though he had been hiding in a cellar.

"Monsieur Guillaume, this lady—you remember her—has come back asking for her friend. For her friend who was killed. I tell her and I tell her, but she won't believe me. You, you tell her that the lady was certainly dead."

"I assure you, she was dead."

There was a heavy groan from Madame Guy. On his lips it became so palpably a lie.

"Aha! They are lying to you just as they lied to me! She was alive enough when they carried her off, alive enough to cry out with pain, for I heard her. They are sparing your feelings, that's all."

It was a woman's voice, young, speaking in a tone of such imperious despair that it seemed to Sophia that it might well have been her own voice speaking.

"She was alive, right enough! She was alive, for I heard her scream as they hauled her up from the ground where she lay. But whether she's alive now, that's another matter. For maybe they grew tired of pulling her along, and knocked her over the head like a dog. Or threw her into the river. Or sabred her, as they did that good Ingelbrecht. But dead or alive, they took her and they've got her. And if she's still alive, then God help her, I say, for then she's herded into some barracks, or some prison, or some cellar, yes, with hundreds of others, mad with thirst, mad with pain, suffocating in this heat, or else down in the vaults below the river level, with the water rising, the filthy stagnant water, and the rats galloping overhead, and . . ."

"Mathilde!" exclaimed the old man imploringly.

"She is my daughter-in-law," he said. "She is half distracted, poor creature. For my son is missing since yesterday, and we fear he may have been taken prisoner. And now she has heard these rumours. There are already these rumours. They spring up, they are everywhere, one cannot prove or disprove them. . . ."

"One cannot prove them?" She came forward, clapping her hands together, taut as a lightning-flash. "One cannot prove them? But if one has seen these things happening, if one has stood outside a building and heard within the shrieking and the shooting?—If one has seen the cobbles spattered with blood, covered, with bits of bone as though bottles had been broken there, as it is in the rue des Mathurins, where they shot the twenty-six prisoners?—One cannot prove these rumours? And if they are only rumours, why do you hide in the cellar?"

She beat her hands together, and stared at them, contemptuously.

"What else could I do?" asked Madame Guy. "Knowing all this, how could I have the heart to tell you she was alive when, after all, it is possible that she is dead?"

"Come with me. Show me where to look for her."

She saw them hang back. After all, it was not their affair. With a last effort of the mind she admitted the light of reason, viewed herself insignificant and powerless, one straw among the thousand straws that danced in the grip of the whirlpool. She sat down on a bench by the door and said humbly,

"Will you keep me a little longer? I can't go on. I am at my wits' end."

For three days she lay in Madame Guy's great bed, awake, and sensible, but powerless to direct her will into her body. She would put out her hand, as she thought, to lift the glass of water by the bedside, and see it instead move wanderingly to and fro, paw at this and that, and fall on the coverlet again. With a perfect intention of what to say, other words would impose themselves upon her tongue; and an hour afterwards, carefully pondering as to how and where the speech failed of its aim, she would realize that instead of asking Madame Guy if there were any news of Mathilde's husband, she had asked what time the chimney sweep might be expected. Every night Madame Guy, her head tied up in a bandanna, would climb into the bed beside her, and lie there, a warm mountain, remote in slumber.

On the morning of the twenty-seventh, body and will came together again. She got up, and made the bed, and went into the kitchen to say good-bye to Madame Guy.

"Are you going to look for your friend?"

"Yes."

"It is better that you should not go alone. As a matter of fact, while you were ill, we thought of this. And Monsieur Guillaume has found a very suitable person who will accompany you—a Monsieur Paille, a notary."

"There is one thing I must warn you of," said Monsieur Paille. "You have been ill, I understand, you have not been in the streets since the first days. You will find a great change of temper since, then, a very great change of temper. There is no sympathy now for the insurrection. I feel it my duty to prepare you for this."

He seemed to apprehend that she would be a dangerously demonstrative companion. But by the end of their search she admired him the more for this lack of courage, since it made the courage he had so much more remarkable. He had prepared a list of all the places where inquiries might be made; and as they went from one rebuff to another, and entry after entry was crossed off in pencil, he remained dry and unflustered and dutiful; and though at every inquiry it was quite clear that no one in authority cared to answer, or indeed, was capable of answering, he renewed the same persuasive tones, and even remodelled his phrases from time to time, as though he feared they might pall on her.

His mood, his moderate unenthusiastic stoicism, still tinctured hers as she walked up the rue de la Carabine. Madame Coton came forward from the lodge, carrying a new piece of knitting which was already more than half finished. No doubt she had added on many more rows to her ruminating hatred also, but that she kept to herself.

"Ah! It is Madame Willoughby. There is someone waiting for you upstairs."

Who could be waiting for her, who was there left to wait for her? Not Minna. It could not be Minna. She allowed her fatigue to go as slowly as it pleased up the winding stairs, neither hastened nor hesitated at the door.

"Sophia, what a joy, what a relief! . . . My poor child, I never thought I should see you looking like this."

In that shocked cry, in that wondering abhorring glance, Léocadie was for a moment perfectly genuine.

"On the contrary, I think you should congratulate me that I have been through these last few days and retained not only my head, but my bonnet."

"I have not even glanced at your clothes, my dear. But to see you looking so tired, so strained, so pale. . . ."

"So old, so dirty. . . ."

"Goes to my heart," continued Léocadie. "Ah, Sophia, I cannot express how anxious I have been, how often I have reproached myself for submitting to this estrangement between us. For the last three days I have come here, sat here waiting for you. That odious good woman downstairs is growing quite accustomed to me."

"I'm afraid you must have been very uncomfortable."

"I do not wonder that you speak coldly, after all that you have been through. You are like me in that. I have always found that catastrophes leave me positively frigid. But where have you been ever since?"

"Ever since when, Great-Aunt Léocadie?"

"No, there is no need to spare my feelings. I have had four

days, my child, in which to accustom myself to the idea of you being lined up for execution. I still do not quite understand by what providence you escaped."

"Because I had been brought up as a lady."

"Thank God!" she exclaimed devoutly.

"But now it is my turn not quite to understand. How did you come to hear of this?"

"Through Père Hyacinthe. The priest who was fetched for that unfortunate misguided young man described to him this lady, so tall and distinguished, so astonishing an object among that crew. He was immensely struck by you, described you with such detail that Père Hyacinthe recognized you immediately. Especially since he noticed that you had a slight, a very slight English accent. And ever since then we have been moving heaven and earth to find you. Poor Père Hyacinthe! He was immensely concerned about you, almost as concerned as I was."

"And was poor Frederick also immensely concerned about me?"

"Poor Frederick, my dear Sophia, poor Frederick . . . he is certainly in a very perturbed state. But at this moment he is not in Paris. A certain Irish lady, a Mrs. Kelly, very beautiful, I believe, and immensely witty, became so agitated at the prospect of being killed in her bed that she left Paris. And Frederick went with her."

With a flush of delight on her withered cheeks, with her eyes dancing and her lips pursed, she gazed at Sophia in an ecstasy of amusement and serene ill-nature.

"Ah, Sophie, what a pleasure to hear you laugh again! You admirable creature, I can forgive you all your vagaries for such a laugh, so candid, so free from affectation. And seriously, my love, I feel I may congratulate you on being—how shall I put it?—on being again released from a bad bargain. For you know perfectly well that I have never considered Frederick fit to black your shoes."

"Yes. I have suspected you felt like that."

"Moreover," continued great-aunt Léocadie smoothly, "I congratulate myself. For now I think you will forget all this shocking business about money, and allow me the pleasure of being both your bank and your hotel. I have always looked on you as a daughter, you know. Except that I have never found you tedious."

"I think I should be very glad of some money. But if you give it to me, you must give it to an ingrate. For I cannot possibly return to the Place Bellechasse, or to anything like my old manner of living."

"Nonsense, my dear. You are overwrought, you see things in an exaggerated light. A little soap and water, if you will let me be so frank, a visit to the hairdresser and to the dressmaker, and you can return to the Place Bellechasse without a scruple."

"No."

"And why not?"

"I have changed my ideas. I do not think as I did."

"Now, my dear Sophie, do not become a prig just because you have been a revolutionary. I have not said, I shall not say, one word about your ideas. Think exactly as you please. Add only this to your thinking: the possibility that other people may even think a little as you do. For myself, I am perfectly disgusted with the spirit shown by some people. Only today I had that upstart Eugénie de Morin assuring me that four hundred criminals have been shot daily in the Luxembourg gardens. Four hundred criminals! Forty misguided working-men, more likely. I detest this fouling of our own nest. It is not patriotic. It is not French. For me, I am heartily sorry for the poor fellows."

"Yes, I am sure you would feel sorry for them, after they had been shot. Death is always an ingratiating act, and we could manage to agree quite nicely over the dead. But we should still disagree over the living."

"For what reason?"

"For one reason, the conditions under which you are prepared to let them live."

"There you go, my poor child, flying away after another fallacy. Naturally, I do not say that we can run in and out of each other's houses like brothers and sisters. But I recognize that we are all the children of one Father. And since I had the advantage of being one of a large family, an advantage so unfortunately denied to you, I can also recognize that in every family some will be more able, some more beautiful, some more fortunate than others. Meanwhile, if I am one of the more fortunate, I perform my obligations, I do what I can for the less fortunate. And I count myself particularly fortunate, particularly obliged to a universal Father, that I happen to be born of a family which has always honoured such obligations. When my dear father lost his estates in 1792 his first cry was, 'Now I can do nothing more for my poor peasants!' "

"But his peasants were poor?"

"Naturally. It is the order of the universe. And let me tell you —I am an old woman, I permit myself to speak my mind—that it is the people of my way of thinking who do most for the poor. While people like your new friends are making indignant speeches about the wickedness of a society in which Madame Dupont lies freezing to death in an attic, people like me, without making any speeches whatever, see to it that she is given a good load of firing."

"Unfortunately, your system does not relieve Madame Dupont from the anxiety of wondering how she will keep warm when your load of firing is burned up."

"It is not impossible that I may send her another load. And in any case, I assure you she does not wonder. It is people like you and me, Sophie, who have never done a day's work in our lives, who wonder, and meditate on society, and ask ourselves what good we can do in the world. But I won't argue with you about these things. I have no arguments, no theories. All this while I have been hobbling along on what I could recall of your own arguments, when we used to discuss your tenants at Blandamer. There! That was a pretty little rap, wasn't it? But seriously, my Sophie, on this matter I have no arguments, no theories. I only know the teaching of religion, I hear only the dictates of my heart. And where you are concerned, my religion tells me to clothe the naked, relieve the destitute. And my heart . . . My dearest child, you will come with an old woman?"

"I will see you home. Then I shall return here."

Great-aunt Léocadie sighed, rose nimbly, gave her a tranquil, a philosophic embrace. On the threshold she turned, surveyed Sophia from head to foot.

"No, my dear. On second thoughts, I refuse your escort. You look too tired."

And too shabby.

Ah, here in this empty room where she had felt such impassioned happiness, such freedom, such release, she was already feeling exactly as she had felt before she loved Minna, and wrapping herself as of old in that coward's comfort of irony, of cautious disillusionment! How soon her blood had run cold, how ready she was to slink back into ignominy of thought, ignominy of feeling! And probably only the pleasure of disagreeing, the pique of being thought shabby and deplorable, had kept her from a return to the Place Bellechasse. She looked round her, dragging her gaze over the empty, the soiled and forlorn apartment. There was the wine that Minna had left for her, the slippers she had tossed off, sprawling, one here, one there, and on the table where she had thrown it down and forgotten it, the fifth of the packets which Ingelbrecht (yes, he was dead too) had entrusted to her. She took up one of the tracts, fingered the cheap paper, sniffed the heavy odour of the printer's ink, began to read.

A spectre is haunting Europe—the spectre of Communism. All the powers of old Europe have entered into a holy alliance to exorcize this spectre: Pope and Czar, Metternich and Guizot, French Radicals and German police-spies.

Where is the party in opposition that has not been decried as communistic by its opponents in power? Where the Opposition that has not hurled back the branding reproach of Communism, against the more advanced opposition parties, as well as against its reactionary adversaries?

Two things result from this fact:

Communism is already acknowledged by all European Powers to be itself a power.

It is high time that Communists should openly, in the face of the whole world, publish their views, their aims, their tendencies, and meet this nursery tale of the spectre of Communism with a manifesto of the Party itself.

She seated herself; and leaning her elbows on the table, and sinking her head in her hands, went on reading, obdurately attentive and by degrees absorbed.

THE CORNER THAT HELD THEM

To Valentine Ackland

"For neither did the corner that held them keep them from fear."
—Solomon 17:4

CONTENTS

I.	Orate Pro Anima	569
II.	The Tuft of Wormwood *(April 1349–July 1351)*	589
III.	Prioress Alicia *(August 1351–October 1357)*	619
IV.	The Spire *(November 1357–May 1360)*	653
V.	The Lay of Mamillion *(June 1360)*	689
VI.	Prioress Johanna *(July 1360–January 1368)*	703
VII.	Prioress Matilda *(February 1368–December 1373)*	714
VIII.	Saint Leonard, Patron of Prisoners *(January 1374–June 1374)*	729
IX.	The Fish-Pond *(July 1374–September 1374)*	741
X.	Triste Loysir *(October 1374–May 1377)*	766
XI.	A Sacrifice to Woden *(June 1377–January 1380)*	799
XII.	A Candlemas Cuckoo *(February 1380)*	825
XIII.	A Green Staff *(March 1380–June 1381)*	853
XIV.	Prioress Margaret *(July 1381–March 1382)*	871

I. ORATE PRO ANIMA

Alianor de Retteville lay on her bed and looked at Giles who was her lover. She did not speak. She had nothing to say. He did not speak either. They were not alone, for in a corner of the room an old woman sat spinning, but she was no more than the bump and purr of her wheel. It was summer, and late afternoon. The rain fell and birds were singing; they had their summer voices, loud and guttural. The rain had come unobtrusively, breaking up a long spell of drought. For leagues and leagues around it was falling on the oak woods, dripping from leaf to leaf and taking a long time, because the foliage was so thick, to reach the ground. It would be pleasurable, Alianor thought, to lie naked in the oak woods now, feeling the rain on her skin. Each drop would be a small separate pleasure. But only the pigs and a few foresters were in the woods, creatures whose skin has little sensitivity.

It is going to thunder, thought Giles, noticing how dusky the room had grown and seeing the leaden hue of the sky above the vivid green of the oak woods, a narrow picture in the window that because of the heat was unscreened. Instead of the thunder which he expected to hear a wood-dove began to croon. He closed his eyes and stretched and fell asleep again.

They were both sleeping when the old woman jumped up from her wheel and hobbled toward the bed, softly calling on them to waken. A moment later the spinning-wheel was knocked over as the door was forced open, and Brian de Retteville and his two cousins, Piers and Richard, burst in. Giles awoke and saw the old woman at the bedside holding out his sword. She proffered it blade toward him, poor old fool, and in snatching it he cut his hand. That was the first bloodshed. Immediately the three were upon him. He fought, not to defend himself, there was no hope of that, but to die fighting and quickly.

After the first start of waking Alianor did not move. Recumbent, stiffening in the posture of her sleep, she watched her lover being butchered. What would have been the use of moving? She could not save Giles and in a little while she would be dead herself. So she stayed as she was, the braid of hair lying across her breast, her long arms and narrow hands spread out on either side as she had laid them for coolness, for the air, cooled with rain, to refresh her ribs and flanks. Even her seaweed-coloured eyes were motionless, attentively watching her lover's death.

It was this immobility which saved her life. Turning to the bedside, Brian de Retteville supposed that now he would kill the woman too. But seeing her lie there, so calm, so arrogantly still, his anger was arrested by the horror a man feels at a woman's immodest individuality. He began to call his wife whore and strumpet. The impulse to kill her was overwhelmed in a flood of reviling, and only emerged later in kicks and blows.

Meanwhile the two cousins were dragging Giles' body toward the stairhead. The old woman reproached them for their unchristianity, saying in her rasping dialect that they should show pity for the dead even if they had none for the living. Looking down on the young man's bloodied face, which seemed to express an indignant and slightly supercilious astonishment, she crossed herself and began to pray. He had given her many presents and joked with her. It was a sorry thought that now for lack of a little grace of time and a priest he was almost certainly damned.

Piers and Richard were in no mood to stomach pious reproaches just then, being excited with bloodshed and embarrassed by Brian's stockishness and Alianor naked on the bed. Bundling the old woman up between them, they tossed her downstairs.

"So much for you, Dame Bawd!"

There was no reply. Peering down, they saw that she lay at the turn of the stair, her head wried to one side, a thin vomit trailing between her lips. She was dying, and they felt relieved, and as if the situation had been bettered. Even if that oaf Brian could not follow the example, an example had been set.

That evening the three men got extremely drunk. The house rang with their brawls. Alianor, listlessly stirring to and fro, trying to find some attitude in which she could forget the pain of her bruises, heard the cousins telling Brian what they thought of him, and Brian shouting out that he knew how to manage his wife, it was no business of theirs.

"Since you've left the slut alive," hiccuped Richard, "you'll have to send her to some nunnery."

"I'll do what I'll do," Brian roared.

He won't do much, she thought. There will be no nunnery, for he will never part from my money. If I had the energy I could soon cuckold him again and serve him right. But remembering Giles and his love and how she had loved him, and how deeply they had embraced and how little they had spoken, it seemed to her that all possibility of love was over, that any other love she might entertain would be flawed with deliberation, and specious; and she wept silently, biting her hair to prevent herself from crying out.

Her forecast was right. Beyond some more outbursts of temper, and dismissing most of the servants, Brian did no more. Life went on in the former pattern. Brian rode out to hunt, the horns squawking through the oak woods. Within doors the long afternoons were silent as ever except for the buzz of the lazy autumn flies and the bump and purr of an old woman's spinning-wheel: only it was a different old woman, and there was no lover. By Christmas Brian had squared matters with his self-respect. If he had omitted to kill his wife it was because such a wife was not worth the trouble of killing: a sensible man does not take women so seriously. The sense of ignominy which might have fretted him he sublimated by seeing the funny side of his misadventure. With roars of laughter he entertained company by recounting how he had sneaked home to find Giles and Alianor snuggling. A rude awakening . . . God's blood, how chop-fallen they had looked! At dinner, at supper, the story was repeated till in the end even the sturdiest senses of humour found it tedious.

And so for another ten years they lived together, Brian countering all suggestions that he should take the cross in defence of the Holy Sepulchre by the plea that he must stay at home to keep an eye on Alianor's virtue; and he would recount again the tale of that summer afternoon to anyone unwary enough not to get away in time. In summer the woods were green, and full of flies and deep shadows, and the wolves lived quietly, the she-wolves bringing on their cubs from the teat to rabbits and badgers. In winter they gathered into packs and ravaged the open country night after night. In snowy seasons their large footprints showed how they moved in companies, where the scouts had gone out from the main pack, and how cunningly they had skirted the wolf-traps; or the blurring of footprints told how a carcass had been dragged back to the outskirts of the wood where it could be eaten in privacy. All night their voices rose and fell, sharpening into quarrels like the voices of men. So time went on, every year a little more draggingly, as though time itself were growing middle-aged. Alianor bore two more children, both girls. Then it was time to find a bride for Gilbert, the eldest son. Aged ten, she came to live with her new parents. She was a high-bred hoyden, wealthy, frank, hating all music except the sound of the horn—a daughter-in-law after Brian's own heart. Once again Alianor was with child, and unwontedly timid, oppressed by the girl's hearty, careless curiosity and pebble gaze. And in this childbed she died, having given birth to a large dead boy.

What followed astonished everyone—perhaps even Brian himself, who had become the astonishment. Whether it was he dreaded Alianor's ghost, or whether in some dull crevice of his heart he still loved the woman who had once dishonoured and always despised him, or whether her death released him from the bondage of feeling and acting like a dolt, no one could say; but suddenly he was a different man. Alianor's funeral was a nine days' wonder. She lay unburied for a fortnight while the preparations were heaped up; and because there were few serfs on the manor, for he had cleared away two hamlets in order to have more room for his wild boars, he sent a general invitation through the countryside for all beggars, scholars, jugglers, and broken men to come and share in the funeral feast and receive alms and new clothes in her memory. He commissioned the best craftsmen in England to carve her tomb, and sat beside the effigist as he worked, telling him that the nose must be a trifle narrower, the left eyebrow a hair's breadth higher than the right, while he watched for the likeness to emerge as sharply as in better days he had watched outside a thicket.

Meanwhile, Alianor's body, in a lead coffin, waited till it could be transferred to the nunnery which he intended to found in commemoration of her soul. For months on end his intercourse was with bishops and lawyers, and through the long negotiations his hunter's patience was inexhaustible and no detail escaped him. He chose to have a priory of the Benedictine Order. All Alianor's fortune he gave to its endowment, and made a will leaving it half his own property, though Gilbert and Adela and Adela's relations complained furiously and threatened alternately to bring a law-suit or to write to the Pope. The site chosen was a manor called Oby. Oby had been part of Alianor's dowry, and in the early days of their marriage they had often lived there, for it was good hawking country along the Waxle Stream; but as his taste in hunting turned to larger quarries the manor house had fallen into neglect and now only the shell of it remained, housing several families of serfs and countless bats. Now this shell was made weatherproof, whitewashed within and partitioned into dormitories and chambers. A chapel was constructed and a bell hung in the squat belfry, the barns were re-roofed and the moat was cleaned. The dedication was made to Our Lady and Saint Leonard, patron of prisoners, and the choice of this saint was perhaps a little acknowledgment toward those acquaintances who had urged Brian de Retteville to take the cross, since several of them had actually done so and still awaited ransom. The nuns arrived, bright as a flock of magpies, and into their keeping he gave his two younger daughters, and then, when everything was finished, he went back to his oak woods and his hunting, and died in 1170.

The Waxle Stream flowed northeast through a poor country of marsh and moorland: a muddy reluctant stream, full of loops and turnings, and constantly revising its course, for the general lie of the land imposed no restraint on its vagaries. In some places it had hollowed for itself long pools where the current seemed to have ceased altogether, in others it skulked through acres of rushes and spongy moss. Every second year or so it spread itself into a flood. When the flood-water went down, the Waxle Stream had changed some part of its course and the former channel was filled up with a false brilliant herbage that had little or no nourishment in it.

Such a stream makes a very contentious boundary; and if the land had been of more value, one generation or another of

Alianor's ancestors might have set their men to embanking. But their manor of Oby was a small part of their possessions and lay far away from any other de Bazingham property, so nothing was done. The only indication of man's will to thwart nature was the high earthen causeway running to the town of Waxelby on the coast. This was made long before the first de Bazingham came into England. It was called the Hog Trail, and people said that long ago all the hogs of Oby, and of Lintoft on the farther side of Oby Fen, had been driven along the trail to Waxelby for slaughtering because in those days men were so foolish that they took their hogs to the salt instead of fetching the salt to the hogs. Whoever made the Hog Trail, and for whatever purpose, it was well made and still serviceable, though the willows, that had rooted in the ditches and grown to huge trees and split and rooted again, had weakened the earthworks and sooner or later would pull them down. When the floods were out the Hog Trail was the only way to get from Oby to Waxelby: a bitter nine miles, with the wind from the sea beating over the floods like a skater. But in summer, when Brian de Retteville came to the manor for some hawking and to remind his bailiff that if the Martinmas beef were to be worth eating the beasts should now be fattening, the place was well enough: he, at any rate, had liked it. When he chose to found his nunnery there it did not occur to him that nuns live in a place all the year round, and must feed through the hungry half of the year as well as through the plentiful half. There was land, and water, and a population of serfs, not many but enough; there were buildings and outbuildings, a fish-pond, an excellent dovecot. What more could women, holy women, desire?

Negotiations with the house in France which was to supply his first batch of nuns enlarged his notions of what holy women desire. The abbess, a notable woman of business, sent him a long list of requirements, including a boat; for the title deeds of the manor, expressing Oby's condition in the more watery past, used the term *insula.* Even with assurance that the manor was on the mainland she extracted a great deal more from him than he had thought to give: yearly loads of timber, carriage free, from his oak woods; half the profit of one of his mills to cover the purchase of wine; a yearly consignment of dressed fox-skins, to make coverlets; a good relic; books for the altar and for account-keeping; the complete furniture for the convent priest's chamber over the gate-house and the tolls of a bridge over the Nene to pay for his upkeep and salary; a litter; tin porringers with lids to them; and a ring for the prioress.

Even so, the nuns arriving to take possession felt that they had come a long way to worsen their lot. They saw their new home at its best, for it was midsummer, and under the enormous vault of sky their manor, perched on the little rise of ground which gave the place its old name and half-circled by a loop of the Waxle Stream, looked like one of those maps into which the draughtsman has put every detail and coloured the whole to resemble life. The river was blue, the fields were striped in the colours of cultivation and fallow, there was a small mill, a large barn, a brewhouse, a fish-pond, also blue, and the house itself, a scramble of low buildings newly roofed with reed thatch, with a small chapel to one side of it and to the other a large dovecot, banded with black-faced flints. Farther along the ridge were the huts and sheds of the hamlet. To the east there was a belt of trees, warped and stunted by the wind from the sea.

Everything was poorer, smaller, clumsier than they had expected. The rooms were dark and poky, and seemed thrown together at random. Food had to be carried across the yard, for there was no covered way between the kitchen and the refectory. They must take their exercise out of doors or not at all, for there were no cloisters. Even their newly built chapel—they had been told it was newly built—was a squat, cramped building with a disproportionately large west door, a low roof supported by stumpy pillars, and a floor two foot below ground level (it was, in fact, a reach-me-down conversion of what had been the dungeon and cattle-hold of the original manor house). Like all people of bad taste, Brian de Retteville had saved on the structure in order to spend on the fittings. Altar, screen, stalls, canopies, were highly ornate and bright with painting and gilding. As for the one bell, it was so clumsy that it took two women to sound it.

With dubious hearts they sang their Te Deum.

A good convent should have no history. Its life is hid with Christ who is above. History is of the world, costly and deadly, and the events it records are usually deplorable: the year when the roof caught fire, the year of the summer flood which swept away the haystacks and drowned the bailiff, the year when the cattle were stolen, the year when the King laid the great impost for the Scotch wars and timber for five years had to be felled to pay it, the year of the pestilence, the year when Dame Dionysia had a baby by the bishop's clerk. Yet the events of history carry a certain exhilaration with them. Decisions are made, money is spent, strangers arrive, familiar characters appear in a new light, transfigured with unexpected goodness or badness. Few calamities fall on a religious house which are not at some time or other looked back upon with wistful regret. "In such an out-of-the-way place as this anything might happen," said the first sacrist of Oby, staring at the listless horizon toward which the sun was descending like a lump of red-hot iron. "Anything or nothing," replied the first prioress. It seemed to her that Brian de Retteville's choice of site had been unrealistically too close to the mind of Saint Benedict—since it was a nunnery he had founded. Men with their inexhaustible interest in themselves may do well enough in a wilderness, but the shallower egoism of women demands some nourishment from the outer world, and preferably in the form of danger or disaster. While appeasing grumbles and expostulations, she realized that the inconveniences of the new house were in fact providential, and that when they were remedied (and for the good name of her order she must strive to remedy them) her nuns, exercising themselves dry-footed and eating meals which had not been spoiled between the kitchen and the table, would complain much more, and with better reason; since they would then be able to give an undivided attention to the mortifying tranquillity of their lives.

As things turned out the providential inconveniences of her house lasted longer than she did. With a manor abounding in reeds and supplied with a sufficiency of timber one might think it an easy matter to make a covered way between kitchen and refectory and some makeshift sort of cloister. But the wood was not seasoned, the reeds were not cut or were not dried, the labour was not available, the time of year was not suitable: in short, the newcomers were unwelcome. The families which had been turned out of the manor house when it was made over for the nuns were, of course, related to all the other families on the manor; and the evicted were scarcely more resentful than those into whose hovels they packed on the plea of cousinship and christian charity. Under an absentee lord and a careless bailiff the manor serfs had achieved a kind of scrambling devil-take-the-hindmost independence. Though the new state of things included fresh livestock, repairs to roofs and carts and ploughs, and all the advantageous pickings which flow from an occupied manor, the Oby serfs unanimously disapproved of the nuns, a pack of foreigners who had come to feed on them, a gaggle of silly women, more tyrannical than any de Bazinghams or de Rettevilles, and ignorant into the bargain. The de Bazinghams had at least known better than to plant fig trees. To this enmity was added, after Brian de Retteville's death, the enmity of Gilbert and Adela, who suffered as sharply as any of the evicted serfs from the pangs of dispossession. Brian's legacy to the convent was indisputably legal and spiritually meritorious; but this did not prevent them from holding on to it as long as they could and wrangling over every piecemeal transfer. Neither did this prevent the convent's mother-house in France becoming increasingly unsympathetic toward an offshoot whose revenues on paper now warranted filial offerings rather than these perpetual begging-letters. Meanwhile the first prioress had died of a fever, and her successor was that same hopeful sacrist who had thought that anything might happen, and still preserved the same illusion (it was she who enfranchised two families, the Figgs and the Torkles, in order to raise enough money to build a new gallows). In 1183, twenty years after its foundation, the convent of Oby was in such a state of confusion and indebtedness that the bishop of the diocese began to talk of dissolving it. Then Richenda de Foley interposed her strong secular arm. Richenda was Alianor's younger sister, a widow and a seasoned harridan, who having quarrelled her way through all her nearer relations had now worked down to quarrelling with Gilbert and

Adela. What love is to some women and needlework to more, litigation was to Richenda. Gilbert and Adela were withholding Brian's legacy, were they, and imperilling the soul's welfare of a beloved sister and, for the nonce, a beloved brother-in-law? She would hunt the last farthing out of them; and in addition she would shame them by finding other and better patrons for the house, and better dowered and more creditable nuns than Gilbert's two wretched sisters. In order to conduct these operations she settled herself in the nunnery, where at that time there was room and to spare for boarders. She brought several servants, a great deal of household furniture, three dogs, one of the Magdalen's tears in a bottle, and twelve chests stuffed with law-papers and inventories. She also brought a great deal of method and efficiency. For the first time the memorial dues were properly enforced, and the serfs, working as they had not worked for years, became almost reconciled to the convent, since one of the old family, who in shrewdness and obstinacy might almost be one of themselves, had taken it under her wing.

In 1194 a wandering scholar, very old and shrill, came begging for a meal. As he sat munching his bread and a salt herring he talked to the wicket-nun about the properties of numbers, and of how Abbot Joachim, analysing the arithmetic of the prophecies, had discovered that the end of the world was at hand. He himself expected much of the year 1221, a date whose two halves each added up to three. In such a year, he said, one might look for the reign of Antichrist to be fulfilled, or else it might betoken the coming of the kingdom of the Holy Ghost, as the number six expressed a completion of two-thirds of the Trinity. Something, at any rate, he said, might be expected. Under his arm he carried a monochord. To make himself clearer to the nuns (for several of them had gathered to pity the old man, so wise and so witless), he explained to them about the Proportion of Diapason, the perfect concord which is at once concord and unity, and showed them how, by placing the bridge of the monochord so as to divide the string into a ratio of one and two, the string will sound the interval of the octave. Thus, he mumbled, was the nature of the Godhead perceptible to Pythagoras, a heathen; for it lies latent in all things. He sat on a bench in the sun, but overhead the wind howled, tormenting the willows along the Hog Trail and clawing the thatch, and the nuns could scarcely hear his demonstration of how the Godhead sounded to Pythagoras. It was really no loss, for his hand, shaking with cold and palsy, had failed to place the bridge correctly, and the diapason of the Trinity was out of tune. Then, brushing the crumbs out of his beard and plucking a sprig of young wormwood to stick behind his ear, he sang a love song to entertain the ladies and went on his way toward Lintoft. The lovesong had a pretty, catchy tune: for some days every nun and novice was humming it. Then Dame Cecilia began to have fits and to prophesy. This infuriated Richenda de Foley, to whom any talk of the end of the world after she had worked so hard and successfully to put the convent on a good footing for the next century seemed rank ingratitude. But the itch is not more contagious than illuminations, and throughout that summer Oby resounded with excited voices describing flaming bulls, he-goats of enormous size floating above the lectern, apparitions of the founder and shooting pains. In a fury of slighted good intentions and outraged common sense Richenda de Foley packed up and went away, but as she was generous as well as authoritarian she left a great deal of household stuff and provisions behind her. The community, after one universal gasp at finding itself unclasped from that strong and all-arranging hand, settled down to enjoy an unregulated prosperity and comfort; and prosperity and comfort wielding their usual effect, the spirit of prophecy flickered out, and by the close of the year they were looking for nothing more remarkable than improvements to the fish-pond.

In 1208 came the Interdict.

In 1223 lightning set fire to the granary.

In 1257 the old reed and timber cloisters fell to bits in a gale. It was decided that the masons who came to build the new should also build on a proper chapter-house. When it was half-built a spring rose under it. Rather than throw money away, the head mason suggested, why not finish the new building as a dovecot, a wet floor being no inconvenience to doves, and convert the old dovecot, so solid and weatherproof, into a chapter-house? This suggestion, too hastily accepted, led to discomfort all round. The pigeons refused to settle in their new house. Some flew away for good, the others remained in the lower half of the old dovecot, whose upper story, remodelled with large windows and stone benches, made a very unpersuasive place of assembly. However, the arrangement was allowed as a temporary expedient, and as such it became permanent.

In 1270 there were disastrous floods, and this happened again seven years later. In 1283 hornets built in the brewhouse roof and the cellaress was stung in the lip and died. In 1297 the convent's bailiff was taken in the act of carnality with a cow. Both he and the cow were duly executed for the crime, but this was not enough to avert the wrath of heaven. That autumn and for three autumns following there was a murrain among the cattle. After the murrain came a famine, and the bondwomen of the manor broke through the reed-fence into the orchard where the nuns were at recreation and mobbed them, snatching at their wimples and jeering at such plump white breasts and idle teats. For this a fine was laid on the hamlet, and the last remnants of the *pax Richenda* broke down. Tithes and dues were paid grudgingly or not at all, and going along the cloisters to sing the night office the nuns would strain their ears for the footsteps of marauders or the crackle of a fired thatch.

In 1332 a nun broke her vows and left the convent for a lover. Misfortunes always go in threes, was the comment of the prioress: they might expect two more to play the same game. But after a second apostasy there was a painful Visitation by the bishop, when the prioress was deposed and Dame Emily, the novice-mistress, a better disciplinarian, nominated to be her successor. Unfortunately Dame Emily was unpopular, being both arrogant and censorious. Dreading the rule of such a prioress, the nuns refused to elect her and chose instead, out of bravado, Dame Isabella Sutthery, the youngest and silliest nun among them. The young and silly can become great tyrants. Dame Isabella proved fanatically harsh and suspicious, scourging the old nuns till they fainted for anguish and inventing such unforeseeable misdemeanours that no one could steer clear of offending. The convent waited, languishing, for the next Visitation, when each nun in her private interview with the bishop could make her report. But though the bishop came and heard, he was still nursing his wrath about their rejection of Dame Emily whom he had nominated, and though Dame Emily herself was the greatest sufferer under Prioress Isabella he answered every plea for a fresh election by saying that the convent having chosen must abide by its choice. It was not till 1345, when Prioress Isabella choked on a plum-stone, that peace and quiet returned, followed by four ambling years of having no history, save for a plague of caterpillars.

In 1349 the Black Death came to Oby.

When Prioress Isabella first began to gasp and turn blue Dame Alicia de Foley framed a vow to Saint Leonard, patron of the convent and of all prisoners, that if their tyrant should die of her plum-stone a spire, beautiful as art and money could make it, should be added to their squat chapel. In her mind's eye it soared up, the glory of the countryside, and she was so absorbed in contemplation that Prioress Isabella's eyes were lolling on her cheeks before Dame Alicia remembered to add to the saint that she would also undertake to pray daily throughout the time of the spire's building for the repose of Isabella's soul.

Persuading the rest of the convent to support her in this vow, working on her relations in the world to contribute toward the expenses, manipulating the bishop into expressing approval (his approval was not really necessary but after the business of Prioress Isabella no one at Oby was going to risk slighting a bishop), arranging for the supply of building materials and making a contract with a band of travelling masons, took three years—though her election as prioress enabled her to do all these things more easily. She had been praying for the repose of Isabella's soul for just under a twelvemonth, and the spire, after several false starts and buttressings of the existing tower which was to be its base, was beginning to rise, when at the news that the pestilence had reached Waxelby the masons with one accord scrambled off the scaffolding and went away.

It had been pleasant to kneel on alone after the end of mass, hearing the noise of her spire growing: the whine of the pulleys, the scrape of trowels, the jar as stone after stone was set in its place, the songs and outdoor voices of the masons. But now there was no sound except the March winds hoo-hooing through the gaps, and the thought that the second part of her vow could still be kept was cold comfort. Besides, could she be sure even of that? The pestilence might stop her mouth. Already her treasuress was making it difficult for her to find much time for praying. In the leanest time of year the convent had to be victualled and provided as though to stand a siege. There was wood, meat, meal, fish, oil, spices, candles, serge, wool, and linen to get in, wine and honey, and medicines in case the sickness penetrated their defences. There was fodder for the beasts to be thought of, vinegar for fumigations, charcoal for braziers, and the roof of the infirmary to be re-thatched. The running of the household must be looked into and tightened up, and dues still owing must be got in, and somehow she must increase the convent's stock of ready money, for in times of calamity people will do nothing unless they are paid on the nail for it. Then, too, there was the problem of how best to prepare for the assaults of the poor and needy: these would troop to the wicket, crying out for food, for medicine, for old rags for their sores: they would bring the pestilence to the very gate, and yet they could not be denied, Christ's poor and the plague's pursuivants. Her musing was interrupted by the sound of horses being halted outside the gate-house and a fluster of unfamiliar voices. William de Stoke, whose daughter was a novice in the house, had sent to fetch the girl away, having heard that the pestilence was already at Oby. He had sent a large retinue of servants, and all of them were hungry and required feeding.

While the de Stoke people ate they talked. Though there had been pestilences often enough there had never been, they said, such a pestilence as this. It travelled faster than a horse, it swooped like a falcon, and those whom it seized on were so suddenly corrupted that the victims, still alive and howling in anguish, stank like the dead. The short dusky daylight and the miry roads and the swollen rivers were no impediment to it, as to other travellers. All across Europe it had come, and now it would traverse England, and nothing could stop it, wherever there were men living it would seek them out, and turn back, as a wolf does, to snap at the man it had passed by.

The roads were filled with people fleeing before it. The riders cursed at the travellers on foot, and lashed at them to make way. A fine litter had gone by, said one of the men, and he had asked who was inside it: it was an old Counsellor, one of the retinue answered, and for a long time he had been dying with a slow death that fed on his vitals; but even so, he wished to preserve the live death within him from that other death. Lepers broke out of their hospitals and crutched themselves along with the rest, and people scarcely feared them. Townsfolk who all their lives had lived in comfort now ran to the forests and fed on snails and acorns and rabbits, tearing them apart and eating them raw; but the Black Death was in the forest too, and the outlaws lay dead beside the ashes of their fires. There had never been such a press of men going to the ports to take ship for the wars in France; for it was better to die in battle than to die of the Black Death. But in the ports and in the crammed holds of the ships the Black Death found them and killed them before they could be killed by their fellow-men.

Wherever they went, another voice broke in, they would find this new Death waiting for them. Better to stay at home than be at so much trouble to go in search of him. For if you went to another town you heard the bells tolling, and saw the kites gathering, and smelled the stink coming from the burial-pits; and if you went afield, the same stink crossed your path, the ploughman lay rotting under a bush and the plough stood near by, with the spring grass growing up around it as though this year were the same as other years. People were fools, he said, to go in search of a death which would come in search of them. Better to stay under your own roof. Yet that was dismal, too, to sit waiting with your hands dangling between your knees, not daring to pull off your shirt or handle yourself for fear of seeing the tokens come out on your flesh: sometimes like spots, sometimes gatherings as big as plums, but always black because of the poisoned blood within. There was no comfort or pleasure in neighbourliness now; friends scarcely dared look each other in the face, for fear of seeing there the look of death or the look of one who looks on it. Death drove the best bargain at the market, drank deepest at the tavern, walked in processions, married the bride at the church door. The priest said his *Ite missa est* and already his lips were parched and blackening. The server's *Deo gratias* slid between teeth that chattered with fear. The congregation hurried away, silent, each man staring before him.

But the footloose have the best of it, the prioress said to herself, hearing all this talk beyond the window. Better to be one of those masons and run into the jaws of death than to sit behind walls and wait for the Black Death to enter. When the little girl was brought in to make her farewells she said to the child, as desperately as to a grown woman, "Remember to pray for us here at Oby." The child burst into tears and clung to her skirts, saying she was afraid. "Afraid of what, my child?"—"Afraid of the horses."

Early in April the pestilence was in Lintoft. It broke out in the miller's house, and immediately the miller of Oby went off with his family and belongings, none knew whither. His departure was no hardship to the peasants: for many years households had dodged the manorial mill-dues, grinding their corn in their private hand-mills; but it was a blow to the convent, and though Dame Blanch, who as cellaress ruled over kitchen and storeroom, said jauntily that when they could no longer make bread they must eat frumenty and be thankful for it, many saints and christian garrisons had thanked God for a handful of parched grain, the other ladies muttered about starvation and the weakness of their teeth. Presently more people in the hamlet began to flit away and another novice was removed by her parents. At each new departure the nuns drew closer together, whispering in corners and hunching up their shoulders as though a cold wind blew in on them, as though they bodily felt the cold breath of rumour, the many stories now current of how the Black Death had dealt with other religious houses. It crept in, and laid a finger on one person; and his sickness spread through the community like fire through a faggot until the smell of death was stronger than the smell of the boiled meat in the kitchen or the incense in the quire. For a while the Rule held out, the imperilled lives were lived to measure, the dark figures shuffled into quire and out again. There were no straying glances, no one spoke to his neighbour: never had the ordinance of silence and self-immurement been better obeyed. But at last the Rule itself faltered, and sagged, and was lost, and the altar was greeted only by desperate visitors, solitary figures grovelling in silence or perhaps suddenly thrusting out a frantic shriek for mercy.

In one house, every monk had died. In another, every monk but one. And that was the worst—that desolate figure on whom the brand of life was scored like an inversion of the brand of death.

If it were I, the prioress thought—if I were left alive and alone under my unfinished spire . . . Overcome by her imagination she forced herself to go and sit in the parlour, where the nuns were telling each other that this pestilence was unlike any other, for it killed men rather than women.

The first two to sicken were Dame Emily and a novice, and they died on the same day. That evening Sir Peter Crowe, the convent priest, walked uninvited into the prioress's chamber, where she sat with the treasuress, Dame Helen, and Dame Blanch the cellaress, talking calmly (as one does when all hope is gone) about the quality of some vermilion paint, newly bought for an illuminated book of hours which had been commissioned by Piers de Retteville, descendant in the sixth generation of Gilbert and Adela.

"I am leaving you," he said.

Her first thought, that he was running away from the pestilence, could not be sustained in the face of his bleak self-assurance. He must have gone out of his mind. He had always been sombre and given to austerities.

"I shall set out tomorrow, as soon as it is light. I am going to Waxelby."

"To Waxelby?"

It was on the tip of Dame Blanch's tongue to say that they did not need any more dried fish. She blushed, thinking how nearly she had said it, while Sir Peter spoke of how heavy the plague was at Waxelby. Since it had declared itself there two rectors had died, the second only ten days after his predecessor. Most of the friars were sick, of the two chantry priests one had gone mad, the other had run away. And the common people were dying unattended.

"You are going to shrive them? It is a most christian intention—but we here may be dying also. Will you leave us to die unshriven?"

"You must find someone else."

The prioress stared at her hands. She had never found it easy to brook bad manners.

"I think you should have consulted us before deciding. Like you, we are sorry for the poor people at Waxelby. But in your anxiety about their souls—"

"It is not their souls I am thinking of!" he exclaimed. "I am thinking of the faith. I can't stay idling here while heresy is spreading faster than the pestilence. Do you know what they are doing at Waxelby? Yes, and all over England! Do you realize what they are doing?"

"Dying without the aid of the Church. But how is that a heresy?"

"They are confessing to each other! Yes, and shriving each other too, I'll be bound."

"I hope not."

"It's bound to follow. Give presumption an inch and it will take an ell. Hodge confesses to Madge and Madge gives Hodge absolution. What is let loose on us, I say?"

"But if there is no priest confession may be made to a secular—for instance, in battle. My father once received a confession on the battlefield from another knight, and if he had not heard it a great wrong would have remained without amendment."

Dame Blanch drew herself up and looked round sternly. It was her pride that she came of a warrior family.

Drawing his hand over his chops, Sir Peter assumed an air of patience and began to expound in easy language the doctrine of the sacraments, of the sacramental virtue which sets the priest apart from the ruck of the world. Pedantic fool! thought the prioress, saying courteously, "Of course. Undoubtedly. How clearly you put it."

"We shall miss your explanations," added Dame Helen with sturdy malice.

"God knows," cried he, "I say this without arrogance. Humility is inherent in the priestly office; what can be more humbling than to know that the sacramental work is efficacious without regard of him who performs it? In the hands of the vilest priest, a fornicator, a blasphemer, a sodomite, the sacrament is as much sacramental as in the hands of a saint. But the distinction must be kept. And if the saint were a layman his administration of the sacrament would be void."

"Surely a saint would know that?" Dame Helen said.

His fingers twitched in his wrath. "All this is beside the point. The point at issue is—"

"Whether you go to Waxelby."

"No. That is decided. The point at issue is whether we are to leave Holy Church undefended while heresy stalks the land. Yes, and when even a pastoral crook is raised against her, when a bishop himself, a bishop! . . ."

In a horrified whisper he told them how the Bishop of Bath and Wells had written allowing that those at the point of death might confess to a lay person if no priest were available.

"But whom shall we confess to?" asked Dame Blanch. "For while you are giving absolutions at Waxelby we shall be dying unconfessed and unshriven."

"That is a secondary consideration. How often must I tell you that I am not concerned with individuals? What matters the ease of a few souls more or less when the faith itself is in danger? It is no longer a matter of who dies shriven or unshriven, comforted or comfortless. What is at stake is whether the Church is to keep her hold over the souls of her children. Think of the future, or try to. Consider the frightful possibility—a future age when all over this country men and women will die, will die quite calmly, without the assistance of the Church!"

They considered it, moved by his eloquence. Such a future was hard to imagine. It was hard to imagine, too, how by leaving the death-beds of Oby for the death-beds of Waxelby, Sir Peter could effectually restrain the future.

Their silence appealed to him. Presently he began to speak on a milder note, saying how deplorable it was that though God's providence sent these catastrophes upon mankind, mankind was not, as a rule, any the better for them. Then, asking for their prayers, he said farewell.

The convent and its manor lay in the parish of Wivelham. The rector of Wivelham was a young man of good family. He had celebrated one mass in his parish church, looking round with horror on the gaunt grey building in the flat, tow-coloured landscape, and then returned to Westminster. His curate, elderly and decrepit, was not likely to have much time to spare for Oby. A mass a week was as much as they might expect of him; and to supply that he must travel seven miles fasting and seven miles back, or wade the short cut through the marshes. A messenger now sent to him returned with the news that he was sick with an ague. As soon as he could get about he would come to them.

The graves were dug for Dame Emily and the novice; and the prioress told Jesse Figg, the bailiff, that he had better send up a man from the village to dig other graves in readiness. "They can always be filled up if they are not needed," she said. The bailiff assured her she need not worry on that score, the graves would soon fill; he added that it would be more satisfactory to dig a large pit, the more so as he could not promise to supply labour for long. After the first two graves had been smoothed over life crept on as usual for a few days. The messenger again returned with word that the curate's ague was abating, that he hoped to come early next week. He did not come, and another nun sickened.

"Sir Peter might just as well have stayed. He would have found plenty to do," remarked Dame Susanna, the infirmaress. Nothing could disabuse her of the notion that Sir Peter had gone to Waxelby to minister to the dying, an heroic but premature decision. She spoke to a nun called Matilda de Stapledon, who was helping her to powder dried newts and centaury roots. Presently they began to discuss the convent's latest difficulty, shortage of labour. Being a poor convent, Oby could never keep its servants for long, and having the village at its door it had come to depend on day-workers. Now these came no longer, the kitchen was reduced to old Mabel and poor Ursula, who was more afraid of what the world could do to her than of any pestilence. Milk was carried as far as the threshold, wood was thrown down in the outer yard, and once some compassionate person left a dozen hens there, but the rats spoiled them. To

Dame Matilda this desertion seemed like revolt. Dame Susanna saw it as lack of christian charity and so was more philosophic. She pointed out that though the Black Death kept away their servants it also kept away beggars. It was some days now since any poor traveller had troubled them for a dole.

II. THE TUFT OF WORMWOOD

(April 1349–July 1351)

Nowhere does news travel faster than among vagrants. For miles around every wandering beggar knew that the pestilence was among the nuns of Oby. If Ralph Kello had not got drunk he would have known it too. Not that he had drunk either well or deeply; but, being cold and hungry, the liquor had mounted to his head, and he had spoken so cantankerously that the company at the alehouse let him depart unwarned, thinking, as they watched him stagger off in the moonlight he mistook for morning, that if a clerk took the sickness it would be one proud beggar the less and a seat by the fire the more.

It had been very bad beer, and after walking a few miles he was sick. During the last mile he had seemed to age with every step, his features growing pinched, his jaw drooping, his eyes sinking into his head. Now, even more rapidly than he had aged, he grew young again. The rabbits coming out to feed in the sunrise looked scarcely more innocent and candid than he. Hunger, and another hour's walking, smudged out this glory, and by the time he reached Oby he looked his true age, which was thirty-five.

Seeing the unfinished spire, he crossed himself and greeted the Virgin, partly in thankfulness that a meal was in sight, partly in thankfulness that this time the pestilence had not got him; for till the vomit had risen in his throat, tasting so unmistakably of sour beer, he had believed himself stricken.

There were some faggots of small wood lying before the gate-house. He stepped over them and knocked. A party of crows flew up from the roof and one by one returned and settled again; but no one answered. He knocked once more. He noticed a tuft of wormwood growing near by, and he broke off a shoot and began to snuff at it—for his head ached violently. A weasel reared up from the grass and studied him.

At length there was a creaking overhead. A window had opened and an old nun was looking down on him.

"A breakfast, my good man? Yes, if you are not afraid of us. We have the pestilence here."

His impulse was to run for his life. But self-esteem compelled him to muster up a few words of compassion.

"Yes, we are all shut up here, like knights in a castle. The enemy has broken in, but we aren't overcome yet."

Later he was to find Dame Blanch's military fantasies as tedious as everyone else did. But now the contrast between the warlike words and the piping voice touched his heart; and looking up (for after her first speech he had stood with head hanging), it seemed to him that the old nun had a face of singular goodness and honesty. She for her part saw a large, raw-boned man with a hooked nose and thick lips; and discerned, as she said later, unmistakable traits of a noble character. He heard himself asking if he could help them. It was a relief to learn that the help required was to carry a message to Wivelham.

"To the curate there, if you will. Beg him to come to us, if only to say one mass. Our priest has left us. For ten days now we have had neither mass nor shriving."

"My daughter, I am a priest."

He had thought to himself, Enough to comfort them, and then be off—off before they rise from their knees and begin to ask questions. Perhaps, too, there entered into this hare-brained falsehood an element of superstition; as though by going to meet the pestilence he would insure that it would fly him. Waiting to be let in he had time enough to examine every aspect of his folly, and to quake with fear and to remember that there is no beast of worse omen than a weasel. And yet at the same time he was saying to himself, Except for that nibble of wormwood I am certainly fasting.

Weeping with gratitude, she let him in.

In the sacristy a thin short-sighted nun awaited him with an armful of clothing.

"Is this your largest chasuble?"

"Forgive me! Our sacrist died last week."

"This one is better. Who will serve the mass?"

She pointed to a boy who stood in the doorway, picking his nose and swaying from foot to foot as he gazed at the silks and embroideries. A nun's child, no doubt: a pupil of the convent would be better disciplined and better dressed. But this was one of those little creatures which trot through a household of women like a pet animal, accepted and neglected as a matter of course. Thirty years ago on just such terms another little boy had picked his nose and stared at gauds—only it was Fat Maggy he watched, or Janet, or Petronilla, instead of a priest. Between their quarrels they were kind, and when his mother died Petronilla replaced her just as Janet would come forward if Petronilla had gone with a client. But a little boy grows lanky and out of place in a brothel, and so, remembering his mother's ambition, the whores of the establishment clubbed together and sent him to the Canons across the way to be educated and made a clerk of.

The sacrist came forward with the stole. My first mass, he thought, kissing it. And my last. And of all my sins the deadliest, and of all the negligent idiocies I have fallen into the most idiotic. If I had not a bald patch it could not have happened, for I suppose not even the shadow of death could blind these ladies to an untonsured head; but causation tunnels like a mole under the surface of our free will, and because of an attack of ringworm in Toledo I am about to say mass in an English convent where they are dying of a pestilence. And here, very probably, I shall die too. The stole settling round his neck seemed to noose him and lead him on into a new life.

A few hours later it was as a matter of course that he sat with the prioress and the older ladies of the convent telling them of his education among the Black Canons, and of his travels and studies; and falling asleep that night, the priest's lodging over the gate-house seemed as familiar as an old cloak.

Long after he was abed Ursula was on her knees in the

kitchen, offering up thanks to the Virgin. The glow of the embers silhouetted the cooking-pots on the hearth and lit up the curve of the boy's cheek as he lay before the fire. Now they were safe again, there was a priest in the house, and a man. Her child had served his mass, and so already he and she were linked. He would certainly take notice of the boy, and so in time become aware of the boy's mother. He would speak to her about Jackie. She would not be able to answer, but he would have spoken to her—priest and man he would have spoken to her about her child.

She was cold, and tired, and ageing, and disgraced. Three times she had left her convent for love, and twice she had crept back and lived in penance. Again a craving for love had haled her out into the world, where with a child in her belly and afterward with the child on her back she had wandered from place to place, the creature of any man who would look at her with a certain look, speak to her in a certain voice. And then, just as before, Christ her bridegroom had waylaid her, more mastering than any man, and she had gone back, cowed, to woo him with abject repentance. This time her convent would not re-accept her: she was sentenced to live in mortification and obedience, but without the veil, and presently she was sent with her child to Oby to live there as a servant. She was a good cook and a feverishly hard worker, and the Oby ladies did not trouble her with any reproaches unless they found insects in the salad—which happened occasionally because lust and tears and wood-smoke had weakened her eyesight—and was serious because in swallowing a live insect one may swallow an evil spirit inhabiting it. Sometimes, when a fit of hysteria took her, Dame Helen would urge her to resist Satan whose bargains, as Ursula must know from experience, were so little worth the purchase; but Dame Helen's exhortations, as Ursula also knew, sprang as much from anxiety lest the convent should lose a cook as concern lest the fiend should gain a soul. This assurance that she was of some value in the world did more than any prayers and fastings to keep her safe in the convent kitchen. For the rest, they were kind enough, and tolerant to the boy; and no one suspected what she suffered at the hands of the Oby laity—the miller's wife with her scorching tongue, the boys who threw stones at the child and scattered dung on her hair. Six years of virtue and security had almost tamed her. Then news of the pestilence came like a yelling of hounds on a renewed scent. At one moment it seemed to her that she had not repented sufficiently and that the hour of death might take her before she had had leisure to win God's mercy (there had never been so much to do, even when the bishop came, as now); an hour later the thought of dying without one more taste of the sweet world drove her frantic. Then Sir Peter left, as a man of no account, but his departure created the most frightful of all voids; for the priest stands in the place of God, and when that place is left empty God steps into it, God unmitigated and implacable.

But now the strange priest was lying in the room over the gate.

She crept on her knees toward the child and began to kiss him, furiously and inattentively. Only by kissing or shrieking could she slack the strain of so much thankfulness. The child woke and struck at her with a sleepy arm.

"Don't kiss me so hard, mother. It hurts."

"Tell me, Jackie, tell me about the new priest. What does he look like? Has he got white teeth?"

"He's got an ugly nose," said the child. Burrowing into her lap, he fell asleep again. For a long while she sat there, staring at the embers with her weak eyes, holding the hot bony immature creature that would one day in his turn become a man.

A man; but being a bastard, never a priest.

"Yes, it is a pity he is a bastard," said the prioress, answering commendations on her server. "As you say, he is a clever child. And what could be better than to return as a priest to the house that nurtured you? Such a priest would feel a son's care for everything about the place, he would be interested in its upkeep, see to the repairs, drive the work-people, carry out, maybe, projects he had seen others begin. Such a priest," she added, smiling, "might even finish my spire."

She liked Ralph Kello. He was educated, and discreet, and she was grateful to him for arriving when he did, and remaining.

"But who can talk about the future now? Yet if any of us are left alive, and if the world remains, and if Sir Peter dies at Waxelby—which I suppose he is very likely to do—how convenient it would be if you should take his place! Why not, indeed, since God has sent you? We are all convinced of that."

"I might have been sent by the devil. How are you to know?" He had woken with a splitting headache and along with it a strange feeling of some inner exhilaration and ferment. It must have been that which allowed him to speak so incautiously.

She looked at him and sighed. "You are too polite to say so. But I can see that you have other ambitions than to bury yourself at Oby."

He let it go at that. Whether he spoke discreetly or recklessly, either way seemed to lodge him more securely in his imposture. For now it was his second week at Oby, and Dame Joan, the short-sighted nun who, all in a flurry at finding herself in the place of the dead sacrist, had tried to fit him with the smallest chasuble, was herself dying. He walked up and down the infirmary, nursing the flask of oil in the crook of his arm. Each time he walked toward her she seemed to have grown smaller and shabbier, like a dying cat. She had lain senseless for many hours; but at the anointing of her feet she had suddenly quivered, making an intense effort to come out of her stupor, and the hand which had been clawing the pallet was extended, blindly caressing the air. That tremor, and that enamoured gesture of the hand, had revealed such an intensity of love that he had stayed by her, thinking that if she recovered her senses it would please her to be God-speeded toward the God she loved so fervently. Or was it that she was ticklish? The vocabulary of the body is full of ambiguities. Be that as it might, he had stayed. The prioress had lingered to thank him, and Dame Susanna, the infirmaress, coming in and out with medicines and linen, gave him esteeming glances. Every action now must fasten him more irrevocably into his perjury.

Perjury, and imposture, and sacrilege. His thoughts, running with unusual lucidity (for by nature he was a heavy and confused thinker), were like a transparent stream. They ran by, and by; and beneath them, like the river-bed, were the facts. He was no priest, and he was here in a house of nuns, absolving the dying, saying mass. The absolutions were void, the rite was sacrilege. He was damning himself and abetting the damnation of others. There, plain enough, was the bottom of the matter, the bottom of the river. But between him and the facts ran this glassy process of thinking, this flow of apprehending how it had all come about.

How could it have happened so?—and again, how could it not? He had not wanted to impose himself on the convent. He had never even felt any particular desire to be a priest. Learning his music-note and his Latin at Holy Cross, enduring so many beatings, so many chilblains, so much hunger and cold and so many bouts of the itch, it had never occurred to him but that he would grow up to be a priest as naturally as he would grow up to be a man. But he had taken it merely as a matter of course, there had been no vocation in it; when he understood the impediment of his bastardy he felt no great regret, and growing up into a man seemed good enough. The Canons had assumed that he would take Lesser Orders or become a friar; but quitting them he had said only that he would bear it in mind and decide later, after he had ripened his judgment by travel and study. In time the impetus of his schooling had carried him on into Lesser Orders; and that was reasonable enough, a tidy completion of a course of learning, a practical measure toward a livelihood. The sow's ear does not expect to become a silk purse, but to become pigskin it submits itself to singeings, tannings, and thumpings. In the same way the thumpings of theology had suppled him, and proximity to the priesthood had coloured him; and some of the pigskin he had seen in Spain was really very fine indeed, and when stamped and gilded almost indistinguishable from damask. So he had travelled on into his middle age, with poverty always at his heels and his wits generally contriving to outpace the beast, until that morning when he had stood knocking on a gate, thinking of nothing more blameful than a breakfast. Then an old woman had looked out of a window, and had spoken some fanciful brave words in a piping voice, and his voice, loud and clear and confident, had answered her. *My daughter, I am a priest.* For no reason; he had not even said it as a jest or a cheat. He had just said it—out of complaisance, as one soothes a squalling child, not even troubling to ask what it squalls for. And then Satan, weasel-shaped behind him, had watched him cross the threshold of Oby, walking with priestly dignity and making large signs of the cross.

The dying nun grew smaller and shabbier, but still she did not die. God makes woman to have more endurance than man, because of childbearing. Even in a virgin this endurance is valid. But was it thus in the original creation, God providing even in his unfallen creatures for the Fall, or was it added to Eve at the time of the sentence upon her to obey her husband and bring forth in sorrow? Again, has the bitch more endurance than the dog? And if so, why? For animals are soulless and without either sin or merit, merely obliging or disobliging, which makes it a simple matter for the devil to go in and out of them whenever he pleases. He turned once more towards her, and still she lived. And here he walked up and down, waiting to comfort her departure with a fraud—out of complaisance, as one parts a squalling child.

He began to think of a sermon he might preach one day, showing how if a man be too timid, too scrupulous, too indolent, to run into any mortal sin, the fiend can trip him in an act of merit: an alms to a beggar, a cloak thrown over a naked back —but damnation lies at the bottom of the cup. *Thou hast made them to drink of a deadly wine.* That could be the text of the sermon he might preach one day—on the day he was made pope, perhaps!

The woman from the kitchen—she was called Ursula—came to the door with a cup of broth. Catching sight of him, she started and dropped the bowl, and began to wring her hands and cry out that she could see the pestilence in his face. The infirmaress came forward. She too stared at him and caught her breath. Ursula's cries brought other nuns hurrying. Not since his childhood had he lived among so many women. That, too, and the begetting in some hasty, forgotten bed, lay at the bottom of the river. But now the river ran too deep. He could see all these things, but he could not plumb to them.

A little before she died Dame Joan became conscious. It seemed to her that she was floating in a dark place and that a very slow and fitful wind was propelling her westward. Somewhere near by a woman was weeping. She thought she knew the voice and said at last, "Is that you, Dame Salome?" But as she could only speak in a whisper the other did not hear her and wept on. Dame Joan began to think that she was dead, in which case the weeper must be some poor soul who naturally would not hear or answer. Yet it did not seem to her that she was rightly dead. Then another noise came into the room, the noise of the death-rattle; and an unmistakable Dame Salome began to call out, "Come, come! She's dying, Dame Joan is dying!"

They hurried in and took their places round her and began to say the prayers for the dying. One and all they were thankful to be on their knees, murmuring the familiar words. There was nothing in this death to shock them, nothing furious or unmanageable. They were still vibrating from their experience with Sir Ralph. It had been as though their recognition of his sickness had in an instant changed him from a man in his senses to a madman. His knees had given way, he had grovelled on the floor, tearing at his bosom and shuddering. Worst of all, he had seemed incapable of understanding anything they said to him, tossing their words out of his ears like a wounded animal. In the end there was nothing for it but to take hold of him and drag him away to his room over the gate, hoisting and hauling him up the stair.

Staring round on the room he suddenly freed himself. "No one is to come near me!" he shouted, and fell face downward on the bed and sank his teeth into the bolster.

He had no idea of sparing them the sight of his agony; it was because he hated them that he roared to them to go away. These women, fluttering and whispering, had done enough with him. It was through them that he had damned himself and lay dying. Even the bolster smelled of them, a shabbily sweet smell.

"No one is to come near me!"

His head was so heavy that he had to lever it up with his fist. The room was almost dark, and it sounded empty. But as he rolled his eyes heavily it seemed to him that a child, a little boy, was there, always flitting away just before his sight could take hold of him.

"No one is to come near me!"

Furious, senseless, melancholy, his roars echoed through the house. It was as though a bull were tethered by the gate-house. Such an heroic man, said Dame Blanch, could be sure of heaven and a good end. Just now Satan was trying him. This only proved how nearly Sir Ralph was a saint, for God constantly permits Satan to have his sport with the saints in their last hours on earth, just as when one has fixed a partridge on the roasting-spit one throws the feathers to the cat.

But shout and command as he might, the kitchen-woman always came back. He knew her by her shuffling gait, and by the smell of smoke and grease that came in with her. She came and went. Her hands were hard, like tongs. Sometimes she cajoled him, sometimes she spilled broth down his neck, sometimes she cried.

She was the kitchen-woman. She came and went. The other one, the black man, never stirred out of his corner. The other one was Death. Death was a burly man-cook, who breathed heavily. His hair was frizzled; between his black lips the tip of a red tongue wandered like a flame among charred logs; at his girdle dangled an iron hook. Hour by hour he watched the cauldron boiling and scumming, and when the right time came he struck his hook into the pot and lifted out a lump of meat. No sooner was the meat lifted up through the steam than it putrefied, and began to quiver with worms, and then to shrivel, and then to fall into dust. Death watched the pot patiently, biding his time. The hook was plunged in again, seeking and finding. Though there was no fire under the cauldron it boiled perpetually, for it was licked invisibly by the breath of hell-fire.

"I am damned, damned, damned!"

They sent for the curate of Wivelham but he was dying: of his ague, said the messenger, laughing foolishly. Dying of ague, think of that!

"How the priest roars out that he is damned," said Mabel the scullion to Ursula.

"It is his fever burning him."

Jackie, chewing a bone in his corner, looked up and asked, "How can a priest be damned?"

"Easy enough," Mabel answered. "Why, have you never seen

the picture in Waxelby church, the picture of the Last Judgment? There is a priest there, tied in a faggot with naked women, and the devils are wheeling them away in a barrow. A priest can be damned."

Ursula wandered about the kitchen, picking things up and wiping them and setting them down again, restless with the mechanical industry of exhaustion.

"Presently he will leave off bawling. Then he will die."

"No!"

The word had broken from Ursula like the twang of a bowstring. It echoed against the smoky roof of the kitchen. She brushed the back of her hand across her lips and crossed herself. With her round eyes, her long face, her long yellow teeth, she looked like a hare.

"Yes, Ursula, he will. Simon Ragge died just so. For three days he bawled and burned. Then on the fourth day he died. He too was a big strong man, just such another as our priest."

Ursula took an iron pot and began to scrape the grease off it. The pot sounded hollowly; as she scraped harder and faster it gave out a continuous groaning boom, and so neither of the women heard Dame Susanna come in. Her face was exceedingly pale, and she crossed herself repeatedly.

"Ursula, Ursula! He is saying it again."

"I'm coming, I'm coming. Leave it to me, madam."

She threw down the pot and hurried after the infirmaress. Still resounding, the pot rocked to and fro like a dying animal.

Half-way up the gate-house stair the infirmaress turned back. She leaned close down over Ursula, and seized her wrist, and cried, "But suppose it were true?"

"That he is damned, madam? How can we tell? Many are damned. Sir Peter told us that out of seven six will go to hell and burn everlastingly. It is God's will, and no affair of ours, if the priest be damned."

"No! Not that! The thing that is worse—the thing he says over and over again: that he is no priest."

"But he talks about a blackamoor cook standing in the corner. He points to him and says, 'Now he has it, now he has it!' That is not true."

"N-no."

"Neither is the other. Now let me go in, for I understand a man."

He was lying on his back, staring at the flies that buzzed overhead. In a reasonable voice he said:

"Ipsa dies alios alio dedit ordine Luna
Felices operum."

She had never been a learned nun: the flesh had given her no time for that; and in the long years of drudgery all her Latin had fallen away and it was as much as she could do to muster up a creed and a *Salve Regina.* There was a louse crawling on his cheek. She pounced on it and nipped it between her nails.

"Septima post decimam felix et ponere vitem
Et prensos domitare boves et licia telae
Addere. Nona fugae melior, contraria furtis."

Dame Susanna would have been edified by all this beautiful Latin. But the cowl does not make the monk. For all his Latin the man who lay there was no priest. The admission came out, tumbled among his other ravings, among the black cook and the Black Canons and the forge where the two Catalans laboured at the bellows, and the bear, and the deadly wine, and the weasel; and there was nothing to distinguish it from the rest of his nonsense, only that it was true. She knew in her bones it was true. She began to smooth his black hair. The fever had scorched it, it was harsh as dried bents, and stank. He moved his gaze and looked at her with a dull half-recognizing mistrust.

"My love, my sweet falcon!" she said.

The bell began to ring for compline. Doors opened and shut, the nuns were going into quire. He started and sat up in bed, striking her away.

"Do not hate me, do not fear me! I swear I will never tell it."

For a moment he seemed to look at her with his full senses. Then wearily he lay down again and turned his face to the wall and began to weep. She squirmed on to the bed and lay down beside him, caressing him and pulling out her breasts as though for a child. For a while he tried to shrug her off, at last he resigned himself to her, and lay sighing in her arms.

"My falcon, my heart's comfort, my love!"

She heard the nuns singing and the wind stirring the willows and ruffling the flood-water in the ditches that bordered the causeway. While compline lasted she could hold him in her arms and be appeased. No one would miss her. And there was no great sin in it for he was no priest and she was no longer a nun.

It was true, no one missed her; and if anyone wondered that Ursula should take such pains over a dying man, the answer was easy; for Ursula, poor soul, was always a hard worker. To scour the grease off a platter that will be greasy again tomorrow, to scrub a board till it is clean enough to be dirtied once more, to wheedle a dying man into swallowing broths that he will presently vomit up again, such labours were what one associated with Ursula. It was true that she persisted in saying that Sir Ralph would recover; but Dame Susanna declared that he would die; and as she was the infirmaress she must be the better judge.

He would die. Everyone would die, for it was the end of the world. The bailiff's wife was dead, Roger the wood-reeve and three of his children, Ragge and his two sons. Two more nuns had died: Dame Helen the treasuress (an invaluable nun, for she kept all the accounts, never forgetting a sum or a date); and Dame Alice Guillemard, who was to have made the book of hours for Piers de Retteville; and another novice was dying.

"Very soon," said Dame Agnes, the novice-mistress, "there will be none left but us old hags."

The prioress started. Though she was in her forties she did not feel herself a hag. Dame Agnes apologized for disturbing her meditations.

"No, no! You did not disturb me. A flea bit me in the breast. As it happens, I was just about to remark that God calls those whom he loves best."

For all that, Dame Agnes's words had startled her from a meditation. She had been reflecting that both the novices had brought good dowries, and therefore the house would be the gainer by their early deaths. Such speculations are unseemly in the shadow of death, yet it is usually in the shadow of death that one is forced to entertain them. Provisioning her household to resist the pestilence, she had bought in a rising market, and to buy at all she had been forced to pay money down. Summer was coming on, but because of the pestilence on the manor no work had been done, and there would be little revenue from crops or livestock this year. She would not get much from the convent's outlying property either: tithes, tolls, rents—the pestilence would be reason or excuse for their nonpayment, and she dared not go to law for them; Prioress Isabella (for whose detestable soul she must still pray God's mercy) had given Oby its stomachful of law-suits. Then Dame Beatrix and the other Dame Helen and the novice Cecily, who had had the sickness and recovered from it, would need dressings, salves, extra diet, and strong beer, and the same must be given out among the work-people. Then there would be the cost of a new priest. This must needs be a considerable item; she would scarcely find another who would tolerate the shabby hangings and broken floorboards of the gate-house lodging, which had appealed to Sir Peter as a mortification and which Sir Ralph had not been granted time to complain about. Indeed, as the pestilence wrought such particular havoc among men, priests would be at a premium and able to demand whatever they wished—and the same would apply to masons and carpenters. She had been counting on the book of hours to bring in a good sum, but this was crossed off by the death of Dame Alice Guillemard, while the colours and the gold leaf had still to be paid for. It was possible, of course, that in this downpour of deaths some legacies would come to the convent, and bequests for the saying of masses for the dead; but these were possibilities only; and at best time must go by and many formalities before they could be paid. Thinking of her spire, she said to herself that jackdaws were likely to be the only builders she would see on it.

Till now she had never had to face poverty. Oby was not a wealthy house, but it generally had a margin between its revenues and its outgoings. Lying far from any city, cut off from the world by marshes and heathland, its expenditure on transport was disproportionately high, and she had often listened to Dame Helen and Dame Blanch discussing whether it was worth while to send farther in order to buy cheaper; but they always concluded by agreeing that isolation benefited them in the long run, for it kept away visitors and pilgrims, and allowed them to be shabby without being shamed.

It had been an easy house to rule; remembrance of Prioress Isabella lasted on and reconciled the nuns to leading a humdrum life, a life stagnant but limpid. So they had lived. So, now, they were dying. For the extravaganza of death that was sweeping their world away suggested no changes to them except the change from being alive to being dead. They kept to the Rule, punctually offering God his regular service of prayer and praise. In the same spirit they also expected their meals to be as plentiful, and punctual as before. "It is bad enough to be without a priest. Surely we need not be without purslane," she had heard Dame Agnes remark to Dame Salome, who answered with a story of the piece of eggshell she had found in her pancake. If they had panicked, she could have been braver. If they had rebelled and disputed, she could have felt sure of her power to rule them. But with a meek, desponding fortitude they went on waiting to die while she with her knees knocking under her was asking herself how they could manage to live.

When the worst of the pestilence was past she called a meeting in chapter. Ninety years' tolerance had not made the converted dovehouse any more tolerable. It was cramped, and full of cross-draughts, and between the lofty roof and the empty room below such an echo was created that it seemed as if every dove ever hatched on the manor were haunting it. Consequently, it was seldom used, and only for the most formal and unpleasant occasions, a bishop's visit, the announcement of a new impost, the administration of rebukes and punishments. The nuns now climbed the stairs and sat themselves down on the cobwebbed benches. No doubt they would hear an admonition on the narrow space of time left them on an earth where, as in the time of Noah's deluge, the waters were rising, and of how that space should be filled with prayers and final meditations. They were surprised to hear themselves urged to be more economical: to darn little holes before they became large ones, to be sparing of fuel, to keep a sharp lookout for moths. Their prioress's voice, which was thin and reedy, contended with the flustering echoes. "Poverty, my daughters, is nothing to fear. As the brides of Christ, it is our portion. We must prepare ourselves for poverty." Her eyes, set shallowly in her pale, plump face, desperately perused their stolid ranks, but saw no answering alarm.

She talked on and on, darting from one precept of housewifery to another, the high price of pins, the extravagance of little loaves, the wastage of candles. She told them how much wood was thieved yearly off the convent lands, and how the cost of living must certainly rise, and how the convent's income must as certainly fall. She spoke of the increase in beggars they must look to face, and of the cost of a priest, which must now be met from their general income as the bridge over the Nene had given way, and the de Rettevilles, not getting the profit of the tolls, naturally refused to repair it. And again she asserted that poverty was nothing to fear. Being so appalled by what she had to say, she found it hard to leave off. When at last she had ended, her senior nuns assured her that they did not fear poverty in the least.

A sensation of irrevocable loneliness crushed her spirit. She lived with these women and she would end her days among them; yet she understood them no better than they understood her. There can hardly be intimacy in the cloister: before intimacy can be engendered there must be freedom, the option to approach or to move away. She stared at their faces, so familiar and undecipherable. They are like a tray of buns, she thought. In some the leaven has worked more than in others, some are a little under-baked, some a little scorched, in others the spice has clotted and shows like a brown stain; but one can see that they all come out of the same oven and that one hand pulled them apart from the same lump of dough. A tray of buns, a tray of nuns. . . .

After a difficult silence Dame Agnes suggested that they should proceed to appoint a treasuress to take the place of Dame Helen. She suggested Dame Salome. Dame Salome begged that she should not be chosen, saying truly that she had no talent for business. But the appointment was unanimously urged: plainly because of a general realization that the position of treasuress was going to be uncomfortable, and Dame Salome one of those mild, pillowy women who can be squeezed into tight places.

Irked by the sense that a responsibility which they had never bargained for had been imposed on them, the nuns left the chapter-house in silence. When they began to talk again it was all of religious matters—relics, vows, and cases of conscience. By the evening it had somehow been agreed that if death spared those still alive they should go in pilgrimage to Walsingham.

Dame Blanch began to rub her hands up and down her thighs, a trick of hers when she felt pleased or excited. In fancy she saw herself riding under an archway, and heard the horse's hoofs ring on the pavement. This, too, would come of the pestilence, just as the pestilence had brought about the chivalrous and miraculous arrival of Sir Ralph. Sir Ralph was still alive. He might even seem to be recovering, Dame Susanna said, but in truth he was only lingering. Though he could not lead their pilgrimage his soul would benefit by their prayers, unless, indeed, already released from purgatory he watched them from some heavenly turret. Craving for adventures, Dame Blanch had enjoyed the Black Death. She had been excited, dauntless, and even sought after. Her chatter about knights and fortresses had suddenly seemed heartening and authentic, and when she assured them that the battlefield smelled much worse than the infirmary because of all the entrails, no one remembered to remember that in fact she had entered religion at the age of ten, having seen no nearer approximation to warfare than a provincial tournament.

The pilgrimage of thanksgiving did not, of course, take place. Except to Dame Blanch it was merely something to talk about and a path of escape from thinking about economies. Sir Ralph's recovery took its place as a subject for conversation, for soon even Dame Susanna admitted that he was better, and well enough to leave his room and sup in the prioress's chamber. They made a little feast for him, and Dame Blanch as cellaress could not be prevented from assuring him at every mouthful how carefully it had been chosen for him and how much good he would gain from it, nor from reminding him jocosely how he had first come to them for a breakfast. He grew paler and paler. His face twitched; he put down a chicken-wing only half chewed. Supper being ended, Dame Salome and Dame Susanna rose and asked leave to retire. Dame Agnes sat on, and so did Dame Blanch. There was an awkward pause.

"Well, well," said Dame Blanch too genially, "now that supper is over, why do we not come to business?"

Thinking of the expenses at stake, the prioress looked at the window where a white cloud sailed peacefully above the insignificant horizon. A little more geniality, a few more encouragements, and he would refuse. Already there had been Dame Agnes's stories of her squirrel, and Dame Salome's conundrums. How could an educated man, fastidious too, with sickness, contemplate a future of such company? Still looking at the cloud, she said in a flat defeated voice that they now had definite confirmation of Sir Peter's death and wished to offer him Sir Peter's place. In a voice equally flat and defeated he accepted the offer. He seemed to be accepting because it was the quickest way to end a painful evening and get to bed.

To Ralph Kello it seemed like that. He had entered Oby on an impulse, and on an impulse he now engaged himself to stay. But the first impulse had been something spontaneous and hardy; this was a mere trickle, as though the last very small drop had sidled out of a tilted cask. He felt like an empty cask. Nothing was left him but an enormous consciousness of fatigue and a few ghostly sensualities: the relief of lying down, momentary pleasures from the smell of wine or spices, a momentary sensibility to colour. In the body's combat with sickness his mind, a poor ally, had gone down and been trampled to death. His conviction of damnation had lost all meaning, and so had his old ambitions, his curiosities, his resentment against that fatality of being a nobody's bastard which had barred the chancel door against him. He would stay quietly on at Oby, doing a priest's duty since that was what they required of him, and being housed and fed. And what would be, would be.

Having secured her priest, the prioress could give a more judicial mind to examining him. Perhaps he was not quite all she had supposed: not so sympathetic, not so capable—in fact, slothful and rather glum. But she had got him, and he seemed prepared to put up with his floorboards till he fell through them, and her nuns liked him, and—perhaps his greatest recommendation—he had become hers with very little trouble. As the Black Death moved northward and its shadow rolled away she looked round on her landscape, summing up what was lost and what remained. Of her twelve nuns four had died, and two novices; and two other novices whose parents had taken them away to escape the sickness had died at home. However, she could reckon on their dowries, their parents could scarcely default on such an obligation. Of the four dead nuns two had been under twenty. As Dame Helen would have said, they had eaten very little of their provender. Were Dame Helen alive now how shrewdly and with what impartial pleasure she would be casting her balance of profit and loss! No doubt she would be allowing for many more losses than were apparent to the prioress; even so, the final balance might not be altogether discouraging. On the manor the Black Death's encroachments were unequivocal. Many of the best men were dead and many of the ablest women: Big Roger, the three Ragges, Baldie Shipperson, the cooper and his boy, Anne and Katharine Noot, the best reapers on the manor, and Emme who washed sheepskins and made candles, and Joan Scole and Joan Pick. Later on, when the hay was in, a requiem must be said for the repose of all these souls. But what sort of hay crop would it be? For months the cattle had been straying where they pleased, eating what they found: hay, rye, or winter barley. Her thoughts having taken a more cheerful turn since the affair of a priest was settled, she supposed that if the beasts had eaten the crops they would at least be the fatter for it, so that what was lost one way was gained another.

She felt less confident, and more than ever regretful for Dame Helen who had been so clever at overcoming difficulties, when she had talked to Jesse Figg, the convent's bailiff. The hay, he said, wasn't so bad. But who was to win it? She ran her finger down the roll whence the names of the dead had been scored off. She repeated the names of the living.

"They wouldn't do it, Madam Prioress. Not now. Flog, flay, or fine, they wouldn't do it."

"Not do it? What do you mean?"

"They're thinking of themselves. They're behind-hand on their own work, and that's what they'll do first. Pease and beans, that's what they'll plant—pease and beans to stay them through the winter."

"But work for the manor must come first," Dame Salome interposed.

"Not this season, Madam Treasuress. If they cheated the sickness one year, they say, it wasn't to starve the next. That's what they're saying. And it's the same everywhere. Ours are no worse than any others. Maybe they'll come along after they've looked out for themselves," he added. "But I darsn't drive them."

Why should they be driven, she thought maternally. They are only stupid children. Persuasion will bring them back. And she took particular pains over the three masses for the souls of the manor's dead. The nave was cleared of its lumber. Garlands were hung along the screen and the boy Jackie was sent up a ladder to dust the rood-loft. The west door was forced open, its rusty hinges whining like an old dog with rheumatism; for the nave was so small, Brian de Retteville having thought only of the nun's quire beyond the screen, that it would not hold all the worshippers, and the later-comers would have to kneel outside.

The summer air streamed in, warm and purifying, and the garlands rustled and tapped against the wood. She heard the people coming in, whispering among themselves. They were comparing the convent's church with their parish church at Wivelham and with the friars' great church at Waxelby. They snuffed approvingly. She had ordered that the incense was not to be spared; but even so it could not mask the odour of sweat and poverty that came in with them. The candles on the altar burned with a pure scent, their smoke and the clouds of incense spun a visible blue on the air. The singing, too, was excellent: a small body of tone but very pure and accurate. Only Sir Ralph did not strike her as doing his part as well as he might. His voice was carelessly pitched, and he gave an impression of being hurried.

Afterward there was a distribution of small mutton pies, and a child was heard crying because he had not seen the convent ladies. "I want to be a nun, I want to be a nun!" he lamented.

This innocence was often recalled among the nuns, the more tenderly because at that time the children on the manor were being peculiarly tiresome and ill-behaved. With parents either dead or still sickly, they were running wild, thieving, maiming, and destroying. They killed the convent's doves and roasted them on spits; they swarmed through the reed-fence into the orchard and broke the trees; they overturned the beehives; they threw a dead dog into the fish-pond; during office hours they marched up and down singing lewd choruses to an accompaniment of bird-rattles and old cauldrons. At first they had come to the convent to hunt Ursula's Jackie. Though he was better grown than most of his peers, being better housed and fed, he was timid and backward. When he heard them coming he turned pale and ran. But one day when his mother was not there to protect him they caught him and dragged him away, saying that they intended to pluck, skin, and roast him. Late that same evening he came back, bruised, filthy, tattered, and a changed boy: bragging of all the mischief he had done and all the enormities he had witnessed. After that there was no keeping him from their company. He feared them as much as ever, but his fear had turned itself inside-out and now he was a ringleader among them.

Ursula's complaints became so tedious to all who listened to them that finally the prioress decided that it was time Sir Ralph took the boy and made a clerk of him.

At this time she was making many decisions. Early in the new year Dame Blanch had a fit, and became childish—a noisy and rollicking childishness which imposed a great strain on the decorum of the younger nuns. As she could not fulfil her post as cellaress she was retired and the other Dame Helen took her place. Dame Blanch's relations in the world had not troubled about her for years, but in that summer, as ill luck would have it, Humphrey de Fanal rode to Oby to visit his aunt and to present a small reliquary containing a tooth of one of the Holy Innocents to the house where his daughter had ended her short life. Dame Blanch happened to be in one of her more rational moments. Humphrey could see no reason why she should have been deposed and put away in the infirmary, and she, in her rambling explanation, chivalrously defending the prioress's decision, did not supply him with one. His aunt was ill-used. His daughter was dead; that too was a form of ill-usage. He left Oby in dudgeon, taking the reliquary with him.

To lose so interesting a relic, even though one had never really possessed it, was bad enough. A more serious loss was to follow. One of the two novices who had been taken away at the time of the Black Death and who had afterward died at home was the daughter of William de Stoke, and Humphrey and William were brothers-in-law. Presumably Humphrey said something to his sister about the treatment of their aunt. The de Stokes, who supplied a yearly provision of wine as part of their daughter's dowry, defaulted. This was the more disquieting as the parents of the other novice who had died at home had from the first demanded her dowry back, alleging that between leaving Oby and dying the girl had changed her mind and been betrothed. These parents were of no great social standing, there was little hope of shaming them into a more religious frame of mind. With the de Stokes it was different. They had a reputation to keep up; moreover, by sending one consignment of wine after their daughter's death they had admitted the obligation. So argued the elder ladies of the house, supporting their prioress in her sharp if rather sketchy conviction that something must be done about it, and could best be done by means of the bishop.

Sir Ralph was asked to give his advice, and said that they had best get a legal opinion. Dame Agnes, who always preferred to disagree with her prioress, now reminded her how in the days of Prioress Isabella, God rest her soul, the bishop had been worse than useless to them.

"That was the old bishop. There is a new bishop now."

"A new broom sweeps clean," Dame Salome pronounced. "Which reminds me, dear Mother, we must have a new broom. The passages are really quite filthy. Of course, Ursula is growing very short-sighted."

"I have treated her with euphrasy water, but I don't think it has done her much good," said Dame Susanna.

"Sea-water is best. If only we were near the sea!" Dame Beatrix exclaimed; and she was telling them how the Cornish fishermen preserve their sight with sea-water when Dame Agnes interrupted, remarking that they seemed to be wandering from the point and adding that as the bishop was a new man he would probably be too busy just now to spare much attention for a nunnery.

The prioress stiffened. She was loath to give up the bishop, because if he would not act for them they would have to pay fees to a lawyer.

"I remember, my daughters, that in the time of Prioress Isabella the bishop was prejudiced against us because he thought we had shown too much independence in refusing Dame Emily. We don't want to get a name for independence."

"But as you yourself pointed out, dear Mother, this is a different bishop. It is unlikely that he would know anything about Dame Emily's affair."

"I still maintain that we were justified in . . ."

Haled back from Cornwall, they were now heading toward a discussion of the rights and wrongs of Dame Emily.

Sir Ralph folded his arms and coughed. "There is another consideration to bear in mind. We do not know how this new bishop feels about dowries. He may not approve of them."

They were silent, their attention riveted by this extraordinary surmise.

"Obviously, dowries are expedient. Ladies cannot lead the religious life with decency if they are to be beggars and paupers. But, nevertheless, there are some extreme churchmen who deny this, and say that monastics should be apostolically poor. Fancies of this sort delight the laity, who are only too willing to learn that they have no obligation to support the religious. All this is in the wind now, and perhaps our new bishop may not wish to mix himself up in a squabble about dowries."

They are all the same, thought the prioress. I might be listening to Sir Peter. She said, "I really do not see how we can live on air."

At the same moment Dame Salome began to explain how very galling it would be for those families who paid dowries to see others going scot-free. In the end, she pointed out, no one would pay anything at all.

"That is why I advise you to consult a lawyer, who is less likely to act opportunistically than a bishop. Make ye friends with the Mammon of Unrighteousness and he will receive you into everlasting habitations."

"And do you really think that the bishop might refuse to take up our case?"

"I think he might even forbid you to proceed in it."

Sir Ralph went back to his lodging and sat down with a sigh of relief. He thought that the bishop had been fended off for the present. He had no wish to obtrude himself on bishops. Having sighed with relief, he grinned with pleasure. It had been enjoyable to throw this cat among his ladies, whom just now he was finding almost intolerable. His grudge against them began when he had to teach Jackie. He did not mind the boy so much; but teaching Jackie exposed him to Ursula's gratitude, and he disliked Ursula a great deal. His dislike was increased by a morbid apprehension that he would come to dislike her more and more. It alarmed him to be feeling such loathing for such an insignificant person, to catch himself avoiding the sight of her, leaping aside from the thought that a hair in the soup might be one of her hairs, or sitting in his room like a prisoner because he fancied he could hear her breathing outside the door. Once, when Dame Susanna had spoken of how devotedly Ursula had nursed him during his sickness, he had been compelled to lean from the window and vomit.

In songs and romances an apostate nun may be a romantic figure. God's Mother becomes her proxy in the convent and pins up the curtain before her frailties; but in real life she is a drab like any other drab, nursing her baby and eyeing her lover and the tankards from the tavern doorway. Ursula at Oby, among loyal nuns, Ursula with her sly sad glances and her hot breath, was an indecency. She was there like a grub in an apple. What about yourself? asked a rapid voice. True enough; and reason enough why he should hate the sight of her. Now she was forever pestering him with hopes that Jackie was a good scholar, and fingering him with gratitude and little services. So it was no wonder that his exasperation enlarged itself, and took in the nun's boy and the loyal nuns as well. When the prioress invited him to make one of the expeditions to consult a lawyer he felt as much relief at a holiday from Ursula as on the score of evading the bishop. The bishop could not be everlastingly evaded, sooner or later he must come to Oby on a Visitation; but half a loaf is better than no bread; and every month that postponed the bishop weathered him more naturally into the Oby landscape. He had done all in his power to encourage the prioress to make this expedition. Being a woman and a natural gadabout, she had not really needed encouragement. Being a woman in authority, though, and a natural featherhead, nothing could nail her to a decision, and not till the morning when they set out, the prioress, Dame Helen, and himself, did he feel secure that things would go as he hoped. For a long time the problem of a suitable bower-woman to wait on the ladies had kept them dangling over the bishop's lap: then in the nick of time came Pernelle Bastable. Pernelle was a widow, childless, and with just enough wealth and more than enough high spirits not to want another husband. She boarded herself at a convent, till the convent was rebuked for keeping too many boarders, when, as Pernelle was only a small-fry person, she was sent away. After trying the amenities of two other convents she applied to Oby. The money she could pay for her board was not much, but the agility with which she took a swarm of bees during her interview of application convinced Dame Salome that Pernelle would prove a good pennyworth. She had, too, her own horse and saddle; and scarcely had she done with exclaiming over the delight of being settled and tranquil at last before the horse was saddled and Pernelle hooded for another journey.

The August sun was climbing lazily out of the mists when they set out. Watching their departure, Dame Blanch received her last disillusionment: Sir Ralph had a deplorable seat. The thought of that pilgrimage to Walsingham returned to her, her fancy of riding under an archway, hearing the horsebells jingle and smelling the wholesome sweat of her mount. Now they were riding toward the Lintoft heath and she was left behind, an old woman supping gruel and supported by pillows. There would be no pilgrimage to Walsingham, no adventures by the way, no fording of rivers, no wandering through forests, no castles. She would end her days still a prisoner, among silly women a silly old woman. She ripped open her pillow and began to throw handfuls of feathers about the room, weeping and screaming as she did so. The feathers flew into her open mouth. Then the usual pattering footsteps came patiently pattering to the infirmary, and Dame Susanna bent over her, holding her wrists with her soft hands and saying that she really must not excite herself, that no harm was likely to befall their prioress even though she was obliged to go on a journey. When she lay back exhausted, Dame Susanna began to pick the feathers out of her mouth.

The prioress had decided that the lawyer should be consulted in York, saying that it would not be judicious to be consulting lawyers in the cathedral city of their own bishop, and adding that though York seemed a long way off she had a cousin there with whom they could lodge with no expense beyond a few gratuities to the household. In fact, she wanted to examine the minster. Though it would be painful to see fine architecture while her spire was halted and unlikely to go further, the pain would be a small price for the pleasure of seeing something new. She looked back. A rise of ground had already obliterated Oby. A spire would be visible from here, giving a soul and a reason to the flat country, and any traveller would bless her for it. But her spire, however lovely from a distance and lovely in itself, might disappoint that traveller as he came nearer, and saw it in its relation to the body of the building. That is the curse of having to work on someone else's foundation. The awkwardness of an earlier generation will assert itself through later additions, like an original sin. It might be possible to lengthen the nave, or seemingly to lengthen it by adding a portail to the west door. If the nave were lengthened, the spire would be more nearly centred and the disparity between height and length less apparent. Meanwhile, Pernelle Bastable was chattering about Lincoln. She had been there, it seemed; but only to eat eels and buy a lined gown and visit a nephew.

"No Jews now," she chirruped, "to waylay poor little lads and hang them up in cellars. It was a good day for England when they were packed off. My grandfather—he was a ship's captain —saw a whole shipload of Jews spilled and drowning off Wittesand. The waves were speckled with their bales and parcels bobbing up and down. My grandfather cast a hook and line, and hauled up one of the bales, and inside it there was a gold cup, and baby-clothes of finest linen, and little padded caps with furred ears, little gloves—christian babies, my grandfather said, had no such gear."

"Poor things!" Dame Helen said.

A hook . . . a hook fastening in a bale and dragging it up from the boiling surge. A hook dragging up a body, and the body corrupting as soon as the air touched it. That is what I dreamed of in my sickness, Sir Ralph thought.

A moment later Pernelle Bastable dismounted, having caught sight of some mushrooms. "They won't be here on our way back," she remarked wisely.

By the next day they were well inland. A light rain fell, the apples shone on the boughs. Their road, mounting and descending through a rich, rolling landscape, continually presented them with new things to admire; and after the sad fen country round Oby to be travelling through this landscape so full of plenty and variety was like turning the pages of an illuminated psalter.

At the inns Pernelle Bastable showed all the wiles of an experienced traveller, calling for hot water, demanding chickens and pillows, following the hostler to the stable.

"It is wonderful what God sends us," remarked Dame Helen. "First a priest, now a Pernelle. We should have done badly without her, for we could scarcely shout and bustle as she does." The prioress agreed, thinking that left to herself Dame Helen would indeed have done badly; for she always agreed with every statement and fell in with every suggestion.

It was a late afternoon when they first caught sight of the minster: dominating the city, as Pernelle pointed out, like a hen brooding her chickens. If it isn't a hen it's a goose, thought the prioress. The journey had been delightful, but now it was over, and the proximity of the lawyer dashed her spirits. She felt exhausted with travelling, and even more exhausted by the atmosphere of rustic inferiority which she must breathe, it seemed, whether she travelled or stayed at home. When her hostess, Marie de Blakeborn, whose first husband had been a de Foley, welcomed her with the news that cousin Thomas, the prior of Etchingdon, had heard she was coming and would sup with them that night, her first impulse was to plead fatigue and take refuge in bed. She had not seen Thomas for twenty years. During those years he had become more and more distinguished, while she had lived at Oby. But when she saw him the prior of Etchingdon was so little changed that she began to think that she might not be much altered either.

"Look at us! How well we've both got on," he said, in the manner she so well remembered: a manner at once warm and insincere, but with an insincerity which was deeply flattering, since it implied a common indifference to what wounded less enlightened self-esteems. She laughed without a shade of mortification.

"The prior of Etchingdon! The prioress of Oby! Solomon and the Queen of Sheba!"

"The goose-girl and the goose-boy! But you are luckier, you don't have to herd a mixed flock of geese and ganders."

He began to mock at the incommodities of the Gilbertine Order, telling of his quarrel with the nuns, who were supposed to see to the victualling of the monks, but supplied them with nothing but soup.

"I reminded the dear creatures of their vow of obedience. The next day the cabbage soup had radishes in it—two and a half radishes (we counted them) for each man."

It was the same old story of kitchen and buttery; but as he told it the greed of his monks, the peevishness of his nuns, was transfigured into the grotesque. Fired into wanting to have something to recount also, and forgetting all about the lawyer, she began to consult him about the spire and the problem of reconciling it to the existing building. He pulled out his writing materials and she sketched the ground-plan with the belfry jutting artlessly from the northwest corner. She might lengthen the nave, he said, and balance Brian de Retteville's old stump by a porch to the south; then she would have balance and yet avoid the pedestrian symmetry which made so many of the new friary churches appear to have been designed not by artists but by grammarians. He went on to say that the transition from the stump to the spire would call for management.

"I thought of doing it rather like this."

The rest of the party saw the resemblance between the cousins, and felt that the tie of blood excused this monopolization of the guest of the evening.

"And your country is flat?"

"Flat as a trencher."

"You will bring it to life. What I like so much about your design is its unanimity. It looks as though from the very first you had seen it as a whole."

"I did."

She told him of her vision when Prioress Isabella choked on the plum-stone and turned blue, adding, "But I shall have prayed her into heaven long before I can get on with the spire."

God forbid, he said devoutly. If lack of ready money were the obstacle, that could be overcome tomorrow. York was full of the most worthy usurers.

She answered that she dared not incur any more debts. "For I know how it would be!" she exclaimed, heedless now whether or no she exposed the poverty of her house. "The interest would fall due, and just at that moment the floods would carry off our corn-shocks, or the King would ask us for three men-at-arms, or the roof would fall in, or our church at Lantock would burn to the ground and we should have to rebuild it."

"I am sure that would be a great improvement. Have you many spiritualities?"

"One at Lantock near Northampton and one in Cambridgeshire."

"That's not enough. I must find you some more."

"I would rather you took those we have. They are the curse of my life. The tithes are never paid us unless we drag them out like teeth, and the vicars are always in some trouble or other. God does not wish his nuns to own spiritualities."

He tapped his bald head with a bony forefinger. "Listen, my dear prioress. All this can be managed. Etchingdon has just appropriated another church. We will do all the business for you, and you shall have half the revenues."

"How much for the vicar?" she inquired.

"Nothing at all. We don't propose to put one in, at any rate for the present. Since the pestilence it is impossible to find a spare priest at a reasonable price. People think of nothing but money," he said, "and what do they do with it when they've got it? Spend it hoggishly on themselves, or endow chantries for their souls, which is really only a rarefied self-indulgence. No doubt we are much pleasanter people than our forbears. But compared to them how mean-spirited we are, how lacking in enterprise! Look at the old buildings! I daresay they seem uncouth, but what a grandiose imagination conceived them! Now we only tinker and ornament and enlarge windows and put canopies over tombs."

"I like modern architecture," she said.

"I like your spire, because it is ambitious. But if you were proposing to smother old Brian de Retteville in pleats and fancywork I would not give you a penny to further it. As it is, I offer you half the Methley great tithe and all the little tithe, for really it's too small to be worth dividing. And if that's not enough, then ask me for more. It will be a great satisfaction to me to think of some portion of a church revenue being properly spent."

"But, Thomas, I am not easy about the little tithe. Surely it is very wrong to leave a parish without a priest?"

"Methley is a great scattered parish, inhabited by long-legged cattle-drovers. It will be no trouble to them to walk elsewhere for their mass. And no priest is better than a bad priest."

"Do you really mean that?"

She had it in her mind to tell him about Sir Peter's departure for Waxelby, an example of a diametrically opposite way of thinking; but he had turned to the others and was telling them how beautifully his cousin's spire would rise out of the melancholy flatness of the moors; and though she felt the falseness of their interest compared with his, their questions and congratulations smothered her uneasiness about the little tithe of Methley. After all, Thomas was prior of Etchingdon and must know what he was doing. To refuse the little tithe would seem priggish and ill-mannered, and be of no benefit to the Methley parishioners either, since there was to be no priest in any case.

III. PRIORESS ALICIA

(August 1351–October 1357)

In his lifetime the Black Death, a sorcerer travelling from China, had shifted the balance of christendom and killed half the folk in England. But to Ursula's Jackie it seemed that nothing new ever happened or ever would. The bell rang and the nuns went into quire. The bell rang and the serfs in the great field paused in their labour and crossed themselves, and then scratched themselves, and then went on working. The little bell rang and Christ was made flesh. One day the thought had risen up in him: Suppose I don't ring my bell—what then? This thought had come on a summer afternoon when the noise of the grasshoppers was everywhere. For an instant the sun had seemed to smite him with a tenfold heat, he felt himself dissolving like wax, and the butts of the mown grass where he lay pricked him like a thousand daggers. What then? The end of the world, perhaps. The bell silent, Christ not made, the world snapped like a bubble. Perhaps. But also a beating. Sitting up, he shook the hair out of his eyes and saw a grasshopper and tore it apart and felt better. The sun was no stronger than before and all round him it was a summer afternoon and the grasshoppers were chirping and the dun horse feeding and everything was as usual.

The willows and alders cast their leaves, the clouds gathered, the earth darkened, the autumn rains began. One morning there would be a great bellowing of beasts. It was Martinmas, when the pigs and cattle were driven to the shed and slaughtered for winter meat. After that it seemed to grow dark very quickly, as though darkness steamed out of the great cauldrons where they made the black-puddings. A frosty day coming in December scratched one's eyes, the sunlight was so suddenly brilliant. Through Christmas and Epiphany there were sweet dishes, pastes of eggs and figs and ground almonds that encrusted the spoon and the mixing-bowls. A pittance of unmixed wine made the nuns a little tipsy, they walked more swimmingly and were unwontedly polite, and when they spoke their voices were pitched as though they were just about to sing. This amiability made it difficult to tell them apart. But each face resumed its particular expression, and through February and March he was glad to stay in the kitchen, watching the wind ruffle the pool of rainwater that spread from under the woodhouse door, and eating the chips of dried cod that flew from under the mallet. Round and round went the days like a mill-wheel, and because it was Lent when penances are remembered, on Fridays his mother went barefooted to the cloisters to repeat the penitential psalms and be scourged by the prioress. No one much pitied her, neither did he; and hearing Mabel say that the bishop's sentence had ordained that the scourgings should continue throughout the year and that only the prioress's laziness restricted them to Lent, he felt defrauded, as though his significance as a nun's child were belittled.

Being a nun's child distinguished him from the other children about the place, and even when they taunted him he knew he was more interesting than they, and that whatever future awaited him he would not, like them, live tethered to the sour soil of the manor. In spring, when all young animals play together, he played with them and was their ringleader, but when the days grew hot he left them and went to lie among the rushes, hidden, as he liked to lie. And so it would be full summer again, and he would be a year older, and this summer, surely, he would be old enough to go to Waxelby Fair.

But no summer is so long, so wide, as the summer before it. Time, a river, hollows out its bed, and every year the river flows in a narrower channel and flows faster. Jackie was old enough to work now, and Jesse Figg, the bailiff, set him to weave hurdles or spread dung or keep the cows from straying into the young crops, and Mabel added that a cowherd has time on his hands, time enough to gather the tufts of wool that the sheep leave on brambles. Now, too, there was this new woman, this Pernelle. Sometimes she was a pleasure, for her clothes were coloured, and she could tell stories, and with a fine comb she would scratch the lice out of his head when they became troublesome. But at other times she was hateful, bustling after him and saying, "Jackie, do this! Jackie, do that! Jackie, Jackie! Where's my little page?" Then he would have to help her set up her loom or pound ginger or pick over feathers for pillows, or she would send him out to collect dew for a facewash; for being a townswoman she was full of such notions. And her stories, after all, were not worth much. Though they were of different places they were all about herself; and wherever she had gone she had always been the same Pernelle, cleverer and more meritorious than anyone else. If she spoke of anyone else, it was always her three nephews, who were such fine brisk boys, no bookworms. You would never see them with their eyes reddened by crying over grammar.

"Grammar, grammar! Who's the better for grammar? The Apostles had none."

"Saint Paul was a scholar," said Ursula.

"So they say. But he was never pope. That was for Saint Peter who was only a fisherman. Saint Paul's grammar never hoisted him so far."

She plunged her smooth hand into the belly of a goose.

"If you had seen as much of the world as I have you wouldn't care to have the priest stuffing your boy with grammar. All this hickorum-hackorum never filled a belly yet. Look at my brother-in-law the armourer. He can neither read nor write but he can afford to pay two clerks to keep his accounts for him, and in his house there are three beds, one of green serge, one of russet, and one of a most beautiful blue. The abbess of Shaftesbury hasn't finer beds. But plenty of poor honest souls lie on rotten straw while these abbots and abbesses loll on goose-down, thinking over their Latin. Let them work, I say! Let them earn a living as other people do! Many's the day my brother-in-law has worked twelve hours at a stretch, forging link after link till the eyes stood out of his head. Quite right, too! We are put into the world to labour. Let them labour like the blessed Apostles, that's what I say. And if your Jackie were my Jackie I'd take him from those books and send him off with the masons."

Jackie's heart assented to these last words. As learning went on it became less agreeable. There were fewer discoveries in it, it lengthened out like a midday road. Sir Ralph had ceased to teach him what he could repeat to the astonishment of others. There were no more anecdotes of the basilisk, the swallow curing her blindness, the virtues of precious stones. Instead, it was all proportions and properties, things impossible to remember. And there sat Sir Ralph, plucking at his lower lip, brooding some thought of his own, or endlessly, scornfully patient.

"The Proportion of Diapente, I said. What is the Proportion of Diapente? Pooh, you will never learn! And why should you?"

Among the masons it was different. They were kind jolly men, they always had a welcome for him, and the fish they caught and roasted in coffins of river-clay tasted better than any food cooked by his mother, or Mabel, or the widow Bastable even. It was in the spring of 1352 that the masons came, and put up their booths in the shelter of Saint Leonard's wood—which had that name because the timber sold from it paid for the candles which burned before the figure of the patron saint. The convent supplied their main victuals, but they eked out the supply with what they poached from pool or thicket. In the convent it was all women living together, and in the masons' settlement it was all men. He liked the men better. For one thing, they made more of him. There was always something to eat and a knee to lean against, and the rough hands that stroked his head stroked uninquiringly, never pausing to ferret after vermin or tweak out tangles. They told stories too, stories of wonder-working shrines and clever animals and the bands of wolves that came down from the Welsh mountains. They made the more of him because he was the only child who visited them. The manor people cold-shouldered the masons. They were strangers and thieves; worse, they were building the new spire with money which should have been spent in repairing houses and supplying ointment for plague-sores. Even now many of those who had recovered from the Black Death were limping about with open sores, though it was two years since the plague had left the manor; or where sores had healed rheumatism had followed, and cramps that disabled a man when he had worked for no more than a couple of hours. Straightening up from their toil in the field, the labourers would see the stonework, white as bleached linen, new as nothing else about the place was new. To cart those stones they had been obliged to spend their days and the strength of their oxen tugging loads across the heath. All for nothing, all for display and vanity! If the prioress must spend her money away from the manor let her buy some relic, something that would cure agues or avert cattle murrain or help a childing woman.

But those proud nuns knew neither the curse of Adam nor the curse of Eve.

Since the Black Death the relations between convent and its manor had been getting steadily worse. The work was still done, the dues were still paid—but with delays, cheats, interminable English arguments. The bailiff became more and more like an ambassador carrying terms from one camp to another.

The older nuns, whose lives had accustomed them to broils within the convent but only compliance from the dun landscape without were troubled at these changes. It was not christian, they said, to have the sulks and grumbles of the working-classes so continually thrust before their noses. How could a nun contemplate when within earshot there was a dispute about whether or no William Scole would yield his ox on the Thursday to bring in a load of firing, whether or no the family of Noot should pay a fine for the loss of their son to the manor?—Mabel, who knew everything, and Jesse Figg both asserted that the boy had gone to find paid work elsewhere, though his family continued to declare that he had been drowned in the flood on Saint Luke's day. It was not seemly. It was not christian. The prioress was to blame for allowing it. It should be reported to the bishop.

But when the bishop next came for a Visitation he took it for granted that Oby should be experiencing labour troubles. Instead of condoling with them he said they were fortunate to have serfs who would still remain on their manor, and congratulated the prioress on being wise enough to know when to give way a little. Dame Margaret, a nun who was transferred to them about this time, bore out what the bishop had said with her story of the nunnery whence she had come. There, the serfs were so unruly that one day they had gone off in a body, leaving only the old and the infirm behind them. The abbess had been forced to hire labour, and this at such an exorbitant rate that the finances of the house had given way and some of the nuns had had to be redistributed, Dame Margaret being one of them. Her reading of the times, however, was opposed to the bishop's. There must be a firmer rule, she said, more penalties and more punishments, or society would fall to pieces and christendom be the prey of heathen invaders.

The younger nuns disregarded these croakings. They said that things had never gone so well as now. There was the spire going up, a pleasure to watch, the exciting visits from the prior of Etchingdon, the revenues that were coming from Methley. Their prioress was really a fine woman of business. Instead of scraping like a hen in the manor acres, scratching up a grain here and a grain there, she had spread her wings in a longer flight and had come back from York with a whole new spirituality in her mouth—as it might be Noah's dove. That was how one should manage: with bold strokes, with a policy that fitted the times. In these days a convent could not afford to turn its back on the world, spin its own wool and wear it, live on eggs and salad through the summer, sleep through the winter like a dormouse, and never receive a novice who had not three aunts and a cousin among the nuns.

"Yet we are told to renounce the world," said Dame Susanna.

"That is not to say that the world is to renounce us," replied Dame Isabel. "Besides, we are also told not to hide our light under a bushel. We cannot forever go on in the old way, booming in our swamp like so many bitterns."

Though she was young, Dame Isabel de Scottow was already a personage, and talked in chapter with as much weight as if she had been a nun for twenty years. She would argue her point so reasonably, so gracefully, that no one felt herself humbled by being talked round. Here, in embryo, was a most eminent prioress—if her fevers and shivering fits did not carry her away first. The prioress had already contemplated resigning in her favour, and was only kept from it by the assurances of some of her elder ladies that a prioress who spent half the year in bed would be worse than no prioress at all. Instead, a new post was created for her—the post of guest-mistress. Now that Oby was seeing so much company a guest-mistress was really quite necessary.

It was a pity that no post could be found for Dame Matilda, who was also of the stuff from which prioresses are made, though she had no outward graces and had come to the convent late, and under a cloud: a novice of eighteen who had been bedded with a husband, and only scrambled out of bed on a plea of nullity, causing Dame Agnes to mutter about fish, flesh, and red herrings. But Dame Matilda was still young and so healthy that she would certainly survive till a death or a resignation freed a post for her. If only Dame Salome would resign! She had proved a wretched treasuress. But people like Dame Salome never resign. Each time she exclaimed "If it were not for love of Our Lady and Saint Leonard I could not keep on!" one knew that only death would detach her from her burden.

Divided on a moral issue—the old nuns so naturally saying that one must be faithful to old ideas, and the younger nuns saying that one must live in the date where God has sent one—the convent was preserved from lesser bickerings. Pernelle Bastable with her considerable experience of convents declared that she had never known such peacefulness, that one might be among holy images rather than among holy ladies. At other times she admitted that such tranquillity made life a little dull and that she felt herself growing old before her time—since without some small dissensions the blood grows thick, as in oxen, who age before bulls do. Fortunately she felt a great benevolence toward the masons, and was out on every sunny morning, warning them to be careful not to fall off the scaffolding. Pernelle's slope of mind toward kitchen and brewhouse made her a convenient boarder. From Pernelle being in the kitchen to oversee the cooking of some particular mess for herself it was a short step to Pernelle being in the kitchen filling sausages for them all. A good useful sort of woman, the prioress thought; suppressing the thought that followed it: that Pernelle among the masons was almost intolerable. It would have astonished the prioress to learn from some incontrovertible source, an angel, say, that next to herself it was Pernelle Bastable who felt the keenest enthusiasm about the spire: muddied, certainly, by pleasure in the masons, excitement to have something going forward, hopes of a day when the completed spire would bring company to admire it; but for all that springing from a true pleasure in fine building.

It was in 1351 that the prioress made her visit to York—where she took a lawyer's opinion on the disputed dowries but went no further. In the following year the prior of Etchingdon made the first of his three visits to Oby. Luckily he came at Martinmas, so there was plenty of fresh meat and stubble geese in good condition; and the darkening weather was really an advantage, for with a spirited fire rooms do not show their shabbiness as they do in summer. But even in a November dusk Sir Ralph's cassock could not pass muster; and among all her other preparations Dame Isabel found time to measure him for a new one, which the novices made up under Dame Agnes's supervision. After so much sweeping and garnishing it was a surprise that the great prior of Etchingdon, a man known throughout England, could be such an approachable figure, talking to everyone, speaking English like any peasant, smiling if he as much as caught your eye, sneezing without dissimulation and apologizing to everyone for having such a frightful cold. At their first sight of this extraordinary prior the simpler nuns could not believe that this was indeed the man. It must be one of the others: the stout one, or the one in a furred hood who looked so very scholarly and ascetic. But, no! The stout one was the secretary and he of the furred hood was the Etchingdon clerk of the works, who had been brought because he was such a good man of business, delighting in costings and estimates. Further inspection of Prior Thomas convinced them that thus, and no otherwise, should a great cleric look, talk, and behave. His eccentricities were the sign of good breeding; his extravagances betokened a heavenly unacquaintance with ordinary cares. One forgot that the house was shabby, that one's skirts were narrow, that one's company manners were rusty, that the noises from the kitchen were too plainly audible in quire, that Dame Salome was again singing much too loud and had lapsed into her old habit of *et in saeclula saeclulolum.* Even his cold was gracious and yielded to Dame Susanna's horehound with poppy-seeds.

Listening to the subsequent praises, Dame Isabel thought, And not one of you suspects that all this simplicity and spontaneity, and all those sneezes, represent the height of arrogance. She was wrong. Sir Ralph, travelling by a coarser route, had arrived at the same conclusions.

Perhaps being put into a new cassock had sharpened his insight. To be put into a new cassock in order to appear with decency before a great man who insists on treating you as an equal can be a mortifying experience. A prior of Etchingdon should not straddle the gulf fixed between him and the priest of an unimportant nunnery like a boy leaping back and forth across a ditch. What call has he to be so ingratiating? grumbled the lesser man. Questioning me about Toledo, envying me my travels . . . he knows well enough that all I saw in Toledo is what a poor man sees anywhere: a glimpse through a doorway, a garden behind a grating, and on a saint's day six inches of a bishop going in procession. So he growled to himself, devouring the fine food which was served because of the visitor and which his resentment distracted him from enjoying.

His third winter at Oby was closing about him. He was lonely, uncomfortable, bored, and damned. For a quiet anteroom to hell he had engaged himself to Oby: a bargain with a weasel, a bad bargain. True, he no longer had to wonder how he should earn, beg, or steal the price of a breakfast; but instead of his own money troubles he listened to the money troubles of the convent. True, he had escaped from the company of rogues, pilgrims, and prostitutes to the company of good women; but he had as little in common with the one as with the other. As for his future, it was no more certain than before; for it seemed to him that he could not endure another year of his present life, and his thoughts trudged in a round of speculation as to how he should live next, whether he should go to a town and hope to pick up a livelihood as a copyist, or follow the plough (there was a demand now for any man who would work on the land), or load a pack with bones and beads and set up as a relic-pedlar, or go to sea, or become a soldier. He must do one or the other, one day or another he must set about it. Meanwhile, he was still bewintered at Oby, and thinking, Tomorrow is Saturday, so we shall have beans and bacon. I hope there will be more bacon in my portion this Saturday.

The new cassock had a wider girth than the old one. He had put on flesh, he was broad now as well as long. All the more to frizzle, he had said, answering Dame Isabel's jokes as she measured him. He could talk so and feel no more than a numb appreciation of the jest. Not that he doubted of damnation. He was as sure about hell-fire as any good simple old woman watching her pot boil. But having gone into his sickness in a frenzy of terror he had somehow come out again with only the formula of fear. From time to time he felt horribly afraid; but what he feared was not the ultimate hell-fire, but that nearer day, sure to come, when terror would rouse up again and take hold of him. Then he would go mad.

The Martinmas visit was a time of plans and talk, and one of the plans was that Prior Thomas and the clerk of the works should come back in the spring to see how the work was going on. Before Easter the nuns were talking of how they should receive their guests. Prior Thomas did not come till August—he had been busy in Westminster. When he came there was not much for him to see. At an offer of higher pay the chief mason had gone off with most of his men to another job. Such things happened now, the pestilence had made wage-earners freer than those who hired them. But what did it matter to Prior Thomas? He was affable as ever, affable as an immortal, telling diverting stories of how projects of his own had been frustrated by such petty accidents as death or disease. And so he was gone again, leaving a strew of gifts and largesse behind him.

"I shall come early next year." The words rang in Sir Ralph's head, reminding him of King Tarquin's Sibyl, coming back with her diminishing offer, her rising fee. In the quick of his reason Sir Ralph knew that the prior of Etchingdon was his last chance. To such a man, insatiably curious in the oddities of human misfortune, he could tell his story. If he could once humble himself and get it out, Thomas de Foley was the man to hear him and help him. He might be quit of his sin yet: confession, contrition, penance . . . it could be done. In the end even he might be made what he was damned by feigning to be—a priest. Prior Thomas was very much his cousin's cousin: he would exert himself to cover up the scandal that for four years Alicia de Foley and her nuns had been without the body of Christ.

For they were like that, all calling each other cousin and sharing England among them. Even in their feuds they were united. They quarrelled among themselves and saw to it that no one should quarrel with them. He had listened to Thomas de Foley explaining to the prioress how deftly things were managed at Westminster, how by statutes and ordinances both wages and prices would be held down, how, though there should be but one labourer left, man and loaf should be as cheap as before.

During the third visit the quarrel blazed up between them. It was April. The party had been walking round the grounds to see how the spire looked from different aspects when the sharpening east wind brought a pelt of rain and they went into the nave for shelter: the prioress, Dame Agnes, Dame Margaret, Dame Salome, Dame Isabel. Thomas de Foley had a new secretary with him, a red-lipped smiling young man, and the clerk of the works. Sir Ralph was also of the party, half unwillingly, for he had been invited to join it by Prior Thomas; and yet it pleased him to be talking about painted windows and discussing the French cathedrals with the clerk of the works. The nave seemed very small and cramped with such a number of people walking about in it, the more so since the masons were using it as their storeroom and had blocked the western end with timber and bits of ready-made carving.

Prior Thomas continued to urge his cousin to lengthen the nave.

"There is nothing here you can want to keep. Your western arch—it is like some country sermon where the priest mumbles out, Good people, I will now begin. And then there is a long pause while he pulls up his hood."

Dame Agnes expressed a hope that new doors would be better fitting. The screen between nave and quire was no protection against draughts. Dame Isabel and Dame Salome took up the theme, describing the painfulness of mattins in winter, the wind howling, the nuns scarcely able to repeat the office because their teeth chattered so.

"The novices stamping their feet and rubbing their chilblains!" Dame Agnes cried.

"The candles wasting!" Dame Salome mourned.

Thomas de Foley glanced from one wrinkled face to another, thinking how much uglier they must look at two o'clock on a winter's morning. Every force of art was strained to beautify God's house and worship, but nothing was done to improve the appearance of his votaries. A religious order where everyone was young and beautiful . . . there would be no place for him in it. A new expedient for the nave sprang into his mind, and he turned to the prioress. Let them abolish that west door, since there would be a south porch in the remodelled nave. Instead, a simple arcading, balancing the screen, and above it a small rose window with modern glass.

"My vow was a spire. The spire brings a south porch, a lengthened nave, a window. All this must be paid for; and we are not Etchingdon."

She spoke lightly, as good breeding demanded.

"Surely you are not worrying about money? If the Methley tithes are not enough . . ."

Dame Salome had begun to pant in a very strange way and was turning purple. She rolled her eyes imploringly toward her prioress. The prioress shook her head.

"What's wrong?" asked Prior Thomas.

"It's nothing." Her tone of voice made nothing as good as a great deal.

"I believe," said the secretary, "at least I understood our treasurer to mention, that though it is perfectly understood that the Methley tithe is earmarked for Oby there are still a few formalities . . ." He paused, and added with a pout, "People are such sticklers."

Prior Thomas beat his forehead with his small fist. "My fault, my fault! My mind was so taken up with your design that I forgot these accursed formalities. But nothing gets done unless I see to it myself. Steven! Make a note of this. Because of the great love we bear to Our Blessed Lady and Saint Leonard, and that the vow of my cousin the prioress of Oby may not be hindered, and so forth: half of the great tithe of Methley and all of the little tithe; for ten years, no, twenty. No, no! That's paltry. In perpetuity."

The faces of Dame Agnes and Dame Margaret expressed at once their admiration of a man who could dispose so easily of a spirituality and their reprobation of such flippancy in money matters. Though they had suspected that the money was not coming in—otherwise, why should Dame Salome have sighed with such portentous secrecy whenever they referred to it?—no one had supposed that its payment had not even been secured. Sweet Trinity, he might have died meanwhile, and we should have been left with the cost of all this! At the thought of the peril they had been in Dame Margaret sat down and crossed herself with a trembling forefinger.

Embarrassed by feeling herself so much relieved, the prioress began to veil the crudity of her sensations by a return of scruples about the lesser tithe.

"I do not like to think of those poor creatures without a priest."

"I assure you the poor creatures wouldn't know what to do with him. When they had one the only use they could make of him was to pay him for charms to hang about the necks of their cattle."

"It seems a shocking state of things in a christian country."

"So it is," he replied cheerfully. "But one must look facts in the face. Say we send a priest to Methley. If he is a good man they will murder him. If not, they will do as they did before: turn him into a sorcerer, a water-diviner, and a weather-witch. I will waste no priests on Methley."

"This is a very stewardly outlook on salvation. One can see that Etchingdon is a great priory, to have so economical a prior."

Everyone looked at Sir Ralph, the speaker. He was leaning against a stack of timber, turning a little piece of carved work in his hands.

Prior Thomas flushed. "As for salvation, I am modest enough to suppose that salvation comes from the Lord. But that is disputable, and if you please you may say it is heretical. As for Methley, you must allow me to know more about it than you do. And I do not intend to cast any more pearls before its swine. I have too great a respect for the priesthood."

"A fine respect for the priesthood! You place a priest here, you withhold him there. What do you suppose you are doing? Playing at checkers?"

The secretary closed his notebook and returned it to his pocket.

"A very striking metaphor," said Prior Thomas. "I think you have mistaken your calling. You should have been a preaching friar. Metaphors are a great comfort to simple congregations."

"And to talk of casting pearls . . . that's not a metaphor, I suppose?"

"Not my own. I content myself with quotations from the scripture. In fact I am, as you imply, merely a humble administrator of the Church's goods. A steward." He spoke with contemptuous good humour and gave a little bow.

"Perhaps you would like to go to Methley yourself?" he added. He had meant to annoy; but he had not foreseen such a glare of resentment. He hastened to add that he hoped that Sir Ralph would think of no such thing, that Oby would be badly off without him. The nuns exclaimed that they could not do without Sir Ralph and the prioress told of how providentially he had come to them in their hour of need. Swept by the general impulse to make talk over an awkward interval, the clerk of the works stirred himself to reply with an anecdote of how a cousin of his had seen, had seen quite plainly, a skeleton hand appear and scrawl *Hic* on the door of a house in Shrewsbury; and the next day plague broke out among the people of the house.

Sir Ralph stared at the floor. His face was of a uniform dull red except for the bridge of his nose, which showed with a sallow whiteness. Even then all might have gone well if Dame Margaret had not taken it on herself to remark profoundly, "Without a priest there can be no mass."

Sir Ralph looked up. The prioress said hastily that no doubt there were masses within reach of the Methley folk. Plenty, said the secretary, and it would do them no harm to walk for the good of their souls. In the old days when masses were not to be found in every corner there was much more true devotion.

Praises of olden days seemed about to tide them to safety when Sir Ralph exclaimed in a loud tone that fury rendered doting, "Feed my sheep!"

Losing his self-control, the prior answered testily, "Oh, very well, very well! Go and feed them yourself."

The little piece of carved stone fell from Sir Ralph's hand. "Why should I stuff up the holes you make?"

"You seem to make a practice of it. You stuffed up a hole here, did you not? By the way, what hole were you shot out of to be so conveniently ready to pop into this one?"

Another hailstorm was coming up. The wind howled, the sunlight was wiped off the window as though a cloth had mopped it. Sunlit no longer, they all seemed to dwindle and sink lower—like blown-out candles, Dame Isabel thought, pulling her veil closer about her face and peering out through the chink. Men fight like so many stags, and to live with them perpetually would be intolerable; but from time to time a male quarrel is refreshing, like hartshorn or catnip.

"No cloister, at any rate," Sir Ralph bellowed. "I did not sit caressing my belly in a cloister, robbing the poor and slighting the body of Christ because I was not able to make it."

"They all talk like this nowadays." Thomas de Foley turned to the secretary with a paternal air. "Every boy, every beggar, can talk like this. It is the growth of learning and the spread of piety."

Sir Ralph detached himself from the heap of timber and lumbered toward the prior. He walked stooping forward, his hands dangled, his mouth hung open. His face was blank of any expression except an intense animal attentiveness.

"A fit! He's going to have a fit!" exclaimed the secretary.

At this moment the bell began to ring for vespers. Beyond the screen could be heard the orderly steps and rustling skirts of the other nuns going in to take their places. With a sudden roar Sir Ralph launched himself on Prior Thomas. The prior stepped nimbly to one side, and simultaneously the clerk of the works and the secretary joined in the fray. The nuns clustered round their prioress, scandalized, excited, and inclined to giggle. It was ludicrous to see Sir Ralph charging to and fro, dragging the clerk and the secretary after him, and the prior so coolly whisking his skirts from under their feet. Then Dame Agnes asserted herself, pointing her lean forefinger to the door in the screen and signing to Dame Isabel, the youngest among them, to open it. There she stood, her snub nose in the air, her face rigidly composed, and marshalled them in their order through the doorway. One by one they went sedately into quire, and the door closed behind them. Just as it fell to, the noise of scuffling ceased and was followed by a pitiable bellowing, the outcry of a beast struck down in the shambles; then that too died away and there was no more to be heard but the chant of the nuns in quire and outside the cry of the first cuckoo calling through a downpour of rain.

Two days later, riding through the flashing landscape, Thomas de Foley said to his secretary how glad he was that the priest had gone mad just then, enabling him to witness this performance: a perfect demonstration, he added, in proof of how women, despite all their weaknesses, perhaps, indeed, because of them, are best fitted to live under Rule. The Rule is a kind of dance to them, he exclaimed, a lifelong dance. The bell chimes, the music strikes up; and with the whole force of their sense of drama, their wilfulness, their terrific vanity, they give themselves over to a formal pattern of obedience.

"Don't doubt it, Steven! Those women going in to their vespers were experiencing a far greater excitement by doing what they were pledged to do every day of their lives than ever they could have procured from watching their maniac trying to strangle me."

The secretary remarked that just as God had called Mary to be the vehicle of the incarnation, he called women to the religious life, choosing the frailest objects and the most unlikely to convey his intentions and to illustrate Our Lady's words about exalting the humble. His head was still throbbing from the blow Sir Ralph had given it, and he could not look back on the visit to Oby with any pleasure. Thomas de Foley's observations struck him as hyperbolical. Everyone knew that nunneries made hay of their Rule and needed constant supervision and rebuke. The house they had left behind was no exception, with incompetent finances, no proper servants, a prioress thinking of nothing but building, and a mad priest.

Sir Ralph had run mad, no doubt of it. What was equally disconcerting was that Dame Susanna chose this moment to run mad too. Instead of welcoming an opportunity to show her skill as infirmaress she refused to go near him, or to give any reason for her refusal, saying she could do nothing but pray. Prayer was all very well; but more than prayer was needed. Fortunately Dame Beatrix came forward, saying with decision that what was needed was a black cock. The message went into the kitchen, and Jackie had laughed till he cried, thinking how funny the priest would look with a black cock crowing in his ear like another Saint Peter. That would rouse him!—for Sir Ralph's madness was of the stupid kind, his bellowings and blubberings had ended as abruptly as though a key had been turned on them, and nothing remained but a heavy doting melancholy. The black cock, however, was killed, and bound to Sir Ralph's head. A black cock tied to the head was, of course, an old and sanctioned remedy, and no sooner had Dame Beatrix prescribed it than others remembered it too. But Dame Beatrix had remembered it instantly. There was a general satisfaction when Dame Susanna resigned her post and Dame Beatrix became infirmaress in her stead.

Till past midsummer Sir Ralph was mad. It was a remarkably fine season, and every morning he was led out to enjoy the sun. There he would trudge up and down, blinking behind his feathers, and sometimes he would stoop and very carefully remove a twig or a pebble from the path before him. Sometimes he just sat still, a waterlogged bulk; or he would stare at a bush and tremble all over, and then utter a long thrilling howl like the howl of a dog which smells the approach of death. At other times he would chuckle and rub his hands together and then trot off to find a hearer, anyone patient enough to listen to him, and very earnestly recount some joke or funny story that had visited his mind. At meal-times he came in of his own accord, clambered to his room over the gate, and sat there polishing his spoon and waiting for his dish to be brought him. Seeing how well he remembered his old habits, they feared he might attempt to say mass, and on Dame Susanna's suggestion the quire door and the door of the sacristy were kept locked. But he never attempted this.

Several cocks had corrupted and been removed, and still there was no change in his condition. A mad priest became part of the routine of the house, an accustomed nuisance, like the wash-house door which for so long had been warped and would not close properly. Dame Helen and Pernelle and the novices were busy all through this fine weather with airing and cleansing the rugs and the furred winter hoods and mantles. Shaking them and beating them, and pouncing on the fleas that skipped out, they laughed and frolicked, and the madman was nothing more to them than his shadow passing and repassing.

When he had his fits of howling the nuns drew together and whispered that it was indeed an approaching death he smelled: the death of Dame Isabel. Throughout her short sickly life she had accepted the idea of an early death; but now she thought that, after all, she would be sorry to exchange the ambiguity of this world for the certitude of the next. There is pleasure in watching the sophistries of mankind, his decisions made and unmade like the swirl of a millrace, causation sweeping him forward from act to act while his reason dances on the surface of action like a pattern of foam. Yes, and the accumulations of human reason, she thought, the proofs we all assent to, the truths established beyond shadow of doubt, these are like the stale crusts of foam that lie along the river-bank and look solid enough; till a cloudburst farther up the valley sends down a force of water that breaks them up and sweeps them away.

Recently the prioress had made many references to the desirability of death, the comfort of being released from worldly cares and disappointments. Part of this, Dame Isabel knew, was on account of the convent's money troubles, the prioress's scruples about that lesser tithe of Methley, her uneasy conviction that the spire, somehow, would be the worse for it; but another part was meant for consolation. Studying the prioress's face, a round moon-face clouded with uncertainties as the moon's disk is tarnished with cloud-rack, the young nun assented to the consolations; but under her assent she reckoned the years she must forfeit, the events which would happen and which she would not see, the many thoughts she might have had—and no one else would think them. The world was deeply interesting and a convent the ideal place in which to meditate on the world. She was twenty-three. If she should live to forty, to sixty, her love of thinking would not be satiated. And yet Dame Agnes, who could remember the Jews in England and the Te Deums that had been sung at their expulsion, and Dame Blanch who was older still, so old that she remembered nothing, had never spent an hour of their lives in speculation.

Meanwhile, she also had to think about her money. The de Scottows had property in Guienne, and though since the war and the increase of pirates in the Narrow Seas the wine trade was not so profitable as it had been, the family was still wealthy, and Dame Isabel had not only brought a great dowry with her, but also received a yearly income from a vineyard of her own. "To pay for a few little comforts," her mother said, semi-apologetically, "since the poor child is so sickly." This was the sheepishness of the lay mind, still nursing an illusion that nuns lived on dew and a little porridge. The convent was less squeamish. Dame Isabel's private property shocked no one there, it was only the state of her health which made alluding to it a little delicate, since to inquire about its disposal was tantamount to talking about her death. Hints and inquiries observed a sideways decorum, as when Dame Agnes and Dame Helen spoke so regretfully of the draughts in the chapter-house which had, they felt sure, undermined her health. That she should bequeath her vineyard for the purpose of building a new chapter-house was the design of the majority. Dame Susanna, however, a chilly woman, attributed Dame Isabel's sickness to the fact that the convent burned so much peat. The smoke had made her cough, and coughing had worn out her lungs. It was peat-smoke, too, which was spoiling Dame Beatrix's eyesight. Was it not distressing to watch her measuring out medicines? She could be sure of nothing unless she held it an inch from her nose, and often the wrong ingredients must have gone into a potion. A little money laid out on improving the convent's woodland. . . . Dame Matilda said bluntly that what the convent needed was better housing for the labourers, and a new bull. "Our own roofs are bad enough, Heaven knows, but good or bad we have to stay under them. But nowadays a discontented serf just walks away from us."

One other speaker matched Dame Matilda in frankness. This was Dame Salome, who urged the dying nun to devote the whole of her vineyard to masses, since of all sins spiritual pride takes longest to expiate.

"And now that Sir Ralph has recovered it can be managed so nicely, the masses said in your own convent where you can be sure nothing will be scamped, for we shall keep our eyes on that. The day he came back to his senses and went off to spear eels I said to the others, Now our poor Dame Isabel can die in comfort! It was my first thought."

A different thought had come to Dame Isabel when they told her how Sir Ralph had suddenly come out of his madness, rosy and blinking like an infant awakening. Though she had never found him a congenial confessor her curiosity started up at the prospect of meeting someone newly returned from madness. Madness was a whole new world, and surely he would have some interesting news of it? Her hopes were dashed. The simile of the waking infant was only too true; he sat smiling at her bedside, saying how wonderfully well he felt, and that in spite of the drought he had never seen the harvest so promising.

A nun has no property, she cannot make a will; but there is nothing to prevent her setting down her dying wishes. Dame Isabel's dying wishes were expressed in a letter to her father, and a signed copy of the letter was retained by the convent. It seemed to her, as it usually does to the dying, that her intentions would inevitably be misunderstood or disregarded. Still holding the copy of her letter she repeated what was in it. She had asked her father to grant to Oby the income from her vineyard for ten years after her death. For these ten years no penny of that income, beyond the charge of a decency minimum of masses, was to be spent. It was to be put out to usury, and the interest as it accumulated was to be put out to usury also.

"And when we get it, what then?" asked the prioress, flustered by all these directions. Sometimes it seemed to her that everyone was in league to talk of nothing but money.

Dame Isabel made a gesture of impatience. Another coughing fit began to shake her, and Dame Beatrix handed her the spitting-bowl.

"Pay . . . off debts," she gasped. A surge of blood swept away anything else she might have been minded to say.

She had a long agony. The weather was intensely sultry. Thunderstorms rattled overhead but did not break the drought. The little rain they wrenched out of the clouds had scarcely touched the earth before it rose up in a steaming mist. The nuns, exhausted by kneeling round Dame Isabel and repeating the prayers for the dying on behalf of a woman who seemingly could not die, found it hard to conceal their weariness and their disillusionment (for it is disillusioning to discover that compassion, stretched out too long, materializes into nothing more than a feat of endurance). The flies made everything worse. The smell of blood and sweat brought them in swarms, houseflies and bluebottles and horseflies. The lulling of prayers and the buzzing of insects were broken by shooings, scratchings, and slaps at the flies which settled on cheeks and foreheads. There lay Dame Isabel, mute as a candle, visibly consuming away and still not extinguished. Every time she opened her eyes they were more appallingly brilliant. It was an exemplary end, but not a consolatory one. Even her patience seemed to take on a quality of deceit and abstraction, it was as though she were calculating the hours that must pass before they would leave her alone. When at length she was dead the reflection that they had done everything they could for her was confused by a feeling that they and not she had stayed too long. To crown all, the drought broke in such torrents of rain that the ready-dug grave filled with water and it was impossible to bury Dame Isabel till it left off raining and the floods drained away.

For many years the death of Dame Isabel, so young, so unusually gifted, was remembered because it coincided with the flood at the Assumption. Crops were spoiled, cattle were drowned, the river broke its banks and settled in a new channel, so that the mill was left high and dry and finally fell into ruin.

After the floods went down there was an epidemic among the masons, and several of them died. All these disasters enforced the disagreeable impression of Dame Isabel's death, and later on a legend grew up of a nun who was so wicked that death himself refused to take her and earth would not give her burial. Her wickedness was an excessive learning; all day she sat reading forbidden books, and sometimes barking like a dog, for such was her knowledge of grammar that she could change herself into animal shape. Naturally, all this was known in Lintoft and Wivelham and Waxelby before it was heard of in Oby, and the convent learned of it only through Pernelle's bringing it back from a lying-in, where, as she remarked, people will say anything to help pass the time. Dame Salome felt herself grow hot and uncomfortable. Once again, she realized, she had been guided by an angel when she had modestly supposed she was only following her own nose.

For the unbelievable had happened. Dame Salome's devotion to Our Lady and Saint Leonard had given out, and she had resigned her office as treasuress the day after Dame Isabel's death, alleging that she had scruples about usury and could not undertake sums *per centum.* Dame Matilda was appointed in her place.

It was high time for a change. At the last Visitation mild Bishop Adlam had observed that even conscientiousness can be carried too far and that Dame Salome's habit of glossing every entry in her books with a recital of how painstaking she had been to make it thus and not otherwise was, in the long run, tedious. He had also been obliged to point out several faults in arithmetic. Besides the relief of getting rid of Dame Salome the prioress was relieved to have Dame Matilda at last among the obedientiaries. She was a Stapledon, a family not to be slighted.

Just as the Scottows were eminently rich, the Stapledons were eminently well-to-do. They had the name of being prudent, self-providing, strong-minded, and full of family affection. That was one version. The other version of the Stapledons described them as miserly, obstinate to the point of pig-headedness, and tribal as the Jews. The mother of Prioress Isabella had been a de Stapledon. To the convent groaning under her rule the arrival of a full-grown de Stapledon, and one who had already got the better of a husband, seemed a menace of the worst kind, and there were many allusions to that text in holy writ which promised that Rehoboam's little finger should be thicker than his father's loins. In the course of time she had plodded down most of the prejudice that met her; but the old nuns who still remembered Prioress Isabella continued to assert that Dame Matilda was only biding her time till she could leap into authority and become as frightful a tyrant as her aunt had been.

In 1354 when she became treasuress Dame Matilda was thirty-six, a tall, heavily built woman, slow of speech and sparing of glance. When she raised her eyelids it was to look: a steady, observing glance, wielded like a weapon or a kitchen implement, and, its purpose fulfilled, put by again. Oddly enough, she was extremely popular with the young.

This might be the reason why the prioress, constantly praising her, and supporting her in her new-broom measures, so plainly did not like her and had kept her so long without an office. Dame Agnes, explaining the convent politics to Dame Margaret, had another theory. The prioress was so absurdly fastidious and finicking that she could not stomach Dame Matilda's loud voice and cart-horse tread. The real explanation was so obscure that the prioress was the only person who could have given an account of it, though she would have been abashed to do so. In 1345, when she first vowed her spire, Dame Matilda was a raw-boned stockish creature, very shy, and looking much younger than her real age. Time went on, and she became self-possessed, massive, even stately, all without appearing to make any especial effort and with no one taking any pains on her behalf. The spire was still unfinished. Why should the most prosaic of her nuns have grown as smoothly as Solomon's temple while the spire lagged and pined like a rickety child? Because of this unfortunate association of ideas the prioress felt that somehow the one had grown at the expense of the other, that Dame Matilda was the spire's rival, and her indifference to it charged with ill-will where the indifference of the other nuns was merely due to stupidity. She had been used to console herself with the thought of Dame Isabel. Dame Isabel would recover her health—at any rate she would grow no sicklier; Dame Isabel would be the next prioress. It was probably God's design that what had begun because of an Isabella an Isabel should complete. While there was a Dame Isabel, Dame Matilda could never amount to much, her common sense could never be more than a foil for the other's brilliance. But Dame Isabel had died, Dame Salome (whom she had only tolerated as treasuress because she was an obliging stopgap) had resigned, and immediately the prioress had found she must submit to depend on Dame Matilda.

Yet the new treasuress showed no enmity toward the spire. It figured in her account-books along with butter and prunes and tallow and cattle-drenches. She made one or two very sensible suggestions about it, and she kept the men at their work, intervening whenever she could do so discreetly in the incessant quarrels that sprang up between the prioress and the head-mason.

"Why was Dame Matilda talking for so long with Edmund Gurney? I wonder she does not climb up on the scaffolding and spend the afternoon with him. What with Dame Matilda and Pernelle Bastable it is a marvel that any work at all gets done on the spire."

"Talking of Pernelle reminds me that . . ." But Dame Beatrix got no further in her tactful diversion.

"You were there, too, for part of the time. What was she gossiping about?"

"She was reasoning with him about the price of this new load of stone."

"I might have known it. That is all it means to her—whether it can be done more cheaply."

"She is reserved. You know she has always been reserved. And naturally she would not try to compete with you in matters of taste. But it is not true that she is uninterested. Only the other day I heard her say to Dame Susanna how much she was looking forward to seeing it finished."

The prioress walked away, red with mortification. Plainly, Dame Matilda was not only indifferent to the spire: she made game of it and rejoiced in its laggard growth. Nowhere could she find a sympathetic hearer for her ambitions, her agonizing doubts. If she consulted the nuns, they agreed with whatever she said. If she consulted the master-mason, he disagreed. Just now she was ravaged with indecision about a crocket. If only Thomas would come!

But he did not come.

In 1356 the work on the spire was suspended, and the masons told to prepare foundations for the extension of the nave. Digging was none of their business. They sat about, chewing grasses, while old Richard Noot, lame ever since the pestilence, and Mary Ragge and Mary Scole spaded and carried earth in baskets. It was impossible, Jesse Figg said, to spare anyone else from the manor, and hired labour could not be had. Inwardly he was resolved that no man of his should waste his strength while those great idle masons lolled in the shade. Though strangers might cheat the prioress they would not get round the prioress's bailiff. Presently the master-mason took his men away, saying that they would do a small job at Waxelby and be back by Michaelmas, he did not suppose the digging would be finished till then. As it was now harvest the diggers also went away. The nuns said among themselves that the prioress would spin out the work till her dying day rather than lose the self-importance and sense of power it gave her. Fortunately there was the Methley money to pay for it, and Dame Isabel's money to come later.

She had now been prioress for almost twelve years—a long time to hold that office. If she had been a really good prioress, good by orthodox standards, she would scarcely have been endured for so long; but her faults made her tolerable: being self-absorbed she seldom interfered, and except where her spire was involved she was quite remarkably free from suspicions. The arrears of the Methley money had been paid, the tithes now came in punctually. Life had become very comfortable, in spite of the rising cost of living—or perhaps because of it. The rise in the cost of living brought a rise in the standard of living. When difficulties with the manor resulted in less home-grown produce, the deficiency was made up by buying more at fairs and markets. What is produced for sale is naturally more luxurious than what is produced for home consumption. The nuns ate more delicate foods, wore finer wool, drank wine and cider when their home-brew ran out. The bad times, too, had increased the number of pedlars, and the competition among the pedlars had improved the quality of their wares. Pins were bought freely—gone were the days when a nun searched on all fours through the floor-strew rushes, saying, Where is my pin? Fur-lined slippers were bought, little cushions to slip behind the loins, comfits to sweeten the breath, and new spoons that did not stretch one's mouth till one looked like a gargoyle. New furnishings were bought, the walls had hangings, the tables had napery. About this time the book of hours, projected so long ago, was carried out by the young Dame Cecily Bovill, and found a purchaser (the de Retteville who had commissioned it had died of the Black Death). With the money that this brought in Saint Leonard's altar was done up in the latest style.

Pernelle Bastable had a say in many of these improvements. She knew where such and such things could best be bought, she travelled to fairs and came back with bargains and novelties. Jackie saw fairs in plenty now, fairs which made Waxelby Fair very small beer. Pernelle needed a strong boy to carry bundles and scare off dogs, and Jackie was just what she needed.

He was now in his teens and by way of working for the masons, a big comely lout, fresh as a new painting with his crimson lips and green eyes. Pernelle had supplanted Ursula with her son just as she had supplanted her in the kitchen. For now, among the many servants which the convent's improved style of living called for, Ursula was a nobody. Almost blind and very rheumatic, she had drifted back toward the cloister and lived pretty much as a nun, spending most of her days before the redecorated Saint Leonard whose lips were as bright as Jackie's. Her carnality had burned out at last, love had no more power over her than fire has over a clinker. And in the Lent of 1357 when Ursula limped into the cloister and knelt down for her penance the prioress, looking at her with embarrassment, said, "The time is past . . . there is no sense in it now. Go in peace, my daughter."

It was notorious that the prioress disliked scourging Ursula; and to Ursula it could have been no pleasure. Yet for some days after, both women looked cast down, and the prioress began to speak of herself as an old woman. Only a week or so earlier Pernelle, riding home from Waxelby with the lenten provisions of dried fish and figs, had been lifted from her pony by Jackie and laid on the grass. She had yielded with little ado, for she recognized a talent. Afterward, resettling her headgear, she studied his indeterminate English profile against the pure green sky of twilight. Watching him stand there in an isolation of bodily contentment, she felt an almost virginal gratitude and humility.

This humility was followed by the reflection that a mature woman has great charms for a boy. What was more natural than that poor little Jackie should make love to her? She in return would bestow her stores of experience, treasures of amorous learning now immensely ripened and subtilized by keeping; for a woman, she said to herself that night, always keeps the best wine till the last. And she had always been kind to Jackie. Later that night she woke again. She heard a shuffling of feet, quiet yawns. The nuns, poor ladies, were coming back from their mattins. They knew no pleasure, their lives never quickened into real life. Taking it all in all, they would have to expiate as many sins as secular women, being greedy, slothful, angry, and proud, and yet have nothing to show for it. Here lay she, still reverberating the pleasure long laid aside and never forgotten. Too long: she was old. Her body was wrinkled, hairs grew from her chin. Very soon Jackie would not want to set his teeth in this old keeping-pear. He would quit her and go off after something of his own age. For two wisdoms never can keep company, and a boy is no sooner made wise in love than he wants to impart his wisdom to some ignoramus of a girl. There are girls everywhere, and here there were the nuns. The conviction seized her that she must certainly lose Jackie to one or other of them. They were ladies, their skins were smooth with idleness, they were virgins. At any moment Jackie might feel the desire for a virgin; and having neither shame nor modesty there would be nothing to restrain him. Neither would the nuns be likely to hold back. Think of Ursula . . . all nuns are the same.

The convent noticed that Pernelle had suddenly lost her looks and was always losing her temper. They also noticed that Ursula wept a great deal, as though the scourgings had been doubled instead of remitted. As for Jackie, they noticed nothing: he was outside their world, the subject of an occasional remark that he was old enough to work as a man, and that Sir Ralph's lessons had been wasted on him. At mid-Lent Pernelle announced that she would have to go to Waxelby to buy provisions for Easter, and that she would take Jackie with her. They were absent for a week.

It was the fifth day of their absence, the nuns, walking in the orchard, were talking about robbers and Dame Beatrix was recounting her dream in which she had seen Pernelle's horse rush out from a thicket, its eyeballs glaring, carrying, not Pernelle, but a tall hairy man in a torn jerkin, when Dame Susanna exclaimed that a man was riding toward the convent. They pressed their faces to the gap in the reed-fence. Sure enough, there was horse and rider. The horse was not Pernelle's horse, neither was it rushing, neither was its rider particularly tall or dishevelled. But Dame Beatrix talked of signs and portents and they listened, half-persuaded, till Dame Susanna spoke again, to say that the rider was Prior Thomas's secretary. They hurried indoors to wipe their faces and set their veils and clean the dirt from under their nails. A breath of festivities was in the air. What a pity Pernelle was not there to whip up one of her custards!

There was no sign of festivities about Steven Ludcott. His manner was cold and hurried, his voice had an edge on it. When they inquired after Prior Thomas he replied that Thomas was prior of Etchingdon no longer. He had resigned his office in order to devote himself to contemplation.

There has been some quarrel, the prioress thought, or some scandal. The partisanship of her girlhood boiled up in her, she felt herself throbbing with protective anger and ready to exclaim that the whole world was in league to flout poor Tom just because he was cleverer than other people. She said:

"My cousin Thomas has always been deeply religious. His retirement will be a great loss to Etchingdon, but christendom will be the gainer, for no doubt he will enrich it with some treatise of inestimable value."

What's more, her thoughts continued, this fellow has had a hand in Tom's downfall. Tom never had any discretion in his choice of favourites.

"Our new prior, Prior Gilbert Botley," he said, "has sent me to you with this letter. He chose me to carry it since I have been here before and know something of the circumstances."

Prior Gilbert greeted his well-beloved sister in Christ, and while deploring the inroads of Mammon upon the religious life yet found it his duty to remind her that the interest on the Methley tithe since 1351 had not been paid. Some very exact and impressive calculations followed, and the letter closed with an allusion to the merit of the serving-man who converted his single talent into ten.

The prioress turned to Dame Margaret, who was present at the interview as a chaperon, and asked her to go and fetch Dame Matilda de Stapledon.

The dreaded name of Stapledon shook Steven Ludcott's reserve. No sooner had Dame Margaret left them than he said, "Actually, the whole of this trouble was brought to a head by the Methley tithes. It was all so unbusinesslike, a family deal between Prior Thomas and yourself. The community objected."

"The community," she said, "has been slow to anger."

"Exactly! The community felt that it was time the whole matter was looked into and regularized. We could not have the late prior disposing of the community's goods as though they were his private property, handing over a considerable part of the Etchingdon income without consultation, without contract. Nothing at all, nothing beyond a mere note that the Methley tithes were to be paid to Oby."

"Which you, I think, drew up? I recollect my cousin asking you to do so. We were all very unbusinesslike, that is true. For instance, I think we omitted any mention of the rate of interest, any mention of interest at all."

"Very probably. We were interrupted, were we not? By the way, what became of your mad priest?"

"Thanks to Our Lady and Saint Leonard he is perfectly recovered."

Entering, Dame Matilda received a meaning glance of comradeship from her prioress. It was with one mind and soul that the prioress and treasuress of Oby conversed with Steven Ludcott. For the cloistered life develops in women infinite resources both of resentment and of intuition; or perhaps it merely develops their sensibility, from which arise both understanding and a delight in being misunderstood. Dame Matilda and the prioress might have been rehearsing their strategy for months. Though Steven Ludcott left Oby with every jot of his errand completed, the interest agreed on and his spleen vented, he rode away with the sensation of having been horribly mauled between the pair of them.

He was no sooner out of the house than a spirited defensive action became a defeat. The prioress had hysterics, Dame Matilda cursed like a crusader, and Dame Margaret, who had sat reading her psalter during the interview, sped off to tell the convent that Oby was certainly ruined and would most likely be dissolved by the bishop.

It was to the aftermath of all this that Pernelle Bastable returned, explaining that the Waxelby merchants were asking such exorbitant prices that she had thought it best to go on to Lambsholme, where she had bought such raisins as had never before been eaten at Oby. The price of the raisins was the only thing in her story that made an impression. Dame Matilda said it was much too high. The convent, she added, had to face an unexpected liability, and for some years to come must practise economy.

To Pernelle this meant one thing only: her Jackie would not be so well fed. There would be fewer little marginal pies and pittances to hand through the buttery wicket. Feeding Jackie had become a precious duty—rather more than a duty, indeed; for she knew that to a young man the elderly woman he loves is sufficiently like his mother for nourishment to be part of the transaction. These virgins might economize if they pleased. They had nothing to lose but their suppers. She would lose Jackie. Reckless with agitation she began to huff and expostulate, saying that if, after all she had done for them, the ladies of Oby questioned her honesty there could be only one ending; go she must and go she would. Dame Matilda blandly agreed.

Even so, Pernelle might have stayed (for travelling is costly, and ruin to a woman's looks, and there seemed little chance that another convent or her brother-in-law at Beverley would welcome her with a Jackie under her wing) if a Lent lily had not appeared behind Jackie's ear. A young man does not wear a Lent lily for nothing—unless he is a poet. It was during Holy Week, when the convent was busy commemorating Christ's death and passion, that Pernelle arranged her departure. While Dame Matilda was nailed down in quire Pernelle could do much as she pleased in the storeroom, explaining to the servants that she was getting ready for the great festival of Easter. On Holy Saturday she staged a quarrel, declared she would live no longer where she was not trusted, and rode off, her saddle-bags swinging, while the bells of Lintoft, Oby, and Wivelham stammered out their *Haec, haec, haec dies,* assuring each other across the moor that Christ was risen. "As for my bedding," she cried over her shoulder, "I will not wait for it. Jackie can ride over with it later to the inn at Waxelby."

By the time Oby realized that Jackie was gone for good and had taken the roan horse with him it was too late to do anything. Several people had seen the woman and the boy riding southward, but, supposing they went on yet another marketing expedition for those spendthrift nuns, had taken no special note of it. Ursula wept. Jesse Figg cursed over the loss of the beast. Dame Salome, with one of those flashes of worldly wisdom which at times emerge from very stupid well-meaning people, said, "Now we can expect a crop of slanders. For when people do you an injury they always slander you afterward."

No one can economize without arousing suspicion and dislike, and an economizing community offends even more than an economizing individual. Presently even the beggars and pilgrims who came for alms went on through the countryside proclaiming that Oby had grown so miserly that it provided nothing but sour beer and barley meal. Such news travels far. The parents of two prospective novices wrote to say that they found their daughters' vocations would be better suited under the Cistercian Rule. The convent's vicar at Tunwold complained to the bishop that Oby, while building fast enough for itself, had allowed the Tunwold parsonage to fall into shameful disrepair.

Tunwold parsonage came up at the next Visitation. The diocesan surveyor, sent to verify the vicar's complaints, had returned with the news that the roof was not only in tatters but sheltered, such as it was, a concubine and five small children. Though the nuns could not be held directly responsible for the concubine, such a state of things bore out the truth of what the prioress had said, half-laughing and in better days, to Thomas de Foley: That God does not wish his nuns to hold spiritualities. The bishop spared them this platitude and went on to tell them how, when admonished, John Cuckow had pleaded that his house was infested by water-spirits, which was why he had taken a woman to live with him, it being better to go astray after ordinary flesh than after dracs and melusines. Smoothing his cheeks, the bishop suggested that as well as having the roof mended the prioress might be well advised to have the place thoroughly exorcised. Dame Beatrix broke in with some hair-raising stories of phantom hounds galloping through Cornwall. Feeling that Dame Beatrix was displaying herself to be quite as silly as John Cuckow, the prioress put in a word to her credit, saying what a skilled doctoress she was, and how she had cured Sir Ralph with a black cock.

This jogged the bishop's memory. He had come intending to find out more about Sir Ralph, whom he had met and taken as a matter of course in an earlier Visitation. The scandal at Etchingdon had been a major one, and Steven Ludcott had felt himself sufficiently implicated in Prior Thomas's vagaries (they had gone as far as necromancy and raising the ghost of Avicenna) to avail himself of any red herrings handy. At the Etchingdon inquiry he had testified that Thomas de Foley had been seriously scratched by a mad priest at Oby, an alteration in his demeanour had been perceptible to the anxious Steven from that day onward: it was his opinion that Sir Ralph, slavering at the jaws, howling like a wolf, and obviously under the dominion of Satan, had infected the prior. As a tailpiece he had added that nobody knew where Sir Ralph had come from. All this had come to the bishop's hearing. He discounted the dominion of Satan (the Black Death had roused up every superstition in England), but a priest from nowhere needed investigation. He questioned the prioress and some of the elder ladies. From all of them he got the same story. Sir Ralph was a man of sober life, a careful counsellor, a comfortable preacher. He had only been mad once, and then quite harmlessly. He was fond of reading and of fishing. Where did he come from? Dame Agnes said roundly, "From God."

She was now of a great age, leaning on a staff and quite bald. No amount of pinning could secure her coif, which sidled on her polished skull with every shake of her palsy.

"From God," she repeated.

"Do you remember seeing his letters of ordination?"

"Dame Blanch de Fanal (God rest her soul!) saw them. She saw to it all. It was a terrible time, nothing but fluster and dying, and our priest had run away. If I live to a hundred I shall not forget it. Dame Blanch looked out of a window, and there he stood, and at the same moment there appeared a rainbow. He cured my squirrel, too, when she was scalded and all her fur came off."

She hobbled away.

I may get more sense from a younger nun, he thought. Presently Dame Susanna Piers came in for her interview. She had been trying to nerve herself to speak of how Sir Ralph had raved in his sickness and had declared himself no priest. Her demeanour convinced the bishop that she was going to be full of scruples, and as he disliked scrupulous nuns and was feeling very tired he questioned her as briefly as possible, said nothing of Sir Ralph, and dismissed her before she could begin any confidences. The Virgin, thought Dame Susanna, smote my lips in the very moment when I was going to speak a slander. She went to the chapel and began to pray forgiveness for harbouring wicked thoughts. Meanwhile the bishop was back in the guest chamber, still puzzling a little about this dull-looking man who had had the heroism to enter a house where the pestilence had entered before him and who an hour before, it seemed, had been wandering about at a loose end. No doubt there was some perfectly satisfactory explanation. The de Foleys were traditionally proud, Alicia de Foley was not reputed lacking in that family grace, she would scarcely engage a priest—even when priests were at a premium—without making sure of his credentials. And though there was no record of the transaction in the episcopal roll of appointments the Black Death had caused many such hiatuses. Perhaps they had neglected to apply to the late bishop for his approval. They were very unbusinesslike, that was obvious.

I will ask the man himself, he thought sleepily, while his chaplain sat at his bedside reading aloud from the Lives of the Hermits. That would be best, it would spare the prioress's feelings and save time. How pleasant to be in Egypt, sitting under a palm tree, plaiting a garment of palm fibre and speaking to nobody. Yes, he would speak to Sir Ralph tomorrow. But during the night his sore throat grew worse, and by the morning his larynx was so much inflamed that it was impossible to speak more than a word or two. All the voice he could muster had to be expended in thanks, in replies to condolences, in assurances that his cold had not been caught at Oby, in reiterated thanks for all the provisions being made to ease his journey. Dame Beatrix, hurrying forward with a linctus, dragged the priest after her. "My Lord, pray take a sip of this every hour. Sir Ralph will tell you I am a good doctoress." "Yes, indeed, Dame Beatrix has much skill in medicine." He looked round, saw Dame Susanna, and added, "Dame Susanna, too, is most skilful. I should have died of the pestilence if it had not been for her care of me."

"No, no! I did nothing, it was not I! It is Ursula you should thank."

A modest nun, shrinking from praise, the bishop noted. A kindly, tactful priest. The man had a loud roistering voice, yet he spoke with a certain crispness, an accent of scholarship. Speech, carriage, demeanour—everything was priestly, and he seemed, too, perfectly sane. A very worthy fellow, no doubt; running to seed a little, growing fat and forgetting his scholarship among all these women, possibly more inclined to follow Peter with a net than with a crook; but a good sort of man, and just where he was needed, and so providentially free from ambition that he might be counted on to remain at Oby.

A healthy man too. One would need to be extremely healthy to withstand such a cold lodging, such draughts playing over the altar, such a melancholy marish climate. No wonder if from time to time he went a little mad. There is no sin in madness, only God's wrath, and God's wrath often falls on the most estimable characters, as on, for instance, the prophet Daniel. Daniel's statements, so inconsecutive, so inconsistent—one must attribute them to God's wrath. When did order and reason slide into the world?—with Christ, *lux mundi?* Perhaps one might say a little earlier, a cool silvery intimation of the light to come glimmering through the heathen philosophers. So the bishop mused, shepherding his thoughts, trying to put off a recognition of an oncoming toothache. The litter creaked and swayed, presently the bishop began to fall asleep—a light sleep of old age in which he could distinctly hear himself snoring. Squeezed uncomfortably into a corner, the chaplain looked at him with a malevolence so habitual that it was almost indifference.

IV. THE SPIRE

(November 1357–May 1360)

This was in 1357. Bishop William Adlam, an unostentatious figure, went home to die, and Sir Ralph remained at Oby. His brief fillip of alarm was over. He did not think there was any further likelihood that an inquiry would rout him out from his place as nuns' priest. He had exchanged the insecurity of being a man for the security of being a function; it was a sound bargain, though he sometimes regretted it.

The cassock in which he had fought Thomas de Foley was now rounded like a grapeskin; even when hanging on its peg it kept a flaccid rotundity like a grapeskin which has been sucked. But he said that it would last him out till the great day when the spire was finished and consecrated. The work on the spire was still going on—for economy's sake in the most wasteful manner possible: with one man and a boy.

"I begin to think there must be a curse on my building," said the prioress, voicing to Sir Ralph what her nuns had felt for a long time already. "Ever since I began it we have met with one disaster after another: the pestilence, the loss of that relic, Dame Isabel's death and those floods, and the vile behaviour of Etchingdon about the Methley tithe, and Pernelle Bastable's robberies, and those two novices being diverted to Culvercombe, and the cost of the repairs at Tunwold. . . ."

Her voice died away. She was tired of hearing herself complain and of hearing Sir Ralph's perfunctory consolations. Her laments rang false, because they always stopped short of the truth: the truth was Thomas. Since Steven Ludcott's visit there had been no news of Thomas de Foley. Thomas was lost and gone, his career ended, his light put out. She would never see him again, he would die and she would not know it. Her spire might be completed, but he would never come to praise it. And here am I, she thought, fixed in the religious life like a candle on a spike. I consume, I burn away, always lighting the same corner, always beleaguered by the same shadows; and in the end I shall burn out and another candle will be fixed in my stead.

She knew, too, who the next candle would be. Dame Matilda would succeed her as prioress, just as certainly as William Holly would follow Jesse Figg as the next bailiff.

In the spring of 1358 Sir Ralph found that he was tired of fishing and wanted to go hawking instead. A strong horse would be needed to carry him, and since Jackie had gone off with the roan, horses were a painful subject. Rather stiffly—he had no talent for asking favours—he consulted Jesse Figg. Having said that it was useless to consult him about a horse, he had neither time nor heart for such frivolities, the bailiff met him a week later with the news that everything was arranged. The horse would be Peter Noot's dun horse, a raw-boned animal, but with feeding it would come into better shape and last for years; a horse taken from field-work is so grateful that it will give you another ten years' service. Peter Noot was due to die at any moment. When he died the convent would claim a heriot, its due of his best beast. The dun horse was not really his best beast; his young ox was better value. "But do I say it is," said Jesse, "old Matilda will believe it. And Widow Noot, she wouldn't complain at losing a horse and keeping an ox, an ox is work now and meat later. My cousin at Dudham has a hawk that will suit you. It's a sparrow-hawk. A sparrow-hawk for a priest." Sir Ralph had looked forward to choosing his hawk; but he saw that he must take both or neither, and a hawk without a horse would be no use to him in this bare country. Peter Noot died, the heriot was claimed and curried, the hawk and her trappings arrived. When he felt her hard feet fidget on his hand Sir Ralph experienced an authentic happiness. At last he had something of his own.

The Oby people were pleased to see him ride out on Noot's horse. They had always liked him pretty well, giving him the meed of approval which an idle man who minds his own business is pretty sure to receive from the working Englishman. Now that he had a hawk they liked him better. It put her in mind of the old days, said Grannie Scole (pretending she could remember them) when the manor had a proper lord on it instead of a parcel of nuns. Those were the days: always something going on, hunting or hawking, hanging or whipping, always something to keep life stirring. Oby had never prospered since the nuns came to it.

Riding out with his hawk, Sir Ralph began to have a hawk's-eye view of his world. The river ceased to be a fisherman's river, a rosary of pools and shallows; from the black of the dun horse he saw it as a progress, winding like some wasteful history, with here and there the record of a forsaken channel, such as a row of alders sulking in a hollow, or a long ribbon of rushes. He began to see the shape of the hamlet, too, and how cunningly the hovels had been plastered to any shelter against the prevailing wind. Round and about them ran a network of foot-paths, tending toward the common field and the common waste. Along one track went the Hollys, along another the Noots, and the girl driving a lame cow past the thorn thicket must be a Scole, for that was the way the Scoles went. The masons' settlement had added new tracks to the tracks of the village, tracks somehow different: one could see that they were made by strangers. Out of this network of foot-paths, purposeful and well trodden, ravelled the three tracks from Oby to the outer world. The southward one led to Wivelham, a wretched place, and to Dudham beyond it. Westward, past Oby Fen, a track went over the rising ground to Lintoft, and later joined the old road which brought you in the end to London, and was called King Street; and to the northeast the Hog Trail and the river twisted on toward Waxelby and the pale seaward sky. The Black Death had dealt hard with Waxelby, and still lingered on there like a dog worrying a carcass. The wharfs were rotting, the export trade of salted herrings had dwindled, the great church built by the friars was botched up and would never be properly finished. In twenty years' time there would be little left of Waxelby, so men said, but a byword.

Waxelby wealthy,
Wivelham wet,
Lintoft plenty,
Dudham sharp-set.

The dun horse and the Dudham hawk had drawn Sir Ralph into the company of the bailiff and his nephew, William Holly. He discovered that Jesse and William knew much more about the nuns than he did, and discussed them and their doings with dispassionate familiarity, always referring to them as Old So-and-So, regardless of whether they were actually old, middle-aged, or young. They might, in fact, have been discussing the peculiarities of the Oby cows—with no more reverence and, equally, with no more intention of disrespect. After the first slight discomfort of adapting himself to this outlook on religious ladies Sir Ralph enjoyed sitting in Jesse Figg's orchard, drinking cider and slapping away midges while the dews fell and the blackbirds sang through the dusk. His appearance was always greeted with the same remark: he must sit down and tell them about his travels. That was as far as his travels took them. Jesse and William then resumed their sober, untiring arguments; sometimes about affairs on the manor or in the convent, sometimes about events that had happened during the time of the Danes. It was an everlasting dispute how far the Danes had travelled up the Waxle Stream. As far as Kitt's Bend, asserted William. Farther by a mile, Jesse maintained; for at that time the Waxle Stream flowed in a straighter course, cutting down through old Wivelham Fen where the ghost of Red Thane's daughter walked to this day through the osier-beds. Wrangling about the place of the landing, both men agreed as to what happened next. Whether at Kitt's Bend or farther upstream, the Danes were welcomed by an old woman who gave them poisoned beer; half of them died forthwith and the rest were so weakened by sicking-up that the old woman's sons came out of the reeds and finished them off. Their boat was all that was left of them, and some of its timber was built into the roof of Lintoft church. If you licked on a wet day you could still taste the salt water in it.

Sometimes Sir Ralph tried to persuade them that they might be descended from these same Danish invaders. Swearing by Saint Olave, they said they were English, nothing but English, and that no Danes had settled hereabouts, for the English had driven them off, as they would have driven off Duke William and his crew if Duke William had not been cunning enough to land in the south where men don't know how to fight. Then Jesse would call for more drink, and his wife would waddle out with it, and stand easing her bare feet in the orchard grass, staring round her with mud-coloured eyes. She was a Wivelham woman, born in the mud, she said. One shapeless garment covered her from neck to knee, and her head was muffled in a dirty green hood. She had no air of being a bailiff's wife; even on saints' days she wore the same dingy clothes and the same dumb looks. For all that, she was a valuable woman to Jesse, the best of his three wives; she had an infallible gift of foretelling the weather. One evening as she stood there listening to the disputes about the Danes with her usual waterlogged expression the fancy came to Sir Ralph that she might have waddled toward them out of those same times, that with the same dull stare she had watched the beaked prow of the warship rearing above the osiers, and that if anyone could say how far the Danish ship had got, she could. The thought was so compelling that he half turned to ask her. But at the same moment she began to sidle away, clumsy and majestic as a goose.

Another drinker in Jesse's orchard was John Ragge, who fifteen years earlier had been one of the three men provided by the manor for the wars in France. An arrow had put out his eye, and though a one-eyed archer is still good for something, when the other eye began to fail he was turned off. There were many disabled men like him, going through the country in gangs, and he joined such a gang. One winter's night when he and his mates were busy in a dovecot a pair of great dogs came bounding out and attacked them. John Ragge, mistaking a frozen horse-pond for solid ground, crashed through the ice into icy water. There he remained; for the dogs sat watching him, he could hear them growl whenever he stirred; and in the morning the servants came out, noosed him, dragged him through the crackling ice to the bank, and thrashed him. To hear him tell this adventure one would think it was the most triumphant moment in his travels. It had taken him over a twelvemonth to beg and cozen his way back to Oby, where of all the tribe of Ragges time and the pestilence had left only his sister-in-law and her two daughters, skinny muscular women who worked as thatchers. They had not much welcome for a blind man who spoke like a foreigner and was too lazy to trim gads or carry bundles of reed; but having once heard the story of the night in the pond, William Holly could not hear it too often, and brought him to the orchard as a minstrel. Sir Ralph gave him an old cloak, and once a day he stumped up to the convent for an alms of bread and leavings.

It was through him that the novices began to practise levitation.

Dame Agnes died early in 1358. The new novice-mistress was Dame Susanna. She had neither the learning nor the deportment of Dame Agnes, but her manners were particularly elegant, she was the cleanest eater in the convent, and her temper was so equable that even singing lessons went by without ill-feeling. Noticing that the plain-chant was no longer urged on with thumps and stamps, and that no cries of "Fool!" and "Blockhead!" no yelps of pain, broke the flow of the melodies, the older nuns were inclined to say that Dame Susanna was no disciplinarian. But no one could dispute that she was a good musician, and that the novices' singing showed it. Another subject which every novice must master is the art of alms-giving: how to serve out doles at the wicket, whom to encourage and whom to snub. Under Dame Agnes, who hated the poor, this had been chiefly a matter of snubbing. Dame Susanna, herself relishing a little gossip, enjoined politeness as part of the performance. Nothing loath, the novices chattered at the wicket like a troop of birds, practising, so they said, their French on John Ragge. Long after he had finished his victuals and turned his cup upside-down he lingered on, talking French and gibberish, and assuring them that the nuns in France were all very haughty and undersized. But it was in plain English (for really he knew very little French beyond the usual salutations and bawdry) that he told them how girls in Brittany have a game called Flying Saint Katharine, and how, if they sing long and earnestly enough, and are pure virgins, the girl sitting on the clasped hands of her four playmates will rise and hover in the air.

"*Fly, good Saint Katharine,*" he sang in his weather-beaten voice. "*Fly up to your tower!* And up she goes like a feather. But it can only be done in Brittany, I think," he added, his quick ears catching a little cough from Dame Susanna.

A few days later Dame Matilda, on her way back from inspecting some repairs to the brewhouse, heard giggles and a breathless singing coming from under the great walnut tree, and paused to ask the novices what wickedness they had hit on now.

Lilias le Bailey answered, rubbing her elbow, "We are learning to fly, Madam Treasuress."

She was thirteen—a tall girl, with burning hazel eyes, and the beauty among them. But they were all fine young women, Dame Matilda thought, straight and well-bred and likely to be a credit to the community.

"And where did you learn all this nonsense?"

"From Blind John. But there are not enough of us, only three. Sweet Madam Treasuress, buy us two more little novices, very little ones would do."

It was one of those fine ripening days which come in mid-July. The air was pungent with the wild peppermint that grew along the ditches, and glancing up into the tree Dame Matilda noticed that there would be a fine crop of walnuts. Relaxed with heat and satisfaction, she looked benevolently on the three girls and forgot to remember that games of this kind lead to torn clothes and sprained ankles.

"Romping and sprawling," she said. "Well, make the most of your time. No more of this when you are nuns, remember."

Only as she walked on did it come into her mind to wonder where Dame Susanna might be. By rights, Dame Susanna should have been with her novices.

Dame Susanna was on her knees among some shallots which had been laid to dry. Her mouth was open, and she was staring upward. Seized with foreboding, Dame Matilda hurried toward her, though when she spoke it was to say rather casually, "I'm sure you would be more comfortable in the shade."

Dame Susanna scrambled to her feet. Dame Matilda's forebodings intensified themselves: only a visionary could look so distraught and so defensive.

"What are you looking at so earnestly?"

"I was watching the hawk—Sir Ralph's hawk."

"And praying it may bring you down a snipe for supper, I suppose. Well, no doubt we shall all be in the air soon. I left your novices trying to fly. Perhaps you might go to them before they all take wing."

As a rule Dame Susanna winced like an aspen under the slightest rebuke. Now she went off with only a surface apology, like a person answering out of a dream. Dame Matilda thrust aside her coif and scratched her head. All her pleasure in the brewhouse repairs, the fine ripening weather, the promise of the walnuts, and the promise of the novices was dissipated. A taint of the supernatural had mixed itself with the healthy odour of the drying shallots. Of all menaces to peace and quiet a visionary nun is the worst, and when that nun is the novice-mistress the worst is ten times worsened.

What had the woman been staring about for? More than Sir Ralph's hawk. How could she be brought back to earth? Dame Matilda scratched and pondered and walked out of the sun and into it again, wishing she could ask someone for advice and knowing that there was no one whose advice she valued—for in this matter she could not consult Jesse Figg. That is the drawback of being so very sensible: one cannot take counsel because it is against common sense to seek it. The metal of common sense is so lonely and unfusable that for people like Dame Matilda there is no career except to be a tyrant or a superlative drudge. In the end she was reduced to the usual expedient of the despairingly practical: she would try what a chance augury might suggest, consulting the first person she met. The first person she met was Ursula, squatting in a doorway and rubbing a censer. Knowing all the household footsteps by heart Ursula did not look up, but asked if the censer were sufficiently burnished.

"Yes, you've put a good polish on it. Poor Ursula, you are almost blind now, are you not? How much can you see?"

"I can see light, and darkness. Sometimes, if I look at the sky, I can see a bird pass."

"Can you see our faces?"

Ursula shook her head.

"I was going to ask you if you had noticed anything about Dame Susanna. She looks changed and sickly, to me."

The blind countenance, attentive as an animal's, looked wise for a moment, and then became blank.

"She is busier now, being novice-mistress, perhaps."

"Not so busy that she need sicken."

"Oh, no, no! But you see her among young ladies. That would make her look older, would it not?"

Ursula kissed the censer, rubbed it where she had kissed it, and shuffled indoors. Dame Matilda knew that she had been put off a scent. She despised Dame Susanna for choosing such a confidant.

Meanwhile Dame Susanna had returned to her novices, and now they were practising an antiphon. The voices extended the tune like a silk canopy, and under that canopy one was safe from hearing the little bells fastened to the hawk's feet, which sounded so much like the little bell at mass. The antiphon was *Quinque prudentes,* from the parable of the wise and the foolish virgins. *And at midnight there was a cry made, Behold the bridegroom cometh; go ye out to meet him. Then all those virgins arose, and trimmed their lamps, and the foolish said unto the wise, Give us of your oil; for our lamps are gone out.*

Presently the sound of the hawk's bells began to pierce the singing like pins pricking through a piece of silk. It was Sir Ralph's hawk. Nine years ago Dame Susanna had stood at Sir Ralph's bedside, watching his hand clench into a fist and strike the wall till the blood spurted. A black stubble bristled from the spotted purple face, the air that steamed from him was foul with fever, and in the voice of someone infuriated by a long argument he asserted that he was damned, damned, damned, no priest and therefore damned. Ursula, who was with her, thrust a cup against his mouth. He whined and quarrelled with it like a child, and then, like a child, frowned and sighed and fell asleep. But later on he had cried out again, maintaining that he was no priest, and damned; and that time she had been by him alone. She had really been alone ever since, excommunicated by this fear she dared not express.

Once she had forced herself to speak of it to Ursula. Ursula had flown into a rage, saying that Dame Susanna should know better than to believe the witness of fever against a good man and a priest. Ursula did not believe it. But then, what is belief? A thought lodges in the mind, will not out, preserves its freshness and colour and flexibility like the corpse of a saint: is this belief, or is it heresy? Many times she had made ready to disburden herself in confession: to harbour such a suspicion was an offence against charity and should be confessed, repented, absolved. But something always intervened: was this intervention diabolical, or angelical? Afterward, looking at her fellow-nuns, seeing the small, familiar mannerisms which each one carried like a coat-of-arms, she had been appalled to think how she might have ruined them by suggesting that for all these years they had been served by a priest who was no priest. Even if it were disproved, and she forever disgraced for having spoken it, how could Oby recover from such a scandal?

"*Exite obviam Christo Domino-o-o.* Shall we do it again, or is that enough?" asked the novice Philippa.

"Once more, I think. And this time try to be rather less noisy at *clamor factus est.*"

The hawk had missed her prey and was mounting for another hover. But those bells only rang for the death of a little bird. One must not give way to accepting omens. One must stop one's ears, like the prudent adder. One must be silent. The sweat broke out on her face as she thought how easily she could ruin Oby. Who would bequeath manors or send novices to a house where such a suspicion could be breathed? The lamp must have oil, or it goes out. A convent must have money. And Oby was now a poor house: for the last ten years there had been talk of poverty, poverty and debt; the words had struck her the harder because she herself had brought a very little dowry, so little that if it had not been for her musicianship they would not have been able to admit her. She had impoverished them; was she to ruin them too? And for nothing more substantial than a fancy based on words spoken in a fever? It could not be true. It could not be possible. Heaven would not allow such a thing, and certainly not for so many years. There would have been a sign. A dream would be sent, a toad would jump from the chalice, the spire would fall. The spire! She turned and looked at it. It was tall now, pure as a lily-stalk in its cage of scaffolding. One could see how long it had taken to grow, this lily, for already the lower stages had begun to weather. It would soon be completed. Then it would be consecrated. The Virgin would accept the lily.

"*Exite obviam Christo Domino-o-o-o.*" The singers prolonged the last syllable till their breaths gave out. They did not want to go through *Quinque prudentes* again. They waited for Dame Susanna to tell them what to do next. But she seemed to have forgotten all about them. She had turned away and was staring at the spire as though she had fastened her very soul to it. The novice Philippa tapped lightly on her white forehead with her white forefinger and gave a condoling nod.

A few evenings later as the elder nuns sat in the prioress's chamber Dame Matilda loosed her arrow.

"By the way, I find our novices are learning to fly."

The prioress frowned, for the arrow had twanged too sharply in Dame Matilda's voice. She made a languid inquiry and was told that Dame Susanna could best answer it. Dame Susanna explained that it was a game.

"There is a song," Dame Matilda pursued. "I don't know how it goes. I have no ear for music. But no doubt Dame Susanna can sing it."

In a timid voice, invincibly in tune, Dame Susanna began to sing. Instantly Dame Salome, not usually very musical, joined in at the top of her voice and sang the tune through several times.

Since it really was not possible to praise such singing, the prioress praised the tune, and said that it sounded as if it were a very ancient one. Dame Beatrix remarked that much the same game was played by little girls in Cornwall, and added that as a child she had played it herself, and that if you were the girl in the middle you felt sick.

"Did you fly?" Dame Salome's voice was so solemn and suspicious that the others were abashed by her silliness. Dame Beatrix began to laugh and answered that she had not been so fortunate. Instead, she had tumbled, bruising herself badly, and had been beaten for dirtying her clothes. The prioress remarked that children lived in pain as in an element, so much so that beating was probably no real change to them. Dame Helen said that she had been a very well-thumped child, and told a story. Conversation had moved elsewhere when Dame Salome harked back and said, "You know, there are certainly some who can fly. At least they remain in the air quite a little while. And was not Saint Katharine herself carried all the way to Alexandria by angels?"

"There are so many stories of flying," said Dame Beatrix, "that no doubt some of them are true. But I think one would need to be extremely young or extremely saintly."

"Not at all," said Dame Salome. "It can happen with quite an ordinary person—a good person, of course. But one need not be anything so very out-of-the-ordinary. Cleverness is not everything."

Dame Helen agreed that cleverness was not everything. Many saints were simple enough. The prioress remarked that it was not till christian times that simplicity became a virtue; the good characters of the Old Testament were ingenious as well as virtuous.

"That was because they were Jews," said Dame Beatrix.

Once more the conversation was turned away from flying. But Dame Salome continued flushed and thoughtful. Dame Matilda watched her. Though well aware that she had made a false step in her attack on Dame Susanna, Dame Matilda saw no reason why she should not follow up the false step with a better one. A dog-day demon had entered into her. She was determined to pull down her quarry, no matter who suffered by it. So she waited till there was a pause in the small talk and then remarked on the scarcity of miracles nowadays. As she had intended, Dame Salome instantly remarked on the scarcity of faith. After a couple of sentences Dame Salome was induced to say that faith could remove mountains.

"Come, come . . . You are not as heavy as all that," said Dame Matilda, and rose, putting back her sleeves. This was the difficult moment. But by exerting all her geniality, her air of good-fellowship and affable tolerance, she conjured Dame Helen, Dame Beatrix, and at last Dame Susanna, into her circle.

"Now then! Fly, good Saint Katharine!"

Amusement turned to embarrassment, embarrassment to a communal frenzy, *"FLY, good Saint Kathar-ine! Fly UP to your Tow-er!"* They sang at the tops of their voices, riotous as vintagers. Each felt another's griping hand-clasp, their wrists ached, their fingers grew slippery with sweat. Thinking of the difficult moment when they must at last let go, they went on and on; and Dame Salome jigged up and down on the swaying net of their hands, her features resolutely composed in a prim smile, like some enormously weighty doll.

"Oh! O holy Virgin!"

Someone had let go. Dame Salome sat on the floor and wept bitterly.

She wept unheeded because the others were looking nervously toward the prioress. The prioress sat with her eyes cast down, and her fingers closed so sharply on her little dog that it yelped and bared its teeth. Out of the past came Thomas de Foley's voice telling of the absurdities of the Gilbertine nuns, the cabbage soup with two and a half radishes for each monk. Out of the present came Dame Salome's sobs, which burst from her like hiccups because she was so much out of breath. At last Dame Beatrix took pity on her, wiping her face and thumping her shoulders.

"Is that better? Shall I get you some dill cordial?"

Dame Salome looked up and said sullenly, "I flew. I know you won't believe it, but I flew."

Dame Matilda looked at Dame Susanna and slowly shrugged her shoulders. That night she fell asleep thanking her prudent saints for a good evening's work. She did not suppose that Dame Susanna would cultivate visions for some time to come.

When, after a decent interval, the question of John Ragge's deservingness was somehow raised in chapter there was a general sense of relief at the decision to feed him no longer. When there are so many cases of real need and genuine desert it was an abuse of alms-giving to nourish such idle roisterers. Throughout the convent there was a noticeable air of decorum and spring-cleaning. The incident in the prioress's chamber had a wholesome after-effect, bracing as doses of wormwood. Everyone felt with relief a tightened bond of discipline and convention, the sturdy tradition of the ordinary which had controlled for centuries and all over christendom the cloistered life. In that life there was no place for aberrations of individuality. One monastic must resemble another, and all go the same way, a flock soberly ascending to a heavenly pasture, a flock counterfeiting as best it could under difficult circumstances the superlative regimentation of heaven. Even Dame Salome was subdued; and in Jesse Figg's orchard Sir Ralph was told how Old Matilda and Old Susanna had had another set-to, and now it was patched up again.

John Ragge's chatter at the wicket was regretted for a while and then forgotten. By the end of August the game of Flying Saint Katharine was forgotten too. There were the apples to gather, and the damsons and the elderberries and the blackberries. The fine weather lasted on into October, with frosts sharpening at night and dissolving in golden mornings. Quantities of wild geese flew over. Sir Ralph said that in all his years at Oby he had not seen a greater flocking of birds. It was a sign of a hard winter, and by such signs God warns his creatures to prepare against it. God's creatures were busy preparing as best they could. A great deal of firing was stolen from Saint Leonard's wood, several geese disappeared, and John Holly's wadded coat vanished from the thornbush where she had hung it to air. She said plainly that Elizabeth and Margery Ragge had stolen it to wrap their worthless uncle in. Now that Blind John was no longer fed by the convent he was less popular with his gossips.

On the eve of All Saints the masons began to take down the scaffolding—for at last the spire was finished; miraculously, one might say, considering all the mischances which had delayed it and, more potent than any mischance, the prioress's creative vacillations. But, just as at the end of a labour the child asserts itself and comes forth, it seemed that the spire had at last escaped from her whimsical control.

Walking in the cloisters, Dame Beatrix and Dame Helen paused to watch the timbers being lowered.

"Who could have believed it? For all these years we have been expecting it. And yet, now that it has come, I feel quite astonished, quite taken aback."

"Wonderful," said Dame Helen more tranquilly.

"It makes me feel very old."

It made Dame Helen feel very old too.

"Another wonderful thing is that we still have the same prioress. When you think of all the changes"—Dame Beatrix began to count on her fingers—"and all the deaths . . . Dame Agnes, Dame Isabel, Dame Blanch. And Pernelle Bastable going away with our horse. And Bishop William. Well, God rest their souls! They were all very good people."

"We must not forget those who died at the time of the pestilence. The spire was begun before that, you remember."

"So it was. Dame Helen Aslack, Dame Emily—"

"Dame Alice Guillemard—"

"That poor little novice—what was she called? She was a hunchback."

"Wait a minute. She was one of the Isabels. Isabel de Stoke."

"No, Isabel de Stoke was taken away and died at home. She was tall and straight. No, I mean the novice who was to bring us the relic. Don't you remember, the tooth we were to have, the tooth of the Holy Innocent?"

"Quite true! The tooth of a Holy Innocent. That was a bad piece of work and I never perfectly understood how it all happened. I can't recollect the novice's name, though. She died first of all, just before Dame Emily. Isabel . . . Isabel . . . Isabel de Fanal."

"Marie de Fanal. Not Isabel at all. The other Isabel was Isabel Goffin who was taken away by her parents and compelled to break her vocation and marry."

"I suppose one can't count her in with the others. Now I am out."

They began to reckon again and had brought the count to eight when Dame Beatrix recollected old Dame Roesia who died before the pestilence and Dame Helen recollected Dame Joan.

"Though she was almost blind even then, you remember. Even if she had lived she would not have seen the spire. I hope that scaffolding will be split into firewood. It grows colder every day, it is as cold as midwinter already. Here comes Dame Johanna."

Dame Johanna was coming to fetch Dame Beatrix. Ursula had fallen downstairs again and cut her head.

She gave the message in a detached, well-mannered tone of voice which conveyed a readiness to overlook. As the infirmaress hurried indoors Dame Johanna paused beside Dame Helen, huddling her hands in her sleeves, and remarked graciously, "How delighted you must be to see your spire finished at last! And how fortunate you are to have the means to build it! At Dilworth we only saw things falling down."

"We have been counting up all the ladies who have died here while it was a-building."

"Indeed. Are they many?"

"Yes, a great many. But of course it cannot interest you, since you have known none of them."

"I imagine that a great many of them must have died of cold," retorted the newcomer. "At Dilworth, even in midwinter, it was not as cold as it is here."

Dame Helen stumped toward the house. Dame Johanna, keeping up with her, imparted a few details about the state of poor Ursula's head.

During these last few months Ursula had aged very fast and simultaneously she had grown tiresome and intractable. Though she was unwieldy with dropsy and crippled by a sore in her leg she would not stay quiet on her pallet, but roamed about the house listening at doorways, mumbling and crossing herself. She had a delusion that some danger threatened Sir Ralph, and this made her bent on sleeping outside his door—crawling up the stairs, bumping her blind head, losing her balance and falling, and making her way up again, uncontrollable as water. He would wake, and hear her snoring and praying in her sleep, and if he were not too sleepy himself he would lead her down again to the nuns; but in an hour or two she would be back. One morning she was picked up dead at the stair-foot. It was a deplorable death—the death of an animal rather than of a christian; but everything to do with Ursula was deplorable, except the kindness she had received: a rather negligent kindness, no doubt, but more than her deserts, since for many years no one had reproached her or forced her to labour beyond her strength.

Perhaps such kindness was a mistaken kindness. Praying for Ursula's soul (about whose welfare Dame Johanna expressed a deal of unsolicited concern), the prioress asked herself if she had acted improperly in remitting Ursula's penance. Another twenty or thirty scourgings might have made a great difference. She submitted these doubts to Sir Ralph, and speaking in his dry professional voice he assured her that she was being overconscientious. Her part in the business was merely instrumental, for since no penance is sacramentally efficacious unless it is accompanied by contrition it depended on Ursula and not on her whether the stripes were salutary. She hastened to agree, and did not add that in beating Ursula she had felt no more sacramental than if she were a laundress thumping dirty linen.

For all men are alike; if one asks a direct question they reply with a treatise. Edmund Gurney, the mason, had been just the same, wrapping himself in long discourses about the natures of different kinds of stone. That is how men are made, and that is what they expect women to put up with. Yet if she had failed to supply Sir Ralph with a dinner, replying to his hunger with a discourse on the breeding of cattle and the difference betwixt beef and mutton, he would scarcely be contented. Beef and mutton, clothing and firing, that is the life-work for a prioress. Not souls. Not even spires.

She did not try to hide from herself the sense of anticlimax which accompanied the completion of her spire. It was beautiful, but it was not as beautiful as she had meant, and her inability to carry out the extension of the nave left it awkwardly placed. It was finished; but "over and done with" was the truer word. The exaltation she had looked for had not kept its tryst; even her nuns, who had never cared for it, and who now went about saying how pretty it was, how neat, and what an embellishment, had more pleasure from it than she. It was her life-work; but her life persisted, a life filled with beef and mutton, clothing and firing, cavils and quarrels. Life as prioress, however, would soon be over, for after the consecration of her spire she would resign her office. They were expecting it. Probably they were looking forward to it. It was impossible that anyone could look forward to it with such longing as she. To be freed from beef and mutton and misunderstandings; to sit silent in chapter; never again to be pursued with those account-books; never again to hear those accursed syllables, *Dear Mother, I am sorry to trouble you, but . . .* Cost what it might—and this present bishop, Giles de Furness, was rumoured to be a much sterner stickler for fees than the kind old Bishop William—there should be an election, and Prioress Matilda should replace Prioress Alicia.

Two dates suggested themselves as suitable for the ceremony of consecration: the patronal feast of Saint Leonard, or Candlemas. Saint Leonard's Day was the favourite choice until Dame Johanna took it on herself to point out all its advantages: this was enough to convince everyone that a late November festivity was out of the question, one could not ask people to wade through the mud. When Dame Johanna said that the mud would be just as much of an impediment in early February she was reminded that she had yet to spend a winter at Oby and could not know what she was talking about.

Dame Johanna was a transferred nun who had come to Oby from the house of The Holy Trinity at Dilworth. For years

Dilworth had been notorious for its debts and confusions, and though Bishop William had been patient with it Bishop Giles had ordered its dissolution and the dispersal of its seven remaining nuns into other establishments. These unfortunate creatures carried no dowry with them, for their portions had been devoured in the Dilworth quicksand. Nevertheless, Oby had undertaken to receive two of them, Dame Matilda pointing out that to gratify a new bishop is always a good pennyworth. The bishop, returning kindness for kindness, had sent them his most advantageous pair. Dame Johanna Pyke was sickly, and not likely to cumber them for more than a year or so, and Dame Alice Sutton, though young and sturdy, was a skilled confectioner—so skilled that the little revenue left to Dilworth had been brought in by her exceptional marzipan.

Dame Alice's sweetmeats bore out the bishop's words. It was to be hoped that time would prove him as accurate about Dame Johanna. For Dame Johanna was disliked by everyone, and the more she tried to ingratiate herself the more she was felt to be an interloper, a meddler, and a bore. "It would be better," said the prioress to Dame Beatrix, "if the poor scarecrow would not force herself to take such an interest in us and our doings. Surely it is quite unsuitable for a woman who is going to die in a year or so to attach herself to a mere temporary lodging-house!" To which Dame Beatrix gloomily replied that being a bishop does not make one a doctor, and that there might be a long step between looking like a death's-head and dying.

"If I hear that woman utter another word of praise I really think I shall strangle her," exclaimed Dame Margaret. "She praises everything and doesn't mean a word of it." Even Dame Helen was driven into a spirit of contradiction, and when Dame Johanna happened to mention that Dilworth owned no more than five books assured her that this could not be so, quite the contrary, the Dilworth library was cited by everybody as excellent.

Having discredited Saint Leonard, Dame Johanna proceeded, all unwittingly, to compromise the coming election. Dame Matilda, she understood, would be elected unanimously: how very nice that would be! Unanimous elections are creditable to all concerned, they demonstrate to the world the favour of God, who makes men to be of one mind in a house. The Oby nuns were fortunate to have been spared such electoral squabbles as had taken place at Dilworth, where the sacrist had got herself elected in the very teeth of the bishop.

"It is so wonderfully peaceful here!" exclaimed Dame Johanna.

She meant it as a commendation, but her unfortunate manner made it sound like a taunt. At Dilworth it was nothing to have half the ladies absent, one on a pilgrimage, one visiting a sick mother, another cheering a lying-in, a fourth searching for a little dog. The home-comings after such absences were as disrupting as the absences themselves: amid talk of heresies, fashions, family disputes, kid served with almonds, law-suits, adulteries, harp-players, and heraldic bearings, the offices were neglected, discipline was thrown to the winds, God was forgotten, and meals were late. Only those who had experienced such a state of things, she concluded, could realize what a comfort it was to find oneself in a house like Oby, where everything went on so quietly, month after month, and the bull *Periculoso* was so honestly observed.

As a result, Dame Johanna's hearers burned to flout the bull *Periculoso* as soon as possible; and when the prioress was invited to stand as godmother to a baby of a cadet branch of the de Rettevilles the indigenous Oby nuns insisted that she must go to the christening and pointed out, as though it were something scandalous, that she had not slept a single night away from her convent since the August of 1351. The prioress, too, had smarted under Dame Johanna's commendations. She was admitting the various advantages of going to the christening—founder's kin, making new friends, picking up new novices perhaps, and making sure of that long-promised, never-secured little Adela de Retteville, whom with any luck she could bring back with her—when Dame Beatrix happened to suppose that on this journey Sir Ralph might as well be left behind, he was really too shabby for visiting. Unquenchably shameful, the recollection of the scene in the nave overwhelmed the prioress: Sir Ralph lungeing and bellowing, Thomas skipping aside, his nose bleached with fury. She exclaimed that going to the christening was out of the question. She was too old to ride through the winter weather, and the litter, a relic of Dame Isabella's days, lay mouldering past repair in the cart-shed, where the hens laid eggs in it.

But she was forced to give way when a grizzled squire brought a letter from Marie de Blakeborn. She too was going to the christening, and it would be only a day more in her journey to turn aside to Oby. "Unless you have grown as fat as I have," she wrote, "the litter will hold us both, and it will be pleasant to talk of old times as we travel."

Marie de Blakeborn arrived soon after sundown with a small retinue of elderly servants. She had grown unbelievably fat. Tottering forward in the January dusk, swathed in furs, she looked like a performing bear. She had also grown very deaf, and deafness had deformed her voice into a stately roar. The nuns found it hard to conceal their amusement. As soon as she had been taken to the guest-chamber they began to mimic her, mouthing hushed imitations of her roars, and Dame Cecily drew a sketch of Saint Michael weighing Marie and Sir Ralph against each other in his scales and staggering under their combined weight.

It did not seem to the prioress that there would be much talk of old times. Marie was absorbed in the present, bellowing about the latest shaping of gold hair-nets, a new sort of little woolly dog, and the progress of her law-suits and her grandchildren. Well, so much the better! Ten years had passed since their last meeting, and now she shrank from the prospect of any intimacy with this noisy, affable stranger. They set out immediately after mass. It was a dark morning, the sky was covered with smoky vapour, all the pigs were screaming in their sties. Deafened by the pigs, the shrill good-byes of her nuns, Marie's torrential directions to her retinue, the prioress sat with closed eyes, cursing the moment she had consented to this expedition. As well drag a corpse out of its grave, she told herself, prop it up with cushions and send it off to stand godmother! Who wants a *larva mundi* at a christening feast?

She was aroused by an exclamation.

"Why, there's your spire! You never told me it was finished. Stop, stop, Denis! Stop the horses! We want to look at the spire."

From the rise of ground they looked back across Oby Fen, darker than ever under the smoky sky. White and sharp-cut, the only thing with a definite outline in all the shaggy, formless, sad-coloured landscape, the spire seemed to be sinking, to be sucked down into the mud.

"Charming!" roared Marie. "I should have known it was yours anywhere. You always have such good taste."

The prioress was thinking, This is the first time I have seen it from a distance, seen it as others will see it; and it needed Marie's litter and the birth of a child to get me here. I had the enterprise, once, to begin it, and now I have not the enterprise to come out and look at it.

"Tell me, is Thomas dead?"

"Dead, my dear? Our Thomas dead? Very much alive, I assure you, and a great man again. Why, didn't you hear how he outwitted them all?"

She gave the order to ride on and settled down to relate how Thomas had emerged from his spell of penitence as merry as a marmot and as vindictive as a hornet; how he had stayed at Etchingdon long enough to pay off all old scores, had got himself offered the priorship again for the satisfaction of refusing it, and now was in Lombardy, negotiating a loan for the King.

"They think the world of him at Westminster. And you really supposed him dead? Well, your convent is a most exemplary convent if you know so little of what's going on outside as to think Thomas was dead."

To the deaf ears, to the sighing breeze, Alicia de Foley allowed herself to say, "I see how wrong I was. I see now that it is I who am dead."

Only good breeding enabled her to endure the christening festivities, the feasting, the display of gifts, the women exchanging child-bed stories in one corner of the hall, the men getting drunk in a devil-may-care, no-business-of-mine fashion in another. Like a ghost she listened to the singing in Saint John's church, like a ghost she fingered the embroideries on bed and baby, half expecting to see her fingers leave a blight on what they had touched. The only thing like real life was the incessant tipping. Wherever she turned someone started up, expecting a gratuity from a godmother, and by the third day she was compelled to borrow from Marie de Blakeborn. She saw her new novice, Adela de Retteville. The girl was very pretty, so pretty that it was a wonder that her parents had finally consented to part with her; but no doubt there was some sufficient reason why she should be given to God. Laying her finger—that blighting finger—under the warm chin and staring at the parted crimson lips, the prioress said, "You will be very happy with us, my child. There is more contentment in the cloister than in the world."

"And that there is!" said the child's mother, with a bitter expression on her discouraged face. "And I hope you will be grateful to us, Adela, and pray well for our souls. It's time you did something more than romping and spoiling. When will you be going back to Oby?" she added.

"On the Tuesday."

On the evening of the christening a band of musicians was hired, and the young ones of the party danced. Relieved of their company the elders had the supper table set close to the hearth and sat there quietly, drinking and eating nuts. Conversation turned on the infirmities of the flesh. Marie spoke of the encumbrance of her fat, describing her struggles on the close-stool, the terrific purges that were needed to drive a way through her bowels. Adam de Retteville replied that fat would be a comfort to him. His teeth had rotted in his gums, he could bite nothing without anguish, he was forced to live on broths and decoctions, and no spices, no peppercorns, could mask the taste of corruption that haunted every mouthful he swallowed. But that, said his brother Steven, was better than a fistula. A man with a fistula could not be easy on a horse or on a cushion, and must wait, for all his pride and all his prowess, on the good pleasure of a body servant. Yes, but a flux of the lungs, imagine that! cried his neighbour: to spit, to stifle, to have not only food and exercise, but the more common air denied you. An old de Retteville widow, yellow as saffron, continued to assert that the pains in her head would astonish anyone who could experience them, for sometimes it was as though the devil were stirring up her brains with a red-hot spoon and at other times as though three worms, bred in the nose, were eating their ways toward eyebrow and ear and jaw.

Since people will boast of anything and be glad to have the wherewithal, conversation in the ingle was happily competitive. The prioress took no part in it. She sat eating nuts with her eyes cast down.

"And you, my dear gossip?" inquired Adam de Retteville in a burst of cordiality, "You too must have something to tell us, some hardening in the breast, some twinge in those white knees that are bent for us sinners on the cold stone?"

Marie answered for her. "Not she! Look at her! Look at her colour, look at her smooth chin, smooth as a page's. Look how she sits there, stuffing herself with nuts, and not so much as a belch."

Raising her eyes, the prioress looked round on her contemporaries: on cheeks veined with purple or pinched and sallow, on rheumy eyes, grey hairs, brown teeth, knotted joints. How fat they were, or how thin! How hot, or how cold! How they belied their grand clothes and their grand manners!—a crop of toadstools could not look more garishly death-like.

"I must thank Our Lady," she said correctly, "for my good health." And just as though she were running over her beads she felt herself reckoning up sight, hearing, touch, taste, smell, all perfect, her limbs wholesome, her blood pure.

"Look at her teeth," continued Marie. "The whole set of them, white as wolf's teeth."

"One of them is chipped." She could hear the affected modesty of the words. Parting her lips she pointed to an eye-tooth that was minutely flawed.

"It's the same with all you de Foleys," said Marie. "There's Thomas, as brisk as a young hound. Not a grey hair in his head —nor in yours, I daresay."

"We nuns are supposed to last out well, you know. There were two ladies in our house, both were near four-score, and except that one of them grew a little forgetful . . ." Growing a little forgetful herself, the prioress gave a coy description of

Dame Agnes and Dame Roesia. Her companions listened with delight, melting with sentiment, nudging each other, rolling their bleared eyes, and saying that there was nothing so pleasant as the religious life and that they wished they had given themselves to God instead of remaining in the world to be battered to pieces with care and sickness.

"Well, then, you must give me my god-daughter."

Adam de Retteville pinched her arm. "Nothing would please me better. But you must settle it with her father, you know, the dowry and all that. The girl is founder's kin, you ought to take her for nothing. You agree to take her for nothing—you can always get a double dowry from some scrivener—and she's yours."

"But vocation . . . One must not forget vocation."

Adam de Retteville looked across the table at the group of dancers at the other end of the room. "What you eat's vocation," he pronounced.

Marie de Blakeborn had planned to carry the prioress and little Adela back to Oby and make a short visit there. It had been raining heavily, the floods were rising, and Marie's horoscope declared that she would die by water. When Tuesday came she refused to set out. If the prioress were bent on swimming back to her nuns, she said—who no doubt were doing very comfortably without her—the litter was at her service, and one of Marie's waiting-women, a big, hook-nosed Fleming, could go with her and look after the child. Painfully aware that she was disobliging a number of people, the prioress paid the last gratuities and departed, farewelled by assurances that she would soon regret being so dutiful and scowled on by Marie's retinue. It was a relief to look into Adela's beaming daisy-face, so very pink, so very white, so gaily turned toward the future. The floods were wide and turbulent. Clots of foam and swans speckled the water, and in the half-light of the January day the child amused herself by her inability to distinguish between them until a swan melted or a clot of foam rose into the air. The Fleming stitched on at a piece of embroidery, growling under her breath when a jolt or a stumble jerked the needle from its aim. The litter creaked and swayed and the prioress drowsed as if in a roughly rocked cradle. Awakening she would find in herself a sensation like a wound, a sensation of being exhausted with bitter weeping; and then she would wake a little further and remember Thomas de Foley, who was alive and flourishing, and careless whether she died or lived on. Careless? No, it was more likely that he had deliberately put her out of his mind, she, and her spire, and her crazy priest, all detestably associated with his reverse at Etchingdon. But perhaps careless. She stroked one edge of the sword and then the other against her heart and it was impossible to decide which was sharpest.

On the second day they made better speed. The wind had got into the north, it had begun to freeze and the ways were harder. On the third morning it seemed likely that they would reach Oby before vespers, but flakes of snow began to glitter in the air, then the sun went in and the snow fell in earnest. The Fleming put by her embroidery and took the child into her arms, holding her close to warm her. Twice, bemused by the snow, the horsemen lost their way. At last they reached Lintoft, where the priest's housekeeper came out with a drink of hot beer. The floods had not been so bad, she said, no worse than any other winter; but the wind had been terrible, a biting north wind. During the night it had risen to a tempest, screaming down on them like a troop of horses. Her master was sick of a fever, stifling, and black in the face. He would die tonight, she fancied . . . would the prioress and her nuns pray an easy death for him?

"I will, I will!" exclaimed Adela, dancing up and down.

The prioress asked if he had been shriven. Yes, said the housekeeper; by a lucky chance Sir Ralph had ridden over yesterday, inquiring about his lost hawk, and had shriven him. He will be desperate if he has lost his hawk, she thought. He should never have loosed her in a north wind, hawks lose heart in a north wind. Thinking of a distracted Sir Ralph and of the prayers she must order for the Lintoft priest, she felt herself suddenly re-knit to her convent, and interested to be returning. It always looked pretty in snow, a white landscape was a grateful change after the sallow monotony of the moors. Tomorrow they would throw out crumbs for the birds and she would ask the cellaress to provide some little extra delicacy for a dinner to celebrate her home-coming with one de Retteville novice in her hand and the prospect of another. If it continued to snow the litter could not be sent back to Marie for some days. Possibly the Fleming, so skilful with her needle, might be beguiled into mending the Trinity Cope.

"The sacrist must show you our vestments. We have one or two fine old pieces. But just now we are poorly off for needle-women, none of our novices seems able . . ."

The litter canted over as the front horse swung aside. The beasts were halted with kicking and shouting. A voice said, "There's something here across the track. One can see nothing for the snow, but I can see something there."

The hinder horseman replied, "You see and you can't see. I was nearly off."

"It's a great heap of thatch. What a place to leave it! Now how are we to go on? The track is so narrow that we can't edge past it, and there seems to be a ditch here and a ditch there."

"Well, we don't need to go on, do we? Here we are at Oby, in my opinion, for I can see a building in front of us, and people are coming out with lights."

A moment later he added, "Here comes such a nun! By God, she's fatter than our mistress!"

It was Sir Ralph. "Which roof?" she began. Grunting out something about the depth of the snow, he carried her indoors and set her down in the parlour. All the nuns were there, looking oddly formal, she thought; but of course nuns would look formal to an eye which had been studying the de Retteville christening party. She glanced round for the de Retteville novice. The Fleming had just carried her in and was unwinding her from her mufflers.

"See who I have brought."

Dame Matilda came forward, kissed her ring, and drew her toward the fire. "Dear Mother, you are very welcome to your poor daughters."

"How solemn you all look! You must have been getting into some scrape."

Up came Dame Beatrix with a bowl of mead. "Drink this, dear Mother. Such . . . such a cold night!"

She sipped and looked round on them. After all, there was one missing. "Where is Dame Susanna? I have brought her a novice. Half-frozen, but a novice for all that."

Something was wrong. Not one of them could look her in the face. Now here was Dame Salome standing before her, crimson, opening and shutting her mouth like a fish. The instant I am back, she thought, this sort of thing begins. I suppose they have been flying again.

"Somebody must give the girl her supper and put her to bed."

Dame Salome flapped out of the circle, looking as pleased as a fish that slips out through the net, and beckoned Adela and the Fleming away.

The prioress finished her mead and then turned to her treasuress.

"Well? What has gone wrong now?"

"During your absence God has sent us a great sorrow. Dame Susanna is dead."

Released by these words, the nuns now began to cross themselves flutteringly, to sigh, and to commend Dame Susanna's soul.

"How? When?"

"She died last night."

"But how? How did she die?"

"She died suddenly. By an accident."

"Unshriven!" The word was screeched out in Dame Johanna's most calamitous hoot.

"Where was that fat beast, then? Out hawking, I suppose?"

"No, he was in bed."

"It was in the middle of the night."

"He came at once, but it was too late. She was dead already."

"She was buried!"

Together they could do what no one had the courage to do singly. Interrupting each other, contradicting, referring, harking back to make something clear, having theories as to how it happened and other theories as to how it might have been prevented, they pieced out the story of Dame Susanna's death.

They were in quire for the night office, scarcely able to hear themselves chant for the force of the gale. Then, following on a strong gust of wind, there came a noise of rending, and a crash. They looked round, they could see nothing to account for it; but at the same moment several candles were blown out and the air became icy cold. They went on with the office, and finished it, and were just about to leave the quire when the rending noises began again, and this time, because the wind was not blowing so violently, they heard them more plainly and realized that they were close at hand. Dame Matilda opened the screen-door and peered into the nave, supposing that a window had been blown in. The nave was flooded with moonlight, and overhead through a hole in the roof they saw the bleached clouds hurrying, the frosty stars, the outburst of the full moon. The nave floor was heaped with timber and rubble and blocks of stone. While they stood gazing, there was a sharp patter, and fragments of mortar showered down, and then tiles and pieces of stone-work. Then came a terrible noise, like a lion's roar—no, said Dame Beatrix, like the noise a wave makes as it rears up against the shore and sucks back the shingle—and then, answering it from among them, a shriek that made the blood run cold, a shriek that was more horrible than anything else in all that horrible night, just such a shriek as a soul must utter when plunged astonished into hellfire; and with the strength of a madwoman Dame Susanna forced her way through them and ran into the nave. Whether she fell on her knees or whether the falling masonry caught her and felled her it was impossible to say, but in that instant she had disappeared, lost in a cloud of dust, crushed under the falling spire.

The story was told but not finished. Dame Margaret had to recount all that was done afterward, how comfortable Sir Ralph had been, how well Dame Matilda had kept her courage, how all the manor folk had heard the crash of the falling spire but not one had come near to help. Dame Johanna had to say how remarkable it was that within a minute or two of the calamity the wind had gone down, though bits of stone kept falling at intervals for some hours after. Having begun to talk, they were afraid to leave off. No one wished to bring on the silence into which their prioress must speak. Flustered, compassionate, embarrassed, they chattered on, eking out their stock of narrative, remembering to add that the thatch had been blown off the gate-house, that a roof-tile had been blown as far as the walnut tree.

The prioress sat by the hearth, turning the empty bowl in her hands. When at last she spoke it was to say, "Where is Sir Ralph? Why is he not here? I must see him at once."

When he came, entering the room with a wary animal composure, she began to discuss with him the arrangements for Dame Susanna's burial and the masses that must be said for the repose of her soul. Such arrangements were ordinary enough, a commonplace to both of them, and scarcely needed discussion; but she spoke as though she were a commander issuing directions in the heat of battle. For the last eighteen hours he had been sweating with anxiety as to how she would take the news that her spire was in ruins and her novice-mistress dead with every appearance of self-slaughter. He had allowed for fury, dejection, misery, weeping and wailing and gnashing of teeth, and even for fortitude and magnanimity—since he knew her to be capable of almost anything. The one thing he had not expected was what she presented: this front of trivial authority, like a plaster representation of a carving in stone. It threw him out, and he resented it, and felt for the first time in their mutual relations that she was a thoroughly disagreeable woman.

He was not alone in feeling so. If the prioress had shown a sociable grief her nuns would have been very willing to grieve with her; but she wrapped herself in a mood of cold sulks, and left them to turn their compassion on themselves—the victims of a calamity which her ambition had provoked. Not only had the spire fallen, and killed Dame Susanna; but it had fallen piecemeal, and so incompetently that it would be cheaper to rebuild than to pull down, which meant a further expense and all the dust and clamour of building to be endured over again. The masons were aggrieved at being fetched back, and a quarrel arose between the convent and the master-mason, for naturally the nuns blamed him for the fall of the spire. He for his part asserted that the fault lay with the convent; if the ladies had been able to make up their minds so that he could have gone ahead with the job the mortar would have dried out evenly, the weight of the stone-work would have settled. But ladies never can make up their minds.

Then one of his boys, clumsy with cold, tripped, fell off the scaffolding, and broke his thigh. The masons left the work and stood about saying that there was a curse on the spire and that it would be against God's will to finish it. The Oby people who worked with the builders, carting stone and loading and carrying the hods, now added their witness. Floods, pestilence, murrain, scarcity: there had been one misfortune on the heels of another since the spire was begun. If the nuns were so wealthy, they should spend their money on succouring the poor, as Christ bid. Succouring the poor, indeed!—why, they had even turned away blind John Ragge, poor soul, and as a result no one in Oby could call his hen his own, for since the convent had turned him away he had fallen back on the tricks he had learned in the wars; even a blind man must live. Of course there was a curse on the spire. Who could wonder that God had toppled it over, for what right had nuns to be building spires?—keeping them from their work by extortion of cartage and labour dues, and wasting the manor in order to heap stone on stone and feed a pack of strangers. From abuse of the nuns they turned to abusing the masons. Young Scole swore that if he saw another mason perched in the scaffolding like a crow in a winter tree he'd send an arrow through him. That night the men of Oby mobbed the masons' settlement, kicking down their huts and scattering their gear. After that they marched round the convent singing at the tops of their voices, and in the midst of the procession was John Ragge, twanging an old viol and lovingly supported—for he was popular for the nonce. Next morning the masons took down the scaffolding. By that same evening they were gone, William Holly taking it on himself to arrange transport for them and their stuff as far as Dudham, where his cousin's homestead was soon the better for several repairs and innovations.

While the people of the neighbourhood were saying how chop-fallen the nuns must look, the nuns were warming themselves over the possibility of a law-suit. Oby had not had a law-suit since the stirring days of Prioress Isabella, but most of its ladies had hearsay experience of the law: family litigations about dues, dowries, maimings and slayings, neglect of floodgates, encroachments on land, abduction of heiresses, poaching of deer, and contested legacies. Law, they all knew, is tricky and costly, and much depends on knowing the right people; but this was no sooner admitted than it appeared that a great number of the right people were known: a cousin, an uncle, a talented and rising nephew, a prodigiously hoary and crafty kinsman by bastardy, a stepniece at court; and both Dame Margaret and the novice Philippa came of legal families. "And we must not forget the de Stapledons," put in Dame Salome, turning courteously to Dame Matilda, who acknowledged this tribute with an uneasy shifting of her bottom. It seemed to her that there was little hope of averting a popular form of ruin.

For the moment there was too much to say for anything to be agreed, for each nun had her own view as to what ground the action should lie on. Dame Margaret was for breech of contract. What could be plainer? There stood the unfinished spire to prove it. Dame Beatrix objected that Edmund Gurney might plead that the spire had been finished, and that the wind which threw it down was an act of God and no fault of the builders; surely it would be better to catch him on an accusation of scamped work; an honest piece of building would not have been overthrown by a mere winter's gale. Dame Helen was all for manslaughter. How else had Dame Susanna died? What a loss to the community! Something must be due to them for that, surely? They had never had such a novice-mistress, and who could tell what novices might not be lost to them by losing her. Her fame was spreading far and wide, such a good musician, such delicate manners, and such piety! In old days such a nun would have been canonized, if only for her piteous death. There she had knelt, her hands stretched to heaven as if to ward off the disaster, praying aloud that the convent might be preserved. And sure enough, a minute later the wind fell, the air was as still as midsummer. Dame Johanna had remarked on it at the time. If they were to lose such a nun and not get exemplary damages, there was no justice in England. And another thing . . . what about those repairs at Dudham, that new roof on the Hollys' granary? As plain a theft as ever finger pointed at! At times they even remembered to put in a word of regret for the spire, which had been so beautiful and their cherished ambition for the last twenty years. It was useless for Dame Matilda to remind them that they had constantly grumbled about the spire. It was useless for Dame Johanna to explain that she had never said or supposed that the wind fell because of Dame Susanna's prayers. They were united in longing for a law-suit, and only waited for the prioress to lead them to it.

But the prioress seemed to have lost all interest in life. She lay in bed, or sat in her chamber listlessly teaching her bullfinch to pipe the *De Profundis.* Loyal, though fraying with impatience, they maintained that she was stunned by the shock.

On Holy Thursday a pittance was distributed among the old people of the hamlet, and since John Ragge could not be kept out and might make trouble Dame Matilda had asked Sir Ralph to be present. Afterward he and she stood for a while dawdling in the sun, before the gate-house. Spears of young grass were poking up through the winter mud-banks. The clump of wormwood that grew by the threshold had put out its sharp new green.

Feeling the sun warm on his back, Sir Ralph remarked that it had been a wonderfully peaceful Lent.

"Peaceful?" said she, stopping short and staring at him.

"The peacefullest Lent I have ever experienced. I have never confessed such a sequence of untroubled consciences, souls so free from wrath and worldly agitation."

"It is the peace before the storm then," she said, "for they are all set on a law-suit."

"Ah, that accounts for it. I thought there must be some reason. Lent is usually acrimonious. Ladies, I think, find it particularly trying. It really is extraordinary," he continued, "quite extraordinary, to reflect on the means employed by God's providence to . . ."

Tough and evasive as a snake, he was sliding away from any share in the convent's temporal concerns.

"I find man's improvidence quite as much as I can reflect on," she said. "What if we are all ruined by this law-suit?" Her voice, escaping from its usual control, was harsh and tremulous, like the chirp of a fledgeling bird.

He turned and looked at her. She was almost as tall as he, and she looked back at him steadily, though her cheeks were flushed with resentment and angry tears brightened her small eyes.

"It will not happen," he said. "I assure you, it will not happen. The things which one dreads never come to pass."

She had never heard him speak with such authority. It might have been a stranger who spoke. Abashed, and yet comforted, she hurried away, making off before this astonishing being should decompose into their familiar, shabby, bulky, running-to-seed Sir Ralph.

Left to himself, he continued to walk about in the sun, feeling the gay air, admiring the sharp tint of the wormwood, and reflecting on the means employed by God's providence. Here, for instance, was another springtime. At any moment now he might hear the cuckoo. At any moment, too, he might hear some little rattle inside him, or some twang in his brain, and know that death was after him. As you are when you hear the first cuckoo, whether busy or idle, merry or sorrowful, so you will be the year through; so Magdalen Figg had said, standing mud-coloured under the apple trees in bloom. He asked no better from the first cuckoo than to be found here, walking and thinking before the gate-house at Oby. For life on every springtime confirmation of it was sweet, and would be sweeter still with Dame Matilda as prioress. Life was durably sweet, it improved like a keeping-apple. If he could live to be old, live tranquilly and keep his health, he might yet get such enjoyment out of life as would astonish the devils when they came to unpick him. He gathered a spray of wormwood and rubbed it between finger and thumb. It was an old acquaintance. These sproutings were the tenth generation that he had seen put forth since that morning when he first stood here so lean and fretful. Not damned then, and yet so fretful. Damnation had taught him tranquillity and resignation to God's will. Not damned then; and yet, God being timeless, as much damned before God then as now, damned before his birth, damned before his begetting, native to hellfire as a salamander. What would Dame Matilda say, that sensible prudent woman, could she know that with the prioress-ship of

Oby she would inherit the services of a damned man? And yet he had been within an inch of telling her.

Dame Matilda was so powerfully impressed by Sir Ralph's assurance that the things which one dreads do not come to pass that she preserved her equanimity even when Dame Johanna, speaking in chapter, said she wished to say a few words about the proposed law-suit.

It was plain that Dame Johanna had learned her few words by heart, and her hearers resigned themselves to a sermon. Pitching her voice too high, she was checked by a coughing fit before she finished with her views on submission tempered with zeal; then she had to clear her throat; then she went on to her *Imprimis. Imprimis* was that nuns should not go to law, it being their part to live in the world as though the world were not. *Distinguo,* the world may so press upon nuns that law-suits must be undertaken; but if so undertaken, the nuns must go to law in a spirit of charity—which some present yet lacked. *Secundo,* it is forbidden to covet. She had nevertheless overheard the nuns of Oby talking about the damages they hoped to gain. Such hopes were both wrong and fallacious, for at Dilworth it had been shown—then followed several anecdotes from Dilworth. *Tertio.* . . .

The prioress had been sitting hunched up, listlessly turning her ring. Now she raised her hand as though to brush away a fly and said, speaking in a faint voice, brittle with exasperation, that she for one was already convinced by Dame Johanna's eloquence, and begged there might be no more talk of the law-suit. There was a murmur, if not of agreement, at any rate of sympathy and understanding. Was it possible? Dame Matilda asked herself; could Sir Ralph have been right? But at that same moment Dame Johanna began to talk again. Now she was congratulating the prioress on so wise a decision.

"For as I was about to say, dear Mother, *tertio* . . ."

The prioress sunk her head in her hands.

". . . *tertio,* it is forbidden to bear false witness. Yet with my own ears, dear sisters, I have heard you say that we are certain of our suit because the stones fell and killed Dame Susanna, and no court of law can remain unmoved by a dead nun. But this is not true. I saw, and so did you all, how Dame Susanna sought her own death. If she had stayed quietly with the rest of us she would be alive now, as we are. Furthermore . . ."

A clamour of disagreement arose, most of it quite sincere, for by now Dame Susanna's exemplary death was canonical.

"Furthermore . . ."

The prioress leaped to her feet and boxed Dame Johanna's ears. Her first blow loosened Dame Johanna's coif, the second dislodged it. Fastening one hand in the short grizzled locks, the prioress began to scratch Dame Johanna's face. Dame Johanna screamed, moaned, called on the saints, and choked. With no expression beyond a sort of sleep-walking attentiveness the prioress clawed on in silence. Her silence was more alarming than anything else; it was as though she had forgotten speech, or felt no need for it, and had become an animal, killing without malice and almost without thought. No one knew what to do. The hopeful confidence that Dame Matilda would deal with it died away. Dame Matilda sat biting her finger; her eyes were shut, her face was green. They remembered that Dame Matilda always felt sick at the sight of blood, and at the regular blood-lettings was as regularly sick. It was Dame Alice, the other nun from Dilworth, who, with an "Excuse me, dear Mother," seized the prioress in her sturdy arms and carried her back to her seat. Dame Beatrix and Dame Helen approached to mop and tidy the victim. The prioress looked on approvingly and advised them to carry her away, adding in a voice airily resigned, "We shall never have any peace while she is with us."

From that day onward the prioress, awakened from her trance, persecuted Dame Johanna with remorseless artistry, inventing one derision after another as gleefully as a stone-carver inventing a set of gargoyles. She decided to enforce the rule of a good book being read aloud during dinner, and appointed Dame Johanna to be reader because, she said, of her scholarship. Perched in the reading-desk, Dame Johanna coughed and stifled, while her appetite—she had a punctual appetite—proclaimed itself in unseemly rumbles. Dame Johanna, too, was peculiarly unhandy, one of those women doomed to drop, fumble, tear, dishevel, crumple, and soil. But because of her piety, her particular piety, Dame Johanna, said the prioress, must have the post of sacrist.

Candles fell from their sticks, vestments caught on nails, incense spluttered, stains spread on the altar linen. Worst of all, there were the altar breads to make. Sweating with anxiety and desperately praying, Dame Johanna thumped and rolled an intractable lump of greying dough, scattered flour everywhere, and burned herself on the oven-tray. Finally she was set to repair the Trinity Cope. The Trinity Cope was one of the few treasures of Oby, and the nuns plucked up courage to defend it from Dame Johanna's puckers and gobble-stitches.

"Look how she is ruining it! And it is so beautiful."

The prioress looked at it. Indeed, it was very beautiful. All her life she had loved beauty. Her spire was broken; since Dame Susanna's death the singing had become screeching; her nuns were ugly; Adela, the de Retteville novice, was a half-wit. In everything she attempted she was mocked and frustrated, and she could make nothing out of her despair but an exhibition of spite and vulgar malice.

Biting back her sobs, she said, "Very well. No one shall repair it. Since you wish, it can go to ruin, like everything else. I have been thinking about the law-suit, too, and I have come to the conclusion that it would be useless to go on with it. I cannot carry it through alone, I have neither the health nor the spirits for such an undertaking. And I know by experience that I cannot count on any of you to help me. We will get the spire botched up somehow—sufficiently to prevent the draughts blowing down on you, that is all that matters. And everything shall go on as usual."

V. THE LAY OF MAMILLION

(June 1360)

On Holy Thursday Sir Ralph had walked in the sun, thinking of the peacefulness of Oby. By midsummer he wondered if he would ever know peace and quiet again. Just as when two dogs fight to the death all the dogs within earshot fly at each other, the affair between the prioress and Dame Johanna set everyone by the ears. Through the bland spring weather the nuns bickered, the servants fought, and his new hawk was unmanageable. He could not even find repose in Jesse Figg's orchard. Jesse and William had fallen out too, about the repairs at Dudham. Though the quarrel had not parted them, for they were as inseparable as ever, they were now inseparably locked in reproaches and recriminations. Beyond bringing them out cider in a large jug—for quarrelling is thirsty work—Magdalen Figg took no part in their wrangles. She flowed on like the Waxle Stream, slow, calm, impenetrably muddy, foretelling the weather as indifferently as a river reflects the sky. Sometimes Sir Ralph found himself thinking that carnal pleasure with Magdalen might be very pleasurable, and that one would come away from it feeling refreshed and suppled like a washed shirt. But the fancy remained fancy; he knew that he would not be thinking of her at all if he had not failed to make William Holly more attentive to his troubles with the hawk.

He would have to find another hawk unaided. Unaided, too, he must somehow fit the convent with a new prioress. Things could not go on like this: sooner or later the prioress would kill Dame Johanna; and that would be a great pity, for the prioress was an exceptional woman and Dame Johanna invincibly a nonentity. So he must procure a hawk, a prioress, and the bishop; for the three novices were clamouring to make their final vows, and though a bishop was not really necessary for this, parents prefer a bishop.

It was Brother Baltazar, one of a pair of friars who lodged for a night at Oby, who told him of the hawks at Brocton.

Sir Ralph knew Brocton by hearsay. It was a small manor lying westward of Lintoft. The Lord of Brocton, though a young man, was blind. He had inadvertently ridden into a Corpus Christi procession, and his horse, alarmed by the singing and the banners, had taken fright and trampled down the priest carrying the pyx. Thus involved in sacrilege and already head over ears in debt, the Lord of Brocton had despaired and hanged himself—as if, said Brother Baltazar, that would make things any better. His goods, of course, had been seized; but friends can always find a way round the laws. Sir Ralph had only to ride to Brocton, offer his ghostly comfort to the widow, turn the conversation to falconry, and the hawk would be his. Brother Baltazar added that he should not delay. The widow, it seemed, was being difficult, and there was talk of an excommunication pending to bring her to reason.

A few days away from Oby was such a heavenly prospect that as Sir Ralph on the dun horse looked westward from Lintoft and saw before him the oak woods through which he would ride so pleasantly all day he almost forgot about the hawk. It was enough to be on a holiday. The smell of the fern, the squirrels, the hares leaping about the glades, the buzzing of flies, the screams of the woodpecker, everything delighted him. He seemed to himself to be a hundred miles away from Oby, and restored to the days of his youth. Nightfall found him still wandering in and out of woods. A woman in a forester's hut to whom he described his route assured him that he must twice have been within a stone's throw of Brocton. Now he was a good five miles away from it. But in the morning, she said, her little boy should sit on the saddle-bow and guide him.

The next day's sunrise waxed into a day of burning heat. The little boy was not so good a guide as he had been promised to be, and the sun was high before they came to the manor house. Seeing himself reflected in the moat, Sir Ralph realized how fat he had grown. He had often seen his image in the pools of the Waxle Stream, but the Brocton moat, reflecting him among sharp details of architecture, was more revealing of his shapelessness than the Cow Pool or Kitt's Bend. *Here comes such a nun!* Among all the unpleasantness of that night when the prioress returned to her broken spire he had not failed to notice this mortifying exclamation; and, watching the porter lead away the dun horse, he could imagine the comments that would be made on its rider. The Dame of Brocton, the porter told him, would see neither priest nor friar. He wondered if this was a pretext to conceal that a sentence of excommunication was already in force; but having got so far he asked if he could see the hawks.

"I will not go beyond a sparrow-hawk." He had been saying this to himself ever since the conversation with Brother Baltazar, but handling the birds, seeing the love-lorn way they tilted their heads and poked with their wings, he forgot all prudence. Come what might, cost what it might, he must have a tiercel. While he gazed at them he heard a quick step and a rustle of skirts behind him. The falconer bowed and fell silent. Sir Ralph had to hoist himself from his contemplations to salute the Dame of Brocton. Though he was dazzled by the beauty of the birds he saw that she was young, and very handsome, though her face was deformed by weeping and her lip swollen with the bites she had given it to stop her tears. She greeted him frankly and began to question him. Why she had changed her mind about seeing neither priest nor friar she did not explain, but it did not appear that she had sought him out for any religious reason. When she bade him come into the house and dine astonishment spread over the falconer's broad face. The house was furnished with great elegance, and so clean that he could not believe himself in England. It was no wonder these people were in debt. She led him into the solar where an elderly woman, some sort of aunt, made the third at table. A little while after they had begun to eat a fourth member of the party came in—a boy about thirteen, a brother to the Dame of Brocton. His countenance showed how beautiful hers would have been if grief had not marred it.

With the same arrogant directness as when she had questioned him about himself and his journey the Dame of Brocton now began to question him about poetry. Many of the poets she mentioned he had never heard of, and to defend himself, and also because it was truly his opinion, he replied that the poets of the present age were of little account in comparison with the great men of the past.

"That is because you do not know them," she replied.

"That may be true. It is many years since I have been amongst poets." The admission cost him something, but he hoped a hawk would come of it.

She continued, "And why do you mention only such old poets? All poetry is not in Latin."

"No. But it might be better if it were. Since God and man between them have given us the Latin tongue and the Latin mode of poetry, it is waste of time to turn aside and scribble in the vernacular. That sort of thing can be left to old nurses, and jugglers at wakes and fairs, and those who cannot think how to go on unless a rhyme prompts them to their next thought."

"Do you call the great Dante an old nurse? He wrote in the vernacular, and used rhymes."

There was a sauce flavoured with ginger that he would have liked to give his whole attention to; but he thought of the hawk. Italian, he said, French too, for that matter, being dialects of the Latin tongue, were more musical and better suited for poetry. The fallacy of the vernacular was exposed as soon as the tutelage of Latin was lost. In Norway he had heard a man declaiming parts of an epic in the dialect of that country, and it had sounded like the snuffling and growling of bears.

At this the boy looked up, and laughed.

"Yet some poet wrote it," she said. "And perhaps he was as great as Virgil."

"If he were—which I cannot believe, for language is a great part of poetry, where the language is imperfect the poem must be imperfect too—if he were, none but his own countrymen would know it."

The Dame of Brocton frowned and fell silent.

His mind was returning to the sauce when the elder lady asked him if he were skilled in music. She had been told that the ladies of Oby were renowned for their singing of the plain-chant.

"There again!" he exclaimed. "Another example of what I maintain. These vernacular tunes, sung and forgotten in the space of a lifetime, and these descanters with their flourishes—how trivial they are by comparison with the classical modes of the Church!"

The aunt now inquired about the nuns' needlework. It seemed that she was trying to divert the conversation from the question of poetry in the vernacular. He replied that the nuns embroidered very prettily, and that the convent had also possessed a fine illuminator. Unfortunately the house was damp and much of their work was already impaired by mildew. She asked if there was a moat. A moat was the only hope for a dry house.

He explained that Oby stood on a rise of ground where no moat was feasible.

Meanwhile the Dame of Brocton sat biting her lip. Presently she began again, constraining her voice into amiability.

"I cannot help thinking that you might change your mind about poetry in English if you heard more of it. My husband . . ."

The boy looked at the aunt and folded his hands as if to say, "The same old story!" Sir Ralph found that he was to spend the afternoon listening to a reading of the dead man's verses. There was a long poem, the widow explained, long, but unfinished, which her husband had considered to be his finest work. He had brooded over it for many years, sometimes coming home with a score of stanzas, sometimes with a line or two: for he found his invention worked most freely when he was on horseback, and he would ride hour-long over the waste, a groom going with him to pull the horse away from the thickets or out of the quagmires. On his return he would repeat his day's work and she would write it down. Before their marriage he had used a secretary; but the secretary had thought himself a poet also, his copies were not reliable, and at other times he was drunk when he wrote and his script could not be deciphered.

"And is it all in English?—and all in rhyme?"

"Of course. It is an English epic."

He resigned himself. A hawk might have been purchased elsewhere at a less exorbitant price. But he was at Brocton, his adventure had mastered him, and till it released him there was nothing for it but to submit.

Yet the afternoon was not entirely unpleasant, for his seat by the window was cushioned and he could look out and see the dragonflies darting over the moat, or the aspen quiver of the reflected sunlight on the mossed wall, or a water-rat swimming across and dragging its wheat-ear pattern of ripples after it. It sharpened his appreciation to remember that all this was in the hands of the law, and that at any moment the summoner might ride across the drawbridge. His adventure had brought him here just in time. A few weeks later and there might be no hawks, no cup of wine, nothing but sunlight and water-rats and dragonflies. As though no calamity had befallen or ever would befall, she sat reading aloud, her voice persisting through the flies buzzing and the haymakers calling for drinks. Though the poem was unfinished there was a great deal of it, he could tell that from the bulk of the manuscript. Its chief character was someone called Mamillion, a giant, it seemed, or perhaps an enchanter; but a gentle giant, for his power was of small use to him and he did little but ride from one place to another, often pausing to hold long conversations with birds, or to wash his hair and beard in enchanted fountains. The poem was full of bird-songs and voices of water. No doubt the author's blindness had sharpened his other senses, so that the tweedle of a wren or the taste of a bilberry meant more to him than to the sighted.

"I wonder that your lord did not write a poem about Samson," he remarked at the close of a section. She answered that Samson was a person with no attributes of chivalry and quite unsuited to be the subject of a poem. To the best of Sir Ralph's remembrance Samson was well-born, at any rate Samson's parents were people of substance, but not being sure of it he did not care to commit himself. He thought, too, that Samson, if not a good christian, was at any rate nearer to christianity and more deserving of an epic than Mamillion. Whoever Mamillion might be, he was certainly a heathen. Though the Lord of Brocton's verses referred from time to time to the Virgin or the saints, it was obvious that this was merely because the poet himself chose to do so. Even when Mamillion came on Christ in the depth of a yew forest, bewailing, and hiding his face in the bitter yew boughs, no conversion or judgment came of it; Mamillion only gazed, and pitied, and rode on.

The sunlight quitted the water, reflected light danced no longer on the wall of the moat. A swarm of midges rose and fell, a minute chaff fanned by some mysterious breath of living. Somewhere overhead a thin wailing arose. After a while he realized that it was a baby crying. So there was a child in the house. This was natural enough, yet for some reason it surprised him. When next Mamillion fell asleep under a thorn tree, or came to a castle, or found a boat of stretched skins and paddled off in it among the reeds, so putting a colon to his unadventurous adventures, he would speak to the Dame of Brocton about her child. Possibly she would then go off and see to it, leaving him free to look again at the hawks. He had lost hope of getting away before nightfall.

Yet in such a house there would be a good bed. Though he itched to be gone he was also pleased to be staying. All his life he had wondered how it would feel to live as the rich do. Now he was in a way to find out. God in heaven, what happiness to be rich!

Mamillion's wanderings halted where they would forever halt, on the brink of a blood-stained river and a blank page, but Sir Ralph remained at Brocton. By force of acquaintance he had come to like the poem and even to find pleasure in the sound of English rhymed verse. The sharp consonants, the rebellious false quantities, put him in mind of a wide mere bristling with reeds and flawed with a choppy wind. Taking the manuscript, he began to read aloud to himself, experimenting with the scansion, trying to find some reason in it. One might as well try to scan the paces of a hare. Sometimes it loped, sometimes it ran: all one could say of it was that it had its own ways of moving.

"And what became of Mamillion? Did he find a kingdom, did he marry, was he slain?"

"It was to end with a piece of mistletoe," she replied. "He was to find the mistletoe growing on an oak tree and lop it off with a golden sword."

"An imitation of the golden bough in Virgil, no doubt?"

"I do not know."

Though she had a child (true, it was only a girl-child), all her maternal feeling seemed to be fastened upon this unfinished poem. Having compelled him to listen to it, having persuaded him into liking it, she led him on to her main purpose, which was to make the poem known. Would the fact that it was unfinished make the world reject it? He answered soothingly that there was a great deal of it already: an unfinished epic would have a better chance than a few lyrics. If it had been in Latin, he muttered to himself; but there was no object in going through all that again. He pointed out that thanks to her scholarship and her wifely devotion the story of Mamillion was already in writing, the first step toward being known. She said that being written down was not the same thing as being read. A happy thought struck him. Very earnestly he advised her to make a second copy. The boy and the aunt also asked him what he thought of the poem. The boy mocked gracefully, the aunt seemed to be consulting him as though he were a physician and the poem something he might prescribe a cure for. She thanked him too effusively for his interest and was sure that the Virgin had sent him to Brocton. It was evident that unless he were careful he would find himself saddled with the obligation of introducing Mamillion to the world of letters. In their different ways, the boy with his derision, the aunt with her hypocrisy, the widow with her sincerity, they were easing the burden on to his shoulders. It was very silly of them, for of course he could do nothing about it. How was he to go among the writers and poets, saying, Here is an unfinished English epic which you must admire? Perhaps he had misled them, mentioning during that first meal the countries he had visited, the notabilities he had seen; yet even the nuns at Oby, those simple ladies, had known such talk to be the ordinary brag of the penniless travelling student, and took it for no more than it was worth. Brocton swallowed it whole. He marvelled at the unworldliness of these worldlings, till he remembered that far away in the past he had seen the same thing. Apparently if one were sufficiently rich and sufficiently well-born one need have no worldly cunning, it was enough to exist—in which case the lilies commended by Jesus were several degrees higher in the social scale than King Solomon. Even these Brocton people, and Brocton was not a great manor, were too sophisticated to distinguish between a poor priest on the lookout for a hawk and a fashionable scholar: all they knew of the world was that it could and would support them, as kings and dukes travel from one estate to another, eating up a year's food in a month and, when everything is eaten, travelling on. Yet the poem of Mamillion stayed in his mind, and he began to wonder about the character of the poet, that lord as attentive as any shepherd to wild berries and signs of rain, who had so haughtily and impractically hanged himself. There was a parish priest, a red-faced, sharp-eyed little Welshman to whom he had been introduced after mass on Sunday (the ban of the Church had not fallen on Brocton after all), and Sir Ralph began to question him. Indeed, yes, it was very sad, a great pity, said the little man, his black eyes dancing in his red face. He was very sorry for them, the poor women, the poor servants who would so soon be trotting. His lamenting sing-song was belied by an undertone that it was no great loss after all. Presently he said that the Lord of Brocton was a bad young man: proud, harsh, luxurious, an unkind lord to his people.

"Yet the serfs look thriving," said Sir Ralph, thinking of Oby.

"No wonder, indeed! He granted them whatever they asked. That is one reason why his debts were so many. He was a bad lord, and much hated. He had no consideration, and people like to be considered. It makes a serf feel silly to be given whatever he asks."

He marched Sir Ralph off to the parsonage and showed him his geese, his pigs, his bees, his little cow. Everything told of neatness and management—the beds heaped with goosefeather pillows, the flitches drying in the chimney, the bee-skeps smoking among the bean-rows, the loom, taking up half the room, where Sir Jankin sat weaving blankets on rainy days. Learning that Sir Ralph was only a nuns' priest, Sir Jankin condoled with him. No glebe, no goods of his own, no occupation: life on such terms must drag heavily.

Learning that Oby lay among reeds and osiers, he urged Sir Ralph to take up basket-making.

As busy as the Georgics, thought Sir Ralph, walking back through the silent Sunday landscape, hushed with Sunday and dinner-time. One might be very happy in such a life, jostled through the sameness of the days by a hundred small thrifts and contrivances. In spring one sows, in autumn one garners, there are nuts to pick and little pigs to geld, and morning and evening one milks the cow and looks about for eggs. There is no time of year when one cannot bring home something profitable, and that is how nature would have one live, as attentive as a lover.

Sir Jankin proposed basket-making. The Dame of Brocton proposed Mamillion. Everyone had a plan for him, he only had no plan. "What ails me?" he said, stopping under an oak tree as though the question must be answered there and then. "What ails me that I can never have a plan for myself?" Was it lack of ambition? Was it lack of desire? In his youth he had been ambitious. Desire had not failed him even now. Desire for a hawk had brought him to Brocton, and certainly his faculty of desire had not perished, for he was capable as ever of disgust, and disgust is the inversion of desire. He had as much ability as other men, as much endurance, more health and strength than many. If he could get rid of his fat he would be in excellent condition. But his life had been aimless as an idiot's, in his youth running from place to place with an idiot's delight in motion, and now, like an idiot, set down in the chimney-corner. He was a bastard and penniless? Other penniless bastards had done well enough for themselves, so why not he? But he was damned—and can a man who despairs of salvation in the next world frame desires in this? A bird hopped in the tree, and before it had settled, his mind had tossed away this answer as worthless. Long before he had come to Oby and damned himself he had lacked whatever it is that holds a man to his purpose.

What impulse, what little puff of wind, had sent him toward Oby? The thought of a breakfast. Clear as in a dream he saw the track rising to a knoll with trees on it and the colour of the moonlight as the dawn began to tarnish it, and felt once more the physical desolation which had preceded his vomiting. I am stricken, he had thought. I shall die here, alone and unfriended. And nobody will know or care.

Perhaps that was the answer: his stubborn lifelong loneliness, a celibacy costing no effort and earning no approbation, cold as the devil's loins when he genders with a witch. And suppose he were indeed begotten by Satanas, and came into the world inheriting damnation as all others inherit original sin? The devil might have come stamping into the brothel as the rest of them did, someone must have fathered him, so why not Satanas? Here was a thought to run mad with. He stood snorting under the tree, waiting to feel the blood climb into his neck and the hairs bristle on his scalp. A brilliant hope flashed before him. If he ran mad at Brocton as he had run mad at Oby he might wander away in his madness; and when his wits came back to him he would be far away with no one knowing who he was, far away and free to begin another life.

He wrung his hands in an agony of hope. But nothing happened. At last he began to walk on, for there was no sense in staying.

That same afternoon he saw that the days of his popularity at Brocton were over. Though his hostess continued to thank him for all he would do to make known the poem of Mamillion, she thanked him without conviction, and though the aunt continued to heap his platter and fill his cup he saw her exchanging glances with the boy and imagined her slow, furry voice saying, "One might as well fodder that great beast Leviathan." But melancholy now made him as stupid as a baby; it took the news that the summoner and his officers were within a day's journey of Brocton to dislodge him. Nothing like damnation to disgrace a man, he thought, hearing himself say that his absence would now be more comfortable to them than his presence.

"You must not go without your hawk," she answered. Stumbling over her long-tailed gown, he followed her to the falconry, and while he was biting his knuckles she chose out a couple of falcons.

"Can you carry them both, or shall I send a man along with you?" One such bird would cost a fortune, a pair of them was out of the question. He must avail himself of the excuse of priestly orders and get off with a sparrow-hawk. Then the thought of his inadequacy, his disgraceful departure, smote him, and he resolved not to flinch before any price she asked. The money must be raised somehow. He could sell his books. He could make baskets as the Welshman had advised.

Her voice cut through his expostulations. The falcons were a gift.

He rode away, a clumsy candelabra for the two birds. The dun horse neighed and looked back toward the manor of Brocton as though he were riding it out of Eden. The poor brute also had a taste for high living, for clean water and sweet hay. There was actually a gloss on its coat. I am riding like Mamillion, he thought, riding through woods and past little woodland meres.

But it was not possible to conceive Mamillion riding to Oby, to that epitome of humdrum, a provincial nunnery. Topping the rise of ground between Lintoft and Oby, he looked down on his bishopric. The corn was ten days yellower, the beans were ten days rustier. The Hollys' dwelling was being re-thatched, and bristled like a boy's head. There was the Waxle Stream, winding in its green sleeve. There was the convent, with the spire cased in scaffolding—so the masons must have come back. Within it were his ladies, all at sixes and sevens, no doubt, just as he had left them.

He spoke to his two falcons.

"Now you are going to live in a convent and become two holy nuns."

Their demeanour was so composed, they were so gentle and dignified, that he was constrained to add, "God forbid it!"

But something had resolved the sixes and sevens. Voices were low, brows were smooth, and the prioress had resigned. Seemingly this had been achieved without a struggle, for she told him the news with a satisfaction only triflingly enhanced by her natural art.

"You know how often I have said that my one wish was to be relieved of my office. Only the thought of the expense held me back. Now our good treasuress tells me we can perfectly well afford an election. You cannot imagine how thankful I feel! Saint Leonard has never freed a more delighted prisoner."

What was more, she meant it. Her eyes were clear, she had the washed, girlish look of a convalescent.

What had effected this miracle? There was a new cook, a good one. A good cook can do much, but surely this was beyond the mediation of cookery? Dame Salome had fallen and broken her leg, and at her age and with her bulk it was unlikely that she would survive it; but Dame Salome had never been a nun of any importance, the prospect of losing her could not have brought about this mysterious millennium. During his absence the convent had been served by the new priest at Lintoft, whose name was John Idburn. But there was nothing to suggest that John Idburn's ministrations had spoken peace to Oby. Questioned, the nuns reported that he was a very quiet young man, that he looked weakly, and stammered.

At Brocton Sir Ralph had congratulated himself on being out of earshot of his ghostly daughters. Now, racked with curiosity, he wooed them to converse with him, but wooed in vain. To Dame Matilda he remarked that it must be a relief to her to have the election fixed at last, and that there could be no doubt as to the succession. She answered that whoever was chosen could at best only hope to be a poor copy of such a distinguished prioress. When he grinned she gave him a look so austere that he began to revise his cheerful anticipations of her term of office. When he condoled with Dame Margaret on the headaches which the renewal of work on the spire must be causing her, she asked him if he had seen the revised design?—it had several notable improvements over the other. Nothing came of a visit to Dame Salome, who lay in the infirmary, mildly delirious and mistaking him for Prior Thomas. Even Dame Johanna, with whom he cautiously strolled in the cloister, said no more than how much she was looking forward to meeting the bishop. They had some secret; but as she-cattle put the calves in their midst and confront the wolf with a ring of lowered horns and trampling hoofs, his nuns kept him at bay with primmed-up lips and lowered eyelids. He would never know.

He had never learned, either, how a game of Flying Saint Katharine had ended so awkwardly. So how was he to guess that Dame Salome, increasingly put about by the quarrels of the convent, quarrels in which she was quite unfitted to play a distinguished part, had been re-creating that incident in a shape more favourable to her self-esteem? She might be a fat old woman, and of no account. Yet if the truth were known, the truth which envy tried to conceal. . . . The nuns were in chapter and only gave half an ear to Dame Salome's grumbles. They went on with their interchange of more topical accusations while Dame Salome worked herself up with complaints of how she had always been slighted, her opinions disregarded, her age unhonoured, her plate constantly heaped with bones when it was well known that she had not the teeth to deal with them. Then came some quotations from the Magnificat and an allusion to stones which the builders rejected, and developing from stones and builders a reminder that she had always said the spire was too tall to be safe. The prioress, who remained sensitive about the spire, bade her hold her tongue. Dame Salome then harked back to envy and conspiracy, saying that if a man should rise from the dead the nuns of Oby would not be convinced. No, they would declare that nothing had happened, that he had been mistaken and had better drink a little soup and forget about it. The nuns failed to see the import of this hypothetical man who rose from the dead and was given soup. It was not till Dame Salome cried out from the head of the steps that they should see for themselves whether or no there was a flying saint among them that they grasped her intention. By then it was too late. Flapping her arms and screaming, she launched herself off the topmost step, rolled to the bottom, and lay stunned, one leg projecting at an unnatural angle from her dusty petticoats.

This shocked them out of their quarrels. If they had been rooks they would have migrated. Being nuns, they revolted. After compline Dame Matilda, Dame Beatrix, Dame Helen, and Dame Margaret followed the prioress to her chamber and said, speaking one after another as if it were a liturgy, "Dear Mother, we ask you to resign." The prioress with a gasp of relief replied that that was exactly what she wished to do. Then and there the letters of resignation were written, one to the bishop, the other to Adam de Retteville, the secular patron of the house, and Sir John Idburn rode with them to Waxelby, whence they would be carried on by the friars.

VI. PRIORESS JOHANNA

(July 1360–January 1368)

To John Idburn, who, like everyone of his generation, had heard countless stories of the indecorum and flightiness of nunneries, Oby had seemed like something out of the age of faith. He was deeply touched. Being a young man and still inclined to literature, he wrote a long account of his visits there to an Oxford friend. "In such a house," the letter concluded, "so uncontaminated by strife and worldly cares, so peacefully set like Mary at the feet of Christ, one might even expect to see a miracle take place." He wished that he could have served Oby rather than his parish of Lintoft; though he had not been six months at Lintoft he was already disheartened, afraid of his parishioners, and very lonely. Soon after Sir Ralph's return he invited him to dinner. He had seen the nuns' priest once or twice and had not been prepossessed by the fat old man balanced like a bag of soot on the dun horse; but he might after all find him the friend that he craved for, and at any rate he came from Oby.

After the first interchange of professional conventionalities Sir John had the luck to ask the right question. His sexton had told him that the timbers in the Lintoft church roof had been taken from a Danish galley, and that the sea-salt could still be tasted on them. Could this be true? Sir Ralph discovered that all those boring disputes he had listened to in Figg's orchard were in truth the material for his own antiquarian researches. He was able to tell Sir John everything about the voyage up the Waxle Stream, where the galley grounded and why, how the old woman brought her poisoned cup, how most of the Danes succumbed, how the others, surviving but disheartened, remained to work for the inhabitants, ingratiated themselves by introducing a new kind of wolf-trap, intermarried with the natives, founded red-haired families and bequeathed a number of Danish words to the local speech. He had no hesitation in assuring Sir John that the timbers in his church roof had grown in some Scandinavian forest. On their second meeting Sir John began with another lucky opening. He spoke of hawking. But when that subject was exhausted his own plight came to his lips and he broke out into a complaint of his isolation at Lintoft.

"What else can you expect?" cried Sir Ralph briskly. "A strong young man like you must do more than preach and say masses if he is to earn the esteem of his parishioners. You should work, young man, you should work! If you want to be a good priest you must have the best sow, the best beans, the sweetest honey, the cock that crows loudest. You will do nothing with books and prayers. Turn your mind to pigs."

As though his words had summoned them a number of pigs

just then rushed screaming and grunting into the parsonage cabbage-yard. Screaming and grunting the priest's housekeeper rushed out and drove them away by jabbing at their noses with an iron-shod staff.

"I hate pigs!"

"Very well, then!" Sir Ralph's voice was injuriously tolerant. "Why not take up basket-making? But in God's name, do something! It is better to work than to whine and grow costive. Most of your troubles are the common lot of man, if you will allow an old man to say so."

They parted with civility, but each knew that civility would be the limit of their acquaintance. Riding home, Sir Ralph trounced himself for his aspirations. He had actually looked forward to telling John Idburn about his travels, had prepared phrases and rehearsed anecdotes. Bah! What would his old stories mean to a young milksop, absorbed in his own troubles and thinking that there was nothing notable in the world until he had opened his eyes on it?

Smoking his hands over a wet fire, Sir John exclaimed, "*Turn your mind to pigs!* You've done it to some purpose, haven't you, with your paunch and your greasy gown and the bristles starting from your skin. Turn your mind to pigs!" And when his housekeeper came in and idled into gossip about Oby he listened greedily, stuffing the wound in his heart by stories of how Sir Ralph was no priest at all but the paramour of an old nun called Dame Agnes who had smuggled him into the convent to stay her lechery, though she was thrice his age; and how another of the nuns, young, and very rich, was with child by him, but the old nun, frantic with jealousy, beat her so terribly that she died, spitting up blood by the pailful, and not even her own spells could save her, though she was a sorceress; and how a very honest woman, a widow, called Pernelle Bastable, had tried to lodge with the nuns but their gross behaviour had driven her away; and how the bishop had come and scourged all the nuns and ordered Sir Ralph to be gelded, which was why he was now so fat. Though he did not credit these stories he listened to them, drooping his head over the smoking brands and vaguely wondering when she would remember to clear the dinner-board.

Though Sir Ralph's main mind was given to his new falcons it tickled him to hear stories about the insufferable tediousness of the priest at Lintoft, who would follow his parishioners into the field to tell them of his poor health and his bad dreams. But after a little indulgence he would stop the stories, saying that whatever sort of fool the young man might be, he was a priest and should be respected as such: people who allowed themselves to mock at a priest were but a half a step from beastly Lollardry. This went down well. The hamlet was in a ferment of loyalty to the Church knowing that a bishop was imminent. Other bishops had come and gone and the hamlet of Oby had been none the better for it; nevertheless, the advent of a bishop aroused pleasurable expectations. If a bishop did nothing else he improved the quality of the broken meats served out at the wicket. Bishop William had been half a roast goose to old Granny Scole.

The permit to proceed to an election came in August 1360, and in the convent, as in Jesse Figg's orchard, there was a cheerful certainty that Dame Matilda would be elected. In Dame Matilda's heart, too, there was a cheerful certainty. She had served the convent well as treasuress, she looked forward to serving it better as prioress. Above all, it pleased her to see the novices looking forward to the day which would make her a prioress and them her nuns. Lapsing from her usual realism, she saw herself ruling an Oby from which all the elder nuns had conveniently disappeared, leaving her a household of the young, the open-countenanced, the practical.

Two nuns had been chosen as tellers: one was Dame Cecily and the other Dame Alice, the second of the Dilworth nuns. She it was who had intervened when the prioress was killing Dame Johanna, and from that hour Dame Matilda had conceived an esteem for her, and had tried to bring her forward as something more than a set of stout arms and sturdy legs coupled to a willing disposition. After prayers and a special mass for a good decision the tellers set out to collect the votes. Each nun spoke her choice in private. At the close of her round Dame Cecily looked flushed and uneasy. She scrutinized the countenance of the other teller but learned nothing from it. Together they went to the chapter-house where, having given their votes, the nuns had assembled to hear the result.

Dame Johanna was elected prioress with a majority of one vote.

Dame Cecily glanced from face to face, and her distress at the miscarriage was swallowed up in a more personal regret: that she could not at once use her sketch-book and her silver style. Such physiognomies would supply initials for the whole length of Jeremy's Lamentations. What had happened was one of those accidents that overtake the righteous in the midst of their prosperity. Feeling sure of Dame Matilda's election, grateful to be relieved of the old prioress whose temper had grown so disturbing, nun after nun had yielded to the thought: Why not vote for that poor Dame Johanna?—one vote can't upset the result, and it would please the poor wretch.

Speeches of congratulation and joy were made in the gloomiest tones, and the meeting broke up. In the general mortification no one appreciated how very suitably the prioress-elect was behaving, nor did anyone surmise that for many years Dame Johanna had contemplated exactly this happy event, and so walked into her new dignity with the calm and decorum that come from long practice in day-dreaming. Her humility, her courtesy, her affability—everything was irreproachable, and stale as a treatise.

Seeing her so bleak and so meek, every soul in and about the convent groaned at the thought of the future and of the revenges which Dame Johanna could be expected to take. Jesse Figg cursed and swore, William Holly was silent but prepared to move himself with all that was his, and a little over, to Dudham, and Sir Ralph in his chamber over the gate lamented as feelingly as King Saul. The servants trembled. They foresaw that the new prioress would set Dame Alice over them, Dame Alice who would expect everyone to be as active as herself. "That skinny one?" said the masons. Edmund Gurney said nothing but looked at the spire. It was again almost finished and now more beautiful than ever, at any rate to his mind, since in the rebuilding he had been able to go ahead with it, unhampered by his employer's second thoughts. Though it was beautiful and almost finished he looked at it with pursed lips. He knew the goings-on inside the convent as well as though he were (Heaven preserve him from it!) a nun of Oby himself. What more likely than that Dame Johanna would have it pulled down in revenge for the beatings and floutings she had endured? Even in the bishop's palace the news of the Oby election was heard with paternal grief. "They have elected a Dilworth nun!" exclaimed the bishop. "Am I never to be rid of those Dilworth nuns?"

Only the old prioress was serene, absorbed in designing a new cope. This had begun as a work of reparation, a copy of the Trinity Cope which her malice had handed over to Dame Johanna, so much to its detriment. But in the course of copying the original so many new interpretations of the design, and then so many variants and improvements, crowded into her mind that it became clear to her that no mere copy would do, and that what God willed of her was an original penitential tribute to His glory.

The Trinity is a boon to the designer. It gets over all those difficulties of antithesis—light and shade, man and woman, good and evil—which, however proper they may be in nature and philosophy, are monotonous in art. Dame Alicia, as she again heard herself called, often paused to give thanks to the Godhead for having, somehow or other, outwitted the dualism of the moralists and insinuated the idea of a threefold unity. Perhaps her thanks were not quite so explicitly theological as that. The best minds of christendom had travailed, fathers of the Church had fought, bishops had fallen into heresy, deacons had been martyred, saints had imperilled their sainthood, councils had taken to fisticuffs, all in order to arrive at this doctrine which she was now sketching in charcoal on six ells of the best linen; and whole sections of that seamless garment, the Church of Christ, had been rent away by misunderstandings of what was now a commonplace to every novice at Oby. Dame Alicia by luck of time and place was nearer to the novice than to the fathers of the Church. She accepted the doctrine of the Trinity and found it just what she needed.

"I hope you will work in some Herb Trinity," said Dame Beatrix. "I have been using it on our poor prioress, and really I believe her breathing is easier. At any rate she doesn't seem to me to snort quite as loudly as she did."

Like many other artistic people, Dame Alicia did not know one flower from another. She asked what colour Herb Trinity was.

"Three colours, yellow, purple, and white . . . a little flower that grows in stony pastures. Some people call it Three Faces under One Hood."

Of course, of course! Three faces under one hood, three faces in one glory, a right and a left profile developing from the full face instead of ears, four grey eyes, one crown, three beards. Purple, yellow, and white: the robe purple, the crown golden, the white beard of the First Person flanked by golden beards in profile; and the purple, yellow, and white of the little flower acknowledged in a surrounding garland. Whistling under her breath like a schoolboy, she began to erase the centre of her design, which had followed the more ordinary Crucifixion Trinity of the old cope, and to sketch in the three-fold countenance.

She had never been so happy in her life as now. Officially a retiring prioress returns to the standing of a simple nun, but civility softens this regulation, and Dame Johanna wished particularly to be magnanimous. Blithely accepting magnanimity, Dame Alicia had a room of her own, meals on trays whenever she wanted them, her bullfinch and her posset-cup, a stuffed mattress and a recorder; for when she tired of stitching, or waited for a problem of design to thaw out, a little music refreshed her. In summer the open window gave her a view of her spire. In winter she had the best brazier. Her ageing lap-dog snored at her feet, and Adela stroked the lap-dog.

Adela, poor child, was a disappointment. Released from her mother's biddings and beatings she proved to be noisy, arrogant, and unbiddable; even her sweet temper was like a kind of obstinacy. She was, however, very pretty; and when she was newly arrived and still regarded as an acquisition it had delighted the nuns to compare her little hooked nose with the profile of her ancestress Alianor, whose effigy had gazed toward the altar of Saint Leonard since the convent's foundation. Alianor was ugly and had no waist, the child complained. Her feet were big and rested on a cushion instead of on a dog. When she, Adela, was a nun she would have fifty dogs. Why could she not have a dog now? Please could she have a dog? Please would

Dame Cecily draw her some dogs? There was one little dog too many in the convent already, said Dame Cecily snappishly, a little she-dog called Adela. They wanted no more. A noisy little dog with no tail, Dame Philippa added. If Oby was disappointed in Adela, Adela was no less disappointed in Oby. A house of nuns was a place where everyone was cross, where doors were closed against one, where skirts were twitched out of one's hands, where Our Lady was displeased. "Look, Adela! She is frowning at you!" The child would whisk round and study the wooden countenance; but it had always resumed its cold and rather threatening smile, and she grew to feel that a frown would be better. The only escape she could find was to creep off to the old prioress, where she could warm her chilblained hands, stroke Mouton, and pair the strands of bright embroidery silk. Even this was not reliably secure. Sometimes the sight of the de Retteville novice would recall to Dame Alicia the occasion of their first meeting: the sounds and the smells of the christening feast would recur, and all her suffering and melancholy amid the clashing of dishes, the laughter and belching, and elderly boasting. She would turn savagely on the child and drive her away. But as the new cope came to life and was her only responsibility, Dame Alicia accepted the position of being fond of Adela: one of her failures, admittedly, but not a very painful one.

Adela's dowry, too, seemed to be a failure: the rents which had looked so well on paper were badly paid, and the promise of victual had resolved into a cartload of stinking venison. But these things which formerly would have roused her to an intensity of vexation passed over her like thistledown.

They did not much trouble the new prioress either. She was accustomed to insolvency: Dilworth had taught her that. Had Dame Matilda remained treasuress many items in Edmund Gurney's final bill would have been challenged. But in her pursuit of magnanimity the new prioress decided that it would be painful for Dame Matilda to retain a post which brought her so continually in contact with the person who had supplanted her: Dame Dorothy, a dull nun, was hoisted up into being treasuress, and Dame Matilda, complying with a delicacy of feeling which she did not herself feel, became sacrist. If she had had a shred of saintliness in her character the mortification of this change of occupation might have burnished her into something quite remarkable. But no such outlet was possible, for she was incapable of religious feeling. She burnished the altar plate with energy and spent her spare time unwieldily larking with the young nuns. Prioress Johanna frowned and sighed to see her sacrist rolling along the cloisters arm-in-arm with Lilias and Eleanor le Bailey like a Silenus among the nymphs. She could not forget that Dame Matilda had been married. The marriage had not been consummated, Dame Matilda was a virgin; but through no fault of her own, the prioress opined.

Perhaps the spectacle of Dame Matilda, so red in the face and so rowdy, encouraged the prioress to develop her scruples about four-footed beasts. Saint Benedict had forbidden his monastics to eat the flesh of four-footed beasts; yet beef, pork, and mutton were served as a matter of course in the refectory of Oby, just as they had been at Dilworth, and just as they were in any Benedictine house. At Dilworth there had been frequent outbursts of carnality. No doubt such outbursts would happen at Oby too. Dame Alice, the cellaress, was commanded to reform the dietary, at least to modify it by making more use of eels and dumplings. Dame Alice said that a dumpling is nothing without gravy, and that for a good gravy there must be meat. She appealed to Sir Ralph as an authority on gravy. The prioress appealed to him as an authority on discipline. To the cellaress he recommended a freer use of mushrooms, and confused the prioress by citing other prohibitions in the Rule. She was not entitled to pick and choose. Further, if Holy Church had learned from heaven that a reversal to the original rule was desired, Holy Church would have informed its children *ex cathedra.* Having wound her up in heresy, he judged that he had done all that was needed, and went out with his falcons after some partridges; for he disliked mutton.

Presently the nuns were tapping on Dame Alicia's door with a new story. The prioress had turned her mind to another aspect of the Rule. Surely her nuns were very idle? Oby was commanded to delight in labour, and everyone was set to spin. Dame Cecily was taken from her illuminating, Dame Alice from her marzipan: only Dame Alicia was left in peace with the Trinity, for the prioress would do nothing that might seem vindictive. Though no one span very industriously, a certain amount of yarn accumulated and was sent to the Dudham weavers. Back came a scanty quantity of bad cloth. But it was not too scanty for the prioress's ideas; for now her scruples had fastened on apparel. Gowns, she saw, were too wide, and far too long. Sleeves were too ample and frontlets not ample enough. A nun should be covered, but no more. As for Dame Lilias, who laced her kirtle on both sides in order to show off her long weasel waist, she must have a new and conforming gown made from the convent's homespun immediately.

Yet none of these vagaries provoked rebellion. It takes a strong character to create an opposition; and there was an inherent mediocrity in all the prioress's ordinances which made them tolerable, and almost welcome. She supplied her community with something to talk about, and beguiled the tedium of convent life as a jester beguiles the tedium of life at court. Besides, all this was an interlude. She could not possibly live beyond another six months. When she was dead it would be time to take life seriously.

She lived on for seven years, coughing and creaking: an extraordinary figure whose skeleton head and hands emerged from an apparent corpulence; for she was so thin that Dame Beatrix kept her wrapped in layers of raw wool, like a seven-month child. Dame Beatrix, who could love anything provided it was sickly and needed her help, used to come away from wadding the prioress weeping real tears and crossing herself as though she were returning from a visit to the sacrament. Then she would take Dame Lilias on one side and describe to her the staring bones, the sores, the veins that showed through the yellow skin like illuminations faintly remaining on an old parchment. For the infirmaress had diagnosed her successor in Dame Lilias, and was now acclimatizing her.

Even after the prioress's death they still heard her cough, or thought they did so. Dame Alicia remarked, "What a noisy house this will be when I have died too. What with Dame Johanna's cough and my recorder you will not be able to hear yourselves think."

"No matter. We are nuns, we don't think," Dame Cecily answered.

Dame Cecily was nearing thirty now, and had grown ugly and shrewish. Her eyes troubled her. A discharge came from them, and none of Dame Beatrix's remedies helped her. To be properly cured, said the infirmaress, Dame Cecily should bathe her eyes at Saint Winifred's shrine. But that was a long way off, at Holywell in the marches of Wales; and however cheaply the journey was made, even if Dame Cecily and her companion were to go on foot across England, such a journey, and the thank-offering that must accompany the cure, would entail a considerable outlay. Besides, added the infirmaress, how could she have left the prioress, who needed her so badly?—for Dame Beatrix was determined that Dame Cecily's fellow-traveller should be herself. But when the prioress was dead Dame Matilda would soon get her hands on Isabel de Scottow's legacy: then there would be money enough for journeying to any shrine.

Dame Isabel de Scottow's bequest of the ten years' profit on her vineyard and the interest at ten per cent on that profit had fallen due in 1364, three summers before the death of Prioress Johanna. After a year's expectation the nuns began to urge their prioress to look into the matter. But nothing was done. A few months later Etchingdon sent in a claim for half the cost of repairing the church at Methley, which had been struck by lightning. Since Oby still received the Methley tithes this liability could not be shirked; and a letter was sent to John de Scottow, nephew to Dame Isabel and now the head of the family. After some time he replied to it, saying that the funeral expenses of his parents had cost a great deal, and that at present he could not part with the large sum of money involved in his aunt's legacy (how much that sum amounted to he was too wary to say). He begged the honoured house of Oby to be patient for a month or two longer. Six months later Oby sent a second application, and again John de Scottow wrote, temporizing. In due course Oby wrote once more. It seemed as though these letters would become part of the yearly routine, like the feasts of the Church and the quarterly blood-lettings. Then Fulk de Scottow, Dame Isabel's brother, poked his head out from under a Cistercian hood and wrote to the prioress austerely inquiring how she could make such a claim. Did she not understand that in becoming a nun his sister had renounced the goods of this world and was therefore incapable of bequeathing anything except her immortal soul? If, indeed, Dame Isabel had, in her infirmity, so far forgotten her vows as to sully her death-bed with thoughts of money, or if she had been regrettably influenced to do so, then at least christian charity demanded that the living should speak no more of it.

This was a difficult letter to answer. Custom winked at legacies by people in the religious life provided that the money was not alienated from the Church; but custom was not canonical. Just what one would expect of a Cistercian, said the ladies of Oby. For what made Fulk de Scottow's interposition so particularly ill-natured was that he himself stood to make nothing by the diversion of the legacy. Malice, flat black Cistercian malice against a Benedictine foundation, must lie at the bottom of it! (Here, in fact, they were wrong: Fulk had compounded with his nephew for half of the disputed sum, as a price for getting him out of parting with the whole of it.) Things were at this pass when the prioress died.

This time at least there should be no mistake in the election. The votes were unanimous, except for the favourite's own vote, politely given to Dame Alicia, and Dame Matilda was prioress.

VII. PRIORESS MATILDA

(February 1368–December 1373)

The installation took place in February 1368, during a spell of bitterly cold weather. Treasuress Matilda's thrift had been proverbial. Prioress Matilda's installation was unprecedentedly magnificent. There were new clothes, new hangings, an abundance of candles, sweet rushes strewn on the floors so thickly that it was like walking through a meadow; and as she had had the prudence to work up to these splendours gradually the nuns had become accustomed to them before the guests arrived, and did not discredit the fine feathering by staring at it as though they had never seen its like before. For once the house was tolerably warm, good fires having been kept up throughout the previous week, and on the day of the installation the prioress ordered a great bonfire to be lit at the convent gate so that all those who came to watch the show and wait for pickings should do so in comfort. At intervals servants came out with trays of hot mutton pies and roasted apples whose blackened hides were daubed with honey and poppy-seeds: there was not a child in Oby who had not got a scorched mouth by midday. The old and the infirm were given clothing, and two girls belonging to the manor received marriage portions of bed-furniture to celebrate the spiritual espousals of the newly made Dames Adela and Lovisa. There was a procession; and just after the bishop had given a general blessing a great thumping of drums introduced a party of professional entertainers from Waxelby with a performing bear. For one day at least the manor of Oby was devoted to its convent. The bishop remarked on it, and Sir John Idburn, thinking of his own surly parishioners, wished to God there were nuns in Lintoft rather than pigs. His horse had a sprain, he had walked the freezing miles from Lintoft to be present at the installation; but his cares were exorcised by the puffing incense and the smell of warm wax. On this festal day even Sir Ralph seemed to look at him with good-nature.

Sir Ralph was in a state to be good-natured. He was counting de Stapledons. During three days they had been arriving to witness the glorification of their kinswoman, and more had arrived this morning. The air rang with greetings and family jokes, and Dame Matilda's short barking laugh seemed to echo from every corner of the building. Wherever one looked one's eye fell on the red faces, the large noses, the three badgers couped proper of the de Stapledon coat. The family was one of those everlasting families out of the North: litigious, tenacious, unprincipled with prudence, living in small houses on large manors. If they had lived rather farther north they would have made a loyal livelihood by forays across the border; as it was, their position was very convenient for disposing of Scots' cattle, for some they passed onward and some they kept and fattened, and all they handled at a profit. Even with one's eyes shut one could tell what manner of folk they were by the smells that came from their garments: an uncle's lined boots, a grandfather's hat, the velvet gown a great-great-grandmother had bequeathed. Looking round on the antique finery whose trusty material preserved the bulges of dead and gone wearers, Sir Ralph thought that it was just as though the de Stapledon effigies had come south from their freezing chapels; and at the end of the holiday my uncle's boots, my grandfather's hat, Lady Edith's gown faced with wild-cat, would have the dust of travel switched out of them and be put back in chests and presses, or hung in the wardrobes where the stink of healthy de Stapledon piss would keep the moths away.

Nowadays such families had grown rare. Nowadays one went to court and made one's way by a pleasing son or a handsome daughter, or turned, as the de Rettevilles were turning, to this new sort of parasitic trading, buying and selling of tolls, rights, and monopolies. He thought the prioress's resort to the de Stapledons was a gamble: even if they continued to prosper it would be touch and go between family loyalty and family close-fistedness. But gamble or no, it was a policy; and after seven years of Prioress Johanna and eleven years of the old prioress, any policy was a refreshing change. His interest in how Prioress Matilda would tackle the legacy affair (it was certain to come up when the formalities were over) overcame the modesty he was wont to feel in the presence of bishops. Quite patently he hung about, inviting the invitation to our good priest to join the party in the prioress's chamber.

She must have primed Hugh de Stapledon, for it was he who opened the matter.

". . . and a sorry botch you seem to have made of it, knowing that you had the Scottows to deal with. Though I daresay you were not able to do much to guide it at the time, she was dying, I understand, and no doubt everybody was praying and screeching, death-beds are always the devil."

The bishop sighed.

"Women should never be allowed to do business," Hugh concluded. Hugh's wife, Arbella, a hard-featured dame, settled her gold buckle and smiled.

"But something written is something written. I'd like to look at it, if you have it at hand."

The prioress handed him the little scroll with a bloodstained corner.

"I can't make it out. Here, wife, this is more in your line."

Arbella's beady eyes whisked to and fro. She began to read aloud. " 'The vineyard which by love of my good father has always been accounted mine; its revenues for the space of ten years and the usury at ten in the hundred thereon accumulating. And I beg my good father, or his true heir should he be no more living, to give freely to the house of Oby,' "

"For chantries, no doubt," interposed Bishop Giles.

" 'for love of Our Lady and of Saint Leonard, and of kindness to me, Isabel, now in my last agony and awaiting the deliverance of God . . .' No. Nothing about chantries."

"Well, have they accepted it? It will hang on that," said her spouse.

Now the bishop was reading Dame Isabel's document for himself. He was a handsome man in a sheeplike, saintlike way, and the attitude of study became him because it concealed the fact that he squinted. He read carefully and attentively, without a vestige of expression.

Arbella de Stapledon now spoke.

"I do not pretend to know anything about business, I know nothing of the law. But speaking as a simple christian it seems to me that Fulk de Scottow might be unwilling to enter on a law-suit. He is a monk, he has abjured the world's wealth. Would there not be something of a scandal if it were made known that he is contesting a legacy?"

The bishop raised his head and gave Arbella a thoughtful squint.

"But even if he withdrew his objection," said the prioress, "we should still have John de Scottow to deal with."

"Make no account of him!" said her brother. "I know him, he hasn't the stomach for law-suits."

"No, no, no!" cried the bishop. "It must not come to that. No law-suit!"

"Why not? She would win it. You Church folk always win your law-suits against us wretched laity."

"Oh, no, indeed!"

Whether the bishop was repudiating the law-suit or denying that the Church always won hers it was difficult to say.

"The house, I suppose, is in debt?"

Andrew de Stapledon asked this. The prioress nodded. Simultaneously Hugh said of course it was, all nunneries were in debt, though heaven knew why, for they were rich enough. The bishop looked pained.

"Dear son, do not say such things. They are not true, and they are exceedingly harmful. In the past, I do not deny it, the piety of our ancestors enriched many of these establishments. But then think of the commitments, the many outgoings, the alms, the decorations of the altar—"

He paused. Dame Alicia had moved out that he might have her chamber, but she had left the new Trinity Cope behind. Should he speak of it? If so, what should he say?

"—many of which are wrought by the nuns themselves with exemplary devotion. In this very house I have seen a cope which, considering the advanced age of the lady who made it, is most creditable. No one can say that our nunneries are places of idleness. But unfortunately there are some so envious, so impious, that they do say so."

He looked around with the triumph of a rhetorian. "And that, my dear prioress, is why I must beg you to proceed in this matter with circumspection. The world is full of wolves, all ready to rend the garment of Holy Church. Lollards, Poor Men, and worse. Let us do nothing to provoke them."

"Any Lollard," said Hugh, "who comes on my manor goes off it again with my dogs after him. For all that, there is something in what they say. No christian who leaves property to a religious house likes to think of it running to waste, and squandered by thriftless ladies or monks who sing all night and sleep all day and leave everything to bailiffs."

"None of us is faultless," said the bishop firmly. "Meanwhile, my daughter, do not think that I will forget you. I will do what I can. I will consider. I should like to examine these letters, all the letters, if I may."

She gave them over and he rolled them up with an air of relief and remarked that the wind seemed to be rising.

Breasting the ridge half-way to Lintoft, John Idburn felt the tears freeze on his cheeks. He sat down in the lee of a furze-brake and stared through the whirling darkness toward Oby, seeing the embers of the bonfire flap into a blaze and sink again.

Jesse Figg had put two men of the manor to sit up with the fire till daybreak in case it should rear up out of its ashes. Fire, he remarked, is a good serf but a bad lord. At other times he would say the same thing about water and about wind. In his old age he repeated himself most tediously: everyone was weary of his proverbs, his anecdotes, his wife's gift of foretelling the weather. But though he was old and his wits sprawled, he was still a sharp bailiff, shrewd as ever about earth and beasts and men. For instance, for this night's watch he had picked the two men of the manor who most hated each other, knowing that neither cold nor liquor would send them to sleep while they had each other to glare at. In the slaty dawn they were still wakeful, sitting on either side of the ashes like two beasts disputing a carcass. At the inquest each could testify that the other had borne him company all night and so could have had no hand in Figg's death. Sometime between the first and second cockcrow, the widow said, Jesse had gone out to ease himself. She had heard him groan and cry out, but she had not thought anything of it as he was pained with a strangury. Then she had heard the thud of feet running hard over frozen ground. No one else had heard footsteps. Oby lay in a blissful drunken slumber, dreaming of bishops and sweet singing. Even Magdalen Figg's outcries (she had gone out with a lantern and found the old man lying wounded and past speech) had been heard as psalmody. So it was never established who had murdered the bailiff, only that the deed must have been the work of several men, for no one man could have stabbed him in so many places. It was a hard winter, such a season as brings wolves and outlaws from the forest. Probably the installation, with its press of visitors and abundance of pickings, had fetched some outlaws to Oby; and while they were dividing their spoil the old man had tumbled into their midst.

Now there was a new bailiff, William Holly, to match the new prioress. She was sorry to lose old Jesse's counsel, but he could not have lasted much longer, and if the murder had to take place (and all things are in God's hand) at least it befell at the least inconvenient time of year, when there was nothing much to be done but threshing and mending up harness. William Holly's first concern was where to bestow the bailiff's widow. A woman with her gift for smelling rain must not be lost to the manor. "Someone will carry her off within a month, do you don't seize hold on her!" he exclaimed. It was clear that he felt she should be taken as a heriot. Magdalen said she would marry no one on the manor. She wanted to be a nun. That was out of the question, but finally it was agreed that she should come as a corrodian. The prioress was in two minds about it, for though Magdalen brought a good portion she was under forty and might well outlive it. Besides, corrodians are always a dubious speculation; they live in the convent, yet outside its discipline, and can't be got rid of. In the past there had been a terrible corrodian at Oby. She filled the house with gossips and nephews, she got drunk and played on a trumpet, and at the most unsuitable moments she would appear with no clothes on, declaring that she was the Patriarch Job.

Yet to refuse Magdalen Figg would be to alienate William Holly, which she could not afford to do. For similar reasons of policy she must relinquish all hopes of Dame Isabel's legacy. Bishop Giles had carried off the papers, saying he would consider them. She knew that his considerations would begin and end with the expediency of doing nothing, for to a scandal-fearing bishop a convent in debt, however irksome to itself, is less irksome than a convent claiming a nun's legacy.

Matilda de Stapledon soon discovered that a prioress of fifty feels very differently about economy from a treasuress of forty. It is the business of a treasuress to attend to the time being: a prioress must attend to the future. For herself, she thought she could carry both parts, and so, appointing Dame Dorothy to be sacrist, she chose for her treasuress the agreeable Dame Helen, who had a neat handwriting and no views of her own. Oby, she thought, would never become prosperous by mere saving; something bolder was needed; and as one must throw a sizable sprat to catch a whale she had spent lavishly on her installation. For the rest, she largely relied on family loyalty.

The first reaction came from one who was only by marriage a de Stapledon. Arbella was a hard woman of business, long-clawed and tight-fisted—even the de Stapledons said she was niggardly. She was half-way a Lollard, and in addition she had taken a vehement dislike to the bishop. Being more passionate than logical, she expressed this by an Easter gift of three coverlets of fox-fur, a bale of the best wool, a parcel of spices, a dozen horn spoons, and six pieces of gold money. The two hard-featured serving-men who brought these gifts also brought a letter in which Arbella urged her sister-in-law to be firm with the de Scottows, and promised her a pair of novices. *Both girls are straight and sound and will do you more credit than that young rat with leprosy whom you were forced to put before the bishop.* The young rat with leprosy was the newly made Dame Lovisa, a de Stapledon bastard; and it had to be admitted that she was a blot on the ceremonies at the installation, for she was undersized and crooked, and her face was scarred with scrofula. She looked the worse being paired with the newly made Dame Adela—grown so beautiful a girl that her parents had tried to snatch her back into the world. She had been willing enough to go with them, chattering about how she would wear a dress of white satin and ride a horse with blue harness, and hunt with a pack of white hounds, each hound to be trimmed with bells and blue ribbons. Perhaps it was her chatter which in the end made her parents decide that God should keep her: too beautiful for the cloister, she was too silly to be safely invested in the world. She was, indeed, almost an idiot; but in the convent no one quite said so. At the most, it was said that Lovisa, poor little crooked thing, had wits enough for two. Only Lovisa loved Adela, loved her seriously and without delight. Only Lovisa was indignant when Dame Alicia suddenly turned against her pet and boxed Adela's small ears, crying out furiously, "Zany, zany, zany! Would to God I had never set eyes on you!" This flash of former days ensued on a letter which brought the news that Marie de Blakeborn was dead, dying of dropsy. The old prioress stared at the letter, mouthing and twisting her face. Then she burst into violent weeping. All her placid light-hearted senility was scattered like the leaves of a Saint Luke's summer. She wept as a young woman weeps, stamping and clawing her bosom; and from that hour she either grieved or raged till a flux ended her. It seemed an unaccountable degree of mourning for Marie de Blakeborn.

This was in 1370. Dame Beatrix, who was dying of cancer, staggered from her own sick-bed to nurse the old prioress and lay her out. "You force me to do it," she told the prioress. "I can't lie still and think of anyone I loved being bungled by Dame Alice. If you had made my Dame Lilias infirmaress it would have been a different matter."

In every community there must be someone who is odd man out. Now this position was shared by Dame Lilias and Dame Cecily. Both in their beginnings had been brilliant young nuns. Both had brought very good dowries and had advantageous relations in the world, both were virtuous and well behaved. Blindness had snuffed out Dame Cecily. Quite naturally she had declined from being the most profitable member of the house to being a sad cipher: a mouth to be fed, a voice in quire, a patient countenance to be turned to the light and poulticed. The decline of Dame Lilias was harder to account for, and it was tenable to argue that she had not declined at all, that she had merely grown sulky and unsociable.

That was how the prioress argued when Dame Beatrix—who had suddenly become cantankerous, as though the arrogance of her cancer had infected her character—reiterated her complaint that Dame Lilias had been slighted in not being chosen to succeed her as infirmaress.

"But it is no slight to be made cellaress. Cellaress is a very responsible position."

"I tell you this, she is breaking her heart."

"Most nuns break their hearts between twenty-five and thirty. They lose their complexions, and a tooth or two, and break their hearts. Then they settle down and are no more trouble to themselves. Besides, Dame Lilias is not the only nun to be considered. Dame Alice had been cellaress for ten years, it was time we hauled her away from the kitchen. And she is doing very well."

"She can pat pillows and season purges just as she could pat pastries and season broths. Wait till there is another pestilence! Then you will see what Dame Alice is worth. I hate the sight of that Dilworth dumpling. How can I have any piety in my death while she is simpering at me as though I were a skinned eel?"

At this juncture the Dilworth dumpling came in, together with a strong odour of boiled fennel. In a manner modelled on Dame Beatrix's own she whisked off the lid of the bowl, saying, "Now drink this while it is hot, and the virtue is still in it. It will ease you wonderfully."

"I am a dying woman, not a baby with wind," said Dame Beatrix.

The prioress broke into laughter. "You are growing as cross as old Agnes! Do you remember . . ."

Waving away Dame Alice and the fennel, she sat down by Dame Beatrix and took her hand.

"How far away it seems! How badly we used to behave, and how light-hearted we were! The young are different nowadays, they are as melancholy as though they were living in the world. And do you know why? It is because we ourselves are not so strict with them as the old nuns were in our day. When I think how Roesia used to thump us, and how Dame Blanch starved us for the least little fault . . ."

She exerted herself to put out all her charm: to be quarrelled with by a dying woman afflicted her sense of propriety. Her charm, when she took pains over it, was considerable, and Dame Beatrix laughed and forgot Dame Lilias. Feeling more at ease, the prioress became more natural, and began to talk of their indebtedness.

"But the spire has been paid off?"

"Yes, by raising the loan on our land at Tunwold. But there is still this wretched church at Methley. Now they have sent us a bill for glazing its windows. That is the worst of being tied to Etchingdon, they do everything as royally as though they were doing it for themselves. Glass windows for a parish church, whoever heard of such nonsense? And now there is this new levy. If only . . ."

She hesitated. An angry colour rose into her cheeks.

"All these years Sir Ralph has been with us, living at rack and manger. He has his horse and his falcons, two years ago we had to strengthen the stairway to his chamber with new wood, now he wants a hat. He might do something for us in return."

"He has been very faithful to us."

"You defend your nursling. There is another thing he owes us. If it had not been for your skill in curing him he would have been turned out on the road as a madman twenty years ago. He might very well give us part of his savings as a thank-offering instead of buying books—and worse."

"Yes, I cured him with a black cock. The cock is the bird of the resurrection, you see, and a melancholy madness is like the grave. But it must be a black one. Black overcomes the moon, whereas the moon at her full has dominion over lunatics. How black his hair was then!—as black as the cock's feathers."

"There is no fool like an old fool. I wish we had never taken the Widow Figg. My corns can tell me when it is going to rain quite as well as she can. And Sir Ralph does not lust after my corns."

"I don't believe half of it," said Dame Beatrix.

"Nor do I. He is too fat to do more than fondle. But she will bleed him of his money, poor old man! Now if he would lend it to us . . ."

The bell began to ring for nones. Dame Beatrix crossed herself with a look of relief. How many uncomfortable conversations, boring confidences, protracted jokes, that blessed bell had cut short!

"And with thy spirit, dear Mother!"

Swish-swish, shuffle-shuffle, yap-yap-yap from Dame Adela's little dog. The bell ceased and the chanting began. It was loud and hearty, dominated by Dame Alice's oversweet soprano. Hearing it, Sir Ralph reflected that one could distinguish the changing moods of a convent by the way its nuns performed the unchanging chant of the office. In the days of the old prioress the singing had been elegant, reedy, almost insubstantial, like the notes of water-birds secluded in some distant mere. In the time of Prioress Johanna it had grown ragged and strident. Now the tone was full and saccharine, the cadences were reposed on as though they were cushions, and Dame Alice executed the ornaments exactly as she executed the marshmallow roses on her sweetmeats: a whisk, a twirl, a tapering, and there you were! He had looked forward to the reign of Dame Matilda. It had come, and he was satisfied, and yet he was not satisfied.

To his surprise, his pleasures with Magdalen Figg had awakened his spiritual man. From every possession of her he emerged with a rediscovered sensibility, a sensibility such as he had not known since he was a very young man. But now it was better. In his youth he had only a piecemeal enjoyment of his senses: ambition and necessity shouldered him on and away. Now he was old. His manner of life remitted him from hope and anxiety. He could live in the present, and be as poetical as he pleased. No one would suspect it, no one, not even himself, would mock him for being so; and there was no compulsion (ambition having released him) to turn away from the delight of feeling poetical to the distracting labour of constructing poetry. "As free as a fish," he repeated to himself, watching the willow-boughs moving so easily against the wet sky, waiting for the wren to burst into another flourish of song. Sometimes, remembering the manor of Brocton, he would alter the words and say to himself, "As free as Mamillion." But, on the whole, freer. Mamillion might seem to have the completer freedom; he had no obligations to a nunnery, he traversed a wider landscape and encountered more adventures; but Mamillion, however eludingly, was tethered to a quest, sooner or later he must remember the mistletoe and take the golden knife in hand and end the story. Ralph, happier than Mamillion, sought for nothing. He had only to make his mind a blank and some interesting speculation would enter it. He had only to turn his back on God to be flooded with appreciative gratitude to his Maker. It was God the Maker he praised, not Magdalen Figg. She, like the water of baptism, was instrumental. At night, lying awake as the young do, for the pleasure of remaining conscious, he admired the discernment which had led him from the moment he first set eyes on her to think of this heavy uncomely woman in metaphors of water or of the creatures of the fourth element. She was smooth as an eel. She walked like a goose. She goggled like a carp. She was dumb as a fish. She smelled of stagnant water and the river mud-banks. She was the water of baptism. She was the source of joys as reliably as the convent's fish-pond was the source of dinners.

The pleasure he had felt at Brocton was a stammering prophecy of what he now enjoyed. At Brocton there had been much that was delightful, but he had been too far self-absorbed, and too gross of palate, to be more than outwardly delighted. Brocton with a delicate finger had stroked his skin. Now, in his dusty chamber or walking his accustomed rounds, a mere thinking could pierce his heart with pleasure. A boy riding down to the river, his thick tow tresses rising and falling with the movement of his beast; a yoke of oxen turning at the furrow's end and confronting the winter sun with mild faces; the mists wallowing inland at the day's end, towering with the reflected rose of sunset above the poor dusky heath; the intonation of a voice, some fragment of peasant speech, clumsy and true, like a coarse instrument skilfully played on, the enskied speaking of the plain-chant, the eloquence of gospel or collect, Saint Paul's transfigured faith suddenly bursting out amid his polished argument as the face of the satyr looks out from the laurel bush: all these ordinary things were new and entrancing to him, and his alone. For privacy was a great part of his pleasure. If Magdalen Figg, that Eve made of cool clay, had enjoyed this paradise with him, it would not have been paradise.

But, though he was an unfallen Adam in paradise, he was also nuns' priest at Oby, and where his awakened sensibility could not make him appreciative it made him critical. Thus he was both satisfied and not satisfied with Prioress Matilda. As the upholder of his world she could not be bettered. She carried every responsibility, her nuns were well fed, well clothed, contented, and in all his years at Oby he had not been so free from the trouble of troubled consciences. Her eye (except that it was blind to the Widow Figg) roved into every cranny, oversaw his dinners, and noted his need for a new hat. All this was admirable. Everything would have been admirable if he had remained the same Ralph Kello. But now, just as meals became regular and dishes clean and consciences calm, he found that he did not live by bread alone, and in a house that was a model of sober carnality he began to worship the spirit. That was why he sometimes felt disappointed in Dame Matilda and censured her in that among all her healthy, creditable virgins there was not one who could sing like Dame Susanna, or distinguish like Dame Isabel, or dream of beauty as the old prioress had dreamed.

Prioress Matilda, too, was shrewd enough to know that her performance was falling short of what she and others had anticipated. It was well enough; in time to come Oby would number her among the good prioresses; but it was not excelling, and she had meant to excel. More distinctly, she had meant to be popular. The long years during which she had seemed to be stuck forever in an ungainly immaturity, her sojourn in the post of treasuress where she had so often to be disobliging in order to be esteemed, had bred in her an immense appetite for popularity. Now she was popular, just as she had intended to be, and in just such a way as she had intended: a pedestrian, unspectacular popularity with no nonsense about it. But in practice such a popularity seems slovenly, and she was beginning to resent being approved of as a matter of course by a household that increasingly struck her as lacking in discrimination.

Every death entails an audit. When Dame Beatrix died in 1371 the prioress contemplated a vista of very mediocre nuns. Dame Helen, Dame Margaret, Dame Dorothy, Dame Alice, the extinguished Dame Cecily—there was nothing of interest till one came to the three nuns who as novices had played at Flying Saint Katharine. Then, they had seemed of exceptional promise, as promising as that year's crop of walnuts. The walnuts had proved admirable; she could still remember them. Seven years of Prioress Johanna's blow-hot, blow-cold climate must be held to account for a less perfect development of the nuns: for Dame Philippa's nonchalance, Dame Eleanor's obstinacy, Dame Lilias's exasperating detachment. Last came Dame Adela, who had no wits, and Dame Lovisa, who had wits enough for two, but was ugly enough, unfortunately, for seven. There, if it had not been for the prohibitive ugliness, one might look for the next prioress of Oby.

God willing, Oby would not need another prioress for many years to come. There is more to being a prioress than ruling a household of nuns; beings who are, in any case, much less interesting when seen from above than when studied sideways. There was, for instance, the rule of the manor. In the realm of crops and cattle such words as *satisfactory* and *thriving* possess their full weight, they do not have the heart eaten out of them by considerations of whether or no their objects lack distinction. The manor was doing very well; and as she was magnanimous it did not spoil her pleasure to know that the performance was more William Holly's than hers, and that William Holly very plainly said so. The prioress was seldom heard to praise her bailiff; but then she did not praise the sun either. She had found in him the sort of friend she had once hoped to find in Sir Ralph: a more trenchant and active version of herself, a Matilda not encumbered by vows and the female gender.

But most of all she enjoyed finance. Little by little, here by a cautious envelopment and here by a bold stroke, she was pulling Oby out of its insolvency. The work was so congenial that she was glad to think it would go on for a long while yet; for when your feet are once set on the right path you can guide them as you please, even a few steps backward is no more than a prudent measure for getting up your strength to go forward more advantageously a little later. Thus she had raised two loans; and the indebtedness was nothing because she secured them at a rate of interest which proved that usurers now considered the house of Our Lady and Saint Leonard a sound investment. Such loans are not debts: they are demonstrations of solvency, stairways to other loans on even easier terms, a stairway, in particular, to the loan which in 1373 she began to negotiate with Hugh de Stapledon. The family connection was already in good working order. It had transmitted encouragement, good advice, gifts in kind and promises of better gifts to come, with return of thanks, assurances that advice was followed, reciprocal gifts and promises of prayers (Arbella, oddly enough, was extremely susceptible to being prayed for). Now the moment she manœuvred for had come. Hugh de Stapledon, sympathetically comprehending her dislike of raising money from strangers, had suggested lending her enough to pay off the other two loans and leave a little over for improvements, a loan which he would grant on terms no higher than she was paying already and which would be all in the family.

Her first letter of acceptance was so incautiously eloquent that on second thoughts she did not send it. A more circumspect acceptance was composed and despatched. Sooner than she expected the hard-featured serving-man brought a letter from Hugh. It was almost as eloquent as the letter she had not sent. Hugh was engaged in a new law-suit, a law-suit of compelling intricacy and far-reachingness, against his brother Andrew and Andrew's son Nigel. He described it at length, and in the course of his description he made it clear that she need not expect the loan, or any other financial assistance beyond good counsel. This was calamitous, but it was not surprising. She had always foreseen that if it came to a choice between family litigation and family affection, litigation would have it. What she had not foreseen was that Hugh would ask her to contribute toward the expenses of the litigation.

She gave a loud brief laugh. It was a pity that she had no one to share this joke with. Presently she told herself that she was really no worse off than before. She must go on rather longer, that was all; and why should she regret the extension of what she found so congenial? Dame Cecily's expedition to Holywell must be postponed for a while longer. Saint Leonard must be patient for his new coat of paint. She turned to reckoning up possible small gains. The tenant of the saltings along the River Alde (part of Dame Lilias's dowry) could very well be asked to pay a higher rent. Lovisa's peace-loving father could generally be squeezed for the good of his soul; and then there was Sir Ralph's private purse, which must have something in it besides comfits for the Widow Figg.

VIII. SAINT LEONARD, PATRON OF PRISONERS

(January 1374–June 1374)

Day by day, season after season, Dame Lilias, walking in the cloisters, looked at the spire, and her mind experienced the same train of thoughts. There was the spire, and here was she:

the same day had ceremonialized them both into the fabric of Oby, and a long, a too long novitiate had preceded that day. The spire had tried to get away. It had broken itself in the gale and fallen and killed Dame Susanna in its fall. But it had been rebuilt, and here it was, so much a part of Oby that now it was not even grudged at. No one remembered what a nuisance it had been, and with the death of the old prioress went the last thought of the time when it was still only a project and the dearest preoccupation of a mind. For that matter, the old prioress had lost interest in it long before she died. But she, Dame Lilias, had never tried to escape her destiny, and no gale had thrust such an idea upon her. She had been a novice, and now she was a nun; and in all her life she had known nothing more impassioned than what came to her from a narrow highly specialized sensuality. She had an extreme sensibility to sweet smells and the warmth that nurses them, and to certain aspects of light, as when it lies trembling in a bowl of water. Underlying this, as the grim root underlies the flower, she had a less explored sensibility to what was harsh, foul, and noisome. It was this latent sensibility that Dame Beatrix had discerned and exploited, ignoring everyone else's Lilias to elicit the five-year-old child who had trotted, attentive and forgotten, through a castle where the Black Death had usurped any other ownership. It was sickness and not the sick, death and not the dying, which drew Dame Lilias toward the infirmary: as the sick must have perceived, for when the post of infirmaress was given to Dame Alice there was a general outcry of relief.

Appointed instead to be cellaress, Dame Lilias sometimes asked herself why this veer in the wind should be so chilling. She had not lent more than half an ear and half a heart to Dame Beatrix's persuasions; and as appointments go, cellaress was the less disagreeable post—it is better to smell stale fish than sores. But from the hour that snapped off her rather indefinite intention she was overcome by a sense of coldness and stagnation. Little by little the sensuality which had quilted her wore thin and fell away. No one would have guessed it. She was still fastidious about her food, she dodged physical discomfort as dexterously as ever, and now that she had command of the spice cupboard she castled herself in sweet scents, was never without a couple of cloves or a bayleaf in her pocket, and rubbed powdered cinnamon into her veil. But scents must be nursed by warmth, and she was cold: cold to pleasure, cold to her own coldness even. When she lounged in, late as always, for the night office, yawning and shrugging her shoulders, no one could have guessed that she came, not from sleeping, but from a frigid and boring wakefulness.

Among her companions her languor was diagnosed as pride. She was too proud to speak, they said; and if one asked her a direct question she was too lazy to give back more than a bare Yes or No. It became a current pastime to address remarks to Dame Lilias—the sillier the better; when she replied, one exclaimed at the wit of her answer or thanked her for replying so graciously. Dame Adela put a great deal of energy into this sport, but she was not so skilful as Dame Lovisa. It was Dame Lovisa who hit on the device of consulting Dame Lilias on matters of beauty and the toilet, magnanimously exposing her own ugliness for the pleasure of the community by asking Dame Lilias how often she should wash her face, how best she could improve her complexion, what she must do to grow long eyelashes; or thrusting her ill-odoured face under Dame Lilias's nose she would inquire if her sores were not wonderfully mended by the rose-water.

If the sores had not been vizored by so much hatred and derision this particular sport might have mended Dame Lilias. The sensibility to what was foul and noisome had made a better resistance than the sensibility to light conversing with clear water or strawberry leaves trodden by the sun, and reacted to this young, pitiable, and intelligent little monster. Looking down on the sores and the pimples and the weak glaring eyes, Dame Lilias felt as though she had turned from a painted landscape to a window giving on the whole real world, the world of our first parents as they walked away from Eden gate under trees whose fruits were unmystically wholesome or deadly, a world where serpents were sufficient in being mortal serpents, no more, no less. But an artificiality of malice and the routine amusement of the other nuns interposed between her and what she might have got from her tormentor, and presently she was insensible even to Dame Lovisa.

It was God's will, she supposed. God's will had taken away Dame Cecily's eyesight, God's will had taken away her sensuality, and with it the sins of the flesh which nourish the life of the spirit. She could feel neither pleasure nor disgust, neither rebellion nor contrition. For a while she tried if austerities and mortification would revive her. Nothing revived her: austerities and mortification fell on her like ashes on the dead.

At length, and almost inadvertently (for she did not doubt that her wretchedness would be quite as boring to others as it had become to herself), Dame Lilias in confession spoke of her state of mind. To her astonishment, Sir Ralph roused up and seemed interested. It was accidie, he said; a malady of the soul that in its final intensification of wanhope is one of the seven deadly sins.

"Accidie," she repeated. "Dame Susanna spoke of it when she taught us our sins."

"Dame Susanna!" he exclaimed. "A lot she knew about it."

The convention of the confessional seemed to have broken down, here was Sir Ralph talking to her as if she were a person. Recovering his manners, he went on to say that accidie was not so very rare, though unusual among women; and, with patience and God's help, curable. She rose from her knees with an impression of having pleased. It was momentary: as though, travelling through an endless cavern, a ray of sunlight had for an instant touched her cheek. A moment later the laconic voice of her intelligence was assuring her that since the majority of mankind will be found among the damned the addition of herself to that number could not be remarkable, and that if Sir Ralph were interested it could be only because wanhope was rather more of a rarity than sloth or anger. But to Sir Ralph it appeared as though his last prayer were about to be granted. In addition to the pleasures of the senses he enjoyed with Magdalen Figg and the pleasures of sensibility he enjoyed with himself, he was, it seemed, in a way to enjoy the pleasure of conversing with a spiritually minded nun. She had touched his heart. The words, so inadequate and true, in which she had described her wasting misery were like a descant on his own revival. Her dreariness was the antipodes of his delight. Everything he had, she lacked; and the antithesis drew him to her because it completed his self-realization.

His first fear was that she might recover too quickly and become as dull a penitent as the rest. Time went on, she made no step toward recovery. She was too wretched for eloquence. His sincere attention drew from her little more than a glum, "It is no better. I can feel no hope." But the few bare words seemed to him to have a classic grace. And so he continued to reason with her and admonish her, genuinely concerned for her state and at the same time snuffing up her odours of clove and saffron, the sweet scents that breathed from this barren fig tree.

As for what went on in the convent, it was really no affair of his. But one day Magdalen Figg said to him that the nuns would murder Dame Lilias among them, and he plucked up his resolution and went to the prioress, telling her that Dame Lilias was in a state of perilous melancholy and should be handled with consideration. Immediately it sprang into her mind how abominable it was that Mary can always catch a man's ear while Martha grunts unheeded.

"Dame Lilias has always been singular. It is just what I should have expected of her—to choose this moment to doubt of her salvation while all the rest of us are worrying night and day how to pay off the convent's debts."

He had happened to approach her on the day after she had received Hugh de Stapledon's repudiation of the loan. He could not know this, but he realized that he had chosen a bad hour. It struck him that the prioress was growing vulgar and uncongenial. If she would not listen to him about Dame Lilias he would not listen to her about debts. He ignored her hints about a little loan from a friend, some old friend who could be trusted, and she grew angrier than ever and more confirmed in her prejudice against the nun.

Christmas passed, the days grew lighter, colder, barer. It seemed to him that Dame Lilias and he were wading through some classical Styx, a cold corner of hell that Christ had never harrowed and where the writ of christianity did not extend.

When he said, "Why do you not pray to Saint Leonard? He releases prisoners," he thought how falsely the words rang and how her silence made mincemeat of them. For months she had been incapable of prayer, he might as sensibly have told a lame man to put on red shoes, and see what that would do for him. That same evening she knocked on his door.

"Saint Leonard has heard me. He has shown me the way out."

Even now she was not eloquent. Her narrative was broken by long pauses during which she seemed to be falling asleep, but it was plain and coherent. She had done as he had bid, escaping from the afternoon recreation to go and pray before the statue of the saint. She had done her best, but no sense of devotion had come to her. Instead, she had been submerged by resentment against her companions, remembering all the pricks and gibes they had given her, until the last convention of charity was torn away from her mind. She had felt, she said, all of a sudden such a force of loathing that it was as though a headsman's axe had fallen on the nape of her neck, and she had tumbled face forward on the ground. Then she was aware of Dame Dorothy standing behind her and saying, "What a pity to disturb such devotion! But the rest of us are such dull grovelling creatures that we have to live by the Rule; and it is time for me to light the candles."

"And while she was still speaking," she concluded, "I heard another voice. And it said, 'Now see the reason of all this hating. Go, and become an anchoress.'

"An anchoress!" she repeated. "Saint Leonard bade me become an anchoress."

"You did not see the saint?"

"No, for I was lying on the ground when he spoke. But I felt him. It was he who struck me that blow. See if there is not a bruise." The bruise was not large, but there was no doubt of it. Saint Leonard must have a small fist and a strong arm. Saint Leonard, or Dame Dorothy. It looked like woman's work to him.

"And when you felt this blow . . ."

"I was free, suddenly free. It broke a chain."

Even if the blow came from Dame Dorothy, one might say that Dame Dorothy must be accounted instrumental, a signet snatched up in a hurry while the wax was in perfection, as one seals with a groat or a dagger-hilt.

"There is a bruise, certainly. But do not speak of it."

She gave an adjusting shrug of her shoulders and winced at the real pain of the real bruise. Her veil fell, her spices flowed forth. He would miss her. But she must go to her anchoret cell, and he must help her departure.

After she had quitted him he remembered the dried plums in his cupboard and began to munch them, grateful to be eating. He had always dreaded something like this, now it had happened. Dame Lilias had heard a voice from heaven, and the voice she had heard was now reverberating in him, and assuring him with the greatest distinctness that it takes a sacrament to make a priest. Learning, custom, the habit of years, all that is of no avail, the tinted water does not make the wine: here he was, reacting to Dame Lilias with as much simplicity as a ploughman. Dame Lilias had heard a voice from heaven, and so little a priest was he that he thought none the worse of her, and even took her at her word. The bruise, he supposed, was Dame Dorothy's handiwork. She was a dull unnoticeable creature; in all the years he had known her she had been a nonentity. But every nonentity must have a moment when it flashes into something positive, the immortal soul is not housed in flesh for nothing, and very probably Dame Dorothy's soul had had its moment of necessity in striking that blow from behind. The blow was necessary if Dame Lilias was to be freed. Everything is planned by divine intelligence: a cipher is begotten and born and lives for thirty years in religion in order to deliver a blow on the neck; and after that, naturally, it lives on, according to the law of its kind. Whether or no Dame Dorothy's soul must suffer the penalty of nursing malice and giving way to anger was a fascinating speculation, but one to be deferred. Her part was played, a "Here beginneth" to the voice of Saint Leonard, a supernatural voice released by the natural instrumentality of her blow, like the waters which sprang from the rock when Moses struck it. *Now see the reason of all this hating. Go, and become an anchoress.*

All in the imperative as usual. A model of conciseness, as well struck as Dame Dorothy's blow. But it is not enough for heaven to speak—the supernatural for its completion must be adequately accepted, otherwise the work is not worked out. Dame Lilias had matched her moment. She had heard and believed. As for himself, he really could do no less.

He had eaten two more plums before he recalled his own part in the affair, his advice to Dame Lilias that she should pray to Saint Leonard, patron of prisoners. He too had been instrumental, a figure balancing Dame Dorothy's. Everything is planned by divine intelligence.

But now came the formalities; and his heart sank as he contemplated the morass of tact and negotiations through which he must move. Dame Lilias could not become an anchoress without the bishop's permission. Her application must be made through the prioress, which meant that the voice of Saint Leonard would reach the bishop at third hand. In theory his own voice, as the professional witness, should outshout that of the prioress, but it was questionable whether this would be so in fact. Above all, the voice of Dame Lilias must be pitched very low.

As a first step he commanded her to say nothing about it. Then he set about the prioress, who pointed out that no letters could be sent from Oby till the floods went down, and added that it would be best if for the present Saint Leonard's speech remained a matter of confidence. "For I am sure you don't want to have everyone chattering about it, and plaguing you for advice on how to hear voices. No doubt many of them would enjoy a word or two with a saint."

"It is her own wish that nothing should be said of it," he replied artfully.

"I am glad she is so sensible."

Sir Ralph was glad that the prioress was so sensible. He had not expected her to take the news so indulgently.

It had been an exceptionally wet season. The watery skies were mirrored in acres of water, flocks of water-fowl cried and swooped across the floods, and in the hamlet people were laying bets as to what course the Waxle Stream would be found in when the floods withdrew. Pigs, poultry, and cattle, men, women, and children, all the livestock of Oby were gathered on the rise of ground. Lowings and gruntings, cock-crowing, shouting and chattering, the thump of the flails and the hymns of the nuns, all resounded together as in some jovial ark; for this winter there happened to be plenty of victual, so the prevailing mood was cheerful and rather childish.

Feeling that Dame Lilias might be the better with something to divert her mind after all she had been through, he lent her his copy of the *Georgics.* It was a cheap copy, the scribe had used his worst ink and saved space and time by employing all the recognized contractions and some others of his own invention; though Dame Lilias was a fair scholar, he wondered how much she would be able to make out. He thought, too, that a book so appreciatively devoted to the active life would make odd reading for a woman who proposed to spend the rest of her days in a cell fastened, like a moth's coffin, to the side of some church. Yet her cell would have its window-slit, and she would see, as in the compass of a pentameter, oxen at plough, a tom-cat courting its female, the cloud retreating behind the rainbow. Meanwhile her mind was at rest. Her outer life too had become easier, so Magdalen reported, for the prioress had called off the tormentors.

The prioress had done so for a sound reason. She had not forgotten the affair of the old prioress and Dame Johanna, and she knew that only a thick universal plaster of good manners could save her from expressing a most impolitic annoyance. An anchoress, even more strictly than a nun, forswears worldly goods; but would Bishop Giles allow them to lose Dame Lilias and retain her dowry? He had behaved scurvily over the de Scottow legacy, ten to one he would behave as scurvily now and rule that the revenues of those water-meadows and saltings should be diverted to some almshouse or some altar. First the failure of the loan, now the loss of a considerable revenue. . . . Fury shook the prioress as she saw her work jeopardized by this nonsense of Saint Leonard and a discontented nun. But if the situation were to be retrieved she must not show her fury. She must seem to believe, and she must seem to approve. Even in her letter to the bishop she must somehow combine disparagement of Dame Lilias with piety toward the saint and indifference to a possible reduction of income.

She made many drafts of the letter. Fortunately the floods gave her a breathing-space; and when they went down William Holly could not spare a man to carry letters. Regretting this to Sir Ralph, she added that the Etchingdon bursar would shortly come to collect the interest on the Methley tithe, and that the letters could be entrusted to him. He came, stayed a night, and went away. Only after he had gone was it discovered that in the turmoil of trying to persuade him to take part of the interest in kind the prioress had forgotten to give him the packet. But a week later when Brother Baltazar called for a meal she gave him the packet herself.

"The bishop?" said Brother Baltazar. "But he has gone. He has been appointed to the see of Auch, a great advancement, and they say that Pope Gregory will soon make a cardinal of him."

"What a loss to us!" she exclaimed. "Has the new bishop been chosen?"

"Not that I know of. But many wish that it may be Sir Walter Dunford, the archdeacon. He is a poor man's son, and a very holy clerk, and much loved by the poor."

It was a friar's answer. Friars ramble everywhere and are as slippery as coins rubbed smooth by all the hands that have transmitted them. She had no doubt that Brother Baltazar knew something of Walter Dunford which it pleased him to keep from her; and since it pleased him to withhold it, that something must be something which it would advantage her to know. At the same moment the companion friar, a great hulking youth with lips like sausages, cried out in a strong west-country accent, "Oh, he's a lovely clerk! He will make a lovely bishop."

So Walter Dunford was the man.

But even friars may be misinformed, and Oby continued to speculate until the eve of Palm Sunday. The nuns were out gathering willow-palm. It was a sudden hot day, as hot as summer; bees were lolling from one golden tuft to another and followed the cut boughs into the chapel. Light-headed from the conjunction of lenten abstinence and this luxurious weather the nuns were frisking about and pretending to beat each other with the willow boughs when a messenger rode up amongst them. Where was the prioress? There was the prioress, trying to put a bee down Dame Philippa's neck. But she came up with her usual sturdy dignity to receive the letter. The new bishop was Walter Dunford, who greeted his beloved daughters and begged for their prayers.

In a fine springtime there is always a lot of coming and going; before long more was learned about the new bishop. Yes, it was true, he was a man of low birth: his father had been a candle-maker, his mother a midwife, and between them with great piety they had reared up a long family. The father's connections (he supplied candles to the great Abbey of Holy Cross in Middlesex as well as to the house of Our Lady at Barking) helped him in getting an education for his children, and he had placed many of them either in religion or near by it. By the time Walter, the youngest son, entered the priesthood, the Dunfords in their small way were a dynastic family. Yet he had much to contend with, for he was sickly, diffident, and unprepossessing: up to his fortieth year no one would have thought him the stuff of a bishop. Then came the Black Death and cut a swathe for him. In that time when so many priests died and others hid themselves in routine, the sickly diffident Walter Dunford became known as a man almost angelical in energy. He ministered, he comforted, he organized. Respectable witnesses averred that he had been present, at one and the same time, beside a death-bed and at the altar. Some had felt healing flow from his fingers with the holy oil, others had seen him, whilst running to catch the confession of a dying outlaw, caught up by his zeal as if on wings, and wafted across the empty market-place like a bird. In the year 1351 many people were saying that Walter Dunford was a saint. Five years later twice that number were saying he was a man with a future. He became eminent enough to have slanderers, the retinue of eminence. He had the evil eye, it was said; he was leprous, he was crazy, he was a plotter, he was a sorcerer. Beyond doubt he was undersized, pious to eccentricity, ludicrously thrifty. His reputation spluttered and hung fire. It did not seem likely that he would ever win more than a local fame. He was made an archdeacon, with every expectation that he would die of the office, but he did not die. All of a sudden, as startlingly as a grounded heron displays its wing-span, he was in every mouth as a man who should by every right be a bishop. There is only one statesmanly answer to this sort of challenge, and in 1374 he was given a mitre.

The reports that came to Oby by pedlars and palmers, people who carry rumours as naturally as they carry fleas, told a rousing tale of Bishop Walter's austerity and industry. He drank only water and slept on a mat. He journeyed incessantly, dismounting to kneel at every wayside cross. He listened to the poor talking among themselves, he plucked young girls out of brothels, he visited leper-houses and poor parish priests. He asked rich ladies how much they paid an ell for velvet and how many ells it took to make a mantle. He had not changed his shirt since his ordination. He had an open sore on his left side but no one was allowed to look at it. His sister cooked all his food for him, for he feared to be poisoned.

Roger Salhouse, Dame Cecily's lawyer cousin, staying the night on his way to Bury Saint Edmunds, confirmed much of this, and added that Walter Dunford was a hard and shrewd man of business, and that so far no one had found a handle to him; but that he would probably wear himself out in a year or two. Meanwhile, he was extremely popular, with the wealthy praising him even louder than the poor, and thronging to hear his sermons against luxury and vanity.

Such a bishop, thought Dame Lilias, who kneels before the Christs of the wayside, would understand my wish to become an anchoress; and such an industrious functionary will not fail to read that request. Her patience took heart. Patience is an easier merit under Taurus, when cold does not drive one to the chattering fireside. Dame Cecily liked to hear the birds singing, and during recreation she and Dame Lilias sat in the orchard, the sighted nun winding silk off the blind nun's hands. Dame Cecily listened to the birds and Dame Lilias thought of her cell and wondered to which quarter its window would face. She still kept her word not to speak of her calling.

Such a bishop, thought Sir Ralph, will blow like an east wind through Oby. What with our debts and our dinners we shall certainly feel the admonitory end of his crozier. But such a bishop, rating austerity so high, will be more inclined to favour Dame Lilias, if only as a slap in the face to the remainder of the establishment.

The prioress also thought about the new bishop; and among weightier considerations she recalled her letter to Bishop Giles about Dame Lilias's vocation. The former bishop would have read it sympathetically, but this one might not be so responsive to her disparagement of the kind of nun who hears voices, especially if he believed himself to have been whisked over a market-place. But there had stood Brother Baltazar, eyeing the packet in her hand and ready to tell the world that the prioress of Oby wrote letters to a Bishop Giles which a Bishop Walter might not read, and so she had let him carry it off. How silly of her!—any woman with her wits about her would have said it contained a recipe for a febrifuge. But when Bishop Walter's answer came it was pretty much as though Bishop Giles, that prudent man, had written it. For a nun to quit her convent and become an anchoress, he wrote, demanded so clear a vocation and such special gifts of the spirit that he could not consider the application without further evidence and a personal interview. He would go into it when he visited the house of Our Lady and Saint Leonard, which he proposed to do, God willing, before the feast of Saint Michael and all Angels.

IX. THE FISH-POND

(July 1374–September 1374)

Sooner or later everyone has his turn. During that spring and summer the nuns of Oby noticed that the prioress was making a favourite of Dame Alice. Dame Alice noticed it herself: she had sharp eyes. There was a certain sharpness in her gratification too. She had been a nun of Oby since 1358, always cheerful, always obliging, and bringing in a tidy little profit by her marzipan: it seemed to her high time that her merits should be acknowledged. Perhaps the merits might have been acknowledged more flatteringly. However much one may boast oneself as being just practical and sensible, one would like (if only for a change) to be commended for something more celestial. But the prioress continued to express pleasure in Dame Alice's common sense, candour, and lack of imagination, so Dame Alice continued to manifest common sense and lack of imagination.

Dame Alice was the first nun to be told that the bishop had fixed on the second week in September for the date of his Visitation.

"Which gives us nine weeks to prepare in, dear Mother."

"I think we will entertain him quite modestly. He is said to be very austere. If he seems vexed we can always explain that we are living in a poor way because of our debt."

Dame Alice said concurringly, "Goose?"

"Goose, I suppose. Goose with forcemeat. And some fish, something out of our own fish-pond. And some sweet eggs with whipped cream. And your marzipan, of course. If he says it is too much we can explain that it is only what the manor provides. In fact, we had better say at the start that it is all home-grown, no bought dainties. And the quire must concentrate on singing loudly and pronouncing the words plainly, for they say he is rather deaf."

"And Sir Ralph?"

"Yes, he must be tidied up. But he looks more creditable now that his hair is so grey."

After a pause Dame Alice said, "And the Widow Figg?"

Though she kept her voice level, and said no more than any of the others might have said, a view-halloo sounded through the words. The prioress coloured angrily, but she said with a laugh, "The Widow Figg is a corrodian, so we can keep her in a cupboard till he's gone."

She began to speak of their debts again—more philosophically than she was wont to do—saying that they were no worse than anyone else's, and that they had the spire to show for it, which was more than most houses could put forth in extenuation. They walked up and down in the sunshine, dashed by the shadows of the martins hawking round the spire, and nothing more was said of Sir Ralph and the Widow Figg. But as the bell sounded and they turned toward the quire door Dame Alice exclaimed, "Do not say I have not warned you, dear Mother!"

It was plain enough what the woman meant. A new-broom bishop who slept on a mat would certainly take exception to a convent priest living in fornication with the convent's corrodian. It would be a damaging disclosure. But who was intending to disclose it? She had not a nun who was not good and loyal—unless it were Dame Lilias. Wrath bounced her in her stall at the thought of Dame Lilias justifying her wish to leave Oby by tales against Sir Ralph. But Dame Lilias depended on Sir Ralph's testimony, she could not at once invoke his advocacy and denounce his incontinence. Might it be Dame Alice herself? Dame Alice was a Dilworth nun, and a woman of low breeding. Imported nuns are never reliable. The prioress recalled—and turned cold at the recollection—how surprisingly Dame Alice had risen up in chapter, laid hands on the old prioress and carried her off from beating Dame Johanna. But that was long ago; and since that day Dame Alice had never surprised anyone, knowing, if ever a nun did, on which side her bread was buttered, and avoiding unpleasantness as a cat avoids puddles. Was it not to avoid unpleasantness that she bore away the old prioress?

Arguing herself in and out of confidence, the prioress arrived at two certainties: that she must question Dame Alice, and that she dreaded doing so. The affront of the second certainty stung the old woman into action. Dame Alice was summoned.

"Shut the door, my daughter. On the day before yesterday you told me to remember that you had warned me. Against what?"

"We were speaking of the bishop's coming, dear Mother."

"We were. We spoke about our debt, and of a goose stuffed with forcemeat. Were you perhaps warning me that a goose might be too rich for the bishop's stomach?"

"No," said Dame Alice. "I spoke of something fatter than a goose."

The prioress swallowed.

"Of something fatter than a goose," Dame Alice repeated, raising her voice, "and more foul-feeding. I spoke of Sir Ralph and the Widow Figg."

The prioress put her hands into her sleeves, for they were trembling. Hammering inside her was an unwonted girlish fear, such a fear as she had not known since those nights when she had been thrust into the same bed as a naked, hairy, and angry man. Then she had screamed and fought. Now she sat still and said:

"We will speak no more of them. To anyone. Do you understand?"

"Speak of it? Not I! But do you suppose, dear Mother, that we, your poor loyal nuns, are the only people who can talk of this? If Bishop Walter has not heard of it already, he soon will. The nearer you are to earth, the quicker you hear these stories. And the bishop is only a candle-maker's son, you know. He is quite a low-bred gossiping sort of person—like me, dear Mother."

She paused, watching this arrow sink in. Like an animal that runs wild as it smells the blood of its quarry, she showed her teeth and cried out savagely, "We are simple people, the bishop and I. We think like the common folk we are. We have no patience with fornicating priests and their strumpets! . . . . They will bring down God's vengeance on the house," she whispered. She crossed herself with a shaking hand. Her berry eyes stared bolting from her round face.

The prioress told her to sit down. For the moment that was all she could do. Her composure staggered under Dame Alice's assertion of her own and the bishop's kindred morality. But inside that great mass of heated and quaking flesh the habit of ruling persisted, calm as a compass in its binnacle. Under an appearance of dignified grief she collected herself and began to think.

She could afford to discount Dame Alice's moral indignation. Moral indignation at its most powerful, the indignation of a Bishop Walter, could not really inflict more than some hard words, a penitential contribution to the diocesan money-chest, and Sir Ralph being put away to muse on his indiscretions, as Prior Thomas had been, and then, like Prior Thomas, fished out again to be a credit to holy contrition. The teeth of the threat lay in Dame Alice's blackmail of God's vengeance. For now, in these bad days, it was not only the Pope who could impose an interdict: the people could do it themselves. First the cook goes, and then the scullions follow the cook; piously removing themselves from the neighbourhood of an avenging God, the workers begin to leak away, the hind leaves the plough, the thatcher makes excuses not to come and mend the roof; the harvest is not gathered, sheep are not shorn, calves are not gelded; and presently dues are not paid, novices are diverted elsewhere, and the moneylenders demand their capital. Only an indubitably solvent establishment, a house built on a rock, can afford to disregard rumours of God's vengeance. And Oby was not solvent.

On the other hand, Oby was by no means so insolvent that an incontinent priest should bring the house down.

The flies buzzed, and Dame Alice panted. Her outburst had left her short of breath. She pants like a dog, thought the prioress: like a mad dog. Perhaps that was the explanation of her extraordinary behaviour, and the no less extraordinary perturbation felt by the prioress herself; for one is instinctively afraid of madness. The prioress peeped hopefully. One glance at Dame Alice was enough to do away with any such hoping. A leg of mutton could not look further from madness than Dame Alice did. What's more, she had seen the peep. The situation suddenly presented itself to the prioress in a new light. She saw it as comical. With this, her courage returned, and she felt sure of her next move. Since Dame Alice had become the mouthpiece of the common people, who are the mouthpiece of God, she should be treated as such. Mouths, thought the prioress, can be shut.

She looked up and sighed suitably. "H'm, h'm. It's a sad business, my daughter. If it comes to his knowledge we cannot expect the bishop to overlook it."

"I do not expect God to overlook it."

"No, indeed. That would be impiety. God sees all and judges all. A bishop's position is a little different."

Dame Alice made no reply.

"In many ways I should be sorry to lose Sir Ralph."

"Would you be sorry to lose the Widow Figg?" inquired Dame Alice in a voice of tremendous insolence and burst into tears.

A parleying castle and a listening woman are both ready to give in. The prioress knew this saying and had often proved its truth. Disregarding the sobs and the snuffles, she launched into an account of the convent's finances and why at this juncture it would be injudicious to dismiss Magdalen and part with the remainder of her money.

"If she were a healthy woman it would be different. But she has a swollen neck, she faints, she goggles like a sleep-walker. Anything may finish her."

Dame Alice had undoubtedly begun to listen.

"People like yourself and Bishop Walter may despise these considerations. I'm sure I should be very glad to despise them myself and give over my mind to considering heaven and hell and so forth. But we cannot all be saints. Some of us have to be stewards. Where do you suppose Oby would be if I were to fall on my knees every time something happens that calls for God's vengeance?"

Dame Alice had left off crying and was thoughtfully licking the salt off her upper lip.

"I am like a man pursued by a bear," said the prioress, "and who carries twelve small children on his back, and a horsefly settles on his face. He might like to knock off the horsefly, but how can he?—for with both his hands he supports the children, and if he stops to put the children down the bear will catch up with him. Do you suppose that I like to have this scandal in my house? Do you suppose that I am so devoted to Sir Ralph that I keep the Widow Figg to pleasure him? Do you suppose that I would not prefer a new clean priest instead of this greasy gobbler? But who's to pay for it, eh?"

The listening woman listened harder.

"So the horsefly sucks and I trudge on. And let me tell you, the Widow Figg is not the only sting that Sir Ralph has given me. He won't lend us a penny, though I have told him how things are with us and promised him good interest. And now he stings me in a new place and plans to steal away my nuns."

Carried away by her own eloquence, the prioress had told everything about Saint Leonard, Dame Lilias, and the dowry before she remembered that this was a secret. But the castle had yielded; Dame Alice was once more her usual unimaginative self. She caulked up the disclosure with a command of silence and sent off the mouthpiece of God with an affable, "Now, remember! One of our secrets, my daughter."

"One of our secrets, dear Mother."

Left alone the prioress wondered why at the onset this interview should have seemed so portentous. Really she had worked herself up for nothing. Too long taken for granted, too suddenly favoured, Dame Alice was suffering from nothing more than an indigestion of self-importance. Better now than two months later, when all this might have been poured out to the bishop.

Two months to go, thought Dame Alice: there is no need to hurry. I will not do anything yet, while her memory is still raw. If I leave it a little longer she will forget that I threatened her, and only remember what a blessed thing it would be to lose the Widow Figg. Then, when the Widow Figg goes, she will thank God for it and ask no questions. For that matter, she as good as urged me to it herself. Did she not call her a horsefly and talk about her dying? Two months . . . anyone might die in two months. She might die suddenly, and in all her sins, and yet not get further than purgatory, if at the last moment she remembers to invoke God's mother. I mean no harm to her soul. And then the bishop will come and go and harm nobody, all will go on quietly. Not, O God, as at Dilworth, that hell on earth!

Only exceptional characters, or very imprudent ones, murder for a pure motive. Dame Alice had a retinue of motives for wishing to help on Magdalen's death—the word, murder, she did not admit. There was the motive of being spiritually inconvenienced—how could she not fall into unchaste speculations while this example of unchastity was forever under her nose? There was the motive of averting scandal—for it was quite true, she really had overheard a great deal of kitchen comment, and though so far it had been indulgent, it might change at any moment to condemnation. There was the motive of the new bishop. Above all there was the motive of preserving Oby from becoming like Dilworth. But with all these motives for wishing Magdalen out of the way, Dame Alice would not have gone beyond wishing if the prioress had not armed her with those words: "anything may finish her." And what could be easier for an infirmaress than just to hasten the parting between Sir Ralph and his whore? The woman was sickly, always pleased to take a medicine. Dame Alice let time wag, the warm days falling one after another like wild raspberries, dropping from their own ripeness, confused in a rotting, unregarded sweetness underfoot. Every day someone, prompted or unprompted, would speak of Bishop Walter's coming; and Dame Alice would glance at the prioress, and the prioress would remark that they must put their best foot foremost. In August Dame Alice felt secure enough for her first attempt. First attempts are often failures. So was this one. So was a second, and a third. It was as though Magdalen Figg, mysteriously weatherwise, had a similar power for nosing out death in a drink.

William Holly now came every day to consult his oracle, and followed her advice, though it strained his faith to do so. In spite of the intense brooding heat, the dewless nights and the dull stars and clouds that boiled up every afternoon, Magdalen continued to assure him that it would not rain yet. Many of the strips in the great field were cleared already, for in spite of Magdalen's reputation the harvesters could not believe her. But the manor corn had been left to ripen to the uttermost, and the shocks were still standing in the field, bold as castles.

Dame Lilias was the only nun who did not complain of the heat. The weather that was like a trance, the enormous unstirring noontides that lay on the face of the earth as a snake lies basking in a cart-track, the hot breath of wheat that filled the air at dusk as though it came out of a baker's oven, had brought her to a speechless acquiescence. She had ceased to hope, to fret, to pray. She waited. The pother about the Visitation had no more relevance to the bishop's coming than the smell of hot women that was constantly in her nostrils had anything to do with the sun's journey overhead. This placid, pregnant state she had fallen into was a relief to Sir Ralph, who felt the heat acutely and would have found it hard to support any troubled soul just then. His gate-house chamber, in winter as cold as a cage, was hot as a furnace. He skulked out of doors, lying under the willows of the Long Pool, trailing his hand in the tepid water.

The midges would have driven him away, but he carried his brazier with him and a faggot of lavender stems. Being this year's stems they burned slowly and gave a strong odour. A fat man sweltering under Leo and carrying a smoking brazier: he must look like the emblem of Fatuity, he told himself; but for many years now it had not mattered what he looked like, he was as familiar as a way-mark. Sometimes Magdalen would sidle through the willows and sit down beside him, with a pretext of looking for a strayed hen, or gathering the wild watermint whose smell keeps flies from the larder. She dangled her feet in the water to wash off the dust and the chaff which sweat had plastered on them, and sometimes she carried a cluster of the little corn-bindweed which is like a pink star and smells of almonds. Though it was too hot for desire he liked to have her beside him, talking slowly of commonplace things; for life in a convent had taught her to speak, though in Jesse's orchard she had been dumb as a fish. Like all the rest of them she was besotted with the bishop's coming. She was to help with this and to oversee that. Dame Lilias had asked her to rub down the dried fleabane which was to be scattered in the bishop's bed. Tomorrow morning she and Dame Alice would carry water to refresh the fishpond: already they were throwing bread to the carp twice a day, so that they might be well flavoured when they came to table. There was to be a dish of carp as well as the stuffed goose and the sweet eggs, and she would have a taste of all these, and a good view of the bishop, wearing her black hood. Next to a virgin a widow has the approval of heaven, she had heard this in her wedding sermon at Wivelham.

"A virtuous widow," he put in mechanically.

"I shall wear my black hood," she repeated, gazing at him with mud-coloured eyes. There was no more reproach in them than in the water that went so gently by, and suddenly his heart smote him, not for the offence he had done her, for indeed she seemed unwrongable as water, but because of her simplicity. In his hours with her he had come to be able to speak without fear or supervision of his words, and now he heard himself asking her to pray for him. She promised that she would do so. She spoke in her usual placid voice, and he might have been asking her to sew on a button. Yet he could see pleasure moving under her muddy skin like a sun through a mist.

After she had gone he sat looking at the squashed grass where she had sat, and enjoying the sensation she had left with him: the sensation of being a philosopher and his own man. A reed-warbler's nest came twirling down the river. It was so dry that it floated like a coracle, and as it twirled on out of sight he wondered if it would sail as far as Waxelby, and how long the journey would take it, and if it would get there before the bishop made his portentous arrival at Oby. But he did not dread Bishop Walter. When a dog has slept in the same corner for so many years no one is likely to inquire into its pedigree. The nest went out of sight and Sir Ralph fell asleep. When he woke he had the impression that something fortunate had happened, and presently he traced this to the fact that Magdalen would be praying for him. On his way back he met her. She was looking rather perturbed and walking hurriedly, like a goose that had snuffed a fox behind the hedge.

"I feel water rising," she said, "I must go and tell William."

Neither of the two Frampton novices (Arbella's sending) had set eyes on a bishop. Destined from their cradles for the religious life, they had stayed at home at the tail of a long family while their elder sisters were taken to solemn masses and banquets. Now they pestered Dame Philippa with their expectations. Would he come riding, or in a litter? Would he have a jewel on his shoe? Would he bring his best crozier? Was he going to be a saint? Did he sleep in his gloves? Would he make them nuns? No, indeed! No bishop would give the veil to girls who slopped their soup and forgot half the saints in the calendar, she answered admonishingly. Unabashed, the younger one asked if the bishop would poke with his crozier in the pork-barrel as Saint Nicholas had done. Nothing likelier, she said, turning aside to smile. For the younger nuns saw with amusement the fuss their prioress was in about this Visitation, and laughed among themselves at Dame Alice lugging buckets of water to refresh the fish-pond, and Dame Dorothy blowing dust off the images, and Dame Helen and Dame Margaret hurrying with pursed lips to unburden themselves to Dame Cecily. Tormented with an incessant face-ache, Dame Cecily now spent most of her time in the infirmary. But her curiosity flickered on. Though she was subject to the usual calamity of the bedridden, to be visited only by bores, she liked to hear what was happening, and anything that could make a picture roused her into asking question after question. Now she asked how Dame Alice carried the water. Did she carry it on a yoke? They answered that the Widow Figg went with her, carrying the second bucket.

"I see. And so they stand on the rim, emptying the buckets at arms' length in order not to get splashed. And do the fish put up their heads in gratitude?"

"I don't suppose so. Dame Alice has said nothing about that."

"She is joking, Dame Helen. I must say this seems to me a great waste of water, for they do it twice a day. But when I suggested this to our prioress she flew into a huff and said that Dame Alice knew what she was about. I thought of saying, Then why has she never done it before?—for we have had other droughts, you know. But now it seems that Dame Alice can do no wrong."

"Do you know what I think it is? I think it is a plan, and that the prioress herself invented it, a plan to keep the Widow Figg out of our priest's way, so that he may be preserved from falling into sin until the bishop has come and gone. They say that this bishop is remarkably acute. Which of the saints was it, Dame Cecily, who was so chaste that he could smell unchastity just like cheese? Was it Saint Thomas Becket? We don't want that to happen here."

"And does the Widow Figg wear her russet kirtle?"

"Oh, no, it is too hot for that. She is wearing a kirtle of grey canvas and going about barefoot. It grows sultrier every day. When the storm comes it will be a terrible storm."

Dame Cecily saw in her mind's eye the barefoot walking of those who are accustomed to walk unshod; the widespread toes, powerful as fingers, taking hold of the ground, scattering the burned gold of the camomile, twitching aside from a thistle.

Meanwhile Dame Helen was remarking in her most oracular voice, "Sometimes I think the storm will not break until we have received the bishop."

They could tell Dame Cecily nothing about the weather that her own senses could not tell her more lucidly, and her imagination returned to Magdalen Figg's bare feet and the ground they trod, to the spurts of dust, the litter of broken snail-shells round the thrush's stone, and the conversing shadows of the two water-carriers. Suddenly their talk gave her a new picture.

"I have never seen anyone in such fear."

"She is afraid of thunder."

They were talking of Dame Adela. Dame Adela's countenance was one of the last things Dame Cecily's eyesight had pulled out of the dull broth into which her world was dissolving. When the girl was at a loss she drooped her lower jaw, and this gave her flowerlike face the additional vacancy of a flower, of a rose so fully expanded that in a moment a petal will fall.

"There she sat with her mouth open, gasping. And when I took hold of her to give her a shake, she was cold with fear. Cold in this weather! I told her to pray to Saint Barbara, to ask Saint Barbara to take our spire under her protection. I shan't be in the least surprised if the lightning brings it down."

"Is Dame Adela as pretty as ever?" the blind nun asked.

"Yes, I think so," said Dame Helen, and at the same moment Dame Margaret said, "No, no! Nothing like so pretty. Her teeth are beginning to decay."

"Well, to my eyes, she is still pretty. Though she spoils herself by walking in the sun and getting freckled."

"Yes, and now she is growing thin."

Finally they agreed that Dame Adela was by no means the beauty she had been, and that by her twenty-fifth year she would be positively haggard. Dame Margaret added that no one could expect to keep her beauty in the climate of Oby; the most one could hope for was to maintain a pleasant expression.

After they had taken themselves away Dame Cecily began to despise herself for the entertainment she had found in them. While she still had her sight she had preferred beyond anything else to draw caricatures and grotesques; and perhaps it was for this that God had blinded her. She tried to hold in her mind's eye the beauty her bodily eye had slighted, but it was not much use: the recollection of Adela's novice loveliness wavered out before the image of Dame Margaret maintaining a pleasant expression. She lay gasping for breath, sometimes waving a branch of elder to drive away the flies. Guiltily—for there is no more abject sense of guilt than that which is born from recurrent bouts of pain—she felt another spell of her face-ache coming upon her. If they had been able to find any alleviation she would not have felt so guilty; but nothing overcame it, neither draughts nor plasters nor pulling out her teeth nor change of season. It persisted like an original sin, and the kindest thing they could do was to overlook it.

She waved her branch toward the sound of the flies and tried to direct her thoughts elsewhere. Poor Dame Adela!—so lovely, so stupid, and so much afraid of thunder. For days now she must have been dragging herself about in an agony of apprehension: straining her ears for the first growl of thunder, starting in terror if the sunlight should happen to flash back from some reflecting surface, a bowl of water or a dangled key. Of course she expected the lightning to strike the spire, and talk of Saint Barbara would increase the apprehension to a certainty, just as the thought of Saint Lucy's eyes on a platter wrenched Dame Cecily's own eye-sockets.

The air was stifling as ever, yet something told her of a diminution of light. Clouds must be covering the sun. She heard the men in the field shouting to each other, dogs barking, the creaking of axles. The sounds were like pictures in a psalter, brilliant and minute. Excitement heightened them like gold-leaf. Below the window she heard the Widow Figg's slow mumbling tones, and Dame Alice's sharper note replying, "No, no! Not yet. It will threaten and go past, just as it did yesterday. I won't have my poor fish defrauded."

She heard them come back from the well with their clattering buckets and go toward the fish-pond. Far away, so far away that it seemed to be something sighing in the room, there was a long puff of sound. It might be thunder, it might be a gust of wind. A door banged.

Though she was blind she saw the first lightning-flash. It had traversed her senses and left her gasping before she heard it confirmed by Dame Adela's wailing cry and the bellow of thunder overhead. The house began to resound with footsteps, questions, orders, exclamations. There was another terrific thunderclap, and the rain fell in torrents. A voice somewhere outside the building called out, "Help! Help! Here—at the fish-pond."

They've fallen in, thought Dame Cecily. Apparently she was the only person to hear Dame Alice's outcries. An obligation of compassion overcame her amusement, she went to the door and said to someone going by that Dame Alice seemed to be in the fish-pond and needing help. The footsteps were stayed. There was a pause, a breath drawn in, and the prioress exclaimed in a loud sharp voice, "What's that you say?"

"Dame Alice, dear Mother. I heard her calling for help. I think she must have fallen into the fish-pond."

Without answering, the prioress walked slowly away. Dame Cecily supposed, but without much surprise, that she had said the wrong thing: such mishaps had been frequent since her blindness. She stood about hoping that someone else would come by, for her face-ache was less acute, and she would have liked to discuss the storm. But there was only a gabble of voices, calling for cloths and basins for the rain was coming through the dormitory ceiling, and Dame Margaret saying, "The prioress? Where is the prioress? We should ask her what to do."

The prioress had gone out by the side door and into the hedged walk leading to the fish-pond. She walked slowly, setting her feet with deliberation on the puddled path. She was so fat and the hedges so overgrown that she had to fold her veil and her skirts around her in order to pass.

"Help! Help!"

Dame Alice crouched by the fish-pond, bending forward as though she were landing some enormous fish. But it was Magdalen's feet that she was clasping to her bosom, and the rest of Magdalen lay face downward under water. Clasping Magdalen's feet as though in a frenzy of prayer, she looked at the prioress and continued to scream. Sir Ralph, sheltering under the walnut tree, had heard the screams, saying to himself that Dame Alice screamed just as she sang—with hearty efficiency and without a trace of sensibility.

For a minute or two the prioress looked at Dame Alice. She

wanted to go away and leave the woman to get on with it; but she could not afford to retreat a second time. She drew a deep breath, stooped down, and unclasped Dame Alice's hands. It was as if she were pulling open the lock of a fetter. Magdalen's legs dropped into the water, their descent propelled her body a little farther from the rim of the pond. The ripples spread and subsided, the raindrops speckled them. Dame Alice's hands settled heavily on the wet grass. The prioress became aware that she had left off screaming. In silence they looked at Magdalen's body, which lay, unnaturally large, unnaturally still, under about a foot of water.

The prioress said with profound conviction, "Fool!" Her face puckered up into the grimace of a thwarted baby and became scarlet. Without another word she turned and stumped back into the house.

Dame Cecily supposed that a fresh outburst of scurrying and exclamations was caused by another leak. Even when the door of the infirmary opened and let in shuffling footsteps and heavy breathings, the noise of dripping water that came in with them only bore out this supposition.

"I don't know why we bring her in here," said Dame Eleanor's voice. "She is certainly dead. Lord, what a weight she is!"

"Lay her face downward, so, and help me to rock her. No, not so hard. Gently, like a cradle." This was Dame Lilias. "Where are the hot cloths?"

"They are bringing them."

Water splashed on the floor. From her corner Dame Cecily asked, "Who is dead?"

For a long time Dame Eleanor and Dame Lilias laboured over the dead woman. The monotonous creaking of boards and rustling of garments, the rhythm of their breathing, the smell of hot linen and hot wine, became soothing as a lullaby. Away to the eastward, over the ocean now, the thunder growled softly. From time to time the nuns spoke of Sir Ralph, wondering when he would come to do his part for the dead. The situation embarrassed them, they were careful to speak of him only in terms of his office. Only Dame Dorothy, coming in to report that he was still being searched for, spoke out what they all were thinking, saying that no doubt he would now run mad again, an awkward thing to get over when the bishop was so imminent.

The storm broke the drought. But on the morrow it was as hot as ever—a steaming, oppressive heat. Everything began to go wrong. The cream soured. The food in the larder spoiled. Doors stuck. Patches of mildew came out on the walls. The house was invaded by hordes of ants. Feeling as though she had been hit over the head by a pole-axe, the prioress drove on through these various calamities, hearing of each new disaster with the grinning patience of despair. She was even patient with Dame Dorothy, who pursued her everywhere, saying that as the Widow Figg had drowned in the fish-pond it would be impossible to serve the bishop with carp.

Every report of something gone wrong, every demand, every inquiry, ended with a comment on how unfortunate it was that Dame Alice should choose this juncture to go to pieces. For Dame Alice, prostrated by shock, had become as worthless as Adela. She did nothing but weep, pick quarrels, do all over again what someone else had done already, and complain of Dame Lilias—who had usurped, she said, her function in the infirmary and so mismanaged the Widow Figg that she had died. For how could anyone drown in the fish-pond? It was not deep enough to drown a dog in. Again and again she told her story of how the Widow Figg, dazzled by the first flash of lightning, had uttered a great shriek, declaring that the fiend was upon her; and had slipped, and fallen into the fish-pond, where she lay wallowing, too frightened to help herself, and too heavy to be pulled out, though Dame Alice had strained her arms trying to lift her. Then Dame Alice would roll back her sleeves and show her swollen arms.

Her story and her big arms were disgustingly exuberant in such hot weather. Though as a rule a person with a story is popular, Dame Alice aroused nothing but dislike and avoidance; and because she expressed a strong desire to have an interview with the prioress, only the prioress could understand her feelings and soothe them, Dame Margaret and Dame Helen took special pains to thwart this desire. Dame Alice, feeling their ill-will, and seeing them so constantly called to consult with their

Superior, could draw only one conclusion: that they had been told the true story of Magdalen's death.

For the first time in her term of office the prioress was finding it natural to turn to her two senior nuns for support. Their sympathies were no wider than a coffin—but wide enough to lie down in. Being themselves old and stiff and pained by any departure from the normal, they could understand something—not all—of what it had cost her to tell Sir Ralph of Magdalen's death. Breathless, and red in the face, she had blurted it out to him—like an order. "Drowned," he had said, drawing out the word as though he would never come to the end of it, as though the word were itself some dark pool in the Waxle Stream which he would never plumb to the bottom. "Drowned." She hastened on to talk about the burial and requiem masses. "Drowned," he said again; and it was almost as though he spoke with some kind of assent and approval.

It is an old observation that the drowning never drown alone: they take something along with them, if possible the would-be rescuer, if not him, then a reed, a handful of turf, a handful of ice. Magdalen Figg had taken away the prioress's only sentimentality: her sense of kinship with the young. Completely old, she stood on the threshold of Oby to welcome Bishop Walter.

But at her age it takes more than a shock and a few days of self-reproaching to alter the long habit of the body. Saying to himself, "So you are the Prioress Matilda!" Bishop Walter saw what he was prepared to see: a burly old woman whose air, at once imperious and jovial, made her seem better fitted to rule a brothel than a nunnery. Meanwhile to the Frampton novices it seemed that Saint Nicholas himself had come to Oby. Dame Cecily, present with the rest, was soon able to put together a mind's-eye picture from such whispered exclamations as "A bishop out of the Golden Legend!" "What dignity for such a small man!" "Oh dear, they should not allow him to get wet!" Snuffling Dame Lilias beside her, she asked in an undertone, "What is he like?" "White as thistledown," was the answer. The bishop's voice, however, was unexpectedly resonant. It was a golden, rather syrupy voice with a chanting intonation. It puzzled her to find it sound so familiar until she recognized that it had much in common with Dame Alice's singing. During the Te Deum she was able to make sure of this, for Dame Alice sang loud and sweet. Too loud, indeed, and too sweet—but if it betokened that she had recovered from her tempest of nerves they could be glad of it. Through all the hubbub of the final preparations there had run an undeclared dread that Dame Alice would make some sort of scene before the bishop; but with his coming she became useful and cheerful, just as usual.

The dinner, thought Dame Lilias, went off very well—except that there was rather too much of it. The bishop had arrived with an unexpectedly small retinue: two secretaries, his chaplain, and a body-servant. But the surplus food went to the poor so it could not be called wasted. Immediately after dinner the bishop hoisted himself nimbly into the chapter-house and got to work.

Outside fell the rain, a persistent small rain. Inside, the bishop asked questions in a voice of persistent sweetness. His two secretaries sat beside him, writing steadily, and in addition he took notes himself. His questions went into the minutest detail and covered everything: the number of vestments, their age and state of repair; the number of cows and how many were in milk; the number of household servants, their wages and perquisites; the state of the quire books and of the brewing-tubs; what became of the nuns' old clothes, how often the nuns were let blood, how often their heads were shorn; how many fires were lit during the year, how many doles given at the wicket, who mended the casks, what precautions were taken against fire. Coming to the subject of revenues and expenditures the questions ramified and became yet more searching. The account-books and all the more recent business papers had been put out in readiness for him; but from time to time there were others he wished to examine. While these were being fetched he sat with his head in his hands, his fine white hair stirring in the draughts that scourged the chapter-house; but the moment the new document was before him he came out of his abstraction with a smile and began gently, politely, patiently, to ask questions again. Such an interrogation was impressive but not intimidating. He was so lucid, so methodical, that each obedientiary came out of her examination with the sense that she had given a good account of her ministry, while the listeners felt that they were assisting at a very fine sort of performance. Only when the sitting was broken off did the nuns realize how exceedingly tired they were and how their limbs ached, as though they had been taking some violent and unaccustomed exercise.

Supper had been made ready in the prioress's chamber, a suitable supper—light but reviving—for a frail old man. But he excused himself with childish simplicity, saying that he was sleepy, and went to his bed with some bread and milk. Rosy and refreshed as a child, he reappeared to attend the night office, wrapped in a white woollen gown.

His chaplain and his two secretaries spoke of him almost with adoration. They had more time to bestow such confidences the next day, for after a morning with the account-books he sat alone in the chapter-house receiving each nun in turn for her private interview.

When Dame Lilias went in it seemed to her that she carried with her all the fluster of housewifery and would be unable to speak except of geese and brewing-tubs and the price of almonds. He held out his cold ring for her kiss. When she gave her name he recalled that she was cellaress, and made her somewhat of a lecture about the responsibility of such a post; only after this did he begin to poke about among his papers for the letters dealing with her application to become an anchoress. She repeated the tale of her long melancholy, of how Sir Ralph had bade her pray to Saint Leonard, of how poorly she had done so; and of how the saint had felled her to the ground and then spoken to her. It was disconcerting to see the bishop make a note of his words. But the words of a saint, however memorable to the hearer, may be less striking at second hand; besides, he was an old man, and made notes of everything. He manifested neither surprise nor disbelief. Saints often speak, he said—more often than they are attended to. He told her of his sister, a nun at Barking, who had twice been addressed by heavenly voices. On the first occasion the voice warned her that the tap of a wine-cask had not been properly turned off, so that the wine was wasting. On the second occasion, when his sister had cracked a nut and found nothing inside it but dust and a fat white grub, a voice had rebuked her disappointment by exclaiming, "You should thank God for this picture of a good nun!"

Without a change in his tone of voice he began to question her about Oby. She admitted that there was often talking at meals and after compline, that sometimes the nuns ate sweets in the dormitory, and gossiped, and took the name of God in vain, and kept pets. As she answered these inquiries the triviality of the offences overwhelmed her with boredom and melancholy; and when he asked her if there were no graver offences, no fornications or abortions, her voice was almost apologetic as she replied that no such things had happened within her memory.

At intervals the bishop sniffed. Perhaps he had caught a cold. Bishops visiting Oby usually caught colds. He had the abstracted look of one who feels an ailment gathering within him. He sat sideways to her, his mantle shrugged round him, his eyes averted.

"And you wish to become an anchoress. Why? What gave you this idea?"

She could only say over again and with less confidence what she had said before. Would he once more make a note of the saint's words? But instead he turned on her suddenly and fixed on her a long rigid stare. It struck her that she had seen exactly such a look from King Matt, an old lunatic beggar whom she had served at the wicket. It was part of his madness to believe himself a monarch, and while his hand clutched at the dole he would stare angrily out of his red-rimmed eyes as if to enforce his delusion of might and majesty. But then the bishop smiled, and lost all resemblance to King Matt. In a murmuring voice he said, "When God gives me leave, I, too, shall look for some hermitage," and dismissed her.

When Dame Philippa entered after Dame Lilias the bishop was still abstractedly smiling, so much lost in contemplation that he did not appear to notice her. Dame Philippa, a nun of considerable shrewdness, immediately said to herself, No one looks like that for nothing. I must not be led away into criticizing anything.

Says all is well, noted the bishop. *Obstinate and a liar.* His handwriting grew neater as his mistrust and indignation grew. Even before that worthy honest nun, Dame Alice, gave him her report, he had suspected that he was in the midst of a conspiracy to pull wool over his eyes. No nunnery could be so pleased to welcome a bishop on a Visitation as this nunnery had pretended to be. That dinner; those too evident regrets that he had not brought a pack of young clerks with him; that red-faced prioress, with her recollections of all the other bishops who had held the see before him; those undisciplined little novices, staring at him as though he were a monkey or a unicorn, even peeping round the door of his chamber. . . . Where was virgin trepidation, where was the mortified life. Where was the oil? It was a house of foolish virgins, lacking prudence, propriety, solvency. The bookkeeping was scandalous, and the priest—though more to be pitied than deplored—really ought to be replaced by a younger man. For in her determination to cover her tracks Dame Alice had represented Sir Ralph as a good, simple man, worn out by his unavailing struggle to correct the levity of his flock. Being so simple he had been completely hoodwinked by Dame Lilias who, repudiating even the featherweight discipline of Oby, had invented a vocation to become an anchoress. But did she look like an anchoress? Even the prioress (Dame Alice continued) was shocked and incredulous at first; but Dame Lilias had talked her round, promising that her water-meadows and saltings along the River Alde should remain in the convent revenues. Burdened with debts, the prioress had given way. But was it not outrageous that Dame Lilias could talk of *her* water-meadows, *her* saltings, as if she had never forsworn the world's goods? She was always like that, however, in great things and in small. There was a little comb she used (the bishop noted the comb), and once when Dame Alice had also made use of it Dame Lilias picked it up, turned as red as a soul in hell-fire, and cried out, Whose hairs are these in my comb?

"Oh, I am as wretched among them as a pelican on the housetops!" exclaimed Dame Alice. The bishop only responded with a slight frown; but no doubt he disliked learned nuns. She glided on to how the nuns despised her for her lack of learning, and thought her only fit to work in the kitchen. "To labour is to pray," replied the bishop, but only as one says an amen; there was no malice in the words.

This plain, honest, good woman made a most congenial impression on the bishop, and he noted and underlined her desire to leave Oby for some simple God-fearing nunnery where she could live as inconspicuously as possible.

On the third day he went away. Talking him over, they decided that he was not so remarkable as rumour had made him out to be, neither so saintly nor so eccentric—certainly not the kind of man to fly over a market-place. A few hours after his departure the wind changed, the low roof of cloud broke into towering masses of vapour. It was a pity that he had not seen the place at its best, with the clouds sailing through the intense blue of the sky and seeming to set their course by Dame Alicia's spire. It was a pity, too, that the second key of the convent chest should not have turned up till after he had gone, for he had been rather pettish about it being mislaid. But things always fall out that way, and the Visitation was over and might well have been worse.

Sir Ralph walked out and stood in the sun, sighing and hearing his gown flap about him. He supposed he was thinking of Magdalen until he discovered that it was Mamillion he was thinking of. On such a day, the first day of autumn, Mamillion would have set out on another of his wanderings. On such a day the blind Lord of Brocton would have mounted his horse and ridden past the blackberry thickets and the sodden beanstacks, knowing the one by the smell of hot wine and the other by the stink of decay. Magdalen was lost, and little remained. Yet he could re-read the poem of Mamillion. The Lady of Brocton had sent him a copy some time since. It was beautifully written, he had no excuse not to have read it. Well, he would read it now. This coming winter he would read it, spinning it out. Then he remembered that he must get back his copy of the *Georgics* from Dame Lilias. Poor woman, her affair was scotched, no doubt of it. Observation of Bishop Walter had filled Sir Ralph with forebodings—a religious cockatrice, a man with neither meat nor mercy in him.

William Holly came by, slackened his pace, and remarked

that Sir Ralph might do worse than think of getting himself another saddle.

"Too stiff," said Sir Ralph. "It's a cushion I need. If your wife has any feathers to spare she can remember me."

William Holly's glance roved over the spire, the gate-house, the yellowing tufts of wormwood, the rain-plumped islands of moss on the thatch, as if to see whether the bishop had made any difference in them. Then he looked along the track toward the point on the horizon where the bishop's party had disappeared from sight some hours before and said, "Well! Now we've got Martinmas to think of."

Having thus expressed his condolence on the loss of Magdalen Figg and his mistrust, tempered by scorn of all bishops, of this particular bishop, he walked on. So he, too, smelled something in the wind.

For his next sermon Sir Ralph took as a text: *For the foundations shall be cast down. And what hath the righteous done?* To him the implication seemed so clear that there was no need to labour it; accordingly the bulk of the sermon was devoted to classical examples of calamity, such as Job, Tobit's father slumbering, Caesar on the Ides of March, Roncesvaux, and the Gadarene swine, which got in by accident and had to be driven out again. Dame Helen recalled her uneasiness about the spire. Dame Lilias tried not to recall that King Matt stare from the bishop. Of the two Frampton novices the elder thought with detestation of Brutus and the younger wondered if fish gall would cure Dame Cecily. Only Dame Lovisa snuffed out an application, and sat flicking her eye from the preacher to the prioress. But she kept her own counsel, and as a warning the sermon fell flat. It was not even given credit for being a portent or a coincidence, for when the bishop's letter came it caused a stir in which no one had time to remember a sermon.

Before reading the letter aloud in chapter the prioress studied it by herself and digested her feelings enough to have a certain anticipation of amusement. At any rate, she would show them that she was not so much run to seed as they might suppose.

Greeting his dear sisters, Bishop Walter informed them that he had earnestly considered the plight of their house, which was like a house builded upon sand. As a house builded upon sand is liable to be inhabited by imps, apes, and serpents, the house of Oby was full of pride, sloth, greed, falsehoods, worldliness, pet animals, and private property. His grieving eyes had beheld spiced meats, soft cushions, perfumed and flowing mantles, better befitting harlots than the brides of Christ whose joy it should be to feed on roots and wear narrow garments. Instead of the silence of the tomb, which to the ear of religion is music, his hearing had been tormented by the yelpings of little dogs and the clattering of egg-whisks. Even more had it been wounded by overhearing such words as, Where is my brooch? or, Who has taken my spoon? Yet among all this care for worldly things he had discerned no care for convent property. Keys were mislaid and could not be found. Windows did not fasten securely. Account-books were deformed by such entries as *sundries, one shilling and one penny,* or *things bought at Waxelby:* entries shocking and inarticulated as the young of bears. Furthermore, he had noted an entry for October eleventh, in the year of Our Lord thirteen hundred and seventy, saying only *Rabbit.* No mention of the cost nor the purpose of the rabbit, no record even of whether the rabbit had been bought or sold.

The prioress drew breath and read on.

As Mary was preferred before Martha for having chosen the better part, a household of nuns might be forgiven their careless stewardship (the more so since women are ordained the weaker vessel and have no business sense) if those same nuns neglected the goods of the world by reason of their devotion to heaven. But at Oby he found no such excuse. The office was performed with worldly glibness, the song was too loud, the words were not fully pronounced. He had seen no traces of true piety, no fear, no trepidation. All was blighted by complacency, and an old incense-boat had been sold without permission. Also, he had seen in the poultry yard a peacock without a peahen, reprehensible both as wastefulness and thwarting the purpose of God, who framed the animal creation to multiply the food of christians. With even greater concern he had noted the unfitness of the prioress to hold her office. Supine, and weak of purpose, gullible, and a groveller (the prioress remitted this passage with particular elegance of diction), she was a toy in the hands of her nuns, and cheated by her servants. Her incompetent stewardship was reflected in the state of her house: burdened with debt, failing to call in its rents and dues, selling sacred vessels, and not keeping up a sufficient intake of novices. The bishop, therefore, grieving paternally, would apply remedies. First, he would nominate three additional nuns; second, he would commission two psalters, which he would pay for at a just and reasonable price when they were completed and in his hands; third, to restore the finances of the house and yet avoid the scandal of a prioress deposed for mismanagement and levity, he would appoint a custos, to oversee the temporal affairs of the house of Our Lady and Saint Leonard till all its debts had been paid off.

Raising her voice above an outburst of horror and indignation, the prioress read the bishop's final assurances of the prayers and personal austerities he would offer up on behalf of her establishment. There seemed no reason to doubt their sincerity.

"The crocodile!" groaned Dame Margaret. "This, after all our trouble to please him!"

"That rabbit—if only he had asked me about the rabbit I would have explained about it, for I remember it perfectly. It was a rabbit . . ."

No one ever hesitated to interrupt Dame Helen, and Dame Eleanor exclaimed, "If a bishop were Antichrist he would have to assert himself in his first Visitation. Let him say what he pleases! But these nominated nuns!"

"But the bursar!" said Dame Dorothy. "Surely that is the worst of all. Such a slight to you, Dame Helen! Such a slight to our dear Mother!"

"As if convents never had a debt! All convents have debts."

"Yes, and three nominees arriving with no dowries and enormous appetites. That will better it!"

"Three new novices for you, Dame Philippa!"

"Three bishop's pets, ready to grow into tattletales. I'll novice them!" The colour rushed into her long face, mild as a sheep's.

"I wish we had roasted the peacock," said Dame Cecily, adding, "The perfumes must be you, Dame Lilias."

"I'm afraid so."

It was the first time she had spoken. Dame Alice looked at her searchingly and said, "I wonder who told him all this. Someone must have given him a bad report of the house. Very unfortunate!"

"There's worse to come," remarked the prioress amiably. "Do you know what I have been thinking all this while? That I shall have to tell William Holly about the custos."

Dame Adela's wild-flower countenance was shaken with a thought. "Why should not William Holly be our custos?"

The nuns laughed and clapped their hands. Not for years, thought the prioress, have they been in such good humour. Holy Bishop Walter had been catnip to them—and to herself: she had not felt so alert for years.

Meanwhile, Dame Lovisa was saying that she would undertake a psalter.

"But who is to put in the pictures and the decorations?"

"There will be the text, he must put up with that. After all, a book is for reading, not for admiring."

She spoke with such decision that no one felt inclined to contradict the statement, though no one agreed with it. Dame Helen whispered to Dame Lilias, "Another de Stapledon prioress."

Another de Stapledon prioress, thought Dame Lilias, looking at her persecutor. And I shall be here to endure her. In five years, in ten, in twenty: as plain as the voice of Saint Leonard another voice now spoke in her bosom, saying, You won't get away.

X. TRISTE LOYSIR
(October 1374–May 1377)

Quare fremuerent gentes, wrote Dame Lovisa in her heavy, undistinguished script. The first psalm was behind her, and already the distaste for David which became so marked in her later years had begun to form itself. The man talked like Dame Helen: he said what he had to say, often silly enough, and then immediately said it all over again in rather different words. As something to sing it might be well enough, but as a statement from one rational being to another—and God is the sum of rational being—it was poor. The sunlight fell on the page and lit her scarred face and the few light eyelashes stuck in her swollen eyelids. Her hand, moving in the sunlight, displayed all its defects, the toad-skin, the misshapen nails, the look of being ingrained with dirt which overlies unwholesome blood. Her attitude and expression showed a slow-burning thrifty happiness, and she resembled a virtuous wolf. Wolfishly, she had got her teeth into the psalter, she was at last doing something positive and profitable. Thus Dame Lovisa, unwittingly, was a confirmation of what Bishop Walter was writing on that same morning in the peroration which closed the first book of his treatise *De Cantu.*

> *The song of David tempers the clarion of the victor; accords the inharmonious cries of the oppressed; awakens the slothful; mollifies the furious; rebukes the luxurious; exalts the despairing; purges the glutton; abashes the proud; confutes the envious. It instructs the ignorant and refreshes the scholar. And as the psaltery is made of reeds of differing lengths, varying from the most treble to the most grave and yet all by the lips of the player breathe forth a melody, even so doth the psalter conform itself to every mood of man and melodiously control and express them.*

He leaned back and shivered. In spite of the warmth of the day and the sound of the two wasps buzzing over a dish of pears which lay on the window-sill, he was cold with the effort of expressing his thoughts and controlling that metaphor of the psaltery. Now he looked at the two wasps and smiled vaguely. Wasps, he thought, are the laity of bees. It was remarkable, he had noticed it before, how one metaphor puts you in train for another. He began to think of how the wasps and the bees could find their place in the second book of his treatise. Both make a noise, and that would bring them into the fold of the title. The bees are the religious, no doubt of that, leading chaste lives, obedient, constantly industrious, storing honey in such abundance that they can feed both themselves and the laity with sweetness: the wasps on the other hand . . . The wasps had been the laity of the bees in the first conception of the metaphor, but two laities would be troublesome and lead to confusion. The wasps should be . . . The door opened. His chaplain showed in a short man with a snub nose and green eyes that were staring and sorrowful like those of a hungry cat. He was Henry Yellowlees, a clerk in lesser orders. He had been recommended to the bishop by the abbot of Revesby (whose distant relation he was) as being honest and mathematical and the sort of man the bishop would find useful. The bishop disliked recommended men and so far had not found a use for him. But now on the report of his chaplain he thought Henry Yellowlees might do very well for Oby, and no doubt his mathematics would make him a sharp accountant.

Opening with a reference to the valued opinion of the abbot of Revesby, the bishop went on to his Visitation of Oby and its shortcomings. Henry Yellowlees interrupted him to say that he was sorry to hear it. The establishment had a good name in the locality as a nunnery that went along quietly and had no scandals. He had a soft diffident voice—a voice that the bishop, if he had been more attentive to humankind, would have recognized as the kind of voice that goes with an obstinate character. But while noting that Henry Yellowlees had implied better knowledge of his diocese than he had himself, the bishop exclaimed, "A whited sepulchre! And the buildings are in very bad repair. That must be one of the first things you look into."

Henry Yellowlees said that he remembered hearing that the spire had fallen shortly after its building but that he understood it had been replaced by a much finer spire. Why the chaplain should have put forward this fellow, thought the bishop, qualifying the fellow as an upstart fellow, he would subsequently inquire into; but he went on to explain, with great smoothness and clarity of diction, all that Henry Yellowlees must do as custos: which amounted to discovering all that was or was not done at Oby and reporting it to Bishop Walter. He then rang for the secretary and told him to bring the documents relating to Oby, and spent some time reading them aloud with comments. Then he handed them over, saying that he could spare no more time and that Henry Yellowlees must study and digest them at leisure, and bring any doubts or queries to him.

Henry Yellowlees went away with a mind divided between loathing the bishop and looking forward to Oby. The appointment was not congenial: he knew nothing of domestic administration and hated fiddle-faddle; yet it was an appointment. He was tired of hanging about waiting for his cousin's recommendation to take effect, and being jostled by secretaries. He was in debt too. Though this appointment carried no salary with it his expenses would be paid, one can always make a little out of that; and an unpaid appointment may lead to a paid one, and the prospect of being led to a paid appointment improves one's credit. His spirits, sharpened by disliking the bishop as an appetite is sharpened by pickles, took an upward turn. He began to think well of a future in which he would clear up the usual nuns' tangle at Oby and become Oby's champion against that sanctimonious old gadfly.

Henry Yellowlees was too poor to have a lodging of his own. He slept in a hostel for poor travellers and spent wet days in the nave of the cathedral, fine days among the stumps of masonry and grassy hummocks which had once been a Roman temple and now was the city's rubbish-tip. Today was fine; but a wind was blowing which would toss the papers about, so he turned into a tavern, ordered some beer, and sat down to read about herrings and vestments and rents of meadows and repairs of roofs and bequests for masses. He read with such concentration that he was scarcely aware of the lad who came in and sat down beside him, except that he continually scratched himself. Only when a louse crawled across the details of the Methley tithe did Henry Yellowlees move himself a little away: he had picked over his shirt the day before and did not want to be at that trouble again before the week's end. Other lice, however, had already established themselves; and that, though he did not know it, was why he presently sickened with typhus, and had to squeeze through an interminable thicket where every thorn that pricked him struck at the same time a loud iron bell and every bell-stroke must be counted, instead of riding across the cheerful October landscape to Oby.

It was not till Saint Stephen's Day that he was well enough to set out, riding a horse provided by the bishop, a very poor beast. He was to lodge with the priest at Lintoft—"to spare the house of Oby any temptation to distraction and needless expense," was Bishop Walter's message; but to Henry Yellowlees, his temper worn threadbare by sickness, it was patent that he would lodge at Lintoft in order not to be bribed by the nuns.

For his part, Sir John Idburn was very ready to welcome a visitor. Sixteen years at Lintoft had exhausted his sensibility, he had settled down, come to terms with his parishioners and even with their pigs. Nothing remained of the earlier Sir John except a liking for company, the scar on his thigh where a boar-pig had ripped him, and the scar on his memory where Sir Ralph had snubbed him. He told Henry Yellowlees that the Oby nuns were proud, heartless, and cared for nothing but eating and drinking. He also recounted the old tales that had so much disgusted him when he first heard them from his housekeeper: the sorceries of Dame Isabel, the babies strangled at birth, and so on. Time had mellowed them into being good stories, and he told them with every intention of pleasing, but they fell on drowsy ears, for Henry Yellowlees was overcome with a day's hard riding and a supper of raw onions. By the morning he remembered little beyond an impression that Oby was a very unpleasant establishment, and that only such malice as Bishop Walter's could have made him its custos.

Expecting a cold welcome, he got it. As it had not occurred to Oby that anyone sent by the bishop could be less ill-intentioned than the bishop himself, there had been an unanimous agreement among the ladies to cold-shoulder him. Accordingly, a very ill-favoured nun who introduced herself as Dame Lovisa met him at the door, inquired after the bishop's health, excused the prioress from attending on the grounds of sickness, and suggested that he should begin by going round the outbuildings. With this he was handed over to William Holly.

Through the chinks in the window-screens the nuns watched this peregrination. Nothing could have been better, they agreed, than Dame Lovisa's reception. Even her singular ugliness was recognized as providential, a putting of Oby's worst face forward. First Dame Lovisa; next William Holly: the new custos would spend a nasty forenoon. Plastering Dame Adela's mouth to stifle any indiscreet cries of pleasure, they moved round the inside of the house as the two men walked round its outside.

The custos stared upward so intently that Dame Margaret said he must be looking at them. He was looking at the spire. As the web of low-lying cloud scurried under the wind it seemed to breathe like a living thing. Sometimes it inhaled the light of day, and then its pallor enriched to the colour of a primrose; a moment later it waned, and pulled the misty air over it like a veil; and whether it brightened or waned it seemed to be flying toward him against the scudding sky, so that he felt that in a moment it would bend down to his embrace. The bailiff stood beside him drawing his attention to a faulty piece of guttering, a wet wing of thatch that beat against the rafters, the damaged coign on the brewhouse, the crack that ran down the granary wall, the great puddle that lay stinking and soaking outside the kitchen door and ought to be filled up, the tattered reed fencing, the well-head which had been nothing but a trouble since the men who came about the spire started mucking it about, the rot in the beams, the doors off their hinges, the scandalous condition of the barns. He looked where he was bid; but the spire, or the thought of the spire, distracted his attention, and at every lightening in the atmosphere he turned to stare after it, to see it breathe in the daylight and come to life.

Now they came to some pigsties. Pigs, he had learned from the priest of Lintoft, meant a great deal in this locality: he must assert himself and say something about the pigs. Remembering that three hours earlier he had ridden past droves of Lintoft pigs snorting among the oaken scrub, Henry Yellowlees remarked on these pigs still being in their sty. William Holly, his bark brightening at a prospect of contradiction, replied that he had always given his pigs a long lie, and would continue to do so. Henry Yellowlees recalled that sloth was one of the accusations against Oby. He said that the pigs must be half-starving. William Holly said that a long lie in the morning fattens a pig. Henry Yellowlees remarked that this was mere legend and against nature. The pig by nature is a foraging animal.

"Not my pigs!" exclaimed the bailiff. "My pigs don't need to go round poking their noses in where they have no call to! My pigs aren't clerks and custoses!"

Up to the knees in mud the two men glared at each other, then they waddled stiffly off in different directions.

When Henry turned to enjoy the spire in solitude it wrapped itself in vapour. A tooth began to ache in his upper jaw and immediately a confederate tooth in his lower jaw ached in sympathy. The pain shuttled from one to another. In the barn they were threshing. The noise of the flails resounded, clouds of chaff blew by. It was starvingly cold, lifeless and lightless. It was as though the sun held such a day so cheap that it would scarcely trouble to light it. An Egyptian Day, thought Henry Yellowlees, a day blasted in the calendar. See into everything yourself, the bishop had told him. Now, with nothing to rely on but the bishop whom he hated, he obeyed the instructions, wandering about the outbuildings, peering into sheds, and finding the wind round every corner. The inventory rattled in his hand. Sometimes a woman hurried by him, or a child, muddy to the thighs, blear-eyed and snivelling. "Good woman, can you tell me . . ."—"My child, where shall I find . . ." It was no use. They ran past him as though deaf and blind. Already the news that the bailiff had quarrelled with the custos had flown through the manor, and with the loyalty of fear no one would be seen speaking to the man whom William Holly had quarrelled with.

Presently he found his horse. It had been moved from a clean stall to a dirty one. His hand on the bridle-rein shook with rage as he led it out. He would stay no longer, to be blown around with the chaff. He would ride off and make a formal complaint to the bishop.

"Surely you're not going away without eating something? It's a cold ride from here to Lintoft."

The voice came from overhead, from a fat old man who leaned from a window above the gate-house.

Henry Yellowlees dismounted, hitched his horse on the lee-side of the gate-house, and went unwillingly up the crazy stairs. He did not wish to stay, but he did not wish to be seen riding away defeated either. The priest's lodging was as small as a nutshell. Its walls were hung with faded red canvas that rippled as the wind blew through the chinks. A bed took up half the floorspace. His host poured out some beer and cut some hunches of bread and fetched a handful of raisins from a cupboard. The two men sat down side by side on the bed. The thump of the flails seemed to fill the room.

"You've come on a busy day. How do you find things?"

Henry Yellowlees shook his head. He was trying to remember what the bishop's chaplain had told him about the Oby priest. But he could only remember that whatever it was it had prejudiced him against the man.

"What? You don't think much of the corn? The heads were well ripened, at any rate. I have never known a hotter harvest."

Ashamed to say that fear of William Holly had kept him from the threshing floor, Henry Yellowlees remarked that they were late in the threshing.

"Two of the best men are sick."

"This is a time of year when one buries strong men. In summer one buries children. Children die under Leo."

"Children die at all times of the year. The curate at Wivelham buried two of his a little before Christmas. Of course, one might say he should not have had them. But he grieved, like any other sinner."

"Indeed."

This cat-headed fellow, thought Sir Ralph, is no great acquisition. Can he do nothing but munch and drum with his heels on the bedstead?

"Oby seems an unhealthy place. I understand that the prioress and the treasuress are also unwell."

"Ah, yes, poor ladies!" Sir Ralph answered imperturbably.

Henry Yellowlees half-rose from the bed. The room had been growing colder and darker, and now a storm hit the house. Hailstones pattered against the window-screen, the red hangings fluttered. He had to sit down again. To depart at this moment would look petulant; and though he disliked the fat man beside him, he still hoped to find in him—being a man—an ally against this household of invisible women.

Sir Ralph got up and creaked over to the brazier and put on more charcoal.

"There is one thing," he said, "that I hope you will see to now you are our custos. We are wretchedly off for firewood. And the wood-reeve sells it off the manor to anyone who'll pay him a good price for it."

"Poor people must have fires, I suppose. They can't be left to die of cold."

"If anyone is left to die of cold it will be the nuns of Oby. They can't go about from manor to manor wherever an extra penny whistles them."

"If landowners did not offer more than the statutory wage the labourers would not wander," said Henry Yellowlees.

"Young man, that is very true," said Sir Ralph. "Nevertheless, and as I was saying, labourers now move about and live on the country, just as kings do. For if your house has no roof, you can leave it without regret. And if you have no land, you do not have to stay on it. How perspicaciously the scriptures say: The poor ye have always with you. Whoever else is ruined and undone, the poor will always scramble out with something they have managed to snatch from the wreck."

His guest remarked that he did not believe the text about the poor was intended in that sense.

Just what the bishop would send us, thought Sir Ralph. He went on to be as annoying as possible.

"Consider another thing. The poor, being loved by God, are miraculously enabled to love one another. In themselves they are as full of rancour and mistrust as the rest of us, but the grace of God teaches them to be mutually loving and helpful even while their own hearts persuade them to act with malice. And when a poor man rises in the world, it is his own kind who hoist him up. Consider our bishop, for instance. He would be nowhere if he had not started as a nobody. But being a nobody . . ."

It took him aback to hear Henry Yellowlees chuckle. They turned to face each other. Intelligence flashed from one to the other, and then they began to look rather sheepish, embarrassed at the sudden discovery of a common bond.

"H'm," sighed Sir Ralph, the first to recover. "He's a good man of business, they tell me. That's what's needed in a churchman, nowadays."

Having found a mutual dislike they settled down to be affable. They talked of food, pestilence, women, weather, the likelihood of a papal schism and the date of a Last Judgment. Sir Ralph did not consider that a plurality of popes would accelerate the coming of Christ.

"But, on the other hand, the Last Judgment may have happened already," he said in an obliging tone. "In any case, it would be a mistake to expect too much from it. What's done can't be undone, you know."

It began to dawn on Henry Yellowlees that the priest of Oby might be a little crazy.

Smoothing his vast belly, the old man continued, "Take, for instance, the position of the Holy Innocents. As far as they were anything, they were Jews. As such they died in a state of damnation. Are they in hell? I do not see where else they can be. Yet we invoke them and celebrate their martyrdom."

Henry Yellowlees blinked. Sir Ralph looked at him kindly and went on, "That's what you say. But I am convinced they are both blessed and in hell. Such a state is quite possible, and an intelligent man like you should realize it. Hell, you know, must have its saints as well as heaven."

Holding on to the bedstead, Henry Yellowlees asked if Sir Ralph would advance the converse proposition.

"God save us, yes! Paradise is full of the damned. It is their doom and their torment to be in the presence of God. Where else could they feel such infelicity?"

Henry Yellowlees said that damnation was more than infelicity. Infelicity was the common lot of man, and the expectation of continuing to exist in eternity as he had existed in mortality would give man a quite insufficient motive for repentance. Sir Ralph said that on the contrary it would be amply sufficient: if mankind could be brought to believe that the state of damnation would be merely a continuation of life in this world, mankind would be forced to take steps to improve its present living conditions. Why else should God give man the art of logic?

There could be no doubt but that the priest of Oby was mad, riddled with heresies and speculation and quite unfit to be holding his post; but reporting on dilapidated priests was no part of a custos's duty, and he would say nothing to the bishop.

His horse was stamping, the brief January day was closing. He made his farewells to Sir Ralph and found that he did so with regret.

"By the way—the bishop wished me to inquire how his three nominees are settling down, and if you are satisfied with their spiritual estate. Though really it is none of my business."

Presumably habit imposed some kind of sanity, for Sir Ralph's answer was quite ordinary and correct.

Of the bishop's three nominees two had yet to make their profession. But there could be no hope that they would not make it, they were delighted at the good fortune which had transplanted them to the religious life. It was a step up in the world for both of them. Joan Cossey was the daughter of a small tradesman, Amy Hodds a bastard. To be called Dame and live in a cloister was a better prospect than their natural future of scrubbing trenchers, clacking at a loom, and bearing great hordes of hungry children. Dame Sibilla, the third nominee, was a Dunford. To look at she was the image of her great-uncle, with the same slight build, small prim mouth, receding chin, and vehement eyes. Unlike him, she had a loud discordant voice. She was twenty-one and had been for nine years a nun in a small house called Allestree. Pestilence and a cattle plague had brought the house to the brink of ruin, and to readjust its finances two of its nuns had to be farmed out elsewhere.

Joan Cossey and Amy Hodds came with only the minimum of dowry. Their thrifty nominator had seen to that. Dame Sibilla, being a transferred nun, brought no dowry at all. Bishop's kin, and foisted upon them, she did not seem likely to make many friends at Oby. Yet in a little while she was popular; for she brought what to the bulk of the convent was almost as good as a dowry: a narrative. Oby was enlivened by the misfortunes of

Allestree: first came the portents which had foreshadowed the pestilence, the spots on the milk, the horde of invisible swine which flew over during a storm, the mysterious beggar, superhumanly tall and with blue teeth; and then the starving spring, when the nuns wandered about gathering nettles in fields strewn with rotting sheep and oxen, and the two friars who helped them get in the rye harvest, two friars who had seemed rough simple men, full of ordinary jokes, yet when they went on their way a light from heaven trailed from their dusty heels. Whether one believed her stories or no, such stories were pleasant to listen to; and as well as stories Dame Sibilla had a stock of practical wisdom, and could darn and mend and was full of expedients and contrivances.

Being friendly to everyone, she was friendly to Dame Lilias, too.

"Have you noticed," said Dame Alice, "that our Dame Lilias has become quite talkative—to Dame Sibilla?"

There was no need for Dame Alice to insinuate the obvious. Everyone could put two and two together and perceive what part Dame Lilias had played in the catastrophe of the Visitation. Everyone had noticed that for some months previously she had been bland and abstracted, like one who ripens a revenge. Everyone had observed that her interview with Bishop Walter had lasted nearly half an hour and that she had come out looking like a cat coming away from the dairy. When the bishop's letter came it was easy to guess whose malice had subjected them to insults and the ignominy of a custos. Who would have thought Dame Lilias capable of such treachery? It appeared that many would have thought it.

So now more than ever they were banded together to cold-shoulder her. No one wished to sit by her, to pass her the bread at dinner, to tie the fillet on her arm after the blood-lettings. It was remarkable how many elbows jostled her, how many spits happened to land on her back and bosom. Her short sight was nobody's concern. Dame Margaret, seeing her about to stumble over a brazier, said no word of warning, said no word of condolence when Dame Lilias and the brazier together pitched down stairs; said nothing at all until a few days later when during the chanting of the day's psalms she was heard to sing with particular clearness, "What portion shall be given unto thee, thou lying tongue? Even hot burning coals."

The prioress thought it very likely that Dame Lilias had complained (others, no doubt, had also complained); but as Dame Alice had blown up this fresh persecution she took no part in it. Excellent as it might be to dwell together in unity, she could not see herself being pleasurably united with Dame Alice in anything. But it is one of the inconveniences of convent life that though you may suspect your fellow-nun of being a murderess you are obliged to live cheek by jowl with her for the rest of your days, and make the best of it as best you may. The best the prioress could do was to turn her attention elsewhere.

Fortunately there are always practical considerations, and Bishop Walter had supplied her with several new ones. His three nominees stretched the accommodation of the house, the Visitation had somehow cost more than she had meant it to, and though he had inflicted a custos on them the custos had no silver lining, the Oby finances were just as they had been before, the only difference was that now she was hampered in any attempts to set things to rights. A further consideration hung over the future—the question of Sir Ralph. The loss of Magdalen Figg had certainly shaken him, and she thought he was going mad again, though not with such a madness as can be cured by a black cock. This was a different affair, a kind of misty eccentricity into which he might altogether vanish. Against all this she could set nothing but the profits of Dame Lovisa's unappetizing psalters, and the money owing from Esselby. Esselby was a small property lying inland, bequeathed to Oby a hundred years before. It had been profitable then, but the Black Death had almost unpeopled it. The land was not tilled, the mill, since no one brought corn there, paid no dues and fell into ruin. During the prioress-ship of Dame Johanna the convent was glad to rent the old manor house to a family of iron-workers. Being so far away their payments were never reliable, and for the last three years they had paid no rent at all.

One day she spoke of this in chapter.

"Sue them," said Dame Margaret.

"It would cost almost as much. Yet if we do not recover it soon we shall never recover it. These little properties, here, there, and everywhere, are more trouble than they are worth."

Dame Lovisa looked up. "Should we not ask our new custos to collect the Esselby rent for us?"

"Never!" exclaimed Dame Margaret, while at the same moment the prioress laughed and said she might think of it.

This was in February, after Henry Yellowlees' first visit (he had said nothing injurious about Oby, only reporting that the bailiff neglected the pigs, whereon the bishop, knowing more about pigs, told him he was a fool); but it was some time before Dame Lovisa's suggestion was put into effect, for on the first day of April Henry Yellowlees appeared once more, bringing a letter which created such a stir that the Esselby rent slipped everyone's memory until after he had ridden away with Dame Alice behind him. For Bishop Walter informed his dear sister in God that he wished to remove Dame Alice to another house, where her simple piety would be better placed than among the broils and superbities of Oby. Since the Visitation, he said, her plea to be removed had echoed in his ears like the plaint of a turtle-dove; and as she was healthy and active he supposed she could quite well make the journey riding behind Henry Yellowlees.

So she had pleaded to be removed, had she? It was a movement of conscience the prioress had not expected, supposing that murder would lie as quietly under Dame Alice's self-assurance as a dead rat at the bottom of a cream-bowl. She accepted the current indignation with a grave countenance, though she wished that it were possible to have someone to whom she could confide her relief, and her amusement at finding herself obliged to this sweeping and scouring bishop.

Meanwhile, Dame Alice was performing a very creditable *Nunc Dimittis,* tripping to and fro with farewells and parting solicitudes, and at the same time making up a considerable bundle to carry with her to the new house whose austerities would render it so much more congenial to her than Oby. Her parting with the prioress, her kneeling for a last blessing, was exemplary. Both women played their parts with relish, each tendering her performance to the other like a final testimonial of mutual hatred and self-control.

So departed the second Dilworth nun.

In the course of her farewells Dame Alice deposited one parting gift. Breathing on Dame Lilias's cheek she had whispered, "Two women grinding at the mill, the one shall be taken and the other be left." And with a final kiss of peace she added, "Who would have supposed that the bishop would have favoured my request and not yours?"

Thus it became clear to Dame Lilias that the prioress had betrayed her secret. She saw Dame Alice ride off with the same bleak vision as she now saw everything. Everything was visible and everything was lost. Even her melancholy had forsaken her. She was a quite ordinary nun, who would lead an ordinary nun's life, no better than the others and no worse, and dying, would suffer the ordinary pains of purgatory, no sharper and no lighter.

About this time Dame Helen began to fail; and this became another reason to defer mentioning the Esselby rent, for as her wits—scattered at all times—weakened, she was preyed on by doubts and frets about her account-books; though she would not hand them over to anyone else, saying that there was just one thing she must be sure of, one column she must add up again. While they prayed round her death-bed they heard her wandering through income and outgoing, and anxiously explaining to the bishop about that unaccounted-for rabbit. Coming out of her distraction she looked at them gathered round her and reckoned them up with a shaking finger.

"One less; and Dame Alice gone, that's two less. It will be more manageable now," she said hopefully.

By dint of coming regularly once a quarter; praising their singing and taking their medicines; bringing them news of the world and stories of the bishopric; doing little errands and commissions; showing the novices geometrical puzzles, and interfering as little as possible in the convent's management, Henry Yellowlees had become acceptable and was on his way to becoming dear. Sir Ralph was always brisker after his visits too; and that was another reason for welcoming Master Yellowlees, for no one wanted to admit that Sir Ralph was past his usefulness. For his part the custos of Oby also enjoyed his inspections, though as time went on he asked himself what good came of them. Though the day-to-day management was good enough, the long-term muddle was as bad as ever, and worse, and he did not see how it could ever be remedied. If he could get the bishop to attend . . . but the bishop now avoided any mention of Oby, even in his dislikes he was fickle; and as Henry Yellowlees disliked the bishop as steadfastly as ever, he could not bring himself to a degree of intimate conversation which might make the bishop attend. He had been reporting the Esselby debt since 1375, nine times in all, as his reports were quarterly. He supposed it would go on like this forever, that is to say, it would last out his time.

Receiving the bishop's orders to go to Esselby, Henry Yellowlees felt wings break from his shoulders. To travel into a new county, to see strange towns and the unwinding of strange road and the glitter of unforeseen rivers, to hear people talking in a different dialect about things he had no concern with, to be overtaken by dusk in an unfamiliar place: all this made his blood quicken. Yet routine and its slow mildewing of the mind had so far decayed him that to break with his work even for a week or so seemed like a break in the earth's surface, and a minute later he was asking what would become of his scholars —for he now taught in a school for pious poor boys which had been founded by Bishop Walter; and an uncommonly dull set they were, being chosen on merits of piety and poverty without regard to intellectual promise.

That, and everything else, had been arranged for. His route was planned, his expenses reckoned; so much for lodgings, so much for stabling, so much for tolls, and a small sum for gratuities and incidental expenses.

"Please count it," said the treasurer's clerk, pouring out small money from a bag, "and sign the receipt. You will start on the day after the feast of Saint Pancras. We shall recover the money, of course, from the convent of Oby."

The convent of Oby had been lightly taxed. Everything was planned with the greatest economy. For the first night he must lodge with the chaplain of a leper-house, and on the morrow he must ride several miles out of his direct route in order to avail himself of a midday dole at Killdew Priory.

"You will need to ride hard on the last day in order to reach Esselby by nightfall. See that they give your horse a good feed and a good rub down, he will need it. And as these debtors are blacksmiths, they might very well re-shoe the beast."

"What sort of place is Esselby?"

The clerk shrugged his shoulders.

The weather turned wet. All through Saint Pancras' day the rain dripped through the schoolroom roof. The patter of raindrops mixed with the clatter of his pupils' abacuses, and random peals of thunder rumbled in the cold air. But he did not think so much of what a detestable journey lay before him as of the certainty that the school's warden was too much devoted to Bishop Walter to ask for the roof to be mended.

When he set out the sky was still a heavy slate grey, darkening to purple where the sun slashed through the clouds. The night's rain still dripped from the house-eaves, young leaves and immature fruits floated in puddles. Before he had left the bounds of the city he was splashed to the thighs.

Once beyond the gate, riding became easier. He could choose his path, and by keeping to the outer edge of the track he escaped being more muddied than he was muddied already. The sun was now above the horizon, the air was growing warmer, the thatch of the suburb hovels and the dung-heaps before their doors were steaming. This was the brothel quarter. Vice had lately been put out of the city and had settled down philosophically just beyond the gate, waiting till the alarm died away and it could go in again. He remembered hearing a whore in a tavern declaiming at the injustice of this. Within the city walls, she said, clients came and went quickly, as easy as a Hail Mary; but once a poor whore was put outside the wall a client who outstayed the shutting of the gates at nightfall would make it an excuse to stay till morning. How could a whore make a living that way? she asked; and for all the young men, thwarted by this ordinance, what was there but to turn to sodomy?—which was grievous, the more so since many of them had given their lives to God. It would distress the bishop if he knew how hardly his virtuous intentions bore on poor girls. He was so kind a man, and loving to all the poor. Sure enough, as Henry Yellowlees rode by one steaming hovel a young clerk came out from it, yawning and stretching.

Everywhere the cuckoos were screaming. It was a senseless noise, and turned his thoughts to how Francis of Assisi had preached to the birds. Did he number many cuckoos among his devotees? "Would to God I had made you a holy friar and got you off my hands!" his mother had said to him as she lay dying. Afterward he had thought pretty seriously of becoming a friar. Black, though, not grey. He could forgive Francis his cuckoos, preaching so cheerfully from other birds' pulpits, opening their jaws so deedily in the bosom of Mother Church. What, after all, had the saint of Umbria done but lay a new egg in an old nest? No wonder that the laity, seeing the friar begging so hard, staggering under the weight of his bag, streaming with sweat, whisking from door to door, and comparing him with the monk in his cloister, should think the friar the honester of the two. He could forgive Francis his friars. But not his nonsense: not those birds, that wolf, that jackass brotherhood with grass and thistles, sun and moon.

At the summit of a long rise he drew rein and stared out over the landscape. The clouds were gone, only a few shadows were left, hastening to the northward. Brilliant, senseless, irresponsible, the landscape stretched before him. What soul was there, what trace of praise to its Maker? What trace of reason, what trace of purpose, except where man's sad hand had etched it? Alongside the river water-scars like old burns showed where the winter floods had run. Now it was spring. Everything was new, was remade. The night's rain glittered in every runnel, flashed from bush and bramble, lay pearled in the clasp of daisies and liverwort leaves. Rain had washed the face of the earth like the waters of baptism. And the young leaves on the oak tree were not more bright than those which the storm had torn off and cast on the ground, and in the furrows the weeds were growing up with the corn. How can this praise God? he said sternly to the ghost beside him; all this beauty and promise is barely a month old, and already it is full of ruin and has not the sense to know good from evil.

His horse tossed its head, jerking away the flies. Having despatched Francis, he rode on till he found an elder bush, and broke off a handful of twigs and fastened them in the headband. He was beginning to feel pleasure in his journey. It was pleasant to sit with his back against a thorn tree, eating cold bacon while the horse cropped the young grass. Though a cuckoo sat in the branches it did not irk him. Before vespers, he said to himself, I shall be in country I have never seen before. So it was; though he could not be certain where the familiar changed to the unknown, the change had taken place. Presently he began to meet groups of labourers, their tired legs moving in time to the gait of their oxen, and when he asked them if he were going right for the leper-house their accents were strange to him.

The chaplain of the leper-house, a burly man with tow-coloured hair and a mincing manner of speech quite out of keeping with his looks, welcomed him warmly enough: that is to say, he continued to repeat that he was delighted, though at the same time he yawned and stared at the horse as if it resembled something he knew of by hearsay. Supper was scarcely on the table before he asked if his guest could read music at sight.

"What sort of music? I can read church-note, of course."

"No, no! Music in measure. Do you understand the prolations? Well, I can soon teach you."

He laid out a music-book among the mutton bones and the bread crumbs and began to explain.

"See, these red notes are to be sung in the triple prolation. And these red minims, following the black breve, show that the breve is imperfect. Bear that in mind, and the rest will be simple. You have only to get the knack of it. Let us begin with an easy one. This is charming: *Triste loysir.* Suppose I just run through your part to give you an idea of it? When it comes to *mors de moy* the longs are perfect, and you will be enraptured."

His voice was slender as a reed, but accomplished. As he sang he thumped the measure on Henry's shoulder. Though written out with such complications, the music itself seemed simple, almost like a ballad tune, and before long Henry interrupted, and rather scornfully at that, saying that he was ready to take his part.

He began loudly and steadily, but after half a dozen notes it seemed to him that he must have gone wrong and he broke off.

"Go on, go on! You were doing excellently."

"But surely there was something wrong? It sounded very odd."

"No, there was nothing wrong. Perhaps the interval unsettled you. You expected a fourth, no doubt. This is composed in the style of the *Ars nova,* it is disconcerting at times. Let us begin again. And hold on: you will soon become accustomed to it."

This time he held on, though he felt himself astray, bewildered by the unexpected progressions, concords so sweet that they seemed to melt the flesh off his bones. Coming to *mors de moy,* where the chaplain's voice twittered in floriations high above his tolling longs, he could hardly contain himself for excitement.

"But this is astonishing," he said. "Are there others like this?" He began to turn the pages of the book.

"Yes, most of the things in this book are in *Ars nova* style. This Kyrie by Machault, for instance. . . . Unfortunately, it is for three voices. Of course, we could sing it without the middle voice, but you would not get a true idea of it. The bishop's message did not tell me to expect a musician."

Henry Yellowlees realized with certainty how strongly Bishop Walter would dislike *Ars nova;* and if anything could deepen his dislike of the bishop, this did.

"Out here, one has so few chances of meeting a competent musician. It is a stroke of good fortune for me that you should come. That is why I wish you could hear the Machault. Of course . . ." The chaplain paused, staring at his hand as it lay on the music-book. "One of my lepers here has an extremely fine voice and is a skilled singer. He used to be in the Duke of Burgundy's chapel. I don't know if you would object—he is not an advanced case of leprosy. He and I often sing together. To him, too, a third voice would be a godsend."

Not knowing whether he turned hot or cold, Henry Yellowlees answered, "No, of course not. I should like to hear the Kyrie."

The chaplain slid back a panel in the wall and called, "John! Will you come and sing?"

Shuffling footsteps approached. The leper came in. In the dusk of the doorway he seemed to glimmer like bad fish. He stank too. He stationed himself at the farther end of the room; it was clear that he knew his place as a dog does. There he stood, rubbing his scaly hands together, drawing preparatory breaths. His expression was professionally calm.

"Now, John! The Machault Kyrie."

The three voices sprang into the air.

If *Triste loysir* had seemed a foretaste of paradise, the Kyrie was paradise itself. This was how the blessed might sing, singing in a duple measure that ran as nimbly on its four feet as a weasel running through a meadow, with each voice in turn enkindling the others, so that the music flowed on and was continually renewed. And as paradise is made for man, this music seemed made for man's singing; not for edification, or the working-out of an argument, or the display of skill, but only for ease and pleasure, as in paradise where the abolition of sin begets a pagan carelessness, where the certainty of Christ's countenance frees men's souls from the obligations of christian behaviour, the creaking counterpoint of God's law and man's obedience.

It ended. Henry Yellowlees raised his eyes from the music-book. The rays of the levelling sun had shifted while they sang and now shone full on the leper. His face, his high bald head, were scarlet. He seemed to be on fire.

"Again! Let us sing it again!"

"I told you so," said the chaplain. "I tell you, there has never been such music in the world before."

All through the evening they sang, the leper standing apart and singing by rote. And Henry thought how many an hour these two must have spent together, the leper at one end of the room, the chaplain at the other; or perhaps they bent over the same music-book, their love of music overcoming the barrier between life and death-in-life. What did the other lepers think of it, those who could not sing, sitting in their straw, mumbling their sour bread (for if the food given to a guest were so bad the food given to the lepers must be worse), and hearing the music go on and on? Most of the night Henry lay awake, recalling the music, humming it over again to the burden of the chaplain's snores, with half of his mind in a rapture and the other half wishing that there were not so many and such ferocious bugs. It struck him that every bug in the place must have heard the good news and forsaken the lepers for flesh that was a novelty.

"You will come again?"

"Yes, indeed. In a week's time, perhaps."

"I hope you slept well?"

"Excellently, thank you."

The morning mist was just floating off the meadows. It would be a hot day, and he had started late. But the heat of the day was as yet only a theory, and he huddled his cloak round him, chilled by lack of sleep even when the mist had cleared and the sun filled the long narrow valley. Singing and whistling he rode on, and presently came to the valley's head and a hillside where the track showed out clearly in the poorer grass.

A mile or so farther on he met two of those happier travelers he had been considering (for still occupied by the music of overnight he had been thinking that in this world, where all lives are subject to so much discommodity, and death muddies the bottom of every cup, golliards and wanderers probably make out the best). A man was leading a chained fox and a woman staggered after him with a bundle on her back and a harp slung across it. He asked them the way to Killdew Priory, while saying to himself that it was waste of time, he could leave it to the horse: any horse from Bishop Walter's stables would know by instinct the detour that led to a free meal. The man directed him, dragging the fox this way and that as he swung his arms explaining the way to be taken, the way to be avoided, while the woman looked on with a satirical expression on her sweaty face; no doubt she was thinking of the dole for travellers, and perhaps with experience of it, for her look conveyed that he was going a long way for very little.

It might be better to have some settled habitation, and to live, like the chaplain at the leper-house, with enough routine to ward one from the reflection that a man's fate is no one's concern but his own. The chaplain might sometimes regret the lack of a bass, but otherwise he had not much to sigh for; and though in the end he might catch leprosy the shock would not fall on him with such astonishment as on other men. I could be happy living like that, thought Henry: nursing the music-book among the mutton bones, having forsaken this world to live in the fifth element of sound . . . Ah, that Kyrie, and the rondeau they had sung after it, and the song with the bass part descending with iron tread at *mors de moy!* Such music, and such squalor! . . . never had he seen a house so dirty, or slept in a more tattered bed. But out came the music as the kingfisher flashes from its nest of stinking fishbones.

From the brow of the hill he looked down on Killdew Priory, a modern building, ostentatiously symmetrical, and at the priory church, cluttered with scaffolding where the nave was being built higher. They'll run into debt for it, he said pleasurably, and be colder into the bargain. He passed the vineyards and the fish-ponds without envy and asked for his free dinner without humiliation. It was just such a meal as a flourishing community provides, clean, adequate, and disagreeable, with a strong flavour of fennel to mask the mustiness of the dried fish. He told the serving brother he would be back in a few days' time. He reckoned without his host. Wild hyacinths and wild garlic had taken the place of windflowers in the copses before he saw Killdew again.

For at Esselby the worst of a visitor's misfortunes overtook him: he became indispensable.

At first sight the house seemed calm enough, a house fit for the end of a journey, sheltered under a little craggy hill. There was a well-head and some sheds near by, and a smithy, and in the dusk he saw great hammers leaning against the anvil. It should not be difficult to get the money from such a thriving concern. He entered the house and explained his errand. There was a handsome child crawling on the floor, and, feeling that some civilities should garnish the rent-collecting, he complimented the young woman on its sturdy looks.

"It's no brat of mine," she cried out furiously.

Absorbed in its own life, the child pulled up its smock and began to make water. The young woman began to whimper, an old woman chimed in. He discovered they were telling him a story. What it was about, and why they should be telling him, he could not make out, for they had told it so often that they mislaid the tale in the telling, going off at a tangent to argue whether something or other had happened on a Tuesday or a Wednesday, in one or another Lent. Meanwhile, he seated himself at the board, hoping his attitude would suggest a supper. No food came, and the man of the house went out, talking about bedding down the horse.

Presently two nuns appeared in the story. They came seeking something, but while they were still parleying at the door a mastiff burst into the narrative and mauled the older nun so savagely that if some workmen had not run to her rescue she might have died. Then came a long wrangle as to whether it was before or after this affair that the lightning struck the great oak at the foot of the pightle. This they could not determine, but harking back to the nuns and the mastiff, they explained how a sentence of excommunication falling on a household that traded in iron-work, and specialized in church furniture—here again was an excursion to a neighbouring chantry whose screen had not been paid for—was reason enough, as Master Yellowlees must see, for an inability to pay one's rent.

"So this house is under the ban of the Church?" asked Henry hopefully; for if it were, it would give him an excuse to go elsewhere to a better likelihood of a supper.

God forbid, they cried out: no such thing. And after a long account of how the mastiff was hanged for sacrilege they quieted down to explain that the ban of the Church had fallen upon Roger Longdock, the old woman's husband, and on their daughter, the mother of the child there. She was a nun. But when she appeared one day with the child in her belly Roger had harboured her, and it was after barring the door against the nuns who arrived to reclaim her that the mastiff had been let loose.

Appalled by the sentence of excommunication, the nun had craved to submit herself and go back to her convent, but the old man had kept her and the child under lock and key for almost a year. At last she escaped and fled to the parish priest. Finding her gone, Roger walked out of the house and ever since had been living as a wild man in the woods; and now, old as he was, he had a woman with him.

By the time all this was told and the daughter-in-law had remembered that their guest must be hungry, the fire had gone out. Long past hunger, his head throbbing, his eyes smarting with sleeplessness, Henry wanted nothing but to lie down and sleep. But the two women had now persuaded themselves that he would get them out of all their troubles and not be exigent about the rent, and this being so it followed that they had to keep him waiting for another couple of hours while they poked up the brands into a smoke and roasted some eggs for his supper.

In the morning the household was reinforced by other members of the family: a married daughter, two swaggering cousins, and the old woman's brother, who somewhere or other had picked up some tags of law Latin, and bowed incessantly. With one accord they thanked God for his arrival; with one accord they were ready to accompany him to the woods, where he would talk Roger Longdock out of his contumacy. By then Henry Yellowlees had taken a look at the son of the house: a young man with the frame of an ox and the bolting eyes of a fanatic. He remembered that he had come to collect a debt, not to call sinners to repentance, and said he was ready to be taken round the buildings in order to make an inventory.

What overnight had seemed so thriving was only a husk of prosperity. Walls and roofs needed mending, the wood-stack was overgrown by moss and ferns, thick curtains of cobwebs hung on the anvil, the tools were rusted. No one, young Longdock bewailed, would commission as much as a poker from them now, because of the ban of the Church. But the Church, said Henry, had discriminated between the guilty and the guiltless, and surely the parish priest had only to make this clear for trade to return? All the Longdocks began with one voice to say how kind, how good, how considerate the village priest had been. While they expatiated a little old man, wrinkled and very thin, began to appear and disappear at the back of the workshop, flitting about like a lizard.

"Now I come to think of it," said Henry Yellowlees, "my horse needs re-shoeing—" the old man at the back of the shop showed his broken teeth in a grin—"though it is a small matter to kindle up your forge for."

The old man darted forward and began to pull out the embers of a long-cold fire.

"Yet one piece of work may bring another. The sight of your smoke will tell your neighbours that you are ready to work."

The old man gave an exploratory pull at the bellows. They wheezed with disuse, and quantities of dead flies fell out of their foldings. Henry continued to talk of industry and the value of a family business and secrets of handicraft passing from one generation to another.

At last the fire was going, the ingot melted and laid on the anvil. Mouthing woefully, young Longdock picked up a hammer, sighed, swung it and let it fall. It fell awry.

"You seem to be out of practice. But it will soon come," Henry observed.

At the same moment the old man, speaking for the first time, cried, "Spit on your hands, master! Spit on your hands!"

"So you tried to get Sim to work," was old Longdock's greeting on the following morning. Accompanied by troops of Longdocks, Henry had looked for him in vain the day before. This time he had gone to the woods alone and found him quite easily. "You'll get no work out of my son Sim, I can tell you, unless you thrash him." He was an alarming old man with quantities of shaggy hair and one eye. He lolled under a tree, eating the leg of a goose and childishly dabbling his enormous bare feet on a cushion of moss. "Seeing as you've come so far, I'll tell you this much. There are two ways to get the rent for your good ladies. One is, put me right with the Church, so I can finish that screen for the Congress chantry. T'other is, to squeeze my wife's brother for it."

Henry felt no love for the brother-in-law, but it seemed to be his duty to press the first expedient. He did his best to reason the old man into submission, but unavailingly. Perhaps the thought of the mastiff tied his tongue. The wood was a frowning place, full of old quarry holes, and looked as if it might contain any number of fierce dogs. When he had finished old Longdock remarked, "Best thing you can do is turn them all out. Let them go to my good brother."

Hatred of his brother-in-law seemed to be his fixed star. For the rest he rambled on about the gates and shrines and fetters he had made in the old days. In his snarling way he was hospitable; probably he enjoyed having a stranger to talk to. When his woman came out of the bushes driving a couple of nanny goats, he told her to make a meal for the visitor.

The parish priest, who did not appear till the fourth day, for he had been away looking after a law-suit, was no help. All his thoughts were given to the child, whom he had snatched away, he said, from under the ban. Now the boy would grow up a good christian and if things went well become a friar—priest he could not be, being a bastard—and so be serviceable to God and atone in some measure for the sins of his family. Henry remarked that the younger Longdocks seemed pious enough. Pious, oh, yes, certainly; but troublesome parishioners and exceedingly covetous. Covet, indeed, was the root of the whole trouble. Settling down to a story (for it was a wet afternoon and he was pleased with a new listener), he related how, many years before, a friar had passed through Esselby, pausing to preach a sermon on the heinous sin of taking usury. Quite uncanonical, Henry commented. The friar must have been old-fashioned. Aye, but so was Esselby, replied Sir Robin. Most of Esselby had borrowed money at some time or other from Cuthbert Ledwidge, old Longdock's brother-in-law, whose terms were extortionate, so the sermon had been heard with enthusiasm. Half-way through the sermon, continued the priest, Ledwidge had thought it best to steal away. But what he had heard had wrung his conscience, and when a couple of his debtors defaulted and his house was set on fire, he surmised that God's wrath would not wait till eternity but was snuffing round him already. So he arranged for his younger niece to become a nun, paying down a good dowry with her. With a niece in a nunnery, it seemed to him, he would stand better before God, and with any luck she would make such a virtuous nun that her merits and mortifications might help to shorten his years in purgatory. But instead she fell in love, was got with child, ran home to her father, and became the cause of all this trouble. Ledwidge would have been better advised to lay out his money on masses, said Henry, and Sir Robin warmly agreed; but these people were as wrong-headed as strayed pigs: they had no conception of God's will.

"As for the upshot, you have seen it for yourself. Roger Longdock will not submit, the Church cannot give way. Sim Longdock, between ourselves, will never do a stroke of work, your rent will never be paid. The water will not quench the fire, the fire will not burn the stick, the stick will not beat the dog. Now tell me about Bishop Walter. I hear he is a very holy man, and in his youth even did miracles."

That Bishop Walter should wing his way hither and collect the rent would be a timely miracle. But Henry Yellowlees' obstinacy was now engaged. The rumour spread that a man had come to Esselby who could get money out of the Longdocks, and presently he found himself charged with half a dozen hopeful furious creditors. The tangle yielded where the knot had seemed toughest: Roger Longdock suddenly declared himself ready to submit to the Church. Henry haled him off then and there to repeat this good news to Sir Robin. The stick would beat the dog, after all. His work was done, and he told the Longdocks that he would start on the morrow. They were profuse in praising God, though he observed that Sim Longdock's praises had a pensive note in them, as though he already foresaw his father back and the cudgel lifted. This supposition must be his reward for a most unpleasant sojourn; expensive too, for they whined him into paying more than above for his lodging and his horse's stabling. Not even a pair of horseshoes, he said to himself; but here he was wrong, for he found that the goblin old man who haunted the smithy had made and fitted them.

When the morning mass was over he waited to say good-bye to Sir Robin. Holy Church would thank him, piped the old man, wrinkling his eyelids in the pure sunlight. Thanks to him, another soul would be safely cupboarded in religion.

"In religion?"

"Aye. In religion. Roger came to me last night, he is set on it, nothing will appease him but to spend the rest of his days in a religious order."

"A religious order?"

"Yes, indeed! Nothing else will serve. He swears that he cannot go back to his old life, for if he were to do so he would only damn himself over again by murdering Sim and Cuthbert. So he will flee from temptation."

"And the rent?"

Sir Robin began to cackle. Willy-nilly, Henry Yellowlees had to laugh too. They laughed and dug each other in the ribs, till Sir Robin became so weak that he had to be propped against a buttress.

"God bless you, my son. God be with you on your journey, and forevermore. I shall always thank God that you came to Esselby."

A good story to tell the bishop, Henry said to himself; though not so good a story to tell at Oby. In a little while rents and bishops were forgotten, for now he was riding toward the leper-house and *Ars nova.* At last, early in the afternoon of his second day's travelling, he looked down from the ridge, where he had met the musicians and their fox, into the valley, where now the buttercups had come fully into bloom. They were blooming so richly, their colour was so burnished and intense, that by contrast the green of the meadow-grass seemed almost blue. Riding through them, he felt himself growing dazzled and giddy, as though he might fall into this whispering golden sea and drown there. At every turn of the valley he stared ahead, searching for the shabby building which encased such music. Bishop or no, errand or no, he would stay two nights, perhaps three. He saw a building. But it was not the one he looked for. It was roofless: some ruin, some old cattle-shed which he had not noticed when he rode by before because of the mist. Then through the hot pollen-scented air came a whiff of burned thatch. It was heavy and fulsome, the stink of a recent burning. The mare put back her ears, and snorted, and made to turn away; but he drove in his spurs and set her onward. Riding nearer, he saw that the elder bushes and the young nettles growing around the ruined building were newly blackened. And while he was still staring, and not believing, a figure sprang up from the threshold and came uncertainly toward him, crying out, "Pity! in the name of the Virgin, have pity!" Then he saw that this was the leper who had sung in the Duke of Burgundy's chapel. The mare reared, and the leper stopped, shielding his face with a shapeless hand. "Have pity!" he said again. Peeping out from behind his hand he recognized the rider. "I am John of the Chapel. We sang together. Do not forsake me, do not slay me! I swear before God I had no part in it."

There was stale blood on his clothes and flies swarmed about him. Still warding his face, and turning his head to listen this way and that, he came a step nearer.

"They set on us while we were singing. We were singing, we did not hear them come. They had armed themselves, some with sticks, some with bones. They struck him down and beat him, and one of them thrust a bone into his mouth and down his gullet, and worked it to and fro till his gullet split and the blood ran out. Then the others set fire to the roof, and they all went away.

"The lepers that could not walk they put in a cart, and the rest went alongside with clappers and bells, saying that now they would beg and be well filled," he said, his eyes staring down the valley as though he were watching still. "But the men went that way." He turned and pointed up the hillside.

"What men were they?"

"I do not know. They had carts, and booty, and some had blackened their faces."

"They were robbers?"

"They called themselves the Twelve Apostles, they said they were going about to right the poor. One of them had been here before, and had heard the lepers complain, I suppose. They were always complaining and saying that he spent all on music-books that should have been spent on them. And it is true, there was often nothing to eat. It was the lepers who killed him, they had hated him for a long time. The others only shouted and destroyed."

"And when was this?" The question was partly answered by the stink of decay that now seemed the only smell in all the rich valley. The brook chattered to itself, and presently he rode off toward it with an indistinct purpose of cleansing himself, and dismounted and rinsed his mouth and wiped the sweat off his face with a handful of water-cresses. He had no sooner done so than he was again sweating with fear and feeling sick, for it seemed to him beyond any doubt that just here was where the leper had lapped the water and pulled the cresses which, so he said, had been all his nourishment for three days. The leper—what was to be done with him? He looked back and saw the man standing in the same place, staring after him in a desolate doubt. He thinks I shall ride on and leave him, thought Henry; and so I might, and not cause him much more distress, since already in his mind I have forsaken him.

He beckoned, and the man came on, at first in a flurry of relief, then more slowly as his doubts gained on him; he stopped within hailing distance.

"What became of the music-books?"

"They poked them into the thatch to burn."

He threw to the leper what food he had. Then he asked him how well he could walk. The leper's assurances that he could walk as well as a sound man Henry discounted by half. But as there was nothing else to be done he mounted again, jerking his disbelieving beast back into the way they had come, and rode slowly on toward the head of the valley, telling the leper they would be at Killdew before nightfall, and that at Killdew he would be well cared for. Killdew would not be best pleased, he thought; but the news of the Twelve Apostles being abroad might quicken their loving kindness. At intervals he paused and looked back. The leper was still following, dragging his shadow over the buttercups. The hillside would have been too much for his strength if Henry had not remembered the length of cord that fastened his wallet to the saddle. Throwing one end to the leper and fastening the other to the saddle-bow he hauled the man after him as the musician had hauled the fox. So at last they came to the brow of the hill and looked down on the Priory, and heard the bell ringing for compline. Its reiterated notes rose up straight and slender as a row of poplars. The leper hawked, and crossed himself, and began to sing *Te lucis ante terminum,* and as Henry took it up he deserted the plain-chant and sang a descant. The horse wandered about, cropping the hill-top turf, and Henry and the leper sat on the grass, the leper sitting a dozen paces away, but near enough to prompt Henry in the bass part of *Triste loysir* until he could sing it steadily enough for the tenor to be added. They sang it three times through, and if in the beginning Henry remembered the chaplain, from whose stinking body the chill of evening had now swept off the flies, by the third repetition nothing remained but the delight of the two voices answering and according, and a regret that they could not sit singing all night through. But they could not delay; as it was they would arrive after the hour of the great silence, the porter would be grumpy and might stand on the rules. As they went downward past the vineyards and the silvered fish-ponds, John of the Chapel talked with excitement of hearing the singing at Killdew. To him music was something which could be found here or there indifferently, like a mass.

They reached the Priory. The porter came out, protesting, but also boasting that late-comers were nothing to such an establishment as Killdew. The leper was disposed of, a subinfirmarian conveying him away as efficiently as a river swallows a pebble. As for the news of the Twelve Apostles, it was stale news.

"They are not likely to trouble us," said the guest-master. "If they do, we have made our preparations and no doubt God will defend his servants. It is only small establishments that need fear them—like that unfortunate Hospital of Saint Sepulchre, which in any case was scandalously mismanaged. Still, as our cellarer is riding to Ingham Fair tomorrow, I suggest you make one of his party. In any case, to ride in company is pleasanter than to ride alone."

The cellarer's party was so stately and so well mounted that Henry Yellowlees, riding the bishop's provision of a horse and depending on the very small residue of the bishop's provision for gratuities, wished at first that he had said he would travel alone. The cellarer's clerk, however, a Lombard, was an easy talker, a man with so large an acquaintance with religious establishments that he seemed to find all of them about equally criticizable. To such a man, Henry realized, the shifts of poverty were so far removed as to be entertaining. So he recounted the story of the Esselby rent. The cellarer's clerk was delighted with it, and at dinner Henry was called on to tell it all over again, and again it gave much pleasure. Then the cellarer remarked that it was just what one would expect of Oby, he feared Henry Yellowlees must have nothing but annoyance in the custos-ship of such an ill-managed house. The bishop had succeeded in blackening Oby as far as the exalted ears of Killdew, had he? Henry at once launched into an eulogium of Prioress Matilda, her nuns, so discreet and well connected, and the good old priest who had served them so long and devotedly and who was despite his years a most discriminating theologian.

"I heard he was out of his wits," said the cellarer's clerk.

"I seem to have heard he was no priest," said another. The cellarer remarked that if one believed all that one heard one would despair of the providence of God. Fortunately one need not take such rumours seriously. He had heard some odd things about Bishop Walter too, for that matter. The librarian, who was also of the party, travelling to the fair to buy oak-galls and vellum, said more seriously that the most damaging rumours about Bishop Walter were those telling of his poverty and abstinence. Such talk suggested to the poor and ignorant that the majority of churchmen lived inordinately richly. Personal austerities were all very well no doubt, but to obtrude them was disloyal to the tonsure. He added that if Bishop Walter ate two dishes at dinner instead of one, in all likelihood the unfortunate chaplain at Saint Sepulchre would not have been clubbed to death.

The next day they separated. Riding on by himself and nearing his journey's end, Henry Yellowlees began to think of his errand and of what he should report. His fruitless errand, which had been to the monks of Killdew a story for dinner, and to himself a nut to crack, like a problem in mathematics, would be to the ladies of Oby a matter of bread and bacon. For each one of us lives in his microcosm, the solidity of this world is a mere game of mirrors, there can be no absolute existence for what is apprehended differently by all. And if he could have brought back the music-books his fruitless errand would have been as rich for him as a return from the lands of Saba.

The fruitless errand had lasted much too long: this was the first comment of the bishop's secretary, who went on to say that during his absence his class had mislaid the large compasses while roasting larks on them. Tell the bishop that money is the root of all evil, he replied. Some new element, perhaps *Ars nova*, perhaps the conversation of that sophisticated Lombard, had made a new man of Henry Yellowlees, and the secretary reported to the bishop that Master Yellowlees had been away for so long because he had been consorting with the Lollards.

XI. A SACRIFICE TO WODEN

(June 1377–January 1380)

Riding out to Oby, Henry Yellowlees looked over the landscape with sunlike benevolence. The hay was newly cut and lay in swathes on the meadows as orderly as a mackerel sky, the spire laid its delicate shadow across the green ground, the willows drew their silvery foliage across the enamelled red of their bark. In returning to Oby he was returning to something he might love; and the thought that he might love it and the thought that he had no hold upon it swept over him together, so that he saw it as imperative that he should at once apply for priest's orders and be ready to succeed Sir Ralph as convent priest. The old man could not last forever; indeed, would he last long enough to fill those comfortable shoes until Henry was ready to step into them? Yet how foolish and impetuous to plight himself to Oby because it was enjoying a moment of midsummer beauty!—for the rest of the year what was it but mire and mist, boredom, loneliness, a worthless soil, and the wind ruffling the winter floods?

Sir Ralph rose out of the Waxle Stream to greet him, splashing and snorting through the reeds like a cow or a rivergod. He had been poking about with a net for perch, his gown was bunched up round his thighs and his face with its deep wrinkles and tufted eyebrows and features shaped for wrath wore an expression of silvery innocence like the full moon. Full of pleasure at seeing Henry again, he questioned him about his journey.

Soon his attention slid away. He began throwing grasses into the river and drawing designs on the mud-bank with his toes.

"Since Whitsun," he said abruptly, "I have been thinking about the sacrament of baptism."

Henry Yellowlees resigned himself. Sir Ralph's thoughts on baptism had led him to conclude that the rite did not go far enough, what was squirting a baby? Well enough for a beginning, but for the full-grown man there should be a full immersion, for such was the baptism of John. For the sake of conversation Henry Yellowlees represented that there is no evidence in the scriptures that John had immersed Jesus, and that the tradition of the Church, as expressed in art, was that John had scooped up the water of Jordan, perhaps with some vessel, perhaps with his hand, and had poured it on Jesus' head. Meanwhile Sir Ralph was beating the Waxle with his net and fidgeting. Suddenly he threw off his gown and waded back into the stream. "Let me baptize you," he begged. "You look very warm, a good sousing is just what you need. Come, off with your clothes! The nuns will not see you, they are all asleep."

Moving a little farther up the bank Henry asked if the prioress were in good health, if Dame Philippa were still coughing. But he asked in vain. The old man waded to and fro, happy as a cow, and rambled on in praise of water, water, he said, which was the innocent element. Why was the Redeemer of mankind forever faultless and incapable of sin? Because he was a fish and forever immersed in the flood. He swam for eternity in the waters which are above the earth. And in those waters, Sir Ralph continued, wading and splashing, in those waters there swim with Christ the souls of all His blessed; for heaven is a great fish-pond, and there you can see the Bishops and the Confessors nosing about like carp, and the Martyrs with bright bloody spots are trout, and the Virgins in their silver mail of chastity are dace. Whoever loves holiness must love water by natural inclination, he shouted, and whoever dies by drowning goes straight to God, filled to human bursting with the innocence and absolution of water. Scooping up a handful of water and pouring it on his head, he threw himself under with a splash and displacement which sent the ripples over Henry's feet.

With such a madman the only way was to humour his fancies. When he came up again Henry called out, "And what are the eels?"

"The Doctors, the learned Doctors!" cried Sir Ralph. "Are they not full of small bones and fatness? Wade in, young man, and receive the baptism of John!"

He showed no ill-feeling when Henry Yellowlees excused himself. His madness was akin to childishness: he was so perfectly convinced by his nonsense that he felt no need to proselytize.

Yet what if he should begin to throw the nuns into the Waxle Stream? If he did so, and a nun died, her death would be upon Henry's soul. I am a custos, he said to himself, riding along the track between the willows; my only concern is with their temporalities, and if I say to the prioress that in my opinion her priest is mad she may ask me what my opinion has to do with it, and if I speak of it to the bishop he will have Sir Ralph out and a new man in; and what then will become of my plan of being priested myself and following Sir Ralph, and growing, I daresay, after ten winters as mad as he? It was clear to him that he would say nothing either to prioress or bishop. He also had a pretty strong impression that Sir Ralph was totally uninterested in the souls of his nuns.

By the time he reached the convent the picture of Sir Ralph tossing nuns into the Cow Pool seemed very unlifelike. It lost all validity when Dame Lovisa's face looked out of the wicket. She raised—not her eyebrows, she had no eyebrows—but the roughened tracts of skin above her eyes, and remarked that he was quite a stranger. Though women arouse the lusts of the flesh they atone for it by quelling any vagaries of the imagination.

He made his report to the prioress. It struck him that he would not make her many more reports. In spite of her massive bulk and her straight back she seemed hollowed by some inward decay. She would drop suddenly, as the limb of an elm tree drops. She heard the news from Esselby with imperturbability, laughed, and turned the conversation to ask about the management of the vineyards at Killdew. Her gruff good manners made him realize for the first time how completely he had disgraced himself in his errand. But *Ars nova* had waylaid him: the man who arrived at Esselby was not the man who had set out on the morrow of Saint Pancras' Day. Like those who fall in with fairies, he had been conveyed under the green hill; and *Triste loysir* was the tune of that place. He would never be his own man again, *Ars nova* had worked its will on him only a little less commandingly than on the chaplain of the leper-house. One man it had killed and the other despatched without death into another world. If he seemed to come back, and be the same custos of Oby, who had miscarried of a business errand, it was only by force of habit, and with such inattentive freedom of mind that he was now asking himself whether Sir Ralph's madness or the materialism of the nuns was furthest from real life. Yet what was real life? Not his own life assuredly. He felt no pavement of reality under his feet, wandering among a chance assemblage of geometry, hunger, sickness, loaned horses, debts and shifts and other people's intentions. Whose life was real?—old Longdock's in the wildwood, the chaplain's at the leper-house, the suave Killdew clerk's? Each of them in his way knew what he wanted and sought it with self-will, and for that matter, with self-denial; for no doubt the Killdew clerk must have denied himself something in order to live with such a rotundity of worldliness, he must have trampled down some artless predisposition such as wishing to recite his own poems.

On the morrow there was William Holly waiting to go round with him, and the usual litany of this needing doing and that ill-done. William Holly was one of those small, tight men like a knot of wood, his cross-grainedness seemed a warrant of longevity; while there was a young man to snub, a new opinion to confute, a youthful hope to disparage, one would expect William Holly to be at his post. But today he had scarcely a contradiction in him, and in a manner quite unusual to him he stopped and pointed out the grave of the elder Frampton novice, who had died of measles, and Henry saw with amazement that tears were standing in his eyes. They finished their round and were looking at a spotted ox which had recently come in as a heriot when William Holly suddenly remarked that something in his inwards was gnawing and biting him, which he opined to be a toad, swallowed small in a salad; for nothing less malicious than a toad would have withstood the purges he had been taking. Henry Yellowlees foolishly allowed himself to say that he did not think a toad could live within a man. William Holly replied that every fool knew that a toad can live inside a stone for a hundred years if it pleased to.

The crab, the archer, the man with the water-pot—there is not a sign in the zodiac which has not its patronized malady, there is death, thought Henry, staring up past the spire, death in the firmament. Prioress, priest, bailiff, they were all growing old in this midsummer air. Another prioress would follow, another priest would be found; it would be harder to replace the bailiff; for William Holly was one of those yew-tree characters which do not allow younger yew trees to grow up in their shade. He rode away thinking of the pretty child who had outgrown them all in her dying, and that she would not have to suffer another winter's chilblains, or a new-broom priest imposed by Bishop Walter. And as for the Esselby rent, let the bishop deal with it, he said to himself.

Any such hope was wiped out when he next saw the bishop. Here was another old age under sentence from a sign in the zodiac—in Bishop Walter's case perhaps the sign of the scales, for his eyes were netted in wrinkles of calculation, and the word *judgment* continually recurred in his talk.

"It is a judgment!" he exclaimed of the non-payment of the Esselby rent. "Why should I intervene when God has judged? Oby is judged, I assure you. We can do nothing. It is taken out of our hands."

His chaplain signed to Henry to say no more of it, and primmed up his lips as if to contain something unspeakable. No sense could ever be got out of that chaplain. Henry Yellowlees went to Humphrey Flagg, the bishop's doctor. Humphrey Flagg was also devoted to Bishop Walter, but his love had more secularity in it. Besides, he was a Yorkshire man, a fellow-countryman of Henry's.

"It is no use. And I beg you not to vex him with any more talk of your nunnery. It only upsets him. And after all, what is one nunnery?"

"But what has he got against it? What maggot is all this? What has anyone got against it? I suppose it is the most respectable nunnery in all his bishopric."

"I can only say that it made a bad impression on him. I have felt his pulse jump like a ram when someone has mentioned Oby."

"But why? The ladies of Oby don't skip like lambs when someone mentions the bishop."

Evading this, Humphrey Flagg continued, "The bishop is not like other men. His will is stronger than other men's, his sensibilities are much more acute. His body is at the mercy of his soul, and the soul is a hard master. For some reason or other his soul flogs him with Oby, that is all I can tell you."

"Some prejudice," Henry grumbled. "Well, he sent his Dame Sibilla to Oby, anyhow. Why did he do that if Oby is such an offence to him?"

When Bishop Walter asked himself that same question, though he found many answers he could not hit on one that silenced it. At first the question had been no more than any other question, an exercise of a conscience which fed on scruples; for the bishop was a man who constantly asked himself questions and as constantly resolved them to his own satisfaction. But the Dame Sibilla question came back and back, and grew more urgent and more mysterious. Correspondingly, his first dislike of Oby, the dislike he had so naturally and properly conceived on discovering that the Oby nuns supposed they could throw dust in his eyes, had deepened into an apprehension of something quite unusually baleful, a wickedness beyond all the faults he had been able to catalogue and rebuke, a wickedness so wicked that it transcended his diagnosis, and only God could put his finger on it. That, of course, was why his first dislike had been so much sharper and more quivering than an intention to deceive a bishop might warrant. Oby was not singular in hoping to deceive a bishop, any more than in being luxurious, frivolous, worldly, and insolvent. Under these everyday offences a deeper abomination lay in wait.

Having got thus far in his surmising, the bishop naturally went on to seek out more information, keeping his ear to the ground; and naturally he heard a good deal. Though everything he heard could be construed to Oby's disadvantage, he really heard nothing at all telling until just before Henry Yellowlees came back from Esselby. Then, in the course of conversation with a newly appointed summoner whose uncle had been clerk of the works at Etchingdon, he learned the true story of the Methley tithes: which was that Thomas de Foley had given them to Oby as a price for the carnal pleasures he had enjoyed with his cousin, the Prioress Alicia. Hard on the heels of this enlightenment the bishop made a Visitation to the convent to which he had transferred Dame Alice. In many ways the Visitation was grievous, he noted, for instance, a shocking degree of gluttony, and the nuns were bristling with quarrels and slanders; but amidst all this Dame Alice's simple, homely pleasure at seeing him warmed his heart. In the course of their private interview she told him how she and Dame Johanna had always believed that the spire had fallen, and Dame Susanna had thrown herself under it, as a plain manifestation of the wrath of God. She also recounted the deaths of the boy who fell off the scaffolding, Ursula who fell down the stairs, the corrodian, Magdalen Figg, who fell into the fish-pond, and Magdalen's husband, the old bailiff. Did it not seem as though God would scarcely allow a christian death-bed at Oby? How could she express her gratitude to the bishop for having delivered her from such a place?

And how, she added, was Dame Sibilla?—that sweet lady, the pattern of what a nun should be.

He stared at her, not daring to turn aside the question he dreaded to hear.

"I have often asked myself why you sent Dame Sibilla to Oby." Her eyelids closed down, as though the sight of his distress were something that must be eaten in private. Sighing appreciatively, and gently wagging her head, she murmured, "I should not be so presumptuous. But it seemed to me you were sending a lamb among the wolves."

"Yes, yes!" he answered, and hastily blessed the understanding creature.

Dame Alice was perfectly satisfied with this interview, and lived on in peace of mind. It was not in any case likely that the prioress of Oby would denounce her; but if she did Bishop Walter would not now be inclined to listen with any favour. That goose was cooked. The bishop's satisfaction did not last so long. By the evening the answer supplied by Dame Alice to the inexorcisable question had shrivelled into no answer at all. It is a function of lambs to be sent among wolves; such a sending would have been pious and meritorious, and God might have been expected to bless it. But this was no such thing. He had placed his great-niece at Oby in order to chasten an extravagant house by compelling it to take in three unprofitable newcomers. Dame Sibilla had not been so much sent as a lamb as applied as a leech.

Yet God had permitted it. Perhaps God even had designed it. It was in God's hands, and there he must leave it. He had repeatedly tried this answer, and whenever he tried it, it led to Abraham and Jephtha. Abraham had been ready to sacrifice Isaac, Jephtha had not been ready to offer up his daughter but had done so nevertheless. Of the two, it seemed to Bishop Walter that Jephtha's case was nearest his own. With Abraham, God proceeded directly and with the authority of a father, but in his dealings with Jephtha he availed himself of a stratagem, at the last moment substituting Jephtha's daughter for what Jephtha very likely expected to be a ram. Preaching on the duty of obedience, the bishop perplexed his hearers, for it was unlike him to enter so feelingly into the emotions of pre-christian characters. Yet the lesson was clear, and several fathers went home to beat their children with renewed zeal and confidence.

Why had he sent Dame Sibilla to Oby?

In his crannies of spare time and in his wakeful nights the bishop brooded over the girl and over his kinship with Jephtha and over the curse accumulating about the house of Oby. Suppose that the spire, bought by incest and profanation, should fall again, and Dame Sibilla be underneath it? . . . but the death of the body is of no importance, he could not consider withdrawing her for such a light reason. Suppose the miracle of the Esselby rent (it could hardly be less than a miracle that a hardened excommunicate should be melted by the exhortations of Henry Yellowlees) should be repeated and repeated till Oby became insolvent? . . .

why then, of course, the nuns would have to be dispersed, Dame Sibilla among them. But suppose that while remaining at Oby Dame Sibilla fell under the power of whatever mysterious evil accumulated there, and by some mischance or the dire deliberation of God's will were damned? . . . would it not be his doing, and would not God require her soul at his hands?

He thrust the thought away. It was a sleight of Satan's, who also tempted Job. But after a while the speculation would creep back again, hooded in the guise of an omen, or lurking in the pages of a book, or dancing in a candle-flame. Throughout his life Walter Dunford had availed himself of his naturally strong sense of the supernatural, and had been constantly assisted by visions and by voices, sometimes almost believing, and never quite disbelieving, and always convinced that even if he did a trifle enhance and exploit these adjuncts from another world it was by God's will and for God's purpose that he did so, just as he allowed his authentic mortifications to play their useful part in the world's eye. Now he was nearing three-score, and the visions and the mortifications had done their work on him. The Dame Sibilla question, which had entered his mind as no more than a whet to his prejudice against the house of Oby, had become his meat and drink, his scourge and hair-shirt, his prayer and his sentence. In reality, he might have been hard put to it to recognize her among his other nieces and great-nieces in religion; but she was the sole grandchild of his dead brother Thomas, whom once he had loved; and the remembrance of this, jangling his rusty affections, enforced her on his imagination and made her dear, and terrible, and like a vow.

Meanwhile, Oby was due for a Visitation. A date was fixed. He became accustomed to hearing Oby spoken of: it took its place with other commonplaces, it assumed a covering of other people's fears, his doctor's fears of ague and unsuitable diet, his secretary's fears of finding a great deal that would be troublesome. It eased him to hear such talk of Oby, and to reply that the Visitation was a painful duty which he must at all costs fulfil. The day before he was due to set out an attack of fever and vomiting prostrated him, and Henry Yellowlees was sent off to tell Oby that the Visitation must be postponed.

He did not recover till after the equinox. By then the weather made going to Oby impossible, so Humphrey Flagg said, and the secretary remarked that a few months more or less could not make much difference to an establishment like Oby. Their fears muffled Oby no longer, and the bishop was left to contemplate his own, until the November evening when his brother's voice spoke in his ear, louder than the north wind and the sleet that rattled on the windows of the lady chapel, saying, "Deliver my darling from the power of the dog!" It was a plain command. But he could not obey it, because of the terror it roused up in him, and because he failed to obey he feared the more.

"You think too much of Oby," his secretary said, when on the morrow he was told to make arrangements for Oby to be visited by a proxy.

A few nights later another gale got up. This night he was in bed. He rose, saying he must pray, and dismissed his attendants. Presently they heard him shuffle out of his chamber and along the gallery from which stairs led down into the cathedral. At the head of the stairs he saw that they were following him, and turned on them so furiously that they stayed where they were, eyeing each other uneasily, and saying that one must not intervene in such manifestations of piety. The wind was shouting in the north porch like the sea struggling in a cavern, and it seemed to him that he was walking on the cold pavement of ocean. There, like the bones of a wreck, was his tall throne: he paused for a moment and looked at it. Then he went on into the lady chapel, and threw himself on the ground as a dog casts himself down in his kennel. The gale gathered up more strength, the first handful of sleet struck against the windows, and Thomas's voice spoke in the wind; using the words indeed of David, that same David whom the bishop had praised so handsomely in the last paragraph of the first book of his treatise *De Cantu,* but uttering them in the voice of a character much less venerable and amenable than the son of Jesse, a character dark, frightful, and unknown, some god of the ancient Britons, perhaps, whom Walter Dunford's ancestors had appeased with living sacrifices.

The gale died down a little before dawn, and it was then that the sleepy group in the gallery heard their bishop's footsteps on the stairs. They took him up in their arms, and he looked at them, but could say nothing for his teeth were chattering with cold. Whatever it was that Walter Dunford had heard in the north wind it had wholly delivered him over to the supernatural on which he had so long and so confidently relied. His faculties of piety and imagination were at work with him as they had never been at work before, and the people about him began to say that he had fallen suddenly into dotage. What else could they say, seeing him sit groaning, with his hands wandering through his white hair?

After this he allowed himself to be treated as a sick man, to be kept warm in a little room, and fed on wine-whey, and to have his feet washed in warm water. Christmas went by, and Epiphany, and Candlemas, and he grew no better and no worse. Then Humphrey Flagg remembered the only weakness that Walter Dunford had ever indulged himself with: an affection for other Dunfords.

"Would you not allow one of your nieces to come and nurse you?"

The old man looked up with a sudden watery brilliance like a dash of November sunlight.

"My great-niece Sibilla. Let her come."

The doctor suggested that one of the intermediate generation of Dunford nuns might be more comfortable and have more leechcraft.

"No, no! Let it be Dame Sibilla. She is the nearest, she would travel at the least charge. I will have no unnecessary expense."

Humphrey Flagg congratulated himself on finding the right stimulant for the poor old man. It was extraordinary how at the thought of seeing another Dunford he roused up and became almost his former self. He even remembered that the custos of Oby could combine fetching Dame Sibilla with his customary visit of inspection. However, Henry Yellowlees was not troubled with this errand. The occasion called for something more ceremonious, and a litter and a discreet escort set out for Oby to bring Dame Sibilla away.

Still clasping her bundle of remedies and delicacies, she fell on her knees beside the great chair where the bishop sat, huddled in a white woollen gown. All through the darkening afternoon he had sat before the fire seeing her image among the flames which were alternately the flames of hellfire and the flames of the seraphim. Sometimes a log fell to bits, sometimes the missel-thrush in the pear tree set up its song against the gusty rain-pelts. At intervals his doctor or his chaplain came to his side and glanced at him.

Now he turned and looked into her very face. It seemed to him that he had never seen such a worldly countenance. Her cheeks were flushed with the sudden change from the cold journey to the heated room, her eyes flashed and twinkled, her teeth, protruding under her short upper lip, gave her smile an expression of carnal alacrity—and she smiled a great deal. The world, which he thought he had forsworn, gazed up in his face, patted his arm, fingered his ring, as confidently as though he had never slighted it.

Still on her knees, she began to rummage in her bundle, pulling out one thing after another, misnaming and mislaying them, and littering the floor with waddings and wrappings. Here was some honey, broom honey which never fails to allay a cough. Here was some of Oby's marzipan, specially made on purpose. Here was a bottle of mead. Here was a little pillow. Here was a most remarkable salve for stiff joints, and here was an ointment for chilblains, and here was a plaster to be laid over the heart. Here were some comfits, and here was a distillation of mugwort, and here was another psalter from Dame Lovisa, and here were some candied stems of angelica, and here was a towel embroidered by the novices, and here was some damson jam. Everything had a recommendation or a message or had been specially made or had a history of healing. And in the confusion of giving she displayed and explained at random, so that the pillow was to be laid over the heart and honey was sovereign for stiff knees.

The doctor came forward and whispered that the bishop was extremely weak and must not be tired with talking.

"Of course, of course, I quite understand," she replied; and out came more damson jam, and a long story of how the tree had been pruned by a passing friar, and had responded with a wonderful crop, but after all not so many had been gathered because the magpies came and pillaged it; but next year they would throw a net over it, a fishing-net which had been bought at Waxelby at much below the usual price because the vendor was a fisherman's widow who had been thankful to close with Dame Lovisa's offer of half the price in money and the rest to be made up in prayers for the fisherman's soul. For Dame Lovisa managed such things cleverly, and would make an excellent prioress.

"What? Another de Stapledon prioress?" inquired the dying man.

"Yes, indeed! We have quite made up our minds, she is certainly what God wishes. And Dame Eleanor will still be treasuress, and Dame Philippa will stay with the novices, and Dame Dorothy will be cellaress, and . . ."

"And you, my child?"

"Sacrist, perhaps. Unworthily, but you see there are so few of us." But the first two words had sufficiently proclaimed a violent spiritual ambition socketed in complacence. In due course, a Dunford prioress.

"A solemn charge," he said.

The flask of mead, set working by its journey, had been placed injudiciously near the fire, and now it blew its stopper out. The bishop started and crossed himself. While Dame Sibilla mopped and talked, and mingled the goodness of the mead and the privilege of being sacrist and how much mead was lost and yet how much was spared, all with a kind of tranquil flurry, he stared at the flask with his jaw trembling and his thin hands fidgeting. The doctor rose from his bench in the corner and began mixing something in a little bowl. He was too late. The bishop staggered up from his chair, and fell on his knees, howling. The doctor ran with his bowl, the chaplain snatched up a crucifix, exclaiming, "These accursed women!" and held it before the bishop's eyes. But he eluded them both, dragging himself about the room on his knees, howling and knocking on his breast. It was Dame Sibilla, getting in front of the chaplain, who stayed him. Kneeling herself, and clasping him round the waist, she wrestled with him until she had him down on the floor with his head in her lap.

"How you frightened us!" she said. "You mustn't pray so loud, nor so suddenly. You must tell us when you wish to pray, then we will all pray together, like Abraham and his household."

"Not Abraham, not Abraham! Jephtha!"

"Who was it? Did you see a vision?" she asked.

"An omen!" he said, gasping and whistling. "God's wrath!"

"Tuba mirum spargens sonum
Per sepulcrum regionum,"

intoned the chaplain.

"I saw a vision," said Dame Sibilla. "Just when the cork flew out and I was blaming myself for my carelessness in putting the flask so near the fire and wasting all that good mead that Dame Margaret showed us how to make, just then I saw Saint Magdalen spilling the ointment from a vase and smiling, as much as to say one need not worry about a little waste."

"Quid Mariam absolvisti," said the chaplain, glaring at Dame Sibilla but following her lead.

"But it is not the first time I have seen one of the saints," Dame Sibilla continued soothingly. "At Allestree I saw Saint Jerome several times. He used to sit in the cloisters with a book on his knee. The Allestree priest was unable to believe it, and told me that nuns had no business to see visions. But how can one help it, if heaven sends them? However, I do not talk about it. How do you feel now? Perhaps you might eat a little angelica. It is the best kind, the kind that is prepared with vine-leaves."

The chaplain laid down the crucifix and said in an undertone to Humphrey Flagg that they would have to get rid of her somehow. The doctor replied that she seemed to be doing him good. Shrugging his shoulders, the chaplain remarked that it was no sort of death-bed for a bishop to lie with his head in a nun's lap mumbling angelica, and that he would not have expected a doctor, a professional man, to be so tolerant of convent quackeries, little pillows and what not; to which the doctor retorted that speaking as a professional man he did not look to see the bishop die for several days to come. They were still wrangling in their corner when Dame Sibilla announced to them that her great-uncle was now in a peaceful sleep and that she thought he should be carried to his bed.

The way she oversaw this operation and particularly the ineffable little pats she gave to the pillows drove Humphrey Flagg to the chaplain's way of thinking. With single-hearted courtesy they conducted her to her lodging, where a respectable widow was in readiness to wait on her. But a couple of hours later they were compelled to call her back, for the bishop had started up in bed, declaring that he had seen her carried away by a piebald dog as large as a horse, that she was lost and God would require his soul for it. Now for more visions, the chaplain observed sombrely. This time Dame Sibilla quieted the bishop with a long account of the finances of Oby. But the chaplain was no better pleased. He had taken a prejudice against her.

Meanwhile, all the poor in the city knew that Bishop Walter was dying, and with the irrational hopefulness of the poor were praying fervently for his recovery. They trooped in processions to the cathedral, they knelt in prayer at the palace gate, they clamoured for relics to be brought from all parts of the kingdom immediately. Children were beaten to make them pray more fervently, for the prayer of a child has more power than any grown person's prayer; women vowed the babe in the womb to God's use provided God would spare them the bishop; and hunchbacks, who are known to be luck-givers, were seized on by the crowd and rubbed against the palace walls. For he was the poor man's bishop, he had considered the poor, he was their father, their treasure, their only warm garment, their champion before God and man, their only flatterer. The crowd wept and swayed, telling each other how even now, at death's door, he would not lie in a bed but lay on the ground with nothing but straw beneath him. None was more fervent than the harlots whom he had cast out of the city, and who now came in a procession, combed and clean and wearing their best clothes, to pray for the man who had taken them seriously. Walking among these crowds, Henry Yellowlees felt himself someone apart, a ghost perhaps, or more truly a figure in geometry, a stalking, displeased triangle among these swelling curves of emotion. The death of Walter Dunford, whom all these people were so passionately and so pleasurably lamenting, and whom he had for so long so violently hated, roused in him nothing but a kind of quiet, despising astonishment at having hated so violently. In the same way, a stink which has half-choked one, when run to earth becomes no more than the shrivelled body of some wretched rat.

Since his scholars were constantly being called off to sing litanies he had time on his hands, and spent it wandering in and out of the crowd as one wanders in and out of a forest. It amused him to hear all the talk about the nun who was in constant attendance on the dying man. She was a nun of extraordinary saintliness, and in a vision of the Virgin she had been commanded to go to him. She was a doctoress of renowned skill and was keeping him alive by a secret remedy. She was a witch, and killing him as fast as might be. Who would believe him if he had said that he knew all these remarkable ladies and had discussed the price of salt fish with them? He noted that it was quite untrue to suppose that men will fight for their beliefs. All three schools of thought about the bishop's nun heard one another's heresies without the slightest movement of ill-will. Mankind untutored and savage will fight for bread or a bedfellow, but must be schooled by theologians before it will fight for a faith.

He had tired of watching the crowds (which anyhow had grown less as the bishop's dying delayed) and was sitting in his old haunt among the scattered masonry of Jupiter's temple when the note of the passing-bell clashed out. It was evening. The dew was falling, the scent of the gorse blossom hung on the chilling air like the ghost of the day, the birds had left off singing and were settling themselves for the night with occasional screeches of alarm. A little while before, a party of vagrants had come into the enclosure, where they pulled up some gorse stakes and kindled a fire. He had watched the first twine of smoke stain the pure dark blue of the sky and listened to their quiet grunting voices as they sat unbinding their feet before the blaze. The smoke veered aside, and where it had been he saw the first star, and a moment later the first stroke of the bell expanded in the air and died trembling.

Walter Dunford was dead. But every other consideration was lost in a transport of gratitude for his part in the elegy, for the death which had set the bell tolling in the innocent solemn dusk with notes as apt and compelling as the longs in *Triste loysir.* If he knelt to pray for the bishop's soul it was because his pleasure was so intensely physical that he must buttress it by some constraint of asceticism, and the discomfort of his knees on the cold turf would substantiate his delight.

Closer within the circumference of the bell's vibration the news was heard with rather different ears. The clerics hurrying to take their part in the prayers glanced at each other with a flash of eye, admitted man's poor mortality with small shrugs. "At last!" said the glances, and the shrugs replied, "We are well out of it."

For Bishop Walter's last days on earth had been painful and unedifying, and his vitality was so obstinate that no one could feel assured that he would not contrive to exert himself in some irreparable dying scandal. Twice he had broken out of his chamber, saying that he must go out and repent in the face of the poor (for he was acutely aware of the vast audience waiting outside); and only the deftness of that nun had turned him back. Repentance is proper. But Bishop Walter repented beyond all decorum, raving with fear of death and fear of hell and with a self-hatred that slashed out to include all mankind. What it was all about no one had leisure to surmise, any more than when a house is burning the men fighting the fire have time to speculate what caused it. He raved like a madman, they agreed; but the madman was a madman in full possession of his wits, able to rip up the sophistries of would-be comforters, able to recall in their utmost niceties the intrigues of half a century before. Theological acumen had never been attributed to him, even by his backers. He had made his name by simple piety, personal austerities, industry, saintly eccentricity, and a marvellous head for business. But now in the process of demonstrating himself damned no schoolman could have bettered him. He argued like an eel; and the force of all his arguments and of his natural acerbity was directed against the consolations they offered him. Nothing would persuade him to lie down and die in quiet, trusting to the church to manage his affair for him. The devils they exorcised were no sooner disposed of than they came back reinforced with more devils. The relics they brought him he greeted with computations of how much they had cost, how much they had earned, how much they would be worth in ten years' time at that rate of earning. They brought in strangers (against better judgment, but his misery was so authentic that they were ready to try any remedy), summoning friars, anchorites, pious children, even an old woman of the locality who had been whipped for declaring that the Virgin was so familiar with her as to have picked the lice out of her head. But these were no more effective than the people of his household. For a minute or two he welcomed them with craving submission, clasped their hands, whispered in their ears; but the welcome would turn into satire, confutation, abusive home-truths, and mockery. They had waited till he seemed past speech before giving him the holy oils. Half an hour later he began to writhe, and muttered that the oil was burning him, was eating his flesh away; and to their horror they saw his dry skin redden and rise up.

After his death the marks were as plain as if branded with a hot iron. The chaplain, exhausted beyond endurance and beyond tact, pointed them out to Dame Sibilla, saying, "There they are. What do you make of it?" She replied that to her they looked like roses. The doctor, who had really loved Walter Dunford, and was half-dead from watching him die, turned aside with a groan at such silliness.

Yet when he was an old man, and the death of the bishop had taken its place in his memory as one of many deaths, he often quoted Dame Sibilla as an example of the medicinal virtues of virginity. For the bodily heat of a virgin, he said, is at once purer and more vehement than the heat of a deflowered creature, and when the physicians put Abishag into King David's bed they were applying this knowledge, and put her there with no carnal intention but exactly as they would have poured virgin honey into a wound or bound virgin wool about an inflamed joint. And the brain of an old man, he continued, is vexed with cold humours, and chafes and maddens like a river impeded with ice, so that meekness itself becomes irascible and breaks out in furies and contentions. In such cases a virgin, the more simple-witted the better, can do more than any other medicine. She need not be put into the sick man's bed; her mere presence is enough.

That was how, twenty years after, Humphrey Flagg accounted for the efficacy of Dame Sibilla. Of all those taking part in the bishop's last days, she alone remained confident and serene. As his fits grew worse, as he raved more savagely and feared more abjectly, she seemed to be in her element, like a water-spaniel in the flood. She was clumsy, she was obtuse, she was insufferably trivial in the remedies she suggested and the consolations she offered. But her devotion to the dying man was unquestionable, and in the face of his agony her obtuseness took on a quality of intrepidity. Nothing daunted her competence. Did the bishop see devils? She saw them too, in gross and in detail. Naturally, at the death-bed of a bishop the powers of hell would make the most of their opportunity of such a catch. Repentance? But of course! The greater the saint, the greater the repentance. Reproaches and revilings? Again of course. What could be more distressing to the eyes of a dying man than the sight of the world's wickedness, and how could a bishop spend his last breath more valiantly than in rebuking sin and confounding the vainglorious? Doubts, self-damnings, despair? Yes, yes, that was how the dying must feel, but it was all quite natural and nothing to be alarmed at. Besides, think of God's mercy, and of all the poor folk outside, all praying for his soul. The crowd was larger than ever, she said, stepping back from the window with her eyes enlarged as if they had spread to contain the sight of such a multitude. So she flattered and consoled, and belittled this and magnified the other, holding her conjuror's mirror before his eyes. And in the intervals of peace that she won for him he lay with his head in her bosom, clutching at her veil to cover him and sometimes murmuring that he could die in peace for he had saved her from the power of the dog, and at other times listening with a drowsy satisfaction to her chatter about Oby. After he was dead she began to weep, and shook as if an ague shook her; but almost in the next breath she was supping hot wine and patronizing Humphrey Flagg, her tears splashing into the cup as she assured him how interested the ladies of Oby would be when she told them of his prescriptions.

By the time the funeral had taken place (naturally she stayed for the funeral), reports of the bishop's manner of dying had got out; and this was spread about as the doing of the nun who had bewitched him, calling up devils to torment him and prolonging his agony by knots tied in the fringe of the counterpane. Such a person should be got rid of expeditiously and with as little show as possible. But when the steward sent for Henry Yellowlees and told him that he must take Dame Sibilla back to Oby, Henry expostulated that if she were to ride openly through the streets she would be stoned: let her stay a while longer, he urged, while he himself rode to Oby and arranged for an escort of some of her own community with whom she could travel back, a nun among nuns. But no one at the palace cared what became of Dame Sibilla, all they cared for was to be rid of her and rid of the last Dunford. Fortunately the old widow who had been told off to wait on her admired her profoundly; by her arrangements and connivance Dame Sibilla slipped out before dawn, dressed like a serving-woman in short petticoats and a hat with a flapping brim. By the time the sun rose they were well away from the city, riding over the green turf speckled with primroses. It embarrassed him to see her dressed like a secular person, but she took it very lightly and enjoyed the hat. He was relieved when later in the day she went into a thicket and came out in her nun's clothing.

When they got to Oby all the nuns were standing in front of the house to receive her. Looking for the spire to prick the horizon, Henry had wondered how she would be feeling, returning after those weeks of violent emotion to a future flat as the landscape that lay before them. Such a life was comfortable, creditable, happier, probably, than the lives of most other women; and of course in accordance with God's wishes; but after her part in the drama of Walter Dunford's death-bed it must seem tame. She jumped nimbly to the ground and dived in among the others and disappeared.

During Dame Sibilla's absence a new voice had been added to the familiar voices. There had always been plenty of owls round Oby, but this spring an owl established somewhere near by had taken to hooting by day. It was astonishing to hear its *tu-whoo* come floating out from amidst the pink and white of the apple-blossom or tranquilly joining in the midday office. Because this is the kind of thing that frightens servants and excites novices, the ladies of the convent took the line that such behaviour on the part of an owl showed a wrong-headed playfulness; and Dame Philippa's comment that the poor creature must be kept awake by the thought of its sins was often repeated. Possibly Dame Lovisa, so coolly attentive to every hint of a prioress-ship hastening toward her, may have thought otherwise of the owl. But she was quite as discreet as Dame Matilda had been toward the old prioress thirty years earlier, and when Dame Adela (as usual voicing everyone's silliest thought with an added personal tactlessness) said that it was a good thing that Dame Margaret was too deaf to hear the owl hooting for her, Dame Lovisa left it to Dame Eleanor to retort that deafness saved people from hearing a great deal of silliness besides owls, and only remarked that living in a damp climate often renders people hard of hearing.

The convent was full of old women: there was the prioress, Dame Margaret, Dame Dorothy, Dame Cecily—true, she was not really old, but she was blind and sickly; the owl had plenty to choose from before it hooted its *Come-away!* for Adela; but death, even the death that takes someone else, is frightening, and Adela feared the owl. Her fear expressed itself in bravado. Perhaps because the de Retteville blood ran in her veins, and from Brian onward the de Rettevilles lived for hunting, and were more in sympathy with the beasts they slew than with their own kind, Dame Adela was what in later days came to be called a nature-lover. Birds perched on her hand, lizards ran up her wide sleeves, she had pet toads and spiders as well as her troops of pet dogs; though she had never learned her plain-chant she could bark like a fox, whistle like a blackbird, and imitate perfectly every noise in nature. Now when the owl hooted she answered it; and if it did not hoot she would hoot herself and provoke it to reply. No one troubled to check her. Perhaps they even inclined to encourage her. If there was anything alarming about an owl hooting in broad daylight, there was nothing alarming about Dame Adela, so the one was approximated to the other. And when Sir Ralph, poking out from under his abstraction as a tortoise pokes out its head from under its shell, remarked in his Whitsunday sermon that there seemed to be a great quantity of owls about this season and that no doubt owls had their own language as much as the Parthians, and Medes, and Elamites, and the dwellers in Mesopotamia, but that as there was no record that the Apostles began to understand owls christians must wait till the second coming of the Paraclete before they tried to do so, his hearers paid no special attention to this observation.

Then one noontide, to make conversation, Dame Sibilla asked when the daylight owl had begun to hoot: she had not noticed it before she left Oby. One remembered one thing and one another, the date was hunted through remembrances—it was when Dame Amy had a whitlow, it was just before the pear tree blossomed, it was round about the time when the refectory was whitewashed. Then Dame Cecily recalled that it was on Saint Bennet's eve.

Dame Sibilla changed colour, and presently asked another question about something else. She need not have troubled. Conversation flowed on, Bishop Walter was dead and gone from their minds, the fact that the midday owl had begun hooting on the day he died struck no one, nor would anything have been made of this, had it been recalled. If the midday owl hooted for any purpose it hooted for Oby.

Seeing that no one put the owl and the bishop together, she felt relieved. Not to anyone, not to herself even, would she quite admit that there had been anything unseemly in the bishop's manner of dying; but though in the main she was zealously self-deceiving, she had filaments of shrewdness floating from her, and it was with one of these that she sensed that other people were willing enough to be scandalized, and that there was plenty to scandalize them. What had been the likeness of roses to her, for instance, the chaplain had seen with impurer eyes. So hearing the owl—or Dame Adela—she was grateful that no one at Oby was so ill-natured as to suppose that these untimely cries voiced the uneasy estate of her great-uncle's soul. Why should they, why should they? Unfortunately, by combating the idea that anyone should think so, she began to think so herself. To admit such a thought was disloyal to a man of saintly character and unjust to herself: what would become of the shining part (she knew it had been shining) she had played at the vexed death-bed of a saint if in reality that death-bed had been the death-bed of a reprobate? One must flee from temptation. Becoming convinced that this was a temptation, Dame Sibilla fled from it to the best of her considerable abilities, smothering it in prayers, industry, and sociability. For all that, it was soon remarked on that Dame Sibilla could infallibly distinguish between the real owl and Dame Adela—she had such a fine ear.

It was about this time that Dame Lilias plucked up enough resolution to follow Dame Sibilla into a corner and go through with what she wanted to ask.

"While you were attending Bishop Walter I suppose you and he sometimes talked of Oby."

"Yes, indeed! He asked me many questions, and even when he was too weak to question me he liked to hear me talk about it. It is astonishing how much he remembered about us, what an interest he took in us. Truly a father to his poor nuns!"

"Did he happen to say anything about me?"

"Oh, yes, I told him how you made the salve and the distilled betony water."

After a bitter swallow Dame Lilias brought herself to ask if that were all. Umbraged, Dame Sibilla replied in the tone of voice most commonly used toward Dame Lilias, a brisk, rallying tone of voice, "I think that was all. He was very weak, and suffering much, and he had a great deal to think of besides us and our little affairs."

Dame Lilias straightened herself out of her habitual drooping posture and looked fixedly at Dame Sibilla.

"When your great-uncle made his Visitation here I asked him for permission to become an anchoress. He then said he would think of it and send me word. That was five years ago. I wondered if, in his last hours, he had time to remember this."

Out in the orchard Dame Adela hooted.

"But perhaps he had too many things on his mind to give a thought to me."

The owl replied to Dame Adela.

Dame Sibilla said warmly, "An anchoress! I never knew that you wished to be an anchoress. How did it happen, how did you come to wish it? An anchoress! How well I understand such a wish!"

When Dame Sibilla wished to please she could put a great deal of skill and determination into it. Willy-nilly, Dame Lilias had to tell the whole story. Willy-nilly, she received from Bishop Walter's great-niece the sympathy she had hoped for in vain from Bishop Walter. Everything in the story, the long desolation, the voice of the saint, the bruised neck, assailed Dame Sibilla in her core of romantic and real piety. Overlooking the implied disparagement of the bishop, she exclaimed:

"You really heard his voice? How wonderful, how satisfying! I have sometimes seen saints myself but I have never heard one." (For it was also wonderful and satisfying that these supernatural experiences should be thus diversely distributed.)

"Bishop Walter did not think so well of it, you see," said Dame Lilias.

"He had so many things to think of, he had so much on his mind," reiterated Dame Sibilla, but in a graver voice.

Sometimes God sends a death-bed, sometimes a martyrdom, sometimes, as at Allestree, a pestilence. Now God had sent a mission. In a flash Dame Sibilla realized that she and she only could put through this affair of an anchoress and carry out the spoken command of a patronal saint. The notion of making an anchoress glowed in her imagination; perhaps, later on, she would become an anchoress too. Meanwhile, she would give an anchoress to God and the Church.

"If only I had known in time," she sighed, "I would have spoken to my dear uncle. He would have listened favourably, he would certainly have found time to give his blessing and order the preliminaries. Well, we must do what we can without him. I shall always feel that it has his approval, that we are carrying out his wish."

It was not so much a moral scruple as personal fastidiousness that made Dame Lilias say, "I cannot feel sure that he wished it. He did not give me such an impression. And during five years he did nothing about it."

"It slipped his memory. He was so desperately busy. He never slept more than four hours, he snatched his meals, his whole time was given to God and the Church. Or perhaps he did remember it, and gave directions to a secretary, and it was the secretary, not he, who forgot. That seems much likelier. It took four secretaries to keep up with him and anything may be mislaid among four secretaries. No doubt that was it. My uncle would not have forgotten anything to do with Oby."

"He was not very well pleased when he came here."

"Oh, but all that was quite changed, you know."

Dame Sibilla knew that this was not exactly true. But then there are two truths, perhaps three truths, perhaps a dozen. In any case there is the exact and mortal truth which marches with the living and there is the other truth whose dominion opens out with death, a more insighted truth which enables the survivors to give a tranquillizing variant, to anoint the waves with oil. It was the mortal truth that when Bishop Walter gave his attention to Dame Sibilla's talk about Oby he usually did so with an appearance of reservation and mistrust. But then all she had told him must have combated his prejudice and led him to change his mind. And as his features up to the moment of death had been vexed and furious and after his laying-out were the image of an austere repose, so his suspicions of Oby, she felt sure, must have changed to a discerning benevolence. Thus her statement to Dame Lilias which neither of them could mortally and exactly credit was true nevertheless, and not to have spoken it would be impiety and injury to the dead. Surely the souls blessedly afflicted in purgatory need not endure the further pang of hearing themselves misrepresented by truths merely mortal and occasional. In the same way the owl, more often than not, was only Dame Adela. She could not really believe that some little mishap like slighting Dame Lilias's vocation could compel her great-uncle's soul to hang hooting round Oby; but in the light of the post-mortal truth now shining so clearly on Walter Dunford it was plain that he would wish poor Dame Lilias to achieve her ambition, and so one must endeavour, if only as a simple piety to the dead, to bring it about.

It was a thousand pities that the first movers in the business were now so ineffective. The bishop was dead, the prioress heavy with age, and it was impossible to get any sense out of Sir Ralph. Though he remembered everything to do with Dame Lilias and was full of good will, nothing developed from the good will but more good will, and speculations as to the view Dame Lilias would have from her slot window and if the angels, which in a marish country are winged like herons, might not be winged like pigeons in a more comfortable type of landscape. There remained Dame Lilias and Saint Leonard. Dame Lilias was almost as ineffective as the others. The long decline of hope deferred, hope disillusioned, hope slighted and put away, had left her in a state of apathy. She was so apathetic that she did not even oppose Dame Sibilla's intentions. She was like a weed in the water. As for Saint Leonard, another word from him would have put everything in train. But he did not speak it. And the image of Our Lady gazed at the crucifixion of her son, intent as a child at a fair with her blue eyes and pink cheeks, and could think of no sorrow like unto his sorrow.

All this was very discouraging. If Dame Sibilla had not possessed her full share of the Dunford suppleness and resolution she might have abandoned her project. But she persisted, with here a step and there a tweak, praying intemperately and hinting discreetly until she actually contrived to fan up a sort of community pique that Oby, possessing a nun called by heaven to adopt the mortified career of anchoress, could not have been better attended to. Yes, really, it was a great slight! Not every convent can make such an offer, not every convent wants to; yet for five years Oby had been offering its Dame Lilias and was offering her still.

In order to establish this frame of mind Dame Sibilla had had to yield a little ground in the matter of Bishop Walter. A new truth was made plain: that saintliness and episcopacy cannot abide under the same hood, and that a bishop as saintly as Bishop Walter left too much to his secretaries, and was flouted by his underlings, who disregarded his intentions and hoodwinked a good old man with stories of, "Yea, immediately, it shall be seen to tomorrow." Witness the case of Dame Lilias's vocation, trampled and forgotten under the feet of these officials.

"They should have left him in peace among his poor," she

grieved. "They should not have compelled him to become a bishop. He was not meant for a bishop. If they had not bishoped him, I daresay he would be alive and with us to this day."

She was about to add, "And making Dame Lilias an anchoress," but she remembered that the presentation of anchoresses is an appurtenance of bishops.

XII. A CANDLEMAS CUCKOO

(February 1380)

A wolf dead is half-way to being a lamb. Bishop Walter Dunford dead was emerging as the mild admirer of Oby, the more easily since a new bishop had taken his place, a complete novelty, and so to be dreaded. The new bishop was Perkin de Craye, a Fleming of a great moneylending family, who was said to be a fat, smooth, proud man with a stammer, caring only for Our Lady, works of art, ritual, and foreign cheeses. Such a bishop would look with little favour on Dame Lovisa's magpie psalters. He would be more efficaciously wooed with an embroidery. When next Henry Yellowlees came on a custodianly visit he was questioned about Perkin de Craye's views on gold thread and *opus anglicum.* As for Perkin de Craye's views on anchoresses, that subject was put by for more immediate considerations.

In a convent any long-term strategy is at the mercy of the present. In the excitement of blue satin, white sarsenet, silks and fine needles, gold thread and spangles, Dame Sibilla forgot to hear the owl, and Dame Lilias, who was always admitted to have very good taste whatever her failings might be, was suddenly gathered into the life of the community to animate the party which favoured a design of white ostrich plumes, naturalistically treated, rather than the gold and white lilies advocated by the traditionalists. It was many years since the convent had undertaken a large needlework. The prioress possessed no skill as a needlewoman, Dame Lovisa's broken nails made it out of the question that she should handle an embroidery: needlework had become involved in the politics of the community, and its laying-by was a sign of the de Stapledon ascendancy. Now the enthusiasm for the proposed altar-hanging nursed up an opposition party, brought Dame Lilias into popularity, and kindled a revival of admiration for the Trinity Cope embroidered by the old prioress, Dame Alicia de Foley the spire-builder.

Unnoticed for years, this was now brought out and studied in all its details. One stitch used by Dame Alicia baffled every needlewoman of the current generation; there was some trick in it, some manipulation of the thread, which they could not reproduce; and then came a dramatic turn when Dame Adela paused by the group of nuns puzzling over this stitch and said that she knew just how it was done, for she had often watched the old prioress doing it. Give her a needle, she said. Unbelievingly they gave her a scrap of canvas and some cheap green thread; and before their eyes she performed the old prioress's stitch, so exactly that only by the materials could you tell the new from the old. Dame Adela being a de Retteville this discovery strengthened the anti-de Stapledon party. It was agreed that the way Dame Adela was neglected and allowed to wander hooting about the grounds was part and parcel of the de Stapledon usurpation of power, and Dame Adela was made miserable by finding herself kept at needlework instead of being left to her own out-of-door devices.

When William Holly took to his bed only the prioress was sufficiently detached from the politics of the altar-hanging to think that Oby might lose an invaluable servant. The peril of her contemporary roused up her faculties, she wept and fretted and lay awake at night fingering her beads and reckoning incomings and outgoings much as she had used to do in her treasuress days and often confusing the calculations of those days with the calculations of the present. But now she saw all with the despondency of the aged: the interest on the Methley tithe, the debt on the Methley repairs and the interest on the loan which had been raised to pay part of that debt, the rise in the cost of living, the expenses of the next Visitation (God be thanked, Perkin de Craye made no move so far to come to them but sooner or later come he must), the expenses of her own funeral and the cost of installing Dame Lovisa as her successor (but who could say?—there might yet be a schism, an Eleanor prioress debating with a Lovisa prioress, election and counter-elections), the repairs needed at Tunwold, the deadlock over the Esselby rent, the diminishing returns from the river-dues at Scurleham, caused by the silting up of the estuary and the lessening value of the water-borne trade, the burden of Henry Yellowlees (he was not so bad as he might have been, but every custos is economically bad, for he authorizes expenditures too easily and corrupts the community he is put in charge of by lifting the sense of responsibility from the nuns in chapter themselves, this or that is granted, agreed, neglected, because the custos wills it or because the custos will see to it), the burden (another legacy laid on them by Bishop Walter, might he burn in hell-fire, God rest his soul!) of those two healthy, eating gawks, Amy Hodds and Joan Cossey (who had lived through the measles which had killed Lucy Frampton), and an undowered Dame Sibilla, the fact that these three nominees took up room that might otherwise be given to advantageous novices, the difficulty, though, of getting a good novice nowadays, the alarming increase in convent servants, nuns and servants alike now grew so luxurious that more servants were needed to wait on the nuns, and more servants to serve the servants, the cost of a new priest, for Sir Ralph was so senile that really he was a scandal and something must be done about him and in any case he would die, the blindness of Dame Cecily and the cost of the opiates that must be given her for mere pity's sake—and now all this expenditure on blue satin. And nothing to put against it but William Holly's heriot if William Holly died. And a new bailiff to choose and train who would never be a patch on William Holly.

So the old woman lay awake, grunting and grieving. There was another thing on her mind too, though she managed to keep it from getting into the inventory. Dame Alice had drowned Magdalen Figg in the fish-pond. It was all long ago, Magdalen had drowned in water and now was decaying in earth, and Sir Ralph was out of his wits and remembered nothing; but earth and water are but two elements, there are also fire and air to reckon with, and air can body a story and fire can burn the soul.

The nuns heard their prioress grunting and sighing, and the bedstead creaking and the dry rattle of the beads, and since they heard such sounds every night thought nothing of them.

Having twice been anointed for death, William Holly recovered. Soon he was snapping round the manor again, boasting of how he had squelched his toad with a great blow he had given himself in the belly. His sickness had left no mark on him except that he was rather thinner and considerably more fault-finding. Everything had gone to rack and ruin, he said, during his illness; the prioress herself could not persuade him to admit that many of the deficiencies he complained of were long-standing and had been complained of by him for years. The vivacity of his complaints compelled them to face the fact that nowadays a manor was not what it used to be, and little more than a rather tiresome way of supplying oneself with milk and poultry, bread and firing. More tiresomely, a manor in these days was a camp of malcontents, and one must be on good terms with one's people, and not press them too much, lest they should take part in the rebellions which were jumping up, here, there, and everywhere, like a fire in the stubble. Anything is better than being burned out or murdered in one's bed.

"But should we not aim," said Dame Lovisa, "to do something more than please William Holly? That will soothe no one, since they all detest him for his prosperity and his extortions. We should find some means of seeming to serve them all."

"Then we must first make a fortune," answered Dame Eleanor. "Food, clothing, new thatching, the gleaning bell rung an hour earlier, a remission of dues—there is no way of pleasing people that is not costly."

"There is one way. We can teach their children. That would cost very little except time and trouble. People like you to make a fuss of their children, nothing pleases them so surely."

"Teach them? Teach them what?"

"Really, as little as you wish. A few hymn tunes, the names of the patriarchs, a little hearsay Latin, how to wipe their noses . . . it is the attention that pleases, the learning is no matter."

She could read a *non-placet* in their looks even before they began to make objections. "Where should the children be put?

—in the nave? Their fleas won't stay in the nave, Dame Lovisa, their fleas will come leaping into the quire."—"And who is to teach them, are the novices to be neglected on their behalf when heaven sends us novices?"—"And if we have them here, how are we to get rid of them? They will stay all day, we shall never be free of them."—"And if we teach them they will all go off the manor to become friars and clerks, nuns and jugglers, they will never stay at work once they begin to think themselves scholars. Besides, how are we to teach children when our hands are full of the altar-hanging?" Such were the answers, and Dame Margaret lifted up her ancient croak and recalled how Oby had once educated a boy, who had gone off with their best horse and a quantity of spices.

Dame Lovisa's project got no further. Thinking of her own project, Dame Sibilla sighed with relief. The anchoressing of Dame Lilias, the appeasing of the owl (it was still there, for owls are constant in their haunts, and in the dusky vapours of a November forenoon its tranquil disembodied note was quite as sinister as in high summer), were not proceeding as fast as she had hoped, and another distraction might be ruinous. It was now almost two years since Walter Dunford's death. But the great needlework would soon be completed: then would come a pause, an idle interim when she could command their attention.

And then everything was overturned by the affair of Dame Adela. Twenty years before it had been axiomatic that Adela would need to be watched; and her profession had been postponed for some time since a seduced novice is less scandalous than a seduced nun. But a short watchfulness sufficed. Her apple-blossom beauty had not been substantiated by the slightest carnal intellect, she was as chaste as a parsnip; and now, nearing thirty, she was faded, awkward, gap-toothed. It was strange to reflect that the wonderful de Retteville novice, procured with such triumph by the old prioress and fought for as briskly as though she were Helen of Troy, should have turned into this harmless incubus, rather greedy, terrified of thunderstorms, who tamed mice and could hoot like an owl. Nobody reflected on it, however, for nobody gave Dame Adela a thought—except Dame Lovisa, who had never lost the protectiveness which she, the ugly novice, had so oddly displayed for her lovely contemporary. Her concern showed itself by harshness where the unconcern of the others was indulgent. She scolded her, tidied her, hunted her out of the kitchen court, discouraged the fellowship with toads, kites, and spiders. When it came to light that Dame Adela remembered the old prioress's trick stitch, Dame Lovisa rejoiced in this opportunity to put Dame Adela on a level with the other nuns, though, as she knew, every stitch copied from the second Trinity Cope strengthened the de Retteville faction and injured her own prospects of becoming the next prioress.

In carefulness, in anxiety, in unpopularity, she was already almost a prioress, and it was strange that having so real a foretaste of the wormwood of office she should be so determined to drink it out of the official cup. Throughout that second winter the work on the altar-hanging was carried forward, and everyone who could thread a needle was engaged on some part of it. Since needlework cannot be done with cold hands all available fuel went to keep up a good fire in the parlour. The prioress sat there, and Dame Cecily was led in, to enjoy the warmth and the conversation and the sense of something in the making. Though Dame Lovisa could not take part in the embroidering because of her broken nails and her chilblains, there was no reason why she should not sit there with the rest and be warm and sociable, and to do so would have been politic. But she was no sooner settled among them than an uneasy austerity drove her out. There was always a pretext to leave them: a message to the kitchen, a beggar to be relieved, a traveller to be interviewed. There was always a reason to go and never a voice to bid her stay. There was not even an open antagonism to challenge by remaining. Hers was a cold unpopularity. So she left the fireside: sometimes to stand at the wicket handing out food and drink, listening to the stamp or shuffle of feet, gulpings and whisperings and fragmentary news of another world; sometimes to hear long-winded complaints and give good advice which would never be heeded; sometimes to check account-books, sometimes to roll pills, sometimes to pray in the quire—where she would no sooner be settled on her knees than she would notice something amiss and get up to right it. Coming and going, she would hear the voices flowing from the parlour, or the thump of the flails from the granary, or from Sir Ralph's chamber a sudden gusty bellow as the old man, lying a-bed for warmth, would recall a tavern song of his student days, or from the kitchen a clatter of dishes and a steady rattle of narrative. Everyone had a voice and a will to use it except her. She could only think, unconversational as a snake.

And yet it was Dame Lilias who wished to become an anchoress and Dame Lovisa who willed to become a prioress.

Peering out through a crack in the window-screen, she stared at the thin-lipped landscape, foggy with long frost, and sought in herself the reason. In her heart were two wishes: to become prioress and to make another psalter. The copying of those psalters had been the only pleasure she had known; to be prioress was the only ambition she could conceive.

Among the voices in the parlour she could hear Dame Adela's —a querulous note, interrupted by a yawn. Adela might weary of the needlework, but she must be kept to it. Every stitch she dragged through the blue satin fastened her a little more into the life of the community, and buttressed Dame Lovisa's fantastic resolve that when she became prioress Adela should be treated with more respect, should even be given some office. But what office?—since she had neither discretion, demeanour, industry, nor common wit. Nunneries, unfortunately, have no call for a verderer. The voices grew louder, someone had opened the parlour door; and at the same moment a figure came into her narrow view of the world, and by its coming, its dark shuffling approach, made that world twice as cold, twice as sombre. Man or woman she could not say; but certainly a beggar. Today it was Dame Eleanor's turn at the wicket, but she was a poor hand with beggars, alternately scorning and scornfully indulging them; besides, she would not wish to leave the fireside. Dame Lovisa went to the wicket herself and waited for the beggar to knock. She heard the footsteps pause, and the sound of a spit. The beggar knocked.

Disconcerted by being so instantly opened to, the woman stared at the nun with a look of antagonism. Then she began her complaint. She was penniless, she said, and hungry; she had been poisoned by eating bad fish, and was seven months gone with child. In the austere air her stink was almost intolerable.

But hungry she certainly was not, thought Dame Lovisa, watching her inattentive mouthing. More likely she had come to the wicket from loneliness. Loneliness is often the beggar's worst affliction, and thinking of this Dame Lovisa now opened the door to her. Sprawling on a bench with her hands over the brazier, the woman began to tell of her rambles from shrine to shrine, misfortune to misfortune. It was at the shrine of Saint Cuthbert, at Durham in the north, that she had been got with the child she carried, a cruel thing to befall a virtuous woman, and certainly it must have grieved the saint. But if it proved a boy she would name it Cuthbert. As ill-luck would have it, Dame Adela now joined them, yawning and stretching and complaining of the fatigue of needlework, and took it upon her to remark that it was a pity the child could not be born a monkey, for a monkey would be diversion and better able to fend for itself. The virtuous pilgrim gave her a displeased look. Dame Lovisa said hastily that she knew something of the north country, since she had been born there.

"Ah well, you're out of it now," said the woman, "and snug in the Virgin's lap. You convent ladies do not know how lucky you are."

Dame Adela exclaimed that a nun's life was not so easy. There was the night office, the lenten fast, all day you were kept at needlework and the gold thread was sharp and cut the fingers. The woman replied that there was nothing she loved better than to see holy needleworks; whether on the priest's back or on the altar it did you good to see so much richness in a poor world, and every stitch of it put in by pure virgins, she daresayed. She began to describe copes and hangings she had seen, the white and the gold and the scarlet, the bullion standing out in lumps as big as your fist, the pearls like drops of mutton fat. Meanwhile her lice, enlivened by the warmth, crawled out over her neck and forehead and at intervals she caught one with a practised hand and inattentively bit it.

This altar-hanging now, she asked, what colour was it? Was

it crimson? Blue, said Dame Adela. Our dear Lady's own colour, said the woman knowledgeably. Instantly Dame Adela offered to fetch it.

"Don't be a fool!" exclaimed Dame Lovisa. Dame Adela giggled and moved toward the door. Dame Lovisa boxed her ears, and Dame Adela began to weep.

The woman put on a discreet expression and busied herself with her lice.

A box on the ears is not much in a convent, yet Dame Lovisa sickened with a feeling of guilt. Alone at Oby she was conscious of Dame Adela as an immortal soul, a thing in which God's intention, however hooded by imbecility, stirred and chirped and was refreshed by the sacraments. Because of this she was harsh and irritable while the rest were tolerant. Now Dame Adela wept with her uncontrollable half-wit's weeping. Her laments would be heard, and some hearer would say, "Listen to the poor wretch! Really, it's a shame," and the shrieks of a pig-killing would not mean less to them.

Pulling herself together, she turned to the woman, who met her glance with a grimace of understanding and tapped lightly on her forehead. With so much knowledge of the world and of needlework, thought Dame Lovisa, this unpleasant pilgrim must be some cast-off bower-woman.

"And to what shrine are you travelling now?" she asked.

"We are going to Waxelby."

There was no shrine at Waxelby, but she went on smoothly to say that she was in hopes that from Waxelby some ship's captain would be charitable enough to give her a passage southward, so that she could visit the shrine of Saint Osyth.

"Then you do not make this pilgrimage alone?"

The thought of other pilgrims straying about the hen-roosts, plunging their hands into corn-bins, made Dame Lovisa's voice sharp.

"How dare one travel alone in these bad days?" said the woman defensively. "The others have already gone on. It was my sickness that kept me lagging behind."

"You had better make haste after them."

Seating herself more squarely on the bench, the woman said

that among the pilgrims there was one brought up in these parts—nearer home, maybe, than it would be convenient to say. After pausing aggressively, she added, "His mother was a nun in this very house."

Dame Adela looked up, all eyes, and said roundly that it could not be true.

"Ah, my poor lady!" said the woman with condescension. "You sit embroidering, you do not know all that passes."

"As if I should not know if a child were born! No such thing, I tell you. It is true our priest used to fondle Magdalen Figg, for I have seen him at it. But she was no nun, and had no baby, she was too old for that."

"I know who you mean," Dame Lovisa said. "He was called Jackie or some such name. He went off on a stolen horse with other goods he had stolen. I have heard the older ladies talk of it. He is well advised to go on toward Waxelby. I do not wonder he made such haste."

She stood over the woman, willing her to depart. The woman rose. In her bosom, tucked into her dirty wrappings, was the bowl from which she had eaten.

"I have a message for that same priest," said the woman, rolling her eyes, "whom some say is no priest at all. Jackie bid me say . . ."

"And our bowl?" Dame Lovisa inquired.

The woman handed it over with a kind of dignity. Then loyalty to her Jackie (from Pernelle Bastable onward many women had been too loyal to Jackie for their own profit) overcame her. She began to rant and scream, saying that such hospitality would choke her, and that the nuns of Oby were no better than their priest, shams all of them, cheats, wantons, greedy-guts, oppressors of the poor. The noise brought Dame Eleanor. Instead of being grateful that another should have borne the stress of entertaining this visitor, she turned on Dame Lovisa and reproached her for usurping everybody's business, "Though why you should be so anxious to poke your face out of the wicket I do not know. Unless it be to scare people from our door. That would be thrifty, of course. That would appeal to you."

"More thrifty still to leave them knocking with never an answer! But you were gabbling by the fire, forgetful of everything except your own ease. If I had not heard her and gone at last to receive her she would be knocking still."

"And a pretty piece of work you seem to have let in."

While the two nuns quarrelled in an undertone the woman had worked herself into a frenzy—the worse since she could get no attention but Adela's—and now she was beating on the walls and crying to be let out of this place, worse than a prison, worse than a brothel, worse than hell itself since every soul in it was black-damned. What else but damned could they be?—idle, devouring caterpillars listening to a mass that was no mass since a priest that was no priest performed it.

"How much longer do you propose to entertain this trull?" inquired Dame Eleanor.

"Now that you are here I will not trespass on your office. I am waiting for you to turn her away," replied Dame Lovisa.

Dame Eleanor advanced on the woman, who instantly turned on her.

"Trull, do you say? True enough, true enough, I am no lady, so any word is good enough for me. I do not sit all day by a fire embroidering in gold thread upon satin. Yes, and deny the very sight of it to a poor woman," she added, turning upon Dame Lovisa. "You will stir your white fingers for God's altar, but when did you ever prick your fingers for God's poor? We go in rags. And you waste on one yard of your fancywork as much gold as would clothe and feed ten of us for a year's length. Where are the words of Christ when he said, Clothe the naked? When do you sit down and spin for us? Spin! You cannot as much as spin for yourselves, you are not worth as much as spiders.

"But you won't laugh for ever," she continued, having noticed Dame Adela's countenance brighten at the mention of spiders. "You may laugh now, but you will weep sooner than you look for. You will have a fine fire to warm yourselves by one night, the red hen will scrabble in your thatch. Mark my words! I know what I know, I know what I've heard, and I tell you it won't be long before they come to smoke you out. We have been eaten up long enough with lewd monks and idle nuns, we have lost patience with you. You have worn out the patience of the poor!"

On the threshold she turned back for a last look. By now half the convent had gathered, flustering, questioning, threatening. She spat, and marched away, holding forth her belly as if it were a shield.

The substance of her words was really nothing new. For many years the nuns had been accustomed to the hearsay of such talk, and could refer to themselves as "we idlers," and "us worthless nuns." Threats of destruction were no novelty either; the more romantically minded would sometimes discuss where they would go, what they would do, when the Lollards came and set fire to the convent. None of them had any distinct ideas as to their plans, and certainly their relations would not welcome them home; but that did not spoil the conversation. The more sophisticated among them, such as Dame Philippa and Dame Cecily, at times contemplated a more gradual kind of destruction, a day —beyond their own day, of course, but within reach of speculation—when well-dowered novices would be so few and expenses so heavy that convents would perish for lack of means. But there is a difference between hearsay and hearing with one's own ears; the woman's fury and insolence had genuinely fluttered those who heard her, so very naturally they fell into a violent squabble among themselves, some blaming Dame Lovisa for letting the woman in, others blaming Dame Eleanor for not being there to keep her out. Thanks to one or other of them the nuns of Oby might well find themselves murdered in their beds. Fortunately the prioress, asleep in her chair, knew nothing of it.

As they broke off their altercation to go in to vespers Dame Eleanor paired with her adversary and said in a low voice, "Why did she say that about Sir Ralph?"

Dame Lovisa shrugged. "It is one of the things they say—I suppose because when he first came here he was a stranger and spoke with an accent; and then there was that business with Figg's widow, and heaven only knows what he may have said himself, for he is quite irresponsible in what he says."

"But do you suppose there is any truth in it?"

"No, no!"

"But it would be fearful. He has been here since the great pestilence."

"Yes, he is older than the prioress. I wonder which of them will go first. Sir Ralph, I imagine. He is failing fast."

Even so Dame Eleanor said, "I think we ought to look into it." She meant what she said. For one thing, she was a proud woman; and at the thought that for years she had been fooled with a spurious sacrament all her pride was up in arms; for another, she was aware that as the router-out of so frightful an imposture she would become a leading figure, the only nun at Oby acceptable as prioress—unless, of course, they chose to jump in someone from elsewhere: that very real danger must be borne in mind.

"We must talk this over, you and I," she said. "I thank my saints that I have you to consult with, one responsible person among this pack of feather-pates."

Full of dejection and foreboding Dame Lovisa temperately agreed.

But all this was blown away when it was discovered that Dame Adela was gone, and the altar-hanging gone with her. Then it was remembered that Dame Adela had excused herself half-way through supper, had been absent from compline, absent from the midnight office. No one had noticed it, and the dormitory was so ill-lit by its one rush-light that her unoccupied pallet was not noticed either. Then, too, it was remembered that in their flurry over the quarrel at the wicket they had forgotten to put away the needlework.

Not till midday did they dare tell the prioress. They feared that the shock might be the last blow to her faculties. She flared up into her old competence, genial and cold-hearted, wasting little time in reproaches and none in lamentations, and at once sent out searchers and messengers and had the house protected against thieves.

Thieves seemed the likeliest hypothesis. The woman was the spy for the gang, and after she had made sure that the altar-hanging was worth stealing (had she not fished to see it?) her companions had broken in under cover of the winter darkness and stolen it. How and why they had also stolen Dame Adela was less apparent; but possibly she, alone absent from quire, had found them breaking in, and they had gagged her and carried her away before she could raise an alarm. Why they should carry rather than kill seemed unaccountable; but no one could find her body, or any bloodstains or signs of a struggle.

Much was said of the ingratitude of Ursula's Jackie, plundering for the second time the house which had reared him—for he, no doubt, was at the bottom of this theft. Dame Margaret, crackling like a holly fire, recalled what a dirty, spoiling, impudent, thievish, forward, and ugly child he had been. Sir Ralph, peering into the past, remembered him as a sullen and unimprovable pupil. Dame Cecily dwelt on him as a distasteful hobbledehoy who used to draw obscene pictures on the walls and torment Dame Salome. The prioress said less, but nursed a deeper resentment. Four days later, when news came that a vagrant man called Jack Nonesuch, also Jack the Latiner, also Jackie Pad, had been seized in Waxelby and cast into jail, her satisfaction was terrible to witness. She guffawed, she cracked jokes, she scratched herself, she suggested having a Te Deum sung for the occasion: it was as if all her de Stapledon forbears, so pious over property, so ruthless over flesh and blood, had come wassailing into the convent. That night at supper she ate and drank inordinately, and went to bed singing. A few hours later she was stricken by an apoplexy. Too tough to die, she lay motionless, a vast senseless ruin, a sounding-board for her stertorous groans.

But questioned and threatened and eventually maimed of his right hand as a known thief, Ursula's Jackie vouchsafed nothing about Dame Adela and the altar-hanging—only that in Waxelby he had met his leman, who had a woman with her whom he had taken to be such another as she, and that he had quarrelled with her and had not seen her or heard of her since. As it would have been to his advantage to help towards the finding of a strayed nun, there seemed no reason to disbelieve him.

All this had come about because Dame Lovisa in her self-importance must needs run to the wicket when it was no business of hers. Cowed by so much calamity, she agreed with the common sentence. It was all her doing, her wretched doing. Her misery was so abject that she did not even forecast the consequences of the event, the loss in money, the loss in reputation with its contingent loss of more money, the death of the prioress, the impossibility that she should now succeed her. Among all these losses she brooded over yet another loss, in the common estimation the loss of least account, the lost Adela. The wind had changed, it blew from the southwest, and brought a rainy thaw. A white mist like steam from a cauldron billowed round the house. Out of this uncertain daylight the daylight owl hooted: hearing it, she was transfixed with a hope as agonizing as if a sword had been thrust between her ribs. Adela had come back! But it was only the owl. Adela was gone, in her last hours cuffed and abused and overlooked. Reduced to foolishness by her grief, Dame Lovisa told herself that Adela had run away because of wounded feelings.

The fears of the half-witted drive them toward what they dread. As the rabbit runs toward the weasel, and the mouse presses itself to the cat's flank, Dame Adela's first impulse had been to follow the beggar woman and hear again and again those threats of a burning roof and the angered poor. But she had not spent her life in a convent for nothing, some shreds of policy had been compelled into her mind; and while the nuns were quarrelling she sat down in her corner to think how best to purloin the altar-hanging. If she took it along with her the woman would receive her with more favour; and then it could be sold and with the money ten of those dreadful poor could be clothed and fed, and so for a whole year (the woman had said ten could be clothed and fed for a year) the roof of Oby would not burn, the poor would go elsewhere, Sir Ralph would be the same Sir Ralph as ever, and no blood start from the wafer as he handled it.

She went into supper with the rest, and made her excuse half-way through it. But instead of going to the necessary house she went to the parlour and collected the gold thread, the silks, the pearls, and parcelled them in the altar-hanging, and wrapped it all in a towel. There was an old furred cloak, it had belonged to Dame Alicia de Foley, which had long lain as an extra wadding under the cushions of the present prioress. She pulled it out; and out with it came a complicated smell, compounded of wildcat, old spices, and fleabane. As she put on the cloak it seemed to her that she was creeping for warmth and shelter into the skirts of the old prioress as she had done when she was a child. She saw the old woman's hand, dry and waxen-white, with the ring that fitted so loosely that it was always slipping round, the light of its jewel shining inward on the palm, and felt herself dutifully turning it right way about again. It was there, it was gone. A brand broke on the hearth, the shadows of the room were re-made with a new shape, peaked and wolfish. It was her own hooded shadow she saw but she did not stay to recognize it. While the voices sounded and the spoons clattered beyond the partition, she pulled the cloak over her bundle and went lightly to the little side-door and out across the orchard to the gap in the reed-fence. Beyond was a stretch of marshy meadow. The cat-iced puddles glittered in the moonlight, and crackled under her tread. Beyond the meadow was the Hog Trail, the causeway to Waxelby.

She began to run.

The bundle was heavy, it slipped and sidled under her arm. Her running settled into a dog-trot.

Two horses were standing at the side of the causeway, nose to tail, pressed together for warmth. As she ran by, one of them pricked its ears and neighed, and a moment later they both came trotting after her. For a quarter-mile or so they kept up with her. Then they stopped, their curiosity at an end, and she ran on alone. The moonlit sky seemed to be made of blue ice. Ice glittered in the crotches of the old willow trees that grew on the banks of the causeway. Their shadows laced the ground before her. She had no fear of the night and no sense that she was doing anything surprising. To be running along the Waxelby causeway was natural, the only thing she could be doing. The bundle under her arm was a nuisance, that was all. But her trot had fallen into a walk and the shadows of the willow boughs had lengthened with the dropping moon before she saw a figure going along the causeway ahead of her. She began to run again. The figure also began to run.

The quarry was heavy with child, it would not be hard for Adela to outstrip her. But some obscure hunting inheritance set her differently to work. She left the causeway, pulled off her sandals, and ran on under the cover of the willows till her ears told her she had drawn level with the woman. Then she steadied her breath and cried, *"Cuckoo!"*

She heard the woman stop and say bewilderedly, "The Saints have mercy!"

"Cuckoo!" repeated Adela.

"You fool, Annis," the woman remonstrated with herself. "Whenever was there a Candlemas cuckoo?"

It was certainly the beggar-woman's voice. Adela scrambled up the bank and came out on the causeway beside her. Now all her sureness and invention left her, and all she could do was to hold out the bundle and look at Annis with a smile.

Annis stared her up and down, from the round simpering face to the bare feet. The feet were so white, white beyond any bleach of moonlight, the face was so wild and vacant. . . . Annis crossed herself and said softly, "Is it you in your flesh and blood?"

Adela nodded and smiled wider than before.

"And your feet as bare as meadow saffron," Annis continued, feeling her way between flesh and ghost. "It's pitiful! But why are you here?"

"I've brought it," said Adela. "I've brought it for you, and all the silks, and the pearls. It's nearly finished, you know. We can soon finish it between us. I'll teach you the stitch."

The woman did not answer.

"Aren't you glad? Look!"

Before Annis could stop her she unrolled the bundle and the altar-hanging was spread on the ground. Annis recoiled, crossing herself. Loosened by the journey, the little bag holding the pearls gaped open. Some pearls rolled out. Annis threw herself down with a hoarse cry and began to scoop them up. Still on her knees, she held one up in the moonlight, scanned it closely, put it to her lips.

"They are not real pearls," she said.

The shapes of the hungry and naked poor started up threateningly on every side. Once more the familiar sensation of having made a fool of herself descended on Adela, and she reacted with fear and fury.

"May your teeth drop out, ungrateful beast! How dare you say my pearls are not real pearls? I brought it because you are poor and I was sorry for you. I ran all this way after you, and now you say they are not real pearls. I'll take it all back!"

She crumpled up the altar-hanging. With a cry of compassion Annis thrust her aside and began to smooth the ill-used satin.

"What a way to treat it! I marvel you don't dance on it. There, so—that's better. What a way to use you!"

The consolations addressed to the altar-hanging had their effect on Adela. She picked up a few pearls and handed them to Annis. The two women crawled about on their hands and knees peering into the ruts and hoof-prints. Annis was still half under the spell of this dreamlike encounter. A Candlemas cuckoo had turned into a ghost, the ghost into a half-wit, the half-wit into a furious child; and lying at the side of the track was the Oby needlework, which might mean a great sum of money and equally might mean a hanging. If this were not enough for her wits to contend with, there was also this mad nun.

The lesser risk would be to take them both back where they belonged. But after her outburst the nuns would not be likely to receive her with much favour, at the best she would come off with some old rags, a clipped shilling, and some more of that soup. And once more the causeway to Waxelby would stretch before her and at Waxelby Jackie would be growing tired of waiting as he was growing tired of her—for he tired easily. Some other woman might get him, or he might give her the slip, for a man can always get himself on to a boat whereas only a very drunken captain will welcome a woman far gone with child. Yet if she went forward, taking Jackie the altar-hanging, she must needs take the nun too.

In the end she decided to go on, with the hope of getting rid of her companion between now and daybreak. Let her get tired out, thought the hopeful Annis. Let her fall asleep, nicely tucked up in her cloak a little aside from the causeway, and leave her. Nuns would rather sleep than walk.

But the virgin capered along beside her, singing and showing off her bird-calls. It was Annis who flagged, it was Annis who could go no farther, it was Annis who fell into a heavy slumber, lying with Adela under Dame Alicia de Foley's cloak. When she woke it was broad daylight and Adela was tickling her nose with a rush. And there, little more than a mile away, was the town of Waxelby, with the great Friars' Church standing up like a ship above the reeds and the waterways, and the round tower of Waxelby Old Church seeming no more than a net-stake beside it.

After one glance Annis lay down again and shut her eyes. The daylight reality of the night's crazy dream appalled her. She wanted to scream, to scratch out those blue eyes, to scream again and again. She prayed with intensity that the pains of her labour might take hold of her here and now, and by their majestic anguish release her from having to think about anything else.

The prayer was vain. She sat up and began to comb her hair with her fingers and to smarten up her garments. Then she pulled a little pot out of her wallet, and reddened her cheeks and her lips. Adela watched with interest.

"You must trim yourself up a little," said Annis. "We cannot go into Waxelby looking like scarecrows."

But Adela had nothing to trim herself up with. By degrees, by lending a kerchief, by stripping off her petticoat and her ornaments and putting them on the nun, and by reddening her cheeks, she made Adela into a passable imitation of a whore. By adapting some of Adela's clothes to her own use she made of herself a more convincing representation of a bawd. All this touch-and-go exchange she carried through with admirable tact and wariness, though she was dizzy with exhaustion. But when it was done, even as she was congratulating herself on having done it so well, the thought of what would happen next almost broke her courage. There would be so many nexts!—to get Adela into Waxelby, to hear a mass, to find a breakfast, to find Jackie, to put him into a good humour and yet not into too good a humour; for dressed as a whore the mad nun had developed a sort of mad beauty, a tattered faded crumpled beauty, as if beauty were a garment that had been left hanging for years on a hedge and now were put on again. But Jackie would relieve her of the altar-hanging, and that would be one care off her mind. There should be no difficulty there, for the nun still prated about how it was to be sold for the relief of the poor.

Annis's thoughts considered the poor as they walked on to Waxelby. Her overnight's rant was nothing but beggar's rhetoric, as she knew well, the noise one hears in every alehouse, every jail, every ditch. It is not hunger and nakedness that worst afflict the poor, for a very little thieving or a small alms can remedy these. No, the wretchedness of the poor lies below hunger and nakedness. It consists in their incessant incertitude and fear, the drudging succession of shift and scheme and subterfuge, and labouring in the quicksand where every step that takes hold of the firm ground is also a step into the danger of condemnation. Not cold and hunger but Law and Justice are the bitterest affliction of the poor.

Entering Waxelby, she hurried her companion to the Friary Church, and fell on her knees, thankful for the sense of respite that came with the rows of pillars so strong and upright, the reiteration of mouldings in triforium and clerestory, the echo that sanctified every sound. Adela knelt beside her, staring about her, but momentarily quiet. Then she rose and began to walk up the nave. When Annis went after her she said placidly that she was going to take her place in quire. Hearing this astonishing statement, an old woman looked round, and was the more astonished when she saw the tattered appearance of the owner of that imperious voice.

"Do you think yourself a friar, then?" she asked.

"I am a nun," Adela replied. While Annis sickened, some obscure whim of grandeur impelled Adela to continue, "We are both nuns."

"Friars' nuns, I daresay," said the old woman, "the pair of you. Whipping's what you need."

The echo could not do much for this. Abashed at having injured the friars in their own church, the old woman turned around and addressed herself to Saint Blaize. Before Adela could get into any more mischief a mass began. Her readiness with the responses made more heads turn towards them, and

Annis could think of no better expedient than to exaggerate her own devotion and hope they might be taken for pilgrims. But as they left the church some stones were thrown and the phrase of "Friars' nuns" was hooted after them.

Adela's dread of the terrible poor returned. She clung to Annis. Annis was in no mood to be clung to. Her short cross answers completed Adela's dejection, and though the ships at the quayside interposed themselves between her and her alarm she was not allowed to gape at them but found herself shoved through a doorway into a narrow room full of men and men's loud voices.

A few looked up, one or two spoke; no one moved to make room for her. Here were the poor again, more and poorer and more intimidating. But the woman who kept the alehouse had already exchanged glances with Annis and now without a word she pushed the two women into a sort of lean-to chamber beyond. It had a couple of trestles in it, some cobwebbed fishing-gear and rags in bunches hung on the walls, it smelt fusty and sleepy; and indeed there was someone sleeping in it even now, an old man with a bald head covered with warts and scabs, who slept fretfully, grunting, and burrowing in his straw for the warmth that had left his limbs. Annis pulled away some of his straw and sat down composedly with the straw round her feet. Then she pointed to her mouth and rubbed her stomach. The alehouse woman nodded and went off, and came back with some bread and beer and two hunks of black-pudding. The beer was stale and the bread sour, but the black-pudding, violently flavoured, seemed to Adela the most delicious and appetizing food she had ever tasted. After her first impetuous gulps she set herself to make it last out as long as possible. Absorbed in this she did not observe all the dumbshow proceeding between the other two (which was as well for her vanity, for it began with Annis making it plain that her companion was a half-wit, and negligible). But she looked up in time to see the dumb woman straddle her legs and set her arms akimbo. Annis nodded delightedly, and fetched her arm about in a wide gathering gesture and finally pointed to her bosom; and the woman, falling back into herself, hurried away.

They were in Waxelby, they had heard a mass and had breakfast; and Jackie was still in the town. Feeling that matters were not so bad after all, Annis turned to Adela and said they would undo the bundle and look at the embroidery by daylight. There was not much daylight in the room, only what came in through cracks in the walls and by the chinks of an outer door, which seemed to open into a yard or garden since no footsteps went by it; and the space was so limited that they could only unroll part of the altar-hanging at one time. But neither at Oby where it began nor in any of its later wanderings was the needlework so truly admired. Dame Lovisa had guessed too high: Annis was never in such comfortable circumstances as to be a bower-woman; but she had a natural bent for works of art which she had cultivated during a long course of visiting churches—sometimes for pleasure and devotion, at other times for more practical reasons of sanctuary. The Oby hanging was beyond all she had ever set eyes on. It was new. No incense smoke had tarnished it, no sacristans had torn it, no candle-grease had spotted it. The blue of the satin was as pure as the blue of heaven, the ostrich feathers were so freshly stitched that they seemed to wave and billow upon the ground-colour, the gold was unfrayed, the tinsel was bright as dew. And she could see it intimately, she could stare into every detail of its workmanship. When they unrolled the corner that was still unfinished she groaned and looked at Adela as though she would strike her.

There was a needle quilted into the stuff, and Adela as a matter of course re-threaded it and wiped the grime off her hands and went on embroidering. Annis watched sharply, having a suspicion that she might begin to gobble-stitch some nonsense of her own devising. But the nun worked as dutifully as though she were in her cloister, and yawned and complained as though a task-mistress were over her.

More than an hour went by. When Annis pulled the needle from her hand and parcelled up the hanging, it seemed to Adela that it must now be time to go into quire. Instead, the dumb woman reappeared, pushed in a man, and went out again. Annis scrambled to her feet.

"Jackie, my good Jackie! How have things been with you,

Jackie?" Her voice was the voice she had used when she first spoke to Adela on the causeway. He stood with his legs apart in the middle of the floor, so bulky that he seemed to fill the room, and surveyed them with a broad dull grin. There was no doubt that this was the man the dumb woman had mimicked. The mimicry had frightened Adela, the original was worse. She shrank into the corner where the old man lay drowsing and clutching at his straw.

Annis was half-way through her story before Jackie troubled himself to speak, and then it was only to ask her where in the devil's name she had been and why she had not come to Waxelby till now. She began her story over again, and this time she got it as far as the meeting on the Waxelby causeway, and the stranger who had started up before her like a ghost and given her the altar-hanging from Oby for pity of God's poor.

"Aha! And where is it now?" he asked scornfully.

"Here!" said Annis. "Here!" echoed Adela.

Then the hanging was again spread out. He looked at it hard and appraisingly. His face showed no animation till the unfinished corner was displayed, and then he rounded on Annis and said that only a fool would steal a half-licked piece of work. Did she think she could finish it?

"No, but here is one who can and will. This—this damsel here. We have the silks and the pearls and all we need, and she can work as fast as a spider. And while she works, Jackie, you must think how best we can sell it, and where. I have heard say that this sort of work fetches a high price among the French and the Flemings. If we all went to France together she could sit at her work while the ship carried it to market. But you must decide, Jackie, you must decide."

Groping around for more straw, the old man took hold of Adela's hand, and feeling its warmth he pulled it savagely towards him and held it on his breast. But she did not struggle, for all the sense she had was concentrated on this conversation between Annis and Jackie. After a glance at her, Jackie turned back to Annis and asked her what he would do in foreign parts with two women tagged to his heels and neither of them worth a penny-piece; and by that token there would be a brat too by then. Yet it seemed as though he were making objections more for the pleasure of making them and to keep himself in practice than for any real purpose; for it was plain that the altar-hanging pleased him and was accepted in his mind as a thing he could dispose of. Annis said they could sell the needlework in England, anywhere out of earshot of the bell of Oby would do. Yes, and be hanged for it, he replied thoughtfully. Annis went on to say that a fair might not serve their turn, for what you sell at a fair is every fair-goer's business; but wherever there is a prosperous shrine you can find a dealer in the neighbourhood who will buy anything he can sell again as an offering, and not bargain too much over it either, since he can be sure of making his price from some customer newly healed or full of a recent gratitude for a grace or a miracle. There was Walsingham, Bromholm, the great shrine of Saint Edmund; going farther south there was Waltham Holy Cross in the forest or the Shrine of Saint Thomas Beckett itself, and by taking a passage in a boat going to London . . . She was rambling on, her mean, worn face lighting up with a gadabout's pleasure, when he interrupted her with the same animation as he had shown when he found the embroidery was not complete.

"And what is to warrant me that she can finish the work? I do not see her working, all she does is to sit fondling that old carcass in the corner there. Let me see you work!" he said, addressing Adela for the first time.

"Yes, dear, show Jackie how cleverly you do it," said Annis.

Once more Adela wiped her hands and took up the needlework. But she was flustered and the silk slipped from the needle.

"She an embroideress, she finish it! She will be a year at it and make a bungle of it when all's told. She knows no more of embroidery than you do."

"That's all you know about it," exclaimed Adela, nettled. "I was the only one among us who knew the secret of this stitch. They all had to learn it from me, Dame Lilias and Dame Eleanor and Dame Philippa and Dame Sibilla and . . ."

"Dame Meg and Dame Peg," he said scornfully. "And where did all you fine dames sit stitching?"

"In the parlour at Oby of course."

He stared at her, at her foolish face and her smooth white hands. Satisfied that she had put him down, Adela smiled primly and went on embroidering. Annis sidled up to him and began to stroke his cheek and whisper.

"I wouldn't hide it from you, Jackie. How could I? You're so clever, you nose out everything. But I dressed her up pretty well, don't you think? No one but you would guess it."

"I'll have nothing to do with her. Since you brought her, you can take her away."

"But I had to bring her, she was bent on coming with me. Besides, she can finish the embroidery, you see, something I could never learn."

"I'll have no nuns," he said.

"No, no! But just let her finish the work. I'll keep her at it, she'll be no trouble to you. The poor creature, she's as harmless as a sheep."

Pulling at his lower lip, he turned for another look. His swagger had evaporated, a mottle of fear overspread his face. He crossed himself.

Annis chuckled. "I thought it would be another game with you, Jackie. You to be afraid of a nun?—I was looking for something different."

"I'll touch no nun!" he burst out, so loudly that the old man sat up and stared at them, and the clash of voices in the next room seemed to be stayed.

"Hush, hush!"

There was no need for Annis to hush him. That exemplary sentiment if overheard might be construed very differently and to his disadvantage. He leaned trembling against the wall, and his eyes rolled dismally in their sockets as he looked from the embroidery to Adela, from Adela to the embroidery.

"Cold, cold," said the old man, lying down again. Adela, pleased to assert herself further after having quelled this rough man of Annis's, took an armful of the altar-hanging and lapped it round him. Annis and Jackie cried out together that she was to do no such thing.

"I'll do what I please," she replied. "It's mine, it's my work. I brought it away to clothe Christ's poor. This old man is poor and needs a garment. When he's asleep perhaps I'll take it away again, but while he's cold he shall have it, poor old man!"

She spoke with the simple arrogance inherited from her forbears, and Annis turned to Jackie with more confidence and said, "She's quite crazy, you see. Just listen to her!"

"She's none the better for being crazy," he answered. "If a woman's in her senses you can beat her. But that one—"

"And who's to know she's a nun unless you go shouting it? Once we're at sea—"

"No, no!" He crossed himself vehemently, and began to sweat. "Nuns bring ill-luck, nuns out of their cloister. I won't set foot on a ship with her for company."

"Well, what are we to do? Stay here?"

"Yes, that's it! You stay here, you and she, and you keep her at it till the work's done. And then send Mum Margaret after me as you did this morning."

"And where will she find you?"

He hesitated. "No, that's not so good. Wait! I tell you, when it's finished, have Margaret put a fresh bough in the sign, a bough of yew. I'll watch for that."

"And the three of us stay here in Waxelby, where every man will be looking for us? Because you are afraid to go to sea with a nun? What is there to fear, what is a nun when all's said? What was your mother but a nun?"

"The devil flay her!" he said. "She reared me in a kitchen to be everyone's kick and flout. Do you wonder I sicken at nuns?"

"If you sicken at nuns the devil will flay you," remarked Adela tranquilly.

"Once we're done with her we'll rub her off," whispered Annis.

Jackie saw the problem otherwise: he would rub them both off if he could. Yet to do so with any satisfaction he must keep the altar-hanging, and to have it at its best it must be finished by the one and the other must be kept as his overseer. And every hour in Waxelby was dangerous. And yet he did not want to go to sea, and least of all with a nun. Any fool of a woman can stitch, he supposed. And if he could rid himself of these two, and find a third. . . .

He sat chewing and sweating in a cage of considerations. At last he said he would go and see what could be done about a passage for the three of them. But the captain would need a sweetener, Annis must hand over her crown-piece, and he would take a few of those pearls.

"And take the hanging off that old dotard," he said, "and roll it up in the towel. For if we can get on the *Barbara*, there will be no time to waste. She's loaded already."

"Don't tell the others," said Annis.

He put a good deal of feeling into the exasperated kick he delivered in reply, and as Annis picked herself up she admitted to herself that the advice had been foolish and uncalled for.

The old man cursed and grumbled when they removed the altar-hanging, and Adela protested that she wanted to go on embroidering. Annis spent no words on either. She made up the bundle and sat down on it. They waited for a long time. The shafts of light shifted from midday to afternoon and sloped in by the door which gave into the yard. A thrush was singing there very sweetly. At intervals Adela complained of being bored and demanded to have the bundle undone so that she could go on with her embroidery. A day with no offices to break it seemed interminably tedious. She began to say some Hail Marys, and fell asleep. The old man rustled in his straw, the thrush sang. Annis sat in a prick-eared anxiety, feeling the child lumber against her backbone, biting her lip as she went over the things she had said to Jackie and saw how she could have mended them.

She started up when the door flew open. Jackie was on the threshold.

"They're after me! And the *Barbara* is weighing anchor. But if you slip out by the yard . . ."

"And leave her?"

"You think of nothing but your nun! No, bring her too."

She shook Adela and got her to her feet. Then she stooped for the bundle.

"I'll see to that. Get along with your nun. Turn to the left, then by the alley towards the quay. On the quay you'll see a sailor with one ear. Follow him, and when you are on board, go straight below and stay there and speak to no one till I come."

"But you will come, Jackie? You will come?"

"Will I stay here to be hanged? But I must wait till I know they have gone past."

It was not easy to get Adela to stir, she seemed unable to comprehend the notion of danger, and she had none of the uncloistered woman's instinct to obey the male. It took all of Annis's powers to move her and keep her moving.

Jackie followed them to the foot of the yard, cursing and encouraging. When he had watched them out of sight he relaxed, leaned against a paling, and began very quietly to whistle. The thrush answered him, or seemed to. He answered the thrush back. For now, with both women off his hands, he had time for a little fancy and poetry. It was one of those February dusks that seem to leap forward into spring, that melt and are complaisant and full of promise and even have a few midges.

Meanwhile, the old man had come nimbly out of his corner. He undid the bundle and took the altar-hanging and buried it under his straw. Then he collected all the rags that were hanging on the walls and made up the bundle again, reproducing its shape and knotting with great accuracy. Then he returned to his corner. After a while Jackie strolled in, picked up the bundle, laughed, spat, strewed a curse or two on the sleeper, and went away. The straw rustled as the old man shook with senile laughter. Not all his difficulties were over, of course. There was still his hostess to overcome, whose eyes were all the sharper because she had not the use of her tongue. But the altar-hanging lay safe beneath him, and he reckoned—rightly, as it turned out—to be able to make a pretty penny by it.

Below decks in the *Barbara* Adela was experiencing her first qualms of sea-sickness and Annis, listening to her moans and groans, began to know herself made a fool of, with a child kicking in her belly, a mad nun on her hands, and a sea voyage before her. As one puffs a green fire her invention patiently breathed on the circumstances before her, and she wondered to whom and for how much or how little she could dispose of this foolish virgin who was now her only asset in a harsh world, and her only friend.

XIII. A GREEN STAFF

(March 1380–June 1381)

The people on the manor heard considerably more of Dame Adela's fate than the convent did; as was natural, since they enjoyed all the tale-bearing resources of cousins at Waxelby, aunts in Wivelham, and Brother Bartlemy dropping in so comfortably with talk of this world and the next. They knew, for instance, how Dame Adela had attempted to enter the quire of the Friary Church by force and had been prevented only by the resolution of old Emme Sampson, who was born a Holly of Dudham. They knew that Katharine Trump, one of the Waxelby whores, had a pearl bracelet which was not honestly come by. They knew that the *Barbara* had left port with a cargo of virgins, all destined for the King of Hungary. They knew that within an hour of the *Barbara* leaving port Jack the Latiner had tried to strangle the dumb woman who kept the alehouse and that in the fight which ensued five men had been injured and a whole cask of beer wasted because no one had time to turn the tap off. They knew that Dame Adela had spent most of the day shut up in an inner room at the alehouse where she had sung as sweetly as a captive bird and eaten inordinately of black-pudding. They knew that when she was dragged on board a vessel which was not the *Barbara* at all but the *Boy of Whitby,* she was speechless with exhaustion and had three dogs with her. They knew that Annis was wearing the altar-hanging as a petticoat. They also knew that it was hidden in a dry well somewhere beyond Wivelham, that Jackie had given it to Katharine Trump, and that it had never left Oby where the nuns, in one of their quarrels, had torn it to shreds among them. Finally they knew, on the assurance of the old night-watchman who lodged by day at the alehouse, that Annis, contrary to appearances, was no woman but a short thick-set man with a red beard; but this was known rather later, and by the report of Sir John Idburn, who had encountered the old fellow crutching himself along to Walsingham in pursuance of a vow.

Meanwhile, the prioress, palsied and senseless, lived on. Her mere survival was a kind of support to her nuns; for while she lived they could defer the problem of an election, and as she might die at any moment it was not worth while to choose a deputy. Throughout Lent the choice of the next prioress was endlessly and languidly canvassed, and by twos and threes they made up and unmade their minds. Dame Lovisa, long accepted as inevitable, was out of the question, since it was she who had let the enemy in among them, and Dame Eleanor, her natural rival, was now felt to be out of the question also; for if you choose the lesser of two rivals you create a schism, and though under some circumstances a schism can be enlivening, it is a fair-weather luxury; one cannot afford it in times of misfortune. Dame Margaret was too old. Dame Dorothy was in her middle forties and healthy, but she was totally without initiative, she would be no better than an image carted about by one party and then another. Dame Philippa was neutral, discreet, and well connected; but she flatly refused to have anything to do with it and said that if they elected her she would certainly resign. This left Dame Cecily who was blind, Dame Lilias who was unwanted, and Dame Sibilla. Dame Sibilla was too young, and she was not an Oby nun, and she was a busybody and her piety was like no one else's piety, and a house ruled by anyone so nearly related to Bishop Walter would not know an easy moment; besides, all her relations were in religion, which would make her an unprofitable prioress, since everyone throws his herring-guts to his own dog. Yet from the variety of reasons alleged why Dame Sibilla would not do, it was obvious that she was generally and seriously considered. If one did not consult expense, the best plan would be to elect Dame Margaret, endure her ill-humour like a Lent, and when she died choose—who? Dame Lovisa with her talent for business, or Dame Eleanor who was the senior of the two and extremely personable. They were back where they had started from.

Never had an election been contemplated with so little spirit. Never had Dame Cecily heard so many sentences left unfinished, so many dubious sighs, so many desolate yawns, and such a general consent that it was too much for them, that it must be left for God to decide. She knew just what they must be looking like: sallow, sluttish, dispirited. Who would have thought a mere apple should undo the world? Who would have supposed that Dame Adela, that negligible being, should have created this cavernous absence? But that was because she had taken the altar-hanging with her—at any rate their disappearances had coincided. The loss of the altar-hanging was beyond the loss of money expended to no purpose, beyond the frustration of their hope of making a good impression on the new bishop. During the months they had worked on it together the nuns of Oby had become a community. Though in its early stages the needlework had been an instrument in the usual convent factions, a de Retteville banner waved against de Stapledons, as time went on it had become everyone's interest and everyone's purpose; and the satisfaction which Dame Lovisa had found in her lonely black-and-white psalters, and which the old prioress had felt with the second Trinity Cope, and which she herself (but how long ago!) had known with her paint-brushes, her cobalt and vermilion, had been felt by all, whether they worked or watched the workers. Something was being made, they had a reason for living together, the blue satin roofed them like a tabernacle.

It was gone. They were at sixes and sevens again, idle, dejected and afraid; and years would pass before they would entertain such another project, for they had been bubbled, and once bit is twice shy.

Prioress Matilda lasted out for another twelvemonth. The permit to elect came on Shrove Tuesday, and the election gave the prioress-ship to Dame Margaret by a majority of three voices. Even those who had voted for her felt considerable qualms when they heard the result, and pitying glances were turned toward Dame Lilias, who would now have the liveliest reasons to wish she had got safely away into her anchoress's cell before this turn of events. Yet though the election chilled most hearts, it expressed the general mind. Dame Margaret, so old, so cut and dried, with nothing to offer but her formalism, her shallow-moulded perspective of convention, was the only co-ordinating element in the community. They could believe in her because she was so incapable of suggesting anything they did not know already.

On his springtime visit to Oby, Henry Yellowlees hurried up the stairs to Sir Ralph's chamber and bemoaned himself to his friend.

"It is ruin! It is lunacy! Whatever possessed them to choose that withered thistle? And then to let her appoint that blockhead Dame Dorothy as treasuress! They neither of them know a rent from the grace of God, and the books are in such a state already —I shall tell the bishop that I cannot go on."

For Henry Yellowlees was now a very different person from the hungry clerk whom Bishop Walter had made custos of Oby.

Perkin de Craye had come to his see resolved not to be scrambled over by a troop of disorderly English clerics, and resolved, above all, to winnow away the retinue of his predecessor. Among his earliest discards were the secretaries, the chaplain, and the doctor. When he had cleared his immediate surrounding he had a list drawn up of all the late bishop's nominations. In it he found the name of Master Henry Yellowlees, custos of Oby and teacher of mathematics at the school of the Holy Innocents. With his winnowing-fan in his hand Perkin de Craye came in due course to this particular threshing-floor, where he found Henry Yellowlees in one of his worst tempers, damning all bishops and in especial this new bishop who had dismissed his crony Humphrey Flagg. Being confident that his own dismissal would follow, Henry Yellowlees began to criticize the cathedral music in a very liberated spirit. As it happened, Perkin de Craye was a considerable musician; and though the two men almost immediately fell into a violent wrangle about Machault (whom Perkin de Craye thought to be too mellifluous and lacking in technical ambition) his opponent disagreed with him so intelligently that Perkin de Craye found himself saying that what Master Yellowlees needed was to hear some of the compositions of Landini, and promising in the next sentence that he should hear them as soon as he could get the parts copied and the quire thrashed into performance. As this could not be unless the winnowing were postponed, Henry Yellowlees remained in his post at the Holy Innocents until the bishop decided that it would be better if he were fanned into a personal secretaryship.

"Tell the bishop?—Oh, yes, this bishop. H'm, certainly! Yes, I should tell him if I were you."

Sir Ralph was lying on his bed with a rug over him. Though the spring air puffed into the room he looked wintry, he looked like the snow-banks which lie on the north side of a baulk and will not melt.

"This is my seventh year as custos of Oby," said Henry, beginning to excuse himself. "It's a long time. At least it is a long time in which to have got nothing done. Really, I have no talents for management."

"The patriarch Jacob served seven years for Leah and another seven years for Rachel. And I don't know that he got much out of it," remarked Sir Ralph.

"I suppose seven years seems no time at all to you?"

"No time at all," said the old man airily. "Some deaths, of course. Some births. Lambs, and so forth."

Though prosperity had set him up Henry was not altogether ruined by it. There was concern as well as patronage in his heart when he suggested that Sir Ralph himself might well think of retiring, that a word to the bishop, who appreciated scholarship, would translate him to some pleasant sinecure. Without affectation he added that he thought Sir Ralph would like the bishop.

Sir Ralph looked at him with affectionate inattention and said, "So you'll be leaving us? Well, I'm thinking of going away myself."

Reflecting that the new prioress must be even worse than he supposed if she had loosened Sir Ralph from his red-arrased nutshell, Henry asked where he thought of going.

"To London, to London," replied Sir Ralph as though it were the most natural reply in the world.

"To London? But that is a long journey."

"The only place for my purpose. I want to make sure of

finding intelligent men, men of culture. I should only waste my time if I trudged about to the lesser places, Oxford and Cambridge and what not. I can't afford to waste time. I have let too much time go by as it is."

Whatever he was raving about, he raved in a new manner. Henry had never heard him speak with such decision nor in such a magistral tone of voice.

"Now in London they understand such matters."

What matters, Henry inquired, and Sir Ralph replied, Poetry. He raised himself on his bed, pulled out a manuscript, and began to read aloud. His reading voice was strong and pompous, he read with old-fashioned gusto, twanging off the words like a jongleur. Who or what he was reading about was hard to say, except that there was a yew tree and a weeping man whose tears dripped through its dark boughs. It was a poem in English, and apparently it was intended to rhyme, though the rhymes observed no obvious pattern. Henry's attention soon slid away from the reading and fastened upon this surprising new aspect of the reader, roaring like a schoolmaster, with his black eyebrows sitting astonished among his dishevelled white locks. What had changed him? Was it the approach of death which had kindled this vigour of mind in the old man? If only he had known him when he was young! The young Ralph Kello must surely have been like this, thought Henry Yellowlees, for the first time realizing that Sir Ralph had once and authentically been a young man.

"What do you think of that, Henry?"

"I—I'm not quite sure. I should have to hear more of it before I could form an opinion."

"Exactly! That is why I am going to London."

Henry said meekly that if Sir Ralph would read on, or if he could borrow the manuscript and study it. . . . His meekness was of no avail. Sir Ralph replaced the manuscript under his bolster and dismissed him as though he were a schoolboy—a dull one at that.

Riding into Lintoft that same evening, his mind still occupied with Sir Ralph, Henry Yellowlees heard the same words: *To London.* It might have been his fancy repeating Sir Ralph's words; but the voice was nothing like Sir Ralph's, and the words had come from beyond his thoughts, as though they had been thrown like a stone and hit him. A moment later he heard another voice reply to the first voice: "Aye, to London. That's where we must go."

A group of labourers was standing under an ash tree. His horse carried him on and he could hear no more of what they were saying.

That night at supper the rector of Lintoft was full of stories about Oby, the extortions of the bailiff, the meanness displayed at the funeral of the late prioress and the haughtiness of the new one. Another thing which was causing a lot of talk, continued Sir John, was the fact that the two novices sent to Oby eight years before were still waiting to be given their veils. No fault of theirs; but they were both of mean birth and the Oby nuns were too proud to admit them. Such behaviour alienated the common people, and no wonder. Henry Yellowlees replied that both novices had been nuns for the past four years. He marvelled that Sir John's parishioners, who were so well informed, did not know of it. Sir John muttered that there had been no feast for them, at any rate. He hastened on to suppose that there was no news of that unfortunate imbecile nun who had been kidnapped by the red-bearded man who had been seen by old Eustace the watchman; and before Henry Yellowlees could answer he went on to say that there could be little doubt as to what had become of her: people could stand so much and no more, and the new poll-tax had broken their patience. Kings should pay for their own wars, it was too much to ask the poor man both to fight in the King's armies and pay for them. What a war, too! Why must the English war again with the French for no purpose but to be beaten by them when our fathers had beaten them once for all thirty years before? Henry Yellowlees was unable to see what the French war had to do with the disappearance of Dame Adela, for surely not even the rector of Lintoft could suppose that she had been carried off to fight for the King? Raising his voice—John Idburn had grown somewhat hard of hearing—he asked if the woman who turned into a red-bearded man had been by any chance a soldier.

No, of course not, why should he be? replied Sir John wonderingly. If a soldier wanted a nun and an altar-hanging he could find them in France. No doubt who he was: one of a band, and the band one of the many bands of the workless and dispossessed who were going through the country to sack and pillage. No doubt either that they had intended more that night than God had allowed them to do; but on the afternoon before Dame Adela was kidnapped a woman, a pious pilgrim, had forced her way into the nunnery and warned the nuns that they would be burned in their beds. Simon Maggs's daughter, who worked in the Oby kitchen, had heard her warning them. So they were prepared and had their doors and windows barred, and all the kidnappers could find when they came was Dame Adela coming from the necessary house. Henry Yellowlees asked how it was that Dame Adela should have the altar-hanging with her at such a time, but he omitted to raise his voice, and Sir John had rushed on to say that he, for one, did not wonder at this state of things. Look at Lintoft, for instance. It was twelve years since the Dambers had visited their manor house, for twelve years he had not preached to an educated hearer: they lived at court, they fought in the wars, they skinned the place and put nothing back into it; now they were felling their woods for sale, and soon there would not be as much as an acorn left for the swine to fatten on. Then on top of all this, the taxes, and on top of the taxes, this last poll-tax. He did not wonder that his parishioners were full of resentment. Starve a dog and it will grow wolf's teeth was an old saying and a true one. He, for one, would wish them God-speed when they set out for London.

"God's bones! Is everyone going to London?" cried Henry.

"No, not everyone. Some are not strong enough, and some must stay behind for the beans and the hay and to look after the cattle. You cannot expect they should all go. But the stoutest are going."

"But why? What are they going to London for?"

"To tell the King. Why else should they go?"

"But what will they tell the King?"

"That nobody else will listen to them," replied Sir John.

If it had not been for those men under the tree Henry would

have discounted this as another piece of the Lintoft priest's nonsense. As it was, he thought enough of it to send a letter to Sir Ralph begging him not to set off for London until he could arrange to go with him. *I would fain go to London where I have never been, yet I fear to go to so great a city alone and untutored lest I be cozened there,* he wrote artfully. It alarmed him to think that the old man might really set out with his manuscript and fall into the hands of such travellers as he had seen scowling under the ash tree. If Sir Ralph persisted in going he would milk the bishop for a conveyance and a couple of men for an escort. Possibly the bishop on his next journey south . . . but on second thought Henry had to admit that his old friend and his new friend would have little in common; though Perkin de Craye would make nothing of taking an old nuns' priest along with him, for his highly intellectual form of christianity regarded no social distinction save the distinction between the Church and the world.

Sir Ralph put the letter carefully away in his Aquinas—a handsome volume which he used mainly as a repository. He need not answer it. There would not be time for that. Lately he had been subject to singular lapses of memory. Not just ordinary forgetfulness, for in recollecting names, verses, dates, his memory served him as well as ever—indeed, it even seemed to be improving, for it was quite surprising how sharply he could remember every detail of events happening forty and fifty years ago. But with an odd inconsistency this good, willing, serviceable memory constantly failed him over things of the present. He had quite forgotten, for instance, till Henry's letter came to remind him, that he must go to London with the poem of Mamillion. Yes, Mamillion must set out on a new series of wanderings, taking the track to Lintoft and westward till it crossed King Street, there turning southward and on through Peterborough and Cambridge and Saint Albans—a long journey; but no longer than pilgrims go, or troops of jugglers and tumblers; and no doubt he would fall in with many lifts in carts and waggons, for people are kind to an old man, an old priest travelling on a good errand. He would meet scholars too, going fastidiously from place to place in search of newer teaching, as he had done in his day; and to them he could speak of the poem of Mamillion, and of his obligation, so long ago incurred, to make it known among the poets and scholars of the world. It had taken him a long time to come to a full appreciation of the poem: a course of time during which the poem's poet, that unfortunate Lord of Brocton, had almost faded from his mind. But while the poet waned the poem waxed, and now he knew it for what it was —one of the great epic poems of mankind, a poem that would wander through one generation to another, sometimes pausing, Like Mamillion himself, in a deep wood or at some welcoming castle, but never abiding there, for its destiny was to wander everlastingly through the hearts of men. Yet the delay was not such a bad thing, after all. By so many desultory readings he knew it through and through. There was, for instance, that passage about the wild man, who capered up to Mamillion and smote him with a flowering branch, filling his nose and eyes with pollen-dust; and before Mamillion could clear his eyes and leave off sneezing the wild man had capered away again, uttering a loud booming Halloo. How many times he must have sauntered through it without seeing its quality!—and at last came a reading which became a first reading, and he had been as much astounded as if he too had been smitten over the nose with a flowering branch.

He took up the manuscript and found the wild man once more. The poets and scholars in London would be quick to admire such imagination. He looked out of his window: the screen was down, the sweet air and the light came fully in. Why should he not start tomorrow? Yes, and make sure of his purpose! Otherwise, his memory might play him another trick; and he could not expect to have a second letter from Henry Yellowlees to remind him that he meant to go to London. It was very obliging of Henry Yellowlees: an excellent, kind-hearted fellow, if for the moment rather too much taken up with his bishop.

If he started tomorrow, what must be done first? He must of course explain to Dame Margaret that he was obliged to go to London. There was always a Wivelham curate whom she could call on. Dame Margaret was so deaf that it would be fatiguing to explain for any length of explanation. He would have to bellow in her ear; and without being a voluptuary he very much disliked Dame Margaret's ear from which the short coarse hairs bristled out so hungrily. Why should he not explain to her by means of an intermediary? He would send her a message by one of the nuns: by Dame Lilias, who was always very kind to him. There was something about Dame Lilias too, which he knew he ought to remember, but just now it slipped his memory. One cannot remember everything and at present he must concentrate on carrying Mamillion to London. What else? A good staff was essential, and he would see about it at once.

He thrust the manuscript into the pocket of his gown and left his chamber. As the door closed behind him a brimstone butterfly fluttered in at the open window.

An ash plant was best. He set off for the copse in the eastern corner of the common field, there were ash stools there, and there in the old days he had often cut himself a staff. As good fortune would have it Thomas Scole was at work in the copse. They searched together, trampling the bluebells, until the right ash plant was found, and the staff cut there and then and its handle shaped and smoothed. Young Scole was an excellent workman. It was a pleasure to watch him, though as the last slow touches were given to the staff Sir Ralph could barely contain his impatience. At length it was in his hands, and with thanks and a blessing he turned away.

If they were all as civil as he, thought Thomas Scole, there would be less to complain of. He watched the old man walking over the furrows and getting along very nimbly considering his age and his bulk. A rabbit ran out of its burrow. Turning his attention to the rabbit, which is meat and clothing both, Thomas Scole failed to notice that Sir Ralph had turned westward along the track to Lintoft. Even had he noticed it, it would not have made any particular impression on him. An old man with a green staff likes to ramble about with it.

For a long time Dame Amy had been summoning up her courage. Seeing the priest's luncheon of bread and beer on the buttery shelf, it seemed to her that this was the moment the Virgin had sent. So she said she would carry it up to his chamber. At the head of the stairs she knocked and waited. At last she pulled the latch and looked in. The chamber was empty. She set the meal down on the stool, and was turning away when a light sound caught her hearing, and she saw a yellow butterfly struggling in a cobweb. She freed it, and watched it fly out of the window, and was about to go when it struck her that there were a great many cobwebs about the room, and since she was alone in it and no one needed her she might pull some of them away. So she wandered about the room collecting cobwebs in her hand till she came to the opened cupboard where Sir Ralph kept his books. Here temptation overcame her. She took one down and opened it at random, mouthing the Latin which she could pronounce but could not understand. It was this which had brought her here. She longed to read the Latin authors, and she had brought up the bread and beer meaning to ask Sir Ralph if it were wrong for a nun to learn Latin. For some nuns it was certainly permissible. Dame Lilias could read Latin as easily as she could read French or English, Dame Philippa also, and the elder Frampton novice had been writing Latin exercises before she sickened with measles and died. But these were all nuns of good family, who had had books put into their hands as early as she herself had been taught to hold a distaff or the thumper of a churn. She was afraid to speak of her desire to Dame Lilias, who everyone said was proud; still less could she speak of it to Dame Philippa, who could with such good reason raise her fine eyebrows and say, "You should have thought of this while you were a novice." Through her novitiate Amy had been idle and inattentive, for at first she could think of nothing but the pleasure of eating such delicate food and the discomfort of always feeling hungry, and afterward she was so constantly sickly and sleepy that even with a new will to learn she could not profit by her lessons. Dame Philippa had said that it was useless to waste any more time on such a dunce, she knew enough to scrape through the office with the lead of the others, and that must suffice. Yet it was just in that last year when she was dismissed to run errands and be useful that she began to know herself clear-witted and to long for learning, and at the same time to be overcome with shyness.

She waited but Sir Ralph did not come. At last, still clutching the cobwebs in her hot young hand and with the Latin murmuring in her head like a charm of bees, she went away.

At that time Sir Ralph was mounting the ridge whence he had so often looked back to admire the spire. But now he walked with his eyes to the ground, warily; for he had all but stepped upon an adder. This had frightened him, his heart still felt bruised by the leap of blood which had assaulted it, and when he poked the ground with his staff the staff wavered with his wavering hand. Turning at last for his look at the spire, he found that it was already out of sight, sunk below the watershed. No matter! What was one spire more or less to a man who was going to see so many, and at his journey's end, among the ships and spires of London, the spire of Saint Paul's?

Most old women are somnolent, but the new prioress of Oby was as wakeful as an aspen. On this hot afternoon when the common wish was to sit still and be shaded she had been taken with a desire for exercise. Accordingly, the nuns were playing at battledore and shuttlecock. It was years since anyone at Oby had played this game, and it seemed that they might yet be saved by Dame Philippa's statement that it was so long since any of her novices had played at it that she fancied the bats and the cocks had been mislaid.

"Mislaid? I suppose you mean thrown away? And who gave you leave to throw away our property? Mislaid, indeed. There is no such thing as mislaying. Either they are here or they are not here. I suppose I must look for myself."

Before anyone could intervene she had looked for herself and found—an easy matter, since they were lying where they had lain for the last ten years. Remarking that it was bad enough to have Dame Cecily cumbering the establishment, but that was nothing, every nun in her house was blind as a bat, and none so blind as those who wouldn't see, the prioress added that they would now spend a pleasant recreation together.

In her youth when battledore and shuttlecock had been fashionable the prioress had excelled in it. Even now she played with grisly agility; the more grisly because her style of playing preserved all the bygone graces of the early century—the upright carriage with the head a little on one side, the arched wrist and the alert expression. She pranced to and fro like a shuttlecock impelled by some invisible bat. Dame Eleanor incautiously remarked to Dame Lovisa that the prioress looked like an old shuttlecock herself. Dame Lovisa incautiously smiled. Immediately they were bidden to play a match. As Dame Eleanor was tall and stout and Dame Lovisa short, crooked, and narrow-chested, their match gave opportunities for a great deal of mortifying comment. Like many deaf people, the prioress spoke her thoughts aloud, and scattered disparagement and insult with no intention to be wounding. As the air grew hotter, and even she began to be jaded and dizzy from so much exercise, she quite genuinely felt that she was suffering to forward the general good, and that they were all having a pleasant recreation together, or should be; and if they disliked it, it was no fault of hers. Speaking her thoughts aloud, she remarked that it was a pity that nowadays no one enjoyed simple pleasures or knew how to move gracefully, really there was nothing to choose between the clumsiness of Dame Philippa and the clumsiness of Dame Amy, whose build and breeding would make her clumsy anyhow.

"Now then, now then!" she cried out. "Why do you all stand puffing and sweating, my daughters? This is the hour of recreation. We must play."

In the latest reshuffle of posts Dame Lilias had been appointed infirmaress. Nailing herself to her office, she now came forward and bellowed politely that doubtless their dear Mother remembered that the spring blood-letting had recently taken place. Many of the nuns were still feeling its effect and found it painful to play games.

"We do not come into nunneries to pamper the flesh," said the old woman, drawing herself up. Raising her voice, she said that they must do without Dame Lilias, who rather than play at battledore and shuttlecock preferred to sit in the shade and await another message from Saint Leonard.

Sir Ralph had told himself that when he got to Lintoft he would stop at the priest's house and rest for an hour or so. Then it would be pleasant to walk on through the cooling evening. Though at the moment he could not remember the priest's name, he remembered the man well enough—a lanky young man, fretful and impulsive, who was inclined to pity himself and to think he was the only scholar set down among the barbarians since Ovid. But as Sir Ralph approached the parsonage he saw a strange priest in the garden engaged in taking a swarm of bees: a middle-aged man with pursed lips and a waddling gait, a man who was a stranger to him and yet somehow called up the recollection of some distant mishap. So avoiding him and the bees, Sir Ralph went on till he met a boy herding a flock of geese, and asked him where he could buy a drink. The boy said that his mother sold cider, and directed him to a hut near by. It was a tumble-down dwelling, and so stinking that Sir Ralph preferred to sit on a bench outside. Bringing him the cider, the woman of the house greeted him by name and asked him where he was going.

"To London," he told her.

"To London?" she said. Her voice was heavy with stupidity and stupid surprise. Presently she called to another woman and said, "Look, he's going to London. But what would take him thither?"

"There are some priests of our way of thinking," the second woman answered. "And what a great staff he has!—if he's strong enough to use it." Together they came over and stared at him, and the second woman asked him why he had not set out before—with the others, she said. But the westering sun shone full in his face and the cider was heavy, so he blessed them and hoped they would go away; and presently they did so.

He woke with a start, feeling bemused and stiff. But his staff was to hand and the track lay before him. After he had walked for a while he began to recollect the talk in the alehouse. It had been about Death. Death was travelling through England, faster than those who travelled to escape it. Whichever road you took, said one man, Death went by you on that road and sat grinning to await you at your journey's end. There was no outwitting such a Death. This Death, said another, was an old woman; for it killed more men than women, and more men in their strength than children or the aged: only an old woman would have such a degree of malice. A third said that Death had come into England by a port in the south called Mamillion Regis, and travelled by the old grassroads, the roads which had been before the time of the Romans. "You frighten yourselves with this nonsense," he had said, striking his hand on the board. "Do you suppose Death wears boots?" Yet this much was true, the Black Death had come; and that was why they were all going to London. He too was going to London; and yet it seemed to him he had another errand.

This much he certainly knew: that he had been this way before. Presently he would cross a small brook and after that he would be sick. Then he would be lightened of the pain in his head, a pain that beat against his temples and hung an obstacle of darkness between him and the growing light in the east. He had only to traverse this last belt of woodland where the flies buzzed among the trampled fern; then he would come to the brook; then he would see the sun.

He saw it: a scarlet disk in a black sky. He tried to lift it from the paten but somehow it eluded his grasp and sank below the horizon. Uttering a heavy sigh, he pitched forward and lay still.

Sir John was in his first sleep and taking swarms of mild gigantic bees when he was disturbed by knockings and shoutings which presently turned into a voice bidding him to come at once to the Oby priest, who was dying. "Saddle my beast!" he shouted; but the voice replied that he would get there as quickly on foot for the dying man was at Mary Kettle's house. Another voice chimed in, saying that they could carry the man no farther because of his great weight. The voices were unknown to him though they were voices of the locality, and when he hurried from the chancel door carrying the oil and the holy elements his first question (for he was a man of methodical curiosity) was, who were they? Thomas Scole from Oby and his cousin Sylvester Scole, they replied. They had found the priest lying across the trackway a matter of a mile beyond Lintoft. He lay like a dead man, and a weasel was sporting around him, but as they turned him over and stared at his round pale face in the moonlight he had begun to groan. They had dashed him with water from the brook to revive him, but he only groaned the more, and so terribly that they decided he was beyond all ministrations save those of a woman and a priest. Staggering under the load of his bulk they had carried him back as far as Mary Kettle's house, and there he lay.

"I wonder how he came to be going that way," mused Sir John. "For that matter, how did you come to be there, and after sundown, since you are both Oby men?"

"He must have had some journey in mind," said one of them evasively, "for I cut him a staff this very forenoon." The other man added that many were travelling at this time, both young and old.

"But some started later than others," Sir John replied meaningfully. Though neither answered he could feel their confidence warming the silence, and he went on to speak of the Lintoft men who had already set out for London, and of the common distress and the common hope that the King might take pity on the plight of poor labourers.

"If it were not for William Holly we might have gone along with the Lintoft men," said the one called Sylvester. "One thinks twice and thrice of leaving wife and children behind at the mercy of that old extortioner."

"That's as may be," said the one called Thomas. "To speak for myself, it's the thought of William Holly that brings me here. To hear the way he overrules all in the court of the manor you'd think he was judge and accuser, king and council, God and the devil. That's not justice!"

"They say he cheats the nuns beyond all measure," said Sir John.

"He cheats us worse," Thomas said, and his cousin added that they were skinned by both alike. Thus talking cheerfully of the wrongs of the poor they came to Mary Kettle's house.

Though it was so mean a hovel she welcomed them with composure. The homes which are too poor for any other entertainment are always prepared to give hospitality to death. Mary Kettle had brought out her stumps of candle, her Palm Sunday cross, her cup of holy water, and the sprig of box to sprinkle with. There was a sheaf of clean straw under Sir Ralph's head. As the priest entered she fell on her knees with as much air of leisured dignity as if she had been a countess in her castle.

Something of the same grand manner had fallen on the dying

man. It was as though Mary Kettle's conviction that everything was taking place exactly as it must and should take place had extended itself to him. He was the wax which she had modelled into its final form before it cooled and set. The mad priest of Oby was dying as decorously as a prince of the church, giving a tenuous assenting consciousness to the ceremonies of his departure. He made only one request, and that was really more a suggestion than anything else. There was a nun of Oby, he said, to whom he wished to say something; what, he could not remember; but if he could see her, her presence might prompt him.

Mary Kettle's neighbour had come in to bear a hand, and after Sir John had finished and gone the two women sat down to watch out the night. They talked of deaths gone by and deaths to come, of storms and snowfalls, miraculous cures, charms to aid cows and children, which woods to burn green and which to burn dry, taxes and tithes and the cost of living, the signs of a hard winter, and how to foretell the sex of the unborn child. They remembered old times, and the people who had gone from the manor either by death or departure, they unravelled cousinships and marriages and traced the long story of the blue cloak which Anne Hamlet, who had been Sir John's first housekeeper, had won by a wager from the miller's wife. They talked of the men who had gone from Lintoft to join in the peasant's march, and of John Ball, the poor man's priest, and of the wickedness of London, and the wickedness of Waxelby. Sometimes a groan or a mumble from the man they watched would intervene in their conversation, and they broke off, and said a Hail Mary. Then their talk began again, and they laughed from time to time, not because what they spoke of was particularly merry, but because of the oddness of the world and the surprisingness of mankind.

The room lightened, the lark began to sing, then the wood-dove, then all the birds together. Where one had seen a star through a hole in the roof one now saw the blue of day. Mary Kettle bent over Sir Ralph and smoothed his hair and considered him. He would last many hours yet, she said, perhaps even to another morning. Her neighbour said that however long he lasted she would stay within call to give a hand at the last. She had noticed it before, said Mary Kettle: just as a child will be born and then be a long time before it will take the nipple, there are dying folk who are in a manner of speaking already dead and yet it is a long time before the soul knows what it wants and leaves them. Looking more attentively at Sir Ralph, she exclaimed, "Why, it is the same man who drank the cider and gave us his blessing!"

"Well, of course it is. Who else should he be?"

"I never thought to ask. It was dark, he was dying . . . that's all I thought of. What a numbskull I am!" And she laughed at her own oddity.

XIV. PRIORESS MARGARET

(July 1381–March 1382)

When the messenger came in the first purity of the morning to say that Sir Ralph was dying at Lintoft and had asked for her, Dame Lilias grieved to think that the rambling mind which had once been so near hers and then had rambled off again should be troubled in its last moments by any compunction at having forsaken or failed her. How should she speak? It would be easy to say that she had outgrown her wish to be an anchoress, and that to be a nun at Oby now contented her. It would be easy to say and easy to see through. He had treated her too well in the past to be lied to now. She must tell him that between them they had failed, that heaven had put some fault in both of them which had prevented the design and which they must forgive each other. Not for a moment had she foreseen that the prioress would refuse her permission to go to the dying man.

In the shock of this refusal she remained unaware of the turmoil that ensued. Dame Sibilla had been the first to expostulate with the prioress. That might well be expected. But when she came away, hoarse with upbraiding and shaking with temper like a wren in song, who would have supposed that Dame Amy, the young, the dull, the negligible dumpling, should be the next to take up battle? Dame Cecily followed on Dame Amy, and was perhaps the most menacing of the three, for her blindness was like an armour to her, and she threw herself into the fight with the added passion and resentment of her personal deprivation. By this time Dame Sibilla had recovered enough to be inflaming the others, and while Dame Cecily was still inveighing against the formalism and malice of the old, who might come to know, sooner than they reckoned, the sensations of the dying, and the prioress was still quoting the bull *Periculoso,* and asserting that this was yet another example of Dame Lilias's anxiety to gad, all the nuns gathered in a body to protest, and even compelled Dame Dorothy to go along with them and to give her valuable opinion that the wish of a dying man merits some attention since it is in all probability the last wish he will ever conceive.

They harassed the old woman with the less mercy because she herself showed no weakness. She had the frank and infuriating obstinacy of a young child or an animal. They were quite surprised when all of a sudden she broke down and began to weep and wail and declare herself worn out by their attacks. This it was, she said, tears leaping off her old nose with youthful vehemence—this it was to uphold discipline and good report among the young. And was it for this that they had elected her, only to make her a target for their scorn and satire? God pity the old in a world that had no pity for them! She wept and panted so violently, and trembled so much and grew so red in the face, that Dame Lilias was called for. Dame Lilias had been at her prayers, and her eyes were sunken with bitter weeping. But she dealt skilfully and gently with the old woman, putting hot cloths to her feet and cold cloths to her head, and gave her a sedative, disguising the bitter taste of the poppy-seeds with honey and spices. She was long past any thoughts of returning good for evil. Someone was sick, and must be dealt with, that was all she knew. The others watched her with curiosity and unwilling admiration. Afterward they attempted to express their partisanship. She answered them without knowing what they said, and supposed that these were further expressions of the old dislike, but wrapped in a new weed. Undoubtedly she is proud, thought Dame Amy. She looks meek, but she is proud at heart.

But she herself would be proud, she reflected, if she were so learned a nun that a dying priest called for her to help him in dying.

When a messenger came on the following day with the news that Sir Ralph was dead they began to think of other things. The prioress was reclothed with considerations of what was proper to do: the provision of a new priest, the funeral of the old. She looked forward to these interesting opportunities of doing things correctly and with decorum. Dame Lovisa, who for a whole day had ceased to think about Dame Adela and was much revived by the change, gave her mind to Sir Ralph's will: Dame Matilda, she knew, had expected a legacy to the convent. Dame Joan thought how delightful it would be if her cousin Oswald could be appointed as the new priest. She was painfully lonely in this place, where now even Dame Amy was turning away from her; if a Sir Oswald were to replace a Sir Ralph she could at least be sure of a familiar countenance to watch during the sermon, not to speak of the consideration which must accrue to the convent priest's cousin-german. Dame Dorothy also meditated on the empty post. There was her nephew: a good quiet man of exemplary conduct and full of sound sense, but unfortunately without the flashiness which procures a man advancement. He had such a loud, clear voice too, just what the prioress would enjoy. Dame Sibilla with so many living relations in the Church thought with concentration of a dead one. She had no doubt that Sir Ralph had some last counsel to give Dame Lilias about becoming an anchoress. Now he was dead, dead as Walter Dunford; and though for some time she had not heard the owl, her mind was not at ease.

In spite of all their planning Sir Ralph was buried at Lintoft. Lintoft had no men to spare for bringing his body across the heath, and William Holly refused to send men from Oby to fetch it. This was no time, he bellowed to the prioress, for rambling to and fro with corpses, Sir Ralph could lie at Lintoft and thank his stars that he lay securely, and that he would not wake up and hear the sods crackling over his head. The living had no such assurance.

The prioress blinked and sniffed and bridled her stiff neck.

"I see no insurrection unless it is yours," she said crossly. "I have never heard such nonsense in my life. What? Set fire to the monasteries? Pillage the religious houses? Let them try that here, and they shall soon learn whether or no Holy Church is above them. Go away, I don't wish to hear another word about it."

Dame Matilda, Dame Helen . . . William Holly sighed for the good reliable treasuresses of former days. He knew that it would be waste of breath to carry his troubles to Dame Dorothy, for though he could soon frighten her into fits the prioress would frighten her out again. He waited for an opportunity to talk to Dame Sibilla. He had always found her a sensible body. The difficulty would be to get her to himself; but seeing her walking in the orchard with Dame Philippa, he decided, since time pressed, to tackle the pair of them. As he approached he heard Dame Philippa say, "If only I could pack off my novices! But where could we send them?"

"They will be in God's hands like the rest of us—if it really comes to the worst."

Dame Philippa shrugged her shoulders.

"Of course they will. But it is easy enough to expect the worst. What I expect is something far more troublesome: half a dozen louts with their faces blacked, everyone screaming and bawling, a cold kitchen, no proper meals, everything in a hurly-burly, and my little girls running wild through it all. If I had no responsibility I daresay I could look forward to having my throat cut as piously as you do."

Meanwhile Dame Sibilla had beckoned him to come forward.

"We were saying how sad it is, good William, that Sir Ralph had to be buried at Lintoft. However bad the times, surely people would respect the corpse of a priest and give it safe conduct."

"I can't say what they do for the dead, Madam Sibilla. I've got to concern myself with the living. Do they come this way we shall need every man on the place, not that I say that more than half of them will be either leal or willing. I'd as soon trust a toad as any Scole, and Noots no better. But how did you hear these stories, ladies both? The prioress, she make no account of them."

"It was the Wivelham curate."

"What's he? I'd never believe a word from Wivelham, the only true tongue ever came from Wivelham was Jesse Figg's Magdalen. The Wivelham curate! I daresay his knees were knocking under him. What did he say?"

"Pack of lies!" he ejaculated when she had finished her recital of the curate's report. But his lip twitched and the fixed red colour on his cheekbones stared out of a yellowing face. The curate's story bore out in detail what he had heard himself.

"And the prioress, she won't hear of it? Well, I'll tell you what I've done. I've sent to Dudham for two of my nephews to come over here, either one of them would be worth a dozen of Oby fellows. But what about the gold and silver, the altar-ware and so forth? That's what they'll be after, they'll think of that before they think of driving away the cows or cutting your throats. Do you take my advice, you'll hide it. Burying would be best. Leave no more than the old pewter stuff for the Wivelham curate. Good enough for him. He make out with nothing better at Wivelham."

"I think they will be more likely to cut our throats if they find nothing worth stealing," said Dame Philippa.

"They'll never do that, not they! Where they find no riches they do no harm. It's the rich houses they set on. By the mass, I'd like to see the prior of Etchingdon this day. He sing small, I'll be bound."

He cackled with abrupt laughter, and Dame Philippa smiled. Dame Sibilla crossed herself, saying correctly that sacrilege was no laughing matter. When William left them she repeated this more earnestly. By some means or other, she said, the altar vessels must be preserved from falling into unhallowed hands. If on a pretext of cleaning them . . . Dame Philippa gave an unconvinced assent. True, they had suffered loss enough with the altar-hanging, they did not want to lose more. But what could be done while the prioress refused to stir?

That night Dame Lovisa helped Dame Sibilla to carry out the chest to William Holly. One of his renowned nephews was with him, and the burying-place, William explained, would be known to him and the nephew alone, for the hen that cackles least rears most chicks. The night was warm and so still that they could hear the Waxle Stream gurgling among the rushes, and the desultory cry of a water-bird. Then a bright light twitched on the southward horizon. They all started with terror, not realizing till it flashed on them again that it was only summer lightning. Dame Lovisa said conversationally that it was early in the season for thunder-storms, but that the tuft of seaweed (by which they now guessed at the weather since Magdalen Figg could no longer foretell it to them) had been moistening for a coming rain.

"That rain may quench some hot ashes," said the nephew from Dudham, speaking for the first time.

The two nuns crept back to the dormitory, but no one was asleep. Dame Joan had seen the flash of lightning and was sure, silly creature, that it was some roof that burned. She lay face downward, bewailing, and Dame Eleanor knelt beside her, trying to stifle her cries by pressing her face into the bolster; for Dame Philippa had come in to say that the noise could be heard in the novices' chamber and that they would all awake and scream in sympathy unless Dame Joan could be hushed.

"Amy, I want Amy," lamented the poor wretch. "Oh, Amy, why did we ever let ourselves be made nuns of? We would be alive now if we had been left in the world."

Dame Lovisa went across to the window, where Dame Amy's snub profile was silhouetted, and pulled at her arm. "Since for once you are wanted, I think you might bestir yourself," she said. But Dame Amy continued to kneel by the window, shaking her head and muttering the prayers for the dying. They might talk of lightning, but she knew better.

The demeanour of these two nuns gave a dreadful sanction to the forebodings of the others. Nothing could dislodge them from a conviction that if the insurgents came to Oby they would be merciless in vengeance; and it was hard to refute an inner voice which reasoned that if anyone were likely to know how the peasants would behave Dame Amy and Dame Joan were the likeliest. "Well, well, I'm afraid you will have to suffer with the rest of us," was Dame Lovisa's ill-judged taunt. Dame Joan burst into renewed howling, and when Dame Lovisa glanced round for approval she saw only pale and noncommittal looks.

Meanwhile, though everyone spoke of precautions, none was

taken. Dame Dorothy, being both the prioress's crony and treasuress, seemed the natural go-between. But nothing could be done with her. Self-importance stiffened her as frost stiffens a rotten board, and to no more effect. She would neither listen nor act. Though she was as much afraid as any of them, her fears evaporated in vanity and fluster. Her only contribution to the common concern was to be meticulously accurate about the stories which now came in day after day, each louder and nearer than the last. "They did not kill five at Blyberwick. They killed three," she would say, or remind them that a house was not set on fire on the Eve of a Saint but on the Saint's Day itself, since the flames were not kindled till after midnight.

Rumour is a poison that carries its own medicine. After the alarms of the first few days it became as animating as a fever to hear stories, to compare one version with another, to reckon up ravages and calculate where the insurgents would strike next. It was remarkable that everyone now spoke of the labourers as though they were some unknown kind of beings, people from under the earth or over the sea. No one now remembered what a few weeks before every one had known and feared: that the revolt sprang up from the soil as naturally as nettles, and that men from every manor who had gone out in hope and desperation were now coming back in despair. Perhaps this was natural. It went against the grain to identify such familiar useful shapes, figures at the plough's tail or at sheep-shearing, with the actors in these stories of wild and efficient vengeance, and to think of those wind-bitten red hands as reddened with blood. It was easier to listen to the stories from the other side: stories of reprisals, executions by scores, miraculous escapes, and the immense popularity of the young King, whom one and the same breath reported as loved for his clemency and dreaded for his ruthlessness. On the whole the most comforting rumour, and the most pervading, was that the rebels were powerless because no one supported them, that they were riven by internal jealousies, had neither weapons nor leadership, and were dying in thousands from hunger, thirst, and exposure.

Oby, though possibly no sillier than any other threatened community, became so drunk with rumour that quite a small impact with reality sent them reeling. Sunday brought the Wivelham curate. Absorbed in his personal preoccupations of fear and hay-fever, he went through the mass without noticing any change in the altar vessels. The prioress was better disciplined, and had more elevation of mind. Before the Kyrie she noticed the substitution of pewter for silver, and the instant that mass was ended she sent for Dame Sibilla to learn the reason for this. Dame Sibilla lost her head and replied that the better vessels were being cleaned. The prioress demanded to see them. Dame Sibilla had to change her tune to a more heroic note. As sacrist, she said, she had commissioned William Holly to bury them. She had made an inventory, and here it was. Dame Lovisa, looking as sour as a sloe, then came forward and added her witness. The two offenders were immediately locked into the infirmary, to remain without their dinners and meditate on their effronteries while the prioress carried out a thorough investigation.

As Dame Sibilla and Dame Lovisa had been unusually skilful in keeping their own counsel the investigation, though as discursive and acrimonious as investigations commonly are, and extending till long after the normal dinner-hour, yielded no result except a general hardening of opinion against the prioress for not having safeguarded the treasure herself. Dame Dorothy said at intervals that if William Holly had buried the chest he was likely to know where it was, but had no reward for her pains except to be told by the prioress to hold her tongue, since in times like these—the first admission the prioress had made that these times were not like other times—it was essential to keep any lapses from cloistered serenity private from the outer world, lest some scandalous advantage be taken of the scandal. Thus it was not till early in the afternoon (by which time Dame Philippa had also been despatched to the infirmary for unseasonably demanding that her novices should no longer be kept without their dinner) that a messenger was sent to call the bailiff. The messenger came back saying that Master Holly had ridden to Dudham for a christening feast and was not expected back till nightfall. Clear as day it was revealed to the prioress that he had absconded and taken the altar plate with him. Her dinnerless rage soared to new heights and descended on Dame Amy, who selected this moment to wander into modernistic speculations and to ask why the rite of the mass could not be as efficaciously celebrated with pewter vessels as with gold or silver ones. She was still trying to beat Dame Amy, the nuns still at liberty were whisking to and fro in order to thwart her, the nuns in confinement were banging and kicking against the infirmary door, and the three little novices, having plundered the kitchen, were wandering up and down outside the building in pursuit of an escaped goldfinch, when Henry Yellowlees arrived in his capacity of custos.

He had been in London with Perkin de Craye. Though they had travelled back unharmed he had seen enough to make him uneasy for Oby, and where the track through Lintoft turned off from King Street he had parted company and ridden eastward. At Lintoft he learned of Sir Ralph's death.

Yet the news did not really become true to him till he halted before the gate-house and looked up at the old man's window, where the shutter knocked in the easy summer wind. He looked away from the window to the spire, which seemed to nestle against the blue sky. Unforeseen tears rushed to his eyes and blinded him. He was still weeping when the novices came up and began to tell him their news. Naturally they did not say a word of Sir Ralph—they were taken up with more recent events; but their forgetfulness reproached him like a comment on his forgetfulness. That vague project for getting Sir Ralph to London in the bishop's retinue . . . he had considered it and rejected it and had gone to London himself with never a further thought of the old man. Now he might consider as much as he pleased, it would all be in vain, it was all and forever too late.

Remembering what he had come for, he dismounted and hitched up his horse and knocked on the door. When he had knocked for some time he tried it. It was not barred, and he walked in.

To the prioress his arrival was susceptible of only one explanation: he had come to ask about the altar plate. Wasting no time on formalities, she swept into her account of what had happened. Rage had so much renewed her faculties that he could hardly reconcile her with the Dame Margaret of the past, she was not even very hard of hearing till he, beginning to understand what it was all about, remarked that Dame Sibilla and Dame Lovisa had taken a very sensible precaution.

"Aye, indeed, I am glad you agree with me. Who knows what else they might have chosen to purloin away? I have a great mind to keep them shut up till the vessels are found again."

Finding that he could not force any sense into her, he thought he would try what fear might do. He began to roar out news of the rebellion, describing the ruined houses he had seen, and saying that they took it very seriously in London. But all she would hear was such words as *riot* and *rebellion,* and these she applied to the state of things in her own household, assuring him with tossings of the head that she would soon put an end to it, for with the ringleaders shut up she could soon master the other malcontents, adding that it would be better for the people in London to mind their own business—what happened at Oby was no concern of theirs. Dame Dorothy plucked at her sleeve, and screamed about fire-raising and murder, but was briefly bidden not to make mountains out of molehills, a household of insubordinate nuns was bad enough without rushing on to suppose they would begin killing and burning.

He looked round for someone who might hear reason, and tried to speak to Dame Lilias. But Dame Eleanor shouldered her aside and began to give him her account of the quarrel; Dame Cecily, ejected from the infirmary, clung to his arm and poured out her indignation because the prioress had prevented Dame Lilias from going to see Sir Ralph on his death-bed; Dame Amy demanded the release of the prisoners; Dame Joan implored to be taken away immediately in order to safeguard her virginity. Dame Lilias, too, was telling him something, but what she said was lost in the uproar, worse now because the prioress was again assuring him that she needed no assistance to restore order and that he was wasting his time listening to her nuns: listening to them only made them worse. At length he lost patience and walked out, thinking he would find William Holly. Learning that William Holly was at Dudham he rode back to Lintoft. He had meant to ask for a night's lodging at Oby, but now the thought of an evening with Sir John seemed as soothing as an evening with Seneca.

And after all if he had been there that night his presence would not have made much difference. It would have taken more than he to prevent Dame Joan from being raped, her fears were so implacably bent on that catastrophe; nothing he could have said to the prioress would have shaken her conviction that these men were in a conspiracy to release the three imprisoned nuns, so that as long as she could keep them away from the infirmary it was immaterial where else they ransacked; this being so, it was inevitable that Dame Lovisa, the hardiest of the prisoners, should have wrenched her stomach trying to squirm out through the window-slit; and as for the fire, the rain quenched it before it had done any substantial damage. So he told himself, having ridden with Sir John to offer what help and consolation they might. They had been listening, deploring, inspecting, reassuring, advising, for some hours before anyone remembered to tell them that William Holly had been killed. He and the nephews and some of the older men on the manor had run to the defence of the convent: to begin with, a battle of words, for the raiders had been placable enough, saying that they were only in search of food and intended the nuns no harm; that every dog has his day and this was the day of the drovers' dogs against the lap-dogs—a sentiment in which most of the defenders concurred. But William Holly, finding his authority made a joke of by both his opponents and his followers, flew into a rage and attacked the ringleader, who hit back with a mortal blow. It was after this that the fighting began, in which the defenders soon had the worst of it and gave way, leaving the raiders to have their will of the place.

These calamities, which had put the prioress to bed, brought the released Dame Sibilla very much to the fore. She looked uncommonly like her great-uncle as she tripped to and fro, ordering this and commending that, and speaking to all and sundry with a particular trustfulness and simplicity. If she were not actually in two places at once she got very near it; and she was Bishop Walter to the life when she turned to Henry, saying how thankful she was to whichever of the saints had put it into her mind to hide away the altar vessels, and what a cordial it would be to the poor prioress to think that they were preserved from falling into unsanctified hands. The protection of the altar, the safety of the novices—those were the essentials, and both, she thanked God, had been granted. As for poor Dame Joan, one must thank God, who had preserved her senses from any soil of complicity; such was her fear, she had not known what was happening to her until it had happened.

"And what have you to say about my stomach?" interposed Dame Lovisa, looking uglier than ever because she was in such pain.

"That you should be lying down with hot cloths on it, as Dame Lilias prescribed," replied the Dunford with ready sweetness.

But a portion of Dame Sibilla's gratitude was premature. William Holly was dead and the Dudham nephew who had helped him bury the chest could not identify the place. They had carried it a long way, so much he could remember and that he had said to his uncle that it would be daybreak before they had disposed of it. But William Holly, full of obstinacy, had held on till they had come circuitously to the field lying fallow, and there, on its northern edge, the chest was put down while William Holly turned around and around like a dog searching. At last he had chosen a place to his mind. The chest was buried, the tussocks replaced, any loose earth scraped up and scattered about. The nephew had said at the time that it would be hard to find the place again, but the old stiffneck had answered there was no need of any mark, he had not lived so many years at Oby to be at a loss in finding what he had hidden.

Such was the nephew's story. Whether or no one believed it, one could not disprove it. Next year's ploughing, he added consolingly, would uncover the chest. It must have been buried deep, beneath the reach of a plough-share. It was never found.

This was a serious loss to the community. It was also a setback to Dame Sibilla. Though she retained her post of sacrist (the prioress remarking that since there was nothing valuable left Dame Sibilla might safely be left in charge of it), her chances of rising further were small indeed. Dame Lovisa was also in disgrace for her part in the misadventure. But no one could put much energy into these recriminations, and the discrediting of Dame Sibilla and Dame Lovisa seemed only part of the general melancholy and loss of lustre. Oby had not even a distinction of ill-fortune to support its self-esteem. The loss of their altar plate, three tubs of butter, two sides of bacon, part of a roof, and one virginity was a small item in the general tale of outrage and spoliation.

By common consent this was no time to make outlays or take on new responsibilities. Sir Ralph's chamber remained empty, and its red hangings were taken down to replace the scorched hangings in the infirmary. The Wivelham curate, Sir John from Lintoft, sometimes a friar from Waxelby, shared out the duties of his post amongst them—to the disappointment of Dame Joan, who had wistfully appointed cousin Oswald not only priest to the convent but godfather to the child she would bear in the new year. As for the bailiffship, it fell by default of a better to William Holly's son: a bad appointment, for Adam Holly was the usual dynastic heir, inheriting all his father's unpopularity and none of his ability. The harvest, however, was no worse than usual, the Martinmas cattle no thinner, and Henry Yellowlees made several attempts to convince the nuns that they were really no worse off than they had been before; for the loss of their plate, he explained, made no difference to their income, and they certainly had not thought of selling it. These sophistries consoled no one. Every time they looked towards their shabby altar they felt themselves poor and knew themselves come down in the world, and the words of Jeremy, *How is the fine gold become dim,* wailed through their minds.

A little before Epiphany he forced himself to pay them another visit. It was just such a day, cold and foggy, as the day he first came to Oby, quarrelled with William Holly and all but quarrelled with Sir Ralph. Eight years had gone by since then, years in which his circumstances had bettered almost beyond belief. Then he had felt this post of custos an advancement. Now he only continued in it out of complaisance. Then he had been a nondescript poor clerk with nothing to back him but a cousinly recommendation, which was only a politer form of the recommender washing his hands of him. Now he was secretary to the bishop, and a bosom-secretary at that; he helped young scholars and wore leather boots. But today his own rise in the world presented itself to him in inversion, telling him that everyone else had gone down, and was either dead or impoverished and dwindling. Adam Holly walked beside him, and instead of William's sturdy grumbles he heard a vague and complacent talk of what was going well and no complaints at all.

Indoors they were subdued as ever, and Dame Cecily was dying. The house was cold. It smelled of dejection and incompetence. Partly from compassion, partly to be quit of a sense of responsibility, he told himself that they must be fitted out with another priest, and on an impulse he told the prioress that the bishop intended to appoint one. She flushed and said sharply that she was in treaty for one herself. This was plainly a lie. But it would serve; for having told her lie to keep the bishop from interfering in her domain, the proud old woman would feel obliged to substantiate it, a priest would be got from somewhere, and with the stimulus of a newcomer Oby would creak into life again. He was not surprised when, a couple of weeks later, Perkin de Craye handed him a letter with the words, "Here is a cackle from your henhouse." The letter, after a great deal of preamble about decorum and necessity and the will of God and obeying the Rule and making exceptions, came to the point of asking the bishop's permission for two nuns to solicit alms in the cathedral city, because of the poverty of the house and especially to buy new altar vessels to replace those which had been lost. It was clear the prioress could not brook that a new priest should find nothing but pewter.

What a deal of discussion, he thought, must have gone to the framing of that letter, what a shaking of heads and pulling down of upper lips, how much sighing and summing and sideways peeping!—and he wondered which of the nuns would be chosen to go begging.

That was soon settled. Having haled herself to the ignominy of begging, the prioress found a cordial consolation in ordaining that Dame Sibilla who had lost them their plate should stand soliciting for alms to buy new. As for Dame Sibilla's companion, Dame Dorothy soon settled that. "Let it be Dame Lilias. She is the one we can most easily spare." Dame Eleanor bestowed a commiserating grimace on her cousin. All this, she meditated, was the height of silliness, and they might beg till their feet were too swollen to carry them before they would ogle the cost of a chalice from the faithful. When she was prioress she would set about it properly, and a fine new set should be presented by her gratified relations or the anxious parents of some socially half-baked novice. Meanwhile, let it run as badly as they pleased. It would be all the more glory to her when she took over and guided things in her way. She had lived under four prioresses, each one of them a bungler of opportunities: it would be a strange thing if she had not learned how to do better.

Tossed between pride and panic, the prioress could not for some time decide whether her expeditionary nuns should travel creditably or economically. Economy won. During Lent the Waxelby fish-merchants sent a string of waggons inland. By dint of riding to Waxelby along the Hog Trail the nuns could take their place with the fish in Master Bilby's waggon, and make their journey without further trouble to anyone. As for their lodging . . . Dame Sibilla here intervened to recall the widow she had lodged with at the time of her great-uncle's death. Such a good woman; so pious; so well-thought of: without actually saying so Dame Sibilla managed to make it plain that the widow's piety was so exemplary that she might even put them up for nothing. If Dame Sibilla compared this impending departure with the splendour of her journey to Bishop Walter's deathbed she was too discreet to mention it. She seemed wholly occupied with practical preparations for their journey and with asking the prayers of those remaining at home for the success of the mission.

The convent had bought its herring and haberdine from Master Bilby for many years, and during that time no one had suspected that Master Bilby had any special devotion to the house of Our Lady and Saint Leonard. But when Dame Sibilla and Dame Lilias dismounted in the freezing early morning (they had set out soon after mattins in order to reach Waxelby in good time), they found themselves caught hold of, greeted in loud voices, supported on their staggering frozen feet to a warm room, their backs slapped, hot drinks poured down their throats, and an enormous breakfast laid before them. Dame Sibilla took it easily enough. Dame Lilias was almost overset by gratitude. Since the death of Dame Beatrix, and that was now twelve years ago, she had not felt physical kindness. Her indifference to opinion and her susceptibility to strong smells simultaneously tumbled off her. These rough Bilbys seemed like angels, and their red faces, glowing in the firelight, like the faces of seraphs incarnadined with love. She became speechless as a child, obediently swallowing whatever they gave her, and leaving the expression of thanks to Dame Sibilla. Yet oddly enough it was she whom the company afterward chose to praise; and to his life's end young Edmund Bilby remembered the nun who had come in the early morning, and who had looked so careworn and spoken so gently that she might have been the Mother of God in the midst of her sorrows.

When the convoy started they found that after all they would not have to travel among the fish. Master Bilby showed them to their place in a waggon which was carrying a load of Spanish wool recently landed at the port; here, he said, they would journey both warm and soft. Then for a long time the carters shouted one to another, the horses stamped and snorted, jingling their bells. At last they set out.

The sun was now rising. Dame Sibilla pulled back the curtain of the waggon-tilt and called to her companion to admire the great bulk of the Friars' Church, slowly assuming its real stature above the housetops. Kites, daws, and seagulls were wheeling and screaming around it. A few minutes later the convoy slowed down. They had come to the bridge over the Waxle Stream, and there were tolls to be paid. Dignified with a bridge, the familiar river looked quite different, its current more determined, its waters more brilliant. The two nuns said a prayer for the soul of the bridge-builder. After crossing the bridge the going became easier, for the waggons now travelled over the turf beside the sprawling, rutted track; and Dame Sibilla hollowed herself a bed among the bales and settled down to sleep.

Dame Lilias continued to stare out on the strangeness of the world, noticing the purpled leaves that hung on the bramble-clumps, the mild white face of the foremost horse drawing the waggon that followed theirs, the slow whirl of the horizon where a windmill was now taking predominance over the Friars' Church. Her mind was full of contending impressions: excitement at beholding novelties, gratitude to the kind Bilbys, awkwardness and trepidation at the prospect before her. She shrank from the thought of begging. For many nights her dreams had been vexed with throngs of faces all regarding her with contempt and ill-will. She held out her begging-dish and they heaped it, not with alms but with pebbles, dying crows, and poached eggs. Somehow the dish would be cleared of these, and again she proffered it, and now a hand poured in gold pieces, more and more of them, till the dish tilted in her hand and amid cries of, *Clumsy! Look what you are doing!* the gold pieces spilled off and rolled away down a gutter and dissolved. But in reality, she said to herself, it will not be anything like that, for I shall stand as befits a nun, with my eyes cast down, and so however scornfully they look at me I shall not see them, I shall only see their feet. Yet feet too can express abhorrence. They can pause for the malevolent survey, they can trample past in anger. Caught back into her dreams, she had indeed lowered her gaze and was conscious of nothing but the wheeltracks leaving dark bruises on the frosty turf. At last with a sigh she wrenched herself out of her preoccupation and looked round for something which might speak to her of comfort, or at least of resignation. She looked, and it was as if new eyes had been put into her head.

The rough ground stretched for a little way and there broke off in a line of stiffened tussocks, heath bushes, and close gorse-clumps. Beyond this, half the world was hung with a blue mantle criss-crossed with an infinity of delicate creases, and the whole outspread mantle stirred as though a separate life were beneath it. Coming to her senses, she knew that this must be the sea.

But nothing that she had seen in pictures or read in books or heard in sermons was true to what she saw. Their sea was dark, turbulent, vexed with storms, a metaphor of sin, and exiled from heaven. This was calm. It lay as blissfully asleep as though it still lay in the trance of its first creation, its colour was like an unflawed virtue; it lay there and knew of nothing but the

God who had made it. Remembering how she had heard a preacher declare that in heaven there would be no more sea, she broke into spontaneous laughter.

Dame Sibilla, waking with a sense of something unprecedented, sat up and inquired, "What was that? Who was laughing?"

"Me," said Dame Lilias.

"Why? How extraordinary! I mean, you don't laugh very often, do you? Why were you laughing?"

"For joy. Look! That is the sea."

"So it is! Heaven save us, how close it is! And what a long way up the sky it goes! It is certainly a very pretty colour. And this smell . . . I suppose that comes from the sea too. It's like the smell of fish."

"Doesn't it make you feel very happy?"

"Yes. Yes, in a way it does. Look, that must be a ship. Do you see? But it is so calm I don't suppose any mischief will happen to them. I wonder where it goes to—this sea, I mean. Do you suppose it goes to France?"

The line of land began to dip and fall away. Now they saw a beach, with long waves running towards it and breaking there in solitude. They fell lightly, twirling like a skipping-rope, and the ripples ran scalloping up the beach and sank into the brown sand. The nuns continued to hang out of the waggon, staring and exclaiming. A sharp wind blew on their faces, but the sea did not look cold. Its pure colour, its air of nakedness, its leisured movement, all spoke of summer, and the foam scattering so gently from the folded blue of the waves looked no colder than cherry-blossoms.

Even when the track bore inland and the last snatch of blue was lost the sea remained in their minds, and on their faces too, for they continued to look somehow cleaned and quieted. Then they found that they were extremely hungry, and Dame Sibilla undid the bundle that held the food for their journey. Seeing how scanty it was they were at first dismayed, and then began to laugh.

"I wish we could always travel and never beg!" cried Dame Lilias, and added, "Unless we begged for food."

"When we are there we will do more than beg," Dame Sibilla answered, speaking primly and yet cunningly.

"Why? What else?"

"What else, Dame Lilias? Why, with God's blessing and the help of Our Lady and Saint Leonard, we will manage your affair. What, did you think I had forgotten that you are to become an anchoress?"

"I? No . . . It is not to be."

"Not to be? What nonsense! Just because there has been a little delay and because we have an old stick for our prioress? Surely you are not so faint-hearted?"

"I know I shall never be an anchoress. Let us talk of something else."

"Never be an anchoress? But what is there to prevent it? The letters are there, we know that they reached my uncle. He spoke of it to me. He wished it, I know he wished it. You must not turn back now, it would distress him, even in heaven. And here we have this chance sent us by God, all that is needed is a little poke, we have only to make friends with some proper person who will set it all going. Why, if needs be I myself will speak to the bishop about it. Perhaps that would be the best plan. I will say to Master Yellowlees that I wish to . . ."

"No!"

"No? But your vocation, your vision? Can you disobey that? Yes, yes! I know it was not a vision. But you heard the saint speak, you felt his hand strike you—why, there was even a bruise! You cannot doubt such a token as that."

Dame Lilias's hands rose like birds fluttering in a net. "Listen," she said. "I hoped I need never speak of this, but I see I must. You remember how when Sir Ralph was dying he sent for me? And how the prioress forbade me to go?"

"Of course I remember it. It was shameful! I told the prioress so myself, and she has borne me a grudge ever since. Not that I mind. I did it gladly, doing it for your sake, and knowing that Sir Ralph must have wished to say something more to you about your anchoressing."

"It was very kind of you. I am very grateful. But when I went to the prioress Dame Dorothy was there too. She did not speak till the prioress had dismissed me and I was coming away. Then she called me back."

"Well? What had she to say that you need take to heart? You must be used to her taunts by now."

"Yes. So I thought. But she had something to say, after all. It was not the saint who struck me. It was she, Dame Dorothy. I was in her way when she came to light the candles. She had always despised me and, finding me in her way, her hatred overcame her and she hit me with all her strength. She confessed this before the prioress, holding a crucifix in her hand. I can have no reason to doubt she was telling the truth. After her confession she begged my pardon for having yielded to her hate of me, and then for misleading me, for allowing me to go on imagining that it was the saint who struck me. She knew of all that, you see. She knew I hoped to become an anchoress."

"I swear I never told her!"

"Dame Alice told her."

"Dame Alice? How did she know?"

"She heard it from the Prioress Matilda."

It was Dame Sibilla who was overcome and wept, Dame Lilias who comforted; though not very well, for those experienced in despair are seldom good comforters, though the world prefers to believe otherwise. Indeed, with the levity of the wretched, Dame Lilias regretted that this confidence should have been drawn from her just at a time when the sea had given her something new to think about. Dame Sibilla was incapable of any such calculating considerations. She was absorbed in a perfectly straightforward turmoil of regret, indignation, and uneasiness of conscience—for how was she to avoid the thought that if only she had exercised a more reckless zeal to forward Dame Lilias's anchoressing Dame Lilias might by now be safely in her cell and Dame Dorothy's confession of no account to alter anything? The more she reflected, the more she became convinced that Dame Dorothy's interposition could and should be disregarded. If one looked at things in their true light, it really could have no bearing at all on the fact of Dame Lilias's vocation. Because an angry woman had dealt a blow, could the words of a saint be invalidated?

"But the Saint's very words! You heard them!"

"Yes, I heard them."

"Well?"

"It was I who spoke them. They came from me, from my heart, not from anywhere beyond me."

"But your feeling of relief, of heavenly consolation?"

"Very much what Dame Dorothy felt after she had hit me."

Dame Sibilla cried out that she could only call this blasphemy.

Dame Lilias said mildly that she was sorry.

"But Sir Ralph believed it?"

"He saw the bruise and did not know how else to account for it. We were both misled through not knowing all the facts."

After a pause Dame Sibilla said, "Do you know what I think? I am convinced that Dame Dorothy has made up all this story. She pretends out of malice that it was she who hit you—having heard it all, you see, from that shameless Dame Alice. What could be more probable?—she has always persecuted you, and now she is doting. Very likely it is the devil speaking through her, to shake you in your vocation."

"I heard her, you know. She had the very voice of truth."

"You are so simple, so candid. You would believe anything. You always believe the last person who speaks to you."

Dame Lilias looked at Dame Sibilla.

"Not always."

Her angel told Dame Sibilla that it would be fruitless to continue the discussion just now. Just now she would do better to pray and, having prayed, to be kind to her unfortunate companion, and to pick up some wayside crumbs from the distractions of their journey. She prayed fervently while Dame Lilias continued to look at the world. Mixed in with her prayers were skirmishing cogitations as to how best—by persuasion, by bargaining, by holy intimidation?—Dame Lilias could be conjured into taking up the vocation she had relinquished. It was so particularly perverse of her to lose her faith at this juncture when everything had suddenly become so propitious and when the hand of God was so notably evident; for hearing of the begging expedition, and that she was to be made chief beggar, the heavenly intention had instantly been manifest to Dame Sibilla, delivered to her, as it were, in a little bundle; and she had seen exactly why she should have been called on to endure so much unmerited reproach because of the altar plate. By no other means—at any rate by no other means so satisfactory—could she and Dame Lilias have found themselves so well placed to approach the private ear of the bishop. There they would be, herself, and the bishop, and Dame Lilias; and the speech would be made introducing Dame Lilias's vocation and her own resolution—really only one degree short of a vocation in itself—to carry it to fulfilment. To end the speech her uncle would be introduced giving his blessing—though one would not stress this unduly, since no shepherd likes to hear too much made of his predecessor's skill with the crook and tar-box. Then some secretary would be sent off to rummage, and the papers would be brought in, confirming all she had said. Thereafter it would be as good as done, with nothing more needed than to find some vacant anchorage and install Dame Lilias. Perhaps this might even be done forthwith, so that she would return alone to Oby to recount the story, thus gloriously receiving on her own shoulders all the thumps which would otherwise have been Dame Lilias's portion.

All this was jeopardized by Dame Lilias's refusal to proceed. It was difficult indeed to be perfectly in charity with her companion. She had to tell herself repeatedly that Dame Lilias, puffed up by her doubts and scruples, could not appreciate all the planning and good intentions which had been devoted to her cause, nor guess how much Dame Sibilla had counted on its success as a counter-charm against the painful recollections which must burst on her as she saw once more the scene of Bishop Walter's death.

How very painful these recollections might prove Dame Sibilla did not like to assess. The comforter of Walter Dunford's vexed death-bed was by no means confident that she could sail through the shadow as easily as she had sailed over the substance. Shadows can be much, much worse—as much worse as is an owl's hoot in broad daylight. A dead man decaying under a flagstone can lay a much more alarming hand on one than that same man when alive. So she prayed harder and harder, hearing the axles creak, the whips crack, the wheels rumbling over the frozen ground.

That night's bustle at the inn, the satisfaction of shielding Dame Lilias, the mass heard in a strange church, all helped to raise her spirits. As they neared the end of their journey she very much enjoyed pointing out the features on the skyline: the cathedral, the palace, the lesser churches, the hospital of the Holy Innocents where Henry Yellowlees set his foot on the first rung of the ladder. The widow, too, was extremely sustaining: most warm in her welcome and skilfully building a bridge between the bishop's dearest niece of 1377 and the begging nun of 1382. Alas! was not everything changed for the worse?—here, too, as elsewhere. For her, at any rate, there could never be such another bishop as Bishop Walter. A little later Henry Yellowlees looked in on them, bringing a box of sweetmeats and inquiring if they were comfortable. On the morrow he would call for them and show them their begging-station.

"And so, unless the wind blows from this quarter, I think you should be fairly comfortable here," he said, having settled them in the south porch of the cathedral. "The mats will keep your feet warm, and if you want anything or are molested Lambert the sacristan will be within call. He still talks of your uncle, Dame Sibilla, and disapproves of everything we have done since by way of improvements. He is a most excellent, trustworthy old man, and the bishop delights in his sour sayings."

So that is what he is like on his own perch, thought Dame Lilias, gazing at the custos of Oby. Well, it is very considerate of him to veil his glory when he comes among us. Catching her glance, he smiled, and she thought better of him. After all, every man will climb if he can, and not many of them continue so kind to old acquaintances.

He turned back to say that on Thursday they should make a particularly good collection. A band of pilgrims from the north would hear their mass in the cathedral that morning, and as they had not been long on their pilgrimage they should be in a state to give generous alms. Dame Sibilla asked where the pilgrims were going, and he replied, to Jerusalem, taking ship at Venice.

Taking ship at Venice. . . . All day Dame Lilias's thoughts sailed to Jerusalem over a blue transparent sea, blue as a flower and wide as a sky. And though in spite of Henry Yellowlees' assurances and the mats it was very cold in the south porch, and though old Lambert pestered them with conversation and inquiries, and though her arms ached with holding out the begging-dish and her face felt scorched with strangers' glances, at the day's end her fatigue was almost like refreshment. Unfortunately they were no sooner alone than Dame Sibilla began once more to persuade, expostulate, argue, and lament about the anchoressing. She was so faithful and so noisy that it was hard not to think of her as a little dog.

On the first day their takings were promising enough—considering, the widow remarked, that it was a Friday. By the second day they were already ceasing to be novelties, and those who had given did not give again, so the result of the second day was not so good. Dame Sibilla grew morose, and said that Master Yellowlees could very well afford to give them a new set of altar vessels, and that really it was the least he could do for the memory of poor Sir Ralph whom he had pretended to be so much attached to. On Sunday the number of alms given went up considerably, but when they came to count the day's winnings the bulk of it was in small money and there was a high proportion of clipped coins, tokens, and forgeries; for the increase in the congregation was made up from the city poor, old women, weavers, and day labourers who did not go to mass on ordinary days. Dame Sibilla was much distressed by the bad coins. When Dame Lilias remarked that she supposed their givers felt compelled by courtesy to give something even though that something was known to be worthless Dame Sibilla flew into a rage and delivered herself of a sermon on the theme of comforting Christ in his poor. It was a good sermon; better than the sermon they had heard from the black friar who had preached that morning. But if he had preached like an angel he would have been a disappointment to them, for they had expected to hear the bishop. By the close of the next day Dame Lilias was almost praying for some sort of notice from Perkin de Craye. It had been her terror that by some chance or other Dame Sibilla should get his ear and perform her design of telling him all about the Oby anchoress; but now, seeing Dame Sibilla so quiveringly mortified, so childishly foiled of all her glorious intentions, she felt that she could endure any exposure if it would contribute to Dame Sibilla's peace of mind. But nothing happened, they continued to stand in the porch watching people get quite accustomed to them and able to walk by them with no more concern than they would have felt for two images to which the sculptor had given the posture of beggars.

It was on Tuesday night that Dame Lilias woke up to find herself being half-strangled by her bedfellow. Her first thought was that some murderer had broken in, for she could not believe that Dame Sibilla, so much smaller than she, could grasp her with such force, nor utter such animal-sounding groans.

"You must, you must, you must!"

Half-stifled, and confused by this strange waking, and with the murderer still in her mind, she gasped out, "Where is he?"

"He's here!"

It was a cry to curdle any blood, and from her bed at the other end of the chamber the widow called out, "Holy Virgin! Who is here?"

Dame Lilias felt the desperate body beside her relax. Dame Sibilla's voice, prim and awed, said, "*Libera nos!* I have had a terrible dream."

"I should think so," said the widow testily. "You shrieked like a lost soul. *He's here,* you said. And then you yelled as if the wolves had got you. What was the dream, who was it you saw that was so terrifying? God save us all, I feel as if there were someone or something in the room at this moment."

"Hush, you'll frighten her. She's still only half awake," said Dame Lilias, feeling the small body beside her convulsed with renewed terror. Interested in her own alarms, the widow now got up and unfastened a shutter. The moonlight shone in.

"The door's barred, just as I left it. I don't see how anyone could have got in. There's no one behind the hanging, is there? Or hidden in the chest?"

She poked and muttered about the room. Then she began to snuff and to think of fire, and presently creaked away to make sure of the kitchen hearth. As soon as her back was turned Dame Sibilla clutched hold of Dame Lilias again, and began to whisper.

"Listen! I have had a frightful dream, and in it I saw—I saw the devil, standing on your side of the bed and threatening you. Do you know why? Because of your pride, your pride, you know. You are so proud that you will not do as our Saint Leonard bid you, and all because it may have been Dame Dorothy who struck you and not he. It is quite true what they all say of you, you are eaten up with pride. You are too proud to take anything on trust, you are too proud to ask for anyone's help, you won't stir a finger to become an anchoress. But you must, you must! You have no idea how much hangs on it, you think of no one but yourself, you sulk and do nothing. And all will be lost! I tell you, this is your last chance, your last chance. You must, you must!"

Here the widow came back, munching something she had found in the kitchen, and got into bed, saying Hail Marys and complaining of the cold. For a while she talked about other midnight alarms she had known. When she had fallen asleep and was safely snoring Dame Sibilla began again to threaten and to implore.

"No! Once for all, no," said Dame Lilias.

There was a silence. Then, in a completely altered voice Dame Sibilla said, "Very well. I have done all I can for you. Whatever happens now, remember, it is on your head."

A minute later she was tranquilly sleeping.

Nothing more was said about this. Dame Sibilla appeared to be rather the better for her nightmare. She exerted herself to be agreeable, and instead of grieving over the fall in their takings she dwelt on the good harvest they would get from the pilgrims. During the afternoon the pilgrims began to come into the city. They walked about examining the sights, begging, and making little purchases. One and all, they were marked by a certain manner, an airiness and inconsequence that grew out of their detachment from the everyday cares of life. Perhaps if they had been going to settle, the citizens might not have liked them so well, for their comments were not always flattering and they drove very hard bargains with shopkeepers, instancing how much cheaper or better such goods had been elsewhere; but as transients they had a cheering effect, and to the two nuns in the south porch they were a most welcome diversion.

That evening the widow's hall and kitchen were full of pilgrims. Some were frying fish for their supper, others patching their clothes or repacking their scrips or doing a little washing. The house was gay with their songs and their stories, and the widow was flushed and boastful as she ran to and fro attending to their needs. These were the people who would take ship at Venice for Jerusalem. In the herring-reek and the bustle Dame Lilias did not at first remember this: recalling it, she loitered in the doorway, wishing that she might pluck up enough audacity to speak to one of the more travelled ones, who had, it appeared, made this voyage once already. But Dame Sibilla pulled at her, saying that she had such a splitting headache that she must instantly lie down. Full of conscience and anxiety and remembering the nightmare, Dame Lilias did all she could for her companion. Presently the widow came in and suggested various remedies. But it was balm-water that Dame Sibilla craved for, and unfortunately there were no balm leaves in the house.

"On any evening . . ." cried the widow. "But tonight I really cannot leave the house."

"Never mind, never mind! Better now than tomorrow."

"Yes, but will you be cured by tomorrow? Tomorrow, too, the great day, when you will need all your wits about you not to let any of the pilgrims slip by without giving an alms. For they'll be sly, you know. They're not like our own quiet, stay-at-home folk. They'd steal the chick from under the fox's paw. That's why I am so loath to leave the house unguarded while I go out for balm leaves."

"If you will tell me where to buy them, I will go," Dame Lilias said.

"What!—alone, with the town full of pilgrims? Well, it is not far, only a little difficult to find. But you must ask for Master Peter Hiddlestone, living next to Sim the Glover at the sign of the Bird and Hand. There are other apothecaries, but he is the honestest. Stay, I have a better plan! I will pick out a pilgrim to go with you, nun and pilgrim is the next thing to nun and nun.

There is an excellent woman below, she has had thirteen children by the one husband and stuffs pillows, she too has some small shopping to do, and you will be none the slower for going hand in hand. And while you are gone I will make a posset for this poor dove."

Master Peter Hiddlestone took some finding; the excellent woman, too, had several commissions and was a most scrupulous buyer; by the time Dame Lilias returned Dame Sibilla had somewhat recovered and was eating supper off a tray. The balm-water eased her wonderfully, and she soon fell asleep. But in the morning her headache was worse than ever and she felt such dizziness and such intimations of vomiting that she was compelled to let Dame Lilias set forth alone.

"On this morning of all mornings!" lamented Dame Sibilla.

"Well, she must rattle the dish so much the louder, and stand well forward, and look them in the face, so that they will be ashamed to sneak by her," said the widow. "But it's a pity."

"Why, where's the other one? Sick? You'll need to look sharp, then," said Lambert the sacristan. "For six who'll give there will be half a dozen who'll take. Here they come."

"Who? The pilgrims? Already?"

"No, no. The executioner's servants, and the men with the faggots for the pitch-barrel. There's a thief being punished this morning. They will chop his hand off and dip the stump into pitch, you know. Yes, and you'll see the bishop. He's going to bless the pilgrims."

"Are they punishing the thief near by? Shall I hear the screams?" Dame Lilias asked apprehensively. His glance fell on a boy who was filching a candle-end, and he hurried off without answering her.

Because of the headache Dame Lilias was a little late. She scarcely had time to feel the wretchedness of being alone and reflect on the screams of the mutilated man before the first mass-goers began to pass by. As awkwardly as if she had never begged till this hour she held forth her dish, wagging it up and down and saying, "An alms, good people. An alms for God's poor nuns at Oby." Her look was so piteous that one or two kind-hearted people gave her a good alms, and others paused to encourage her and to advise her to beg louder. But while these were talking more slipped by, and in her conscientiousness she went too far, leaving her place to run after them. Then one of these said crossly that he had given her an alms but the day before and that she might have the gratitude to remember it; but these nuns had no more consideration than the horse-leach. Abashed she went back into her corner again, and stood there biting her lip and with such shamed cheeks that Lambert came bustling up to ask who had offended her.

"No one, no one."

"Then what are you making such a pother about? The other one, Dame Sibilla, isn't too proud to beg. And she is blood-kin to a bishop."

Now the pilgrims were arriving, spruced up for their mass and their blessing. Inside the cathedral the first disconnected noises of a congregation were amassing into a steady purr, and the newcomers felt themselves to be late-comers, and hurried by without stopping to give alms. Presently she heard like a gnat's noise the voice of the officiating priest, and the responses of the quire following it like a caress. She did not dare look at the contents of her dish. Holding it under her veil, she went to the cathedral door. Never in all her life had she seen so many people gathered together, and this was more marvellous to her than the quantities of the incense, the amplitude of the ritual. Perkin de Craye was sitting on his throne, her short sight could just discern him. Ah, poor Dame Sibilla! But her thoughts only brushed Dame Sibilla's dejected ambitions, going back to the pilgrims, to their incalculable journey, the fatigues and the dangers they must undergo, the long leagues, the mountains, the strange cities and unknown languages. So they would come to Venice, and take ship for Jerusalem.

She was still on her knees when Lambert came up and jogged her.

"Here, Dame Nun! Are you having a vision? Don't you see that they have had their blessing, that they are coming away? Don't let them slip through your fingers this time."

She hurried back to her station. The shuffling feet approached, and the voices, taking hold of the tune, sang more loudly and fervently. Singing, they streamed past her. Though she held out her dish and now and then a coin was dropped in it, the business of begging was quite out of her mind. These people going by her now, so many of them and all unknown and none to be met with again, dizzied her imagination, and it seemed to her that inevitably she would be drawn to go with them as a tuft of dry grass is pulled from the river-bank and carried with the travelling waters to the sea. To Venice, and thence to take ship for Jerusalem, and in Jerusalem to lay her empty sorrows in the empty Sepulchre. . . .

But her dream depended on their going by, and now they slowed down and stopped, some block beyond the porch impeding their progress. Her dream snapped, she remembered herself and held out the dish.

"An alms, good people. An alms for God's poor nuns at Oby."

A sense that she was being scrutinized made her look up. The pilgrim who had been halted just in front of her was examining the contents of the dish, and Dame Lilias received an instant impression that this pilgrim had a cast of countenance which she very much disliked. In the same moment she saw that the pilgrim was Dame Sibilla.

Their eyes met. Dame Sibilla gave a little nod, as much as to say, *I told you so.* Dropping an alms into the dish, she leaned forward and said rapidly, "Do not betray me. Do not say that you have seen me here among the pilgrims."

"But you will be sought for. And if they find you, you will be brought back, an apostate nun, and . . ."

"I shall not be sought for. And no one will ask you what has become of me, not for a long time, not till I am beyond seeking. I have seen to all that. It will be no trouble to you, you will only have to keep your own counsel. I have written a letter, and by now it is being carried to Oby, telling the prioress that my aunt Anna, the nun at Ramsey, the one who sent us the mock ginger, is dying a slow death, and that her convent has sent for me to nurse her. And that I met their steward here, coming in search of me, and have gone with him, because of the escort, and the saving of expenses. You will find everything arranged when you get back. One of us had to go, you would not be an anchoress, so I am a pilgrim. I see you do not understand, but I assure you, it is all God's will. I am a pilgrim, I am inexpressibly happy. I shall pray for you in Jerusalem. And you can rely on the widow. She understands everything, she will arrange . . ."

The procession began to move forward.

"Remember, I trust you," said Dame Sibilla.

Joining in the hymn she moved on. The stoppage had been caused by the executioners going past with the man who was to have his hand struck off. Now they had turned aside, and the pilgrims swept on unimpeded. Their singing swelled out like a banner on the wind as they fell into step and marched southward.

A NOTE ON THE HISTORICAL BACKGROUND

The Black Death—that epidemic of bubonic plague which sent the storytellers of Boccaccio's *Decameron* to lodge in the country, away from plague-stricken Florence—came into Europe along the trade route from Constantinople in 1347 and reached England in the late summer of 1348. It is estimated that in the next eighteen months it killed one-third of the English population. The contemporary estimate was one-half; and for some thriving and well-populated districts such an estimate may be the true one; in any case, as many of those who had the plague and recovered from it were disabled by sores and weakness, it is reasonable to assume that the working population was halved.

The economic consequences of this catastrophe were intensified by the structure of society. A minority—court, nobles, the great clerics, scholars, friars, and outlaws—were so footloose that they can be classed as nomadic; but the base of that society was the manorial serf, who was tied to the place of his birth. For such, and for the monastic communities, there was no running away from infection.* Thus the system designed to provide a regular supply of labour for the manors now prevented redistribution of a greatly diminished labour force. The lord of a depopulated manor saw his land untilled, his crops ungathered, and himself on the brink of ruin; for he, at a remove, was as much dependent on his land as the serfs it carried, whether the feudal due was paid him in actual labour or in commutation fees. Such lords were driven to hire labour, which they could do only by bribing men to come to them off other manors; at the same time the lords of manors who still commanded a sufficiency of labourers could keep it only by counter-bribing. The old cumbrous sleepy bargain of the manorial system, in which the serf was tied to his lord's land while reciprocally part of that land was tied to the serf—the common field supplying his bread, the common grazing his meat and fuel—was replaced by the suppler but more cut-throat bargain of capital and labour.

In the years immediately following the Black Death the labourer had the best of it. By the next generation the situation had changed. The population was rising again. Many landowners had adjusted themselves to the labour shortage by converting their acres from arable (which needs many hands) to sheep-rearing for the woollen trade (which needs few), and in so doing had made over common fields and grazings into sheep-walks. And though wages had risen, the cost of living had risen more. Serfs who had welcomed the opportunity to move about and strike their own bargain found themselves at a disadvantage, and Parliament, which had disapprovingly watched the crack spreading through the old feudal structure, now applied a plastering legislation of wage-fixing and price-fixing (the former, as always, more adhesive than the latter), and pressed for a reversion to the *status quo ante.* Yet the crack had been made and was kept open by a pressure of dissatisfied thinking.

*NOTE: The Court Rolls of the time show what happened when the Black Death got to work on a stationary population. At the manor court of Heacham, in Norfolk, for instance, a suit was postponed from February 1349 to the next sitting, two months later; at that sitting the suit had to be postponed *sine die;* during the interval all the witnesses on the one part, and the litigant on the other, had died of the pestilence.

In practice, the Church had always accepted the feudal obligation to hold landed property. St. Peter had his fief, bishops had their manors, a provision of land and labourers must support any monastic foundation, whatever the personal austerities of the order. Gifts and legacies, charged with a burden of masses to be offered for the dead, accrued to the monastic houses, and an establishment that allowed itself to become insolvent could be, and sometimes was, dissolved. But this massive body of common sense contained, like an element of quicksilver, the doctrine of Evangelical Poverty, and as the Church grew richer this doctrine shone out in more sparkling contrast. Where it displayed itself in a single mind, as with St. Francis, it might be tolerated; where it formed part of the teaching of a sect, as with the Albigenses, the Lollards, or St. Francis's strictest followers, it was cast out as heresy (the doctrine that Christ and his Apostles possessed no property was denounced as heretical by Pope John XXII in 1323). Side by side with Evangelical Poverty went the doctrine of Natural Right (the *ius naturale* of the Stoics, which had passed into christian theology through the patristic writers) that the material gifts of God, being given to all men, should be held in common. Logically, these two opinions are incompatible, for if all men are to share alike there should be no especial poverty to be especially evangelical: Langland, in his *Piers Plowman,* is vehement for Evangelical Poverty, but very wary about Natural Right; but both opinions, like the cat and the rat in La Fontaine's fable, had ears of the same shape, and were often treated as being complementary.

Thus the Church contributed twice over, on the one hand by canvassing these doctrines, on the other by the exasperating richness of its great establishments and its harshness in manorial administration (Church-land serfs were the last to be freed), to the moral indignation which fired a mass of material grievances into the Peasants' Revolt of 1381. Froissart records one of the speeches of John Ball, a priest who led that revolt:

> *"For what reason have they, whom we call lords, got the better of us? If we are all descended from one father and one mother,*

> *Adam and Eve, how can they assert or prove they are more masters than ourselves—except perhaps that they make us work and produce for their spending. They are clothed in velvet, ermine, and furs, while we wear coarse linen. They have wines, spices, and good bread, while we get rye bread, offal, straw, and water. They have mansions and fine manors, and we bear the toil and the trouble, and must endure the wind and the rain out of doors. And it is from us and our labour that they get the wherewithal to keep up their pomp."*

This assertion of *ius naturale* might be within the theological pale, but it was heresy in any monarchical state. The revolt was savagely quelled, and John Ball was put to death.

The art of this period expressed similar impulses of speculation and revolt. In architecture the floridity of Decorated Gothic gave way to the purely national Perpendicular style, at once more lucid and more ambitious. Literature became more expressive of personality. In music the *Ars nova* discarded a good deal of clutter and long-windedness in favour of ease of movement and euphony. The spiritual informality of Eckhart is echoed in the writings of such mystics as Richard Rolle and John Hilton. All these tendencies were apparent before 1350. Even without the shock of the Black Death, fourteenth-century England was concerned with readjustments, but that impact intensified change into conflict.

SOME DATES

Edward III reigned 1327–1377. Richard II reigned 1377–1399. Hundred Years War began, 1337. Battle of Crécy, 1346. Battle of Poitiers, 1356. Treaty of Bretigni, 1360. Treaty overthrown, and successes of French forces under Du Guesclin, 1369–1377. Great Papal Schism, 1378.

Lantern of Ely Cathedral, *c.* 1335. Choir of Gloucester Cathedral, 1337–1357. Chaucer born, *c.* 1340. Richard Rolle died, 1349. *Piers Plowman, c.* 1362. New College, Oxford, founded, 1379.

NOTES

The courtesy titles of *Sir* and *Dame* for clerics and nuns carried no significance of noble birth.

A *heriot* was a feudal due taken by the lord of the manor at the death of the eldest male of a manorial family.

Impediment of bastardy. Before a clerk in Lesser Orders could be ordained as a priest he had to satisfy the bishop as to his moral, scholarly, and worldly fitness. Bastardy was considered as a disqualification unless the candidate could produce a patron of good standing who would be responsible for his upkeep so that he would not become a financial burden on the diocese.

Corrodians. A corrodian was something like an annuitant. In return for a payment of a lump sum a lay person was assured of support by a chosen monastic house, without being subject to its discipline. The system was popular, but not smiled on by ecclesiastical authorities.

Visitations. It was part of the duty of a bishop to pay regular visits of inspection to the religious houses in his diocese, when he heard complaints, inspected account-books, and rebuked errors in conduct and administration.

Spiritualities. It was an act of piety for a lay patron to give a benefice to a religious house, or some other ecclesiastical body, which would then supply the parish with a vicar or curate. Such a gift included the revenues of the benefice and the tithes paid by parishioners. The upkeep of priest and church was a charge on these revenues, but it was allowable for part of the revenues to be appropriated by the new authority. These presented benefices could be farmed or transferred, provided they remained in the possession of the Church.

Periculoso. A Papal Bull of 1300, forbidding nuns to quit their convents.

SYLVIA TOWNSEND WARNER

Sylvia Townsend Warner was born at Harrow on the Hill in Middlesex in 1893. Her father was a housemaster at Harrow School. Though a genuinely erudite woman, she had no formal education but was taught at home by her father and by governesses. During the First World War she worked in a munitions factory and then spent ten years in London editing, with three other musicologists, a monumental collection of Tudor church music. Her first novel, *Lolly Willowes,* was the first Selection of the Book-of-the-Month Club, in 1926. She wrote, in all, seven novels, eight collections of short stories, four volumes of poetry, a biography of T. H. White, a book about Somerset and a translation of Proust's *Contre Ste.-Beuve.* If the Moncrieff heirs had not made difficulties, she would have retranslated the whole of his *Remembrance of Things Past.* Her heart was deeply committed to the cause of the Spanish Republic, and she made two visits to Spain in wartime as the guest of the Loyalist government. During most of her adult life she lived with the poet Valentine Ackland in a house by the River Frome, outside the village of Maiden Newton, in Dorset. She died in 1978, at the age of eighty-five. Two volumes of stories and her *Collected Poems* have been published posthumously, as well as her collected letters.

WILLIAM MAXWELL

William Maxwell is the author of six novels, the best known being *They Came Like Swallows* (a Book-of-the-Month Club Selection in 1937), *The Folded Leaf, Time Will Darken It, The Château,* and *So Long, See You Tomorrow,* which won the William Dean Howells Medal of the American Academy of Arts and Letters and an American Book Award. He is also the author of a collection of tales, a collection of short stories, a family history and a book for children. His stories have been reprinted in the annual "O. Henry" and "Best American Stories" collections and in Martha Foley's *200 Years of Great American Short Stories.* For forty years he was an editor, first in the art and then in the fiction department, of *The New Yorker,* where one of the authors whose stories he edited was Sylvia Townsend Warner. He is also the editor of *Letters of Sylvia Townsend Warner* (Viking, 1982). He lives with his wife in New York City.

The text of this book was set in a film version of Bodoni Book, a popular typeface cut in 1907 by the American type designer Morris Fuller Benton. He based it on original type by Giambattista Bodoni, an Italian printer born in 1740.

Design by Janet Odgis.